Advanced PRACTICAL GEOGRAPHY

— a Laboratory Manual

Dr. Partha Basu

CELEBRATING 60 YEARS 1960-2020
Since BOOKS AND ALLIED 1960

[Covering CBCS Syllabus for B.Sc (Hons) & M.Sc. students of Geography.]

Advanced PRACTICAL GEOGRAPHY

— a Laboratory Manual

Dr. Partha Basu
Reader, Department of Geography
Bhairab Ganguly College.

BOOKS & ALLIED (P) Ltd.
No. 1E(1) "Shubham Plaza"
83/1, Dr. S.C. Banerjee Road, Beliaghata, Kolkata 700010
Tel : (033) 23740062 • ***e-mail*** : booksandallied1960@gmail.ccm
website: www.booksandallied.com

Advanced PRACTICAL GEOGRAPHY

— a Laboratory Manual

First Published : January, 2004
Second Edition (thoroughly revised) : 2006
Revised Reprint : 2007, 2008
Third Edition : 2009
Revised Reprint : 2010
Reprinted : 2011, 2013, 2014, 2015, 2017, 2018
Fourth Edition : 2021
Reprinted : 2022

Publisher	: Ruba Sen BOOKS & ALLIED (P) LTD. No. 1E(1), 'Shubham Plaza' 83/1, Dr. S.C. Banerjee Road, Beliaghata, Kolkata 700010
Typesetter	: BOOKS & ALLIED (P) LTD. No. 1E(1), 'Shubham Plaza' 83/1, Dr. S.C. Banerjee Road, Beliaghata, Kolkata 700010
Printer	: EUREKA 91/A, Baithakkhana Road, Kolkata 700009
Project Supervisor	: Sudhangsu De

ISBN 978-81-946982-4-1

Price : ₹ **690.00**

This book is

dedicated to the pioneers,

who paved the pathway for Geographical studies

Preface to the Fourth Edition

This is the fourth edition of Advanced Practical Geography. In view of incorporating the new additions to the syllabus of Practical Geography at Degree Level this edition has been deemed necessary. The trend of the new syllabus in different universities, following the guideline set by U. G.C., is to make a student of Geography more thorough through practical applications in the fields of Cartography as well as data based Cartographic Analysis, Statistical Analysis, Demography, Soil Properties, Regional and Social Geography and so on. Many of the new additions are not matching with the contents and structure of the previous edition. Hence a new chapter has been annexed along with substantial addition of relevant topics in different existing chapters. This edition also stresses on the theoretical bases of various practical lessons of Geography. Moreover,interpretation of the practical works has been particularly addressed, as interpretation is the most essential part of such practical lessons.

A few more discourses on statistical analysis have been added in connection with further advanced analysis of geographical data. The knowledge of Research Methodology being an essential component in geographical as well as other researches, has been given an elaborate discussion in the new chapter (Chapter 11).

Furthermore, some of the practical works based on real data, as included in this book, have such in-depth analysis as befitting a research paper.

And last but not the least I need to mention that though this book was initially authored by two of us, Dr. Pijushkanti Saha and myself, Dr. Saha departed from this world about two years ago. Whatever additions and changes are incorporated in this book since the Second Edition, I myself have done it with utmost sincerity, though limitations are always there in terms of availability of real data and my limited capability. I hope, by dint of my long experience in teaching of Geography this edition of Advanced Practical Geography will be of immense help to the students.

Kolkata
Kali Puja, 2020

Partha Basu

Preface to the First Edition

The horizon of geography is expanding. Geography is now considered a science interpreting space in terms of human activities. With explosion of population the space on the surface of earth appears to be constricted. We need optimum utilisation of space for sustenance. Such utilisation demands precise measure and understanding of space with application of geographical knowledge. In recent times various innovative tools have come to the aid of geographers.

ADVANCED PRACTICAL GEOGRAPHY : A Laboratory Manual — Outlines various measures and tools in understanding geography and its application with different perspectives. The technological development in the past few decades of 20th Century had been tremendous and created many new devices for use in practical geography. A practical geography without modern techniques will never be considered useful in this new millennium.

This practical handbook in geography incorporates different methods and tools in geography. These include map making; instrumental study for land surveying; morphometric analysis; weather information; map analysis for geological map, weather map; thematic map; topographical map; statistical methods; study on rocks and minerals; remote sensing techniques and interpretation of air-photo and satellite imageries and application of computer in geographical studies with particular reference to Geographic Information Systems (G.I.S.). All such techniques have been outlined with large number of illustrations and explained lucidly for easy understanding of the students. Though this practical geography book is primarily intended for graduate students in Indian Universities, the post-graduate and research students will also be largely benefited. Our mission will be successful if the students can reap appropriate knowledge of practical geography from this book. We will also appreciate any criticism and suggestions from the experts, teachers and students for improvement of this book.

We have received suggestions from many of our colleagues, who have shown keen interest during the preparation of this book. It is not wise to mention a few names. But we owe our indebtedness to all of them. Mr. Arunabha Sen, Executive Director, Books and Allied (P) Ltd. deserves our thanks for his keen interest in the publication of this book.

Kolkata
25th December, 2003

Pijushkanti Saha
Partha Basu

Acknowledgements

We express our sincerest thanks to our teachers whose methods of teaching and spark of knowledge inspired us so deeply that it has ultimately compelled us to write a book on practical geography.

The same inspiration we owe to our students, whose inquisitiveness has guided us in detailing of this book.

We are sincerely indebted to Sangita Chaudhuri and Ratna Mukherjee, who helped us in preparing the press copy of the manuscript and in drawing of sketches.

CONTENTS

CHAPTER 1

TECHNIQUES IN MAP MAKING

MAP AS A TOOL

Dr. H. R. Mill once wrote, "In Geography we make it as axiom that what cannot be mapped cannot be described". We consider Geography simply and directly as the descriptions of earth's surface and its areal variations. Map is the basic tool of a Geographer in understanding the problems and presentation of such variations.

Definition of a Map

The map is the graphical and true representation of varied information regarding the earth surface on a piece of paper in reduced form.

All these information relate to different attributes at a particular location on the ground surface. Different attributes comprise different aspects like geological information, relief depiction, climatic information, socio-economic information etc. All such data are observed/ surveyed, stored and analysed. Different topologic and geometric properties are manifested in maps.

The task is not easy in representing the information from a spherical earth surface on a piece of flat paper. The spherical earth is three dimensional, whereas the flat paper is two dimensional. A technique is to be evolved for conversion of three dimensional information into a two dimensional set-up.

The amount of curvature of the earth surface is expressed in terms of actual distance between a curved line on the arc of spherical earth and a tangent straight line originating at the same point. This distance is called the ***divergence***. The divergence increases with increasing distance between the points. Since the days of Eratosthenes it is of continued interest in finding a solution in measuring the curved distance of the earth surface to be properly fitted on a flat paper (fig no. 1.1). We will discuss the problem in detail in the study of Map Projection later on.

The measured distance on the earth surface (ground surface) can only be represented in a reduced form. Consider the radius of the earth as 250,000,000 inches or 640,000,000 centimetres. A degree of longitude is equal to 70 miles or 112 kilometres. It is necessary to decide some measure for the true representation of the ground surface on a flat paper in a much reduced form. The relationship between the measured ground distance and representative depiction of true distance is expressed in terms of a Scale. The Scale thus controls the area available for representation of detailed features and hence influences the design and appearance of a map.

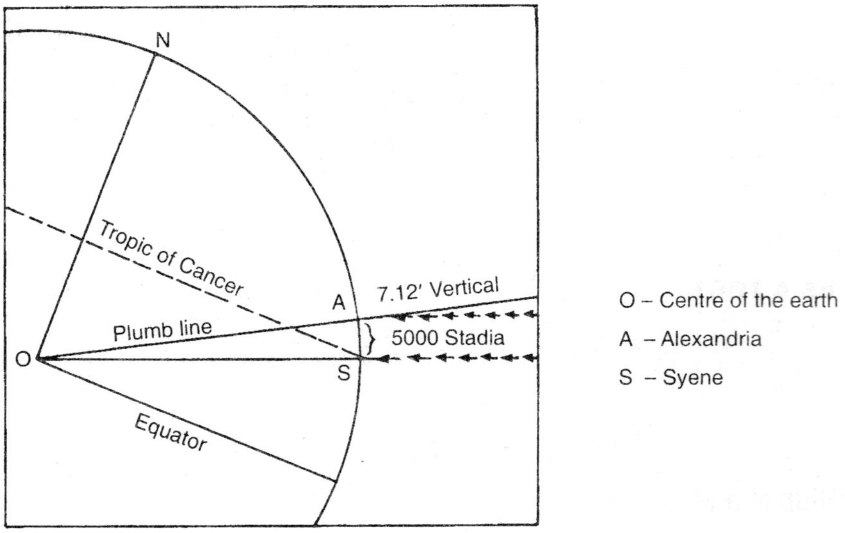

Fig. 1.1 Measurement of earth's surface after Eratosthenes

SCALE OF THE MAP

Definition of Scale

The Scale is the measure for proportional and true representation of the reduced earth on a paper. The Scale expresses the relationship between the size of object on the ground and its image on the map, in terms of measurement made on one to be restated in terms of the other.

For the purpose of constructing diagrams the scale may be defined as the ratio between map distance and the real world data represented by it; e.g. 1 cm represents 10,000 persons in a graph.

The Scale may be expressed in two ways : either in the form of a statement or in the form of a fraction, known as **Representative Fraction (R.F.)**. When we state that a map is on a scale of 1 inch to a mile, it is the statement that one inch on the map will represent one mile on the ground. We can also express this one inch to a mile scale in the form of a fraction. We know that :

> 1 mile is equal to 63360 inches. The ratio of the unit on the map with the unit on the ground comes to 1/63360. We can say that one unit of the numerator (on the map) will represent several units of denominator (on the ground). Thus the Representative Fraction (R.F.) is shown as 1:63360.

Sometimes for better understanding of the distance between two points on a map it is covenient to draw a line-scale or linear scale. Thus the scale may also be represented graphically on the map. This scale becomes very useful for the production purposes, particularly in the reduction and enlargement of the map. If we retain the R.F. scale only the area of the ground will be greatly distorted by reduction and enlargement of the map, but the change will not be reflected in the scale.

The Line-scale or Linear Scale has the advantage of enabling direct measurement of distances on the map denoting in terms of distances on the ground. It is advisable that all maps bear a line-scale. In case the original drawing (map) is likely to be reduced or enlarged photographically, it is not advisable to show the R.F. scale on the original drawing. It is obligatory to be expressed in line-scale.

In cases of showing dual form of the scale in figures, one written as fraction and the other as whole number, may result in confusion when calculations involving scale have to be made. G.C. Dickinson has introduced a new device, known as ***scale factor***.

"The scale factor is the number which must be used in all calculations concerning scale and can be defined as either the denominator of the scale written as a fraction or the second part of the scale written as ratio." (Dickinson, 1979)

For example in maps on the scales 1/50000 and 1:60000 the scale factors are 50000 and 60000 respectively. It is always to be remembered that (i) the scale factor is a number not a fraction and (ii) the map distance is smaller than the ground distance. Another important point we must always note :

Scale is (as a fraction) Map Distance /Ground Distance, while the Scale Factor is the inverse of this i.e. Ground Distance /Map Distance.

CONVERSION OF SCALES

In any conversion such two of the three basic elements must be known and the procedure is easy.

Step 1 : Firstly two known elements are identified and defined in the same unit of length. If these are expressed differently, the smaller of the two units may be chosen. This will help in the identification of the third element.

Step 2 : Two known values are put in the appropriate formula and the third unknown element is identified.

Conversion of a Scale in Words to a Scale in Figures :

Problem : Express 6 inches to 1 mile as a scale in figures.

First Step : 6 inches shown on the map = 1 mile on the ground
So Map distance = 6 inches
Ground distance = 1 mile = 63360 inches
Missing element is Scale Factor

Second Step : Scale Factor = Ground Distance/Map Distance = 63360 inches/
6 inches = 10560
Scale in Figures is therefore 1:10560

Conversion of a Scale Figures to a Scale in Words :

Problem : Express 1:5,000,000 as so many X miles to an inch.

First Step : Expression indicates so many X miles on ground to an inch on map.
Hence ground distance is unknown = X miles = $X \times 63360$ inches
Map distance = 1 inch
Scale Factor = 5,000 000

Second Step : Ground Distance = Map Distance × Scale Factor
$63360 \times X$ inches = 1 inch × 5,000,000
So $X = 5{,}000{,}000/63360 = 79$
Hence the Scale is 79 miles to an inch.

Problem : Express 1:10,000 as so many X inches to a mile.

First Step : Here expression is so many inches on a map to 1 mile on the ground
Hence Map Distance is unknown = X inches
Ground Distance = 1 mile = 63360 inches
Scale Factor = 10,000

Second Step : Map Distance = Ground Distance/Scale Factor
X inches = 63360/10,000 = 6.336
Scale is therefore 6.336 inches to a mile.

Use of Scale to measure Distance on Map :

We know that :

Ground Distance = Map Distance × Scale Factor
Map Distance = Ground Distance/Scale Factor

We can apply this principle to measure the distance on a map by using the scale.

Problem : Measure the width of a 50 ft. road on a map, where the Scale is 1 inch to a mile.

First Step : The Scale of the map in figure is 1:63360
The Scale Factor is 63360

Second Step : We know, Map Measurement = Ground Measurement/Scale Factor
Hence Map Measurement = 50 ft./63360 or 50 × 12 inches/63360 or
600 inches/63360 = 0.01 inch.

CONSTRUCTION OF LINE SCALE

In most of the maps where Line Scale or Linear Scale is shown, it facilitates to measure distance on the map in terms of ground distance as per Scale of the map. More the reduction or enlargement of the map does not distort the area, where the Line Scale is given. It is customary to draw Line Scale in maps, used for reproduction.

The scale line is drawn either as a single or double line, i.e. calibrated in more than one unit of length (say in miles or kilometres) and sub-divisions are marked within the line. The sub-divisions may be of two types - *major* or *minor*, but only one major sub-division is divided. This is marked at the left hand end of the scale line and zero is placed on the right hand end of this division - one unit in from the end of the scale, and the sub-divisions are numbered to read backwards from zero so that map units which are not a whole number of major units can be distinctly read. In some maps the scales are often shown 'diced' for decorative purpose, but this is not essential. Simple calibration drawn neatly can illustrate easy and more accurate readings.

For the construction of a Line Scale it becomes necessary to compute preliminary calculations. Firstly a maximum length for the Line Scale is determined within the space of the map and calculations are made to determine the greatest whole number which may fit within the available space.

Case 1 : Calculations for drawing the Line Scale having major units of one mile for map in the scale of 1:50,000. The available space on the map for the Line Scale is 7 inches long.

First Step : Compute the length of one major unit (i.e. one mile in this case) true to scale. Using the formula (Map Measurement = Ground Measurement /Scale factor), we get,
Map Measurement = 1 mile (63360 inches)/50,000 = 1.26 inch.

Second Step : At about 1.26 inches per mile 7 inches space will accommodate only four whole units. The Line Scale will therefore be of four major units, i.e. four miles long.

Third Step : Next the exact length of the Line Scale is to be calculated. By using the same formula as in First Step we get,
Map Measurement = 4 miles (253440)/50,000 = 5.07 inches
A line of length 5.07 inches is to be drawn.

Problem : Draw a comparative scale showing miles and kilometres, where R.F. is 1:50,000,000 and fit the scale in available space of 10 cm. or 4 inches on the map.

First Step : The map distance is to be determined with reference to mile. The Scale Factor is 50,000,000. Let us choose *Major division* in the unit of 1000 miles.
Say 50,000,000 inches is equal to 1 inch on the map
or 50,000,000/63360 miles is equal to 1 inch on the map
Conversely 1 mile is equal to 63360/50,000,000 inch on the map
or 1000 miles = 63360/50,000 = 1.267 inches (approx.)

Within the available space of the map we can show 2,000 miles in major and 1,000 miles in minor divisions which will cover 3 × 1.27 = 3.81 inches on the map.

Second Step : The map distance is to be determined with reference to kilometre. The Scale Factor is 50,000,000. Let us choose *Major division* in the unit of 1,000 kilometre.
Say, 50,000,000 cm. is equal to 1 cm. on the map
Or 50,000,000/1,000 km. is equal to 1 cm. on the map
Conversely 1 km. is equal to 100,000 x 1000/50,000,000 = 2 cm. on the map.

Within the available space of the map we can show 3 units of 1000 km. in major and 1 unit of 1000 km. in minor divisions (fig. 1.2).

CONSTRUCTION OF PARALLELS AND MERIDIANS

The location of any place on the earth surface is determined by latitude and longitude.

Definition of Latitude

The latitude is defined as the angular distance from the Equatorial plane. The latitude of the Equator being 0° the 40°N latitude is drawn as a line parallel to the Equator on the north, spaced at an angular distance of 40°.

Hence a line of **latitude is an imaginary line drawn around the earth parallel to the Equator and lies at a constant angular distance.** Only the Equator as a latitude appears to be great circle, whereas all other parallels are small circles.

Definition of Longitude

The longitude is defined as the angular distance in east-west direction from the Prime Meridian. The Prime Meridian has been chosen for the longitude of Greenwich and referred as 0°. It is also measured along the equatorial plane covering 360 which is divided into two hemispheres in the east and west having 180 each.

The meridian of a longitude is a line that encircles the whole sphere and passes through the poles. All meridians are great circles.

All parallels and meridians intersect at right angles.

To draw the outlines of any country or region it is necessary to construct the parallels and meridians on a flat paper true to scale. Such network or mesh is considered as geo-reference. The construction of networks of parallels and meridians is a subject of Map Projection.

On the globe the lengths of the parallels are not the same. The parallel at the Equator is a *great circle* and others are *small circles.*

The length of a parallel on a latitude $\phi°$ is expressed as $2\pi R \cos \phi°$, where R is the radius of the Reduced Earth and $\phi°$ is the latitude. The length of the Equator = $2\pi R$ (as $\cos 0° = 1$)

All meridians of longitude are great circles and equal in length. The length of any meridian is, thereby, equal to πR, where R is the radius of the Reduced Earth.

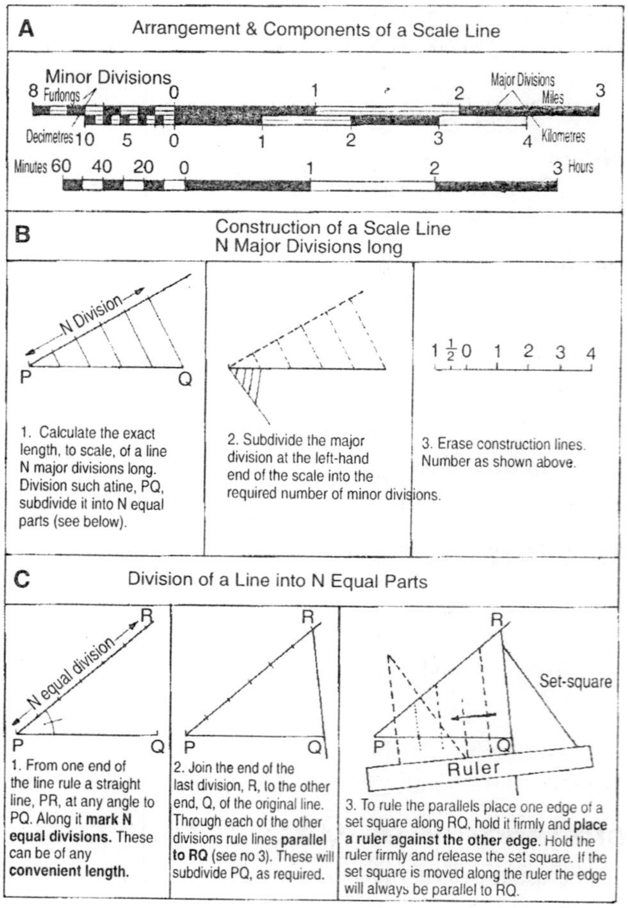

Fig. 1.2 Construction of a Line Scale

Radius of the Reduced Earth

The radius of the Reduced Earth can be computed on the basis of scale of the map. The mean radius of the earth is calculated at 3960 miles or 250,905,600 inches. For practical purpose the radius can be taken as 250,000,000 inches.

Where a map is to be drawn in the scale of 1:50,000,000 the radius of the Reduced Earth can be computed as follows :

Imagine a globe having a radius of 250,000,000 inches. As per scale 1 inch on paper will represent a length 50,000,000 inches of the globe.

50,000,000 inches on globe = 1 inch on paper

1 inch on globe = 1/50,000,000 inches on paper

250,000,000 inches on globe = (1/50,000,000 × 250,000,000 inches) on paper.

= 5 inches on paper

The radius of the Reduced Earth is thus computed to be 5 inches on a scale of 1:50,000,000.

The radius of the Reduced Earth can be simply calculated in dividing the radius of the earth (250,000,000 inches) by the Scale Factor.

Spacing of the parallels and meridians

For a map projection the network of parallels and meridians are drawn on a flat paper true to the scale of the map. The network of parallels and meridians drawn on a flat paper true to scale is called **graticule of the map**.

For parallels :

Say, the latitude is θ. Then the radius of the latitude is R cos θ.

The length of the line of latitude $\theta = 2\pi R \cos\theta$ (R is the radius of the Reduced Earth)

1° of longitude along this line = $2\pi R \cos\theta/360$

Hence, the division along the parallel for spacing the meridians = $2\pi R \cos\theta/360 \times i$ where θ = latitude and i = interval of meridians.

Standard Parallel

In a particular projection when the projection plane is supposed to touch the generating globe, the parallel drawn along the projection plane is known as **Standard Parallel**. In some cases more than one projection planes, known as developable surface can be created to touch the generating globe and more than one Standard Parallels can be drawn. In the construction of map projection the Standard Parallel is to be chosen through the meridians spaced. As the standard parallel is drawn at its correct length, the scale remains correct along this parallel. However, distortions of area, shape, distance etc. increase away from the standard parallel. This is why it is usually chosen at the middle of a given extension of the parallels of latitude, but there is no hard and fast rule in this and it can be selected at any other parallel also.

Problem 1

For the construction of a map projection choose the standard parallel at 50 N, calculate the length of the standard parallel and divide it for spacing the meridians 10 E to 70 E at 10 interval, where R.F. is 1:40,000,000.

Solution

R.F. is 1:40,000,000

The radius of the Reduced Earth = 250,000,000/40,000,000 inches

= 6.25 inches

The length of the standard parallel (50°N) = $2\pi R \times \cos 50°$

= 2 × 3.142 × 6.25 × 0.642 inches

= 25.21 inches

Division along the standard parallel for spacing the meridian

= 25.21/36 inches

= 0.7 inches

The length of the standard parallel for spacing the meridians 10°E to 70°E = 0.7 × 6

= 4.2 inches

Problem 2

Divide the central meridian for spacing the parallel 30°N to 70°N at 10° interval. Choose the central meridian for the extension of longitudes 10°E to 70°E. R.F is 1:40,000,000.

Solution

R.F. is 1:40,000,000

The radius of the Reduced Earth = 250,000,000/40,000,000 inches

= 6.25 inches

The central meridian has been chosen as 40°E.

Division along the central meridian at 10° interval = $2\pi R/36$ or $\pi R/18$ = 1.09 inches

The length of the central meridian will be 1.09 × 6 = 6.55 inches.

Problem 3

Construct graphically the graticules as stated in problems 1 & 2. Scale 1 : 40,000,000

Solution

Step 1 : Draw first the central meridian. Mark the length of the central meridian as 6.55 inches. Divide the central meridian at an interval of 1.09 inches.

Step 2 : Draw line intersecting perpendicularly through the divisions of the central meridian. The lines are spaced at equal interval of 1.09 inches and will be the parallels.

Step 3 : Mark the standard parallel as 50°N and divide it equally at an interval of 0.7 inch for spacing the meridians.

Step 4 : Mark out a boundary of the graticules neatly. Label each parallel and meridian.

Note :

The graphical construction is a simplified representation of graticules. But in the construction of different types of map projection the methods and computation of graticules will be different. We shall explain it in the following discussion on map projection.

Excercise

Q.1. *Draw a linear scale to read 2 miles in the primary division and 4 furlongs in secondary division when the given the given RF is 1:85000.*

Ans. The given RF is 1 : 85000

1 inch on map represents 85000 inch on ground

or, 1 inch represents $\frac{85000}{63360}$ miles = 1.34 miles

∵ 1.34 miles is represented by 1 inch.

1 " " " " $\frac{1}{1.34}$ inch

2 " " " " $\frac{2}{1.34}$ inch = 1.49 inch

Suppose the scale will be shown for 6 miles

∴ 3 ×1.49 = 4.47 inch is the total length of the scale.

Number of primary division = $\frac{8 \text{ miles}}{2 \text{ miles}} = 4.$

Number of secondary division = $\frac{2 \times 8 \text{ Furlongs}}{4 \text{ Furlongs}} = 4$

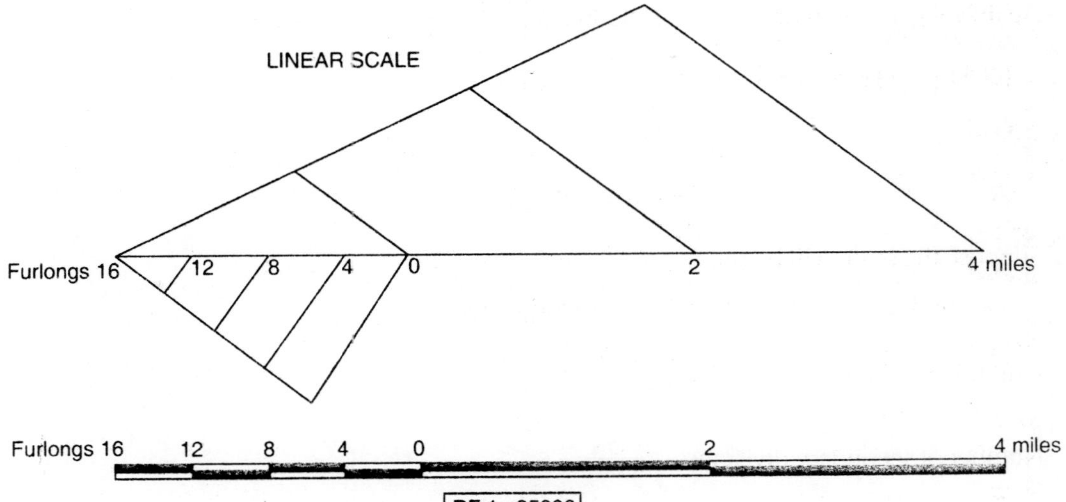

COMPARATIVE LINEAR SCALE

When two line scales showing comparable units of ground length are attached to each other, it is known as a **comparative linear scale.** This scale helps visualizing the difference in length between the comparable units such as mile and kilometre, yard and metre, inch and centimetre etc. The construction of both the scales is done on the basis of the same R.F. (representative faction); e.g. 1:63360 indicates that inch on map represents 63360 inch or 1 mile on ground, and if the same R.F. is used to determine the kilometres, it will come to 1 cm to 0.63360 km or 1.57 cm to 1 km. As we know that 2.54 cm (approx.) is equal to 1 inch, we can easily understand that 1 kilometre indicated by 1.54 cm is much smaller in length, than 1 mile shown by 1 inch. Hence understanding of the difference between various comparable units of length is easy in a comparative linear scale. Moreover, a map with a comparative linear scale showing both miles and kilometres may be readable for both USA and India who use two different systems of length units.

Q.2. *Draw a comparative linear scale to read 5 miles and 5 kms in the primary division and 1 mile and 1 km in the secondary division when the given R.F. is 1:269280.*

Ans. 1 inch represents 26980 inch = $\frac{269280}{63360}$ miles = 4.25 miles

$\because$ 4.25 miles is represented by 1 inch

1 " " " " $\frac{1}{4.25}$ inch

5 " " " " $\frac{5}{4.25}$ inch = 1.18 inch

Suppose the scale will be shown for 20 miles

$\therefore$ 4 ×1.18 = 4.72 inch is the total length of the scale.

Number of primary division = $\frac{20 \text{ miles}}{5 \text{ miles}}$ = 4.

Number of secondary division = $\frac{5 \text{ miles}}{1 \text{ miles}}$ = 5.

Again we get 1 cm representing 269280 cm $= \frac{269280}{100000}$ km = 2.69 km.

$\because$ 2.69 km is represented by 1 cm

1 " " " " $\frac{1}{2.69}$ cm

5 " " " " $\frac{5}{2.69}$ cm = 1.86 cm

Suppose the scale will be shown for 15 kms

$\therefore$ $3 \times 1.86 = 5.58$ cm is the total length of the scale.

Number of primary divisions $= \frac{15 \text{ kms}}{5 \text{ kms}} = 3.$

Number of secondary divisions $= \frac{5 \text{ kms}}{5 \text{ km}} = 5.$

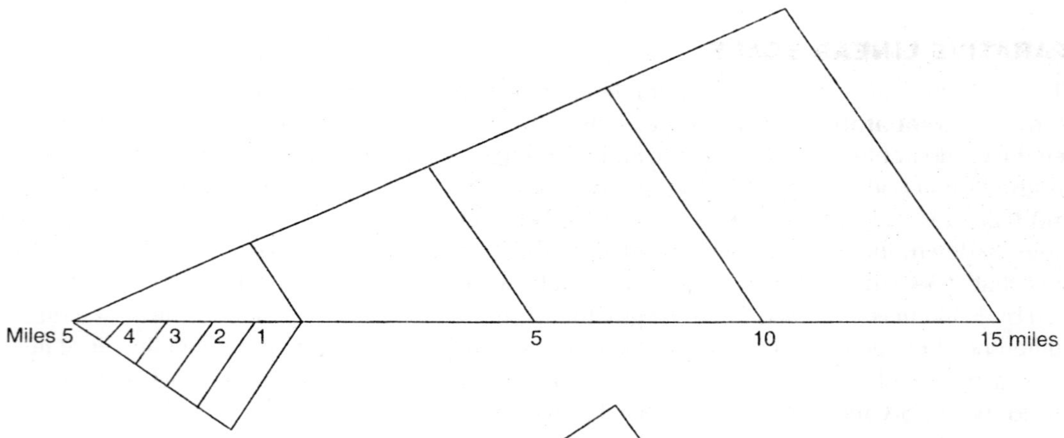

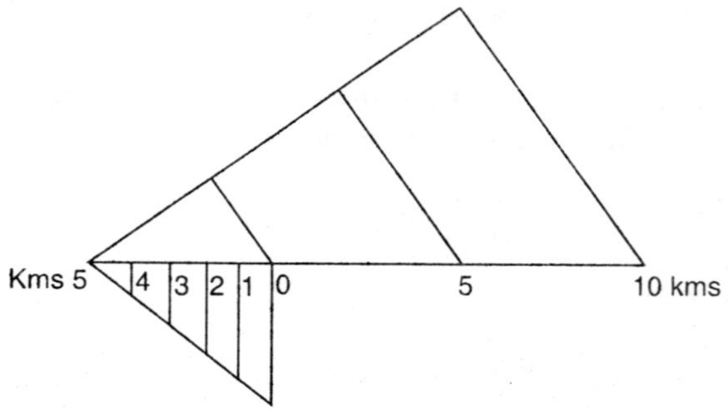

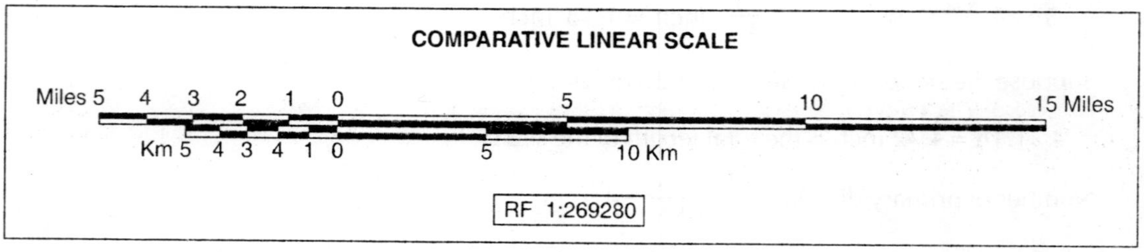

Q.3. *A map of 100 inch² has been enlarged to a size of 456 inch². If the R.F. of the original map is 1:80000, what will be the R.F. of the enlarged map? Draw a linear scale to read miles and yards on the basis of the R.F. of the enlarged map.*

Ans. A map of 100 $inch^2$ has been enlarged to a size of 456 $inch^2$.

$$\therefore \quad \frac{456 \text{ inch}^2}{100 \text{ inch}^2} = 4.56 \text{ times of enlargement has been done}$$

The R.F. of the original map is 1:80,000

$$\frac{\text{New Scale}}{\frac{1}{80,000}} = \sqrt{4.56}$$

$$\text{or, New Scale} = 2.14 \times \frac{1}{80,000}$$

$$\text{or, New Scale} = \frac{2.14}{80,000}$$

$$\therefore \text{ R.F. is } 2.14 : 80,000 = 1 : 37383.177 \approx 1 : 37383$$

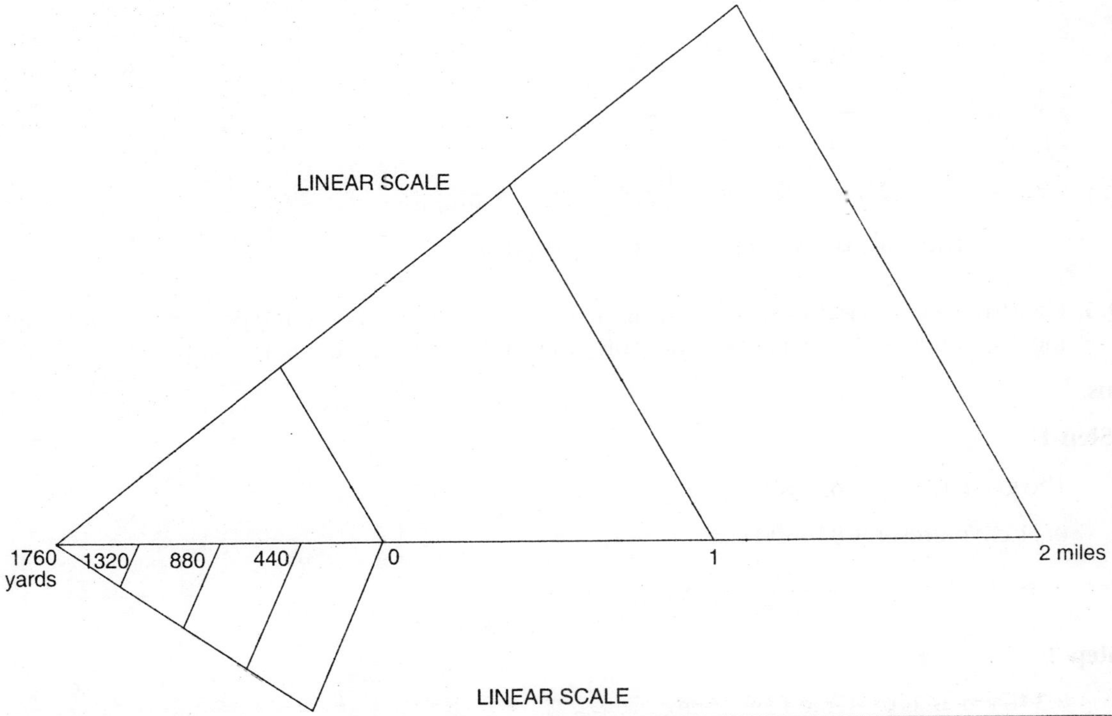

1 inch = 37383 inch $= \frac{37383}{63360}$ miles = 0.59 miles.

0.59 mile is represented by = 1 inch

1 " " " " $\frac{1}{0.59}$ inch = 1.69 inch

Suppose the scale will be shown for 4 miles

$\therefore$ 1.69 × 4 = 6.76 inch is the total length.

Number of primary divisions $= \frac{4 \text{ miles}}{1 \text{ mile}} = 4.$

Suppose the secondary division will be taken for 440 yards each

Number of secondary divisions $= \frac{1760 \text{ yards}}{440 \text{ yards}} = 4.$

Q.4. *A map of 400 cm² has been reduced to a size of 84 cm². If the scale of the original map is 1:48000, what will be the scale of the reduced map?*

Ans.

$$\frac{\text{The size of the original map}}{\text{The size of the reduced map}} = \frac{400 \text{ cm}^2}{84 \text{ cm}^2} = 4.76 \text{ time of reduction}$$

$$\frac{\text{New Scale}}{\text{Old scale}} = \frac{1}{\sqrt{4.76}}$$

$$\frac{\text{New Scale}}{\frac{1}{48{,}000}} = \frac{1}{2.18}$$

$$\text{New Scale} = \frac{1}{2.18} \times \frac{1}{48{,}000} = \frac{1}{104640}$$

$\therefore$ The scale of the reduced map is 1 : 104640

Q.5. Construct a comparative linear scale to read 10 km and 10 miles in the primary division and the 2 km and 2 miles in the secondary division when the given R.F. is 1:834600.

Ans.

Step-1

The given R.F. is 1 : 834600

or, 1 cm represents 834600 cm

$\therefore$ 1 " " $\frac{834600}{100000} = 8.346$ km.

Step-2

$\because$ 8.346 km is represented by 1 cm

1 " " " " $\frac{1}{8.346}$ "

$\therefore$ 10 " " " " $\frac{1 \times 10}{8.346} = 1.19817$ cm

Suppose the scale will be taken for 60 km.

$\therefore$ the total length of the scale $= 1.19817 \times 6 = 7.18$ cm.

Step-3

Number of primary divisions $= \frac{\overset{6}{\cancel{60}\ \cancel{km}}}{\cancel{10}\ \cancel{km}} = 6.$

Step-4

Number of secondary divisions $= \frac{\overset{5}{\cancel{10}\ \cancel{mile}}}{\cancel{2}\ \cancel{mile}} = 5.$

Calculation for the mile scale :

Step-1

The given R.F. is 1 : 834600

or, 1 inch represents 834600 inch

$\therefore$ 1 " " $\frac{834600}{63360} = 13.17234$ mile

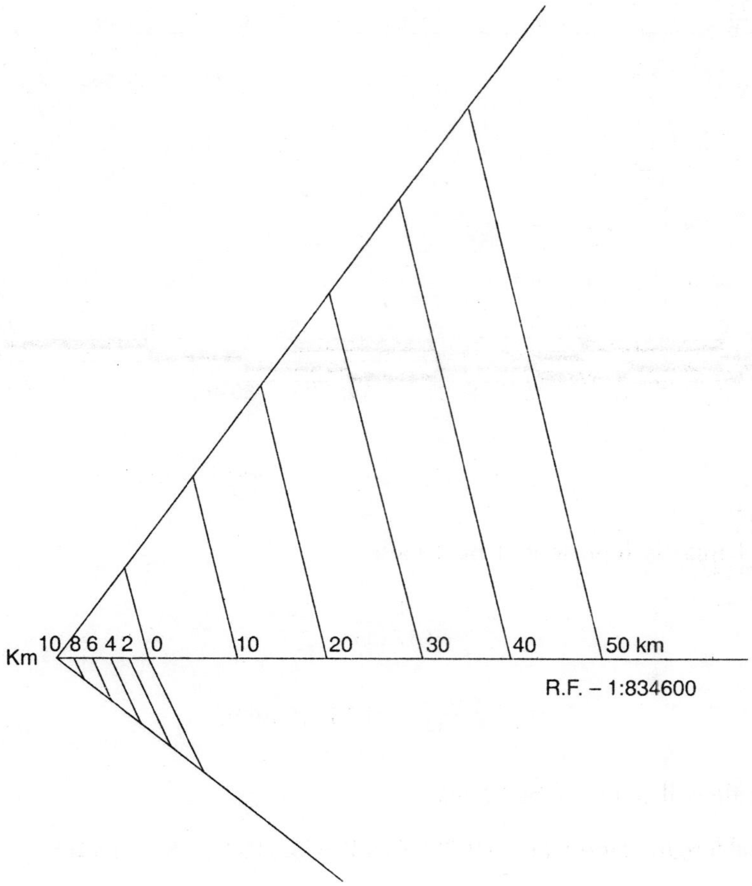

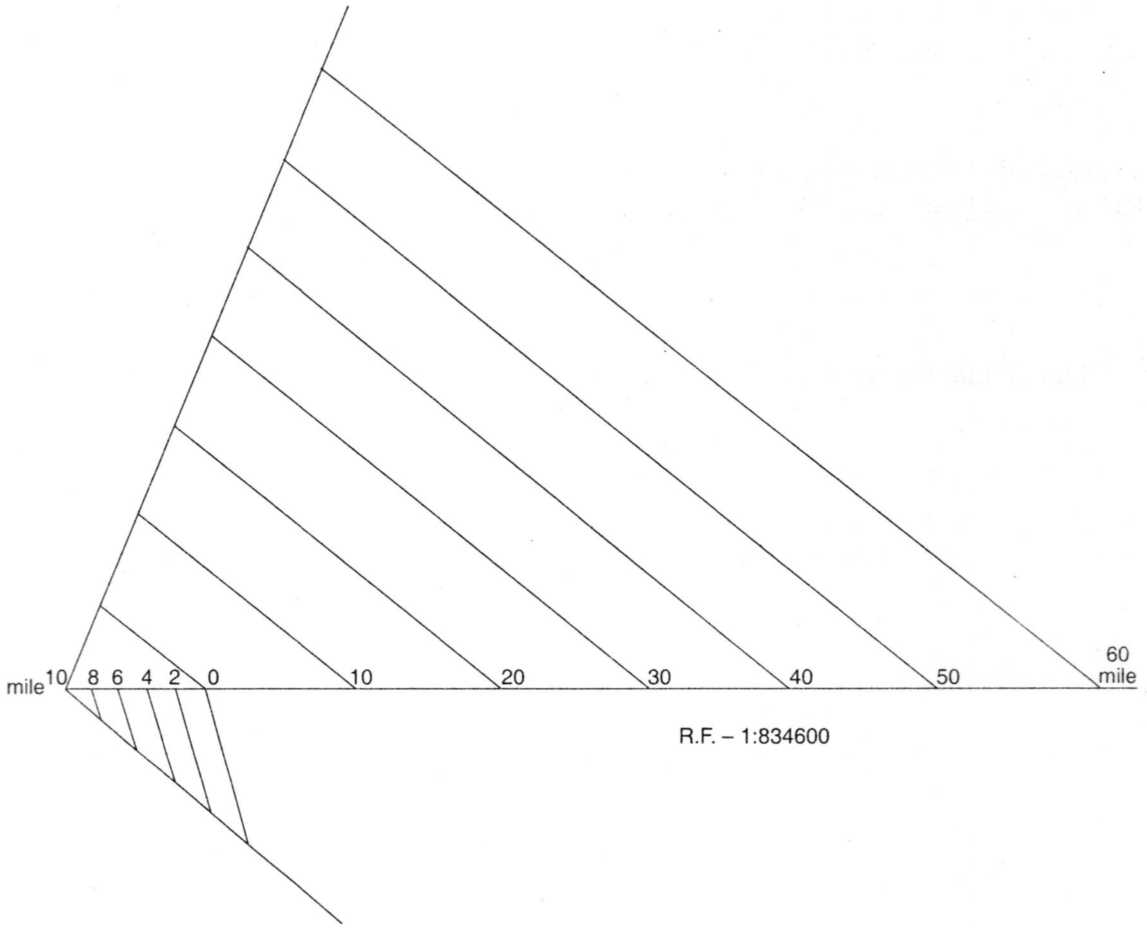

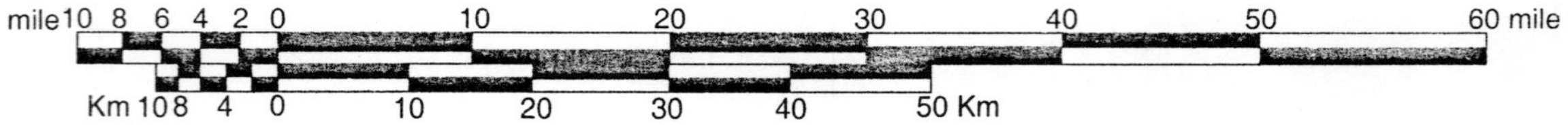

Step-2

13.17234 mile is represented by 1 inch

$\therefore$ 1 " " " " $\frac{1}{13.17234}$ "

$\therefore$ 10 " " " " $\frac{1 \times 10}{13.17234} = 0.75946$ inch.

Suppose the scale will be taken for 70 miles.

$\therefore$ the total length of the scale $= 0.75946 \times 7 = 5.31622 = 5.32$ inch

Step-3

$$\text{Number of primary divisions} = \frac{^{7}\cancel{70}\ \cancel{\text{mile}}}{\cancel{10}\ \cancel{\text{mile}}} = 7.$$

Step-4

$$\text{Number of secondary divisions} = \frac{^{5}\cancel{10}\ \cancel{\text{mile}}}{\cancel{2}\ \cancel{\text{mile}}} = 5.$$

For the advantage of drawing first, one of the two linear scales will be drawn. Then the '0' (zero) line of this scale will be extended at a further lower position so as to mark the zero line of another scale. After that take the length of one primary division of the second scale and mark the length towards left from the zero line to indicate the length of secondary divisions below the previously drawn scale. Then from the end of this primary division mark the total length of the second scale towards right across the zero line and below the previously drawn scale. Mark the divisions.

VERNIER SCALE

This is a device invented by French Cartographer Pierre Vernier to measure the fractions between the small divisions of any length or any angle measuring instrument. Many instruments used by geographers, geologists, physicists have this device attached to the instruments, such as, Theodolite, Abney's Level, Brunton Compass, Slide Calipers. Fortin's Barometer etc. Students of Geography are trained to construct the graphical method of marking this tool. The principle followed in the construction of a vernier is to divide one small division of the main scale by the number of small vernier divisions into which the length of small main scale division is equally distributed. For instance, 19 small divisions of the primary units are divided into 20 small vernier divisions. The number of vernier divisions required to find out the fractional reading left in excess of the direct reading from the main scale is obtained from :

Total reading to be shown minus Direct reading on the main scale divided by the vernier constant of the instrument, which is the difference between the value of one small main scale division and one small vernier division obtained from $^{d}/_{n}$, where d = the value of one small main scale division and n = number of vernier divisions.

Excercise

Q.1. *Construct a vernier to read 177°32′ when the degrees on the main scale is divided into 3 equal divisions and 19 small main scale divisions are equally divided into 20 small vernier divisions.*

Ans. Vernier constant $= \frac{d}{n} = \frac{20'}{20} = 1'$.

$$\text{Required number of vernier divisions} = \frac{\text{Total reading} - \text{Direct main scale reading}}{\text{V.C.}}$$

$$= \frac{177°32' - 177°20'}{1'}$$

$$= \frac{12'}{1'} = 12$$

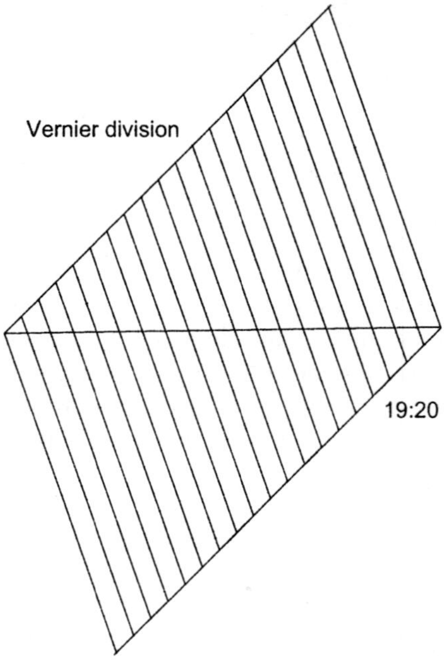

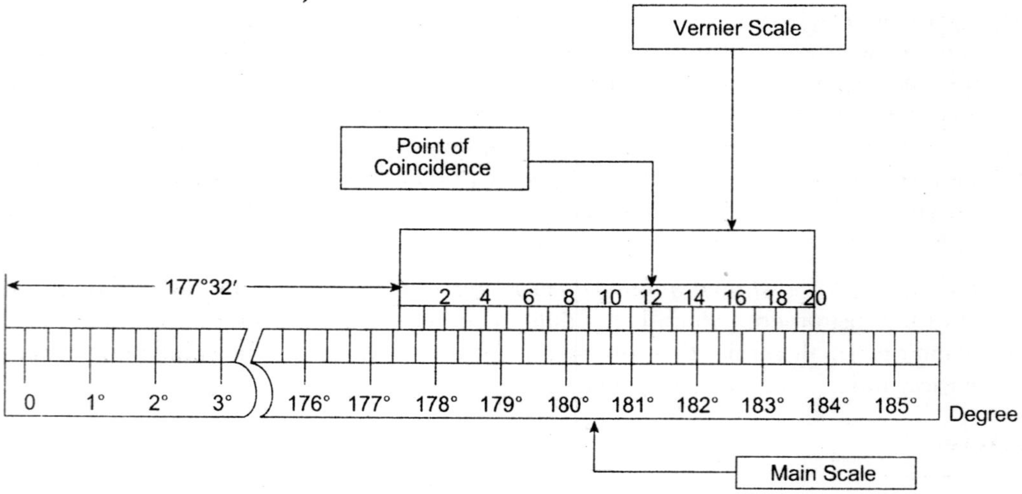

Q.2. *Draw a linear vernier to read 7.40625 inch when the least count of the main scale in 1/8 part of an inch and 19 small main scale divisions are divided into 20 equal vernier divisions.*

Ans. Vernier constant = $\frac{0.125''}{20} = 0.00625''$.

$$\text{Required number of vernier divisions} = \frac{7.40625'' - 7.375''}{0.00625''}$$

$$= 5$$

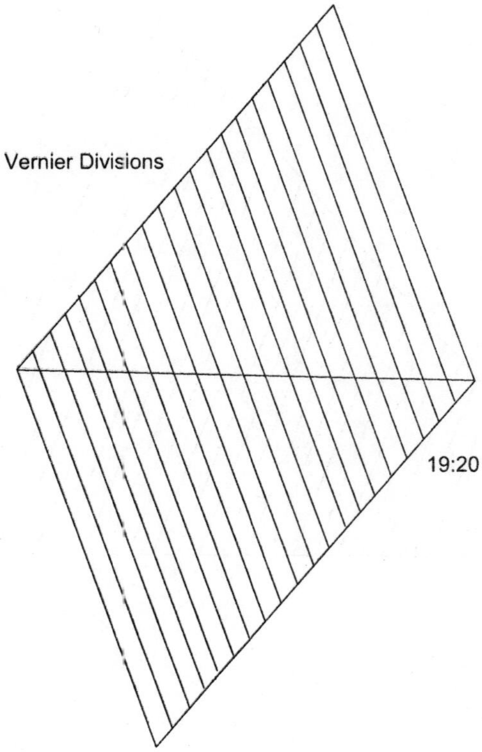

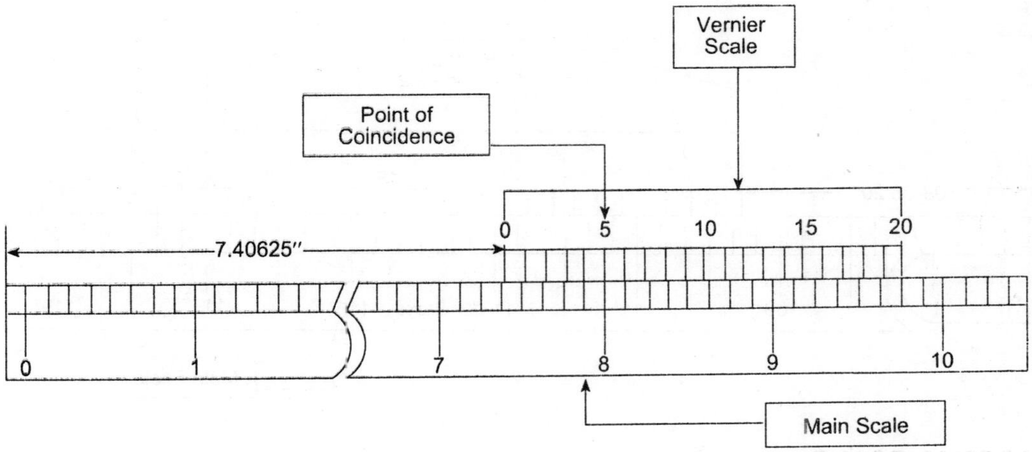

Q.3. *Construct a vernier where the least count of the main scale is 20′ and the least count of the vernier is 19′20″. Show a reading 109°35′20″. Find out the number of vernier divisions also.*

Ans. Vernier constant = 20′ – 19′20″ = 40″

$$\text{Number of vernier divisions} = \frac{20'}{40''} = \frac{20' \times 60}{40''} = \frac{1200''}{40''} = 30 = \frac{109°35'20'' - 109°20'}{40''}$$

$$\text{Required number of verner division} = \frac{15'20''}{40''} = \frac{(15' \times 60) + 20''}{40''} = \frac{920''}{40''} = 23$$

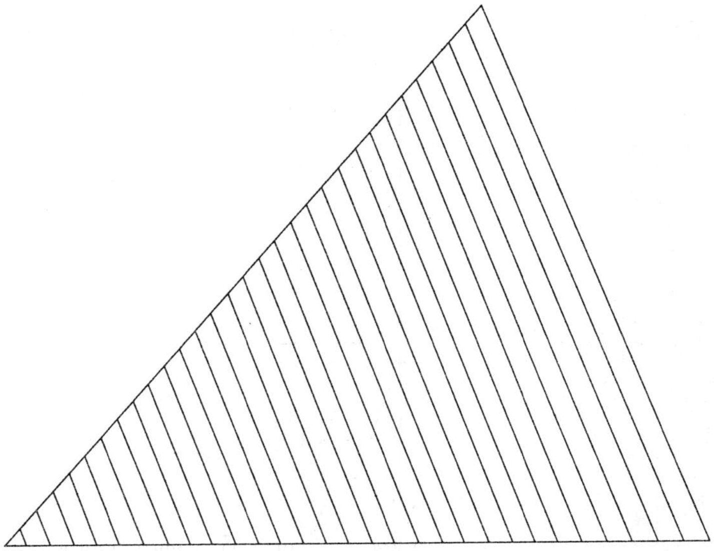

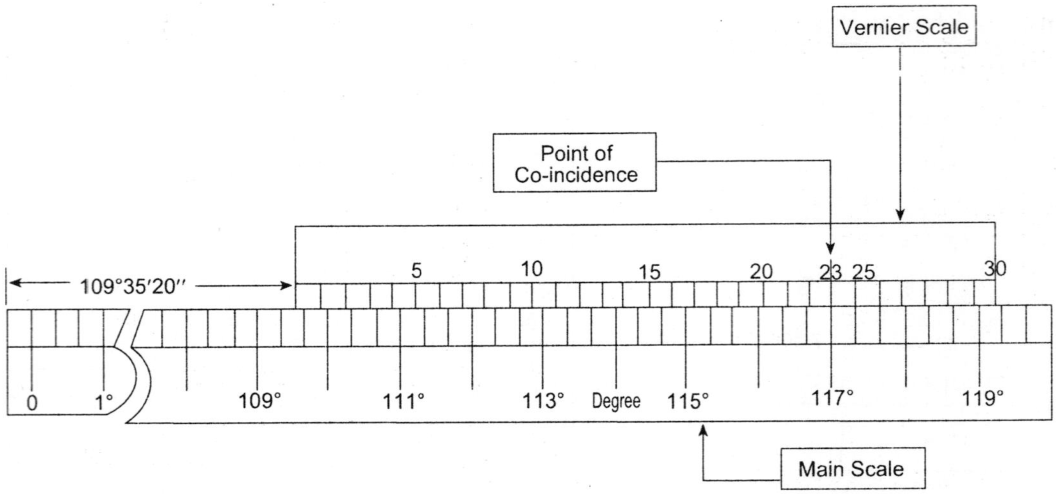

DIAGONAL SCALE

It is a graphical scale in which one primary division is divided into $^{1}/_{100}$th parts in the tertiary divisions, which are marked along the diagonals of the secondary divisions. Various small units, such as, inches, centimetres can be shown on this instrument. Hypothetically, considering various R.F. values, many other units can be shown on this instrument which are then known as composite diagonals.

Q.1. *Draw a diagonal scale to read 2.68 miles when the given R.F. is 1:63360.*

Ans. The given R.F. is 1: 63360

or, 1 inch represents $\frac{63360}{63360}$ = 1 mile

1 mile is represented by 1 inch

∴ 2.68 " " " 1 × 2.68 = 2.68 inch.

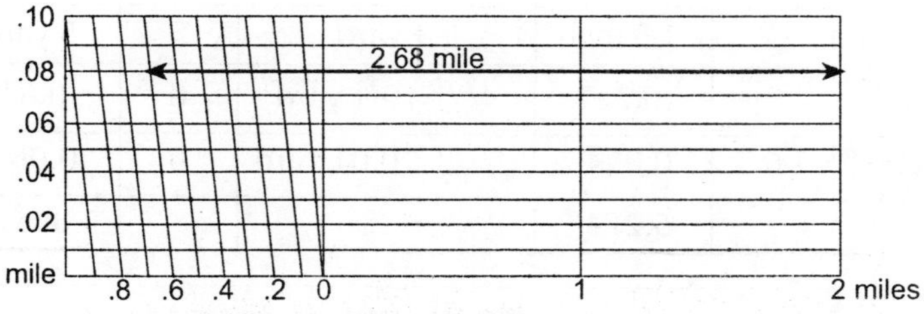

R.F. = 1:63,360

Q.2. *Draw a diagonal scale to read 3.47 inches when R.F. 1:1.*

Ans.

Division	Length	Units	Total
Primary	1 inch	3	3 inch
Secondary	$\frac{1}{10}'' = 0.1''$	4	0.4 inch
Tertiary	$\frac{0.1}{10}'' = 0.01''$	7	0.07 inch
			3.47 inch

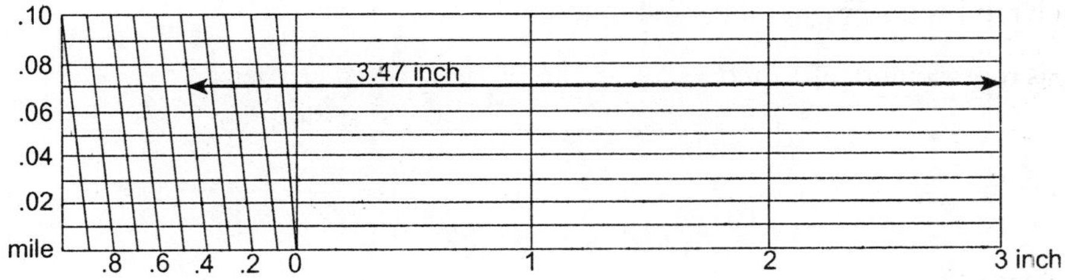

R.F. = 1:1

Q.3. *Draw a diagonal scale to show 5 yard 2 feet 7 inches, when the given R.F. is 1:40.*

Ans. The given R.F. is 1: 40

∴, 1 inch represents $\frac{40}{36}$ yard = 1.11 yard. (∵ 1 yard = 36")

5 yard 2 feet 7 inches = 5 yard + 0.67 yard + 0.19 yard = 5.86 yard.

1.11 yard is represented by 1 inch.

∴ 1 " " " " $\frac{1}{1.11}$ inch = 0.9 inch.

∴ 5.86 " " " " $\frac{5.86}{1.11}$ inch = 5.27 inch.

Table for distribution of units :

Division	Length	Units	Total	Value	Units	Total
Primary	0.9 inch	5	4.5 inch	1 yard	5	5 yard
Secondary	$0.9/10'' = \dot{0}.09''$	8	0.72″	$1/10'' = 0.1$ yard	8	0.8 ″
Tertiary	$0.09/10'' = 0.009''$	6	0.054″	$0.1/10'' = 0.01$ yard	6	0.06 ″
			5.274″			5.86 yard

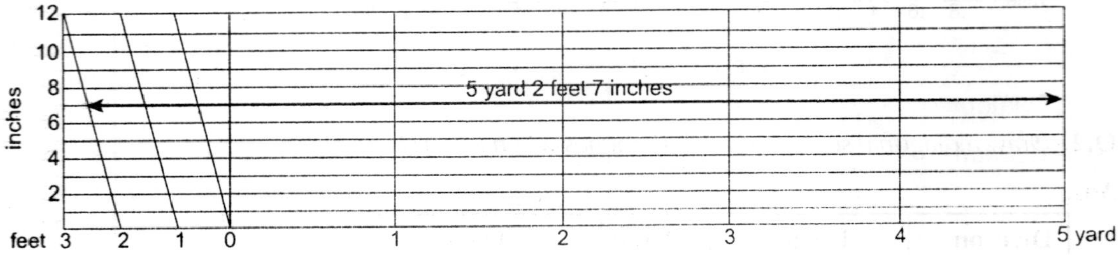

R.F. = 1 : 40

Q.4. *Draw a composite diagonal scale to read 1.4375 mile, when the given R.F. is 1:25344 and 1 inch is divided into 32 tertiary divisions.*

Ans. The given R.F. is 1:25344

Or, 1 inch represents $\frac{25344}{63360}$ mile = 0.4 mile.

0.4 mile is represented by 1 inch.

∴ 1 " " " " $\frac{1}{0.4}$ inch.

∴ 1.4375 " " " " $\frac{1.4375}{0.4}$ inch = 3.59375″.

Distribution of units :

Division	Length	Units	Total	Value	Units	Total
Primary	1 inch	3	3 inch	0.4 mile	3	1.2 mile
Secondary	$1\text{ inch}/4 = 0.25''$	2	0.50″	$0.4/4'' = 0.1$ mile	2	0.2″
Tertiary	$1\text{ inch}/32$ = 0.03125	3	0.09375″	$0.4/32$ mile = 0.0125	3	0.0375 ″
			3.59375 inch			1.4375 mile

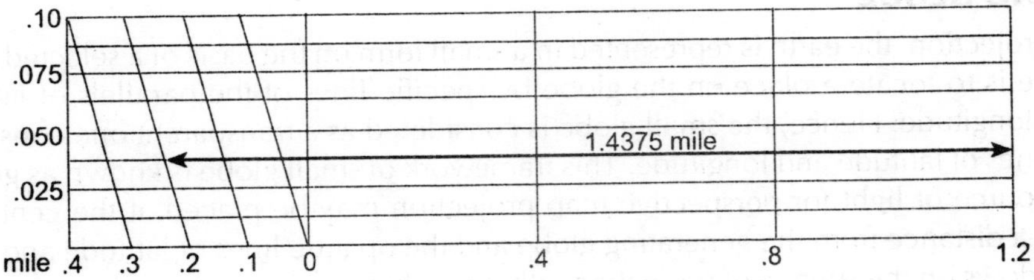

R.F. : 1.25344

Q.5. *Draw a diagonal scale to show 3 kilometres 8 hectometers 90 metres, when the given R.F. is 1:50,000.*

Ans. The given R.F. is 1:50,000

$\therefore$ 1 cm = $\frac{50,000}{10,0000}$ km = 0.5 km.

3 kilometre 8 hectometre 90 metres = 3.89 km.

0.5 km is represented by 1 cm on the map.

$\therefore$ 1 " " " " $\frac{1}{0.5}$ " " " "

$\therefore$ 3.89 " " " " $\frac{3.89}{0.5}$ " " " "

= 7.78 cm.

Distribution of units :

Division	Length (cm)	Units	Total (cm)	Value (km)	Units	Total
Primary	2	3	6	1	3	3
Secondary	$^{2}/_{10} = 0.2$	8	1.6	$^{1}/_{10} = 0.1$	8	.8
Tertiary	$^{0.2}/_{10} = 0.02$	9	0.18	$^{0.1}/_{10} = 0.01$	9	0.09
			7.78			3.89

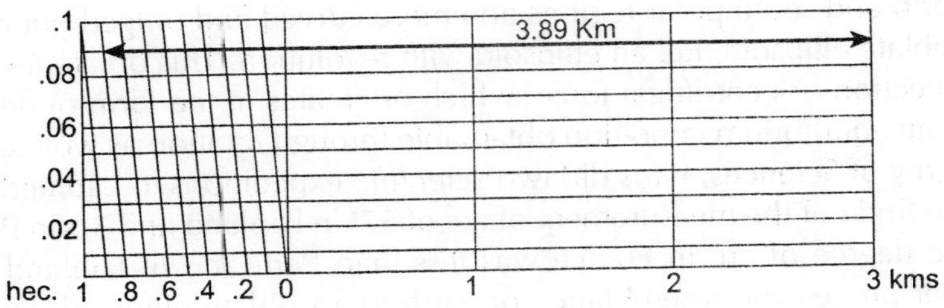

R.F. : 1:50,000

GENERATING GLOBE

In map projection, the earth is represented in a small form on the basis of a selected scale. The basic purpose is to locate a place on the globe by specific lines of the parallels of latitude and meridians of longitude. Hence, the small globe is considered as a transparent one constructed by the opaque lines of latitude and longitude. This framework of small globe is known as **generating globe**. The source of light for perspective map projection may be placed at the centre, on the surface, or at a distance from the generating globe and the opaque lines of latitude and longitude cast their shadows on the surface of projection, otherwise known as developable surface.

Geoid and Spheroid

In early times of Greek period, people did not have a specific idea about the shape of the earth. During 3rd Century B.C. Eratosthenes, the famous Greek philospher and mathematician considered that the earth has a speherical form through a direct measurement of the supposed angle between Syene of Egypt and Alexandria on the basis of the angle formed by the rays of the mid day (noon) sun. This angle was 7°12′ which he supposed as 150th part of the circumference of the earth. The distance between Alexandria and Syene was about 5000 stadia (1 stadium equivalent to 185m). However, two other Greeks of high reputation, Pythagoras (540 B.C.) and Aristotle (384-322 B.C.) believed that the shape of the earth is spherical. Eratosthenes' measurement was an astronomical method. Much later, from Sir Isaac Newton we came to understand that the shape of the earth is slightly bulged out in the middle or equatorial part, whereas the polar regions of north and south are slightly flat.

The French astronomer Jean Richer was sent to one of the islands of French Guiana, the island of Cayenne, to compute some astronomical measurements concerning the shape of the earth. This island is located close to the equator. He was technically equiped with a clock which was adjusted in such a way as its 99.4 cm. long pendulum could beat the exact seconds to be shown in Paris. Jean Richer noted that where he arrived on the island of Cayenne, the clock was losing about $2^1/_2$ minutes a day. This deviation was considered as a lower force of gravity close to the equator. He then realised that the equatorial part of the earth is more distant than its northerly locations. He applied the following formula for his measurement :

$$\cos \alpha = \frac{R}{R + h}$$

[Where,
α = the angular distance in degrees;
R = the earth's radius;
h = the height above earth's surface in same units of measurement as for the radius.]

Richer's observations were confirmed through similar measurements of further refined nature. Such measurements altogether indicate that the earth is not truly a spherical globe, rather a compressed north and south polar regions and more curved and bulged out equatorial region marked it as an oblate ellipsoid, i.e. an ellipsoid with revolution. This oblateness is explained by the course of deflection or centrifugal force, which originates in the form of deformation of the plastic earth into an equilibrium condition obtainable through rotation as well as force of gravity. The Royal Academy of Sciences, Paris did two scientific expeditions to Lapland in 1736-37 and to Peru in 1735 to find out the measurement of arc of 57′ in Lapland and 3° in Peru respectively. The length of the degree of arc in France was less than Peru and in Lapland still lesser. This experiment further proved the resemblance of earth to an oblate ellipsoid. Finally, the earth's equatorial diameter was determined to be 12,757 km (7927 miles) and length of polar axis to be

12,714 km. (7900 miles). The equatorial circumference is determined as 40075 km (24900 miles) [Strahler, 1975].

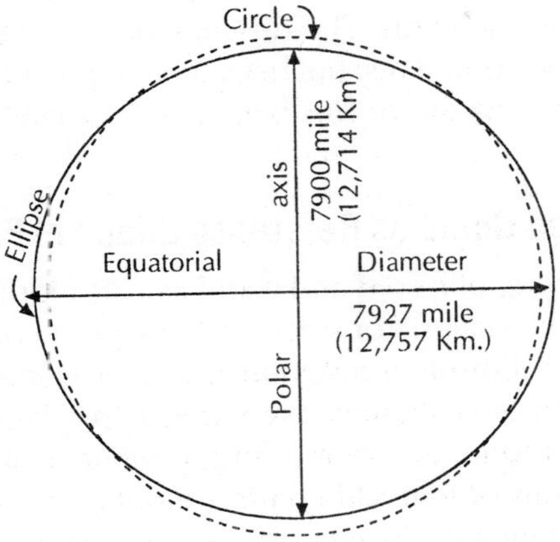

Slightly Elliptical Shape of the Earth in a Cross Section passing through the Polar Axis (Hayford, 1909), in Strahler, 1975

This concept of oblate ellipsoid describes the earth in a better way than a complete sphere, but geodesists and cartographers are not totally statisfied with this form because the earth's surface is much irregular with huge depressions in oceans and much elevations in continents. A better expression is considered to be a **geoid**. A geoid deviates from a perfectly symmetrical ellipsoid. This geoid indicating an earth-like-figure is distinguished from an ellipsoid because of its irregular surface. It is a three dimensional shape which is averaged by mean sea level in the oceans. It is imagined that series of canals at sea level criss cross under the continents like tunnels, as if even in the heart of continents the sea level exists . In some parts of the earth where the elevation is low, the plumb lines may intersect at a much smaller radius of the earth, whereas at some others, the plumb lines intersect at a much greater radius than that of the earth. Thus the plumb line deviates from the true vertical direction from the zenith to the centre of the earth.

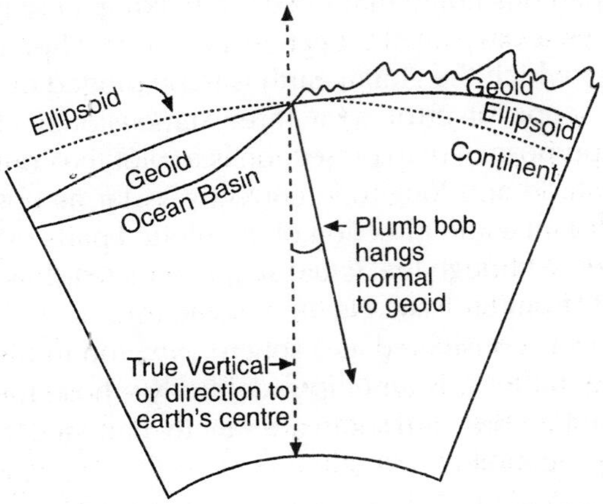

Relative Positions of Geoid and Ellipsoid are reversed from Ocean Basin to Continent

In the continental areas, there is much excess of rock mass with reference to the sea level surface, whereas in the oceanic areas there is much less rock mass and sea level is only reached by ocean water which is less dense. Hence, the force of gravity at the sea level surface is greater than it is in the continents. This course of undulations of the earth's surface considers it a geoid which is an irregular form like the earth. The distance obtained between geoid and ellipsoid is meagre, only 20-30 m. over the continents, but between the polar and equatorial diameters of two forms, it is about 43 km. The variation occurs because of variable density of rocks and variable relief forms.

Use of Sphere, Ellipsoid and Geoid as Reference Shape of Earth

These three shapes of sphere, ellipsoid and geoid as earth-form are used as reference form at the time of mapping on different scales. For small scale maps of countries, regions, continents the difference between sphere and ellipsoid is insignificant. Hence, spherical equations for drawing of a particular map projection give almost same results between sphere and ellipsoid and small scale maps can safely use the earth-form as sphere. On the other hand, when large scale maps like topographic sheets, preparations of nautical charts are done, the difference between spheroidal and ellipsoidal forms are significant. So in order to get nearly correct measurements in map projections, for distance, area and direction, the ellipsoid as earth-form in considered for computation of latitude and lognitude as well as elevation through GPS fixing salellite receivers. However, in such cases World Geodetic System 84, ellipsoid is taken as the reference surface of the earth. The reference surface of geoid is considered for ground surveying determining horizontal and vertical postions, but when a map projection is done, ellipsoid surface is usable as a geoid form would make the mathematical calculations unnecessarily complex. In this context, it may be noted that cartographers use both sphere and ellipsoid as having the same area of surface. This reference sphere is otherwise known as authalic sphere.

Coordinate Systems

The concept of the shape of the earth initially came into the mind of people during the Greek Period. About 250 BC Eratosthenes, the librarian of the Library of Alexandria determined the circumference of the earth to be 28750 miles, 25000 Stadia on the basis of the location of the noon sun. This figure is only about 15% greater than the actual. The shape of the earth was considered to be a sphere. However, Hipparchus noted that the earth making a complete revolution within 24 hours rotates for 360 degrees a day, i.e. 15 degrees per hour. Hipparchus also developed the concept of map projection in which the global earth is to be plotted on a flat sheet of paper. Map projection itself has some scope of error as a three dimensional globe is plotted on a two dimensional flat plane. The purpose of map projection is to plot the continental and oceanic areas on a network of lines of latitude and longitude correctly as far as possible. Errors occur in the correctness of shape, size, distance and direction of the plotted parts of the earth's surface as well as of the network of graticules. Although the actual shape of the earth is to some extent ellipsoidal which was known afterwards from Sir Isaac Newton, sometimes in 1670, for the purpose of map projection initially the earth was considered as a sphere. Newton in his theory of gravity marked that the earth is not a sphere, rather it is an ellipsoidal body whose middle or equatorial part to some extent bulges out and polar north and south are slightly flattened. He also calculated the rate of flattening by the following equation :

$\varepsilon = E - P/E$ [ε = Amount of flattening; E = Equatorial radius; P = Polar radius]

$$= \frac{6378.1370 \text{ km} - 6356.7523 \text{ km}}{6378.1370 \text{ km}}$$

$$= 0.00335281289$$

However, flattening is expressed as 1/ε. Hence, the amount of flatten ng is 1/0.00335281289 = 298.26. Thus the bulging in the equatorial part produces the flattening at the north pole and south pole as 1/298 of the radius of the equatorial part.

Geographical Coordinates

During the Greek Period of 2nd century B.C. Hipparchus introduced the knowledge of geographical coordinate system for the location of a place through the concept of latitude and longitude measureable on the equatorial plane considering the earth as a sphere. The crossing of one line of latitude, which is a circular horizontal line, with one line of longitude, which s a semicircle connecting two poles, drawn as a vertical line on a flat plane.

The lines of latitude and longitude are determined on the basis of north-south and east-west angular distance from the centre of the earth on the equatorial plane.

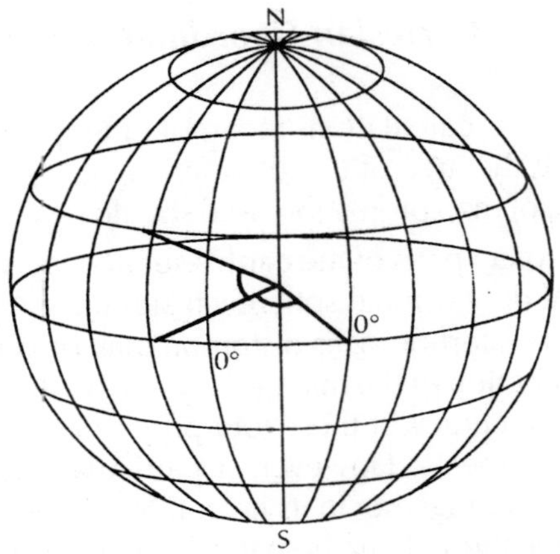

Geographical Coordinates

Plane Coordinate System

As we know, the location of a point on a plane can be determined on the basis of vertical and horizontal distance of the point from a known reference point, plane coordinate system uses a graph with a net of vertical and horizontal lines. Plane coordinate system may be discussed under two subtitles : Cartesian coordinates and Rectangular coordinates.

Cartesian coordinates

In this coordinate system there is a known natural origin which is the initial point of the coordinates. From this point towards left and right and above and below the distance of a point varies unitwise. At the origin on a plane, the two axes intersect each other perpendicularly . The horizontal axis is known as 'X' axis or abscissa, and the vertical axis is known as 'Y' or ordinate. The origin being 0, 0 the distance changes with positive or negative sign. The square nets formed at the four quadrants mark a point on any of the quadrants having a combination of signs. The quadrants are numbered I, II, III, IV in an anticlock-wise direction start ng from the northeastern quadrant. Thus for quadrant I, X and Y values are '++', for quadrant II it is '–+', for quadrant III '– –' and for quadrant IV '+ –'. In the given figure, point P is having a value of 2,3 ; for point Q it is –2, 2; for point R it is 3, –3.

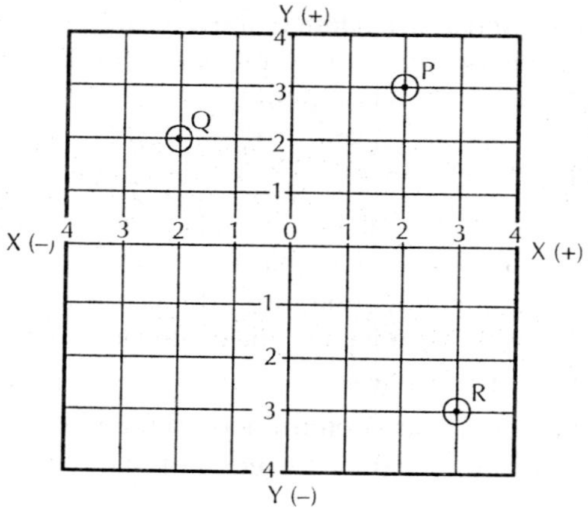

Cartesian Coordinates

Although the earth is a sphere, calculations incorporating spherical character is not necessary for small distance on maps . If the area of calculation is large which requires the accuracy, the distortions inherent in the type of map projection used should be considered.

Map projections plot or project parts of the earth's surface, oceanic or continental or both, on a flat plane. Projecting a three dimensional sphereical surface on a two dimensional flat surface naturally includes the scope of distortion. This distortion may be observed in connection with the actual area, shape, size and direction of the mapped surface on the real globe. A particular type of map projection maintains the accuracy of these four properties, though none of them can really avoid distortion in these four aspects. However, a particular projection tries to maintain the accuaracy of one or two properties together in its layout. Necessary corrections for distance, area, shape and direction can be done through mathematical calculations.

Rectangular Coordinates

Rectangular co-ordinate system in its properties is almost similar with that of cartesian coordinate system, only the plane on which the coordinates are drawn is limitless and it does not have a natural reference point as its origin. Here, each of the points are similar in nature. In this coordinate system too perpendicular axes X and Y determine the location of a point. For the purpose of using such rectangular coordinate system, initially the spherical surface of the globe is plotted on a map projection. Then an abitrary rectangular coordinate system is placed on the projection net of graticules. This net of perpendicular lines should be necessarily referred to a place of origin which is the centre of interest on the mapped area. X and Y axes should coincide with the lines of parallels of latitude and meridians of longitude. Then the location of a place will be obtained on the basis of X and Y values. As the grids of X and Y lines may be some distance apart, the location between two such consecutive horizontal and vertical gridlines can be determined by dividing the distance into decimal values. Thus, a pinpoint location can be obtained. To designate a particular location grid reference can be given for X and Y coordinate with a six figure reference number of which the first three indicate easting and second three indicate northing. Students using grid references should always keep in mind the thumb rule 'right up'. The last one of the first three digits is a decimal value. Similarly, the last one of the northing values is decimal in nature.

This coordinate system may give a false origin where no negative value is obtained. To do so only the upper right hand quadrant is used to locate a place. Hence, it gives a false easting and a false northing. Such grids are normally done at an interval of 1000 metres. This grid system has been very useful for the purpose of war where pinpoint locations are necessary. Thus we often refer to them as military grids which are found plotted on topographic sheets.

Polar Coordinates

Polar coordinate system is also a two dimensional coordinate system. It involves the location of a point on a plane as determined by its distance from a reference point or origin and the angle obtained from the reference direction. The reference point here is known as the pole and the reference direction is known as the polar axis. The difference of this coordinate system from that of the Cartesian or Rectangular coordinate system is the use of angular direction of the location from the pole. If we present this concept diagramatically, it is somewhat of the following figure.

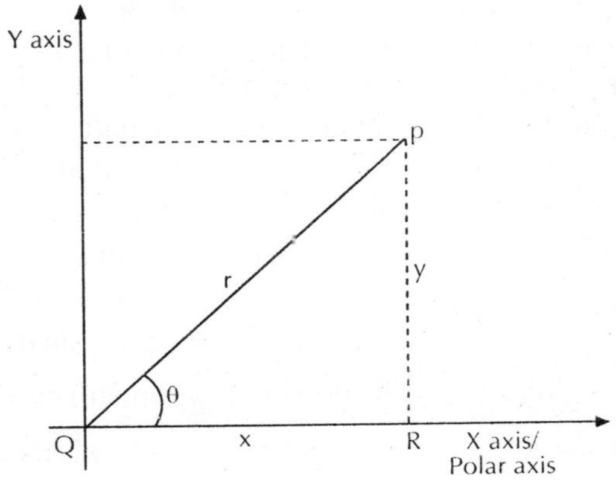

Polar Coordinates

In Cartesian coordinate, the location of point P is simply determined by the values of X and Y. In this Polar coorcinate system, it is r, θ (in radian), as radian is the value of an angle subtended within an arc which is a part of a sphere.

In the ΔPQR, PR is determined by r Sinθ, whereas QR is r cosθ in which sin θ = y/r or RP/r and cos θ = x/r or QR/r. The distance of point P from pole in the reference direction is known as the polar axis and the angle θ is known as angular coordinate, or polar angle or azimuth, whereas the distance of P from the pole is the radial distance or simply radius.

Conversion of Cartesian coordinate to Polar Coordinate

The conversion from Cartesian coordinates to Polar coordinates can be done as X, Y of Cartesian coordinates is r, θ in Polar coordinates, where r is a distance and θ is an angle. Hence, the following formulae (Robinson et. al., 1995) can be used to do so.

On the basis of simple calculation, the location and direction of points with respect to origin can be determined. A distance between two points on the net of cartesian coordinate system can be obtained by two values of X and Y each and the computation can be done with the help of the following formula:

$$d = \{(X_1 - X_2)^2 + (Y_1 - Y_2)^2\}^{1/2}$$

For getting the direction of one point from another the angular distance can be calculated on the basis of the following formula :

$$\tan\theta = \{(Y_1 - Y_2)/(X_1 - X_2)\}, \text{ i.e. } Y/X$$

Rotation of Coordinate System

The axes of coordinate system, say Cartesian coordinates can be rotated on the basis of ϕ angle . With reference to the origin and location of a point P whose location has been determined in Cartesian coordinates, the rotation of X and Y axis may be assumed. The concept can be made clear on the basis of the following diagram

Here the X axis as well as Y axis has rotated for an angle of θ in counter clockwise direction and thus the position of X, Y changes to X′, Y′. However, the point of origin 0 in Cartesian coordinates and P are fixed.

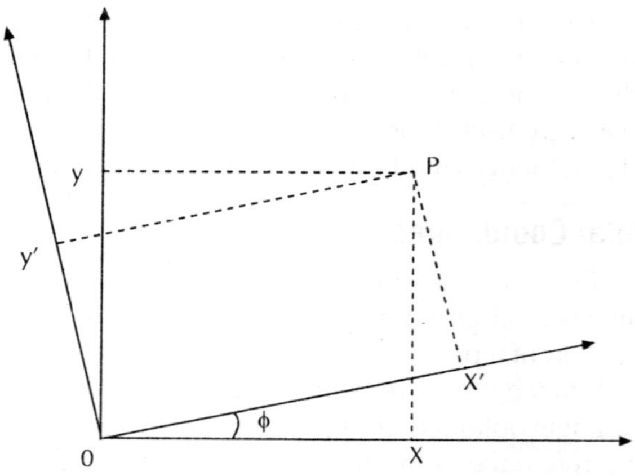

As we know in Polar coordinates it was r, θ, in this new rotated system of X′, Y′, the location of P should have Polar coordinates r, $\theta - \phi$. Previously, we had $X = r \cos \theta$............ (i), and $y = r \sin \theta$ ....(ii).

$x' = r \cos (\theta - \phi) = r \cos \theta \cos \phi + r \sin \theta \sin \phi$ .... (iii)

$y' = r \sin (\theta - \phi) = r \sin \theta \cos \phi + r \cos \theta \sin \phi$ .... (iv)

Substituting the equations (i) and (ii) into equations (iii) and (iv) we get :

$$x' = x \cos \phi + y \sin \phi$$
$$y' = -x \sin \phi + y \cos \phi$$

WGS 84 and its use

To determine correct locations on a spheroidal earth, the equatorial radius at two points A and B on the basis of plumb line of geodetic survey, repeated measurements have been done since 1830, the geodetic survey done by George Everest (1823-1843), the then Surveyor General of India. However, World Geodetic System done in 1984 is basically a global datum indicating that the coordinates may change over time for the objects which remain fixed in the ground. Such changes of coordinates occur because the tectonic plates move. New Zealand, for instance, moves constantly at a slow rate. The speciality of WGS 84 is that the co-ordinates of this system also change constantly and are known as dynamic co-ordinates. Multiple realisations of data are thus obtained for WGS 84. According to WGS 84 ellipsoid datum realisations obtained on different dates from 1984 are as follows :

Datum Realisation	Implemenation Date	Reference Epoch	Network Accuracy in m. Relative to ITRF, 2008
WGS 84	1987, 1st January	NA	1– 2
WGS 84	1994, 29th June	1994.0	0.10
WGS 84	1997, 29th January	1997.0	0.05
WGS 84	2002, January	2001.0	0.01
WGS 84	2012, 8th February	2005.0	0.01
WGS 84	2013, 16th October	2005.0	0.01

Source : www.linz.govt.nz/data

The measurements done for determining the equatorial and polar radius have been carried out repeatedly from the beginning of 19th century to the present. More than 20 measurements were made. Those have shown slight variation of the two radii. The ratio of polar flattening obviously varied too. The following table incorporates a few of such results of calculations for equatorial and polar radius and also includes the changing obtained ratio of flattening.

Title of Measurement	Year	Equatorial Radius (m)	Polar Radius (m)	Ratio of Polar Flattening
WGS 84	1984	6378137	6356752.3	1/298.257
WGS 72	1972	6378135	6356750.5	1/298.26
Australian	1965	6378160	6356774.7	1/298.25
Krasovsky	1940	6378245	6356863	1/298.3
Clarke	1880	6378249.1	6356514.9	1/293.46
Airy	1830	6377563.4	6356256.9	1/299.32
Everest	1830	6377276.3	6356075.4	1/300.8

[Source : J. Snyder, Map Projections — A working Manual in Elements of Cartography; 6th ed.; Robinson et. al.]

DEFINING AND DETERMINING POSITION

Defining position by Latitude and Longitude

The position of a place can be simply defined by latitude and longitude. In normal practice latitude is stated first, then comes the longitude. The latitude and longitude of a place can be expressed in the units of degree, minutes and seconds. All maps including the topographical maps usually indicate latitudes and longitudes. It becomes advantageous particularly in the fieldwork where the location of a place appears to be significant. With the help of a toposheet, either in the scale of 1:50,000 or 1:63,360 it is possible to locate a place by latitude and longitude though the values obtained are not absolutely correct and only approximate values can be obtained. Conversely the location of any unknown place can be indicated by the values of latitude and longitude from the map. In recent years the application of Global Positioning System (G.P.S.) has become important tool in defining a position in the field with reference to latitude and longitude.

Difficulties in defining position by latitude and longitude

Except in the field of navigation or some other fields where latitude and longitude are used in determining the position directly, the use of latitude and longitude in defining a position is not very common. The difficulties are faced as the maps on their margins indicate upto five or 2.5 units of minutes. So the estimation of a second, sixtieth part of a minute appears to be a practical difficulty. Moreover, the latitudes and longitudes are shown on the margins of the map. To determine a place inside the map one will have to draw coordinates from the margin. Direct determination by latitude and longitude from the map will not be possible. Another difficulty is confronted particularly in the small scale maps, where latitudes and longitudes are represented not as straight lines but as various curved lines due to different construction of map projections.

Grids and Grid References

The difficulties in defining a position from a map by latitude and longitude can be conveniently understood by the use of Grid references. Many topographical sheets show Grid references for practical uses. The principle of laying the grids is simple. Within any rectangular area, such as a blackboard the position of a point can be shown with reference to distance from the left hand edge of the blackboard, and up from the base of the blackboard. In the construction of grids also two base lines are drawn, which are called *axes* of the grid. The intersections of these baselines is termed ***origin***. The distances to the east and north of the base line determine the position. These distances east and north are respectively called ***eastings*** and ***northings***, while the eastings and northings of a point are collectively called its ***co-ordinates***. For a six figure grid reference the first three will determine the easting and the last three will be for northing. The third and sixth number indicate fractional distance of one full grid towards east and north respectively.

For easy reading of the coordinates lines are spaced at regular intervals on the map marking distances east and north of the *origin*. The intersection of these two lines produces the network of squares, which we call *grid*. The spacing of the grid will depend on the scale of the map. The variation of grid line is observed in maps of different scales.

For the British Ordnance Survey Maps the following spacings are observed :

Map Scale > 1:10,000 – Grid lines are spaced 100 m. apart.

Map Scale 1:10,000 to 1:63,360 – Grid lines are spaced 1 km. apart.

Map Scale < 1:10,000 – Grid lines are spaced 10 kms. apart.

The Survey of India Toposheets also follow the British Ordnance Survey Maps in spacing the grid lines.

The *Grid Reference* is made by full coordinates. The position of any point on grid is defined by stating its full coordinates. The full distance is marked for the point first lying to the east (*eastings*) and then to the north (*northings*). The distance may be marked in convenient unit. The distance of the point from the grid line is usually estimated, but for accuracy it is necessarily be measured. The measurement can be done either by using a scale line shown at the bottom of the map or by a *romer*, supplied with the map.

Relationship between Grid North and True North

All grid lines run from the origin as North-South lines from which *eastings* are measured. At the origin the grid lines coincide with the meridians. But the grid lines have the parallel form and the meridians have the converging form. This pattern produces a small difference between the direction of the grid north (i.e. the direction of the vertical lines) and true north. The difference in direction (y) increases with distance away from the origin (Fig. 1.3).

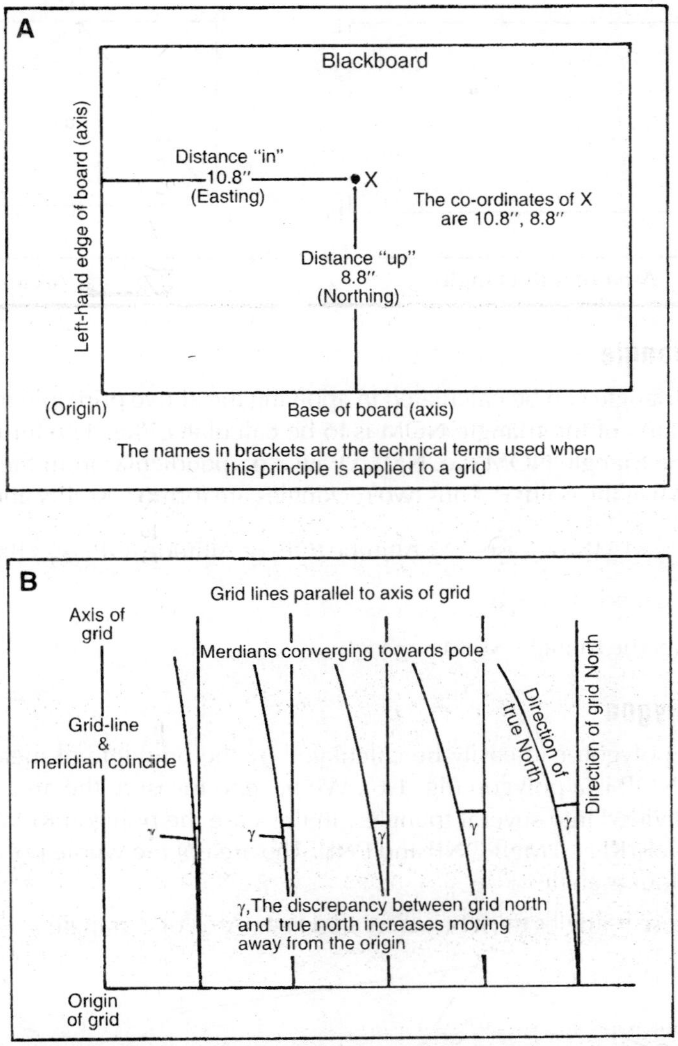

Fig. 1.3 Relationship between Grid North and True North

MEASURING THE AREA ON A MAP

The measurement of area is a key factor in any spatial study or analysis. We have to calculate the ground areas from the map true to scale. For measuring the areas on a map different methods are employed. All such methods are based on geometric principles. We must learn basic knowledge on area of a rectangle, area of a triangle, area of a polygon, area of circle, area of a sector, area of a parallelopiped, area of a pyramid, area of a cylinder, area of a cone. etc.

The Area of a Rectangle

It is very simple to calculate the area of a rectangle. If the length of two adjacent sides of a rectangle are known the area can be calculated. Say in the given rectangle KLMN (fig. 1.4), the side KL has length x and the side LM has length y. (In a rectangle KL = MN, LM = NK).

The area of the rectangle KLMN = KL × LM or KL × NK or MN × LM or MN × NK = x.y

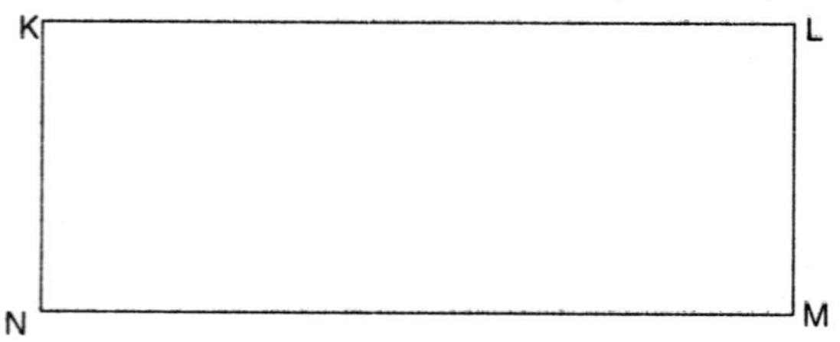

Fig. 1.4 Area of a Rectangle

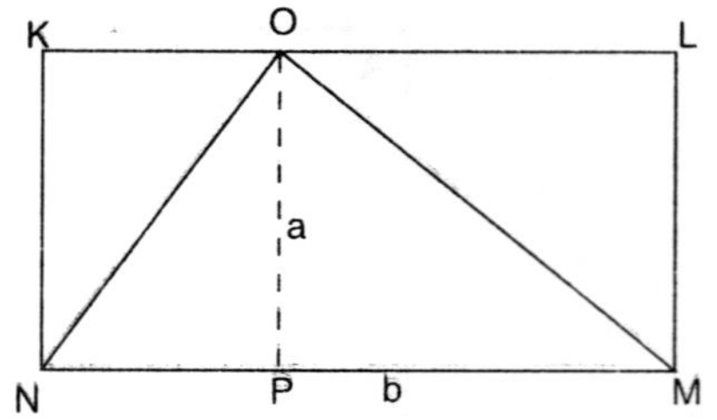

Fig. 1.5 Area of a Triangle

The Area of a Triangle

The area of a triangle can be calculated in applying the above principle in measuring the area of rectangle. The area of the triangle NOM is to be calculated (fig. 1.5) form a rectangle KLMN with the base of the triangle NOM (i.e. NM). Draw a perpendicular from the apex of the triangle (O) to the base (NM) at the point P. Thus two rectangles are formed, KOPN and OLMP.

Now, NOM = $\frac{1}{2}$KLMN or Base × $\frac{1}{2}$Altitude (OP) or Altitude (OP) × $\frac{1}{2}$Base

Say Altitude = a and Base = b

Then the area of the triangle NOM = $\frac{1}{2}a \times b$

The Area of a Polygon

The area of a polygon can easily be calculated by the principle of measuring the area of a triangle. Say KLMNOP is a polygon (fig. 1.6). We have to measure the area of the polygon. The polygon may be divided into several triangles. In this case the polygon KLMNOP is divided into four triangles, namely KLN, LMN, ONP and PNK. The area of the whole polygon is thus equal to sum of the area of four triangles.

The area of these triangles must be calculated first. (Area of a triangle = $\frac{1}{2}$ Base × Altitude).

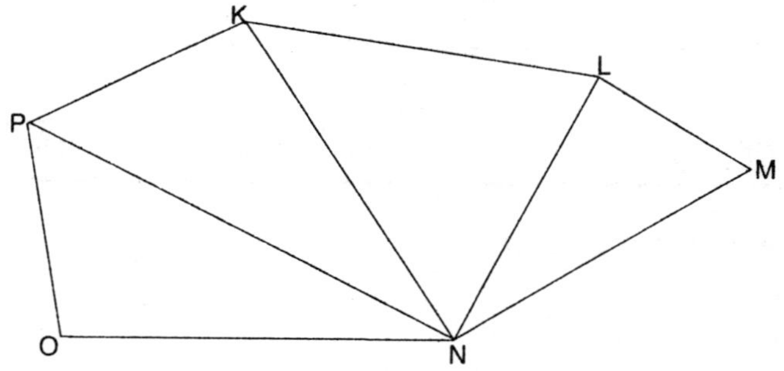

Fig. 1.6 Area of a Polygon

The Area of a Circle

To find the area of a circle the application of the principle of measuring the triangle can also be applied. Let KLM be a circle with the centre O (fig. 1.7). The circumference of the circle is to be divided into n equal parts. Say, KL be one of them. Draw perpendicular ON on KL, which will be the altitude of the triangle OKL. Then the area of the triangle OKL = KN × ON ($\frac{1}{2}$Base × Altitude).

Thus the Area of the Polygon = þπ × KN × ON or $\frac{\pi}{2}$ × KL × ON.

If infinite small number of chords are drawn, each chord will coincide the length of small circumference. Finally the perimeter of the polygon will coincide with the circumference of the circle, which is equal to $2\pi r$ (r = Radius of the circle). The perpendicular ON also finally coincides with OL and OK.

Therefore the area of the circle = Area of polygon of infinite number of small sides

$$= \pi \times KL \times \frac{ON}{2}$$

$= 2\pi r \times \frac{r}{2}$ (As finally × KL becomes the circumference and ON becomes a radius)

= þπr^2.

The Area of a Sector

We know that the area of a whole circle is equal to πr^2 . Consider OLK as one sector divided into n equal parts, such as OLM (fig. 1.8). Let ON be the perpendicular on LM

Assume the area of the triangle OLK= LM × ON = $\frac{1}{2}$LM × ON

The area of the other triangle KOM can be similarly calculated.

As in the circle the part LM may become infinitely small, when the arc LM will be equal to the chord LM. Thus the area of the whole sector is equal to the area of the constituent triangles :

Area of a sector = π × LN × ON

And as in the final stage ON is equal to r (the radius of the circle)

Area = π × LN × r = r × $\frac{1}{2}$length of arc (i.e. LK)

Let O = circular measure of the angle LOK

Then Trigonometrically arc LK = rO and area of sector = $\frac{1}{2}$rO × r = $\frac{1}{2}$r^{2}O

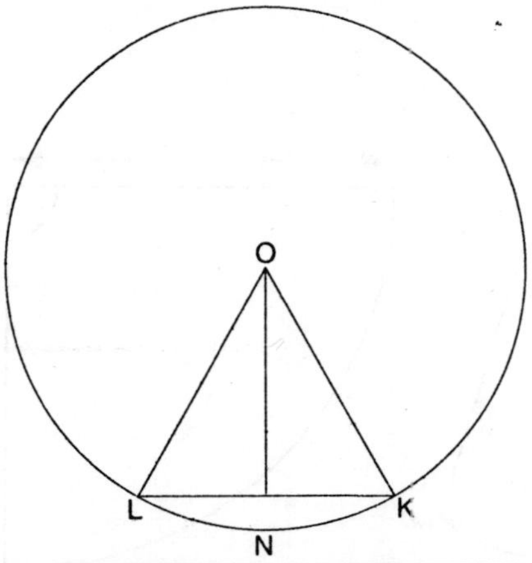

Fig. 1.7 Area of a Circle

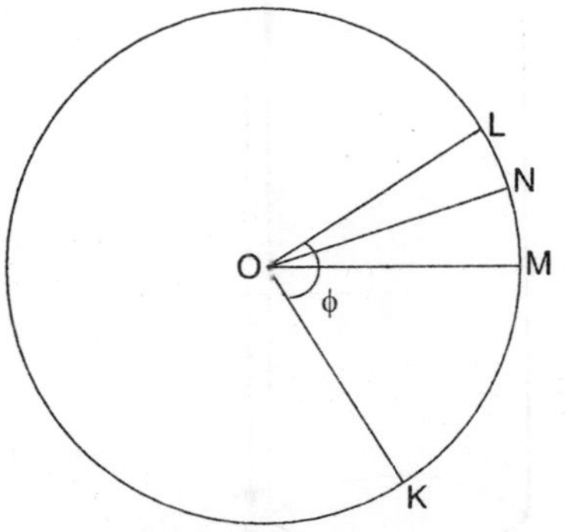

Fig. 1.8 Area of a Sector

The Area of a Parallelopiped

The area of a parallelopiped can be simply calculated. The parallelopiped is a figure bounded by three pairs of parallel planes (say a cube). The area of each face of the cube can be calculated by multiplying length by breadth. The area of the parallelopiped is thus calculated by finding the area of each face and sum of the results.

The Area of a Pyramid

A pyramid is a figure having all the faces except one meeting at vertex. All the faces except the base (in most cases) of pyramid are triangles. The area of each face can be calculated and sum of these areas will indicate the area of the pyramid.

The Area of a Cylinder

In the given figure (fig. 1.9) the area of the base is πr^2. The height of the cylinder is AB or h. If the cylinder is cut along AB and unfolded we find a rectangle. This rectangle has the equal height AB or h like the cylinder and the length is equal to the circumference of the base or top of the cylinder (i.e. $2\pi r$).

Hence the area of the curved surface of the cylinder = $2\pi rh$ and the area of the base + top of the cylinder = $2\pi r^2$.

So, the total area of the cylinder = $2\pi rh + 2\pi r^2$

The Area of a Cone

Consider ABC be a cone, where V is mid-point of the base and AV is perpendicular to the base (fig. 1.10). Assume AB as l and VC as r. The surface of the cone is assumed to be aggregate of infinite number of triangles of which AXY is one. The vertex of all triangles is A and the altitude of all triangles is l, the slant height of the cone.

Thus the curved surface of the cone = the sum of the triangles = $\frac{1}{2} \times 2\pi r = \pi rl$

The area of the base of the cone = πr^2

Hence the total area of the cone = $\pi rl + \pi r^2$.

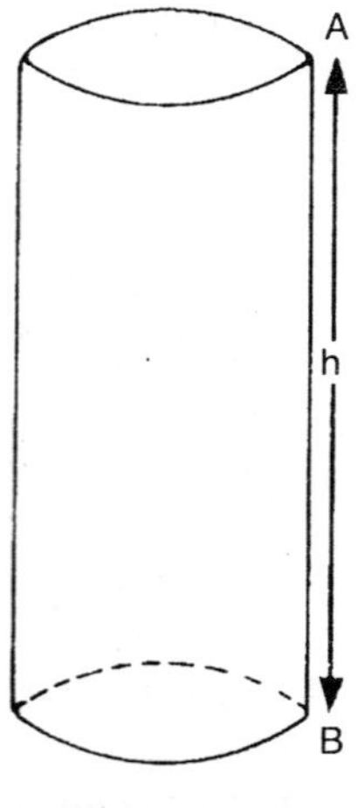

Fig. 1.9 Area of a Cylinder

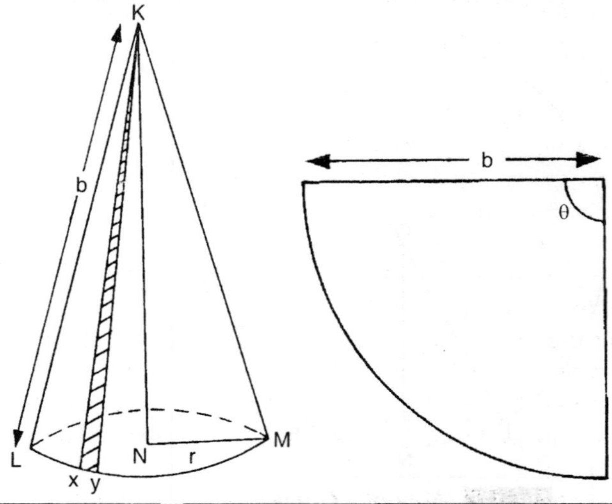

Fig. 1.10(a) Area of a Cone

The Area of the Surface of the Sphere

The area of the surface of the sphere (fig. 1.11) is very useful in the construction of map projection. It can be proved that the surface area of a sphere is equal to the area of a circumscribed cylinder, i.e. = $4\pi r^2$. It can also be stated that the area of a sphere is equal to four times the area of the great circle. The great circle is a circle passing around the sphere and the plane of which passes through the centre of the sphere.

The Area of a Zone

The area of a zone at latitude θ can be calculated on a globe of radius R by the equation : Area of a zone on a globe of radius R = $2\pi R \times R \sin \theta = 2\pi R^2 \sin\theta$.

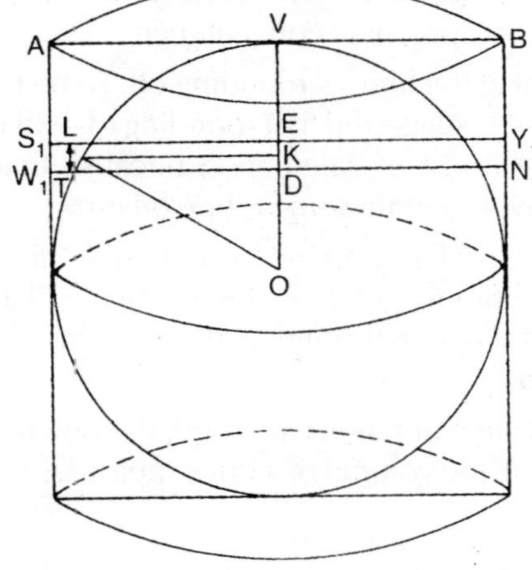

Fig. 1.11 Area of the surface of the Sphere

ROUNDING OF NUMBERS

We often come across certain fractional numbers in our real life as well as in our calculations, as we know that the basic currencies used in different countries are further subdivided into smaller fractions. For instance, a Rupee is divisible into 100 Paisa. In a similar way, US Dollar is divisible into 100 Cent, Pound has smaller values of currency as Shilling and Pence. These smaller currencies are used as coins. However, in these days of metric system, often there are fractional values of prices towards the right hand side of decimal points. In our mathematical calculations also, fractions appear as decimal values. Sometimes the results obtained after a division or multiplication may be very long with several numbers after the decimal point. For further calculation and for practical use we need to make them smaller in length though we can not ignore the numbers which have appeared after decimal point. To make such long numbers into smaller usable numbers, we round off them considering the first or first and second numbers as significant, leaving the rest. During such rounding off and before leaving the rest of the numbers we consider the numbers being 5,6,7,8,9 as significant and add 1 full digit to the last numbers of the result. In doing so, 0 to 4 numbers are considered insignificant and are left out as such. The rule is , if it is 5 to 9, round the number up, and if it is 0 to 4, round the number down. Let us take some exercise on rounding off in the following numbers with fractions.

232.52783 = 232.53 = 232.5

(Original Number) (Rounded off Number)

Similarly, when it is

340.37248 = 340.37 = 340.4

The numbers after the decimal point are known as **trailing numbers.**

The concept of rounding off has been more practised in real life to avoid the inconvenience of using small currencies. This way often we find out that at the time of some transactions, the digits left out or added in terms of the consideration of the nearest 10. For instance, 24 should be considered as 20 because 20 is nearer the digit than 30. If it is 36 or 37 etc. that is, 5 or above, it becomes 40, because 40 is the nearest 10 in comparison with 30 which is at a greater distance.

At present, even the small calculations are done through calculators or computers and rounding off becomes a necessity for practical convenience.

It should be kept in mind that at the time of rounding off, some fractional changes may appear in the final result and that is why it is suggested that rounding off will only be done at the final stage of obtaining a result, not in the midst of calculation because that may affect the final result. However, rounding off will always entertain some round off error.

For rounding off, sometimes a range is given in particular cases. Thus if the rounding off is required upto tenth, only one number after decimal point will be rounded off; if it is upto hundredth, two numbers after the decimal points will be rounded off; for thousandth it will be three numbers after decimal point.

For the calculation of area if such notations are used, the power values will be added and the figures will be multiplied. Suppose the volume of a brick measures :

7.62 cm. (height)

25.4 cm. (length)

12.7 cm. (width)

If the values are converted into metre, it is :

0.0762 m. $= 7.62 \times 10^{-2}$

0.254 m. $= 2.54 \times 10^{-1}$

0.127 m. $= 1.27 \times 10^{-1}$

The base figures will be multiplied and power values added for obtaining the volume.

$7.62 \times 2.54 \times 1.27 = 24.580596 \times 10^{-4}$

$= .0024580596$

$= .0025 = 2.5 \times 10^{-3}\ m^3.$

To use power values in calculator a sign (^) is used. Hence, 2.5×10^{-3} = 2.5 × 10^–3. In scientific notation it is 2.5×10^{-3}. The speed of light is 299792458 m./sec. It can be conveniently written as 2.99×10^8 (rounded off).

Examples :

17.25734 = 17.3 (Up to tenth)

17.25734 = 17.26 (Up to hundredth)

17.25734 = 17.257 (Up to thousandth)

As we consider the nearest full digit as the rounded off value, though it is not truely the exact number obtained, a different sign in a wavy form of equal to is used to indicate that the rounded off value is considered in the place of the exact value as being equivalent. For instance,

$$7.27 \approx 7.3,\ 9.56 \approx 10$$

Alfred George Greenhill introduced this sign in 1892 to mark the process of rounding off.

For the students of geography this method of rounding off is essential for geographical calculations. Pie (π) is a fractional value being a ratio of circumference and diameter of a circle. Truly, it is 3.14159265358, but students of geography either write it as 3.1416 or use it as π as an input in the calculator for calculations. At the time of considering population density similar rounding off becomes necessary. The density of population of West Bengal in 2018 is actually 91347736/88752 Km^2 = 1029.24707, but for practical purposes and to simplify the figure the students of geography can consider it as 1029 per Km^2.

SCIENTIFIC NOTATION

Scientific notation is the way of writing a very long number in a convenient way into a smaller space. In scientific calculators it is given as 'Sci'. It can be applied for small numbers also.

Suppose a given number is 5000000

It can be written as 5×10^6.

Such a notation can be used because 5×10^6 means

$5 \times 10 \times 10 \times 10 \times 10 \times 10 \times 10$.

If there is a number with a decimal point, and it is scientifically written, the decimal point will move towards right when the power of 10 is positive. For a negative power the decimal point will move towards left, according to the value of the positive or negative power above 10. Thus

$5.26 \times 10^7 = 52600000$

In this case two 10s have been used for the two numbers after the decimal points.

For a negative power when the decimal point will move towards left it is :

$3 \times 10^{-8} = 0.00000003$

In the other way, if the given figure is 0.000000057

Its scientific notation is 5.7×10^{-8}

For a small number also this notation can be used.

$7.2 \times 10^0 = 7.2$

$7.2 \times 10^1 = 72$

NATURAL SCALE AND LOGARITHMIC SCALE

Natural Scale

The term natural scale is considered here as a change in the abscissa as reflected in the corresponding scale of ordinate, where scale is the range within which the given values can be measured between two horizontal and vertical range of differences. It is linear in nature as the corresponding change in ordinate is proportional to the change in abscissa. Thus for a change of 1 in X axis may correspond to a change of 2 in Y axis, 2 is corresponding to the change of 4, 3 is corresponding to the change of 6. In such a scale, when data is plotted on a graph, normal graph

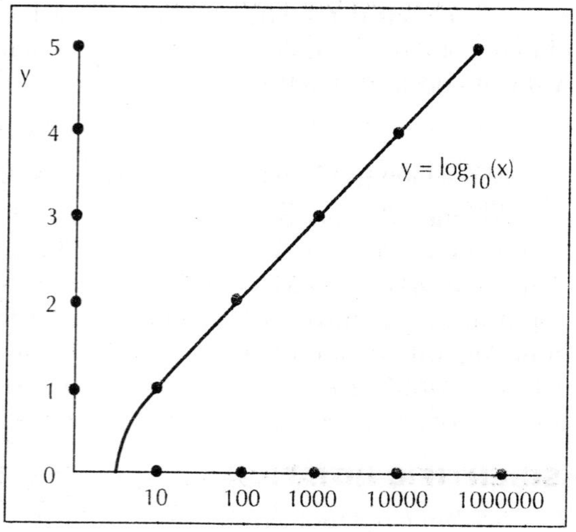

can be used. What will be the graphical interval along the X axis and Y axis corresponding to ground units should be decided by the plotter.

As the interval is regular here, a high range of data can not be plotted conveniently. When a topographic profile is constructed on natural scale, some exaggeration of scale along the ordinate may be required to show the topographic details. This sort of exaggreration should not exceed 2 to 5 times, otherwise a false impression will be developed in the mind of the reader. It should be kept in mind that the nature of the natural landscape of, which the profile is drawn, should be maintained. In a natural scale, the source of the graph may start from zero unit and may not also. In certain cases a datum is taken at the base line and not zero.

Logarithmic Scale

A logarithmic scale shows the variation of units along X and Y axis in terms of logarithmic intervals. It is irregular, as in different cycles of logarithm, the scale will be increased by 10 times when the base is 10. Each of the cycles will have a range from 1 to 10 raised to 10s of times in subsequent cycles. Thus in the second cycle, it may be 10 to 100, in the third cycle 100 to 1000 and so on for the same graphical interval.

In logarithmic scale much high values may be shown starting from very low values, but in no case the source of the graph or the base line will be zero. In double-log graph papers, both X and Y axis may indicate logarithmic intervals, but in semilog graphs one of the two axes has logarithmic intervals, whereas the other has regular intervals.

In a bivariate data set, if one set of variates is geometrically variable and another is regular or arithmetically variable, semilog graph paper can be used. The arithmetically variable data will follow regular intervals in the graph and the other will follow logarithmic change. For instance, in morphometric analysis of a drainage basin, stream orders change arithmetically, whereas the number of streams in different orders may range from 1 to any high value of 100s, 1000s etc.

On the other hand, if in a bivariate data set both of the variables are of very high range, double-log scale can be used. The logarithmic scale will vary on the basis of the base figure, meaning for base 2 mutiples of 2 will be multiplied, if the base is 10, multiples of 10 will be multiplied.

Logarithm and Antilogarithm

Logarithm, as defined in dictionary, is 'a quantity representing the power to which a fixed number or the base must be raised to produce a given number.' The word logarithm has been derived from Greek '*Logos*' meaning ratio. Raising a base means that the logarithm of a given number, suppose 'n' is the exponent to which a fixed number, that is the base will be raised. Truly speaking, **logarithm** shows repeated multiplication of the same number. Thus it may be the repeated multiplication of the base. Suppose, when we consider logarithm to the base 10, it becomes repeated multiplication of 10.

For 10 = 10 × 1, or Log of 10 is 1. This way

For 100 = 10 × 10 or Log of 100 is 2.

John Napier introduced the concept of Logarithm in the early 17th century. The purpose of introducing the concept was to simplify mathematical calculations. In 18th century, Leonhard Euler connected the concept of logarithm to exponential function.

As mentioned earlier, one of the main purposes of using logarithm was to simplify calculation. For instance, large multiplications can be done simply by summing up logarithmic valus of the two numbers involved. In the following multiplication it can be observed.

57.383 × 79.254 = log 57.383 = 1.75878325

log 79.254 = + 1.899021191

3.657804441

Antilog of 3.657804441 = 4547.832291. This figure is equal to the product of multiplication of the two given numbes. Thus the tedious job of doing large multiplication can be avoided by simple addition of the log values and then coming back to the normal number through antilog. For large divisions, it is simply the subtraction between the log values of two given numbers and antilog of that. Such an exercise will seem to be futile to students in the present world where scientific calculators, advanced computers and modern smart phones are at their hands, but when such gadgets were not invented, a student could calculate large sums with the help of logarithmic tables where logarithmic values as well as antilogarithmic values are given. However, even in these days of electronic advancement, the importance of logarithmic values is still there in different exercises of different branches of science. Moreover, it should be kept in mind that for graphical representation of large values of a wide range, logarithmic scales are very useful as it reduces the quantities to tiny figures.

Antilogarithm is the inverse function of log values. Thus antilogarithm of $\log_b X = f(X) = b^x$. It should be kept in mind that antilog through its inverse function brings the logarithmic values to the normal digits. Hence, in all logarithmic calculations, the result should be obtained through antilogarithmic values.

Characteristic is the whole number of a logarithmic value. It is always 10 times less in terms of number of digits in 10s, 100s, 1000s etc. Hence, the characteristic of 57.383 is 1, characteristic of 123.789 is 2. Such determination of logarithmic values reduces it for 1 digit or 10 times. At the time of doing antilogarithm this reduction is again compensated in the normal value. Thus in the multiplication given previously the sum of two log values of 57.383 and 79.254 was 3.657804441. When the antilog was determined, the characteristic of log value being 3, the decimal point was to be placed after four digits, as it was :

Antilog of 3.657804441 = 4547832291 = 4547.832291

Hence, the decimal point will move one digit more to the right side than the characteristic value of logarithmic figure.

The log value of 360 = 2.556302501

When the antilog value is determined, it is 360.0000002 = 360. From 5 Figure log table only 5 digits can be taken.

Antilog of .556 = 35975

Mean difference of 3 = + 25

36000

= 360.00

In 360, as there are 3 digits, the characteristic will be 2. On the other hand, in the antilog of 2.556302501, the decimal point is placed after 3 digits as the characteristic was 2. Antilog values will be taken for the right hand side digits of the decimal point.

Mantissa is a part of logarithm after the decimal point. In these terms, in a log value of 2.55630, 2 is the characteristic and the rest after decimal is mantissa .

In the logarithmic tables 3 digits to the left side of a given figure can be seen as reference, and the rest should be seen in the mean difference table and should be added. Therefore, in 5 figure log table, the log value of

5136 = log of 5.13 = .71012 (from main table)

mantissa of 6 = 50

.71062

As there are 4 full integers, the characteristic will be 3. Hence, the log value of 5136 = 3.71062.

The values obtained in mantissa should be added from extreme right hand side of the previous logarithmic value obtained from main table. If there are 2 digits to be seen, both the figures will be read from the table of mean differences and the first one will be added as it is from the extreme right hand side of the main figure, whereas the mean difference for the second one should be positioned moving 1 digit towards the right. Thus, if the mean difference is a single digit value for the second one, it will be left out and if it is double digited, only first one will be placed at the extreme right hand side leaving the second digit out. If the seocnd digit is 5 or more 1 may be added to the taken value. For instance, the log value of 75128 is

87564 (log of 751)

12 (mean difference for 2)

5/6 (mean difference of 8 for row 75 is 46, hence 6 is left and 1 is added to 4 for approximation of the left out digit)

87581

with characteristic 4 it is 4.87581.

The natural logarithm is indicated by 'e' , i.e. the base ≈ 2.718. The binary logarithim normally uses base 2 or b = 2. Thus in binary logarithm the number 2 should be raised to obtain value of n. For any real number x it is, $x = \log_2 n \leftrightarrow 2^x = n$.

In binary logarithm how many 2s are required to reach a particular n value is to be obtained. The binary logarithm of 2=1, the binary logarithm of 8=3, the binary logarithm of 64 is 6 with base 2.

Thus it is $2 \times 1 = 2$

$2 \times 2 \times 2 = 8$

$2 \times 2 \times 2 \times 2 \times 2 \times 2 = 64$

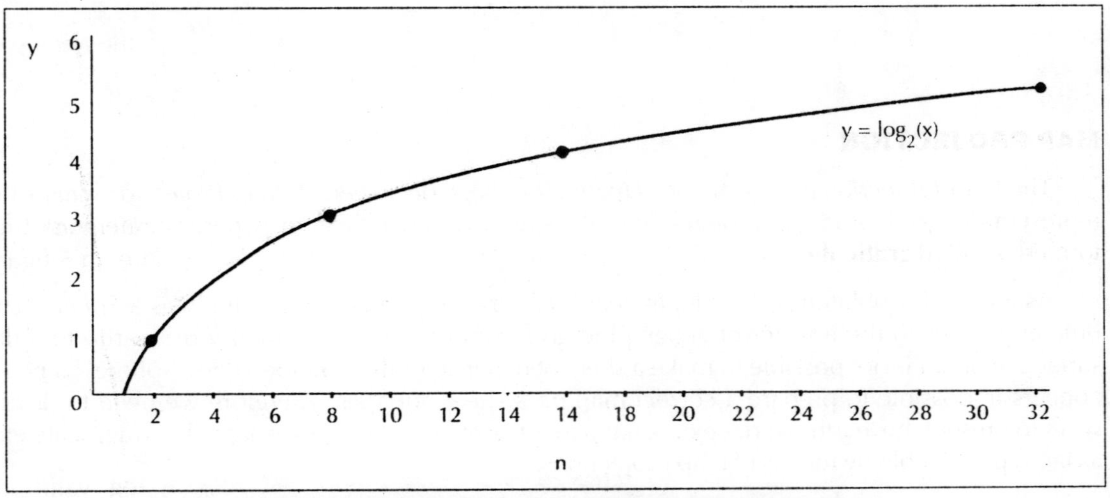

GRAPH OF BINARY LOGARITHM WITH BASE 2

C H A P T E R 2

MAP PROJECTION

MAP PROJECTION

The term *Projection* means the presentation of image on screen. A *Map Projection* means the representation of latitude and longitude of the globe on a flat sheet of paper. The network thus formed is called **graticule**.

As the earth's oblateness is little, the earth can be considered conveniently as a *Sphere*. The difficulty arises in the transfer of geographic grid from its actual spherical form (earth) to a flat surface (map). It is not possible to make a sheet of paper smoothly rounded like a sphere. Hence it appears impossible to prepare a correct map on a sheet of paper. Therefore we need to devise ways to present the earth's surface on a flat paper maintaining the area, shape, bearing, scale etc. as far as practicable by means of map projections.

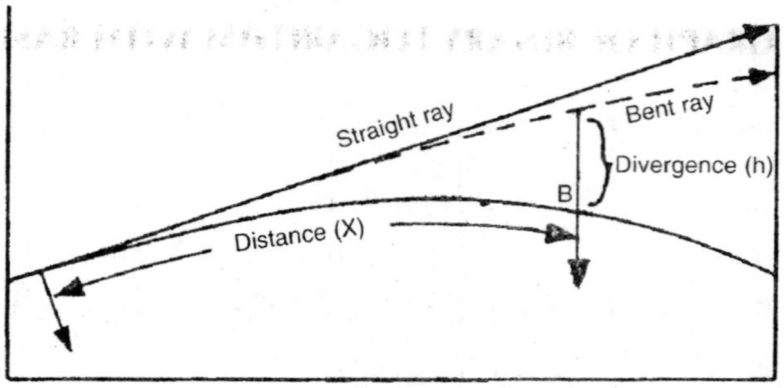

Fig. 2.1 **Oblateness of the earth's surface—divergence of the bent ray from the earth's surface increases with distance**

Developable and Undevelopable Geometrical Surfaces

The paper or cloth on which a map projection is developed is known as a **developable surface**. Some geometrical surfaces appear to be *developable*, as by cutting along certain lines they can be unwrapped to make a flat surface. The *Cone* and the *Cylinder* are such forms (fig 2.2 & 2.3). Had the earth been a conical or cylindrical form, there would have been no difficulty in representing the earth on a flat paper. Then there would have been no distortion of shape and area.

The sphere, on the other hand, can not be developed into a flat surface by unfolding and unrolling. Hence the spherical earth appears to be *undevelopable* geometrical surface. In order to have the parts of spherical surface lie perfectly flat, it must be unwrapped more in some places than others. Due to such unique characteristics of a sphere deformations are inevitable and the surfaces and planes of the projections are not geometrically possible.

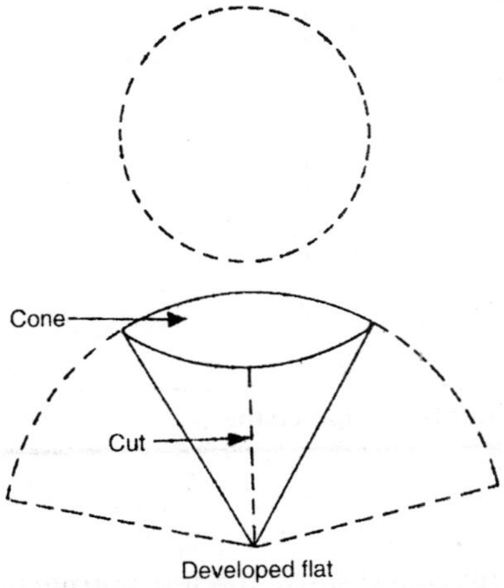

Fig. 2.2 Developable Geometric form – Cone

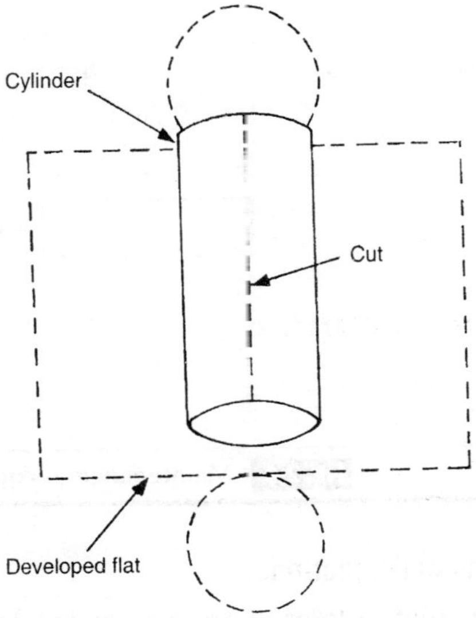

Fig. 2.3 Developable Geometric form – Cylinder

Properties of Map Projections

Although it seems impossible to construct a correct map of any part of the earth's surface, efforts have been made to reduce the distortion to a reasonable limit over certain parts of the earth's surface. This has resulted due to application of different methods of projection where one can preserve specific qualities of the projection. These qualities are namely :

1. Preservation of Area – The projection is called **Equal Area Projection**
2. Preservation of Shape or Form - The projection is called **Orthomorphic Projection**
3. Preservation of Bearing – The projection is called **Azimuthal Projection**
4. Preservation of Distance – The projection is called **Equidistant Projection.**

In some projections where neither of the four above mentioned properties can be maintained we call such projections as **Aphylactic Projections.**

It is easier to maintain the *equal area* of any part of the globe on a map true to scale by neglecting the *shape.* For example, the area of a square on a base of 4 cm. (area 16 sq. cm.) can be expressed in a rectangle having two sides of 2 cm. and 8 cm. (area 16 sq. cm.). Two parallelograms on the same base and between the same parallels are equal area. The area of a sphere can be transformed into an equal area circle by simple computations.

However, it is impossible to maintain the *shape* of large area of the globe (fig 2.4). To certain extent in smaller areas the shape can be preserved. So orthomorphism applies to only small areas. In order to preserve the shape two factors must be considered :

1. The meridians and parallels intersect at right angles on the globe.
2. At any one point the scale is uniform in all directions, but may differ from point to point.

The map projection becomes useful in navigation, where the *true bearing* or *azimuth* is maintained. In simple case it is done by preservation of true bearings from the centre of the map. When this centre coincides with the pole (North or South) the meridians appear as lines of true bearings.

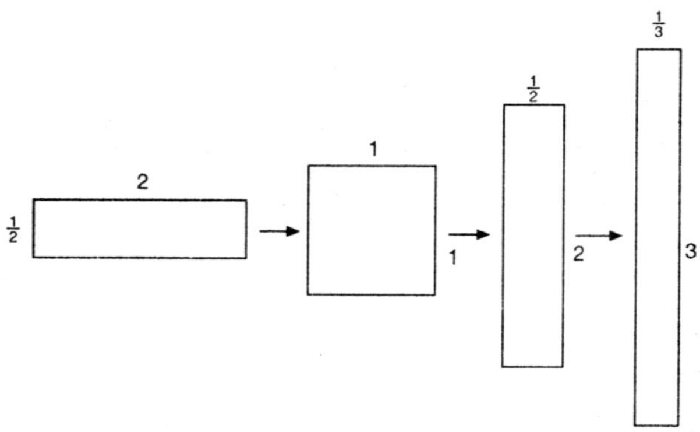

Fig. 2.4 **Maintenance of equal area property, but the shape changes**

Systems of Projections

Different systems of projections can be developed. In restricted sense the term projection is *perspective* or geometrical projection. But *non-perspective* projections can also be developed cartographically on the basis mathematical calculations.

In perspective projections by shifting either the source of light at the centre of the globe or placement of paper in touching the globe (as projection plane) the 'shadow' map could be generated. In this way we can generate *Zenithal Projections.* The bearings are all true in Zenithal projections. Hence these are also known as *Azimuthal Projections,* where azimuth or true bearing is maintained. The projection plane can touch the poles, the equator or any point between the equator and poles. When the projection plane touches the globe at poles, we get *polar* case or *normal.* The projection plane touching the equator and any point between the poles and the equator are called *Equatorial* and *Oblique* cases respectively.

Where a sheet of paper in the form of a cone touches the globe it rests on a particular parallel, we get *Simple Conical Projection.* This is a *normal* case. The cone may be placed in other positions on the globe, but it is difficult to construct the *Equatorial* or *Oblique* cases unlike Zenithal Projections. Conical Projections may either be perspective or *non-perspective,* but the non-perspective forms are more important.

In some cases a sheet of paper rolled in the form of a cylinder or tube is placed around the globe. These are called *Cylindrical Projections.* The Cylindrical projections may be conceived as both *perspective* and *non-perspective* forms touching the globe at different points creating *Polar (Normal), Equatorial* and *Oblique* cases. But the most common types include non-perspective equatorial cases, as the area and shape can be well preserved near the equator.

As a result of continued effort in the improvement upon the preservation of properties (i.e. area, shape, bearing etc.) the various types of projections have been developed. These types of projections are categorised as *Conventional Projections* . Of these types the *Oblique Mollweide* and *Oblique Mercator* are most common.

Thus we have a generalised classification of projections as noted in Table 2.1.

PRINCIPLES OF CONSTRUCTIONS OF PROJECTIONS

It is not intended to discuss all the possible types of map projections here. Students interested in Cartography can learn in detail about the map projection from any standard book on

Cartography. Many of the map projections, though theoretically conceived are difficult to construct and are of very limited use. We will discuss in this chapter a few principal map projections, which are frequently used and easy for construction.

TABLE 2.1

Classification of Projections

Projections	Forms	Types
1. Zenithal Projections	(i) Perspective (ii) Non-Perspective	(i) Normal (Polar) (ii) Oblique (iii) Equatorial
2. Conical Projections	(i) Perspective (ii) Non-Perspective	(i) Normal
3. Cylindrical Projections	(i) Non-Perspective	(i) Equatorial (ii) Transverse (iii) Oblique
4. Conventional Projections		

The Gnomonic or Central Projection

This is a commonly used Zenithal Projection. It is a perspective projection. The source of light is at the centre of the globe and the projection plane touches the globe as tangent at some point, normally at one of the Poles (North or South) or on the Equator. However the point may lie elsewhere.

Polar Case

Graphical Construction (fig. 2.5)

1. Calculate the radius (R) of the Reduced Earth (The radius of the reduced earth is calculated as dividing the earth's radius (2,50,000,000 inches) by denominator of R.F.)*
2. Draw a circle to scale to represent the globe.
3. Draw radii at required angles (given interval) i.e. OD, OA, OB etc. and stretch the lines to the projection plane DD′. The plane DD′ is drawn as a tangent touching the point N (Pole).
4. Take the radius NB′ to draw the parallel (B′B′). As <NOB = x, i.e. the complement of (B′B′) = (90°–x). Say, <NOB=10°, then the parallel has been drawn for 80° (i.e. 90°–10° = 80°). Similarly other parallels can be drawn.
5. Draw the meridians with the help of a protractor at the given interval of longitude from the point N as centre.
6. Label the parallels and meridians conforming the text.
7. Put the scale at the bottom and label the map projection with its title at the top.

---

* In all constructions for projections radius of the reduced earth shall be calculated accordingly.

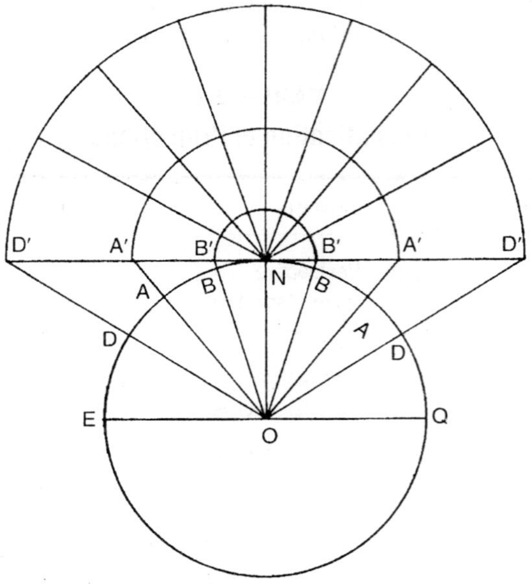

Fig. 2.5 Construction of Gnomonic Projection – Polar case (Graphical)

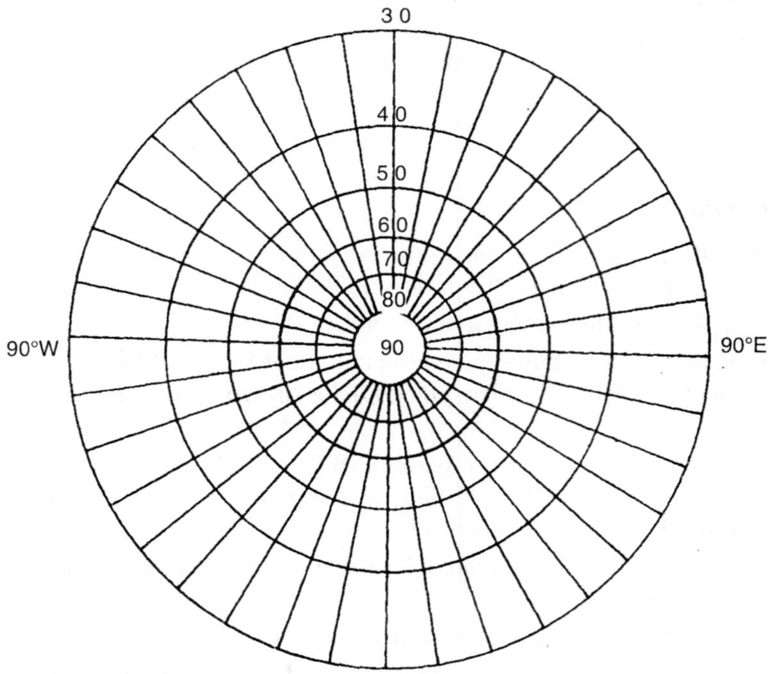

R.F. 1 : 250,000,000

Fig. 2.6 Construction of Gnomonic Projection – Polar case (trigonometrical)

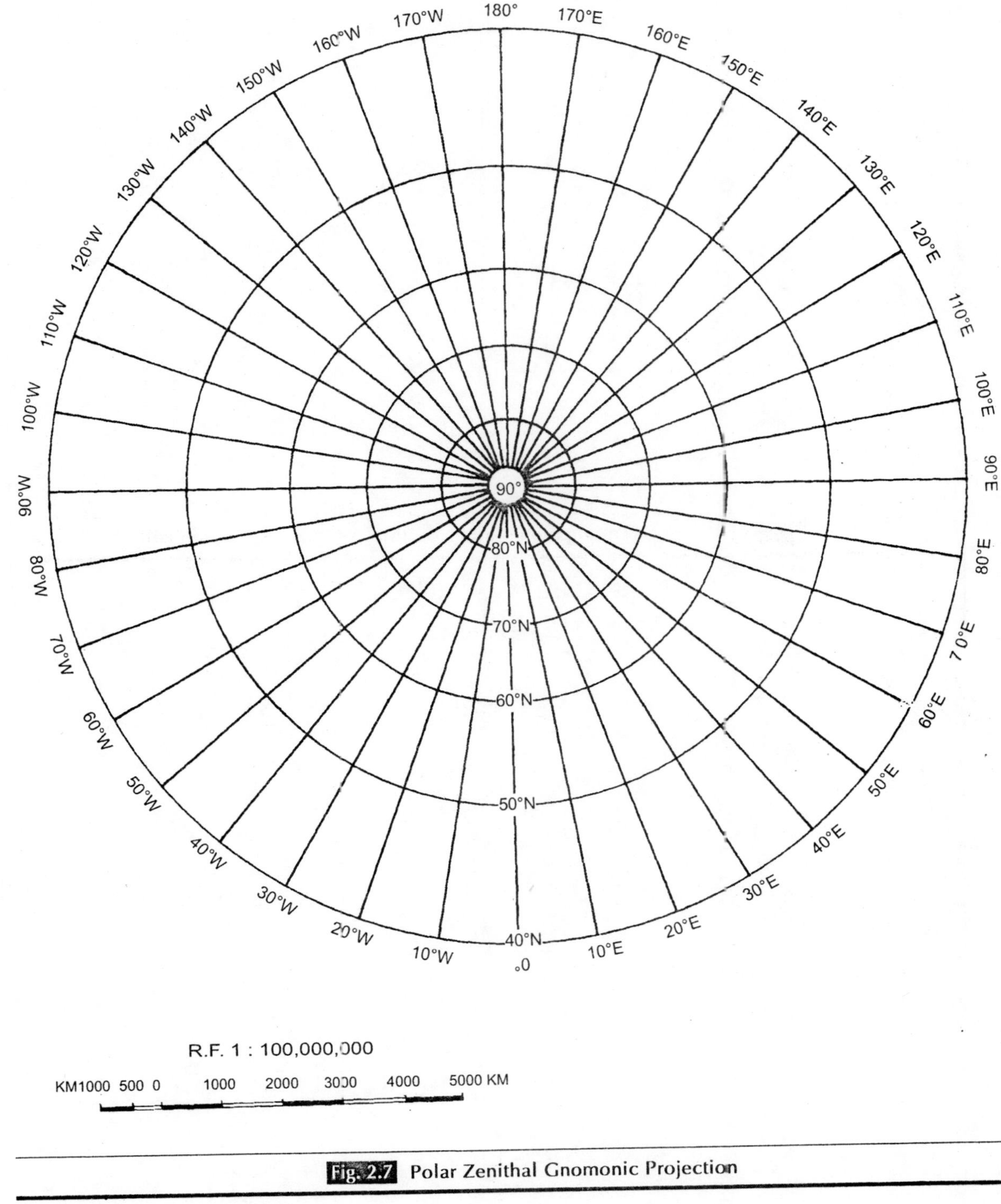

Fig. 2.7 Polar Zenithal Gnomonic Projection

Trigonometrical Construction

The Gnomonic Projection (Polar Case) can be conveniently drawn trigonometrically (fig 2.6).

1. Calculate the radius (R) of the Reduced Earth.
2. Draw a pair of straight lines intersecting each other at right angles (cardinal points are 0°, 90°E, 180° & 90°W).
3. Draw the parallels as concentric circles with the calculated radius from the centre N. The radius to draw the parallel of 30° will be R tan 60° (as the distance of 30° from the pole is 90°–30°).

From the Fig. 2.5 it can be seen; ND′ = NO tan< NOD or R tan60°

The other parallels can be drawn in the similar way. Calculate rϕ (radius to draw parallels at latϕ).

— Lat ϕ	30°	40°	50°	60°	70°	80°	90°
— rϕ	R tan60°	R tan50°	R tan40°	R tan30°	R tan20°	R tan10°	—

4. Starting from O (i.e. pole) divide the quadrants with the help of a protractor at given interval and draw the lines to represent the meridians.
5. Label the parallels and the meridians conforming the text.
6. Mark the boundary. Put the scale at the bottom. Label the title of the map projection on the top.

Properties

1. All parallels are represented as concentric circles.
2. All meridians are straight lines radiating from the pole.
3. The spacing of the parallels and the meridians increases away from the map centre.
4. The meridians indicate true bearing.
5. The direction between two points is truly maintained.
6. All great circles are straight lines and all straight lines are great circles.
7. The Equator cannot be shown in this projection.
8. The plotting of great circle is accomplished by connecting any two desired points by a straight line. For this reason this projection has the advantage for navigation and is known as *Great Circle Sailing Chart.*

EXERCISE

Q. Draw graticules on a Gnomonic Projection (Polar Case) with latitudinal extension 90°N–40°N. R.F. 1:100 million and interval = 10° (fig. 2.7).

Ans. 1. $R = \frac{640,000,000 \text{ cm}}{100,000,000} = 6.4$ cm.

2. Selected parallels are 90°N, 80°N, 70°N, 60°N, 50°N, 40°N.
3. Radii of the parallels — R tanθ

Parallels	θ (90°–Lat)	R tanθ	Result (incm)
40	50	7.62722	7.63
50	40	5.37024	5.37
60	30	3.69504	3.70
70	20	2.32944	2.33
90	—	—	—

Derivation for Polar Zenithal Gnomonic Projection

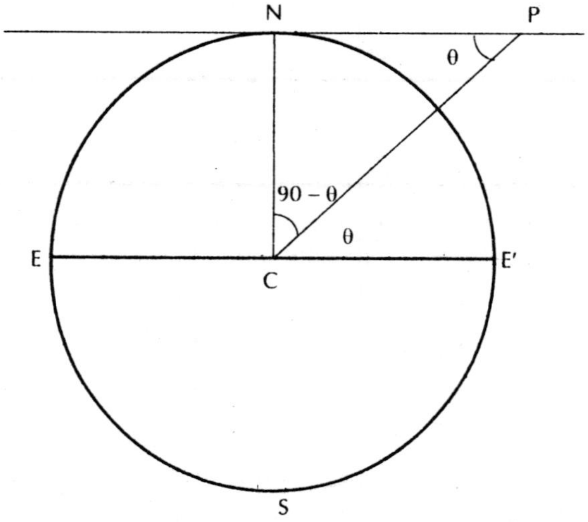

NESE' is the generating globe.

NP is a tangent at north pole on CN radius of the globe.

$\angle PCE' = \theta$

As ECE' and NP are parallel to each other,

$\angle CPN = \theta$; $\angle NCP = 90 - \theta$

The length of NP is to be derived.

$$\frac{NP}{CN} = \tan(90 - \theta)$$

or, $NP = CN.\tan(90 - \theta)$

$= R \tan(90 - \theta)$

Thus, radii of the parallels of latitude can be derived as $R \tan(90 - \theta)$, where θ is the angle of latitude. With the help of protractor the meridians of longitude can be obtained at given intervals and they radiate from the centre i.e., one of the poles.

Equatorial Case

The equatorial areas can be shown on Gnomonic Projection (Equatorial) by both means – graphically and trigonometrically.

Graphical Construction (fig. 2.8)

The graphical construction of Equatorial Gnomonic Projection is more difficult than the polar case. The undernoted steps are followed in the construction of Equatorial Gnomonic Projection.

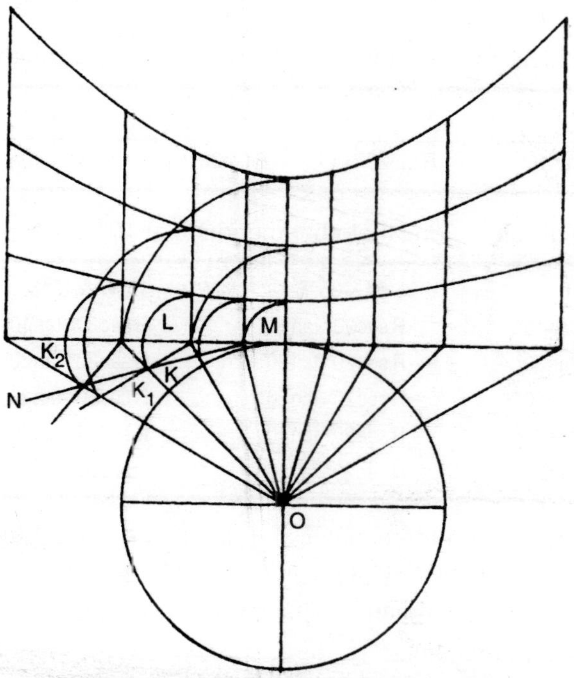

Fig. 2.8 Gnomonic Projection Equatorial case

1. Calculate the Radius (R) of the Reduced Earth.
2. Draw a circle to scale to represent the globe.
3. Divide at angles (given interval) from the centre by a protractor and stretch the lines to meet the projection plane.
4. The projection plane is drawn as a line to be tangent at the point M.
5. The division along the equator and the central meridian are obtained as in the polar case.
6. To obtain the division along the other parallels draw lines perpendicular to the lines radiating from the centre O; such as NM on OM at the point M. Divisions MK, MK1, MK2 etc. will mark the divisions on the parallel. Thus for other parallels also divisions for spacing the meridians are marked and a complete graticule can be constructed.
7. Label the parallels and meridians conforming the text.
8. Mark the boundary. Put the scale at the bottom. Label the title of the map projection on the top.

Trigonometrical Construction

Trigonometrically it is easier to draw the graticules of Equatorial Gnomonic Projection.

1. Calculate the radius (R) of the Reduced Earth.
2. Draw a pair of straight lines intersecting each other at right angle (0° and central meridian).
3. Calculate the division along the central meridian for spacing the parallels.

φ	10°	20°	30°	40°	50°
Distance	R tan10°	R tan20°	R tan30°	R tan40°	R tan50°

4. Calculate the division along the other meridian (at 10° interval).

	5°E & 25°E	5°W & 35°E	15°W & 45°E	25°W & 55°E
10°	R sec10° tan10°	R sec20° tan10°	R sec30° tan10°	R sec40° tan10°
20°	R sec10° tan20°	R sec20° tan20°	R sec30° tan20°	R sec40° tan20°
30°	R sec10° tan30°	R sec20° tan30°	R sec30° tan30°	R sec40° tan30°
40°	R sec10° tan40°	R sec20° tan40°	R sec30° tan40°	R sec40° tan40°
50°	R sec10° tan50°	R sec20° tan50°	R sec30° tan50°	R sec40° tan50°

5. Space the meridians on the equator and divide the central meridian for spacing the parallels as per calculation at Step 3 and draw the parallels as straight lines.
6. Divide the respective meridian for spacing the respective parallel as at step 4.
7. Join the points by curve lines.
8. Label the meridians and parallels conforming the text.
9. Mark the boundary. Put the scale at the bottom. Label the title of the map projection on the top.

Properties

1. All meridians are straight lines.
2. The parallels are drawn as curve lines through fixed points which represent intersection of the meridians and parallels.
3. The spacing of the parallels and meridians increases away from the map centre. Distortions appear large on the outer margin of the map.
4. Equatorial areas are shown in this projection. A map of Africa can be well drawn on this projection.
5. As the value of tan 90° is infinity, the pole cannot be shown on this projection.
6. All great circles are straight lines.
7. For navigational purpose the plotting of great circles is done by simply connecting two divided points. Hence it is known as *Great Circle Sailing Chart.*

Exercise

Q. Draw graticules on Equatorial Gnomonic Projection on a scale of 125,000,000 with latitudinal and longitudinal extension of 40°N to 40°S and 25°W to 55°E respectively, interval being 10° (fig. 2.9).

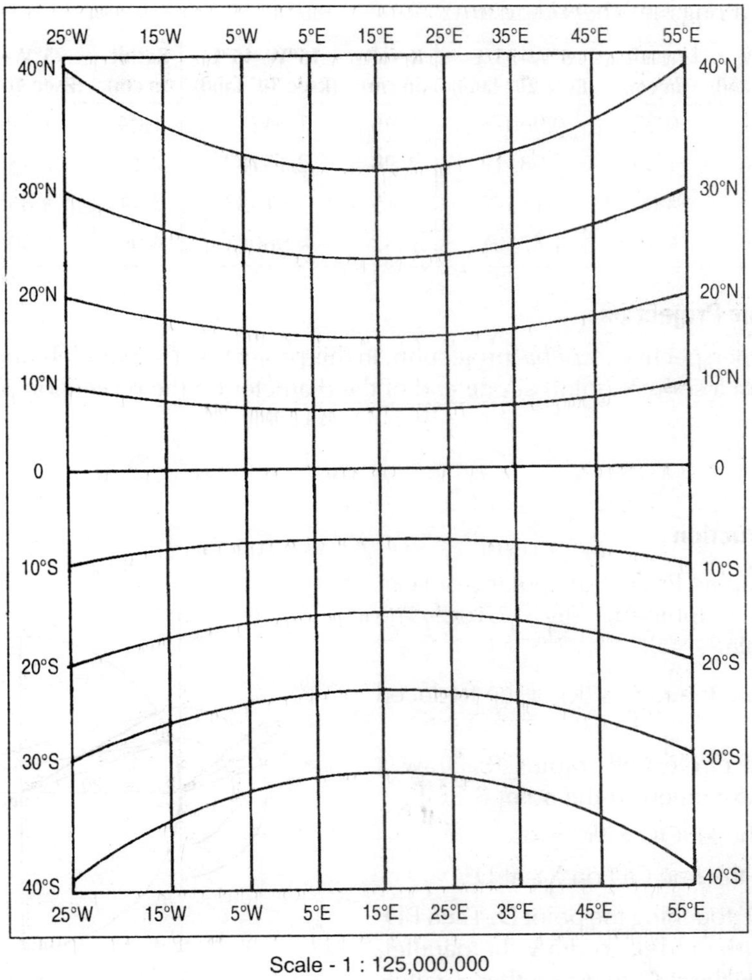

Fig. 2.9 Gnomonic Projection – Equatorial case

Ans. 1. $R = \frac{640,000,000 \text{ cm}}{125,000,000} = 5.12$ cm.

2. Selected parallels are 40°N, 30°N, 20°N, 10°N, 0°, 10°S, 20°S, 30°S, 40°S.

3. Selected central meridian is 25°W, 15°W, 5°W, 5°E, 15°E, 25°E, 35°E, 45°E, 55°E. 15°E is selected as central meridian.

4. Division along the central meridian for spacing the parallels = R tanθ

θ	R tanθ	Result (in cm)
0°	—	—
10°	0.902794	0.90
20°	1.863528	1.86
30°	2.95603	2.96
40°	4.29619	4.30

5. Division along the other meridians :

θ	5°E–25°E (Rsec 10° tanθ)	Result (in cm)	5°W–35°E (Rsec 20° tanθ)	Result (in cm)	15°W–45°E (Rsec 30° tanθ)	Result (in cm)	25°W–55°E (Rsec 40° tanθ)	Result (in cm)
10°	0.91672	0.92	0.96073	0.96	1.04246	1.04	1.17851	1.18
20°	1.89228	1.89	1.98312	1.98	2.15182	2.15	2.43266	2.43
30°	3.00163	3.00	3.14575	3.15	3.41333	3.41	3.85883	3.86
40°	4.36247	4.36	4.57191	4.57	4.96081	4.96	5.60828	5.61

The Stereographic Projection

This is also a perspective *Zenithal* projection. In this projection the parallels and the meridians are projected from a source (point) at one end of the diameter on the projection plane tangent at the other end.

Polar Case

Graphical Construction

The Stereographic Projection (polar case) can be constructed graphically (fig. 2.10). The methods are simple.

1. Calculate the radius (R) of the Reduced Earth.
2. Draw a circle with radius R. Draw a plane XY tangent at the point B.
3. Draw the ∠BOD = 90° – ϕ.
4. Project the line OD on XY at D′.
5. Join CD′ touching the point D. Then BD′ will be the radius to draw the parallel. Similarly the radii to draw other parallels can be constructed. All parallels will be drawn as concentric circles of varying radii with the centre at B.
6. From the point B with the help of a protractor draw the meridians at the given interval. All meridians will be the straight lines converging at the pole (i.e. point B here).

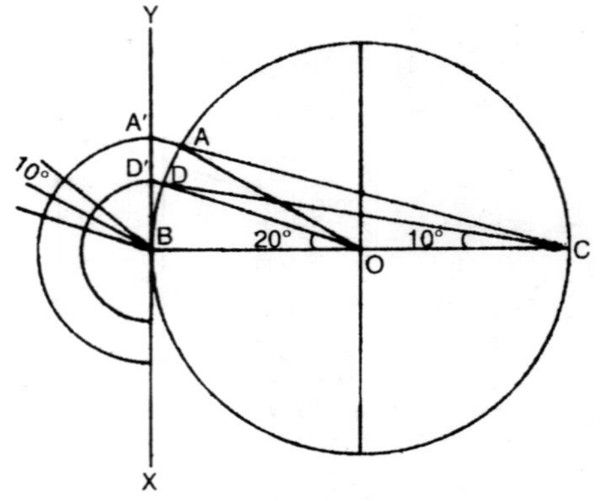

Fig 2.10 Construction of polar stereographic projection

Trigonometric Construction

The trigonometrical construction of Stereographic Projection is very simple and can be drawn faster.

1. Calculate the radius (R) of the Reduced Earth.
2. Draw the pair of straight lines intersecting each other at the point N at right angle. The centre will be considered as the pole (90°). The cardinal meridians are 0°, 90°E, 180° and 90°W.
3. Calculate the radius to draw the parallel of the given latitude (ϕ) by the following equation. Radius of any parallel (rϕ) = 2Rtan(90 – ϕ)/2

[From the fig. 2.10 it can be seen that ∠BCD′= $\left(\frac{1}{2}\right)$ ∠BOD or ∠BOD′ = 90° – ϕ/2, as the angle at the centre will be twice the angle at the circumference subtended within the same arc.

Also BC = 2BO or 2R.

We know, BD′/BC = tan ∠BCD′ or BD′= BC tan ∠BCD′ = 2R tan(90° – ϕ)/2]

4. Divide the quadrants at the given interval by placing the protractor at the point N to draw the meridians. All meridians will be radiating from the pole (i.e. the point N here).
5. Label the graticules (parallels and meridians) as per text.
6. Mark the outline. Put the scale at the bottom and label the title of projection on the top.

Properties

1. All parallels are drawn as a concentric circles with varying radii.
2. All meridians are straight lines radiating from the centre (pole).
3. The spacing of the parallels increases away from the pole.
4. So maximum distortion of shape is near the equator. The polar areas nearly maintain the shape.
5. It can be constructed as a plane tangent to the globe at any point and the tangential scale is true.
6. The whole hemisphere can be shown on this projection.
7. As any circle in the sphere remains a circle on the projection, it is commonly used for graphical solutions in field astronomy.

Exercise

Q. Draw graticules on Polar Stereographic Projection in the scale of 1:250,000,000 of the Southern Hemisphere. Interval of parallels and meridians = 10° (fig. 2.11).

Ans. 1. $R = \frac{640,000,000 \text{ cm}}{250,000,000} = 2.56$ cm.

2. Selected parallels are 0°, 10°S, 20°S, 30°S, 40°S, 50°S, 60°S, 70°S, 80°S, 90°S.

3. Radii of the parallels $2R\tan\left(\frac{90°-\theta}{2}\right)$

θ	$\frac{90°-\theta}{2}$	$2R\tan\left(\frac{90°-\theta}{2}\right)$	Result (in cm)
0°	45°	5.12	5.12
10°	40°	4.29619	4.30
20°	35°	3.58506	3.59
30°	30°	2.95603	2.96
40°	25°	2.38750	2.39
50°	20°	1.86353	1.86
60°	15°	1.37189	1.37
70°	10°	0.90279	0.90
80°	5°	0.44794	0.45
90°	0°	—	—

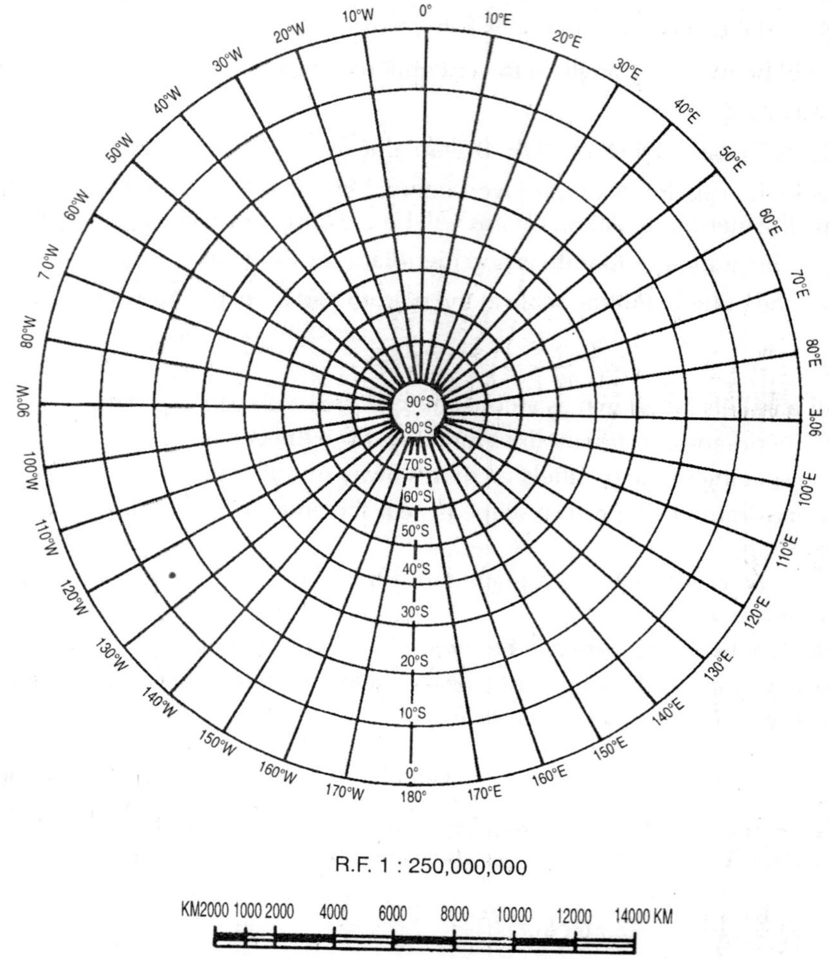

Fig. 2.11 Polar Zenithal Stereographic Projection

DERIVATION FOR POLAR ZENITHAL STEREOGRAPHIC PROJECTION

NELE′ is the generating globe,

$<PCE' = \theta$

As NP tangent and ECE′ diameter are parallel to each other

$<NPC = \theta$

$\therefore <NCP = 90° - \theta$

L is the source of light which is in an antipodal position to N.

In Δ NLP, $<NLP = \frac{90°-\theta}{2}$, as the angle at the circumference is half the angle at the centre, subtended within the same arc.

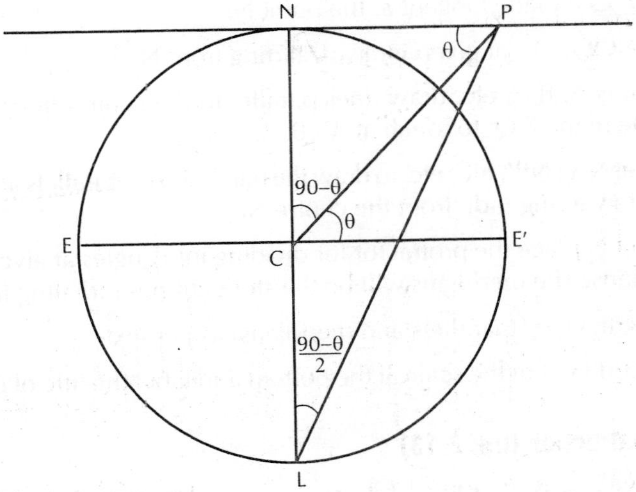

Again in ΔNLP, $\frac{NP}{NL} = \tan\frac{90°-\theta}{2}$

or, $NP = NL. \tan\frac{90°-\theta}{2}$

$= 2R. \tan\frac{90°-\theta}{2}$

Hence, Radius of parallel of latitude is $2R. \tan\frac{90°-\theta}{2}$

The meridians of longitude can be obtained with the help of a protractor at given interval and they radiate from the centre of projection outward.

The Orthographic Projection

This is also a zenithal perspective projection in which the source of light or the point of projection lies at infinity. The rays of light are therefore parallel. The parallel rays or lines project the graphic grid of one hemisphere on a tangent plane. The parallels appear as a concentric circles with varying radii. The meridians are straight lines having true bearing and radiate from the pole.

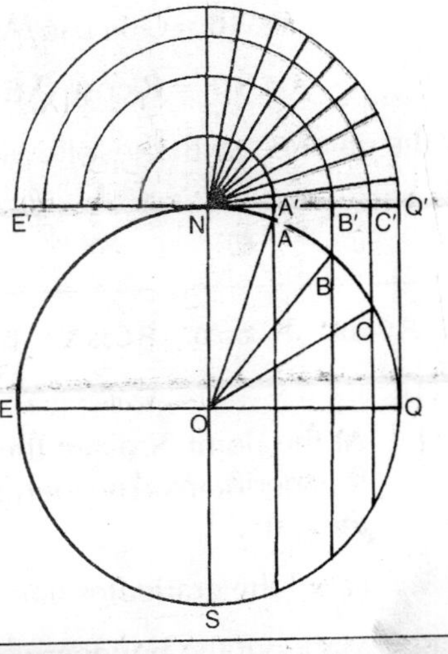

Fig. 2.12 Graphical Construction of Polar Orthographic Projection

Polar Case

Graphical Construction (fig. 2.12)

The graphical construction of Orthographic Projection is simple.

Steps

1. Calculate the radius (R) of the Reduced Earth.
2. Draw a circle with radius R. Let EQNS be the circle.

3. Draw E′Q′ as a plane tangent at the point N.
4. Divide ∠NOQ(90°) at given interval starting from N.
5. At the points A, B,C, etc. draw lines parallel to the central line ON and project these lines to the plane E′Q′ to touch at A′, B′, C′ etc.
6. Thus we get NA′, NB′, NC′ etc. to draw the parallel. The parallels are drawn as concentric circles with varying radii from the centre N.
7. At the point N place the protractor for dividing into angles at given interval for spacing the meridians. The meridians will be the straight lines radiating from N (i.e. pole).
8. Label the graticules (parallels and meridians) as per text.
9. Mark the outline. Put the scale at the bottom and label the title of projection on the top.

Trigonometrical Construction (fig. 2.13)

The trigonometrical construction of Orthographic Projection is also very simple.

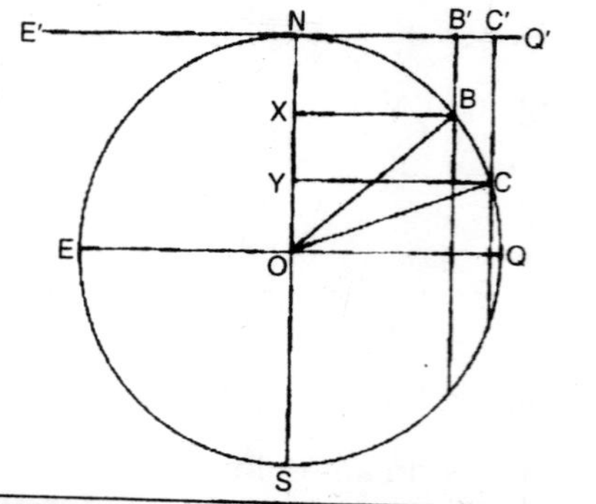

Fig. 2.13 Trigonometrical Construction of Polar Orthographic Projection

Steps

1. Calculate the radius (R) of the Reduced Earth.
2. Draw a pair of straight lines intersecting at the point N. The cardinal points are 0°, 90°E, 180° and 90°W.
3. Calculate the radii to draw the parallels at latitude f by the equation :

$$\phi r = R \cos\phi$$

[From the fig. XB/OB = cos∠XBO = cos ∠BOQ (as ∠XBO = ∠BOQ)

or XB = OB cosϕ (As ∠BOQ = ϕ)

or NB′ = R cosϕ (XB = NB′ and OB = R)]

Draw the parallels with the following radii for different latitudes :

ϕ	90°	80°	70°	60°	50°	40°	30°	20°	10°	0°
ϕr	R Cos 90°	R Cos 80°	R Cos 70°	R Cos 60°	R Cos 50°	R Cos 40°	R Cos 30°	R Cos 20°	R Cos 10°	R Cos 0°

4. At the point N place the protractor, and draw angles at the given interval for spacing the meridians. The meridians will be the straight lines spaced apart at true bearing from the pole.
5. Label the graticules (latitudes and longitudes) as per text.
6. Mark out the boundary. Put the scale at the bottom and label the title of projection on the top.

Properties

1. All parallels are concentric circles with varying radii.
2. All meridians are straight lines spaced apart from the pole with true bearing.
3. The parallels become crowded near the outer margin.
4. The projection is neither equal area nor conformal. The area becomes larger near the centre than in the outer margin. The shape is thus distorted more near the equator.
5. The tangential scale remains true.
6. The projection imparts a visual effect of a globe in three dimensions and appears like a photograph of the globe taken from the space.
7. The projection can be drawn for the whole hemisphere.
8. It is useful in the study of field astronomy.

Exercise

Q. Draw the graticules (latitudes and longitudes) of Southern Hemisphere on Orthographic Projection (Polar case) in the scale of 1:125,000,000. Space the parallels and meridians at 10° interval (fig. 2.14).

Ans. 1. $R = \frac{640{,}000{,}000 \text{ cm}}{125{,}000{,}000} = 5.12$ cm.

2. Selected parallels are 0°, 10°S, 20°S, 30°S, 40°S, 50°S, 60°S, 70°S, 80°S, 90°S.

3. Radii of the parallels : R cos θ

θ	R cosθ	Result (in cm)	θ	R cosθ	Result (in cm)
0°	5.12	5.12	10°	5.04222	5.04
20°	4.81123	4.81	30°	4.43405	4.43
40°	3.92215	3.92	50°	3.29107	3.29
60°	2.56	2.56	70°	1.75114	1.75
80°	0.88908	0.89	90°	—	—

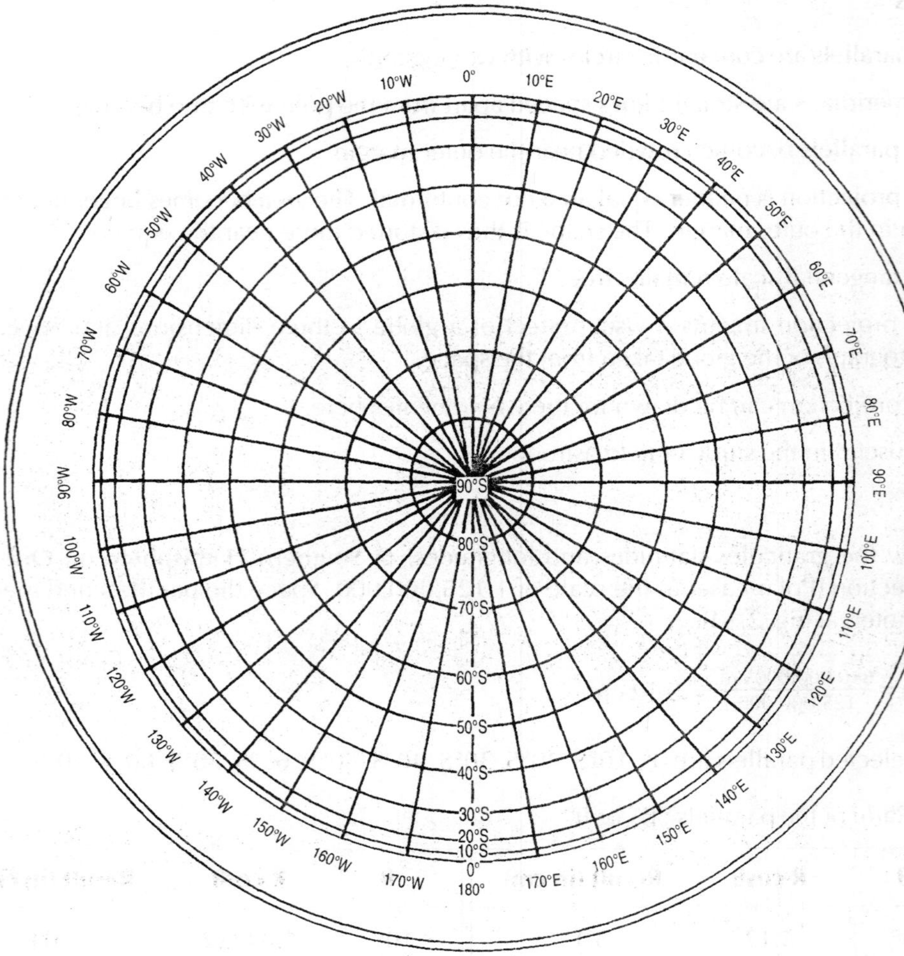

R.F. 1 : 125,000,000

KM1250 0 1250 2500 3750 KM

Fig. 2.14 **Polar Zenithal Orthographic Projection**

Derivation for polar zenithal orthographic projection

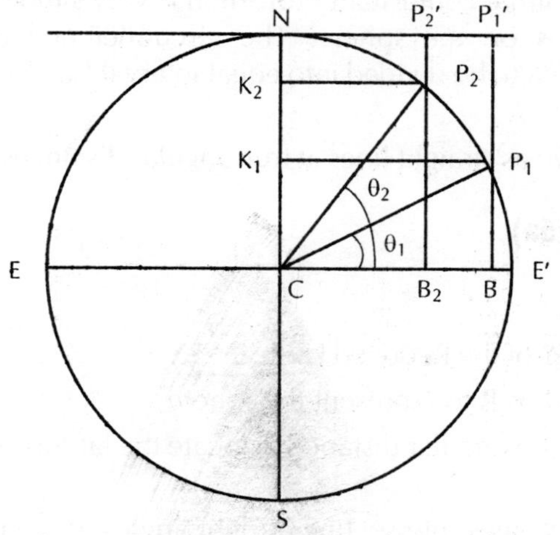

In generating globe NESE′

ECE′ is the equator on which CN is perpendicular (radius) intersecting tangent at N.

θ_1 is angle of latitude of parallel P_1.

θ_2 is angle of latitude of parallel P_2.

K_1P_1 is perpendicular on CN intersecting P_1.

K_2P_2 is perpendicular on CN intersecting P_2.

In ΔCP_1K_1,

$$\frac{CK_1}{CP_1} = \tan \theta_1$$

$$\text{or, } CK_1 = CP_1 . \tan\theta_1$$

$$= R. \tan\theta_1$$

In ΔCP_1K_1,

$$\frac{K_1P_1}{CP_1} = \cos \theta_1$$

$$\text{or, } K_1P_1 = CP_1 . \cos \theta_1$$

$$= R. \cos \theta_1$$

$\therefore K_1P_1 = NP_1'$ (Radius of the parallel of latitude θ_1)

This way $K_2P_2 = NP_2'$.

The meridians of longitude are drawn with the help of protractor.

The Zenithal Equidistant Projection

This projection is commonly used for the map of polar areas. The Zenithal Equidistant Projection is a non-perspective projection. The pole is considered as the centre of the map and all meridians are plotted as straight lines at desired angles. The parallels are spaced at true distances apart equally from the pole. All parallels are drawn as concentric circles.

Construction

The construction of Zenithal Equidistant Projection is very simple. The intervals are to be the same on the projection as on the sphere. The circumference of the sphere = $2\pi R$. The circumference of the sphere is to be divided into equal interval (say X) for spacing the parallels, i.e. $2\pi R/360° \times X$.

The meridians are drawn as straight lines at true angular distances apart from the pole.

Graphical Method (fig. 2.15a)

Steps

1. Calculate the radius (R) of the Reduced Earth.
2. Draw a circle with radius R to represent the sphere.
3. Divide the circle at given angular distance to locate the latitude (f) on the sphere (i.e. A=80°, B=70°, C=60°etc.).
4. Draw a pair of straight lines intersecting at right angles at the point N (i.e. pole). The four cardinal points are 0°, 90°E, 180° and 90°W.

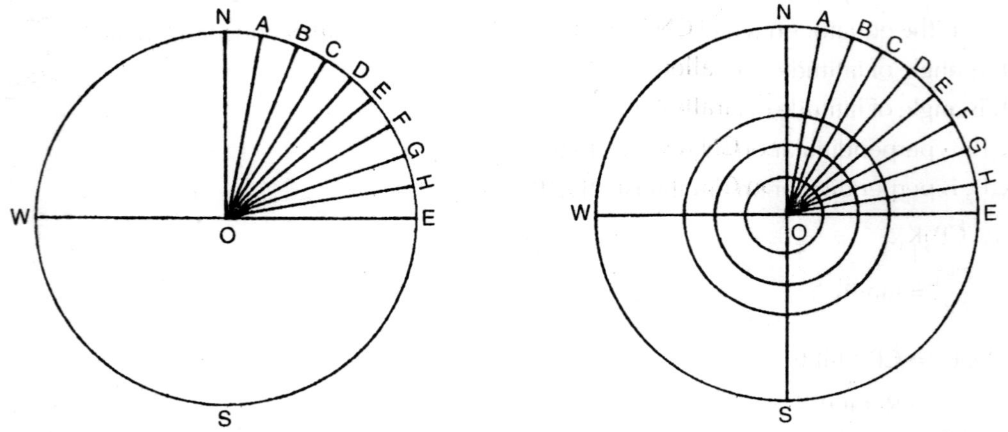

Fig. 2.15(a & b) Construction of Polar Zenithal Equidistant Projection

5. Mark out the arc distances from the pole as NA, NB, NC, etc. Draw concentric circles at N with the radii to represent the parallels.
6. Place the protractor at N and divide the circle with angular distance X to draw the meridians as straight lines.
7. Label the graticules (latitudes and longitudes) as per text.
8. Mark out the boundary. Put the scale at the bottom and label the title of projection on the top.

Trigonometrical Method (fig. 2.15b)

Steps

1. Calculate the radius (R) of the Reduced Earth.
2. Draw a pair of straight lines intersecting at right angles at the point N (i.e. pole). The four cardinal points are 0°, 90°E, 180°and 90° W.

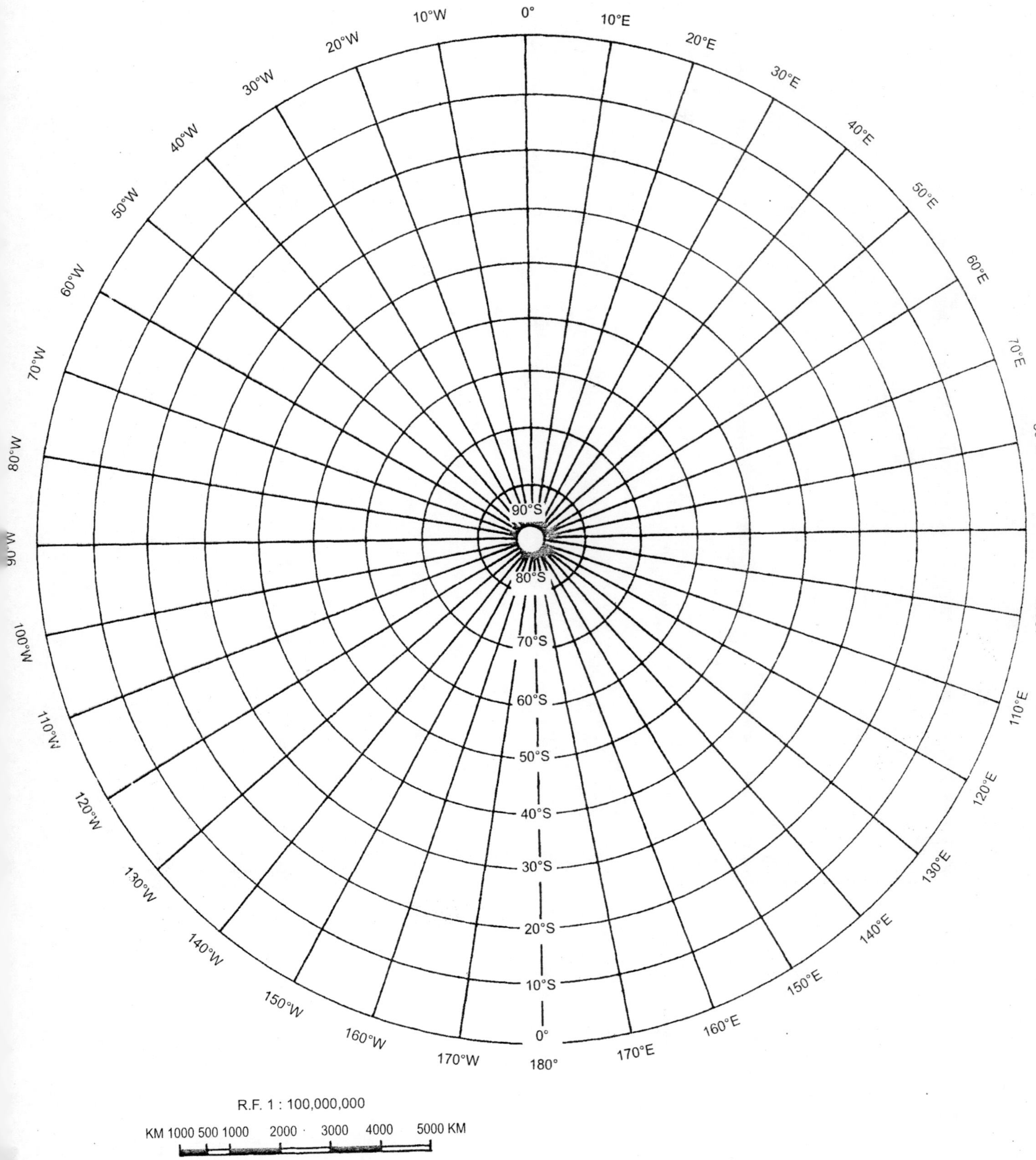

Fig. 2.16 Polar Zenthal Equidistant Projection

3. The distance (d) for spacing the parallels are marked out on the central meridian.

   $d = 2\pi R/360° \times i$ (where i = interval)

Distance from the pole to draw the parallels : = (90–ϕ) × 2þR/360°

ϕ	80°	70°	60°	50°	40°	30°	20°	10°	0°
Dist.	2πR/36	2πR×2/36	2πR×3/36	2πR×4/36	2πR×5/36	2πR×6/36	2πR×7/36	2πR×8/36	2πR×9/36

Draw the parallels as concentric circles with the calculated distances for different latitudes as radii.

4. Place the protractor at the pole and divide the circle with the given angular distance for spacing the meridians. The meridians will be the straight lines radiating from the pole.
5. Label the graticules (latitudes and longitudes) as per text.
6. Mark the boundary. Put the scale at the bottom and label the title of projection on the top.

Exercise

Q. Draw the graticules of Southern Hemisphere on a *Polar Zenithal Equidistant Projection* in the scale of 1:100,000,000 with an interval of 10° for spacing the parallels and meridians (fig. 2.16).

Ans. 1. $R = \frac{640{,}000{,}000 \text{ cm}}{100{,}000{,}000} = 6.4$ cm.

2. Selected parallels are — 0°, 10°S, 20°S, 30°S, 40°S, 50°S, 60°S, 70°S, 80°S, 90°S.

3. Distance from the pole to draw the parallels $(90° - \theta) = \frac{2\pi R}{360°}$

θ	(90°–θ)	$(90° - \theta) \times \frac{2\pi R}{360°}$	Result (in cm)
0°	90°	10.05310	10.05
10°	80°	8.93609	8.94
20°	70°	7.81908	7.82
30°	60°	6.70206	6.70
40°	50°	5.58505	5.59
50°	40°	4.46804	4.47
60°	30°	3.35103	3.35
70°	20°	2.23402	2.23
80°	10°	1.11701	1.12
90°	0°	—	—

Derivation for Polar Zenithal Equidistant Projection

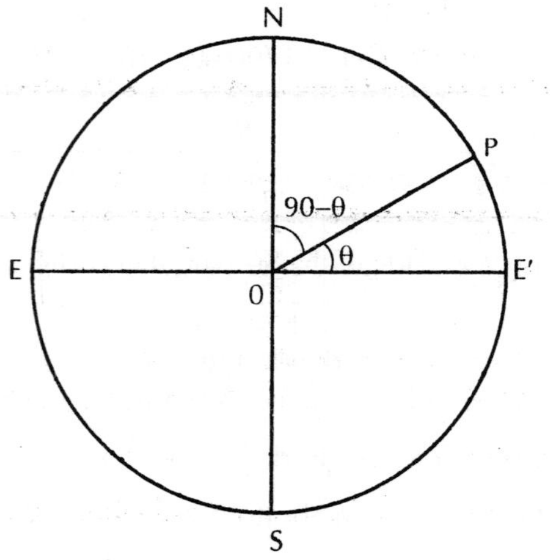

NESE′ is the generating globe, in which <POE′ = θ and <NOP = 90 – θ

$\therefore$ NP = R(90°–θ)^C [Radius for parallel of latitude P]

In another way,

NESE′ = 2πR

$\frac{2\pi R}{360} \times (90° - \theta)$ = NP [Radius for parallel of latitude P]

The meridians are obtained with the help of protractor as radial lines at given interval.

The Zenithal Equal Area Projection

This Zenithal Projection has the property to maintain equal area. The area between any two parallels on the projection is drawn equal to the corresponding area on the globe. Like other Zenithal projections the parallels are concentric circles, but they are drawn with varying radii. The parallels become closer away from the pole. Meridians are all straight lines radiating from the pole and stretch at true angular distances from the pole. The Polar Zenithal Equal Area Projection is a non-perspective projection.

Polar Case

Graphical Construction

The Zenithal Equal Area Projection (polar case) can be constructed conveniently by graphical means (fig. 2.17).

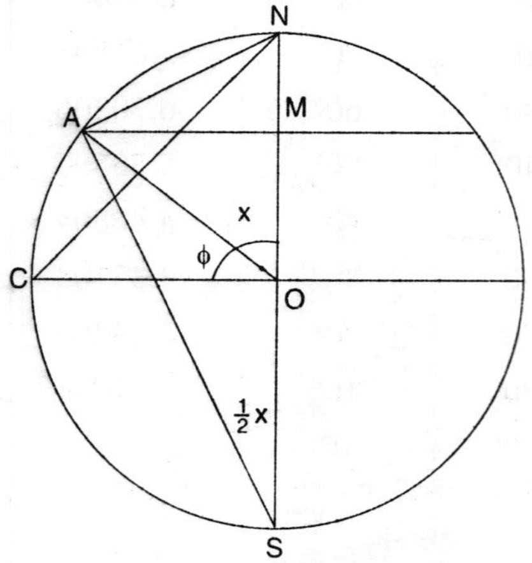

Fig. 2.17 Graphical Construction of Polar Zenithal Equal Area Projection

1. Calculate the radius (R) of the Reduced Earth.
2. Draw a circle with radius R to represent the globe. Draw OA as radius to represent the parallel (say latitude ϕ).
3. Join NA. NA will be the radius to draw the (lat. ϕ). Similarly other radii NB, NC etc. will draw the other parallels.
4. Draw a pair of straight lines intersecting each other at right angle at N. The four cardinal points are thus found namely 0°, 90°E, 180° and 90°W.
5. Draw concentric circles with radii NA, NB, NC etc. to represent the parallels.
6. The meridians are spaced with the help of a protractor as in the polar cases of other zenithal projections.
7. Label the graticules (latitude and longitude) as per text.
8. Mark the boundary. Put the scale at the bottom and label the title of projection on the top.

Trigonometrical Construction

The trigonometrical construction of Zenithal Equal Area Projection can be done by the following steps.

Steps

1. Calculate the radius (R) of the Reduced Earth.
2. Draw a pair of straight lines intersecting at right angle at N. The four cardinal points are 0°, 90°E, 180°, 90°W.
3. Calculate the radius $r\phi$ to draw the parallels by the equation :

$$r\phi = 2R\sin 90° - \phi/2$$

[In the given figure NA is the radius to draw the parallel at latitude ϕ.

Let $\angle AOC = \phi$, $\angle AON = x$ and $\angle ASN = \frac{1}{2}x$; also $AN = SN \sin \frac{1}{2}x = 2R \sin \frac{1}{2}x$

We know $x = 90° - \phi$; So $AN = 2R \sin \left(\frac{90° - \phi}{2}\right)$

Radii ($r\phi$) to draw the parallels for different latitudes (ϕ) will be :

ϕ	0°	10°	20°	30°	40°	50°	60°	70°	80°	90°
$r\phi$ =	2R sin45°	2R sin40°	2R sin35°	2R sin30	2R sin25°	2R sin20°	2R sin15°	2R sin10°	2R sin5°	2R sin0°

4. Draw concentric circles with the calculated radii to represent the parallels.
5. Meridians are spaced with the help of a protractor radiating as straight lines from the pole at given angular distance (interval).
6. Label the graticules (latitudes and parallels) as per text.
7. Mark the boundary. Put the scale at the bottom and label the title of projection on the top.

Properties

1. This projection is a non-perspective projection.
2. All parallels are concentric circles, but spaced at varying distances. The circles become closer away from the pole.
3. All meridians are straight lines spaced apart at true angular distances at the pole.
4. The area between any two parallels on the projection is equal to corresponding area on the globe. Hence it is an Equal Area Projection.
5. Azimuths from the centre of the map are true. So it is an Azimuthal Projection.
6. The Zenithal Equal Area Projection is commonly used in most atlases to represent the polar regions. The graticules for these areas are easy to draw.

Exercise

Q. Draw graticules of Northern Hemisphere on *Polar Zenithal Equal Area Projection Scale* – 1:125,000,000 and interval – 10° (fig. 2.18).

Ans. 1. $R = \frac{640,000,000 \text{ cm}}{125,000,000} = 5.12$ cm.

2. Selected parallels are — 0°, 10°N, 20°N, 30°N, 40°N, 50°N, 60°N, 70°N, 80°N, 90°°N.

3. Distance from the pole to draw the parallels $\left(\frac{90°-\theta}{2}\right)$

θ	$\frac{90°-\theta}{2}$	$2R \sin\left(\frac{90°-\theta}{2}\right)$	Result (in cm)
0°	45°	7.24077	7.24
10°	40°	6.58215	6.58
20°	35°	5.87342	5.87
30°	30°	5.12	5.12
40°	25°	4.32761	4.33
50°	20°	3.50229	3.50
60°	15°	2.65031	2.65
70°	10°	1.77816	1.78
80°	5°	0.89247	0.89
90°	—	—	—

Derivation for Polar zenithal Equal Area projection

NESC is the generating globe, in which <AOC = θ

$\therefore$ <NOA = 90° – θ and <NSA = $\frac{90°-\theta}{2}$

NA is the chord subtended within arc NA.

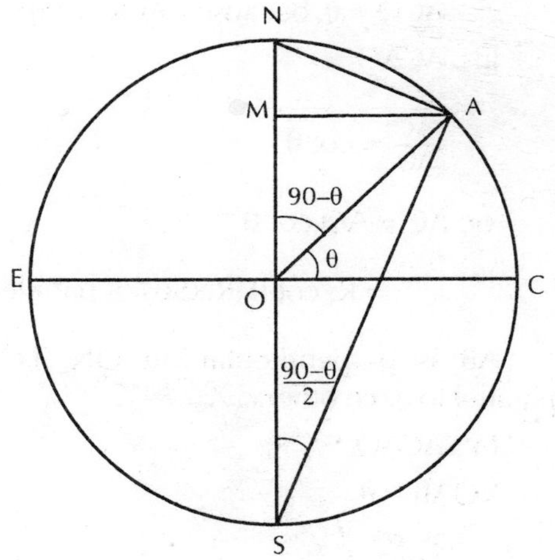

In Δ NSA,

$$\frac{NA}{NS} = \sin\frac{90°-\theta}{2}$$

or, $NA = NS.\sin\frac{90°-\theta}{2}$

$= 2R.\sin\frac{90°-\theta}{2}$ (Radius of parallel MA)

MA is perpendicular on ON

<MAO = θ as MA and OC are parallel to each other

In Δ MAO,

$$\frac{MA}{OA} = \cos\theta$$

or, $MA = OA.\cos\theta$

$= R.\cos\theta$

The total length of parallel of latitude $MA = 2\pi R.\cos\theta$

Comparison of Polar Zenithal Projections

1. In all polar zenithal projections parallels are drawn as concentric circles.
2. In Equidistant Projection parallels are spaced equally at true distances. But in other zenithal projections distances vary. In Gnomonic Projection and Stereographic Projection distances increase away from the pole. In Gnomonic Projection the exaggeration of scale is such that the equator cannot be shown. In Zenithal Equal Area and Orthographic projections distances for spacing the parallels decrease away from the pole. In the Orthographic Projection the parallels become crowded near the Equator.
3. In Zenithal Equal Area Projection the equal area property is maintained in between the two parallels, but the shape is largely distorted in this projection. In Zenithal Orthographic Projection areas near the Equator are exaggerated on the projection while the areas away from the pole become constricted.
4. All meridians are spaced at true angular distances apart at the poles. So all zenithal projections are azimuthal.
5. All zenithal projections are tolerably suitable for the areas 30° or so from the pole. Hence these are common projections for the polar areas in most atlases.
6. The Gnomonic and Stereographic projections are used for the graphical solutions in Field Astronomy.

DERIVATION FOR CONICAL PROJECTION

NESE′ is the generating globe, on which cone AC touches the globe along AB parallel of latitude.

∴ AB is the standard parallel.

<AOE = θ and <CAO = 90°, as AC is the tangent on OA radius.

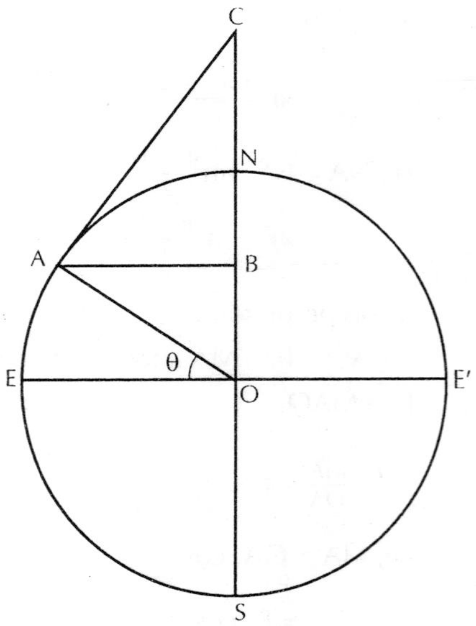

$\therefore$ <ACO = θ, because <AOC = 90°– θ

In ⊥ΔCAO,

$$\frac{AC}{AO} = \cot\theta$$

or, AC = AO.cot θ

= R. cot θ [Radius of parallel of latitude AB]

AB is perpendicular on ON; EO and AB are parallel to each other.

In ⊥ΔCAO,

<OAB = θ

$$\frac{AB}{OA} = \cos\theta$$

or, AB = OA.cos θ

= R. cos θ

The total length of parallel of latitude AB = 2πR.cos θ

Division along the standard parallel AB $= \frac{2\pi R.\cos\theta}{360} \times i$

[Where, i = the interval]

Constant of cone

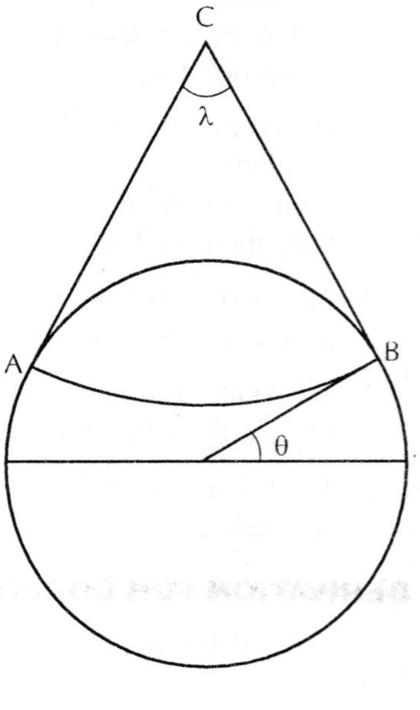

CAB is the cone which touches the reduced globe at AB.

The angle at the apex of the cone is <ACB (λ)

The constant of the cone is the ratio between <ACB and the angle at the pole of the reduced globe.

This angle at the pole is 360°.

On projection the meridians can not be at their true distance apart, as it has been reduced.

The reduction occurs as the ratio between the angle at the apex of the cone when developed and true angle of the generating globe at the pole i.e. 360°. This ratio is known as the constant of the cone.

$\therefore \frac{\lambda}{360^\circ}$, when we know the value of λ

The value of $\lambda = \frac{\text{length of AB (standard parallel)}}{\text{radius of AB parallel}}$

For polar zenithal projections, it is $\frac{360^\circ}{360^\circ} = 1$.

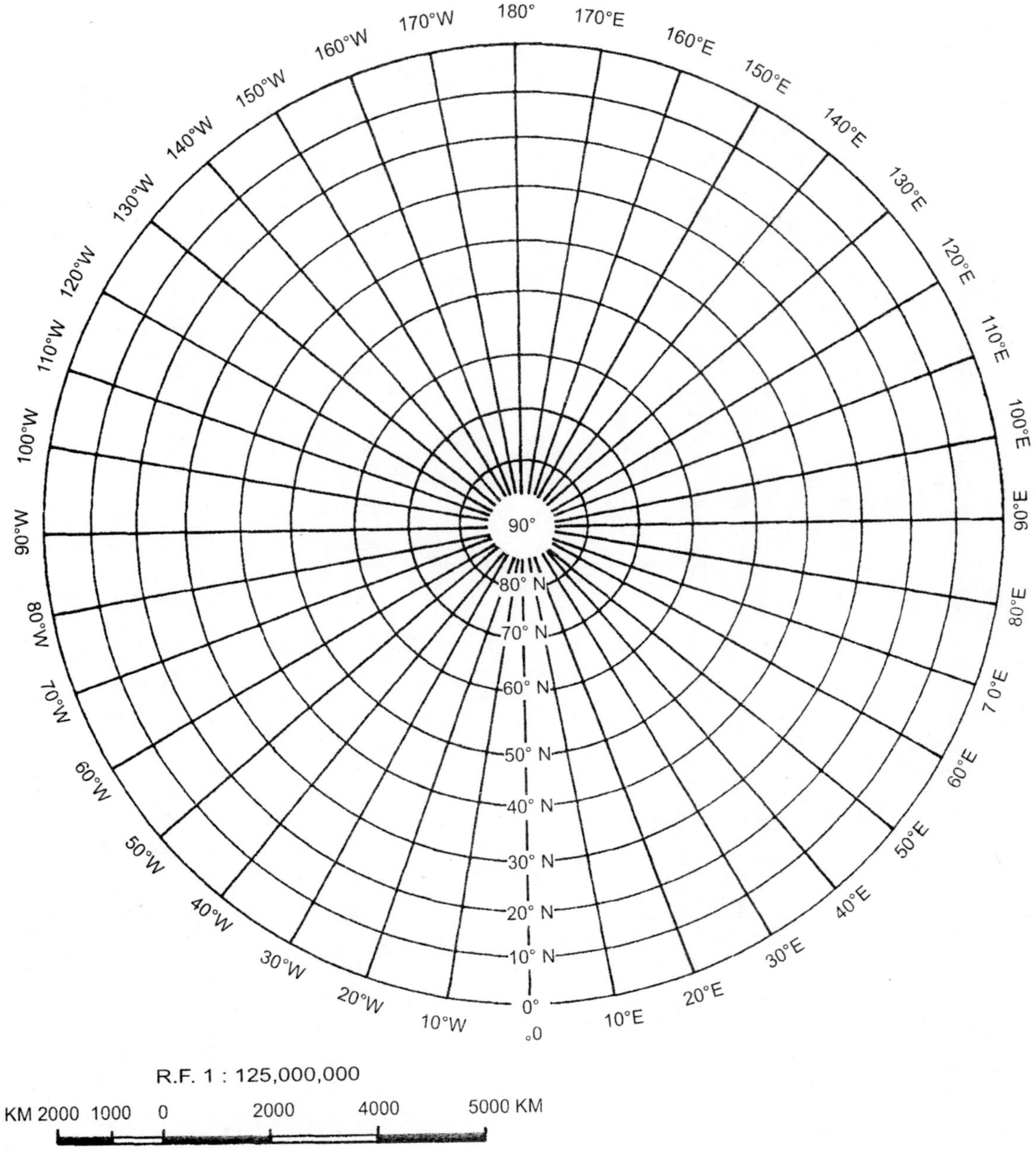

Fig. 2.18 Polar Zenthal Equal Area Projection

Simple Conic Projection with One Standard Parallel

Simple Conic Projection with One Standard Parallel is a simple type of conical projections. In this projection a single parallel is chosen as the standard parallel. Normally the mid-latitude areas are better represented by this projection. **A standard parallel is the parallel along which the cone of developable surface touches the generating globe.** Usually, it is selected at the middle of the given extent of latitudes to maintain a parity between the distortions in the north and south of the parallel. It can be selected elsewhere too.

Construction

The Simple Conic Projection with One Standard Parallel is a **non-perspective projection**. It can be drawn both graphically and trigonometrically.

Graphical Method (fig. 2.19)

1. Calculate the radius (R) of the Reduced Earth.
2. Draw circle with radius R to represent the globe.
3. Select the standard parallel as the line AB and draw a tangent AC at the point A (touching the standard parallel). AC meets the extended line of the central meridian at the point C outside the globe. The line CA will be the radius to draw the standard parallel having its centre at C.
4. Draw an arc XY which subtends 10° at the centre. Divide the central meridian on both sides of the standard parallel at equal distance of XY to draw the other parallels from the point C.

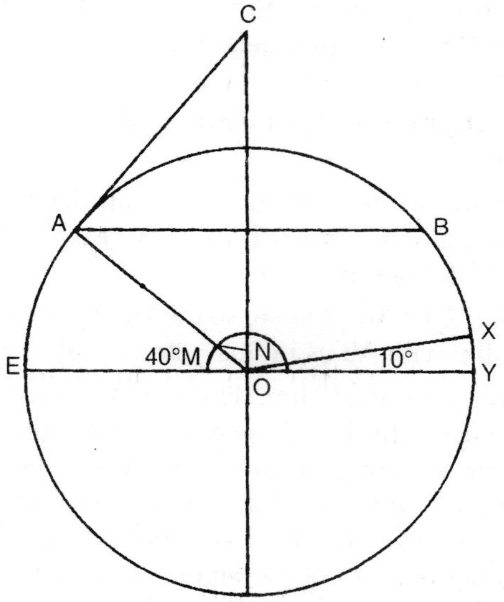

Fig. 2.19 Graphical Construction of Simple Conic Projection with one standard parallel

5. With XY as radius draw an arc with centre O. This arc cuts the lines AO at M. Draw a perpendicular MN from the point M on the line CO. MN will be the division along the standard parallel for spacing the meridians. Divide the standard parallel at equal distance of MN on both sides of the central meridian. Join all the points with C and extend these lines. These will become the meridians.
6. Label the graticules (latitudes and longitudes) as per text.
7. Mark the boundary. Put the scale at the bottom and label the title of projection on the top of the projection.

Trigonometrical Method (fig. 2.20)

1. Calculate the radius (R) of the Reduced Earth.
2. Choose the standard parallel (say 40°N) and central meridian.

3. Calculate the radius $r\phi$ to draw the standard parallel (ϕ) by the equation: $r\phi = R \cot\phi$

[In the right angled triangle CAO

$\angle CAO = 90°$[as the angle between radius and tangent]

$\angle AOC = 90° - \theta$ [θ or angle of latitude = M or 40° here]

$\angle ACO = \theta$ or ϕ as $CA/OA = \cot \angle ACO$

$\therefore$ $CA = OA \cot \angle ACO = R \cot\angle ACO$ = Radius for the Standard Parallel

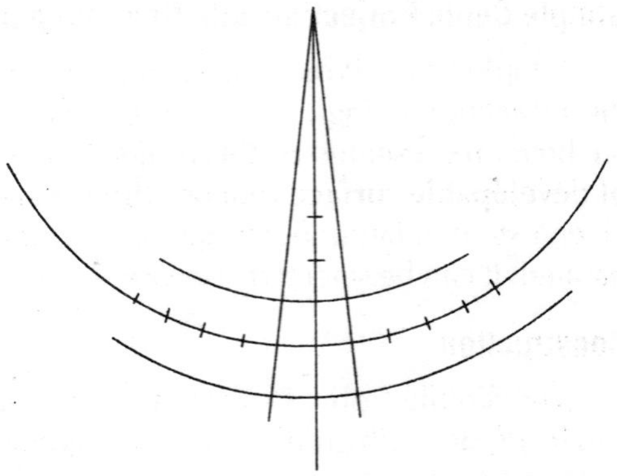

Fig. 2.20 Trigonometrical Construction of Simple Conic Projection

4. The division along the central meridian to draw the other parallels $= 2\pi R / 360° \times i$, where i = interval.
5. The length of the standard parallel $= 2\pi R \cos\phi$.

   Division along the standard parallel for spacing the meridians at interval (i) $= 2\pi R \cos\phi/360° \times i$.

   [In fig. 2.19 $AB = R \cos\phi$, so the length of the parallel with AB as radius $= 2\pi R \cos\phi$]
6. Draw a central line. Having its centre outside on this line draw an arc with radius $R \cot\phi$ to represent the standard parallel. Then divide the central meridian on both sides of the standard parallel at equal distance of $2\pi R/360° \times$ interval. Draw other parallels as concentric circles.

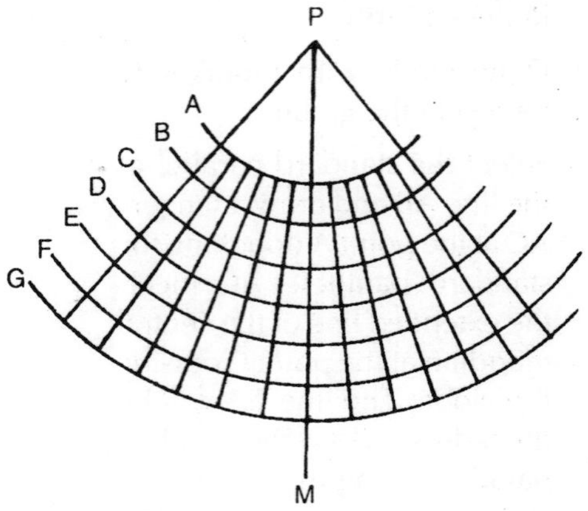

Fig. 2.21 Graticules of Simple Conic Projection

7. Divide the standard parallel for spacing the meridians at a distance of $2\pi R \cos\phi/360° \times i$. Join all these points with C and extend the lines to form the meridians.
8. Mark the boundary conforming the extension of latitudes and longitudes.
9. Label the graticules. Put the scale at the bottom and label the title of projection on the top (fig. 2.21).

Properties

1. This is a non-perspective conic projection and easy to construct.
2. In this projection poles of the earth and apex of the cone do not coincide.
3. The cone touches the globe along a parallel known as standard parallel and the tangential scale is true along the standard parallel.
4. By construction the scale is also correct along the central meridian.
5. All parallels are concentric circles and meridians are straight lines.
6. The scale becomes distorted on north and south away from the standard parallel. The projection is neither equal area nor orthomorphic. So it is called *Aphylactic Projection.*
7. It is desirable to draw maps of smaller countries in middle latitudes.

Exercise

Q. Draw graticules on *Simple Conic Projection with one Standard Parallel* with extension of latitudes and longitudes as 48°N to 60°N & 10°W to 6°E. R.F. is 1:15,000,000, at an interval of 2° (fig. 2.22).

Ans. 1. $R = \frac{640,000,000 \text{ cm}}{15,000,000} = 42.67$ cm.

2. Selected parallels are 48°N, 50°N, 52°N, 54°N, 56°N, 58°N, 60°N [54°N is selected as standard parallel].
3. The radius of the standard parallel $R\cot\theta = R\cot 54° = 31.00$ cm.
4. Selected central meridian is 10°W, 8°W, 6°W, 4°W, 2°W, 0°°, 2°E, 4°E, 6°E (2°W is selected as central meridian).

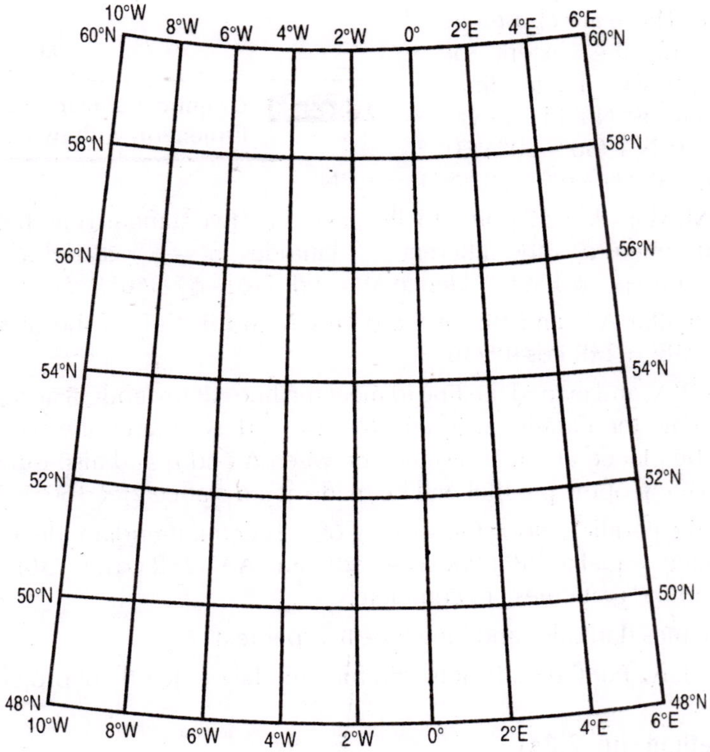

Fig. 2.22 Simple Conic Projection with one Standard Parallal

5. Division along the central meridian for spacing the parallels $\frac{\pi R \times \text{interval}}{180°} = \frac{\pi R \times 2}{180°}$ = 1.49 cm.
6. Division along the standard parallel for spacing the meridians $\frac{2\pi R \cos\theta \times \text{interval}}{360°}$

$= \frac{2\pi R \cos\theta \times 2°}{360°} = 0.88$ cm.

The Conical Projection with Two Standard Parallels

By modification we can have two standard parallels correct to scale as well as all the meridians in this conical projection. This projection is known as the Conical Projection with Two Standard Parallels. It has a distinct advance in the conical group and is useful for wide areas.

Construction

Graphical Method (fig. 2.23)

1. Calculate the radius (R) of the Reduced Earth.
2. Choose two standard parallels at latitude ϕ_1 and ϕ_2, so that they lie equidistant from the highest and lowest latitude. These are chosen in consideration of the extent of latitude and interval. If latitudinal extent is 20°N to 80°N and interval 10°, then ϕ_2 = 20°N + (80°– 20°N/3) = 40°N and ϕ_1 = 80°N – (80°– 20°N/3) = 60°N.

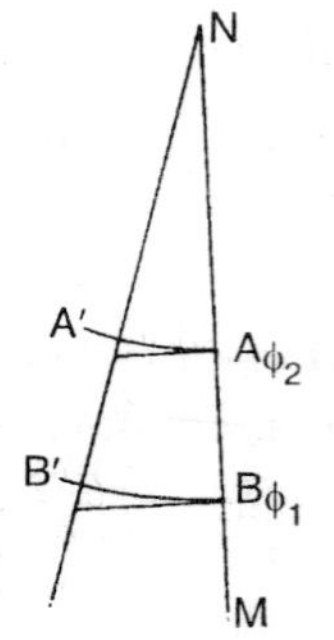

Fig. 2.23 Graphical construction of Conic Projection with two Standard Parallels

3. Draw a line NM. Mark A and B points for the position of two standard parallels. Distance AB is equal to $2\pi Rd$, where d is the difference in latitudes $(\phi_1 - \phi_2)$, stated as a fraction of the circumference [i.e. $(\phi_1 - \phi_2)/360°$]. Hence AB = $2\pi R \times (\phi_1 - \phi_2)/360°$.
4. Draw perpendicular AA′ and BB′ at the points A and B. Cut off the distance AA′ = $2\pi R$ cos60°/36 and BB′ = $2\pi R$ cos40°/36.
5. Join the points B′A′ and extend the line to meet the line AB (extended) at N. Then NB will be the radius to draw the parallel at ϕ_1 and NA, the radius to draw the parallel at ϕ_2. Other parallels may be placed at equal distance between A and B and also outwards towards N and M. The spacing of the parallel will be made at a distance $2\pi R/360° \times$ interval.
6. After drawing the parallels along the spacing of the central meridian, divide the parallels ϕ_1 and ϕ_2 at distances equal to BB′ ($2\pi R$ cos40°/36) and AA′ ($2\pi R$ cos60°/36) respectively. Join these points and the graticules are complete.
7. Label the graticules (latitudes and longitudes) as per text.
8. Mark the boundary. Put the scale at the bottom and label the title of projection on the top.

Trigonometrical Method (fig. 2.24)

Trigonometrical method is more convenient to construct the Conical Projection with Two Standard Parallels.

1. Calculate the radius (R) of the Reduced Earth.
2. Choose the standard parallels ϕ_1 and ϕ_2 as stated in the Graphical Method.
3. Calculated the radii ($r\phi_1$ and $r\phi_2$) to draw the standard parallels ϕ_1 and ϕ_2 by the following equation :

$$r\phi_2 = SA_2 = 2\pi R/360° \ (\phi_1 - \phi_2) \times \cos\phi_2/(\cos\phi_1 - \cos\phi_2)$$

$$r\phi_1 = SA_2 + A_1A_2 = r\phi_2 + 2þR \ (\phi_1 - \phi_2).$$

[In the Fig. 2.24 the sectors SA_1B_1 and SA_2B_2 are exactly similar on the projection.

So, $SA_2/SA_1 = \cos\phi_2/\cos\phi_1$ or $SA_1 = SA_2 \times \cos\phi_1/\cos\phi_2 = r\phi_1$

We know $SA_1 - SA_2 = A_1A_2 = 2\pi R/360° (\phi_1 - \phi_2)$

Substituting SA_1, we get $SA_2 \times \cos\phi_1/\cos\phi_2 - SA_2 = 2\pi R/360° (\phi_1 - \phi_2)$

or $SA_2 (\cos\phi_1/\cos\phi_2 - 1) = 2\pi R/360 \times (\phi_1 - \phi_2)$

or $SA_2 (\cos\phi_1 - \cos\phi_2/\cos\phi_2) = 2\pi R/360° (\phi_1 - \phi_2)$

and $SA_2 = 2\pi R/360° (\phi_1 - \phi_2) \times \cos\phi_2/(\cos\phi_1 - \cos\phi_2)$]

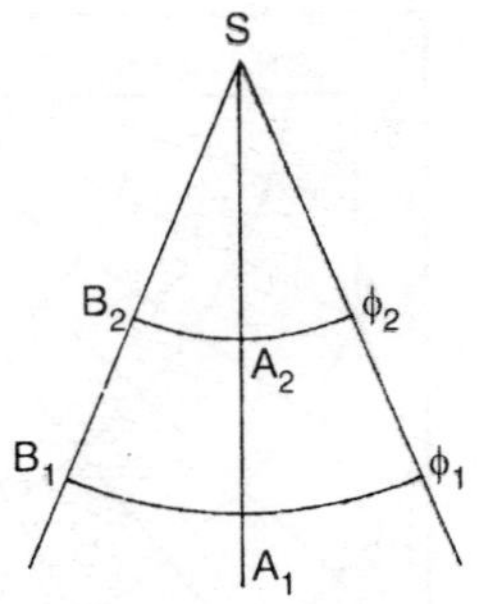

Fig. 2.24 Trigonometrical construction of Conic Projection with Two Standard Parallels

4. Division along the standard parallels ϕ_1 and ϕ_2 for spacing the meridians :

Along $\phi_1 = 2\pi R \cos\phi_1/360° \times$ interval

$\phi_2 = 2\pi R \cos\phi_2/360° \times$ interval.

5. Draw a vertical line as central meridian. Along the central meridian draw the standard parallels ϕ_1 and ϕ_2 with radii $r\phi_1$ and $r\phi_2$.

   Space other parallels on the central meridian equidistant in between the standard parallels and outside it.
6. Divide the standard parallels ϕ_1 and ϕ_2 as per step 4. Join these points and complete the graticules.
7. Label the graticules (latitudes and longitudes) as per text.
8. Mark the boundary. Put the scale at the bottom and label the title of projection on the top.

Properties

1. This is a modified conical projection. Two standard parallels are chosen in order to distribute the error.
2. In this projection meridians are radial lines and parallels are concentric circles.
3. Two standard parallels are true to scale as well as all meridians.
4. The parallels lie equidistant from the standard parallels.
5. All meridians appear as straight lines truly spaced on the standard parallels.
6. The latitude scale between the standard parallels becomes negative (smaller), but outside them becomes positive (greater). So by judicious choice of the standard parallels the error over the whole map can be minimised.
7. This projection is neither orthomorphic nor equal area, but as the meridians and parallels are at right angles to one another, it becomes nearly more orthomorphic than Bonne's projection.

Exercise

Q. Draw graticules on *Conical Projection with Two Standard Parallels* having extension of latitudes 20°N to 80°N and longitudes 90°E to 90° W with 180° as central meridian, Scale – 1:125,000,000 and interval = 10° (fig. 2.25).

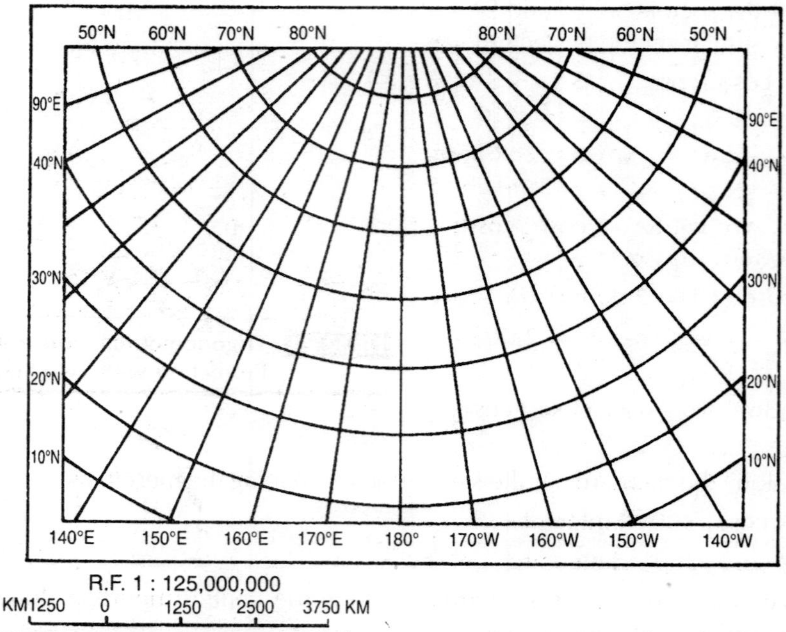

Fig. 2.25 **Simple Conical Projection with two Standard Parallels**

Ans. 1. $R = \frac{640,000,000 \text{ cm}}{125,000,000} = 5.12$ cm.

2. Selected standard parallels are :

$$\theta_1 = 20°N + (80°–20°N/3) = 40°N$$

$$\theta_2 = 80°N – (80°–20°N/3) = 60°N$$

3. Radii for Standard Parallels :

(a) $r_{ø_1} = \frac{\pi R}{180°}(ø_1 - ø_2) = \frac{\cos ø}{\cos ø_1 - \cos ø_2}$

$$r40° = \frac{\pi 5.12}{180°}(60° - 40°) \quad \frac{\cos 40°}{\cos 40° - \cos 60°} = 5.146087 = 5.15 \text{ cm}$$

(b) $r_{ø_2} = \frac{\pi 5.12}{180°}(60° - 40°) \quad \frac{\cos 60°}{\cos 40° - \cos 60°} = 3.35887 = 3.36$ cm

3. Division along the standard parallels θ_1 & θ_2 far spacing the meridians :

$$\text{Along } \theta_1 = \frac{2\pi R \cos \theta_1 \times \text{interval}}{360°}$$

$$= \frac{2\pi R \cos 40°}{360°} \times 10° = 0.45 \text{ cm}$$

$$\text{Along } \theta_2 = \frac{2\pi R \cos \theta_2 \times \text{interval}}{360°}$$

$$= \frac{2\pi R \cos 40°}{360°} \times 10° = 0.68 \text{ cm}$$

Bonne's (Conical) Projection

This is a modified form of conical projection. In Bonne's Projection all parallels are true to scale and in that sense all parallels are standard parallels. In this projection one parallel has the radius equal to R x cotangent of latitude, others are drawn as concentric circles with radii touching the divisions along the central meridian spaced at equidistance true to scale. The construction of this projection is similar to that of Simple Conic with One Standard Parallel Actually, this projection is a modification of simple conic projection with one standard parallel. In this projection the parallels of latitude are intesected by lines of meridians at correct intervals.

Construction

Graphical Method (fig. 2.26)

Steps

1. Calculate the radius (R) of the Reduced Earth.
2. With radius R draw a quadrant of the globe. Let it be NOE.
3. Divide the quadrant NOE at equal interval (10°).
4. Choose the standard parallel at the point M (say $\phi = 50°$) . VM will be the tangent at M and the radius to draw the standard parallel.
5. With one division of angular distance (say KE) on the arc, draw a small arc with centre O. Join the points of intersection of this arc with different lines radiating from O at an angle 10°. These will mark the divisions on different parallels for spacing the meridians.
6. Draw a central and vertical line, say VO. With centre V draw a concentric circle with radius VM. Mark the central line (i.e. central meridian) equally on both sides of the standard parallel with division equal to KE and draw other parallels through these points.
7. Divide the central parallel and other parallels with divisions as derived in step 5 for spacing the meridians. Join the respective points by curve lines. The graticules are thus completed.
8. Label the graticules (latitudes and longitudes) as per text.
9. Mark the boundary. Put the scale at the bottom and label the title of projection on the top.

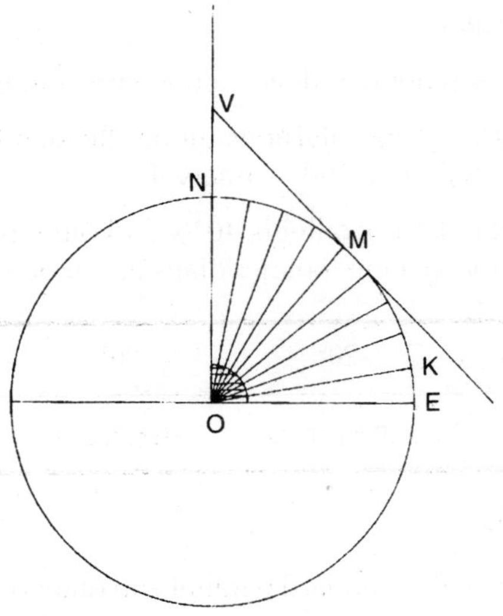

Fig. 2.26 Graphical construction of Bonne's Projection

Trigonometrical method

The trigonometrical method is also very convenient to construct the Bonne's Projection.

Steps

1. Calculate the radius (R) of the Reduced Earth.
2. Choose the standard parallel (ϕs). The standard parallel should be chosen as the mid-value of the latitudinal extent. The radius to draw the standard parallel is
$$r\phi s = R \cot \phi s.$$
3. Draw a central meridian and draw the standard parallel with radius R cotϕs. Divide the central meridian at equal distance of $2\pi R/360° \times$ interval on both sides of the standard parallel.

   Draw other parallels as concentric circles from the point V passing through these divisions.
4. Mark out the divisions along the standard parallel and other parallels by the equation : $d = 2\pi R \cos\phi/360° \times$ interval.

Say the standard parallel is 40°N and other parallels are 20°N, 30°N, 50°N and 60°N. Then the distance for spacing the meridians at standard parallel and other parallels will be :

ϕ	20°	30°	40°	50°	60°
d	$2\pi R \cos 20°/36$	$2\pi R \cos 30°/36$	$2\pi R \cos 40°/36$	$2\pi R \cos 50°/36$	$2\pi R \cos 60°/36$

Interval = 10°

5. Divide the standard parallel and other parallels as per above calculations and join the points by curves.
6. Label the graticules (latitudes and longitudes) as per text.
7. Mark the boundary. Put the scale at the bottom and label the title of projection on the top.

Properties

1. This is modified Simple Conic Projection with One Standard parallel made by R. Bonne, a French Cartographer.
2. All parallels are true to scale and in this sense all are standard parallels.
3. All parallels are drawn as arc of a circle.
4. The radial scale is true along the central meridian.
5. All meridians are curve lines and obtained by joining the points truly divided on each parallel.
6. The obliquity of the meridians to the parallels increases towards the edge of the map. For the above reason areas with a great extent of latitude and longitude are not suitable.
7. The choice of standard parallel is very important in the Bonne's Projection. The parallel selected as standard parallel to govern the curvature of all other parallels will be different in different cases. The principle of choosing the standard parallel is that the nearer the countries

is to the Equator, the lower the selected parallel. Conversely, the nearer the countries is to the Poles, the higher the selected parallel.

8. This is an equal area projection.

Exercise

Q. Draw graticules on *Bonne's Projection* with latitudes extending from 20°N to 60°N and longitudes extending from 40°E to 100°E. Scale 1:62,500,000 and interval at 10° (fig. 2.27).

Ans. 1. $R = \frac{640{,}000{,}000 \text{ cm}}{62{,}500{,}000} = 10.24$ cm.

2. Selected standard parallels are 20°N, 30°N, 40°N, 50°N, 60°N [40°N is selected as standard parallel].

3. The radius of the standard parallel R Cotθ = 12.20 cm.

4. Division along the standard parallel & the other parallels for spacing the meridials

$$\frac{2\pi R \cos\theta \times \text{interval}}{360°}$$

θ	$\frac{2\pi R \cos\theta \times \text{interval}}{360°}$	Result (in cm)
20°	1.67943	1.68
30°	1.54778	1.55
40°	1.36909	1.37
50°	1.14880	1.15
60°	0.89361	0.89

5. Division along the central meridian for spacing the parallels :

$$\frac{\pi R \times \text{interval}}{180°} = \frac{\pi \times 10.24 \times 10°}{180°}$$

$$= 1.787217154 = 1.79 \text{ cm}$$

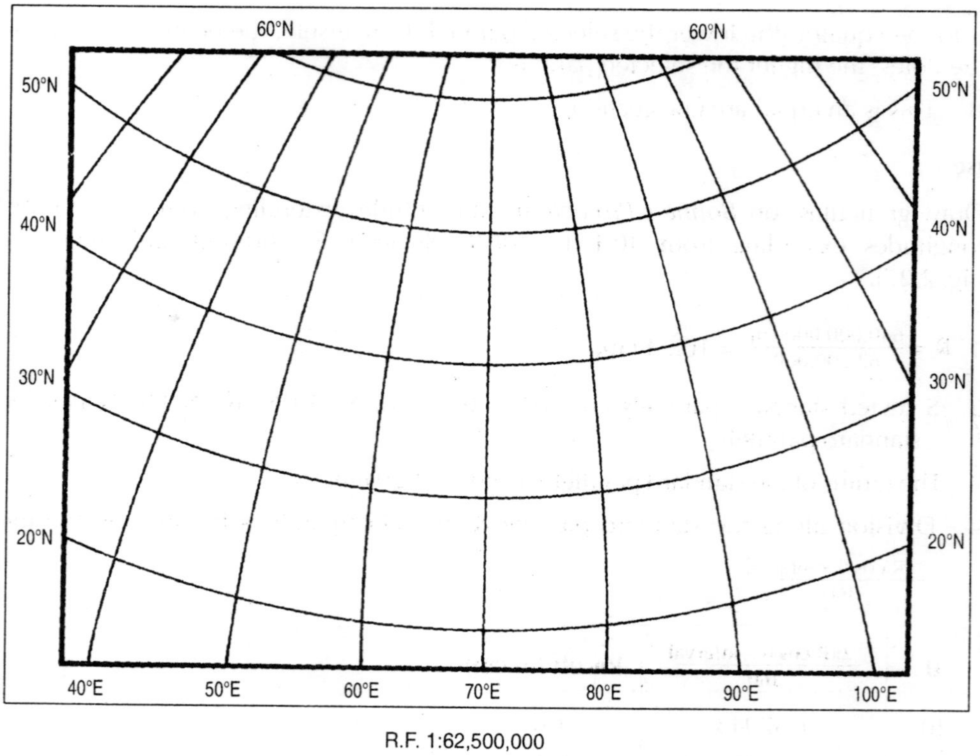

Fig. 2.27 Bonne's Projection

The Sinusoidal Projection

Sanson and Flamsteed developed this special type of Bonne's Projection. In this projection the Equator is chosen as the standard parallel and is a straight line true to scale. The central meridian is also a straight line perpendicular to the Equator, but half of the length of the Equator. Other parallels are spaced equidistant and all are straight lines. The meridians are drawn as curve by lines through the points of the parallels. All the meridians thus become sine curves and hence the name *Sinusoidal* is derived.

Construction

Graphical Method (fig 2.28)

The construction of Sinusoidal Projection by graphical method is very simple.

Steps

1. Calculate the radius (R) the Reduced Earth.
2. Draw a circle with radius (R) of the Reduced Earth.
3. Divide the arc PN at regular interval (i) with the help of a protractor.
4. With radius MN draw an arc at the centre O. Draw parallel lines to the arc joining the intersecting points of each angle with the small arc at the centre. These are divisions along the respective parallels for spacing the meridians.

5. Draw a straight line as the Equator. At the mid-point O draw a perpendicular line to represent the central meridian.
6. Divide the central meridian equally with distance MN for spacing the parallels. Draw straight lines parallel to the Equator. These will form the parallels.

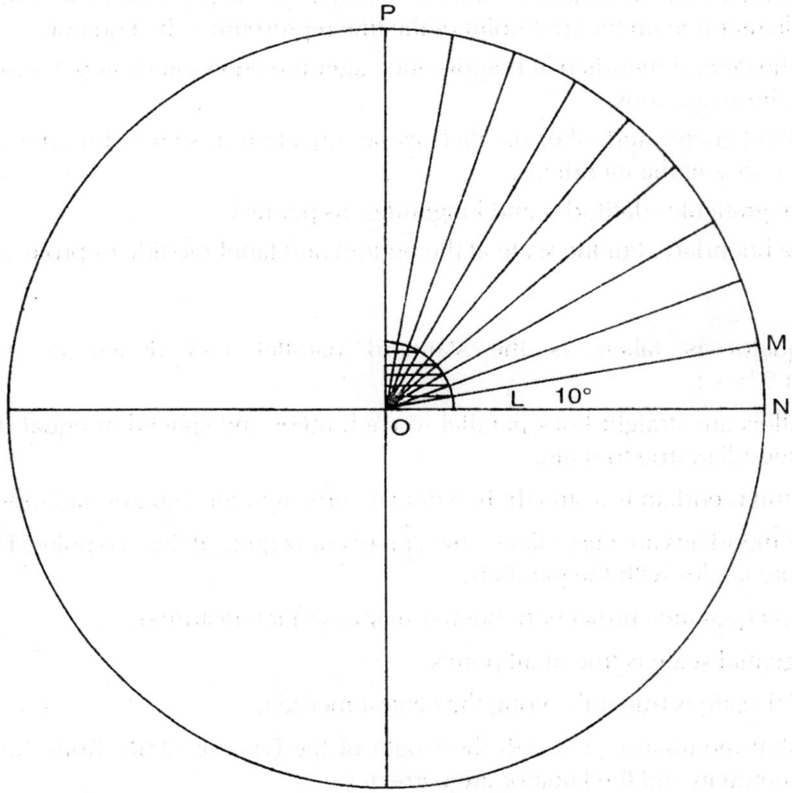

Fig. 2.28 Graphical construction of Sinusoidal Projection

7. Divide the Equator with distance MN and other parallels with distances as derived by step 4 for different parallels. respectively for spacing the meridians. Join all these points by curve lines. These will form the meridians.
8. Label the graticules (latitudes and longitudes) as per text. Put the scale at the bottom and label the title of projection on the top.

Trigonometrical Method

The Sinusoidal Projection can also be constructed conveniently by trigonometrical method.

Steps

1. Calculate the radius (R) of the Reduced Earth.
2. Calculate the length of the Equator = $2\pi R$.
3. Calculate the length of the central meridian = πR
4. Division along the central meridian for spacing the parallels at interval i = $\pi R/180 \times i$ (as latitudinal extent in both hemisphere = 90° + 90°= 180°)

5. In a limiting case of Bonne's projection radius to draw the Equator is infinity or straight line ($R \cot 0° = \infty$)
6. Calculate the divisions along the Equator and other parallels by the equation : $2\pi R \cos\phi/360° \times i$.
7. Draw a straight line as Equator. Mark the length as per step 2. Draw the central meridian as perpendicular line on the mid-point of the line representing the Equator.
8. Divide the central meridian at equidistance after the equation in step 4 and draw parallels through these divisions.
9. Divide the Equator and other parallels as per equation in step 6. Join the points by curve lines to represent the meridians.
10. Label the graticules (latitudes and longitudes) as per text.
11. Mark the boundary. Put the scale at the bottom and label the title of projection on the top.

Properties

1. The Equator is taken as the standard parallel and drawn as a straight line (as $R \cot 0° = \times$).
2. All parallels are straight lines parallel to each other and spaced at equal distance on the central meridian true to scale.
3. The central meridian is a straight line drawn vertical to the Equator and other parallels.
4. All other meridians are curve lines (sine curve) converging at the two poles. These meridians form acute angles with the parallels.
5. This is an equal area projection, but the shape is much distorted.
6. The tangential scale is true at all points.
7. The radial scale is true only along the central meridian.
8. The central meridian is half (πR) the length of the Equator ($2\pi R$). Both the lengths of the central meridian and the Equator are correct.
9. The whole sphere can be drawn on this projection, but is preferred for the equatorial areas, particularly to draw maps of Africa, Oceania and South America.

Exercise

Q. Draw graticules on a Sinusoidal Projection between 75°N and 75°S for the whole earth on a scale of 1:125,000,000 at an interval of 15° (fig. 2.29).

Ans. 1. $R = \frac{640{,}000{,}000 \text{ cm}}{125{,}000{,}000} = 5.12$ cm.

2. length of the equator = $2\pi R = 32.17$ cm.
3. Selected parallels are 75°N, 60°N, 45°N, 30°N, 15°N, 0°, 15°S, 30°S, 45°S, 60°S, 75°S.
4. Selected central meridian is 180°EW, 165°EW, 150°EW, 135°EW, 120°EW, 105°EW, 90°EW, 75°EW, 60°EW, 45°EW, 30°EW, 15°EW, [0° is selected as central meridian].
5. Division along the central meridian for spacing the parallels

$$\frac{\pi R \times \text{interval}}{180^{\circ\circ}} = \frac{\pi R \times 15^\circ}{180^{\circ\circ}} = 1.34 \text{ cm}$$

6. Division along the parallels for spacing the meridians = $\frac{2\pi R \cos\theta \times \text{interval}}{360^\circ}$

θ	$\frac{2\pi R \cos\theta \times \text{interval}}{360^\circ}$	Result (in cm)
0°	1.34041	1.34
15°	1.29474	1.29
30°	1.16083	1.16
45°	0.94782	0.95
60°	0.67021	0.67
75°	0.34692	0.35

The Polyconic Projection

The construction of this projection is fundamentally identical with that of the Conical Projection with One Standard Parallel. In this projection each parallel is drawn with radius R cotϕ, where ϕ is the latitude. The central meridian is divided at equal space for drawing the parallels. But all parallels are not concentric like the Simple Conic Projection. Each parallel is divided truly for spacing the meridians. Hence all meridians except the central meridian appear as curved lines. But the central meridian stands as a straight line in this projection. The central meridian intersects the parallels at right angles, but towards outer areas the obliquity of the angles of intersection increases. This projection is only suitable for small sheets.

Construction

Graphical Method (fig. 2.30)

The Polyconic Projection can be conveniently drawn by Graphical method.

Steps

1. Calculate the radius (R) of the Reduced Earth.
2. Draw a circle with radius R to represent the globe.
3. Set off the angles from the centre at interval i (say 10°) for the required extension of latitudes. Say they touch the arc at A, B, C. Draw tangents at these points and extend the lines to A_1, B_1, C_1 etc. Thus AA_1, BB_1, CC_1 etc. will be the radii to draw the parallels.

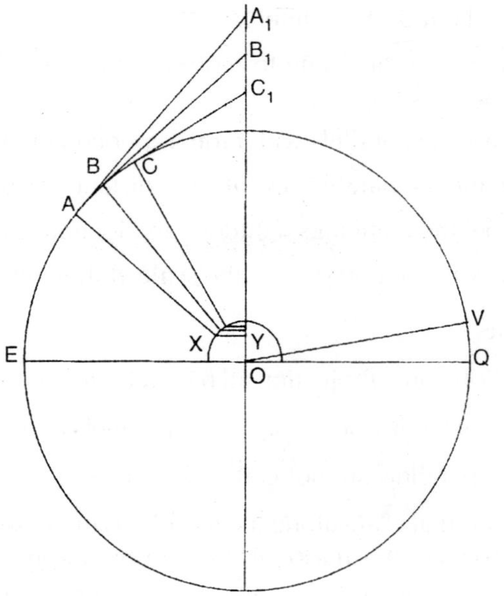

Fig. 2.30 Graphical construction of Polyconic Projection

4. With the radius of an arc subtending i angle, i.e. 10° draw an arc at the centre. Also draw different lines from the points of intersection to the central perpendicular line (central meridian) parallel to EO. These are namely XY, X1Y1, X2Y2 etc. and are represented as divisions along the parallels for spacing the meridians.
5. Draw a vertical line as a central meridian. Cut off the points a, b, c on the central meridian with distance VQ.
6. Draw the parallels along these points with radii AA_1, BB_1, CC_1 respectively with centre A_1, B_1 and C_1.
7. Divide all the respective parallels at equal distance with the distance XY, X1Y1, X2Y2 etc. Join these points and the curve line will represent the meridians.
8. Label the graticules (latitudes and longitudes).
9. Mark the boundary. Put the scale at the bottom and label the title of the projection on the top.

Trigonometrical Method

The Polyconic Projection can also be drawn easily by Trigonometrical method.

Steps

1. Calculate the radius (R) of the Reduced Earth.
2. Calculate the radius $r\phi$ to draw the parallels by the equation : $r\phi = R \cot\phi$
3. Division along the central meridian for spacing the parallels $= 2\pi R \times i/360°$ (i = interval).
4. Division along the parallels for spacing the meridians $= 2\pi R \cos\phi \times i/360°$ (ϕ = latitude & i = interval).
5. Draw a vertical line to represent the central meridian. Divide it at equal distance as per equation at step 3.
6. Draw the parallels with radii as per equation at step 2.
7. Divide the parallels evenly at a distance as per equation at step 4.
8. Label the graticules (latitudes and longitudes).
9. Mark the boundary. Put the scale at the bottom and label the title of projection on the top.

Properties

1. In Polyconic Projection all parallels are considered as standard parallels.
2. The Scale is true along all the parallels and also along the central meridian.
3. The parallels are not concentric circles.
4. The radial scale along the meridians increases away from the central meridian affecting the shape. For this reason it is less orthomorphic than the Bonne's Projection.
5. However the tangential scale is true along all the meridians.
6. It is unsuitable for large areas, but adoptable for smaller areas, particularly for the topographical maps.

7. For topographical maps its principal advantage lies in the facts that (i) by means of tables each sheet may be plotted independently and (ii) the separate sheets fit exactly along their north and south edges and have a rolling fit along their east and west edges. The modified form of Polyconic Projection is known as *One-in-a-Million Map* (also known as International Projection).
8. As being neither equal area nor orthomorphic it is classed as Aphylactic Projection.

Exercise

Q. Draw graticules on a Polyconic Projection on a scale of 1: 60,000,000 with extension of 35°S – 60°S latitudes and longitudes 165°E – 165°W. Interval is 5° (fig. 2.31).

Ans. 1. $R = \frac{640{,}000{,}000 \text{ cm}}{60{,}000{,}000} = 10.67 \text{ cm}$

2. Selected parallels are 35°S, 40°S, 50°S, 55°S, 60°S.
3. Selected central meridian is 165°E, 170°E, 175°E, 180°W, 175°W, 170°W, 165°W. [180° is selected as central meridian]
4. Radii for the parallels R cotθ.

θ	R cotθ	Result (in cm)
35°	15.23358	15.23
40°	12.71204	12.71
45°	10.66666	10.67
50°	8.950396	8.95
55°	7.46888	7.47
60°	6.15840	6.16

5. Division along the central meridian for spacing the parallels

$$\frac{\pi R \times \text{interval}}{180^\circ} = \frac{\pi R \times 5^\circ}{180^\circ} = 0.93 \text{ cm}$$

6. Division along the parallels for spacing the meridians $\frac{2\pi R \cos\theta \times \text{interval}}{360^\circ}$

θ	$\frac{2\pi R \cos\theta \times \text{interval}}{360^\circ}$	Result (in cm)
35°	0.76250	0.76
40°	0.71307	0.71
45°	0.65820	0.66
50°	0.59833	0.60
55°	0.53391	0.53
60°	0.46542	0.47

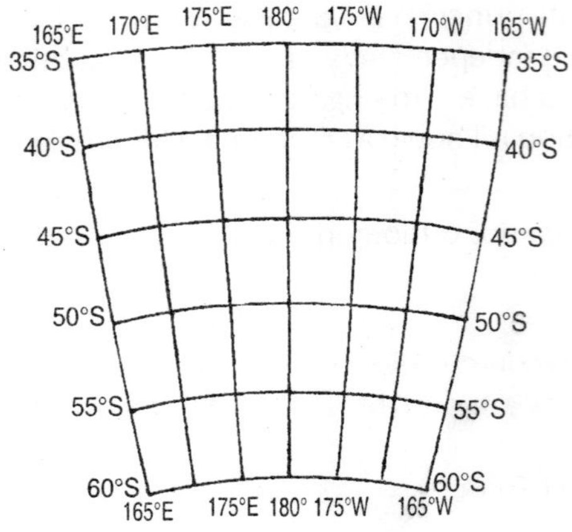

R.F. 1:60000000

Fig. 2.31 Polyconic Projection

Cylindrical Equal Area Projection

The Cylindrical Equal Area Projection was designed by Lambert. In this projection a simple right circular cylinder touches the globe at the equator. All parallels and meridians are drawn as straight lines. The length of the parallels between the poles and the length of the equator remain the same. The area between two parallels and the corresponding area on the globe are made equal. The vertical distance between any two parallels (say h) is equal to $R \sin\phi$. Hence the distance between two parallels decreases away from the equator resulting in north-south compression. On the other hand, the meridians are equally spaced and exaggeration of scale results in east-west direction.

Construction

Graphical Method (fig. 2.32)

The Cylindrical Equal Area Projection can be neatly and simply drawn by Graphical method.

Steps

1. Calculate the radius (R) of the Reduced Earth.
2. Draw a circle with radius R to represent the globe.
3. Divide a quadrant of the circle (þ/2 radian) by laying off angles at equal interval (i).
4. Draw a line tangent at the point E′.
5. From the points A, B, C, D, E, F, G, H draw lines perpendicular to the tangent and project these lines to represent different parallels.
6. Divide the equator at equal distance for spacing the meridians by the equation : $d = 2\pi R/360° \times i$ (where $2\pi R$ = length of the equator and i = interval).

   Draw vertical lines at right angles through these points on the equator which will form the meridians.

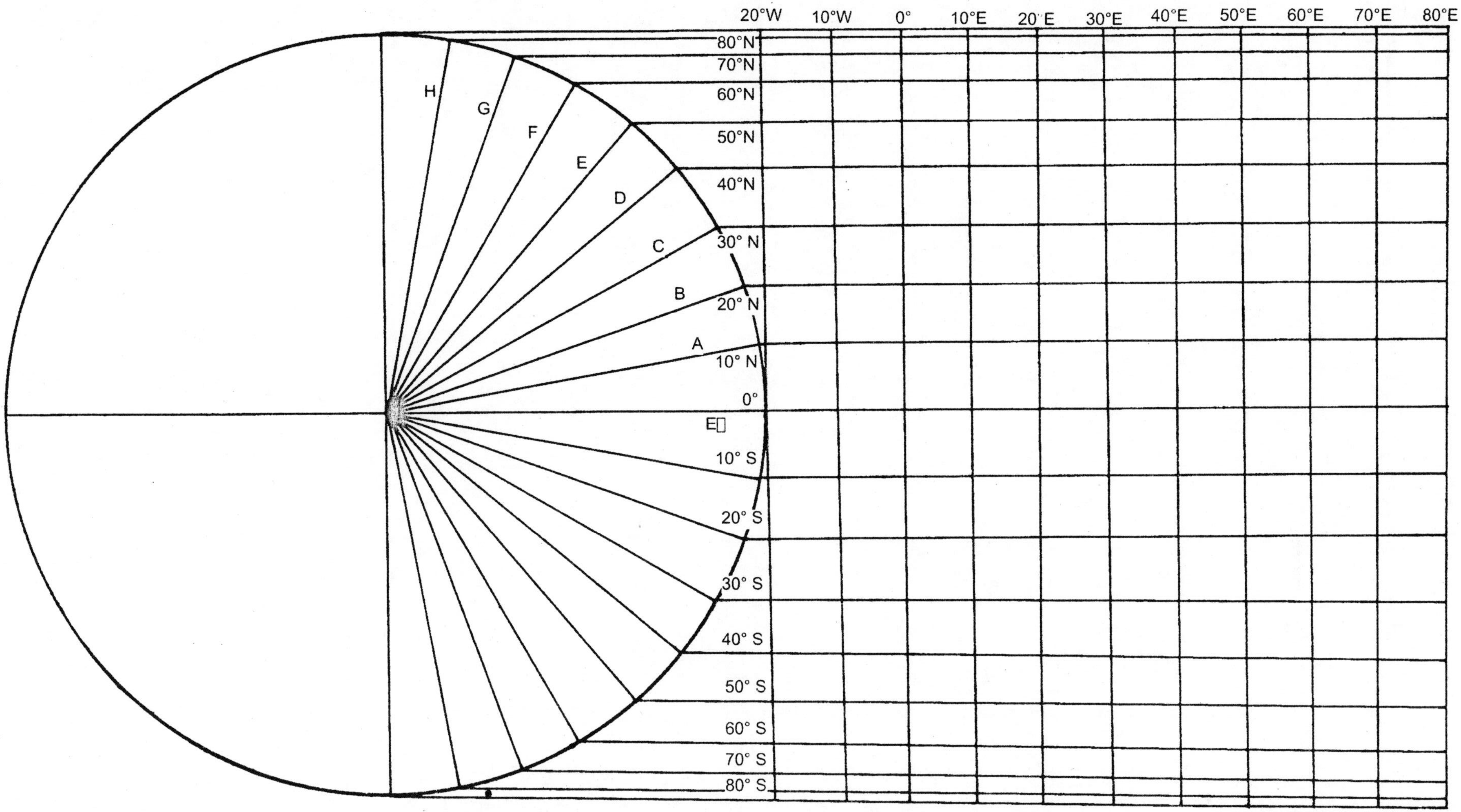

Scale : 1 : 100,000,000

Fig. 2.32 Graphical construction of Cylindrical Equal Area projection

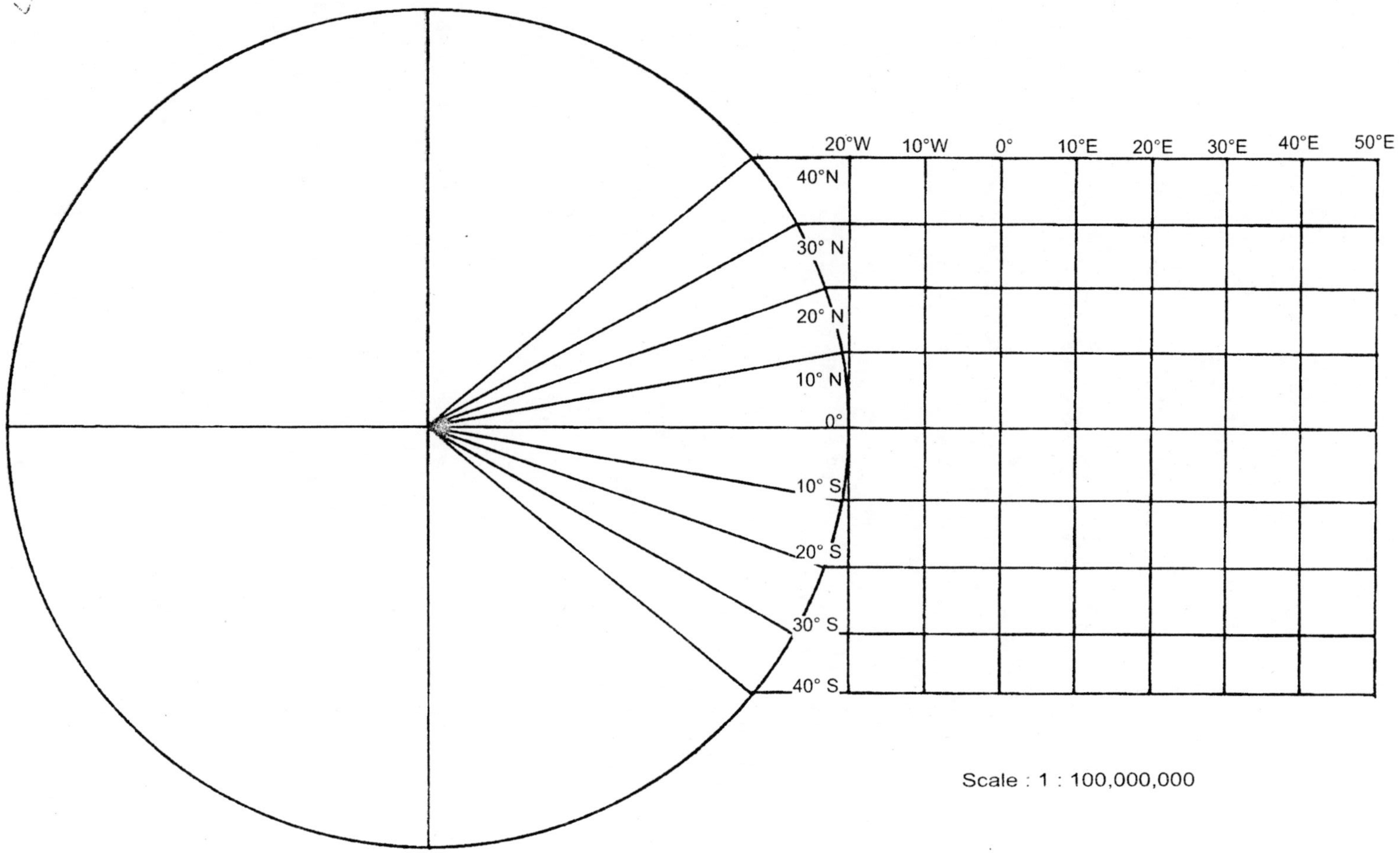

Fig. 2.33 Cylindrical Equal Area Projection

7. Label the graticules (latitudes and longitudes).
8. Mark the boundary . Put the scale at the bottom and label the title of projection at the top.

Trigonometrical Method

The construction of Cylindrical Equal Area Projection by Trigonometrical method is also convenient.

Steps

1. Calculate the radius (R) of the Reduced Earth.
2. Draw a horizontal straight line in W-E alignment on the paper to represent the equator.
3. Divide the equator ($2\pi R$) at equal space : $d = 2\pi R \times i/360°$ (i = interval).
4. On the points such divided draw perpendicular lines to represent the meridians. Choose the central meridian.
5. Calculate the height (h) of the parallels at different latitude (ϕ) above the equator by the equation : $h = R \sin\phi$.

ϕ	10°	20°	30°	40°	50°	60°	70°	80°	90°
h	R sin10°	R sin20°	R sin30°	R sin40°	R sin50°	R sin60°	R sin70°	R sin80°	R sin90°

Mark the height of the parallels above the equator along the meridian (any) and draw lines through these points parallel to the equator.

6. Thus the graticules are constructed. Label the graticules (latitudes and longitudes).
7. Mark the boundary. Put the scale at the bottom and label the title of projection on the top.

Properties

1. All the meridians and parallels are straight lines and perpendicular to each other.
2. The length of all parallels is the same as that of the equator ($2\pi R$).
3. The poles have the same length as that of the equator and other parallels ($2\pi R$).
4. The equator is drawn true to scale.
5. The vertical distance between two parallels decreases away from the equator. As a result the shape is distorted due to compression in N-S direction. Distortion is maximum near the poles.
6. The meridians are truly spaced on the equator.
7. All meridians are equally spaced over all parallels. To compensate the N-S compression and to preserve the area there is stretching of the meridians in E-W direction.
8. It is an Equal Area projection, but not Orthomorphic.

Exercise

Q. Draw graticules on cylindrical equal area projection for an area extending 40° N to 40° S and 20° W to 50°E. Space the meridians and parallals at 10° interval. Choose the scale R.F. 1:100,000,000 (fig. 2.33).

Ans. 1. $R = \frac{640,000,000 \text{ cm}}{100,000,000} = 6.4 \text{ cm}$.

2. Selected parallels are 40°N, 30°N, 20°N, 10°N, 0°, 10°S, 20°S, 30°S, 40°S.

3. Selected meridians are 20°W, 10°W, 0°, 10°E, 20°E, 30°E, 40°E, 50°E.

4. Distance of any parallel from the equator = R sin θ

θ	R sinθ	Result (in cm)
10°	1.11135	1.11
20°	2.18893	2.19
30°	3.2	3.20
40°	4.11384	4.11

5. Distance along the parallels for spacing the meridians $\frac{2\pi R \times \text{interval}}{360°} = \frac{2\pi \times 6.4 \times 10}{360°} = 1.12$ cm.

Derivation for Cylindrical Equal Area Projection :

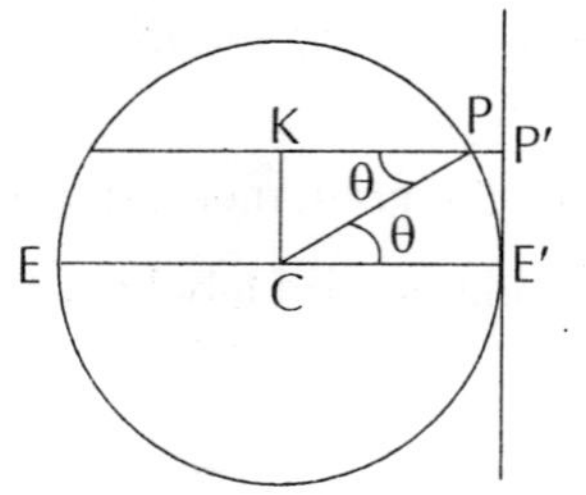

In Δ KPC

<KPC = θ (<of latitude)

$\frac{KC}{CP} = \text{Sin } \theta$

or , KC = CP Sin θ

∴ KC = R Sin θ

Mercator's Projection

This is one of the best known projection in the world. Mercator's Projection is an Orthomorphic Cylindrical Projection, but the polar areas are greatly exaggerated on this projection. Though Greenland is actually one-tenth of the size of South America, but it is shown as larger than south America on this projection. On Mercator's Projection all parallels are equal to the equator in length. As a result the latitude scale increases with increasing distance from the equator to maintain the shape. Hence the parallels are spaced at variable distance from the equator, whereas the meridians are equispaced on the parallels. The meridians and the parallels intersect each other at right angles.

The spacing of the parallels is done in a way that at any point of intersection of parallels and meridians the scale remains the same in all direction. It has thus one advantage. Any straight line drawn in any direction in Mercator's Chart crosses the parallels and meridians at constant angle. Such a line is defined as a *Rhumb line* or *loxodrome*.

Construction

Principles

The construction of Mercator's Projection is simple. However it requires the knowledge of *Calculas* to find the distances of the parallels from the equator.

The exaggeration of latitude scale varies with the secant of latitude.

Let X be the scale. Then X = Length of the parallel on projection/True length

$$= 2\pi R/2\pi R \cos \text{lat.} = 1/\cos \text{lat.} = \sec \text{lat.}$$

Consider y be the distance of any parallel (ϕ) from the equator.

Then by differential equation ; $dy/Rd\phi = \sec\phi$ (R = Radius of the reduced earth and ϕ = latitude)

By integration we have :

$$\begin{aligned} y &= R \int \sec\phi \, d\phi \\ &= R \log_e (\sec\phi + \tan\phi) \\ &= R\ 2.3026 \log_{10} \tan (45° + \phi/2). \end{aligned}$$

From this equation the following table has been prepared to find out the distances of the parallels from the equator in terms of R (radius of the reduced earth).

ϕ	10°	20°	30°	40°	50°	60°	70°	80°	90°
y	.1755R	.3563R	.5493R	.7632R	1.0112R	1.3171R	1.7358R	2.4366R	Infinity

Drawing

Steps

1. Calculate the radius (R) of the Reduced Earth.
2. Draw a pair of straight lines intersecting each other at right angles. These lines will represent the equator and the central meridian respectively.
3. Space the parallels at varying distances from the equator as per calculations shown in the table.
4. Divide the equator at equal pace by the equation ($2\pi R \times i/360°$) for spacing the meridians. Draw perpendicular lines through these points to represent the meridians.
5. Label the graticules (latitudes and longitudes).
6. Mark the boundary. Put the scale at the bottom and label the title of projection on the top.

Properties

1. All parallels are straight lines and equal in length to that of the equator (i.e. $2\pi R$).
2. All meridians are also straight lines, drawn parallel to each other.
3. All parallels and meridians intersect each other at right angles.
4. All meridians are spaced at equal distance on the equator ($2\pi R \times i/360°$). But the latitude scale increases with the increasing distances from the equator.
5. The spacing of the parallels is so arranged that at any point of intersection of parallel and meridian the scale remains the same in all directions.
6. Any straight line drawn in any direction on a Mercator's Chart passes all parallels and meridians at constant angle or constant bearing. Thus it has the advantage for

navigation, where it is easy for sailing along a series of constant bearing (rhumb line or loxodrome).

7. The Mecator's Projection is commonly used to show large extent of the earth surface, as it is easy for construction.
8. The orthomorphism is maintained as the exaggeration in latitude scale at any point is made equal to that of longitude scale. The exaggeration of latitude scale varies with the secant of the latitude.
9. However the area property in this projection is greatly distorted. The areas lying the higher latitudes are shown larger than the true scale. Greenland being truely $\frac{1}{10}$th of the size of South America is projected even larger than South America in Mercator's Projection.
10. The poles cannot be shown on this projection.

Exercise

Q. Draw graticules on *Mercator's Projection* covering 70°N – 70°S and 180°W – 180°E on a scale of 1:250,000,000 at 10° interval (fig. 2.34).

Ans. 1. $R = \frac{640{,}000{,}000 \text{ cm}}{250{,}000{,}000} = 2.56$ cm.

2. Selected parallels are 70°N, 60°N, 50°N, 40°N, 30°N, 20°N, 10°N, 0°, 10°S, 20°S, 30°S, 40°S, 50°S, 60°S, 70°S.
3. Selected meridians : 180°EW, 170°EW, 160°EW, 150°EW, 140°EW, 130°EW, 120°EW, 110°EW, 100°EW, 90°EW, 80°EW, 70°EW, 60°EW, 50°EW, 40°EW, 30°EW, 20°EW, 10°EW, 0°.
4. Distance of the parallels from the equator $R\ 2.3026 \log \tan\left(45° + \frac{\theta}{2}\right)$

θ	$45° + \frac{\theta}{2}$	$R\ 2.3026 \log \tan\left(45° + \frac{\theta}{2}\right)$	Result (in cm)
10°	50°	0.44910	0.45
20°	55°	0.91233	0.91
30°	60°	1.40623	1.41
40°	65°	1.95306	1.95
50°	70°	2.58737	2.59
60°	75°	3.37143	3.37
70°	80°	4.4427	4.44

5. Division along the equator for spacing the meridians :

$$\frac{2\pi R \times \text{interval}}{360°} = \frac{2\pi \times 2.56 \times 10°}{360°} = 0.45 \text{ cm}$$

Mollweide's Projection

Normal case

Mollweide's Projection is grouped in the Conventional Projection. It is an Elliptical Projection, where all meridians except the central meridian and the 90th meridians are all ellipses. The central

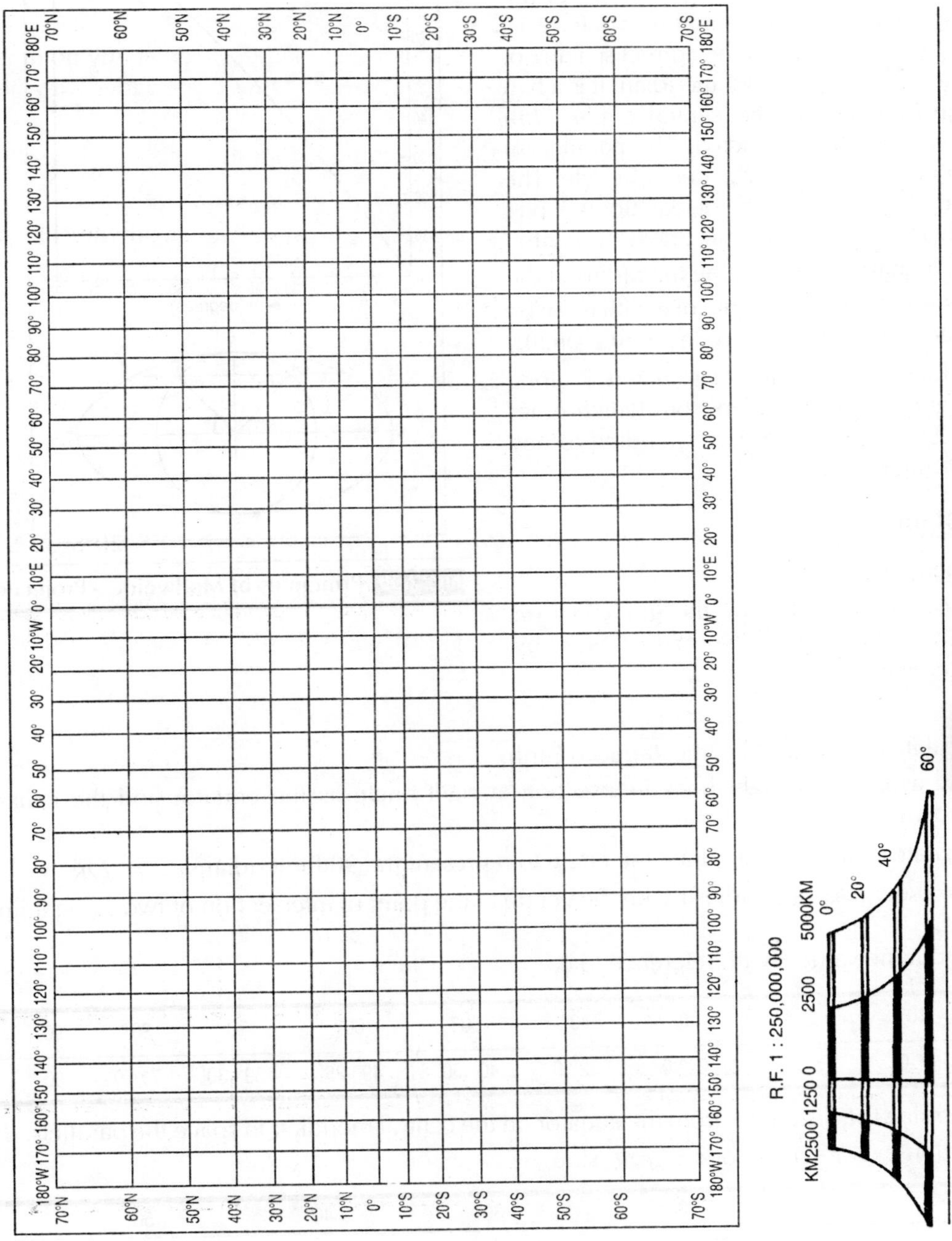

Fig. 2.34 Mercator's Projection

meridian becomes straight line and the 90th meridians become circle. The meridians are equally spaced along the true distance of the parallels. All parallels are straight lines, but not equally spaced along the central meridian. It is, however, difficult to obtain the correct spacing of the parallels along the central meridian. It is a two part projection. Firstly, the central circle (90th meridians) is to be constructed. The parallel (ϕ) will form an angle θ with the central circle. The distance of the parallels from the equator will be r sin ϕ, where r is the radius to draw the central circle and equal to $\sqrt{2}R$ (R being the radius of the reduced earth). The relationship of ϕ with θ can be ascertained by the equation : $n \sin\phi = 2\theta + \sin 2\theta$.

By plotting the values of selected ϕ along with θ a graph can be drawn from which other values of θ can be found corresponding to any value of latitude ϕ (fig. 2.35).

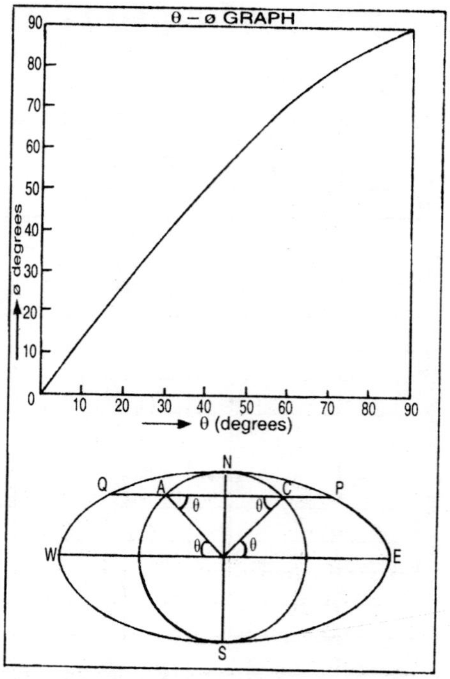

Fig. 2.35 **Principles of Mollweide's Projection**

Construction

Trigonometrical Method

It is convenient to draw the graticules on Mollweide's Projection (Normal Case) by Trigonometrical method.

Steps

1. Calculate the radius (R) of the Reduced Earth.
2. Draw a pair of straight lines intersecting at right angle as the equator and the central meridian.
3. Calculate r, the radius to draw the circle to represent the 90th meridians : $r = \sqrt{2}R$.
4. Draw the circle with radius r with the centre at the point of intersection of two straight line (i.e. O).
5. Find out the value θ with reference to ϕ.

ϕ	10°	20°	30°	40°	50°	60°	70°	80°	90°
θ	8°.0′	15°.45′	24°.0	32°.0	40°.30′	49°.25′	59°.30′	71°.0	90°

6. Determine the distance x from the equator on the central meridian to space the parallels. By equation : $x = r \sin\theta$ or $x = \sqrt{2}R \sin\theta$

For ϕ	10°	20°	30°	40°	50°
X =	$\sqrt{2}R$ sin8°	$\sqrt{2}R$ sin15°.45′	$\sqrt{2}R$ sin24°	$\sqrt{2}R$ sin32°	$\sqrt{2}R$ sin40°.30′
For ϕ	60°	70°	80°	90°	
X =	$\sqrt{2}R$ sin49°.25′	$\sqrt{2}R$ sin59°.30′	$\sqrt{2}R$ sin71°.0	$\sqrt{2}R$ sin90°	

Draw parallel lines along the marked distance as parallels of the respective latitudes (ϕ).

7. Mark the length of each parallel by the equation : $l = 4r \cos\theta = 4\sqrt{2R}\cos\theta$,

   and also divide the parallel for spacing the meridians at i (interval) by the equation : $d\phi = 4\sqrt{2R}\cos\theta \times i/360°$
8. Join these divisions along the parallels to draw the meridians.
9. Label the graticules (latitudes and longitudes).
10. Mark the boundary. Put the scale at the bottom and label the title of projection at the top.

Properties

1. This is an equal area projection of the whole sphere.
2. This projection is an ellipse and hence it is termed Elliptical Projection.
3. The parallels are represented as straight lines but spaced at varying distance from the equator to maintain the equal area property.
4. The meridians are drawn as curves passing through corresponding points of each parallel. The meridians are all elliptical except the central meridian and at 90th meridians.
5. The central meridian is a straight line and at 90th meridians the ellipse becomes a circle.
6. The spacing between the two parallels decreases away from the equator.
7. This projection is drawn in two parts : Firstly cosntructing the 90th meridians circle and then constructing the ellipse. Hence it is known as Two-Part Projection or Double projection.
8. The central meridian is half in length ($2\sqrt{2R}$) than that of the equator ($4\sqrt{2R}$).
9. The distortion towards the poles is less than that of the Sinusoidal Projection.
10. It is the most commonly used projection to show the world maps in most atlases.

Exercises

Q. Draw graticules on *Mollweide's Projection* to show the world R.F. 1:100,000,000 and interval of latitudes and longitudes = 30° (fig. 2.36).

Ans. 1. $R = \frac{640,000,000 \text{ cm}}{100,000,000} = 6.4$ cm.

2. Selected parallels are 90°N, 60°N, 30°N, 0°, 30°S, 60°S, 90°S.

3. $r = \sqrt{2R} = 3.58$ cm.

4. The value of θ with reference to ϕ.

θ	30°	60°	90°
θ	24°0′	49°25′	90°

5. Distance from the equator on the central meridian to space the parallels $\sqrt{2R}$ Sin θ.

φ	θ	$\sqrt{2R}$ Sinθ	Result (in cm)
30°	24°0′	1.45519	1.46
60°	49°25′	2.71713	2.72
90°	90°	3.57771	3.58

6. Length of each parallels $4\sqrt{2R}$ Cos θ.

φ	θ	$\sqrt{2R}$ Cosθ	Result (in cm)
30°	24°0′	13.07360	13.07
60°	49°25′	9.30996	9.31
90°	90°	—	—

7. Length of the equator $4\sqrt{2R}$ = 14.31 cm.

8. Division along the parallel for spacing the meridians $\frac{4\sqrt{2R}\ \text{Cos}\ \theta \times \text{interval}}{360°}$

φ	θ	$\frac{4\sqrt{2R}\ \text{Cos}\ \theta \times \text{interval}}{360°}$	Result (in cm)
30°	24°	1.08947	1.09
60°	49°25′	0.77583	0.78
90°	90°	—	—

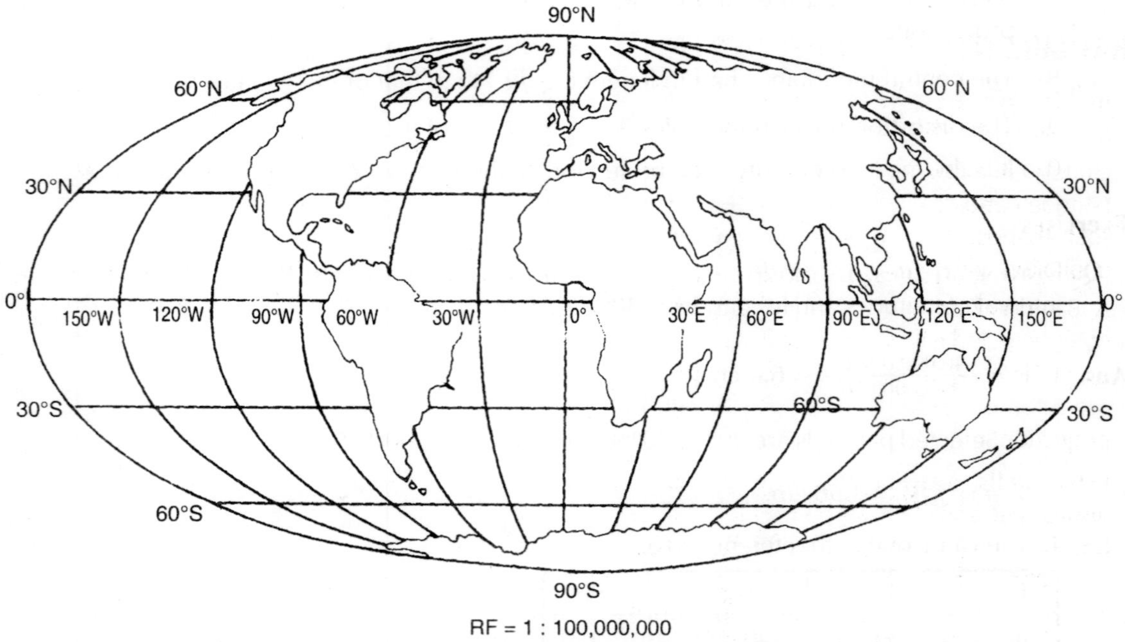

Fig. 2.36 World Map on Mollweide's Projection

UNIVERSAL TRANSVERSE MERCATOR PROJECTION

Universal Transverse Mercator (UTM) Projection is a map projection which can include maximum area of the earth's surface though it does not have a total global coverage. In that sense it is not truly universal, because the latitudinal extension is restricted to 84°N and 80°S. This projection also considers the earth as a flat ellipsoid. Naturally it may invite some distortions also, though the measures taken in this projection minimize the distortions. Transverse Mercator flattening series were originally derived by Johann Heinrich Louis Kruger in 1912.

Properties

- UTM is a conformal projection in which shapes are correct but area is highly distorted.
- It is a cylindrical projection.
- Multiple numbers of cylinders are supposed to be used in this projection as developable surface.
- All the meridians of longitude and parallels of latitude intersect at right angles and rectangular zones are developed in UTM.

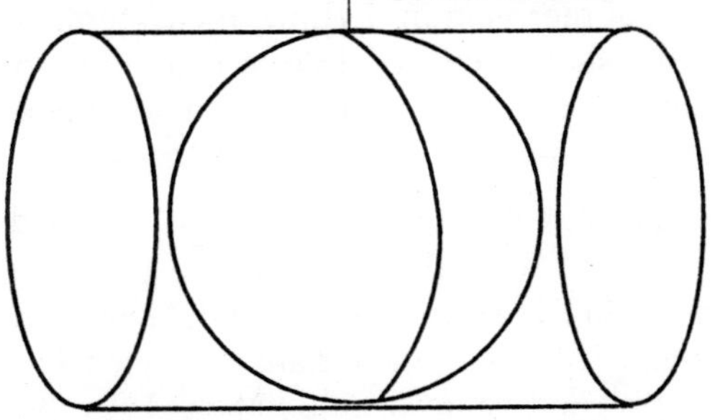

Fig. 2.37 **Secant Cylinder**

- UTM has 1200(60 × 20) projection units for mapping. These are known as cells or zones.
- Each of the cells has a central meridian of its own.
- In UTM projection the unit of measurement is metre instead of degrees, minutes, and seconds.
- Scale is constant in north and south along central meridians, but varies towards east and west along parallels.

GRATICULE NET OF UTM PROJECTION

- In this projection the earth is divided into 60 zones for 6° of longitudinal extent. The zones are numbered 1 to 60 from west to east.
- Latitudinal extension of each zone is for 8°, except for the northern most zone which is 12°. These latitude bands are named by alphabet, C to X leaving I and O in between. Hence there are 20 of such bands. I and O are left to avoid confusion with numbers 1 and 0.
- A, B and Y, Z are also used for latitude bands of western and eastern sides of Antarctic and Arctic regions respectively, but those are projected on Universal Polar Stereographic projection.
- UTM cells are named with meridian zones first and then alphabetical latitude bands. For instance, 42Q locates Kathiawar Peninsula.
- To memorize the latitude bands for northern and southern hemisphere it may be kept in mind that any letter before 'N'

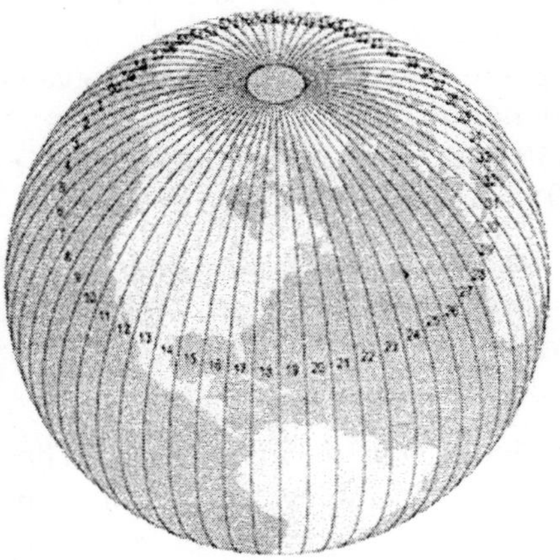

Fig. 2.38 **Logitudinal Zones of UTM Projection**

should be meant for southern hemisphere, whereas any letter from N and after N should be meant for northern hemisphere.

- As the projection considers the earth as a flat ellipsoid, slight distortions occur in various measurements of distance between the central meridian and boundaries of each cell. A scale factor 0.9996 is used for central meridian in distance measurement and a scale factor of 1.0004 is applied to compensate for distortion in distance measurements near zone boundaries.
- In each cell the central meridian is assigned a value of 500000 m. This feature gives the points in the west of central meridian a false origin. To the east the distance is referred to an assigned value of 500000 m. Thus the cell boundary towards west of central meridian is 166,000 m. and along the eastern boundary it becomes 834,000 m. If a map extends across one of the cell boundaries into the neighbouring cell, the distance measurement will follow the trend of the boundary of the cell which contains larger part of the map area.
- The point of origin of each UTM zone is the intersection of the equator and the central meridian of the zone.
- To avoid negative values for distance measurement the equator is assigned a value of 10,000,000 m. south. For determining the position in northern hemisphere the equator is assigned a value of 0 m. north. The northing value at 84° N is 9,350,000 m. At 80°S it has a value of 1100,000 m.
- Each of the UTM zones of 6° longitude tapers from 666,000 m. in width at the equator to a minimum of 70,000 m. at 84° N. AT 80° S it is 116,000 m.
- For finding a position in UTM projection 'Easting' and 'Northing' are required, no questions of Westing or Southing are there.

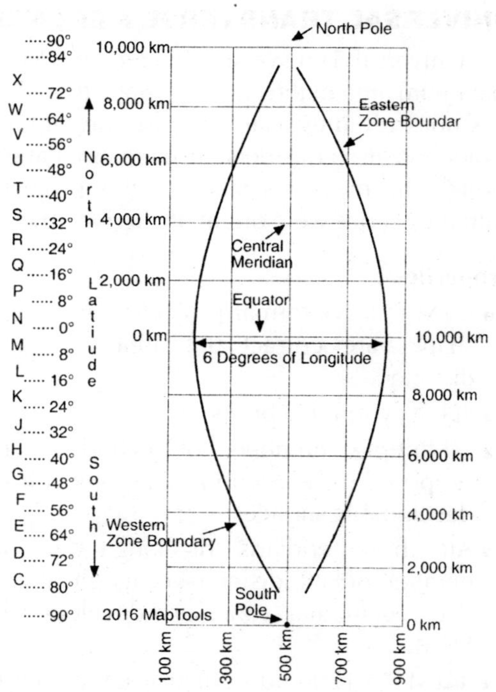

Fig. 2.39 **Scheme of Zoning in UTM**

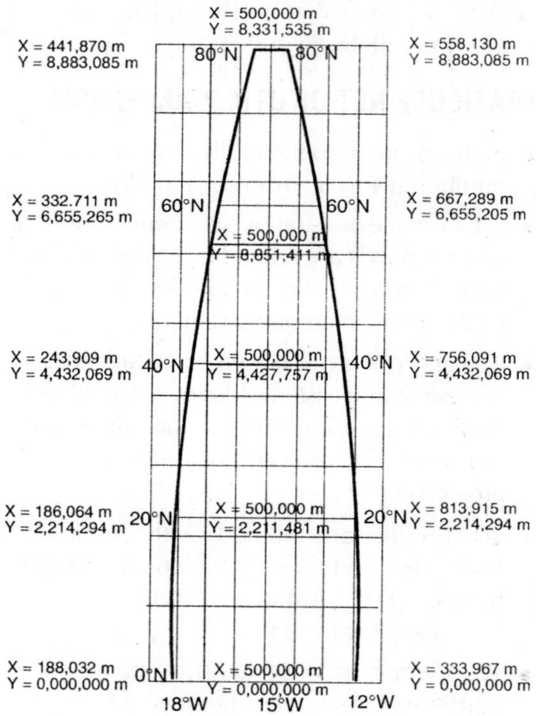

Fig. 2.40 **UTM Zone tapering toward North**

EASTING AND NORTHING

- As in each UTM zone the central meridian is 500000m.E, a location of 35m. to the east of central meridian has an easting value of 500000+35= 500035m.E. If a given location is 400000m. West of central meridian, the easting value is 500000-400000= 100000m.E. The distance between the two points is 500035-100000=400035m.
- In the case of northing the equator is the base line. For the northern hemisphere it is considered as 0m.N, whereas for southern hemisphere the equator has an assigned value of 10,000,000m.N. A point 325m. North of equator has a northing value of 0000325m.N, as it will be 7 digits. On the other hand, a location 75m. South of the equator has a northing value of 10000000-75=9999925m.N.

WORLD MAP ON UTM PROJECTION

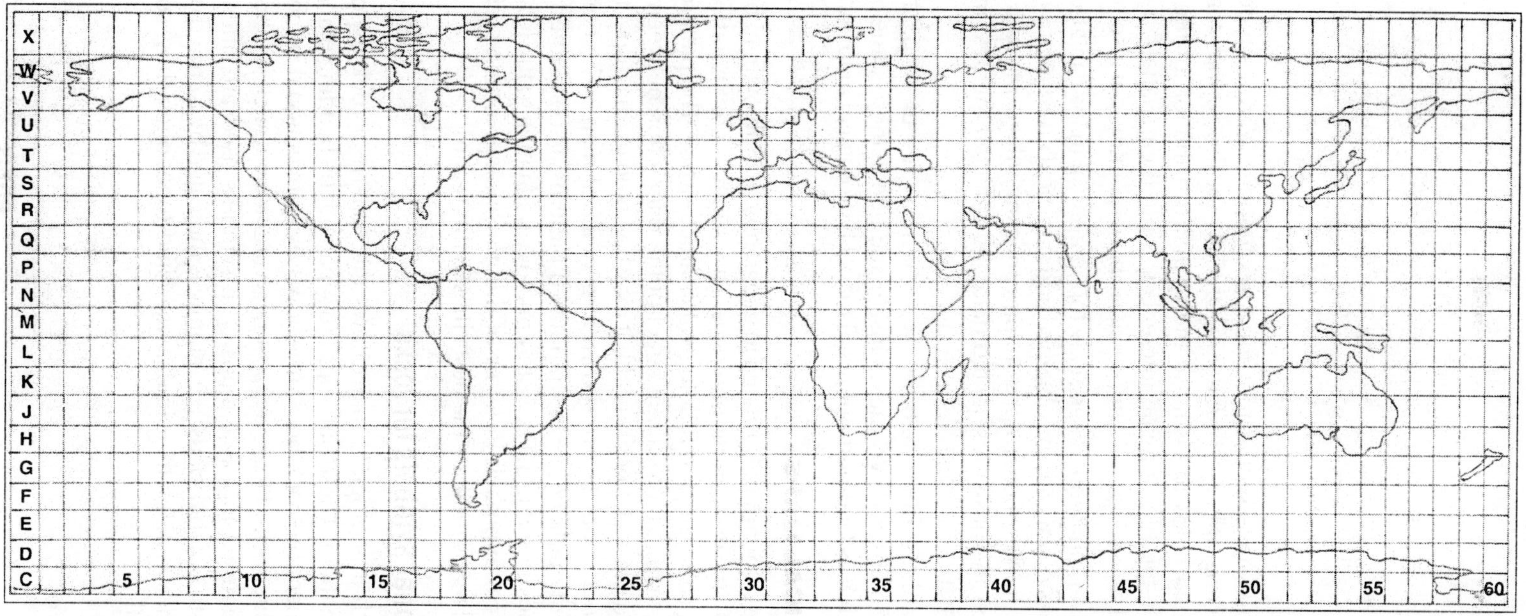

Unlike other map projections, UTM projection cannot be readily drawn manually on the basis of given latitudinal and longitudinal extensions. For this purpose, particular values of latitude and longitude are to be sought from internet search engines. Hence, this projection needs a computerised software management (GIS, DGPS, GPS etc.) for drawing of graticules.

C H A P T E R **3**

MAP ANALYSIS

A map is an essential tool for a geographer. Various types of map are regularly used by practising geographers. By reducing the size of the various features of the surface on different scales, a map helps to visualise the spatial distribution of the features contained in it. This is obviously helpful in drawing inferences about their spatial arrangement, their associations and their actual sizes. A general impression about quantity can also be obtained from maps.

Moreover, authentic large scale topographical maps can also act as the data-bank from which various types of data can be obtained and statistical co-relations can be established between them. However, unlike photographs maps can camouflage many truths also and as they are often prepared on the basis of selected data and selected themes, informaton are often limited on a particular map.

Geographers often handle three basic types of map. These are Topographical maps, Geological maps and Weather maps. In addition to these some other maps are also regularly used by them, such as Geomorphological map, Hydrological map etc.

GEOLOGICAL MAPS

Geology is intimately related to geography as both of them belong to Earth science and have a common field in Geomorphology. The surface configuration is largely influenced by the underlying structure and lithological characteristics. The pattern of rock exposures, as shown in geological maps, is a resultant effect of the interaction between the operating geomorphological process and the rock beds present. It may be noted in this respect that actual surface exposures are never so continuous as are shown in geological maps. The continuous exposures of geological maps are interpolated and extrapolated patterns as configured by the geologist from patchy or pocket exposures. (Fig 3.1) Geomorphology pertaining to the legacy of geological studies includes the analytical approach in terms of the morphology of the surface and drainage configuration. Geological maps indicate the best clues in this regard.

Conventional Symbols for rocks

As such a geological map shows the pattern of rock exposures and topographic contours overlain on them. These outcrops are separated by bedding planes or outcrops of bedding planes. Between them the rock beds are shown by conventional symbols of igneous, sedimentary and metamorphic rocks. However, arbitrary variations of such symbols from the International code are also encountered in a few maps. The symbols used are often thematic representatives of the characteristics of rock beds, e.g. granite is indicated by a crowd of plus sign, whereas gneiss shows broken bands in them. In a similar way, limestones often show some compact symbols resembling a brick-wall.

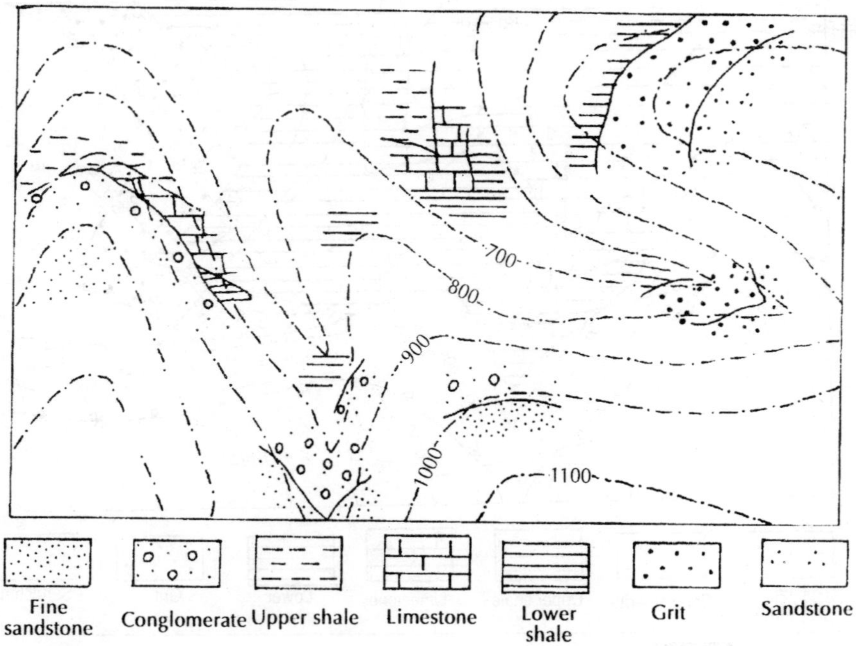

Fig. 3.1 Patchy exposures of rocks

Let us confess here that most of the exercises done for understanding a geological structure from a geological map are usually done on the basis of sedimentary strata, though structures of igneous rocks and metamorphic rocks are also common place on earth's surface.

The forms of igneous bodies, we often encounter with, are dykes, sills and batholiths. Other forms are not very common in occurrence. A dyke and a batholith are discordant plutons. They form across the bedding planes or trends of the country rocks. A dyke may be vertical or inclined and may have branchings. A batholith is a huge massive igneous body which penetrates across the country rocks. The orientation of symbols in them helps to recognise them. On the other hand, a sill is a concordant pluton which form parallel to the bedding planes or to the trend of country rocks. It may be vertical, inclined or horizontal depending on the trend of bedding of the country rocks.

Metamorphic rocks are also not the usual features of geological maps, though the formation of a metamorphic rock bed is often observed among the beds of a sedimentary succession in a geological map. However, in real situation the surface occurrence of metamorphic rocks is more sporadic is nature. Metamorphic rocks may also occur at the base of a sedimentary succession as the lonely member of the sequence.

Among the features of the sedimentary family clay, alluvium, mudstone, shale, various grades of sandstones, coal seams, conglomerate, breccia and limestone are common. These rock beds have variable dips, ranging from horizontal to vertical along with various types of folds, faults, homoclinal and horizontal structures formed by them.

Choice of section line

The understanding about a geological map can be made clear with the help of a geological section drawn across the map. Students are often confused about the selection and drawing of the

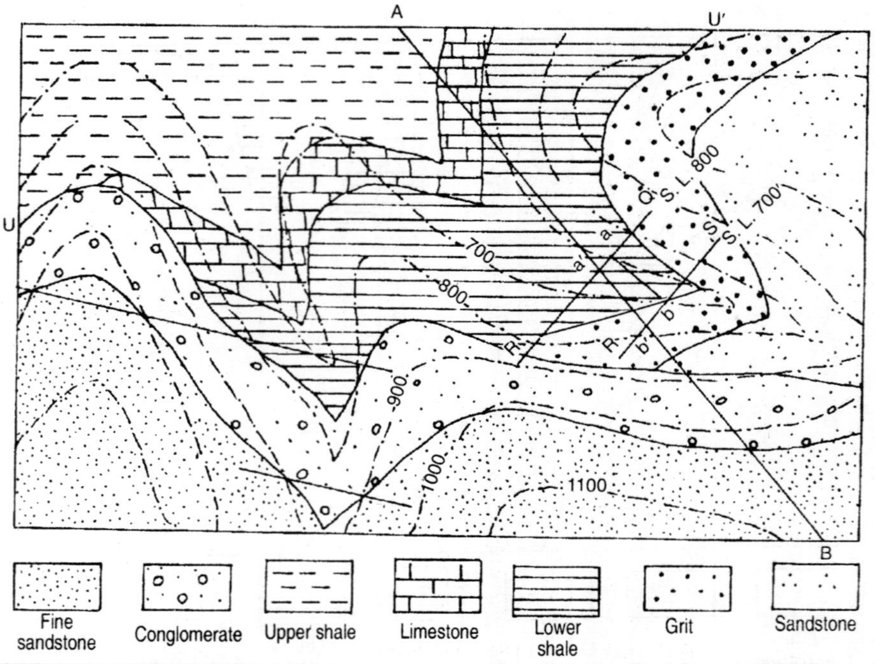

Fig. 3.2 Completion of geological map through extrapolation

section line. It may be suggested here that ***a section line should run across maximum number of rock beds shown in the map as outcrops***. But at the same time it should be kept in mind that ***the section line should run across the direction of strike of the rock beds*** as it is AB in fig. 3.2. Therefore, before the selection of the section line a preliminary idea about the direction of strike of the rock beds should be obtained. *The section line should never run parallel to the direction of strike.*

Series and Unconformity

The rock beds formed during a single sequence of lithogenesis are usually conformable and form a series; the attitude of these rock beds are found to be similar to each other, if not exactly the same. Therefore, the rock beds of the same series have almost the same dip and strike. This idea, of course, entertains the scope of slight variation in dip and strike and the differences in the direction of dip as observed in a folded structure.

We often come across certain geological maps which have two or more series of outcrops, either for a small portion or for a greater part of the map. These two series are separable along the lower most bedding plane of the upper series. This bedding plane forms the unconformity which is the submerged erosional surface of lower series of rock strata. Alike the other bedding planes the unconformity too may have a curvilinear outcrop. However, ***a student should look for this unconformity where there are tri-junctions of bedding planes and where the outcrops of the lower series abruptly end along an outcrop of bedding plane of the upper series***, as it is uu' in fig 3.2. The detection of unconformity will help the student to understand the map in an easier way.

Strike and Dip

After identifying the unconformity, if there is any, or finding out a single series of rock beds a student should draw the strike direction, popularly known as strike line. Drawing of strike lines is a meticulous job. *A strike line should join two points of intersection between a contour and a bedding plane. The strike lines of the same series usually run parallel to each other,* though not at regular horizontal intervals or at any specified vertical interval. However, for finding out the dip-direction and amount of dip two strike lines are required to be drawn on the same bedding plane. Here we may face a problem of not finding out two points of intersection between the bedding plane and another contour. In such cases the strike line should be drawn across the single point of intersection making it parallel to the primary strike line on the same bedding plane, provided the previous one is properly drawn across two or more points of intersection.

Dip and strike of rock beds remain at right angle to each other. The perpendicular distance between the two consecutive strike lines determines the true dip as $\tan^{-1}\theta$ being the ratio between the vertical distance and perpendicular distance of the two strike lines on the same bedding plane (fig. 3.2). From this value the angle of dip (θ) can be calculated :

$$\tan^{-1}\theta = \frac{\text{Vertical distance between two consecutive strike lines}}{\text{Perpendicular distance between two consecutive strike lines}}$$

In figure 3.2 two strike lines S700′ and S800′ have been drawn on the basis of the two points of intersection between 700′ and 800′ contours and the bedding plane between the lower shale and grit. The perpendicular distance between these two strike lines is 0.48″ (ab) i.e. 480′ on a scale of 1″ to 1000 feet, and the distance between them along the section line AB is 0.50″ (a′b′) or 500′. The vertical distance between S700′ and S800′ is 100′. Therefore, the true dip is $\frac{100'}{480} = .208$ or 11°.46′; and the apparent dip is $\frac{100}{500} = .2$ or 11°.18′.

If the difference between the perpendicular distance and diagonal distance increases, the difference between the true and apparent dip will also increase.

The direction of dip will be at right angle to the direction of strike towards the strike line of lower value. Such an amount of dip will be considered as true dip, but the section line may not always follow a perpendicular direction of the strike lines. Such oblique section lines across two consecutive strike lines can give the value of apparent dip as the ratio between the vertical distance and the diagonal distance of the two strike lines. An apparent dip is always less than the true dip (Fig. 3.3). However, geological sections can also be drawn on the basis of apparent dip of rock beds. But if the oblique distance is twice or more than the perpendicular distance, it may result in an erroneous dip in the geological section. The amount of true and apparent dip may be determined by graphical method also.

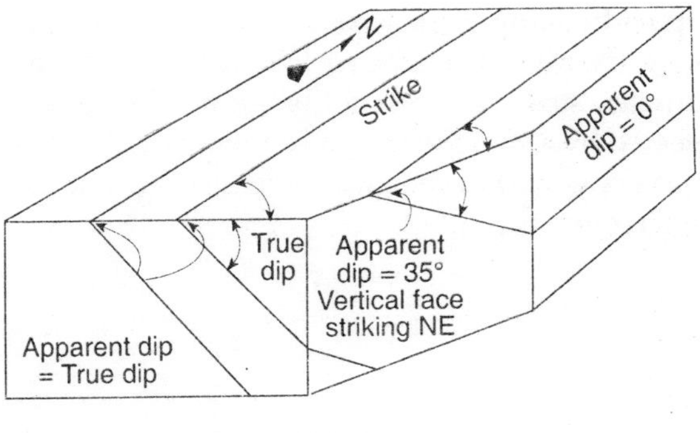

Fig. 3.3 True and apparent dip

For igneous formations, i.e., dyke or sill, the amount of dip can be measured in the same way as it is in the case of sedimentary strata. However, regarding the sill the dip of the bedding plane is the same with that of the inclination of concordant pluton. For batholiths such determination of dip and strike are required in connection with the determination of the two sides of the pluton. **At the time of drawing of such igneous formations in a two series sequence the student should examine which series of rock beds has been penetrated by the intrusion.**

Fault

Faults appear as lines on surface outcrop maps. Along these lines beds are dislocated. A fault may be vertical or inclined. For vertical faults horizontal dislocation is negligible. In such cases only the vertical slip is measured. The wall below the plane of fault is known as foot wall. The wall above the plane of fault is known as hanging wall. In a normal fault the foot wall is dislocated relatively upward and in a reverse fault the hanging wall is dislocated relatively upward. However, it is very difficult to measure the actual amount of upthrow or downthrow from geological maps, if the knowledge about the country structure is not complete. But the amount of displacement can be measured, either from the cross section or from the notional strike lines drawn across the fault affected bed or bedding planes.

For inclined faults the dip of the fault is measured in the same way as is done for the measurement of the dip of rock beds. The drawing of vertical fault is a simple procedure. The point of intersection of the fault outcrop with that of the section line is placed on the base line and the vertical fault is drawn as a vertical line. The beds follow their dip on either side of the fault and automatically the vertical displacement becomes graphically measurable on the basis of the vertical distance between two counter parts of a fault-affected bedding plane or rock bed.

For the measurement of displacement on the basis of notional strike lines the distance between two consecutive strike lines across a bedding plane is taken as the notional distance for other imaginary strike lines and they are drawn until one of them coincides with another actual one on the same bedding plane on the opposite wall of the fault. The difference between the values of the notional strike line and the actual strike line on the line of coincidence gives the amount of displacement (fig. 3.4). For the measurement of thickness of beds similar co-incidence between a notional strike line and an actual strike line or co-incidence between one strike line on the upper bedding plane and another on the lower bedding plane is considered as the thickness between the two. When the rock beds are intersected by contours for a single point of intersection, the primary strike line can not be drawn. For getting the strike line two points of intersection are connected by a straight line and a perpendicular from the convenient intersection at the middle of the two upper and lower values will be drawn on the straight line. This perpendicular will give the strike direction (fig. 3.6c).

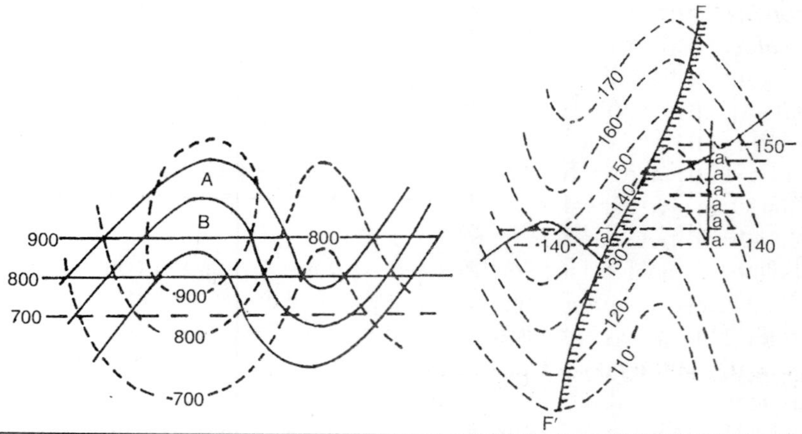

Fig. 3.4 Notional strikelines for measurement of thickness and displacement of bed

Topography

After finding out the direction of strike and the direction as well as the amount of apparent and true dip of rock beds the topographic profile along the section line should be drawn on the given map-scale. It may be noted here that the topographic profile, if not properly drawn, may interfere with the position and thickness of rock beds. Moreover, from the overlying contour plan the relief characteristics of the entire map-area should be understood. Otherwise, the concept of geomorphology of the area will not be clear. However, the hill tops and valley floors should be given slight oval and slight concave shapes respectively. The drainage plan of the area is also important in this regard. Being one of the two major component factors of landform development the drainage plan often reflects the influence of structure and lithology on itself, as is observed in a trellised network of streams. The explanation about topography remains incomplete unless the effect of drainage network and its consequent interaction with rock-structure are understood. However, many of the geological maps do not show the exact location of streams on them, though the contour plan depicts the configuration of valley, spur, dissected topography etc.

Rules of 'V's

Moreover, the stream-gradient, when compared with structural gradient, gives the clue about the direction of dip in terms of the 'V's of rock-outcrops. For such an idea the rules of 'V's should be applied. The rules are as follows :

1. Horizontal strata, while crossing a valley, form a 'V' in the outcrop pattern the apex pointing towards upstream.
2. The topography does not have any impact on the pattern of vertical beds and the outcrop pattern of vertical beds are straight, parallel to the strike of the beds.
3. The outcrop pattern of rock beds that dip upstream forms a 'V' that points upstream.
4. The outcrop pattern of the rock beds dipping downstream at an angle greater than the stream gradient forms a 'V' with its apex pointing towards downstream.
5. The outcrop pattern of the beds of rock dipping downstream at an angle less than the gradient of the stream forms a 'V' which points upstream (fig. 3.5).

Application of these rules helps to determine the approximate dip of rock beds from the pattern of outcrops. This also reveals a relationship between the dip of rock beds and outcrop pattern.

Three point problems for measuring dip

Dip and strike of a rock bed can be determined on the basis of three points, if the altitude of the points on a plane are known. Of these three points two will be having the same altitude and another will be at a different altitude. The line connecting the two points at same altitude is the strike of the plane, as a strike connects points of equal altitude on the same plane. The dip is measured at right angle to the strike. From the third point on another plane a perpendicular is drawn on the strike. On this perpendicular another perpendicular parallel to the strike is drawn. Now following the difference between two altitudes a point on the second perpendicular is marked on scale. From this point the base of the first perpendicular on the strike is connected. The angle between this connector and the first perpendicular forms the angle of dip as it is <OPQ in fig. 3.6a. In fig. 3.6b [In fig. 3.6b, three altitudes are given with horizontal distance between them. Point P is to be found out having same altitude as M. The equation is : Altitude of M–N/Altitude of O–N=Distance PN/Distance NO = 0.647058823 = $\frac{NP}{1700}$ = 1100ft. This horizonal distance from point locates P on NO distance] MP is the strike.

The topographic expression of rock-beds may act as a clue to the structural attitudes. Folds in rock-beds are often well understood by the repetition of the same strata on both sides of a central bed. But that does not necessarily mean that any such repetition is a clear evidence of folding. The

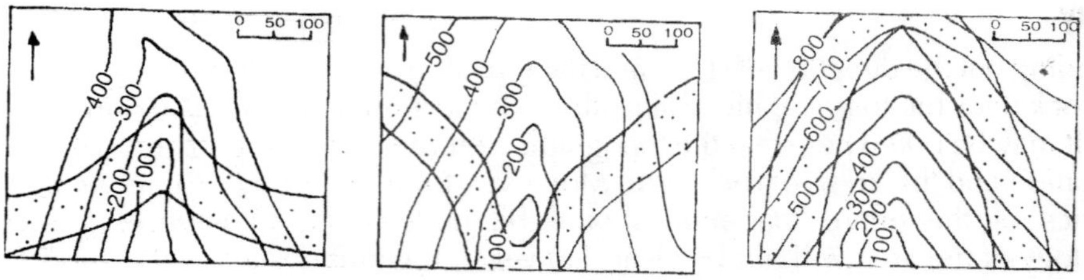

Fig. 3.5 Rule of 'V's

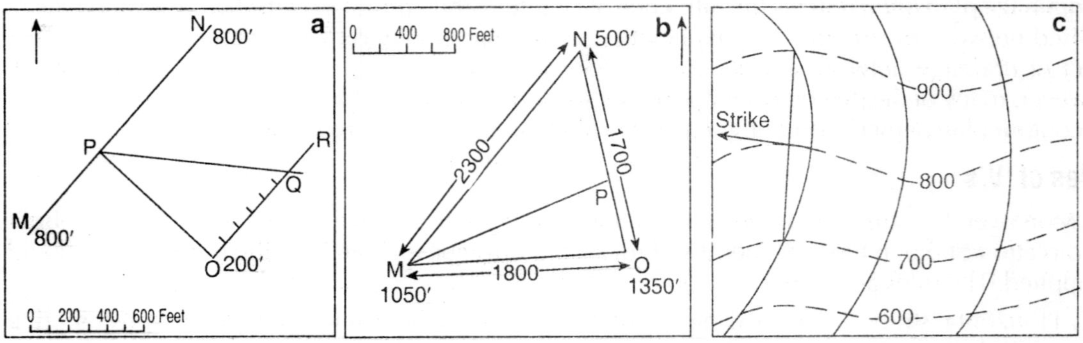

Fig. 3.6 Three point solution

final judgement should be made on the basis of the attitudes of the beds involved and interpretation of the same to observe if any folding has really taken place. Otherwise, mere repetition of outcrops may be misleading.

But it may be stated at the same time that the regular and continuous rock-exposures, as are seen in geological maps, are not the true pictures of the actual surface conditions. On the surface of the earth, even on a rocky mountainous terrain, the rock- exposures of any particular formation are often patchy in occurrence. Geologists, while mapping such exposures, often interpolate and extrapolate after making it sure that the patchy exposures of a rock-bed are of the same formation, and at the same time finds out if the stratigraphic position and their attitudes are matching.

INTERPRETATION OF GEOLOGICAL MAPS

Drawing of Geological section

Interpretation of geological maps should follow a few objective studies on the basis of the given geological maps.

After the line of geological section is chosen, a strip of paper with one straight edge should be placed along the line of section. Along the straight edge of the paper the points of contour intersection and rock contacts will be taken at first. Then drawing of the necessary strike lines will be made complete and the intersections of the strike-lines on the section line should be taken as necessary points for drawing of the angle of dip.

Then the strip of paper should be placed along a straight base line having the same length with that of the section line. The points of contour intersection and rock contacts should be plotted on the base line and the point of altitudes at respective vertical distances on the given scale above the base line should be determined. A line joining these points will give the topographic profile along the section line.

Then the the rock contacts will be taken along vertical direction from the base line to the topographic profile. The dip angle of rock-beds either calculated graphically or by trigonometric ratio, will be placed at strike intersections on the section line or at respective points of rock contact. From the topographic profile downward the rock contacts will follow the dip angles and will terminate at the base of the section. If the structure is folded, the bedding planes drawn from the rock contacts may meet each other in the case of a syncline.

For the two series maps the structure of the upper series will be drawn at first. Then the lower series should be constructed, but a portion of the lower series may remain hidden under the upper series and if that part is not taken into consideration, the structure may remain incomplete.

However, for the construction of such hidden beds the extended strike line intersections of the beds of the lower series on the section underlying the upper series will be used for drawing of dip angles of the beds of the lower series. In that case the points from which the hidden beds will be drawn will be taken at the base of unconformity, i.e. at the lower contact plane of the lowermost bed of the upper series. Then the hidden beds will be drawn below the unconformity. For the three series map the same principle will be followed.

For transferring the contact planes of the partly hidden lower series the strike lines as well as the notional contact planes which are supposed to be present below the upper series can be used. For drawing of notional contact planes care must be taken so that they follow the trend of their exposed counter parts and they should match the fellow-beds of the same series.

After drawing of the geological section the student should notice which beds in particular have formed the surface topography. The vertical scale should be properly shown along the ordinate with the respective units mentioned. The direction of the section line should be given at the top or below the section line. The sequence of beds of all the series present in the geological section should be given along with the unconformity, if there is any, on the right hand side or below the section. The respective symbols should be used and dip and strike be given. The sequence should follow the stratigraphic order of succession. The bed which is not present in the geological section but whose order of occurrence has been understood, should also be incorporated in the sequence.

For a folded structure in particular, the projection of the possibly eroded portion or the portion underlying the base line may be done, so that the completion of the folded structure appears before the viewer.

Interpretation of the Geological Section

The geological section should be interpreted on the basis of the following topics :

a) Topography
b) Sequence of beds
c) Attitude of beds
d) Structure of beds
e) Correlation between structure and topography
f) Geological history

a) Topography

The topographic expression often gives a hint about the underlying structure as it is the product of the sum total effect of the interaction between the structure and process. Moreover, the nature of surface may depict the advancement of planation in terms of maturity. The relief is also determined by such interactions, the highest altitude is formed by a relatively more resistant rock bed and wide valley floors are carved out on less resistant rocks. Other parameters, besides this interaction, cannot be indicated by these geological maps. However, wider exposures are formed in relatively less resistant beds and vice versa.

b) Sequence of beds

The stratigraphic succession should be mentioned with complete sequence, according to the directions mentioned earlier. In this connection a better presentation will be to add the approximate thickness of beds.

For the calculation of approximate thickness of rock beds three procedures may be followed :

(i) If any strike line of the upper or lower contact plane of a bed coincides with another of different value at the lower or upper contact plane of the same bed, the vertical distance between the two strike lines in feet or metre will give the thickness of the bed.

(ii) In the second method notional strike lines are drawn at fixed horizontal and vertical intervals as obtained from the two consecutive strike lines on the lower/upper contact plane of a bed and thus any one of the successive notional strike lines of lower or higher value may ultimately coincide with any other strike line at the upper/lower contact plane of the same bed. Then the difference of two strikeline values at that plane, i.e. between the notional strikeline and actual strikeline will be considered as the thickness of the bed. If perfect coincidence does not occur between the notional strikeline and the actual strikeline, the intermediate distance between the nearest notional strikeline and the actual strikeline can be added with the difference between the nearest strikeline and the actual strikeline.

(iii) The thickness of a bed can also be measured from the perpendicular distance between the upper and lower contact planes of a bed drawn in the geological section.

c) Attitude of beds

Under this title the strike directions, their respective levels should be mentioned. A geological map should have multiple sets of strike lines, if so required. The dip of the rock beds at right angle to the direction of strike should be depicted.

d) Structure

After calculation of dips from the strikelines the structure will be determined, i.e. if it is folded, homoclinal or horizontal should be mentioned. In a folded structure the anticline, syncline, isoclinal or recumbent etc. should also be mentioned.

e) Correlation between structure and topography

The separation of an outlier from its fellow rock beds may occur in an advanced stage of dissection which is indicated by cap rocks and closely spaced 'V' - shaped contours along the line of dissection.

As such, the forms of topographic units may be depicted from the impression and shape of contours, such as, upland, plateau, valley, spur etc. The relief-form along the section line may be mentioned too. Steeper and gentler sections of topography may also be identified.

The structural control on topography may be indicated by the following clues.

(i) An anticline may form a ridge or upland.

(ii) A syncline may form a valley.

(iii) Under the sequence of an inverted relief the anticline may occupy the valley area and the syncline may occupy a ridge or upland successively.

(iv) A less resistant rock bed may form a gentle slope and a more resistant rock forms a steeper slope.

(v) Relatively less resistant rock beds of the upper series may be eroded earlier and valley inliers may contain the exposures of the lower series beds.

(vi) A folded or homoclinal structure may form a strike valley along the direction of strike of the beds.

(vii) Flanking such valleys dip and anti-dip or obsequent streams may join the strike stream.

(viii) A dip stream may follow the dip slope of the beds.

(ix) A gentler dip slope and a steeper scarp slope may form a cuesta.

(x) If the amount of dip of a homoclinal structure is high, the dip slope and scarp slope being nearly equal may form a hogback.

(xi) Horizontal or near horizontal structures may give rise to mesa or butte when separated by scarp slopes.

(xii) A folded or homoclinal structure may develop a trellised network of drainage with dip and anti-dip streams joining the strike stream at right angle.

(xiii) A dendritic network does not comply much the with underlying structure.

(xiv) A dome may give rise to a radial and an annular drainage network, whereas a basin may give rise to a centripetal pattern.

(xv) A rectangular network is controlled by the presence of joints in beds.

(xvi) A parallel pattern develops due to lithological control and presence of faults, as the case may be.

(xvii) Harder and more resistant beds will occupy the highest elevation of the area, if exposed.

(xviii) A drainage channel may follow a fault.

(xix) A parallel pattern of drainage may evolve, if parallel faults are there.

(xx) The uplifted block may bring forth greater amount of energy and may result in more intense erosion.

(xxi) An uplifted block or elevated foot wall may develop a fault scrap.

(xxii) An obsequent fault scrap may form if the uplifted block is less resistant.

f) Geological history

Rock beds and structures are good story-tellers. What was the environment during the deposition of sediments, did sedimentation occur under a calm or a turbulent condition, was the energy for sedimentation of the geomorphic agent fluctuating—all such questions are answered by the beds and their general characteristics. The structure obviously signifies the tectonic conditions under which the structure was formed. A folded structure obviously indicates the horizontally active compressional forces, whereas, a horizontal structure is least disturbed.

If the beds formed are from coarser to finer upward the environment under which sedimentation took place seems to be quiet, and a reverse order indicates an upside down condition which may be due to tectonic inversion or due to variation in energy.

However, the basic stress will be given on the chronological order of events, i.e. which bed was formed earlier and which later. If the particular geological age is known, care must be taken not to mention anything on the basis of the theoretical knowledge about the fossils of flora and fauna. Nothing should be mentioned about the tectonic events of which no proof is there in the given geological map. Sedimentary beds are formed under a submerged condition, but that does not necessarily mean that a marine condition should prevail at the time of sedimentation. A change in sequence of beds requires an unconformity which is an erosional surface formed due to sub-aerial denudation when the beds of the lower series were exposed before geomorphic agents. This should be mentioned also chronologically. The final surface is again a product of sub-aerial interaction between erosive forces and beds of rocks.

If there is any fault present on the section line, it should be specifically mentioned when and which series has been affected by the fault.

EXAMPLE INTERPRETATION

Map no. 1

On the given geological map (fig. 3.7 and 3.8) a section line AB has run across the outcrops of rock beds from SW to NE.

Relief : The relief along the section line has shown an undulating topography with uplands interspersed with valleys. The summits of the upland varies from 900 to 1000 feet or slightly above it.

The contour spacing is not uniform and it has given rise to the formation of scarp-slope and dip-slope. A number of streams are flowing through the area and the tributaries have joined their master stream at right angles.

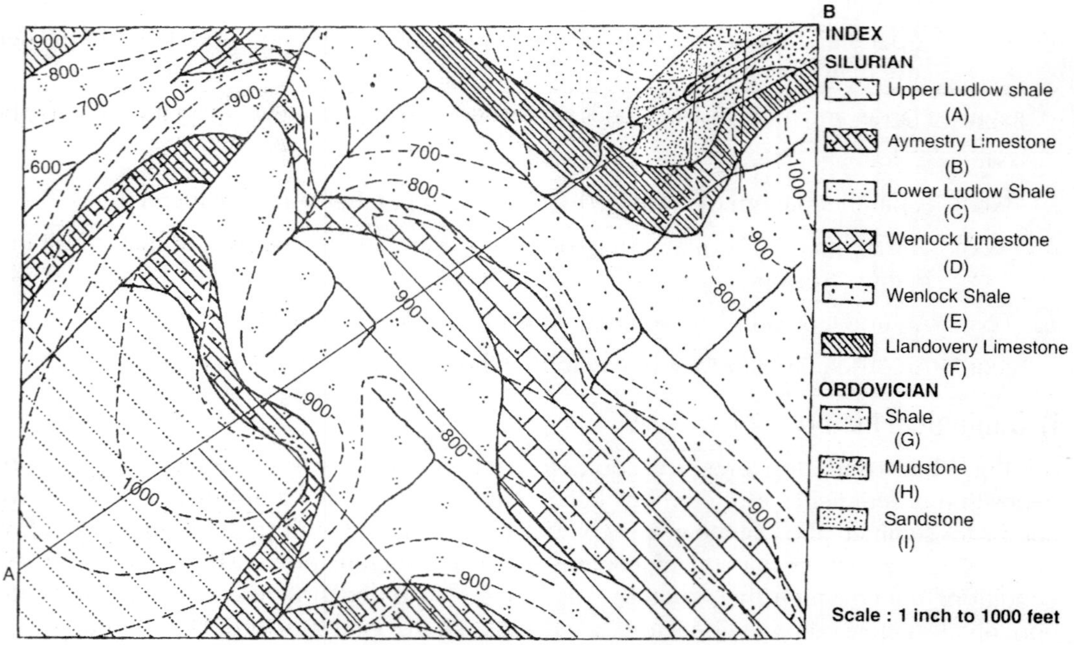

Fig. 3.7 Geological Map 1 (reduced)

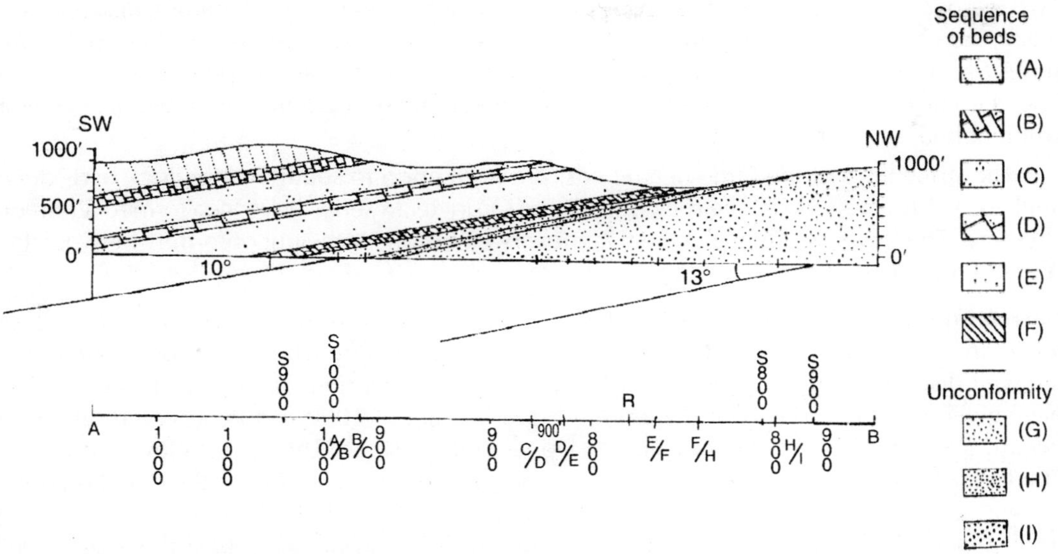

Fig. 3.8 Geological section along AB for map 1 (reduced)

Sequence of beds : As revealed in the geological section there are two uncomformable series of rock beds separated by an unconformity. The sequence of beds in the two uncomformable series of the Ordovician and Silurian period is incorporated in the following table (3.1):

TABLE 3.1

Name of Series	Name of Rock Beds	Signs	Approximate Thickness
Silurian	Upper Ludlow Shales		> 200′
	Aymestry Limestone		100′
	Lower Ludlow Shales		300′
	Wenlock Limestone		100′
	Wenlock Shales		250′
	Llandovery Limestone		100′
	UNCONFORMITY		
Ordovician	Shale		>200′
	Mudstone		100′
	Sandstone		Not known (oldest bed)

Structure **:** The strike lines on the rock beds of the Silurian series run from NW to SE direction. Two sets of consecutive strike lines on different bedding planes are having uniform distance between them , thereby indicating the same amount of dip of the rock beds. The six rock beds of the Silurian series thus dip at an angle of 10° toward SW. As the strike lines are perpendicular to the section line, the true dip has been followed. The beds of the upper series (Silurian), however, have formed a homoclinal structure.

The strike lines of the Ordovician beds, run from north to south and the rock beds dip at the angle of 13° towards west. The rock beds of the Ordovician series have also formed a homoclinal structure. The lower bedding plane of Llandovery Limestone is the unconformity between the two series of rock beds.

Correlation between structure and relief **:** As revealed from the geological section the relief forms an undulating topography with alternate ridge and valley. The scarp slopes and dip slopes are well distinguished and they vary in steepness. The gentler dip-slope and steeper scarp-slope have given rise to curstas. The highest elevation, i.e. about 1000 feet is observed on an upland toward SW, which is mostly occupied by Upper Ludlow shale. The lowest elevation is less than 700 feet. Along the section line it is expressed by a strike valley. Following the direction of the dip a few streams have joined the subsequent at right angles and along the scarp slope a few others have joined the subsequent at right angles too. Hence, the drainage network shows a trellised pattern with a profound control of structure on drainage network.

In the lower series the slopes have followed the direction of dip. The lower series, however, forms higher relief than some areas of the upper series exposures. Perhaps the higher relative hardness of the sandstone bed of the Ordovician series has favoured a higher relief formed by this bed even after being located at a lower stratigraphic position than the overlying beds of the same series and beds of the upper series.

Geological history **:** The three beds of the Ordovician series and the six beds of the Silurian series were deposited unconformably during the geologic past. The Ordovician beds are composed of clastic sediments with sandstone at the bottom and shale at the top. The variation in composition indicates the change in energy of the depositional agent. The coarser sediments occupied a lower position and the finer occupying the upper position indicates a calm condition at the time of sedimentation. However, these beds were deposited under a submerged condition. The beds were tilted at the time of upliftment.

After the development of a levelled surface through erosion, the surface was submerged again and the Silurian beds were deposited with Llandovery limestone at the bottom.

Alternate sequence of shale and limestone indicates a change in the environment as the beds have an alteration of clastic and bio-chemical deposition.

Beds were tilted at the time of upliftment and the present state of drainage network carved out the present undulation in topography with considerable adjustment to the structure.

INTERPRETATION OF FAULTED STRUCTURES

Map no. 2

Relief

In the given map (fig. 3.9 and 3.10) a section line XY has been selected running across the area from west to east.

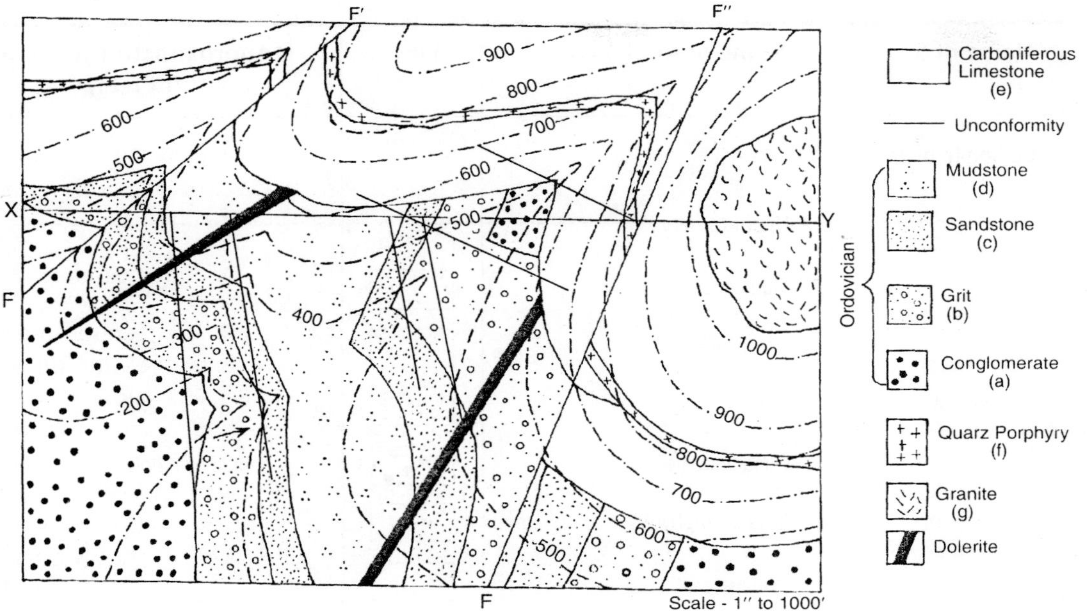

Fig. 3.9 Geological map 2 (reduced)

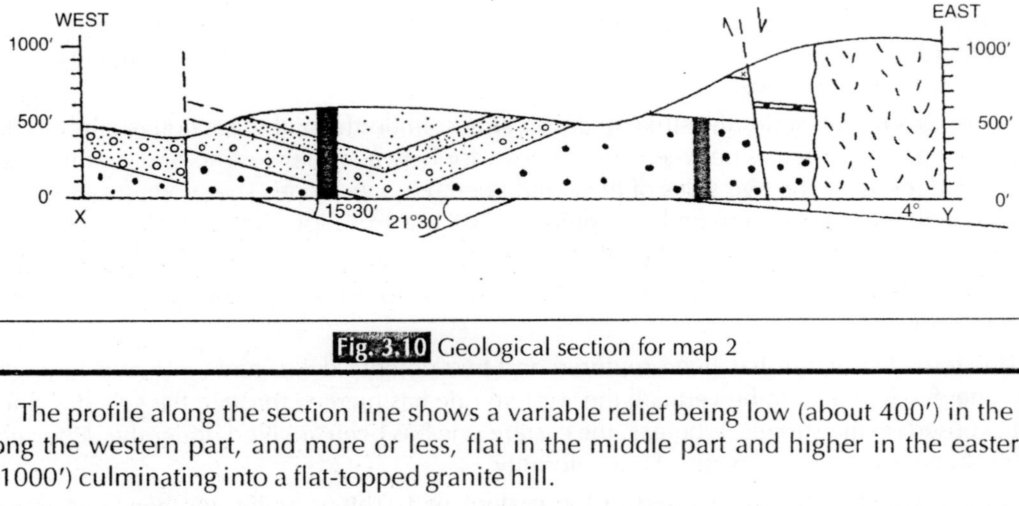

Fig. 3.10 Geological section for map 2

The profile along the section line shows a variable relief being low (about 400') in the valley along the western part, and more or less, flat in the middle part and higher in the eastern part (> 1000') culminating into a flat-topped granite hill.

In other areas shown in the map the elevation goes down to <200' in the extreme south-western corner at the wide expanse of a river valley. In fact, there are two river valleys, both of them facing towards south-west, as it appears in the configuration of topographic contours.

Sequence of beds

As revealed in the geological section along XY there are two series of unconformable rock beds separated by an unconformity at the lower bedding plane of the limestone bed in the Carboniferous series. However, the sequence of beds may be tabulated in the following manner (Table 3.2) :

TABLE 3.2

Name of Series	Name of Rock Beds	Signs	Approximate Thickness (In feet)
Carboniferous	Limestone		> 700 ′
	Unconformity		
	Mudstone	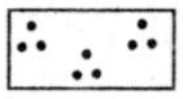	> 300 ′
	Sandstone		100 ′
Ordovician	Grit	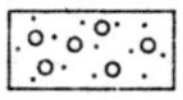	200 ′
	Conglomerate		not known (lower most bed)
	Quartz Porphyry	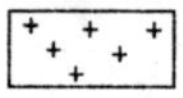	
	Granite	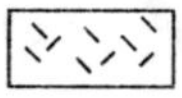	
	Dolerite		

Structure **:** In the upper series (Carboniferous) the strike lines run form WNW to ESE. The apparent dip of the limestone bed along the section line is about 4° towards north-east. The true dip is about 9°. Hence the rock bed of the upper series has developed a homoclinal structure. However, a Quartz porphyry has formed a sill being concordant with the limestone bed and having the same dip as the rock bed assumes.

In the Ordovician series the strike lines run almost in north-south direction (slightly NNW to SSE), although the distance between strike lines vary between the western and eastern counter parts of rock beds on the two sides of the central bed, i.e. mudstone. Therefore, it seems to be a folded structure as the western limb is dipping 15°30′ towards east (slightly ENE) and the eastern limb is dipping 21°30′ towards west (slightly WSW).

Thus the two limbs dipping towards each other or towards the inner side have formed a synclinal fold.

This folded structure has been ruptured and two dolerite dykes have intruded through the beds. The dykes appear to be vertical; the western one has pierced through the syncline and has been exposed on the surface, whereas, the eastern one has been covered under the deposition of the limestone bed along the plane of unconformity.

A huge granite body is exposed in the eastern part. This is again another large intrusion through the eastern flank of the conglomerate bed of the lower series and limestone bed of the Carboniferous series. This intrusion forms a stock or batholith.

Fault **:** Two faults have ruptured the entire sequence of rock beds. Both the faults are normal, vertical , the western one affects the lower series and the eastern one affects both the series. The amount of throw or displacement is about 200′ along both the faults. The middle block, i.e. the central part of the syncline seems to be thrown relatively upward, whereas, the blocks on the two sides seem to move downward. The presence of two dykes in the middle block supports this idea.

Correlation between structure and topography

The topography along the geological section is highly influenced by structural attributes. The highest elevation has been occupied by the granite exposure which is undoubtedly more resistant that its neighbouring sedimentaries of limestone and conglomerate. The steep surface slope on the eastern side of the syncline is controlled by the elevation of the batholith. The topography along the limestone bed is highly influenced by the height of the exposed intrusion.

The syncline, on the other hand, has formed a horst between the two faults and the surface is not very undulating. However, the level of this surface is maintained by the elevation of the dykes intruding into it. Here also the higher resistance of the igneous rock-beds has controlled the height of the levelled surface. As such, mudstone is less resistant and is supposed to form a concave surface, and its flattish expression is only acceptable in terms of the height of the exposures of intruding dolerite dykes. However, the recession of the limestone bed towards east and exhumation of the previous erosional surface along the plane of unconformity is also another instance of differential erosion depending on variable resistance of rockbeds.

Towards further west, in the western flank of the western fault the topography occupies the lower most elevation along a valley. The stream forming this valley is controlled by the alignment of the fault. But the eastern valley does not truly follow the eastern fault. This one does not follow the dip of the limestone bed either. It seems to follow rather an antidip direction across the limestone bed of the upper series. The synclinal horst has formed the ridge, whereas the anticlinal part has formed a valley. This indicates an inversion relief.

However, the lowermost elevation on the geological section has been formed by the exposures of grit.

The 'V's of the outcrop of limestone are pointing towards upstream as the dip of the rock-bed is towards upstream.

The 'V's of the eastern limb of the syncline point in the downstream direction as the dip-slope is much higher than the stream-slope and the rock beds dip downstream.

The 'V's of the western limb of the syncline point towards upstream as the dip of the rock beds is towards upstream.

Geological History

The area was submerged during the Ordovician period when the rockbeds of the same series were formed through depositional processes. The sequence of the beds follows that the grains of the rockbeds are finer upward. This pertains to a calm environment under which sedimentation occurred. Later on, compressional forces resulted in the formation of a synclinal structure. At the time of folding some fractures developed in the rockbeds that gave rise to the scope of intrusion and as a result of that two dykes were formed by intruded dolerite. The upliftment might have been related to faulting (western one) which caused relative displacement of rock beds on either side of the fault. Planation on the Ordovician rocks resulted in a flat surface, the level of which was dictated by the height of the two dykes.

A stream following the alignment of the fault continued its erosive action which carved out a valley.

During the carboniferous at least the eastern part of the area was submerged again and bio-chemical deposition took place on the submerged erosional surface. As a result the limestone bed of the upper series was formed. Due to some tectonic disturbances a major rupturing in the crust was developed and that resulted in the growth of a granite pluton well within the thick limestone bed. A fraction of the magma formed a quartz prophyry parallel to the plane of unconformity.

This was followed by another faulting on the eastern side. This fault affected both the lower and upper series of rock beds and the porphyry bed was also made displaced by it.

A stream was initiated on the surface and erosive action continued through the limestone bed to expose the granite which after exhumation took over as the major control of the landform lowering action of the area.

Gradual sub-aerial denudation resulted in recession of the limestone bed towards east except for the neighbouring part of the granite bed.

Erosion through the lower series rock beds in the west carved out the present landform.

Map no. 3 : Example Interpretaiton of Faulted Structure

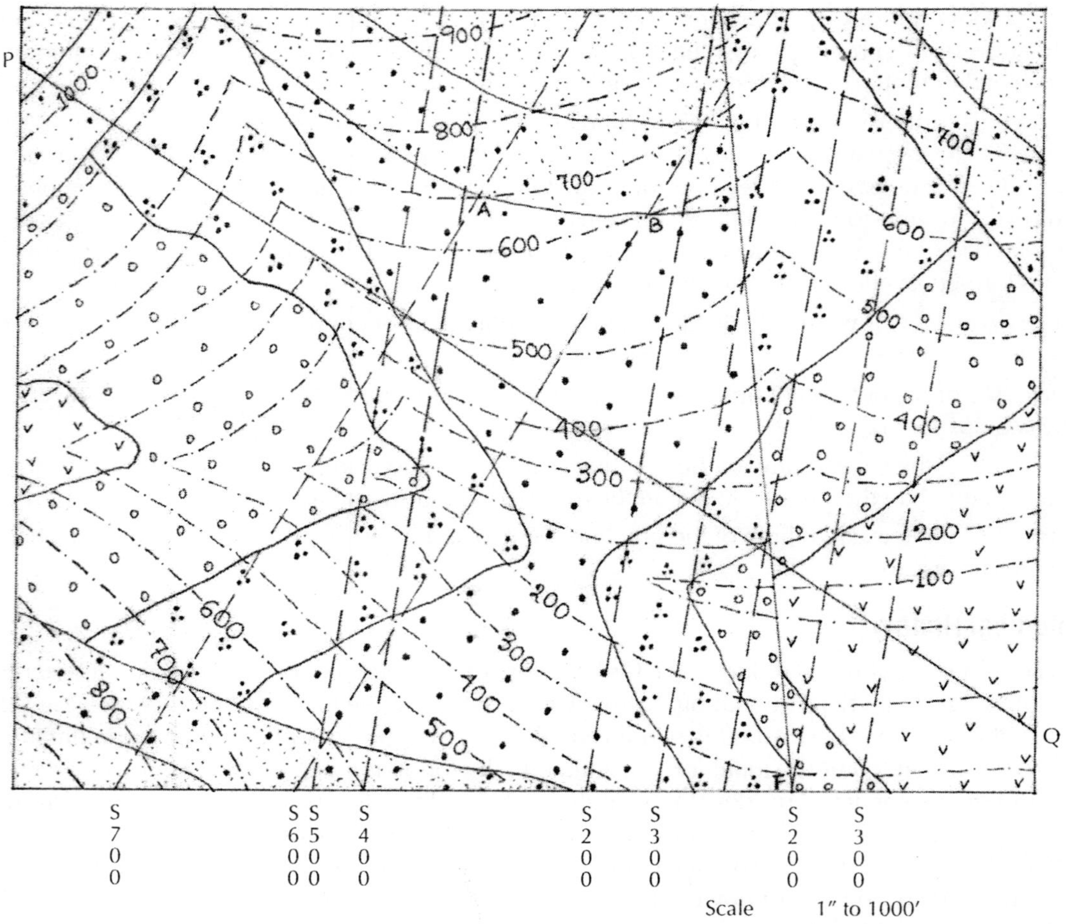

Fig. 3.11 Geological Map 3

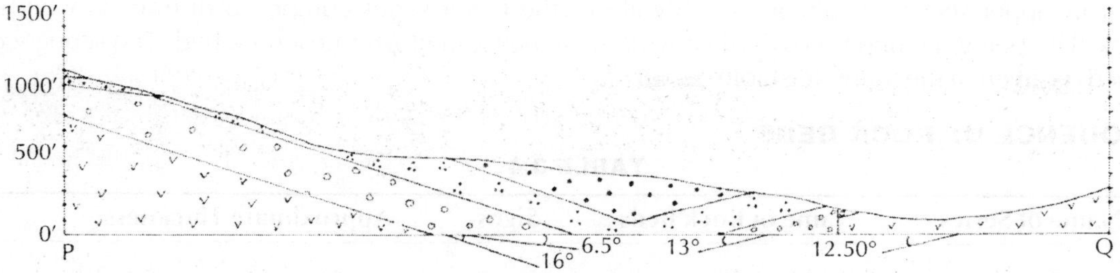

Fig. 3.12 Geological Section for Map3

TABLE 3.3

Name of series	*Name of Rock Beds*	*Signs*
Upper	Middle Oolite	
	Lower Oolite	
Unconformity		
Lower	Black Slate	
	Grey Shale	
	Mudstone	
	Conglomerate	

Interpretation

The given geological map (Map no. 3) has been interpreted on the basis of a section line PQ running from WNW to ESE.

Topography

The contours on the geological map under discussion vary from 1000 ft. in the northwestern corner to 100 ft. in the southern part of the eastern boundary. Thus, a relief of about 900 ft. covers the entire map-area.

The contour pattern shows the occurrence of a stream valley from west to east. Two left bank tributaries join the stream from north and northwest. The section line PQ having higher elevation towards west-northwest and lower towards east-southeast shows the topographic slope from west-northwest to east-southeast. However, the form of the stream valley is observed towards the eastern end.

Sequence of Beds

Altogether there are six rock beds in the geological map, as revealed from the section line PQ. Of them, middle oolite and lower oolite of the upper series are separated by an unconformity occurring at the base of lower oolite. This plane of unconformity crosses 600ft. contour at the lowest. The strike lines S700 and S600 cross the unconformity at two points A and B. Thus the unconformity dips for about 6°20′ towards southeast. However, near P the contours run parallel to the unconformity and thus the two beds of the upper series seem to be horizontal partly.

This upper series lies unconformably above the lower series composed of four rock beds, black slate being the uppermost and conglomerate being the lowermost rock bed. The sequence of beds is given in the following table.

SEQUENCE OF ROCK BEDS

TABLE 3.4

Name of Series	Name of Rock Beds	Signs	Approximate Thickness
Upper	Middle Oolite		> 100 ft (Uppermost Bed)
	Lower Oolite		100 ft.
	— Unconformity—		
Lower	Black Slate		> 700 ft. (Uppermost Bed)
	Grey Shale		200 ft.
	Mudstone		300 ft
	Conglomerate		Not Known (Lowermost Bed)

Geological Structure

As mentioned earlier, the unconformity has strike lines running from SW to NE and the unconformity dips towards SE for 6°20′ . The bedding planes of the upper series follow this inclination and the structure is homoclinal.

The strike lines in the lower series run, more or less, in north to south direction, though they differ in horizontal distance in the west and east of black slate, as well as in the west and east of the fault line running in north-south direction. The strike lines in the west of black slate indicate west to east dipping rock beds, whereas in the east of black slate they indicate a westward inclination of rock beds. Thus in the lower series, there is a syncline, the central bed being black slate.

The western limb of the syncline dips for about 16° towards east, whereas in the eastern limb it varies from 12.5° to 13°. Thus the syncline is slightly asymmetrical.

The Fault mentioned earlier is vertical in nature, as the fault line is a straight line from north of south. However, the occurrence of the fault has very slightly changed the dip of mudstone rock bed. In the west of the fault it is about 13° and in the east it is 12.5°. In general, it may be said that the vertical fault has not caused much distortion in rock beds. The throw of the fault is about 100 ft.

Correlation Between Structure and Relief :

The upper series occupying a higher stratigraphic position marks the highest altitude of the area. The same thing is reflected in the geological section PQ also. The oolite bed occupies an elevation of above 900 ft.

On the other hand, the lowermost elevation is attained by the conglomerate bed of the lower series and the main valley in the lower part is formed in the conglomerate bed. Between the highest and lowest elevation there is variable relief in which the black slate at the core of the syncline occupies the higher position. Thus it seems that, the synclinal core is more resistant than the conglomerate bed. However, of the four beds in the lower series, the black slate is the only metamorphic bed which may have a higher resistance to erosion. This is the reason why it forms a higher elevation, where the surface is more levelled.

RULE OF 'V'S :

The fault does not have any specific impact on drainage system, though it has imposed horizontal displacement of rock beds. Thus is has caused an abrupt change of surface exposures of the beds of the lower as well as the upper series. However, in the eastern side of the fault rock beds are relatively upthrown for about atleast 100ft. The nearly horizontal beds of the upper series form 'V's in their outcrops the appex of which points towards upstream. In the lower series, the western limb of syncline forms 'V's of outcrops pointing towards downstream; in the eastern limb such 'V's point towards upsteam. In the western limb, the stream gradient is lower in inclination than rock beds; in the eastern limb, the rock beds dip upstream and form 'V's in the outcrop pattern pointing upstream.

Geological History

The rock beds of the lower series were deposited under marine condition. The conglomerate occupying the lower most position and being coarse grained seems to be formed at the base. The round pebbles which compose a conglomerate bed are usually observed in the coastal landscape and finer materials are deposited further seaward. It seems that under marine transgression the coastal landscapes were submerged under ocean water and further deposition of materials continued under this marine condition.

During a later phase tectonic movement led to the occurrence of folding where the beds of the lower series were transformed into a syncline. At the time of folding the core bed might be a sedimentary one which during a later period was transformed under pressure metamorphism and turned into slate, but this change may be related to the deposition of the beds of the upper series. The beds of the lower series emerged through tectonic uplift and came under the process of sub-aerial denudation. This set of geomorphic processes created a nearly levelled surface at a lower elevation.

On a later occasion transgression took place and the bio-chemical deposits of calcium carbonate occurred. Thus the two beds of the upper series were formed. Later the entire sequence of the two series of rock beds emerged out of water, the lower series being covered under the upper series of rock beds which were laid uncomformably above the lower series of rock beds. Sub-aerial denudation included strong fluvial action and after the partial removal of the upper series rock beds, the beds of the lower series were exposed. The drainage network formed on the upper series continued even across the exposures of lower series without a good correlation with structure. Thus the drainage system seems to be superimposed above the beds of the lower series.

Faulting occurred at a much later period with both the series of rock beds being affected by it. As the rock beds of the upper series have their present outcrop pattern displaced by fault, it seems that faulting occurred after geomorphic processes turned them towards the present form of surface configuration. However, the valley slope is not much affected by the occurrence of fault. Ultimately sub-aerial denudation with predominance of fluvial action led to the formation of the present surface configuration.

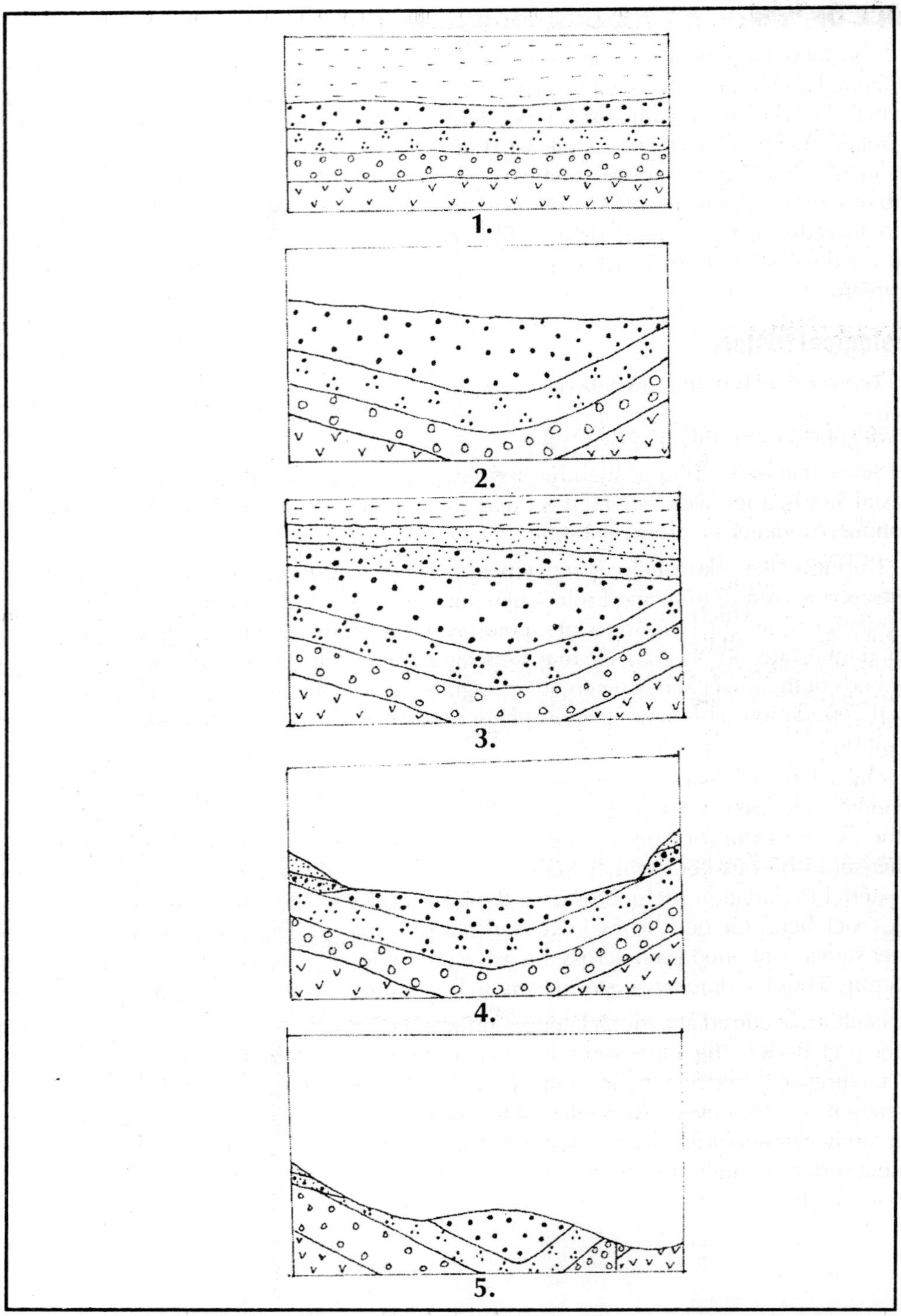

Fig. 3.13 **Hypothetical Phases of Change in the Geological History**

INTERPRETATION OF TOPOGRAPHICAL MAPS

Topographical maps are planimetric in use though they have contours, which may develop a third dimension besides the two others, which are usual for all maps. They depict relief features in terms of contours, spot heights, and conventional signs. The spacing of contours becomes relevant for determination of topographic slope. Various types of linear features such as, man-made features like roads, railways, embankments, etc., and natural features, such as, drainage network, cliffs, etc., pointed features like settlements, ponds, wells, temples, mosques, churches, many office buildings etc., and areal features such as forest patches, reservoirs, mining areas, swamps, hills, plateaus, ridges, erosional and depositional plains etc. are incorporated in topographical maps. Therefore, these maps may act as sources of information about the cultural landscapes as well as for the physical features. Obviously they will act as major tools for the geographers as well as for persons of any other discipline requiring spatial analysis and correlation between various objects placed on the surface of the earth.

Projections of Topographical Maps

Different countries have prepared topographical maps on different scales and on different projections, e.g., the French topographical maps are prepared on Polyconic projection, Indian topographical maps are prepared on Modified Polyconic or International projection.

The table 3.3 shows the projections and scales employed by different countries for topographical maps (Close and Cox, 1913).

Such maps have been prepared on various scales , though almost all of them belong to the medium scale group. The most suitable scale for the topographical map of a country depends on a variety of conditions, such as, the state of development of its various districts, the density of its population, the nature of the physical features, and the funds available both for the actual survey and for the publication of maps. The most useful scales for defence and administrative purposes are 2.5 inch, 2 inch, 1 inch, $\frac{1}{2}$ inch and $\frac{1}{4}$ inch to a mile or from 1:25000 to 1:250000.

Survey of India Topographical maps

The topographical maps prepared by Survey of India have also been published on various scales. Their areal extent has also varied depending on the scale on which they are prepared. As such, there are three different scales used for imperial units, and on metric scale they have been prepared on three other scales. The size of the topographical sheet remaining constant the scale and the extent of latitude and longitude have varied proportionately. The basic grid for preparation of the topographical sheets have an extent of 4° of latitude and 4° of longitude. These squares are divided into 16 sheets of 1° × 1° rectangles, each of which is further subdivided into 16 rectangular sheets. All of these sheets have been designated by a letter and a number. The table below shows the system of topographical sheet hierarchy. The reference number allotted to various categories of sheets is itself an indicator of the scale and surface-extent of the sheets. In table 3.4 below the map hierarchy has been shown according to the system adopted (fig. 3.11).

TABLE 3.5

Country	Scale	Projection
Austria-Hungary	1:75000	Polyhedric
	1:750000	Bonne (Old Edition) Albers' conical equal area (New Edition)
Belgium	1:20000 and reduction	Bonne
British colony & Protectorates		Simple Polyconic
Denmark	1:40000 1:20,000 (Old Map)	Bonne a Modified Conical
Egypt		Conical Orthomorphic
France	1:80000	Bonne
	1:200000	Bonne
	1:100000	Polyhedric
	1:50000	Polyconic (New map)
Germany	1:25000 and reductions	Polyhedric
Italy	1:100000	Polycentric or Natural
	1:500000	Bonne
Netherlands	1:25000	Bonne
Norway	1:100000	Conical with two std.// (?)
Russia	1:126000	Bonne
	1:420000	Conical Orthomorphic
Spain	1:50000	Polyhedric (probably)
	1:200000	Bonne
Sweden	1:100000	same as Norway
Switzerland	1:25000	Bonne
	1:50000	Bonne
England	1:10560	Rectangular (Spheroidal)
	1:63360	co-ordinates
	1:126720	
	1:253440	
	1:633600	Airy's projection
Scotland-Ireland	1:63360 and smaller	Bonne
United States	1:62500	Polyconic
	1:125000	
	1:250000	

S.O.I. 1 Million Maps & their subdivisions

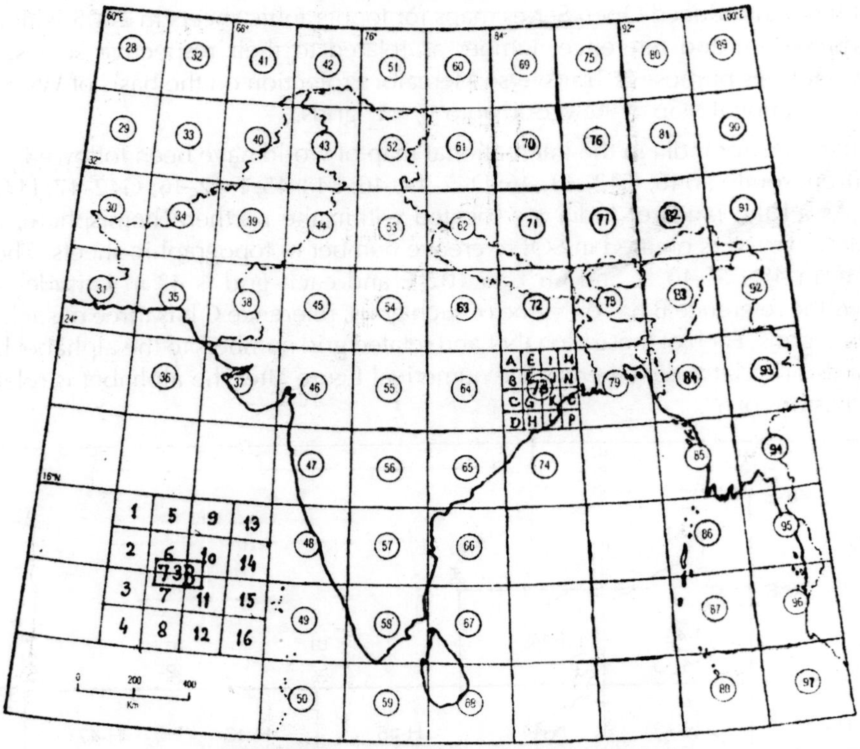

Fig. 3.14 Index Map for S.O.I. Toposheets

TABLE 3.6

Name of sheet	Extent covered	FPs scale	Metric scale	Reference No. (Example)
Million sheet	4° × 4°	1 inch to 16 miles	1 cm to 10 km.	65
Quarter-inch or degree sheet	1° × 1°	1 inch to 4 miles	1 cm. to 2.5 km.	65 G (one of A to P)
Half-inch sheet	30′ × 30′	1 inch to 2 miles	1 cm. to 1 km.	65 G/SE (one of 4 quadrant sheets)
Inch sheet	15′ × 15′	1 inch to 1 mile	2 cm. to 1 km.	65G/15 (one of 1 to 16)
Special	5′ × 7′ 30″	—	4 cm. to 10 km.	65G/15/3 (one of 6 sheets)

Reference Number of Scale of Open Series Topographic Sheets of Survey of India

Survey of India introduced Open Series maps for topographic sheets in 2005 with a different method of grid system and reference number as related to their respective scales. The map projection used for this purpose is Transverse Mercator Projection on the basis of WGS 84. It has followed the International Map of the World upto 1° × 1° grids.

The grid numbers for India in the international map of world have been followed. These grid numbers are (from south) : B46; C42, 43, 46; D42-44, 46; E43-45; F 42-46; G42-47; H42-47; I43, 44; and J43. As all the lands of India are located within the northern hemisphere, the initial marking of reference 'N' is omitted in SOI reference number of topographic sheets. The grids for India extend from 4°N to 40°N and 66°E to 102°E and each grid is 4° in latitude and 6° in longitude. Thus the reference B has only one of such grids, reference C has three of such grids and H has six of such grids. Each of these alphabet and related grid numbers to the alphabet belongs to horizontal bands of 4° latitude, whereas the numerical figure after the alphabet is related to the longitudinal divisions of 6°.

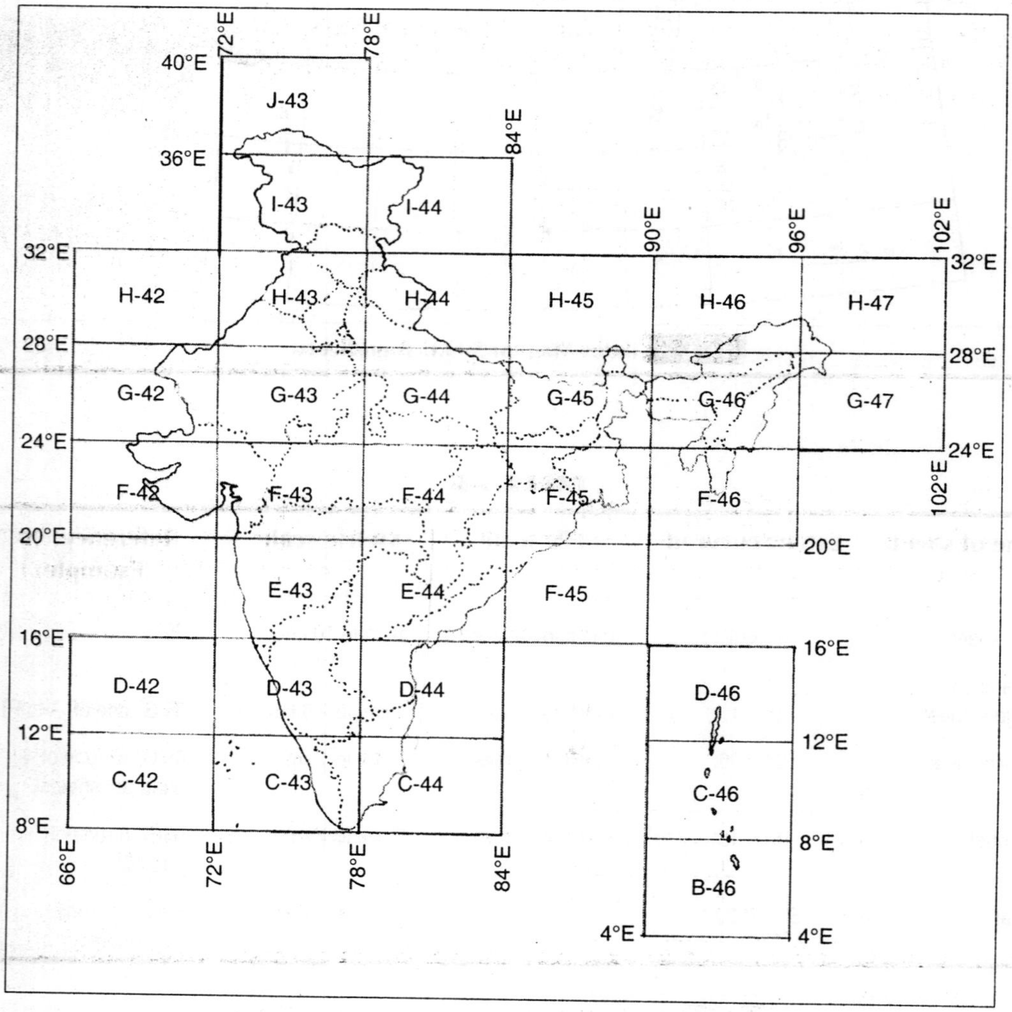

Fig. 3.15 Grid numbers for open series Maps of SOI

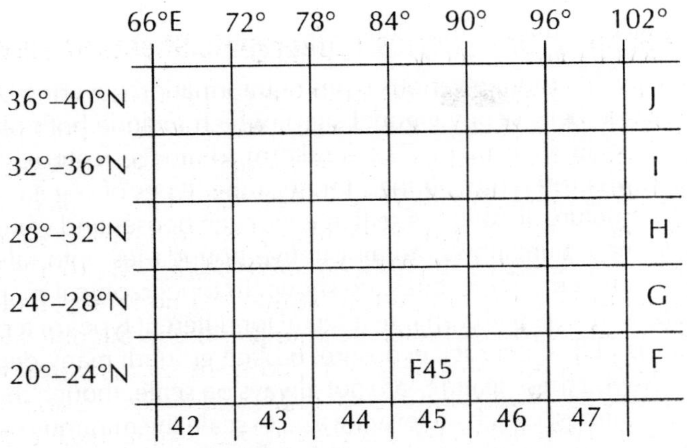

Fig. 3.16 Distribution of Grids from F–J

Each of these grids (4° × 6°) is divided into 24 rectangular grids of 1° × 1° extension of lalitude and tongitude. These grids are numbered alphabetically A to X extending horizontally from A to F, G to L, M to R and S to X.

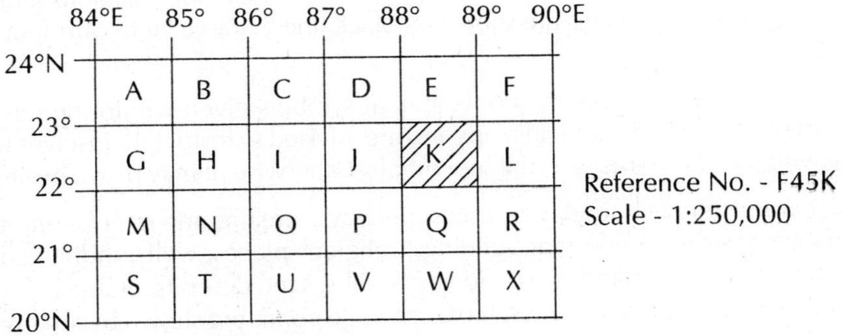

Fig. 3.17 Alphabetical reference number of Grid F45

These 1° × 1° grids are further divided into 16 15′ × 15′ grids assigned with a scale of 1:50,000 each.

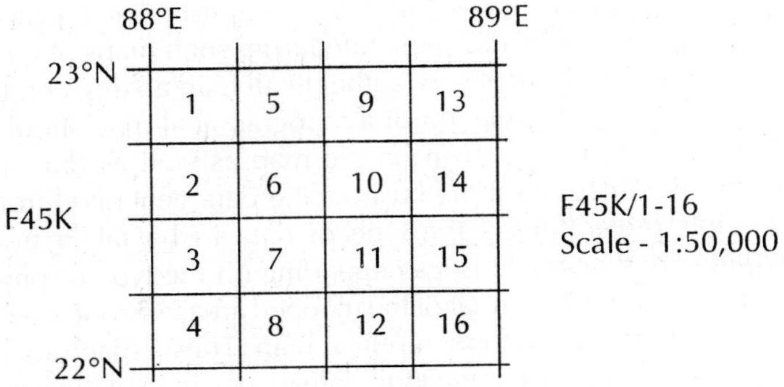

Fig. 3.18 Numerical reference number of grid F45K

Conventional signs

Such topographical maps incorporate various types of information covering both physical and cultural landscape. A good number of conventional signs, which include both physiographic and cultural information, are used in such maps. The landform, drainage features, various types of detention storage, artificial water reservoirs, springs, forests, other types of vegetative covers, arable lands, communication infrastructure, location of settlements, even houses and various other types of office buildings and government bungalows, administrative boundaries upto taluk level and still many other special physical and cultural features are shown in topographical maps. The landform characteristics expressed by contours with variable interval for different types of terrain along with a few special symbols featuring cliff, sheet rock exposure, broken ground, many deposional features etc. are shown in detail. Areawise these features are not always on scale, though the scale for length is maintained, and for other features, which are exactly true to scale the minimum size of the feature to be taken into consideration will depend on the scale of the map. Different colours are used for different sets of conventional symbols. Various types of administrative boundaries are shown in black, though the thickness of lines and patterns of symbols vary at different levels. Forest boundaries are shown in black, though they often have a green riband on themselves. Contours are shown in brown, and so are the other special landform features. Hydrological features in general are shown in blue and seasonal as well as ephemeral streams are shown in black. Vegetative covers are coloured green. Man-made features, such as, roads and tracks, settlements, other religious and government buildings are coloured red. Railways are shown by black lines. Arable lands are shown in yellow. All names are given in black.

Students are required to follow the conventional symbols given within the reference boxes below the format of S.O.I. topographical maps and are advised to restrict themselves to the sizes of symbols along with particular fineness of line symbols. Otherwise, it may prove misleading.

In general, administrative boundaries, roads, railways, streams and rivers, contours are given as line symbols, homesteads, important buildings, religious places, wells, individuals plants and trees are given as point symbols and forests, jungle, scrubs, sand deposits, arable lands, sheet rock, bouldery landform, reservoirs, sand dunes, moraine, large ponds are shown by area symbols made up of dots of colours. Some other numbers indicate height above mean sea level, alphabets indicate names of govt buildings (Fig 3.19).

Interpretation of Topographical Map

The interpretation of a topographical map should be accomplished on the basis of the features shown in the map and on the basis of the data generated from such maps. As the topographical maps include details of topographic features very authentically, an analysis on the basis of such features may prove significant. An interpretation of a topographical map should be a balanced one, highlighting the significant features shown on the map as well as drawing of significant statistical and morphometric correlation on the basis of the data generated from the map. The particular interest of the interpreter selects the type of data to be taken from the map. As topographical maps exhibit varied characteristics depending on the type of physical landscape and cultural layout present in a particular format of the mapped area, any one sheet does not cover all the aspects expected to be present in a topographical map. Thus a map of the middle Ganga plain differs significantly from that of the Chotanagpur plateau, or a map of the Brahmaputra valley is totally different from that of another on Banas-Kantha district. The interpreter should have some primary knowledge about the area of which the map is to be interpreted. Thus in Rajasthan

Fig. 3.19 Conventional signs

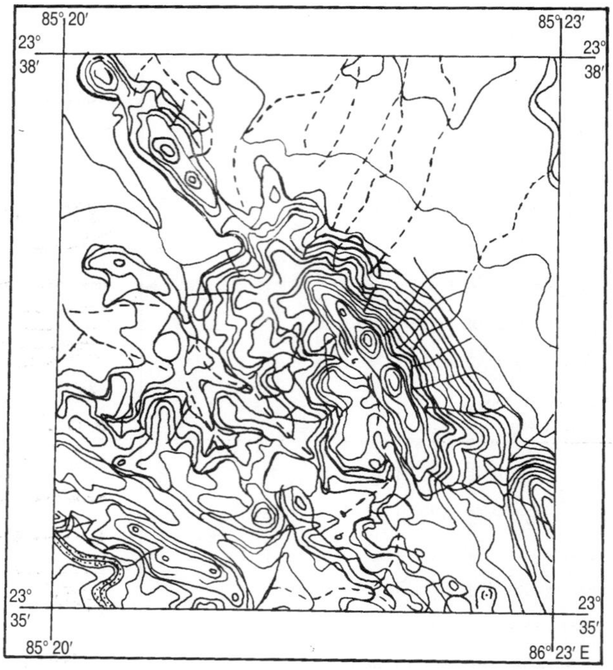

Fig. 3.20 **Ridge (reduced)**

ephemeral streams, sand dunes may be important, whereas in, Assam the braiding of the Bramhaputra and mountain torrents may be significant for the interpreter.

Landform features seen on Topographical Maps

As mentioned earlier contours depict the landform features on such maps along with a few specific conventional symbols. The shape of the contours and the spacing between them is more important for the study of landforms.

Ridge : A ridge is shown by closely spaced elongated contours with a few enclosed contours of higher value in the middle with or without any spot height or triangulation point in them. A ridge is often depicted in terms of its alignment along the axis. Significant correlation can be drawn from the similarities of alignment between an isolated lonely ridge and other ridges in the undissected part of the plateau or mountain. Moreover, ridges often act as water divide on various spatial scales (fig. 3.13).

Spur : Spurs are commonplace in hills, plateaus and mountains. Some of them are interlocking, while some others are non-interlocking. In topographical maps spurs are shown by contours with hairpin bends closed towards the valley-side. These are projected parts of mountains and hills, carved out at the bottom by a stream or river. The bent contours which form a valley with their wide-open side towards downstream section are exactly opposite in trend in the case of spur. Sinuous streams in high-relief area carve out interlocking spurs, whereas, straight channels and streams with wide valleys have shown non-interlocking spurs (fig. 3.14 a & b). A glaciated valley may show truncated spurs.

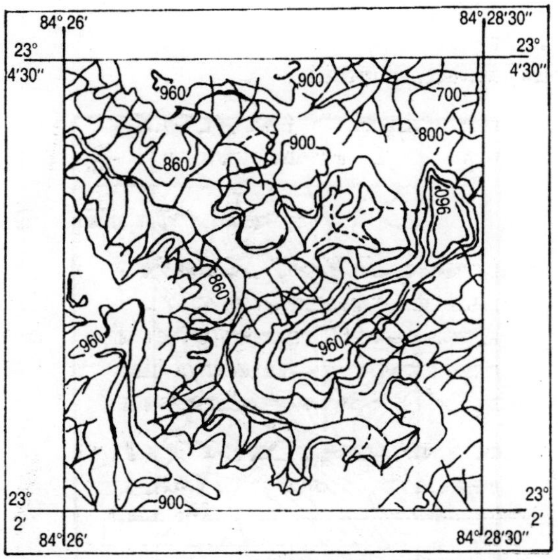

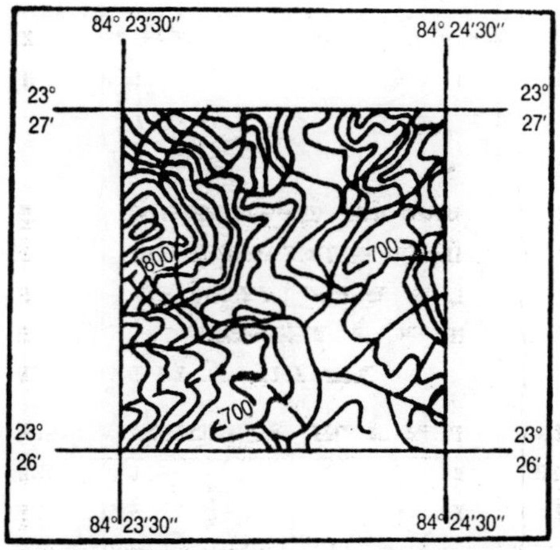

Fig. 3.21 a & b Spur & Interlocking spur (reduced)

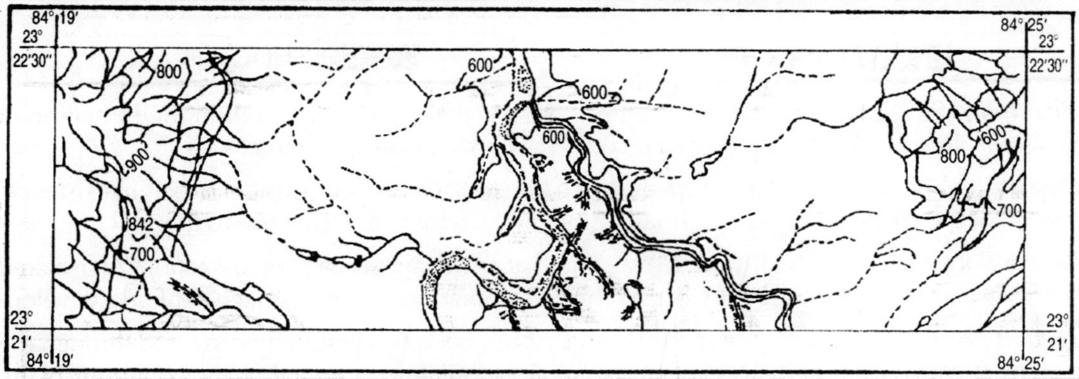

Fig. 3.22 Valley (reduced)

Escarpment : As escarpment is a steep slope which has a gentler counter part. The spacing of contours is different on the two component parts of the slope. Dip streams often flow along the gentler part of the slope, whereas, minor anti-dip streams may flow along the scarp slope in a trellised drainage pattern.

Valley : A river-valley (fig. 3.15) being a flattish strip flanking a stream between two uplands shows wider spacing between contours. The valley-walls, on the other hand, have closely-spaced contours, much closer than a valley. Cross sections between the opposite valley-walls may assume the representation of a valley in a better way.

Summit level : In plateau areas the summits are often accordant in elevation. At the top of the plateau they occur at a low range of variability indicating an erosional surface present, more or less, accordantly at peaks of the ridges, hills and flattish top of a plateau. A cross section or a series of cross sections connecting a few of such accordant summits may be useful in identifying the presence of an erosional surface occurring on a regional scale.

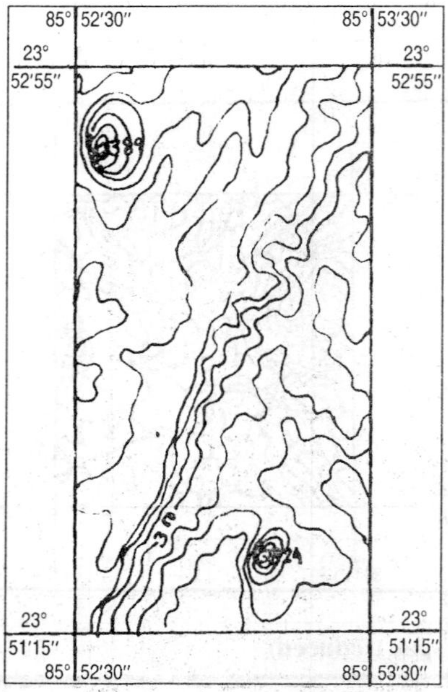

Fig. 3.23 Conical Hill

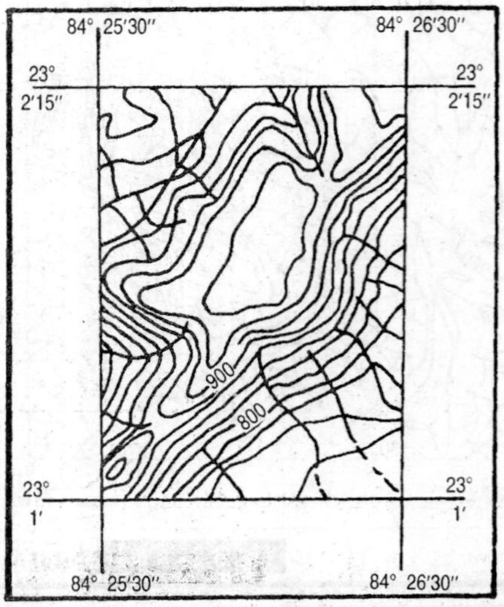

Fig. 3.24 Flat top hill

Conical hill : (fig 3.23) Occasionally, uniform resistance of rocks may result in the formation of conical hills. Residuals hills and volcanic cones may also appear as conical hills.

Flat top hill : Hills (fig 3.24) are flat topped when a horizontally bedded resistant rock is in existence. Recession of the erosional faces of a small unit of plateau may also give rise to them.

Isolated hillock : These hillocks (fig 3.25) are found at an advanced stage of dissection. An isolated hillock may be a monadnock too. Over such hillocks radial pattern of drainage networks develop.

Dissection : A plateau or a hilly or mountainous region becomes gradually dissected through the erosion by streams and their process of valley development. In course of time the continuity of the high relief terrain gets broken and they become separated into segments by the interspersed valleys. A mature stage of dissection causes isolation of such segments.

At a further advanced stage of planation the valleys become wider and the higher resistant core portion of the isolated segment of the plateau or mountain stays as an erosional remnant, usually with a lowered height than the main mass of the plateau or mountain.

A cross section showing such dissection and valley formation and a sketch of the isolated remnants may prove significant in identifying the stage of dissection and planation (fig. 3.26).

Saddle : A saddle (fig. 3.27) is a low lying area between two hills or two ridges. This is otherwise known as a pass when it allows to cross the ridge or hills at a much lower elevation and along a gentler slope through a passable gap. Roads and foot tracks are often constructed across the saddles. This is an erosional feature usually carved out by streams on two sides of a mountain. This pass is also known as a col.

Knoll : These are small mounds, usually round in shape. Only one or two round contours amidst erosional plains indicate these features. Perhaps some minor exposures of more resistant rocks develop these features.

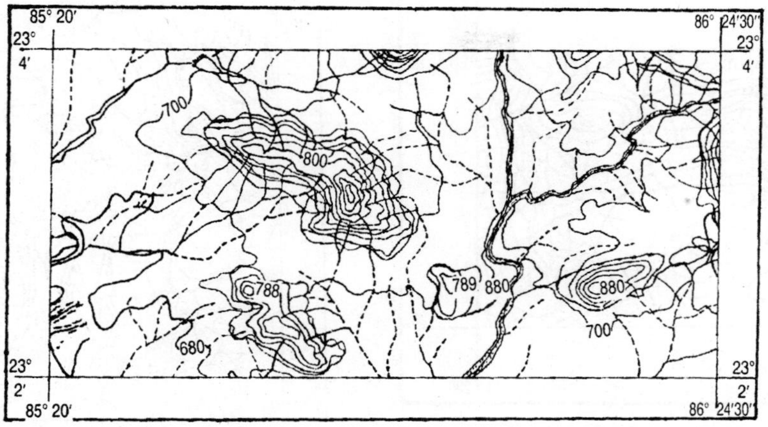

Fig. 3.25 Isolated hillocks (reduced)

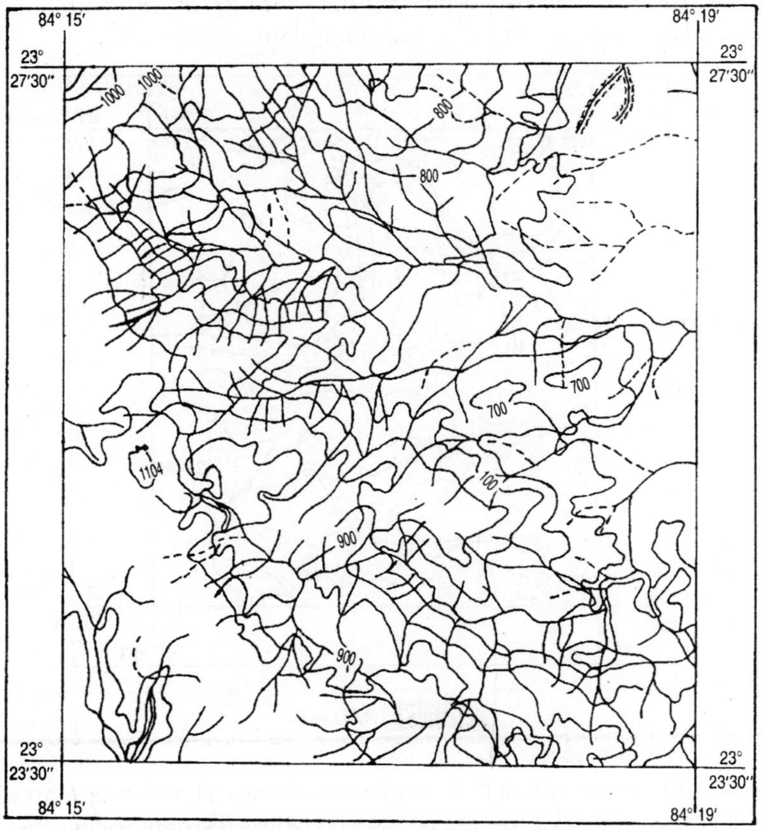

Fig. 3.26 Dissected pleateau (reduced)

Sheet rock : On erosional plains sheet rocks are often exposed in patchy occurrence. These are found in parity with the level of the surface slope. Such features may be taken as criteria of an erosional plain and hence are found in valleys.

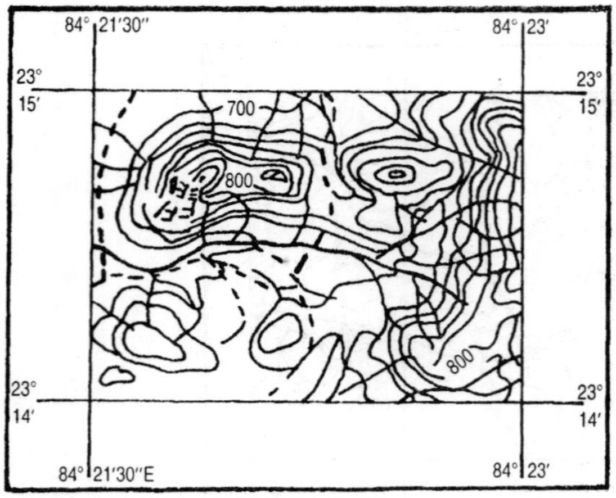

Fig. 3.27 Saddle

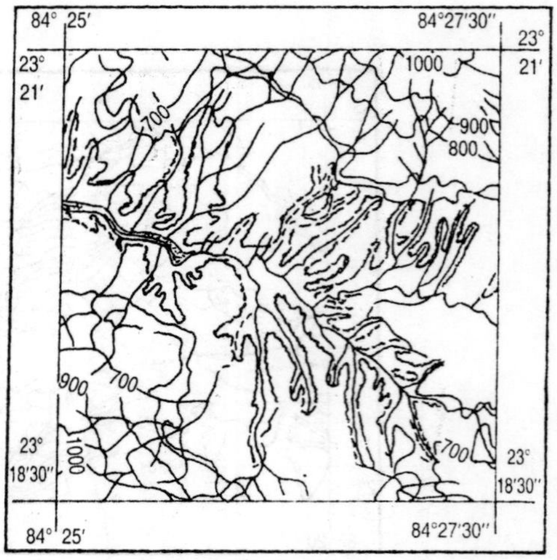

Fig. 3.28 Badlands (reduced)

Boulders : Igneous intrusions, when exposed on surface through erosion, are often weathered into boulders. These are also taken as criteria of erosional plains.

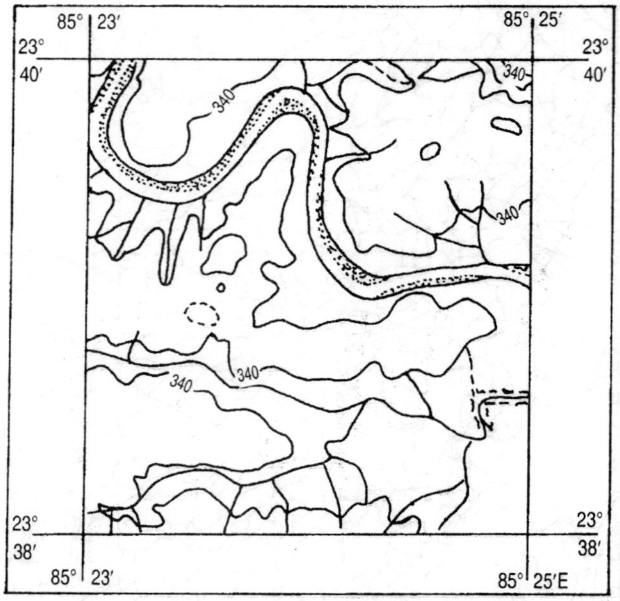

Fig. 3.29 Terrace

Badlands : Areas of gully erosion along bare surface give rise to badlands in minor basins of sub-tributaries or tributaries. Such landforms are composed of less resistant rocks. The areas with slight undulations favour such features (fig. 3.28).

Break of slope : Although the break of slope is a localized phenomenon and varying erosional intensity on different parts of a terrain may give rise to breaks of slope (i.e., the break between a plateau or mountain and a valley) at variable elevations, revelation of such things are necessary for the total understanding of the map.

River terrace : A river terrace (fig. 3.29) is an erosional feature formed along the sides a river which is partly or totally incised into its valley. This being a step-like feature shows two or three closely spaced contours towards the side of the river, whereas, on the hill side the contours are widely spaced. River terraces may indicate planation history of the fluvial cycle.

Incision : An incised stream with more vertical corrasion is flanked by closely spaced contours, whereas, away from the river the contours have wider spacing between them within the outer part of the valley.

Cliff : A cliff is a (fig. 3.30) near vertical face of slope (usually more than 40° which may be erosional or tectonic in origin. However, long cliffs are often favoured by tectonic upheaval or subsidences.

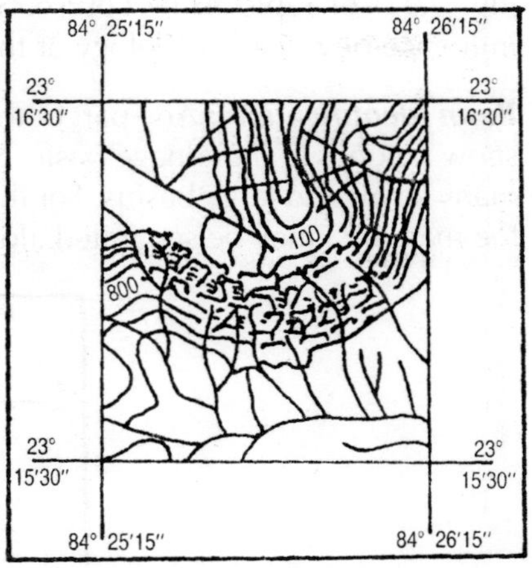

Fig. 3.30 **Cliff**

Gorge : A gorge (fig. 3.31) is a 'V' shaped cross profile of a river valley with closely spaced contours flanking the river. The presence of a gorge indicates active down-cutting by the river in a youthful terrain.

Wide & Shallow 'V' : A valley cross profile being a wide and shallow 'V' in shape indicates considerable lateral corrasion at an advanced stage of planation.

Oscillation : A river may oscillate considerably developing symmetrical bends or meanders at an advanced stage of planation. The channel may expand in width and depositional features such as point bars may appear in the channel.

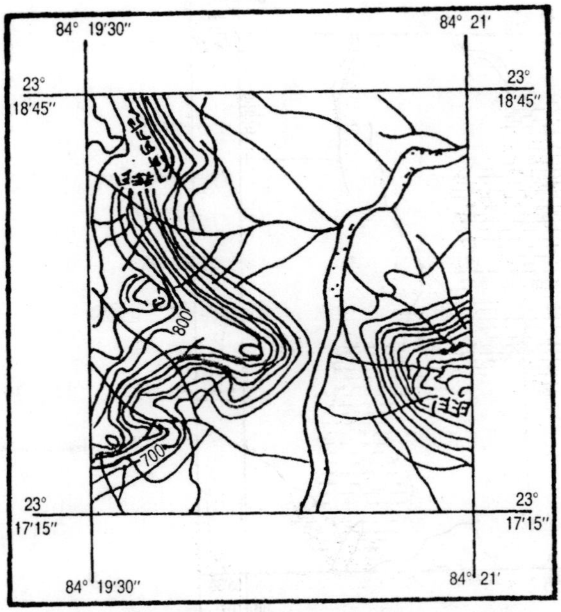

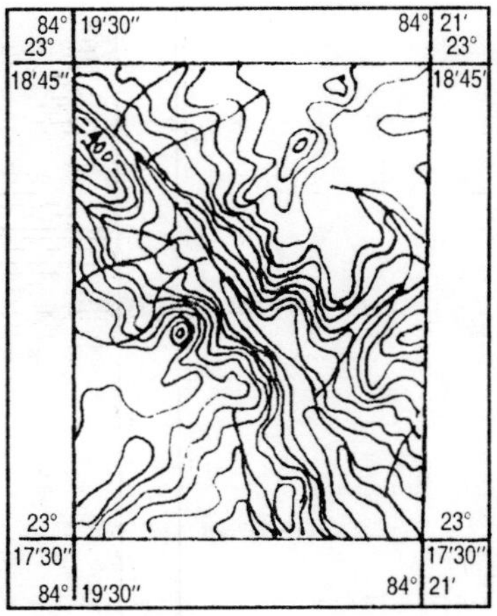

Fig. 3.31 a & b **Flow in a narrow section of valley & Gorge (reduced)**

Waterfall : A river or stream in its course over the mountain or plateau may have a waterfall (fig. 3.32) or rapid in its course. Such a feature should be highlighted as it reveals either the influence of variable lithology or the impact of tectonics.

Basin Identification : Any part of the earth's surface except for the waterless desert and perpetual snow belongs to a drainage basin. Similarly, areas shown on a topographical map also belong to many small and large basins. For the sake of convenience of interpretation the drainage basins of the map-area may be separated along boundaries of water-parting.

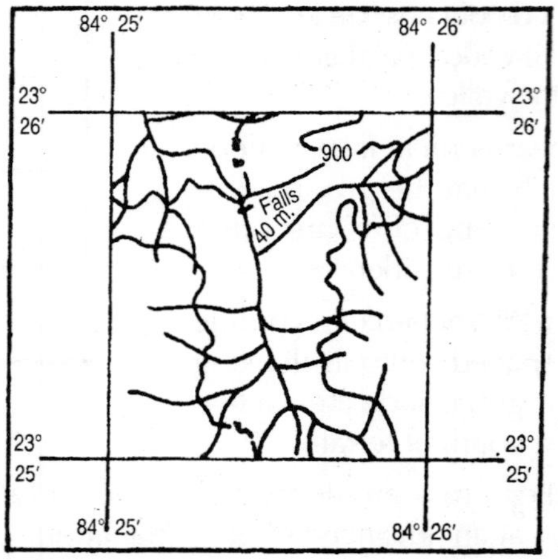

Fig. 3.32 **Falls**

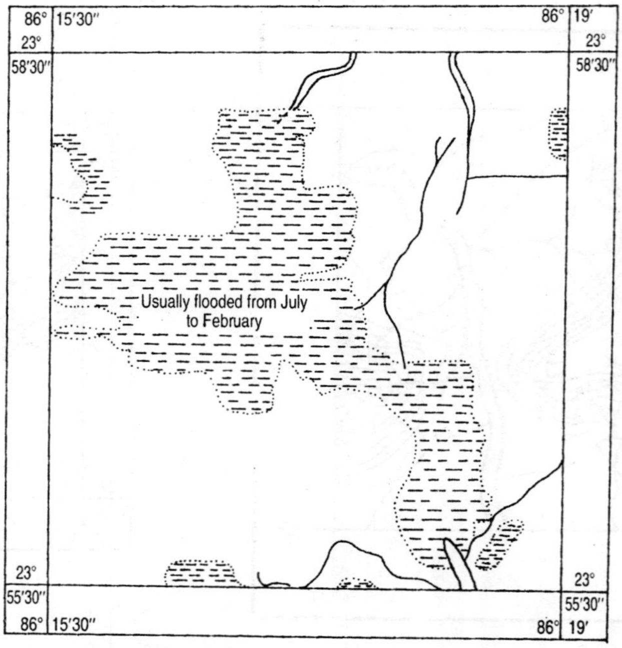

Fig. 3.33 **Flood prone area (reduced)**

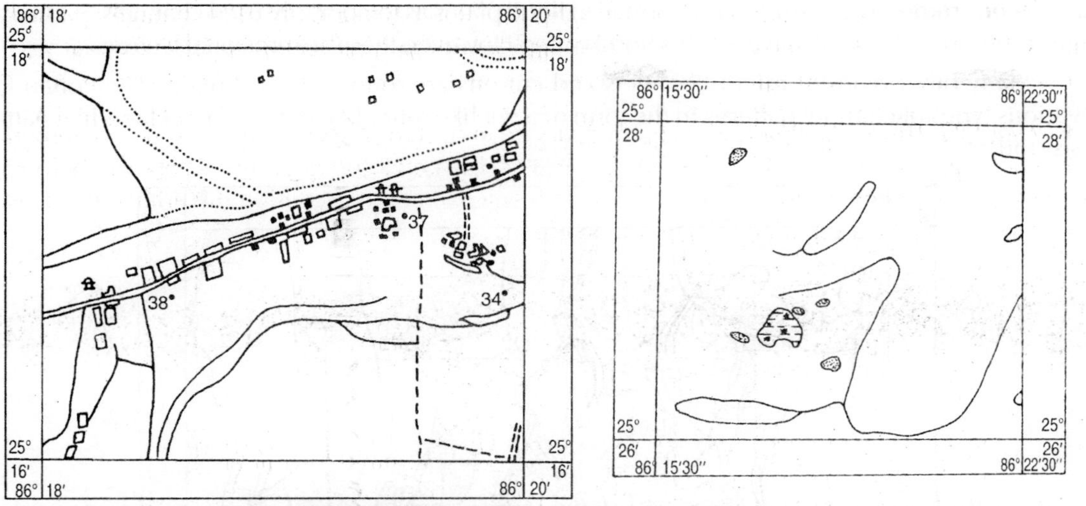

Fig. 3.34 (a) & (b) Levee & Back swamp (reduced)

Flood Plain Features

Flood plains (fig 3.33) are characterised by wide rivers, flat lands with minimum local relief and various types of in-channel and out-channel depositional features related to the accumulation of water and sediments.

Levee : Levees, as such, do not have any conventional sign for S.O.I. topographical maps. Moreover, as their elevation above the flood plain seldom exceed 10 metres and the maps have either 10 or 20 metre interval for contours, levees or the natural embankments on maps of flood plain do not have any mark of direct identification (fig. 3.28a). They are rather indirectly identified on the basis of the roads built along them and their running in nearly parallel alignment with the flood plain forming major river. Such roads are often swarmed with settlements of compact-linear type. Moreover, to mark the local relief spot heights are often incorporated in such maps. Thus spot heights varying locally for a few metre between the low lying flood plain and the narrow strip of levee may also indicate these natural embankments.

Back swamp : It is a swamp (fig. 3.34) formed by accumulation of flood water into the minor depression of the flood plain. They are often marked by the word 'mud' in them and the period of flood is also mentioned. Grassy vegetation is often shown in them.

Slough : A slough is a shallow lake in a flood plain formed by the accumulation of flood water in a deeper depression of the flood plain (fig. 3.35a).

Bils are also similar features but elongated in nature as they are often formed by the abandoned part of a channel (fig. 3.35b).

Cut-off : A cut-off is (fig. 3.30)an abandoned part of a channel. Various types of cut-off are there, viz. chute, neck cut-off, ox bow lake etc. Rivers in their floor plains leave them at the time of oscillation and channel shifting. A ***chute*** (fig. 3.37)is a low angle cut-off with a narrow water body which divides a point bar into two parts. A ***neck cut-off*** (fig. 3.38) forms prior to the formation of an ox bow lake when the river makes nearly a circular loop. After that the river breaches through the neck of the bend and deposition of sediments gradually separates the near-circular bend from the main channel and thus an ox bow lake is formed (fig. 3.39).

Some other elongated or small cut-off may be left as *dry bed* in the flood plain.

Scour routes (fig. 3.40) are also formed in flood plains as temporarily used channels, particularly during flood for the disposal of excess flood water. However, these are erosional features.

Many other types of minor channels and cut-offs are found in flood plain. They often form various types of channel patterns in the form of a net like reticulate pattern , necklace-like pattern, sisi-fork etc.

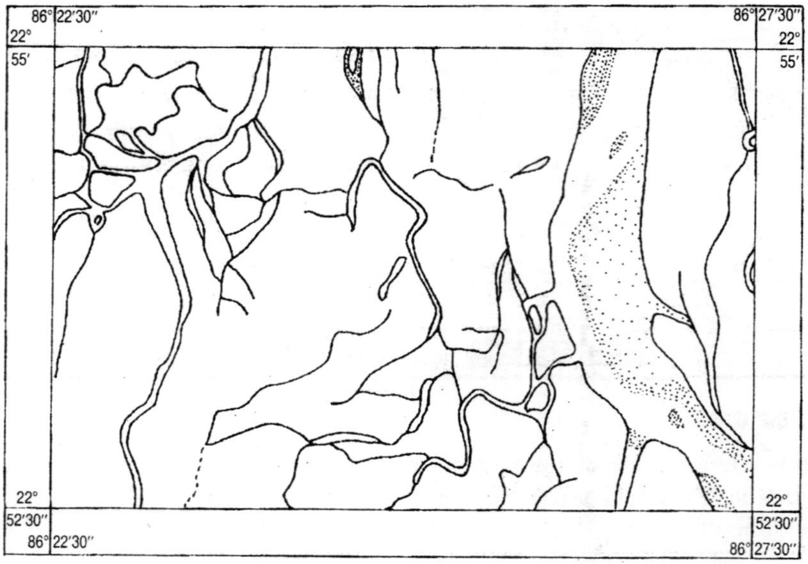

Fig. 3.35 (a) **Reticulate pattern (reduced)**

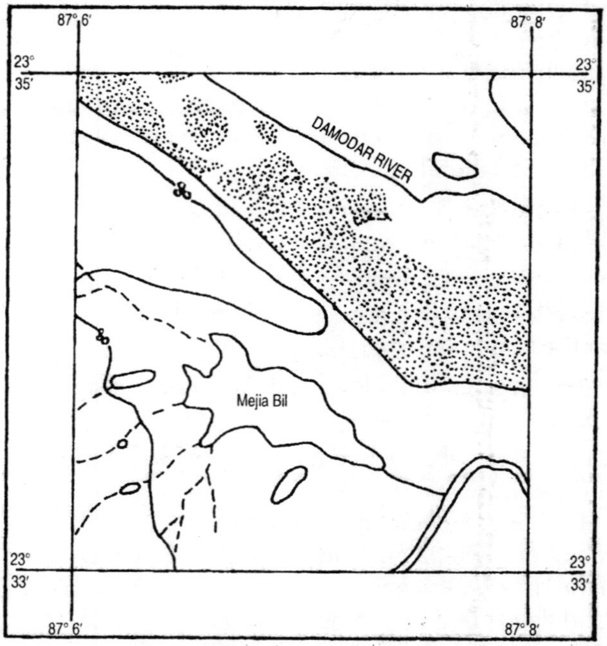

Fig. 3.35 (b) **Bil**

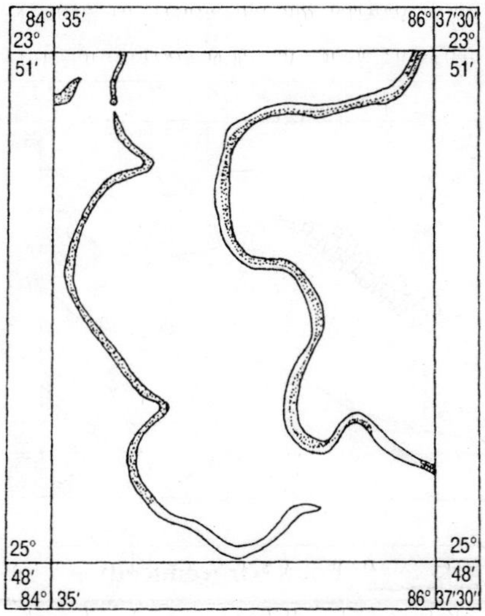

Fig. 3.36 Meander scroll (reduced)

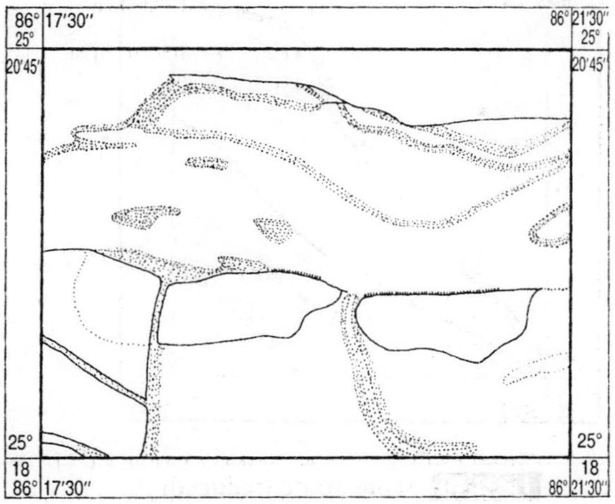

Fig. 3.37 Chute & Sand plug (reduced)

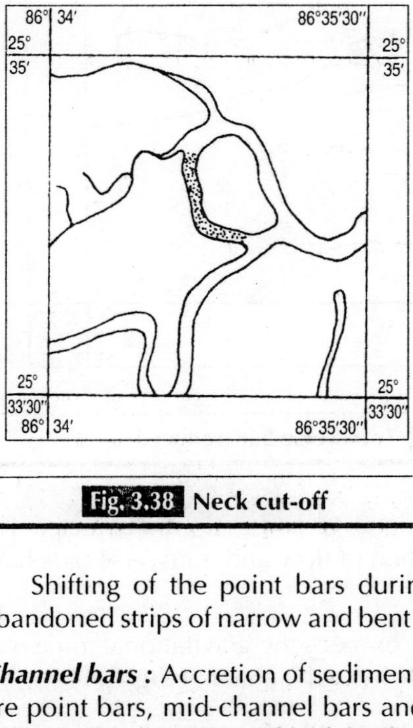

Fig. 3.38 Neck cut-off

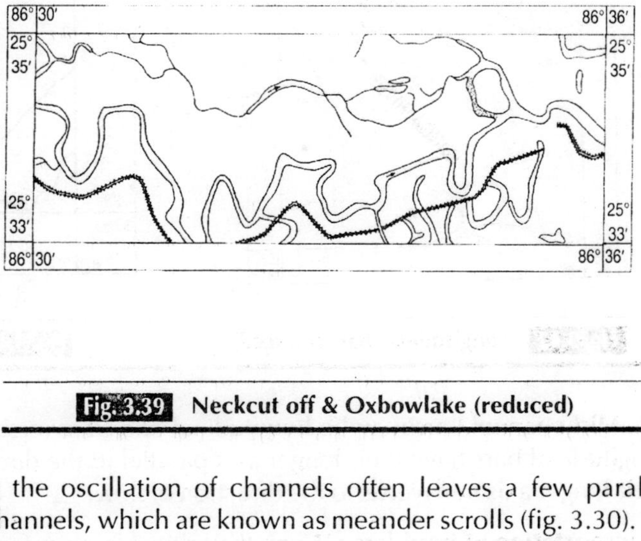

Fig. 3.39 Neckcut off & Oxbowlake (reduced)

Shifting of the point bars during the oscillation of channels often leaves a few parallel abandoned strips of narrow and bent channels, which are known as meander scrolls (fig. 3.30).

Channel bars : Accretion of sediments often forms various types of bars within the channel. These are point bars, mid-channel bars and shoals. Of them a shoal remains mostly submerged under water except for its central high back which is tapered in both up stream and down stream direction. It is formed in the middle of the channel. From such shoals point bars gradually develop.

A point bar (fig. 3.41) is a depositional landform attached to the bank. In a meandering channel crescent-shaped point bars are formed along the inner bank of the channel.

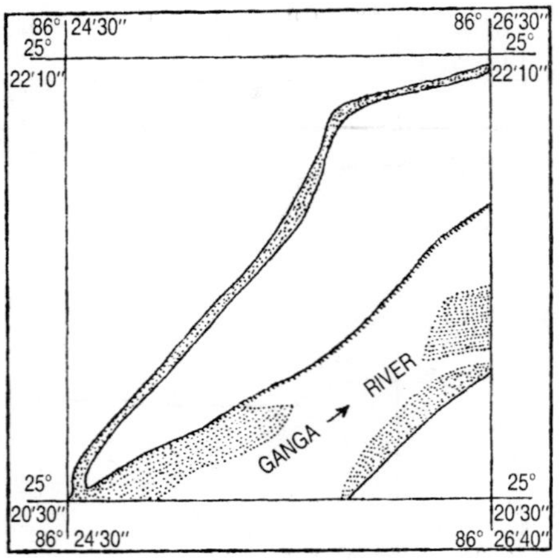

Fig. 3.40 Scour route (reduced)

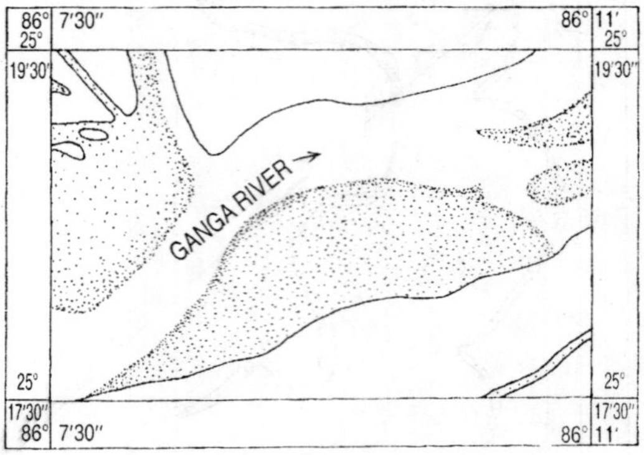

Fig. 3.41 Point bar (reduced)

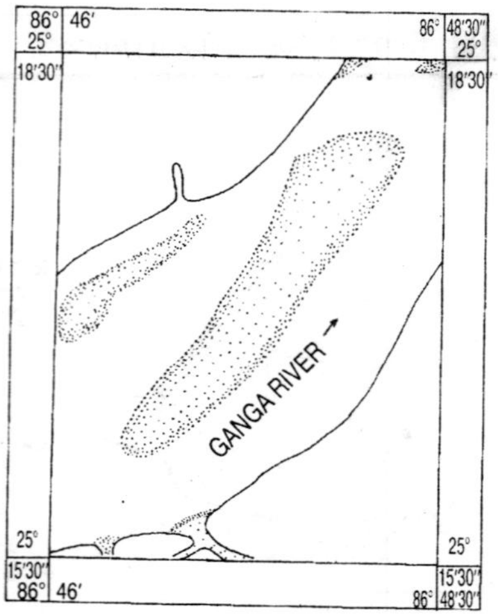

Fig. 3.42 Longitudinal bar (reduced)

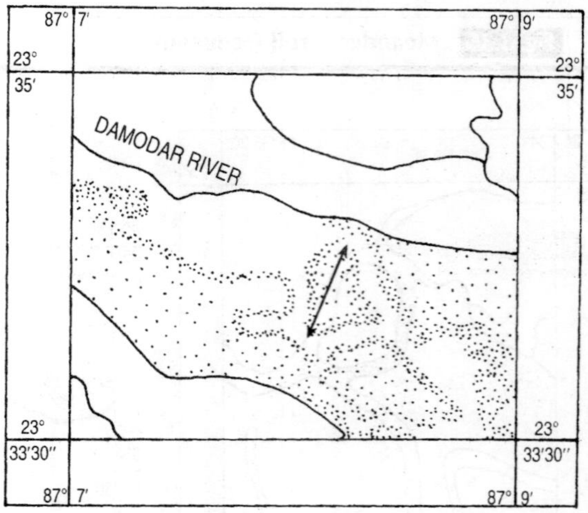

Fig. 3.43 Transverse bar (reduced)

Mid-channel bars may be longitudinal and transverse (fig. 3.42 and 3.43) in character. The longitudinal bars have their longer axis parallel to the direction of flow and transverse bars have their longer axis transverse to the direction of flow.

Transportation of boulders : When the critical tractive force exceeds the gravitational force on a large grain, it is transported. It depends on the erosional velocity of the channel (fig. 3.44).

Necklace of channels : In a deltaic landform a river often branches out into various forms, such as, a necklace, a sisi fork etc. (fig. 3.45).

Anabranching : When a portion of a major river branches out from itself and flowing for a few kilometres separately again drains into the main channel, it is known as anabranching (fig. 3.46)

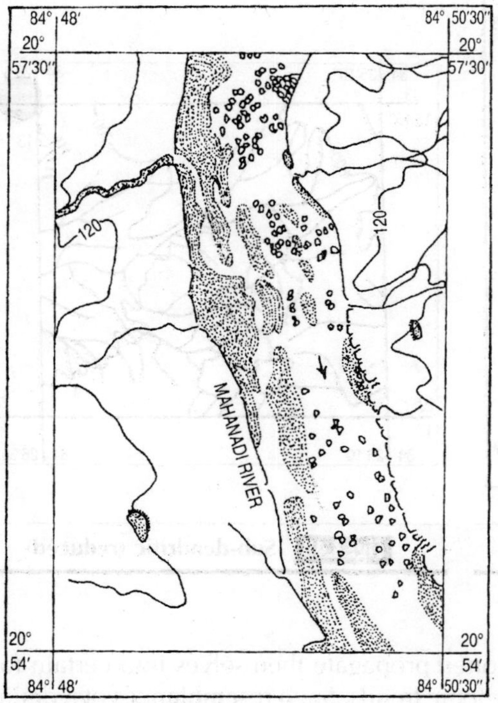

Fig. 3.44 Transportation of Boulders (reduced)

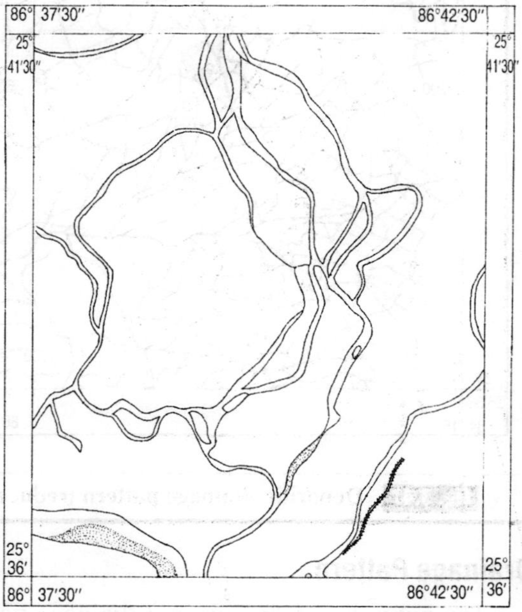

Fig. 3.45 Nacklace of channels (reduced)

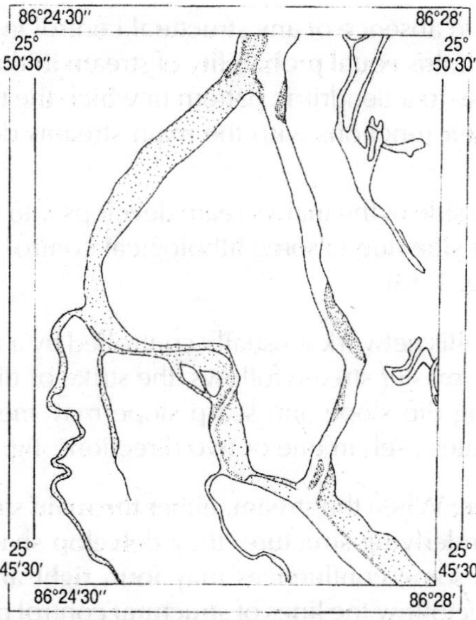

Fig. 3.46 Anabranching (reduced)

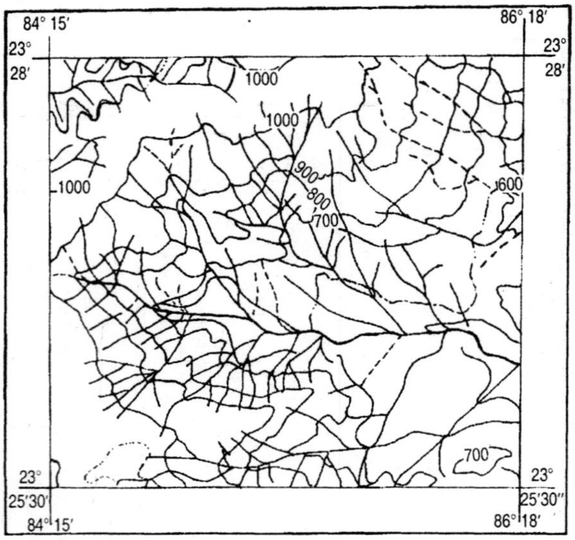

Fig. 3.47 Dendritic drainage pattern (reduced)

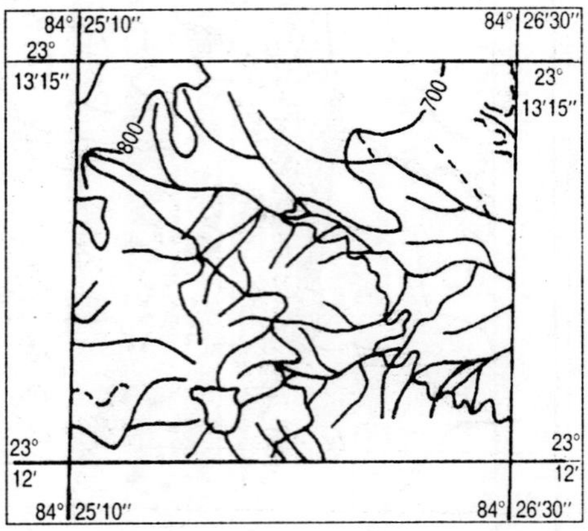

Fig. 3.48 Sub-dendritic (reduced)

Drainage Pattern

The networks of streams in a drainage basin often propagate themselves into certain forms which resemble certain object or follow some geometric trends. Such resemblances of a drainage network on a planimetric map is known as drainage patterns. Drainage patterns are often controlled by the underlying structure to a great extent. Where it is not controlled by structure, a state of uniformity in lithology and structure is expected. The following drainage patterns are generally recognised.

Dendritic Drainage Pattern : In absence of any structural control in terms of lithology and layout of rock beds a drainage basin holds equal probability of stream initiation everywhere in the basin. Such a uniformity may give rise to a dendritic pattern in which the tributary streams branching in a wide variety of angles at their junctions with the main streams develop a resemblance with a 'dendron' or a tree (fig. 3.47).

When the network on one side of the main stream develops into the propagation of a dendritic pattern, whereas, on the other side due to some lithological control the network is not developed properly, it is sub-dendritic (fig. 3.48).

Trellis Drainage Pattern : A trellis network is usually controlled by a folded structure, either simple folds or homoclinal ones. The master stream follows the strike or dip direction, whereas, the dip and anti-dip streams following dip slope and scarp slope may meet the master stream at right angles. A trellis pattern elongates itself in one or two directions (fig. 3.49).

Rectangular Drainage Pattern : When the stream, either the main stream or its tributaries, or both follow joint patterns of the underlying structure, they delvelop sharp rectangular bends in their courses. Following the joints some confluences may form right angled junctions also. In such networks streams which do not follow the lines of structural control may meet their master streams at acute angles (fig. 3.50).

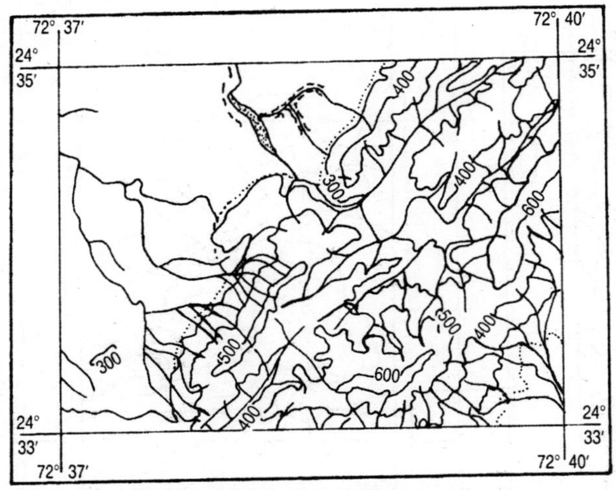

Fig. 3.49 **Trellis (reduced)**

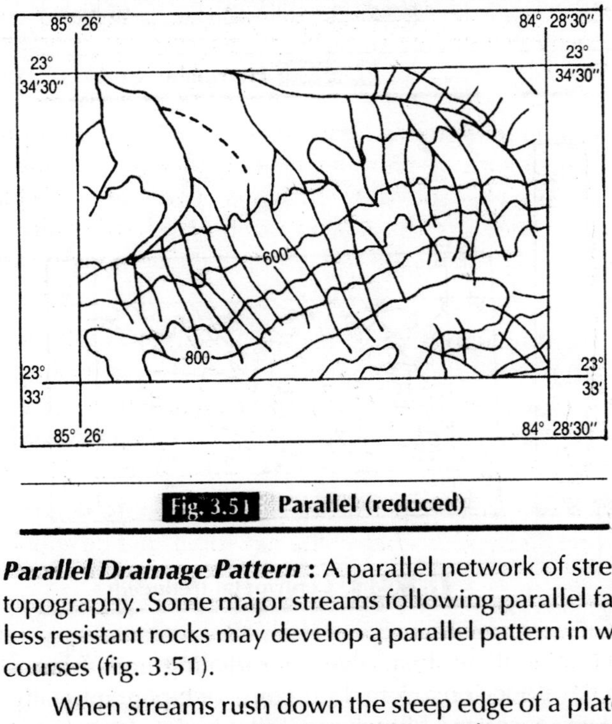

Fig. 3.51 **Parallel (reduced)**

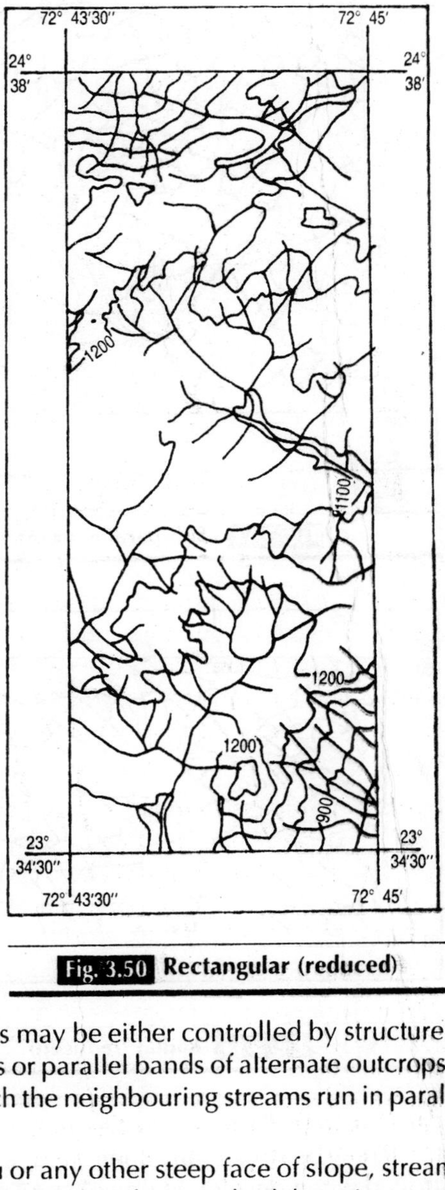

Fig. 3.50 **Rectangular (reduced)**

Parallel Drainage Pattern **:** A parallel network of streams may be either controlled by structure or topography. Some major streams following parallel faults or parallel bands of alternate outcrops of less resistant rocks may develop a parallel pattern in which the neighbouring streams run in parallel courses (fig. 3.51).

When streams rush down the steep edge of a plateau or any other steep face of slope, streams, mostly belonging to the first order, without getting any scope of network elaboration run in parallel courses. Slight decrease in slope may give rise to sub-parallel courses also (fig. 3.52).

Herringbone Drainage Pattern **:** Such a pattern also develops on steep mountainous or plateau slopes. Usually the tributary streams are of first order category and due to steepness of slope they meet the master stream almost at right angle and in straight courses being the shortest route to the main stream. However, the tributary streams, on opposite banks show more trans links than cis links, because the network develops on a slope of small spatial dimension and neighbouring streams require a reasonable catchment area for their initiation (fig. 3.53).

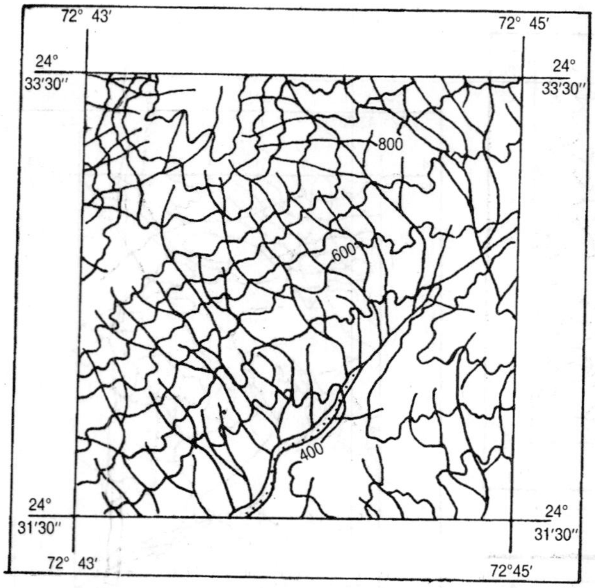

Fig. 3.52 **Sub-parallel (reduced)**

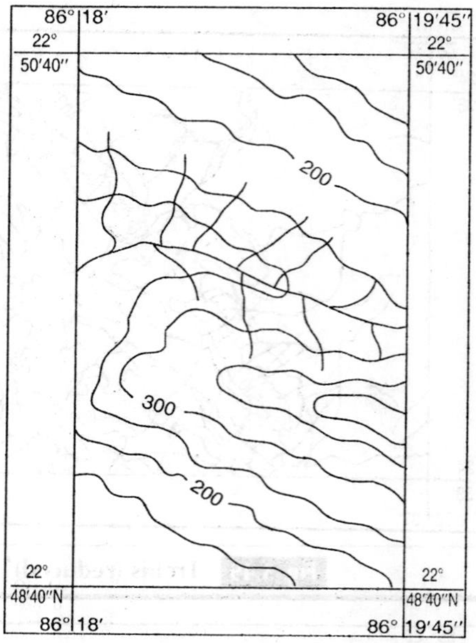

Fig. 3.53 **Herringbone**

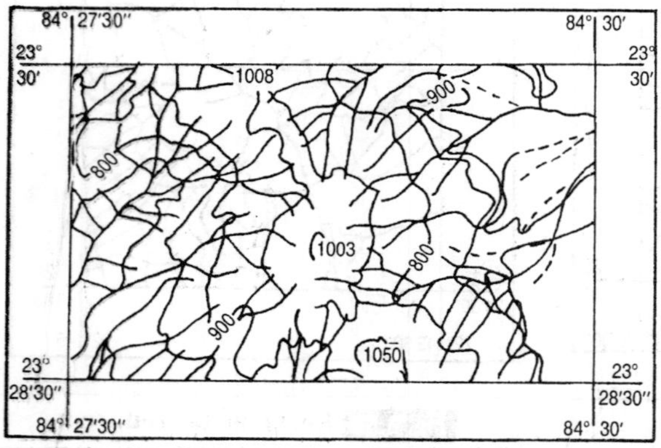

Fig. 3.54 **Radial (reduced)**

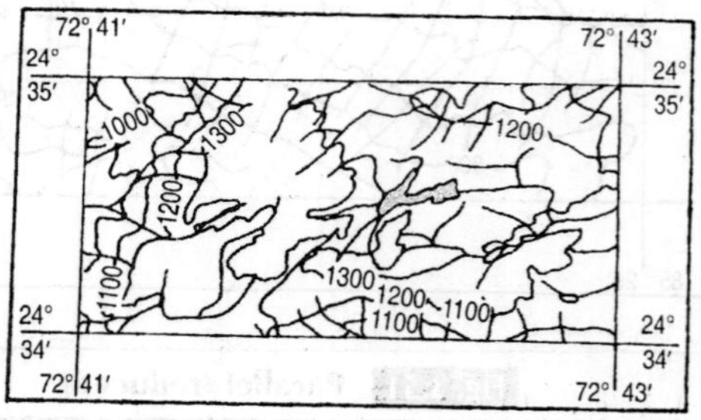

Fig. 3.55 **Centripetal (reduced)**

Radial Drainage Pattern : In this pattern streams initiate themselves as radiating lines from a centre. It may be structurally controlled, when developed on a domal structure, or topographically controlled when developed on volcanic cone or an isolated hillock or a hill which is higher and centrally located on a rugged terrain of lower altitude (fig. 3.54).

Centripetal Drainage Pattern : A centripetal drainage network develops in the surroundings of a centrally located depression preferably a lake or a playa, The formation of the lake may occur due to the presence of a tectonic depression or a structural basin (fig. 3.55).

Annular Drainage Pattern : This drainage pattern shows a ring–like propagation of the major streams which surround a centrally located hill, preferably a dome. The central part of the network

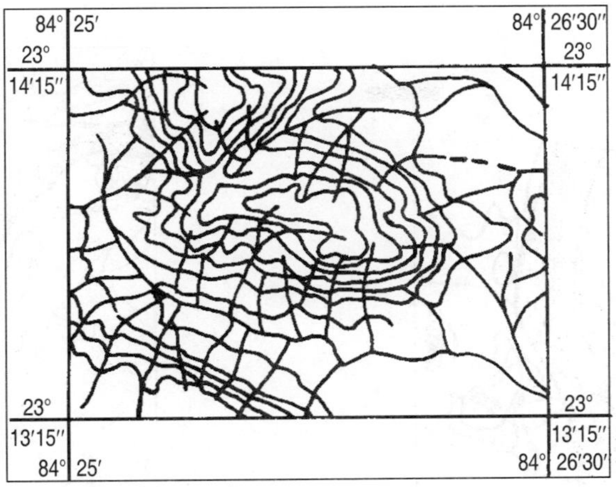

Fig. 3.56 **Annular**

may exhibit a radial pattern in which minor mountain torrents rush down the slope of the hill in all directions in order to meet their master streams at lower slopes, usually at the foot of the hill, following the less resistant outer layer of rock beds in a circular fashion, at the periphery of a domal structure (fig. 3.56)

Deranged Drainage Pattern : This pattern develops on a landform where the previous network of streams of a drainage basin has been effaced and a total disorder has occurred due to invasion by a continental glacier. In such cases streams do not follow any particular trend and they drain into lakes, swamps etc. here and there.

Reticulate Drainage Pattern : A reticulate pattern also does not follow any order and it often develops when on a homogeneous flood-plain the distributary streams initiate themselves at certain impetus in a very irregular net-like fashion following a flood or due to the weak resistance of the bank material (Fig. 3.35a).

Distributary Drainage Pattern : In the deltaic landform a river often bifurcates in its down stream course and thus a network of distributary links or creeks develop, in which fork joiner and outlet joiners are observed.

Channel Pattern **:** A channel pattern is different from a drainage pattern as it refers to the particular pattern developed by the geometry of flow direction within an individual major channel. However, it also indicates the resemblance of the geometry of channel flow with certain object or a geometric shape. The particular types of channel pattern are often defined in a quantitative way as mentioned in the discussion on sinuosity index in the later part of this chapter (p 140). Keller (1972) has shown that the number and length of pools and riffles will increase in the course of journey of a river from a straight course to a meandering one. A *sinuous pattern* has asymmetrical bends, whereas, the bends are symmetrical in a *meandering* channel. If the bank materials are of very low degree of resistance and the channel flows on a homogenous flood plain, it may develop tortuosity (fig. 3.57–3.60 ; see colour plate).

A *braided pattern* resembling a braid (fig 3.63 ; see colour plate) with certain amount of widening of the channel, to accommodate the extra load of silt and water, develops when number

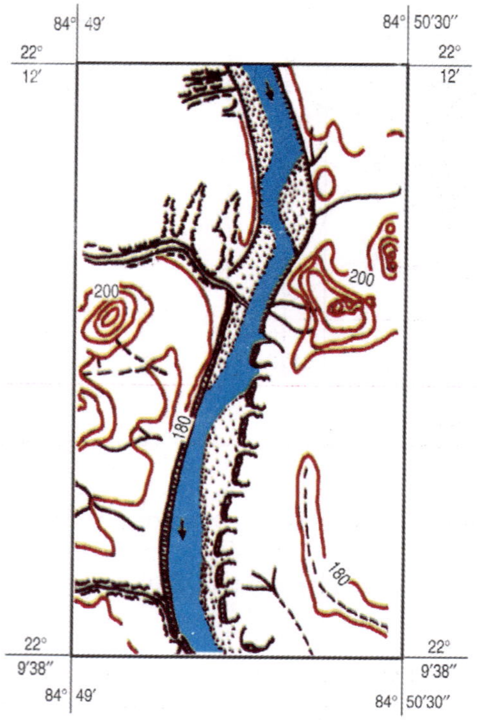

Fig. 3.57 Straight course of Brahmani*

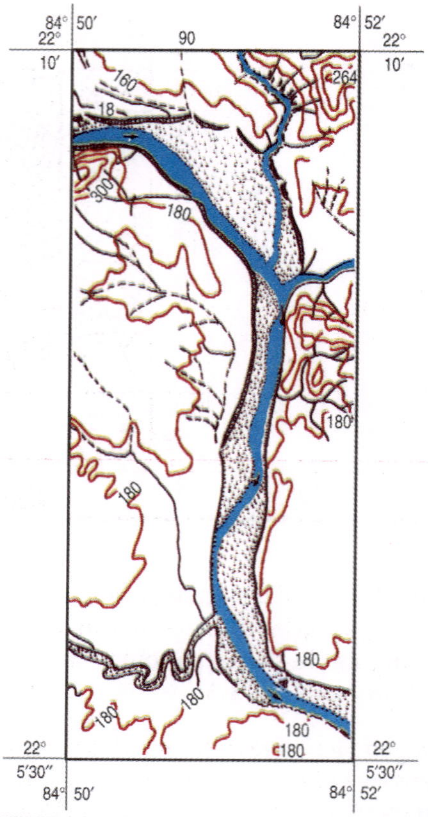

Fig. 3.58 Sinuous course of Brahmani*

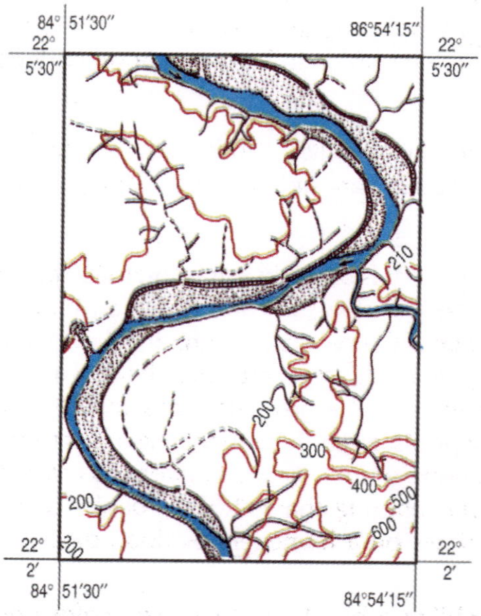

Fig. 3.59 Meandering course of Brahmani*

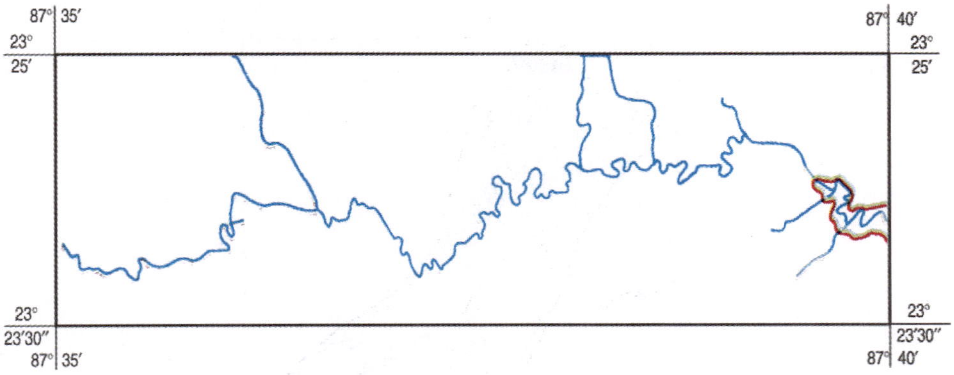

Fig. 3.60 Tortuous course of Khari nadi

of bifurcations of the flow occurs. Such flows are usually separated by islands, made of channel deposition, which are usually submerged during the annual flood.

An *anastomosing pattern*, as the term is derived from the physiological discipline, develops when the flow-separating islands are stable and vegetated (fig. 3.62 ; see colour plate). A channel is well sedimented for a long time at this stage. However, the width, depth and velocity of the channel differ significantly in such channel patterns, as in a straight stream there is minimum width and maximum depth, whereas, it is maximum wide and minimum deep in a braided channel.

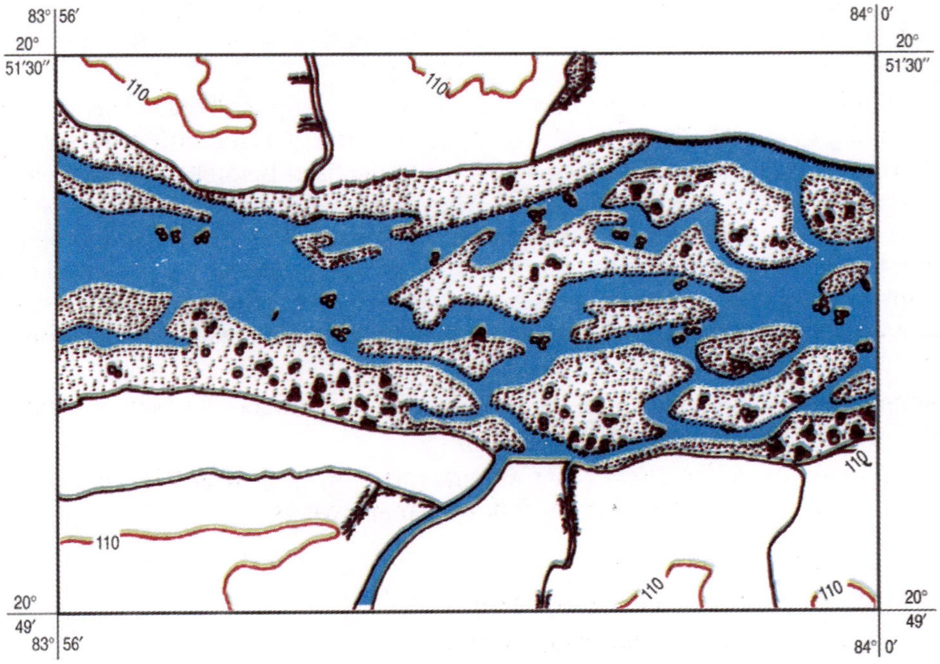

Fig. 3.61 Braided course of Mahanadi river

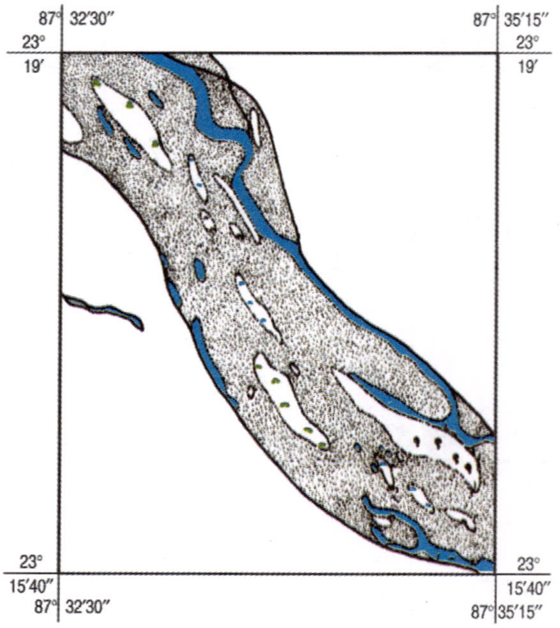

Fig. 3.62 Anastomosing course of Damodar*

Morphometric measurement

Morphometry is the measurement of geometry of a drainage basin or of a part of it. Significant numerical values for the linear, areal and relief properties of the area concerned can be obtained from such measurements.

Efforts have been taken by the geomorphologists since the first half of the twentieth century to find out techniques which will specifically evaluate the status of a landform in the entire gamut of an evolution process. Qualitative assessments were practised beforehand, but they could not reveal the exactness of the landform character. Thus a trend of quantification has been in progress in order to draw very indifferent and imperative inferences. The science of morphometry has evolved in this regard comprising the aspects of identifying landform status as well as drainage network relationship. The quantitative assessment as well as morphometric methods are applied and measured from the topographical maps, which provide us with detailed information about the landform.

A comprehensive classification of the morphometric techniques for landform evaluation as suggested by Dury (1952) involves 5 major groups.

1) Graphical, 2) Arithmatical, 3) Cartographical, 4) Statistical, 5) Drainage network relationship. These five groups include the following major works.

1. Graphical methods
   a) Serial Profiles (Monkhouse, 1948)
   b) Superimposed Profiles (Truman, 1938)
   c) Projected Profiles (Barrel, 1920)
   d) Composite Profile (Barrel, 1920)

e) River & Valley Profiles
   (i) Composite longitudinal slope profile (Broscoe, 1959)
   (ii) Valley cross Profile
   (iii) Crest line Profile (Hammond, 1958)
   (iv) Staggered Spur Profile (Brown, 1952)

2. Arithmetic methods

a) Altimetric or height frequency curve (Baulig, 1928)

b) Area-height diagram
   (i) Hypsometric curve (Hannon-Lowe, 1935)
   (ii) Percentage hypsometric curve (Strahler, 1954)

c) Clinographic curve (Hannon-Lowe, 1935)
   (i) Hypsoclinographic curve (Finsterwalder, 1890)
   (ii) Average slope curve (Wentworth, 1930)
   (iii) Average slope curve (Strahler, 1956)

d) Average channel slope curve (Broscoe, 1959)

3. Cartographic methods

a) Relative relief map (Smith, 1935)

b) Dissection index map (D. Nir, 1957)

c) (i) Average slope map (Wentworth, 1930)
   (ii) Average slope map (Raisz & Henry, 1937)

4. Statistical methods

a) Linear aspects
   (i) Stream ordering (Horton, 1945)
   (ii) Bifurcation ratio (Horton, 1945)
   (iii) Stream length ratio (Horton, 1945)
   (iv) Stream sinuosity index (Brice)

b) Areal aspects
   (i) Basin area ratio (Horton, 1945)
   (ii) Basin circularity ratio (Horton, 1945)
   (iii) Basin elongation ratio (Miller, 1953)
   (iv) Drainage density (Horton, 1945)
   (v) Drainage frequency (Horton, 1945)
   (vi) Drainage texture (Smith, 1950)
   (vii) Basin texture ratio (Horton, 1945)

c) Relief aspects

(i) Basin relief ratio

(ii) Dissection index (De Smet, 1951)

(iii) Roughness index (Hook, 1953)

(iv) Form index (Gravelius, 1914)

(v) Ruggedness number (Horton, 1945)

(vi) Basin slope ratio (Horton, 1945)

(vii) Basin relative relief (Melton, 1957)

5. Drainage network relationship

Horton constructed four laws of drainage composition and Schumm and Morisawa prepared one each on stream number, stream length, basin area, stream slope, constant of channel maintenance and basin relief. Apart from the laws of drainage composition the network relationship can also throw some light in the evaluation of landform status of a drainage basin and methods put forward often prove significant. One of such methods involves using binary connotation for the internal and external links (Shreve). Another uses cis and trans link identification (James and Krumbein, 1969). Equalisation of the number of links indicate the randomness and topology of links in the first method and space constraint in the second.

1. ***Graphical Methods :*** This is a diagrammatic approach.

a) ***Serial Profile :*** A set of simple profiles when arranged serially, is known as serial profiles. When closely spaced, they give visual impression about the characteristics of the landform. Raised beaches, terraces, spurs etc. can be identified on such profiles.

b) ***Superimposed Profile :*** Plotting of a set of serial profiles covering an area on a single frame is known as superimposed profiles. Grouping of lines help in identifying plateau tops, high lavel erosion remnants, the major break of slope (where profiles coincide and intersect), amount of lowering etc.

c) ***Projected Profile :*** A sketch of profiles with a complete shape of the nearest one and peeping of the other profiles behind the former one is known as projected profile. This gives a panoromic view.

d) ***Composite Profile :*** Drawing of the upper most line from the diagram of superimposed and projected profiles produces a composite profile. It is a line of greatest height across the strip. It illustrates the ruggedness of the skyline.

e) ***River and Valley Profiles :*** Channels being the main line of erosional activity and the valley being the product of channel erosion or erosion by any other agency are well indicated in their profiles.

(i) ***Composite Longitudinal Slope Profile :*** Longitudinal profile constructed on the the basis of stream order shows the average slope of the streams in different orders.

(ii) ***Valley Cross Profile :*** Simple profiles across river valley being arranged serially, Illustrates the width of the river valley and configuration of the valley bottom. In the rejuvenated part the steps of the profile indicate terraces.

(iii) Crest Line Profile : Heights plotted against distance along the crest on the axis of interfluves, show breaks of slopes on valley spurs.

(iv) Staggered Spur Profile : Serial profiles along two spurs with one intervening valley shows breaks of slope on valley spurs which might not be apparent on valley side.

2. Arithmetic Methods :

a) Altimetric or height frequency curve or histogram : The spot heights shown in the map are classed into groups and frequency as well as frequency percentage are determined for each group. Then a histogram is constructed. The highest frequency group will indicate the most important erosional surface. Relative relief can also be used in the same method provided grid squares are drawn for a suitable area unit.

b) Area Height Diagram : Area calculated in terms of percentage of total area are plotted against height on a suitable scale. Columns proportional to the area are drawn against relevant vertical height giving a histogram. It gives the visual impression of area-height relationship.

(i) Hypsometric Curve : In this diagram areas enclosed by each contour are plotted against height as proportion to total area and proportion to total height i.e. a/A and h/H, which is derived by

$$\frac{\text{Total area} - \text{area below any particular height or contour}}{\text{Total area}} \quad \text{and}$$

$$\frac{\text{Total relief} - \text{Difference between the lowest point and any height or any particular contour}}{\text{Total height}}$$

It gives a hypsometric integral which is defined as the proportion lying below the curve to the total square graph. When it lies within 0.6-1, it indicates youthful stage of dissection, when the integral lies between 0.35 & 0.60 it indicates maturely dissected landform and less than 0.35 indicates equilibrium or old stage of dissection (fig. 116a & b).

Calculation for Hypsometric Curve

$$\frac{a}{A} = \left[\frac{\text{Total area} - \text{Area below a respective contour(a)}}{\text{Total Area (A)}}\right]$$

(i) $\frac{30.18 - 0}{30.18}$ .. (Respective 285m) = 1 (ii) $\frac{30.18 - 0.938}{30.18}$ ≡ (Respective contour 300) = 0.97

(iii) $\frac{30.18 - (0.938 + 8.54)}{30.18}$ (Respective contour 350) = 0.686

(iv) $\frac{30.18 - (0.938 + 8.54 + 12.875)}{30.18}$ (Respective contour 400) = 0.26

(v) $\frac{30.18 - (0.938 + 8.54 + 12.875 + 7.83)}{30.18}$ (Respective contour 450) = 0

$$\frac{h}{H} = \left[\frac{\text{Total relief} - (\text{Value of any contour} - \text{Lowest point of the basin}}{\text{Total Relief}}\right]$$

(i) $\frac{165 - (285 - 285)}{165} = 1$ (ii) $\frac{165 - (300 - 285)}{165} = 0.91$

(iii) $\frac{165 - (350 - 285)}{165} = 0.61$ (iv) $\frac{165 - (400 - 285)}{165} = 0.30$

(v) $\frac{165 - (450 - 285)}{165} = 0$

Interpretation of Hypsometric curve :

Here, Hypsometric integral is 69.50% or 0.69. It indicates a youthful stream, as 69.50% of basin landmass is yet to be eroded or levelled.

TABLE 3.7

DATA FOR HYPSOMETRIC CURVE

	$\frac{a}{A}$		$\frac{h}{H}$
(i)	1	(v)	0
(ii)	0.97	(iv)	0.30
(iii)	0.686	(iii)	0.61
(iv)	0.26	(ii)	0.91
(v)	0	(i)	1

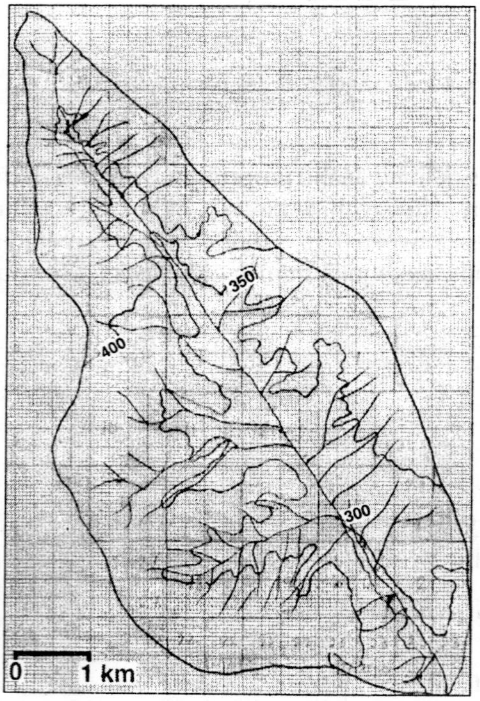

Scale : 1cm = 1 km
Total Area : 30.175 sq. km/30.18 sq . km

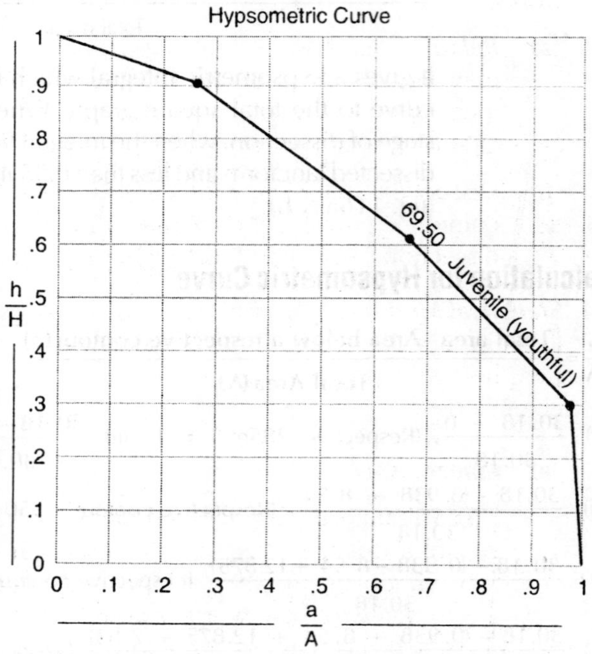

Fig. 3.63 a & b **Measurement of basin area, Hypsometric curve and Integral**

(ii) ***Percentage Hypsometric Curve :*** This is a cumulative frequency curve which involves plotting of two ratios of relative height and relative area with respect to total height and total area of a drainage basin in percentage.

c) ***Clinographic Curve :*** In this method the areas enclosed between adjacent contours are treated as areas for circles and radii are calculated. Difference in radii for adjacent contours is treated as inter-contour distance which being plotted against the contour interval gives the average slope for the area between the two contours.

d) ***Average Slope Curve :*** In this method the map is meshed into a pair of rectangular grid lines at right angle to each other. The number of contour crossing per mile is computed for each segment of area and it is multiplied by contour interval and divided by a constant 3361 for 1inch to a mile maps to give the average slope for each segment of the area. Another set of grids at 45° angle to the perpendicular grid lines may improve the quality of data.

For metric scale maps the constant is ($0.6366 \times 1000 = 636.6$). After dividing by the constant the result will give $\tan^{-1}$ from which the slope in degree can be measured.

e) ***Average Channel Slope Curve :*** For drawing of this curve the streams are designated in orders following Strahler's system. Slope segments are plotted as average vertical drop against average horizontal distance. The hypotenuse thus derived gives average stream slope curve of the basin. This curve can be used further for verification of Horton's law of mean stream slope.

3. ***Cartographic Methods :*** These methods portray the characteristics of individual landform elements and they may give meaningful regional synthesis in the form of cartographical works.

a) ***Relative Relief Map :*** In this method the area is gridded by perpendicular grid lines, then the difference of altitude within each grid is calculated. After computing such local relief per unit area isopleths may be drawn to show regional distribution of relief characteristics.

b) ***Dissection Index Map :*** This is the ratio between relative relief and maximum altitude computed for each grid and then isopleths are drawn. This reveals variable amount of dissection in gently rolling uplands and in the mountainous areas particularly.

4. ***Statistical Methods :*** The statistical indices for topographic evaluation are essential because they produce the standardised measures to find out the essential differences and similarities. Morphometric analysis in this regard is the powerful tool in investigating landform characteristics.

a) ***Linear Aspects :***

(i) ***Stream ordering :*** Horton formulated a system of ordering to arrange the streams of a drainage basin in a hierarchical order. According to this scheme a stream without any tributary is a first order stream. Two first orders join to form a second order, two second orders joins to form a third order and so on. He then extended the highest value of order towards the head. (fig. 3.64 Horton's, Strahler's, Shreve's, Scheidegger's method) Thus a renumbering of streams in terms of order as well as loss of lower order streams take place.

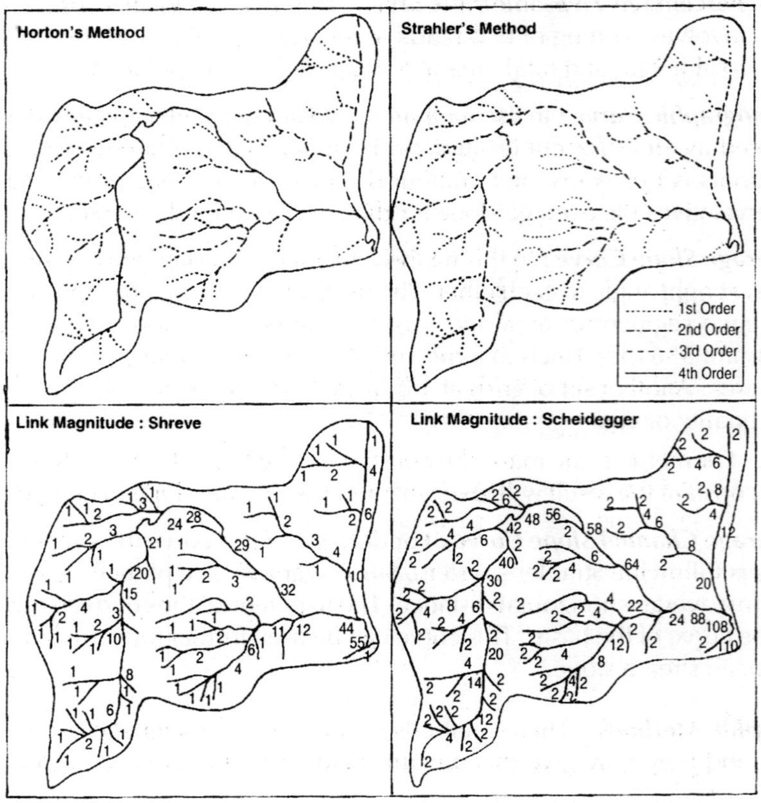

Fig. 3.64 Horton's, Strahler's, Shreve's, Scheidegger's method of stream ordering

Strahler modified the scheme by increasing the number of order segmentwise toward the downstream direction. It can avoid Horton's renumbering and loss of tributaries, but at the same time the higher order segments may decrease in length than the lower ones. Shreve observed that any addition of a new stream to the main channel will enhance its energy and therefore amalgamation of any number of streams will increase the order proportionate to the number of streams. He designated any stream of the basin as 1. Scheidegger formulated almost a similar method of stream ordering and preferred a proportionate rise in stream order with addition of new tributaries, but he contended that any stream of the basin on a topographical sheet should be designated as 2 as they crossed the initial rill and gully stage. Thus the value obtained in Scheidegger's method will double the value obtained in Shreve's method.

(ii) Bifurcation Ratio : It is defined as the ratio of the number of stream segments of any order to the number stream segments of the next higher order. It gives the idea about the rate of bifurcation towards the water divide. R_b is 2 when streams of a given order combine only with another stream of same order. It is 4 when half of the streams combine with the same order and half with the others. In natural and otherwise uncontrolled drainage basins it varies from 2 – 5. If it is well above 5, precise influence of lithology or climate is indicated.

(iii) ***Stream Length Ratio :*** The mean length of the stream of a given order to the mean length of the stream of the next lower order gives this ratio. It is approximately constant for the same drainage basin under uniform lithology and climate.

(iv) ***Stream Sinuosity Index :*** It is the ratio of channel length to the length of the meander belt axis. Particular values of this ratio identify channel pattern. Grading of tortuous, irregular, regular, transitional and straight channel pattern are indicated when the sinuosity indices are 2.1, 1.7, 1.5, 1.2 & 1 respectively. Brice has given 3 specific values such as >1.5, 1.5—1.05 & <1.05 as indication of meandering, sinuous and straight channel (fig. 3.51, 3.52, 3.53) pattern respectively.

b) Areal Aspects :

(i) ***Basin Area Ratio :*** The mean basin area of successive stream orders tend to form a geometric series beginning with the area of 1st order basin and increasing according to a constant area ratio. [Equation : $A_R = \frac{\bar{A}_u}{\bar{A}_{u+1}}$]

(ii) ***Basin Circularity Ratio :*** It is the ratio between the basin area and the area of a circle having the same perimeter. It expresses the basin shape for a basin of circular measurement. If the basin is a circle, it is unity. [Equation : $C = \frac{4\pi A}{P^2}$]

(iii) ***Elongation Ratio :*** It is the ratio between the diameter of a circle with same area as basin and length of the basin. Fault controlled elongated basins have high value. [Equation : $L = \frac{2\sqrt{\frac{A}{\pi}}}{L}$]

(iv) ***Drainage Density :*** It is defined as the length of stream per unit area of a drainage basin. It is independent of order and varies inversely with the size of the basin. It is also fairly correlated with average slope of the basin. The rock character and the influence of vegetation cover may be revealed from the study of drainage density. Coarse grained hard rocks may give a drainage density of <5, whereas shales forming badlands may give values ranging from 50—1300. [Equation : $D_d = \frac{\Sigma l_c}{A_d}$]

(v) ***Stream Frequency :*** It is defined as number of streams per unit area of a drainage basin. It is useful for the study of texture of drainage. It is independent of the drainage density for the same basin. [Equation : $D_s = \frac{N_s}{A_d}$]

(vi) ***Drainage Texture :*** It is defined as the product of drainage density and drainage frequency. The scale of drainage texture is as follows :

4.0 & below → coarse,

4.0 – 10.0 → intermediate,

10.0 – 15.0 → fine, [Equation : $D_d \times D_s$]

> 15.0 → ultra fine, *i.e.*, badlands

(vii) ***Basin Texture Ratio :*** It is the ratio of the maximum number of crenulation in the basin contour to the length of the perimeter of drainage basin. It is directly proportional to the drainage density of the basin.

c) ***Relief Aspects :***

(i) ***Basin Relief Ratio :*** It is defined as the ratio of maximum basin relief to the axial length of the basin. This index is important due to its direct relation with flood magnitude.

(ii) ***Roughness Index :*** It is defined as

$$\frac{N \times \frac{M}{4}}{4} \times 10$$

N = Total no. intersection of contour lines with two sets of perpendicular grids, set at 45° to each other. 4 & 10 are constant.

M = Distance in miles between grid lines.

It is an index to the surface configuration and it is used also to find out a correlation with land use.

(iii) ***Form Index :*** It is the ratio of average width of basin to axial length of the basin. The average width of the basin is equal to the area of basin divided by its axial length. [Equation : $R_{BS} = \frac{S_u}{S_{u-1}}$]

A basin with less form index is less likely to have an intense rainfall over the entire area. Form index gives some indication to the tendency of flooding.

(iv) ***Ruggedness Number :*** It is defined as the product of relative relief and drainage density. It is a combined expression of relief, texture and slope steepness, although a precise index is yet to be worked out. [Equation : $N_R = \frac{H \times D_d}{1000 \text{ or } 5280 \text{ (for FPS)}}$]

(v) ***Basin Slope Ratio :*** The average channel slope of a particular order to the average channel slope of the next lower order gives this ratio. It is always less than 1 and values from 0.3 – 0.6 are typical. [Equation : $H_{BH} = \frac{H}{P}$]

(vi) ***Basin Relative Relief :*** The relative relief of the basin is divided by the perimeter of the basin in order to distinguish between two basins having same local relief.

Transect Chart

The correlation between the physical and cultural features can be comprehensively accomplished through a transect chart which is a vertical correlation. For this purpose five strips of graphical representation can be made, in which relief, drainage, vegetation and arable land, communication and finally, settlement are shown along a strip of land. As a transect chart usually represents a vertical correlation above a topographic profile, it is based on a line in the topographic sheet along which the relief is shown. But a settlement or a road does not stay just on the line and they may be located at fractions of centimetre apart, just by the side of the line. In that case also the settlement should be included within the transect chart. For this purpose it is better if at least one centimetre above and below the line the strip for cultural features is chosen, though the relief, drainage as well as vegetation can be shown on the single line. It is better if for the entire set a two centimetre strip can be taken. In that case two or three relief profiles may be prepared either as superimposed profile on separate profiles. The villages which are located across the line should be enclosed by a pencil-line and the boundary is to be marked for the spread of the settlement. Within the selected strip the features of drainage, communication and settlement can be shown as they are on the map. This will be helpful for spatial correlation.

The correlations are deterministic and relief is considered as the main determinant factor which is supposed to influence other physical and cultural features over itself through the influence of altitude and slope. However, the usual correlations found in a transect chart are as follows:

1. if the relative relief and slope are high and steep, the number of non-perennial minor streams will be high ;
2. on flat terrain major rivers are located;
3. usually high relief and steep slope are covered with forest, whereas, gentle slope and low relief show scattered vegetation as well as arable lands;
4. flat topography is preferable for the construction of metalled road or major unmetalled roads, whereas, high relief and rugged areas show foot tracks, pack tracks etc.,
5. high relief areas usually possess dispersion of settlements, whereas, on flat valley areas there are concentrations;
6. major settlements usually develop in contact with major roads.

Some other correlations can also be established through the study of particular transect charts.

Overlay of physical and cultural features

Apart from transect chart some other visual correlations can be obtained through the overlay of maps showing physical and cultural features. For this purpose the following overlays may be proved effective, though there is no absolute nature in such deterministic correlation, as almost everywhere cultural interactions may distort the original relationship.

1. overlay of the map of drainage density on relative relief or average slope map;
2. overlay of percentage vegetation cover map on average slope or relative relief map.

In these cases usually positive correlations are observed and that can be graphically shown by bivariate analysis of scatter diagrams. For the following cases usually negative correlations or even neutral correlations are observed.

1. overlay of road density values on slope or relative relief map;
2. overlay of settlement density maps on average slope or relative relief map.

Cultural features

Various types of cultural features are shown on topographical maps and many of them are very significant for the purpose of interpretation. That is why whenever any one of such features is shown, the relevance of correlation with some other physical or cultural features should be maintained. The following list of selected cultural features may prove significant in the interpretation of topographical maps.

1. alignment of a major road along the length of a valley;
2. zigzag roads on rugged topography, though in some cases it may be spiral in alignment while climbing up a hill;
3. linear settlement parallel to a ridge or sand dune;
4. dispersed settlement on rugged topography;
5. linear settlement by the side of a river;
6. major agglomeration on valley areas;
7. nucleated settlement at junction of village roads;
8. nucleated settlement near water-point (i.e. a spring) in dry areas;
9. linear settlement along strips of narrow valleys and forest clearance;

10. star-shaped settlement at the junction of major roads or at nodal points;
11. compact nucleation at or near railway station;
12. agglomeration of settlement in mining areas;
13. nucleated settlement at confluence of rivers;
14. planned colonisation at or near mining areas, industrial sites etc.;
15. nucleated settlement at centres of pilgrimage;
16. temporary homesteads on flood-prone areas ;
17. deserted or ghost settlement at abandoned mining areas or industrial sites;

This way many other cultural features may be traced in terms of the guiding influences of the factors which favoured their growth and development, be it physical or cultural.

EXAMPLE INTERPRETATION

This topographical map of Survey of India is referred to as 73 B/16. The area covered belongs to Singbhum district of Bihar and partly to Sundargarh district of Orissa. The rectangular area of the map extends from 22°0′ north to 22°15′ north and from 84°45′ east to 85°0′ east. This map was published in 1972, though the area was surveyed in 1967 – 68. The scale of the map is 1:50,000, whereas, the contour interval is fixed at 20 metre.

Relief

The highest altitude of the area shown in the map is 681 metre located at 23°40′ north 84°46′30″ east at a hill top in Kusumdihi R.F. The lowest altitude, i.e., 168 metre is observed on the left bank of the Brahmani river, at the confluence of Suidihi nadi. Therefore the total difference of altitude is 513 metre. As such, this is a map of a plateau area with a major valley in the middle.

Relative relief

The relative relief of the 9 grids from A_1 to C_3 has been incorporated in the following (table 3.5) :

TABLE 3.8

Grid no.	Highest altitude	Lowest altitude	Relative relief in m.
A_1	310	179.7	130.3
A_2	400	202	198
A_3	681	253	428
B_1	353	175.9	177.1
B_2	324	168	156
B_3	525	176.5	348.5
C_1	425	213.6	211.4
C_2	580	288	292
C_3	594	397	197

Although such an evaluation of relative relief on the basis of large 5′ grids may not prove a matter of much significance, a broad idea about planation and maximum incision can be obtained from such a table. It reveals that grid no. A_3 has the maximum value of relative relief and A_1 has the minimum value. The highest part of the plateau is located in grid no. A_3 and valley development below 260 metre contour is found in the area. On the other hand, the area belonging to A_1 is nearly levelled with the confluence of Sankh and Koel located within the grid. Therefore, the table gives , more or less, acceptable values of relative relief as they are in tune with the present condition of planation of the area. C_3 grid, on the contrary, shows less than 200 metre of relative relief as the gridded area has been least levelled and valley development as well as lowering is also negligible.

Altimetric frequency histogram

The spot heights of the entire map area have been incorporated in table no. 3.6 and 6 classes have been chosen to locate the grouped frequency of the spot heights at regular intervals. On the basis of the frequency percentage obtained, a histogram (fig. 3.65) has been constructed. It shows that about 58% of the spot heights occur below 300 metre, whereas, beyond 500 metre the plateau summits occupy only about 8% of the spot heights. Therefore, it may be inferred that the most significant erosional surface of the area occurs below 300 metre. Moreover, the plateau summits are escaped for only a small part. Another significant range of altitude, where the present erosional activities are actively concentrated in is 301-400 metre, which occupies about 22% of the spot heights. Still less significant is the level between 401 and 500 metre 11%.

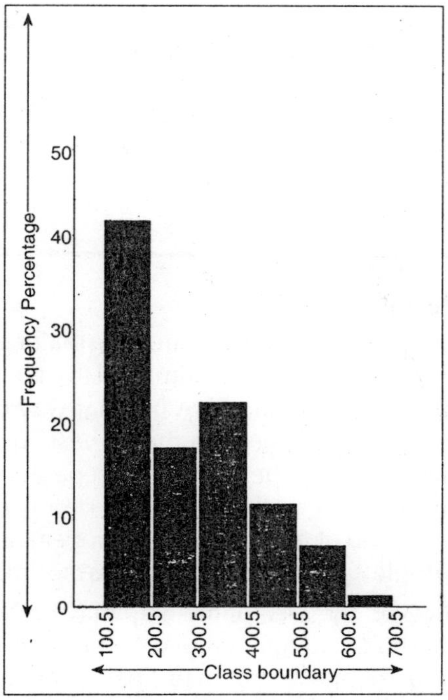

Fig. 3.65 Histogram of spot heights

TABLE 3.9A

Grid No.	Spot Heights
A_1	240, 320, 180, 200, 265, 320, 180, 180
A_2	400, 360, 180, 200, 340, 376, 200, 180
A_3	681, 480, 200, 280, 335, 540,200, 200
B_1	380, 293, 196, 200, 353, 316, 180, 200
B_2	360, 219, 168, 180, 238, 264, 180, 180
B_3	565, 463, 176.5, 200, 318, 500, 180, 180
C_1	425, 316, 220, 200, 380, 348, 200, 213.6
C_2	600, 426, 220, 240, 323, 500, 200, 200,
C_3	594, 480, 200, 280, 580, 481, 180, 200

TABLE 3.98

Class	Class Boundary	Tally marks	Frequency	Frequency Percentage
101 – 200	100.5 – 200.5	~~IIII~~ ~~IIII~~ ~~IIII~~ ~~IIII~~ ~~IIII~~ ~~IIII~~	30	41.7
201 – 300	200.5 – 300.5	~~IIII~~ ~~IIII~~ II	12	16.7
301 – 400	300.5 – 400.5	~~IIII~~ ~~IIII~~ ~~IIII~~ I	16	22.2
401 – 500	400.5 – 500.5	~~IIII~~ III	8	11.1
501 – 600	500.5 – 600.5	~~IIII~~	5	6.9
601 – 700	600.5 – 700.5	I	1	1.4

Physiography

Physiographic study identifies the major geomorphic units of a topographical section and finds out interrelations between them, and thereby analyses the landform characteristics and the role of erosional process on them. (A popular way of identifying broad physiographic units is to draw a topographic profile between the highest and the lowest elevations of the area and to locate the particular break of slope from which separate units may be identified (fig. 3.66). But a probe into the nature of contours and their spacing simply reveals the particular valued contour from which the main valley and plateau or plateau-proper and plateau-fringe may be separated. Thus the highest to lowest profile can be avoided because they may be located at two opposite corners of the map.)

However, the area of the map may be broadly divided into the Brahmani valley (below 200 metre) and plateau area (above 300 metre). It may be noted here that a plateau conventionally starts from 300 metre, but in this particular map the steep edge of a plateau fringe starts right from 200 metre contour and below that the contours are widely spaced on the valley floor. A plateau fringe has been observed between 300 and 200 metre contour. But such strip occurrences are often lost if a broad physical division on the basis of 200 or 300 m. contour is accomplished. The map of physiographic divisions or major geomorphic units is shown in figure 3.67.

Features of the plateau and plateau fringe

The plateau has been characterised by many typical landform features.

Summits of the plateau : As mentioned earlier the plateau summits have escaped the hands of ruin for a small part in the south-western and south-eastern corners of the map-area. A cross section connecting a few of such summits is drawn in figure 3.68.

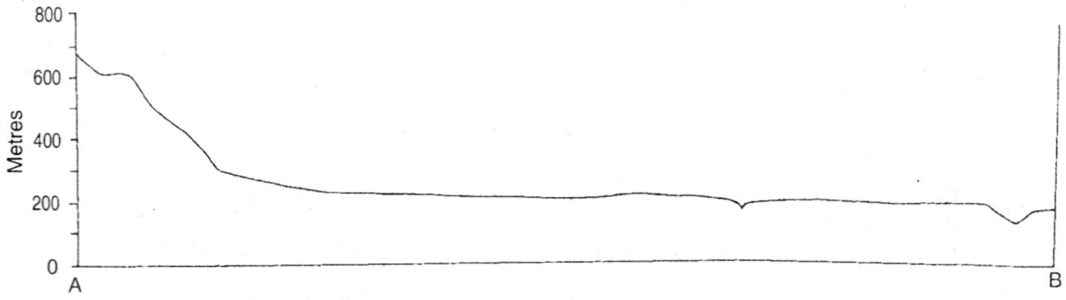

Fig. 3.66 **Topographic profile between the highest and lowest point**

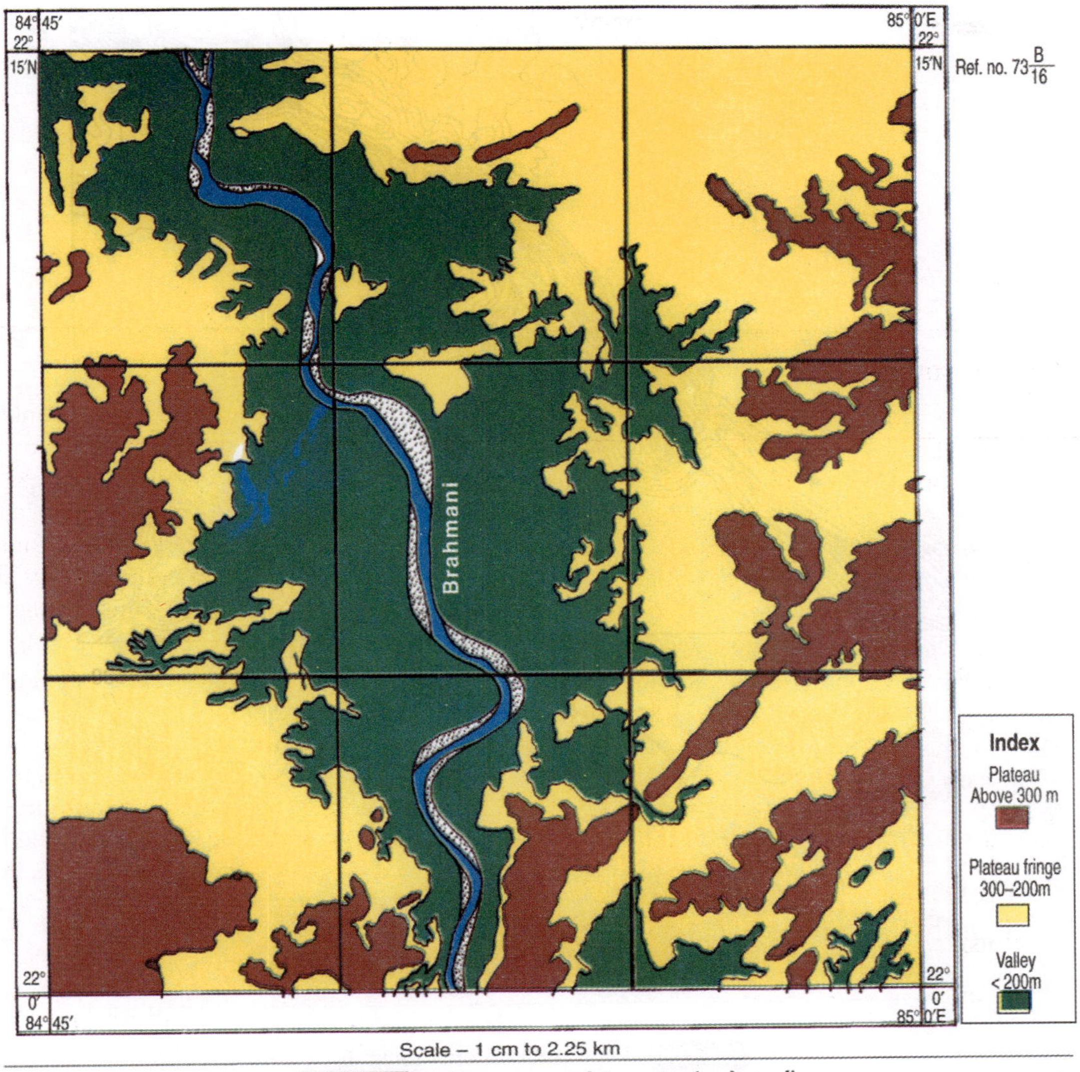

Fig. 3.67 Major geomorphic units (reduced)

Ridge : A major ridge as aligned in south-west to north-east direction through south and north Champajharan R.F. acts as an important micro water-divide of the area. The summits of the ridge top have more than 500 metre elevation. Many of the left bank tributaries and some of the sub-tributary streams of the Brahmani river have their origin in this ridge (fig. 3.68).

Dissection : The plateau has been dissected into a few segments by the Brahmani river and its tributaries such as the Chandri nala and Hathibura nala. The valleys formed between the plateau segments are not very extensive. A cross section of such a dissected area along with a rough sketch depict the status of dissection here (fig. 3.69).

At an advanced stage of dissection isolation of a few lowered plateau segments has occurred. Such isolated masses are scattered here and there in the area. One such is Jhumla pahar on the left bank of the Brahmani. The part of the plateau in the north of the Chandri nala with the location of

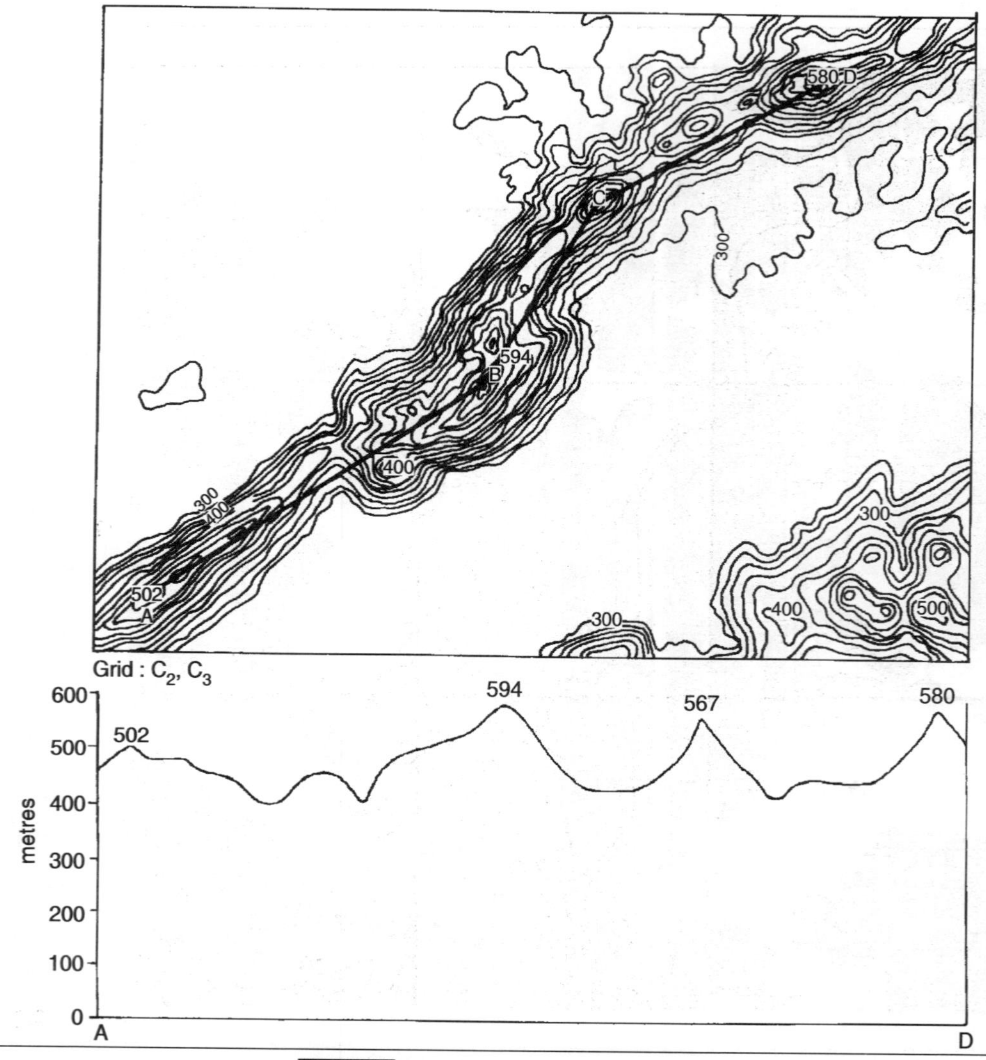

Fig. 3.68 **Ridge and erosional summits**

Chandri pahar within Rutkupiri R. F. is another large isolated mass. This massive part lies below 400 metre, where major erosional activities are being carried out at present.

Residual hill : Jhumla pahar can also be considered as a residual hill (fig. 3.70) amidst the erosional plains of the Brahmani valley. Towards the north another of such residual ridges with an east to west alignment has been found. This ridge is very narrow and at places has escaped for only a minor part. The hilltop at Jhumla pahar is 264 metre in elevation, whereas, in the northern ridge it is 353 metre. However, the ridge is covered with scrubs. A few other small mounds in the form of residual hillocks have been observed elsewhere in the map.

Badlands : Intensive gully erosion has resulted in the formation of badlands (fig. 3.71) within the Suidihi nala drainage basin. This is of course related to the low degree of resistance of the earth materials where gully erosion has taken place.

Fig. 3.69 **Dissection (reduced)**

Fig. 3.70 **Residual hill (reduced)**

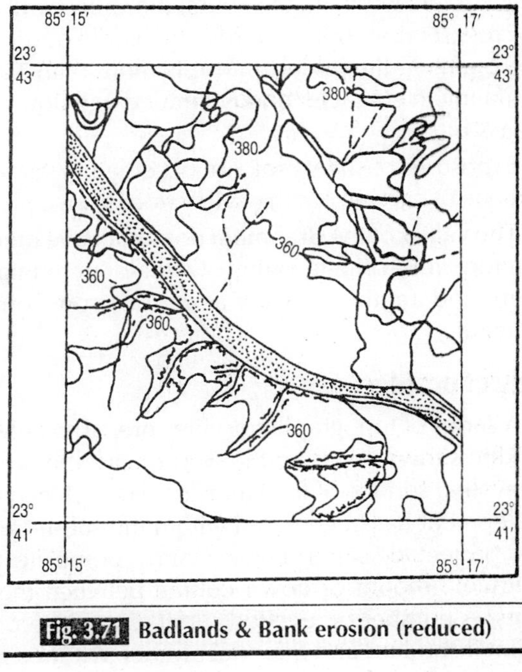

Fig. 3.71 **Badlands & Bank erosion (reduced)**

Cliff : A few small areas of steep slopes have formed cliff-like features with contours adjacent to each other. Such cliffs may be related to collapse of the lower part of the slope or to any other structural cause.

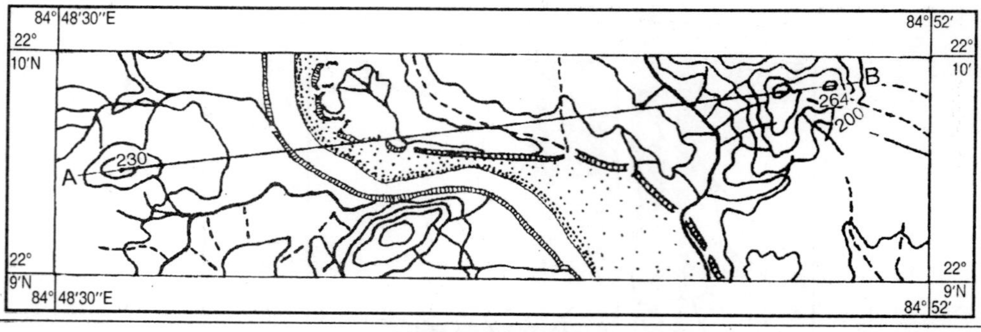

Fig. 3.72(a) Valley

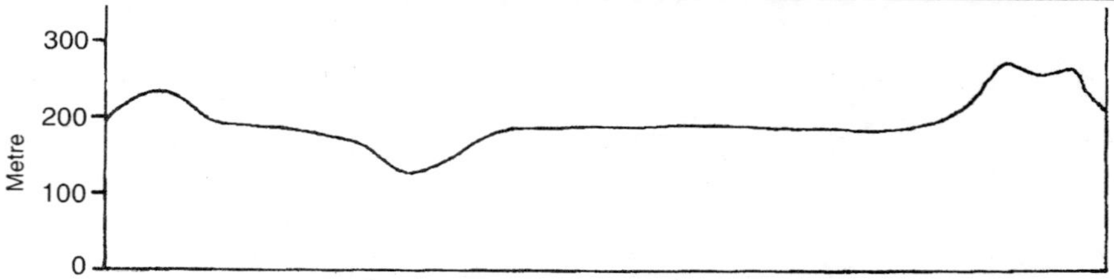

Fig. 3.72(b) Cross profile of the valley

Main valley

The valley of the Brahmani river seems to be forming the main valley of the area. This valley has a variable width. In the South, the valley walls are closer and the river has run through a gorge-like cross section. But, towards the middle portion of the map and further northward, the valley is wide open. At the widest part it is more than 10 kilometre wide. The surface is to some extent undulating in character and is studded with low mounds, ups and down and residual hillocks (fig. 3.72a & b).

Exposures of sheet rock are observed in some sections of the valley. Such exposures bear the evidence of carving out the valley floor from a previous higher rocky surface.

The valley of the Brahmani does not have much corridor within its neighbouring plateau area. Therefore, it is a single valley of a major perennial river without much elaboration except for one eastern and another western strip of narrow corridor carved out by two tributary streams of the Brahmani.

Study of profiles

A series of topographic profiles prepared between 84°56'30"E and 84°59'20" E at an interval of 1 km., shows that from the west to east the profiles become increasingly rugged and gradually the levelled surface of the valley side is replaced by a hilly terrain. However, considerable valley development has been noted within the sub-tributary basins also. The profiles have been used to draw projected, superimposed and composite profiles. The superimposed profiles show the maximum amount of down cutting between the summits of the 6th profile amounting to 480 metres. A number of levelled surfaces at close proximity to each other, reveals the existence of erosional surfaces and their occurrence within a small range of elevation signifies the lack of any great variability of resistance of the terrain in the interaction between the geomorphic processes and the surface materials. Moreover, in the superimposed profiles most of the profiles have shown a common break of slope at 200 metre. The summits of the profiles also have similar altitudes and they occur as a group of hills and ridges in northern and southern parts (fig. 3.73 – 3.74).

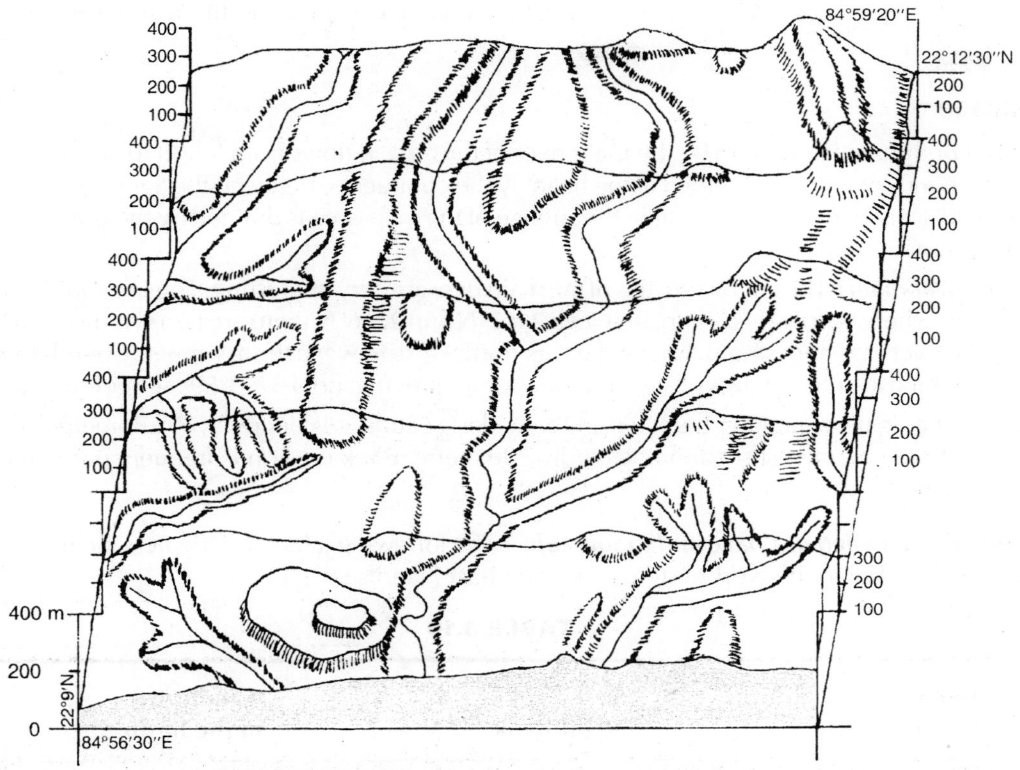

Fig. 3.73 Non-perspective Block diagram by Serial profiles

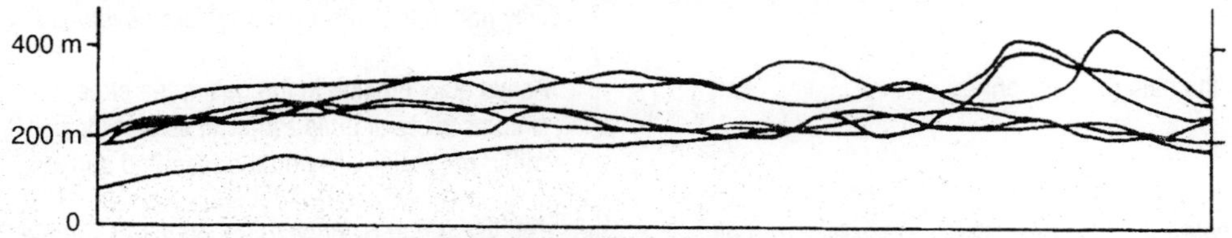

Fig. 3.74 Superimposed profile

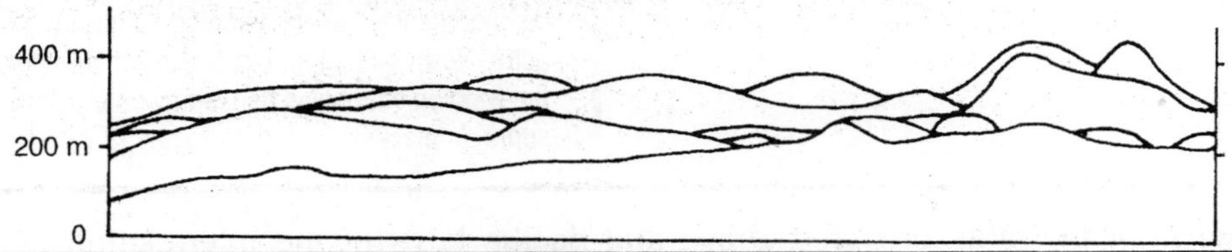

Fig. 3.75 Projected profile

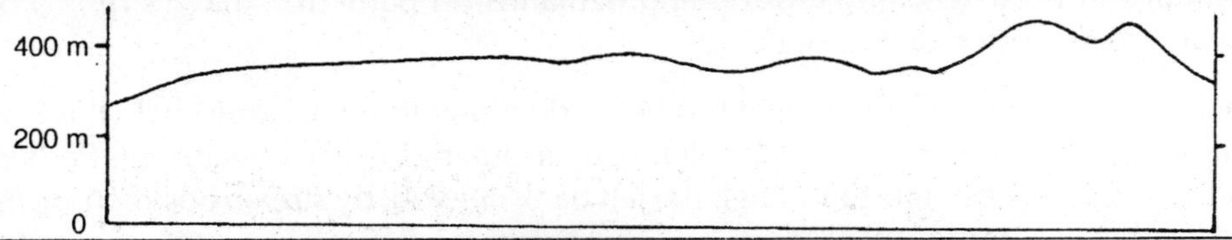

Fig. 3.76 Composite profile

In the composite profile the sky line is not very smooth except for northern and southern flanks (fig no. 3.76).

Drainage

The Brahmani happens to be the main river of the area. It flows from North to South through a winding course which was formed at the head by the confluence between the Sankh and the Koel. Almost 80% or even more than that of the surface of the map-area is drained by the Brahmani river network system.

***The Brahmani*:** The characteristics of the main river are very interesting. Towards north the river is sinuous, whereas, towards South, between 22°2′ N and 22°6′ N there are two symmetrical bends giving the river a meandering character. Further northward between the asymmetric bends there are sections which are more or less straight for a few kilometres (fig. no.3 57–3.59 : see colour plate).

The river is perennial in character. In the widest section it is nearly 0.75 kilometre in width, whereas, in the narrowest section it is hardly 200 metre. Bank erosion is frequent particularly on the left bank (fig. no.3.57).

***Correlation between drainage and topography*:** The following table (3.7) depicts the relationship between the tributary network systems and their basin landforms.

TABLE 3.10

Name of Tributary	Nature	Left bank/ Right Bank	Landforms in the Basin
Chandri nala	Perennial (main stream)	Right	Plateau fringe between 200 and 300 metre contours is being eroded actively towards planation; only right bank sub-tributaries are developed.
Hathibandha nala	Perennial	Left	Active gully erosion in the basin; the stream circumscribes Jhumla Pahar at its foot located within the main valley on the planated surface.
Suidihih nala	Perennnial	Left	The lower part belongs to the planated surface of the main valley, whereas, most of the basin area is characterised by dissected plateau; valley development is constricted along a narrow strip; active down cutting and gully erosion are indicated; the winding channel is flanked by interlocking spurs at places.

Therefore from the table prepared above and on the basis of the interrelation between drainage network and landform characteristics we may assume an intimate correlation between relief and drainage at present. Gully erosion and badlands, in particular, have stressed on the active nature of stream erosion in the area.

***Drainage patterns* :** A *sub-dendritic pattern* has been identified in the Chandri nala basin where only the right bank network is developed and left bank tributaries are nearly absent. Perhaps the left bank tributaries have been effaced through the left bank network by stream abstraction, though some of the 'V's of contours are still present.

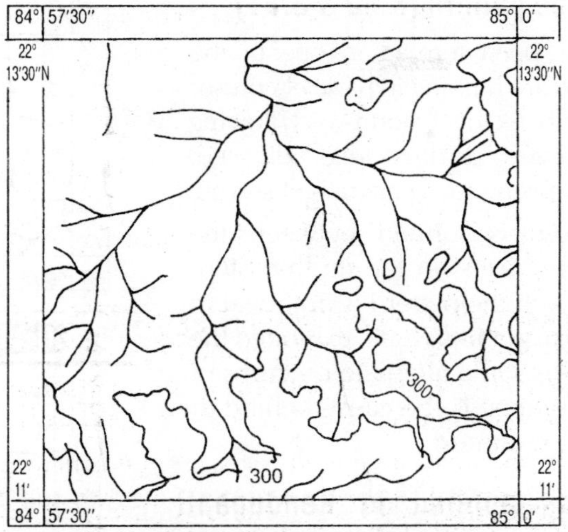

Fig. 3.77 **Dendritic pattern**

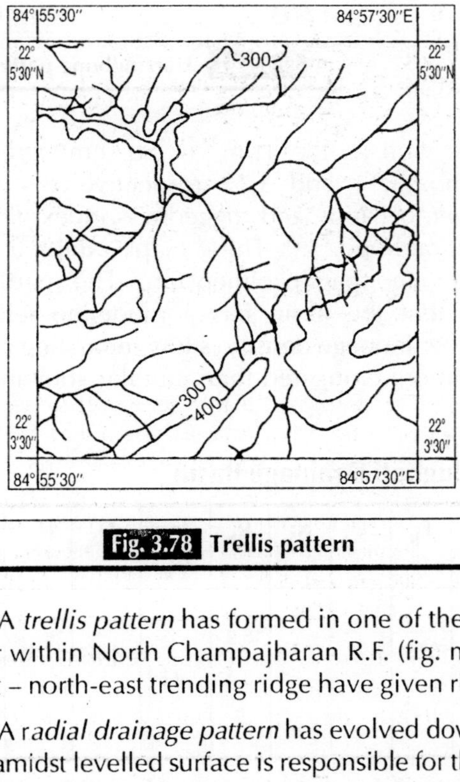

Fig. 3.78 **Trellis pattern**

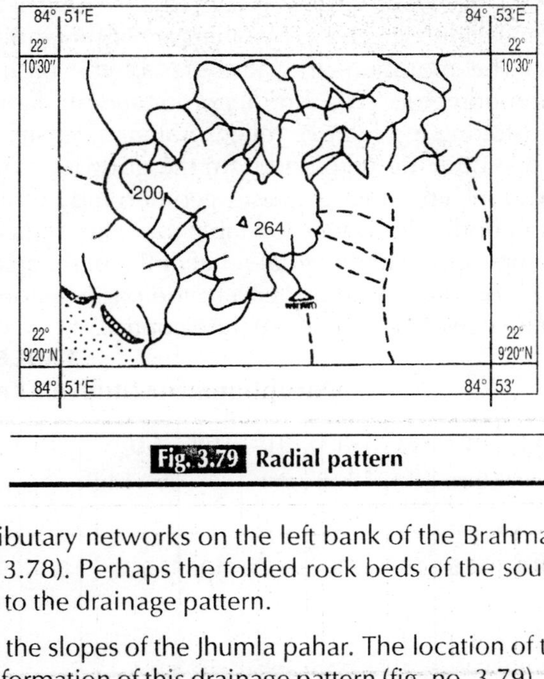

Fig. 3.79 **Radial pattern**

A *trellis pattern* has formed in one of the tributary networks on the left bank of the Brahmani river within North Champajharan R.F. (fig. no. 3.78). Perhaps the folded rock beds of the south-west – north-east trending ridge have given rise to the drainage pattern.

A *radial drainage pattern* has evolved down the slopes of the Jhumla pahar. The location of the hill amidst levelled surface is responsible for the formation of this drainage pattern (fig. no. 3.79).

A *dendritic pattern* has been noted in the north-eastern corner of the area within the Pathalmaca drainage basin (fig no. 3.77). Equal probability of stream orientation in all directions due to uniform lithology may have given rise to such a pattern.

Parallel and Herringbone pattern (3.80 & 3.81)

A *parallel pattern* has been formed in one of the subtributary basins. Streams are running in parallel courses particularly along the left bank of a north-west flowing subtributary. These are more or less relief dictated. However, on the opposite bank no such pattern is observed.

A *herringbone pattern* is formed between the translinks in a subtributary basins in the north-eastern part of the map area. Though the pattern is not ideal in disposition, at least four pairs of links have exhibited the herringbone shape. Perhaps some alternate outcrops of rocks having variable resistance is the cause behind the development of this drainage pattern.

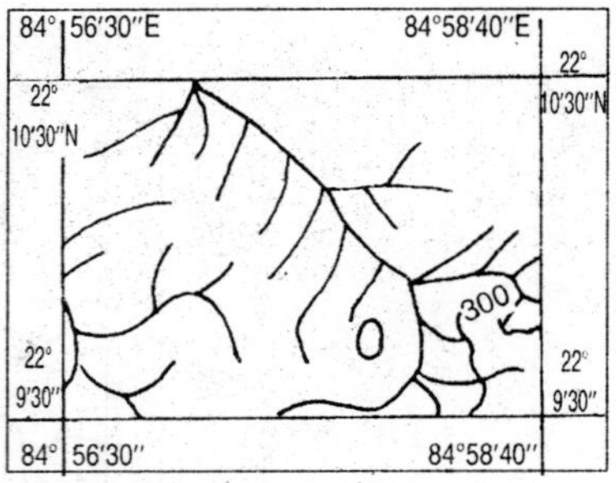

Fig. 3.80 Parallel pattern

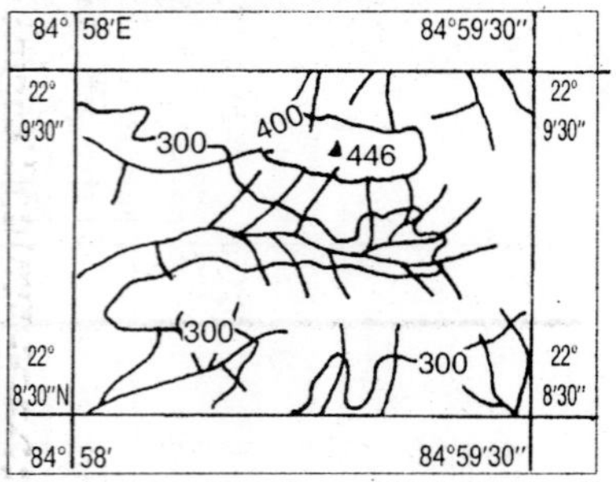

Fig. 3.81 Herringbone pattern

Morphometric methods applied to Kendughati Nala Basin :

The Kendughati nala (named after Kendughati village in the basin) is a left bank tributary to the Brahmani river. The stream rises from the south-west to north-east trending ridge within Champajharan reserve forest.

As such, the landform within the basin is hilly in character. These hills are not very high. Some of them are conical in shape and some others are low mounds.

The morphometric attributes of the basin as well as the 1Km^2 (4 Sq. cm.) gridwise morphometric data are incorporated in table no. 3.11 and 3.12 respectively. 4 maps illustrating the relative relief, drainage density, average slope and ruggedness index (fig. no. 3.82–3.87) are prepared from the gridwise data of table no. 3.9. These maps exhibit a close relationship among these geomorphic attributes in spatial dimension. The particular morphometric values of table no. 3.8 indicate that the basin has a moderate relief in comparison with the total relief of the basin area; the drainage density is low indicating a hard rock or more resistant terrain; the basin shape is more elongated than circular showing the influence of moderate structure control.

TABLE 3.11

Morphometric Study of Kendughati Drainage Basin

A_d (km^2)	P (km)	SL_c (km)	L (km)	H (m)	H/P	D_d (km/km^2)	C	C_R	E_R	U	N_S	R_b	Avg. (R_b)	D_S	D_T	$\bar{L}$
										1	95	5.9				0.46
24.0	27.5	86.0	8	387	14.07	3.58	0.39	0.46	0.69	2	17	3.4	4.8	4.92	17.61	1.18
										3	5	5				2.3
										4	1					11

As such, the D_d being low revealing a hard rock terrain in the basin, the D_S is not very high. The D_T being >10.0 reveals a reflection of the D_S and D_d indicating a fine texture. The sub-tributaries being closely spaced has given a moderate D_S . The L_u shows a gradual rise. The relation between N_u and u as well as between L_u and u being opposite to each other is shown in a graph (fig. 3.82)

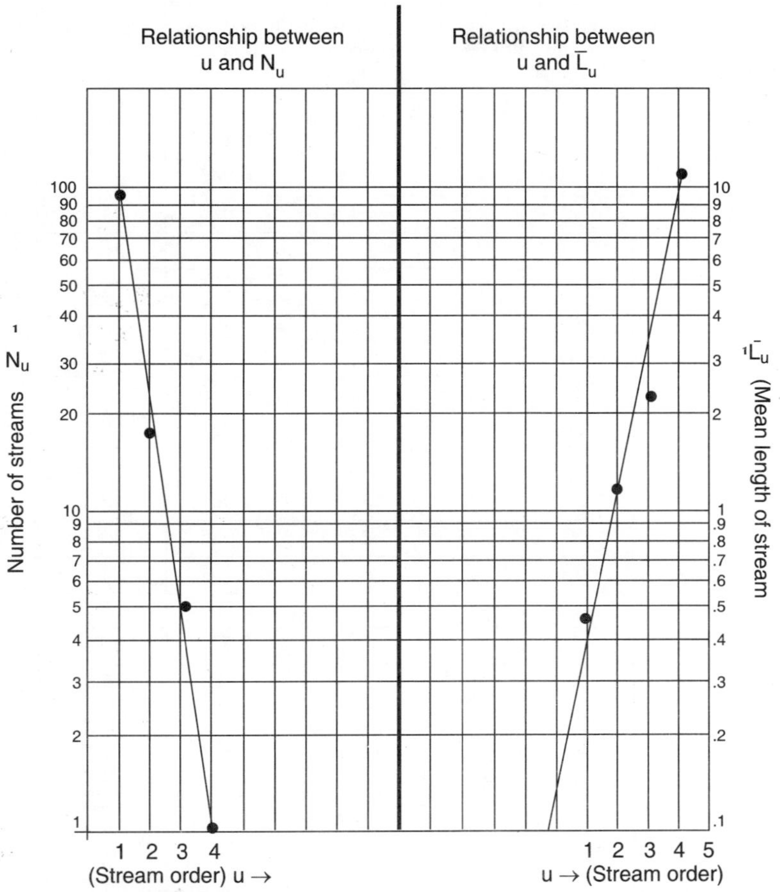

Fig. 3.82 Relationship between u and N_u / u and $\bar{L}_u$

TABLE 3.12

Morphometric Study of Kendughati Drainage Basin

Grid no.	Highest Elevation	Lowest Elevation	Relative Relief (m/km^2)	Channel Length in cm	Drainage Density (km/km^2)	Ruggedness Index	Avg. no. of Contour Crossing per km	Slope in Degree	% of Forest Cover
A_1	180	160	20	5	2.5	0.05	0.5	0°53′	0
A_2	190	180	10	2	1	.01	0.75	1°20′	0
A_3	200	180	20	4	2	0.04	3	5°23′	0
A_4	238	180	58	6	3	0.174	2.75	4°56′	0
A_5	190	180	10	3	1.5	0.015	1.5	2°41′	0
B_1	220	180	40	5	2.5	0.1	1.5	2°41′	45
B_2	190	180	10	7	3.5	0.035	1	1°47′	15
B_3	220	200	20	4	2	0.04	2.5	4°29′	30
B_4	220	200	20	3.5	1.75	0.035	1.5	2°41′	10
B_5	200	180	20	6.5	3.25	0.065	1.75	3°8′	0
C_1	240	180	60	4	2	0.12	3.5	6°16′	10

Contd. table next page

Grid no.	Highest Elevation	Lowest Elevation	Relative Relief (m/km^2)	Channel Length in cm	Drainage Density (km/km^2)	Ruggedness Index	Avg. no. of Contour Crossing per km	Slope in Degree	% of Forest Cover
C_2	240	180	60	5	2.5	0.15	3	5°23′	60
C_3	220	200	20	4.5	2.25	0.045	2	3°35′	25
C_4	220	200	20	7.5	3.75	0.075	1.5	2°41′	15
C_5	200	190	10	3	1.5	0.015	1.75	3°8′	0
D_1	200	180	20	5.5	2.75	0.055	2	3°35′	0
D_2	220	180	40	4	2	0.08	3	5°23′	50
D_3	210	200	10	5	2.5	0.025	3.25	5°49′	80
D_4	220	200	20	3.5	1.75	0.035	2.5	4°29′	40
D_5	220	200	20	6	3	0.06	4	7°9′	25
E_1	260	200	60	6	3	0.18	4.5	8°2′	75
E_2	220	200	20	6	3	0.06	3.5	6°16′	80
E_3	240	220	20	4.5	2.25	0.045	3.25	5°49′	60
E_4	280	200	80	4	2	0.16	4.5	8°2′	85
E_5	300	200	100	6	3	0.3	6.5	11°32′	90
F_1	300	200	100	6	3	0.3	6.75	11°58′	90
F_2	280	200	80	8	4	0.32	4.5	8°2′	75
F_3	260	220	40	5	2.5	0.1	3.75	6°43′	40
F_4	300	220	80	5.5	2.75	0.22	4	7°9′	75
F_5	300	220	80	4.5	2.25	0.18	7.5	13°15′	90
G_1	335	220	115	5.5	2.75	0.31625	6.0	10°40′	40
G_2	340	240	100	7	3.5	0.35	6.75	11°58′	25
G_3	340	240	100	6	3	0.3	9.5	16°37′	70
G_4	380	280	100	4	2	0.2	7.25	12°49′	100
G_5	340	260	80	5.5	2.75	0.22	5.5	9°48′	95
H_1	300	240	60	5.5	2.75	0.165	7.5	13°15′	70
H_2	320	240	80	5.5	2.75	0.22	5.75	10°14′	25
H_3	400	280	120	3.5	1.75	0.21	7.75	13°41′	90
H_4	420	280	140	3	1.5	0.21	7.25	12°49′	95
H_5	380	260	120	5.5	2.75	0.33	7.5	13°15′	90
I_1	567	300	267	7.5	3.75	1.00125	12.5	21°26′	100
I_2	340	280	60	5.5	2.75	0.165	4.5	8°2′	60
I_3	360	300	60	5	2.5	0.15	6	10°40′	60
I_4	340	260	80	6.5	3.25	0.26	5.25	9°21′	70
I_5	340	240	100	6	3	0.3	8	14°6′	95
J_1	500	300	200	6	3	0.6	10.25	17°50′	100
J_2	440	300	140	5	2.5	0.35	8.75	15°22′	95
J_3	320	280	40	3	1.5	0.06	8.5	14°57′	40
J_4	380	300	80	5.5	2.75	0.22	7.25	12°49′	70
J_5	280	240	40	7	3.5	0.14	6.25	11°6′	70

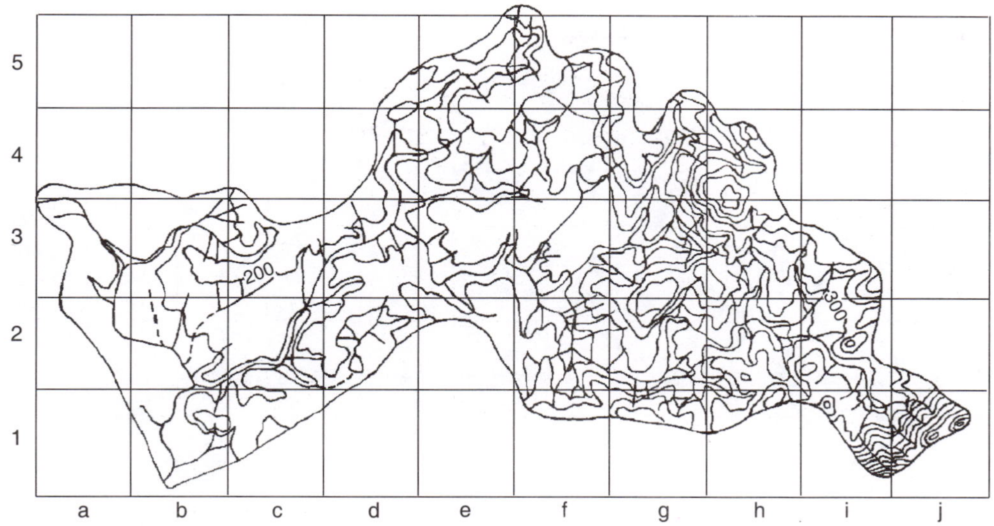

Fig. 3.83 Kendughati drainage basin (grids reduced from 2 cm × 2 cm)

Vegetation : Almost two thirds of the map area are covered with reserve forests. Only the valley floor has scattered trees and arable lands which are coloured yellow. Some forests are there lying outside the R.F. boundaries. These are perhaps unclassed state forests. The table below (table no. 3.10) incorporates the information about the forests in the area.

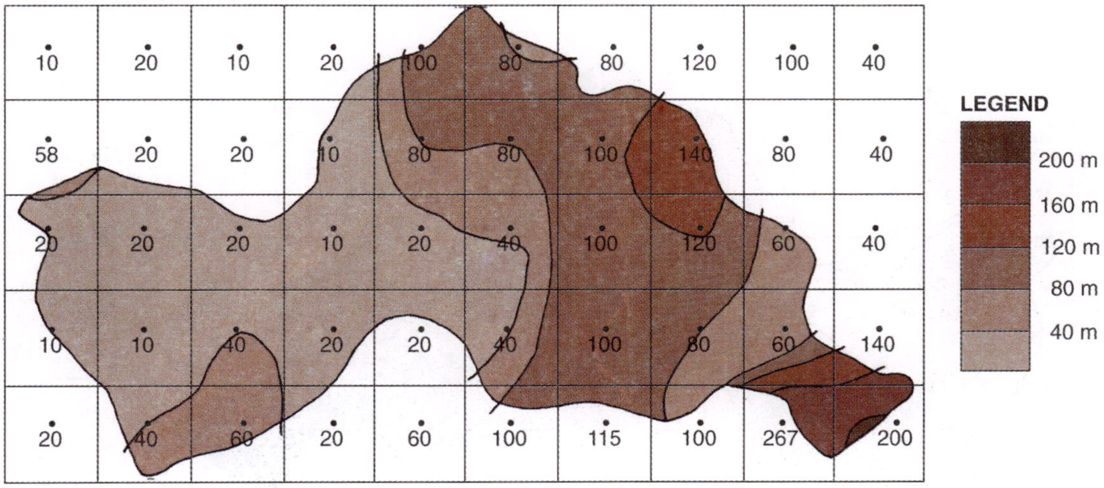

Fig. 3.84 Relative Relief Map

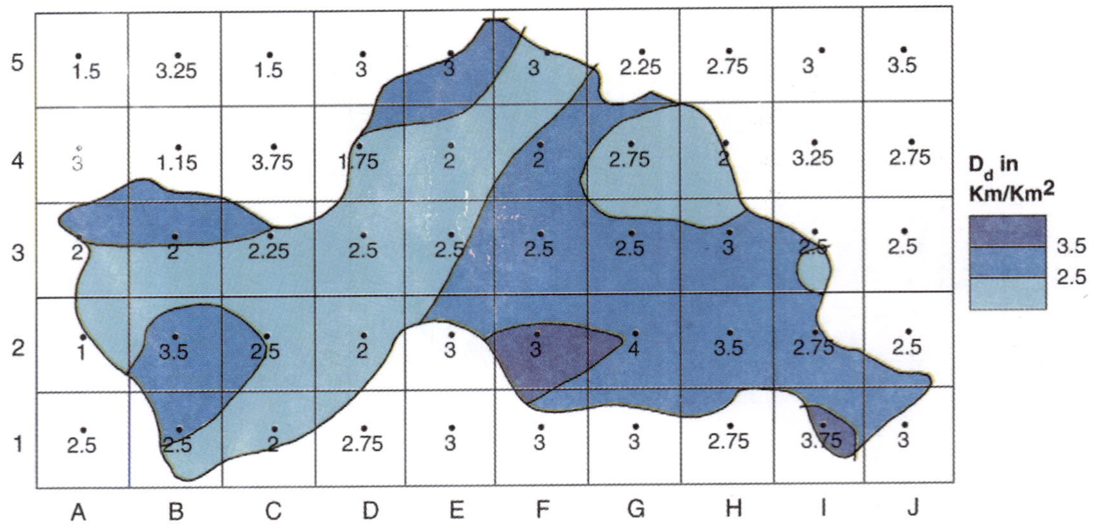

Fig. 3.85 Drainage Density

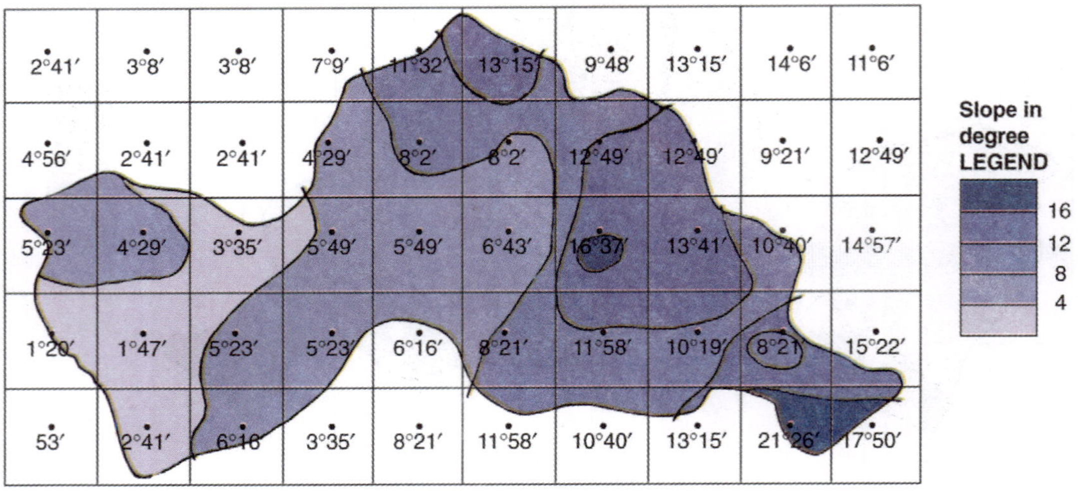

Fig. 3.86 Average Regional Slope Map

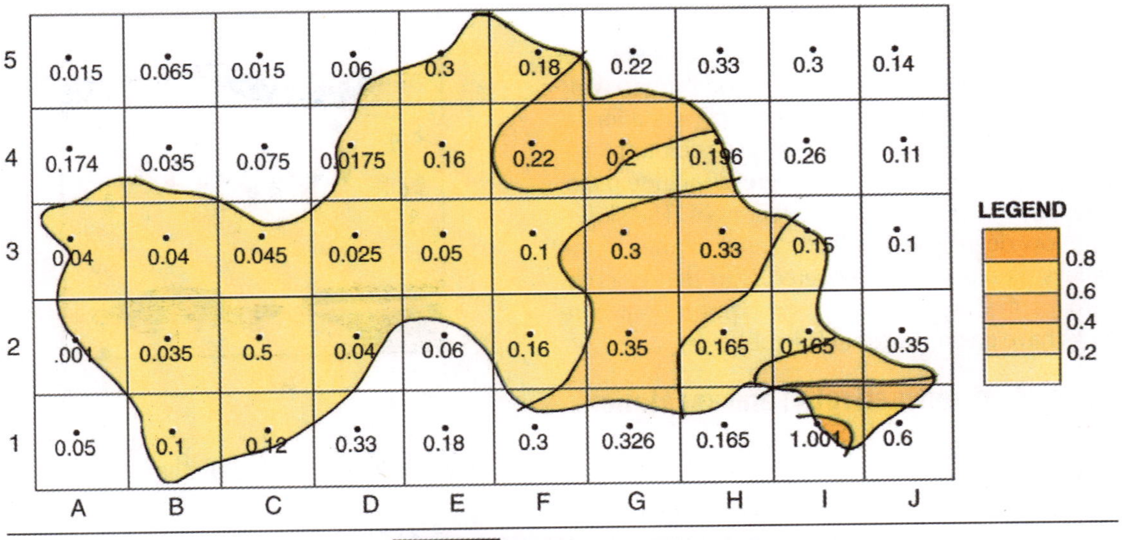

Fig. 3.87 Ruggedness Index Map

From the table (table no. 3.13) it appears that most of the reserved forests are of mixed type and Sal is the predominating species in these forests. They are either open or dense in nature.

TABLE 3.13

Name of forest	Status	Nature	Main Species
Jaltarang	Protected		
Veduyas	protected		Eucalyptus
Balanda	Protected	Dense mixed jungle	
Ruthupiri	Reserved	Dense mixed jungle	mainly Sal
Bhainsamunda	Reserved	Dense mixed jungle	mainly Sal
Kusumdihi	Reserved	Dense mixed jungle	mainly Sal
Dhenkiam	Reserved	Fairly dense mixed	
Rangamatia	Reserved	Fairly dense mixed	
South Champajharan	Reserved	Dense mixed jungle	
North Champajharan	Reserved	Dense mixed jungle	mainly Sal
Mahura	Reserved	Dense mixed jungle	mainly Sal
Jharbeda	Reserved	Dense mixed jungle	mainly Sal
Kuchaita	Reserved	Open mixed	mainly Sal
South Chirobeda	Reserved	Open mixed	mainly Sal
Ergeda	Reserved	Open mixed	
Lathikata	Reserved	Open mixed	
Baribeda	Protected	Open mixed	
Mankd	Protected	Open mixed	
Sona parbat	Reserved	Open mixed	
Karalakhaman	Protected	Open mixed	
North Chirobeda	Reserved	Open & dense mixed	
Hathibandha	Reserved	Dense scrub	
Unclassed unnamed		Open mixed	
Bad marain	Reserved	Open mixed	

In the settled areas of valleys trees are, in general, scattered, but in the surroundings of villages the combination of plants comprises a wide variety of species. One of such combination is found in village Lungai (fig. 3.79, see colour plate). The trees present in the village-grove include palm, coconut, bamboo and some other trees. The slopes with low degree of undulations on the fringe of the valleys, knolls etc. are covered with dense scrub. Perhaps the dryness of soil or exposures of bare rocks have given rise to such scrublands.

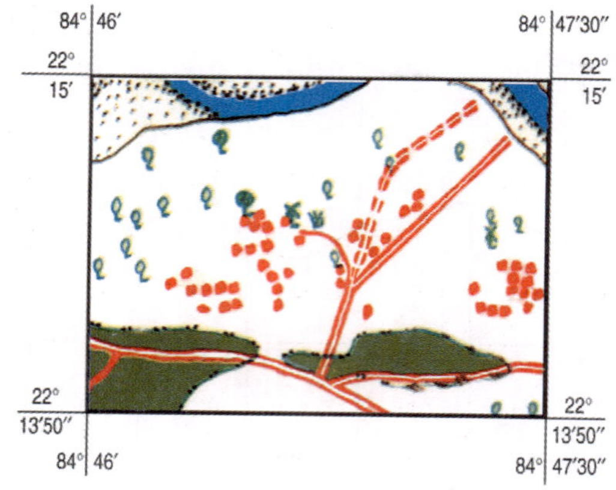

Fig. 3.88 Plant combination in villages

Correlation between relief and vegetation :

As mentioned earlier the valleys have scattered trees on them. On the contrary, high relief areas are covered with forests, steeper the slope, greater the amount of forest cover on them. Such a relationship is observed in the scatter diagram for the Kendughati drainage basin (fig. no. 3.89) expressing a positive relationship between the percentage of forest cover and relative relief (Table 3.12).

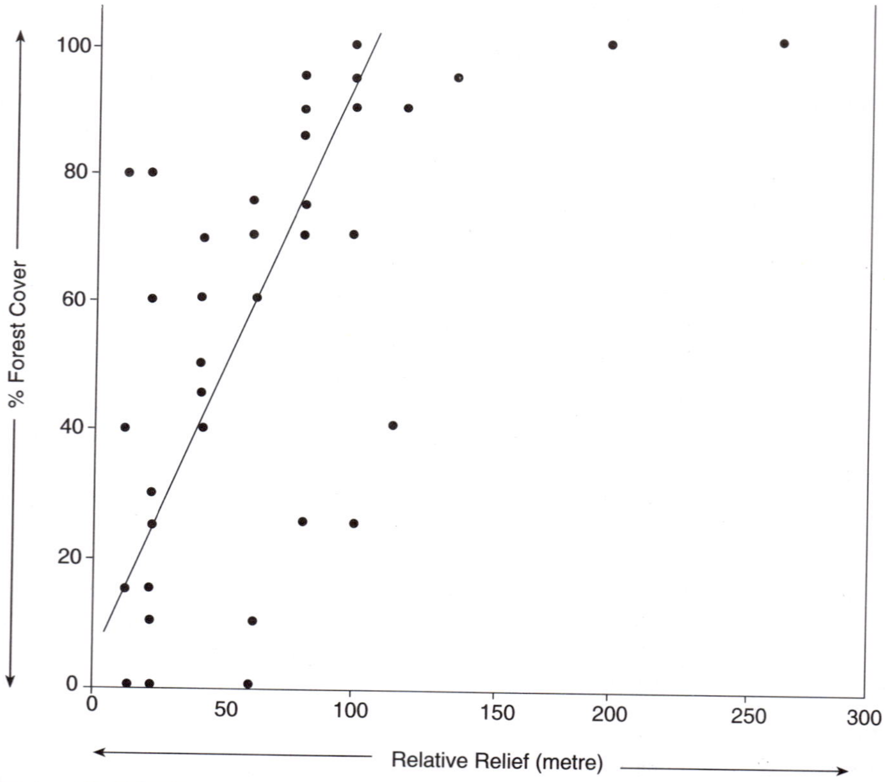

Fig. 3.89 Scatter Diagram showing relationship between relative relief and forest cover

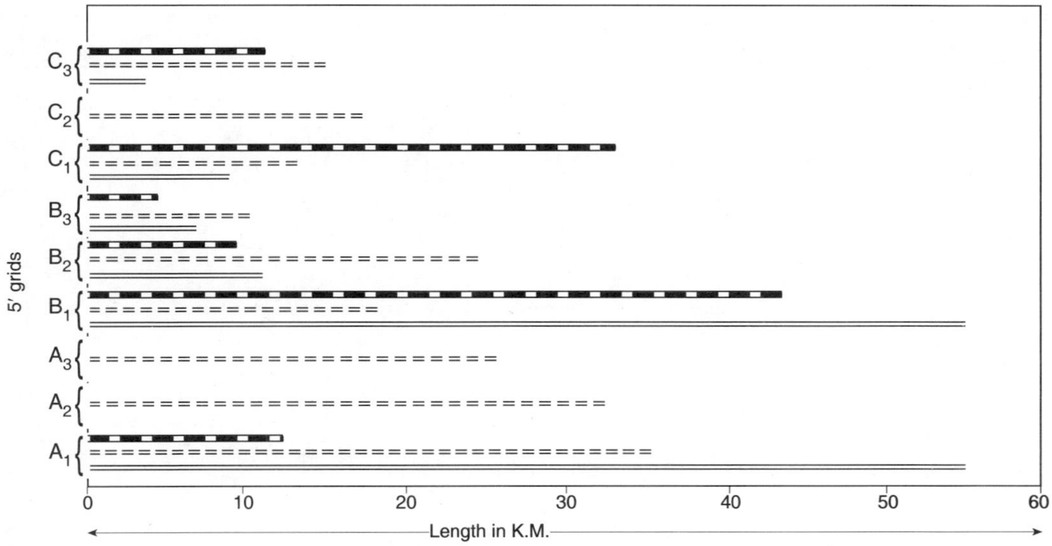

Fig. 3.90 **Major transportation links**

Communication

The area shown in the map has been traversed by a number of railway tracks and metalled roads. Between the villages the links are made by some major unmetalled roads and foot tracks. Some of the roads are under construction, whereas, some others are motorable during dry season .

On the basis of the chart (fig. no. 3.81) and table no. 3.11 prepared to show the length of railway, metalled road and major unmetalled roads, it has been observed that the average density in B_1 grid is 0.92 km./sq. km. On the contrary, in B_3 grid the lowest density of roads is found. Here we may note that the township of Rourkela, one of the major Steel cities of India, is located within B_1 grid. The C_1 grid, on the other hand, has shown very rugged topography and valley development is least advanced in the area. Villages are also very few in number and most of the area belonging to the grid are included within reserved forest. Thus the influences of relief and economy as well as urbanisation have been revealed in the variable density of roads. One major trunk road of the area runs from north to south. Moreover, the main line of south-eastern railway and the Bandamunda-Barsua branch has run through the area, the former in west to east direction

TABLE 3.14

Grid no.	A_1	A_2	A_3	B_1	B_2	B_3	C_1	C_2	C_3
Major Metalled Road (km)	29	0	0	55	11	7	9	0	3.5
Major Unmetalled Road (km)	35	33	26	18	25	10	13	17.5	15
Railway (km)	12.5	0	0	43.5	10	4.5	33	0	8
Road Density (km/km^2) (for major roads)	0.81	0.42	0.33	0.92	0.48	0.21	0.28	0.22	0.23

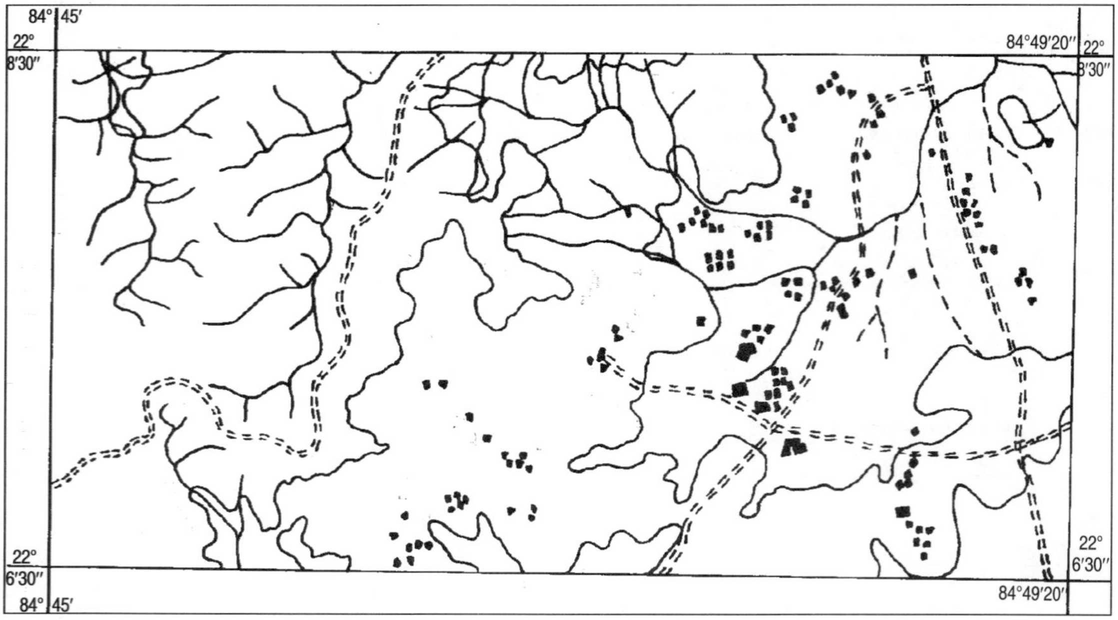

Fig. 3.91 Zigzag road along the ridge

and the latter has a north to south alignment. The north to south alignment of the major metalled road as well as of the railway has mostly followed the narrow strip of the Brahmani valley. Here also the influence of relief is marked. Apart from them the electrified Birmitrapur branch of south eastern railway is also present there.

The impact of relief on roads is further noted in terms of the trend of road alignment. On the erosional plains the roads are, more or less, straight, whereas, they are zigzag or spiral on steep slopes and ridges (fig. no. 3.82).

Foot tracks are very few in number, the cart tracks are fewer. Rourkela and many of the important settlements have been linked up with telephone and telegraph lines also. The length of roads per Km^2 in the Kendughati drainage basin is an effective expression of communication and development. Road density being a cultural feature is not a continuum like natural features and should not use an isopleth mapping method, because that may include some value in a grid, where there is no roads at all (Fig. 3.80a).

Settlement

Except for the town Rourkela all other settlements are rural in character. However, Rourkela has a very widespread development in the northern part of the map-area and planned colonies are being developed at many places in the surroundings.

In general, settlements are few in number over the rugged topography and concentration is particularly noted along narrow constricted valleys.

Settlement patterns : As the given toposheet covers a vast range of concentration of settlements varying from a single homestead amidst forest to a dense and major urban agglomeration over the plains, the patterns of settlements also vary greatly.

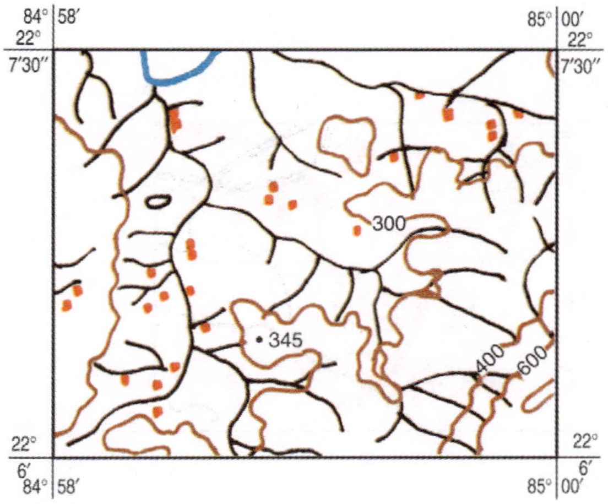

Fig. 3.92 Dispersed settlement on undulations

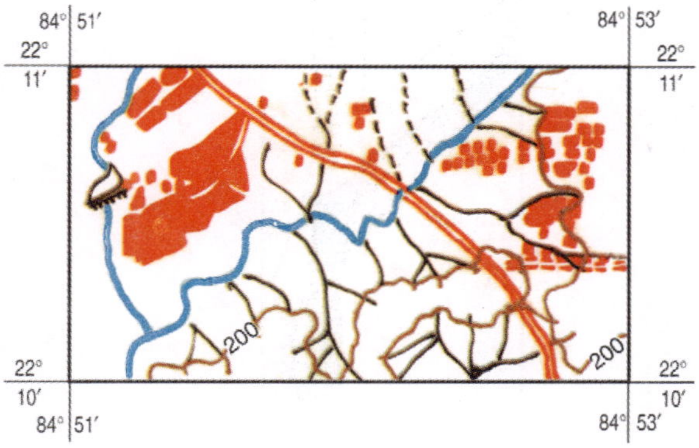

Fig. 3.93 Village at road junction

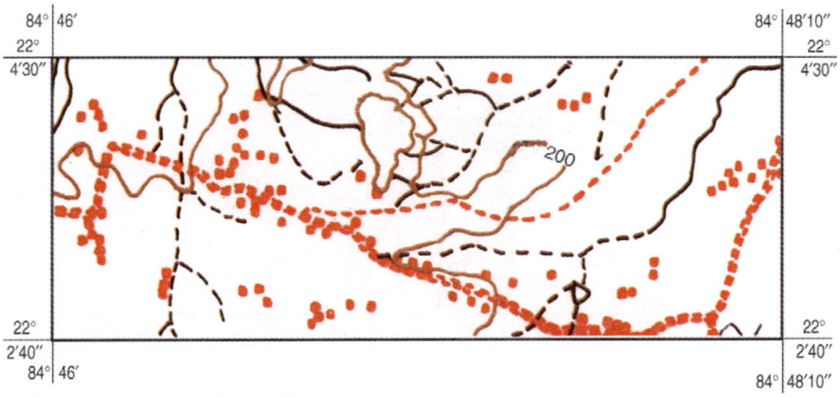

Fig. 3.94 Linear settlement along road

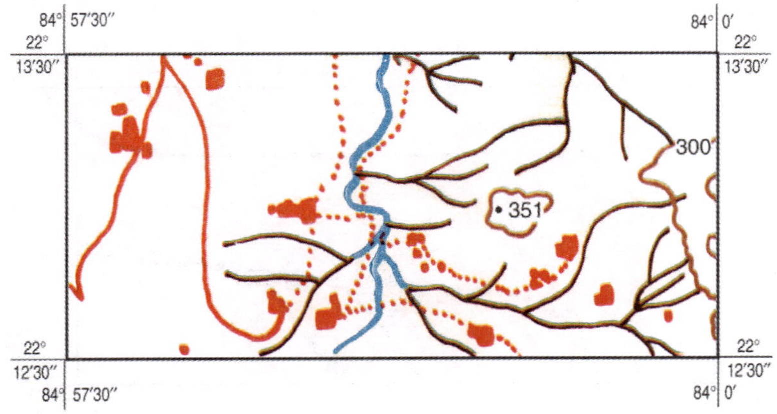

Fig. 3.95 Isolated hamlets

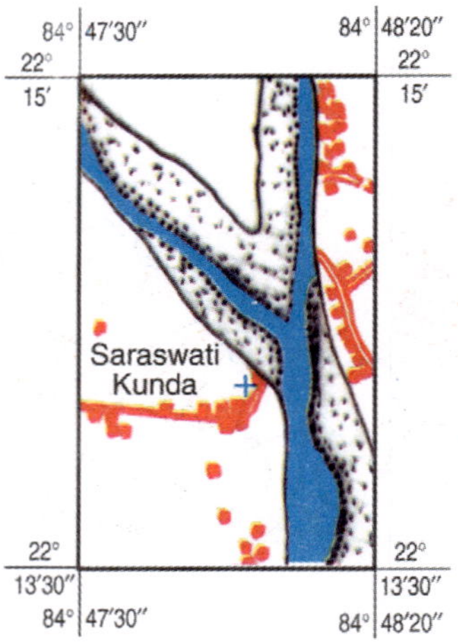

Fig. 3.96 Village near the spring

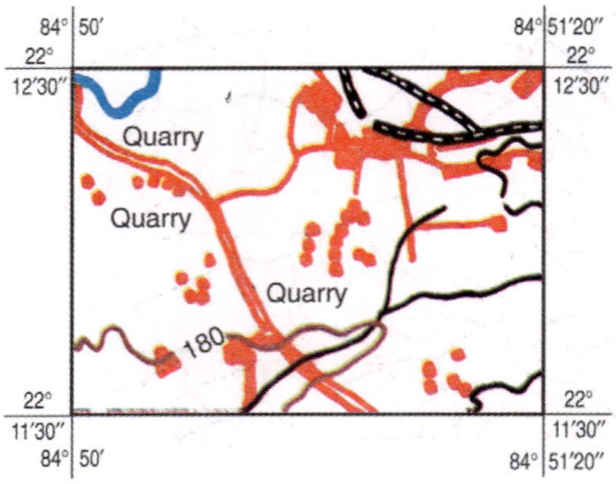

Fig. 3.97 Village near quarry

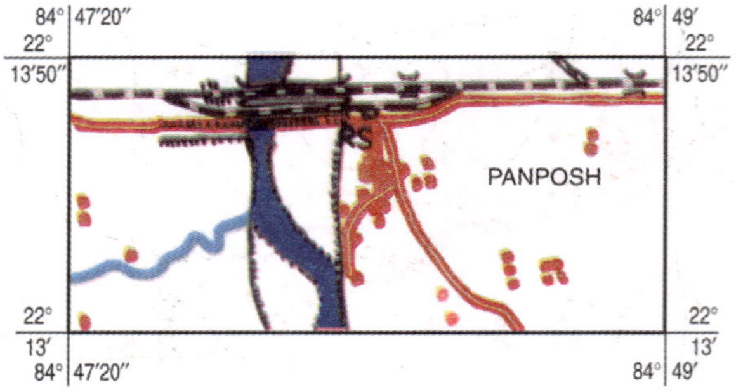

Fig. 3.98 Nucleated settlement near railway station

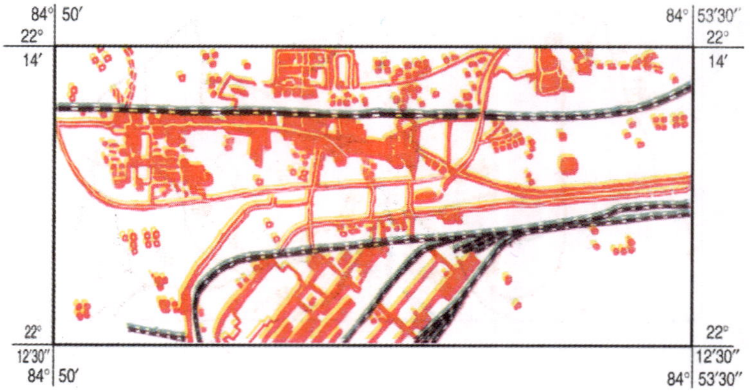

Fig. 3.99 Urban agglomeration of Uditnagar and Rourkela

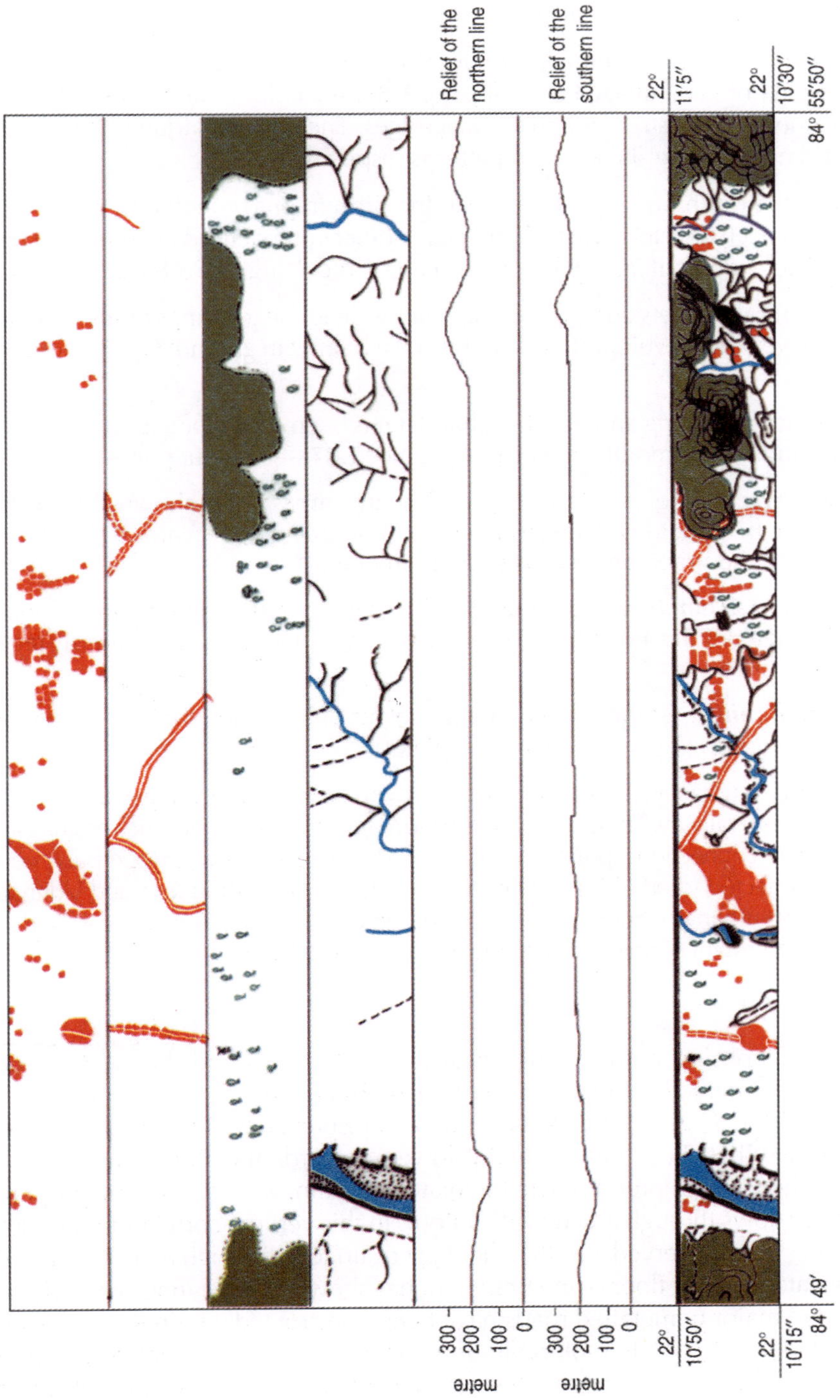

Fig. 3.100 Spatial Co-relation between relief and cultural aspects

Dispersed pattern : Settlements are particularly dispersed on the rugged plateau, which is, more or less, covered with forests. The villages likes Jamjharia in grid A_2 and Jangidiri in grid C_2 exhibit such a pattern (fig. no. 3.83, see colour plate).

Linear Pattern : Linear pattern of settlements are usually observed along the road side. In A_3 grid such a pattern has been noted in village Patua (fig. no. 3.84, see colour plate). This linear trend is again marked along the banks of streams and sides of ridges. The village Garjan in grid no. A_1 and village Manka in grid no. C_2 have shown such patterns respectively.

Compact Pattern : In the north of Panposh between the Birmitrapur branch and the Koel river a compact settlement has been developed at Chhend. Some other compactions are observed between physical and cultural constraints at Jalda B block and Jalda C block (fig. no. 3.85, see colour plate).

Rural Hamlets : Small rural hamlets comprising a few homestead, near springs or reservoirs within the forest clearance have been developed. Birkera is such a hamlet in grid no. C_1 (fig. no. 3.86, see colour plate).

Near Saraswati kunda or spring another small hamlet has been developed (grid A_1). An annual fair is held near this kunda in the month of February (fig. no. 3.87, see colour plate).

Settlement near Quarry : Some of the mining and quarry areas have shown the location of nucleated settlements in their vicinity. Deogaon (fig. no. 3.88, see colour plate) at the confluence of a left bank tributary to the Brahmani river is such a settlement.

Rural agglomeration at road junction : Hathibandha village is located at the junction of two major metalled and unmetalled roads (fig. no. 3.85). The scope of communication has obviously facilitated this settlement.

Nucleated settlement at railway station : A compact nucleus of settlement has been developed at the railway station of Panposh (fig. 3.89, see colour plate).

Urban agglomeration : Two urban agglomerations as twin towns have been developed along the side of the main line of south-eastern railway. These urban units have many urban amenities such as, infrastructure of metalled roads, railway connections, police station, post and telegraph office, dispensary, court etc. Rourkela has also shown factory sheds with railway connection. However, Rourkela and Uditnagar are practically two ends of an urban continuum (fig. no. 3.90, see colour plate). Towards east and west as well as towards south the growth of planned settlements are well marked.

Transect chart

To find out the relationship between the physical determinants and the cultural set up a transect chart has been prepared between two points at 240 metre in A_1 grid and 340 metre in C_1 grid (22°10′15″ N/84°49′ E & 22°10′30″ N/84°55′50″ E) respectively. This chart (fig. no. 3.91, see colour plate) shows that the relief gradually lowers towards the Brahmani valley. Non-perennial streams of short length predominate the plateau terrain, whereas, the major perennial river like the Brahmani flows through a wide valley floor. In this vertical correlation on a selected spatial dimension it has been observed also that the rugged surface with high relief is covered with forest, whereas, the flattish valley floor of the Brahmani has shown arable lands. Similarly most of the metalled roads and major unmetalled roads have been constructed within the valley and the plateau has shown mostly seasonally motorable unmetalled roads. Settlement concentration is markedly high in the valley area, whereas, the forested plateau is nearly without any major settlement (fig. no. 3.91, see colour plate).

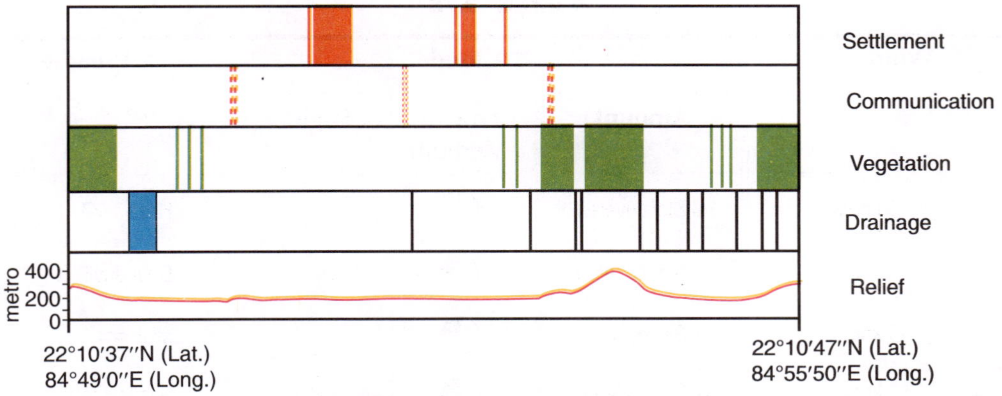

Fig. 3.101 **Transect Chart (reduced)**

Conclusion

On the whole this topographical map covering small parts of Bihar and Orissa has shown both rural and urban sectors in the cultural landscape. The expansion of the urban agglomeration shows a distinct trend of urbanisation in the northern part of the area. The growth of the large rural agglomeration in the vicinity of urban centres have indicated the process of urban development. However, the rugged hilly and ridge-like areas are avoided by people. The extension of railway towards south and the location of quarries signify the good resource base of the area.

WEATHER MAP INTERPRETATION

Weather map and synoptic chart

Weather map is another tool for a geographer. It contains the state of condition of various weather elements (Table no. 3.12) at a particular hour of a day. The hour of the day at which the observations are made is given at the top of the map. The date is also mentioned along with it.

However, the map, as such, does not include the information about all the elements of daily weather. It incorporates the isobars drawn at 2 millibar interval and related location of high and low, the amount of cloud cover present in the sky, the direction and velocity of wind, the amount of rainfall, and some other weather phenomena, such as, haze, fog, mist, squall, depression, limit of south-westerly monsoon wind, sandstorm, thunderstorm, dust devil etc. Over the oceanic and sea-areas the condition of the sea is also marked.

TABLE 3.15

Wind		Cloud: Amount	Cloud: Low or Medium	Cloud: High	Weather
5 knots		1/8 Sky covered	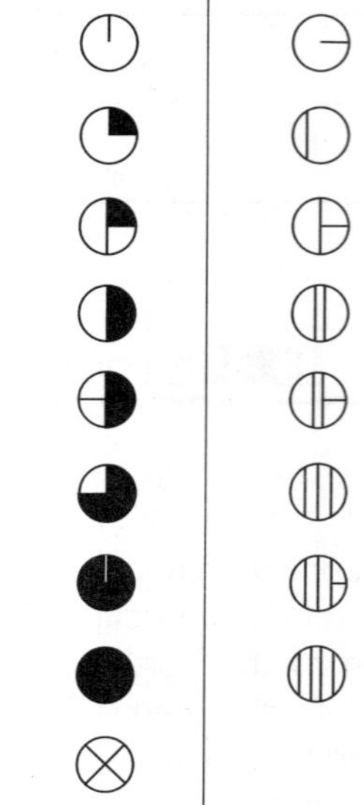		Haze ∞
10 knots		1/4 Sky covered			Dust devil
15 knots		3/8 Sky covered			Mist =
50 knots		1/2 Sky covered			Shallow fog = =
		5/8 Sky covered			Fog ≡
SEA CONDITION		3/4 Sky covered			Squall ▽
Cm	Calm	7/8 Sky covered			Dust or
Sm	Smooth	Overcast			Sandstorm
Sl	Slight	Sky obscured			Hail Δ
Mod	Moderate				Drifting snow
Ro	Rough				Drizzle ,
V. Ro	Very rough				Rain •
Hi	High				Snow ✳
V. Hi	Very high				Shower ▽
Ph	Phenomenal				Thunderstorm
					Lightning

Although the information in a weather map about various weather elements seem to be comprehensive, they do not include anything about the present or past temperature conditions, about the types of clouds covering the sky at various levels, about the humidity and about many other pertinent information. To obtain a more elaborate data about the conditions of all other weather elements usually a synoptic chart is used with station models prepared for different I.M.D. stations. Such station models include about 15 information of the past and present weather condition giving the amount of temperature, pressure, rainfall, type of cloud cover etc. The synoptic information sheet (table 3.13) depicts both past and present weather (fig. no. 3.92).

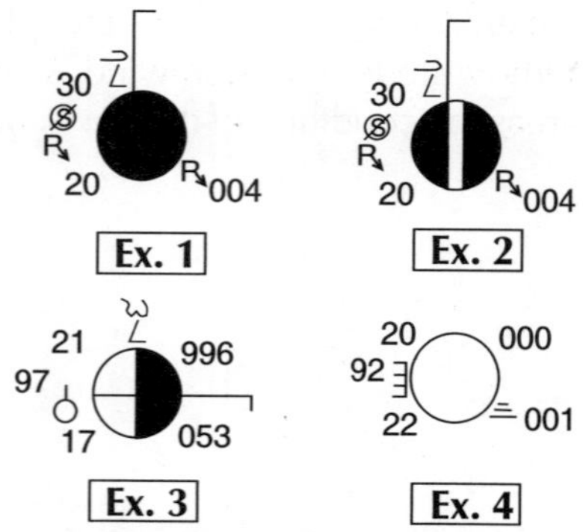

Fig. 3.102 **Station models**

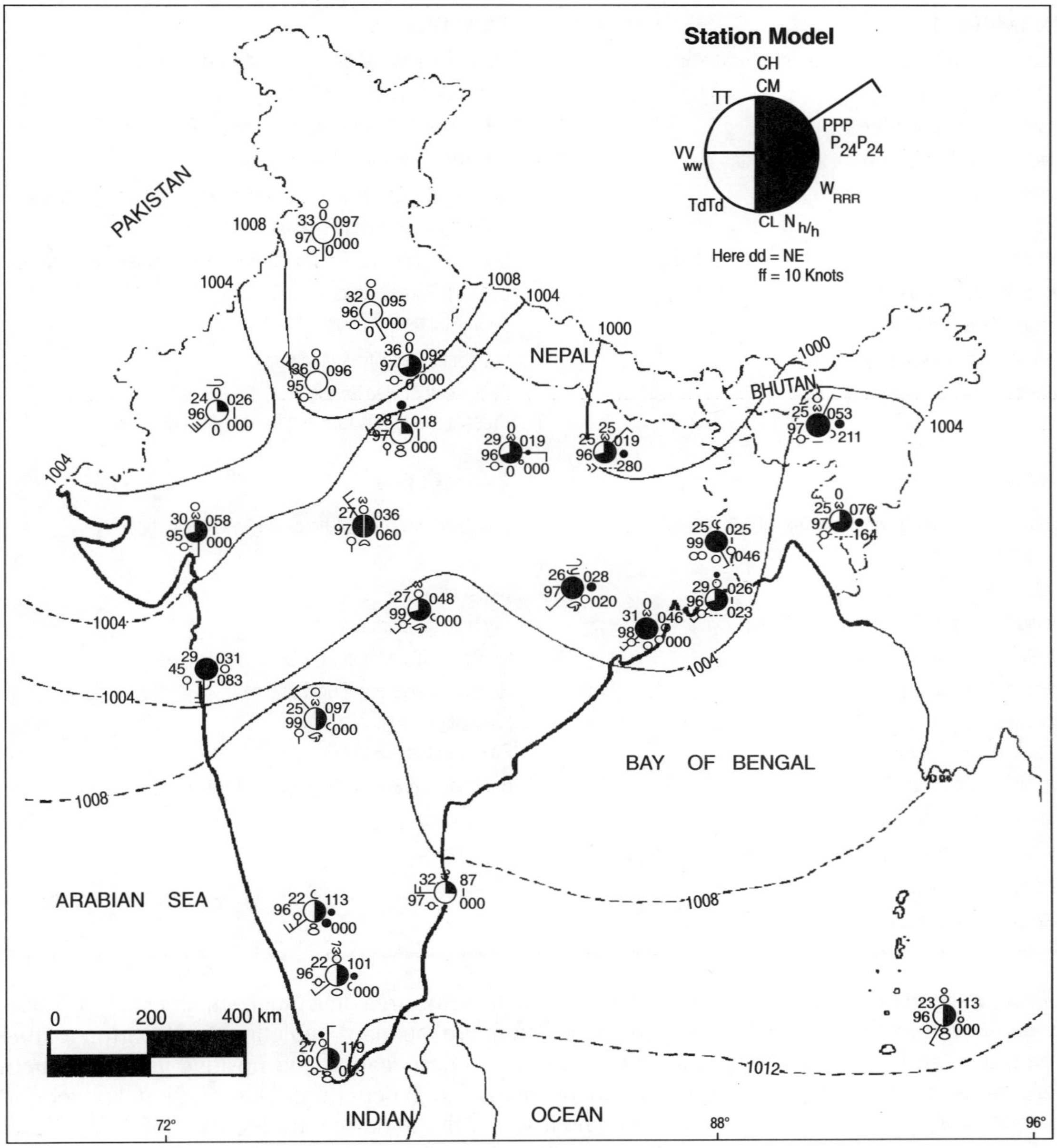

Fig. 3.103 **Synoptic charts for Different Stations in India (isobars in millibar)**

The purpose of using weather map is different from that of using a synoptic chart. In the former a broad regional pattern is evolved in connection with the pattern of isobars, cloud cover and rainfall. For synoptic chart it is more specific, more technical and the nature of elements is elaborate and station-based (fig. no. 3.93), but determining a regional pattern becomes more difficult and complex in that, though it is more informative than a weather map.

TABLE 3.16

EXAMPLE 1 Rainfall during last 24 hours ending at 8.30 hours I.S.T. 0.4 mm High cloud – Thin cirrus Medium cloud – Cirrus in the form of oktas Low cloud – Nil Total cloud amount – 8th of the sky Wind direction is from north with a speed of 10 knots. Dry bulb temperature is 30°C Present weather – Thunderstorm Past weather was thunderstorm Dew point Temperature is 20°C	**EXAMPLE 2** Rainfall during last 24 hours ending at 8.30 hours I.S.T. 0.8 mm High cloud –Cirrostratus gradually grading the sky Medium cloud – Semi Altostratus Low cloud – Strato-cumulus developing into cumulonimbus. Total cloud amount is 7 octas. Surface direction is from south-west with a speed of 10 knots. Dry bulb Temperature – 25°C Dew point temp. – Nil Horizontal visibility is upto 96 m. Past weather was drizzle Present weather is rain, not freezing, continuous.
EXAMPLE 3 Rainfall during last 24 hours ending at 8.30 hours I.S.T 5.3 mm High cloud – Cirrocumulus Medium cloud is altocumulus at different levels. Total cloud amount is 5 octas. Surface direction is from eastern side with a speed of 10 knots. Barometric pressure reduced to mean sea level & standard gravity is 996 mb. Dry bulb temperature – 21°C Horizontal visibility – 97 m. Present weather is clouds generally forming or developing. Past wather not known Dew point Temperature – 17°C	**EXAMPLE 4** Rainfall during last 24 hours ending at 8.30 hours I.S.T. 0.1 mm Sky is clear Dry bulb temperature – 20°C Dew point Temperature – 22°C Horizontal visibility is upto 200 m. Present weather – Fog Past weather – Fog Barometric pressure as correlated to standard gravity is 1000 mb.

Along with the weather map two other maps of the same area on a much smaller scale are also given just below the frame of the weather map. These are the maps depicting the departure of the minimum and maximum temperature from normal. The negative and positive values of such departures are given and isopleths drawn on the basis of such departures give a regional pattern of increasing or decreasing temperature in comparison with the normal for the day. Zero departure line is also drawn where the temperature remains normal. However, a correlation between the weather map and departure of temperature maps may prove fruitful as the causes of the occurrence of low and high may be matched with such departure zones.

INTERNATIONAL METEOROLOGICAL CODES

The information in this appendix is abbreviated and should be used in the preparation of weather maps only when reference of full standard publications is impracticable.

1. Code Forms

a) Reports from land stations :

99911				
$iiiT_dT_d$	*Nddff*	*VVwwW*	*PPPTT*	
$N_hC_LhC_MC_H$	*(6 japp)*	*(7 RRjj)*	$(8N_sCh_sh_s)$	$(9S_vS_vs_vs_v)$

b) Reports from ships :

$QL_aL_aL_a$	$L_oL_oL_oGG$	*Nddff*	*VVwwW*	*PPPTT*
$N_hC_LhC_MC_H$	d_sv_sapp	$(8N_sCh_sh_s)$		$(9S_vS_vs_vs_v)$
$(O\,T_sT_sT_dT_d)$	$(i\,d_wd_wP_wH_w)$			

2. Significance of Letters

iii	Index number of reporting station.
T_dT_d	Dew point temperature.
N	Total amount of cloud.
dd	Direction of surface wind to nearest to degrees (00–36).
ff	Wind speed in knots.
VV	Visibility.
ww	Present weather.
W	Past weather.
PPP	Pressure in millibars and tenths, initial 9 or 10 omitted.
TT	Air temperature.
N_h	Amount of low cloud.
C_L	Form of low cloud.
h	Height of base of low cloud.
C_M	Form of medium cloud.
C_H	Form of high cloud.
6	Initial figure to characterise barometric tendency group.
j	Regional symbol.
a	Characteristic of barograph trace.
pp	Barometric tendency in tenths of a millibar. When tendency equals or exceeds 9.9 mbs. *pp* will be reported as 99, and tendency group will be followed by an additional group *99ppp* where *ppp* is in tenths.
7	Initial figure to characterise precipitation group.
RR	Amount of precipitation.

jj	Regional symbol.
8	Initial figure to characterise significant cloud group.
N_s	Amount of significant cloud.
C	Form of predominant cloud.
$h_s h_s$	Height of base of significant cloud.
9	Initial figure to characterise special phenomena group.
o	Day of week.
Q	Octant of the globe.
$L_a L_a L_a$	Latitude in degrees and tenths.
$L_0 L_0 L_0$	Longitude in degrees and tenths.
GG	Greenwich mean time.
d_s	Ship's course.
v_s	Ship's speed.
O	Initial figure for sea temperature and dew point group.
$T_s T_s$	Sea temperature.
I	Initial figure for wave group.
$d_w d_w$	Direction from which wave comes (00 – 36).
P_w	Period of waves.
H_w	Height of waves.

3. Code Specifications

(i) Code for Cloud Amount N, N_h, and N_s

0	None	1	1/8th (or 1 okta) of sky covered
2	2/8ths	3	3/8ths
4	4/8ths	5	5/8ths
6	6/8ths	7	7/8ths
8	Sky completely covered	9	Sky obscured

(ii) Code for Wind Direction *dd*

00	Calm	10	100°	19	190°	28	280°
01	010°	11	110°	20	200°	29	290°
02	020°	12	120°	21	210°	30	300°
03	030°	13	130°	22	220°	31	310°
04	040°	14	140°	23	230°	32	320°
05	050°	15	150°	24	240°	33	330°
06	060°	16	160°	25	250°	34	340°
07	070°	17	170°	26	260°	35	350°
08	080°	18	180°	27	270°	36	360°
09	090°						

(iii) Code for Visibility *VV*

Code Figure		*Metres*		*Kilometres*
X0	Less than	20		
X1		20		
X2		40		
X3		60		
X4		80		
X5		100		
X6		120		
X7		140		
X8		160		
X9		180		
00	Less than	200	Less than	0.2
01		200		0.2
02		400		0.4
03		600		0.6
04		800		0.8
05		1,000		1.0
06		1,200		1.2
07		1,400		1.4
08		1,600		1.6
09		1,800		1.8
10		2,000		2.0

Continued up to code figure 80 in same increments as above

Code Figure	*Metres*	*Kilometres*
78		15.6
79		15.8
80		16.0
81		20
82		40
83		60
84		80
85		100
86		150
87		200
88		300
89		500

Code Figure		*Metres*	*Kilometres*
90	Less than	50 m.	
91		50 m.	
92		200 m.	
93		500 m.	
94		1,000 m.	
95		2,000 m.	
96		4,000 m.	
97		10 km.	
98		20 km.	
99		50 km.	

Note : *If the distance of visibility is between two of the distances given in the table, the code figures for the lower distance will be reported e.g. if the distance is 350 m., code figures 01 will be reported.*

(iv) Code for Present Weather *ww*

No precipitation at the station at the time of observation (00–49). No precipitation, fog, dust-storm, sand-storm or drifting snow at the station, at the time of observation or during the preceding hour, except for 09 (00–19).

00  Cloud development not observed

01  Clouds generally dissolving or becoming less developed

02 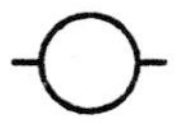 State of sky on the whole unchanged

03  Clouds generally forming or developing

04  Visibility reduced by smoke, e.g. veldt or forest fires, industrial smoke or volcanic ashes.

05  Dry haze.

06  Widespread dust in suspension in the air, not raised by wind at or near the station at the time of observation.

07  Dust or sand raised by wind at or near the station at the time of observation, but no well developed dust devil(s), and no dust-storm or sand-storm seen

08  Well developed dust devil(s) seen at or near the station within last hour, but no dust-storm or sand-storm.

09  Dust-storm or sand-storm within sight of station or at station during the last hour.

10  Mist.

11  Patches of

12  More or less continuous

13  Lightning visible, but no thunder audible.

14  Precipitation within sight not reaching ground at station.

15  Precipitation within sight, reaching the ground, but distant.

16  Precipitation within sight, reaching the ground, near to but not at station.

17  Thunder heard, but no precipitation at the station.

18  Squalls (s)

19  Funnel cloud(s)

Precipitation, fog or thunderstorm at the station during the preceding hour but not at the time or observation (20–29).

20  Drizzle (not freezing)

21  Rain (not freezing)

22  Snow

23  Rain and Snow

24  Freezing drizzle or freezing rain

25  Shower(s) of rain.

26  Shower(s) of snow, or of rain and snow.

27  Shower(s) of hail or of hail and rain.

28 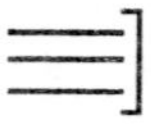 Fog.

29  Thunderstorm (with or without precipitation).

Dust-storm, sand-storm of drifting snow (30–39).

No.	Symbol	Description	
30		Slight or moderate dust- storm of sand-storm	– has decreased during the preceding
31			– no appreciable change during the preceding hour.
32			– has increased during the preceding hour.
33	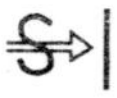	Severe dust-storm or sand-storm	– has decreased during the preceding hour.
34			– no appreciable change during the preceeding hour.
35	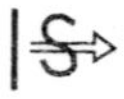		– has increased during the preceding hour.
36		Slight or moderate drifting snow	generally low.
37		Heavy drifting snow	
38		Slight or moderate drifting snow for more than 2 metres	generally high.
39		Heavy drifting snow	

Fog at the time of observation (40–49).

40  Fog at a distance at the time of observation, but not at the station during the last hour, the fog extending to a level above that of the observer.

41 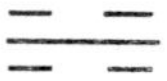 Fog in patches.

No.	Symbol	Description	
42		Fog, sky discernible	has become thinner during the preceding hour.
43		For, sky not discernible	
44		Fog, sky discernible	no appreciable change during the preceding hour.
45		Fog, sky discernible	

46 Fog, sky discernible
47 Fog, sky not discernible
} has begun or has become thicker during the preceding hour.

48 Fog, depositing hard rime, sky discernible.

49 Fog, depositing hard rime, sky not discernible.

Precipitation at the station at the time of observation (50–99).

Drizzle (50–59).

50 Drizzle, not freezing, intermittent
51 Drizzle, not freezing, continuous
} slight at time of observation.

52 Drizzle, not freezing, intermittent
53 Drizzle, not freezing, continuous
} moderate at time of observation.

54 Drizzle, not freezing, intermittent
55 Drizzle, not freezing, continuous
} thick at time of observation.

56 Drizzle, freezing, slight.

57 Drizzle, freezing, moderate or thick.

58 Drizzle, rain, slight.

59 Drizzle, rain, moderate or heavy.

Rain (60–69).

60 Rain, not freezing, intermittent
61 Rain, not freezing, continuous
} slight at time of observation.

62 Rain, not freezing, intermittent
63 Rain, not freezing, continuous
} moderate at time of observation.

64		Rain, not freezing, intermittent	heavy at time of observation.
65		Rain, not freezing, continuous	
66		Rain, freezing, slight	
67		Rain, freezing, moderate or heavy.	
68		Rain or drizzle and snow, slight.	
69		Rain or drizzle and snow, moderate or heavy.	

Solid precipitation not in showers (70–79).

70		Intermittent fall of snow flakes	slight at time of observation.
71		Continuous fall of snow flakes	
72		Intermittent fall of snow flakes	moderate at time of observation.
73		Continuous fall of snow flakes	
74		Intermittent fall of snow flakes	heavy at time of observation.
75		Continuous fall of snow flakes	
76		Ice needles (with or without fog).	
77		Granular snow (with or without fog).	
78		Isolated starlike snow crystals (with or without fog)	
79		Ice pellets.	

Showery precipitation (80–99)

80		Rain shower(s), slight
81		Rain shower(s) moderate or heavy.
82		Rain shower(s) violent
83		Shower(s) of rain and snow mixed, slight.

84  Shower(s) of rain and snow mixed, moderate or heavy.

85  Snow shower(s), slight

86  Snow shower(s) moderate or heavy.

87 

88 

} slight at time of observation.

89 

90 

} slight.
moderate at time of observation.

91  Slight rain at time of observation

92  Moderate or heavy rain at time of observation.

93 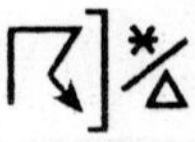 Slight snow or rain and snow mixed or hail* at time of observation

94 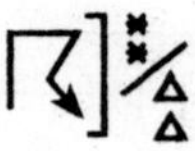 Moderate or heavy snow or rain and snow mixed or hail*

} thusderstorm during the preceding hour but not at time of observation.

95  Thunderstorm, slight or moderate, without hail* but with rain and/or snow at time of observation

96  Thunderastorm, slight or moderate, with hail* at time of observation

97  Thunderstorm, heavy, without hail* but with rain and/or snow

98  Thunderstorm combined with dust-storm or sand-storm

99  Thunderstorm, heavy, with hail*

} thusderstorm during the preceding hour but not at time of observation.

Note : (1) In general, the highest applicable figure should be selected. (2) Whenever the description 'intermittent' is used, the fog or precipitation has not continued without break during the preceding hour.
* Hail, small hail, soft hail.

(v) Code for Past Weather *W*

Code Figure	*Symbol*	*Description*
0		Fair (clear or slightly clouded).
1		Variable sky.
2		Mainly overcast.
3		Sandstorm or duststorm, or storm of drifting snow.
4		Fog or thick dust haze (visibility less than 1,000 metres.)
5		Drizzle
6		Rain.
7		Snow or Sleet.
8		Showers. *
9		Thunderstorms.*

* **Note :** *If with hail, the word "hail" should be reported at the end of the message.*

(vi) Code for Characteristic of Barometer Tendency (a)

Code Figure	*Symbol*	*Description*	
0		Rising then falling.	
1		Rising then steady : *or rising then rising more slowly.*	
2		Unsteady.	Barometer now higher than, or the same as, 3 hours ago.
3		Steady or rising.	
4		Falling or steady, then rising, *or rising then rising more quickly.*	
5		Falling then rising.	
6		Falling then steady; *or falling then falling more slowly.*	
7		Unsteady.	Barometer now lower than 3 hours ago.
8		Falling.	
9		Steady or rising then falling; *or falling then falling more quickly.*	

(vii) Code for Form of, *Low Cloud C_L*

Code Figure	*Symbol*	*Form of Cloud*
0		No low cloud
1		Fair weather Cu
2		Large Cu without anvil
3		Cb without cirrus at top
4		Sc formed by the spreading out of Cu
5		Layer of Sc
6		St
7	- - -	Ragged low clouds of bad weather
8	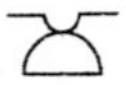	Cu and Sc
9	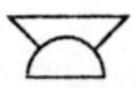	Cb with anvil

(viii) Code for Form of Medium Cloud C_M

Code Figure	*Symbol*	*Form of Cloud*
0		No medium cloud
1		Typical As (thin)
2		Typical As (thick) : sun or moon invisible, or Ns
3		Single layer of Ac or high Sc
4		Ac in isolated bands (often lenticular)
5		Ac in bands increasing
6		Ac formed from the spreading out of Cu
7		Ac associated with As, or As with parts resembling Ac
8		Ac Castellatus (or Ac in ragged fragments)
9		Ac in several layers generally associated with fibrous veils and a chaotic appearance of the sky.

(ix) Code for Form of High Cloud C_H

Code Figure	*Symbol*	*Form of Cloud*
0		No cirriform cloud
1		Fine Ci not increasing : sparse
2		Fine Ci not increasing : abundant but not a continuous layer
3		Anvil Ci (usually dense)
4		Fine Ci increasing : usually in tufts
5		Ci and Cs increasing : still below 45° altitude : often in polar bands
6		Ci or Cs increasing and reaching above 45° altitude : often in polar bands
7		Veil of Cs covering the whole sky
8		Cs not increasing and not covering the whole sky
9		Cc predominating

(x) Code for Height of Base of Cloud *h*

Code Figure	*Metres*			*Feet*		
0	0	to	50	0	to	150
1	50	to	100	150	to	300
2	100	to	200	300	to	600
3	200	to	300	600	to	1,000
4	300	to	600	1,000	to	2,000
5	600	to	1,000	2,000	to	3,000
6	1,000	to	1,500	3,000	to	5,000
7	1,500	to	2,000	5,000	to	6,500
8	2,000	to	2,500	6,500	to	8,000
9	No Cloud below 2,500			No cloud below 8,000		

Note : (1) If there is not cloud at all, figure 9 is reported.

(2) If there is fog, and the sky is discernible through the fog, the cloud form, height and amount are reported as if no fog were present. If the sky is not discernible through the fog the height of the base of the cloud is reckoned as o and, for statistical purposes, the cloud amount is reckoned as 10.

(xi) Code for Height above Mean Sea Level $h_s h_s$

Code Figure	Metres	Feet (Approx.)
00	Lower than 30	Lower than 100
01	30	100
02	60	200
03	90	300
04	120	400
05	150	500
06	180	600
07	210	700
08	240	800
09	270	900
10	300	1,000

Continue in same increments up to code figure 80.

Code Figure	Metres	Feet (Approx.)
78	2,340	7,800
79	2,370	7,900
80	2,400	8,000
81	2,700	9,000
82	not used	
83	3,000	10,000
84	4,000	13,000
86	5,000	16,000
87	6,000	20,000
88	7,000 8,000	23,000 26,000
89	9,000 or higher	30,000 or higher
90	less than 50 m.	
91	50 to 100 m.	
92	100 to 200 m.	
93	200 to 300 m.	
94	300 to 600 m.	
95	600 to 1,000 m.	
96	1,000 to 1,500 m.	
97	1,500 to 2,000 m.	
98	2,000 to 2,500 m.	
99	No cloud below 2,500 m.	

Note :
1. If the height of cloud base is between two of the heights given in the table, the code figures for the lower height will be reported, e.g., if the height is 3,900 m. code figures 83 will be reported.
2. In the decade 90–99, a height exactly equal to one of the heights in the table will be reported by the higher code figures. e.g., a height of 600 m will be reported by code figures 95.

(xii) Code for Day of Week *Y*

Code Figure	*Day*	*Code Figure*	*Day*
1	Sunday	5	Thursday
2	Monday	6	Friday
3	Tuesday	7	Saturday
4	Wednesday		

(xiii) Code for Octant of the Globe Q

Code Figure			*Code Figure*		
0	0 – 90 W		5	0 – 90 W	
1	90 – 180 W		6	90 – 180 W	
2	180 – 90 E	Northern	7	180 – 90 W	Southern
3	90 – 00 E		8	90 – 0 E	

(xiv) Code for Ship's Course, d_s

Code Figure	*Description*	*Code Figure*	*Description*	*Code Figure*	*Description*
0	Stationary	3	S.E.	6	W.
1	N.E.	4	S.	7	N.W.
2	E.	5	S.W.	8	N.

(xv) Code for Ship's Speed in Knots v_s

Code Number		*Code Number*		*Code Number*	
0	0	4	10 – 12	7	19 – 21
1	1 – 3	5	13 – 15	8	22 – 24
2	4 – 6	6	16 – 18	9	> 24
3	7 – 9				

Surface code for inland and coastal stations

R	R	R	D_L	D_M
N	d	d	f	f
V	V	w	w	W
P	P	P	T	T
N_h	C_L	h	C_M	C_H
T_d	T_d	9	P_{24}	P_{24}
6	P_0	P_0	P_0	P_0
7	R	R	T_n/T_x	T_n/T_x

D_L → Direction from which low cloud is coming to the station.

D_M → Direction from which medium cloud is coming to the station.

$P_{24}P_{24}$ → Change of barometric pressure during last 24 hours.

$P_0P_0P_0P_0$ → Station level pressure in mb and a tenth of mb.

RRR → amout of rainfall in mm and tenth of mm.

T_nT_n → minimum temperature in whole degree celsius

T_xT_x → maximum temperature in whole degree celsius to be reported in the afternoon observation time.

(Other codes are given earlier)

Direction of low cloud (D_L) and medium cloud (D_M)

Code No.	Description	Code No.	Description
0	No cloud	5	South-West
1	North-East	6	West
2	East	7	North-West
3	South-East	8	North
4	South	9	No definite direction

Change of borometric pressure during last 24 hours ($P_{24}P_{24}$)

Code No.	Description
00	No change
01	Pressure has risen by 0.1 mb
02	Pressure has risen by 0.2 mb
03	Pressure has risen by 0.3 mb
04	Pressure has risen by 0.4 mb
05	Pressure has risen by 0.5 mb
06 –48	Pressure has risen by 0.6 – 4.8 mb
49	Pressure has risen by 4.9 mb
50	Pressure has risen/fallen by more than 4.9 mb
51	Pressure has fallen by 0.1 mb
52	Pressure has fallen by 0.2 mb
53	Pressure has fallen by 0.3 mb
54	Pressure has fallen by 0.4 mb
55	Pressure has fallen by 0.5 mb
56–98	Pressure has fallen by 0.6–4.8 mb
99	Pressure has fallen by 4.9 mb

RAINFALL AMOUNT (RR)

Code No.	Rainfall Amount in mm.	Code No.	Rainfall Amount in mm.
01	0.5 – 1.5	27	26.5 – 27.5
02	1.5 – 2.5	28	27.5 – 28.5
03	2.5 – 3.5	29	28.5 – 29.5
04	3.5 – 4.5	30	29.5 – 30.5
05	4.5 – 5.5	31	30.5 – 31.5
06	5.5 – 6.5	32	31.5 – 32.5
07	6.5 – 7.5	33	32.5 – 33.5
08	7.5 – 8.5	34	33.5 – 34.5
09-24	8.5 – 24.5	35-49	34.5 – 49.5
25	24.5 – 25.5	50	49.5 – 50.5
26	25.5 – 26.5	51	50.5 – 51.5
52	51.5 – 52.5	65	145 – 155
53	52.5 – 53.5	66	155 – 165
54	53.5 – 54.5	67	165 – 175
55	54.5 – 55.5	68	175 – 185
56	55.5 – 64.9	69	185 – 195
57	65.0 – 75.0	70	195 – 205
58	75.1 – 84.9	71 – 86	205 – 355
59	85.0 – 95.0	87	355 – 365
60	95.1 – 104.9	88	365 – 375
61	105.0 – 115.0	89	375 – 385
62	115 – 125	90	395 – 405
63	125 – 135	98	More than 405
64	135 – 145	99	Measurement not possible

INTERPRETATION OF WEATHER MAP

The interpretation of a weather map is a sequential way of determining the general condition of weather of the day and the preconditions for the next few hours. If the study is made for a few consecutive days, the regional trend of changes of various weather phenomena can be understood.

TABLE 3.17
STATION DATA

Sl. No.	Stations	RRR	N	dd	ff	VV	ww	W	PPP	TT	N_h	C_L	h	C_M	C_H	TdTd	Q	$P_{24}P_{24}$
1	Carnicobar	000	5	23	02	96	03	2	113	28	5	2	5	0	0	24	9	1
2	Guahati	211	8	05	03	97	02	5	053	28	5	6	3	3	0	25	9	0
3	Agartala	464	8	00	00	97	02	2	076	27	3	7	1	3	0	22	9	0
4	Calcutta*	546	8	14	02	94	05	9	025	25	6	3	4	2	—	25	9	1
5	Sagar Island	023	6	20	19	96	03	2	026	25	6	7	5	0	0	27	9	1
6	Cuttak	000	5	23	03	98	02	2	046	21	5	0	9	7	0	27	9	0
7	Sambalpur	020	8	25	01	97	03	6	028	31	4	4	6	2	1	25	9	0
8	Patna	288	8	02	06	96	51	6	006	26	3	7	6	2	7	25	9	0
9	Allahabad	000	6	09	02	96	02	2	019	25	1	0	9	3	0	23	9	0
10	Agra	000	6	00	00	97	02	0	092	29	0	0	9	0	0	20	9	1
11	Delhi	000	1	14	04	96	02	0	095	36	0	0	9	0	0	23	9	0
12	Ludhiana	000	0	18	01	97	02	0	097	32	0	0	9	0	0	23	9	1
13	Jodhpur	000	2	22	24	96	12	0	026	33	6	0	9	0	1	22	9	1
14	Jaipur	000	0	32	14	95	02	0	096	34	0	0	9	0	0	20	9	0
15	Gwalior	000	3	27	19	97	01	6	018	36	4	3	9	4	0	23	9	1
16	Bhopal	060	7	34	11	97	01	2	036	24	2	1	6	0	9	23	9	1
17	Ahmedabad	000	5	18	10	97	02	0	058	27	4	5	5	3	0	25	9	1
18	Bombay	088	8	18	12	95	01	6	031	30	3	5	5	2	—	24	9	0
19	Sholapur	118	4	33	02	99	01	1	087	27	2	4	6	3	0	21	9	1
20	Nagpur	000	6	25	05	99	02	2	048	25	2	4	6	0	—	24	9	1
21	Coimbatore	000	4	23	09	96	02	1	101	27	2	1	6	6	1	20	9	1
22	Madras	000	2	27	15	97	02	0	087	32	0	0	9	0	2	19	9	0
23	Mysore	000	4	21	13	96	03	1	113	22	2	2	4	1	—	19	9	1
24	Trivandrum	030	3	36	02	98	02	0	119	27	3	2	5	0	0	23	9	0

* Kolkata

Pressure condition

Pressure condition is the basic atmospheric control on which the local and regional wind circulation depend. A general trend of isobars, their proximity to each other, loops formed by isobars, the circularity and formation of other enclosing isobars, location of barometric low or high over the continent or ocean etc. help to determine the prevalent control over the weather of the day. Not only that, the location of a low pressure and high pressure over the continent or ocean can also depict the seasonal trend of pressure system over the Indian sub-continent following the northing or southing of the sun, even if the date is not mentioned. It should, of course, take into account the prevalent direction of wind movement and the other associated weather phenomena.

In general, during the summer (pre-monsoon hot weather) there develops a low pressure over the north-west of the Indian sub-continent, whereas, in the south of the sub-continent higher pressure prevails over the Indian ocean. The opposite is true during the post-monsoon season when a high pressure system develops over the Indian sub-continent and a low pressure develops over the Indian ocean. But variations from these general trends are also frequent particularly during the formation of cyclones over the Bay of Bengal or the Arabian sea.

A cross section across the isobars may reveal the nature of pressure gradient which determines the velocity and direction of wind, i.e., steeper the gradient, higher the velocity and vice versa. Moreover, the general direction of movement of winds will be from high to low pressure areas. A very gentle pressure gradient with only two or three isobars on the sub-continent favours a gentle breeze with haphazard direction. A major low pressure with circular and enclosed isobars may give rise to a cyclonic circulation of winds whirling in anticlockwise direction surrounding the low. Similarly, a high pressure over central India during the season of retreating monsoon may cause anti-cyclonic divergence of winds. A trough, on the other hand, during the summer monsoon with its axis being located, more or less, over the Ganga plain is indicated by the opposite direction winds on both sides of the trough axis. If the trough is located towards the foot hills of the Himalayas, the monsoon seems to be weaker than the season when the trough axis is located towards the Bihar-plateau.

The difference of the pressure status between land and ocean may creat loops on isobars with a sudden bend of the isobars along the littoral region.

Wind Condition

As mentioned earlier wind direction and velocity are given in weather maps. Wind flags are attached to the circle of the cloud cover. It comes from the direction of the flag and moves towards the circle of cloud cover. In Indian weather maps the velocity of the wind is given at an interval of 5 knots, i.e., 5, 10, 15, 20, 25 etc. A direction without any bar or flag means that the velocity is so low that it is not measurable. Therefore, it can be taken as a calm condition.

In general, wind movement over the Indian sub-continent is south-westerly in the summer monsoon season, northerly and north westerly during the post-monsoon, north-easterly in the winter and haphazard without any major prevalent direction during the pre-monsoon season. But it does not necessarily mean that all the stations will show such a prevalence of wind direction following the trend of wind movement of the season. Even stations at close proximity may show different directions. However, the prevalence is determined on the basis of the maximum number attained by a particular direction. For this purpose, on the basis of the frequency for eight directions (E, W, N, S, NE, SE, NW, SW) a wind rose diagram may be prepared. This will explain the general trend of occurrence of a particular direction diagrammatically. Stream lining can be proved effective in determining the prevalent direction of wind. For this purpose different symbols may be given to different sets of stream lines. Ultimately from the spread of stream lines and their encroachment the prevalent direction is determined.

Besides, the change in wind velocity may be correlated with the pressure gradient. It is often noted that wind-velocity changes with the change in spacing of isobars, that is, with the change in pressure gradient.The isobar, from which the steeper or gentler gradient starts, may be shown as the boundary on a sketch map between areas of higher and lower velocities. This will show the relationship between the nature of the gradient of slope and wind velocity. The northern limit of summer monsoon is indicated by NLM. That should be mentioned specifically.

Some other small sketches for cyclonic circulation, anti-cyclonic divergence, opposite inward direction of winds flanking a trough-axis, or opposite outward direction of winds flanking a ridge-axis may be drawn for better representation.

A. Beaufort's scale (1806) indicating the various types of wind velocities with a specific range of wind speed associated with a specific observation made about the plants and trees, human beings etc. should be used for understanding and interpreting the effects of a particular wind velocity. The following table depicts the range of wind speed and related observations :

TABLE 3.18

BEAUFORT SCALE FOR WIND SPEED

Beaufort no.	Wind	Arrow	Speed m.p.h.	Speed km. p.h.	Common effects
0	Calm		0	0	Calm, smoke rises vertically.
1	Light air		2	3.34	Direction of wind shown by smoke drift, but not by wind vanes.
2	Light breeze		5	8.35	Wind felt on face ; leaves rustle; ordinary vane moved by wind.
3	Gentle breeze		10	16.7	Leaves and small twigs in constant motion, wind extends light flag.
4	Moderate breeze		15	25.05	Raises dust and loose paper, small branches are moved.
5	Fresh breeze		21	35.07	Small trees in leaf begin to sway, crested wavelets form on in land waters.
6	Strong breeze		28	46.76	Large branches in motion; whistling heard in telegraph wires, umbrellas used with difficulty.
7	Moderate gale		35	58.45	Whole tree in motion ; inconvenience felt when walking against wind
8	Fresh gale	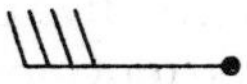	42	70.14	Breaks twigs off trees; generally impedes progress.
9	Strong gale	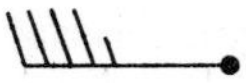	50	83.5	Slight structural damage occurs (chimney, pots and slates removed).
10	Whole gale		59	98.53	Seldom experienced inland; trees uprooted, considerably structural damage occurs.
11	Storm		69	115.23	Very rarely experienced, accompanied by widespread damage.
12	Hurricane		above 75	125.25	Most destructive.

Sky condition

The sky condition in such weather maps is shown by the amount of cloud cover in the sky (in octal), and occurrence of features like haze, thunderstorm, hail, squall etc. However, the actual sky condition is revealed only through the amount of cloud. Whether the type of cloud present in the sky is low, medium or high is also indicated by symbols, for low and medium cloud it is marked by solid black and for high cloud it is by using screen of vertical lines within the circle. These symbols or screens of black have a clock-wise rotation form 1/8 of sky cover to the overcast condition. An obscured sky is also marked symbolically by a cross.

For representation of the nature of distribution of cloud as sky-cover an isoneph map may be prepared. This will identify the zones having the same amount of cloud cover. For this purpose interpolation between the actual cloud covers should be done. The cloud amounts may be converted into percentages which will give a simpler impression.

Zones of cloudless sky and zones of overcast are particularly important because of the extreme variability in the chances of occurrence of rainfall. Moreover, the advent of the summer monsoon and its advancement over the sub-continent is marked by cloud and rain in the areas of its arrival and cloudless sky in the areas yet to be reached by it. Moreover, the overcast sky may cause a rise in night temperature.

A haze is usually developed over an urban area which is highly industrialized. A thunderstorm gives rise to a troubled weather for the next few hours. A squall is another violent blast of wind. Squall and thunderstorms may occur during pre-monsoon season.

Precipitation

The occurrence of rainfall during the last 24 hours is marked by its amount in centimetre. Less than 1 cm. of rainfall is marked by symbols of dot and dash. Rainfall may occur due to the incoming summer monsoon, due to the formation of a cyclone, due to the occurrence of thunderstorm, due to the retreating monsoon over south India, due to westerly disturbances during winter, due to the formation of local convection cell over the southern part of West Bengal etc. So many causes are there. The interpreter is to judge which one is the right cause for a particular sequence of rainfall. As mentioned earlier the limit line for the advancement of summer monsoon is preceded by cloudless and rainless condition, whereas it is succeeded by the overcast sky and occurrence of widespread rain. Rainfall due to cyclone or other depressions may cover considerable areas. Rainfall related to thunderstorm or convective cell is a localised phenomenon. The cyclonic precipitation moves regionally along with the movement of the storm. For instance, a storm may form over the Bay of Bengal and may move towards north, north east, north-west, west or south-west across the coast of Bangladesh, West Bengal, Orissa, Andhra Pradesh or Tamilnadu. Similar cyclonic storms may also form in the Arabian sea and they affect the west coast. However, such storms die out soon or lose their intensity after they encroach over the sub-continent. Drizzle may occasionally precede a cyclone. Many other occurrences of such minor forms of precipitations related to the particular weather condition are often observed.

Hail storm is another form of precipitation which occurs in association with thunderstorm. Snowfall is another form of precipitation particularly observed in the Himalayan mountains during winter season.

For the purpose of obtaining an idea about the regional distribution of rainfall, isohyets at suitable interval may be drawn interpolating between the various amounts of rainfall at different stations. If rainfall occurrences are limited in extent over a part of the sub-continent, isohyets may be drawn only for the region where rainfall has occurred. On a separate sketch map these isohyets will be drawn. Rainfall zones may be identified and tinted with any colour of variable intensity for different lower to higher value zones, higher the rainfall, darker the colour given.

Moreover, if the occurrence of rainfall is very much regional, the zones, where there is no rainfall, should also be marked. In such rainfall distribution maps a distinct regional trend is noticed.

Sporadic occurrence of rainfall should only be marked by their amount and location on a separate sketch map of the Indian sub-continent.

The occurrence of other forms of precipitation may also be shown at their respective locations on a sketch map of the sub-continent. Besides, bar graphs can also be drawn on the basis of the frequency of such events.

Other Weather Phenomena

Solar and lunar halo, corona etc. are a few weather phenomena which are not shown in the weather map.

However, various storms may be given importance as they can cause a substantial change in weather conditions within a short span of time. Therefore, sketches for the distribution of deep depression, thunderstorm, sandstorm, dustdevil etc. should also be prepared. The associated weather phenomena of these storms, such as, rainfall, lightning, hail etc. should be incorporated in such sketches.

During winter fog or mist may form depending on the condensation of the moist air, the difference between them being identified on the basis of the range of visibility, the fog having less than 1000 metre and the mist having 1000 to 2000 metre range of visibility. They have different symbols.

Sea condition

The oceanic areas in the west, south and east of peninsular India are influenced by the impact of the weather features. The tropical cyclones have their origin over the Arabian sea and over the Bay of Bengal. These occur frequently as they are mostly embedded in the oceanic areas of tropical latitudes. From the oceanic areas they move towards the interior of the Indian sub-continent across the west coast and east coast of India and they die out ultimately over the land areas.

Besides, any strong winds blowing over the oceanic areas can cause roughness on the sea. The weather maps identify variable intensity of roughness on the sea surface due to the fetch of strong wind, otherwise, the sea surface remains normal, i.e. 'calm' or 'smooth'. Obviously, predictions about such information of roughness of the sea are of great importance to the sailors and fishermen in particular.

The sea conditions are shown by abbreviations of descriptive terms expressing the variable character of sea surface ranging form 'calm' to 'very rough'.

For representation of such features a sketch map showing the wind flags, sea condition indicated by abbreviations along with curved arrow with an outline of Indian coast may prove useful. Thus both the cause and effect of the particular sea condition may be shown diagrammatically.

Identification of season

If the date of the given weather map is not mentioned at the top, the student may require to identify the season from a broad perspective on the basis of the relevant condition of various elements of weather. For this purpose the particular study should incorporate the following points which will help the student identify the prevalence of one of the four major seasons observed in the climate of the Indian sub-continent.

1. The prevalent direction of wind should be determined and if they follow any particular trend typical for any of the seasons, the season may be easily identified; e.g. prevalent south-westerly rain-bearing winds will indicate the season of summer monsoon;
2. If the northern limit of summer monsoon wind (N.L.M.) is indicated by dashed lines, the season obviously belongs to the summer monsoon ;
3. Summer monsoon will be determined by low pressure on land and high over the Indian ocean preferably with loops and trough over the Ganga plain;
4. Prevalent north-easterlies with high pressure on the sub-continent and low over the oceanic areas in the south indicate the winter season; in such a season fog and /or mist may occur; snowfall over the Himalayan belt is also probable; rainfall over Jammu and Kashmir, Punjab, Haryana is not unlikely ;
5. The season of returning monsoon is dominated by the withdrawal of summer monsoon in the form of prevalent north-westerlies and northerlies. In this season Tamilnadu coast may have cloud cover and rainfall with a divergent wind circulation over central India;
6. During the pre-monsoon season no major prevalence in wind direction is observed as winds are rather haphazard and most of the directions may contribute significantly or almost equally in the frequency of occurrence; sandstorm and/or duststorm may occur over Rajasthan, Uttarpradesh etc.; pre-monsoon squall may occur over northern, central or eastern region, thunderstorm over the eastern region, southern West Bengal is not unlikely; small and localised low pressure systems may develop over northern, eastern and central India and these may coalesce to form a widespread low pressure system;
7. Though the presence of the criteria mentioned above help to identify the season, a given date at the top of the weather map speaks more specifically about the season.

Forecasting

Prediction can be made about the future weather, i.e., what will be the weather of tomorrow, on the basis of understanding the weather of today. Major concentration in this regard should be given on the movement of cyclones and anticyclones as revealed by the pattern of isobars. Forecasts may be of short term, i.e., for the next 12 hours, or may be of long term i.e., for the next 24 to 48 hours. However, a synoptic chart is more useful in this regard as that contains more information about the stations of observation. Weather maps can also give a comprehensive view point towards forecasting the weather. The following aspects should be studied to obtain the idea about the future weather.

Movement of lows and highs **:** Usually the lows and highs move with the prevailing westerlies at an average velocity of about 30 to 35 miles (48–56 km)/hr. in winter and about 20 to 25 miles (32–40 km)/hr. is associated with the cyclones in pre-monsoon, monsoon & post-monsoon seasons. There are large individual variations from the average.

It tends to move with the same velocity and direction as during the next 12 to 24 hours in the absence of other indications. Strong winds in front of a low retard it. A low tends to move parallel to the isobars in the warm sector but to cross the isotherms, that is , to move toward an area of higher temperature it tends to travel towards the area where the greatest fall of pressure is occurring. Highs move towards the area where the greatest rise in pressure in occurring.

The distribution of pressure around the system under consideration influences its movement, the tendency is to move towards a region of gentler gradient and away from a region of steeper gradient. Consideration must be given to whether the low is increasing or decreasing in intensity or is likely to do so within the forecast period. A low with a marked pressure gradient but with weak winds around it will increase in intensity.

Forecasting about other phenomena : An overcast sky covered with low clouds may bring forth showers of rainfall within a few hours if the wind velocity is low. A higher velocity of wind, on the other hand, may take away the clouds elsewhere.

The prediction about the formation of a thunderstorm is not possible from simple weather maps as they do not incorporate any data about the type of cloud or formation of convective cell over an area. However, once the thunderstorm cloud is formed, as indicated by the conventional symbol for thunderstorm on weather map, it is apt to bring one or two showers of heavy rainfall with lightning and thunder. Such storms may bring hail stones if they are large enough and formed near the surface.

A cyclone or depression often brings rainfall. All low pressure systems do not necessarily reach the cyclonic or hurricane velocity. Therefore, the interpreter should check if the gale-velocity is reached. Moreover, how much fall of pressure occurs between the periphery and the centre of a low pressure is also important for a tropical cyclone. However, these maps do not have any information about the amount of dew point temperature which is also significant in this regard. Usually, a well-developed low with low velocity of wind will increase in intensity.

For nocturnal showers along the coast the following observations are important

1. Location of principal build-ups.
2. Time of beginning and dissipation of coast clouds.
3. Periods of principal showers along the coast.
4. Distances that showers cover towards inland.

Forecasts over open Sea : It is usually effective for aircrafts following some route over open sea. The prediction of movement of individual clouds and squall lines can be made for terminal conditions at seaports. The position of individual clouds is of little importance unless the pilot encounters the solid wall of cumulonimbus. But these features are not given in weather maps.

Example interpretation : 1

Monsoon condition

The given weather map (fig. no. 3.94) has shown the condition of various elements of weather over the Indian sub-continent. This weather map may be interpreted under the following sub-titles :

1. Pressure condition
   - a) Extent and range of isobars
   - b) Location of bar-low
   - c) Location of bar-high
   - d) Gradient of pressure
2. Wind condition
   - a) Prevalent direction of wind
   - b) Maximum and minimum velocity of wind
   - c) Special feature of wind system
3. Co-relation between pressure and wind condition

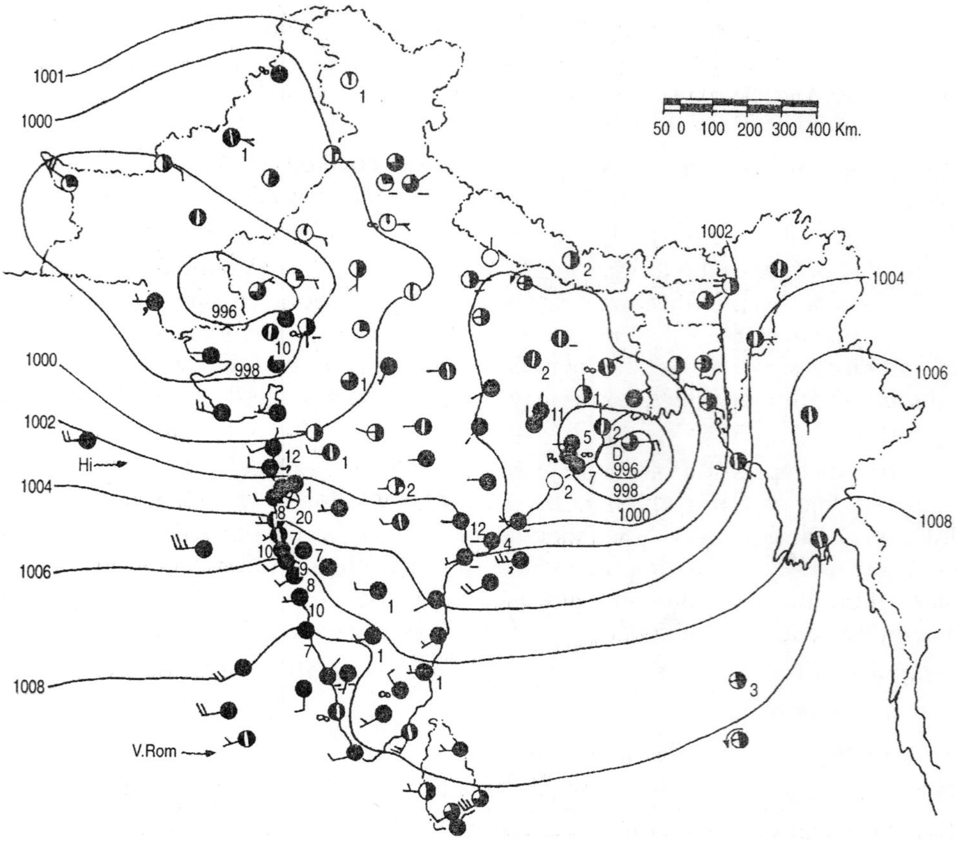

Fig. 3.104 Weather map no. 1 (isobars in millibar)

4. Distribution of cloud cover
5. Occurrence of rainfall and its distribution
6. Co-relation between cloud cover and rainfall occurrence
7. Special weather phenomena and their significance
8. Sea condition
9. Departure of maximum and minimum temperature from normal and their significance
10. Correlation among various weather elements
11. Identification of season

1. *Pressure condition*

a) *Extent and range of isobars :* In the given weather map the isobars range from 996 mb. to 1008 mb. (fig. no. 3.95). The lowest value is observed at enclosed isobars over the northern part of the Bay of Bengal and in the western part of Rajasthan surrounding Barmer, whereas, the highest value is observed over the southern part of the Arabian sea, Kerala, northern part the of Indian ocean and over the Andaman sea.

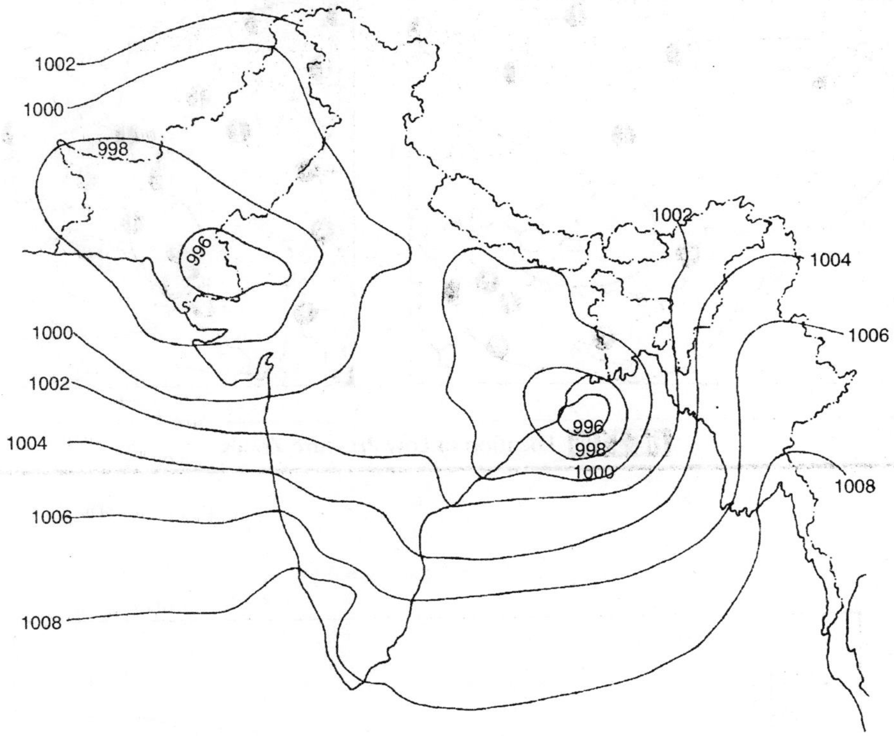

Fig. 3.105 **Distribution of Barometic Pressure (isobars in millibar)**

b) ***Location of bar low :*** Two low pressure zones (fig. no. 3.96) have been recognised over the area by enclosing isobars, one over western Rajasthan and Pakistan and the other over the northern part of the Bay of Bengal off Orissa coast. The low pressure zone over the bay has formed a depression with two other enclosing isobars extending the influence upto the eastern part of Uttar Pradesh. The western low pressure zone is less strong, though well recognised.

c) ***Location of bar high :*** The northern part of the Indian ocean has shown a high pressure zone delineated by 1008 mb. isobar.

This reveals the fact that there was high over the ocean and low over the sub-continent on the day when the weather- observations were made.

d) ***Gradient of pressure :*** In general, the pressure gradient is gentler over the southern part of the Arabian sea and over the Andaman sea in the south of 1006 mb. isobar.

In the north of it, the gradient is steeper and the maximum steepness is observed in the southern periphery of the depression over the Bay of Bengal (fig. no 3.97).

2. *Wind Condition*

a) ***Prevalent direction of wind :*** From the stream lines it is observed that the prevalent direction is from west and south west (fig. no. 3.98).

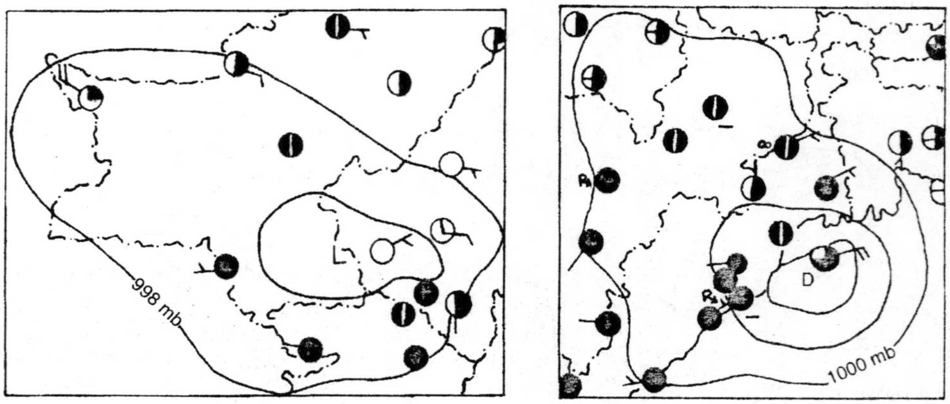

Fig. 3.106 **Location of Low Pressure Zones**

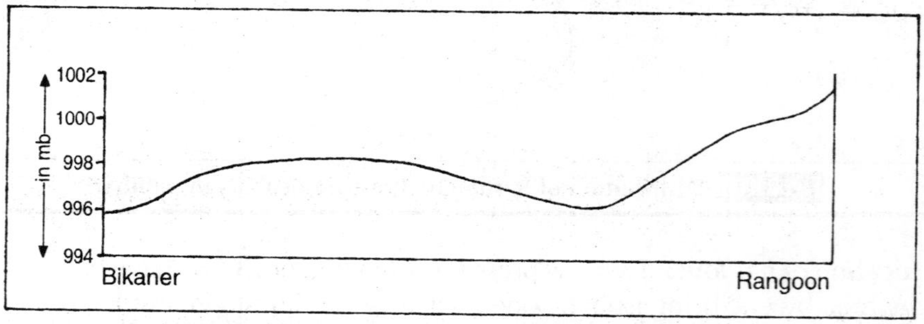

Fig. 3.107 **Profile of Pressure Variation (Bikaner to Rangoon)**

b) ***Maximum and minimum velocity of wind :*** Table no. 3.15 reveals that the maximum wind velocity was 25 knots on the given day. It is observed for the winds from westerly direction (fig. no. 3.99). The minimum velocity (5 knots) is observed in the winds from south-east and north-east. This attaches relatively more importance to the westerly winds over the other winds from other directions.

c) ***Special feature of wind system :*** Over north India, central India, north-eastern India and north-western part of the sub-continent winds are not very strong and have a light breeze character. On the contrary, towards the southern part of the peninsula and also in the middle part, as well as over the northern part of the Bay and over the Arabian sea, winds are stronger and have a strong breeze character.

3. ***Correlation between pressure and wind condition :*** In general, higher velocity of winds has been observed on the areas with steeper gradient of pressure.

In the surroundings of the two low pressure zones, one forming a depression, winds have shown a whirling character. Obviously, these are anti-clockwise in direction.

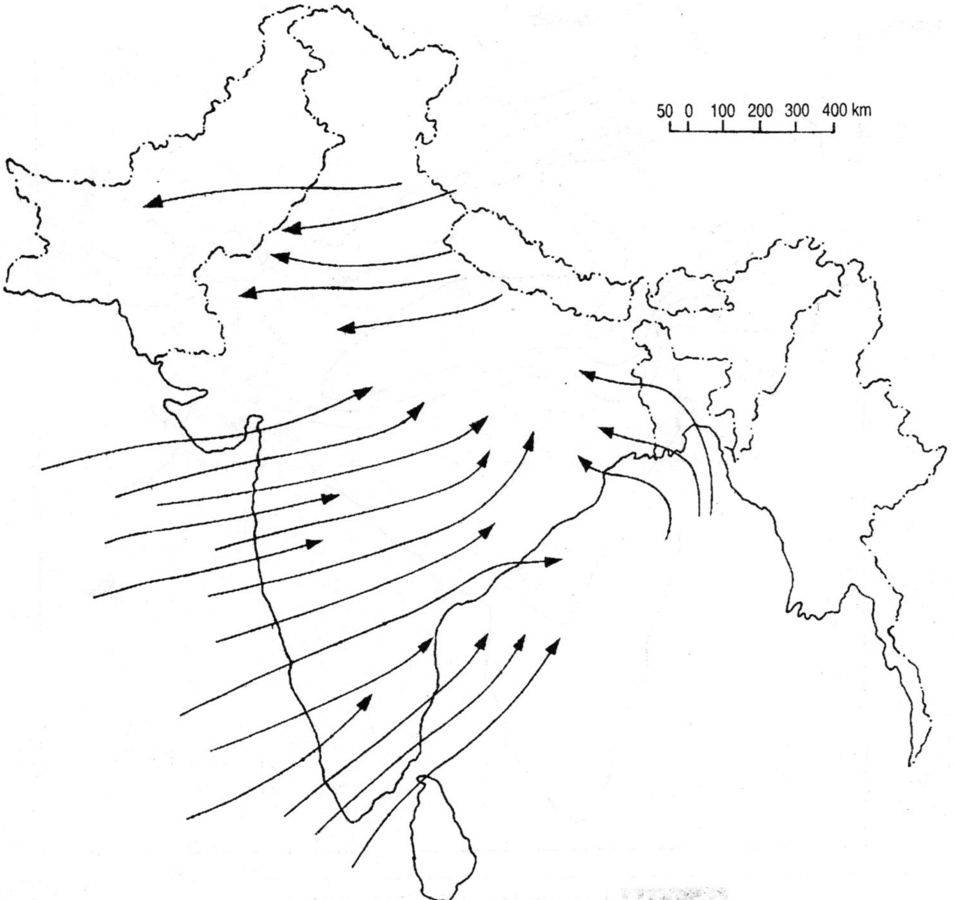

Fig. 3.108 Streamlines of wind movement

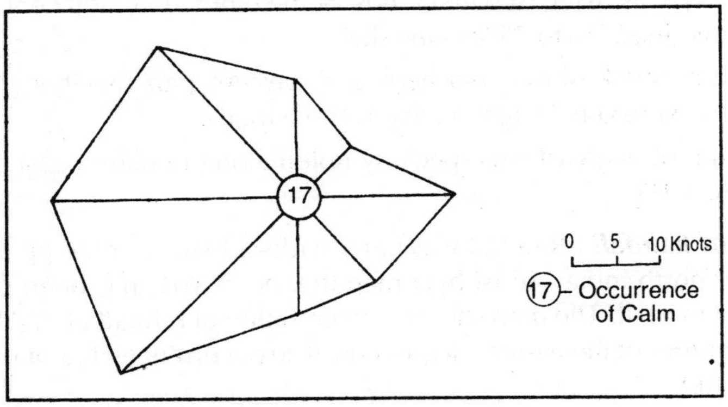

Fig. 3.109 Highest wind velocity from different directions

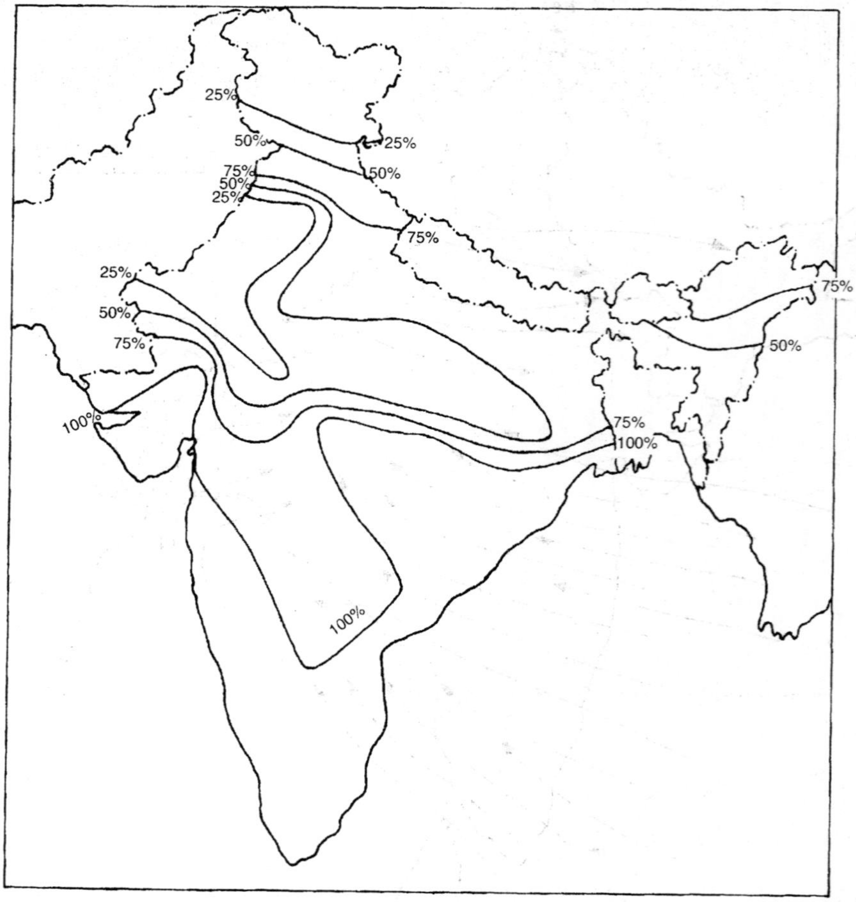

Fig. 3.110 **Isoneph Map (distribution of cloud cover)**

4. ***Distribution of cloud cover :*** On the day when the observations were made, almost the entire southern half of the sub-continent had cloud cover of considerable amount. In most of the areas the sky was overcast with clouds. Some other areas adjacent to them were having low clouds covering 25% to 75% of the sky.

   Over Jammu and Kashmir, northern and western part of Uttar Pradesh, over part of Rajasthan there were very insignificant cover of cloud.

   A continuum of overcast was specially noted along Konkon coast and over the coast of Orissa (fig. no. 3.100).

5. ***Occurrence of Rainfall :*** Rainfall was fairly wide-spread over the peninsula, though it was sporadic over north India. An isohyet map (fig. no. 3.101) has been prepared to show the distribution of rainfall. The map shows concentration of rainfall along the Konkan coast and in the surroundings of the eastern depression. The occurrence of rainfall was also noted over Port Blair (3 cm.).

   The highest amount of rainfall received was 20 cm. in Ratnagiri area, whereas, the lowest was below 1 cm. (less than 0.75 cm.) over north India.

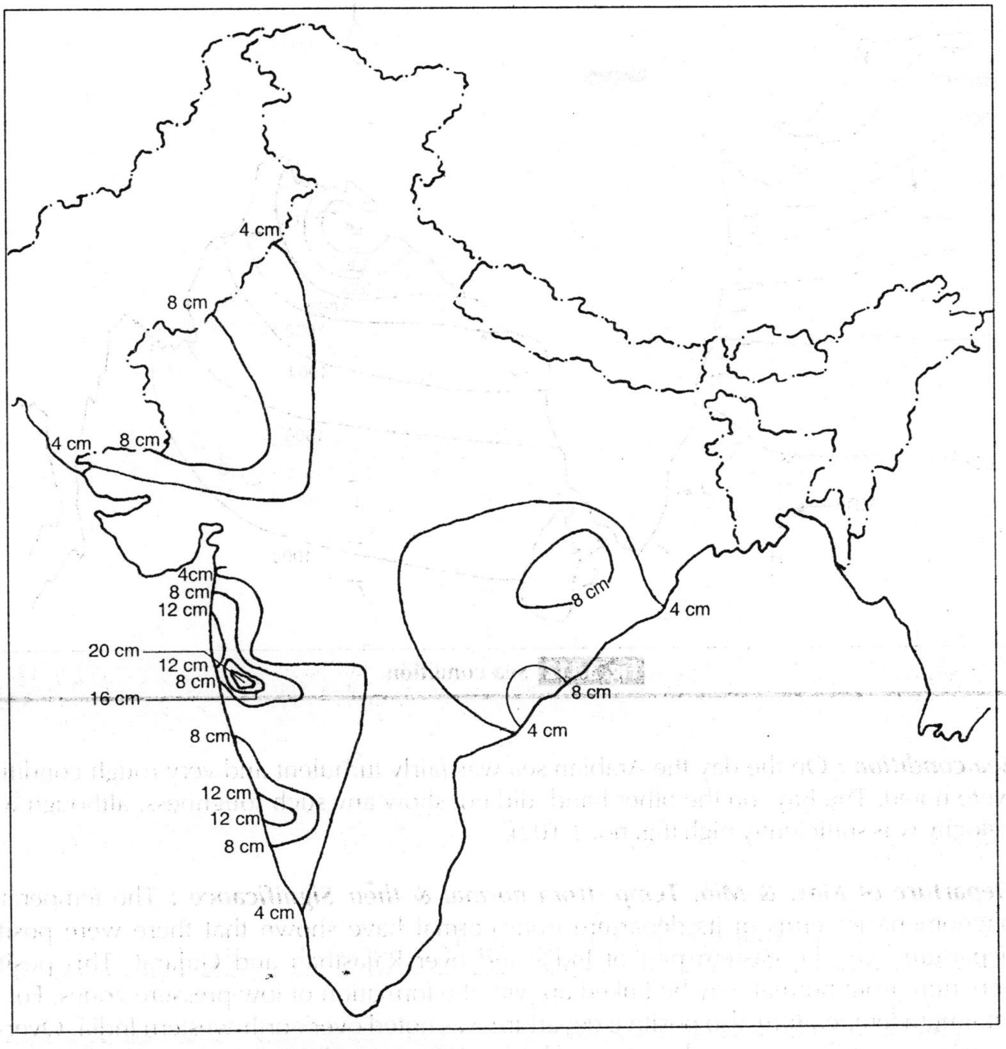

Fig. 3.111 **Isohyet map (distribution of rainfall)**

6. ***Correlation between cloud cover and rainfall occurrence :*** As mentioned earlier the Konkan coast has a dense cloud cover along with another counter part over the Orissa coast. Consequently, these two areas have shown the greatest concentration of rainfall. The areas with low cloud cover did not receive any rainfall in general, except for a few sporadic occurrences.

7. ***Special weather phenomena and their significance :*** The occurrence of a thunderstorm has been noted over the coast of Orissa in north-west of Kataka. This Thunderstorm is perhaps linked with the depression formed over the area. The area has shown sufficient rainfall too.

The occurrence of haze has been particularly noted over Agra, Ahmedabad, Tiruchirapally, Cochin and one or two other areas. This occurrence of haze may be related to industrial pollution in those areas.

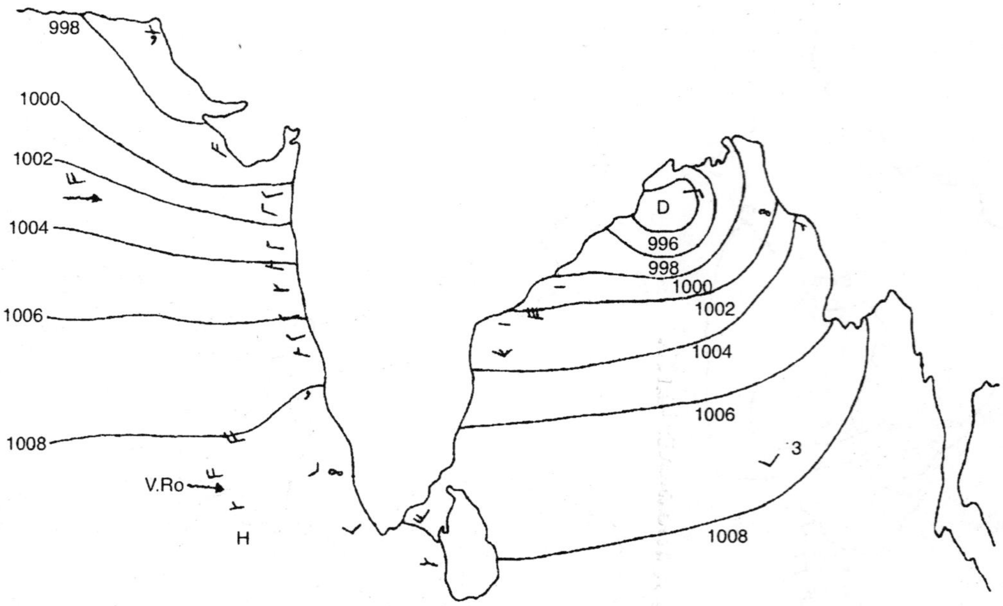

Fig. 3.112 **Sea condition**

8. ***Sea condition :*** On the day the Arabian sea was fairly turbulent and very rough conditions were noted. The Bay, on the other hand, did not show any such roughness, although wind velocity was sufficiently high (fig. no. 3.102).

9. ***Departure of Max. & Min. Temp. from normal & their Significance :*** The temperature phenomena in terms of its departure from normal have shown that there were positive departure over the eastern part of India and over Rajasthan and Gujarat. This positive departure from normal may be linked up with the formation of low pressure zones. For the minimum temperature also positive departure was noted over north-western India. Over the Malabar coast the positive departure of both minimum and maximum may be linked with the loops in the isobars (fig. no. 3.103a & b).

10. **Correlation among various weather elements :** A transect chart showing vertical correlation among various weather elements with pressure gradient at the base shows that the low pressure area has higher velocity of wind and maximum concentration of clouds. A thunder storm is also centred over there with another developed over slightly higher pressure area. Rainfall occurrence is also associated with the areas of greater cloud cover (fig. no. 3.104).

11. ***Identification of season :*** The general prevalence of the south-westerly winds, the location of low pressure over the land and high over the ocean, the occurrence of rainfall over peninsular India, particularly along Konkan coast, as associated with the overcast condition, low cover of clouds over north India indicate that the observations were made during the early part of the summer monsoon period.

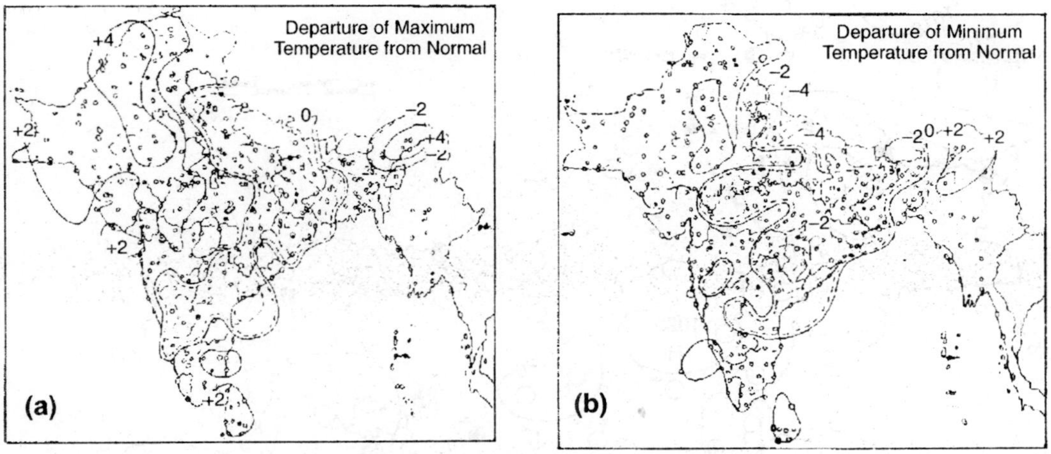

Fig. 3.113(a & b) Departure of maximum and minimum temperatures

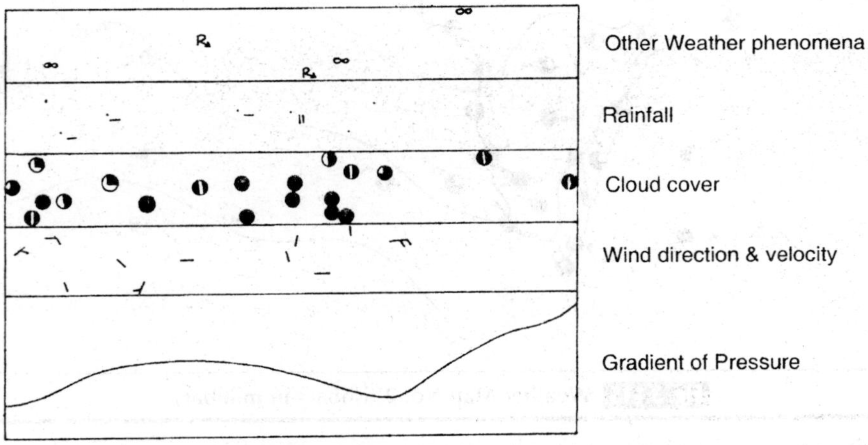

Fig. 3.114 Correlation among various weather elements

Example interpretation : 2

Winter Condition

The given weather map (fig. no. 3.105) shows the condition of various elements of weather over the Indian sub-continent. This weather map may be interpreted under the following sub-titles :

1. ***Pressure Condition***

   a) ***Extent of isobars :*** In the given weather map the isobars range from 1012 mb. to 1020 mb. The lowest value is observed over the Andaman sea, whereas, the highest value is observed at an enclosed isobar over the middle part of the Indian sub-continent.

   b) ***Location of bar low :*** Two low pressure zones have been recognised over the area by enclosing isobars, one over the middle of Pakistan and other over the north-west of the

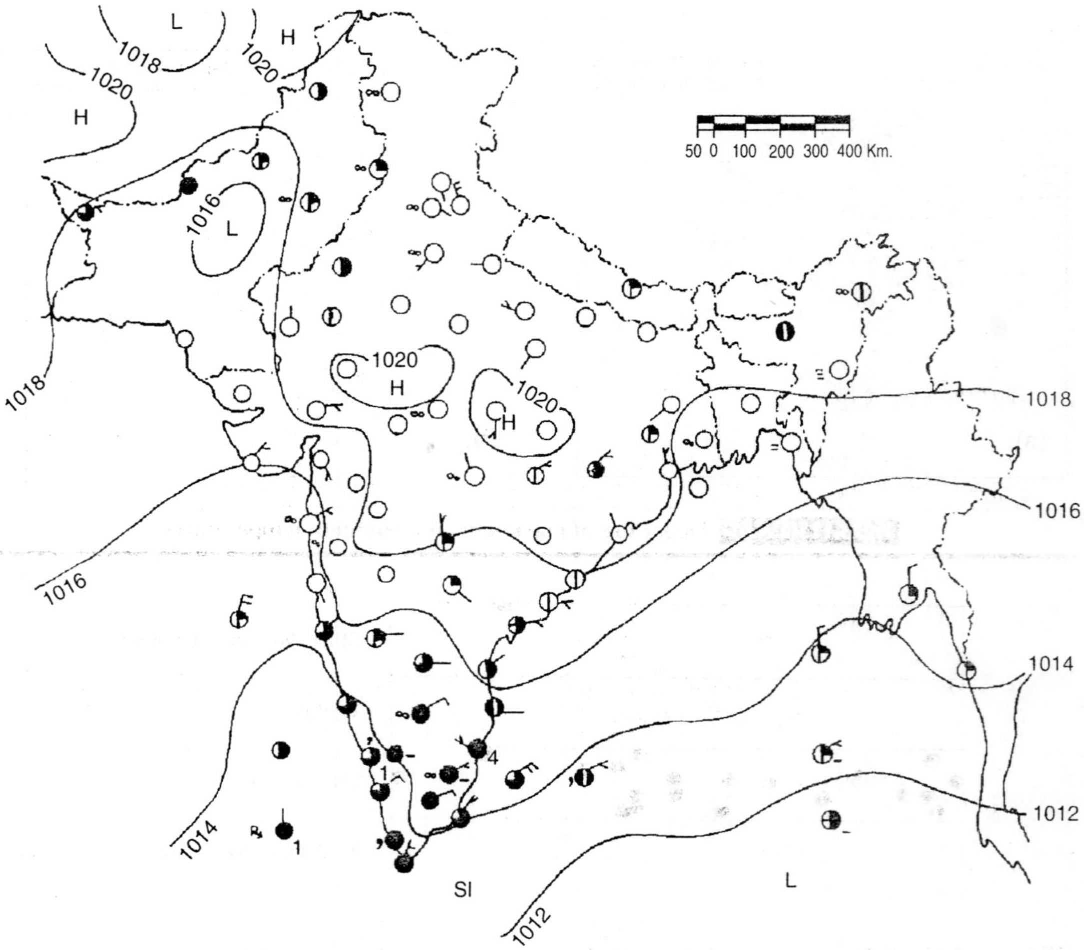

Fig. 3.115 Weather Map No. 2 (isobars in millibar)

sub-continent. Besides another low pressure zone is well recognised at the south of the Bay of Bengal over the Andaman sea as delineated by 1012 mb (fig. no. 3.106 & 3.107).

c) ***Location of bar high :*** The middle part of Indian sub-continent has shown a high pressure zone (fig. no. 3.108) enclosed by the 1020 mb. isobar and two other high pressure zones are shown at the north-western part of this sub-continent as delineated by 1020 mb. isobar.

d) ***Gradient of pressure :*** The gradient of pressure is gentle almost throughout India. The cross section connecting Simla and Tiruchirapally (fig. no. 3.109) has revealed this feature. However, over Madhya Pradesh there is a high pressure marked by 1020 mb. It may be noted here that the pressure gradient across the loop of the isobars along Konkan coast and western Maharashtra is steeper.

2. *Wind Condition*

a) ***Maximum and minimum velocity of wind :*** It reveals that the maximum wind velocity was 20 knots on the given day and is observed from north-east direction. The minimum velocity is observed (less than 5 knots) in the winds from the west. This attaches relatively more importance to the north-easterly winds over the other wind (fig. no. 3.110).

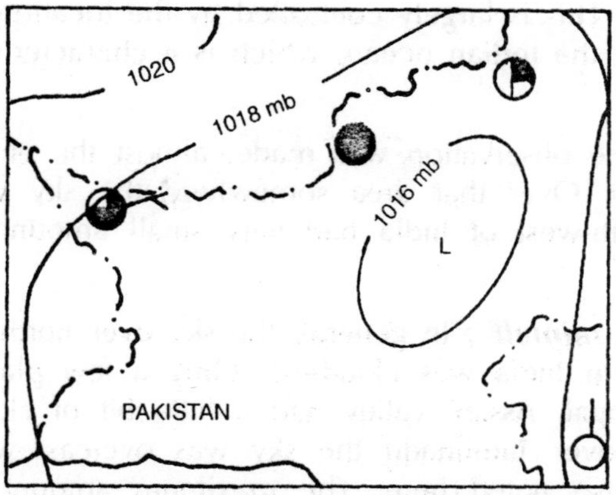

Fig. 3.116 Low over Pakistan

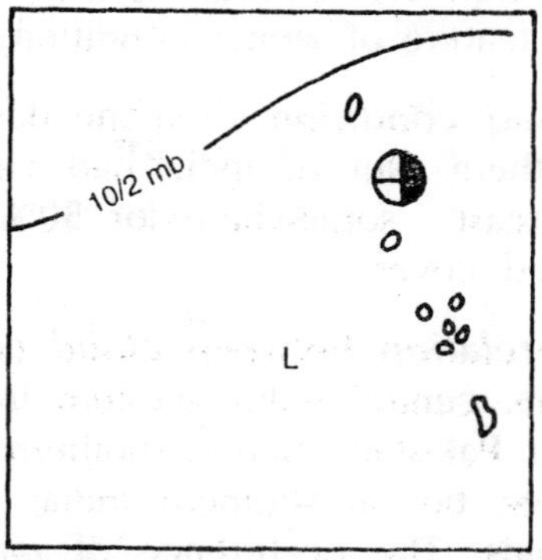

Fig. 3.117 Low over Andaman Sea

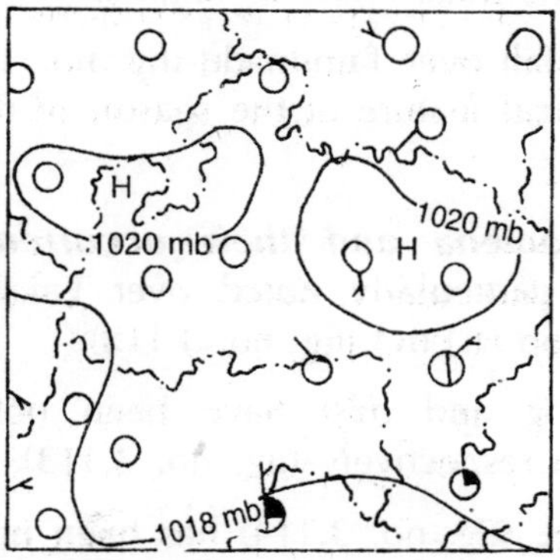

Fig. 3.118 High over Central India

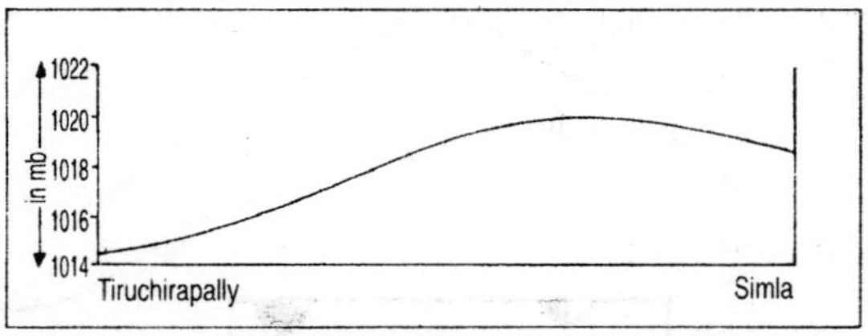

Fig. 3.119 Profile of Pressure Gradient (Tiruchirapally to Simla)

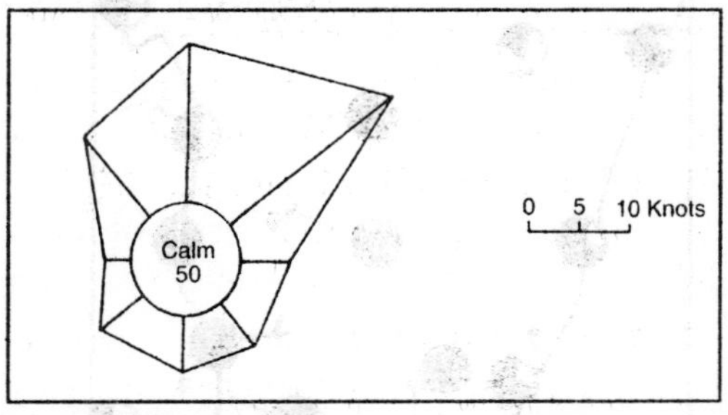

Fig. 3.120 Highest wind velocity from different directions

b) Correlation between pressure and wind condition : The high pressure zone over central India has caused a divergence of wind system. In general, winds are of low velocity being coherent with gentle gradient of pressure. The highest velocity of wind i.e. 20 knots has been observed at two places of which one is off the Konkan coast and another off the Coromondal coast. However, in general, winds are moving from continental area to the Indian ocean. This is largely controlled by the location of high over central India and low over the Indian ocean, which is a characteristic feature of winter condition.

3. ***Cloud condition*** : On the day when the observation was made, almost the entire southern part of India had cloud cover. Over that area somewhere the sky was overcast , somewhere for 50% and north-west of India had very small amount of cloud cover.

4. ***Correlation between cloud cover and rainfall*** : In general, the sky over northern India, central India, western India, eastern India was cloudless. Only a few places over Pakistan, Nepal, southern West Bengal, Assam valley had a little bit of cloud cover, but in southern India, specially over Tamilnadu the sky was overcast with clouds. The occurrence of rainfall is also noted here. The maximum amount of rainfall recorded is 4 cm., which occurred at Kuddalor. Besides, there were a few places such as Trivandrum, Kalikot etc., which had shown drizzles and Madurai, Tiruchirapally recorded less than 1 cm. of rainfall.

   The occurrence of rainfall over Tamilnadu (fig. no. 3.111) and Kerala in response to the overcast sky is a typical feature of the season of retreating monsoon during early winter.

5. ***Special weather phenomena and their occurrence*** : The occurrence of a thunderstorm has been particularly noted over Lakshadwip. The area has shown some amount of rainfall too (1 cm.) (fig. no. 3.112).

   The occurrence of fog and mist have been noted over Imphal of Manipur, Chittagong of Bangladesh respectively (fig. no. 3.113).

   The occurrence of haze (fig. no. 3.114) has been noted over many places of India like Calcutta, Delhi, Bombay, Agra, Pune and Bhopal. It is mainly observed in the Industrial and urban belts.

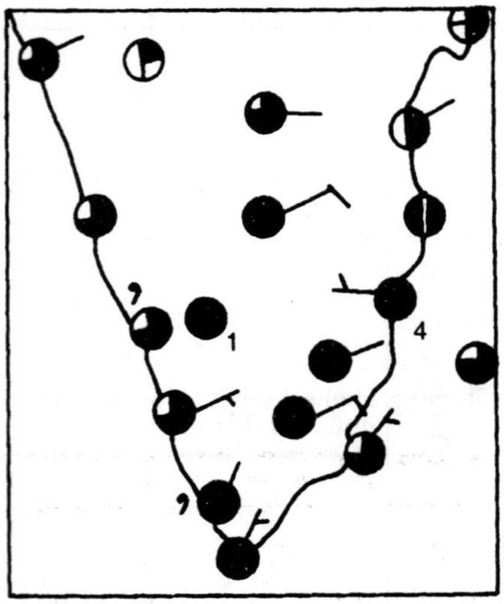

Fig. 3.121 Rainfall over Tamilnadu coast

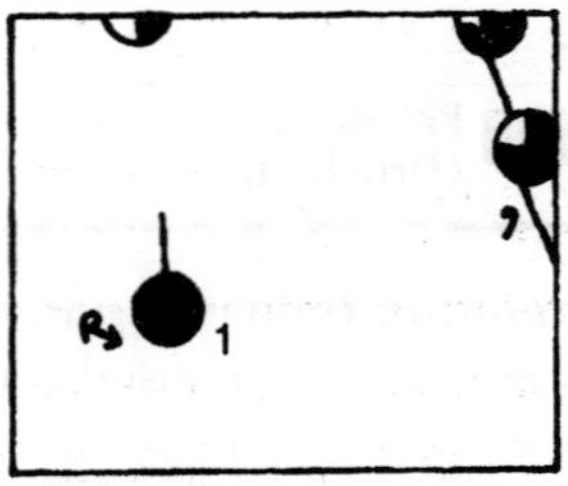

Fig. 3.122 Occurrence of Thunderstorm

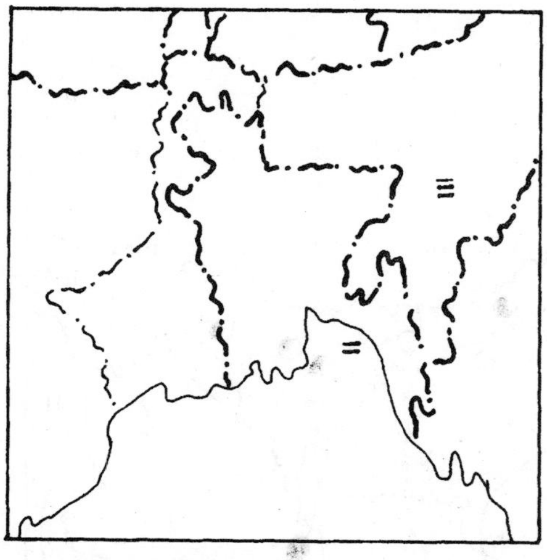

Fig. 3.123 Occurrence of Fog & Mist

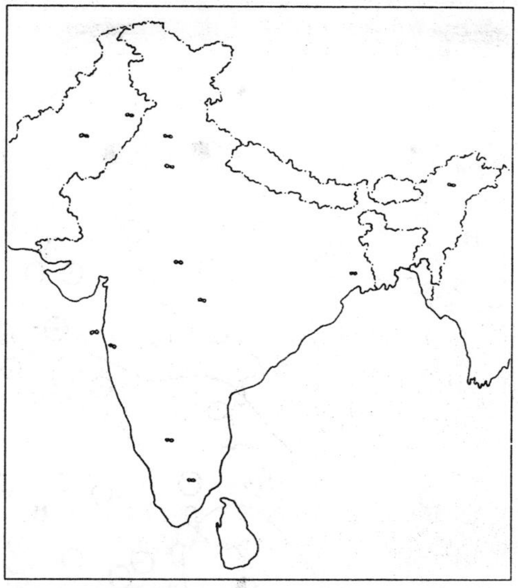

Fig. 3.124 Distribution of haze

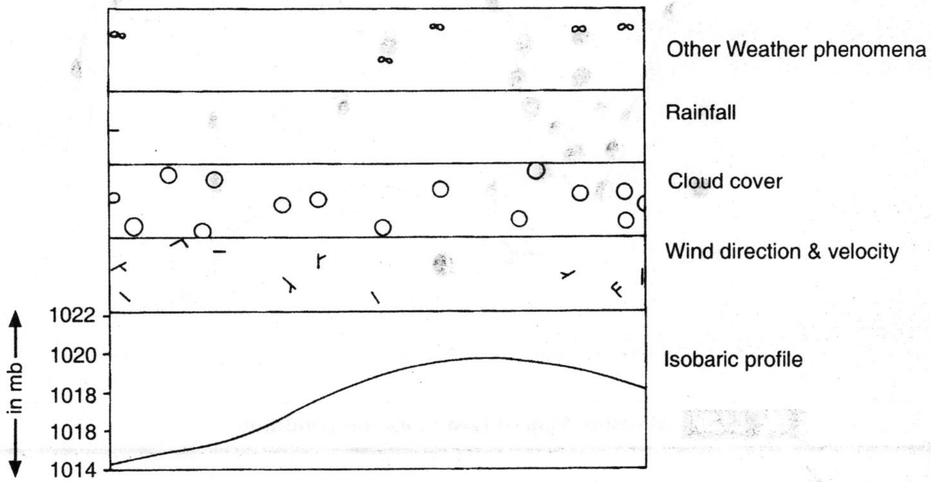

Fig. 3.125 Correlation among various weather elements

6. ***Sea condition :*** On the day the sea was in a calm condition, but between Trivandrum and Colombo sea was slightly rough (fig 3.105).
7. **Correlation among various weather elements :** A transect chart (fig. no 3.115) has been prepared over the pressure gradient between Tiruchirapally and Simla. It show variable direction of diverging winds in the surroundings of central high. Sky is cloudless and rainfall insignificant. The occurrence of haze is more well distributed as in winter the winds are heavy and hold smoke for a considerable time.
8. ***Identification of season :*** The general prevalence of north-easterly winds, the location of high pressure over the middle part of India, occurrence of fog and mist, overcast condition over the Tamilnadu, indicate that the observations were made during the early part of winter season.

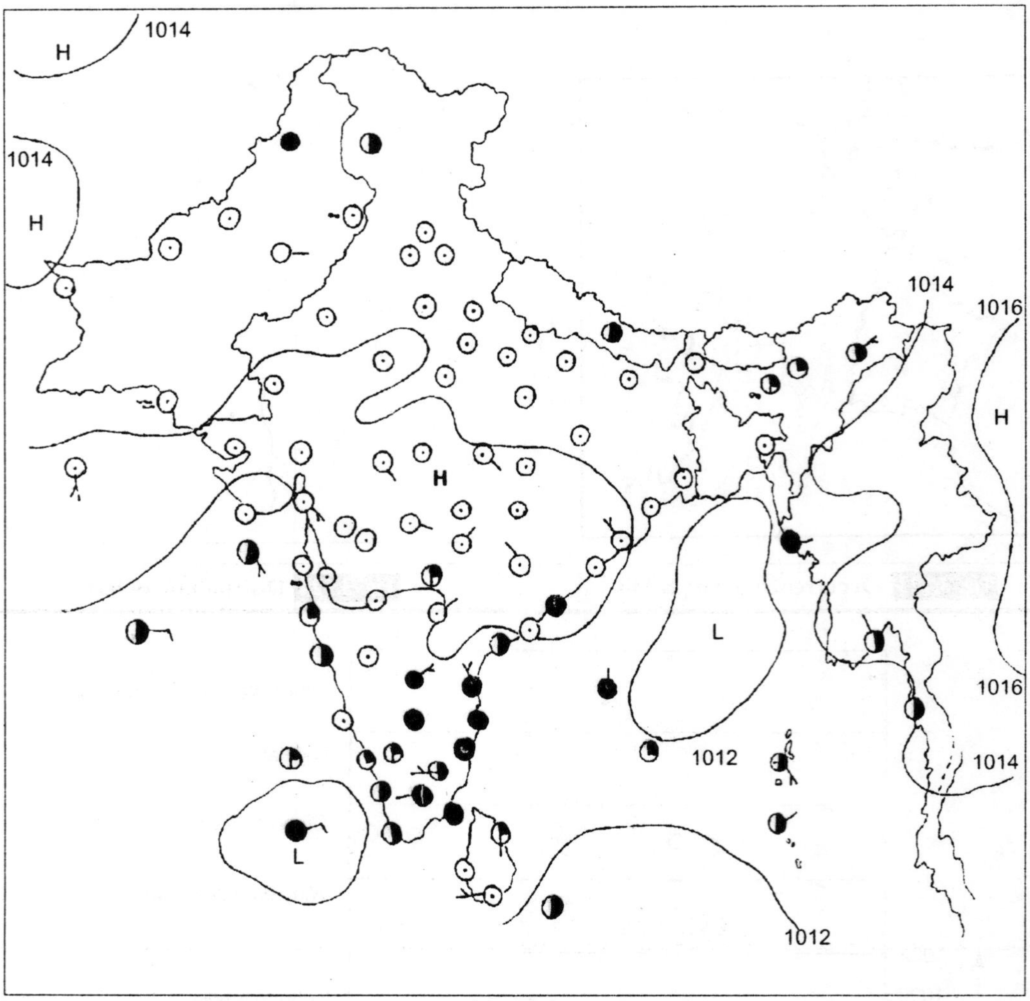

Fig. 3.126 Weather Map of Post monsoon condition

EXAMPLE INTERPRETATION : 3

Post-monsoon season

The given weather map may be interpreted on the basis of the following heads : (Fig. 3.116)

1. **Pressure condition :**

   (a) ***Extent of isobars :*** In this weather map the isobars vary from 1012 mb to 1016 mb. The highest value is observed beyond Myanmar towards further east, whereas the lowest value, *i.e.* 1012 mb is marked over the Bay of Bengal and Lakshadeep area in the southern part of the Arabian sea. The number of isobars are very few indicating very low difference of atmospheric pressure over the subcontinent. It may be noted here that other than the summer monsoon season the pressure condition does not remain very steady over India. (Fig. 3.117)

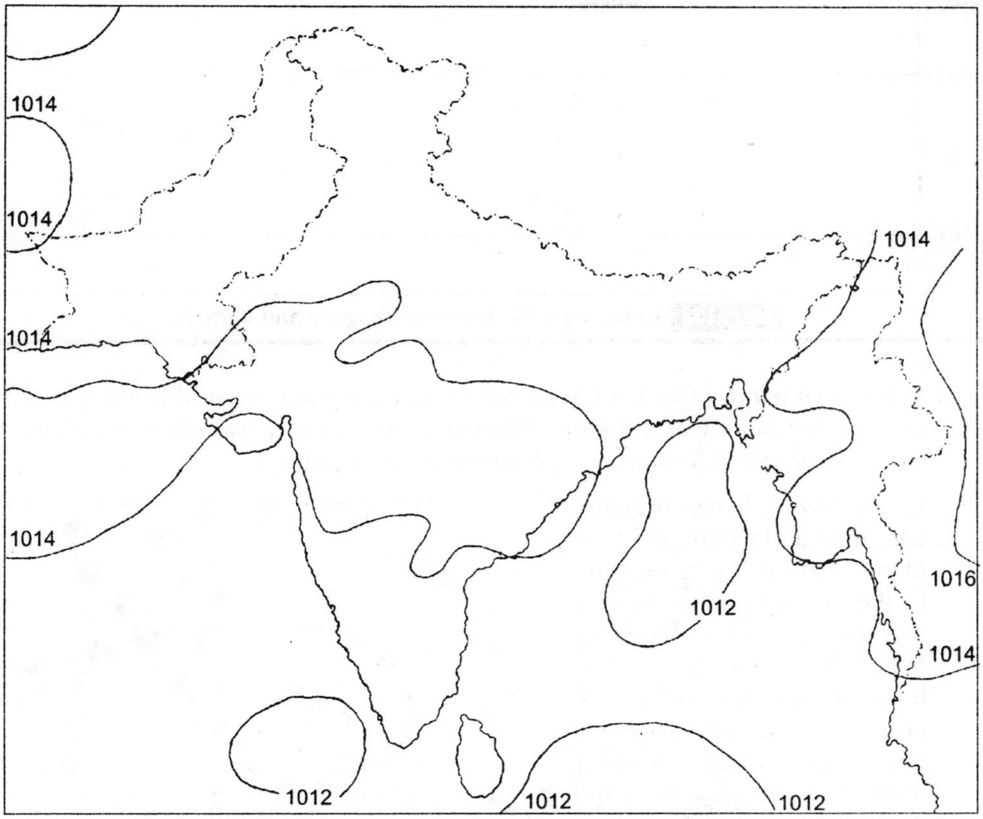

Fig. 3.127 Isobars recognised on that day

(b) ***Location of low*** : Two low pressure zones have been marked on the Bay of Bengal and another has been located over the southern part of the Arabian sea. Two of these low pressure zones are marked with enclosed isobars of 1012 mb. The distribution of low pressure zones indicate that, in general, there is low pressure over occanic areas.

(c) ***Location of bar high*** : A wide spread high pressure zone has been marked over central India and northern part of Indian peninsula. This high pressure zone over central India is an indication of post monsoon season.

(d) ***Gradient of pressure*** : The lack of isobars has given rise to a gentle pressure gradient all over India. The isobaric profile (Fig. 3.118) between Myanmar coast and north western corner of Pakistan Indicates the flatness of the high pressure area with a depression in the low pressure area over the northern part of the Bay of Bengal.

2. **Wind Condition :**

(a) ***Direction of winds*** : On that day winds were haphazard and no major prevalent direction could be marked. Winds were coming from almost all diections. Over the northern part of the sub-continent, however, calm condition prevailed.

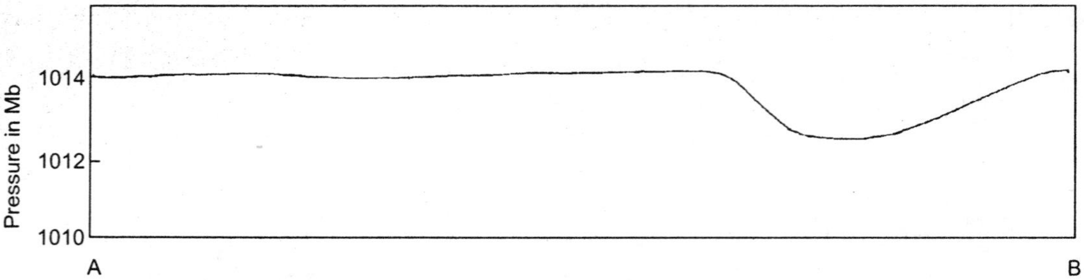

Fig. 3.128 Isobaric profile between Rangoon and Karachi

(b) ***Velocity of winds*** **:** On that day of gentle pressure gradient wind velocity was 10 knots and the minimum was 2-3 knots. The maximum velocity was observed on the Arabian sea, whereas the minimum was observed at many stations.

(c) ***Co-relation between pressure condition and winds*** **:** Because of the location of high pressure in the central part of India a divergence of winds has been noted. The low pressure area, however, did not initiate any convergence or cyclonic circulation though a trend is marked. The haphazard wind direction and low velocity of winds are related to the uniformity of pressure condition over the sub-continent.

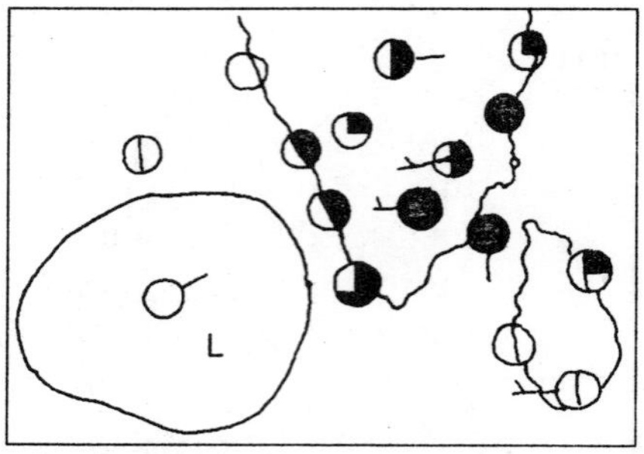

Fig. 3.129 Cloudy sky over Tamilnadu and Kerala

3. **Sky Condition :**

(a) ***Cloud cover*** **:** On that day the sky was almost cloudless through out northern India and northern part of Indian peninsula. Towards north only in Srinargar and towards northeast only in Assam the sky was partly covered with clouds. On the contrary, parts of Maharastra, Andhrapradesh, Karnataka, Tamilnadu and Kerala recorded partial and total cover of clouds. The same is true for parts of the Bay of Bengal, Arabian Sea, Andaman Nicobar islands, Lakshadweep and parts of Myanmar, Nepal and Pakistan.

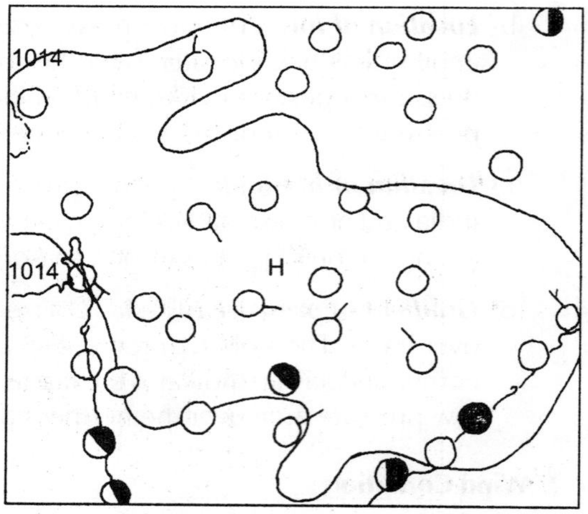

Fig. 3.130 Cloudless sky over high pressure area of Central India

The sky was particularly overcast along the Coromondal coast and over eastern parts of Karnataka. The Occurrence of cloudless sky over most of the northern part of India and high value of cloud cover over coromondal coast is an indication of the season of Retreating Summer Monsoon, when the diverging and retreating summer monsoon winds collect some moisture from the Bay of Bengal and causes the occurrence of cloud and rainfall over Tamilnadu, Andhrapradesh and Karnataka.

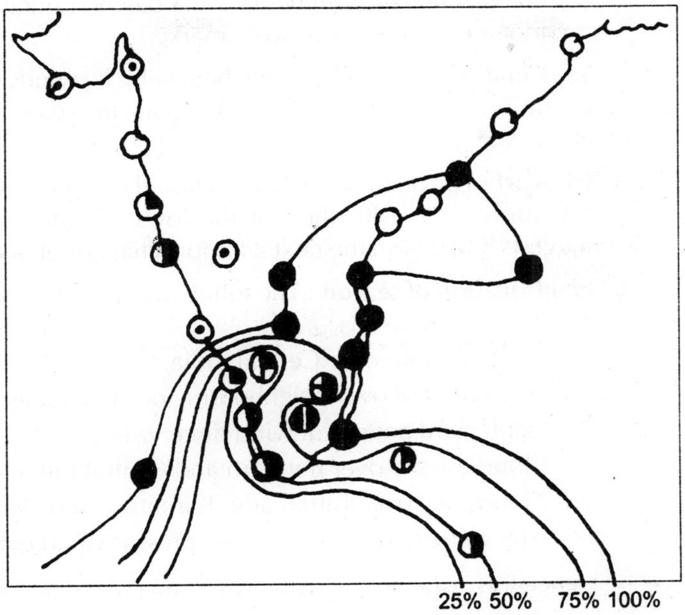

Fig. 3.131 **Isoneph map over South India**

The isoneph map (Fig. 3.121) shows the distribution of cloud cover at a regular interval of 25%. It shows the variable concentration of cloud over south India and neighbouring occanic areas.

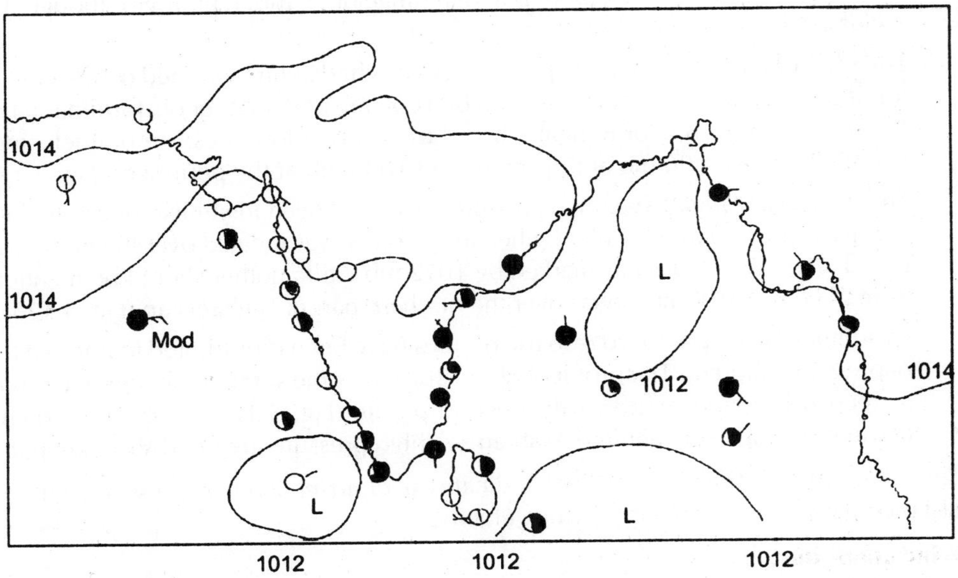

Fig. 3.132 **Sea condition**

(b) ***Occurrence of rainfall*** : On that day no rainfall was recorded during the last 24 hours, though overcast skies were marked.

4. **Sea Condition :** The absence of high velocity winds on the day had given rise to a normal sea condition over the Bay of Bengal, though the sea was moderately rough over the central part of the Arabian sea.

5. **Forecast :** The occurrence of recognised low pressrue areas with low velocity winds indicate that further intensification of the lows will develop. Overcast sky with no rainfall also suggests that within the next 24 hours chances of occurrence of rainfall are there.

6. **Identification of season :** The following criteria suggest that this weather map belongs to the post monsoon season :
   (a) High pressure over Central India;
   (b) Low pressure over neighbouring oceanic areas;
   (c) Haphazard pattern of wind directions;
   (d) Cloudless sky over northern and Central India;
   (e) Cloudy sky over Tamilnadu, Karnataka and Coromondal coast;
   (f) Low velocity of wind and low pressure gradient.

   Hence this is the period of the withdrawl of Indian summer monsoon.

EXAMPLE INTERPRETATION :

Pre-monsoon condition : The given weather map of the Indian subcontinent incorportaties various features of weather elements for which the following interpretation may be suggested.

1. **Pressure condition :**

   (a) ***Extent and Range of isobars*** : The isobars marked on the map extend from 996 mb at the core of a low pressure over the southwestern Bay of Bengal to 1012 mb at the northeastern corner of the India. Hence there is a total range of 16 mb, regionwise though it is highly variable in nature (Fig. 3.123).

   (b) ***Location of bar low*** : Two low pressure centres had been identified on the day, one over the southern part of Rajasthan marked by 1006 mb and another off Tamilnadu coast over the southwestern Bay of Bengal marked by a strong low pressure of enclosing isobars varying between 996 mb at the centre and 1008 mb at the periphery (Fig. 3.124).

   (c) ***Location of bar high*** : Two high pressure zones had been identified, one over the Arabian sea marked by 1008 mb isobar, whereas the other was located over the northeastern part of India and Bangladesh as marked by 1012 mb. Still another should be mentioned here as marked by 1010 mb isobar over the northern part of Afghanistan (Fig. 3.125).

   (d) ***Gradient of pressure*** : Two isobaric profiles have been constructed to find out the nature of pressure gradient. The profile (Fig. 3.126) across the southern low pressure has shown a steep depression, whereas the second profile (Fig. 3.127) shows a gradual change across the loops between the Arabian sea high pressure area and Vishakhapatnam.

   The steepness of pressure gradient indicates a rapid change in pressure within a short distance. This may inspire faster wind velocity.

2. **Wind condition :**

   (a) ***Prevalent direction of wind*** : As studied from the feathers of wind directions over the stations of the subcontinent, it is revealed that there was a haphazard arrangement of

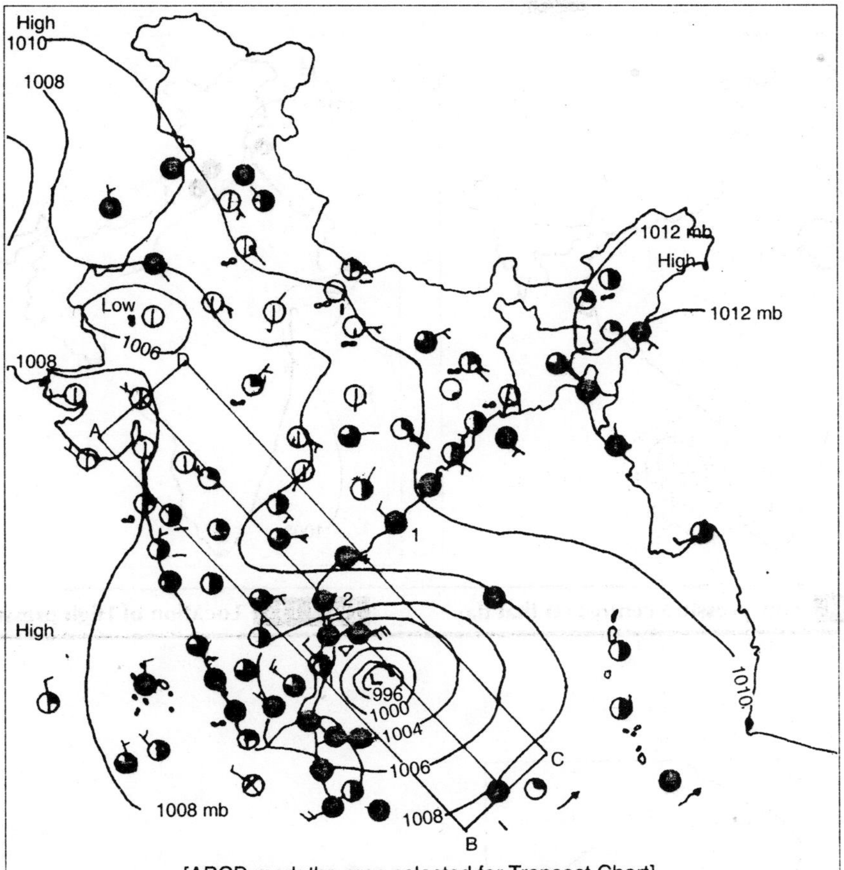

[ABCD mark the area selected for Transect Chart]

Fig. 3.133 Weather map

wind directions on that day. Streams of wind of were coming from almost all directions and no prevalence of wind direction could be identified (Fig. 3.128). However, the eastern India was dominated by easterly winds, Whereas the West coast of India and the stations over the Arabian sea and associated islands were having northerly winds.

(b) ***Wind velocity*** : On that day the wind velocity was of highly, varied nature. The following table (No. 3.14) indicates the particular wind velocities from different directions.

TABLE 3.19

Direction	Velocity (knots)
N	2 – 5
NE	2 – 30
E	2 – 5
SE	2 – 5
S	2 – 3
SW	2 – 15
W	5
NW	2 – 15

From this it reveals that the highest velocity from different directions varied widely (5 – 30 knots), though the minimum velocity is the same from almost all directions. It is also revealed that on the day winds were coming from various directions. The following diagram indicates the highest velocity from different directions. It shows that maximum wind velocity was obtained from northeast (Fig. 3.129).

Fig. 3.134 Low pressure centres on that day

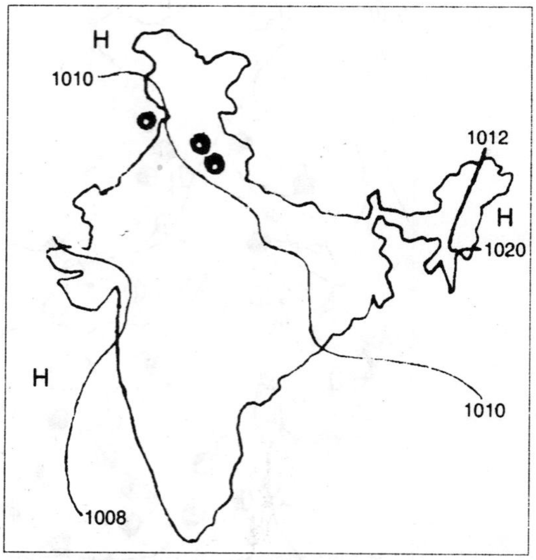

Fig. 3.135 Location of High pressure area

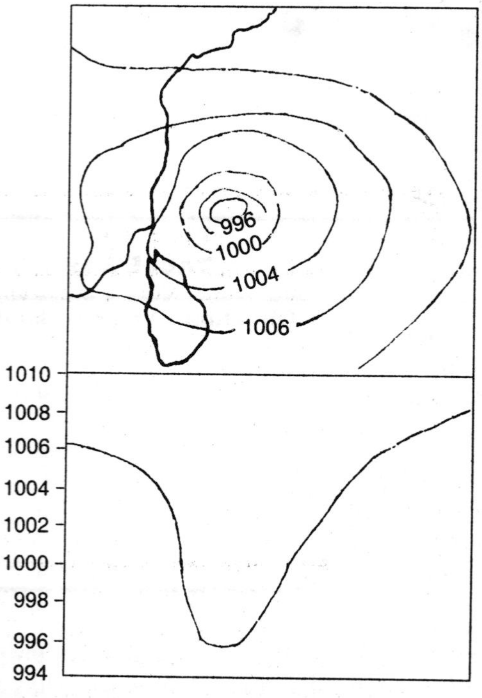

Fig. 3.136 Isobaric profile across low pressure

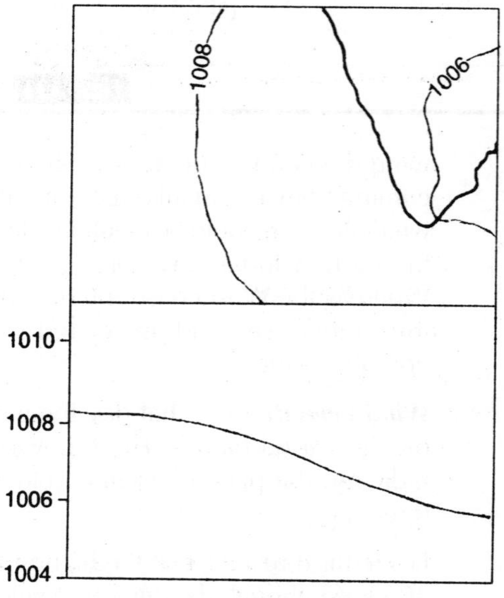

Fig. 3.137 Location of High pressure area

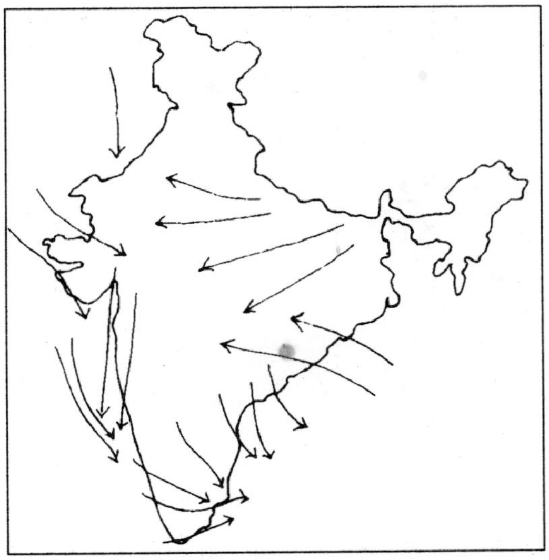

Fig. 3.138 Wind direction

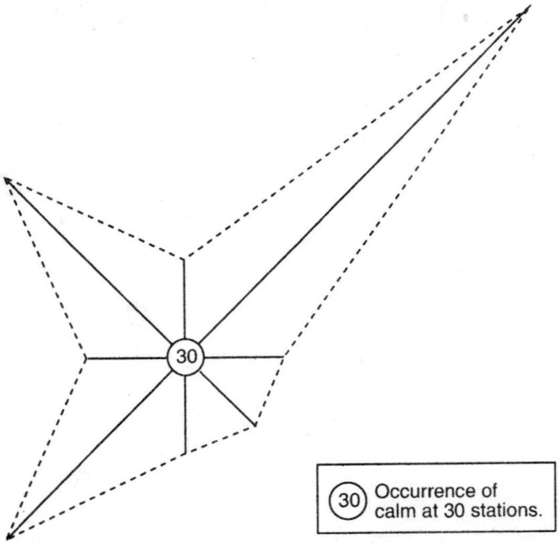

Fig. 3.139 Highest velocity from different direction

(c) ***Correlation between pressrue and winds :*** In general, the gradual change of atmospheric pressure over the subcontinent on that day had given rise to low velocity winds. The only exception was observed in the low pressure area over the Bay of Bengal where steeper pressure gradient inspired higher wind velocity of almost gale nature. Another important correlation can be sought out to observe that there was an anticlockwise cyclonic circulation of winds in the surroundings of the low pressure centre.

3. **Sky condition :**

(a) *cloud cover* : The distribution of cloud cover was very uneven on that day. The sky was either cloudless or covered only for 1/8th part of the sky over central India, upper and middle Ganga plain, Gujarat and Maharastra. On the contrary, Himachal Pradesh and Jammu and Kashmir had shown that 1/2 to 7/8th of their sky was covered with clouds.

The major concentration of clouds was observed over the east coast, Malabar coast, SriLanka and and parts of the Bay of Bengal. In the south of Lakshadweep the sky is obscured. The sky is overcast in almost all the stations. The occurrence of cloud cover over south India, the southern part of the Bay of Bengal and SriLanka may be related to the low pressure developed over the Bay of Bengal (Fig. 3.130).

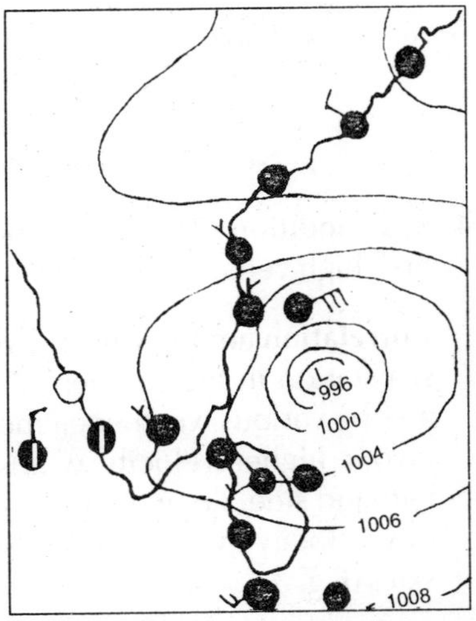

Fig. 3.140 Overcast areas

(b) *Occurrence of Rainfall* : Other than two stations over the northern part of Uttar Pradesh rainfall was mainly concentrated over the southern part of India. It is 0.25 cm to 0.74 cm at Bahraich, Ratnagiri and Pune whereas

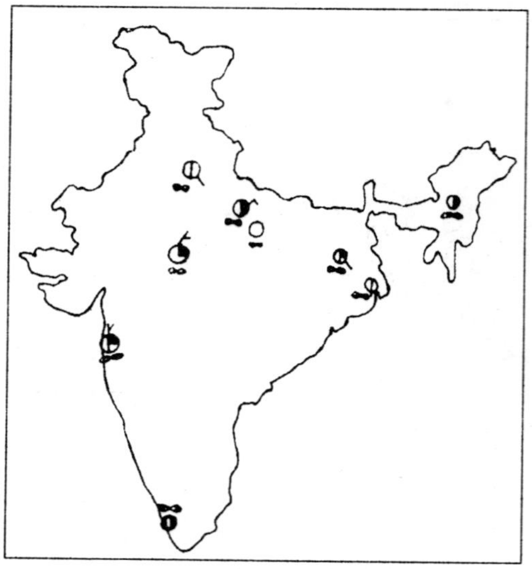

Fig. 3.141 Occurrence of Haze

it is 0.75 to 1.49 cm at Lucknow, Vishakhapatnam and Guntur. The maximum rainfall recorded during the last 24 hours was 4 cm at Kankinada and it was 2 cm at Nellore.

(c) *Correlation between cloud cover and rainfall occurrence* : High rainfall areas have overcast skies, whereas for low rainfall areas the sky is partly covered with clouds.

(d) *Special weather phenomena and their significance* :

(i) Cyclone : The occurrence of a strong low pressure centre and initiation of a cyclonic strom is a very significant weather phenomenon. As such storms bring heavy shower to the coastal districts of India and they often turn into devastating nature. The symbol of shower just off the coast indicates that already a heavy deluge of rainfall is in progress along the cyclone hit coastal areas.

(ii) Haze : The occurrence of Haze (Fig. 3.131) above many of the important urban centres indicates the impact of urban pollution as haze is mostly composed of dust and smoke particles. The particular stations marking the occurrene of haze are New Delhi, Lucknow, Bhopal, Varanasi, Dhanbad, Kolkata, Mumbai and Gauhati.

4. **Sea condition :** Though no specific sea condition was marked on that hour of the day (08.30 hrs), high velocity winds instigated slight roughness in the southern part of the Bay of Bengal.

5. **Correlation among various weather elements :** A transect chart between Ahmedabad and a sea station in the southern Bay of Bengal has been prepared to indicate the inter-relation among various weather elements. It shows that the steeper pressure gradient and depression favour higher velocity winds and occurrence of rainfall. On the contrary, towards the lefthand side, i.e. in Gujarat, Maharastra area the sky is almost cloudeless and winds are of low velocity. Moreover, it also reveals that higher amount of rainfall is related to overcast skies (Fig. 3.132).

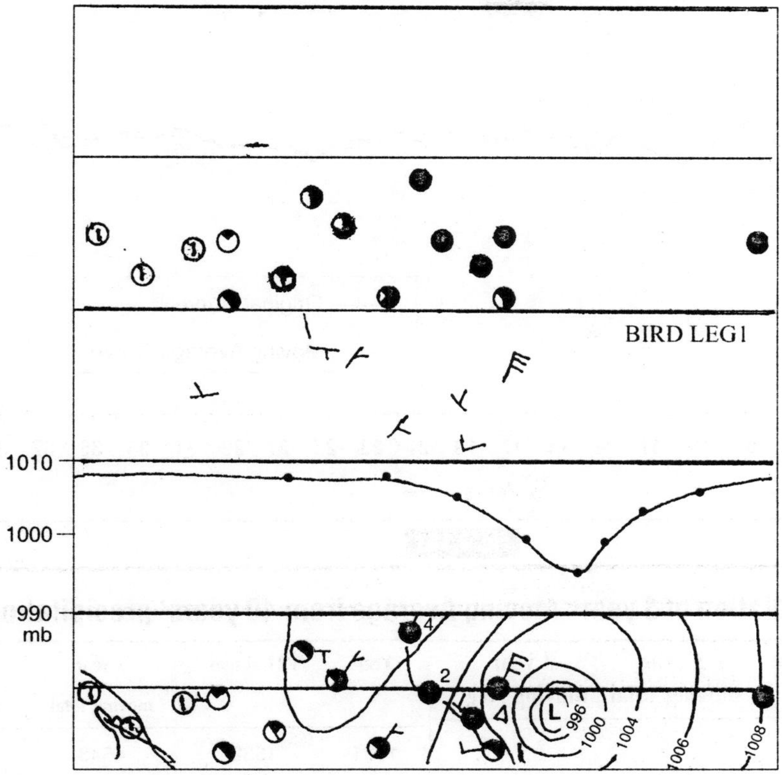

Fig. 3.142 Overcast areas

6. **Identification of season :** The significant conditions of the weather elements may be high lighted here :
   (a) Haphazard direction of winds without any major prevalent direction;
   (b) Occurrence of cyclone over the Bay of Bengal;
   (c) Cloudless sky over northern and central India;
   (d) Cloudy sky in Himachal Pradesh, Jammu and Kashmir because of Western disturbance.

All such features indicate that the weather conditions shown in the given weather map are related to the pre-Monsoon season.

CLIMATIC CHART AND OMBROTHERMIC DIAGRAM

Trend Analysis of Climatic Data by Moving Average Method (3 years)

Trend analysis by Moving Average Method is highly applicable in the analysis of climatic data. Apparently, the precipitation and wind velocity data seem to be highly fluctuating on a current time scale, but if we look at it over a long span of time, we find them indicating an average trend, which is not identifiable in a short span of time with absolute data. Such a trend analysis has been incorporated here.

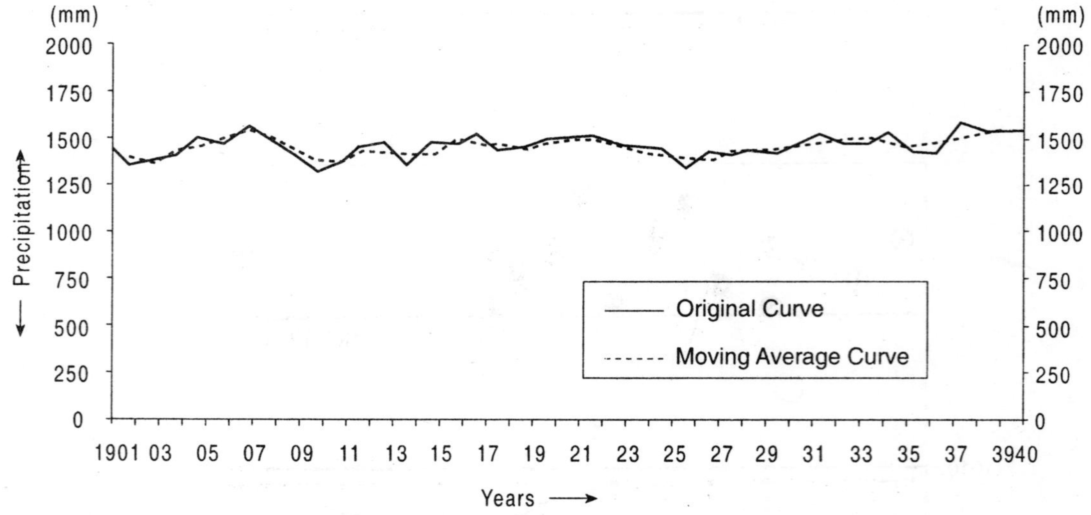

Fig. 3.143

Table for Calculation of 3 years Moving Average from 40 years' precipitation data

Year	PPT in mm	3 year moving total	3 year moving Avg.	Year	PPT in mm	3 year moving total	3 year moving Avg.
1901	1490	—	—	1921	1552	4643	1547.6
1902	1380	4272	1424	1922	1560	4629	1543
1903	1402	4210	1403-33	1923	1517	4566	1522
1904	1428	4351	1456-33	1924	1489	4496	1498.6
1905	1521	4452	1484	1925	1490	4378	1459.3
1906	1503	4640	1546-6	1926	1399	4356	1452
1907	1617	4676	1588-66	1927	1467	4343	1447.6
1908	1556	4625	1541-6	1928	1477	4432	1452.3
1909	1452	4400	1466-6	1929	1488	4436	1478.6
1910	1392	4265	1421-6	1930	1471	4468	1489.3
1911	1421	4311	1437	1931	1509	4567	1522.3
1912	1498	4421	1473-6	1932	1587	4638	1546
1913	1502	4378	1459-3	1933	1542	4683	1561
1914	1378	4395	1465	1934	1554	4693	1564.3
1915	1515	4400	1466-6	1935	1597	4632	1544
1916	1507	4572	1524	1936	1481	4573	1524.3
1917	1550	4528	1509-3	1937	1495	4627	1542.3
1918	1471	4508	1502.6	1938	1651	4747	1582.3
1919	1487	4489	1496.3	1939	1601	4839	1613
1920	1531	4570	1523.3	1940	1587	—	—

Data for Climatic chart of Kolkata for the 3 Summer Monsoon months of 2002 :

Rainfall (in mm.)

July	14.3	—	—	—	—	—	—	—	—	—	2.5	33.5	0.4	—	—	—	—	—	0.9	0.7	0.5	10.2	13.4	1.4	14.3	14.3	14.3	8.0	59.5	—
Aug.	27	68.5	27.1	1.0	—	2.9	10.3	0.9	57.2	25.3	4.1	20.8	2.8	6.1	17.3	0.2	10.4	4.8	4.8	18.7	—	0.5	5.1	4.2	18.1	23.2	23.2	23.2	23.2	—
Sept.	0.4	—	—	45.0	—	3.3	5.9	5.9	1.6	10.7	5.7	6.6	1.6	2.6	7.5	—	—	6.2	—	—	—	—	0.7	0.2	—	—	—	—	—	

Temperature (in °C)

July	31	29	32	34	33	32	31	30	31.5	29	28	28	29	29	25	31	31	31	31	26	29	28	28	29	30	30	28	28	29	29
Aug.	20	30	30	28	28	29	31	29	29	29	29	30	28	29	29	29	29	30	30	29	29	28	29	30	28	30	29	29	28	28
Sept.	28	30	31	31	28	30	29	30	30	29	29	30	29.5	29	30	32	32	30	30	30	30	31	31	30	30	30	30	29	29	—

Pressure (in mb.)

July	998	999	998	1000	1001	1001	1003	1001	1002	1003	1001	1003-1	1003-1	1002	1001	998	998	998	1001-1	1002-1	1003	1003	1004	1002	996-1	997	996	997	997	997
Aug.	996	996	1002	1005-1	1002-1	998	996.8	1001.1	1000-4	1000-1	998	998	998	1000	1001	1000	1000	997-1	998	999	994	999	998-1	1001-9	1001.1	1001	1002	1000	1001	997
Sept.	1007	1006.2	1004	1004	1004	1004	1004	1003	1001	1003	1005	1004	1005	1008	1008	1010	1010	1010	1010	1010	1009	1007	1007	1009	1010.1	1009.1	1007	1007	1001	1008

Relative Humidity (in%)

July	73	83	60	63	71	75	69	65	66	83	73	94	96	88	79	78	66	72	77	97	94	80	77	79	74	74	82	89	93	95	95
Aug.	81	85	97	75	89	96	79	86	77	90	85	85	87	91	81	92	94	83	89	82	92	81	75	83	83	78	83	79	78	78	91
Sept.	79	81	84	78	79	94	76	76	90	92	81	85	83	89	94	95	73	71	77	69	73	75	72	70	71	70	69	63	75	70	

Interpretation of climatic chart : This climatic chart shows that higher temperature has given rise to lower pressure values, which is further related to high humidity and high rainfall. However, relative humidity is more or less high through out the period. It reduces in winter months. During winter, rainfall is very low or nil and the atmospheric pressure rises with lowering of temperature.

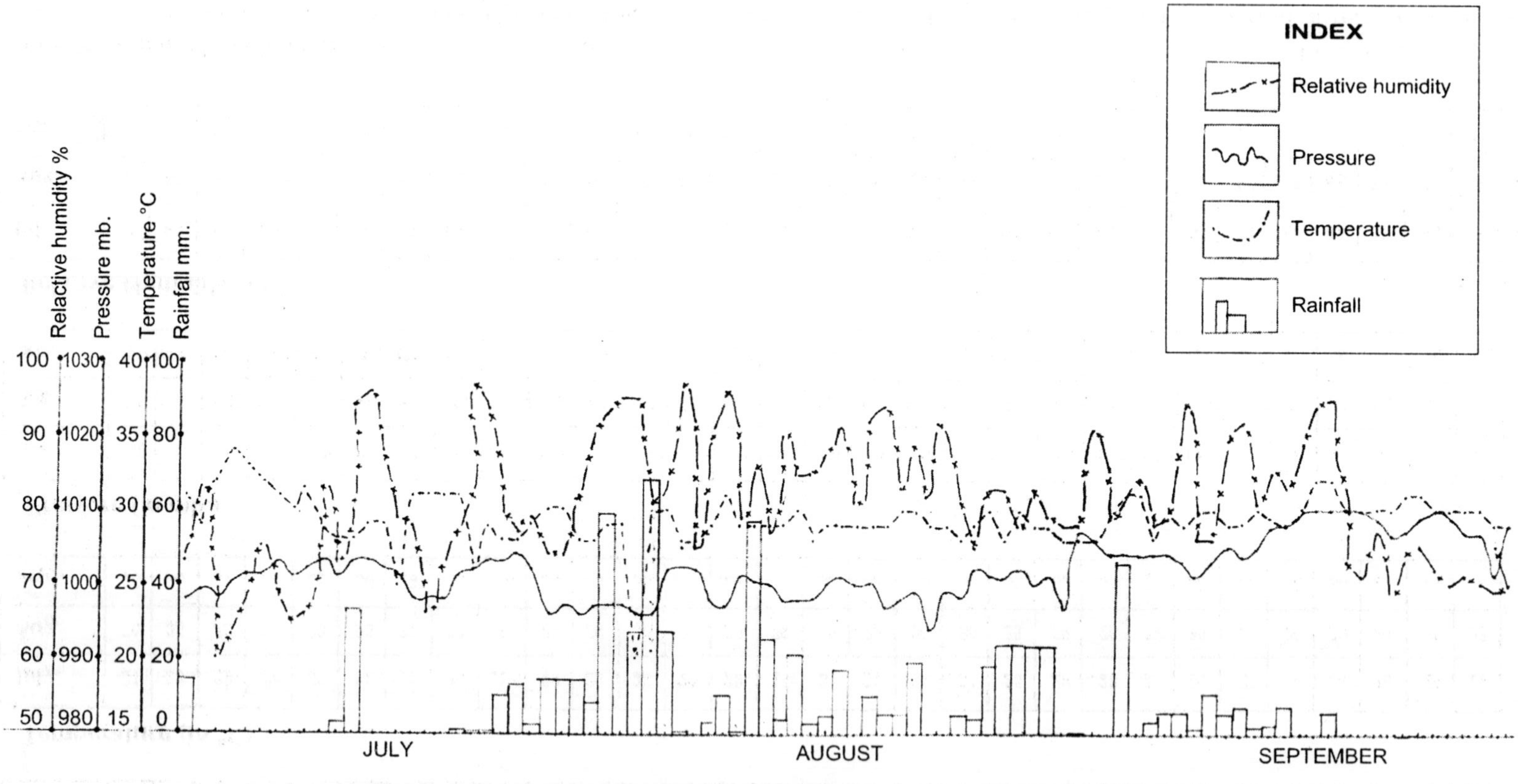

V.S. : 1 cm = 20 mm. Rainfall/5°C Temperature/10mb. pressure/ 10% Relative humidity
H.S. : 2 mm. = 1 Day

Fig. 3.144 **CLIMATIC CHART (Showing co-relation amoung rainfall, Temperature, Pressure, Relative Humidity of Kolkata – JULY-SEPTEMBER, 2002)**

CLIMATIC DATA FOR BOLPUR STATION

Month	Jan	Feb	Mar	Apr	May	June	July	Aug	Sept.	Oct.	Nov.	Dec.	Year
Max. Temp. (°C)	25	28	34	37	39	34	33	32	33	31	30	26	
Min. Temp. (°C)	13	14	21	23	27	26	26	26	26	22	17	12	1996
Rainfall (in mm.)	3	4	9	57	76	247	255	445	139	95	0	0	

Ombrothermic Diagram : Of all the elements of weather and climate temperature and rainfall are the most important ones. The effects of these two elements mutually neutralize each other, though partly, of course. Meterorologists and climatologists have tried for centuries together to find out the exact ratio of such neutralization and also to find out the exact period of season when the influence of temperature overwhelms that of rainfall and vice versa. Such obsrvations are highly significant for the growth of plants. Both V. Koppen and C. Thornthwaite tried to find out the probable correlation between these two elements of temperature and rainfall. An Ombrothermic diagram also signifies the relative overpowering of the influence of temperature on rainfall and

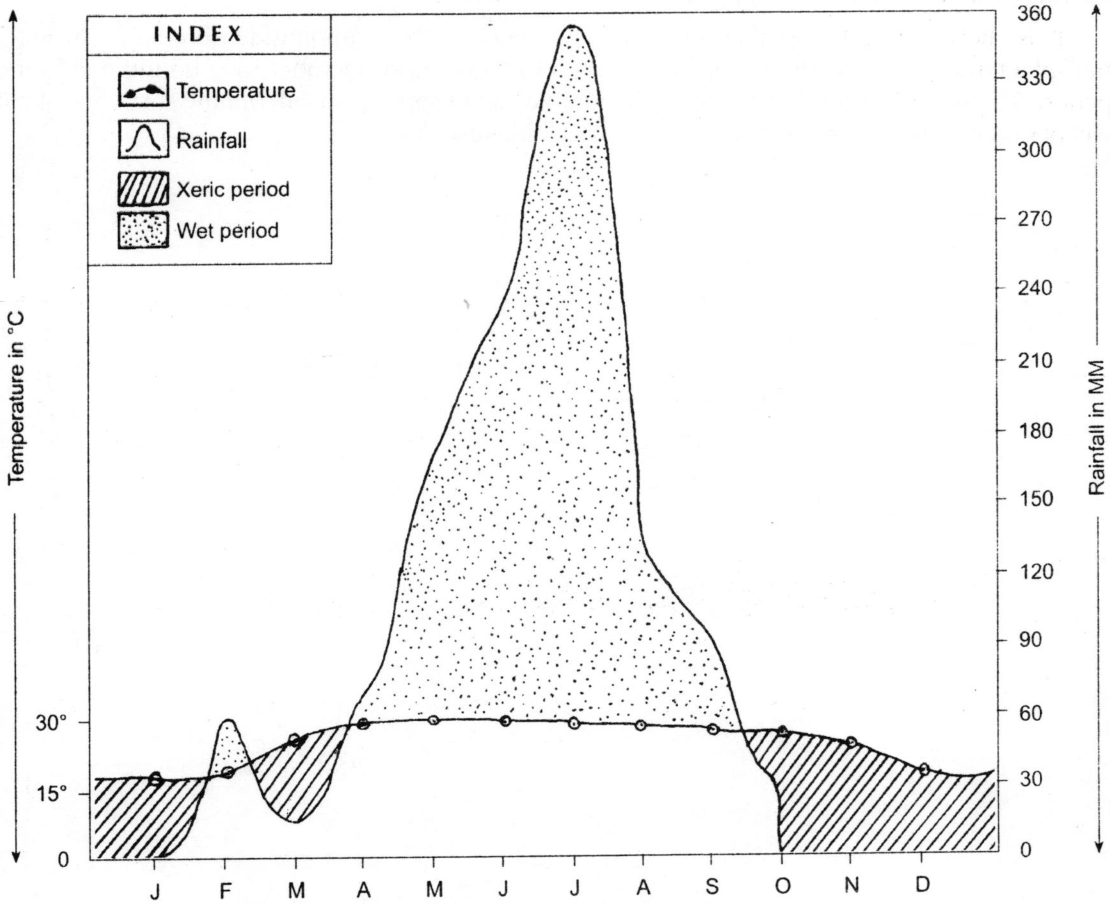

Fig. 3.145 Ombrothermic Diagram of Bolpur, 2000

vice versa. The period identified as of greater influence of temperature over rainfall is known as **Xeric** or dry period and the period when the influence of rainfall overpowers that of temperature is known as **Wet** period. In the former, evaporation exceeds precipitation and in the latter, precipitation exceeds evaporation.

In an Ombrothermic (Ombro = related to precipitation, Thermic = related to temperature) diagram both temperature and rainfall are shown in curves and they superimpose each other. Usually rainfall is shown in mm and temperature in degree celsius.The number of rainfall units are taken as the double of temperature units for the same range of scale length. Temperature units are shown along the left hand ordinate and rainfall units are shown along the right hand. The abscissa marks the months. Usually the mean monthly temperature and mean monthly rainfall are used as data.

Interpretation : An Ombrothermic diagram has been prepared on the basis of the temperature and rainfall data of Bolpur for the year 2000. It shows that a Xeric period is marked from the month of October to March with the exception in February, whereas the wet period extends from April to September. This is typical of a tropical monsoon climate in which there is a distinct dry period followed by a overwhelming wet period. During the peak rainfall period the amount of rainfall is too high which is marked by the peak of the rainfall curve.

It is, however, inferred that April to September is the cropping season, i.e., sowing , transplantation and growth of crops are limited to this period. October may be the harvesting period. The strong winter drought is not favourable as a cropping season, but the small and slight wet period in February may prove useful for vegetables and oilseeds.

CHAPTER 4

IDENTIFICATION OF MINERALS AND ROCKS

Geographers often encounter with problems of identifying minerals and rocks when working on fields, particularly on plateaus, hills, mountains and uplands. A landform is shaped primarily by the tectonic influences, but ultimately it comes under the variable interaction between the geomorphic processes and structures with specific lithological attributes. Quartzite may be more resistant to weathering and erosion, whereas, a shale layer is easily erodible. A geographer or geomorphologist should be able to identify the particular rock involved in the interaction.

Rocks are aggregates of minerals. There are about 20 common minerals which form 99.9% of the earth's crust, though there are more than 1000 altogether. The resistance of a rock depends on the hardness of minerals and their composition and compaction. However, minerals have their independent physical and chemical characteristics on the basis of which they are identifiable. On the contrary, rocks do not have any such specific characteristics though their grain size, particular assemblage of minerals, degree of rounding of minerals present help to identify them. Silicates are the most abundant rock forming minerals. The next important groups in order of relative abundance are oxides, carbonates, phosphates, sulphates etc.

A geographer or geomorphologist often requires to identify rocks on the field megascopically, though microscopic examination in the laboratory gives a more accurate identification. And of course the mark of shearing, the presence of particular minor accessory minerals, puckering etc. are not identifiable megascopically.

The physical properties on the basis of which minerals are identifiable are as follows :

1. ***Colour :*** It is a very important property, but for the purpose of identification the colours of minerals vary greatly and thus it often becomes misleading if much importance is laid on it. For instance, quartz being composed of silicon dioxide is usually colourless or white, but it often appears as pinkish-yellow, green, amethystine brown or even black in colour. The true colour of a mineral in pure form depends on the nature and arrangement of the constituent ions. The minerals containing Al, Na, K, Ca, Mg, Ba, as the main ions are generally colourless or lightcoloured, and Fe, Cr, Mn, Co, Ni, Ti, Va, Cu, are deeply coloured.
2. ***Streak :*** The streak of a mineral or metal is the colour of its dust, e.g. black or steel-grey hematite shows a red powder on the streak plate, a piece of unglazed porcelain.
3. ***Lustre :*** It refers to the brightness which is actually the type of reflection of light that takes place at the surface of a mineral face.

Usually the following types of lustre are observed :

(a) ***Metallic :*** The ordinary lustre of metals, though some of the metals, such as chromite shows a sub-metallic one;

(b) ***Vitreous :*** The lustre of broken glass;

(c) ***Resinous :*** The lustre of resin; e.g. in amber;

(d) ***Pearly :*** The lustre of a pearl;

(e) ***Silky :*** The lustre of silk;

(f) ***Adamantine :*** The lustre of a piece of diamond;

(g) ***Splendent :*** The lustre of a mirror when the mirror is able to reflect any object distinctly.

Minerals with no lustre are described as ***dull.***

4. ***Transparency and Translucency :*** When the outlines of objects are seen through a mineral it is known to be transparent. If the objects are rather indistinct, it is semitransparent. When a mineral is capable of transmitting light, but the object can not be seen through the mineral, it is translucent.

5. ***Taste :*** The character of a mineral is identifiable through taste. If the mineral is soluble in water, the following tastes are common :

(a) ***Saline :*** The taste of common salt;

(b) ***Alkaline :*** The taste of potash and soda;

(c) ***Cooling :*** The taste of nitre or potassium chlorate;

(d) ***Astringent :*** The taste of green vitriol;

(e) ***Sweetish Astringent :*** The taste of alum;

(f) ***Bitter :*** The taste of epsom salt;

(g) ***Sour :*** The taste of sulphuric acid.

6. ***Feel :*** It may be *smooth, greasy, harsh, meagre* and *rough.*

7. ***Hardness :*** It is actually the relative hardness of minerals, usually tested by rubbing the specimen over a fine-cut file and noting the amount of powder and the degree of noise produced.

Usually it is identified on the basis of Mohs' scale of hardness which shows the following grades :

Hardness	Standard mineral	Hardness	Standard mineral
1.	Talc	6.	Orthoclase Feldspar
2.	Rock salt or Gypsum	7.	Quartz
3.	Calcite	8.	Topaz
4.	Fluorspar	9.	Corundum
5.	Apatite	10	Diamond

The intervals on Mohs' scale are about equal, only diamond is more than 30 times as hard as corundum.

Hardness is also tested by scratching with a penknife or even finger-nail. A penknife can scratch up to a hardness 6.5 and a finger-nail up to 2.5.

8. *Form :* Minerals often assume definite geometric forms of crystals which of course favour the identification. Usually the following crystal characters are observed :

(a) ***Crystallized :*** When minerals occur as well developed crystals;

(b) ***Crystalline :*** When no definite crystals are developed but a confused aggregate of imperfectly formed crystal grains have interfered with one another during their growth ;

(c) ***Cryptocrystalline :*** Mere traces of crystalline structure ;

(d) ***Acicular :*** In fine niddle-like crystals;

(e) ***Amygdaloidal :*** Almond-shaped, e.g. zeolite occupying almond-shaped cavities of lava;

(f) ***Bladed :*** In forms shaped like a knife-blade or a lath; e.g. kyanite;

(g) ***Botryoidal :*** In forms of spheroidal aggregations;

(h) ***Capillary :*** In fine hair-like forms as in millerite;

(i) ***Columnar :*** In form of slender columns as in hornblende;

(j) ***Concretionary and nodular :*** The forms being spherical, ellipsoidal or irregular, as in flint nodules of Chalk in England;

(k) ***Dendritic and arborescent :*** In tree-like or moss-like forms by deposition of minerals in very narrow planes or crevices;

(l) ***Fibrous :*** In fine thread-like strands as in asbestos;

(m) ***Foliated :*** In thin and separable lamellae or leaves;

(n) ***Granular :*** In the form of grains;

(o) ***Lamellar :*** In separable plates or leaves ;

(p) ***Lenticular :*** In the form of flattened balls or pellets;

(q) ***Mammillated :*** In mutually interfering spheroidal surfaces as in malachite structure ;

(r) ***Radiating :*** In crystals or fibres arranged around a central point;

(s) ***Reniform :*** In kidney-shaped rounded forms;

(t) ***Reticulated :*** In form of cross meshes like a net;

(u) ***Scaly :*** In small plate-like forms;

(v) ***Stellate :*** In fibres radiating from a centre;

(w) ***Tabular :*** With broad and float surfaces;

(x) ***Tuberose :*** In irregular rounded surfaces;

(y) ***Wiry :*** In thin wires often twisted like the standard of a rope.

9. *Fracture :* The typical forms of chipped surfaces of minerals can distinguish them. These may be :

(a) ***Conchoidal :*** When the mineral breaks with curved concave or convex fracture;

(b) ***Even :*** When the fracture-surface is flattish;

(c) ***Uneven :*** When the fracture-surface is rough;

(d) ***Hackly :*** When the fracture-surface is studded with sharp and jagged elevations;

(e) ***Earthy :*** When the fracture-surface is soft and dusty.

10. *Cleavage :* It is the quality of being splitted along certain definite planes. This is a plane of least cohesion. Amorphous substances show no cleavage. Therefore, it may be closely related to crystallized or crystalline form. There are many good examples of the existence of cleavage, e.g. Calcite produces rhombohedral cleavage-fragments when crushed under blow.

Apart from these tests of physical properties students are often allowed a simple chemical test specially for $CaCO_3$containing minerals and rocks. This is by application of dilute HCl to such minerals and rocks, e.g. Calcite gives effervescence in contact with HCl and after such chemical reaction water and calcium bicarbonate are produced. Students should keep in mind that only unweathered and fresh minerals and rocks behave according to their original properties and any sample for test will be an unweathered one.

11. *Specific gravity :* It is the ratio of the weight of the body to that of a equal volume of water. If W_1, is the weight of the body of mineral in air, W_2 is the weight in water, then $W_1 - W_2$ is the weight of water displaced by the body and the specific gravity will be :

$$\frac{W_1}{W_1 - W_2}$$

The Specific gravity of minerals is dependent upon the atomic weight of the constituent elements and the nature of compaction of the atoms to form the crystal structure. Specific gravity can be determined in various methods, such as, by walker's Steelyard for large mineral specimens, by Jolly's spring balance for very small specimens etc.

However, it is better to be familiar with the relative weights of specimens of approximately same size of common minerals, obviously the heavier one will have higher specific gravity.

12. *Magnetism :* Some of the ores containing iron are generally magnetic, but the degree of magnetism varies and it does not depend on the iron content in all cases. Minerals with no iron content may also be magnetic. Magnetite and to a lesser degree pyrrhotite are only attracted by ordinary bar magnet. Other magnetic minerals are attracted by an elctromagnet.

The minerals with varying degree of magnetism are as follows :

Highly magnetic minerals : Magnetite Pyrrhotite or Magnetic pyrite

Moderate magnetic minerals : Siderite, Iron-garnet, Chromite, Ilmenite, Hematite, Wolfram

Weakly magnetic minerals : Tourmaline, Spinels, Monazite

Non-magnetic minerals : Quartz, Calcite, Feldspar, Corundum, Cassiterite, Hornblende

13. *Radioactivity :* Some of the minerals with high atomic weight are radioactive. They emit radiations which affect a photographic plate. Such radioactive elements are radium, uranium and thorium. Some isotopes are feebly radioactive but they are more frequently and in a greater way present in common minerals, such as, potassium and rubidium.

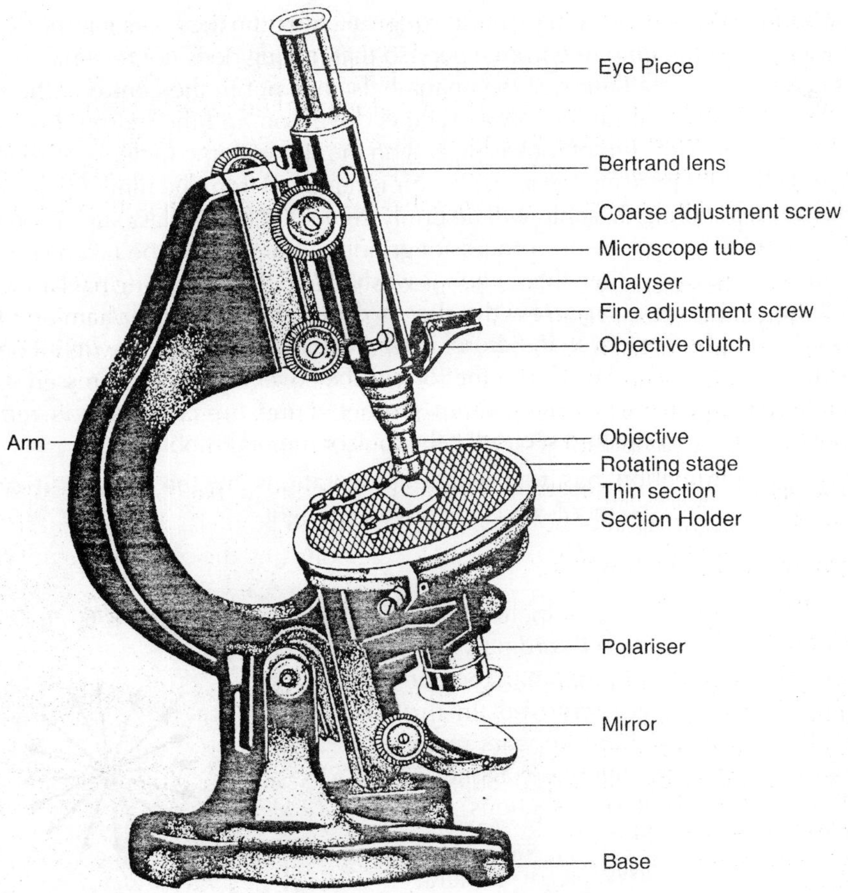

Fig. 4.1 Petrological microscope

However, radioactive minerals are subject to radioactive decay by which unstable *parent* radioactive minerals break down into stable *daughter* elements. The following chart shows the parent *isotopes* and their *daughters* with atomic weights:

Parent		Daughter
Uranium 235_u	→	Lead 207_{pb}
Uranium 238_u	→	Lead 206_{pb}
Thorium232_{Th}	→	Lead 208_{Pb}
Potassium 40_K	→	Argon 40_A
Rubidium 87_{Rb}	→	Strontium 87_{Sr}

Tests under Microscope

Apart from megascopic examination of the physical properties, tests under petrological microscope (fig. 4.1) may give a more complete identification . For this purpose thin sections of minerals and rocks are made. The method of making such sections is as follows. For this purpose a chip of rock is ground perfectly flat on one side with emeri or carborundum powder on a glass or metal plate. The grinding starts with a coarse powder and is continued with fine powder until a perfectly flat surface is obtained. While transferring the chip from the coarser grinding plate to finer, it is necessary to wash the chip free from emeri, so that mixing does not take place. A slip of glass (3″ × 1″) is taken and a small amount of canada balsam is put in the centre of the slip. Then it is heated gently until sufficient turpentine or xylol is driven off and the balsam becomes hard and compact after cooling. The chip of rock is placed on the slip with the flattened side in contact with the balsam and glass. By pressing the rock chip air is removed from the film of balsam between the chip and glass. After cooling this chip will be firmly cemented to the glass slip. Then the thick chip is gradually ground like the previous process of grinding. Care should be taken so that the rock is not completely rubbed away, then the section is washed and the remaining balsam is scraped from the surroundings of the rock chip. Now the slice is covered with fresh balsam and heated again, although to a slightly less extent than before. After the balsam obtains the right consistency very thin sheet of glass is carefully placed over the rock as the cover-slip and is pressed down gently so that no air bubbles are present. Any balsam present round the cover slip is removed by the methilated spirit and finally the thin section of the rock or mineral is obtained.

Microscopic examination has four different operations by the use of (i) ordinary light, (ii) polarized light, (iii) crossed nicols and (iv) convergent light.

Examination for ordinary light

The crystalline form, cleavage, inclusions, transparency, colour and refractive index can be examined through the reflection of ordinary light (fig. 4.2). For this purpose both polarizer and analyser (fig. 4.3 a, b, c) are removed. In this examination the crystalline form appears under microscope. Thus nepheline being hexagonal in shape shows hexagonal cross sections and rectangular longitudinal sections.

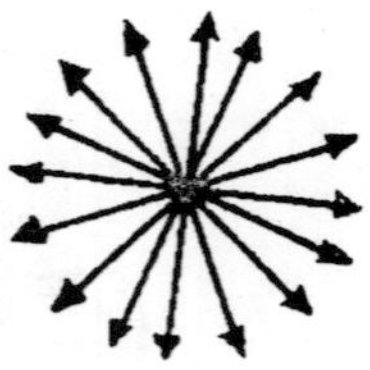

Fig. 4.2 Ordinary light

In thin section the cleavage of minerals appears as one or more sets of parallel cracks, the included materials can be identified as they are often arranged in a definite order. Transparency is a common aspect for minerals whereas magnetite and pyrite are opaque. In most of the cases identification by colour is considered the most distinctive under microscope, though in thin sections they often appear as colourless, as in quartz.

A ray of light striking a surface separating two media passes into the second medium. If the two media are of different properties, the ray is bent or refracted while entering the second medium. The sine of an angle made by the incident and refracted rays, with a line perpendicular to the surface separating the two media, always bear a definite ratio between them. Considering the angle of incidence as I and angle of refraction as R, sin I / sin R is a constant. This constant is known as the refractive index. Air as a medium has a refractive index 1, whereas, water 1.33, fluorspar 1.43, garnet 1.77, canada balsam 1.54, diamond 2.42 etc. It can be determined by the Becke effect or the shadow method. The refractive index increases as the wave length of light decreases.

The relative refractive indices of two minerals in contact of one mineral and a mount may be observed by the *Becke effect.* When a bunch of rays is thrown onto the contact between two minerals, some are refracted and some totally reflected, as they are concentrated within the mineral of higher refractive index. under microscope the narrow line of light or the Becke line travels into the mineral of higher refractive index, when the objective is raised.

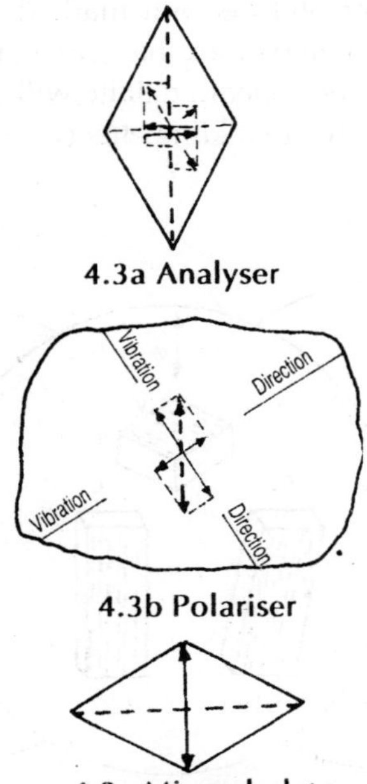

Fig. 4.3 (a, b, c) Analyser, Polariser, Mineral plates

In the Shadow method the rays striking the contact surface between the materials of two different refractive indices, when passing from a mineral of higher refractive index to a lower one, they are concentrated by refraction and form a light band. When they pass from the mount with lower refractive index to a higher one of a mineral, they are spread out by refraction and so produce a shadow.

Examination for polarized light

For this purpose the lower nicol or polarizer is placed between the mirror and the stage. Three tests are important in this regard : pleochroism, plechroic halos and twinkling.

A mineral is pleochroic (fig. 4.4) if it shows changes in intensity and quality of colour when rotated in polarized light. It occurs due to the unequal absorption by the mineral of light vibrating in different places. In a longitudinal section of biotite if the polarized light vibrates parallel with the cleavages the minerals , it is deep brown or even black. On the other hand, if the polarized light vibrates across the cleavages, the mineral is pale yellow. The isotropic substances with the absorption being same in all directions show the same colour and are known to be non-pleochroic.

Surrounding the minute inclusions in some minerals such as, cordierite, very small areas show great pleochroism than other parts of the mineral. They occur due to the bombardment and alteration of the host mineral by radioactive emission from the inclusion.

Twinkling effect is well observed in calcite. In this mineral the refractive index is 1.66 for ordinary light and 1.49 for extra-ordinary light. The refractive index of balsam being 1.54, in a granular mosaic of calcite examined in polarized light, some grains will transmit the ordinary ray and some others extra-ordinary ray. The grain transmitting ordinary ray will have greater refractive index than balsam and their border will be well marked, whereas, grains transmitting extra-ordinary ray and having a lower refractive index than canada balsam will not be so well marked. Therefore, the rotation of the polarizer beneath calcite will cause alternate strongly marked and faintly marked borders and that gives the twinkling effect.

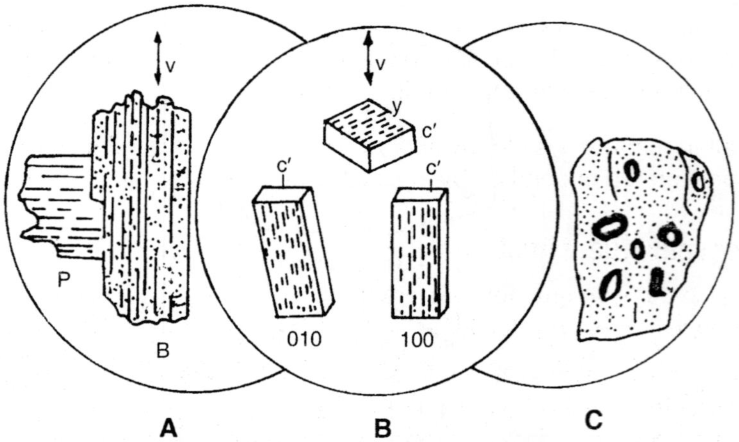

A = Pleochroism in biotite (P = Pale Yellow, B = Dark Brown)
B = Pleochroism in hornblende (y = yellow, c = blue, D = Blue Green)
C = Shows Pleochroic halos around zircon grains in a biotite section.

Fig. 4.4 Pleochroism (Thin section of Minerals in Polarised light under Polarising Microscope)

Examination for crossed nicols

To find out that under the microscope the polarized light is available can be determined by nicol prism or nicol. It produces the light. Usually two nicol prisms (fig. 4.5) are fitted — one below the stage being known as polarizer and the other known as the analyser either above the eyepiece or in a tube between the eyepiece and objective. These two nicols are crossed when the shorter diagonal of one is at right angle to the shorter diagonal of the other. To examine the mineral such an arrangement is necessary because it will make their vibration planes crossed. The particular features identifiable are

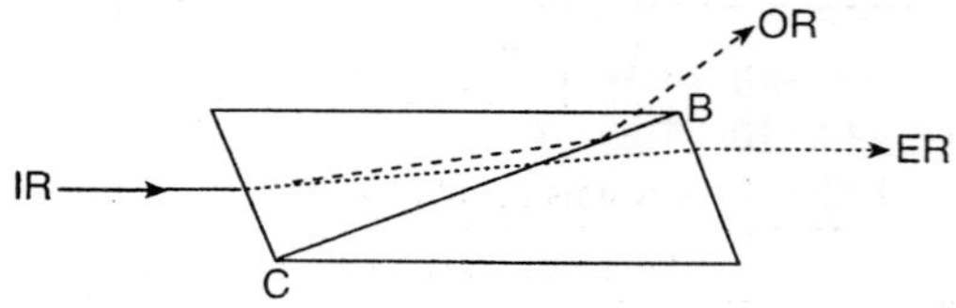

Fig. 4.5 Nickol prism

Isotropism and anisotropism : Isotropic transparent minerals are black between crossed nicols. These minerals have the cubic system of crystals. Other crystal systems are anisotropic.

Extinction and Polarisation colours : When the section of a mineral other than the basal section of a uniaxial mineral is examined between crossed nicols, it becomes black or is extinguished, the four positions being 90° apart. Such an extinction also occurs when the particular crystallographic direction makes an angle with cross wires. This angle is of diagnostic value.

Polarisaiton colour is transmitted by a section of a mineral depending on the thickness of the slice, the direction of the slice in crystal and the character of the mineral. In uniaxial minerals the maximum polarization of colours occurs.

Twinning : This feature is also observed between crossed nicols. In the feature the two halves of the twin or the two sets of twin lamellae give different polarization colours and they extinguish at different angles. Plagioclease feldspar exhibits such twinning effect.

Alteration : An altered mineral is cloudy and the alteration products develop along cleavages. In crossed nicols such altered minerals show aggregate polarization.

Examination for convergent light

For this purpose a converging lens system, i.e. a condenser is placed below the microscope stage. An interference figure is produced due to this light. It becomes visible in three ways :

by inserting the Bertrand lens;

by placing a lens above eyepiece;

by removing the eyepiece.

Crystals of tetragonal and hexagonal nature give a uniaxial interference figure. Such a figure may give by basal sections perpendicular to the optic axis of the c axis, forming a black cross or series of coloured rings. Crystals belonging to orthorhombic, monoclinic and triclinic systems can give a biaxial interference figure. If the stage is rotated the cross which is observed with the optic axial plane being parallel to a nicol plane, breaks up into two hyperbola, one passing through each eye.

Identification of Minerals

The following are the important and common minerals with their identifying features.

Mineral	**QUARTZ**
Chemical composition	SiO_2
Colour	Colourless when pure, coloured by impurities
Lustre	Vitreous
Transparency, Translucency	Transparent to opaque
Feel	—
Form/Crystalline system	Crystals usually hexagonal prisms
Hardness	7 (cannot be scratched by knife)
Fracture	Conchoidal
Cleavage	Nil
Specific gravity	2.65
Magnetism/Special property streak	
Refractive index/other opt. Property	1.553

Mineral	**CHALCEDONY** (Subtypes : agate, plasma, bloodstone, onyx etc.)
Chemical composition	SiO_2 + hydrated silica
Colour	Varied; white, grey, pale blue, brownish, black etc.
Lustre	Waxy
Transparency, Translucency	Opaque
Feel	—
Form/Crystalline system	Crypto-crystalline
Hardness	< 7
Fracture	Conchoidal
Cleavage	Nil
Specific gravity	< 2.65
Magnetism/Special property streak	—
Refractive index/other opt. Property	Less than Quartz and balsam

Mineral	**FLINT**
Chemical composition	SiO_2 + hydrated silica
Colour	Black or grey
Lustre	—
Transparency, Translucency	Opaque
Feel	—
Form/Crystalline system	Crypto-crystalline
Hardness	< 7
Fracture	Conchoidal
Cleavage	Nil
Specific gravity	< 2.65
Magnetism/Special property streak	Generates sparks when struck with steel
Refractive index/other opt. Property	Same as in chalcedony

Mineral	**OPAL**
Chemical composition	$SiO_2 . nH_2O$ (end member of the group)
Colour	Varied; white, grey, red , yellow, brown etc.
Lustre	Subvitreous
Transparency, Translucency	Transparent to nearly opaque
Feel	—
Form/Crystalline system	Crypto-crystalline or radiating fibrous
Hardness	5.5 – 6.5
Fracture	Conchoidal
Cleavage	Nil
Specific gravity	2.2
Magnetism/Special property streak	Internal reflection and opalescence
Refractive index/other opt. Property	1.44, isotropic

Mineral	**ORTHOCLASE**
Chemical composition	$KAlSi_3O_8$
Colour	White, reddish-white, red, flesh coloured, also colourless
Lustre	Vitreous to pearly on cleavage
Transparency, Translucency	Semi-transparent to transparent
Feel	—
Form/Crystalline system	Monocline crystals
Hardness	6
Fracture	Conchoidal to uneven
Cleavage	Perfect parallel to the basal pinacoid
Specific gravity	2.57
Magnetism/Special property streak	—
Refractive index/other opt. Property	Twinning, lower than canada-balsam or quartz

Mineral	**MICROCLINE**
Chemical composition	$KAlSi_3O_8$
Colour	Greyish white or flesh red
Lustre	Vitreous
Transparency, Translucency	Transparent to translucent
Feel	—
Form/Crystalline system	Triclinic crystals
Hardness	6 – 6.5
Fracture	Uneven
Cleavage	Perfect parallel to the basal pinacoid
Specific gravity	2.56
Magnetism/Special property streak	—
Refractive index/other opt. Property	Twinning

Mineral	**PLAGIOCLASE FELDSPARS : ALBITE**
Chemical composition	$NaAlSi_3O_8$
Colour	White with bluish, greyish tint
Lustre	Vitreous, pearly on basal cleavage plane
Transparency, Translucency	Transparent to translucent
Feel	—
Form/Crystalline system	Triclinic crystals
Hardness	6 – 6.5
Fracture	Uneven
Cleavage	Perfect parallel to the basal pinacoid
Specific gravity	2.605
Magnetism/Special property streak	—
Refractive index/other opt. Property	1.535, Twinning

Mineral	**ANORTHITE**
Chemical composition	$CaAl_2Si_2O_8$
Colour	Colourless or white
Lustre	Vitreous, pearly on cleavage plane
Transparency, Translucency	Transparent to translucent
Feel	—
Form/Crystalline system	Triclinic prismatic crystals
Hardness	6 — 6.5
Fracture	Conchoidal
Cleavage	Perfect parallel to the basal pinacoid
Specific gravity	2.74
Magnetism/Special property streak	—
Refractive index/other opt. Property	1.588, Twinning

Mineral	**BIOTITE**
Chemical composition	$K(Mg,Fe)_3\ (AlSi_3)\ O_{10}\ (OH,\ F)_2$
Colour	Black or dark green
Lustre	Splendent
Transparency, Translucency	Transparent to opaque
Feel	—
Form/Crystalline system	Monoclinic pseudo-hexagonal prismatic crystals
Hardness	2.5 – 3
Fracture	—
Cleavage	Perfect basal
Specific gravity	2.7 – 3.1
Magnetism/Special property streak	Thin elastic laminae, decomposes in strong H_2SO_4
Refractive index/other opt. Property	Higher than balsam

Mineral	**MUSCOVITE**
Chemical composition	$KAl_2(AlSi_3)O_{10}\ (OH,\ F)_2$. Al
Colour	White, black, brown, yellow or green
Lustre	More or less pearly
Transparency, Translucency	Transparent to translucent
Feel	—
Form/Crystalline system	Monoclinic six-sided tabular crystals
Hardness	2 — 2.5
Fracture	—
Cleavage	Perfect parallel to the basal pinacoid
Specific gravity	2.76 – 3
Magnetism/Special property streak	—
Refractive index/other opt. Property	Lowest index is not much higher than balsam, yields a biaxial interference figure

Mineral	**CHLORITE**
Chemical composition	$(Mg, Fe)_5Al(AlSi_3)O_{10}(OH)_9$
Colour	Green of various shades
Lustre	Rather pearly
Transparency, Translucency	Sub-transparent to opaque
Feel	Slightly greasy
Form/Crystalline system	Monoclinic tabular crystals
Hardness	1.5 – 2.5 (scratched by finger nail)
Fracture	—
Cleavage	Perfect parallel to the basal pinacoid
Specific gravity	2.65 – 2.94
Magnetism/Special property streak	Flexible non-elastic flakes
Refractive index/other opt. Property	1.56 – 1.60

Mineral	**TALC**
Chemical composition	$Mg_3[Si_4O_{10}](OH)_2$
Colour	White, apple green, greenish grey, dark green
Lustre	Pearly
Transparency, Translucency	Sub-transparent to translucent
Feel	Greasy
Form/Crystalline system	Monoclinic tabular
Hardness	1 (scratched by finger nail)
Fracture	—
Cleavage	Perfect basal giving thin plates
Specific gravity	2.7 – 2.8
Magnetism/Special property streak	—
Refractive index/other opt. Property	1.589, Polarisation colours, delicate high order pink and green

Mineral	**TOURMALINE**
Chemical composition	$XY_3B_3(Al, Fe^{3+})_6O_{27}(OH, F)_4$ [X=Na, Ca, $MgFe^{2+}$, & Y = Mg. Fe^{2+}; Al, Li]
Colour	Black
Lustre	Vitreous
Transparency, Translucency	Transparent to opaque
Feel	—
Form/Crystalline system	Hexagonal prismatic crystals
Hardness	7 – 7.5
Fracture	Subconchoidal to uneven
Cleavage	Rhombohedral
Specific gravity	2.98 – 3.2
Magnetism/Special property streak	Colourless, brittle
Refractive index/other opt. Property	1.642

Mineral	**CORDIERITE**
Chemical composition	$(Mg, Fe)_2Al_3[AlSi_5O_{18}]$
Colour	Blue of various shades
Lustre	Vitreous
Transparency, Translucency	Transparent to translucent
Feel	—
Form/Crystalline system	Orthorhombic granular or massive
Hardness	7 – 7.5
Fracture	Subconchoidal
Cleavage	Poorly parallel to pinacoidals
Specific gravity	2.6 – 2.7
Magnetism/Special property streak	Brittle, colourless
Refractive index/other opt. Property	1.540, pleochroic

Mineral	**CALCITE**
Chemical composition	$CaCO_3$
Colour	Colourless or white, sometimes with grey, yellow, blue etc.
Lustre	Vitreous to earthy
Transparency, Translucency	Transparent to opaque
Feel	—
Form/Crystalline system	Hexagonal with Ca-ions along rhombohedral edges
Hardness	3 (scratched by knife)
Fracture	Conchoidal but difficult to observe
Cleavage	Perfectly parallel to unit rhombohedron
Specific gravity	2.71
Magnetism/Special property streak	Reacts with HCl, white streak
Refractive index/other opt. Property	1.658, in polarized light develops twinkles when nicol is rotated

Mineral	**GYPSUM**
Chemical composition	$CaSO_4.2H_2O$
Colour	Crystals colourless; massive vitreous colourless or white, or grey etc.
Lustre	Shining and pearly on cleavage planes
Transparency, Translucency	Transparent like glass to translucent and even opaque
Feel	—
Form/Crystalline system	Monoclinic crystals as combinations of prism
Hardness	1.5 – 2 (scratched by finger nail)
Fracture	—
Cleavage	Perfect parallel to clinopinacoid, giving thin flexible plates
Specific gravity	2.3
Magnetism/Special property streak	Soluble in dilute HCl
Refractive index/other opt. Property	—

Mineral	**CHALCOPYRITE** (ore of copper – 34.5%)
Chemical composition	$CuFeS_2$
Colour	Brass yellow
Lustre	Metallic
Transparency, Translucency	Opaque
Feel	—
Form/Crystalline system	Tetragonal wedge shaped crystals
Hardness	3.5 – 4
Fracture	Conchoidal, uneven
Cleavage	—
Specific gravity	4.1 – 4.3
Magnetism/Special property streak	Greenish black, slightly shining
Refractive index/other opt. Property	—

Mineral	**MALACHITE** (ore of copper – 57.3%)
Chemical composition	$Cu_2CO_3(OH)_2$
Colour	Bright Green
Lustre	Slightly silky on surfaces parallel with fibrous structure
Transparency, Translucency	Opaque
Feel	—
Form/Crystalline system	Monoclinic fibrous and compact
Hardness	3.5 – 4
Fracture	—
Cleavage	—
Specific gravity	3.9 – 4
Magnetism/Special property streak	Pale Green
Refractive index/other opt. Property	—

Mineral	**GALENA**
Chemical composition	PbS
Colour	Lead grey
Lustre	Metallic, often dull
Transparency, Translucency	Opaque
Feel	—
Form/Crystalline system	Cubic, massive and coarsely or finely granular
Hardness	2.75
Fracture	Flat even
Cleavage	Perfect cubic
Specific gravity	7.4 – 7.6
Magnetism/Special property streak	Lead grey
Refractive index/other opt. Property	—

Mineral	**MAGNETITE** (ore of iron – 72.4%)
Chemical composition	Fe_3O_4
Colour	Iron black
Lustre	Metallic to submetallic
Transparency, Translucency	Opaque
Feel	—
Form/Crystalline system	Cubic octahedron
Hardness	5.5 – 6.5
Fracture	Sub-conchoidal
Cleavage	Poor Octahedral
Specific gravity	5.18
Magnetism/Special property streak	Highly magnetic; black
Refractive index/other opt. Property	Shapeless grains, reflects light

Mineral	**HEMATITE** (ore of iron – 70%)
Chemical composition	Fe_2O_3
Colour	Steel grey or iron black
Lustre	Metallic and splendent when cryatallized
Transparency, Translucency	Opaque
Feel	—
Form/Crystalline system	Hexagonal, trigonal rhomohedron
Hardness	5.5 – 6.5
Fracture	Subconchoidal to uneven
Cleavage	Poorly parallel to the rhombohedron
Specific gravity	4.9 – 5.3
Magnetism/Special property streak	Very low magnetic, cherry red
Refractive index/other opt. Property	—

Mineral	**LIMONITE**
Chemical composition	$Fe_2O_3.\ H_2O$
Colour	Shades of brown on fracture surfaces
Lustre	Submetallic, dull, earthy
Transparency, Translucency	Opaque
Feel	—
Form/Crystalline system	Mammillated or stalactitic forms
Hardness	5 – 5.5
Fracture	—
Cleavage	—
Specific gravity	3.6 – 4
Magnetism/Special property streak	Very low magnetism ; yellowish brown
Refractive index/other opt. Property	—

Mineral	**APATITE**
Chemical composition	$Ca_5Cl(PO_4)_3$
Colour	Pale sea green or bluish green, yellowish green
Lustre	Subresinous or vitreous
Transparency, Translucency	Opaque
Feel	—
Form/Crystalline system	Hexagonal crystals are common
Hardness	5
Fracture	Conchoidal and uneven
Cleavage	Very poor
Specific gravity	3.17 – 3.23
Magnetism/Special property streak	White streak
Refractive index/other opt. Property	1.663 – 1.664; polarisation colours low

Mineral	**BAUXITE** (ore of aluminium)
Chemical composition	Al_2O_3. H_2O + Fe_2O_3, $AlOH_3$ etc.
Colour	Dirty white, greenish, brown, yellow or reddish brown
Lustre	Dull
Transparency, Translucency	Opaque
Feel	—
Form/Crystalline system	Amorphous in granular or pisolitic masses
Hardness	—
Fracture	—
Cleavage	—
Specific gravity	—
Magnetism/Special property streak	Gives aluminium, reaction when heated with cobalt nitrate
Refractive index/other opt. Property	—

Rocks

Rocks, though are aggregates of minerals, develop certain unique characteristics and for the same reason they require different criteria for their identification. However, it should be kept in mind that any rock under examination should be a fresh one preferably without any major impact of weathering. So it is better to have a fresh sample broken from the typical lithological formation.

On the basis of their formation rocks are classified into igneous, sedimentary and metamorphic groups.

IGNEOUS ROCKS

The igneous rocks may be intrusive or extrusive in occurrence depending on their formation as lava flows or as solidified magma formed in the cracks of the earth's crust, e.g. concordant sill, discordant dike etc. Being plutonic in origin they can be formed at great depth of the crust also. On the other hand, the magma solidified in cracks of the crust is hypabyssal, whereas, the solidified lava is volcanic.

Another less significant group is a pyroclastic rock. It forms as dispersed fragments of volcanic eruption either mixed up in adjacent country rocks or solidified in the volcanic pipe and extruded during a later eruption.

The texture of igneous rocks being the composition of various sizes of mineral grains depends on their depth of occurrence, the deeper their zone of formation, the coarser the grains. It further depends on the history of cooling, the faster it cools, the finer the grains and vice versa. Fastest cooling may result in glassy texture.

The nature of magma is another factor for the type of igneous rock formed. Magmas are composed of two components : 1) volatile components and 2) non-volatile components with fusion points up to 1000°C or greater. The volatile constituents in concentration and solidification favour the formation of ore deposits. With gradual cooling magma crystallizes and non-volatile substances form rock forming minerals, which are mostly silicates. The crystallization of non-volatile components leads to the concentration of volatile components made up of fluxes, gases and vapours.

The percentage of compositions of igneous rocks are :

SiO_2	:	35 – 75%	Al_2O_3	:	0 –25%
FeO and Fe_2O_3	:	0 – 20%	MgO	:	0 – 45%
CaO	:	0 – 20%	Na_2O	:	0 – 16%
K_2O	:	0 – 12%			

Of them silica (SiO_2) is the most important mineral. The six other oxides combine with silica to form the significant group of minerals which are known as rockforming silicates. The following comprehensive table (4.1) classifies the igneous rocks on the basis of their constituent minerals, percentage of silica, mode of geological occurrence and general grain size.

TABLE 4.1

Geological occurrence	Plutonic	Hypabyssal	Volcanic	Constituent minerals
General grain size	Phaneritic or phenocrysts	Medium grained	Crypto-crystalline and glassy	
Silica content : ↓				
Acid rocks (> 66%)	Granite, Pegmatite	Micro granite	Rhyolite, Pitch stone, Obsidian	Quartz + dominant orthoclase ± mica
	Granodiorite	Micro granodiorite	Dacite, Pitch stone, Obsidian	Quartz + dominant plagioclase + mica ± hornblende
Intermediate rocks (66% – 52%)	Syenite	Micro syenite	Trachyte, Pitch stone	Dominant feldspar, no quartz
	Diorite	Micro diorite	Andesite, Pitch stone	Sodic plagioclase ± mica ± hornblende
	—	—	Tachylyte	Calcic plagioclase + pyroxene ± olivine
Basic rocks (52% – 45%)	Gabbro	Dolerite	Basalt	Dominant calcic plagioclase + pyroxene ± olivine
Ultra basic rocks (< 45%)	Pyroxenite, Peridotite, Dunite	Rare	Rare	Ferromagnesians

SEDIMENTARY ROCKS

These rocks are known as secondary rocks as they are derived from the rocks previously formed. The name sedimentary is given because its composition mostly includes the materials deposited as sediments. Sedimentary rocks have their various origins and the constituent materials often cover a very wide range of materials, such as various sizes of pebbles in conglomerate and fine grained clay in shale.

These rocks are laid down in layers known as rock beds which are bounded by bedding planes or the planes of contact between two layers of beds. The consolidation of various homogeneous and heterogeneous fragments is favoured either by cementation or by welding. Cementation is done by calcium carbonate, iron oxide or silica. Welding in sedimentary rocks means the mutual attraction between particles because of sufficient pressure exerted by the overlying beds. Under certain typical circumstances evaporation may lead to the formation of gypsum, rock salts, anhydrites and salts of potassium and magnesium.

Sedimentary rocks are classified on the basis of their origin :

(a) ***Rocks of Detrital Origin :*** These rocks, otherwise known as clastic sedimentary rocks are made up of detrital materials of variable dimensions. These are further classified into :

(i) *Rudaceous rocks* composed of pebbly fragments set in a finer matrix; if the pebbles are rounded, the rock is conglomerate, if angular, it is breccia.

(ii) *Arenaceous rocks* composed of sandy materials which are mostly cemented sand grains of rounded nature; if the sands are coarser and angular, it is grit.

(iii) *Argillaceous rocks* composed of crystalline clay materials of alongwith some fine grained detrital materials, as in mudstone.

(b) ***Rocks of Chemical and Bio-chemical origin :*** These rocks are formed by the process of precipitation of mineral matter from solution or by organic processes. Such rocks may be subdivided into :

(i) *Carbonate deposits :* Limestones are formed as deposits of calcium carbonate and calcite contents of shells, hard parts of corals, molluscs etc. Besides, there are chemical limestones and calc-tufa.

(ii) *Siliceous deposits :* The skeleton of silica of some of the organisms such as radiolaria and diatoms, as remains, form diatomite and tripoli. The chemical precipitation of silica may lead to the formation of flint and chert around hot springs.

(iii) *Ferruginous deposits :* Certain iron-depositing bacteria are responsible for these sedimentary rocks, such as, bog iron ore, clayband and blackband ironstones. The formation of laterite is related to the accumulation of ferric hydroxide in the sub-surface as a result of ground water-table fluctuation and drying of iron oxide. Chamosite is hydrated iron silicate which is a constituent of sedimentary iron ores.

(iv) *Phosphate deposits :* Calcium phosphate from skeletons of fish, shells of crustacea, phosphate-bearing bird-droppings form phosphatic sedimentary rocks, such as guano.

(v) *Salt deposits :* When enclosed bodies of saline water are dried up, a sequence of salt deposits, such as gypsum, anhydrite, rock salt are formed.

(vi) *Carbonaceous deposits :* Plant materials may be deposited as carbonaceous sediments, such as, peat, lignite and various grades of coal.

METAMORPHIC ROCKS

The rocks of igneous and sedimentary origin may be altereu due to high degree of pressure and heat. New materials are developed in accordance with the new environment in rocks as the original rock constituents are no more stable. Such changes are known as metamorphism. Thus a layer of shale consisting of quartz, white mica, chlorite, hydrates silicate of alumina and iron oxides will form hornfels composed of quartz, and andalusite, cordierite, biotite and feldspar.

The factors which lead to such changes in rocks are as follows :

High degree of temperature may develop due to the contact with hot magma or deep burial within the crust. This may induce recrystallization of the existing minerals.

Increase of pressure due to the weight of the overlying strata or hydrostatic stress may also develop metamorphism.

Pressure of solution into rock capillaries may cause metasomatism which is another form of metamorphism giving rise to the formation of dolomite from limestone.

Metamorphism may be divided into

1. Contact or thermal metamorphism due to rise in temperature from contact with hot magma, e.g. hornfels containing andalusite and cordierite from shale, spotted slate from shale, marble from limestone, quartzite from sandstone etc.
2. Dynamic metamorphism due to tremendous pressure and related dislocation in areas of faulting e.g., cataclastic breccia from breccia, mylonite from syenite etc.
3. Regional metamorphism due to regionally developed stress in orogenic belts giving rise to variable grades of index minerals (Barrovian trend of metamorphism) such as, chlorite, biotite, garnet, kyanite and sillimanite from argillaceous sediments and forming slate from shale, phyllite from slate, schist from phyllite, gneiss from granite or from sedimentaries.

Textures developed due to metamorphism :

These two important properties of metamorphic rocks, i.e. texture and structure are dependent on the original rock for their development. The important textures formed in metamorphic rocks are :

1. Crystalloblastic, when textures are mainly developed due to recrystallization of minerals;
2. Xenoblastic, when proper crystallographic faces are not developed;
3. Idioblastic, when minerals, assert their crystalline form against resistance of a solid medium;
4. Granoblasic, when minerals are granular or equidimensional;
5. Porphyroblastic, when idioblasts form large crystals in a fine grained groundmass.

The important structures of metamorphic rocks are :

1. Cataclastic structure showing fracturing and warping of rock constituent minerals;
2. Hornfelsic structure giving rise to random orientation of constituent minerals;
3. Granular structure developing equidimentional granular crystals of minerals;
4. Slaty structure producing parallelism of clay minerals and laminated slaty cleavage;
5. Phyllitic structure developing micrograined mica along parallel planes;
6. Schistose structure with foliation or wavy appearance resulting from the birth of chlorite, mica and hornblende;

7. Gneissose structure forming alternate continuous or discontinuous darker and lighter bands of alternate schistose and granulose character;
8. Maculose structure are those in which porphyroblasts of strong minerals, such as andalusite, cordierite, chloritoid, biotite are well developed.

Identification of Rock Samples in Hand specimen

A rock develops certain unique characteristics apart from the physical and chemical attributes of the minerals it is composed of. As we know that the mineral composition helps to identify an igneous rock like granite, a sedimentary rock like shale is better identified by its lamination and smell of clay in moist condition. Therefore, a primary rock is identifiable by mineral composition but a secondary rock requires some what different criteria. However, such identifications are better understood in terms of description, but a comprehensive table in corporating the attributes can also give a, more or less, suitable means of identification. With such an idea in mind the following tables (4.2, 4.3, 4.4) have been prepared. It should be noted in this regard that in the tables below only the major rock identifying attributes have been mentioned.

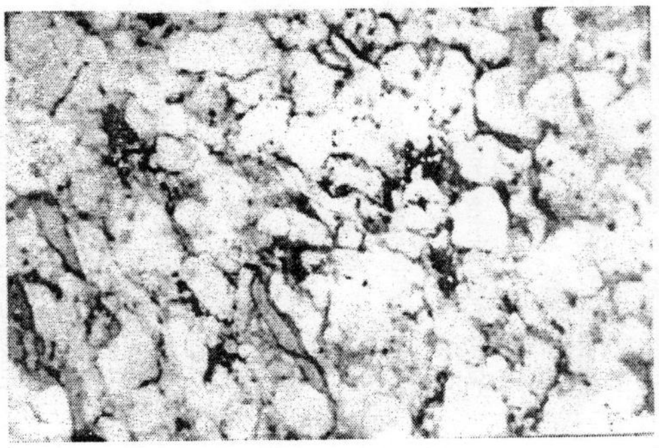

Siwalik sandstone

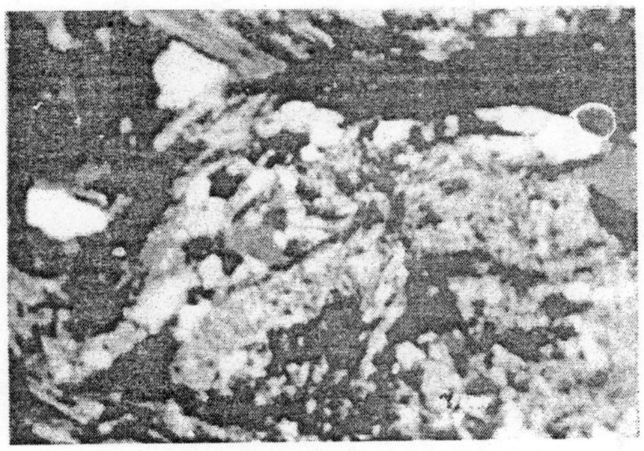

Rangli schist

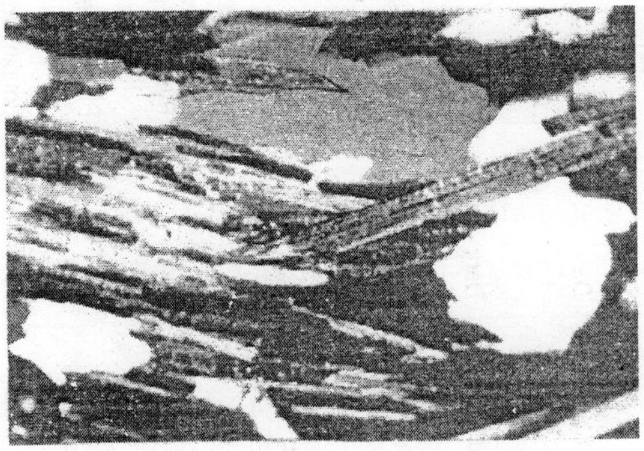

Biotite gneiss

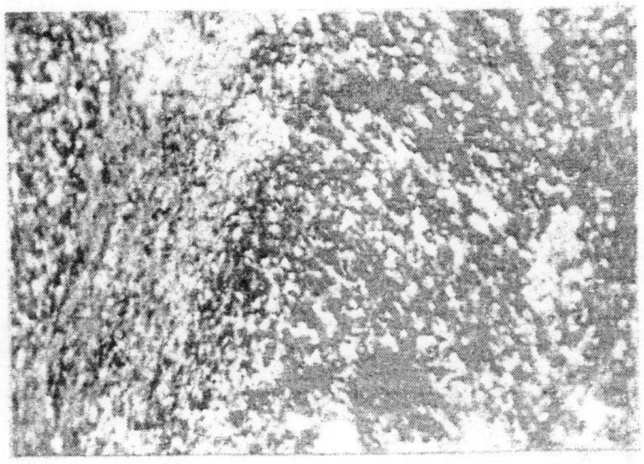

Sheared Daling phyllites

Fig. 4.6 Photographs from microfilm for rocks

TABLE 4.2 — IGNEOUS ROCKS

Physical Characteristics	Colour	Mineral	Composition	Texture	Name of the rock reaction with HCl)
		Essential	Accessory		
Massive, compact, hard, coarse grained and heavy	Light with spots of pink, black, white	Quartz, feldspar, mica, hornblende	Tourmaline, pyroxene minerals, apatite etc.	Medium to coarse grained (holocrystalline)	Granite
Massive, compact hard	Black	Quartz and feldspar	Hornblende, pyroxene, magnetite, potash feldspar	Glassy texture, holohyaline	Obsidian
Massive, hard, compact, lenticular or dike like masses	Light	Quartz, potash feldspar, biotite, muscovite	Topaz, beryls, tourmaline	Very coarse grained	Pegmatite
Compact and hard	Black	Quartz and feldspar	Hornblende, pyroxene, magnetite, potash feldspar	Glassy texture, holohyaline	Pitch stone
Massive, compact hard, heavy	Light	feldspar, hornblende, biotite		Medium to coarse grained	Syenite
Massive, hard, compact	Light to dark	Feldspar	Nepheline, amphibole, pyroxene	Subhedral to euhedral phenocryst	Trachyte
Massive, compact, hard	Dark	Plagioclase, hornblende, biotite	Quartz, feldspathoids, hypersthene, augite	Coarse to medium grained, phanero-crystalline	Diorite
Massive, compact, hard	Dark	Pyroxene, feldspar, magnetite	Hornblende, olivine, chlorite	Poikilitic, interlocking	Dolerite
Hard, compact, heavy, massive	Dark	Plagioclase feldspar, pyroxene, hornblende, olivine	Biotite, hornblende, magnetite	Coarse grained, Phanerocrystalline	Gabbro
Hard, compact, massive	Dark	Pyroxene, olivine	Amphibole	Coarse grained, Phanerocrystalline Phanerocrystalline	Peridotite
Massive, hard, compact	Dark	Pyroxene, plagioclase	Olivine, hypersthene, hornblende	Fine grained, aphinitic, interlocking, poikilitic	Basalt
Massive, hard, compact	Dark	Plagioclase	Orthoclase, quartz, pyroxene	Fine grained, interlocking	Andesite
Hard, massive	Light	Potash feldspar, plagioclase	Pyroxene, muscovite, apatite, magnetite	Medium grained, phanerocrystalline	Granodiorite

TABLE 4.3 — SEDIMENTARY ROCKS

Physical Characteristics	Colour	Mineral Composition	Texture	Structure	Matrix	Cement	Special property (smell/feel/edge/ reaction with HCl)	Name of the rock
Massive, hard, compact unconsolidated	Variable	Rounded pebbles of quartz, quartzite, chert, flint, some carbonate particles	Coarse to fine grained	Massive	Fine particles of quartz, calcareous sand, iron oxide, clay	Siliceous, calcareous, ferruginous		Conglomerate
Massive, compact, hard	Variable	Rock fragments, quartz etc.	Clastic texture, coarse grained	Bedded	Minor amount of clay or silt	Siliceous		Grit
Slablike	Light	Quartz, muscovite or biotite	Clastic, medium to fine grained	Massive	Minor amount of clay or silt	Usually siliceous, rarely calcareous		Flagstone
Massive, hard, compact, heavy	Variable	Angular fragments of chert, flint etc.	Clastic, angular grains	Massive	Fine particles of calcareous sand, iron oxide, clay	Siliceous, calcareous, ferruginous		Breccia
Massive, compact, hard	Variable	Quartz and other rock fragments	Medium to fine grained	Usually massive	Ferruginous	Siliceous	Feel : rough	Sandstone (Ganister) (Fig. 4.6)
Light, soft, laminated	Variable	Clay minerals, minor quartz, iron oxide etc.	Clastic, fine grained	Finely laminated		Poorly cemented (welded)	Gives smell of clay when moist, swells up when water is applied	Shale
Light, soft	Variable, often grey	Clay, silt (50% clay materials in claystone, 50% silt in siltstone)	Clastic, fine grained	Massive, not laminated		Poorly cemented	Swells with water, gives smell of clay when moist	Mudstone
Soft (can be scratched by pencil-knife), massive	Variable	Calcite, dolomite, coral limestone, pisoliths of various composition may be present	Non-clastic, fine to medium grained	Massive, poorly bedded, ripple marks may be present	Calcite, dolomite	Calcareous	Effervescence with dilute HCl	Limestone
Massive, harder than limestone	White or off white	Dolomite, calcite, argillaceous materials, quartz, pyrite etc.	Fine to medium grained, non-clastic, granular	Bedded or massive	Dolomite	Carbonates	Effervescence with hot concentrated HCl	Dolomite
Soft, clayey	Light	Calcareous clay, traces of quartz, mica	Medium to fine grained, non-clastic	Massive or bedded		Carbonate		Marl
Compact, massive, porous	Red, brown	Goethite, limonite with quartz	Fine grained, oolitic, pisolitic, non-clastic	Massive, vesicular	Ferruginous	Ferruginous		Laterite
Banded, light, brittle	Black	Composed of vitrain (brilliant black band), fusain (soft & powderly), Clarain (laminated bright coal), durain (dull bands)	Dense, non-clastic	Massive or banded	Carbonaceous			Coal (Bituminous)

TABLE 4.4 — METAMORPHIC ROCKS

Physical Characteristics	Colour	Mineral Composition	Texture	Structure	Special property (smell/feel/edge/ reaction with HCl)	Name of the rock
Compact, hard, sheet-like	Variable (grey, green etc.)	Quartz, muscovite, biotite, chlorite, feldspar	Fine grained	Cleavable, slate-like	Gives metallic sound under hammer blow	Slate
Soft, glossy	Variable	Micro-grained mica (muscovite), clay, chlorite, feldspar	Fine grained	Cleavable, foliated		Phyllite (Fig. 4.6)
Compact, Hard	Green or greenish	Chlorite, also garnet, staurolite in minor amount	Fine to coarse grained	Foliated, schistose		Chlorite schist
Soft, shiny	White or silvery white	Talc, serpentine, chlorite	Medium to coarse grained	Foliated, schistose		Talc schist
Hard, compact, heavy	Dark	Hornblende, Plagioclase, biotite	Medium to coarse grained	Foliated, granulose, even schistose or gneissose		Amphibolite
Hard, compact	Variable	Muscovite, biotite, quartz, chlorite	Fine to coarse grained	Schistose		Schist (mica) (Fig. 4.6)
Compact, hard	Black or red	Mica, Siliceous material	Sheared, crushed angular grains, granular, granoblastic	Cataclastic, non-foliated		Mylonite
Compact, hard	Grey, black, green	Quartz, plagioclase, pyroxene, sillimanite, andalusite, cordierite, biotite	Non-foliated, fine-grained, porphyroblastic	Maculose, stratified		Hornfels
Heavy, crystalline, compac	Variable (white reddish, black)	Calcite, dolomite pyroxene olivine, garnet etc.	Crystalline, interlocking granoblastic	Maculose, granulose	Reacts with HCl	Marble
Compact, hard, heavy	Dark and light	Quartz, feldspar, biotite, muscovite, hornblende	Alternate granulose and schistose	Gneissose, banded (interlocking or parallel)		Gneiss (Fig. 4.6)
Compact, hard, heavy	Dark	Quartz, feldspar, biotite, hypersthene, hornblende	Medium to coarse grained	Granulose	Oily lustre	Chornokite
Compact, hard, heavy	Light to dark	Quartz, sillimanite, garnet	Coarse grained, granoblastic to porphyroblastic	Banded or foliated		Khondalite
Compact, heavy	Light to dark	Plagioclase feldspar, garnet, quartz, kyanite, pyroxene etc.	Non-foliated, granoblastic, coarse grained	Gniessose		Eclogite
Compact, hard, heavy	Light	Quartz and silica minerals	Granoblastic, compact, non-foliated	Maculose or granulose	Jagged edges	Quartzite

C H A P T E R **5**

CARTOGRAPHIC REPRESENTATION OF DATA

CARTOGRAMS

Definition

Cartograms are certain specific projections of maps which transform topographic space on the basis of statistical factors (Kidron and Sigal, 1984). Statistical values are ascertained on the basis of the variable mapping units. The relationship between units is topological in such maps. In area-cartograms representing countries, the shape of the country concerned can not be maintained and it becomes a puzzle of rectangles, though proportionate to the typical area-data of the country or continent.

Efforts have been made to maintain the correct shape and to reduce the complexity of construction. The disruption of contiguity between units destroying the spatial proximity is also to be removed.

Because of the topological distortions to a high degree the larger units are selected and constructed first. Later the smaller units are superimposed on the larger ones, if so required. Though the shape is not maintained, an effort is made to maintain the affinity and proximity between units. That is why superimposition of smaller units is required. For example, one can not place China, southward across south-Asia, as because there is no area left after placing CIS countries and south-east Asian countries; rather one should try to superimpose China on the south-eastern corner of the Soviet bloc in the west of Korea, Vietnam and, of course, Japan. In such cases, the hierarchy of space concerned should be maintained to obtain a sequential and an advantageous course of placement of countries.

However, in another way of representation Cartograms show statistical data on spatial units with correct administrative or any other type of boundary. In such maps distortion of boundary may not occur, as in a choropleth, but spatial distortion or abstraction of shape is common in cartograms, e.g., the area of a few villages may be shown by proportionate circles or squares, population of a few localities may be represented by bar graph etc.

Various types of mapping techniques are thus shown as cartograms. In this chapter three groups of cartograms are discussed, such as, *Geomorphological map, Climatic maps* and *Diagrams,* and *Socio-Economic maps.*

GEOMORPHOLOGICAL MAPPING

Germination of idea

A geomorphological map is a cartographic product which is little different from other maps of its group. It had a late start, only when its necessity was felt because all other maps of its group proved inadequate to offer a total comprehensiveness as landform maps. Large scale topographic maps, in particular, failed to provide their reader with information about the geomorphic process which has carved out the present form of topography. Someone may feel perplexed with this statement as the topographic maps show streams of various kinds and various dimensions, traces of erosion and deposition; sand dunes, ephemeral streams, gully erosion etc. in drier areas; areas of existing glaciers, moraines, snow clad surface etc. in high mountains. However, it is still inadequate to give a complete geomorphologic background about landform. A piecemeal approach to a special feature as assumed in topographic maps does neither say anything about the rock, its resistance to erosion, nor it can hold any process, in particular, responsible for the formation of the feature. On topographic maps hills, valleys, ridges, spurs etc. are excellently configured by contours, but their delineation is often mixed up in the jargon of contour configurations and many other information about slope, escarpment etc. remain absent in those maps.

Geomorphological mapping in its present form had the initial start in Poland. Since early 1950s in the context of economic planning Poland has been using such maps (Galon, 1962; Khimaszewski 1956). The International Institute of Aerial Survey and Earth Sciences, of the Netherlands (I.T.C.) also made effective use of such maps in the landuse planning for Sumatra of Indonesia, for conservation purposes in southern Italy and northern Spain and for purposes of irrigation on Indus plain (Verstappen, 1970). The Centre de Geographic Appliqué at the University of Strasbourg applied the techniques of geomorphological mapping for acquiring data in connection with a land reclamation scheme on the delta of the Senegal river (Tricart, 1956, 1961). In Venezuela such maps have been prepared and used for an area having limited scope of agriculture as against dangers of erosion, thin and stony soils, excessive local relief, insufficient drainage and flooding. The Centre of Geographic Application also produced geomorphological maps to define the limits of urban development, for planning of routes (Route National No. 2 through the Guil river valley in the Alps), and for understanding river dynamics in relation to occurrence of flood in the Cevennes mountains. UNESCO used such maps as techniques for resource assessments (Franzle, 1966).

Thus it is well understood that geomorphological maps having enormous scope of incorporating various types of physical and cultural data can be exploited in a big way as a geographic tool for planning in various development projects of human society.

Application of geomorphological mapping has a wide scope in planning and economic development. In preparing a comprehensive regional planning in the conservational practices for agriculture and forestry, in civil engineering pursuits on the surface and underground, such as, construction of dams and reservoirs, roads, railways, shore protection, regulation of water level in rives etc., in mining, mineral prospecting, various types of reclamation work etc. (Demek, 1972), geomorphological mapping can act as a useful technique and as a cartographic resource as well.

Compilation

The information we can incorporate into geomorphological maps have three main categories.:

1. Mapping of surface form ;
2. Mapping of surface material ;
3. Mapping of processes .

Mapping surface form

Geomorphological maps can express the form of land in greater detail than they are on contour maps. These maps can recognise the change and break of slope showing 'V' - symbol added to a pecked line pointing downhill. On the basis of orientation of symbols and change of slope convex and concave slopes can be identified. Steepness of slope is shown by an arrow lying normal to the slope and pointing downhill. It carries the angle of slope in degree. Down slope curvature is shown by placing 'X' on the arrow-stem for a convex slope and a vertical '—' for a concave slope. Special symbols are used to indicate a steep cliff, free-face of a bedrock as defined by a solid black symbol along a line marking the crest. Short and steep slope is identified by a pecked line (fig. no. 5.1). Shadings or colours are used to define slope classes. The I.G.U. manual identifies six slope categories, such as, 0° – 2°, 2° – 5°, 5° – 15°, 15° – 35°, 35° – 55° and 55°+ (Demek, 1972). Slope steepness can be measured in degrees, percentage and gradient ratio. Difference of height can be included if it is drawn on a faint contour base.

As regards the scale of the map, if the area is intensely dissected, the map scale may be of 1:10,000, whereas if it is moderate, smaller scale not less than 1:75,000 can be used.

For variable features of similar nature variable thickness of lines may be employed. The features which are not covered by the minimum size to be shown on a particular scale, small symbols should be used for them. Different identification marks should be used for different surface forms. Thus a ridge is marked differently from that of an erosional summit or a solifluction lobe is different from a soil creep etc.

Conventional symbols for landform features (fig. 5.1 a-e)

Mapping of surface materials

As the landforms are composed of various types of materials having distinctive characteristics in their nature and composition, it is necessary to have them mapped differently in order to distinguish the interaction of a less resistant material with geomorphic process from that of a more resistant one.

The geological materials fall into two groups : solid rocks and superficial deposits. The superficial materials may be weathered materials *in situ* or may be transported from elsewhere.

The distinctive characteristics of the bedrock as well as regolith can be mapped in the field in a geomorphological map. The type of bedrock should be distinguished as all of them have distinctive role in the building of country-landform. The structural characteristics of the rocks should also be marked in order to justify any specific behaviour reflected in the landform characteristics.

The superficial materials also behave differently depending on their compaction, composition, porosity, permeability, depth of the weathered mantle etc. Soils also have similar behavioural features. In this regard the information about the compressive strength should also be examined and incorporated in the map. Besides, for any special purpose some other information may be needed in connection with lithology of an area or water retentivity of soils etc. For instance, a geomorphological map meant for agricultural planning should require the knowledge of soil texture, structure, organic matter content, depth of soil etc. However, this information may extend the process of geomorphological mapping further beyond the scope of a field technique and may be used for substantive planning for the purpose of development, that may be agricultural, hydrological, soil conservation, landslide protection or anything else. A comprehensive geomorphological map may be used for prediction purpose also.

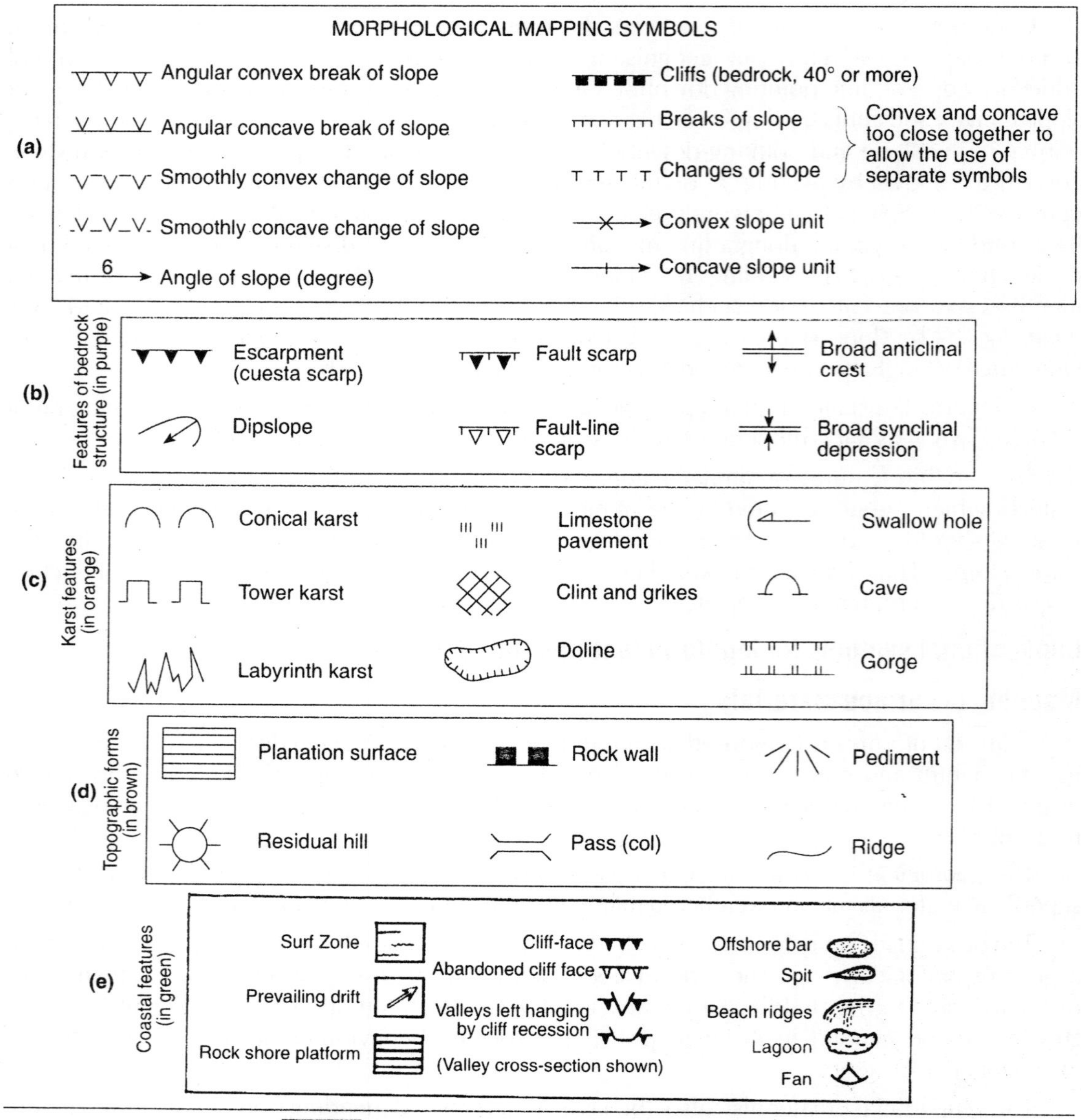

Fig. 5.1 Conventional symbols for landform units

Conventional symbols for surface materials (fig. 5.2 a-c)

Mapping of processes

The ensemble of various geomorphological processes on the surface of the earth and their complicated interactions require detailed mapping. The features of coastal processes are distinctly different from that of mountain glaciers, periglacial processes have totally different set of interactions from that of fluvial processes etc. All such processes in terms of the features produced by them should comprise a major part of geomorphological information in the map.

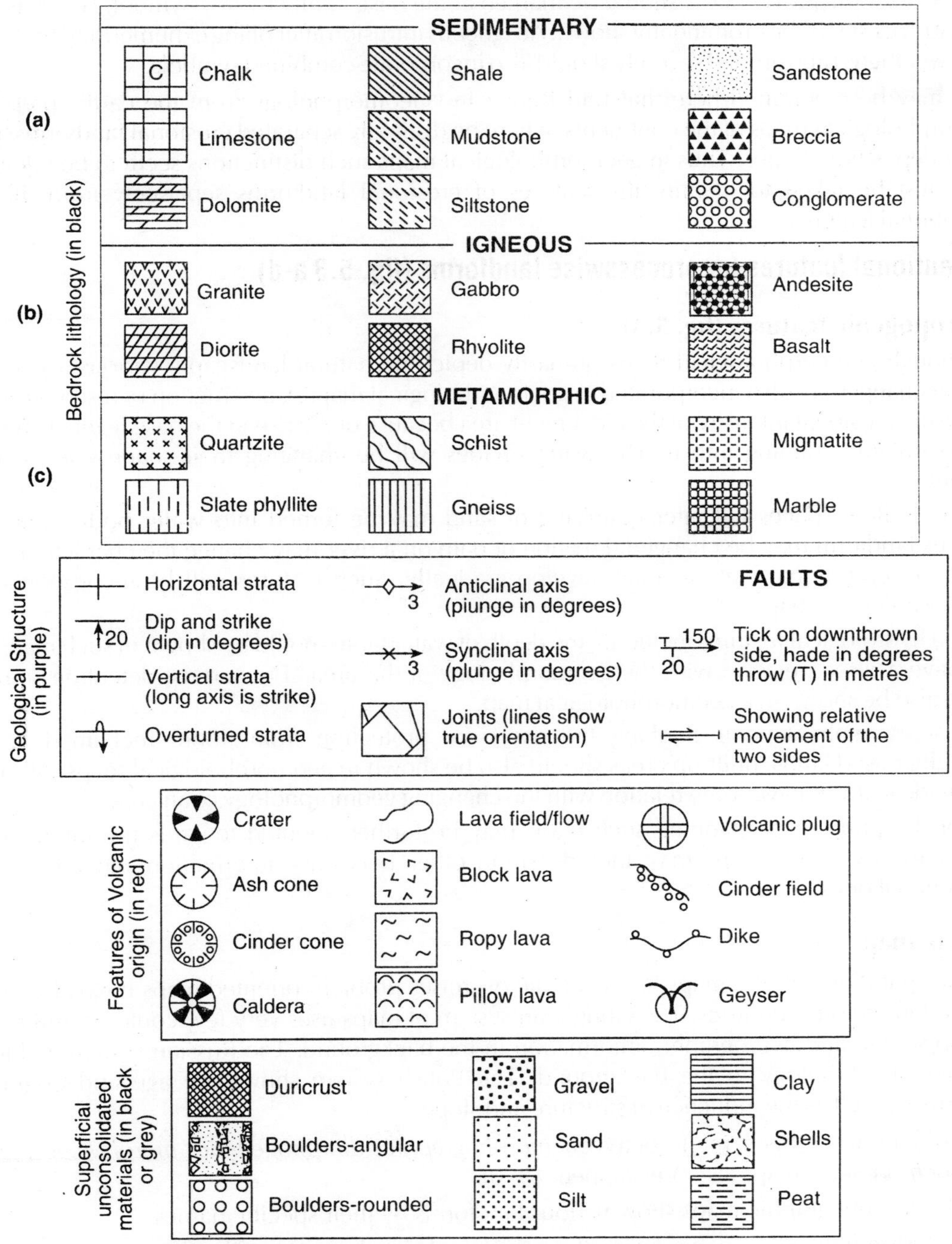

Fig. 5.2 Conventional symbols for surface materials and structure

In this regard it should be carefully maintained that an ancient landform feature largely being formed by any past geomorphological process should be marked in terms of the previous process. For such features the present process should also be mentioned. For instance, a heap of glacial end-moraine, which is a legacy of the last little glacial age, may be presently modified by fluvial process.

In such cases the past process should be marked at the base faintly by any symbol, whereas, the present process will be prominently shown. An igneous intrusion after being exhumed and presently being weathered and eroded severely should also incorporate combined symbols.

It may be mentioned here that Karl Butzar in "Geomorphology from the earth" prepared geomorphological maps of the continents, where he distinctly separated erosional landforms from that of depositional ones. Thus in geomorphological maps such distinctions seem to be relevant. Care must be taken to identify the features of erosional landforms separately from that of depositional features.

Conventional features for processwise landforms (fig. 5.3 a-d)

Anthropogenic features (fig. 5.4)

Though geomorphological maps primarily depict the natural landscape, various aspects of cultural changes are also incorporated in geomorphological maps. Construction of reservoirs may reduce the erosional intensity of the catchment area because of the rise in the base level of erosion for the streams draining into it. The water divides will be changing their shape due to such changes.

The hollow spaces left after quarrying of sand may be turned into water bodies and the previous landform may be changed. Erection of dam on a river may change the character of the river and depositional features may develop gradually. Such features will be incorporated in geomorphological maps.

The hydrological features including the depth of water table should be shown in such maps, as they have a direct relation with the geomorphology of the area. The surface detention storage should also be shown in a geomorphological map.

Besides, embankments flanking the rivers for protection from flood, reclaimed lands, artificially raised lands, built-up areas should also be shown in geomorphological maps. All such man-made features have some relation with the changing geomorphology of an area.

For the purpose of planning such maps may be further oriented towards the information needed mostly. Such maps may include some other necessary information other than the conventional ones.

Types of maps

Thus parallel with the maps for academic exercises problem-oriented maps have also been prepared in various countries. The Hungarian system of maps uses very few contours and show morphogenetic and hydrographic information in the background. The Russian system includes tectonics and lithology in the background. The Polish system shows the age and origin of landforms as well as the influence of structure and slope.

Distinction has been made between *morphographic, morphogenetic, morphometric* and *morphochronologic* maps also (Verstappen, 1970).

1. Morphographic maps show various landforms by their specific names.
2. Morphogenetic maps define the origin and development of landforms with genetic descriptions.
3. Morphometric maps show the dimensions of landforms. The morphometric information are included in such maps.
4. Morphochronologic maps identify landforms according to their time of initiation. Recent forms and those inherited from the past processes are distinctly separated. Age is indicated by a code letter or a code number. It is omitted when age is not known.

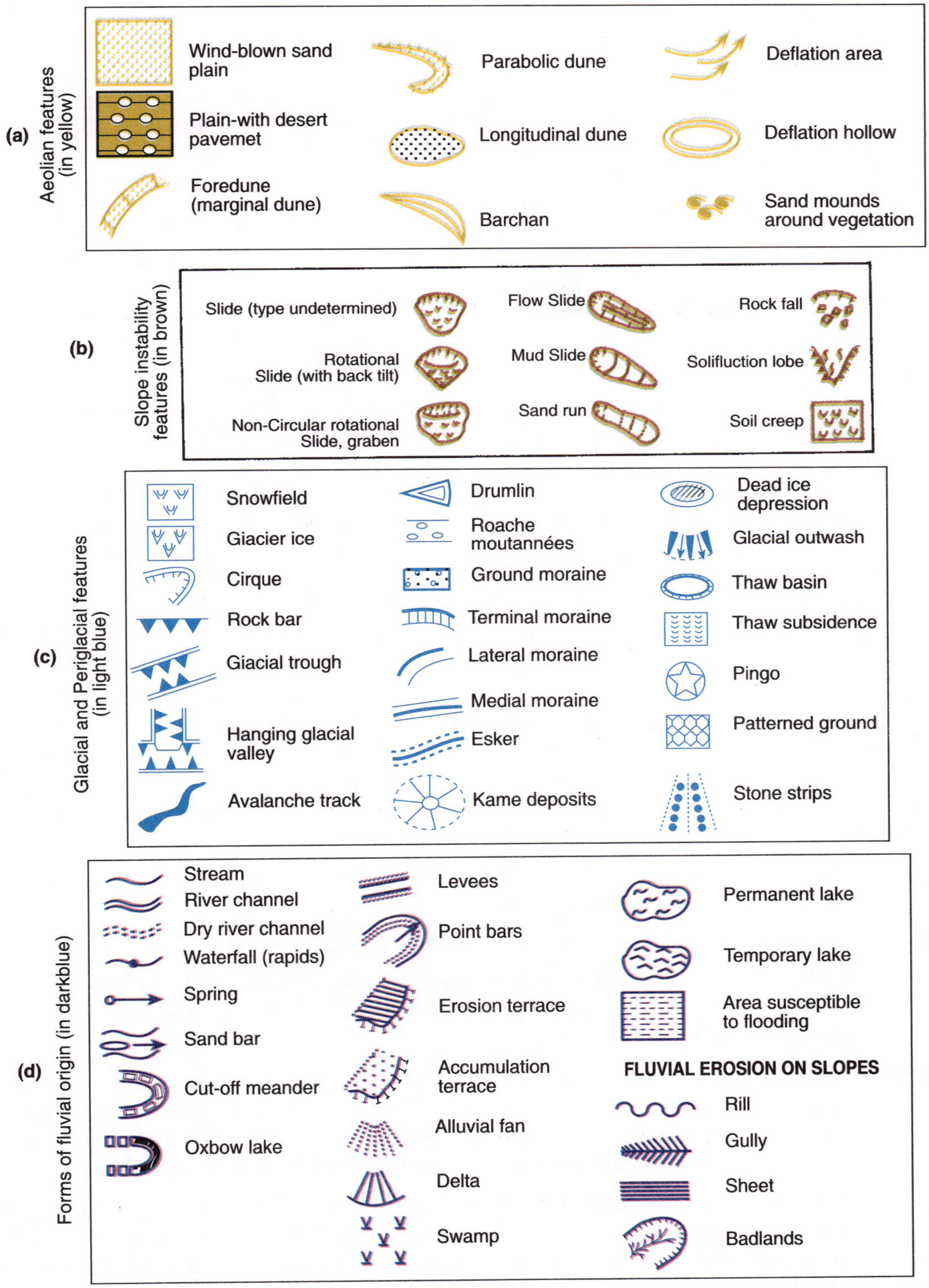

Fig. 5.3 Conventional symbols for processwise landform units

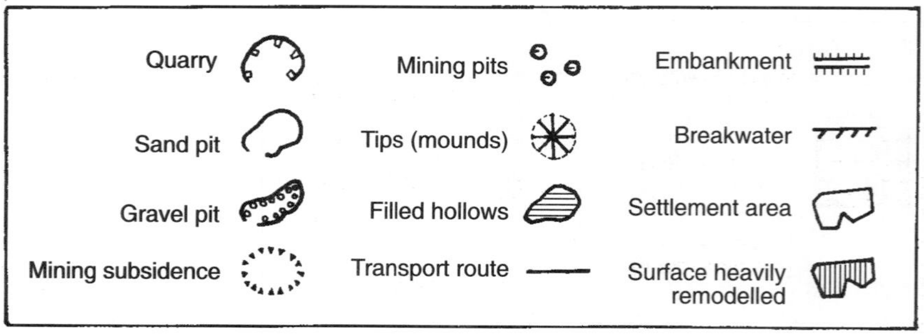

Fig. 5.4 Anthropogenic features

Colours used

I.T.C. has used the following colour system (Table 5.1) for the forms and other aspects of geomorphological maps :

TABLE 5.1

1. Forms of structural origin	purple
2. Forms of volcanic origin	red
3. Forms of denudational origin	brown
4. Forms of fluvial origin	dark blue
5. Forms of marine origin	green
6. Forms of glacial and periglacial origin	light blue
7. Forms of aeolian origin	yellow
8. Forms of solution origin	orange
9. Morphometry	black
10 Lithology	black/grey
11. Chronology	black
12. Topography	black/grey

How to do a geomorphological map

As geomorphological mapping is a comprehensive field technique of incorporating field data with the consultancy of topographic maps side by side, a student or a researcher can aptly apply this to a purpose-oriented planning or making a data-source for future geomorphological works or academic purposes of understanding the present state of geomorphology of an area (fig. 5.5). The following steps will help to prepare such a map for a specific area.

Step 1: From the available published works on the geology and geomorphology of the area have a comprehensive knowledge.

Step 2: Determine the purpose or problem for which the map is needed.

Step 3: Collect copies of the topographical sheets on a scale not less than 1:50,000 for the area to be covered. Prepare a base map on the basis of latitude and longitude given in the topographic map.

Step 4: Study thoroughly the topographic configuration of the area and identify the important landform features on the base map as well as determine the nature and geomorphic divisions of the surface and the major valley axes of the area. Distinguish the landform features process-wise and use separate set of symbols to show them on map.

Step 5: Prepare a slope map by Wentworth or Raisz-Henry method or simply determine the gradient on map to show the general direction of slope. Determine the line of changing slope and break of slope using proper symbols. Superimpose them on the base map as a background by any subdued colour or screening.

Step 6 : If the geomorphological map is morphometric, apply the morphometric techniques to find out the values of significance. For morphogenetic and morphochronologic maps know the origin of landform features from the history of evolution of the area for the former and know or determine the age of the landforms for the latter by any standard method. Compile them into the map placing them at proper places. For morphographic maps name the features.

Step 7 : Visit the area for field study and determine the surface geology including the unconsolidated materials at the valley, at the ridge top, at mid-slope , at erosional summits, at changing point of slope and at break of slope. Superimpose the map of surface geology on the main map using proper conventional signs.

Step 8 : Study the hydrological features in the toposheet and show them with the help of conventional signs. Information about sub-surface hydrology including depth of water table at valley, ridge, plain, plateau etc. may be incorporated by figures, if available.

Step 9 : Locate the man-made features of geomorphic significance on the map.

Step 10 : If the map is meant for any specific purposes, such as, area development planning, study the type of soil for its texture, nature of drainage condition and line of water-divide. Show them on the map using special symbols or alphabets.

Interpretation : A geomorphological map is a composite of geological and topographic features, as incorporated in this geomorphological map (Fig. 5.5). It indicates that the area is

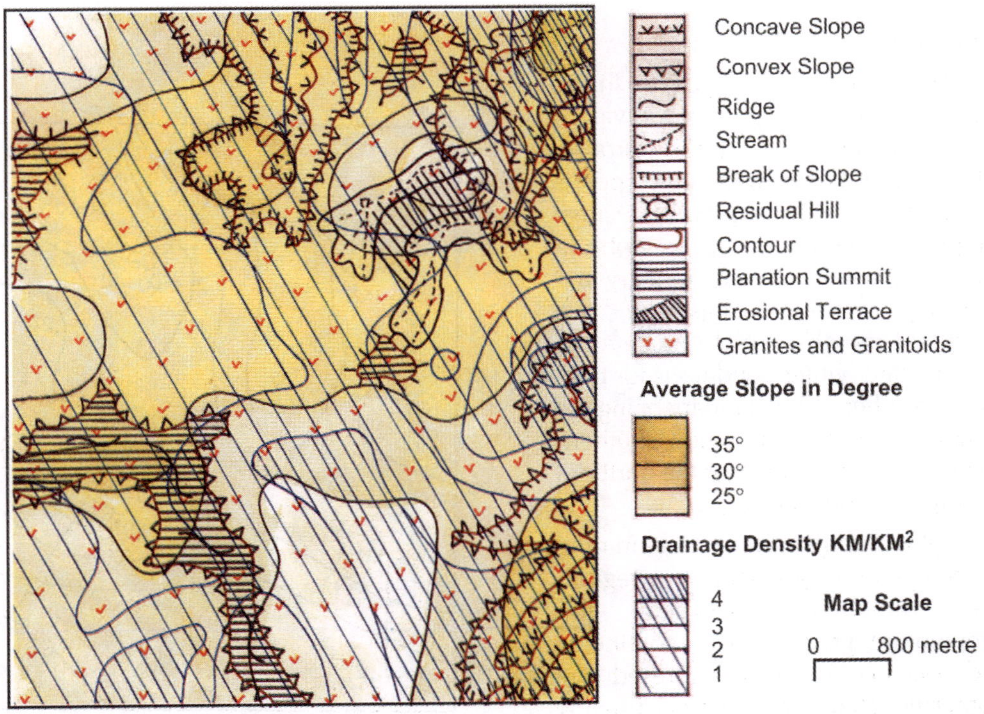

Fig.5.5 A Geomorphological Map

underlain by granites and granitoids. The erosional processes have modified and carved out various types of slope forms and have developed typical landform features. The average slope values are of moderate nature and drainage density is low because of the high resistance of underlying rocks. The accordant summits of the Jot ridge indicates the presence of planation summits. Their slope forms are convex in nature. On the other hand, some eastern and northern valleys have given rise to concave slope forms. Therefore, the area mapped has indicated a complex topographic surface which bear evidences of multiple phases of planation processes.

CLIMATOLOGICAL MAPS

The distribution of various elements of climate and their analysis is often done by climatological maps. The global distribution of temperature, pressure, airmass etc. are shown by such maps. Similarly, many of the critical values obtained during analysis of weather charts, when superimposed on any base of relevant distribution map, makes analysis more significant. Many of such maps use isopleth mapping technique and lines of the same value separates the zones of specific ranges.

Some of the climatological maps being isopleth in character, some others are simple distribution maps for continents, countries or any other smaller area. Isopleth mapping is particularly undertaken where the element or item to be shown seems to be a continuum, as interpolation is required in such maps. But when the distribution is highly localised or zonal in character, the spatial differences still may be shown by isopleths, such as, rainfall distribution over southern India or cloud cover over northern India etc. On the other hand, distribution of airmass may be effectively shown on a continental scale by a simple distribution map without any isopleth method. Moreover, cultural features being controlled by man is discrete and should not be shown by isopleth.

Isotherm

An isotherm map (fig. 5.6) shows the isothermal lines joining the values of same temperature. For this purpose, interpolation between the given points is required. Isotherms depict average temperature condition of the globe in different seasons. Usually, January and July are considered as the two important months, which indicate the summer and winter conditions for both the hemispheres, i.e., January being the summer month for the southern hemisphere and winter for the northern hemisphere and vice versa.

Isotherms are useful in determining the temperature gradient of a region. The variability between the temperature gradient over continents and oceans is also expresed by isotherms. There are northward bends of isotherms over the north Atlantic ocean, whereas, the neighbouring

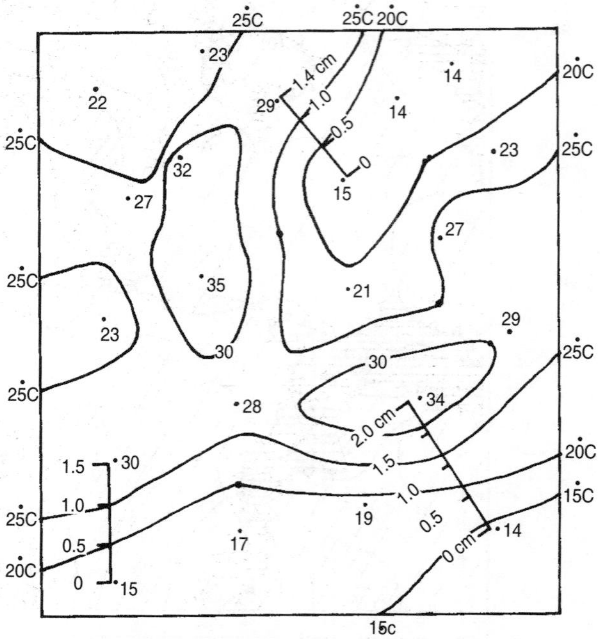

Fig. 5.6 Method of isoplething

continents have more or less straight parallel lines. The following steps should be followed in drawing of isotherms :

1. For drawing of isotherms temperature of selected stations should be known at first.
2. Selected values in the whole range of given temperature should be determined.
3. Selected values of same temperature should be connected. For this purpose the stations showing the selected value should be connected by the isopleth and the line should run between two higher and lower values on either side, positioning itself proportionately in between. That means if an isopleth of 20°C runs between 30°C and 15°C and the horizontal distance between them is 3 cm. on scale, the isopleth should be located at a distance of 2 cm. from 30°C and at 1 cm. from 15°C.
4. After drawing of isopleths different zones will develop between the lines.

   These may be screened or tinted with variable density or intensity increasing from lower to higher values or may be left as such.

   Drawing of isopleths may sometimes prove very difficult. The following precautions may help in this regard :

   a) any specific isopleth should separate the higher and lower values on either side ;
   b) an isolated higher value surrounded by lower values than the isopleth may form an enclosed line;
   c) an isolated lower value surrounded by higher values than the selected isopleth may form an enclosed line surrounding the lower value;
   d) a station with a value of the same amount as that of the isopleth being surrounded by lower or higher values than the specific value should be left as such; such a station should not be connected with the isopleth;
   e) isopleths should not be drawn along the sides of the given area where there is no control on the outer side;
   f) zones separated by isopleths should be successive;
   g) for a gridded map only the immediate neighbouring grids will be considered at the time of interpolation;
   h) for constructing the index for the zones between the isopleths a contiguous column of colours or screens should be made and isopleth values should be marked between the zones; the highest values will be placed at the top and lowest at the bottom.

Isobar

Alike isotherms (fig. 3.95), isobars connect points of same barometric pressure (fig. 3.96). These lines depicting the regional distribution of barometric pressure on a particular day or at a particular hour reveal the structure of pressure systems. They often locate depression and high pressure zones by enclosed lines. In published weather maps, isobars form the base of the control system of the weather features observed. The pattern of isobars not only expresses the trend of spatial pressure changes, but also the gradient may be understood from that. Isobaric patterns may sometimes depict and delineate the formation of fronts also.

Isobars may be drawn on the basis of sea level pressure or on the basis of station level pressure. But in the latter case the variability of pressure due to difference in height cannot be removed. That is why pressure distribution in terms isobar is often shown on the basis of sea level pressure. However, isobaric charts at various millibar levels are also available.

The general pattern of isobars is, more or less, regular in different regions of the earth. Observations made through isobars and inferences drawn have proved significant. For instance, the isobaric pattern over the Indian sub-continent at the time of onset of monsoon is so regular that even the dates of advancement of summer monsoon have matched with them. The trough over the Ganga plain, with loops of isobars enclosing it, is, more or less, a regular observation during the season of summer monsoon.

For drawing of isobars the same method of isopleth mapping will be applied. Usually, on Indian Weather Maps isobars are drawn at an interval of 2 millibar. The density of isobars increases at higher gradient of pressure and they become scarce when the distribution of pressure is, more or less, uniform. Interpolation in drawing of isobars is not very difficult as pressure distribution acts as a continuum.

Isohyet

Isohyets (fig. 3.102) depict the regional distribution of rainfall. An isohyet connects points of same amount of rainfall, but interpolation becomes a practical difficulty for drawing of isohyet, as the occurrence of rainfall may be very localised and never becomes a continuum throughout a large region. Moreover, a few stations may not receive a reliable amount and may be neglected or ignored.

The selection of interval for such maps is difficult, because it depends on the range of rainfall totals to be plotted and within one country, different regions may receive different amounts. The variability in amount is so important that within a small region, the coastal zone and the interior, the east facing and west facing slopes of a mountain may receive significantly variable amounts. The impact of height, the location of a rain shadow area, the windward and leeward sides of a mountain, the coastal and the interior etc. have shown wide variation in rainfall and therefore, an isohyet map should be rationalised with such things in mind.

The drawing of isohyets may be regional in extent. For instance, during the season of retreating monsoon Tamilnadu, Kerala and Karnataka may receive significant rainfall, whereas, the central and northern India may remain dry. On a weather map of such a season isohyets may be drawn only for the southern parts of India. The method of drawing of isohyets is the same with that of other isopleth maps.

Isoneph

The line joining same amount of cloud cover is known as isoneph (fig. 3.101). The amount of cloud on weather maps is shown in octad, i.e., the sky is divided into eight divisions and how much of it is covered by cloud is to be taken into account. This way $\frac{1}{8}$ means only one part of eight divisions of the sky has been covered with cloud, again $\frac{2}{8}$s become $\frac{1}{4}$, $\frac{6}{8}$s become $\frac{3}{4}$s and 1 means overcast. In weather maps specific conventional symbols are there for each $\frac{1}{8}$th part of increase in cloud cover. The increase in the amount of cloud-cover will be shown by the consequent gradual increase in solid or screened portion of the cloud circle in a clockwise direction.

However, at the time of drawing isonephs the octant may be converted into percentage, which may make it convenient for interpolation as fractions will be almost removed. Zones of different ranges of cloud amount may be screened or coloured at variable intensity.

There may be a few area, where the sky is cloudless. Such areas may be categorized as 0% cloud cover. Overcast condition, on the other hand, will be represented by 100% cloud cover. Isonephs may be highly zonal in distribution, as except for the rainy season, the cloud cover may not be present over greater part of the country, though exceptional climatic incidences are always there. Interpolation between two separate zones of cloud-concentration at distant locations from each other should be avoided. As cloud cover is not a continuum and may be highly localized, separate zones of isoneph concentration may be identified.

Drawing of isonephs follows the same method, as in other isopleth maps. Care must be taken to identify the actual zones of cloud concentration. Isonephs may help detection of trajectory of rainbearing winds.

Isanomals

Isanomals are related to the anomalies of temperature with reference to 'normal'. Isopleths drawn on the basis of such anomalies are known as isanomals. The normal for any latitude is the average of the mean monthly temperature of that latitude. The average of mean monthly temperature is reduced to sea-level value. A good number of well dispersed stations are taken for which the data has been obtained. Tables for standard temperature are useful in this regard. The standard temperature (t) is obtained from the following formula :

$$t = -17.8 + 44.9 \cos^2 (\theta - 6.5)°C,$$ where θ is the latitude for any station.

Then the temperature anomaly is derived as the amount of departure of the mean monthly temperature from normal or standard temperature.

After plotting the anomalies isopleth mapping is done through interpolation and isanomal distribution is shown.

In this method regions of positive anomaly and negative anomaly are separated. Regions of considerable positive anomaly are known as *'thermopleions'* and regions of remarkable negative anomaly are known as *'thermomeions'*. For visual effects the positive anomalies may be tinted red and the negative may be tinted blue.

Isomers

In isomers, the mean monthly rainfalls for different stations of a region are 'weighted' and expressed as percentage of the respective mean annual rainfalls. For a year, twelve maps can be prepared to show the distribution of comparative proportions of rainfall for each month by isopleth lines joining places with same percentage. Thus it expresses the regional variations in the relative proportion of rainfall in each month of a year.

It can be effective in understanding the occurrence of drought and flood in a region, as the disparities of monthly variation in a year in terms of its annual rainfall are revealed through it. A comparative study between a particular year and a long term average can clarify the cause of catastrophic incidences related to rainfall.

Isopleths of Aridity and Moisture

Identification of climatic aridity is a long standing question with respect to delineation of climatic provinces and agricultural planning. The following indices were suggested :

(i) R. Lang suggested *rain factor* to serve the purpose :

$$\text{Rain factor} = \frac{\text{Annual ppt. in mm.}}{\text{Mean annual temp. in °C}}$$

(ii) A. Miller prepared an index of humidity as $\frac{T}{R}$

[Here T = Mean annual temperature in °F, R = Mean annual rainfall in inches]

He drew isopleths of this index in a range of 1 to 5. The regions and their respective $\frac{T}{R}$ values are :

<1	=	perhumid
1-2	=	humid
2-3	=	sub-humid
3-5	=	semi-arid
>5	=	arid

(iii) De Martonne's index, on the basis of which a series of maps in the French National Atlas were prepared, is as follows :

$$I = \frac{P}{T + 10}$$

I = Index of aridity
T = Mean annual temp. in °C
P = Mean annual rainfall in mm.

From this the calculation of monthly indices is possible.

$$i = \frac{P \times 12}{t + 10}$$

t = mean monthly temperature
p = mean monthly rainfall

(iv) C.W. Thornthwaite invented the monthly precipitation-evaporation ratio to indicate the relationship between temperature, rainfall and evaporation by the following formula :

$$\frac{P}{E} = 11.5 \left(\frac{P}{t - 10}\right)^{\frac{10}{9}}$$

The summation of the twelve monthly values gives the yearly value. The range of index values varies from 0 to 150. Thornthwaite divided them into 5 humidity provinces : wet, humid, sub-humid, semi-arid and arid.

For the effect of temperature he calculated thermal efficiency from the following formula :

$$i = \frac{t - 32}{4}$$

i = thermal efficiency
t = mean monthly temperature (°F)

In his later classification of climate (1948) he calculated evapo-transpiration with a special formula. Actually he tried to measure the potential evapo-transpiration (PE) for estimating soil-moisture budget, which will be of practical value for agricultural planning. He used the following formula to calculate the potential evapo-transpiration values for the months of a year :

$$PE \text{ (in cm)} = 1.6 \left(\frac{10t}{I}\right)^a$$

I = sum of 12 monthly $\left(\frac{t}{5}\right)^{1.1.54}$
a = a further complex function of I

However, the various types of values estimating aridity and moisture status can be plotted on a distribution map and isopleths can be drawn. Such isopleths will show climatic differences in terms of the degree of aridity between different zones.

Graphs and diagrams

Besides maps various types of graphs and diagrams are used to identify climatic characteristics. Such graphs and diagrams usually do not depict any regional distribution except when those are superimposed on maps. However, comparative studies of such representations may clarify the status of climate at different stations. Very often a single graph incorporates data for different stations. In such cases the comparison is made within a single frame and separate graphs are not required. For instance, temperature graph of the months of a year for different stations can be prepared within one frame of ordinate and abscissa with the help of different symbols.

Composite profiles representing two or three sets of data of different climatic elements or factors or a combination of both can be prepared also, e.g., composite temperature and relief profiles or composite rainfall and relief profiles. Occasionally, a composite of two different elements constructs a single climatic phenomenon, e.g., water surplus graph as suggested by Thornthwaite showing precipitation and evapotranspiration overlapping each other within a single frame.

Line Graphs

Line graphs, in particular, show the trend of rise or fall. Usually, the lines are plotted either as a polygon or as a curve, the curve shows the general trend and the polygon specify the points of bivariate data at each break of the line. Line graphs can depict temperature, humidity, evaporation etc. as ordinate values and months, days, hours as abscissa. Seasonal and diurnal variations are well exhibited in such graphs.

Polygraphs

These graphs incorporate a series of multiple line-graphs to indicate relationships between different sets of climatic or any other statistics at any station. Temperature and rainfall regimes can be indicated by polygraphs, though according to conventional practice rainfall data is shown in columns.

In *composite rainfall and relief profiles* both rainfall and relief, i.e., height above sea level, are plotted along ordinates on a common horizontal scale of abscissa.

Comparison becomes easier when plotted on polygraphs. Data for two or more stations having contrasting climatic characteristics can be plotted on polygraphs. For such comparisons standardization of data can be done by reducing the mean annual data – total of particular climatic element into percentage. Such graphs are known as comparative percentage graphs.

Water surplus graphs superimpose the mean monthly evapo-transpiration on mean monthly rainfall or vice-versa, both plotted along the ordinates. Months are plotted as abscissa. Such graphs help delineation of monthly surplus and deficit of moisture. This was developed and used by Thornthwaite for identifying soil moisture budget. He further clarified the phenomena of soil moisture utilization and recharge in the phase of deficit and surplus respectively. During the deficit period irrigation is needed.

Adjusted profiles are those which incorporate temperature profiles of different places as adjusted in terms of time for regional variations. For this graph all temperature profiles are reduced to the same amplitude by adjusting the mean annual ranges of temperature to an equal size. This can be done for monthly and daily temperature profiles also.

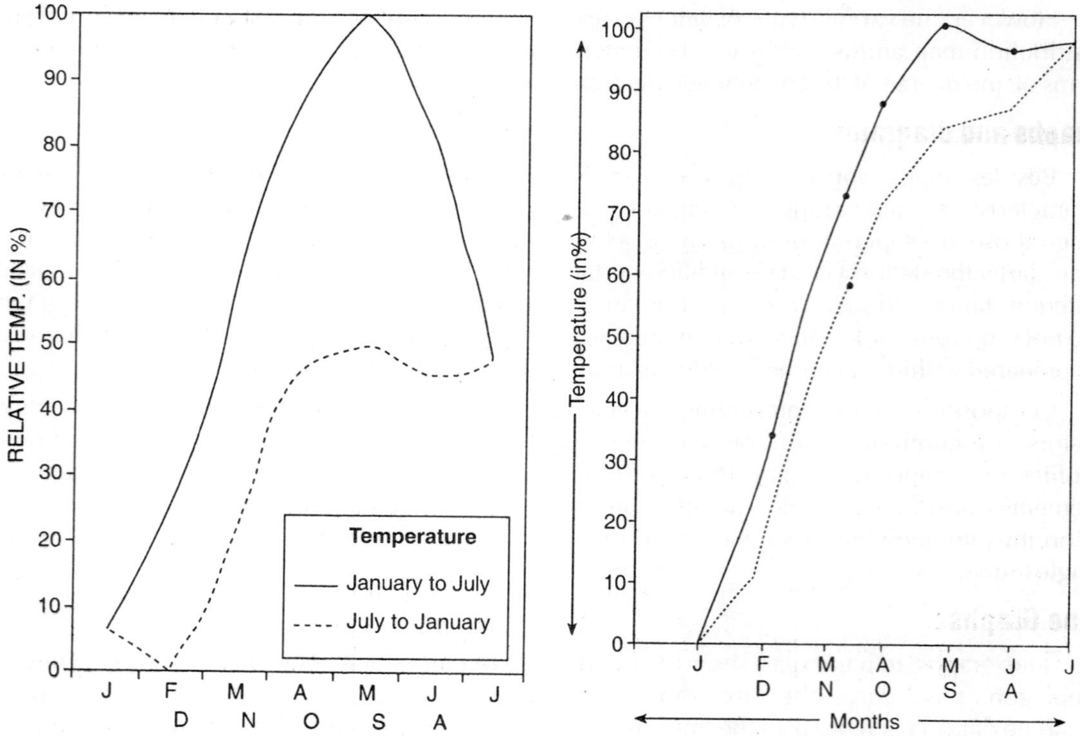

Fig. 5.7 **Relative temperature curve of Bolpur**

Relative temperature curves (fig. 5.7) depict the comparison of temperature curves between the first and second halves of the year, in terms of the amount of mean monthly temperature, which is in excess of the temperature of the coldest month, as expressed in percentage of the difference in average temperatures between the coldest and the warmest month. For instance, if the average temperature of the warmest month is 35°C and that of the coldest month 12°C and the mean monthly temperature of a particular month (say July) is 27°C, the difference from the coldest i.e. 27°C – 12°C = 15°C is considered as 65% of 35°C – 12°C or 23°C. These percentages are plotted as ordinates on the months as abscissa. The horizontal scale is typically graduated as to enable the relative temperatures for the first half of the year to be compared directly with those of the last half. Hence, August is placed along the ordinate of June, October is placed along the ordinate of April and December is placed along the ordinate of February.

TABLE 5.2
CLIMATIC DATA FOR BOLPUR STATION

Month	Jan	Feb	Mar	Apr	May	June	July	Aug	Sept.	Oct.	Nov.	Dec.	Year
Max. Temp. (°C)	25	28	34	37	39	34	33	32	33	31	30	26	
Min. Temp. (°C)	13	14	21	23	27	26	26	26	26	22	17	12	1996
Rainfall (in mm.)	3	4	9	57	76	247	255	445	139	95	0	0	

Contd. next page

Month	Jan	Feb	Mar	Apr	May	June	July	Aug	Sept.	Oct.	Nov.	Dec.	Year
Max. Temp. (°C)	24	28	33	33	37	36	33	32	32	31	29	23	
Min. Temp. (°C)	11	14	20	21	25	26	27	26	25	22	19	15	1997
Rainfall (in mm.)	7	15	4	66	77	183	471	286	384	59	72	18	

Month	Jan	Feb	Mar	Apr	May	June	July	Aug	Sept.	Oct.	Nov.	Dec.	Year
Max. Temp. (°C)	22	27	31	34	36	36	34	33	33	32	30	26	
Min. Temp. (°C)	12	16	18	23	25	27	26	26	26	24	20	13	1998
Rainfall (in mm.)	47	15	75	41	69	196	386	392	269	260	16	0	

Month	Jan	Feb	Mar	Apr	May	June	July	Aug	Sept.	Oct.	Nov.	Dec.	Year
Max. Temp. (°C)	25	30	35	38	35	33	33	32	31	31	30	27	
Min. Temp. (°C)	11	15	19	25	25	26	26	26	25	24	17	14	1999
Rainfall (in mm.)	—	—	—	13	161	320	422	420	438	129	140	—	

Month	Jan	Feb	Mar	Apr	May	June	July	Aug	Sept.	Oct.	Nov.	Dec.	Year
Max. Temp. (°C)	26	25	33	36	36	34	33	33	32	32	31	26	
Min. Temp. (°C)	11	14	19	23	24	26	26	26	25	23	18	13	2000
Rainfall (in mm.)	2	59	18	70	169	233	359	143	93	31	—	—	
5 years avg. of mean temp.	18	21.1	26.3	29.3	30.9	30.4	29.7	29.2	28.8	27.2	24.1	19.5	1996-2000
Temp. (%)	0	24.03	64.34	87.60	100	96.12	90.70	86.82	85.72	71.32	47.29	11.63	

Calculation for Relative temperature curve :

1. Temperature of the warmest month – Temperature of the coldest month = Range of temperature which is considered as 100%.
2. Difference between temperature of any month and temperature of the coldest month expressed as percent value of the Range of temperature.
3. 30.9°C – 18°C = 12.9°C
4. For April $= \dfrac{29.3°C - 18°C}{12.9°C} \times 100 = 87.60\%$

Curves on the basis of statistical techniques

If complete and reliable records over a considerable period of time of one decade or over a longer time is obtained, various statistical techniques can be applied as line graphs to depict such data. A time series analysis on the basis of *moving average* can be done for three, four or five years or of any other value. For such graphs a *scatter diagram* showing the values of the annual means of temperature plotted as ordinates on the abscissa showing the year, may be constructed first. Then the moving average values for three, four or five consecutive years are determined. These average values are plotted on the graph and are connected by straight lines segmentwise. This graph can depict the time based trend or temperature changes. Moreover, it can determine the future trend also on the basis of the yearly trend values between the ranges of two consecutive moving averages. The moving average method has been shown in the chapter of Statistical Methods in Geography.

Deviation graphs depict the cyclic fluctuation and trend in the data of temperature and rainfall. The deviations are obtained from mean annual rainfall or temperature. The accumulated deviations are plotted as cumulative values. Thus, negative deviations can be avoided. But there is no rule that the negative values should be removed. However, for the purpose of comparison the deviations are often plotted as percentages of the accumulated total. The mean value can be taken as the zero percent line in the middle of the ordinate values, and thus it can facilitate to show negative values below the line. Table no. 5.2 shows such accumulated deviation values for a 5 year (1968–1972) annual rainfall data and the deviation graph is plotted as 5.7a.

D. Brunt in "Climatic cycles" (1937) mentioned a form a deviational graph as periodogram in which the amplitudes of temperature in the form of deviations are plotted as ordinates and periods of time as abscissa. A large data for a long period of time can be used for this purpose to identify the exact climatic cycle, either for temperature or rainfall.

TABLE 5.3

Year	Annual rainfall in mm	Mean	Deviation	Accumulated Deviation
1968	2721.6		+ 50.7	+50.7
1969	2597.9	2670.9	– 73	– 22.3
1970	2394.6		– 276.3	– 298.6
1971	3441.9		+ 771	+ 472.4
1972	2198.5		– 472.4	0

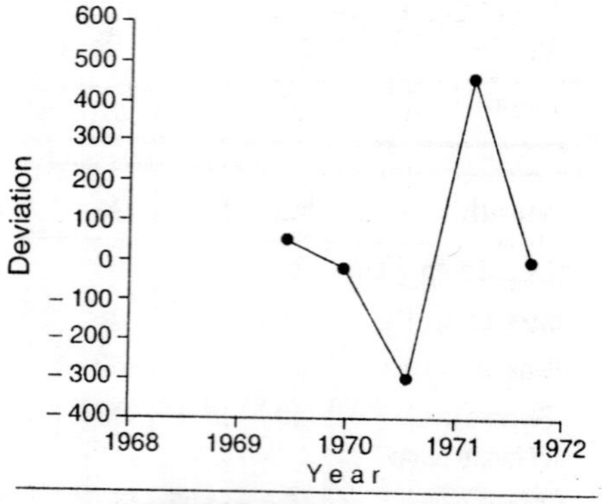

Fig-5.8 Deviation Graph

Frequency graphs

Histogram showing absolute frequency or frequency percentage as ordinates in grouped or ungrouped data above classes of variable amounts of rainfall as abscissa can be constructed. Similarly, it can show the frequencies of extreme temperature, heavy rainfall, hailstorm, thunderstorm etc. on periods of long range. For such data frequency polygons can also be constructed.

Columnar diagrams

These diagrams are very effective in showing climatic data of monthly variation. Yearly distribution of rainfall can also be shown by vertical columns according to the scale about the ordinate giving the amount of rainfall. The horizontal scale is insignificant and the thickness of the columns does not give any indication, only each month occupies certain horizontal length of abscissa uniformly.

When placed at different stations on a distribution map, they can express regional or spatial variations. Humidity can also be represented in such diagrams, but they are more effectively represented in *Percentage bar graphs* as relative humidity is expressed in percentage.

The preparation of columnar diagrams requires to find out the suitable scale along the ordinate, so that the columns shown are not too long for the map or space provided. A compsite graph of rainfall columns and temperature curves on the same frame of abscissa and ordinate is a common method for showing both rainfall and temperature within the same range of time.

Columns representing monthly rainfall and temperature values shown along a curve can identify the nature of climate easily. That is why such graphs are used for academic purposes in schools. A convex temperature curve identifies northern hemisphere and a concave one recognises the sourthern. Mediterranean climate has concentration of rainfall in winter, whereas, monsoon climate has the concentration of rainfall in summer (Table 5.3).

In *hydrographs,* particularly storm hydrograph, the amount of rainfall at different hours of the day or days along with peak rainfall hours are represented by columnar diagram hanging from the top. Such a diagram will have its base at the top horizontal line of the abscissa-ordinate frame and the scale along the ordinate will increase downward. Such a columnar diagram can give the span of lag time or basin lag being the interval between the peak rainfall-hour and peak hour for discharge as the time-based discharge data is plotted in the form of a curve above the bottom base-line showing time. The basin lag varies according to the shape and area of the basin.

TABLE 5.4
DARJILING (1968 - 1972)

Month	Average rainfall in mm	Average Temperature °C
January	5.67	9.4
February	8.78	9.9
March	34.68	13.5
April	79.2	16.0
May	176.84	17.6
June	517.7	19.2
July	720.25	19.8
August	499.81	20.4
September	371.14	20.0
October	226.48	19.6
November	8.38	17.3
December	2.37	12.3

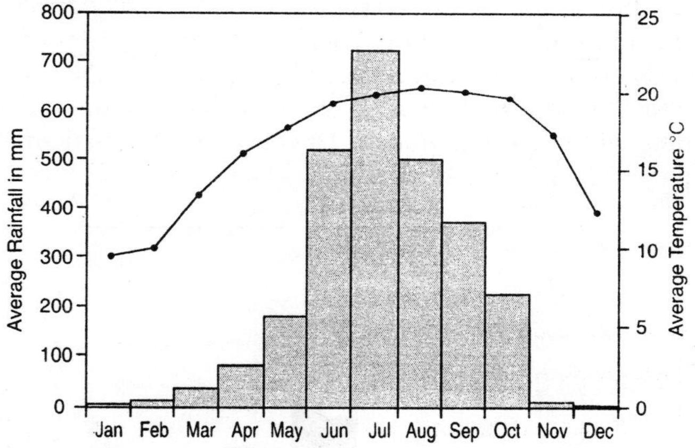

Fig. 5.9 **Rainfall temperature graph, Darjiling**

The rainfall temperature graph of Darjiling (Fig. 5.9) shows marked concentration of rainfall in monsoon months.

When the agricultural calendar as well as the production are shown as horizontal bars below the composite graph of rainfall and temperature, they are known as *Ergograph* (fig. 5.8). Ergographs offer a tangible correlation between the cropping season of various crops and the distribution of rainfall and temperature throughout the year.

Columnar diagram showing only the total amount of rainfall has been known as simple columnar diagram. Similarly, evaporation, run off etc. are also favourably represented in such diagrams. The frequency of the occurrence of fog, snowfall, hailstorm, thunderstorm, rainy days etc. can also be represented by such diagrams.

Percentage columnar diagram

Percentage columns help comparison between inter-regional mean monthly variations of the weather elements. Many other comparisons in terms of component shares of the total, such as, percentage share of monsoon rain in the total rainfall of a year can also be favourably shown in such a diagram. Relative humidity, as expressed in percentage can be conveniently shown in percentage columns.

Superimposed columnar diagrams

When superimposed, a columnar diagram offers direct comparison. Thus the percentage share of run off in the total rainfall, amount of evaporation in the mean total rainfall can be conveniently shown by superimposition. For superimpostion two sets of columns on the same base will be constructed. The longer columns of the total or whole (e.g. total rainfall) can be represented without any screen or colour, whereas, the superimposed ones can be coloured or screened.

Compound columnar diagrams

In these diagrams columns are sub-divided into segments. Various types of climatic data can be represented in such columns, particularly when they represent components, or comparable data of similar nature.

But some other *compound columnar diagrams* are constructed to show deviation of the minimum and maximum rainfall from the mean amount. *Standard deviation* can also be shown in such columns. However, such diagrams are known as *hyetographs*. Dispersion of rainfall may indicate the partition values of *median* and *quarile* and can indicate the variable concentration of data within the total range. To get the mean, median and quartile values the formulae given at page 284–290 can be used.

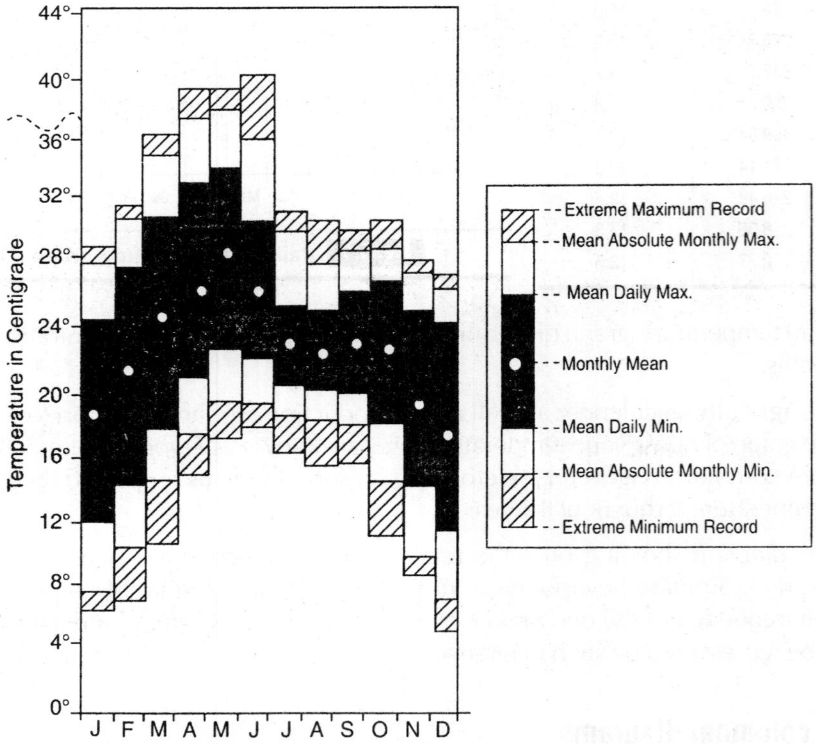

Fig. 5.10 **Compound columnar diagram : Vishakhapatnam**

However, columnar diagrams can be used to incorporate many other types of climatic data, such as, temperature, to obtain a comprehensive idea about the range and variation of data as well as the location of mean amidst the two ends of a range (fig. 5.10).

Circular graphs

In circular graphs the values of various climatic elements are plotted from the centre along the radii in different directions. The points plotted are then joined and closed curves are formed. As a circle contends 360° of angle it can be conveniently divided into 12 months of 30° each. As there are 365 days in a year, even year-round day to day climatic data can be plotted with slight adjustment. A composite of the enclosed graphs depicting various climatic data can give a comprehensive idea about the climate of an area. Seasons can also be identified on such graphs.

For the construction of such circular graphs scales for different climatic elements can be chosen along the radius of the circle. For temperature and humidity the length of the radius from centre to circumference can be taken either as 100°C or as 100% respectively. Some other lower values can also be fixed depending on the place of which the climatic characteristics are to be shown. The area of the circle can also be used to represent the total annual rainfall. A separate scale should be given in the form of a circle to represent the scale of the annual rainfall. The curves drawn can be shown in colours, so that confusions about different curves can be avoided.

Wind-rose diagrams

These diagrams (fig. 5.11) depict wind conditions in the form of a star-like diagram showing the average frequency and direction of wind at different stations. The wind direction is given in terms of cardinal points, although the ordinal points can be used for greater details.

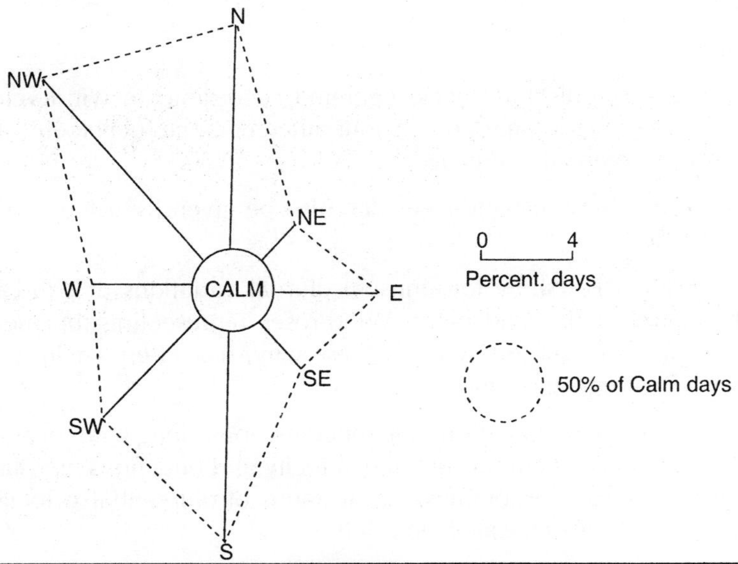

Fig. 5.11 Wind rose

Simple wind-roses represent the frequency of wind movement in eight directions. They can be prepared for one month each. Twelve diagrams are required to represent one year. Two concentric circles, the circumferences set at 12.5% apart, are drawn initially and the percentage frequency of wind in eight directions is shown by columns. The inner circle contains the number representing the percentage frequency of calm conditions.

For such simple wind roses, data for eight directions in terms of days is required along with the days having calm. The number of days from eight directions are drawn as columns based on the inner circle.

Octagonal wind-roses reflect the total mean monthly conditions for wind frequency as well as wind direction at any station. Here two concentric octagons are prepared at such a distance as to represent a frequency of 12.5% between the corresponding sides of each octagon. Each of the sides represents one of the eight cardinal directions of wind movement. The mean monthly frequencies of wind from eight directions are plotted as columns with their base on the inner octagon and apices on the outer octagon. Frequencies being greater than the average value will extend the columns over the outer octagon. The number of calms is represented diagrammatically in the inner octagon.

The data to be shown in an octagonal wind-rose is of the same type as it is in the simple wind-rose. These wind-roses simply identify the frequencies which are above and below the average value in terms of percentage.

In *compound wind-roses* the columns of wind-rose indicating frequency are sub-divided to show the frequency of wind strength associated with any particular direction. Usually, the four velocities used for this purpose are :

i) > 24 m.p.h.

ii) 13 to 24 m.p.h.

iii) 4 to 12 m.p.h.

iv) < 4 m.p.h.

These wind-roses show distinct zones separated according to wind velocity in terms of variable density of symbol or screen used. The four different ranges of velocity are represented by four circles which are differentially screened.

The indication of velocity in wind-roses can also be given by using variable thickness of column for each direction.

Superimposed wind-roses show the unusual diurnal variations of wind for the changing direction of wind between day and night. Wind-roses representing the mean conditions at different hours are superimposed on them. In these wind-roses frequencies are plotted from a central point. They form irregular octagons.

The monthly frequencies of wind from different directions along with mean velocities can be represented in *wind-stars.* The columns of wind velocity and directions are placed on the inner octagon and the thickness of the columns vary in terms of differential velocity. Another outer octagon is placed at a distance of the average value.

But wind-stars are very difficult to construct. The columns of 12 monthly values are so close to each other that determination of any specific value becomes difficult for the interpreter. They do not reduce well. Moreover, when placed on maps they do not depict the regional variations.

TABLE 5.5
CONSTRUCTION OF WIND ROSE

	Wind Speed (m./sec.)							
Direction	<0.5	0.5-2	2 – 4	4 – 6	6-8	8-10	>10	Total
E	0.29	1.07	0.56	0.01	0.00	0.00	0.00	1.93
ENE	0.22	0.77	0.24	0.02	0.00	0.00	0.00	1.25
NE	0.1	0.64	0.15	0.03	0.00	0.00	0.00	0.92
NNE	0.1	0.74	0.32	0.09	0.01	0.00	0.00	1.26
N	0.53	1.29	1.56	1.26	0.72	0.15	0.02	5.53
NNW	0.2	3.12	6.25	5.25	2.63	0.92	0.16	18.53
NW	0.22	2.22	2.42	1.59	0.94	0.2	0.06	7.65
WNW	0.35	1.74	3.07	1.42	0.26	0.02	0.00	6.86
W	0.3	2	2.21	0.7	0.09	0.01	0.00	5.31
WSW	0.49	2.7	2.17	0.49	0.04	0.00	0.00	5.89
SW	0.73	3.55	1.03	0.45	0.07	0.01	0.00	5.84
SSW	1.02	5.76	0.52	0.02	0.00	0.00	0.00	7.32
S	1.21	5.12	0.41	0.05	0.00	0.00	0.00	6.79
SSE	0.92	4.4	1.49	0.65	0.12	0.03	0.00	7.61
SE	0.64	2.22	2.25	1.89	0.92	0.27	0.02	8.21
ESE	0.37	1.45	0.94	0.33	0.11	0.02	0.00	3.22
Total	7.69	38.79	25.59	14.25	5.91	1.63	0.26	
calm				5.88				

Interpretation

16 directions are given in the table 5.4 for wind Rose data. In diagram no. 5.12. Speed for winds varies in seven categories starting from<0.5 m./sec. to >10 m./sec. at different intervals. The data is given in percentage. The total of 16 directions + calm give the total of 100%. The blades of wind rose are constructed on the basis of total values of different directions. The maximum value being 18.53 from NNW and the minimum being 0.92 from NE selects the range of different directions winds are coming from. A scale of 1 cm = 5% has been taken for plotting the blades. The blades are equidistant from the cardinal directions. Then the wind speed variations are marked within the blades proportionate to their frequency. These are shown by different colours. As observed from this wind rose, the NNW is the major prevalent direction of winds, the SE being the next important one. However, the NE gives a minimum value.

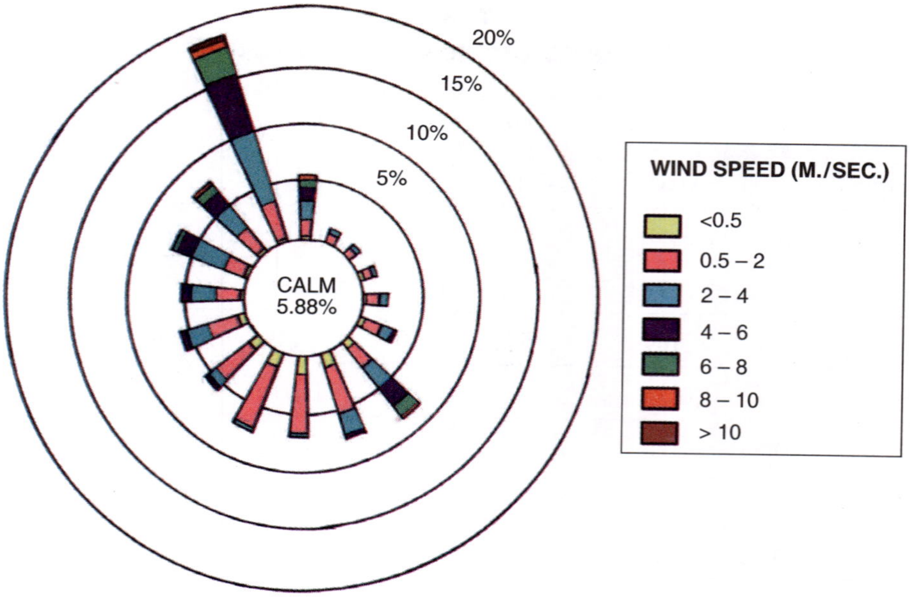

Fig. 5.12 Wind rose Diagram

Climatograph

Various types of impact analysis of the climate are obtained from *climatographs.* These graphs have been prepared for various purposes too. The mode of construction has also varied. The climatograph prepared by E. N. Munns is another type of circular graph. Here mean monthly temperature is plotted from the centre on the basis of a graduated table. The distance from the centre of the circle to 100°F is taken as 10 times the distance from the centre to 0°F. If the distance between the centre and 0°F is x, the difference y for any temperature t°F is obtained from the formula given below :

$$y = x \frac{\text{colog. } t}{100}$$

Such a formula is used so that the temperatures below zero can be plotted. The curve produced by this formula can correctly represent the degree of change in temperature from month to month. If the limiting temperatures of diferent seasons are known, seasons can be identified between the points of intersection of temperature curve and the circles representing limits of temperature on scale.

Climograph

It is a diagram which shows data of various climatic elements of one station plotted against one another and the shape of the graph indicates the general characteristics of the climate of that station.

Researchers have devised a variety of this diagram to depict the nature of different climates. The parameters also vary widely. W. Koppen plotted the temperature of the coldest month as abscissa and temperature of the warmest month as ordinate to indicate the thermal divisions of climates of the world. J.B. Leighly plotted mean annual rainfall in inches as ordinates and mean annual temperature in °F as abscissa. Thus he compared between climatic types of different parts of the world. Critical values of rainfall and temperature were recorded by him to indicate the soil moisture conditions.

Climographs have been used for the understanding the relation between climate and human activities also. Griffith Taylor used climographs to indicate the influence of climate on human activities. He even indicated the phsysiological effect of climate on human beings. Taylor plotted relative humidity values on the abscissa and wet-bulb temperatures on ordinate to prepare this climograph. On the four corners of the frame indicating the vertical and horizontal scale he marked *scorching* in the north-west, *muggy* in the north-east corner, *keen* in the south-west and *raw* in the south-east. The first one shows high wet-bulb temperature and low relative humidity, the second one indicates high wet-bulb and high relative humidity, the third one shows low wet-bulb and low relative humidity, whereas the fourth one gives low wet-bulb temperature and high relative humidity. The mean monthly data plotted on this chart for a particular station indicates each month by the initial letter. The plotted points are then joined and the climograph is prepared (fig. 5.13).

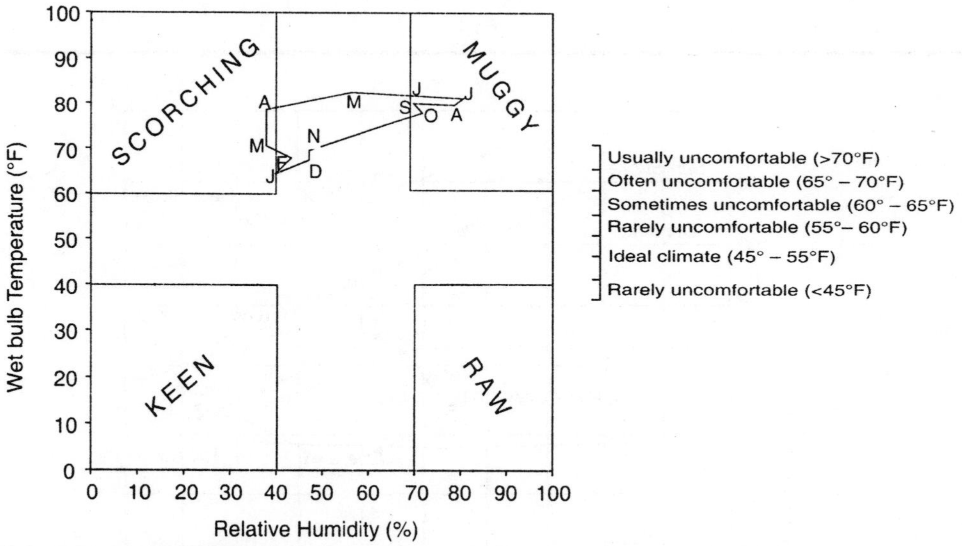

Fig. 5.13 Climograph : Kolkata (After G. Taylor's method)

In this climograph, the middle portion outside the four boxes is the zone of comfort when human activities get a comfortable atmosphere. The climograph done on the basis of wet bulb temperature and relative humidity of Kolkata shows that the months of March and April belong to the scorching zone, and June, July, August, September and October belong to the muggy zone. Hence these months in Kolkata are not comfortable for human beings. On the other hand, the months of January, February, May, November and December belong to the comfort zone. Moreover, the wet bulb temperature is never low in this city indicating a moist and warm climate which is not favourable for working conditions.

Another climograph to indicate human comfort in which dry-bulb temperature in degree Fahrenheit and relative humidity are plotted on the vertical and horizontal scale respectively, was prepared by the United States Department of Agriculture (fig. 5.14).

TABLE 5.6
DATA FOR CLIMOGRAPH, KOLKATA

Month	Wet Bulb (°F) Temperature	Relative Humidity (%)
January	64.8	40
February	68.5	44
March	70.5	38
April	78.1	38
May	82.9	57
June	82.3	69
July	80.8	81
August	80.7	79
September	80.5	75
October	78.0	72
November	68.9	48
December	68.4	48

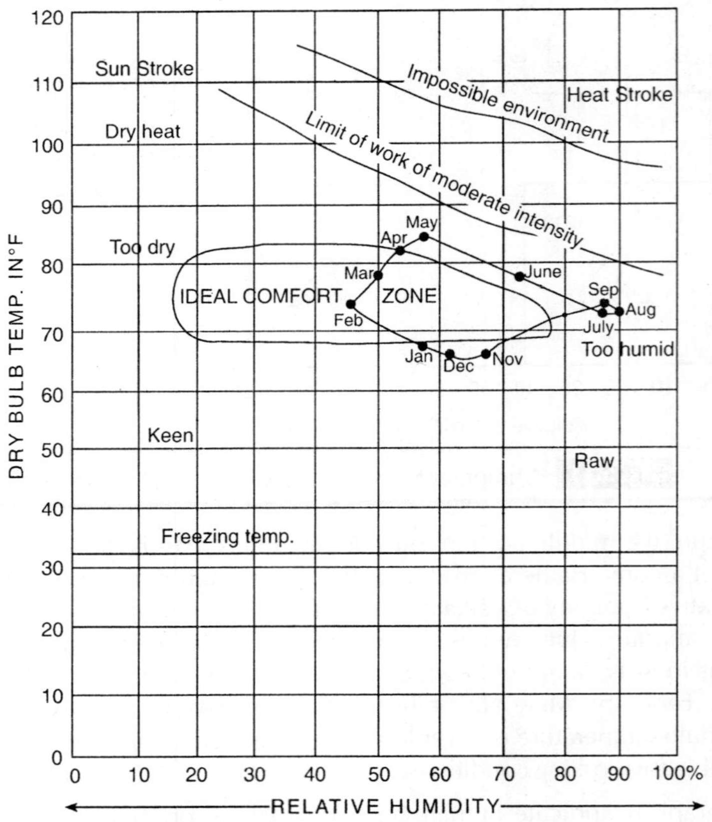

Fig. 5.14 **Comfort analysis : Vishakhapatnam**

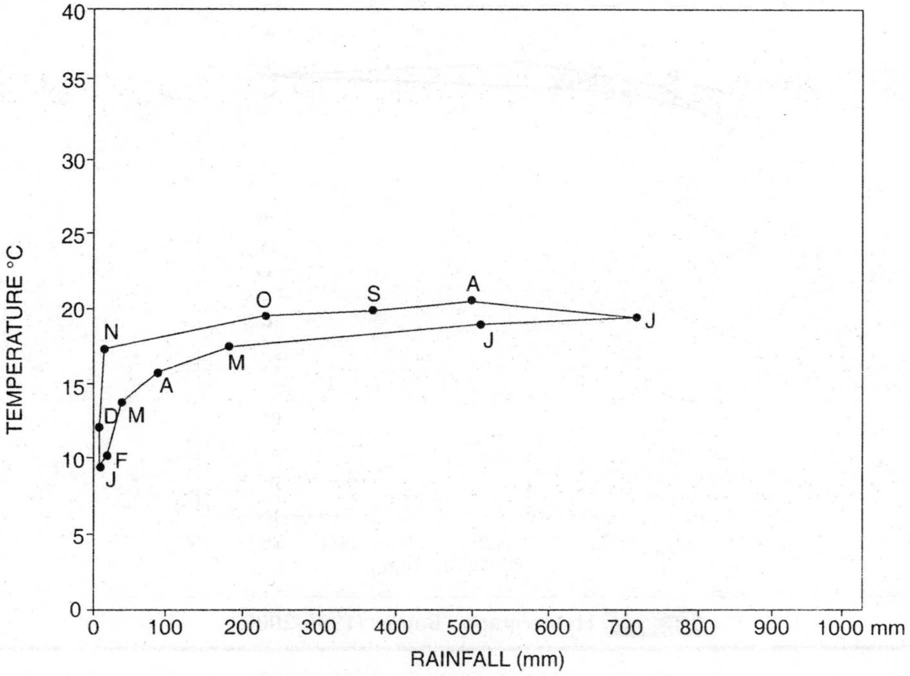

Fig. 5.15 Hythergraph : Darjiling (1968-1972)

Hythergraph

G. Taylor prepared a *hythergraph* (fig. 5.15) which is a variation of climograph with mean monthly temperature on ordinates and mean monthly rainfall as abscissa. He used this hythergraph to understand the influence of climate on human settlement.

Interpretation of Hythergraph (Darjeeling)

This hythergraph, done one the basis of Griffith Taylor's method (1916), shows a twelve sided polygon which extends towards right for a considerable range, though the vertical dimension is short. It indicates a low range of temperature regime and a high range of rainfall regime. As per data (Table No. 5.3), the lowest annual temperature in the month of January is 9.4°C and the highest is 20.4°C in the month of August. Hence, the total annual range is only 11°C. On the other hand, the lowest precipitation in the month of December is 2.37 mm, whereas it is as high as 720.25 mm occurring in the month of July.

Thus the area enclosed within the polygon is small. Had it been having a wide range of temperature with similar concentration of rainfall, it could have enclosed a larger area. The long extension of the polygon towards east or right handside marks the concentration of rainfall over atleast six months. Although temperature is higher during rainy months belonging to summer monsoon regime, it is surprising that the months of April and May are having lower temperature than the period between June and October. Hence, in this mountain resort of Darjeeling, climate, though monsoonal in character, does not follow the typical nature of monsoon temperature range which has the highest annual temperature in the month of May coming before summer solstice. Lower value of temperature is obtained because of high altitude of the area. However, it is note worthy that during rainy months atmospheric air holds a higher value of temperature at Darjeeling and winter is not that severe.

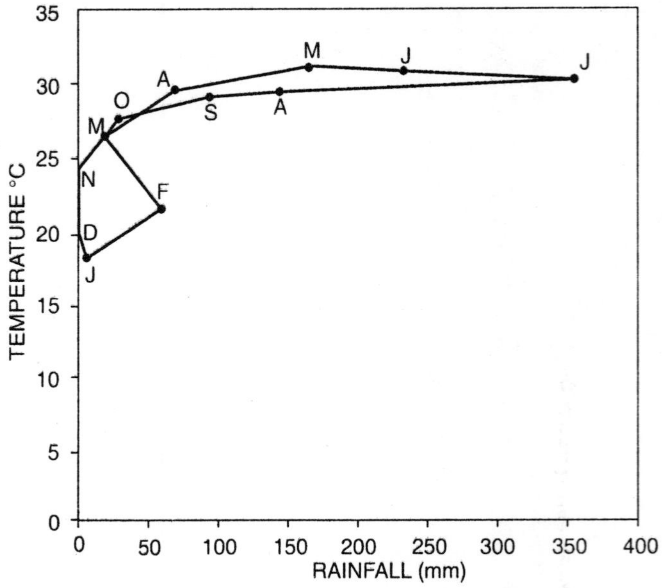

Fig. 5.16 Hythergraph : Bolpur (1996-2000)

Interpretation of Hythergraph (Bolpur)

In the hythergraph of Bolpur, (data given in the climate data for Bolpur station), alike Darjeeling, a similar range of temperature (30.9°C in May-18.0°C in January = 12.9°C) in observed, though in this drier area the range of temperature is slightly higher. Moreover, atleast for two months (November and December) rainfall is zero. The lowest temperature i.e. 18°C is obtained in the month of January, marking it as a typical area of Am climate according to Köppen. Furthermore, highest annual temperatue occurs in the month of May before summer solstice.

This hythergraph again has a strong eastward trend indicating a high concentration of rainfall during monsoon months. Hence, Bolpur gives a typical Am type of climatic regime which is almost an ideal Indian monsoon prototype station. Unlike Darjeeling relief has not modified the temperature regime of Bolpur.

E. Foster devised a climograph consisting of a chart formed by a grid system of rectangular co-ordinates. The vertical scale is graduated from –20°F to 100°F and the horizontal scale varies from 0 to 18 inches of rainfall. This chart shows the following 6 temperature zones.

1. Frigid	:	–20° to 0°F	2. Cold	:	0° to 32°F
3. Cool	:	32° to 50°F	4. Mild	:	50° to 65°F
5. Warm	:	65° to 80°F	6. Hot	:	Over 80°F

The Cool, Mild, Warm and Hot zones are further subdivided into *arid, semi-arid, semi-humid, humid* and *wet* types. The limiting values of these sub-divisions are 32.4°F, 0.32 inch of rain and 83.2°F, 1.03 inch of rain ; 32.4°F, 0.59 inch and 83.2°F, 1.93 inch ; 32.4°F, 1.10 inch and 83.2°F, 3.6 inch; 32.4°F, 2.05 inch and 83.2°F, 6.73 inch of rain respectively.

Another special type of climograph was prepared by P.N.Hore in his study of rice yields and irrigation needs in West Bengal. He used annual rainfall on the vertical scale and number of rainy

days on the horizontal scale. For each of the 35 years under his discussion, a dot was placed according to the given horizontal and vertical scale. The rice-yield per acre for the respective year was given by the side of each dot. Isopleth were drawn on the climograph to indicate the concentration of the points of high yield.

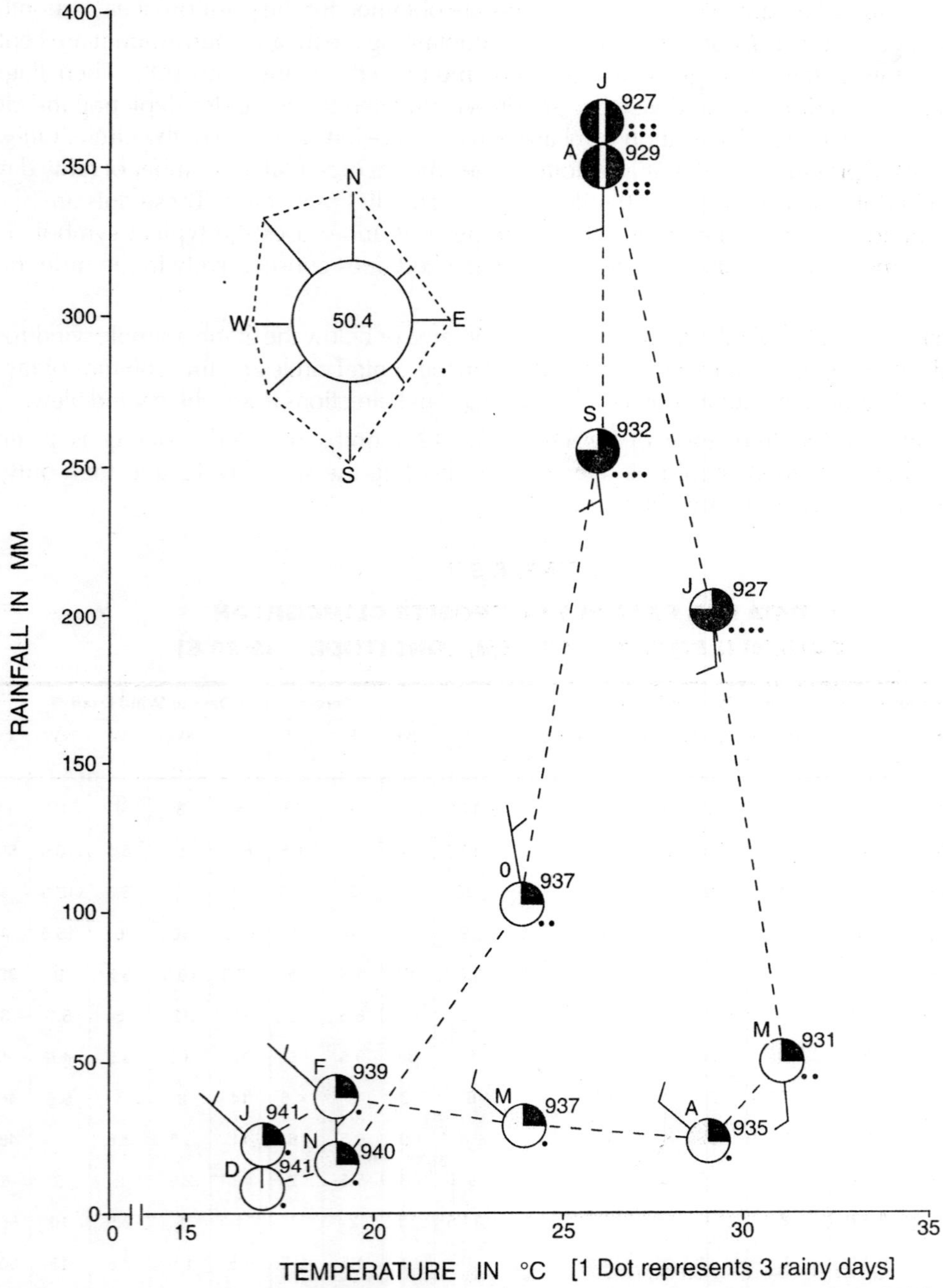

Fig. 5.17 Composite climograph : Ranchi

Composite Climograph

Another composite type of climograph (fig. 5.17) incorporates data of all the important climatic elements and gives a comprehensive idea about the climatic characteristics of a place. Such composite climographs are constructed with monthly mean temperature as abscissa and monthly mean humidity/rainfall as ordinate. Points are obtained for the position of each month on the basis of temperature and humidity data. Circles containing the mean cloud amount are centred on the 12 points obtained (If given in decimals, multiply the value with 0.8). Then flags of predominating wind direction and velocity are drawn attached to the circles depicting the cloud amount. Barometric pressure at station level are placed at the left-hand top of the circle. Only the last three digits of pressure in millibar are plotted. The amount of rainfall or number of rainy days is represented in dot, one dot for each 10 millimetres of rainfall/3 rainy days. These dots are placed at the right-hand bottom of the circle. The lightning or thunder uses the typical symbol. Then finally, all the monthly positions are connected by pecked lines consecutively in the order of the year.

After that either in the blank space within the graph-area or below the graph a simple wind-rose is constructed with number of calm days indicated within the central circle and fine columns or rays on the central circle indicating number of days for eight cardinal directions from which wind blew.

If the data for the frequency of directions for 12 months of wind blowing is given in percentage, their sum total should be averaged by dividing the same by 12 and then only the columns or rays for directions are obtained.

TABLE 5.7

DATA FOR EXAMPLE COMPOSITE CLIMOGRAPH
RANCHI (LATITUDE – 23°23′N, LONGITUDE – 85°20′E)

Month	Pressure	Temp.	Cloud	Rainfall	No. of	Wind	Percentage of Days of Wind From								
	(mb)	(°C)	Amount	(m.m.)	Rainy Days	Speed knots	N	NE	E	SE	S	SW	W	NW	Calm
January	941.2	17	2	24	2	4	14.5	1.5	2	1.5	4	3	4	15	54.5
February	939.3	19	2	39	3	5	10.5	1	2	1.5	6.5	5	6.5	16.6	50.4
March	937.1	24	2	28	2	6	10	1	2	1.5	6.5	7	6.5	18.5	47
April	934.6	29	2	23	2	6	9	1	2	2	10.5	10	6	15.5	44
May	930.8	31	3	50	4	6	7	1.5	4.5	5	17.5	10.5	5.5	9	39.5
June	927	29	6	202	10	7	5	3	6.5	5	18	12	6	5.5	39
July	926.6	26	7	360	18	6	5.5	3.5	9.5	5	17	9.5	3.5	4.5	42
August	929.2	26	7	354	18	6	6.5	3	8	4.5	14	8	4	5.5	46.5
September	931.8	26	6	256	12	5	8	3	8.5	6	11	5.5	3.5	6	48.5
October	937.2	24	3	105	6	3	9.5	3	5.5	2	4.5	2.5	2	6	65
November	940.2	19	2	17	1	3	14.5	1.5	2	1	1	1	2.5	10	66.5
December	941.4	17	1	4	3	3	15	1	1.5	2.5	1.5	1.5	3.6	13	60.4

Socio-economic maps and diagrams

Maps and diagrams represent the socio-economic data in an expressive and analytical style.The character of socio-economic data varies widely. Authors often categorized representations into socio-economic maps and diagrams and population maps and diagrams. However, these two sets of data and diagrams are linked up in many respects, though they are independent in many attributes too. Population maps and diagrams are specifically meant for population data. On the other hand, socio-economic data has a very wide range. It may include a simple data, like the landuse pattern of an area and it may contain the growth rate of a nation's economy as well. Therefore, the range of data covers area, volume, distance, rate, amounts and many other aspects, such as values, ratios etc. Such a data, be it related to a figure of population density or it involves the areas under certain crops or expressed as sex-ratio can be represented through the following techniques. The suitable one is often chosen for the representation of a particular data, e.g. the area data of certain places should be represented by proportionate area diagrams. Thus the square or circle or a rectangular cartogram may suit the representation and dots or columns are not exactly suitable for the purpose. The usual methods are :

1. Chorochromatic maps
2. Choropleth maps
3. Proportional squares and circles
4. Proportional spheres and cubes
5. Shaped symbols
6. Divided circles
7. Dots
8. Dots and circles
9. Dots and spheres
10. Grouped squares
11. Isopleths
12. Columnar diagram
13. Age-sex pyramid
14. Compound pyramid
15. Superimposed pyramid
16. Divided rectangles
17. Star diagrams
18. Isometric block diagrams
19. Directional diagrams
20. Flow diagrams
21. Graphs :
    a) Line graphs
    b) Polygraphs
    c) Frequency graphs
    d) Triangular graphs
    e) Projected curves
    f) Scatter diagrams
    g) Graphs on logarithmic and semi-logarithmic scales
    h) Cumulative graphs
    i) Cartograms
    j) Stereograms
    k) Ergographs
    l) Dendrograms

1. Chorochromatic Maps

The method of representation is related to non-quantitative data which is different from one unit to another in a qualitative way. Different colours are used to show individual units of the map as they are characteristically different from one another, but one particular category should be marked with the same colour, however distant its location may be from its counter parts. Colour or tint is primarily used in chorochromatic maps (Choros = area, chrome = colour), though use of symbols is not very uncommon. As regards the use of colours certain conventions are followed, e.g. an agricultural land may be tinted light yellow and a forest may be dark green. However, minor deviations are not totally uncommon.

Soil maps, geological maps (showing rock outcrops), landuse maps, land capability class maps, maps for cropping pattern etc. can be shown chorochromatically.

Data obtained for this type of map is obviously spatial in character. Large scale base maps are required to prepare such chorochromatic maps. Usually cadastral survey maps on a scale of 16 inches to 1 mile or 8 inches to 1 mile are used as base maps. Such maps show individual plots involved in a particular use, such as, crop cultivation, fallow land, forest, plantation, homesteads etc. In geological maps and soil maps different rock outcrops or soil types are shown within their respective boundaries. For such geological and soil maps usually large scale base maps on a scale of 1:10,000 are required. However, in subsequent reproductions these large scale maps may be reduced to any required size.

The colour used in chorochromatic maps should be transparent and should follow conventions. Preparation of such maps requires an intensive ground survey and a comprehensive knowledge about the ground pattern of the area. For landuse maps detailed information about plotwise data from the land revenue office should be obtained. A local man, perhaps an amin or villagehead, may be consulted in this regard, otherwise, it is often very difficult to recognise and locate a particular plot in the field as the numbers given in the map do not remain the same for a long period of time and often there are fragmentation in terms of inheritance. As regards the preparation of a map depicting urban landuse the concerned town planning department of the respective municipality or corporation should be consulted.

As regards the colour used for a particular landuse type the following chart may be taken as a guide, though depending on the local variations little changes can also be made. In connection with geological maps guidelines of G.S.I. (fig. 5.14) can be followed, NATMO Soil maps can be followed for 'Indian soil types'.

COLOUR SCHEME FOR LANDUSE MAP : — Scale 1 : 6,00,000

TABLE 5.8

Category	Colour Scheme
1. Arable land	Yellow (70% yellow)
2. Plantation	Purple (40% Magenta of 133 lines + 20% Cyan of 65 lines)
3. Forest	Green (70% yellow + 60% Cyan of 85 lines)
4. Non-Agricultural use	Orange (60% yellow + 30% Magenta of 65 lines)
5. Scrub and Grass	Light yellow (30% yellow)
6. Unproductive land	Grey (30% Black of 85 lines)

(As done in NATMO maps)

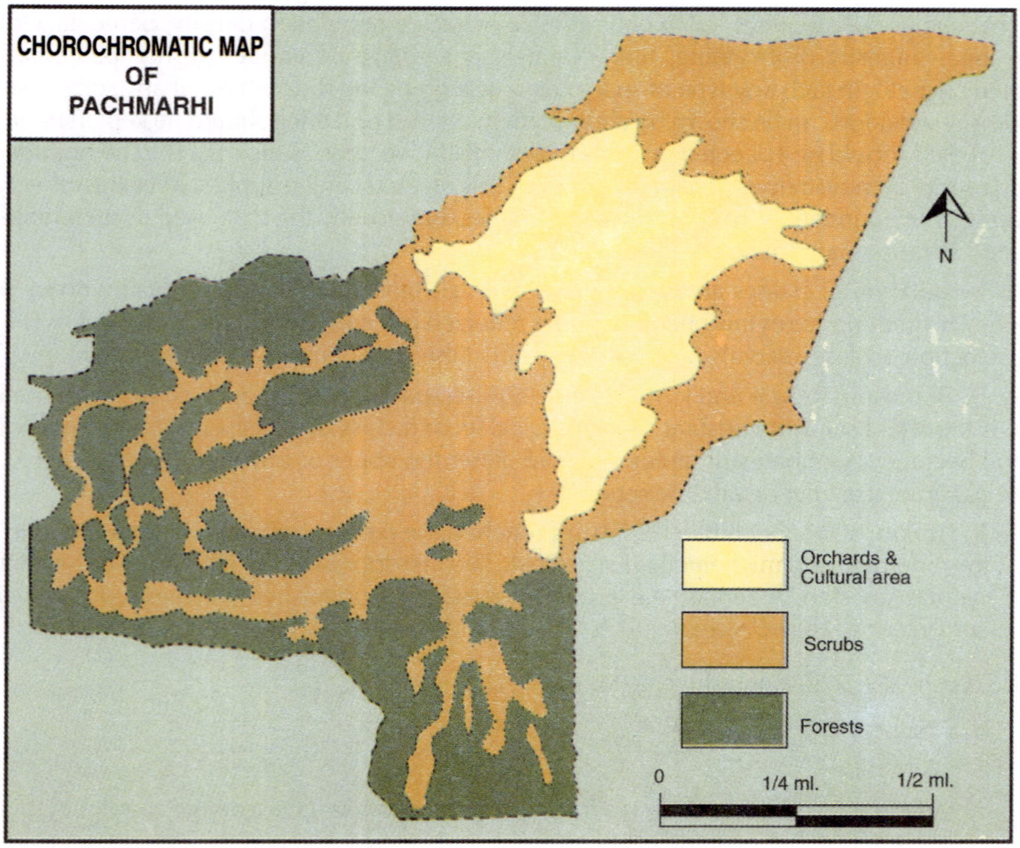

Fig. 5.18 Chorochromatic map

2. Choropleth Maps

A choropleth map is a quantitative expression of spatial data within administrative boundaries. It offers a broad generalisation of the reality as specific local differences are ignored in such maps. A choropleth (choros = area, space; plethos = crowd) map describes a statistical data of varying density or intensity in terms of classes shown by the variation in density of shading or colouring and usually delineated by administrative boundaries. G.F. Jenks and Fred C. Caspall (1971) defined choropleth maps as 'planimetric representations of volumetric statistical distributions and ... normally symbolized by patterns which divided the area into sub-regions', when they are particularly related to volumetric nature of intangible distributions. In such maps each choroplethic class represents a layer or vertical segment of the statistical volume. The classes are obtained by dividing the model in a series of planes parallel to the datum plane. Three of such dividing planes will represent four classes.

The data usually represented in choroplethic maps are population density, percentage of net sown area, intensity of cropping, literacy rates, percentage of various works, percentage of irrigated area etc. In fact, any type of spatial data describing the distribution of any sort of density or intensity variation can be shown by choropleth maps. But one thing should be kept in mind that the areal data should be collected in terms of administrative units as the map is to be bounded by boundaries of administrative divisions. However, this method can be applied for some other types of average not bounded by administratve boundaties, but usually the data used in such maps are obtained at various administrative levels.

Determination of classes and selection of intervals have been variously dealt with by map-authors. The importance of this phenomenon is reflected in a comment made by I.S. Evans (1977): "The selection of class intervals ... can strongly affect the visual impression given by a map ..."

A. H. Robinson, R. Sale and J. Morrison (1978) separated three kinds of class determination : "One is the equal steps or constant series, ... a second class of series includes those in which interval becomes systematically smaller toward either the upper or lower end of the scale ...... a third class is the irregular or variable series."

A. P. Gorkin, V. N. Gochman (1974) approached the problem of class determination in two ways : the empirical and mathemetical-statistical. The first approach involves an intuitive method and a natural division, whereas, the second approach distinguishes between constant range classes and varying range classes.

I. S. Evans (1977) distinguished the following classes :

1. Exogenous
2. Arbitrary
3. Idiographic being further classified into natural breaks, clinographic, contiguity-biased, correlation-biased and nested means.
4. Serial with limits in a definite mathematical relation to each other.

J. Paslawski (1984) identified the following three basic conceptions in determination of choropleth maps.

1. Conception of equal class range — this is most commonly used for geographical phenomena
2. Conception of preserving equal class frequency — this approach is practically a quantile method
3. Conception of uniformity according to an adopted criterion — this approach is an optimalization method

Another approach of preparing classless choropleth maps was earliest in occurrence giving the unit area a tonal value matched to its place on a continuous scale of tones ranging from the lowest to the highest. Such maps have revived further with the use of computer where the electronic device controls the tonal value output.

Choropleths may be constructed on the basis of unequally-stepped class limits also. The two groups of unequally-stepped series are :

I. Arithmetic series : Here each class is separated from the next one by a numerical difference which is not a constant one.

II. Geometric series : Here each class is separated by a stated numerical ratio. The class limits are produced by using the formula :

$L + B_1x + B_2x \ldots\ldots + B_nx = H$

L = the lower most value
B_n = value of the nth term in the progression
H = Highest value

In arithmetic progression the quantity of B_n is obtained by —

$B_n = a(n-1)d$

a = value of the first term
n = number of the term being determined
d = the stated difference

In Geometric progression the quantity of B_n is obtained by

$B_n = Gr^{n-1}$

G = value of first non-zero term
n = number of term being determined
r = stated ratio

Depending on the values of 'd' & 'r' six probable forms may be obtained :

a) increasing at a constant rate
b) increasing at an increasing rate
c) increasing at a decreasing rate
d) decreasing at a constant rate
e) decreasing at an increasing rate
f) decreasing at a decreasing rate

TABLE 5.9
DATA FOR CHOROPLETH

Sl. No.	Name of P.S.	Total Population	Area (sq. km.)	Population density/Km²
1.	Saltora	110929	314.7	352
2.	Mejhia	69294	162.9	425
3.	Barjora	159060	290.0	548
4.	Gangajalghati	143535	371.2	387
5.	Chhatna	156147	448.1	348
6.	Bankura	495173	408.4	1212
7.	Onda	191868	502.2	382
8.	Indpur	125706	300.2	419
9.	Khatra	151630	431.2	352
10.	Ranibandh	109919	428.4	257
11.	Raipur	215870	588.2	367
12.	Simlapal	111308	309.0	360
13.	Taldangra	111573	349.7	319
14.	Bishnupur	115286	321.7	358
15.	Sonamukhi	123665	380.0	325
16.	Patrasair	140680	321.7	437
17.	Joypur	122082	261.3	467
18.	Indas	132344	255.1	519
19.	Kotulpur	144528	250.5	577

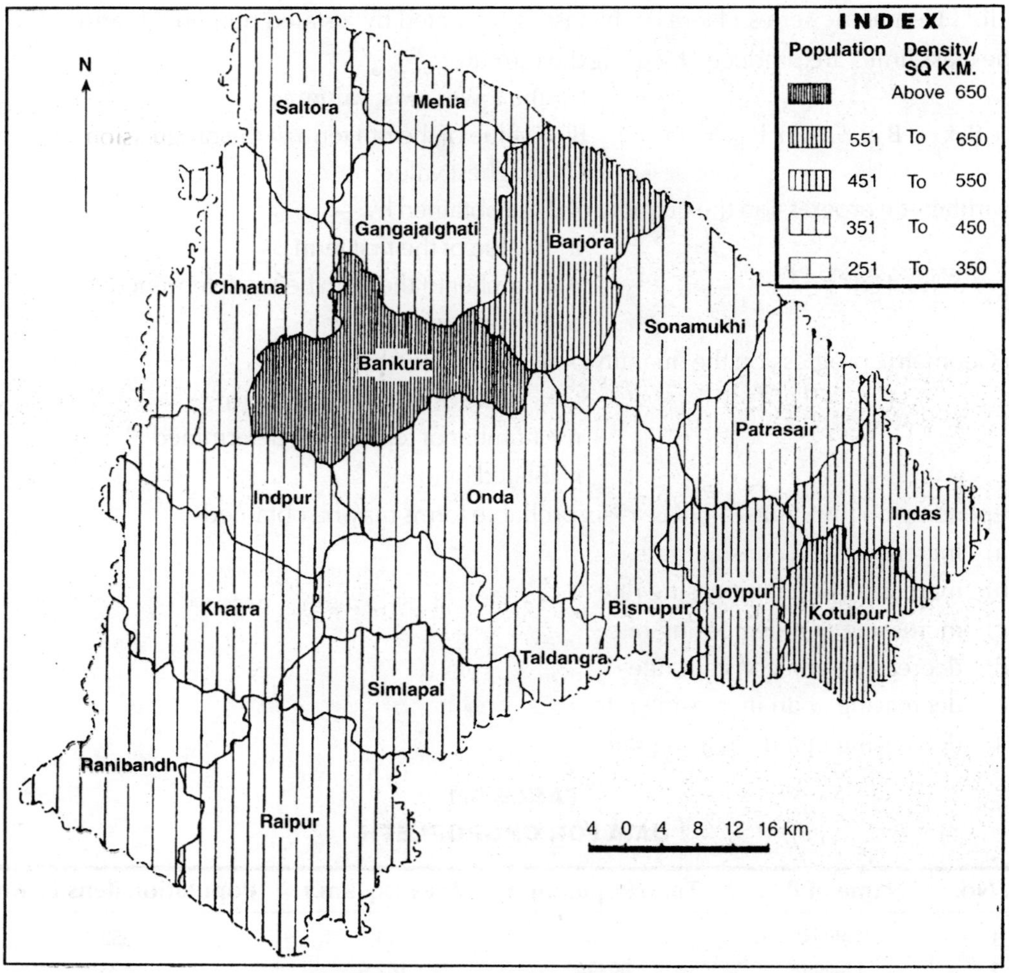

Fig. 5.19 **Choropleth map of Bankura, 1991**

Chowdhury examined the methods of equal-step class intervals for choropleth mapping and surmised that among the five methods (equal step, normal distribution, nested mean, quartile and equal area) for computation of class limits used by her, the equal step method shows minimum mean value and minimum index of diversity as well as the Goodness of Variance Fit also to be minimum. Therefore, this method suits a choropleth map well.

However, if manually done monochromatic choropleth maps allow a few class, but when pattern and value are employed, 5 to 8 classes can be made. As regards the density of colour it should follow the higher the density or intensity deeper the colour; if it uses patterns, denser pattern will represent higher values. Choropleth maps (fig. 5.15) thus give a visual impression by which the difference in the distribution is easily understood.

The steps to be followed in the course of preparation of a choropleth map are :

1. Process the data by finding out the density or intensity as may be the case; for density of population it is P/A i.e., P = total population of the administrative unit and A = area of the administrative unit.

2. Select the required number of classes by fixing their upper and lower limits on the basis of equal step method. For this purpose the exact difference between the highest value and the lowest value of population density (or some other data) will be divided by the required number of classes. The quotient will give the interval which will be added to the lowermost value to get the upper limit of the first class. Then the upper limit of the first class should be added to the interval again to get the upper limit of the second class and so on.

   Occasionally, if the interval is fractional, the nearest round value of it may be considered, but even for that little rounding up the total number of classes may get lowered from that of the required number of classes. So rounding up should be done very carefully.

   To get the possible number of classes in terms of the number of occurrences this formula may used and the nearest round figure will mention the required number of classes that should be obtained for a particular data :

   $1 + 3.3 \log N$ [N = number of occurrence]

3. Find out which administrative division comes within which class-range.
4. Select a shading scheme or monochromatic range for the number of classes and shade or tint each administrative division with its respective type of shade or intensity of the colour selected. Obviously, the administrative divisions categorized under the same class should be shaded or tinted at one time.
5. Prepare the legend on the basis of the colour-variations or shading used. Write the respective values of classes by the side of particular colour or shade. They should be higher upward.

Excercise

In figure no. 5.19 a choropleth map of Bankura district has been prepared on the basis of the area and population data of the district (Table 5.8). The highest density being 1212 and the lowest being 257 the range has been divided into 5 classes. The respective densities 19 police stations can be distributed among these 5 classes (Table 5.9).

TABLE 5.10

Class	Sl. no. of police stations
251– 350	5, 10, 12, 15
351 – 450	1, 2, 4, 7, 8, 9, 11, 12, 14, 16
451 – 550	3, 17, 18
551 – 650	19
> 650	6

Interpretation :

Density of population varies on the basis of the scope economic occupation, amenities for better living, scope of education, stability of political regime, urbanisation etc. In the case of Bankura district the density varies from 257 to 1212 as divided into 5 classes (Table 5.7a). Maximum number of police stations belong to low density classes , which indicates that economic development is not of very high level in the district. Bankura and Kotulpur are exceptions with better standard of urbanisation and economic prosperity.

Dasymetric map **:** When the data for any given region is not sufficiently complete to give an impression about density variations, dasymetric techniques may be applied to ascertain details of distribution on the map which are actually given.

[For such a map it requires to study the topographical and land-utilization maps first and then to locate moorland, marsh, heath etc. on which a settlement develops. Secondly, settlement zones should be delineated on the basis the present layout. The settlement zones should now be superimposed on the base map.]

This way if the density of certain zones or districts are not known, but the total population of the administrative division is known, an average density for the settled areas without any data can be determined and superimposed on the base map, thus offering a logical density to the zones without any data for population density.

However, after determining the unknown densities, the map should be prepared like a choropleth map.

Use and choice of Cartographic symbols : point, line, area and volume

Various types of cartographic symbols are used to represent different types of data. The choice is dependent on the nature of data and the space provided for presentation of the data. In some cases these symbols are highly comprehensive and can represent a large volume or a variety of data within a single diagram, such as a compound bar graph; while in some others it requires scattering of the symbols for realistic presentation of the data, such as, any distribution of population as shown by dots. The scale will determine the size of the symbol, more or less, being proportional to the quantities represented. Thus, dots may have variable sizes, bars may have variable lengths, spheres and cubes or blocks may have variable volumes. For each of them certain method of measurement of scale is there. Even literal symbols will have proportionate sizes in coherence with the amount or quantity represented.

There are some usual and conventional ways of selecting a particular symbol for the presentation of a particular data. It is obvious that the selection is biased on the nature of data to be represented. If the given data is areal in character, it is useless to represent it by a line, although in that case also the proportion can be maintained. Similarly, the length of different roads should be represented by lines, and not by any areal or dot symbol, because the basic purpose is to represent the length and direction of the road. Moreover, depending on the nature or status of road the linear symbol may have varied characteristics in terms of colour, thickness, etc. If the statistical data requires a distribution map of scattered nature dots may be ideal selections. Such dots may have uniform size, each representing a specific value, or they may be variable in size depending on the quantity represented. In such cases dots are practically circles with any solid colour in them. For this purpose, dots with variable diameters are used. Such a symbol should be used if the map-maker is interested to represent the absolute figure of population distribution in rural units.

In some of the maps variable sizes of circles represent the absolute population figure and in some others scattered dots are used for distribution of rural population, whereas, proportionate circles or dots.of variable sizes are used for the urban units in the same map.

As urban areas have smaller areal spread in comparison with the large figure of population residing in that area, it is often required to use more comprehensive symbols with compact nature for the representation of such data. For this purpose spheres are used, the radius of the sphere being derived from a cube root can have a much reduced length in comparison with circles used for the same data. Moreover, a sphere has the smallest surface in proportion to its volume. That is why such a symbol should be used for an urban area having less spatial extent (Fig. 5.16). The radius of any sphere should be derived from $\frac{4}{3}\pi r^3$ which is the volume of the sphere.

Cubes are some types of three dimensional representations. For these diagrams cube roots are also done which again will occupy a lesser area than a circle. A pile of small cubes of the same size are used often to represent number of residential houses in a police station or village. In that case a small cube should represent a small number of houses only. Cubes can be increased in number in all the three dimensions of the diagram. Mere counting of cubes may give the figure of data to the map reader.

The number of houses can be represented by a square also. In that case only the square root of the data on scale will represent one of the four sides of the square and the square of that length will give the number of houses.

Dot and Sphere maps

The simplest form of a symbol is a dot. It is a very useful form for a distribution map representing a quantity or value by dots of uniform size. Such a method is specially useful when values are distributed unevenly and sporadically. The dots are inserted within particular administrative units for which the data is available. The smaller the statistical unit chosen for a dot, the more accurate is the map. The success of the map depends on the choice of this value. The unit to be represented by a dot should not be so small that there will be difficulty in inserting all the dots in the administrative area. It will not be so high too, because that may result in the insertion of a very few dots only (fig. 5.20). A ground information may give a more clear picture because that may introduce variable density of dots. The uniform distribution of dots through out the administrative unit is to some extent erroneous. A Dot map as well as a choropleth map suffer from this problem of uniformity.

Spheres usually represent urban population, because urban areas are small, but they have very high concentration of population. **A sphere occupies minimum space to represent maximum volume.** That is why it is used for showing urban population.

TABLE 5.11

DATA FOR DOT & SPHERE

Sl. No.	Name of the Police Station	Rural Population	Urban Population	Number of dots (1 dot ¾ 5000 person)	Radii of sphere (r) (1 cm = 35r)	Radii of on scale (in cm)
1.	Muraroi	208843	—	42	15.32	0.43
2.	Nalhati	194759	15073	39	20.21	0.57
3.	Rampurhat	224276	34593	45	—	—
4.	Mayureswar	187727	—	38	—	—
5.	Muhammad Bazar	92853	—	19	—	—
6.	Rajnagar	54139	—	11	—	—
7.	Khoyrasole	100817	—	20	—	—
8.	Dubrajpore	113624	—	23	—	—
9.	Suri	115793	40783	23	21.35	0.6
10.	Illambazar	99064	—	20	—	—
11.	Sainthia	129318	24081	26	17.91	0.51
12.	Bolpur	127999	38436	26	20.94	0.6
13.	Labpur	130132	—	26	—	—
14.	Nanoor	142952	—	29	—	—

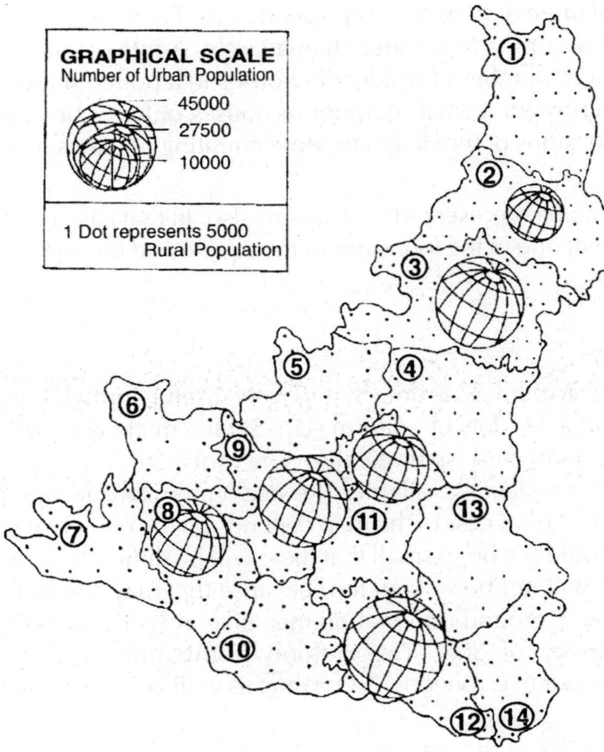

Fig. 5.20 **Dot and Sphere showing the Rural and Urban Population of Birbhum**

Some cartographers claim that coalescence of dots is preferable in areas of higher density, so that the contrast between the white or dot less area and solid black areas can be maintained. But some others insist that the dots should be countable and should not be allowed to merge. Of course, in practice dots are rarely counted because the person in search of more precise information must return to the statistical source upon which the map is based.

The placement of dots should be even and straight rows of dots should be avoided because patterns are not wanted.

The dots may be placed more precisely when detailed information is available concerning the exact location of the values derived from field work. But more generalised information as is provided by relief or climatic maps should be avoided. However, without any precise information the even distribution of dots may, of course, create misconceptions. For instance, a rural unit having a rugged and forested populationless area may show uniform density of dots as in plains, in the absence of any precise information about the location of settlements.

The actual size of the dots to be used presents another problem. The dots must be neither so big that a coarse generalised effect may be produced, nor so small that a blur is produced in areas of dense value. A ball-pointed nib should be used to make dots of uniform size. Care must be taken about the possibility of reduction in size if the final reproduction requires some reduction of the map. Moreover, the same idea of reduction should be kept in mind in connection with the spacing of dots. If several types of distribution are required to be shown in one map, dots of different colours may be used.

Excercise

A Dot and sphere map has been prepared on the basis of the rural and urban population (police stationwise) of Birbhum district as per 1981 census. Each dot represents 5000 persons and the rural population has been represented by uniform distribution of the dots of the same size.

The 5 towns of the district have been represented by spheres proportional to their respective number of population. The radii for the spheres have been derived from the volume of spheres i.e., $\frac{4}{3}\pi r^3$. Example : for Nalhati.

$$\frac{4}{3}\pi r^3 = 15073 \quad \text{or, } r^3 = \frac{15073 \times 3}{4\pi}$$

$$\text{or, } r = \sqrt[3]{\frac{15073 \times 3}{4\pi}}$$

$$\text{or, } r = 15.32$$

Interpretation :

It appears from the spread of dots that the rural population is more concentrated in Dubrajpur, Nanoor and Bolpur police station areas. This might have happened due to better state of agricultural activities, whereas it is more scattered at Rajnagar and Labpur are as indicating the presence of infertile lands, lack of irrigation etc.

As far as the urban population is concerned it is more concentrated in Suri and Bolpur p.s. areas. It indicates better state of urbanisation, education and scope of better living.

Percentage dot map

Instead of using a located dot with a precise absolute value, it may be desirable to let it represent 1.0 or 0.1 per cent of the total value involved in the particular distribution. In other words, such a map will bear 100 or 1000 dots respectively. These are known as percentage dot-maps. They facilitate arithmetical comparisons, and they afford ready information concerning fractional distribution and proportions. Their disadvantage is that a dot will rarely represent a round number.

Proportional symbols

Symbols can provide quantitative as well as locational information if they are drawn on scale. Circles, spheres, squares, rectangles, columns, triangles, cubes etc. may be employed for this purpose. Columns are bars practically representing a single dimension to represent the absolute or percentage data proportional to their length. The two dimensional figures showing area, the three dimensional figures representing the volume are made proportional to the quantity they represent. These symbols may be used as diagrams or may be located on maps. Thus they illustrate the distribution in a more specific way. For determining the size of such symbols on scale particular geometric formula should be used, such as, for a circle the area being πr^2, the 'r' may be calculated on a given scale. Thus the size of different circles representing different areal dimensions will vary and they will be representing their proportional areas.

Computation for Proportional Circles

Circles representing area (fig. 5.21) or population being proportionate in diameter in terms the amount of area or figure of population they represent, are often placed in thematic maps, more or less, within the boundary of the respective administrative division.

The radii of such circles can be computed by considering the respective area or population as πr^2.

TABLE 5.12

Data for Proportional Circle

Location Code	CD Block	Total population	r	r on scale (1 cm ≅ 300R)
1.	Nalhati-1	174541	235.71	0.79
2.	Nalhati-2	89841	169.11	0.56
3.	Muraroi-1	122544	197.50	0.66
4.	Muraroi-2	144908	214.77	0.72
5.	Mayueswar-1	116592	192.65	0.64
6.	Mayureswar-2	98818	177.35	0.59
7.	Rampurhat-1	134329	206.78	0.67
8.	Rampurhat-2	138485	209.96	0.70
9.	Mohammad Bazar	116319	192.42	0.64
10.	Sainthia	155104	222.20	0.74
11.	Bolpur-Sriniketan	152048	220.00	0.73
12.	Labpur	153546	221.08	0.74
13.	Nanoor	168364	231.50	0.77
14.	Dubrajpur	135787	207.90	0.69
15.	Illambazar	120895	196.17	0.65
16.	Rajnagar	61539	139.96	0.47
17.	Suri-1	77430	156.99	0.52
18.	Suri-2	65153	144.01	0.48
19.	Khoyrasol	122081	197.13	0.66

Calculation for the Graphical Scale

$$\pi r^2 = x$$

$$r = \sqrt{\frac{x}{\pi}}$$ x = area or population to be represented

(H) $\pi r^2 = 170000$ (L) $\pi r^2 = 61000$

$\therefore r = 232.62$ $\therefore r = 139.34$

$\therefore$ r on scale = 0.78 cm $\therefore$ r on scale = 0.46 cm

'r's of various lengths worked out will be converted into cm. or inch according to the scale chosen. At the time of selection of the scale care should be taken to see that the circle fits the size of the administrative division on which it will be placed. Neither the circle should cover the entire boundary nor it will be too small for the map. This diagram gives an instant impression of the variable number of total population.

Computation for squares

Drawing of squares (fig. 5.22) also follow the same principle as it is for circles, only the computation is different. Squares usually represent the number households, number of houses etc.

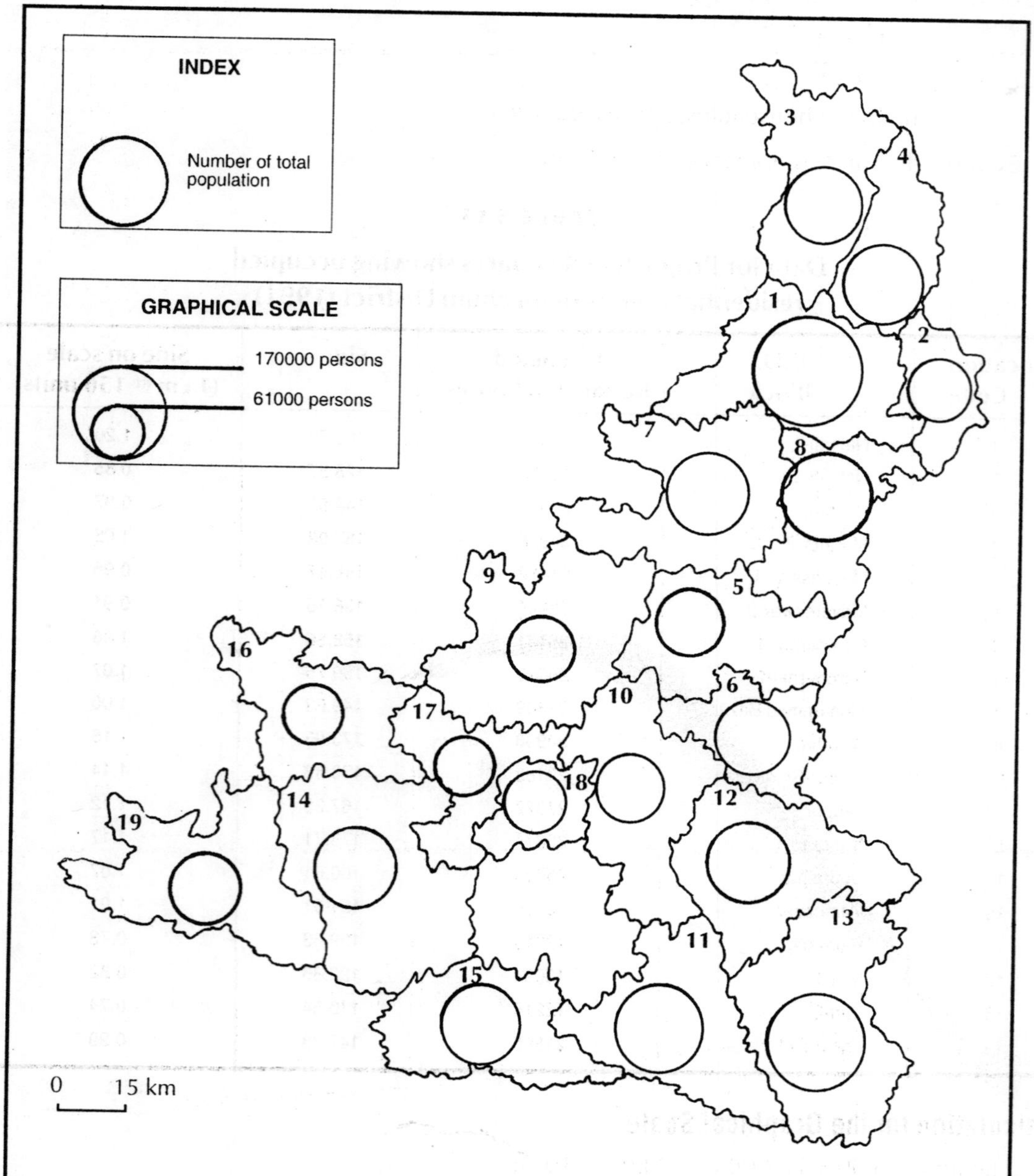

Fig. 5.21 Proportional Circles showing C.D. Blockwise Total Population of Birbhum district, 1991

of any administrative division. Some other types of data can also be represented in squares. One side of the square is simply the square root of the data.

$$r^2 = x$$

$$r = \sqrt{x}$$

x = number of households, houses etc.

Example data and computation (Table 5.10) :

TABLE 5.13

Data for Proportional Squares showing occupied residential houses of Birbhum District (1991)

Location Code	C.D. Block	Occupied Residential houses	Side	Side on scale (1 cm @ 150 units)
1.	Nalhati-1	32528	180.36	1.20
2.	Nalhati-2	16096	126.87	0.85
3.	Muraroi-1	20977	144.83	0.97
4.	Muraroi-2	24958	157.98	1.05
5.	Mayueswar-1	21452	146.47	0.98
6.	Mayureswar-2	18645	136.55	0.91
7.	Rampurhat-1	25141	158.56	1.06
8.	Rampurhat-2	25519	159.75	1.07
9.	Mohammad Bazar	22389	149.63	1.00
10.	Sainthia	29938	173.03	1.15
11.	Bolpur-Sriiniketan	29182	170.83	1.14
12.	Labpur	27972	167.25	1.12
13.	Nanoor	30874	175.71	1.17
14.	Dubrajpur	25796	160.61	1.07
15.	Illambazar	22956	151.51	1.01
16.	Rajnagar	12019	109.63	0.73
17.	Suri-1	15094	122.86	0.82
18.	Suri-2	12218	110.54	0.74
19.	Khoyrasol	21868	147.88	0.99

Calculation for the Graphical Scale

Higher = 32000 = $\sqrt{32000}$ = 178.89 = 1.19 cm

Lower = 12000 = $\sqrt{12000}$ = 109.54 = 0.73 cm

Interpretation :

The number of occupied residential houses of 19 C.D. Blocks of Birbhum district have been represented by square diagrams, proportional to their numbers. The diagram indicates the variable concentration of occupied residential houses. It is observed that maximum concentration has taken place at Nalhati and Nanoor as well as at Bolpur-Sriniketan. Better scope of economic property may account for greater concentration and vice versa.

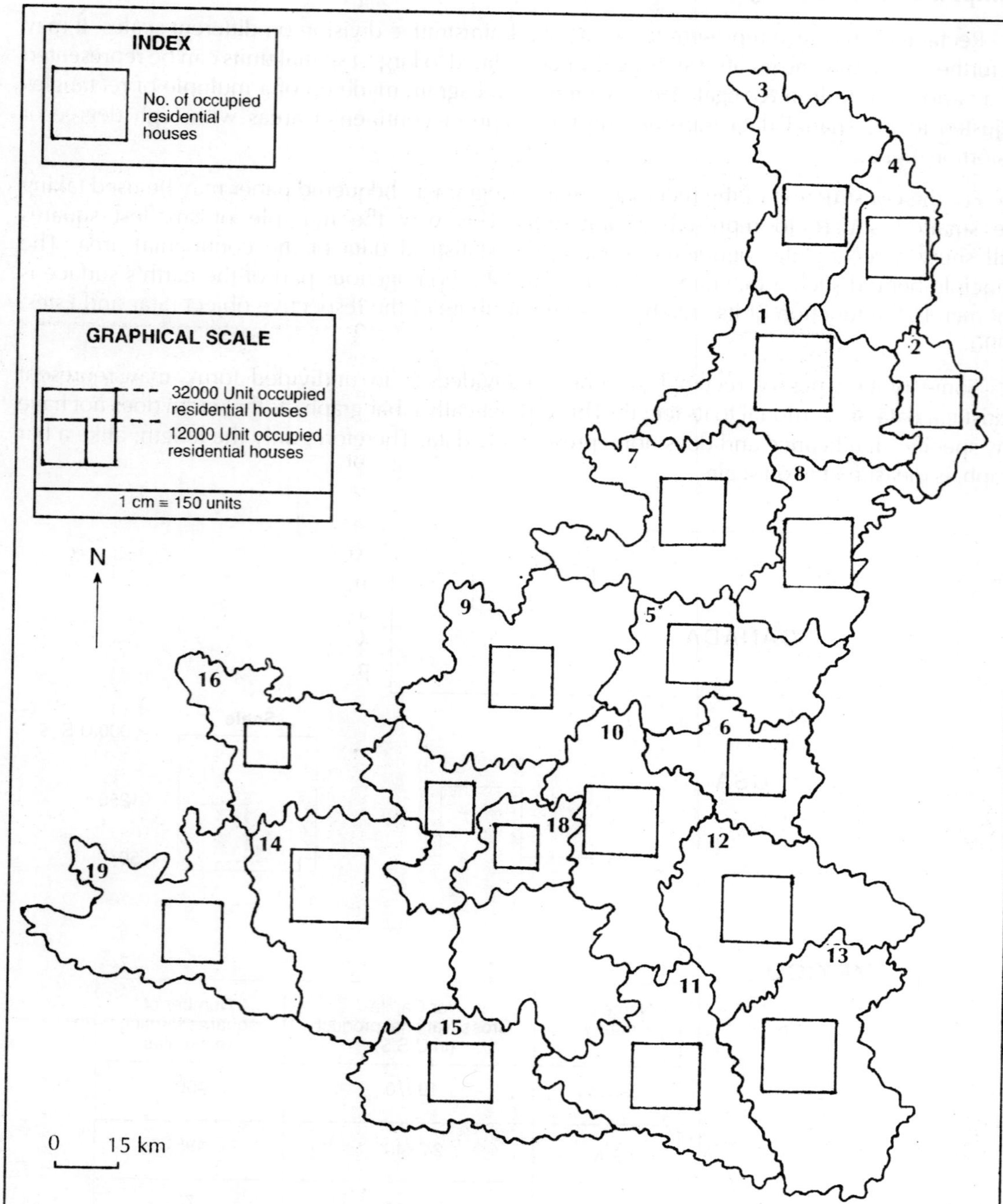

[The diagram is slightly reduced from the computed length of sides in Table no. 5.10]

Fig. 5.22 Proportional squares showing occupied residential houses of Birbhum District (1991)

Computation for rectangles

Rectangles may also represent the areas of administrative division on different scales. It may be further noted that the greatest statistical values related to largest spatial units can be represented by a cartogram (Kidron & Segal, 1984) which is a diagram made up of a multiple of rectangles adjusted to the spatial data transforming the shape of continental areas with high degree of distortion (fig. 5.23).

For the construction of the rectangles in a cartogram a chequered paper may be used taking the smallest square to represent a unit area. This way the multiple of smallest squares will show a rectangular figure representing the statistical data of the continental area. The principle behind such a diagram is that the data of a homogenous part of the earth's surface is not merely the function of its area but of some attribute of the respective object (Star and Estes, 1990).

Some other types of rectangles, either in divided or in undivided form, may represent statistical data proportional to its length. This is practically a bar graph, as the width does not have any specific significance and does not represent any data. Therefore, only the length, alike a bar graph, is measureable on scale.

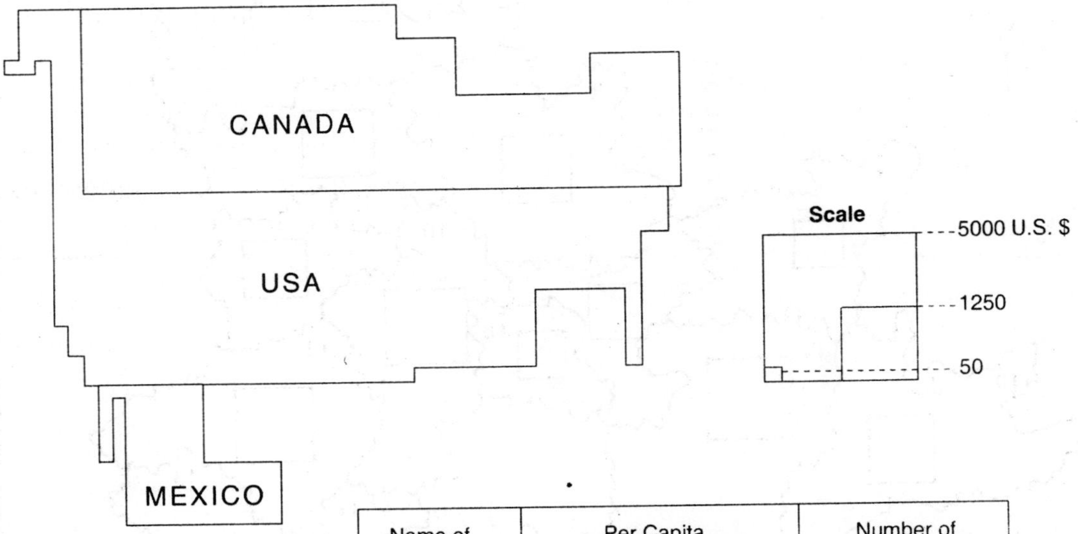

Name of Country	Per Capita Gross National product (in U.S.$)	Number of squares forming rectangles
Canada	19970	400
U.S.A.	24,740	495
Mexico	3610	72

Fig. 5.23 Cartogram or rectangular diagrams

Computation for columns or bar graph

Columns and bar graphs are the same thing, only the columns are always erect.

Only the length of the column is measured on scale. Therefore, what is required is to multiply the data by the ratio of the scale in order to have the length of the column in cm. or inch.

When placed on maps the scale should be chosen carefully, so that the columns or bars are not outside boundary of the administrative division for much of its length.

These columns or bars are of two types :

i) Simple bar or column representing only one item throughout its length;

ii) Composite bar or column representing more than one item as component parts of a whole data.

This second one is more comprehensive as it gives the total as well as its component parts within the same diagram.

However, comparative data can also use such diagrams (fig. 5.24) in multiple of bars and visual comparison seems to be very clear between data for different years, data of male and female etc. For this purpose of comparison both simple and composite bargraphs can be used.

TABLE 5.14

Example Data and Computation

Sl. No.	District	Rural Sex ratio	Length of Bar in cm. (1 cm ¾ 500 SR)	Urban Sex ratio	Length of Bar in cm
1.	Darjeeling	909	1.45	731	1.17
2.	Jalpaiguri	863	1.38	768	1.22
3.	Cochbihar	899	1.39	774	1.24
4.	West Dinajpore	914	1.46	821	1.31
5.	Malda	969	1.55	873	1.40
6.	Murshidabad	979	1.57	920	1.47
7.	Nadia	952	1.52	933	1.49
8.	24-Parganas	932	1.49	737	1.18
9.	Calcutta	—	—	612	0.98
10.	Howrah	940	1.50	644	1.03
11.	Hooghly	948	1.52	749	1.20
12.	Bardwan	898	1.44	699	1.12
13.	Birbhum	984	1.57	844	1.35
14.	Bankura	987	1.58	905	1.81
15.	Medinipur	963	1.54	830	1.33
16.	Purulia	979	1.57	889	1.42

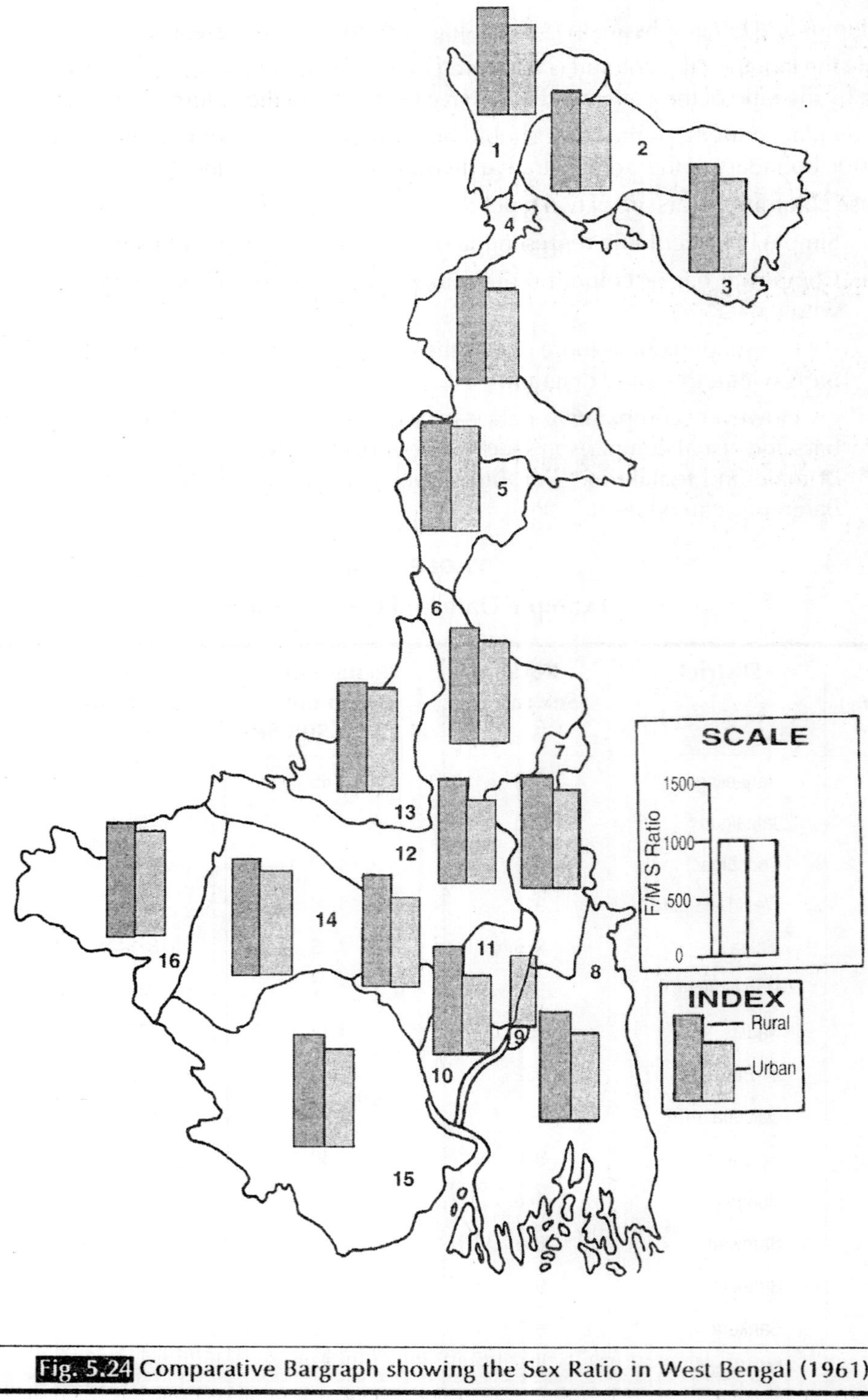

Fig. 5.24 Comparative Bargraph showing the Sex Ratio in West Bengal (1961)

Interpretaion :

The rural and urban sex ratio of the districts of West Bengal according to 1961 Census data have been represented by comparative bargraphs. Basically these columns or bars are simple in nature, as each of them has included only one item or a single component data. It is interesting to note that highly urbanised areas have shown low sex ratio, whereas districts with poor urbanisation have given high sex ratio, such as purulia, Bankura etc. In the case of rural scenario, there is greater parity among the sex ratio values. If indicates that in the highly urbanised areas there is greater concentertion of male population than female population because of the presence of male migrants engaged in various kinds of jobs and business works.

Computation for triangular or Ternary diagrams

Three different sets of data pertaining to three component objects of a whole, such as, percentage of sand, silt and clay for identification of soil texture, can be favourably shown in ternary diagrams. As such, the ternary diagram used by the United States Department of Agriculture and (1938) and Kachinskii (1986) represent the compositional variation of nine major types of soil texture. In this diagram (fig. 5.25a). The three sides of the triangle represents 100% sand, silt and clay. This is practically a graphical work on which combinations of the three components in various proportions will represent textural types.

In terms of the participation of the working population in different types of occupation ternary diagrams can be helpful, as it expresses the percentage people involved in agriculture, industry and in tertiary occupation. Here also the apices of the intersecting triangles formed by 10% lines can gives a state's position in terms of the involvement of its labour force. All a diagram-maker has to do is to draw 10% lines from three bases and to locate the intersecting triangles. Now the state should be placed in terms of its data of labour force, in percentage, participating in agricultural, industrial or any tertiary occupation. The apices of the triangles or any intermediate position can be occupied by a state in terms of which the broad occupational structure may be known.

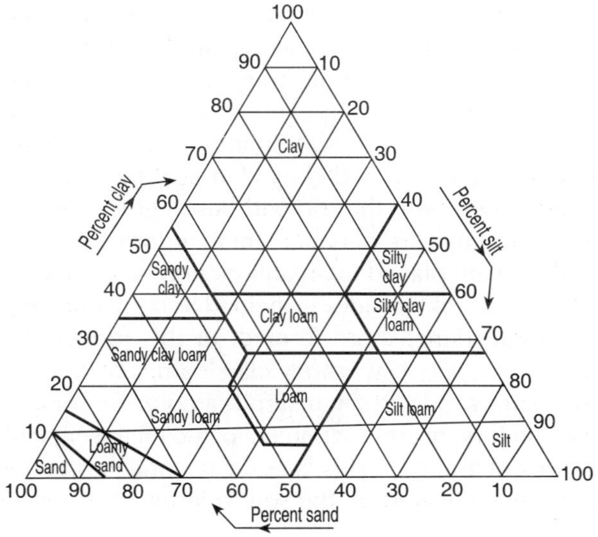

Fig. 5.25a Triangular diagram

Geographical data is often bi-variate, tri-variate and multi-variate. Cartographers have

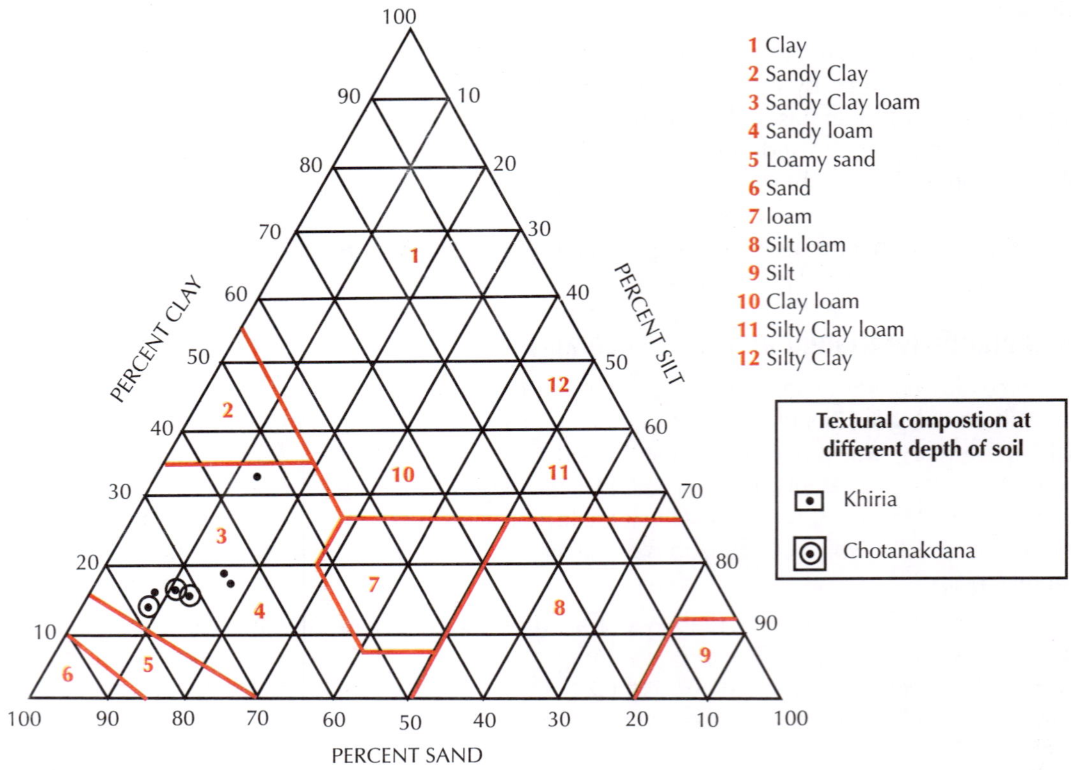

Fig. 5.25b **Ternary Diagram or Soil Texture**

repeatedly tried to find out a proper way of presentation of geographical data. Various statistical analyses have critically examined such data in bi-variate and multi-variate forms. In the case of soil texture various grades are observed starting from coarse sands to colloids at the lowest. However, in determining soil texture which is the proximity of soil forming grains to each other illustrates the physical composition of soils. USDA simplifed soil textrue in terms of three broad classes of soil grades (1938) into sand, silt and clay. Hence, it includes all the sand grades into sand; silt grades into silt and clay. These three broad based grades are presented in a ternary diagram where three sides of a triangle are of equal length to form an equilateral triangle. Along the three sides sand, silt and clay are placed in an anti-clockwise direction as percent which are given in a clockwise direction. Each of the sides is divided into ten parts representing 10% each. Altogether 100 small equilateral triangles are formed. In this format, 12 textural classes are marked. These are clay, sandy clay, silty clay, sandy clay loam, clay loam, silty clay loam, sandy loam, loam, silt loam, sand , loamy sand and silt. In a soil sample, the composition of sand, silt and clay are determined in the laboratory in terms of percent of the total weight of soil sample and then these are placed on the network of triangles. This fixes the textural class of the soil sample. It helps to select a particular crop to be cultivated on the soil in terms of water retention capacity and scope of aeration.

TABLE 5.15

Soil data

District - West Medinipur; Police Station - Garhbeta; Village - Khiria

Depth in inches	Coarse Sand	Fine Sand	Sand (Coarse sand + Fine sand)	Silt	Clay	Total	Percentage of textural components			Total (%)
	(weight in grams)						Sand (%)	Silt (%)	Clay (%)	
0–6"	29.76	34.32	64.08	17.85	16.45	98.38	65.14	18.14	16.72	100
6–14"	36.91	36.46	73.37	8.75	16.3	98.42	74.55	8.89	16.56	100
14–23"	29.71	33.8	63.51	15.68	19.15	98.34	64.58	15.95	19.47	100
23–35"	31.78	20.62	52.4	12.73	31.75	96.88	54.09	13.14	32.77	100
35–48"	23.04	19.91	42.95	15.83	37.40	96.18	44.65	16.46	38.89	100

Village - Chotanakdana

Depth in inches	Coarse Sand	Fine Sand	Sand (Coarse sand + Fine sand)	Silt	Clay	Total	Percentage of textural components			Total (%)
	(Weight in grams)						Sand (%)	Silt (%)	Clay (%)	
0–10"	23.18	47.88	71.06	12.5	14.8	98.36	72.24	12.71	15.05	100
10–17"	22.44	47.7	70.14	10.85	17.18	98.17	71.45	11.05	17.50	100
17–48"	27.71	48.91	76.62	8.35	13.48	98.45	77.83	8.48	13.69	100

Interpretation :

Eight soil samples are taken. Of them five samples are from Khiria village of Garbeta PS, West Medinipur, and three samples are from Chotanakdana village of the same PS. These soil samples are taken from various depths of the two profiles. When the percentage of sand, silt and clay are determined, they are placed on the textural diagram. It shows that all the three samples of Chotanakdana belong to sandy loam category. On the other hand three samples of Khiria are sandy loam in character, whereas one belongs to sandy clay loam and another belongs to sandy clay classes. Profilewise in all the five samples of Khiria, sand is the predominating grade. Clay increases downward, whereas silt is variable and low in percentage. In the three samples of Chotanakdana village, sand is again the predominating component . Clay comes next and it is higher in the second layer, though it reduces further downward. Silt is low in percentage and gradually decreases downward.

FLOW LINE DIAGRAM

In flow-line maps elongated arrows curving to denote the changes in direction are shown. Such maps can be used for the data where showing the linear movement is the major objective of the map. Thus streamlines can be used for wind movement, ocean currents, mass migration etc. In such maps, the flow-lines are equidimentional in width though the length may vary without any specific measurements for scale.

Another type of flow-line diagram may include proportionate representation in terms of frequency, volume, number, velocity etc. Such flow-lines may vary in thickness or may have some symbolic indications representing the variability of data (fig. 5.26).

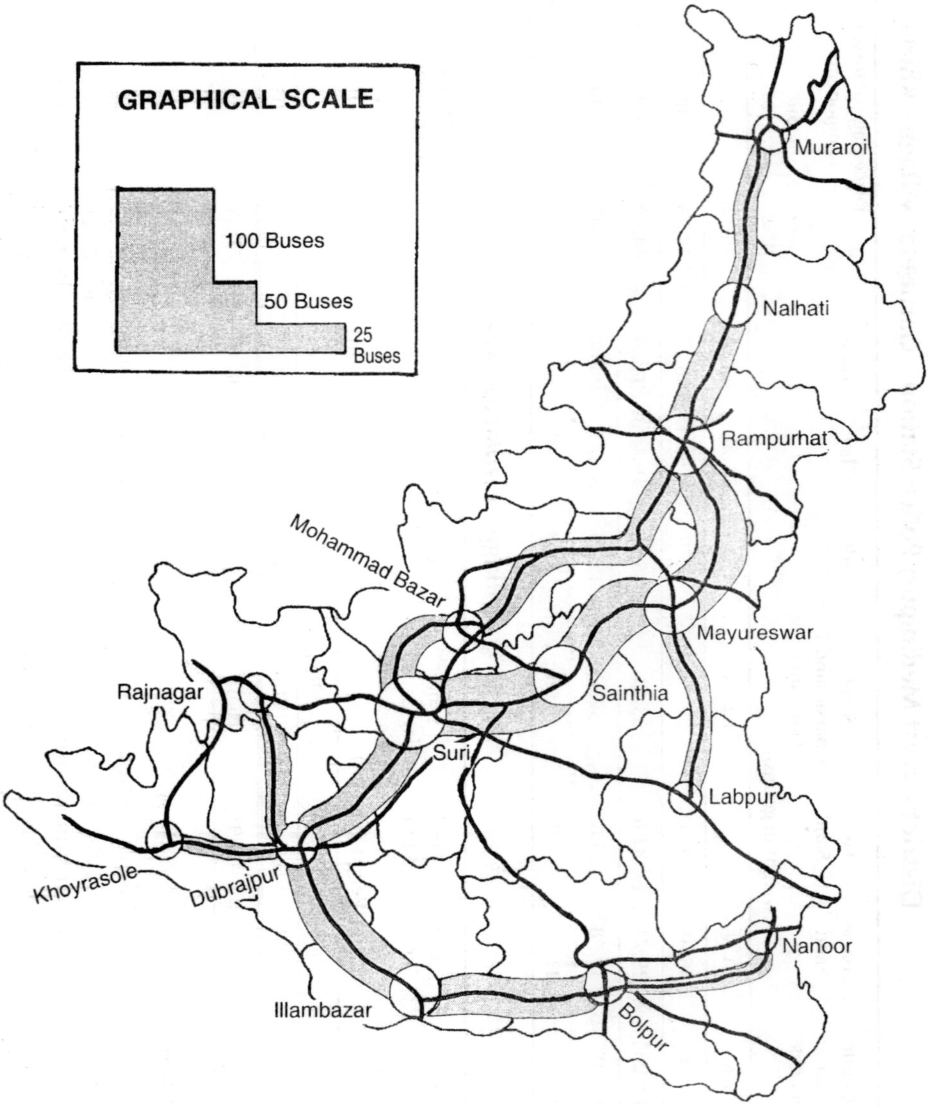

Fig. 5.26 Flow Diagram of Birbhum

TABLE 5.16

Data for Flowline Diagram

	Dubrajpur	Suri	Bolpur	Nanoor	Rajnagar	Saithia	Labhpur	Muhammad Bazar	Rampurhat	Nalhati	Murarai	Mayureswar	Khayrasole	Illambazar
From Illambazar	34	26												
From Dubrajpur		40	11											
From Illambazar			43	9										
From Suri						10								
From Mayureswar						29								
From Suri								51	52	39	33			
From Muhammad Bazar (via Saithia)										12				
From Dubrajpur					2									20

Flow-lines may be used where no specific path of flow is noted. For this purpose a number of arrows are drawn to indicate the flow covering the area over which the flow seems to occur. Thus for migration from one town to another only a single arrow may be shown, but in the case of immigration from a vast rural hinterland to a metropolis any number of arrows can be used over the rural urban interfringe over which the migration seems to occur. Similarly, for wind movement too, no specific path may be discernible and thus the area over which such a movement of winds is predicted or identified, any number of arrows indicating the flow can be used. However, regarding flow diagrams of passenger or traffic or goods as the path of flow is fixed, flow-lines of variable thickness according to scale will follow the curvilinear path only (fig. 5.26).

Construction of cubes and spheres

Cubes and spheres represent volumetric data. Usually when a huge amount of data is to be represented in a small area, these three dimensional diagrams are used, such as, the population of an urban unit, a large number of residential houses in an administrative unit of small spatial dimension etc. Such a diagram represents a great concentration of data.

For the purpose of construction of the sphere the radius of the sphere to be drawn is to be calculated using the formula for the volume of a sphere : $\frac{4}{3}\pi r^3$. Therefore, it involves a cube root of the data and that reduces the data to a small figure. Then on the basis of certain selected scale, chosen on the basis of the space available on map, the radius or radii are converted into radius on scale. With this radius on scale a circle is drawn fixing the centre of the circle at the approximate centre of the map. Then the circle is transformed into a sphere by drawing graticule-like lines to give an impression of a volumetric diagram.

For the construction of cubes simple cube root of the data is derived. The data obtained as cube root should represent one side of the cube to be constructed. For this purpose the values of cube roots should be converted into desired lengths on a selected scale. Obviously, the selection of scale will depend on the space available on map.

For another type, blocks or cubes are piled in one diagram, each representing certain small amount of data, the smaller the unit figure, more close it is to the data represented, though perfect equalization the between actual data and the data represented by the number denoted by piled blocks or cubes can be seldom obtained. However, this diagram exhibits a good expression of a three dimensional diagram as the piling nature of cubes is well understood and the interpreter can count the number of blocks very easily and thus he/ she can get a near-perfect idea about the absolute figure of the actual data.

Computation of Compsite Bar Graph and Pie Graph

Composite bar graphs are constructed to represent a sum total and its components. It represents the components as rectangles dividing the bar into segments. Various types of data representing a whole and its components can be represented in this bar graph, such as, landuse categories of a locality, male-female population, occupational structure of any population, religious composition of the population etc.

For the construction of a composite bar graph (fig. 5.27) only the length of the bar is to be derived by converting the data on a selected scale which varies depending on the space available. However, the proportion of different segments in the bar may be obtained as the conversion of absolute figures on scale or may be derived as proportion of the total. [Dividing the data, be it a component or the sum total, by the scale-unit will give the length of the bar easily.] For percentage bar graphs such proportions may be obtained as percentages by multiplying different fractional proportions by 100. However, the total length of the composite bar will be fixed on the basis of the sum total of different composite figures. Thus two composite percentage bar graph representing different data will be of same length; in both the cases the sum total will be considered as 100%.

TABLE 5.17

Data for Composite Bargraph

Sl. No.	States	Main Workers	Length of bar on Scale1 cm = 200000 workers	Marginal Workers	Length of bar on Scale	Total workers	Length of bar on Scale
1.	Arunachal Pradesh	390976	1.95	88060 (18%)	0.44	479036	2.39
2.	Manipur	708283	3.54	66621	0.33	774904	3.87
3.	Meghalaya	715587	3.58	41735 (6%)	0.21	757322	3.79
4.	Miizoram	290317	1.45	47028	0.24	558897	1.69
5.	Nagaland	511497	2.56	47400	0.24	516237	2.80
6.	Tripura	802063	4.01	56454	0.28	858517	4.29

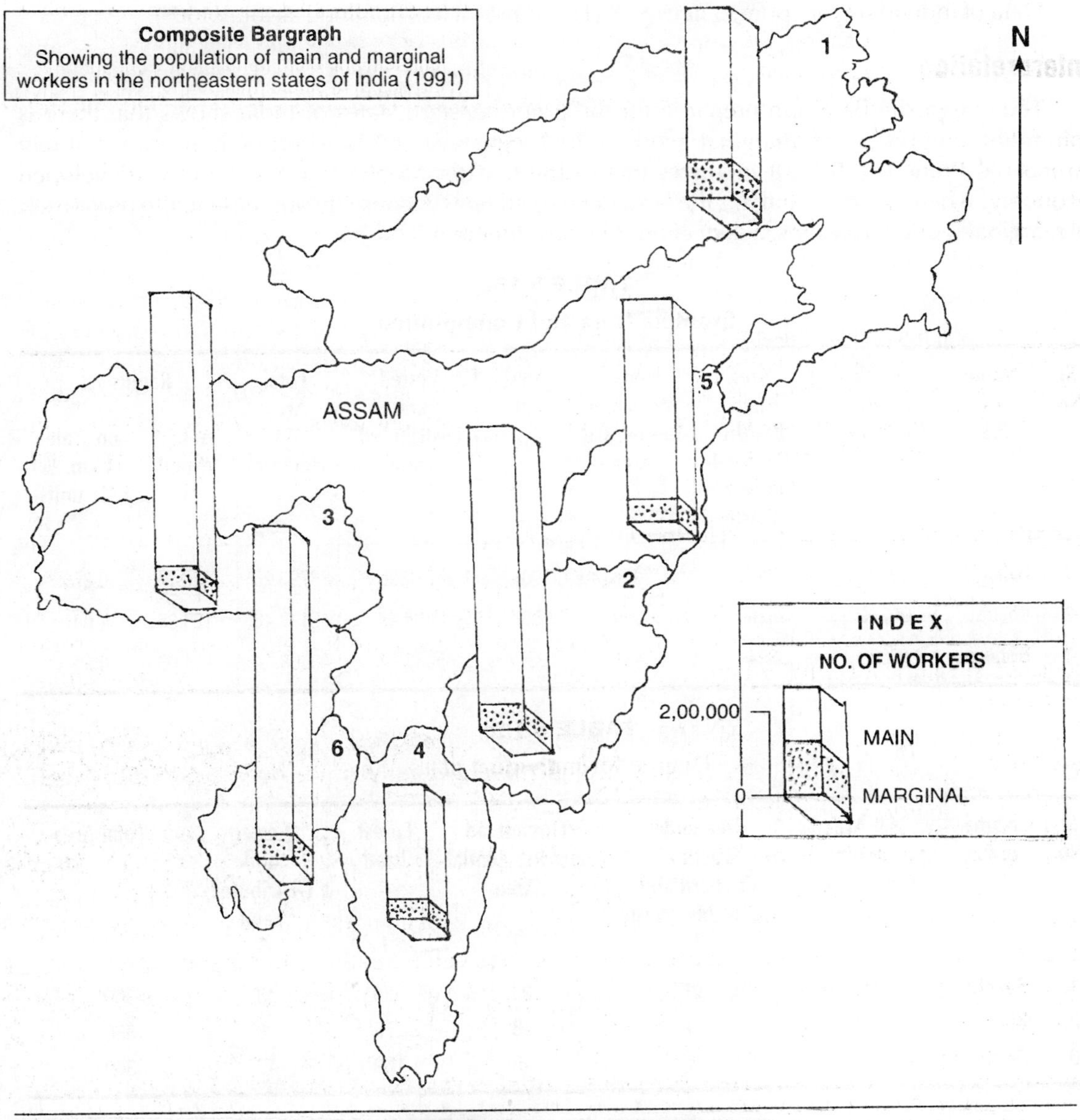

Fig. 5.27 Composite bargraph

Pie-graph or pie-diagram, on the other hand, is a circular diagram representing the component segments as proportional angles within the circle which represents the total (fig. 5.28 See colour plate). The term 'Pie' from Greck alphabet has been used here to indicate the circularity of the diagram, because pie (π) is considered as the ratio between the circumference and diameter of a circle. For the purpose of construction, the radius of the circle should be calculated from πr^2 representing the sum total of the component figures as the area of the circle. The square root value should be taken on a selected scale chosen according to the space available on map.

To obtain the angles in degree representing the components the following formula should be used:

Data of individual component item × K (The constant K is obtained as total/360°).

Interpretation :

The composite bargraph prepared for the 6 northeastern states of India shows that there is minimum proportion of marginal workers in Meghalaya (6%), whereas it is maximum in Arunachal Pradesh (18%). It indicates that of the 6 states Meghalaya has the most developed economy, whereas Arunachal has the least developed one, because the increase in the proportion of marginal worker indicates lack of economic development.

TABLE 5.18a

Example Data and Computation

Sl No.	Name of P.S.	Net Area under Cultivation	Area under Pasture Orchard Cultivable Waste	Home-stead and Residential Area	Forest Land	Vested and Distributed Land	Total Area (in Hectare)	Radius	
								Actual 'r' units	on scale (1 cm. ¾ 125r units)
1.	Saltora	22131	3866	2467	3006	4323.25	35793.25	106.74	0.85
2.	Khatra	29769	420	6050	6883	2305.46	45427.46	120.25	1.00
3.	Bishnupur	17083	894	5431	12377	5083.14	40868.14	114.06	0.91

TABLE 5.18b

Degree for individual class

Sl No.	Name of P.S.	Net Area under Cultivation 1	Area under Pasture Orchard and Cultivable Waste 2	Homestead and Residential Area 3	Forest Land 4	Vested and Distributed Land 5	Total Area
1.	Saltora	223°	39°	25°	30°	43°	360°
2.	Khatra	236°	3°	48°	55°	18°	360°
3.	Bishnupur	150°	8°	48°	109°	45°	360°

Interpretation for Pie Graph

The 5 categories of landuse of the 3 police station areas of Bankura district have been represented by pie diagrams (Fig. 5.28). It may be noted that the proportion of forest land is maximum in Bishnupur and consequently the net area under cultivation is much lower than two other police station areas. On the otherhand, saltora has minimum proportion of forest land and residential area, whereas the proportion of pasture, cultivable waste and orchard is maximum. It seems that Bishnupur has more lands unusable for cultivation and those have been left to the forests. On the contrary, Saltora's undulating topography may not be suitable for living space, but it may be used as pastures and orchards. Khatra seems to be having maximum proportion of fertile lands.

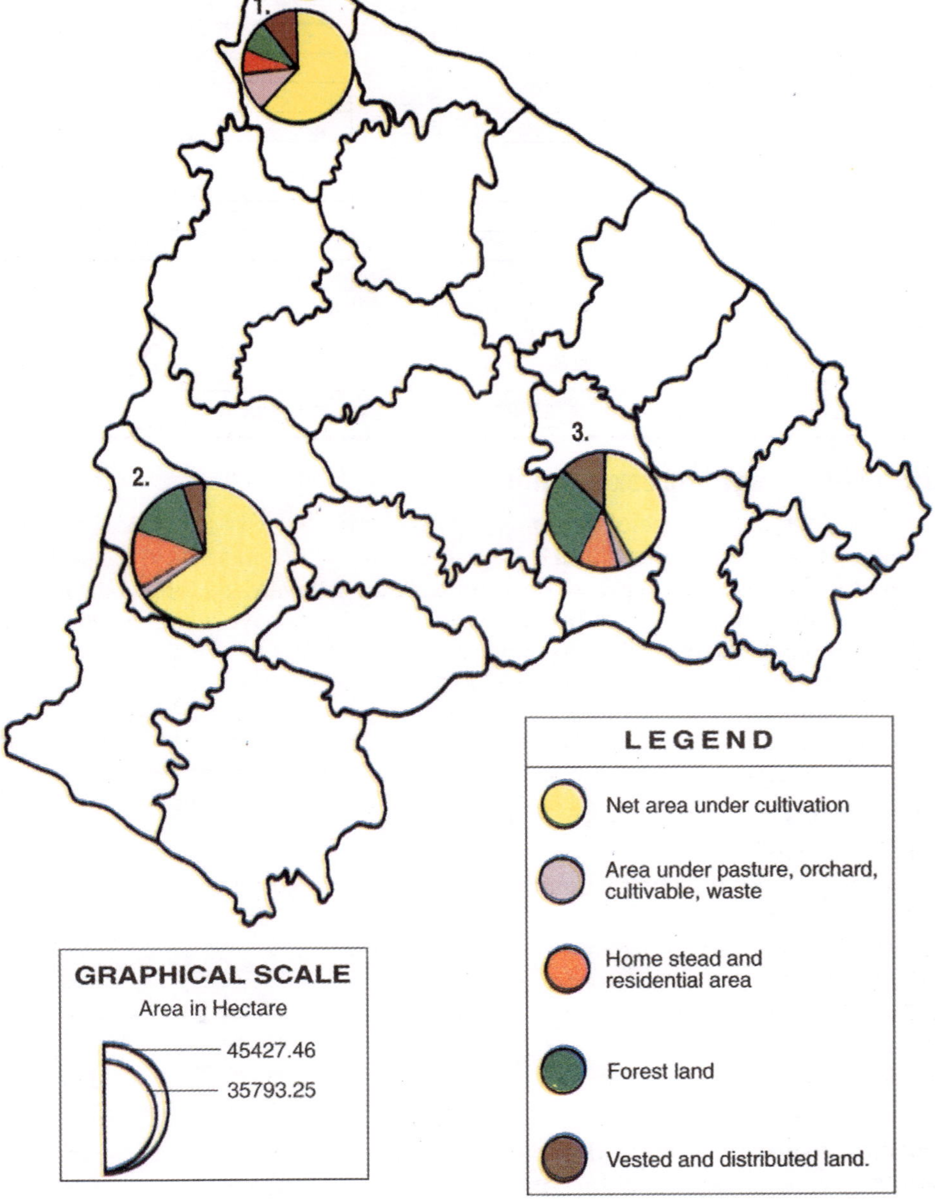

Fig. 5.28 Pie graphs Showing land use pattern of Bankura

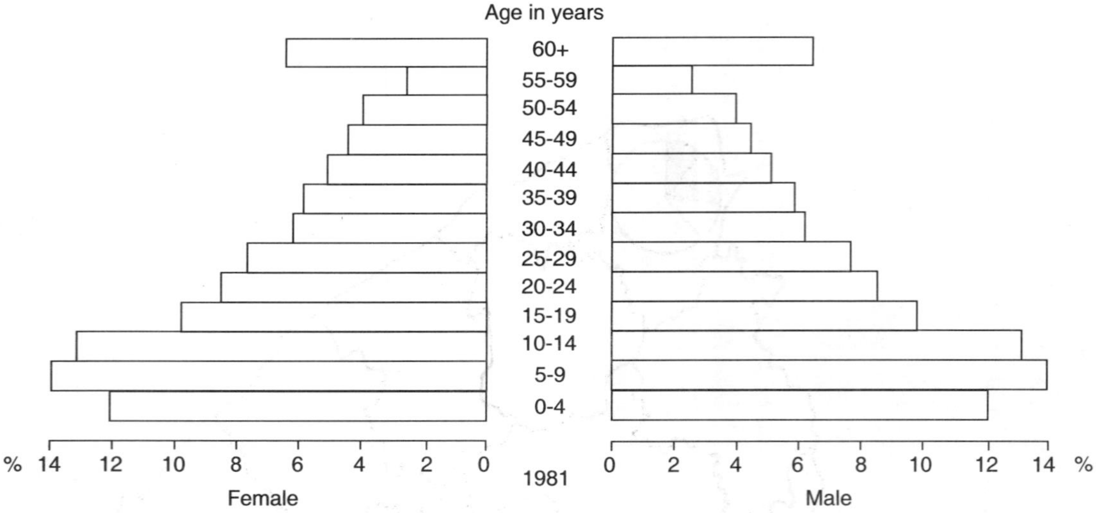

Fig. 5.29 Age-sex pyramid (1981)

Construction of age and sex pyramid

Age-sex pyramid is a useful diagram prepared from table 5.14 (fig. 5.25) can convey important information to the geographer about the age-structure of the two sexes in the particular population of a country. It appears like a pyramidal form narrowing toward the top and broadened toward the bottom. Usually, the younger group of people of a country have a larger number than the highly aged old people. In the pyramid the youngest group forms the bottom whereas, the oldest group forms the top, with successively higher age-groups occupying successively higher positions. Age-grouping can be done at one year interval or it may quinquennial, i.e., 5 year groups. Various other groupings for a particular data can also de done.

For the purpose of construction the male and female population of different age groups are separated and absolute figures are put to scale to obtain the length of consecutive horizontal bars. In stead of absolute figures percentage of the total male and total female can also be used in such pyramids.

The length of bars for male and female population may vary slightly depending on the absolute data, but a large variation is unusual as the number of male and female population varies with only a few exception. The two sets of horizontal bars representing male and female population are usually separated by a gap mentioning various age-groups in tiers (fig. 5.29). The total population irrespective of sex can also be represented in these pyramids. In that case the age-group in year is shown at the side of the bars.

TABLE 5.19

Age-wise distribution (%) of Indian Population, 1981

Age Categories / Class of Age	1981	
	Male	Female
0 – 4	12.33	12.87
5 – 9	14.02	14.12
10 – 14	13.14	12.60
15 – 19	9.85	9.38
20 – 24	8.42	8.82
25 – 29	7.49	7.78
30 – 34	6.28	6.49
35 – 39	5.79	5.90
40 – 44	5.25	5.03
45 – 49	4.48	4.30
50 – 54	4.02	3.61
55 – 59	2.48	2,47
60 +	6.45	6.63
% of Total Population	100.00	100.00

However, the overall shape of age-sex pyramid varies substantially between developed and developing nations, as the number of children in a developing nation is always very high as compared with other age-groups. In a developed nation, on the other hand, the people belonging to working age often have a higher number than the dependent age-group of children and old-age people.

Construction of compound pyramids

Compound pyramids represent data of different categories concerning population within one diagram. The categories pertain to different components of a sum total. Year-wise migration stream with earliest ones occupying the uppermost tier and the latest occupying the bottom-most tier with successive years in between, ethnic structure of a population, decennial changes in the population of different ethnic categories of a nation, wage-wise divisions of the working population of different age-groups etc. can be represented in such compound age-sex pyramids. In these diagrams usually the successive tiers are separated by a regular space in between along which lines are drawn to connect the same category of two different age-group tiers. Such spacing can gives a step-like impression too.

For the purpose of construction the total length of an age-group a tier is obtained on the basis of the sum total of different component categories in male and female groups put to the selected scale. Then individual division of different component categories are separated according their respective proportions of the total male and total female in any age-group and are marked by different symbols.

Superimposed age and sex pyramids

Such pyramids are usually constructed for the purpose of comparison between two sets of data of the same population. They can show temporal changes in population-structure when prepared on the basis of the population of two different important years, such as, the year before partition of India and the year after two or three years of independence with great influx of emigrants from Pakistan. Both the figures of in-migration and out-migration can be used as components of population particularly related to migration in the year after partition of India.

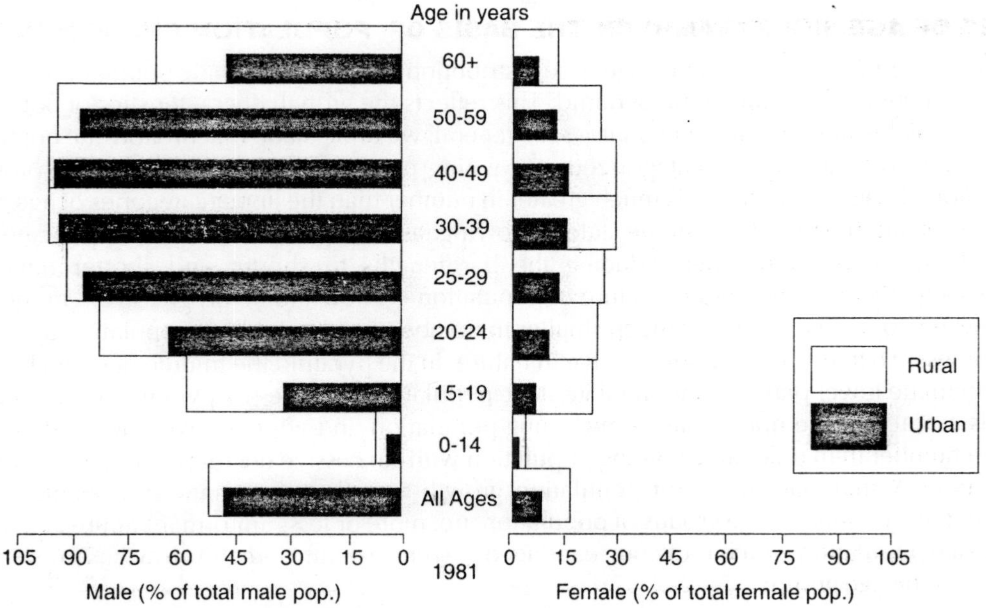

Fig. 5.30 **Superimposed age-sex pyramid**

Such a diagram can also be used for the comparable data of one base year and another successive year after strong imposition of population control measures for a few consecutive years. Therefore, any two sets of comparable data of population can be used to construct such a superimposed pyramid Here it (fig. 5.30) has been constructed on the basis of the data from table no. 5.15).

TABLE 5.20

Data for superimposed Age-sex pyramid 1981
Working Population ratio to total

Age Categories In years	Rural (%)		Urban (%)	
	Male	Female	Male	Female
All Age	52.62	16.00	48.54	7.28
0 – 14	6.30	3.53	2.46	0.88
15 – 19	58.19	22.77	31.54	6.19
20 – 24	82.71	24.29	63.35	9.25
25 – 29	92.79	26.14	86.78	12.17
30 – 39	96.71	28.45	94.93	15.1
40 – 49	97.25	28.90	95.49	15.34
50 – 59	94.08	23.94	86.86	12.42
60 +	67.59	11.29	47.49	5.75

The method of construction is the same as it is in other types of population pyramids. Therefore, only the lengths of the age-group tiers for male and female groups are to be derived. The base year is shown as blank tiers, whereas, the superimposed tiers are tinted or marked by symbols. Where the superimposed tier supercedes the base-tier in terms of length, a very narrow blank space is left on the two sides of the demarcating terminal line of the base-tier, so that the length of the underlying tier can be understood easily.

TYPES OF AGE-SEX PYRAMID ON THE BASIS OF POPULATION GROWTH MODE

Demographers have noted that age wise distribution of male and female population gives rise to some difference in shape of the pyramid. This reflects the growth characteristics of population which is variable among different countries. In general, we understand that broadly the population of a country or state can be categorized into young population, working population and old population. If young population is much greater in number than the upper categories of age group, it indicates that the population of the state is growing fast. In this type when the upper categories gradually decrease in number reducing the bar lengths to shorter and shorter dimension successively, the pyramid and the nature of population is known to be progressive. On the other hand, when young population is much smaller in number that the working population age group, more or less, 18 to 64 years, it is regressive in nature. In the pyramid the middle part will be much wider than the lower part. An intermediate stage population and age-sex pyramid is one in which there is a notch in the upper part of the young population and younger working population is more in number than older age working population with successive decreasing figures for old age population. A stationary phase of population growth as reflected in age-sex pyramid can be identified when different age groups of population are, more or less, uniform in number except for the old age population which is of course reduced to some extent. Here the growth is proportional to the working age group.

TABLE 5.21

Afghanistan (2016)

Age (in years)	Male (in %)	Female (in %)
0-4	7.6	7.2
5-9	7.6	7.2
10-14	7.1	6.7
15-19	6.1	5.8
20-24	5	4.6
25-29	4	3.6
30-34	3.3	3
35-39	2.8	2.5
40-44	2.2	1.9
45-49	1.7	1.5
50-54	1.3	1.2
55-59	1	1
60-64	0.8	0.8
65-69	0.5	0.6
70-74	0.3	0.4
75-79	0.2	0.2
80-84	0.1	0.1

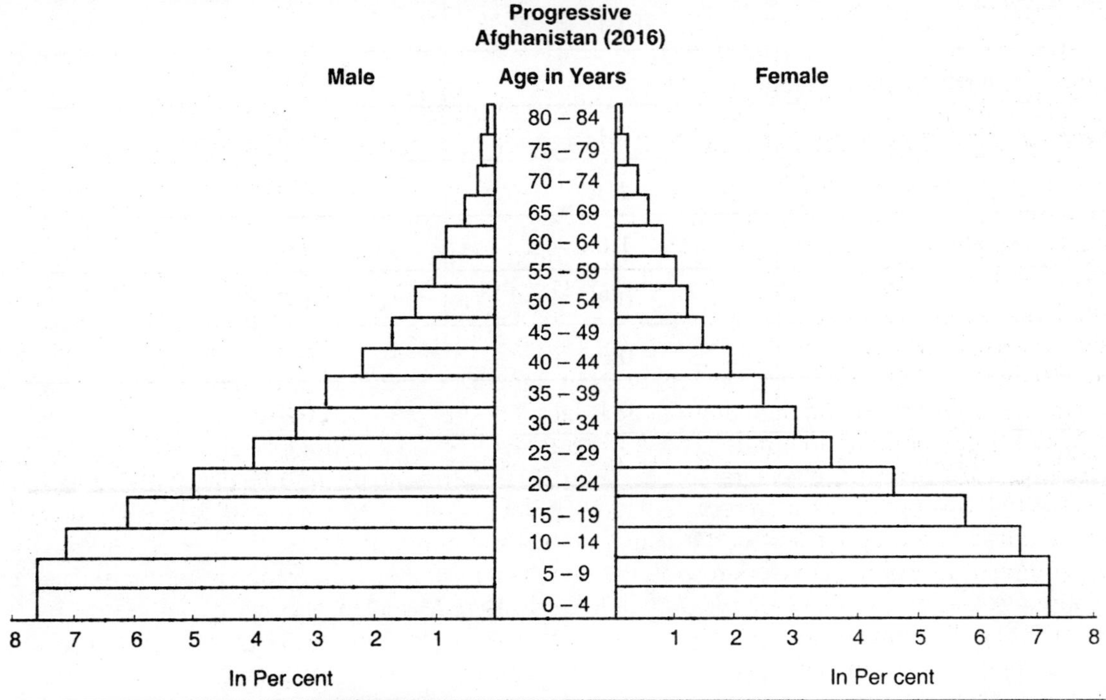

Fig. 5.31 Age-Sex Pyramid of Afghanistan

TABLE 5.22

Japan (2016)

Age (in years)	Male (in %)	Female (in %)
0-4	2.1	2.0
5-9	2.2	2.1
10-14	2.2	2.1
15-19	2.4	2.3
20-24	2.4	2.3
25-29	2.7	2.5
30-34	2.9	2.8
35-39	3.2	3.1
40-44	3.7	3.7
45-49	3.7	3.6
50-54	3.2	3.2
55-59	2.9	3.0
60-64	3.1	3.2
65-69	3.5	3.8
70-74	3.1	3.5
75-79	2.3	2.9
80-84	1.6	2.4
85-89	0.9	1.7
90-94	0.3	0.9
95-99	0.1	0.3
100+	0	0

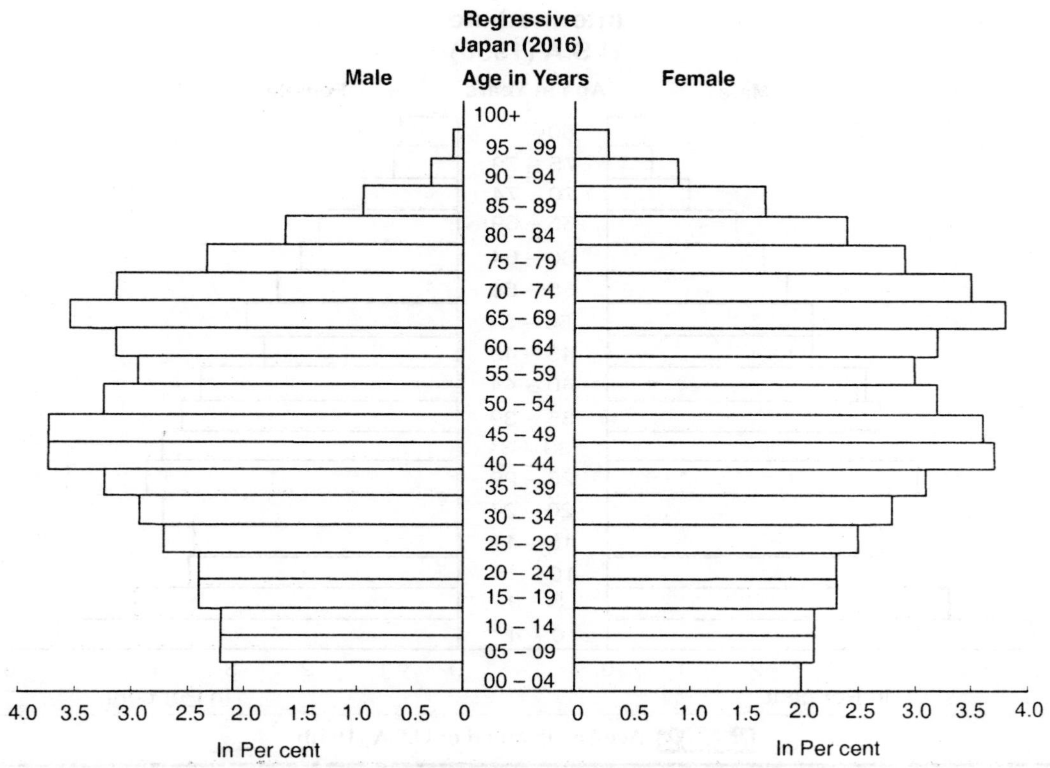

Fig. 5.32 Age -Sex Pyramid of Japan

TABLE 5.23

U.S.A (1950)

Age (in years)	Male (in %)	Female (in %)
0-4	5.6	5.3
5-9	4.5	4.3
10-14	3.7	3.6
15-19	3.6	3.5
20-24	3.9	3.9
25-29	4.1	4.1
30-34	3.8	3.9
35-39	3.6	3.7
40-44	3.4	3.4
45-49	2.7	2.6
50-54	2.7	2.8
55-59	2.4	2.4
60-64	2.1	2.1
65-69	1.7	1.8
70-74	1.1	1.2
75-79	0.6	0.8
80+	0.5	0.7

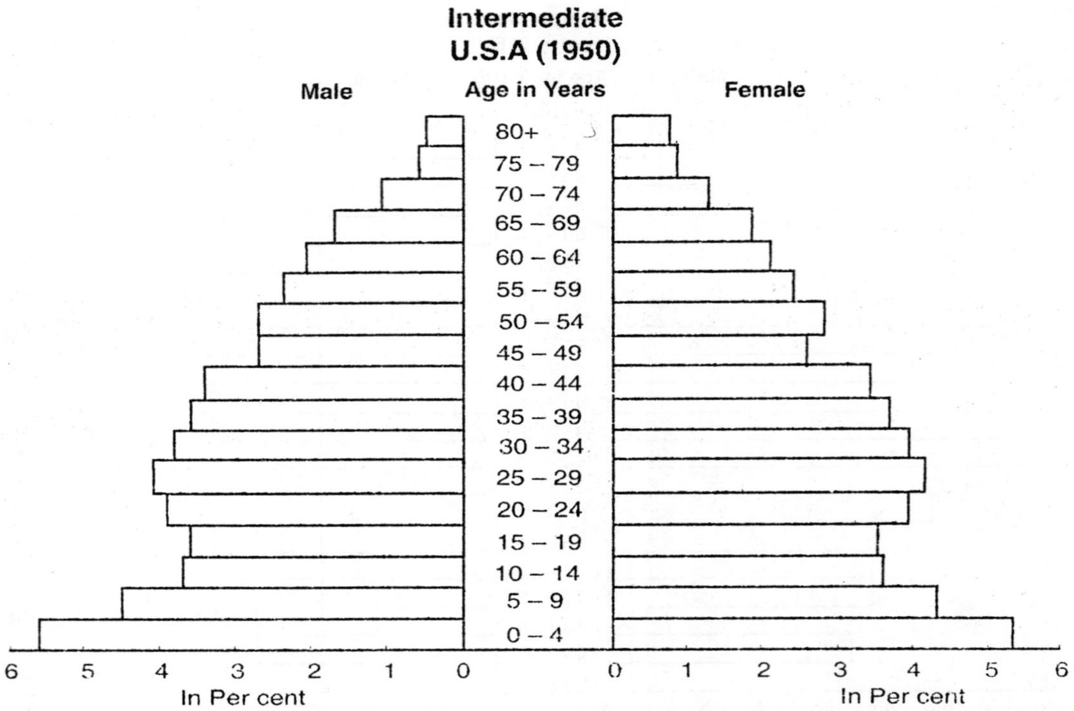

Fig. 5.33a Age-Sex Pyramid of U.S.A (1950)

TABLE 5.24

U.S.A. (2018, July in millions)

Age (in years)	Male (in %)	Female (in %)
Under 5	10.3	9.68
5-9	10.32	9.88
10-14	10.66	10.22
15-19	10.77	10.32
20-24	11.2	10.67
25-29	12.02	11.54
30-34	11.19	10.94
35-39	10.79	10.77
40-44	9.8	9.92
45-49	10.26	10.48
50-54	10.28	10.61

Contd. next page

Age (in years)	Male (in %)	Female (in %)
55-59	10.67	11.27
60-64	9.73	10.6
65-69	8.03	9.05
70-74	6.21	7.19
75-79	4.14	5.12
80-84	2.59	3.54
85 and Over	2.33	4.22

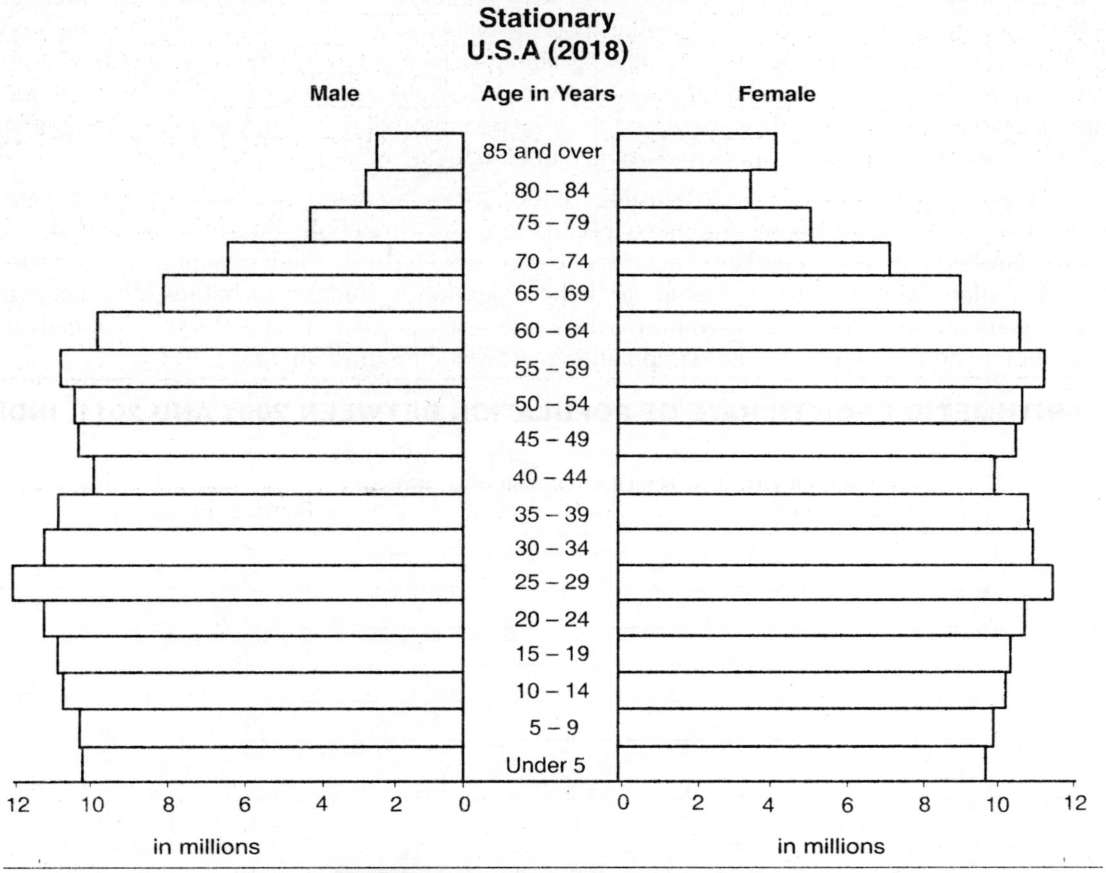

Fig. 5.33b Age-Sex Pyramid of U.S.A. (2018)

Interpretation

The populations of different countries may cite examples of these four types of age-sex pyramid. The true pyramidal shape is reflected in the progressive population pyramid of Afghanistan (Fig. 5.31) where the youngest group of population has the longest bars and it successively reduces with narrowing shape of pyramid towards the upper age groups culminating into the minimum in the top most age group. It may be noted here that in Afghanistan perhaps because of poverty, malnutrition and lack of availability of modern medicines, age groups do not extend beyond 80 to 84 years which is also only 0.1%.

Japan (Fig. 5.32) is an advanced country of the orient. Population is less poverty striken. Modern amenities and medicines are available in plenty. Japanese people are also cautious about the hazards of uncontrolled growth of population. As a result, they have reduced their population growth strongly. The working age population of both younger and older categories dominate the population pyramid. On the other hand, the young non-working age group is getting smaller and smaller in number. Hence, the age sex pyramid has a narrower base than wider middle part. This pyramid is regressive. The country may face a problem of lacking working age population in future.

The population of U.S.A. (Fig. 5.33a) immediately after second world war reflects an intermediate shape of population pyramid in 1950. At that time, the population figures of working age groups were much smaller than highly growing figures of children population. This is because the young American population felt relieved as the war was over and younger working age group of population had a strong trend of making families. As a result, children or new born babies increased much in number than the working group and the adolescents. That was the period of baby boom (1946-1964). This increased the American population substantially and within 100 years American population increased from 76 million to 282 million.

The population of U.S.A. (2018) (Fig. 5.33b) shows a stationary character as reflected in pyramid. After baby boom and huge population growth people became concerned as an uncontrolled growth of population may lead to economic hazards. Hence, population control has been initiated and the trend goes towards the reduction in number of babies. This leads to a stationary phase of population pyramid as the working age population after 2000 was already high in number and the figures for child population were reducing substantially.

ARITHMETIC GROWTH RATE OF POPULATION BETWEEN 2001 AND 2011, INDIA

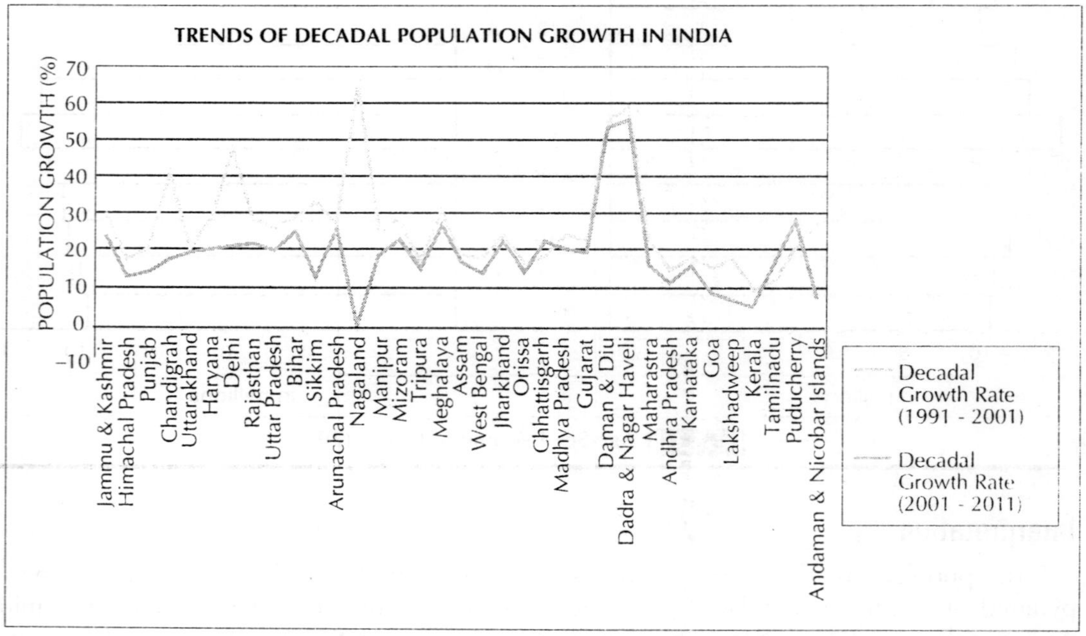

Fig. 5.34 Trends of decadal population Growth in India

During the Greek Period, population census was maintained for individual city-states where direct calculation of the number of population could be made because of small number of population. In large nation states, census operations are done through government departments related to Home Affairs. However, during the Colonial period, colonial rulers used to maintain some form of census of population of the subordinate state.

India was under the British rule for a long period of time. The then ruling government felt the need of preparing and maintaining a set of census data for the population of India as it was relevant to the exploitation of resources. The British Government initiated the first Indian census operation in 1872. The first complete Indian census of population came into being in 1881 under the guidance of British Viceroy Lord Ripon. However, India achieved her independence in 1947. In 1948, the census of India Act came into force. Since 1949 the census of population for independent India has been conducted by Registrar General and Census Commissioner of India under the Ministry of Home Affairs, Government of India.

Here, decadal growth of population has been calculated between the state-wise Indian population in 1991 and 2001 and also between 2001 and 2011. The growth of population has been calculated by simple subtraction of population of previous census year from successive census year population. Then the percentage of increase or decrease has been calculated between these two census years.

Interpretation :

In this study the normal decadal growth rate of population in provincial states and union territories has been calculated (table no. 5.25) for two successive decades, between 2001 and 2011. For the sake of convenience and proper analysis the two decadal growth patterns have been separately treated, so that any increase or decrease in the growth rate of population in the successive dacade can be specifically marked.

Between 1991 and 2001 the decadal growth of population for 35 states and union territories of India varied between 9.43% in Kerala as the minimum and 64.53% in Nagaland at the maximum. This range of population growth has been classified into four classes : <10%, 10% to 20%, 20% to 30% and above 30%, though only a few states and union territories have shown above 40%, above 50% as well as above 60%. Kerala, in particular gives a low decadal growth rate of <10% i.e. 9.43. Between 10% and 20% there are Tripura, Assam, West Bengal, Orissa, Chhattisgarh, Himachal Pradesh, Karnataka, Tamilnadu, Goa and Lakshadweep, altogether 10 states and UTs. Within the range of 20% to 30% the 16 states and UTs included are Jammu and Kashmir, Punjab, Uttrakhand, Haryana, Rajasthan, Uttar Pradesh, Bihar, Andhra Pradesh, Maharastra, Manipur, Mizoram, Meghalaya, Jharkhand, Madhya Pradesh, Gujarat, and Puducherry. Above 30% there are all together six States and union territories of which Sikkim has 33.03%, Chandigarh 40.8%, Delhi 47.02% , Daman & Diu 55.73%, Dadra & Nagar Haveli 59.22% and Nagaland has 64.53%.

The state of Kerala showing minimum decadal growth has controlled its growth of population substantially, as it is observed that in the successive decade it has maintained a still lower rate of population growth (4.86%). May be the cause lies in the enlightenment of people through education. However, the decadal growth rate does not remain the same in the successive decade for these administrative units, for some it has risen and for some others it has gone down.

In the study of the successive dacade, it reveals that between 2001 and 2011, 16 states are having 10-20%, 12 states are having 20%-30%, whereas 4 others maintain their recent decadal growth rate within 10%. It may be considered that the states having low positive growth rate may have a controlled birth rate and state to state migration. It may also be noted that the lack of economic growth and lack of adaptability of tribal population to the present environment might be

TABLE 5.25

Population Data and Calculation

Decadal Growth Rate of Population between two census years

Sl. No.	Name of the State and UT	Total Population			Decadal Growth of Population 1991 to 2001	Decadal Growth of Population 2001 to 2011	Decadal Growth Rate 1991 to 2001	Decadal Growth Rate 2001 TO 2011	Deviation of Decadal Growth Rate in successive Census Year
		1991	2001	2011					
1.	Jammu & Kashmir	7837051	10143700	12548926	2306649	2405226	29.43	23.71	– 5.72
2.	Himachal Pradesh	5170877	6077900	6856509	907023	778609	17.54	12.81	– 4.73
3.	Punjab	20281969	24358999	27704236	4077030	3345237	20.1	13.73	– 6.37
4.	Chandigarh	642015	900635	1054686	258620	154051	40.28	17.1	– 23.18
5.	Uttarakhand	7050634	8489349	10116752	1438715	1627403	20.41	19.17	–1.24
6.	Haryana	16463648	21144564	25353081	4680916	4208517	28.43	19.9	– 8.53
7.	Delhi	9420644	13850507	16753235	4429863	2902728	47.02	20.96	– 26.06
8.	Rajasthan	44005990	56507188	68621012	12501198	12113824	28.41	21.44	– 6.97
9.	Uttar Pradesh	132061653	166197921	199581477	34136268	33383556	25.85	20.09	– 5.76
10.	Bihar	64530554	82998509	103804637	18467955	20806128	28.62	25.07	– 3.55
11.	Sikkim	406457	540851	607688	134394	66837	33.06	12.36	–20.7
12.	Arunachal Pradesh	864558	1097968	1382611	233410	284643	27.0	25.92	–1.08
13.	Nagaland	1209546	1990036	1980602	780490	–9434	64.53	– 0.47	– 65
14.	Manipur	1837149	2293896	2721756	456747	427860	24.86	18.65	– 6.21
15.	Mizoram	689756	888573	1091014	198817	202441	28.82	22.78	– 6.04
16.	Tripura	2757205	3199203	3671032	441998	471829	16.03	14.75	–1.28
17.	Meghalaya	1774778	2318822	2964007	544044	645185	30.65	26.82	– 3.83
18.	Assam	22414322	26655528	31169272	4241206	4513744	18.92	16.93	–1.99

Contd. next page

Sl. No.	Name of the State and UT	Total Population			Decadal Growth of Population 1991 to 2001	Decadal Growth of Population 2001 to 2011	Decadal Growth Rate 1991 to 2001	Decadal Growth Rate 2001 TO 2011	Deviation of Decadal Growth Rate in successive Census Year
		1991	2001	2011					
19.	West Bengal	68077965	80176197	91347736	12098232	11171539	17.77	13.93	–3.84
20.	Jharkhand	21843911	26945829	32966238	5101918	6020409	23.36	22.34	–1.02
21.	Orissa	31659736	36804660	41947358	5144924	5142698	16.25	13.97	–2.28
22.	Chhattisgarh	17614928	20833803	25540196	3218875	4706393	18.27	22.59	+4.32
23.	Madhya Pradesh	48566242	60348023	72597565	11781781	12249542	24.26	20.3	–3.96
24.	Gajarat	41309582	50671017	60383628	9361435	9712611	22.66	19.17	–3.49
25.	Daman & Diu	101586	158204	242911	56618	84707	55.73	53.54	–2.19
26.	Dadra & Nagar Haveli	138477	220490	342853	82013	122363	59.22	55.5	–3.72
27.	Maharastra	78937187	96878627	112372972	17941440	15494345	22.73	15.99	–6.74
28.	Andhra Pradesh	66508008	76210007	84665533	9701999	8455526	14.59	11.1	–3.49
29.	Karnataka	44977201	52850562	61130704	7873361	8280142	17.51	15.67	–1.84
30.	Goa	1169793	1347668	1457723	177875	110055	15.21	8.17	–7.04
31.	Lakshadweep	51707	60650	64429	8943	3779	17.3	6.23	–11.07
32.	Kerala	29098518	31841374	33387677	2742856	1546303	9.43	4.86	–4.57
33.	Tamilnadu	55858946	62405679	72138958	6546733	9733279	11.72	15.6	+3.88
34.	Puducherry	507785	674345	1244464	166560	570119	20.62	27.72	+7.1
35.	Andaman & Nicobar Islands	280661	356152	379944	75491	23792	26.9	6.68	–20.22

the causes of low decadal growth in Andaman and Nicobar Islands. In the case of Kerala, it may be further added that a huge emigration is occurring in the state towards the Middle East countries which may be the cause of low decadal growth of population. The spread of education in the state is another substantive cause behind low population growth.

The phenomenally high deacadal growth rate of population in the two Union Territories i.e. Daman and Diu as well as Dadra and Nagar Haveli may be explained on the basis of their high economic growth, particularly in the industrial sector as a tax concession was given by the central government in 1980. Moreover, tourism and growth of agricultural sector are the other boosters of their economic growth which may be a cause of high decadal growth of population.

The only state indicating a negative decadal growth rate is Nagaland. Surprisingly, the same state had a positive growth rate of 56.08% between 1981 and 1991, and 64.53% between 1991 and 2001. A state having such a high positive growth rate cannot recede to a negative growth rate in the immediate successive decade. However, 64.53% growth rate of population jumping from 56.08% is also not easily understood if a major migrational change is not recorded. Moreover, in the same state, a negative growth rate without mass exodus due to political instability or huge number of death due to break out of war, epidemics etc. is not explainable. As revealed in a report of the Hindu that during the census operation for 2001 census the authorities of rural areas of Nagaland reported enhanced fictitious population figures in the hope of receiving greater amount of financial grant. That resulted in a very high exaggerated figure for 2001 census. This fact was revealed later. During the census operations for 2011 census, the director of census operations, Nagaland, H. Zhimomi made all efforts to get a correct census figure controlling the chances of exaggeration. Thus the population figure of Nagaland in 2011 became much reduced than the previous population figure of 2001 census. Hence, in reality there was no negative growth of population in Nagaland and 2001 census population figure is erroneous.

When the deviation of decadal growth rate of 2001 to 2011 from that of 1991 to 2001 is computed (table no. 5.25), it reveals that except for 3 states and union territories namely, Chhattisgarh, Tamilnadu and Puducherry all other states and UTs show negative change of decadal growth rate. It may be noted that awareness among population through the spread of education and modern trend of small families have perhaps resulted in such control in the gears of population growth. However, the states with positive change of decadal growth rate may have some other causes behind the increase of decadal growth rate. Such causes may be related to migration.

SOPHER'S DISPARITY INDEX

Disparity is a very common phenomenon between different population groups. As far as literacy is concerned, inequalities are very common between male and female groups, and rural and urban groups. David V. Sopher (1974) developed a disparity index to find out the inequality in literacy between male and female groups of population. We know that gender inequality is one of the most common characteristics of all societies, be it a developing or even a developed country. This disparity evolves out of traditional bias, lack of scope to access the knowledge resources, religious supersitition and ofcourse some others. However, the Disparity Index developed by Sopher has been proved useful in measuring specifically the disparities of education, as his formula undertakes the measurement between two contrasting gorups. The equation is given below :

$$D = \log(X_2/X_1) + \log[(Q - X_1)/(Q - X_2)]$$

Where, $X_2 \geqslant X_1$

$Q = 100$

This index uses percent data for literacy whether $Q = 100$ between male and female population or rural and urban population. It can not use absolute figures of population.

Application :

Applying Sopher's Disparity Index on male and female literacy rate in the census years 1991, 2001 and 2011, the changing nature of gender disparity in the scope of education in India can be determined. The minimum value of Sopher's Disparity Index is 0 When there is no gap between male and female literacy and rural and urban literacy. This is a mark of development.

TABLE 5.26

Literacy Rate of India in three census years

Year	Literacy Rate	
	Male	Female
1991	64.13	39.29
2001	75.26	53.67
2011	82.14	65.46

In the following calculation the variable having higher value of literacy is taken as X_2, whereas the literacy rate for the population group having lower literacy rate is considered as X_1, because if the variables are reversed, disparity index will give a negative value though the numerical value may remain the same.

Disparity Index for 1991

$$D = \text{Log}\,(X_2 / X_1) + \log\,[\,(Q - X_1) / (Q - X_2)]$$
$$= \log\,(64.13 / 39.29) + \log\,[\,(100 - 39.29) / (100 - 64.13)]$$
$$= \log 1.63222 + \log 1.69250$$
$$= 0.212277 + 0.22852$$
$$= 0.44129 \qquad = 0.44$$

Disparity Index for 2001

$$D = \text{Log}\,(X_2 / X_1) + \log\,[\,(Q - X_1) / (Q - X_2)]$$
$$= \log\,(75.26 / 53.67) + \log\,[\,(100 - 53.67) / (100 - 75.26)]$$
$$= \log 1.40227 + \log 1.87267$$
$$= 0.14683 + 0.27246$$
$$= 0.41929 \qquad = 0.42$$

Disparity Index for 2011

$$D = \text{Log}\,(X_2 / X_1) + \log\,[\,(Q - X_1) / (Q - X_2)]$$
$$= \log\,(82.14 / 65.46) + \log\,[(100 - 65.46) / (100 - 82.14)]$$
$$= \log 1.25481 + \log 1.93393$$
$$= 0.09857 + 0.28644$$
$$= 0.38501 \qquad = 0.39$$

Interpretation :

As per census data the literacy rate of India has been increasing at variable rate since 1951. However, the gap between the literacy of male and female population persists, though it reduces at variable rates. Male literacy in 1951 was about 27.16%. Since that year it has substantially increased in different census years and in 2011 it became 82.14%.

In the case of female literacy it was only 8.86% in 1951 and since then it has risen to a value of 65.46% in 2011 as per Census Of India data. The so called gap between male and female literacy is also decreasing, though this decrease has become steady since 1981. Previously it was increased in 1961 and between 1971 and 1981 census years. The following table as per census data indicates the changing nature of gap in gender literacy.

Year	1951	1961	1971	1981	1991	2001	2011
Male Female Literacy Gap (%)	18.3	25.05	23.98	26.62	24.84	21.59	16.68

Sopher's Disparity Index has been determined for three census years : 1991, 2001 and 2011 in this work. The values obtained indicate the disparity in literacy between male and female population. In 1991 it was 0.44, in 2001 it was 0.42, whereas in 2011 it was further reduced to 0.39. This changing nature of Sopher's Disparity Index indicates specifically that the disparity gap has been reducing.

Ergograph

An ergograph shows a graphical correlation between agriculture and climatic elements during different cropping seasons of a year. Arthur Geddes of the University of Edinburgh coined the term. The elements of climate taken for this graph are monthly average of maximum, minimum temperature (°C) and rainfall (mm).

Normally, the climatic graph is shown at the upper part, and agricultural data is represented in the lower part of the graph directly below the climatic graph. Agricultural data may include type of crops, their cropping season and area under different crops. Besides, some ergograph may include agricultural production also. Different scales are used for different types of data in this graph. Months of the year are arranged in such a manner as to show the warm and moist season first. Hence months are arranged from April to March instead of January to December.

An ergograph of Krishnanagar of Nadia district of West Bengal has been constructed here. The following tables incorporate the relevant climatic and agricultural data of Krishnanagar.

Data for Ergograph of Krishnanagar, Nadia, West Bengal

TABLE 5.27

Per cent Area Under Different Crops [Average of 1971-1976]

Station	Rice			Wheat	Pulses		Edible	Jute and	Miscellanesus
	Aus	Aman	Boro		Kharif	Rabi	Oilseeds	Mesta	
Krishnanagar	42.08	12.03	2.49	12.33	8.92	7.75	1.74	9.95	2.71
Cropping Season	May - Mid Sept.	Mid July -Mid Nov.	April - May and Mid Feb. - March	Mid Nov. -March	Mid Sept. Mid - January	March-July	October -January	May-August	November-March

TABLE 5.28

Data of Average Monthly Maximum-Minimum Temperature and Rainfall of Krishnanagar

Month	Temperature (°C)		Rainfall (mm.)
	Maximum	Minimum	
April	35.3	25.1	43
May	35.4	26.0	95
June	34.0	26.5	274
July	32.3	26.1	287
August	32.1	26.1	241
September	32.4	25.8	231
October	32.3	23.9	113
November	30.3	19.6	18
December	27.0	14.5	3
January	26.4	13.8	11
February	29.1	16.9	15
March	33.5	21.7	22

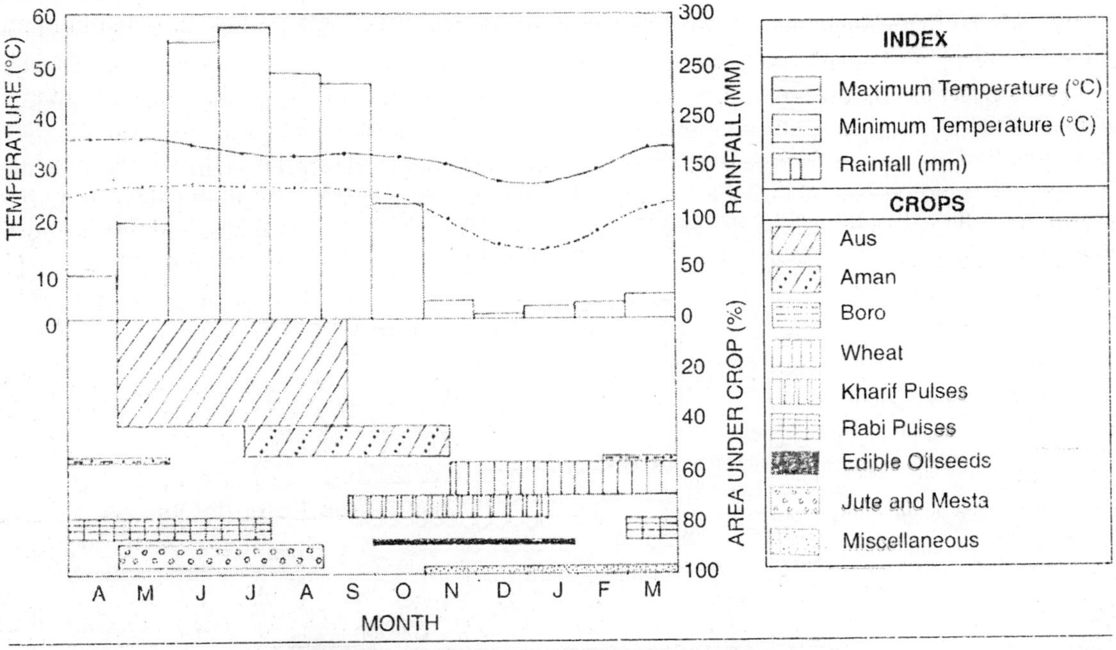

Fig. 5.35 Ergograph of Krishnanagar, Nadia District

Interpretation

In West Bengal, cropping seasons are traditionally divided into two major agricultural seasons : Rabi and Kharif, the former is related to the low temperature dry period, whereas the latter is related to warm and wet summer. However, the cropping seasons are not perfectly compartmental and they overlap partly in connection with the production of a few crops.

Here, in this ergograph (Fig. 5.35), it reveals that the rainy period of the year has maximum diversity of crops and during the dry winter and spring only a few crops are grown. The crops in need of more water are produced during the wet season, whereas wheat with minimum irrigation can be produced during winter. Boro is an exception. It is cultlvated in low lying wetlands where other crops are absent.

This ergograph also indicates that aus paddy has maximum hectarage, wheat comes next being almost equal with aman paddy. Boro is cultivated in small areas. Of the other crops in the area pulses have a significant hectarage. On the other hand, edible oilseeds cover minimum area.

Population potentials

The measurement of the potential of population is done to identify the influence of any concentration of population on another. It is expressed as the number of people in the respective concentration divided by its distance to the spot at which the potential is to be assessed. This method is applied to find out the influence of any major concentration in terms of the probability of migration and spread of concentration. The potential of any point is calculated by :

$$P = \frac{n}{d}$$

[n = number of persons of the point at which the potential is to be calculated
d = distance between the two points of population
P = potential]

If there are two points having two different concentrations, one major and one minor, such as 1,00,000 and 10,000 and the distance between these two points (P and Q) is 50 km. the potential will be .

From Q to P is 10,000/50 = 20 persons per kilometre. On the other side of P if there is another point at R having a population of 12,000 at a distance of 30 km from P the potential will be from R to P 12,000/30 = 400 persons per kilometre can be determined and isopleths can be drawn on the basis of such potentials at variable distances between the population points.This will give a distribution map of potential values (fig. 5.36) and may reveal the extraordinary concentration at particular points.

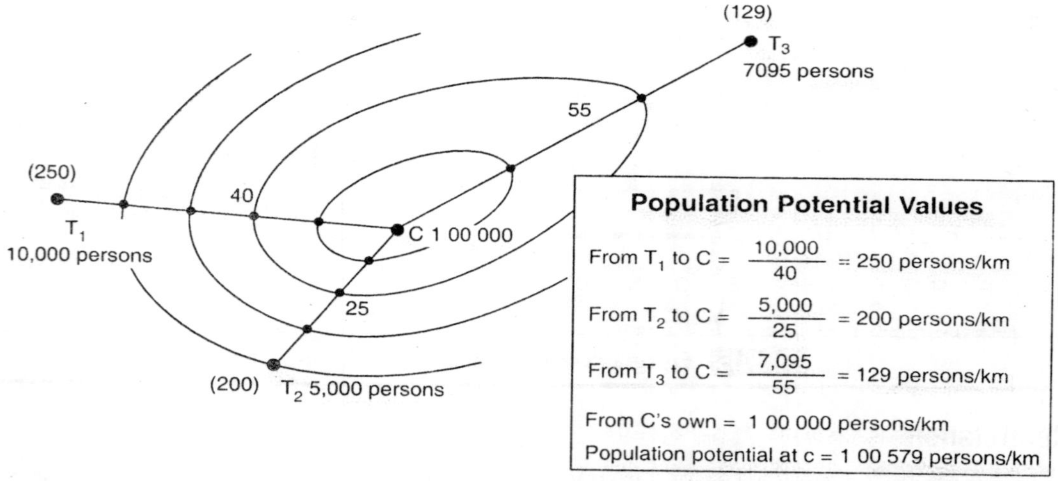

Fig. 5.36 Population potentials

RANK SIZE RULE

In a study of German cities Auerbach pointed out that there is an empirical relationship between the rank of a town and its population size. As such, the rank size rule implies an inverse relation between the number of cities and its size category. He further pointed out that the product of a city's rank and its size tends to be constant. George K. Zipf acknowledged the existence of such a correlation and presented the rank size relationship in the following expression :

$$P_i = \frac{K}{r_i}$$

[p_i = Expected population of a town of rank
r_i = Rank of the city in descending order
K = Population of the largest town]

Following Zipf's formula it is expected that the expected population of the second and third ranking towns will be one half and one third of the population of largest town respectively. Thus there will be a harmonic progression of cities within urban hierarchy.

A great deal of interest has been shown by geographers in the relationships between towns and cities of different sizes and their spacing in the landscape. It is assumed that settlements do not grow up in a haphazard or random manner, and a measureable degree of order is to be found in their size and spacing. So, in this exercise city rank and city population size are examined and the relation between the hypothetical and the actual population. Large towns overlap some of the regional functions of the lower order towns. It has been suggested that effective policy of regional development should rectify this type of anomaly and that the rank size rule can be used as a diagnostic tool in regional planning.

ZIPF'S METHOD OF RANK SIZE RULE :

TABLE 5.29

Estimated Population in Rank order

Towns	Actual Population in rank order	Rank (R)	Estimated Population
Bhatpara	304952	1	304952
Halisahar	114028	2	152476
Barasat	102660	3	101651
Basirhat	101409	4	76238
Habra	100223	5	60990
Kanchrapara	100194	6	50825
Ashoknagar-Kalyangarh	96747	7	43565
Bongaon	79571	8	38119
Panpur	6553	9	33884
Sadpur	5955	10	30495

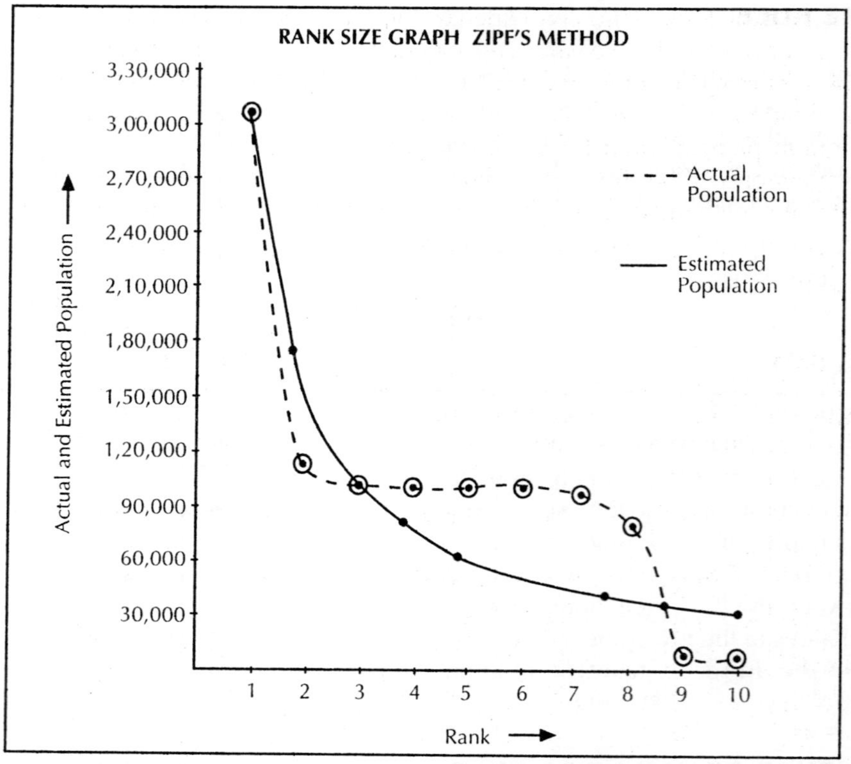

Fig. 5.37 **Rank size population Distribution in Ten Towns of North 24 Parganas**

Interpretation :

In this method of Rank Size Rule, the highest population, i.e. the population of Rank1 town is not an estimated figure. It is the real data of the largest town. All other smaller towns are having calculated proportionate population according to their ranks. However, in the graph for Rank Size Rule, it is revealed that six towns, i.e. Barasat, Basirhat, Habra, Kanchrapara, Ashokenagar – Kalyangarh, Bongaon have higher population than their estimated figures. Hence, economic and infrastructural growth in these towns have led to the growth of population which have exceeded the estimated values according to Rank. On the other hand, three other towns, i.e. Halisahar, Panpur and Sadpur have lower population than estimated values, as lack of economic growth does not attract people in these towns. Hence, these are suffering from negative growth.

In Zipf's method a similar trend of curve has been observed with that of Berry's method. The same towns have exceeded their estimated population. The only difference observed in this case is that the highest value of estimated population is much higher in Berry's method.

Although such methods are best applicable for the countries where the influence of urbanisation is very well-spread, it can be applied to developing nations also. For 10 townships of North 24 parganas the rank size can be calculated in following manner :

At first the rank of the towns according to the actual population is marked. Then 1/rank or reciprocal of the rank (which is obtained as 1 divided by every town's rank) is found out. Now the summation of the actual population is divided by the summation of 1/R. The result is known as Pe_1 or K which is a constant. Other Pe values are calculated as K divided by every town's rank or as K multiplied by reciprocal of rank. Pe of all the towns are calculated by this method. It is the estimated population of the town. For plotting and for finding out a straight progression line a double log graph paper should be used. Ranks will be plotted horizontally and actual and estimated population will be shown as ordinate values of ranks. In logarithmic graph papers the starting point at the left hand corner will never be zero because log 0 is non-existent. This method (Berry) differs from Zipf's method as it considers the population of the Rank 1. City/town as a calculated figure.

TABLE 5.30

Raw data

Sl. No.	Towns	Total Population 1991
1.	Bongaon	79571
2.	Habra	100223
3.	Sadpur	5955
4.	Ashoknagar-Kalyangarh	96747
5.	Kanchrapara	100194
6.	Barasat	102660
7.	Halisahar	114028
8.	Bhatpara	304952
9.	Panpur	6553
10.	Basirhat	101409

Calculated data

Rank (R)	Towns	Acutal Population in rank order	1/R	Pe (Estimated Population)
1	Bhatpara	304952	1.00	Pe_1=1012292/2.93 = 345492.15
2	Halisahar	114028	0.50	Pe_2 = 172746
3	Barasat	102660	0.33	Pe_3 = 115164
4	Basirhat	101409	0.25	Pe_4 = 86373
5	Habra	100223	0.2	Pe_5 = 69098
6	Kanchrapara	100194	0.17	Pe_6 = 57582
7	Ashoknagar-Kalyangarh	96747	0.14	Pe_7 = 49356
8	Bongaon	79571	0.13	Pe_8 = 43186
9	Panpur	6553	0.11	Pe_9= 38388
10	Sadpur	5955	0.1	Pe_{10}= 34549
		Σ A.P. = 1012292	Σ1/R = 2.93	

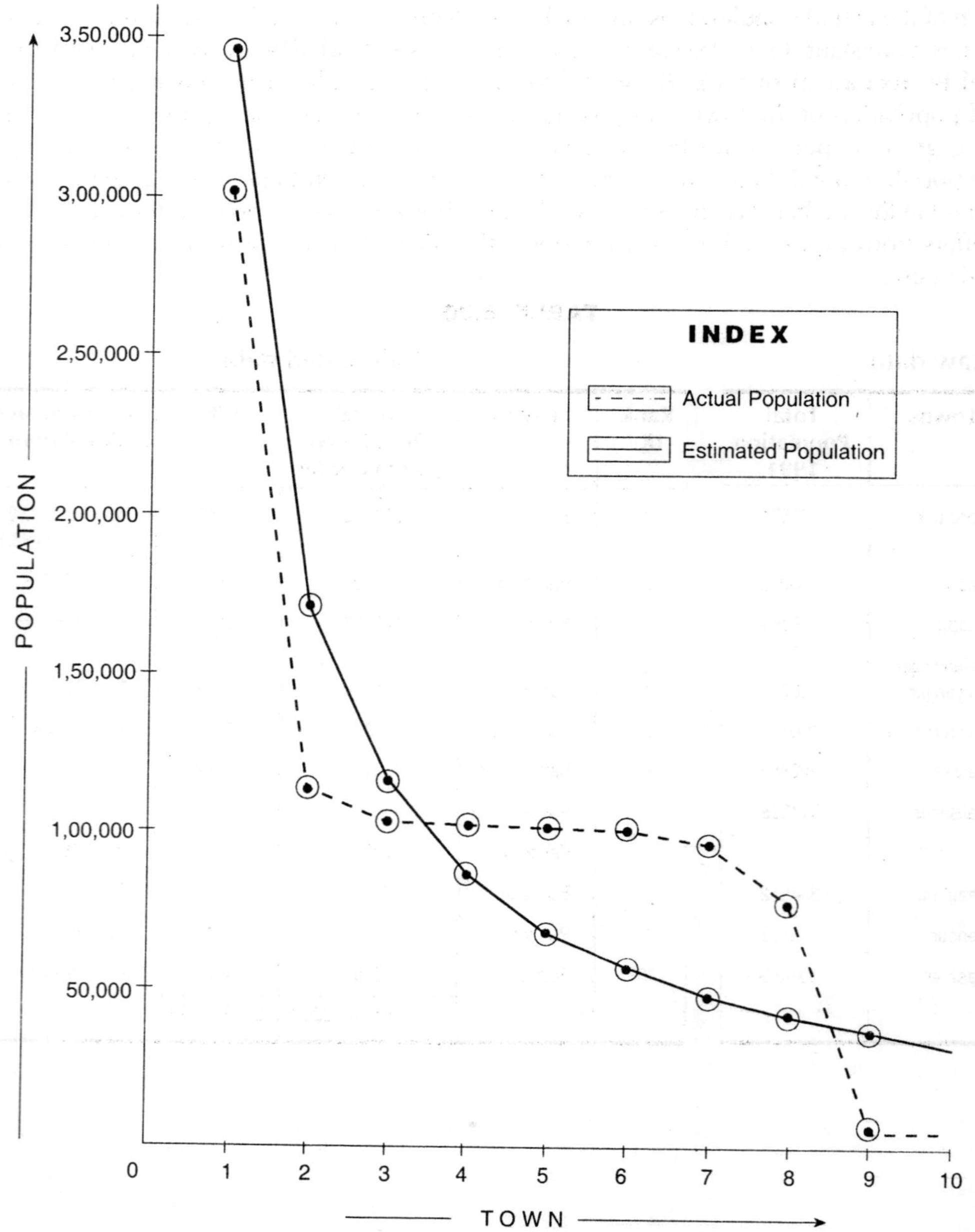

Fig. 5.38 **Rank size graph of 10 selected towns of North 24 Parganas**

Interpretation and inferences

In the graph it is seen that Bhatpara and Halisahar's acutal population is lower than the estimated population. But Barasat, Basirhat, Habra, Kachrapara, Ashoknagar-Kalyangarh and Bangaon have larger population than estimated population. These towns are pirating a few of the regional functions of the lower order towns. Panpur and Sadpur have much lower population than their estimated population. So, other large towns have pirated the functions of these two towns.

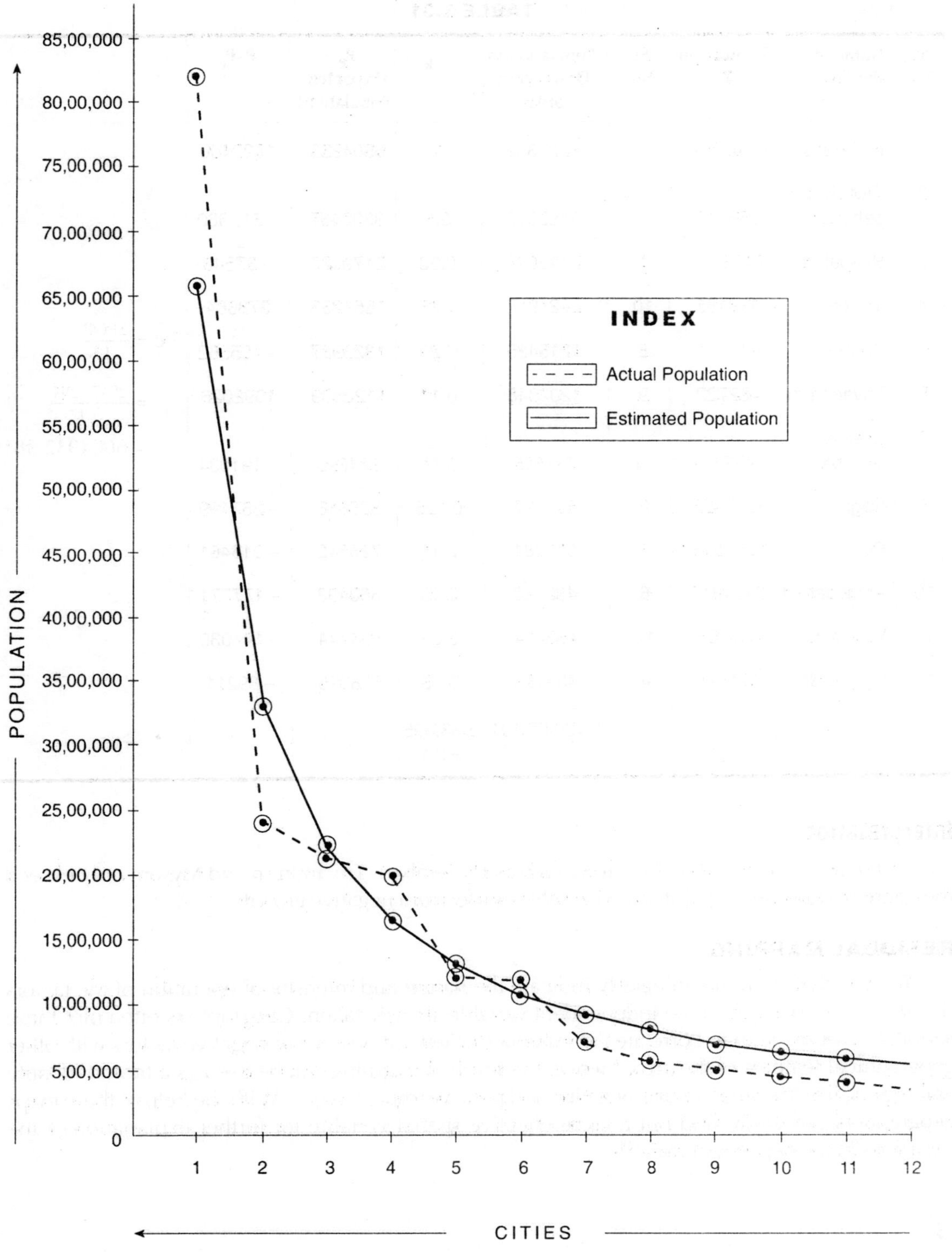

Fig. 5.39 Rank size rule of Twelve selected cities of India

TABLE 5.31

Sl. No.	Name of the City	Population (P)	Sl. No.	Population in Descending order	$^1/_R$	P_e (Expected Population)	$P-P_e$	
1.	Hyderabad	2142087	7.	8227332	1	6604933	1622400	
2.	Vishakha-pattanam	558117	3.	2482507	0.5	3302467	– 819960	
3.	Bangalore	2482507	1.	2142087	0.33	2179627	– 37540	
4.	Mysore	439185	10.	2024917	0.25	1651233	373684	
5.	Kochin	513081	8.	1215425	0.20	1320987	– 105562	$Pe = \frac{\Sigma POP}{\Sigma 1/R}$
6.	Trivandrum	482722	9.	1202848	0.17	1122839	1092026	$= \frac{20475291}{3.1}$
7.	Greater Mumbai	8227332	11.	733656	0.14	924690	– 191034	= 6604932.581
8.	Nagpur	1215425	2.	558117	0.125	825616	– 267499	
9.	Pune	1202848	5.	513081	0.11	726542	– 213461	
10.	Ahmedabad	2024917	6.	482722	0.10	660493	– 177771	
11.	Vadodara	733656	12.	453414	0.09	594444	– 141030	
12.	Vijaywada	453414	4.	439185	0.08	528395	– 89211	
				Σ=20475291	Σ=3.095 = 3.1			

Interpretation

Of the twelve cities of India, a few, such as Hyderabad, Trivandrum and Mysore only exceed the figure of expected population. Nine others suffer from negative growth.

RESIDUAL MAPPING

The residuals very meaningfully indicate the nature and intensity of operation of the factors determining y, other than the independent variable already taken. Geographers often plot these residuals over the map to correlate the influence of left out positive or negative factors with other geographical features of the area. Hence, the residual mapping can be used as a tool to identify and regionalize the areas having negative and positive impact over y. With the help of these maps geographers can easily find out a more effective spatial variable for further explanation of the variations in the dependent variable.

TABLE 5.32

Raw data

Sl No.	Police Stations	Literates Persons	Trade & Commerce	Trade Transport & Storage	Other Service	Literates Persons in '000	Trade. Comm. + Transport + Other Service in '000
1.	Muraroi	69878	4650	1510	3440	69.88	9.6
2.	Nalhati	83623	5141	1359	4205	83.62	10.7
3.	Rampurhat	50556	4709	2924	5032	50.56	12.67
4.	Margram	55761	2122	443	2125	55.76	4.7
5.	Mayureswar	90916	2581	745	3256	90.92	6.6
6.	Mohd. Bazar	41551	1605	408	2079	41.55	4.1
7.	Rajnagar	22780	987	179	1392	22.78	2.6
8.	Khoirasole	31686	1498	329	1485	31.69	3.3
9.	Kankartala	18500	991	122	903	18.50	2.0
10.	Dubrajpur	49977	4352	1148	4514	49.98	10.01
11.	Suri	49136	5759	2631	9698	49.14	18.09
12.	Panrui	35440	1024	200	1588	35.44	2.8
13.	Sainthia	56573	4537	1490	4689	56.57	10.72
14.	Illambazar	38097	1863	301	1690	38.10	3.9
15.	Bolpur	47095	5613	2488	8599	47.10	16.70
16.	Labpur	61605	1636	401	2683	61.61	4.7
17.	Nanoor	70350	2211	584	3193	70.35	6.0

Computation

At first two variables are taken as dependent and independent. The percentage of literates and percentage of tertiary workers are given here. They are considered as x & y respectively. The main equation is : $y = a + bX$, $b = \frac{N\Sigma XY - \Sigma X\Sigma Y}{N\Sigma X^2 - [\Sigma X^2]}$, $a = \frac{\Sigma Y - \Sigma X}{N}$ and calculated a and b are constants.

TABLE 5.33

Calculated Data

Sl No.	X	Y	X^2	Y^2	XY
1.	69.88	9.6	4883.21	96.16	670.85
2.	83.62	10.71	6992.30	114.70	895.57
3.	50.56	12.67	2556.31	160.53	640.60
4.	55.76	4.7	3109.18	22.09	262.07
5.	90.92	6.6	8266.45	43.56	600.07
6.	41.55	4.1	1726.40	16.81	170.36
7.	22.78	2.6	518.93	6.76	59.23
8.	31.69	3.3	1004.26	10.89	104.58
9.	18.50	2.0	342.25	4	37
10.	49.98	10.01	2498.00	100.20	500.30
11.	49.14	18.09	2414.74	327.25	888.94
12.	35.44	2.8	1255.99	7.84	99.23
13.	56.57	10.72	3200.16	114.92	606.43
14.	38.10	3.9	1451.61	15.21	148.59
15.	47.10	16.70	2218.41	278.89	786.57
16.	61.61	4.7	3795.79	22.09	289.57
17.	70.35	6.0	4949.12	36	422.1
	ΣX = 873.55	ΣY = 129.2	ΣX^2 = 51183.13	ΣY^2 = 1373.90	ΣXY = 7182.05

Sl No.	Police Stations	bX	a	$Y_c = a + bX$	$Y-Y_c$
1.	Muraroi	6.29	2.98	9.27	0.33
2.	Nalhati	7.53	"	10.51	0.2
3.	Rampurhat	4.55	"	7.53	5.14
4.	Margram	5.02	"	8	− 3.3
5.	Mayureswar	8.18	"	11.16	− 4.56
6.	Mohd. Bazar	3.74	"	6.72	− 2.62
7.	Rajnagar	2.05	"	5.03	− 2.43
8.	Khoirasole	2.85	"	5.83	− 2.53
9.	Kankartala	1.67	"	4.65	− 2.65
10.	Dubrajpur	4.50	"	7.48	2.53
11.	Suri	4.42	"	7.4	10.69
12.	Panrui	3.19	"	6.17	− 3.37
13.	Sainthia	5.09	"	8.07	2.65
14.	Illambazar	3.43	"	6.41	− 2.51
15.	Bolpur	4.24	"	7.22	9.48
16.	Labhpur	5.54	"	8.52	− 3.82
17.	Nanoor	6.33	"	9.31	− 3.31
					Σ = − 0.08

$$b = \frac{\Sigma XY - \dfrac{\Sigma X \Sigma Y}{N}}{\Sigma X^2 - \dfrac{(\Sigma X)^2}{N}}$$

$$= \frac{7182.06 - \dfrac{873.55 \times 129.2}{17}}{51183.13 - \dfrac{(873.55)^2}{17}} = 0.09$$

$$a = \frac{\Sigma Y}{N} - b.\frac{\Sigma X}{N}$$

$$= \frac{129.2}{17} - 0.09 \times \frac{873.55}{1}$$

$$= 2.98$$

Interpretation

Here it can be observed that Muraroi, Nalhati, Rampurhat, Dubrajpur and Sainthia have medium number of literate persons and teritiary workers. Suri and Bolpur are high positive area which have medium number of literate persons and high number of teritiary workers. But Margram, Mayureswar, Mohammad Bazar, Rajnagar, Khoirasole and Kankartala have few literates but high number of teriary workers. This may be due to socio-economic and political factors. The negative values of residuals indicate that the actual figures of tertiary workers are less than expected, whereas the positive resudues indicate the opposite, meaning that the growth of tertiary sector is lower than expected in negative residuals and higher than expected in positive residuals.

Sl No.	Police Station
1.	Muraroi
2.	Nalhati
3.	Rampurhat
4.	Margram
5.	Mayureswar
6.	Mohd. Bazar
7.	Rajnagar
8.	Khoyrasole
9.	Kankartala
10.	Dubrajpur
11.	Suri
12.	Panrui
13.	Saihthia
14.	Illambazar
15.	Bolpur
16.	Labhpur
17.	Naroor

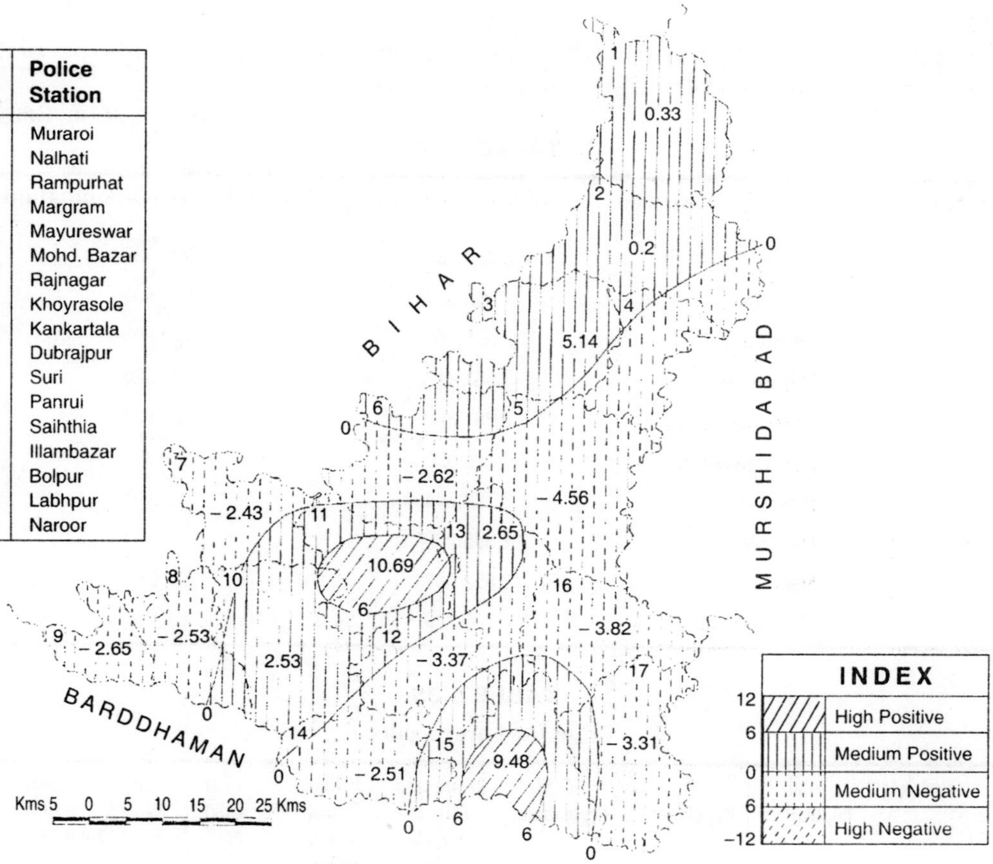

Fig. 5.40 Residual Map

Lorenz Curve

Another type of graph showing a bi-variate data in a cumulative percentage distribution is the Lorenz curve. It shows the dispersion of a set of data in terms of their deviation from a perfect distribution curve, which is, in fact, a diagonal straight line between 0% and 100%. The dispersion is followed by the curve which leaves some space between the diagonal indicating the perfect distribution line and the curve itself, the greater the space, the lesser the homogeneity of distribution between the two sets of variates and vice versa. **This is a measure of inequality.**

Such a curve does not indicate any quantitative deviation, rather it is effectively visual in impression. However, determination of Gini's coefficient can give a numerical parameter.

In such a curve if population is given along the abscissa, and any of the distribution of wealth, land, income, wages etc. is shown along the ordinate, it gives a tangible graphical presentation of inequality. That is why it is widely used in socio-economic surveys (fig. 5.41).

Exercise

Compute and draw a Lorenz curve to show concentration of scheduled tribe population in selected districts of west Bengal in 2001. Interpret the curve.

(year - 2006, Batch - IV)

TABLE 5.34

Sl. No.	Name of the Districts	Total population	Scheduled Tribe population
1.	Burdwan	6,050,605	375,033
2.	Birbhum	2,555,664	177,501
3.	Bankura	2,805,065	289,906
4.	Midnapore	8,331,912	689,636
5.	24 Parganas (N)	7,281,881	169,831
6.	24 Parganas (S)	5,715,030	70,499
7.	Howrah	3,729,644	10,090
8.	Hooghly	4,355,230	176,401
9.	Nadia	3,852,097	90,525
10.	Murshidabad	4,740,149	61,513

TABLE 5.35

Table for Lorenz curve

Sl. No.	Districts	Total Population	ST Population	% of ST Population	Rearranged districts in rank order	Rank order of st. Population	% of Total Pop.	% of ST. Pop	Cumulative % of	
									Total Pop.	ST. Pop
1.	Burdwan	6,050,605	375,033	6.20	Howrah	1	7.55	0.48	7.55	0.48
2.	Birbhum	2,555,664	177,501	6.95	24 Parganas(s)	2	11.56	3.34	19.11	3.82
3.	Bankura	2,805,065	289,906	10.34	Murshidabad	3	9.59	2.91	28.7	6.73
4.	Midnapore	8,331,912	689,636	8.28	24 parganas(N)	4	14.74	8.05	43.44	14.78
5.	24 Parganas (N)	7,281,881	169,831	2.33	Nadia	5	7.80	4.29	51.24	19.07
6.	24 Parganas (S)	5,715,030	70,499	1.23	Hooghly	6	8.81	8.36	60.05	27.43
7.	Howrah	3,729,644	10,090	0.27	Burdwan	7	12.24	17.77	72.29	45.20
8.	Hooghly	4,355,230	176,401	4.05	Birbhum	8	5.17	8.41	77.46	53.61
9.	Nadia	3,852,097	90,525	2.35	Midnapore	9	16.86	32.67	94.32	86.28
10.	Murshidabad	4,740,149	61,513	1.30	Bankura	10	5.68	13.73	100.0	100.0
		Σ= 49417277	Σ = 2110935							

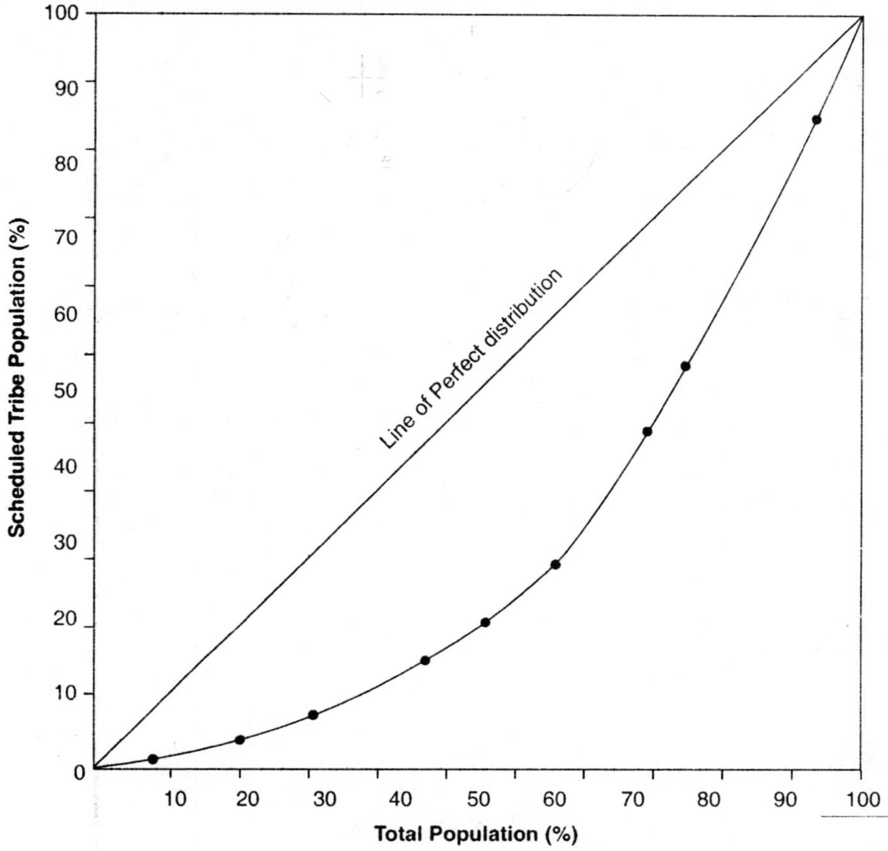

Fig. 5.41 **Lorenz curve Showing total population vs S.T. population**

Calculation for Gini's Co-efficient :

The total area of the square being 100 × 100 i.e. 10000, the area of the triangle considering the line of equal distribution is 5000, i.e. $\frac{100 \times 100}{2}$. In the case of highest concentration or perfect distribution, the area below the curve would be very close to the area of this triangle. An uneven distribution will show much smaller area below the curve. The area is calculated as multiplying the 1st element of X_i with 2nd element of Y_i i.e. Y_{i+1} and the 2nd element of X_i will be multiplied by the 3rd element of Y_i and so on and so forth. On the other hand, for $X_{i+1} \cdot Y_i$ calculation will consider the 1st element of Y_i to be multiplied by the 2nd element of X_i i.e. X_{i+1}.

TABLE 5.36

GINI's Coefficient

Sl. No.	Districts	Total Population	ST Population	% of ST Population to the total population	Rearranged Districts in Rank Order	Rank order of ST Population	% of Total Population	% of ST Population to the total ST pop	Cumulative % of Total ST		$X_i . Y_{i+1}$	$X_{i+1} . Y_i$
									Population (Xi)	Population (Xi)		
1	Burdwan	6,050,605	375,033	6.20	Howrah	1	7.55	0.48	7.55	0.48	28.841	9.1728
2	Birbhum	2,555,664	177,501	6.95	24 Parganas (S)	2	11.56	3.34	19.11	3.82	128.6103	109.634
3	Bankura	2,805,065	289,906	10.34	Murshidabad	3	9.59	2.91	28.7	6.73	424.186	292.3512
4	Midnapore	8,331,912	689,636	8.28	24 Parganas (N)	4	14.74	8.05	43.44	14.78	828.4008	757.3272
5	24 Parganas (N)	7,281,881	169,831	2.33	Nadia	5	7.80	4.29	51.24	19.07	1405.5132	1145.1535
6	24 Parganas (S)	5,715,030	70,499	1.23	Hooghly	6	8.81	8.36	60.05	27.43	2714.26	1982.9147
7	Howrah	3,729,644	10,090	0.27	Burdwan	7	12.24	17.77	72.29	45.20	3875.4669	3501.192
8	Hooghly	4,355,230	176,401	4.05	Birbhum	8	5.17	8.41	77.46	53.61	6683.2488	5056.4952
9	Nadia	3,852,097	90,525	2.35	Midnapore	9	16.86	32.67	94.32	86.28	9432.00	8628.00
10	Murshidabad	4,740,149	61,513	1.30	Bankura	10	5.68	13.73	100.0	100.0		
		$\Sigma =$ 49417277	$\Sigma =$ 2110935								$\Sigma X_i . Y_{i+1} =$ 25520.527	$\Sigma X_{i+1} . Y_i =$ 21482.2406

$$\text{Gini's Coefficient (G)} = \frac{1}{100 \times 100} \times (\Sigma X_i . Y_{i+1}) - (\Sigma X_{i+1} . Y_i)$$

$$= \frac{1}{10{,}000} \times 25520.527 - 21482.2406$$

$$= \frac{1}{10{,}000} \times 4038.2864$$

$$= 0.404$$

Interpretation

Lorenz curve initially developed in 1905, has been considered as a measure of understanding the inequality in the distribution of wealth and income. Being a measure of inequality it can also identify the concentration of a demographic group in the distribution of total population. Thus it has become a measure for dispersion also.

In this lorenz curve, the concentration of ST population has been measured. it is observed that in all the 10 districts of West Bengal mentioned here the concentration of ST population is unevenly distributed , as the curve formed has sufficient concavity with reference to the line of perfect distribution .

To quantify the unevenness in the distribution of ST population Gini's coeffienent has been calculated. The value obtained is 0.404. The perfect distribution line and the Lorenz Curve together bound this area. Now if we multiply the 'G' value, i.e. 0.404 with 100, it gives the unevenness of distribution in percent value. Hence, 0.404 × 100 = 40.4% unevenness in the distribution of ST population is marked.

TABLE 5.37

Dominant and Distinctive Function

Sl. No.	Towns	Total Worker (male)	Culti-vator	Agricultural Labourer	Livestock Forestry Fishing	Mining & Quarrying	Household, other than Household Industry	Cons-truc-tion	Trade & Com-merce	Trans-port & storage	Other services
1.	Bongaon	19647	1603	1954	98	7	2795	717	6479	2578	3416
2.	Habra	25096	761	1416	257	26	4699	968	8976	2393	5600
3.	Barasat	25810	296	1065	330	28	5905	1417	7907	3433	5429
4.	Bhatpara	87110	142	171	301	25	63011	1526	11112	3739	7083
5.	Basirhat	24284	1174	3111	518	14	3746	1032	7568	2707	4414

TABLE 5.38

Sl. No.	Towns	Total Worker (male)	Culti-vator (%)	Agricultural Labourer (%)	Livestock Foresty Fishing (%)	Mining & Quarrying (%)	Household other than Household Industry (%)	Cons-truc-tion (%)	Trade & Com-merce (%)	Trans-port & storage	Other services (%)
1.	Bangaon	19647	8.16	9.95	0.49	0.04	14.23	3.65	32.98	13.12	17.39
2.	Habra	25096	3.03	5.64	1.02	0.10	18.72	3.86	35.77	9.54	22.31
3.	Barasat	25810	1.15	4.13	1.28	0.11	22.88	5.49	30.64	13.30	21.03
4.	Bhatpara	87110	0.16	0.20	0.35	0.03	72.33	1.75	12.76	4.29	8.13
5.	Basirhat	24284	4.83	12.81	2.13	0.06	15.43	4.25	31.16	11.15	18.18
	Mean ($\bar{x}$)	→	3.466	6.546	1.054	0.068	28.718	3.8	28.662	10.28	17.408
	Standard Deviation (SV)	→	2.84	4.42	0.64	0.032	22.01	1.21	8.15	3.30	4.98

Dominant and Distinctive Function

Theory : Localities often have various types of economic functions of which there may be a dominant one along with some other distinctive ones. Indian Census recognises 9 broad types, some of which are composite of many less important functions. While identifying the dominance and distinctiveness among economic functions Nelson used mean and standard deviation of the number of workers engaged in various occupations. For this purpose he converted the number of workers into per cent values and then he calculated the mean and standard deviation for each of the functions for a given number of localities. The scale for identifying the dominance and distinctiveness, however, varies between the developed and developing nations.

TABLE 5.39

Function	Class	Sl. No. of town
Cultivator	3.466 — 6.306	5
	6.306 — 9.146	1
	> 9.146	—
Agricultural Labourer	6.546 — 10.966	1
	10.966 — 15.386	5
	>15.386	—
Livestock Forestry Fishing	1.054 — 1.694	3
	1.694 — 2.334	5
	> 2.334	—
Mining & Quarrying	0.068 — 0.098	—
	0.098 — 0.128	2, 3
	> 0.128	—
Household & Other than household industry	28.718 — 50.728	—
	50.728 — 72.738	4
	>72.738	—

Contd. next page

Function	Class	Sl. No. of town
Construction	3.800 — 5.010	2, 5
	5.010 – 6.220	3
	> 6.220	—
Trade & Commerce	28.662 — 36.812	1, 2, 3, 4
	36.812 — 44.962	—
	> 44.962	—
Transport & Storage	10.280 — 13.580	1, 3, 5
	13.580 — 16.880	—
	> 16.880	—
Other Services	17.408 — 22.388	2, 3, 5
	22.388 — 27.368	—
	> 27.368	—

TABLE 5.40

Sl. No.	Town	Total worker	r	(1 cm = 75 unit r on scale)
1.	Bongaon	19647	79.1	1.05
2.	Habra	25096	89.4	1.2
3.	Barasat	25810	90.64	1.21
4.	Bhatpara	87110	166.52	2.2
5.	Basirhat	25284	89.71	1.2

$$r = \sqrt{\frac{\text{Total worker}}{\pi}}$$

TABLE 5.42

Scale	Ranking for Developing Countries	Ranking for Developed Countries
Mean — Mean + 1SD	1	—
Mean + 1SD — Mean + 2SD	11	1
Mean + 2SD — Mean + 3SD	111	11
> Mean + 3SD	—	111

< Mean = Diverse functions and no distinctiveness (for developing countries)

TABLE 5.41

Degree for individual working category

Sl. No.	Towns	Cultivator	Agricultural Labourer	Livestock, Forestry, Fishing	Mining & Quarrying	Household & other than Household Industry	Construction	Trade & commerce	Transport & storage	Other Services
1.	Bongaon	29°30′	35°48′	1°47′	30′	51°12′	13°8′	119°	47°14′	62°35′
2.	Habra	10°54′	20°18′	3°41′	30′	67°24′	13°53′	128°45′	34°19′	80°19′
3.	Barasat	4°7′	14°51′	4°36′	30′	82°21′	19°45′	110°17′	47°53′	75°43′
4.	Bhatpara	0°35′	0°42′	1°14′	0°6′	260°24′	6°18′	45°55′	15°27′	29°17′
5.	Basirhat	16°42′	44°17′	7°22′	0°11′	53°20′	14°41′	107°45′	38°32′	62°50′

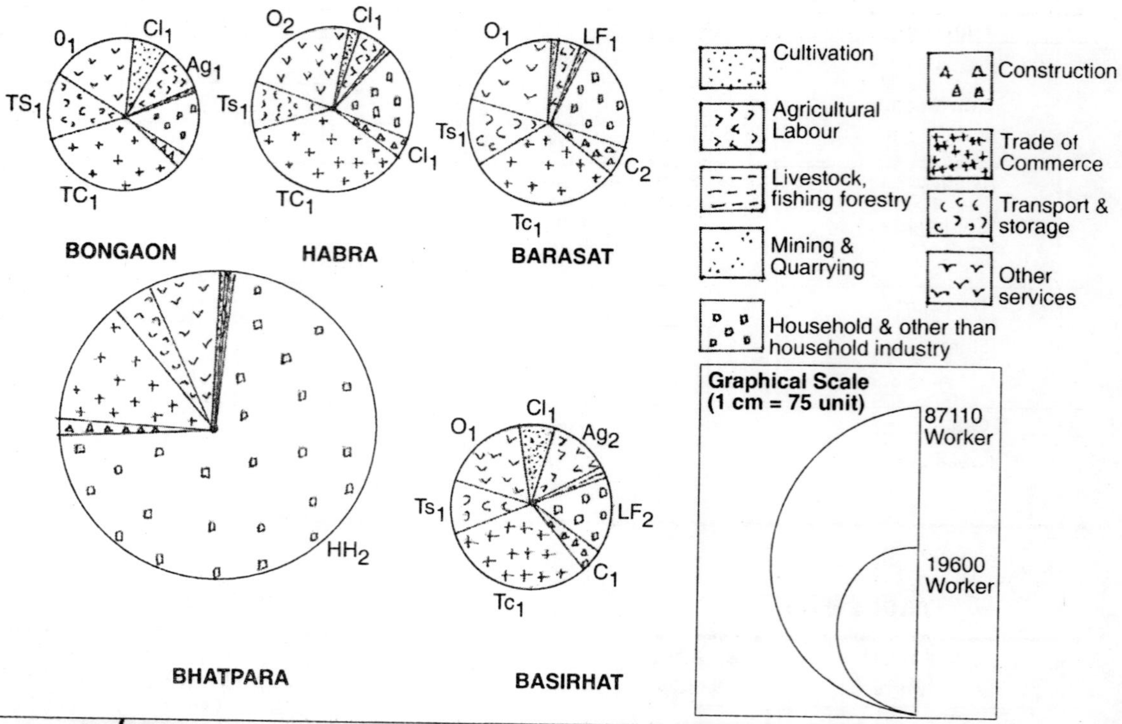

Fig. 5.42 **Dominant and Distinctive Functions of Five Towns of North 24 Parganas**

Interpretation

In these five towns, cultivation and agricultural labour are distinctive functions in Bongaon and Basirhat, livestock, forestry fishing in Barasat and Basirhat; mining and quarrying in Habra and Barasat; industry in Bhatpara; construction in Habra, Barasat and Basirhat; trade and commerce in Bangaon, Habra, Barasat and Bhatpara; transport and storage in Bangaon, Barasat and Basirhat; and other services in Habra, Barasat and Basirhat.

FUNCTIONAL CLASSIFICATION OF TOWNS :

Mr. Ashoke Mitra first used a **Ternary diagram** in 1961 census to classify the functions of a town or city. His motive was to find out the dominant and distinctive functions related to a particular town. For this purpose the workers involved in seven non-agricultural economic functions according to census categories were grouped into three broader Groups as given below :

Group A : Industry, which includes Mining and Quarrying, Household industry and industrial workers in other non-household (other than) industries;

Group B : Trade and Transport involving workers in Trade and Commerce, Transport and Storage etc.;

Group C : Service holders.

At first percentage of different groups of male workers in total male workers minus male cultivators and agricultural labourers and marginal workers is calculated. These per cent values are then plotted on a Ternary diagram divided into six triangles. This Ternary diagram is an equilateral triangle showing 0 to 100% values at 10% interval of three computed groups A, B and C. This Ternary diagram is divided into six sub-triangles, each indicating relative dominance of the three groups of functions.

The sub-triangles are further subdivided into four parts on the basis of three circles drawn from the centre for 40%, 45% and 50% catagories.

The following data comprises the number of male workers in various categories of work for 10 towns of West Bengal. Let us find out which functions predominate in these towns.

Sl. No.	Name of town	Mining of quarrying	Household industry inds.	Otherthan household (Industry)	Total of Group A	Construction	Trade and Commmerce
1.	Bongaon	7	165	2630	2802	717	6479
2.	Habra	26	247	4452	4725	968	8974
3.	Sadpur	3	28	271	302	46	526
4.	Ashokenagar-Kalyangarh	38	430	4891	5359	854	6002
5.	Barasat	28	330	5575	5933	1417	7904
6.	Halisahar	12	287	18594	18893	1151	4606
7.	Bhatpara	25	181	62830	63036	1526	1112
8.	Panpur	1	14	642	657	101	287
9.	Basirhat	14	804	3942	4760	1032	7568
10.	Kanchrapara	5	315	11035	11355	936	5133

Sl. No.	Transport & Storage etc.	Total of Group B (Trade & Transport)	Other services	Total of Group C (Services)	Male Workers in Percentage: Industry (Group A)	Trade & Commerce (Group B)	Service (Group C)
1.	2578	9774	3416	3416	23	53	24
2.	2393	12337	5600	5600	25	45	30
3.	136	708	242	242	32	46	22
4.	2337	9193	4454	4454	33	39	28
5.	3433	12757	5429	5429	31	42	27
6.	1937	7694	3575	3575	65	21	14
7.	3759	6397	7083	7083	82	7	11
8.	91	479	274	274	53	26	21
9.	2707	11307	4414	4414	29	46	25
10.	2165	8234	3535	3535	51	30	19

Once we get the percent values for three groups of workers, those can be plotted on the Ternary diagram. On the basis of their location in the sub-triangles I to VI the pre-dominance of a group of workers can be identified and the town can be designated as an Industrial town, Trade and Transport town etc.

Interpretation

TABLE 5.44

Sl. No.	Name of Town	Predominant function	Sub-triangle location	Secondary functions
1.	Bongaon	Trade & Transport town	V	Highly accelerated trade, Medium industry, Low service
2.	Habra	Trade & Transport town	VI	Moderately accelerated trade, Medium service, Low industry
3.	Sadpur	Trade & Transport town	V	Moderately accelerated trade, Medium service, Low industry
4.	Ashokenagar-	Trade & Transport town	V	Highly accelerated trade, Medium industry, Low service
5.	Barasat	Trade & Transport town	V	Moderately accelerated trade, Medium industry, Low service

Contd. next page

Sl. No.	Name of Town	Predominant function	Sub-triangle location	Secondary functions
6.	Halisahar	Industrial town	IV	Highly accelerated Industry, Medium trade, Low service
7.	Bhatpara	Industrial town	III	Highly accelerated Industry, Medium trade, Low service
8.	Panpur	Industrial town	IV	Highly accelerated Industry, Medium trade, Low service
9.	Basirhat	Trade and Transport town	V	Moderately accelerated trade, Medium industry, Low service
10.	Kanchrapara	Industrial town	IV	Highly accelerted trade, Medium trade, Low service.

Interpretation

As per data (1991 census) 10 selected towns of North 24 Parganas of West Bengal have been taken for functional classification through ternary diagram (Fig. 5.43). Through graphical analysis by ternary diagram in Mitra's method it is understood that on the basis of sub-triangle location 10 towns may be categorized as industrial town or service town or trade and transport town. However, of the 10 towns Bongaon, Habra, Sadpur, Ashoknagar-Kalyangarh, Barasat and Basirhat are trade and transport towns, whereas Halisahar, Bhatpara, Panpur and Kanchrapara are industrial towns.

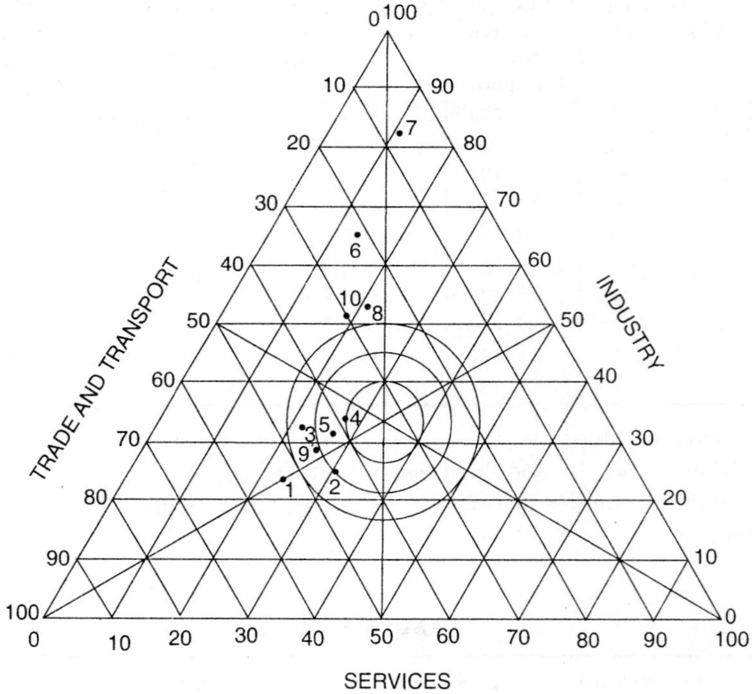

Fig. 5.43 Functional Classification of 10 selected Towns of North 24 Parganas of West Bengal, 1991

NEAREST NEIGHBOUR ANALYSIS

In rural areas, settlements or villages are located at different distances apart. Depending on the locational factors, various patterns of settlement evolve. Although basically rural settlements are either nucleated or dispersed depending on the concentration or dispersion of the resource potentiality, different patterns and nearness between the settlements develop on the basis of some other secondary factors. On a topographic map (sheet), the rural settlements are shown as small clusters of square-blocks and they can be easily delineated by boundary lines enclosing them. Unless the individual homesteads are arranged in a dispersed pattern, a single village can be easily marked this way. Nearest Neighbour Analysis, as worked out by Dacey (1962) and King (1967), analyses the proximity or nearness of settlements in the spatial distribution of settlements and determines if the settlements are clustered, uniform, or random. This analysis marks the nearness of settlements in terms of numerical values.

This method may be applied to some real field based problems also, provided we use it for the determination of nearness of trees in a randomly planted forest, though the factors behind the settlements are not the same as it is for the forest. However, many other man-made and natural features can be analysed for their nearness provided any factor plays a significant role for the nearness of the features i.e. their concentration or dispersion.

Formulae :

As pioneered by Dacey and King, the formula for determining Nearest Neightbour Index (NNI) was developed by the ecologists, Clark and Evans (1954). It determines the deviation of any particular spatial distribution from the point of randomness. It assumes the distribution of points as a random one. The probability distribution of the distances between the points considers the first nearest neighbour as normal, and the estimated mean nearest neighbour distance $\bar{D}r$ between the points of the selected area is calculated by the following equation :

$$\bar{D}r = \frac{1}{2\sqrt{\frac{N}{A}}} \quad \text{[N = number of settlements, A = area or selected area]}$$

The nearest neighbour index 'R' is considered as the ratio of the actual mean distance between nearest neighbour points of a selected area $(\bar{D}_0)$ to the mean expected distance of random distribution of the same number of points within the same area, i.e. $\bar{D}r$.

$$R = \frac{\bar{D}_0}{\bar{D}r} = \frac{\bar{D}_0}{{}^1\!/_2\sqrt{\frac{N}{A}}} = 2\,\bar{D}_0\sqrt{\frac{N}{A}}$$

[R ranges from 0 (zero), when maximum aggregation occurs at one location, 1 being the mark of random distribution, and upto 2.15 representing an even or uniform distribution]

The standard error of the expected mean distance is :

$$\sigma\bar{D}r = \frac{0.26136}{\sqrt{N^2/A}}$$

If 'R' value occurs between 0 and 1, or 1 and 2.15, it indicates an approaching cluster for the former, and an approaching uniform for the latter, considering that the value or $\bar{D}r$ significantly differs from $\bar{D}_0$. The pattern, otherwise, is considered as random, and the difference between $\bar{D}r$ and $\bar{D}_0$ is taken as due to chance factor only. The statistic or the numerical datum is represented as :

$$Z = \frac{\overline{D}_0 - \overline{D}r}{\sigma \overline{D}r}$$

It is the standard normal variate and can test the significance of the difference between $\overline{D}_0$ and $\overline{D}r$.

Important points about the analysis :

(i) As the sub-patterns in the area are averaged in this analysis, each sub-pattern should be studied individually.

(ii) The analysis does not distinguish between a single and a multiclustered pattern.

(iii) The area demarcation is a major problem and as that can affect the 'R' value, the researcher should take the decision of marking that very carefully.

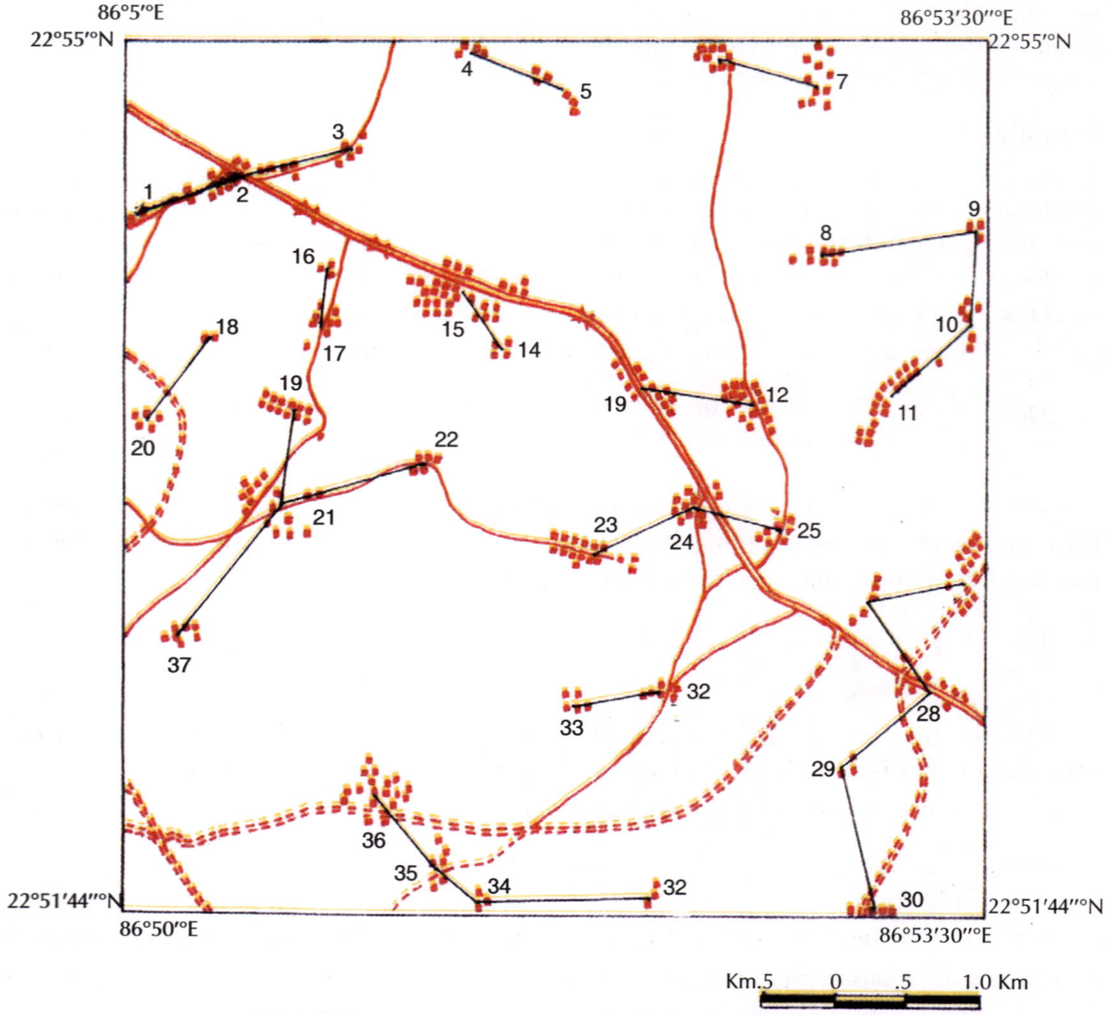

Fig. 5.44 **Map of Nearest Neighbour Distance**

TABLE 5.45

Nearest Neighbour Analysis

Serial No. of stations	Serial no. of nearest neighbour	Distance from nearest neighbour on map (in cm.)	Distance from nearest neighbour on ground (in km)
1	2	1.6	0.8
2	3	1.5	0.75
3	2	1.5	0.75
4	5	1.3	0.65
5	4	1.3	0.65
6	7	1.5	0.75
7	6	1.5	0.75
8	9	2.2	1.1
9	10	1.3	0.65
10	9	1.3	0.65
11	10	1.5	0.75
12	13	1.5	0.75
13	12	1.5	0.75
14	15	1.0	0.5
15	14	1.0	0.5
16	17	0.9	0.45
17	16	0.9	0.45
18	20	1.4	0.70
19	21	1.3	0.65
20	18	1.4	0.70
21	19	1.3	0.65
22	21	2.1	1.05
23	24	1.5	0.75
24	25	1.2	0.6
25	24	1.2	0.6
26	27	1.4	0.7
27	26	1.4	0.7
28	26	1.5	0.75
29	28	1.6	0.8
30	29	2.0	1.0
31	34	2.4	1.2
32	33	1.2	0.6
33	32	1.2	0.6
34	35	0.8	0.4
35	34	0.8	0.4
36	35	1.3	0.65
37	21	2.3	1.15
			$\sum = 26.3$ Km

$$\text{Mean Distance } \bar{D}_0 = \frac{\text{Total Distance (Km)}}{\text{Total no. of settlement}}$$

$$= \frac{26.3}{37} = 0.71$$

$$\text{Expected mean nearest neighbour distance } \bar{D}r = \frac{1}{2\sqrt{\frac{N}{A}}} = \frac{1}{2\sqrt{\frac{37}{36}}} = 0.49$$

[Where, N = No. of settlements; A = Area]

$$\text{Nearest Neighbour Index or } R = \frac{\bar{D}_0}{\bar{D}r} = \frac{0.71}{0.49} = 1.45$$

The standard error of expected mean distance :

$$SE_{\bar{d}} = \frac{\beta_2}{\sqrt{\frac{N^2}{A}}} = \frac{0.26136}{\sqrt{\frac{37^2}{36}}} = \frac{0.26136}{6.17} = 0.04235$$ [where, β_2 = Test statistics for randomness]

$$Z = \frac{\bar{D}_0 - \bar{D}r}{SE_{\bar{d}}} = \frac{0.71 - 0.49}{0.04235} = 5.19$$ [where, Z = Standard normal deviate]

Since value of R occurs between 1 to 2.15, it is expected that a uniform distribution is approaching as, R = 0 means clustered around 1 point, 1 represents random distribution and beyond 1 up to 2.15 the distribution is uniform.

When Z is compared with the probability table of the test of significance, at 1% level it is 4.03, but the value obtained is 5.19. Hence, even at 1% level it is clear that the random distribution is approaching uniformity.

DETOUR INDEX

Sometimes villages near an urban centre are connected to it through such road links as may involve much deteouring in comparison with the aerial distance between the town and the village. The villages surrounding an urban centre may have various lengths of detouring to communicate along raodways. Detour Index can be determined on the basis of such detour values. Detour Index is calculated as :

$$D_i = \frac{\text{Actual Distance in Km}}{\text{Straight Distance in Km}} \times 100$$

The lowest index value is 100. It is obtained when the urban centre is connected along a straight road. The distance is determined from topographic sheet (1:50,000) considering the geo-centre of the patch of a village and a node marked at the central position of road junctions in the urban centre.

TABLE 5.46

Calculation of Detour Index

Sl. No.	Name of settlements	Actual/curve distance from from Ranibandh		Straight distance from Ranibandh		Detour index
		in cm.	in km	in cm.	in km	
1	Pithageria	6	3	4	2	150
2	Jamsol	6.5	3.25	5.1	2.55	127.45
3	Danrkedih	4.5	2.25	4.2	2.1	107.14
4	Chilagara	6	3	5.9	2.95	101.69
5	Khariyasahi	8	4	6.1	3.05	131.15
6	Kashidanga	4.5	2.25	4.1	2.05	109.76
7	Rajakata	5	2.5	4.5	2.25	111.11
8	Birkham	9	4.5	8.6	4.3	104.65
9	Talgara	1.8	0.9	1.6	0.8	112.5
10	Katiam	4	2	3.5	1.75	114.29
11	Maula	5	2.5	4.5	2.25	111.11
12	Garra	7	3.5	5.4	2.7	129.63
13	Ghagra	5	2.5	3.5	1.75	142.86
14	Haludkanali	3.5	1.75	3.1	1.55	112.9
15	Doloibasa	10	5	5.9	2.95	169.49

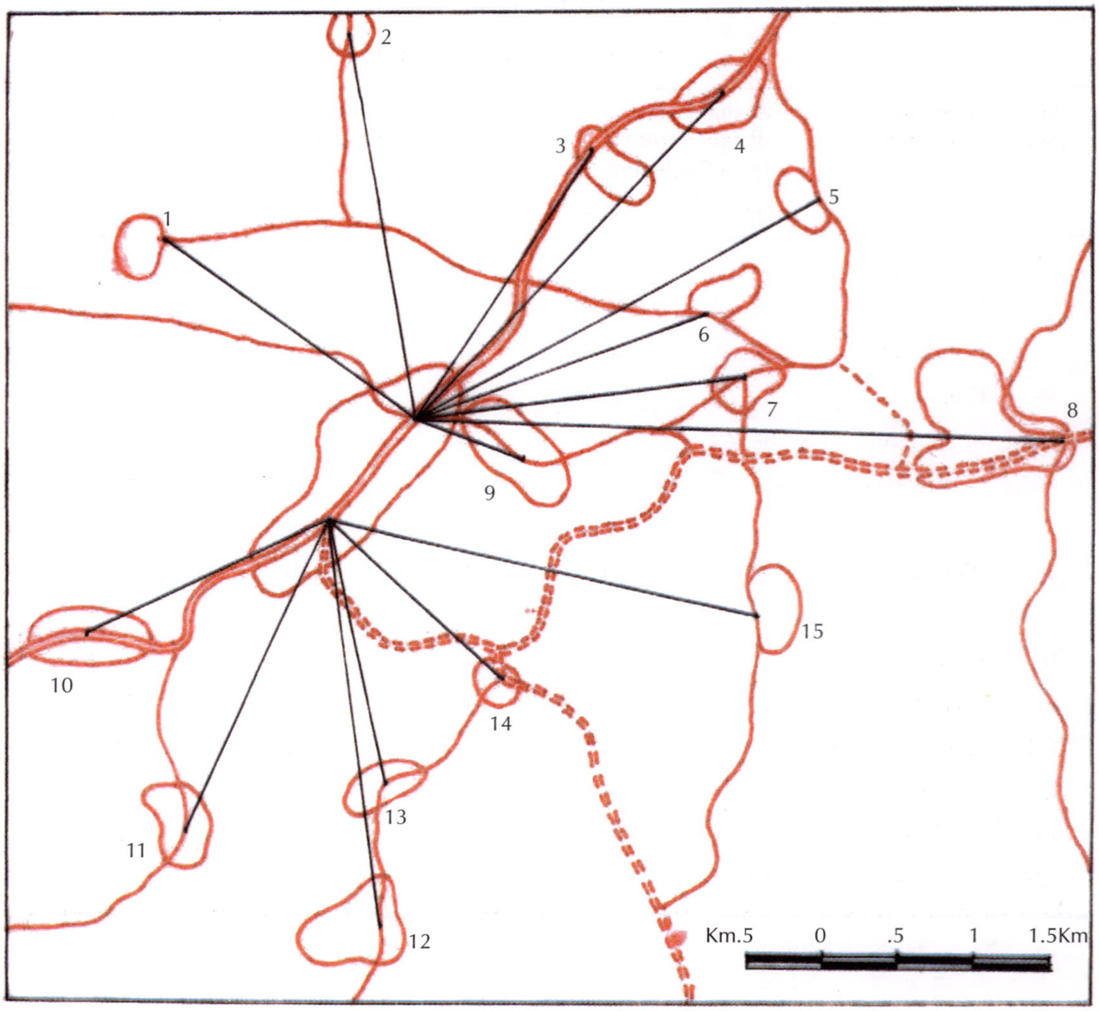

Fig. 5.45 Aerial and Shortest Curve Distance of Settlement from Ranibandh

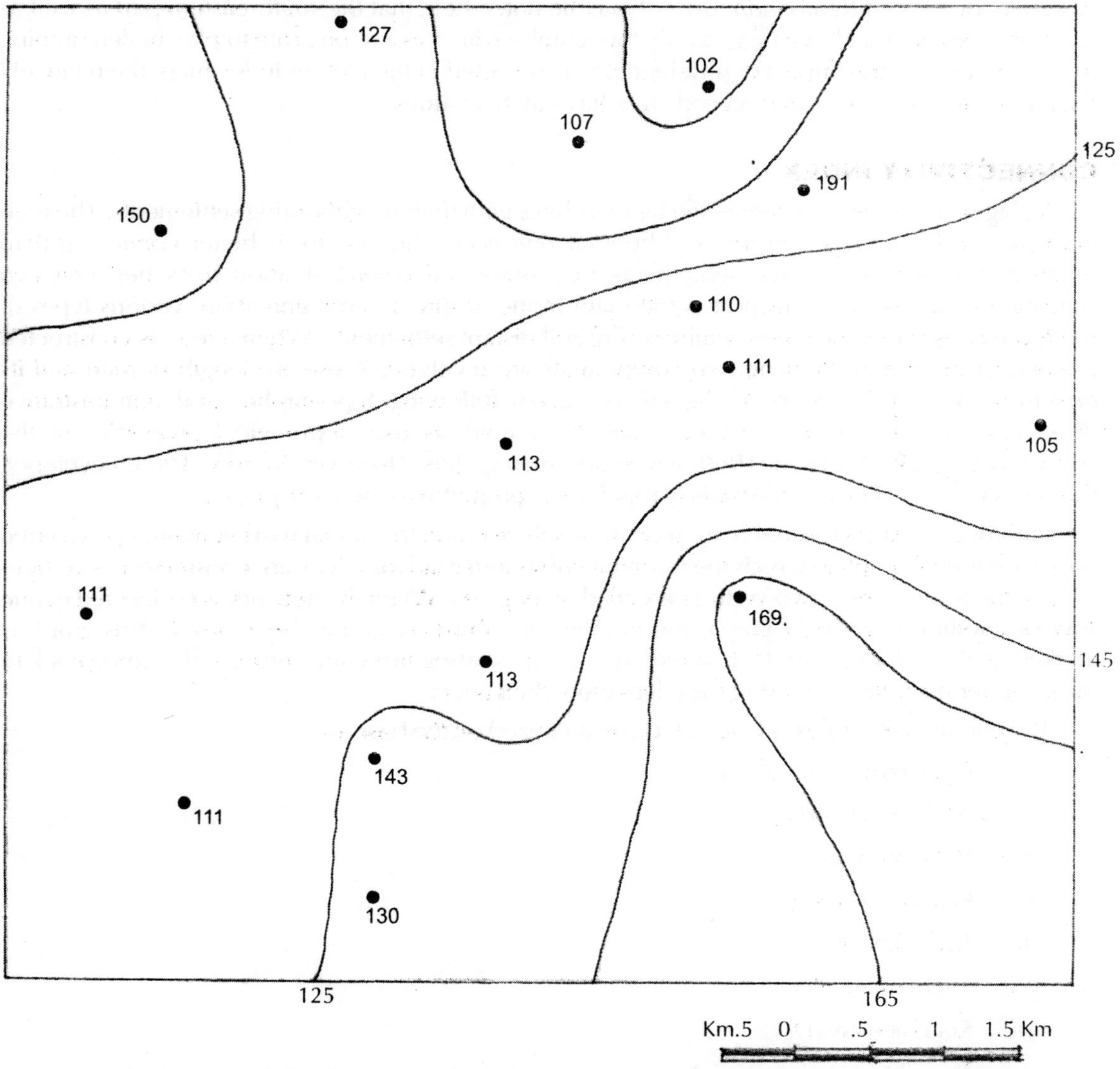

Fig. 5.46 **Isopleths of Detour Index from Ranibandh**

Interpretation :

In the given area of topographic sheet $73\frac{J}{13}$, Ranibadh is a major urban node which is connected by roads with different villages in the surroundings . As Ranibandh has two major road junctions inside the town, two nodes have been taken for measuring the distance of roads. 15 villages (Table for Detour index) have been selected from the surroundings of Ranibandh. The actual road distance which is curvilinear in all the cases have been determined in Km. using a rotameter. Then the straight distance is also determined by a ruler in Km. according to map scale. Then Detour Index values are obtained using the relevant formula. After that within the range of Detour Index values, four isopleths at an interval of 20 have been drawn (Fig. 5.46). The Detour Index Map thus prepared shows that the higher values are obtained towards north-west and south-east, in particular, of Ranibandh town. It may be noted here that the south-eastern part as well as the north-western part have rugged hilly topography which as a strong role to play in determining road plan. Hence, the impact of physiography is reflected in the Detour Index map, the relatively flat areas have low values and rugged areas have higher values.

CONNECTIVITY INDEX

Villages and towns are connected by road-links with their neighbouring settlements. The road network can be analyzed to find out how far one population centre is better connected than another. The nearness to the settlements may introduce communication links between two settlements and as road transport is the main mode of direct communication, various types of roads are constructed between neighbouring and distant settlements. When a road is constructed to connect another settlement, two components are involved. These are length of road and its direction. As roads are often aligned as curves following topographic and administrative directives, direction and length of connectivity analysis uses topological properties of the connectivity graph. Garrison (1960) developed such graphs. However, Kansky (1963) developed the connectivity indices on the basis of topological properties of network graph.

Initially, a well connected road network is selected and the actual road network is converted into a topologial graph in which the terminal points and road junctions are considered as vertices (V) and the route joining two vertices is called an edge (E). When the network is connected in one way or another as a single graph, the number of subsidiary graphs becomes 1. This graph is marked as P and P becomes P=1. A circuit is a path starting from one vertex and coming back to the same vertex without crossing the edges more than once.

The connectivity index is calculated and analyzed on the basis of :

(i) Cyclomatic number (μ)

(ii) Alpha index (α)

(iii) Beta index (β)

(iv) Gamma index (γ)

(v) Eta index (η)

(vi) Theta index (θ)

(vii) Road density (D_n)

(i) Cyclomatic Number indicates the number of circuits present in a network. It is obtained by :

$$\mu = E - V + P$$

(ii) Alpha Index is the ratio of actual number of circuits and maximum number of possible circuits in the network. It is determined as :

$$\alpha = \frac{E - V + 1}{{}^1/_2\,(V^2 - V) - (V - 1)}$$

(iii) Beta Index is the ratio of edges to vertices. The equation is :

$$\beta = \frac{E}{V}$$

(iv) Gamma Index is the ratio between actual number of edges and the maximum possible number of route connections. It is obtained by :

$$\gamma = \frac{E}{\frac{1}{2}(V^2 - V)}$$

(v) Eta Index gives the average length of edges when the total length of edges is m. Thus it is calculated as :

$$\eta = \frac{m}{E}$$

(vi) Theta Index gives average length of edges per vertex. It is calculated as :

$$\theta = \frac{m}{V}$$

(vii) Road Density is the length of road per unit area:

$D_n = \frac{m}{A}$ Where, A = Area

TABLE 5.47

Connectivity index

No. of edges	Length (in cm.)	Length (in km.)
e_1	1.5	0.75
e_2	1.1	0.55
e_3	0.5	0.25
e_4	1.0	0.5
e_5	0.5	0.25
e_6	2.6	1.3
e_7	1.4	0.7
e_8	4.5	2.25
e_9	0.95	0.475
e_{10}	2.4	1.2
e_{11}	0.45	0.225
e_{12}	0.4	0.2
e_{13}	1.75	0.875
e_{14}	5.6	2.8
e_{15}	6.25	3.125
e_{16}	1.15	0.575
e_{17}	1.5	0.75
e_{18}	0.9	0.45
e_{19}	1.1	0.55
e_{20}	2.9	1.45
e_{21}	2.2	1.1

Contd. next page

No. of edges	Length (in cm.)	Length (in km.)
e_{22}	0.95	0.475
e_{23}	2.05	1.025
e_{24}	0.65	0.325
e_{25}	3.8	1.9
e_{26}	0.9	0.45
e_{27}	0.6	0.3
e_{28}	0.35	0.175
e_{29}	1.7	0.85
e_{30}	5.2	2.6
e_{31}	0.7	0.35
e_{32}	0.4	0.2
e_{33}	1.2	0.6
e_{34}	1.0	0.5
e_{35}	1.7	0.85
e_{36}	1.2	0.6
e_{37}	3.3	1.65
		$\Sigma = 33.175$

$$\text{Alpha Index } (\alpha) = \frac{E - V + 1}{{}^1/_2 (V^2 - V) - (V - 1)}$$

Where,
V = no. of vertices
E = no. of edges

$$= \frac{37 - 36 + 1}{{}^1/_2 (36^2 - 36) - (36 - 1)}$$

$$= \frac{37 + 1 - 36}{{}^1/_2 (1296 - 36) - 35}$$

$$= \frac{2}{630 - 35}$$

$$= \frac{2}{595}$$

$$= 0.00336$$

$$\text{Beta Index } (\beta) = \frac{E}{V} = \frac{37}{36} = 1.03$$

$$\text{Gamma Index } (\gamma) = \frac{E}{{}^1/_2 (V^2 - V)}$$

$$= \frac{37}{{}^1/_2 (36^2 - 36)} = \frac{37}{630} = 0.06$$

$$\text{Eta Index } (\eta) = \frac{m}{E}$$

Where,
m = Total length of edges

$$= \frac{33.175}{37} = 0.90$$

$$\text{Theta Index } (\theta) = \frac{m}{V} = \frac{33.175}{36} = 0.92$$

$$\text{Road Density } (D_n) = \frac{m}{A} \qquad \text{Where, } A = \text{Area}$$

$$= \frac{33.175}{36}$$

$$= 0.92 \text{ km/km}^2$$

$$\text{Cyclomatic number } (\mu) = E - V + P, \qquad \text{Where, } P = \text{no. of network}$$

$$= 37 - 36 + 2$$

$$= 3$$

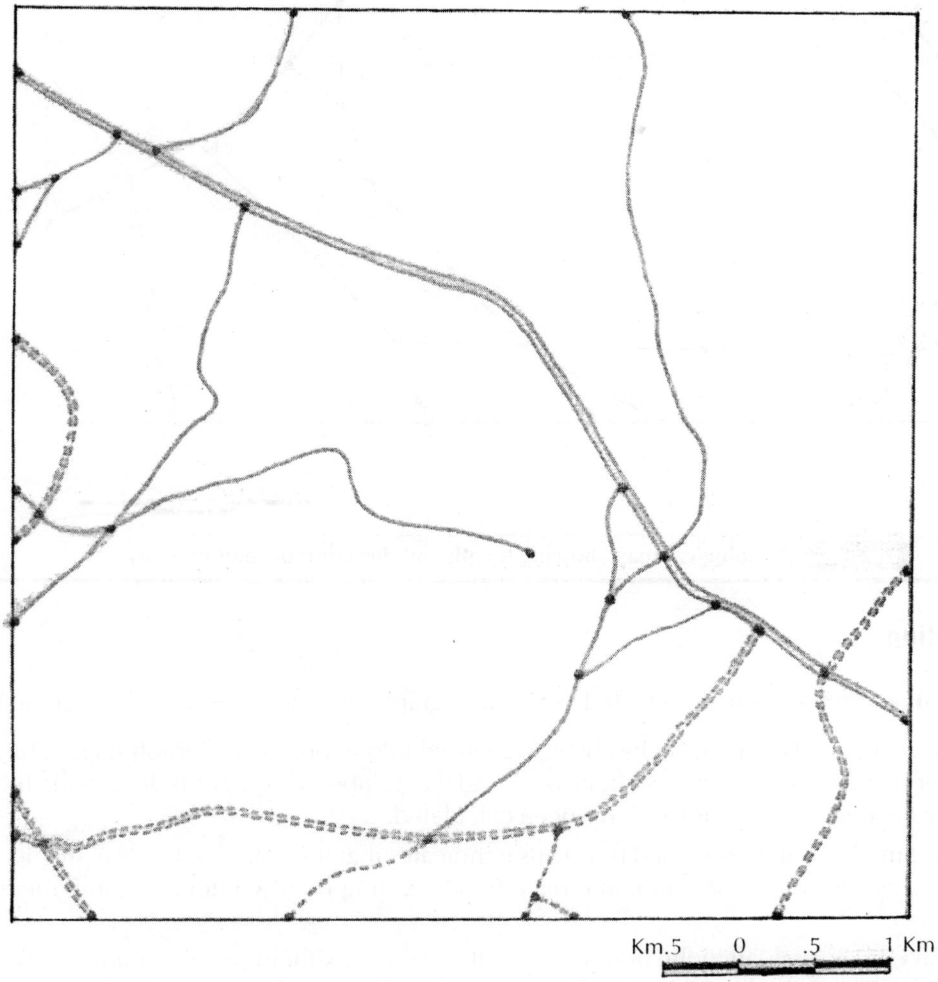

Fig. 5.47 Actual layout of roads on Topographic Sheet

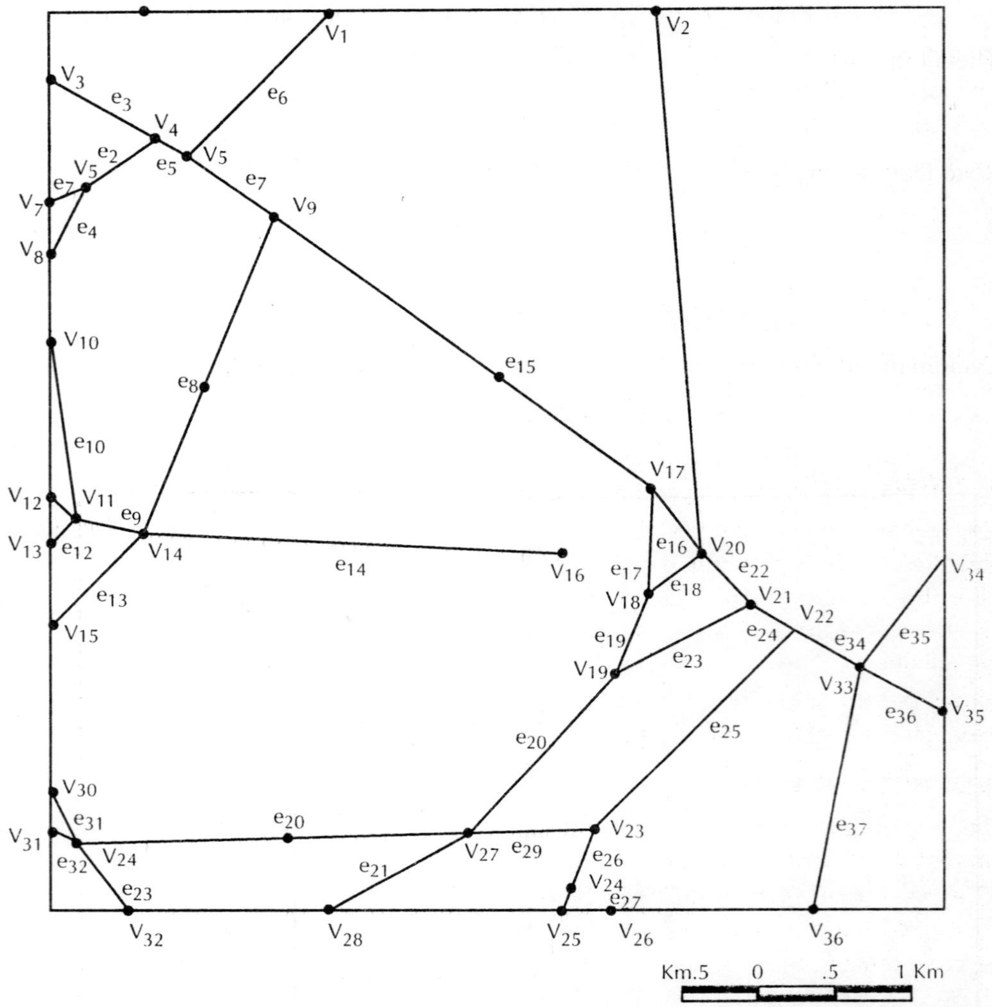

Fig. 5.48 **Topological map showing length and direction of road network**

Interpretation

About 36 km² area has been selected from a topographic sheet ($73\frac{J}{13}$) and the road network between the settlements (Fig. 5.47) has been converted into a topological graph (Fig. 5.48). The total number of edges or route connections is 37 and the number of vertices is 36. On the basis of this network the connectivity indices have been calculated.

The cyclomatic number obtained is 3. Thus it indicates that there are 3 circuits in the network where following the route one can come back to the starting point without crossing the edges more than once.

The alpha index evaluating the number of cycles to the maximum possible number of cycles in the network. The higher the value of alpha index the more connected a network is. The value varies between 0 and 1, when $\alpha = 1$, it indicates that the network is totally interconnected. The alpha index obtained in the given network is 0.00336. Thus the given network is of very low interconnectedness. It has a discrete character.

The Beta value obtained is 1.03. When $\beta = 1$, it indicates that the network has only 1 circuit. If it is >1, it gives a complex network with increased number of edges in comparison with number of vertices. The obtained value indicates that the network has more than 1 circuit. Trees have a beta value of <1. A well connected network may have a value which equals to 1. If the value is >1, the network is supposed to be complex where there is higher number of links of a fixed number of nodes.

The value of gamma index varies between 0 and 1, 1 indicating a completely connected network which is normally unlikely in reality. Gamma value can measure the progression of a network with time. The obtained value in the given network is 0.06. This value being much less than 1 indicates that even if the number of edges is greater than number of vertices, it is not of much higher value as 1 gives the maximum number of connections possible in the network.

Eta index value obtained in the given network is 0.90. Two comparable eta value of two networks can indicate a lower development of transport network and vice versa. However, if the number of links are increased further, the length per edge will decrease and will give a better development of transport system.

Higher theta value indicates the greater load of network. The value obtained here is 0.92 which is very close to 1. Thus it shows that the structure of the network is very close to interconnectedness.

The road density value obtained is 0.92 km per unit area. This is moderate value and enough scope of developing a good transport network is still left.

CONNECTIVITY MATRIX

In the network of roads we often observe some nodal points which are connected by routes from different directions. The importance of the node depends on the number of connections to the node. These nodes are also known as vertices.

From the given network of the roads the vertices and the edges are incorporated in table 5.48 for connectivity matrix. It is revealed that the vertices are joined by different number of edges or routes. It is observed that the maximum number of edges connected to a vertex is 4, whereas the minimum number is one, the latter is observed when an edge connects a node from a terminal point at the boundary of the graph. The relative importance of the nodal points are reflected in this matrix, higher the number of connections, greater the importance. In metropoliton cities we often come across some nodes which have greater number of links connected to it . The linearity and the circularity of network development are also reflected in such nodes with multiple connections.

TABLE 5.48

Connectivity Matrix between Neighbouring Vertices

	V_1	V_2	V_3	V_4	V_5	V_6	V_7	V_8	V_9	V_{10}	V_{11}	V_{12}	V_{13}	V_{14}	V_{15}	V_{16}	V_{17}	V_{18}	V_{19}	V_{20}	V_{21}	V_{22}	V_{23}	V_{24}	V_{25}	V_{26}	V_{27}	V_{28}	V_{29}	V_{30}	V_{31}	V_{32}	V_{33}	V_{34}	V_{35}	V_{36}	*No. of Connections*
V_1	0	0	0	0	1	0	0	0	0	0	0	0	0	0	0	0	0	0	0	0	0	0	0	0	0	0	0	0	0	0	0	0	0	0	0	0	1
V_2	0	0	0	0	0	0	0	0	0	0	0	0	0	0	0	0	0	0	0	1	0	0	0	0	0	0	0	0	0	0	0	0	0	0	0	0	1
V_3	0	0	0	1	0	0	0	0	0	0	0	0	0	0	0	0	0	0	0	0	0	0	0	0	0	0	0	0	0	0	0	0	0	0	0	0	1
V_4	0	0	1	0	1	1	0	0	0	0	0	0	0	0	0	0	0	0	0	0	0	0	0	0	0	0	0	0	0	0	0	0	0	0	0	0	3
V_5	1	0	0	1	0	0	0	0	1	0	0	0	0	0	0	0	0	0	0	0	0	0	0	0	0	0	0	0	0	0	0	0	0	0	0	0	3
V_6	0	0	0	1	0	0	1	1	0	0	0	0	0	0	0	0	0	0	0	0	0	0	0	0	0	0	0	0	0	0	0	0	0	0	0	0	3
V_7	0	0	0	0	0	1	0	0	0	0	0	0	0	0	0	0	0	0	0	0	0	0	0	0	0	0	0	0	0	0	0	0	0	0	0	0	1
V_8	0	0	0	0	0	1	0	0	0	0	0	0	0	0	0	0	0	0	0	0	0	0	0	0	0	0	0	0	0	0	0	0	0	0	0	0	1
V_9	0	0	0	0	1	0	0	0	0	0	0	0	0	1	0	0	1	0	0	0	0	0	0	0	0	0	0	0	0	0	0	0	0	0	0	0	3
V_{10}	0	0	0	0	0	0	0	0	0	0	1	0	0	0	0	0	0	0	0	0	0	0	0	0	0	0	0	0	0	0	0	0	0	0	0	0	1
V_{11}	0	0	0	0	0	0	0	0	0	0	1	0	1	0	0	0	0	0	0	0	0	0	0	0	0	0	0	0	0	0	0	0	0	0	0	0	4
V_{12}	0	0	0	0	0	0	0	0	0	0	1	0	0	0	0	0	0	0	0	0	0	0	0	0	0	0	0	0	0	0	0	0	0	0	0	0	1
V_{13}	0	0	0	0	0	0	0	0	0	0	1	0	0	0	0	0	0	0	0	0	0	0	0	0	0	0	0	0	0	0	0	0	0	0	0	0	1
V_{14}	0	0	0	0	0	0	0	0	1	0	1	0	0	1	1	1	0	0	0	0	0	0	0	0	0	0	0	0	0	0	0	0	0	0	0	0	4
V_{15}	0	0	0	0	0	0	0	0	0	0	0	0	1	1	0	0	0	0	0	0	0	0	0	0	0	0	0	0	0	0	0	0	0	0	0	0	1
V_{16}	0	0	0	0	0	0	0	0	0	0	0	0	1	1	0	0	0	0	0	0	0	0	0	0	0	0	0	0	0	0	0	0	0	0	0	0	1
V_{17}	0	0	0	0	0	0	0	0	1	0	0	0	0	0	0	0	0	1	1	1	1	0	0	0	0	0	0	0	0	0	0	0	0	0	0	0	3
V_{18}	0	0	0	0	0	0	0	0	0	0	0	0	0	0	0	0	1	0	1	1	0	0	0	0	0	0	0	0	0	0	0	0	0	0	0	0	3
V_{19}	0	0	0	0	0	0	0	0	0	0	0	0	0	0	0	0	0	1	0	0	1	0	0	0	0	0	1	0	0	0	0	0	0	0	0	0	3
V_{20}	0	1	0	0	0	0	0	0	0	0	0	0	0	0	0	0	1	1	0	0	1	0	0	0	0	0	0	0	0	0	0	0	0	0	0	0	4
V_{21}	0	0	0	0	0	0	0	0	0	0	0	0	0	0	0	0	0	0	1	1	0	1	0	0	0	0	0	0	0	0	0	0	0	0	0	0	3
V_{22}	0	0	0	0	0	0	0	0	0	0	0	0	0	0	0	0	0	0	0	0	1	0	1	0	0	0	0	0	0	0	0	0	1	0	0	0	3
V_{23}	0	0	0	0	0	0	0	0	0	0	0	0	0	0	0	0	0	0	0	0	0	1	0	1	0	0	1	0	0	0	0	0	0	0	0	0	3

Contd. next page

	V_1	V_2	V_3	V_4	V_5	V_6	V_7	V_8	V_9	V_{10}	V_{11}	V_{12}	V_{13}	V_{14}	V_{15}	V_{16}	V_{17}	V_{18}	V_{19}	V_{20}	V_{21}	V_{22}	V_{23}	V_{24}	V_{25}	V_{26}	V_{27}	V_{28}	V_{29}	V_{30}	V_{31}	V_{32}	V_{33}	V_{34}	V_{35}	V_{36}	*No. of Connections*
V_{24}	0	0	0	0	0	0	0	0	0	0	0	0	0	0	0	0	0	0	0	0	0	0	1	0	1	1	0	0	0	0	0	0	0	0	0	0	3
V_{25}	0	0	0	0	0	0	0	0	0	0	0	0	0	0	0	0	0	0	0	0	0	0	0	1	0	0	0	0	0	0	0	0	0	0	0	0	1
V_{26}	0	0	0	0	0	0	0	0	0	0	0	0	0	0	0	0	0	0	0	0	0	0	0	1	0	0	0	0	0	0	0	0	0	0	0	0	1
V_{27}	0	0	0	0	0	0	0	0	0	0	0	0	0	0	0	0	0	0	1	0	0	0	1	0	0	0	0	1	1	0	0	0	0	0	0	0	4
V_{28}	0	0	0	0	0	0	0	0	0	0	0	0	0	0	0	0	0	0	0	0	0	0	0	0	0	0	1	0	0	0	0	0	0	0	0	0	1
V_{29}	0	0	0	0	0	0	0	0	0	0	0	0	0	0	0	0	0	0	0	0	0	0	0	0	0	0	1	0	.0	1	1	1	0	0	0	0	4
V_{30}	0	0	0	0	0	0	0	0	0	0	0	0	0	0	0	0	0	0	0	0	0	0	0	0	0	0	0	0	1	0	0	0	0	0	0	0	1
V_{31}	0	0	0	0	0	0	0	0	0	0	0	0	0	0	0	0	0	0	0	0	0	0	0	0	0	0	0	0	1	0	0	0	0	0	0	0	1
V_{32}	0	0	0	0	0	0	0	0	0	0	0	0	0	0	0	0	0	0	0	0	0	0	0	0	0	0	0	0	1	0	0	0	0	0	0	0	1
V_{33}	0	0	0	0	0	0	0	0	0	0	0	0	0	0	0	0	0	0	0	0	0	1	0	0	0	0	0	0	0	0	0	0	0	1	1	1	4
V_{34}	0	0	0	0	0	0	0	0	0	0	0	0	0	0	0	0	0	0	0	0	0	0	0	0	0	0	0	0	0	0	0	0	1	0	0	0	1
V_{35}	0	0	0	0	0	0	0	0	0	0	0	0	0	0	0	0	0	0	0	0	0	0	0	0	0	0	0	0	0	0	0	0	1	0	0	0	1
V_{36}	0	0	0	0	0	0	0	0	0	0	0	0	0	0	0	0	0	0	0	0	0	0	0	0	0	0	0	0	0	0	0	0	1	0	0	0	1

LOCATION QUOTIENT

Finding out the concentration of economic features in terms of spatial distribution is one of the major works in geography. Such concentrations may range from industries to a particular community of population in different spatial units. Determination of Location Quotient is one of such measures to indicate the concentration of different types of economic and demographic data. The uniqueness of the place with maximum concentraiton can be identified in such works. It was initially developed by Robert Murray Haig in 1928. He used it in his research work while developing the regional plan of New York City. His study was based on basic and non-basic industries.

Formula of location quotient

The determination of the value of Location Quotient can be done on the basis of the following equations :

$$LQ = \frac{e_i/e}{E_i/E}$$

Where,

LQ = Location Quotient

e_1 = Reference data of the locality.

e = Total reference data of the spatial unit which the locality belongs to .

E_i = Reference data of the entire region (District/State/Nation).

E = Total universe of data which the reference data belongs to (District/State/Nation).

[Reference data = The particular type of data used.]

TABLE 5.49

Calculation of Location quotient

Sl. No.	Name of the Blocks	Total Population (e)	Total Literate Population (e_i)	Percentage of Literate Population $(e_i/e)/100$	Location Quotient of the Literate Population (LQ)
1	Murarai I	190802	89238	46.77	0.777
2	Murarai II	222033	109260	49.21	0.817
3	Nalhati I	204818	133428	65.14	1.082
4	Nalhati II	127785	78390	61.35	1.019
5	Rampurhat I	188435	119769	63.56	1.055
6	Rampurhat II	187823	114999	61.23	1.017
7	Mayureswar I	159782	99993	62.58	1.039
8	Mayureswar II	127661	79749	62.47	1.037
9	Muhammad Bazar	164570	92045	55.93	0.929
10	Rajnagar	77979	46355	59.45	0.987
11	Suri I	111377	71173	63.90	1.061

Contd. next page

Sl. No.	Name of the Blocks	Total Population (e)	Total Literate Population (e_i)	Percentage of Literate Population $(e_i/e)/100$	Location Quotient of the Literate Population (LQ)
12	Suri II	87405	55765	63.80	1.059
13	Sainthia	195349	124849	63.91	1.061
14	Labpur	201901	126842	62.82	1.043
15	Nanoor	218654	133771	61.18	1.016
16	Bolpur-Sriniketan	202553	126779	62.59	1.039
17	Illambazar	168709	109023	64.62	1.073
18	Dubrajpur	181437	107340	59.16	0.982
19	Khoyrasole	153248	91848	59.93	0.995
		$\Sigma = 3172321$	$\Sigma = 1910616$		

[The Ratios are converted into percent values]

$$E_i/E = \frac{\text{Total Literate Population of the District}}{\text{Total Population of the District}} \times 100$$

$$= \frac{1910616}{3172321} \times 100 \qquad = 60.23$$

Interpretation

This work has been done on the basis of literate population of 19 CD blocks of Birbhum district to determine the concentration of literacy in the district. The Location Quotient values are compiled in table no. 5.49.

It is observed that 6 CD blocks i.e. Khoyrasole, Dubrajpur, Rajnagar, Muhammad Bazar, Murarai I and Murarai II are having the LQ value of <1.0, whrereas 13 other blocks are having it as more than 1.0. Murarai I is having the lowest value i.e. 0.777. On the other hand, the highest value i.e. 1.082 is obtained by Nalhati I block. It is notable that , Bolpur-Sriniketan block where Viswa Bharati University is located, Location Quatient of literacy is not the highest. However, the 6 blocks having low Location Quotient value of literacy require a better spread of educational institutions and awareness of people towards literacy.

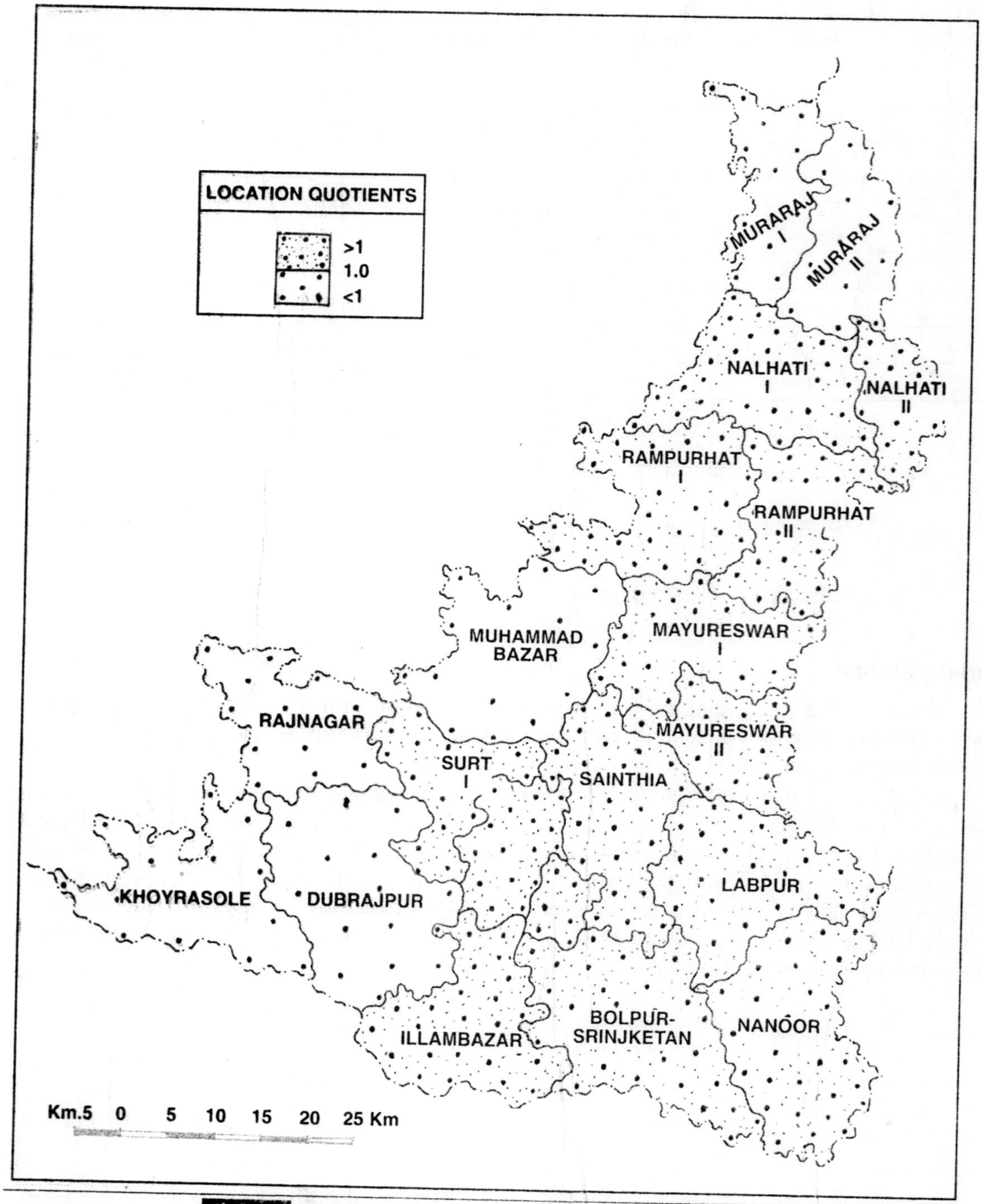

Fig. 5.49 Location quotient map of Birbhum District (2011)

MEAN CENTRE

The growth of population does not remain uniform across the spatial spread of administrative units. Usaually, the economic growth attracts population concentration and in different districts the growth of population varies. When compared temporally between different decades, it is observed that the centre of growth has not remained constant. It may shift spatially depending on the shift of concentraiton points related to urbanization, economic growth etc. The centre of population growth can be determined by mean centre, which is a graphically determined point on the the basis of spatial distance of geocentres from the X and Y axes drawn along the edge of adminsitrative unit in terms of population. A geometric mean of all the geo-centres determine the mean centre of the major administrative unit which may be a state or a district. Calculation for different census years may indicate a shift of the mean centre.

TABLE 5.50

Table for Calculation of Mean Centre

Sl. No.	District	Population 2001 (W)	Population 2011 (W)	Dist. of Geo-centre from axis		Population 2001		Population 2011	
				X (in cm.)	Y (in cm.)	XW	YW	XW	YW
1	Darjeeling	1609172	1842034	8.4	19.4	13517044.8	31217936.8	15473085.6	35735459.6
2	Jalpaiguri	3001173	3869675	10.5	18.6	31512316.5	55821817.8	40631587.5	71975955
3.	Coachbihar	2479155	2822780	11.7	17.1	29006113.5	42393550.5	33026526	48269538
4.	N. Dinajpur	2441794	3000849	7.1	16	17336737.4	39068704	21306027.9	48013584
5.	S. Dinajpur	1503178	1670931	8.1	13.8	12175741.8	207438564	13534541.1	23058847.8
6.	Maldah	3290486	3997970	7.35	12.9	24185072.1	42447269.4	29385079.5	51573813
7.	Murshidabad	5866569	7102430	8	9.3	46932552	54559091.7	56819440	66052599
8.	Birbhum	3015422	3502389	5.9	8.5	17790989.8	25631087	20664095.1	29770306.5
9.	Burdwan	6895514	7723663	7	6.1	48268598	42062635.4	54065641	471143344.3
10.	Bankura	3192695	3596292	4.3	6	13728588.5	19156170	15464055.6	21577752
11.	Purulia	2536516	2927965	1.75	6.3	4438903	15980050.8	5123938,75	18446179.5
12.	W. Midnapur	5193411	5943300	4.8	3.1	24928372.8	16099574.1	28527840	18424230
13.	E. Midnapur	4417377	5094238	6.45	1.7	28492081.65	7509540.9	32857835.1	8660204.6
14.	Nadia	4604827	5186488	9	6.8	41443443	31312823.6	46678392	35268118.4
15.	Hooghly	5041976	5520389	7.4	4.8	37310622.4	24201484.8	40850878.6	26497867.2
16.	Howrah	4273099	4841638	7.5	3.8	32048242.5	16237776.2	36312285	18398224.4
17.	Kolkata	4572876	4486679	8.5	3.7	38869446	16919641.2	38136771.5	16600712.3
18.	N. 24 Parganas	8934286	10082852	9.4	4.45	83982288.4	39757572.7	94778808.8	44868691.4
19.	S. 24 Parganas	6906689	8153176	8.9	2.55	61469532.1	17612056.95	72563266.4	20790598.8
		ΣW= 79776215	ΣW= 91365738			ΣXW= 607436686.3	ΣYW= 558732640.3	ΣXW= 696200095.5	ΣYW= 651097025.8

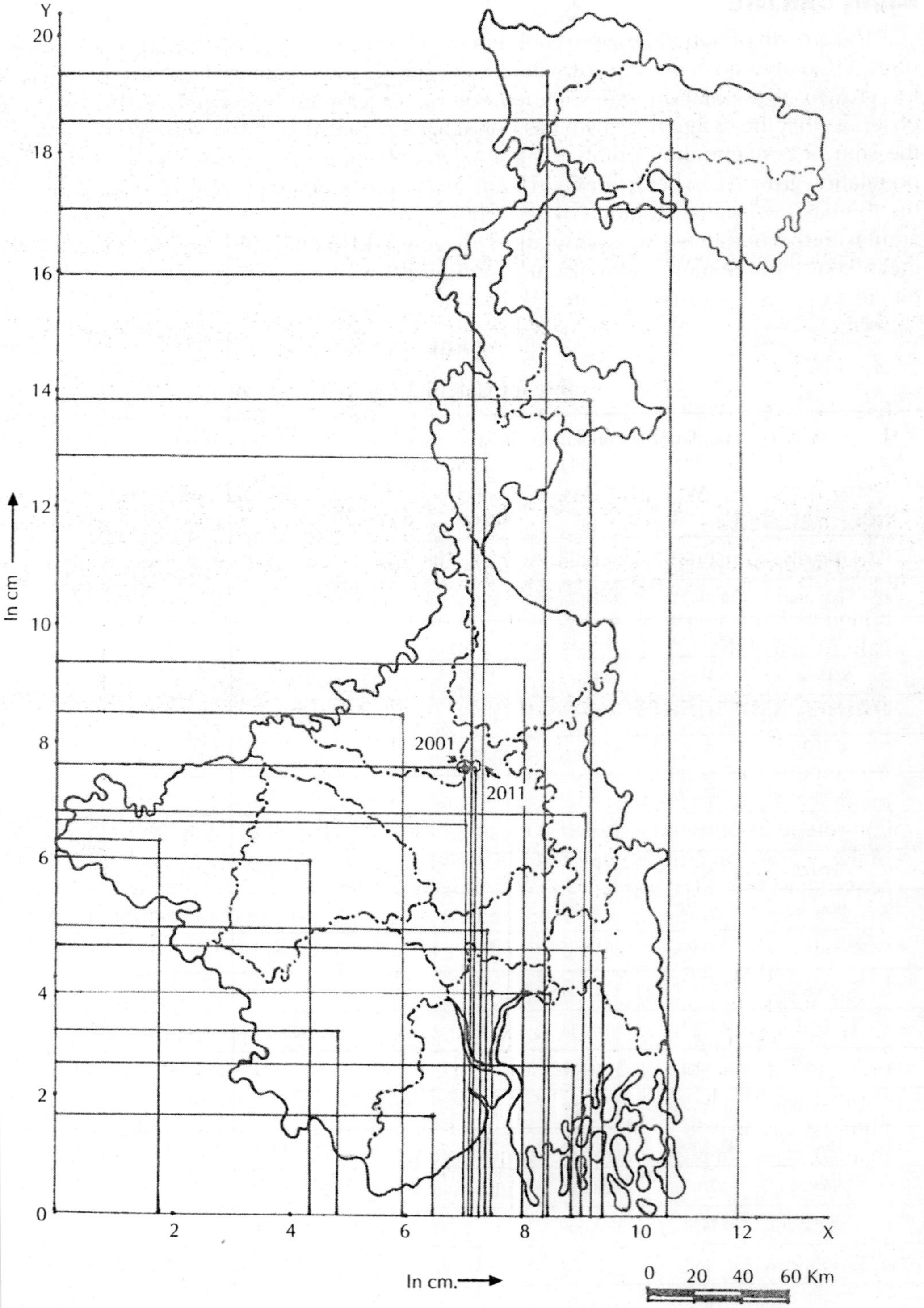

Fig. 5.50 Shift of Mean Centre of Population of West Bengal between 2001 and 2011

Calculation for mean centre, Population 2001 :

$$X_C = \frac{\Sigma xw}{\Sigma w} \qquad Y_C = \frac{\Sigma yw}{\Sigma w}$$

$$= \frac{607436686.3}{79776215} \qquad = \frac{558732640.3}{79776215}$$

$$= 7.61 \qquad = 7.00$$

Calculation for mean centre, Population 2011:

$$X_C = \frac{\Sigma xw}{\Sigma w} \qquad Y_C = \frac{\Sigma yw}{\Sigma w}$$

$$= \frac{696200095.5}{91365738} \qquad = \frac{651097025.8}{91365738}$$

$$= 7.62 \qquad = 7.13$$

interpretation :

Mean centres have been determined (Fig. 5.50) on the basis of census population data of 19 districts and West Bengal in 2001 and 2011. In 2001, the mean centre was located on the boundary between Birbhum and Burdwan districts . In 2011, it shifted towards east in the district of Burdwan perhaps on the basis of the shift of economic growth point.

RAINFALL DISPERSION DIAGRAM

Rainfall Dispersion Diagram is a parametric test which is carried out with a graphical technic. It compares between the dispersion diagrams of neighbouring stations. For this diagram the median and quartile values of each set of data are to be calculated. Three diagnostic values are considered to determine the relative variability in dispersion, i.e. in terms of the relative positions of the quartile and median values. The quartile range. i.e. the difference between the upper and lower quartile is also an important criterion. The comparison is usually made between two sets of records, but it can also be used for multiple sets of records. The correlation becomes significant when the lower quartile value of first set is greater than the median value of the second set, i.e. $LQ_1 > M_2$ and $M_1 > UQ_2$. If such conditions are satisfied, the difference between two sets of records is probably significant though not absolutely so when samples of less than 40 items are taken.

In this diagram, Stations are located along the horizontal axis and rainfall is given along the ordinate. 30 years of rainfall data has been used for 5 meteorological stations of West Bengal, i.e. Darjeeling, Maldah, Bolpur, Bankura and Alipore. As such the stations are located in dry sub humid areas as well as moist areas of the state. However, the number of sample data being less than 40, does not give any absolute impression.

TABLE 5.51

Amount of rainfall in cm of five stations of West Bengal (1901-1930)

Year	Darjeeling	Maldah	Bolpur	Bankura	Alipore
1901	108.54	46.34	54.89	48.11	70.11
1902	150.76	49.35	45.18	46.07	62.28
1903	100.0	40.55	46.08	57.57	54.14
1904	108.01	39.56	54.36	54.90	63.2
1905	151.42	66.38	67.03	48.57	69.76
1906	113.36	49.05	54.68	59.70	57.19
1907	89.42	50.26	42.08	54.65	53.64
1908	90.29	35.86	56.58	53.36	80.77
1909	131.85	48.81	55.63	70.82	72.22
1910	115.93	52.71	45.70	44.26	57.23
1911	134.85	58.92	44.71	61.89	43.37
1912	128.77	53.90	19.04	65.67	56.82
1913	127.03	63.90	51.44	63.54	80.34
1914	127.73	45.09	37.84	57.39	57.23
1915	107.14	42.08	39.45	44.99	65.96
1916	137.18	73.67	67.69	72.82	82.78
1917	142.70	88.10	57.30	82.05	70.68
1918	130.46	90.79	60.75	44.91	58.37
1919	131.17	77.16	28.54	88.37	63.69
1920	107.17	49.37	33.27	53.48	63.78
1921	111.21	67.24	37.48	42.09	56.56
1922	111.47	72.14	36.80	82.41	83.1
1923	101.10	43.17	34.17	50.86	56.5
1924	126.43	56.02	43.33	61.47	51.03
1925	129.81	73.90	35.68	50.25	59.28
1926	114.23	53.39	49.92	60.48	75.25
1927	123.34	42.30	42.94	48.18	45.83
1928	105.48	70.90	54.94	51.71	78.66
1929	131.97	74.11	49.09	77.11	59.64
1930	100.55	45.63	49.85	55.04	59.88

TABLE 5.52

Ranking of data for computation of Quartiles

Rank	Darjeeling	Maldah	Bolpur	Bankura	Alipore
1	89.42	35.86	19.04	42.09	43.37
2	90.29	39.56	28.54	44.26	45.83
3	100.0	40.55	33.27	44.91	51.03
4	100.55	42.08	34.17	44.99	53.64
5	101.10	42.30	35.68	46.07	54.14
6	105.48	43.17	36.80	48.11	56.50
7	107.14	45.09	37.48	48.18	56.56
8	107.17	45.63	37.84	48.57	56.82
9	108.01	46.34	39.45	50.25	57.19
10	108.54	48.81	42.08	50.86	57.23
11	111.21	49.05	42.94	51.71	57.23
12	111.47	49.35	43.33	53.36	58.28
13	113.36	49.37	44.71	53.48	59.28
14	114.23	50.26	45.18	54.65	59.64
15	115.93	52.71	45.70	54.90	59.88
16	123.34	53.39	46.08	55.04	62.28
17	126.43	53.90	49.09	57.39	63.2
18	127.03	56.02	49.85	57.57	63.69
19	127.73	58.92	49.92	59.70	63.78
20	128.77	63.90	51.44	60.48	65.96
21	129.81	66.38	54.36	61.47	69.76
22	130.46	67.24	54.68	61.89	70.11
23	131.17	70.90	54.89	63.54	70.68
24	131.85	72.14	54.94	65.67	72.22
25	131.97	73.67	55.63	70.82	75.25
26	134.85	73.90	56.58	72.82	78.66
27	137.18	74.11	57.30	77.11	80.34
28	142.70	77.16	60.75	82.05	80.77
29	150.76	88.10	67.03	82.41	82.78
30	151.42	90.79	67.69	88.37	83.1
Q_1	107.16	45.50	37.75	48.47	56.76
Q_2	119.64	53.05	45.89	54.97	61.08
Q_3	131.51	71.52	54.92	64.61	71.45

$$\text{Quartile Rank } 1 = \frac{N+1}{4} = \frac{30+1}{4} = 7.75$$

$$\text{Quartile Rank } 2 = 2\left(\frac{N+1}{4}\right) = 2\left(\frac{30+1}{4}\right) = 15.5$$

$$\text{Quartile Rank } 3 = 3\left(\frac{N+1}{4}\right) = 3\left(\frac{30+1}{4}\right) = 23.5$$

Darjeeling :

$$Q_1 \rightarrow \frac{R_1 - R_L}{R_U - R_L} = \frac{Q_1 - L_1}{L_2 - L_1}$$

Where,

R_1 = Rank of 1st quartile

R_L = Previous rank of quartile rank

R_U = Next rank of quartile rank

L_1 = Value of previous rank

L_2 = Value of next rank

$$\text{or, } \frac{7.75 - 7}{8 - 7} = \frac{Q_1 - 107.14}{107.17 - 107.14}$$

$$\text{or, } \frac{0.75}{1} = \frac{Q_1 - 107.14}{0.03}$$

$$\text{or, } Q_1 - 107.14 = 0.0225$$

$$\therefore Q_1 = \boxed{107.16}$$

$$Q_2 \rightarrow \frac{R_2 - R_L}{R_U - R_L} = \frac{Q_2 - L_1}{L_2 - L_1}$$

Where,

R_2 = Rank of 2nd quartile

$$\text{or, } \frac{15.5 - 15}{16 - 15} = \frac{Q_2 - 115.93}{123.34 - 115.93}$$

$$\text{or, } \frac{0.5}{1} = \frac{Q_2 - 115.93}{7.41}$$

$$\text{or, } Q_2 - 115.93 = 3.705$$

$$\therefore Q_2 = \boxed{119.64}$$

$$Q_3 \rightarrow \frac{R_3 - R_L}{R_U - R_L} = \frac{Q_3 - L_1}{L_2 - L_1}$$

Where,

R_3 = Rank of 3rd quartile

$$\text{or, } \frac{23.5 - 23}{24 - 23} = \frac{Q_3 - 131.17}{131.85 - 131.17}$$

$$\text{or, } \frac{0.5}{1} = \frac{Q_3 - 131.17}{0.68}$$

$$\text{or, } Q_3 - 131.17 = 0.34$$

$$\therefore Q_3 = \boxed{131.51}$$

Maldah :

$$Q_1 \rightarrow \frac{R_1 - R_L}{R_U - R_L} = \frac{Q_1 - L_1}{L_2 - L_1}$$

$$\text{or,} \quad \frac{7.75 - 7}{8 - 7} = \frac{Q_1 - 45.09}{45.63 - 45.09}$$

$$\text{or,} \quad \frac{0.75}{1} = \frac{Q_1 - 45.09}{0.54}$$

$$\text{or,} \quad Q_1 - 45.09 = 0.405$$

$$\therefore \quad Q_1 = \boxed{45.50}$$

$$Q_2 \rightarrow \frac{R_2 - R_L}{R_U - R_L} = \frac{Q_2 - L_1}{L_2 - L_1}$$

$$\text{or,} \quad \frac{15.5 - 15}{16 - 15} = \frac{Q_2 - 52.71}{53.39 - 52.71}$$

$$\text{or,} \quad \frac{0.5}{1} = \frac{Q_2 - 52.71}{0.68}$$

$$\text{or,} \quad Q_2 - 52.71 = 0.34$$

$$\therefore \quad Q_2 = \boxed{53.05}$$

$$Q_3 \rightarrow \frac{R_3 - R_L}{R_U - R_L} = \frac{Q_3 - L_1}{L_2 - L_1}$$

$$\text{or,} \quad \frac{23.5 - 23}{24 - 23} = \frac{Q_3 - 70.90}{72.14 - 70.90}$$

$$\text{or,} \quad \frac{0.5}{1} = \frac{Q_3 - 70.90}{1.24}$$

$$\text{or,} \quad Q_3 - 70.90 = 0.62$$

$$\therefore \quad Q_3 = \boxed{71.52}$$

Bolpur :

$$Q_1 \rightarrow \frac{R_1 - R_L}{R_U - R_L} = \frac{Q_1 - L_1}{L_2 - L_1}$$

$$\text{or,} \quad \frac{7.75 - 7}{8 - 7} = \frac{Q_1 - 37.48}{37.84 - 37.48}$$

$$\text{or,} \quad \frac{0.75}{1} = \frac{Q_1 - 37.48}{0.36}$$

$$\text{or,} \quad Q_1 - 37.48 = 0.27$$

$$\therefore \quad Q_1 = \boxed{37.75}$$

$$Q_2 \rightarrow \frac{R_2 - R_L}{R_U - R_L} = \frac{Q_2 - L_1}{L_2 - L_1}$$

$$\text{or,} \quad \frac{15.5 - 15}{16 - 15} = \frac{Q_2 - 45.70}{46.08 - 45.70}$$

$$\text{or,} \quad \frac{0.5}{1} = \frac{Q_2 - 45.70}{0.38}$$

$$\text{or,} \quad Q_2 - 45.70 = 0.19$$

$$\therefore \quad Q_2 = \boxed{45.89}$$

$$Q_3 \rightarrow \frac{R_3 - R_L}{R_U - R_L} = \frac{Q_3 - L_1}{L_2 - L_1}$$

$$\text{or,} \quad \frac{23.5 - 23}{24 - 23} = \frac{Q_3 - 54.89}{54.94 - 54.89}$$

$$\text{or,} \quad \frac{0.5}{1} = \frac{Q_3 - 54.89}{0.05}$$

$$\text{or,} \quad Q_3 - 54.89 = 0.025$$

$$\therefore \quad Q_3 = \boxed{54.92}$$

Bankura :

$$Q_1 \rightarrow \frac{R_1 - R_L}{R_U - R_L} = \frac{Q_1 - L_1}{L_2 - L_1}$$

$$\text{or, } \frac{7.75 - 7}{8 - 7} = \frac{Q_1 - 48.18}{48.57 - 48.18}$$

$$\text{or, } \frac{0.75}{1} = \frac{Q_1 - 48.18}{0.39}$$

$$\text{or, } Q_1 - 48.18 = 0.2925$$

$$\therefore Q_1 = \boxed{48.47}$$

$$Q_2 \rightarrow \frac{R_2 - R_L}{R_U - R_L} = \frac{Q_2 - L_1}{L_2 - L_1}$$

$$\text{or, } \frac{15.5 - 15}{16 - 15} = \frac{Q_2 - 54.90}{55.04 - 54.90}$$

$$\text{or, } \frac{0.5}{1} = \frac{Q_2 - 54.90}{0.14}$$

$$\text{or, } Q_2 - 54.90 = 0.07$$

$$\therefore Q_2 = \boxed{54.97}$$

$$Q_3 \rightarrow \frac{R_3 - R_L}{R_U - R_L} = \frac{Q_3 - L_1}{L_2 - L_1}$$

$$\text{or, } \frac{23.5 - 23}{24 - 23} = \frac{Q_3 - 63.54}{65.67 - 63.54}$$

$$\text{or, } \frac{0.5}{1} = \frac{Q_3 - 63.54}{2.13}$$

$$\text{or, } Q_3 - 63.54 = 1.065$$

$$\therefore Q_3 = \boxed{64.61}$$

Alipore :

$$Q_1 \rightarrow \frac{R_1 - R_L}{R_U - R_L} = \frac{Q_1 - L_1}{L_2 - L_1}$$

$$\text{or, } \frac{7.75 - 7}{8 - 7} = \frac{Q_1 - 56.56}{56.82 - 56.56}$$

$$\text{or, } \frac{0.75}{1} = \frac{Q_1 - 56.56}{0.26}$$

$$\text{or, } Q_1 - 56.56 = 0.195$$

$$\therefore Q_1 = \boxed{56.76}$$

$$Q_2 \rightarrow \frac{R_2 - R_L}{R_U - R_L} = \frac{Q_2 - L_1}{L_2 - L_1}$$

$$\text{or, } \frac{15.5 - 15}{16 - 15} = \frac{Q_2 - 59.88}{62.28 - 59.88}$$

$$\text{or, } \frac{0.5}{1} = \frac{Q_2 - 59.88}{2.4}$$

$$\text{or, } Q_2 - 54.88 = 1.2$$

$$\therefore Q_2 = \boxed{61.08}$$

$$Q_3 \rightarrow \frac{R_3 - R_L}{R_U - R_L} = \frac{Q_3 - L_1}{L_2 - L_1}$$

$$\text{or, } \frac{23.5 - 23}{24 - 23} = \frac{Q_3 - 70.68}{72.22 - 70.68}$$

$$\text{or, } \frac{0.5}{1} = \frac{Q_3 - 70.68}{1.54}$$

$$\text{or, } Q_3 - 70.68 = 0.77$$

$$\therefore Q_3 = \boxed{71.45}$$

ALTERNATIVE METHOD OF COMPUTING QUARTILE

Darjeeling :

$Q_1 \rightarrow L_1$ + difference between R_1 and R_L $(L_2 - L_1)$

$$= 107.14 + 0.75\,(107.17 - 107.14)$$

$$= 107.14 + 0.75 \times 0.03 \qquad = 107.14 + 0.0225$$

$$= \boxed{107.16}$$

$Q_2 \rightarrow L_1$ + difference between R_2 and R_L $(L_2 - L_1)$

$= 115.93 + 0.5\,(123.34 - 115.93)$

$= 115.93 + 0.5 \times 7.41 \quad = 115.93 + 3.705$

$= \boxed{119.64}$

$Q_3 \rightarrow L_1$ + difference between R_3 and R_L $(L_2 - L_1)$

$= 131.17 + 0.5\,(131.85 - 131.17)$

$= 131.17 + 0.5 \times 0.68 \quad = 131.17 + 0.34$

$= \boxed{131.51}$

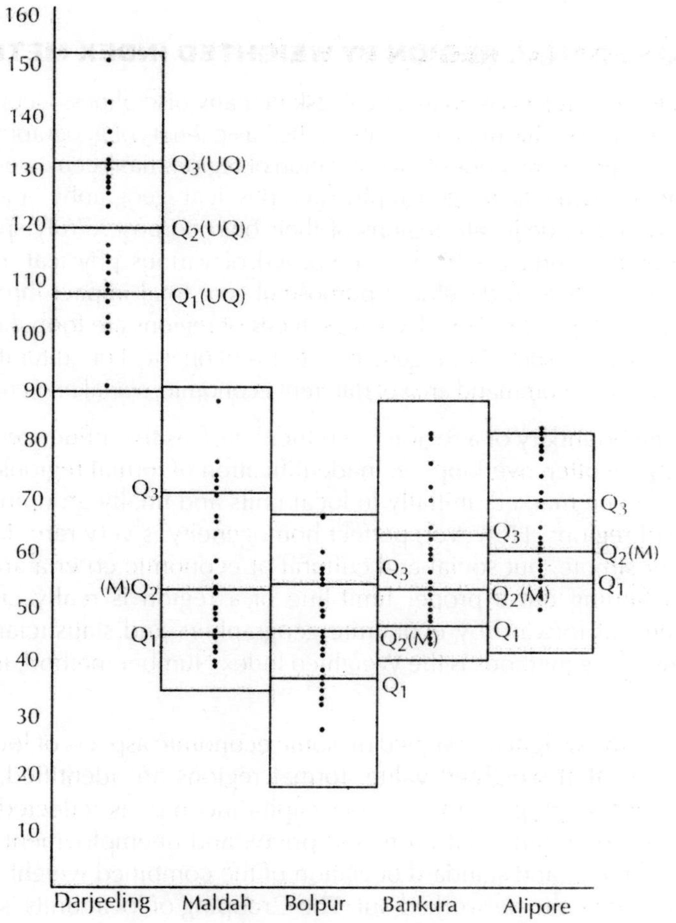

Fig. 5.51 **Rainfall dispersion diagram of five station of West Bengal (1901-1930)**

Interpretation

In this five sets of data of five stations, Darjeeling is the most moist in nature. If we compare the rainfall dispersion of Darjeeling with Maldah or Bolpur or Bankura or Alipore, it is observed that the Median value of Darjeeling, i.e. 119.64 is greater than Upper Quartile of Maldah, i.e. 71.52, greater than Upper Quartile of Bolpur, i.e. 54.92, greater than Upper Quartile of Bankura, i.e.. 64.61 and of Alipore, i.e. 71.45. On the other hand, the Lower Quartile value of Darjeeling, i.e. 107.16 is greater than the Median values of all other four stations being 53.05, 45.89, 54.97, 61.08 respectively. Hence, the difference in the nature of rainfall dispersion between Darjeeling and any other of the four stations is significant.

On the other hand, if we compare between two data sets of Maldah and Bolpur, it is observed that the lower Quartile of Maldah, i.e. 45.50 is less than Median value of Bolpur, i.e 45.89, and the Median value of Maldah, i.e. 53.05 is less than the Upper Quartile of Bolpur, i.e. 54.92. Hence, the conditions of significance are not satisfied and the difference in the rainfall dispersion between Maldah and Bolpur is not significant.

DELINEATION OF FORMAL REGION BY WEIGHTED INDEX METHOD

The identification of a region is an essential task in many disciplines. Geography being a spatial science obviously stresses on this matter, as one of the basic tenets of geography is regional complex analysis. That is why so many methods of identification of regions has been essential in this discipline. Both the component segments of geography i.e. physical geography and human geography relentlessly endeavoured to delineate regions of their own purpose. Truly speaking, a region is a spatial unit of the earth's surface which is composed of various physical and cultural elements interacting among themselves to develop a purposeful sum total impact through which it can be designatd as a particular type of region. Two basic types of regions are formal region and functional region, the former indicating some homogeneity in terms of physical or cultural aspects, whereas the latter indicates the extent of command area of different economic, social and cultural functions.

To determine the boundary of a region is a difficult task as the influences of different physical and cultural aspects are often overlapping. In identification of formal regions, similarities of some selected criteria are to be marked, initially in local units and finally grouping the local units into delineation of broad regions. However, perfect homogeneity is very rare. If the criteria is static, delineation is rather simple, but social and cultural or economic criteria are often dynamic and overlapping. Thus finding out a proper limit-line of a region is really cumbersome. Various methods have been put forward by economic geographers and statisticians for delineation of formal regions. One of the methods is the Weighted Index Number method, initially developed by Boudeville.

In this method, some weight is assigned on some economic aspects of local regional units and finally on the basis of that weighted value, formal regions are identified. The two economic variables selected for this purpose may be per capita income (as reflected in GDP in terms of international standard of a particular base year price), and unemployment rate. This method is purely statistical and mean and standard deviation of the combined weight of per capita income and unemployment rate are to be worked out. The Grouping of local units is done on the basis of upto $\overline{X}$ + 1S.D, $\overline{X}$ + 1S.D. to $\overline{X}$ + 2 S.D and so on.

In this book the delineation of formal region by Weighted Index Number method has been carried out on the basis of districtwise basic economic data of West Bengal in 2013-14 as related to per capita income in US dollars at constant of 2004-05 prices an unemployment rate of the same units in 2009-10.

Delineation of Formal Region by Weighted Index Method

TABLE 5.53

Districtwise Basic Economic Data of West Bengal in 2013-14

GDP per Capita as of 2013-14 at constant of 2004-05 prices (US$) and Districtwise Unemployment Rate in West Bengal (2009-10) converted into Percent values

Sl. No.	Name of Districts	Per Capita Income ($)	Unemployment Rate (%)	Weightage		Total Weight
				Per Capita Income	Unemployment Rate	
1.	Barddhaman	1500	3	10	1.5	11.5
2.	Birbhum	940	4	−2	2	0
3.	Bankura	1100	1	2	0.5	2.5
4.	Purba Medinipur	1700	2	14	1	15
5.	Paschim Medinipur	1000	1	0	0.5	0.5
6.	Howrah	1500	3	10	1.5	11.5
7.	Hooghly	1300	4	6	2	8
8.	North 24 Parganas	1400	3	8	1.5	9.5
9.	South 24 Parganas	1100	1	2	0.5	2.5
10.	Kolkata	2500	3	30	1.5	31.5
11.	Nadia	1100	2	2	1	3
12.	Murshidabad	940	2	−2	1	−1
13.	North Dinajpur	700	2	−6	1	−5
14.	South Dinajpur	870	0.5	3	0.25	3.25
15.	Maldah	940	1	−2	0.5	−1.5
16.	Jalpaigudi	1100	4	2	2	4
17.	Darjeeling	1700	8	14	4	18
18.	Coochbehar	930	1	−2	0.5	−1.5
19.	Purulia	920	1	−2	0.5	−1.5

TABLE 5.54

for Mean value in group data of total given Weight on Percapita Income and Unemployment Rate

Class of Total Weight	Frequency of Total Weight (f)	Mid Value (x)	Deviation (x − 12.5)	$y = \frac{x - 12.5}{5}$	f.y
−5 — 10	6	−2.5	−15	−3	−18
0 — 5	6	2.5	−10	−2	−12
5 — 10	2	7.5	−5	−1	−2
10 — 15	3	12.5	0	0	0
15 — 20	1	17.5	5	1	1
20 — 35	1	27.5	15	3	3
	$\Sigma f = 19$				$\Sigma f.y = -28$

$\bar{x}_0$ = Assumed Mean of Mid values = 12.5

$$\text{Mean } (\bar{x}) = \bar{x}_0 + \text{Common Divider}\left(\frac{\Sigma f.y}{\Sigma f}\right)$$

$$= 12.5 + 5\left(\frac{-28}{19}\right)$$

$$= 12.5 - 7.3684$$

$$= 5.1316 \quad = 5.13$$

TABLE 5.55

Standard Deviation in grouped data on Per Capita Income and Unemployment Rate

Frequency of Total Weight (X)	$\overline{X}$	$(X - \overline{X})$	$(X - \overline{X})^2$
6	5.13	0.87	0.7569
6		0.87	0.7569
2		– 3.13	9.7969
3		– 2.13	4.5369
1		– 4.13	17.0569
1		– 4.13	17.0569
Total = 19			$\Sigma f(X - \overline{X})^2 = 49.9614$

$$\text{Standard Deviation} = (\text{S.D.}) = \sqrt{\frac{\Sigma f(x - \bar{x})^2}{n}}$$

$$= \sqrt{\frac{49.9614}{19}} \text{ mm}$$

$$= 1.621587916 \quad = 1.62$$

TABLE 5.56

Classes for Formal Region

Class	Formula	Value	Serial No. of Districts
I	< Mean + 1 S.D.	< 6.75	2, 3, 5, 9, 11, 12, 13, 14, 15, 16, 18, 19
II	Mean + 1 S. D – Mean + 2 S.D	6.75 – 8.37	7
III	Mean + 2 S. D – Mean + 3 S.D	8.37 – 9.99	8
IV	Mean + 3 S.D – Mean + 4 S.D	9.99 – 11.61	1, 6
VII	Mean + 4 S.D – Mean + 7 S.D	11.61 – 16.47	4
VIII	Mean + 7 S.D – Mean + 8 S.D	16.47 – 18.09	17
IX	> Mean + 8 S.D	> 18.09	10

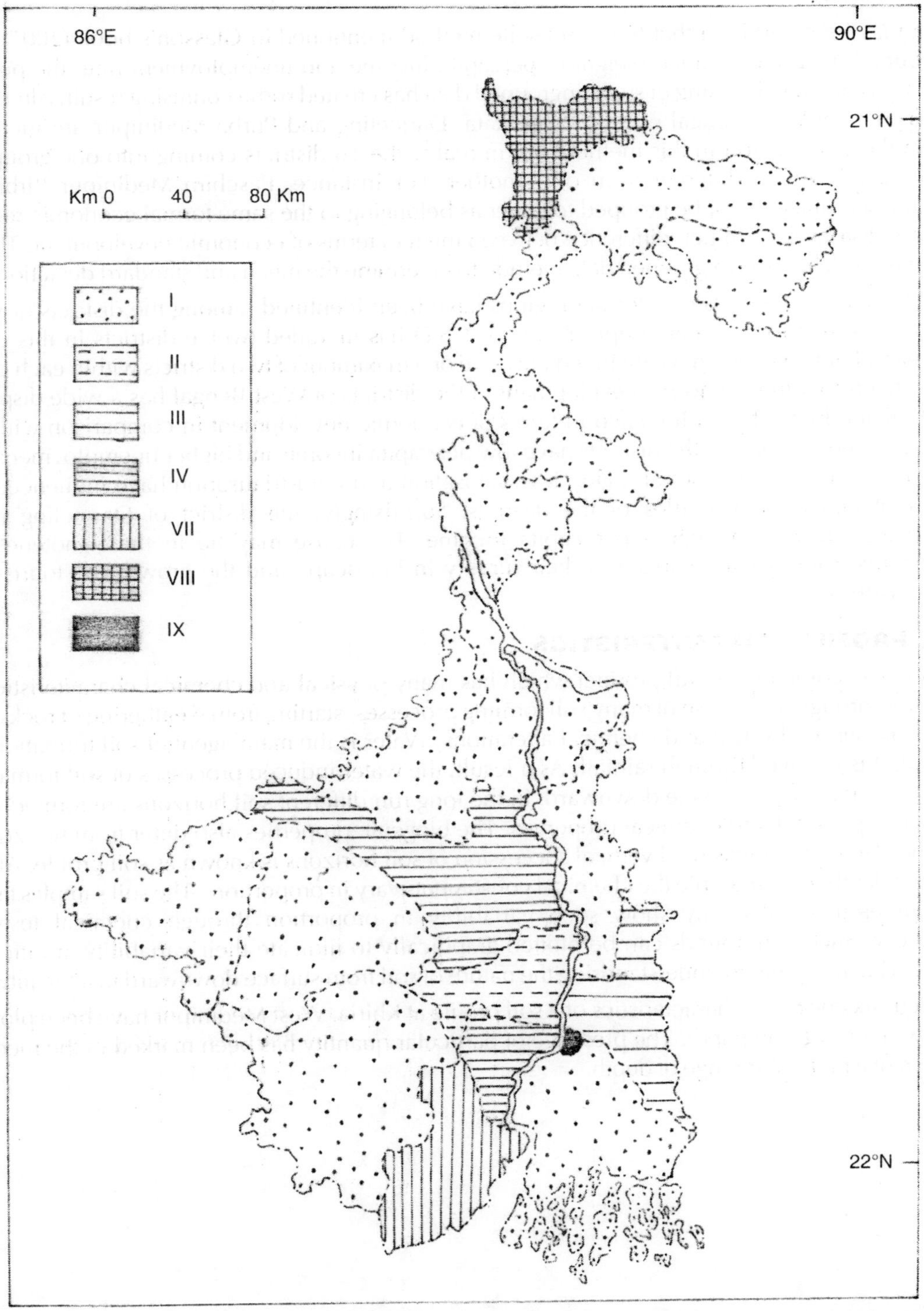

Fig. 5.52 Delineation of formal regions of west bengal by weighted index method

Interpretation

It may be noted here that the Boudeville method mentioned in Glasson's book (2007) uses ungrouped data of combined weight of percapita income and unemployment rate, the present work finds out that the using of such ungrouped data has created some confusing result. Almost all the districts of West Bengal except for Kolkata, Darjeeling and Purba Medinipur are included within the same region in this method, but in reality the 16 districts coming into one group are economically much different from one another. For instance, Paschim Medinipur Birbhum, Bankura, Purulia can not be grouped together as belonging to the same formal economic region, as these districts have much difference between them in terms of economic development. That is why this work has used a grouped data method to determine the mean and standard deviation.

Altogether nine classes of formal regions have been identified among the districts of West Bengal. The first formal region upto mean + 1 S.D has included twelve districts in this class, whereas all other regions have included only one or a maximum of two districts within each class. This reflects that the economic development in the districts of West Bengal has a wide disparity and Kolkata district has culminated in terms of economic development in comparison with the others. Moreover, most of the districts have low per capita income and higher unemployment rate as grouped into the first formal region I. Urbanisation and industrialisation have influenced the values of economic variables of the districts. Surprisingly, the district of Darjeeling (with Kalimpang) shows the highest per capita income. The cause may lie in the remoteness of settlements from urban centres and their rurality in landscape and the growth the tourism at selected areas.

SOIL PROFILE CHARACTERISTICS

Soil is a complex natural product which has many physical and chemical characteristics. it develops through the course of many soil forming processes, starting from weathering of rocks to a good number of physical and chemical alterations. Water is the main agent of soil formation. In general, it is received through rainfall. As a result, the water induced processes of soil formation begins vertically from surface downward. In the long run different soil horizons are formed with distinctive physical and chemical properties. The biogenic properties also differ from horizon to horizon. The two-dimensional vertical succession of soil horizons is known as soil profile. Along different depths of soil profile the chemical constituents vary in proportion . The soil samples taken from different depths may show such variability in proportion through chemical tests in laboratory. Such compounds can be plotted graphically to indicate their variability at different depths. That may help in understandsing the nature of soil from surface downward in a locality.

Here six chemical characteristics of a soil profile at Khiria, West Medinipur have been plotted depthwise on a graph paper. The presence of particular quantity has been marked in the median position of a particular range of depth.

TABLE 5.57
Soil profile characteristics
District : West Medinipur
Village : Khiria

Depth in inches	pH	Organic matter	Nitrogen	CaO (Acetic acid)	CaO (HCl)	Carbon
0–6"	5.68	0.8084	0.056	3.08	0.185	0.47
6–14"	7.0	0.17716	0.017	3.60	0.242	0.103
14–23"	7.14	0.14276	0.014	3.60	0.228	0.083
23–35"	6.9	0.14792	0.018	5.12	0.332	0.086
35–48"	7.54	0.14964	0.017	7.4	0.407	0.087

Diagrams of Soil Profile Characteristics

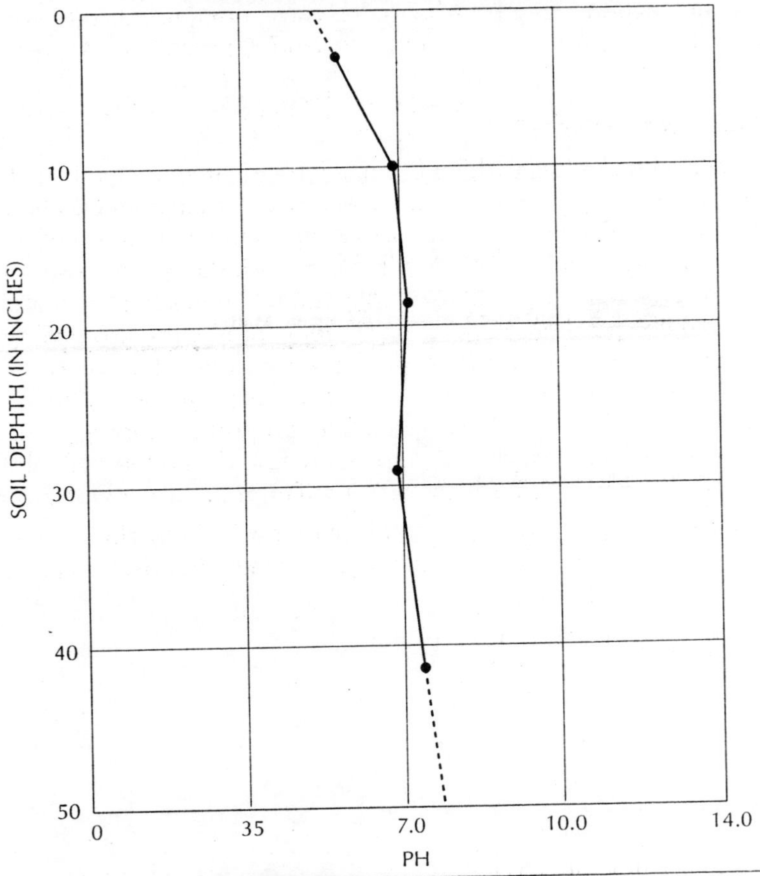

Fig. 5.53 Depthwise variation of pH

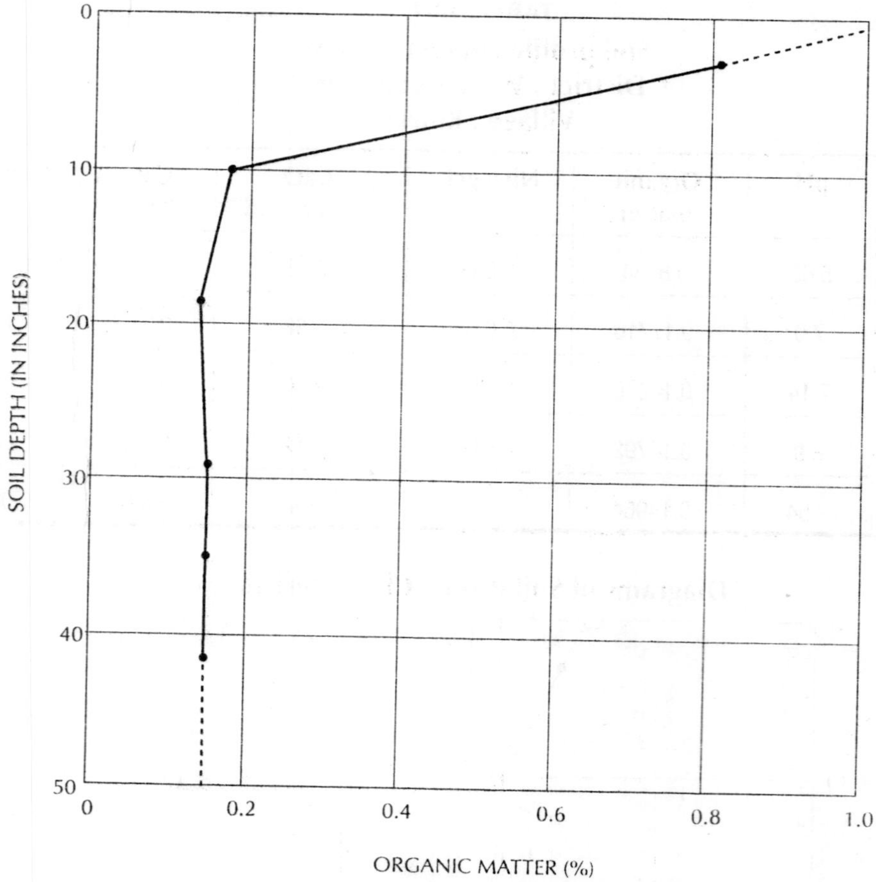

Fig. 5.54 Depthwise Variation of Organic Matter

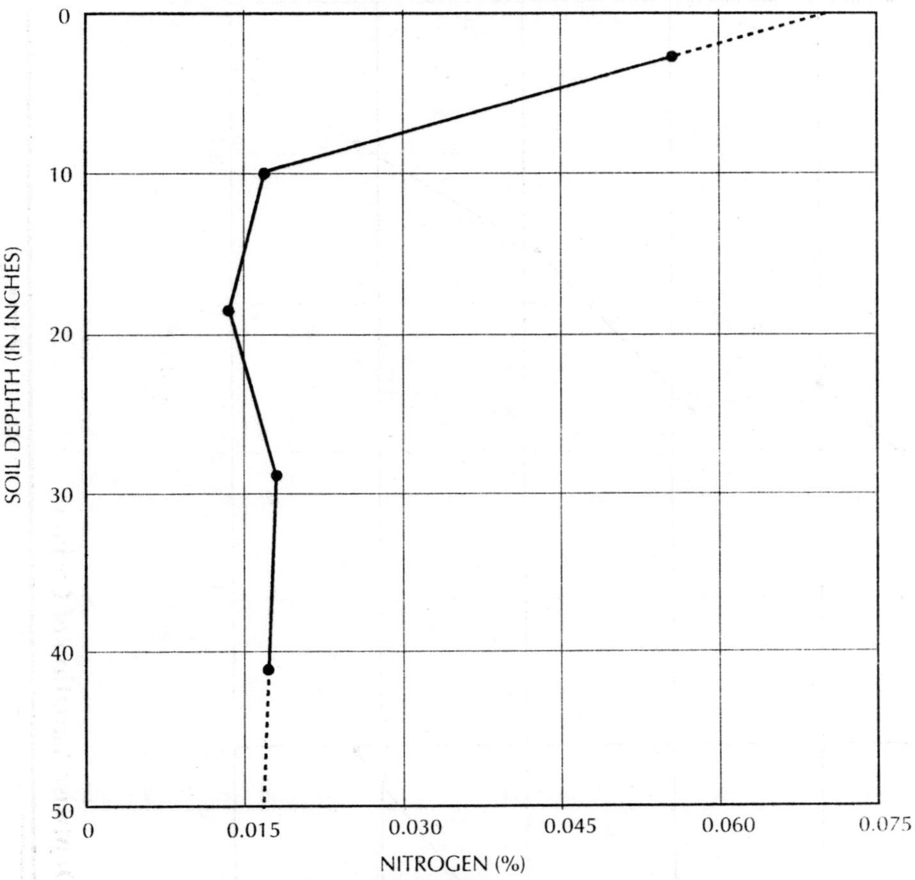

Fig. 5.55 Depthwise Variation of Nitrogen

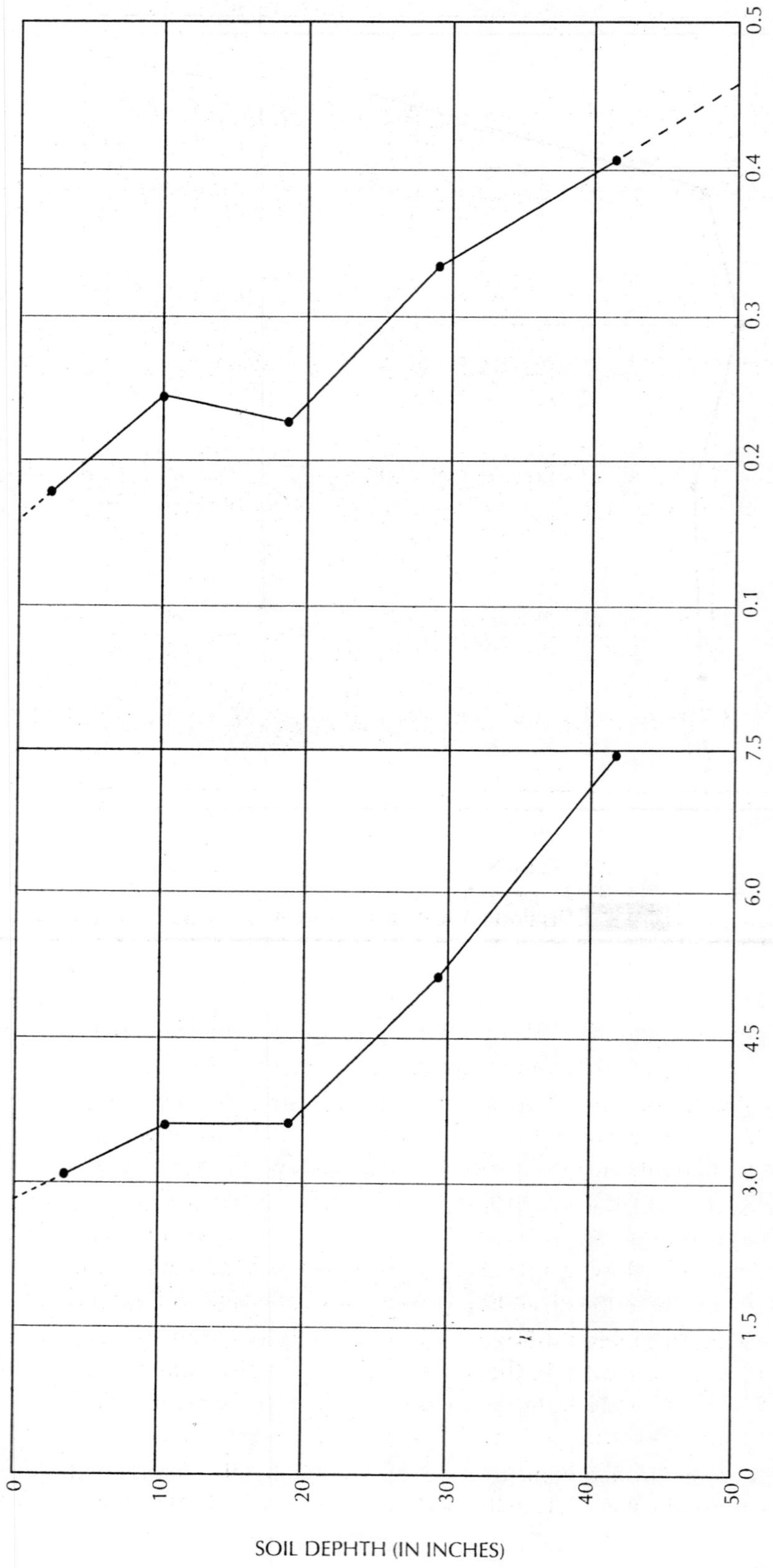

Fig. 5.56 Deptwise Variation of Carbon

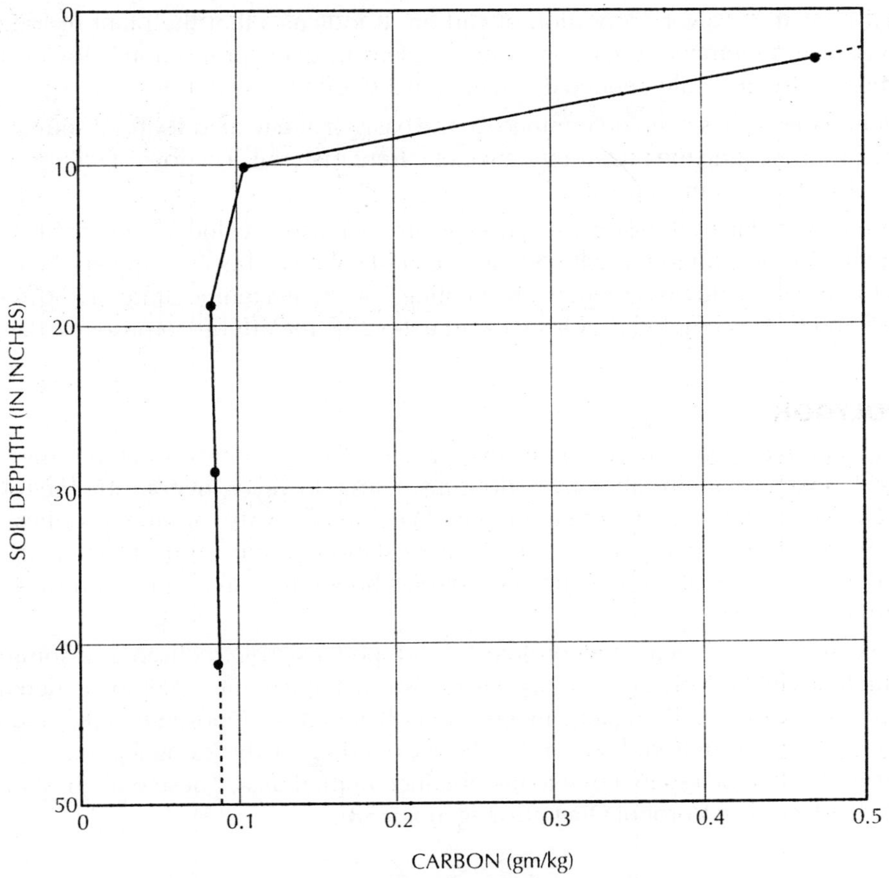

Fig. 5.57 **Depthwise Variation of Carbon**

Interpretation

The six chemical characteristics determined at various depths are pH, organic matter, nitrogen, CaO (acetic acid), CaO (HCl) and carbon.

As far as chemical status of acidity and alkalinity is concerned, the pH of the surface horizon is slightly acidic (5.68), and downward it changes from neutral to low alkalinity (7.54). This soil seems to be suitable for agriculture, even for paddy cultivation.

Organic matter is much higher in the surface horizon (0–6"/0–15cm). Gradually downward organic matter reduces in proportion. This indicates that there is presence of thick vegetation as it is 0.8084 in the surface horizon. Downward decrease of organic matter is a natural phenomenon as is observed in most of the soils of tropical landscape with not so long and well spread root networks.

The nitrogen content of different horizons is obviously lower from surface downward. The greater proportion of organic matter in the surface horizon is also reflected in the quantity of nitrogen which also is maximum in surface horizon and proportionately decreases downward, as organic matter is the source of nitrogen.

Carbon is also produced from organic residues of soil. Practically, in different soils C:N varies with specific values, normally it is 10:1. In this soil sample of Khiria, C:N is 8.39:1 which is a little less than normal indicating lower proportion of carbon. It indicates that the plant residues are highly decomposed and elementary carbon is not present in good proportion. However, the presence of carbon is also gradually redued downward in the soil sample of Khiria.

CaO or Calcium Oxide has been determined on the basis of acetic acid sol base shows that it increases downward indicating the higher influence of parent material. The lowest value is 3.08, whereas at about 48" (121.92 cm) depth it is 7.4.

CaO determined with HCl sol shows also a downward increase in value. However, this value is much lower than that of CaO tested with N/2 acetic acid sol base, because the application of HCl produces CO_2 and the volume is reduced. By heating $CaCO_3$ at a temperature of 550°C, CaO can be produced and CO_2 is emitted. CaO is used in extractive metallurgy to produce slag with the impurities in metal ores.

THIESSEN POLYGON

Normally, rainfall does not occur uniformly everywhere. The quantity of rainfall is measured by a Raingauge. Raingauges are installed by various agencies. However, over a small region the distribution of Raingauge station may not be uniform. We often face also another problem, how much area can be allotted to one particular Raingauge station is uncertain. It means that the measured rainfall of one particular Raingange rxepresents how much area in its surroundings is difficult to determine.

Alfred H. Thiessen, an American meteorologist developed a simple method as a solution to this problem sometimes in the early 20th century. He devised a mathematical method to determine the area meant for one particular Raingauge in terms of polygon. It is supposed that the boundary of the polygon is,more or less, uniformly spaced in the surroundings of the Raingauge station. Thus he assigned the significance of a spatial unit to the obtained rainfall data. These polygons are also known as Voronoi Polygons or Voronoi Diagrams (fig. no. 5.58).

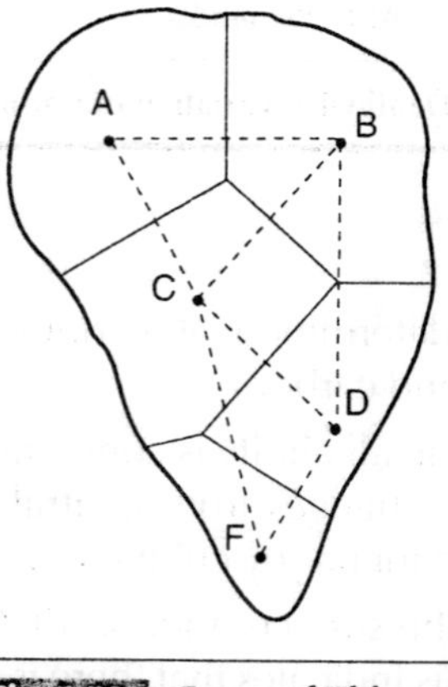

Fig. 5.58 Form of Thiessen Polygon

The polygons are drawn through some simple geometric methods. First, two neighbouring raingauge stations are to be connected by a straight line, then a bisector of this line is drawn perpendicular to the line. This bisector extends up to the boundary of the spatial unit. This way the required number of bisectors are drawn on the lines connecting the neighbouring stations. The bisectors intersect one another in neighbouring areas. These intersection points mark the lines of the polygon with the outer side open marking a part of the boundary of the spatial unit. Hence the outer side of the polygon will have a curvilinear shape, though the inner sides are marked by straight lines. Each of the polygons has some specific area and rainfall amount measured by raingange located in the area of the polygon. Now the average of rainfall amount is calculated on the basis of the following formula :

$$R = \sum_{i=1}^{n} \frac{r_i a_i}{A}$$

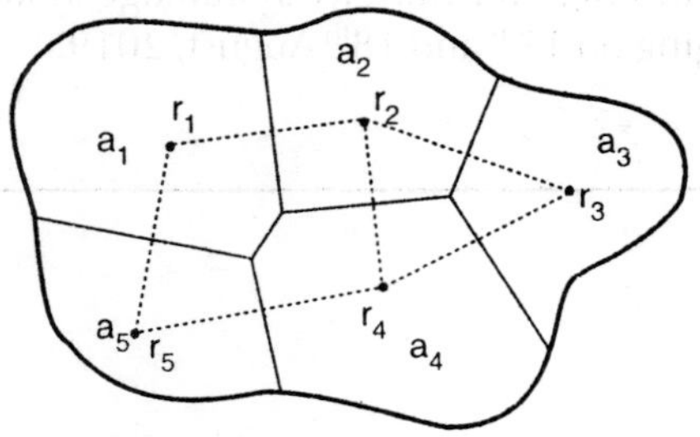

Fig. 5.59 Schematic Diagram of Theissen Polygon

Where, R = Average of rainfall amount; r_i = Rainfall at gauge station i ; a_i = Area of the polygon in the surroundings of raingauge *i* ; A = Total catchment area

Thiessen Polygons have been constructed for KMC area on the basis the excessive rainfall that occurred between 16th and 17th August, 2019, (Fig. 5.60)

TABLE 5.57

Table for rainfall in six wards of KMC on 17-08-2019 and area of Thiessen Polygons

Sl. No.	Ward No.	Name of the Measuring Station	Total Area of KMC (Km^2)	Area of the of pollygon (Km^2)	Rainfall of Individual Station (mm.)
1	14	Ultodanga	185	31.33	140
2	78	Mominpur		35.05	162
3	68	Ballygaunge		36.71	126
4	58	Dhapa		24.92	147
5	116	Behala		40.47	140
6	126	Chaubaga		16.53	155

$$R = \sum_{i=1}^{n} \frac{r_i a_i}{A}$$

$$= \frac{r_i a_i}{A} + \frac{r_{ii} a_{ii}}{A} + \frac{r_{iii} a_{iii}}{A} + \frac{r_{iv} a_{iv}}{A} + \frac{r_v a_v}{A} + \frac{r_{vi} a_{vi}}{A}$$

$$= \frac{140 \times 31.33}{185} + \frac{162 \times 35.05}{185} + \frac{126 \times 36.71}{185} + \frac{147 \times 24.92}{185} + \frac{140 \times 40.47}{185} + \frac{155 \times 16.53}{185}$$

$$= 23.71 + 30.69 + 25.00 + 19.80 + 30.63 + 13.85$$

$$= 143.68 \text{ mm}$$

Interpretation :

Through the analysis by Thiessen Polygon method we understand that on 16th to 17th August, 2019 Kolkata Municipal Corporation area received an average rainfall of 143.68 mm. This amount is too high for our city's drainage system. As a result, Kolkata suffered from widespread water-logging on 17th and 18th August, 2019.

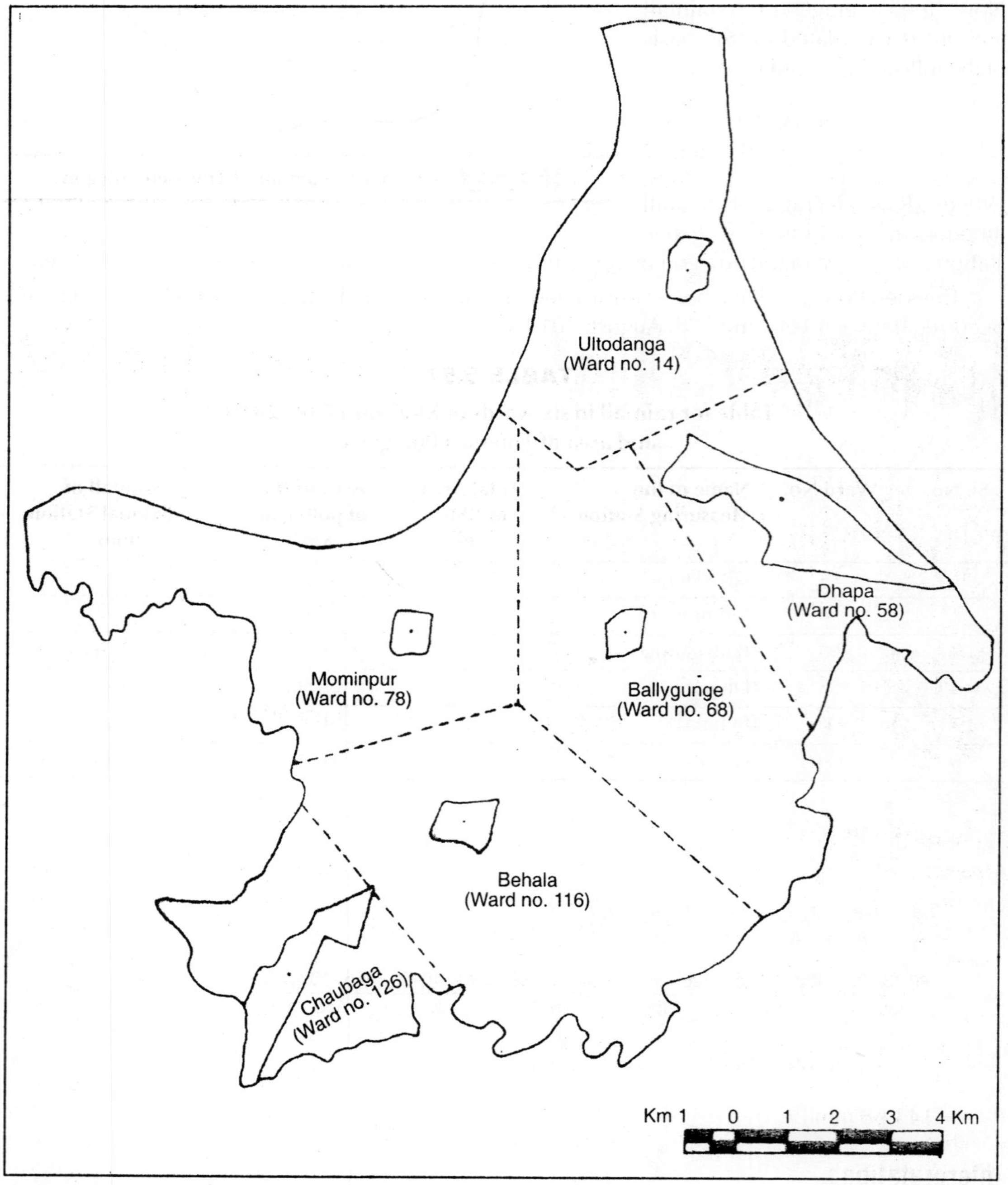

Fig. 5.60 **Area of Thiessen Polygons for KMC Area**

C H A P T E R **6**

INSTRUMENTS

The study of geography includes a lot of field observation which requires the use of instruments. The data collected from the field is processed and used to construct useful and expressive maps, diagrams and graphs. The instruments used in Geography can be divided into the following categories :

1. Survey instruments to measure angle, direction, area, height and distance of objects on ground
2. Instruments for observation of weather elements
3. Instruments for observation of geologic and geomorphic phenomena
4. Soil testing instruments
5. Instruments for measurement of area and distance on map

1. Survey Instruments to measure angle, Direction, area, height and distance of objects on ground

A few survey instruments are used in connection with carrying out a survey work along a traverse on the ground. They can determine the horizontal and vertical angles, distance and height of different objects with reference to another. Practically **the very work of field survey refers to the determination of distance, direction and relative height of any object or station of observation with reference to a known point, line or level respectively. The term traversing refers to the set of connected lines on field along which the surveying is accomplished.**

The instruments mostly used in this respect are Prismatic Compass, Dumpy level, Transit Theodolite, Abney's Level and Plane Table.

a) Prismatic Compass

The Instrument **:** Prismatic Compass (fig. 6.1) is a simple instrument comprising an aluminium ring graduated upto 30 minutes held at the top of a broad magnetic needle set in balance on a hard steel pivot. This compass is fitted in a circular metal box with a transparent glass cover. The glass-top is further covered with a hinged metal lid. On one side of the circular box there is a hinged eye-vane with a prism having convex vertical and horizontal face in order to magnify the marking of degree on the aluminium ring as reflected from the hypotenusal side of the prism. Two coloured sunglasses are set at a hinge to avoid direct sun-rays at the eye-vane.

On the other side of the circular box, there is a sighting vane consisting of a hinged metal frame with a horse hair at the centre. This horse hair in reality may be a fine silk thread or a metal wire. A hinged adjustable mirror is set on the outer side of the sighting vane in order to locate the too high or too low object through reflection.

There is a brake pin or knob which brings the oscillating circular ring to a standstill.

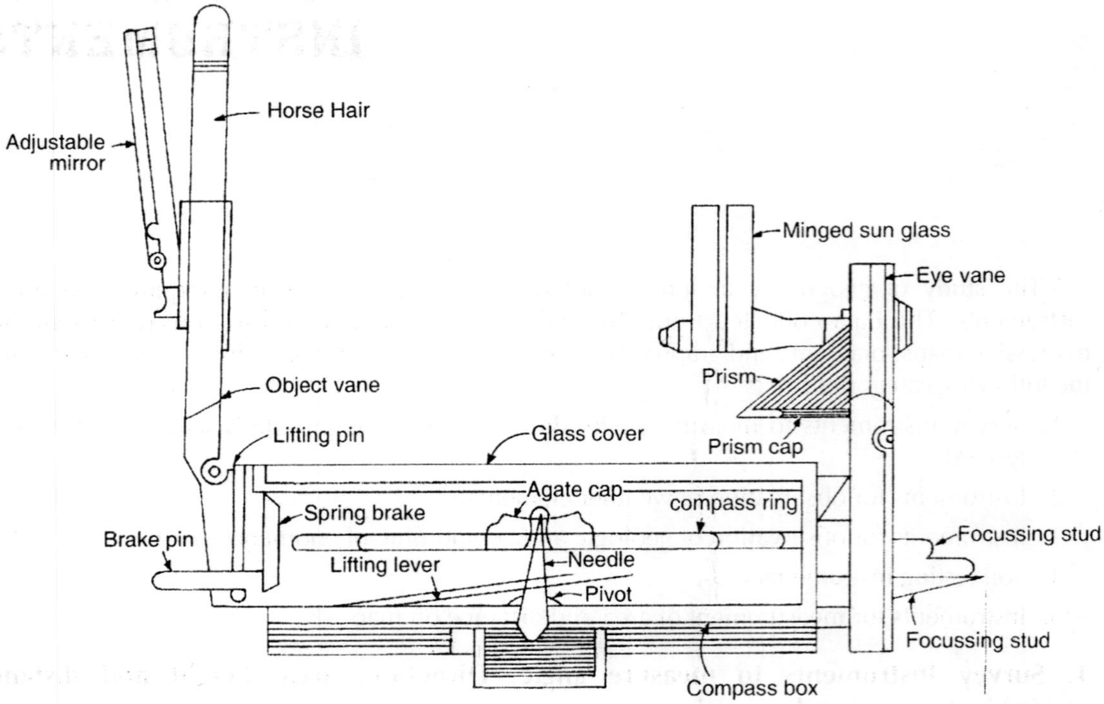

Fig. 6.1 **Prismatic Compass**

The metal box has a threaded bottom which can be screwed in by another threaded knob at the top of a ball fitted and adjustable in a socket of the compass-stand.

Use : Prismatic compass measures the horizontal angle with reference to the magnetic north-line. The bearing thus obtained is a magnetic bearing which is measured as a horizontal angular distance of any line of the traverse from the magnetic north in clockwise direction.

The corners of a plot or a building, bends of a road can be measured directly by prismatic compass. The bends of a meandering channel, if divided into segments, can be favourably determined by a prismatic compass.

Bearing :

Bearing in ground surface survey is a horizontal angle taken by an instrument from a reference direction. It is measured clockwise from the reference line. As the total value of angle in a circle is 360°, bearing can be measured upto nearly 360°, because 360° line marks the reference line. When the range of horizontal angle varies between 0° and 360°, it is known as *whole circle bearing*. On the other hand, if a circle is divided into four quardants, the range of angle is 0°–90°. Such a bearing is known as *quadrantal bearing* , marked with the particular direction of the quadrant from the centre of the circle, as it is NE, NW, SW, SE.

The survey instruments which can measure such horizontal angles are prismatic compass and theodolite. However, for prismatic compass, the reference line being the magnetic north gives magnetic bearing, i.e., horizontal angle from magnetic north direction. As a prismatic compass is controlled by a magnet, it gives magnetic bearing. The true angle between two lines can be determined on the basis of magnetic bearing. For this purpose, taking of two angles may be required.

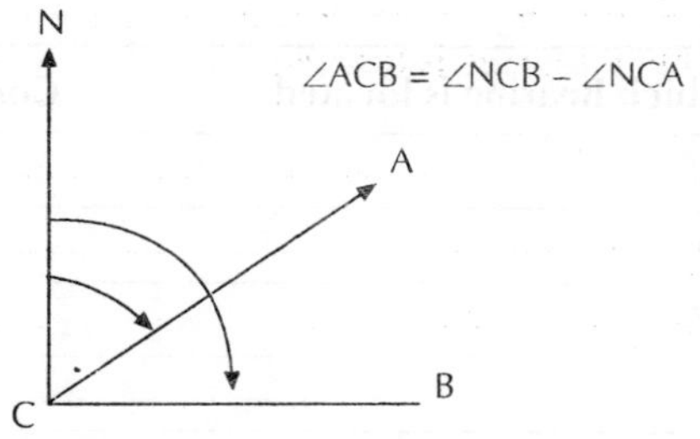

Fig. 6.2 Obtaining True Bearing From Magnetic Bearing

Without taking magnetic bearing we can get *true bearing* between two lines with the help of theodolite. In that case one of the lines is considered as the reference line from which the instrument should be rotated upto the other line giving the angle within the instrument in the two eye vanes A and B. The final angle is measured as the mean of these two angles. At the time of setting the instrument on the reference line the zero line of horizontal circle and vernier circle should coincide and should be adjusted with the reference line fixing the horizontal plate to that direction marking the line on the basis of a ranging rod fixed at the other end and seen through the telescopic lens when the telescope is also set in the horizontal position with the help of vertical circles. However, the telescope as well as the upper plate will be clamped. At the time of taking the horizontal angle the lower plate will be released from the clamp.

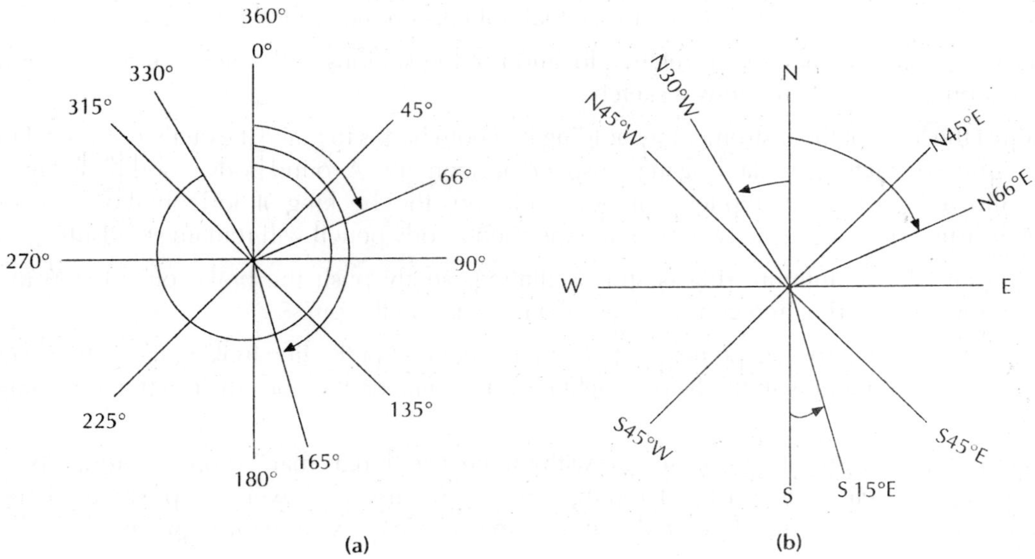

Fig. 6.3 (a) Whole Circle Bearing; (b) Quadrantal Bearing

The whole circle bearing when converted into quadrantal bearing is known as *reduced bearing*. It is defined by an acute angle along a line with reference to the meridian. For quadrantal bearing, the bearing measured is designated by N or S in the beginning indicating if it is from north or south. E and W indicate the reading towards east or west respectively. The conversion of whole circle bearing into reduced bearing can be done on the basis of the conversion relation as follows :

Name of Quadrant in which Bearing is located	Conversion Relation
NE	$\alpha = \theta$
SE	$\alpha = 180° - \theta$
SW	$\alpha = \theta - 180°$
NW	$\alpha = 360° - \theta$

Method of taking reading **:** Taking of reading by a prismatic compass means the determination of magnetic bearing which are truly horizontal angles with reference to the north direction. Each line in the traverse will have two bearings — (i) fore or forward bearing towards the direction of progress of survey and (ii) back or backward bearing in the opposite direction of the former. Actually, the fore and back bearing of a line are taken at two ends of the line in the traverse and the correctness of reading is known when the difference between the back bearing and fore bearing becomes 180°, as a straight line is supposed to subtend a straight angle. **The traverse along which the survey is to be carried out may be either a closed traverse, if the last station of observation coincides with the first one, or an open traverse, if the last and first stations are different.**

Taking of readings in a prismatic compass should be easy if we follow the steps given below :

1. Set the instrument on the station preferably at the initial point at one end of the first line, i.e., if the lines are AB, BC, CA, set the instrument at A station of AB line.
2. Check the exact location of the instrument with the help of a plumb bob, so that the centre of the circular box is exactly above A station. In absence of it, a stone held at the bottom-centre of the circular box can be dropped to see that if it falls on the ground pin of the station.
3. Have a visual idea above the relative location of the stations with reference to the north direction of the field and draw a sketch of it.
4. Adjust the level of the instrument by holding it in both hands to make it exactly horizontal in position, so that the circular ring may suspend horizontally. A round body wood-pencil may be allowed to roll at the top level of the circular box for checking of horizontal position of the instrument (if it is exactly horizontal, the round-body pencil will remain standstill).
5. If the circular aluminium ring is still oscillating, gently push the brake pin to stop the movement of the ring and gently release the pressure on the pin.
6. Locate the ranging rod on the next station at the other end of the line looking through the slit above the prism and with the help of sighting vane coincide the horse-hair with the ranging rod.
7. After fixing the instrument's horse-hair with the next station as marked on the ground by a ground-pin release the prism clamping screw and raise or lower the prism until the graduation values on the circular aluminium ring are clearly visible through the slit.

Then take the reading for the magnetic fore bearing of the first line in the traverse at the point where the horse-hair intersects the image of the circular ring. Slight up and down movement of the surveyor's eyesight will help to locate even the station on the image of the ring.

In a closed traverse the back bearing of the last line can also be taken from the first station. Similarly, the back bearing of the first line will be determined after the instrument is shifted to the next station and the line behind is looked at.

The bearings thus obtained are whole circle bearing (W.C.B.) which varies between 0° and 360°.

The same process of observing bearings will be repeated and continued along the traverse until the surveyor reaches the last line of the traverse (closed) and observes the fore bearing of the last line and back bearing of the previous line.

8. The distances between the stations may be measured with the help of a measuring tape.

Correction of data observed **:** The difference between the fore and back bearings of a line should be exactly 180°, if correct, but in practice it often becomes ±180°. The latter gives an incorrect data as the difference between the back and fore bearings should be a straight angle.

For such an incorrect data a mathematical correction is there for all the magnetic bearings (back and fore) having a difference of ± 180°.

The amount by which the observed data is less than 180° is a minus (–) error, which will be divided into two equal halves and one of the two will be added to the greater value the other will be subtracted from lower value of bearing. In a clockwise circuit usually the greater value is of backward bearing and the lesser is of forward bearing, except for the station at which the north-line is located within the closed traverse. In the latter case the forward bearing is greater by 180° than the backward bearing.

For a plus error (+), i.e., when the difference is more than 180°, the excess above amount 180° is divided into two equal parts and one is added to the lower value, whereas, the other is subtracted from the higher value of bearing.

Open Traverse : An open traverse survey by a Prismatic compass may be useful for marking alignment of a road or the course of a winding and narrow channel. It does not include any area, only directions and distances can be obtained.

For the purpose of drawing the traverse every line will have a forward bearing and a backward bearing. For an open traverse correction of plotting error by Bowditch's method is not required.

TABLE 6.1

Data of Open Traverse Survey

Lines	Distance	Observed		Difference	Error	1/2 Error	Corrected	
		F.B.	B.B.				F.B.	B.B.
AB	5 metre	35°30′	214°30′	179°30′	–1°	– 30′	35°00′	215°00′
BC	8 metre	325°	143°30′	181°30′	–1°30′	+45′	324°15′	144°15′
CD	3 metre	0°30′	220°30′	180°00′	–	–	40°30′	220°30′
DE	6 metre	340°30′	160°30′	180°00′	–	–	340°30′	160°30′

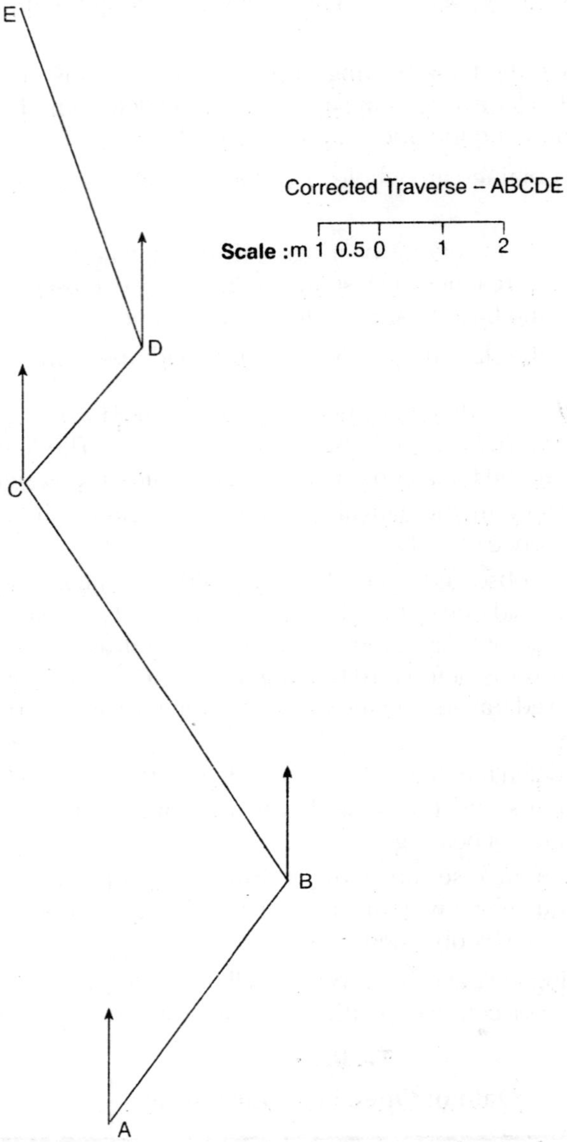

Fig. 6.4 Plotting of an Open Traverse by Prismatic Compass Survey

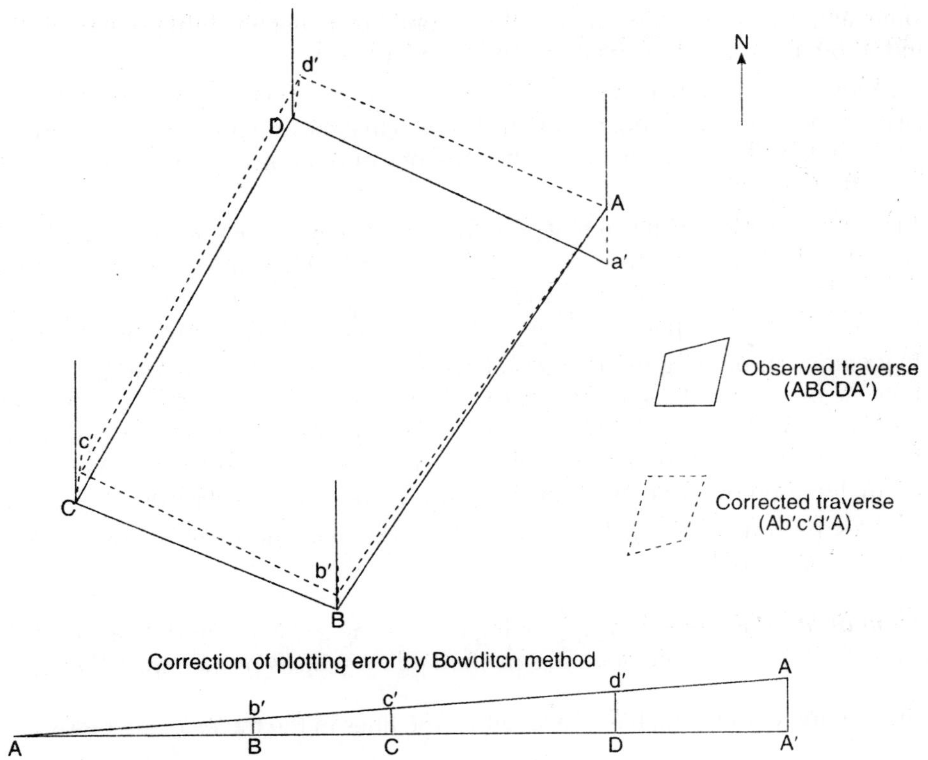

Fig. 6.5 Plotting of closed traverse in prismatic compass survey

TABLE 6.2

(The following is a methodical table prepared during taking readings of a closed traverse)

Lines	Distance in metre	Distance in scale 1 cm ¾ 2 m	Observed Bearing		Difference	Error	$\frac{1}{2}$ of Error	Corrected Bearing		Remarks
			F.B.	B.B				F.B.	B.B	
AB	16.32	8.16 cm.	213°30′	34° 30′	179°	–1°	30′	214°	34°	
BC	9.61	4.80 cm.	294°15′	112° 30′	181° 45′	+1° 45′	52′ 30″	293° 22′ 30″	113° 22′ 30″	
CD	15.13	7.56 cm.	30°00′	208° 45′	178° 45′	–1° 15′	37′ 30″	29° 22′ 30″	209° 22′30″	
DA	11.89	5.94 cm.	116°00′	293° 00′	177°	–3°	1° 30′	114° 30″	294° 30′	

Plotting **:** Plotting of the observed traverse should be done with the help of corrected forward bearing determining the horizontal angle between the north-line and any other line of the traverse. The length of the lines should be drawn on a suitable scale matching the size of paper on which the plotting is to be done. After measuring the forward bearing of the first line from the vertical north-line draw the length of the line according to scale, then at the end point of the line towards the direction of progress of the survey draw another north-line in vertical direction and plot the horizontal angle as well as the length of the second line to get the third point of observation at the end and so on (fig. 6.2) on the basis of data from table 6.1.

In a closed traverse the end point of the last line of the traverse polygon should coincide with the first point of observation, but it is often observed that the end point of the last line deviates from the first point. It happens so because of the presence of *plotting error* which might have generated from the following sources.

1. Inaccuracy in plotting the actual proportionate ground length of the lines in the traverse, e.g. if a line on ground measures 55 feet 7 inches and if the scale chosen is 1 inch to 10 feet, it will reduce the ground length into 5.55833 ...... inch on paper, but such a length can not be correctly plotted on paper, at least with the help of ordinary drawing equipments.
2. Inaccuracy in plotting the horizontal angle or correct forward bearing , e.g. a line in the traverse may have observed fore and back bearings as 92°0′ and 273°15′ respectively; now the difference between the two is 181°15′, which means that there is a plus error of 1°15′ ; this error then divided into two equal halves becomes 37′30″ each. Now the instruments normally used by students cannot measure such an angle correctly.
3. Besides, personal error, lack of parallelism between the north-lines may be another possible source of plotting error.

Correction of plotting error **:** This plotting error being graphical in character can be corrected graphically by Bowditch's method. This method follows the steps mentioned below :

1. Draw a line comprising half the length of the lines in the traverse, i.e., $\frac{1}{2}$AB + $\frac{1}{2}$BC + $\frac{1}{2}$CD, and $\frac{1}{2}$DA in the case of a closed traverse forming a four-sided polygon and mark the end points of the lines as A, B, C, D, A′ (A′ being the non-coinciding end point of DA line);
2. Put the gap between A and A′ of the traverse as a perpendicular on A′ point of the horizontal line as A′ A ;
3. Join A′ with A at the left hand end and draw other perpendicular lines on B, C and D. These perpendiculars will intersect A′A line at b′ , c′ and d′ .
4. Draw parallel lines at B, C and D points of the closed traverse in the direction of A from A′ maintaining their parallelism with A′A line which has formed the gap between first point and the last point.
5. Cut the respective lengths of Bb′ , Cc′ , Dd′ perpendiculars from these parallel lines and name them in the same manner as it was in the perpendiculars.
6. Join Ab′c′d′ A with pecked lines to get the corrected traverse (fig. 6.2).

Interior angles **:** Now this corrected closed traverse forms four interior angles the summation of which will be :

$(2n - 4) \times 90°$, n = number of sides of the polygon.

The interior angles can be determined by subtracting the corrected fore bearing from the corrected back bearing of the previous line, except for the station where the north-line is located within the traverse. For the latter case it should determine the exterior angle at the station first and then this will be subtracted from 360° : Exterior angle = fore bearing for the progressing line – back bearing of the previous line and 360° – exterior angle gives the interior angle.

Source of error and precautions : A Prismatic compass holding a magnetic needle is vulnerable to error particularly in close contact with any iron structure as the magnetic needle cannot show the magnetic north in that position. The particular sites which may instigate erroneous observations due to local attraction are :

1. areas of iron-mountains or exposed iron ore reserves,
2. areas close to or within big concrete buildings containing a lot of steel,
3. areas by the side of iron structure, such as iron pillars, lamp posts etc.,
4. at the close proximity to cables.
5. close to rails by the side of a railway track.

Moreover, the surveyor should be cautious not to hold keys, knife etc., not to wear steel band, iron buttons , steel rimmed spectacles etc. If the difference between back and fore bearings of a line is 180°, it means that there is no distortion due to local attraction at the time of observation.

Levelling

Definition : Levelling refers to determination of relative height of points or objects. The relative elevation or height of any object is obviously related to a reference elevation or altitude. It may be a bench mark or any other known spot height. Situations may arise when only the relative height of any point may suffice to determine the observed point on a vertical plane without any reference to a known elevation e.g., determination of a channel cross profile, where the line of sight may be taken as 'zero level' from which projection of the negative values of vertical height downward may determine the points on the cross profile.

Instruments used : Various types of levelling instruments are there, such as, Dumpy level, Wye Level, Cooke's Reversible Level, Cushing's Level, Tilting Level, Automatic Level etc. Of them the Dumpy Level is the most widely used one, as it is simple, accurate and quick-setting. A Sopwith Staff of folding type is used to get the staff reading of the object.

b) Dumpy level

This refers to a short, stable and compact instrument (fig. 6.3). It has a telescope fixed to its base. Unlike Wye Level, Cooke's Reversible Level or Cushing's Level, this telescope cannot be removed from its base. The telescope cannot be rotated about its longitudinal axis, though it can be moved horizontally around the vertical inner axis of the telescope.

The telescope is attached to the levelling head by three or four levelling foot screws which, by rotation in clockwise direction lowers the level of the telescope and vice versa. These levelling screws are threaded into the upper plate lying immediately below the telescope and their bottom part is a ball set in sockets where they can be rotated easily. The lower plate is made fixed with the tripod head by a tripod-head screw.

A clamp screw between the inner axis and level-base can clamp the telescope at a fixed direction. A spirit level is attached to the telescope by capstan headed screws. These can be adjusted to set the axis of the spirit level parallel to the line of sight.

The telescope is fitted with cross hairs to indicate the line of collimation or line of sight.

To set the telescope in a horizontal position the levelling screws are adjusted, so that the bubble of the spirit level is brought at the centre. The longitudinal axis is made parallel to the imaginary line joining any two of the three screws at the foot-plate at first, and the bubble is taken at the centre. Then the telescope is rotated in the horizontal plane and the longitudinal axis becomes perpendicular to the line previously mentioned. Then the bubble is again adjusted.

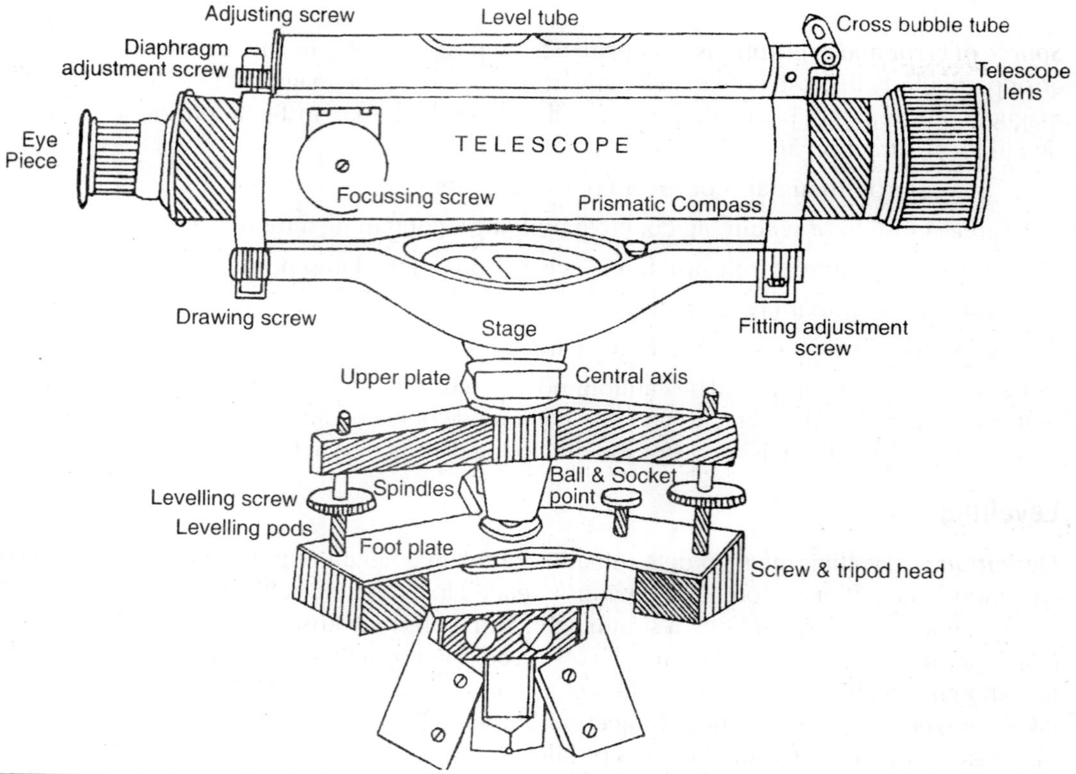

Fig. 6.6 Dumpy Level

The object glass is a lens nearest to the object being a compound of a double-convex crown glass and a convex - concave flint glass lens. This compound lens is achromatic. The eye piece of the telescope is usually a Ramsden type comprising two plane convex lens mounted at a short distance apart in a cylinder, with two convex surfaces facing each other. The cylinder screws in and out of the barrel and this motion enables the cross hairs to be brought into focus. This Ramsden type eye piece shows the final image as inverted although erect image telescopes are also there. It is also free from spherical aberration and curvature of the field.

There are cross hairs in front of the eye piece. The cross hairs are originally made of stretched spider's web filaments or fine silk. At present fine lines are also inscribed on glass. In some of the telescopes the central cross hair is flanked by two other horizontal lines. According to the inverted image the lower one seen throughout the telescope is known as upper stadia, whereas the upper one is known as lower stadia. Either of the two arrangements is termed the graticule which in turn is mounted in a diaphragm. The diaphragm with a graticule is mounted in an interchangeable cell which is pushed into or pulled out of the diaphragm with an extractor tool which screws on to the thread of the cell. A locking pin prevents it from turning when the tool is unscrewed.

The staff

The Sopwith telescopic staff is 4 metre or 14 foot long and it can be dwarfed into a smaller size. At the time of unfolding the inner narrower parts are taken out until a press button fixes the inner part to match the outer lower part. Previously this staff was made up of seasoned wood, but in current manufacture these are made of aluminium.

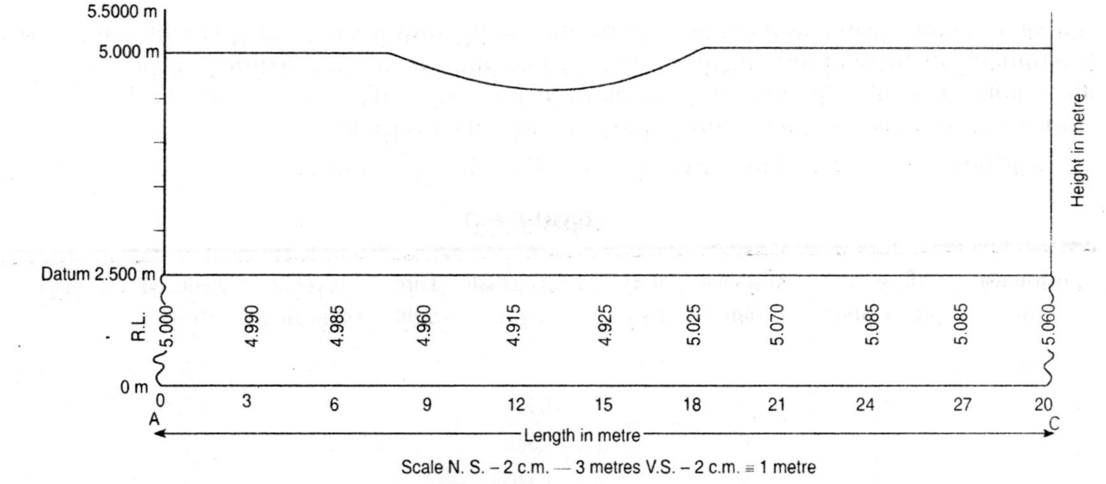

Fig. 6.7 Profile by Dumpy level

In foot staff the staff is graduated into tenths and hundredths part of a foot. The markings are given in black with white space between two black markings.

In metre-staff (fig. 6.7) each metre is divided into tenths and hundredths as staff of one hundredth part. The white space between black lines may give further smaller reading of 0.005m.

The staff should be held erect at the time of taking readings. Slight inclination may give an erroneous reading. The cross hairs show two vertical lines at the middle portion of the glass, so that it may check if the staff is held exactly vertical.

The staff is seen inverted through the telescope, and hence the reading will increase downward. The position of the cross hair in the middle will determine the staff reading, when seen through the telescope. In erect image telescope, however, the staff readings are higher upward.

Taking readings through a dumpy level

The levelling survey considers three types of sights in one set of observations until the instrument is shifted elsewhere. These three sights are known as back sight, intermediate and fore sight. The *back sight* refers to the first observation and the fore sight refers to the last observation keeping the instrument at one place. However, the station for *fore sight* of a set of observation will act as the back sight of the next set of observations when the instrument is shifted. Thus the reduced level at fore sight may act as a link between the two sets of observations with the Level at two different base stations. All other points of observation between the back sight and fore sight are *intermediate sights,* but there may be a particular set of observation in which the intermediate sight may be absent, because there are only two points of observation in that set. The point at which the instrument is shifted is known as *change point.* This station has two staff readings, one as fore sight of the previous set of observations and the other as back sight of the latter set of observations. Linking up the two sets of observations will require to add the staff reading of the back sight with the reduced level obtained as the previous level of collimation minus fore sight of the change point, and thus the new collimation height will be obtained.

The readings during levelling survey are taken setting the instrument at a convenient position wherefrom the points of observation for one set of data are clearly visible. When the instrument is reset at another place for taking readings, it should be noticed if the fore sight of the previous station is clearly visible from the second position of the instrument. Change in the position of the instrument will be required if all the points of observation are not visible from one place, e.g. when the points are set along road sides particularly at any bend of the road. The site of a building at the corner may also require such a shift in the position of the instrument.

The field book for levelling survey should follow the type shown below :

TABLE 6.3

Instrument at	Point of observation	Distance in m.	Back sight	Intermediate sight	Fore sight	Level of collimation	Reduced level	Remarks
A	1	0	1.370			6.370	5.000	5.000 (B.M)
	2	3		1.380			4.990	
	3	6		1.385			4,985	
	4	9		1.410			4.960	
	5	12		1.455			4.915	
	6	15	1.405		1.445	6.330	4.925	C.P.
	7	18		1.305			5.025	
	8	21		1.260			5.070	
	9	24		1.245			5.085	
	10	27		1.245			5.085	
	11	30			1.270		5.060	

Check : ΣB.S. – ΣF.S. = Last R.L. – First R. L.

ΣB.S. – ΣF.S. = 2.775 – 2.715 = 0.060

Last R. L. – First R. L. = 5.060 – 5.000 = 0.060

Types of levelling

Two types of levelling are usually done : 1) *Simple levelling* 2) *Differential levelling*

1. *Simple levelling* refers to the determination of relative height between two points both of which are visible from the position where the level has been set. Usually in such a case the level is positioned between the two points, may be at the midway between the two, if convenient. The staff is erected vertically at the two points and readings taken.

   If the instrument is set at a place from where both the stations are visible, the reduced level of one of the two should be given as reference level. The staff reading of that station should be added to obtain the level of collimation from which the staff reading of another station should be subtracted to get the reduced level of the station.

2. *Differential levelling* refers to a continuous levelling in which every next station is a change point. Such a levelling will require frequent shifting of the level at every next point. This method may be used of determine relative heights in areas of higher relative relief than the Sopwith telescopic staff can cover. The instrument may be positioned between the two stations also; in that case, the second station will act as change point and should be visible from the next position of the instrument, i.e., the staff, when held vertically, should cross the collimation height of the next instrument position.

Determination of reduced level

Reduced level of a particular point is determined by two methods : 1) *Rise and Fall method* 2) *Collimation method*

The principle of determination of the reduced level is to locate the particular point on land on the basis of its relative height with reference to the previous one or with reference to the line of sight at collimation level. It should be noted here that for one set of data starting from one back sight and ending at one fore sight it will have only one collimation level. **Whenever the instrument is shifted, the collimation level changes.**

Collimation level is determined by adding the staff reading of a station with the bench mark or spot height of that station.

1. ***Rise and fall method*** : This method observes the successive negative or positive changes in the elevation of the land with reference to its previous one. An increase in staff reading will indicate a fall of elevation, whereas a decrease will indicate a rise in elevation or positive change. Therefore, the principle is to locate the consecutive changes in elevation of the stations towards the direction of progress of the survey work. For instance, if station 'A' has observed a staff reading of 1.26 metre and 'B' is having a reading of 1.32 metre, it will indicate that there is a fall of 1.32 – 1.26 = 0.06 metre in the elevation of 'B' station with reference to 'A'.

   In this method, as all the observational changes are calculated in terms of a chain line connectedness , any error in computing the observational changes will be reflected in the data the successive of stations also. For instance, if A is having a spot height of 6.25 m and a staff reading of 1.26 m and B is having a staff reading of 1.32 m the reduced level of B will be 6.25 – 0.06 = 6.19 m. Now if C is having a rise and the staff reading is 1.20 m, the reduced level of C will be 6.31 m. Now if the computation of the reduced level of B is erroneous, it will be reflected in C also. Therefore, the chain of error will continue and the entire calculation of spot heights will prove erroneous like a house of cards.

   However, the method is easy and does not claim much theoretical conception.

2. ***Collimation method*** : In this method the collimation height should be determined at first. For this purpose the bench mark or a given spot height or a reduced level at a particular station should be added to the staff reading of that station. Now in the same set of data between one back sight and one fore sight, the collimation height will remain the same and the reduced levels will be determined for all the stations in that set of data by subtracting the staff reading of the station from the collimation height.

   On the change point the reduced level of the station will be added to the back sight of the station to enter into the new set of data and to determine the next collimation height. The reduced levels for the successive set of data will be determined by subtracting the intermediate and fore sights or staff readings from this new collimation height.

   This method has a good theoretical base, as the surveyor knows the level of collimation or the level of sight. Moreover, if one of the reduced levels becomes erroneous by computation, it will not affect the consecutive or successive ones. Great care should be taken in the determination of the collimation height because that is the base from which the reduced levels are determined.

Checking of data

The reduced levels determined can be checked mathematically in both the methods. For the collimation method the difference between the first R.L. and the last R.L. is supposed to be equal to the difference between the summation of backsights and foresights. Truely the rule is ΣB.S. – ΣF.S. = Last R.L. – First R.L.

For the rise and fall method the difference between the first R.L. and the last R.L. Should be equal to the difference between the summation of rise and fall. Any deviation from this premise will mean that the calculation has been erroneous. However, for the collimation method the correction is easier than that of the rise and fall method.

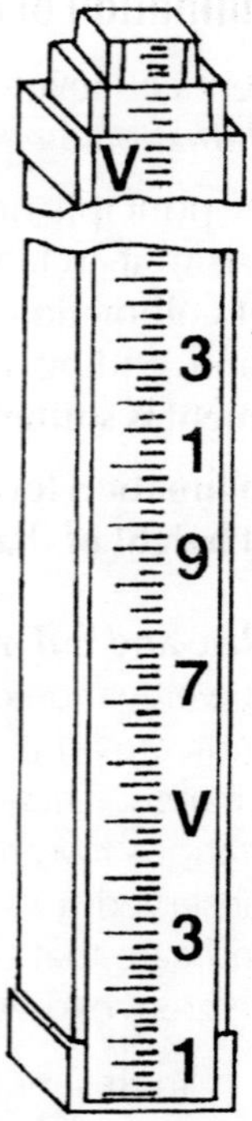

Fig. 6.8 Telescopic Staff

Plotting of data

By levelling survey a topographic profile can be determined in terms of the relative height of any point on the profile with reference to the given reference height or bench mark (fig. 6.5).

For drawing of the profile a datum surface is required. Datum is an arbitrary surface above which relative heights are plotted vertically, on the basis of the scale chosen. Along the horizontal line of the datum surface the distance between the consecutive stations of observation are plotted as points above which the respective relative height is plotted. There is another zero line below the datum surface and the vertical distance between the zero line and the datum is not true to scale. The reduced levels are written below the respective points on the datum surface and the zero line also reflects the same horizontal distances of the respective stations above which reduced levels are written.

Finally, the points of relative height are plotted above the datum surface and are connected by a free hand curve which depicts the profile of the surface along which surveying has been carried out. The scale along the vertical axis can be exaggerated for maximum of ten times the horizontal scale. For an uneven surface little exaggeration is needed, but if the surface is more or less levelled, the minor changes in relative height will only be reflected if the vertical scale above the datum surface is sufficiently exaggerated. The datum can be taken as the nearest height in round figure below the minimum reduced level.

Contouring

Through a combination of prismatic compass survey and dumpy level survey contouring can be done locally. Three methods are used in this respect. These are (1) contours (otherwise known as isohypses) by radial lines, (2) contouring by cross sections and (3) contouring by squares.

1. ***Contouring by radial lines*** : In this method a common point or station is taken at the centre from which a few radial lines are taken in different directions. Stations of observation or points are selected along three or more lines either at equal or at required intervals of distances. The distance between the points can be measured by a tape along a horizontal surface slightly above the original surface. Relative heights of all these stations or points are determined and spot heights are obtained by referring those to the bench mark of the area either by collimation method or by rise and fall method.

TABLE 6.4

Collimation method

Field Book for Dumpy Level survey

Station	Distance	Distance On scale 1 cm = 1 m	Staff Reading			CL	RL	Remarks
			BS	IS	FS			
0	0	0 cm	1.390				4.645	
A_1	3	3		1.400			4.635	
A_2	6	6		1.335			4.700	
A_3	9	9		1.330			4.705	
B_1	3	3		1.390			4.645	
B_2	6	6		1.390			4.645	
B_3	9	9		1.380			4.655	
C_1	3	3		1.370		6.035	4.665	BH = 4.665
C_2	6	6		1.380			4.655	
C_3	9	9			1.360		4.675	

Arithmetic Check :

$\Sigma BS - \Sigma FS$ = last RL – First RL

1.390– 1.360 = 4.675 – 4.645

0.03 = 0.03

TABLE 6.4A

Table for Field Book Prismatic Compass Survey

Lines	Distance on scale	Observed Magnetic Bearing		Error (E)	Half Error (E/2)	Corrected	
		FB	BB			FB	BB
OA_3	9 cm	89°	270°	1°	30′	89°30′	269°30′
OB_3	9 cm	159°	337°30′	−1°30′	45′	158°15′	338°15′
OC_3	9 cm	291°	112°30′	−1°30′	45′	291°45′	111°45′

TABLE 6.4B

Rise and Fall method

Station	Distance	Distance on scale	Staff Reading			Rise	Fall	RL	Remarks
			BS	IS	FS				
0	0	0	1.390					4.645	
A_1	3	3		1.400			0.010	4.635	
A_2	6	6		1.335		0.065		4.700	
A_3	9	9		1.330		0.005		4.705	
B_1	3	3		1.390			0.060	4.645	
B_2	6	6		1.390				4.645	
B_3	9	9		1.380		0.010		4.655	
C_1	3	3		1.370		0.010		4.665	BM = 4.665 m
C_2	6	6		1.380			0.010	4.655	
C_3	9	9			1.360	0.020		4.675	

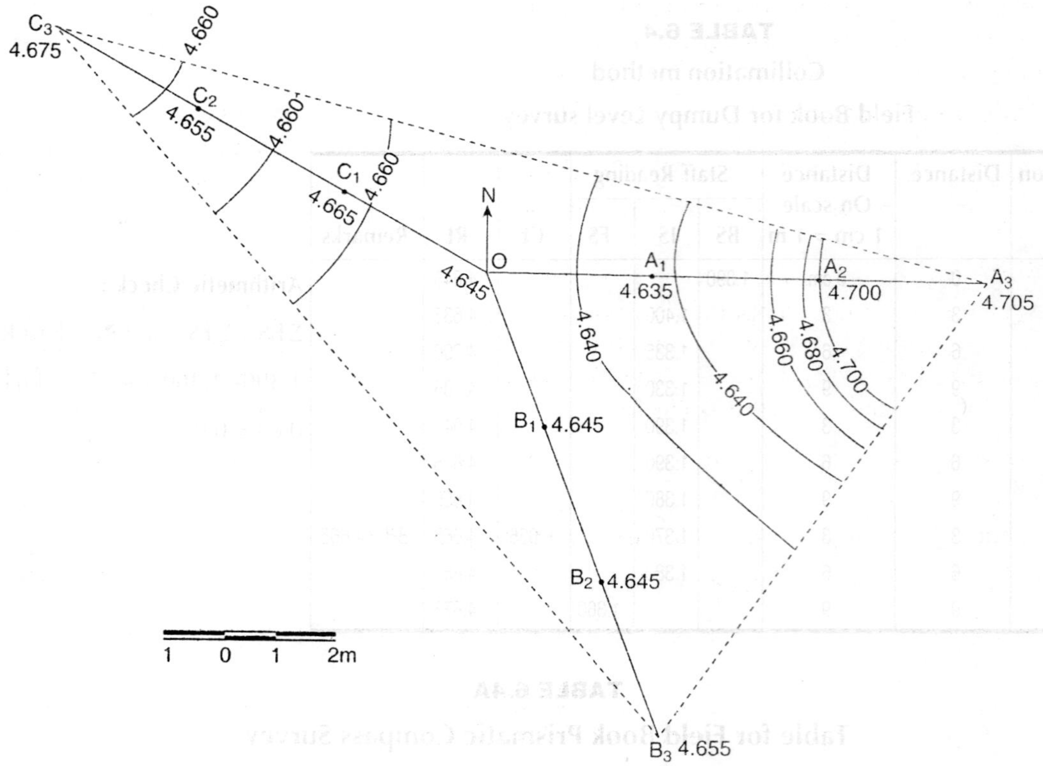

Fig. 6.9 Contouring by radial lines

The locations of the lines can be determined by fixing a prismatic compass (or any other instrument which can measure horizontal angle) at the centre or common point. With the help of a prismatic compass the magnetic bearing of the radiating lines are taken. At the time of plotting the lines, the directions are determind on the basis of respective magnetic bearings with reference to the north line (Table 6.3).

After the plotting of the radiating lines on paper the reduced levels are plotted. Then selected contours are drawn across these lines through interpolation at required intervals. The contour-interval is fixed on the basis of the total range of difference in elevation. For flat topography it may be in terms of centimetres and for rugged terrain it may be in metres (fig. 6.6).

2. ***Contouring by cross sections*** : In this method levelling is done along two sets of parallel straight lines perpendicular to each other. The distance between two consecutive lines is determined according to convenience or requirement. For a flat terrain the distance may be much greater than an undulating surface. The location of the bounding lines can be determined by magnetic bearing of them taken by a prismatic compass. The points of observation are determined on the basis of the particular nature of undulation of topography. Spot heights are obtained at these points.

At the time plotting, the bounding lines are plotted first. Then the intermediate lines are plotted on the basis of the respective interval distances between them for two consecutive lines. The spot heights determined for the selected points are plotted at their respective positions. Then contouring is done for selected values at a selected interval through interpolation.

3. ***Contouring by squares* :** In this method points for determination of spot heights are fixed at corners of the squares. The size of each square will depend on the nature of the terrain, but usually such methods are followed on a flattish topography. After determining and plotting the spot heights contouring is done by interpolation.

Theodolite

Theodolite is another important survey instrument (fig. 6.7) which can measure both horizontal and vertical angles with precision. For this purpose two protractors are there, one for measuring the vertical angle and the other for measuring the horizontal angle. Practically, all modern theodolites are transit theodolites as they can be rotated freely about the horizontal axis.

***Use* :** Traversing by theodolite and measurement of height and distance are common uses of theodolite.

Components : A transit theodolite comprises the following components :

(i) a telescope which rotates in a vertical plane around a horizontal axis (trunnion axis);

(ii) two spirit levels set at right angle to each other, on the upper horizontal surface of the vernier plate;

(iii) two 'A' frames or standards stand upright to support the horizontal axis about which the telescope rotates;

(iv) a vertical circle attached to the telescope measuring the vertical angle, and graduated continuously in four quadrants from 0° to 360° and fitted with a circular vernier at the inner side, that rotates about the horizontal axis;

(v) the standards are supported by an upper horizontal plate or horizontal vernier plate surrounding which there is a horizontal protractor for reading the horizontal angle or the movement of the line of collimation ;

(vi) the two horizontal plates being circular and mounted on two concentric tapered axis, the upper one being integrated with the inner axis are the lower one rotating on the outer axis ;

(vii) these two axes rotate in a tapered bearing which is cast with the levelling head ;

(viii) the levelling head has three (or four) sides at the three ends where there are tapered holes at the end of arms, in which threaded levelling screws are set and the screws are fitted with milled disc, for manual operation ;

(ix) each of the levelling screws is enlarged to a ball at the bottom and are fitted into a socket in the tribach plate or foot plate ; in some of the instruments the levelling screws are not made a ball and socket fit and they just rest on the foot plate with an extending levelling head;

(x) there is a large and vertical threaded hole in the tribach to take the tripod head ; in some of the instruments a threaded bolt passes upward through the tripod-head screwing it into the foot plate ;

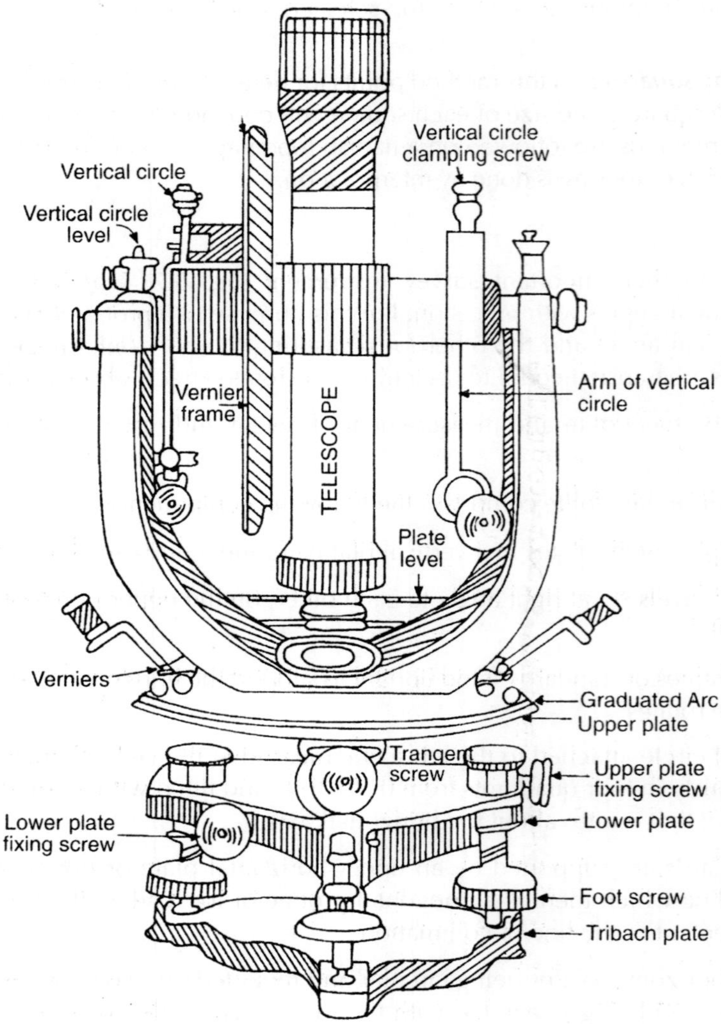

Fig. 6.10 Transit Theodolite

(xi) the tripod head is made fixed with the tripod ;

(xii) some of the tripods are fitted with a bubble and a sprit level to check if the tripod head is horizontally set ;

(xiii) a plumb bob can be suspended by a string from the underside of the levelling head to check if the instrument is properly centred on the station of observation. Besides, a few clamp screws are there to fix the telescope, lower plate and upper plate ;

(xiv) four eye vanes, of which two on the vertical circle and two others on the horizontal circle, are there each pair being at 180° to each other to read the instrument.

Measurement of vertical angle

For the purpose of measuring the vertical angle the following steps are taken ;

a) Set the tripod on firm ground (not cemented or mosaic) and check if the bubble at the tripod head comes at the central of the level.

b) Fix the theodolite on the tripod head by threading it in.

c) . Check with the help of plumb bob if the instrument is rightly centred on the station.

d) Check the sprit levels, if the bubbles are at the middle position which indicates a horizontal setting of the instrument.

e) Turn the theodolite exactly towards the object and fix both the lower and upper plate by clamping screws .

f) Turn the telescope upward until the middle stadia coincides with the top of the object.

g) Clamp the telescope by the vertical circle clamping screw. If at the time of clamping the telescope the middle stadia slightly deviates from the line of coincidence, the slow motion screw can be used to make it perfect again.

h) The reading is taken twice with the vertical circle once at the left and next time at the right of the observer.

i) At the time of changing the face from left to right the clamping screw of the telescope is loosened and the telescope is rotated about 180° ; then the upper plate is unclamped and is rotated for 180° with the help of the 'A' frame. Now the eye piece of the telescope will again come before the observer and the head of the telescope or the viewing glass will again face the side of the object.

j) With the vertical circle at left hand and at right-hand side readings for VC and VD will be taken.

The average of two VC and two VD readings will give the mean and the grand mean of the two will determine the vertical angle of the object with reference to the collimation level.

The table (Table 6.4) for taking data for vertical angle is given below :

TABLE 6.5

Instrument at	Face	Vernier Readings		Mean	Grand mean	Distance	Remarks
		VC	VD				
A	Left	44°30′	44°32′	44°31′	44°33′	25m	
	Right	44°35′	44°35′	44°35′			

Measurement of horizontal angle

The measurement of horizontal angle by theodolite is required mainly for traversing . The following steps may be taken for determining a horizontal angle :

a) As a horizontal angle occurs between two lines on a horizontal plane, one of the two lines is considered as the reference line which may be a 0° line.

However, at first the theodolite is set at the station of observation at the junction between two lines which form the horizontal angle, and perfect levelling is done.

b) The telescope is fixed in a horizontal position. For this purpose the zero mark of the vertical protractor will be made coincident with zero of the vernier C. Obviously on the opposite side (VD) it will coincide with 180° of the vertical protractor. The telescope in the horizontal position is clamped .

c) At an unclamped position both the upper and lower plates (the axis of the telescope being in a horizontal position) are set along the line on the left hand side and 0° or 360° of the horizontal protractor is made coincident with the zero of vernier A. Then both the lower and upper plates are clamped. If the zero coincidence is slightly disturbed, the slow motion screw may be used for a perfect coincidence.

d) The upper or vernier plate is unclamped and rotated clockwise until the axis of the telescope coincides with the other line. Then it is clamped and readings at vernier A and vernier B are taken.

Measurement of height and distance

Theodolite is most frequently used to measure the height and distance of objects from a reference station. The precision of the instrument can allow accuracy upto millimetre level. It can also make distant measurements from a station with the instrument fixed at any point, provided the object is clearly visible from the station of observation. However, the measurement can be done under two major approaches :

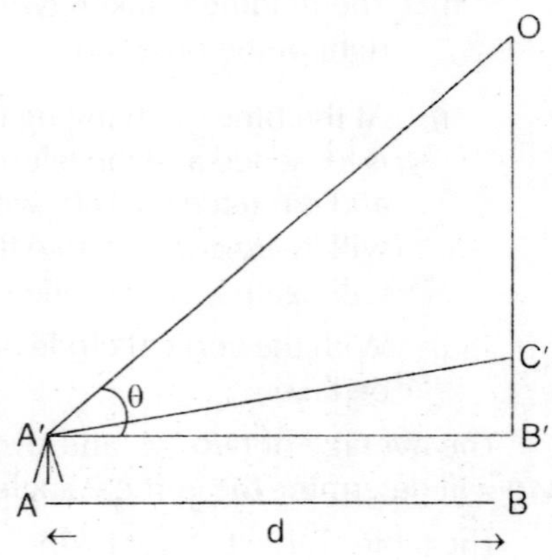

1. ***Base accessible*** : In this case the surveyor can reach at the base of the object and the staff can be held over there. This method is rather easy.

In this diagram O is the object, θ is the vertical angle between the collimation level and the object. AB is the distance (d) between the station of observation and base of the object, which can be measured directly with the help of a measuring tape.

Alternative Measurement of Distance (d) :

In Δ A'B'C' $\quad \frac{A'B'}{B'C'} = \cot 1^\circ \quad$ or $A'B' = B'C' \cdot \cot 1^\circ$ $\quad$ B'C' is the difference of staff reading with middle stadia at 0° and 1°.

∴ A'B' (d) = difference of staff reading at the middle stadia between 0° and 1° × cot1°

Measurement of height of object above base :

In Δ OA'B' $\quad \frac{B'O}{A'B'} = \tan\theta \quad$ or $B'O = A'B' \times \tan\theta \quad$ or $B'O = d.\tan\theta$

Now the height of O above B is B'O + staff reading at 0° (for a nearly levelled surface)

Measurement of height of object above station of observation :

For this the height of the instrument at A i.e., AA' is added with B'O.

Measurement of slanting distance A'O :

For this purpose if B'O and A'B' is known it may be derived as :

$\therefore\ A'O = \sqrt{(B'O)^2 + (A'B')^2}$

If B'O is known only it may be derived as

$A'O = B'O \operatorname{cosec}\theta$, θ = vertical angle at A'

If A'B' is known :

$A'O = A'B \sec\theta$, θ = vertical angle at A'

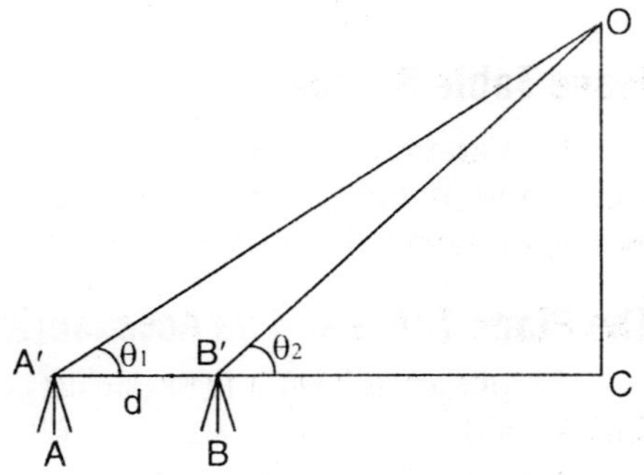

2. ***Base inaccessible*** : If the base of the object is inaccessible, neither the direct measurement of horizontal distance between the stations of observation and base of the object can be done nor any staff can be held below the object. Therefore, two indirect methods are used to find out the vertical height and the horizontal distance.

a) Same Vertical Plane Method :

To calculate the vertical height CO :

In $\Delta CA'O$: $\frac{A'C}{CO} = \cot\theta_1$ or $A'C = CO.\cot\theta_1$ .... (i)

After taking a known distance 'd' along the same vertical plane and instrument at B

In $\Delta CB'O$ $\frac{B'C}{CO} = \cot\theta_2$ or $B'C = CO.\cot\theta_2$ .... (ii)

Subtracting equation (ii) from (i)

$\frac{A'C}{CO} - \frac{B'C}{CO} = \cot\theta_1 - \cot\theta_2$ or, $\frac{A'C - B'C}{CO} = \cot\theta_1 - \cot\theta_2$

or, $\frac{d}{CO} = \cot\theta_1 - \cot\theta_2$ or, $\frac{CO}{d} = \frac{1}{\cot\theta_1 - \cot\theta_2}$ or, $CO = \frac{d}{\cot\theta_1 - \cot\theta_2}$

$\therefore$ The height above station A is

CO + AA' AA' = height of instument above ground

The horizontal distance A'C is calculated as

$\frac{A'C}{CO} = \text{Cot}\ \theta_1$ or, $A'C = CO.\ \text{Cot}\ \theta_1$

b) Oblique Plane Method :

In this method the base being inaccessible another point of observation is taken at an oblique plane, as it is 'B' at the at an angle α_1 and at distance 'd' in the associated geometric figure given below.

To calculate the horizontal distance AC :

In Δ CAO $\quad \dfrac{AC}{\sin\alpha_2} = \dfrac{AB}{\sin\{180 - (\alpha_1 + \alpha_2)\}}$

$$\text{or, } AC = \frac{d \sin\alpha_1}{\sin\{180 - (\alpha_1 + \alpha_2)\}}$$

$\therefore$ CO = AC $\tan\theta_1$ (height of object O).

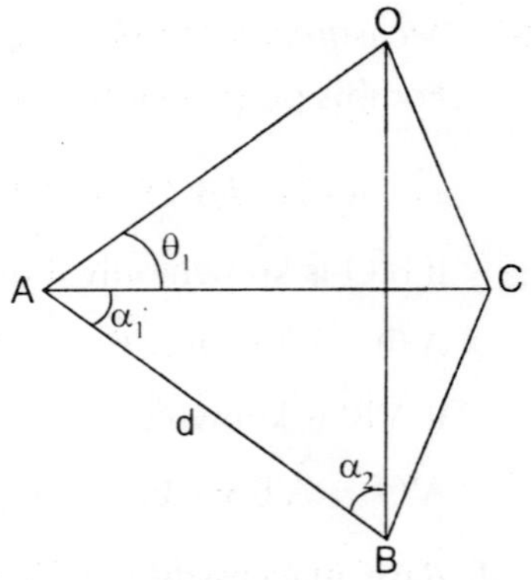

Plane Table Survey

It is a graphical method of surveying through which the field survey and plotting are done simultaneously. This survey is done mainly in connection with traversing and triangulation.

The Plane Table and its Accessories

The plane table (fig. 6.8) consists of a board mounted on a tripod. This table can be levelled and rotated as it is fitted with a levelling head or a ball and socket. The board is usually made of wood, preferably a well-seasoned teak or pine, varying from 40 cm. × 30 cm. to 75 cm. × 60 cm. in size.

An alidade is given to determine the line of sight. Attached to it is a straight edge for plotting the direction of the line of sight. Usually the alidade is made of metal or boxwood. The straight edge or ruler is 50 cm. long. This bevelled edge is known as fiducial edge. The alidade may be plane or telescopic and may either be fitted with sight vanes at both ends or with a telescope. One of the sight vanes has a narrow slit, whereas, the other has a central vertical hair or wire. In both the cases the line of sight occurs in the same vertical plane as the fiducial edge is parallel to it. If it is a telescope, it is provided with a vertical circle and a level tube as well as it has a cross hair and stadia hairs.

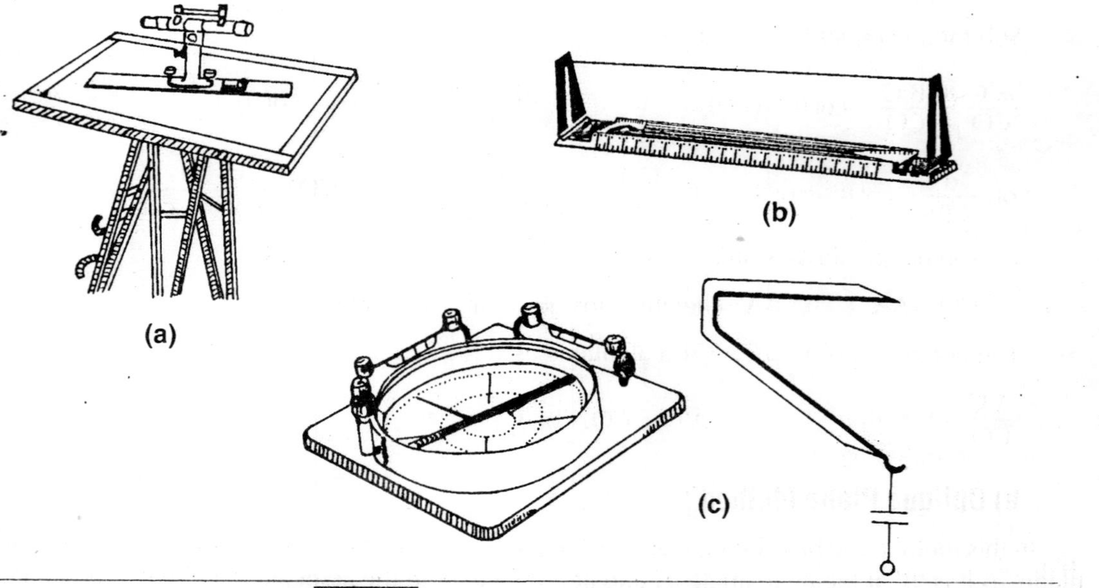

Fig. 6.11 Plane table and Accessories

A circular level or two bubble tubes set at right angle to each other are often attached to the alidade for levelling the table.

A trough compass or circular box compass with two bubble tubes for levelling fixed on a brass plate is used for marking the direction of magnetic bearing on paper.

A 'U' frame with a plumb bob is used for centering the table above the station.

Setting up of the Plane Table : For setting up of the table the following steps may be followed :

a) The tripod should be fixed with legs well apart at a convenient height in such a way as the centre of the tripod will remain exactly above the station.

b) The table should be placed exactly above the ground-station and centering should be done with the help of the plumbing fork or 'U' frame.

c) The table should be properly levelled with the help of level tube or circular level.

d) A good quality paper should be spread on the table.

e) Then orientation of the table for any subsequent station may be done either by the use of magnetic needle or by backsighting.

The trough compass or circular box compass should be placed along the line representing the magnetic meridian which is drawn on paper at the first station and the board is then turned until the ends of the needle are at opposite zero of the scale. Then clamping of the board is done. Usually this method is followed for small-scale mapping.

For orientation of backsighting if the table is set up over the station B on the line AB which has been previously taken as ab from station A, then the alidade is placed along the line ba. The board is turned until the line of sight bisects the ranging rod at A. The board is properly oriented and clamped at this position.

Methods of Plane Tabling **:** Plane Table survey is done by four methods :

a) Radiation b) Intersection

c) Traversing d) Resection

Of them the first three methods are more important.

Radiation **:** In this method the following steps are taken :

- A point 'O' is selected on ground. From this point O each station is visible.
- A point 'o' is fixed on the sheet of paper after the board is levelled and then it is clamped. U frame is used for centering the table exactly above O on ground.
- The direction of magnetic meridian is marked with the help of compass in the corner-top of the sheet.
- Various points at A, B, C, D, E, F, G etc., will be sighted by centering the alidade at O and rays will be drawn along the edge of the alidade pointing towards those points.
- The respective distances OA, OB, OC, OD, OE, OF, etc., will be measured by tape or chain and corresponding rays on scale will be drawn on paper radiating from o and thus a, b, c, d, e, f, g points will be determined on paper at the end of the radiating lines drawn on a selected scale. The points a, b, c, d, e, f etc., will be joined and the outline of the surveyed area will be determined (fig. 6.12a).

Suitability of radiation method: This method of Plane Table survey is useful for small areas which can be surveyed from a single station.

Intersection : For this method the following steps should be taken :

1. Two points O and C are selected. It is to be seen that these points can command the whole area and all points can be seen from these two points.
2. A line to join O and C is known as base line.
3. With the centre of the table on O a point o is taken on paper.
4. The magnetic meridian is determined at this station.
5. With the alidade at O the station C is sighted. Other objects at P, Q, R, S, T are also located. Rays are drawn towards these points along the fiducial edge of alidade.

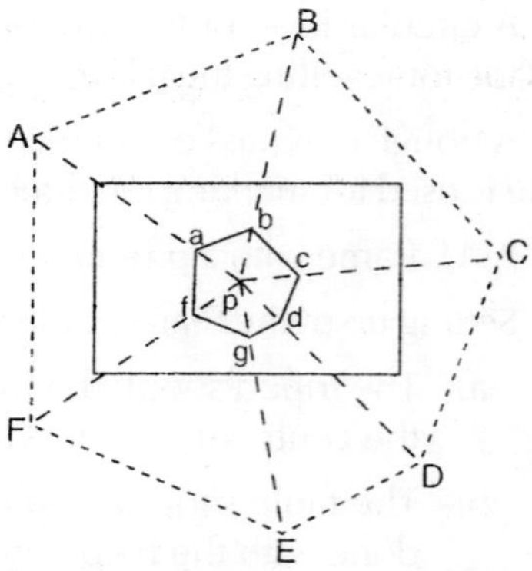

Fig. 6.12a **Radiation method**

6. The exact distance between O and C is measured and c is marked on the sheet.
7. The table is shifted to C.
8. Same objects are sighted from C and rays drawn. The intersections of these rays with the corresponding ones drawn from o determine the positions of the objects PQRST (fig. 6.9b).

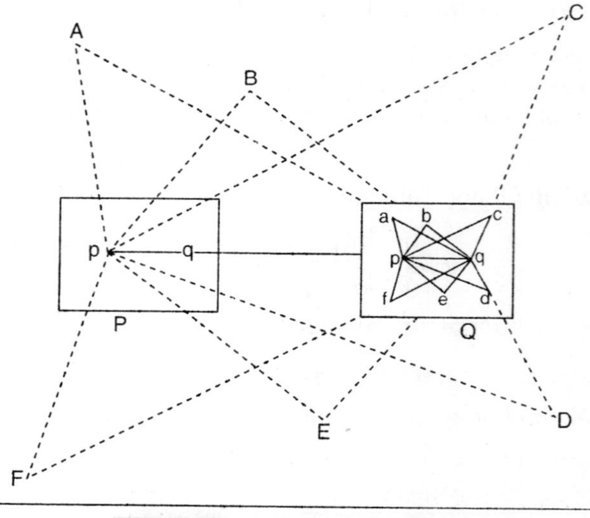

Fig. 6.12b **Intersection method**

Suitability : The method is more accurate. It is commonly used for locating the detail of the distant and commonly inaccessible points.

Traversing : For traversing the following steps may be followed :

a) Table is set at P. A point p is selected on the sheet of paper and the table is centered and clamped.

b) The magnetic direction is marked on paper.

c) Centering the alidade at p the ranging rod is sighted at Q and a ray is drawn in this direction along the edge of alidade.

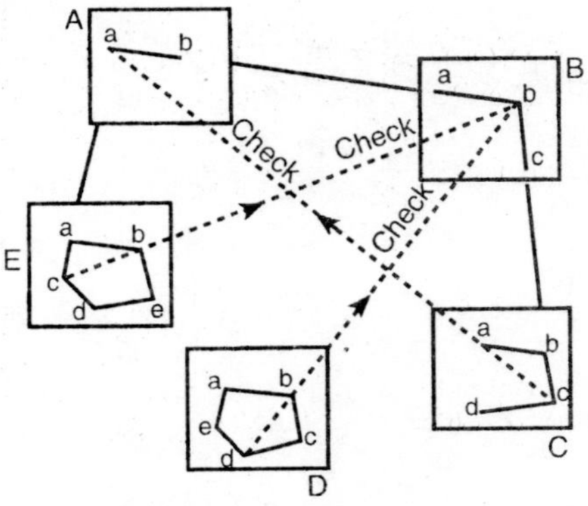

Fig. 6.12c Traversing method

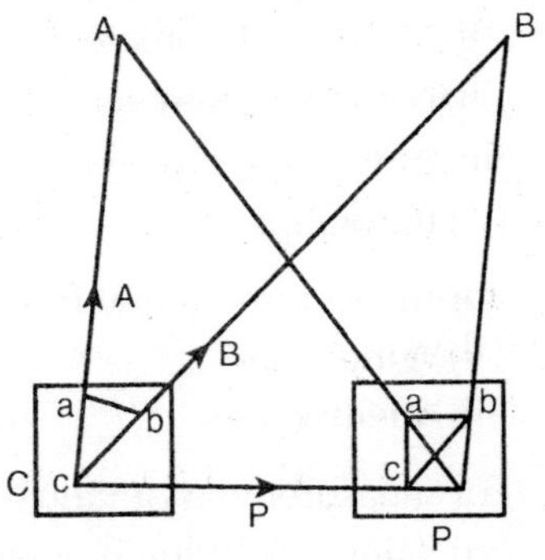

Fig. 6.12d Resection from two known stations

d) The distance PQ is measured by chain or tape and is converted into a scale-distance on a selected scale and is cut off from the ray as pq. Thus q representing Q is determined on paper.

e) The instrument is shifted and set on Q. Centering, levelling are done.

f) With the table centered at Q along QP, P is backsighted by alidade and clamping is done. The alidade centered on Q station and R is sighted and a ray along the edge of the alidade in the direction of R is drawn.

g) The distance QR is measured and set off to scale on the ray determining the point r on paper.

This way the same process will be repeated until all the remaining (fig. 6.12c) stations are plotted. At any of the stations the correctness of the procedure can be checked by taking sights of two or more preceding stations.

Resection : This method is similar to traversing, but only one linear measurement is required. A base line AB is measured and plotted with the table at A, and ac is towards stations C. Then the table is set up at station C, the position being estimated on the board and the table is oriented, so that the plotted line ca is directed towards A. B is sighted with the straight edge touching the plotted position of B and then the positon of C is represented by the intersection of ca and the straight edge. This procedure can then be repeated to determine the position of each succeeding station where it is always necessary to sight B since resection can be obtained by sighting any other previously plotted station (Fig. 6.12d).

2. Instruments for Measurement of Weather Elements

The elements of weather are continuously watched with the help of certain instruments which can keep day to day and hour to hour vigilance and can record very specific observations in order to reveal specific conditions of weather elements at a particular hour of a day. Such instruments are :

A) For measuring temperature

(i) Ordinary thermometer

(ii) Six's maximum and minimum thermometer

(iii) Dry and Wet bulb thermometer or hygrometer

B) For measurement of atmospheric pressure
  (i) Mercury Barometer
  (ii) Fortin's Barometer
  (iii) Aneroid Barometer
  (iv) Barograph

C) For measurement of wind direction and velocity
  (i) Wind Vane
  (ii) Anemometer

D) For measurement of Rain
  (i) Raingauge (Pluviometer)

E) For measurement of evaporation
  (i) Evaporation pan
  (ii) Atmometer
  (iii) Lysimeter
  (iv) Evapotron

F) For measurement of cloud, sunshine and dew
  (i) Sunshine recorder
  (ii) Duv-Devani Dewgauge

A. (i) ***Ordinary thermometer*** : A simple thermometer (fig. 6.10) has a bulb of mercury connected with a glass tube marked with a temperature scale. This scale may be given in Fahrenheit or Celsius. The Fahrenheit shows a range of temperature of 32° to 212°, whereas the Celsius (centigrade) scale marks it between 0° and 100°. It is placed on a block of wood and is kept hanging on wall at a shaded place where there is uninterrupted blowing of wind from outside. Often thermometers are placed within Stevenson's screen which is a wooden box on four legs and ventilated with regular gaps on three sides. Free movement of air makes contact with the thermometer in it.

The mercury in contact with the glass of the bulb get heated up and expands through the narrow slit within the other part of the glass tube. Practically this is a Maximum Thermometer in which there is a constriction in the capillary of the glass tube below the lowest graduation of the scale. The constriction allows the mercury to be forced through with rising temperatures but prevents it being drawn back with falling temperatures. This thermometer is mounted horizontally in the upper part of the stevenson screen. After the reading is taken the thermometer is reset by removing it from the support and holding it firmly in hand by the remote end and swinging it briskly downwards.

The Minimum Thermometer contains spirit as temperature measuring fluid. It is provided with a small dumb bell shaped index in the stem of thermometer. The index is kept inside the column by the surface tension of the meniscus. When the temperature of air goes downward the meniscus retreats towards the bulb dragging with it the index, until the minimum temperature is reached. When the temperature rises again, the index remains stationary. The end of the index farthest from the bulb indicates the minimum temperature recorded since the thermometer was last set.

To reset the minimum thermometer the bulb end is tilted upward which causes the index moving slowly down the tube up to the meniscus.

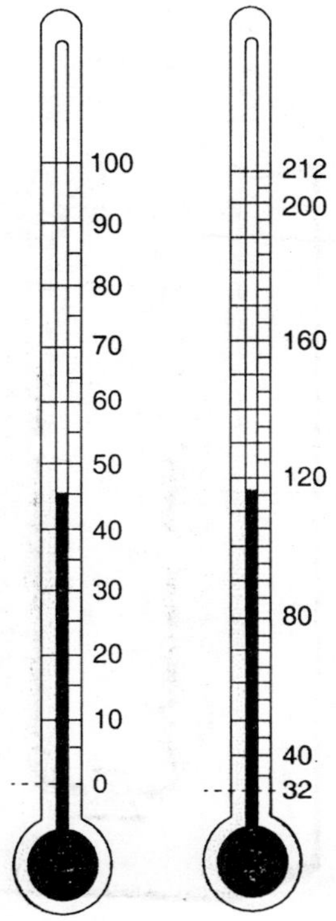

Fig. 6.13 Thermometer

A. (ii) ***Six's maximum and minimum thermometer*** **:** A thermometer which is used for recording maximum and minimum temperatures (fig. 6.14) automatically on the same thermometer, is known as Six's maximum and minimum thermometer. It saves the trouble of keeping hour-long vigil to note the two extremes of temperature for a given day. Daily maximum and minimum temperatures helps in finding out the mean daily temperature which helps us to analyse the weather of a place. They also provide a basis for finding out monthly and annual averages as well as annual and diurnal range of temperature.

Six's maximum and minimum thermometer (fig. 6.14) consists of a cylindrical glass bulb 'A' connected to an U tube with two limbs 'B' and 'C', whose other end is joined to another bulb 'D'. The lower part of the tube 'B' is filled with mercury and above the mercury there is alcohol in both the limbs. The bulb 'D' is partially filled with alcohol. Above mercury level in both the limbs there are iron indices 'I_1', and 'I_2', which are kept in touch with the sides of the tube by spring handles. They can be moved up and down by a small horse shoe magnet. Before taking readings the iron indices are brought in contact with the mercury level.

Both the limbs of the thermometer, 'B' and 'C' have graduations for reading of temperature. Limb 'B' records a minimum temperatu e and limb 'C' records a maximum temperature. When temperature rises, the alcohol in bulb 'A' expands and pushes down the mercury level in limb 'B' and consequently the mercury level in limb 'C' rises upward. When temperature falls, the mercury level in limb 'C' falls leaving the index 'I_2' in the same position. But in limb 'B' the mercury level rises due to contraction of the alcohol in bulb 'A' and the mercury column now pushes 'I_1' upward. The readings against the lower end of the indices 'I_1' and 'I_2' are taken and the maximum as well as the minimum temperature are recorded.

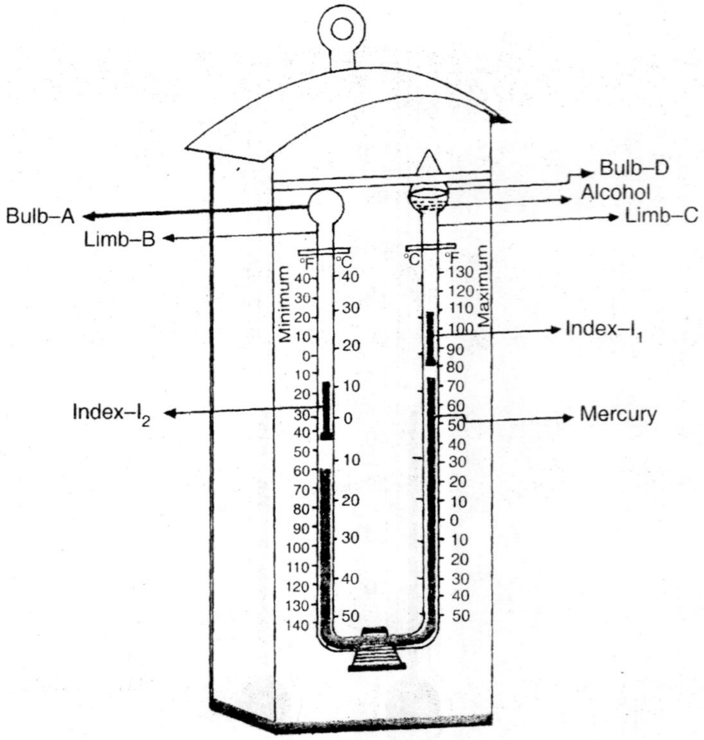

Fig. 6.14 Six's Maximum and Minimum thermometers

A. (iii). ***Dry and wet bulb thermometer or Hygrometer*** : A wet and dry bulb thermometer (fig. 6.15) is used to calculate the relative humidity of the atmosphere. These are two identical thermometers mounted together. The bulb of one thermometer is exposed to the air, whereas the second bulb is wrapped with a piece of muslin which is being kept constantly moist by a wick dipping into a small container with water in it. The wet bulb thermometer gives a lower temperature because the evaporation of water in the muslin requires energy and some of the energy is to be taken from the wet bulb the thermometer. Thus the temperature of the wet bulb thermometer is lower than the temperature of the dry bulb thermometer. When the air is saturated, there is no evaporation and both the thermometers indicate the same temperature but, when the air is dry, there is rapid evaporation and lowering of temperature due to the wet wick of the thermometer. The more rapid the evaporation, the greater is the lowering of the temperature. The difference in temperature indicated by the two thermometers can be used to determine the relative humidity with the help of a hygrometric table and dew point temp. table (6.5). If the altitude of the place of observation is less than 475.5 m (1500'), the 1000 mb. Hygrometric tables are used and if it is higher than that, 900 mb. tables are to be used. Dew point temperature and relative humidity are given corresponding to specific values of Dry and Wet bulb temperatures at intervals of 0.2°C. By interpolation it can be reduced to 0.1°C, if necessary. Computation of relative humidity referring to 1000 mb. Hygrometric table :

		Wet Bulb	
		29.6° C	29.8° C
Dry Bulb	34.4 °C	69	70

It means that at 34.4°C of D.B. temp. and 29.8°C of W.B. temp. the relative humidity is 70%.

TABLE 6.6

Table of Wet of Dry blub thermometer readings with corresponding percentages of humidity

CENTIGRADE SCALE

Dry Bulb C	DEPRESSION OF WET BULB C 0.5	1.0	1.5	2.0	2.5	3.0	3.5	4.0	4.5	5.0	5.5	6.0	6.5	7.0
—1	90	79	69	59	49	39	30	20	10	1				
0	90	81	71	61	52	44	34	25	16	7				
1	90	81	73	64	55	47	38	29	20	13	4			
2	91	82	73	64	57	49	41	33	24	17	9	1		
3	91	83	74	65	57	49	43	36	28	21	14	7		
4	92	83	75	67	59	51	43	35	32	25	18	11	4	
5	92	84	76	68	61	53	46	38	31	24	21	15	8	2
6	92	85	77	70	62	55	48	41	34	27	20	14	12	6
7	93	85	78	71	64	57	50	44	37	30	24	17	11	5
8	93	86	79	72	65	59	52	46	39	33	27	21	15	9
9	93	86	80	73	67	60	54	48	42	36	30	24	18	12
10	93	87	81	74	68	62	56	50	44	38	33	27	21	16
11	94	87	81	75	69	63	58	52	46	41	35	30	24	19
12	94	88	82	76	70	65	59	54	48	43	37	32	27	22
13	94	88	83	77	71	66	60	55	50	45	40	35	30	25
14	94	89	83	78	72	67	62	57	52	47	42	37	32	27
15	94	89	84	78	73	68	63	58	53	48	42	39	34	30
16	95	89	84	79	74	69	64	59	55	50	43	41	37	32
17	95	90	85	80	75	70	65	61	56	52	47	43	39	34
18	95	90	85	80	76	71	66	62	57	53	49	45	40	36
19	95	90	86	81	76	72	67	63	59	54	50	46	42	38
20	95	91	86	81	77	73	68	64	60	56	52	48	44	40
21	95	91	86	82	78	73	69	65	61	57	53	49	45	42
22	95	91	87	82	78	74	70	66	62	58	54	50	47	43
23	96	91	87	83	79	75	71	67	63	59	55	52	48	45
24	96	91	87	83	79	75	71	68	64	60	57	53	49	46
25	96	92	88	84	80	76	72	68	65	61	58	54	51	47
26	96	92	88	84	80	76	73	69	66	62	59	55	52	49
27	96	92	88	84	81	77	73	70	66	63	59	56	53	50
28	96	92	88	85	81	77	74	70	67	64	60	57	54	51
29	96	92	89	85	81	78	74	71	68	64	61	58	55	52
30	96	93	89	85	82	78	75	72	68	65	62	59	56	53
32	96	93	89	86	82	79	76	73	70	67	64	61	58	55
34	96	93	89	86	83	80	77	74	71	68	65	62	59	56
36	96	93	90	87	84	81	78	75	72	69	66	63	61	58
38	96	94	90	87	84	81	78	75	73	70	67	64	62	59
40	96	94	91	88	85	82	79	76	74	71	69	66	63	61
42	97	94	91	88	85	82	80	77	75	72	70	67	65	62
44	97	94	91	88	86	83	81	78	75	72	70	67	65	63
46	97	94	91	89	86	83	81	78	76	73	71	68	66	64
48	97	95	92	89	86	83	81	78	76	74	72	69	67	65
50	97	95	92	89	87	84	82	79	77	74	72	70	68	65
52	97	95	92	89	87	84	82	79	77	75	73	70	68	66
54	97	95	93	90	87	85	83	80	78	75	73	71	69	67
56	97	95	93	90	87	85	83	80	78	76	74	71	69	67
58	97	95	93	90	87	85	83	81	79	76	74	72	70	68
60	98	96	93	90	87	85	83	81	79	77	75	72	70	68

CENTIGRADE SCALE

Dry Bulb C	DEPRESSION OF WET BULB C 7.5	8.0	8.5	9.0	9.5	10	11	12	13	14	15	16	Dry Bulb C
—1													—1
0													0
1													1
2													2
3													3
4													4
5													5
6													6
7													7
8	3												8
9	7	1											9
10	10	5											10
11	14	9	4										11
12	17	12	7	2									12
13	20	15	11	6	1								13
14	23	18	14	9	6	1							14
15	25	21	17	12	8	4							15
16	28	24	19	15	11	7							16
17	30	26	22	18	14	10	3						17
18	32	28	24	21	17	13	6						18
19	34	30	27	23	19	16	9	2					19
20	36	32	29	25	22	18	11	5					20
21	38	34	31	27	24	20	14	7	1				21
22	40	36	33	29	26	23	16	10	4				22
23	41	38	34	31	28	25	18	12	6	1			23
24	43	39	36	33	30	27	20	15	9	3			24
25	44	41	38	35	31	28	22	17	11	6	1		25
26	45	42	39	36	33	30	24	19	13	8	3		26
27	47	44	41	38	35	32	26	21	15	10	5	1	27
28	48	45	42	39	36	33	28	23	17	12	8	3	28
29	49	46	43	40	37	35	29	24	19	14	10	5	29
30	50	47	44	42	39	36	31	26	21	16	12	7	30
32	52	49	46	44	41	39	34	29	24	20	15	11	32
34	54	51	48	46	43	41	36	32	27	23	19	15	34
36	55	53	50	48	45	43	38	34	30	26	22	18	36
38	57	54	52	50	47	45	40	36	32	28	24	20	38
40	58	56	53	51	49	47	42	38	34	30	27	23	40
42	60	57	55	53	50	48	44	40	36	32	29	25	42
44	61	58	56	54	52	50	46	42	38	34	31	27	44
46	62	59	57	55	53	51	47	43	39	36	33	29	46
48	63	60	58	56	54	52	48	44	41	37	34	31	48
50	63	61	59	57	55	53	49	45	42	38	36	32	50
52	64	62	60	58	56	54	50	47	43	40	37	34	52
54	65	63	61	59	57	55	51	48	44	41	38	35	54
56	66	64	62	60	58	56	52	49	45	42	39	37	56
58	66	64	63	61	59	57	53	50	47	43	40	38	58
60	67	65	64	62	60	57	54	51	48	45	42	39	60

CENTIGRADE SCALE

DEPRESSION OF WET BULB C 17	18	19	20	21	22	23	24	25	26	27	28	29	30	Dry Bulb C
														—1
														0
														1
														2
														3
														4
														5
														6
														7
														8
														9
														10
														11
														12
														13
														14
														15
														16
														17
														18
														19
														20
														21
														22
														23
														24
														25
														26
														27
														28
1														29
3														30
7	3													32
11	7	3												34
14	10	7	3											36
17	13	10	7	4	1									38
20	16	13	10	7	4	1								40
22	19	16	13	10	7	4	2							42
24	21	18	15	12	10	7	4	1						44
26	23	20	18	15	12	10	8	5	3	1				46
28	25	22	20	17	14	12	10	7	5	3	1			48
29	27	24	21	19	16	14	12	9	7	6	3	1		50
31	28	26	23	21	18	16	14	11	9	8	5	3	1	52
32	30	27	25	22	20	18	15	13	11	10	7	5	3	54
34	32	29	27	24	21	19	17	15	13	11	9	7	5	56
35	33	30	28	25	23	21	19	17	15	13	11	9	7	58
36	34	32	29	27	25	23	20	18	16	15	13	11	9	60

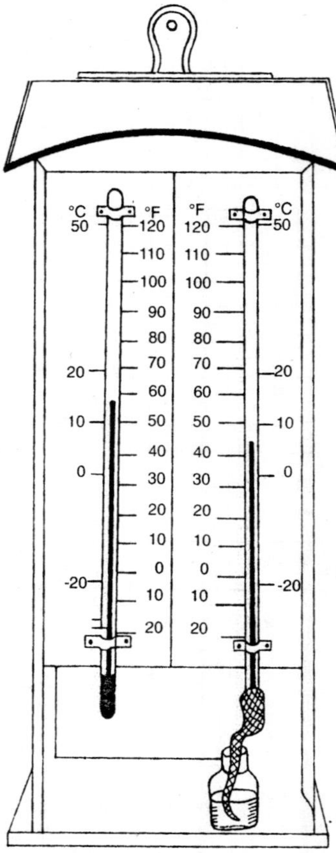

Fig. 6.15 Hygrometer

Computation of dew point temperature :

The values from the tables are as follows :

		Wet Bulb	
		29.6° C	29.8° C
Dry Bulb	34.4 °C	27.9	28.2
	34.6°C	27.8	28.1

Interpolating for dry bulb temperatures, we get :

		Wet Bulb	
		29.6° C	29.8° C
Dry Bulb	34.5° C	27.9	28.1

Therefore, for about 29.8°C of W.B. temp. the dew point temp. is 28.1°C.

In this connection it should be noted that if any digit is followed by fraction of 0.5, it should be rounded off to the next higher digit only when the digit is an even number. If the digit is odd, it remains the same. Therefore, the dew point temperature is 28.0°C.

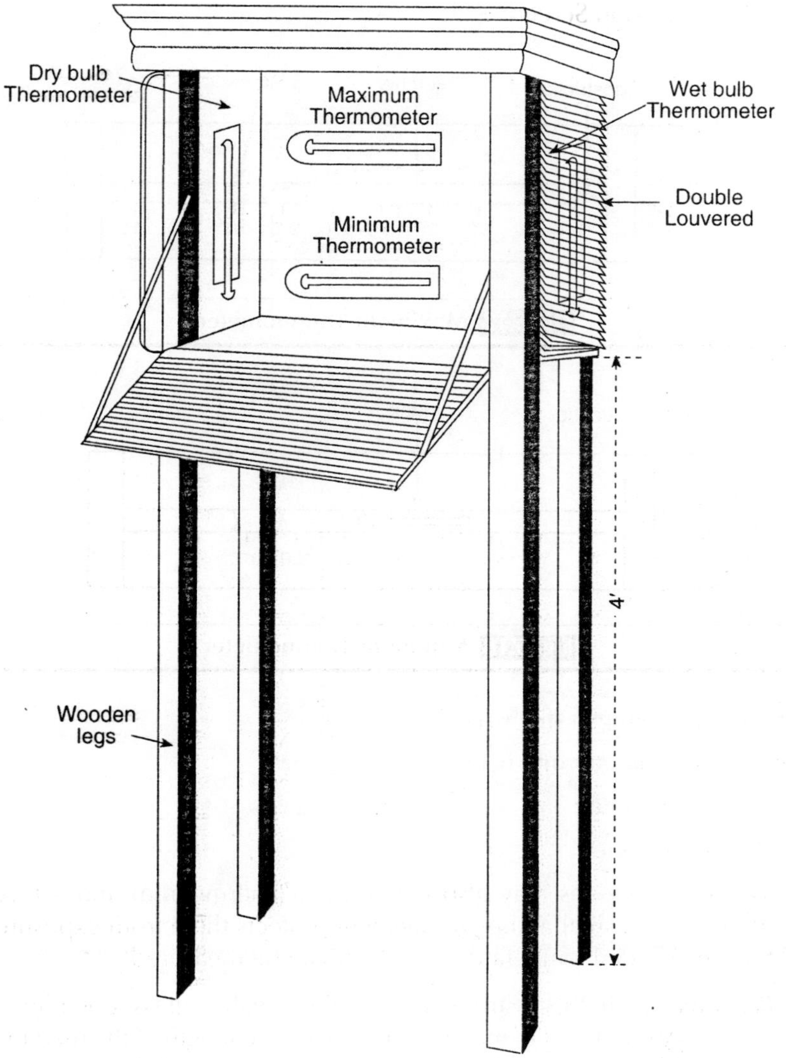

Fig. 6.16 Stevenson screen

A. (iv) ***Stevenson Screen*** : For recording the elements of weather, a meteorological station has an arrangement of a Stevenson screen (fig. 6.16). The screen consists of a wide wooden box whose four walls are double louvered to allow the free entry of air. It is placed on a stand about one and a quarter feet above ground. In order to get the shaded temperature, the roof of the box is made up of double boarding with an intervening air space to prevent the sun's heat from reaching the inside of the screen. The floor of the box is 4ft. above ground. One side of the box is hinged and it acts as a door which can be opened and closed freely for providing access to the apparatus inside the box and note the readings. The box is painted white outside, in order to avoid the direct impact of insolation. In meteorological observatories two separate thermometers are used for recording maximum and the minimum temperatures. The Stevenson screen comprises of the following :

Under present use in Stevenson Screen:

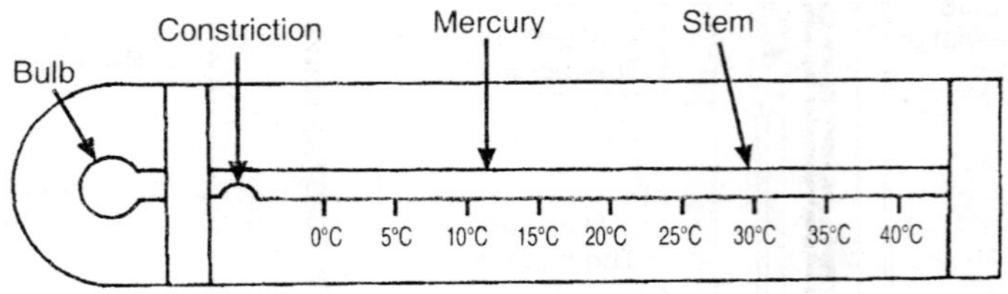

Fig. 6.17 Maximum Thermometer

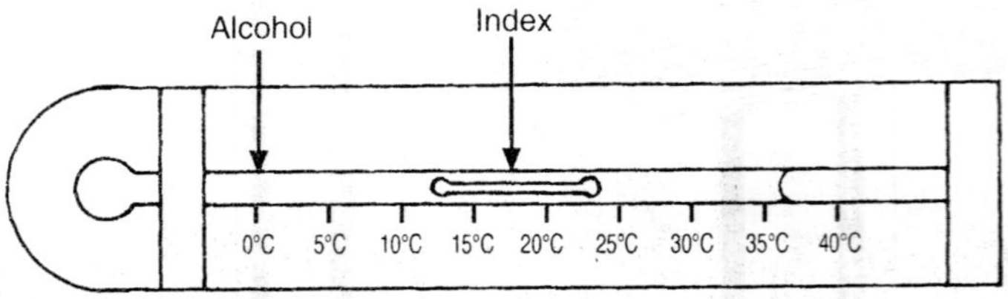

Fig. 6.18 Minimum Thermometer

a) Maximum Thermometer (fig. 6.14);

b) Minimum Thermometer (fig. 6.15) ;

c) Wet bulb Thermometer;

d) Dry bulb Thermometer.

Larger types of Stevenson Screens may also contain is a Thermogram and a Hydrogram. The screen is designed in such a way that the arrangement protects them from exposure to the direct rays of sun, and thus the shaded temperature of the air can be measured.

B. (i) ***Mercury Barometer*** : In this instrument a 33″ thick walled glass tube filled with mercury is inverted and immersed into a bowl of mercury (fig. 6.19). The length of the mercury column will show the pressure exerted by the atmosphere on the mercury of the bowl, the pressure of atmosphere being equal to the weight of the mercury column. The length is measured against a given scale and the atmospheric pressure is known with the conversion of the length in millibar.

B. (ii) ***Fortin's Barometer*** : Fortin's barometer (fig. 6.20) is a modification of original barometer. In this instrument a long glass tube filled with mercury is inverted into a container of mercury the bottom of which is fitted with a leather sack with considerable flexibility and scope of air passage. A cistern is placed at the bottom to push the mercury level upward. An ivory pin is fixed with its pointed head downward at the top of the mercury container. This ivory pin is reflected on the mercury below and when the mercury level is pushed upward with clockwise turning of cistern, gradually the reflected image touches the original ivory pin and then only the instrument is ready for observation. The glass tube is placed in a tube made up of brass to avoid breakage. At the upper part of the instrument a vernier scale is placed in front of the mercury tube by the side of the main scale which measures the length of the mercury column at any particular barometric pressure and at a particular temperature. This vernier can be moved up and down with the help of a screw fitted on the brass tube.

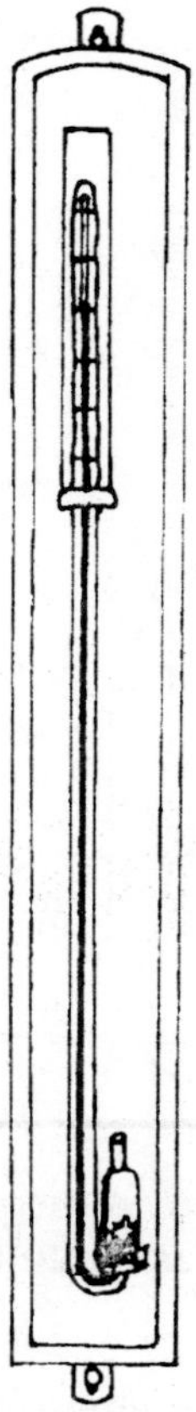

Fig. 6.19 Mercury Barometer

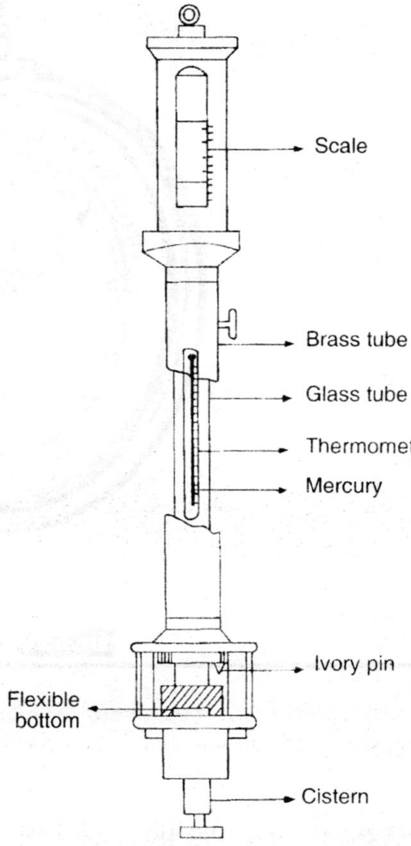

Fig. 6.20 Fortin's Barometer

To measure the length of the mercury column the upper part of the mercury column can be seen through the glass tube. Behind the upper part of the glass tube a white plate is there. In front of the white plate the upper meniscus of the mercury column is clearly seen, when the vernier scale is moved upward. For measurement of the actual length the screw on the brass tube is rotated to bring the bottom of the vernier just at the top of the mercury level. Then with the help of the main scale and the vernier the reading is taken. The length in millimetre, centimetre or inch is converted into millibar, as one inch of mercury column can exert 33.86395 mb. of atmospheric pressure and one centimetre of mercury column can show 13.33171 mb. of pressure.

B. (iii) ***Aneroid Barometer*** **:** An aneroid barometer (fig. 6.21) is dry and does not contain any mercury. It is some type of metallic chamber with a thin lid of elastic metal plate. The air within the box is almost totally extracted and then it is hermetically sealed. The box contains a spring which presses the lid outward against the pressure of the atmosphere. When the atmospheric pressure increases the lid is pressed inward and when it decreases the spring of the box pushes the lid outward. The relative movements of the metallic plate rotates a needle above a dial which indicates atmospheric pressure in millibar. On the basis of the variation of pressure various weather conditions are also marked on the dial.

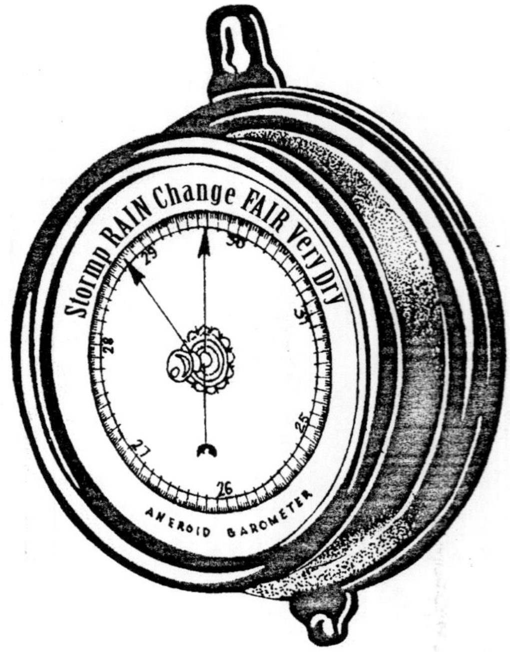

Fig. 6.21 Aneroid barometer

This instrument can be taken conveniently to any place and is frequently used in mountaineering and exploration, but the reading does not remain accurate for a prolonged period.

B. (iv) ***Barograph*** : A barograph (fig. 6.19) makes a continuous record of atmospheric pressure. In this instrument a number of vacuum boxes are placed one above another. A system of levers magnifies the displacement of these boxes and the movement is recorded by an ink-pointer on a paper attached to rotating drum. The displacement of the boxes occurs on the basis of atmospheric pressure on them. However the reading of a barograph is not very accurate.

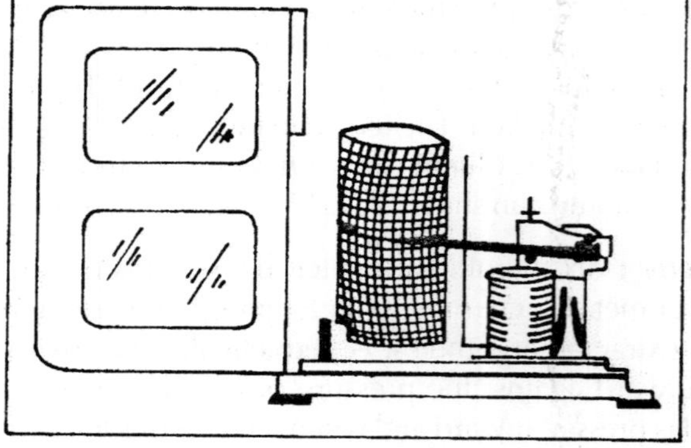

Fig. 6.22 Barograph

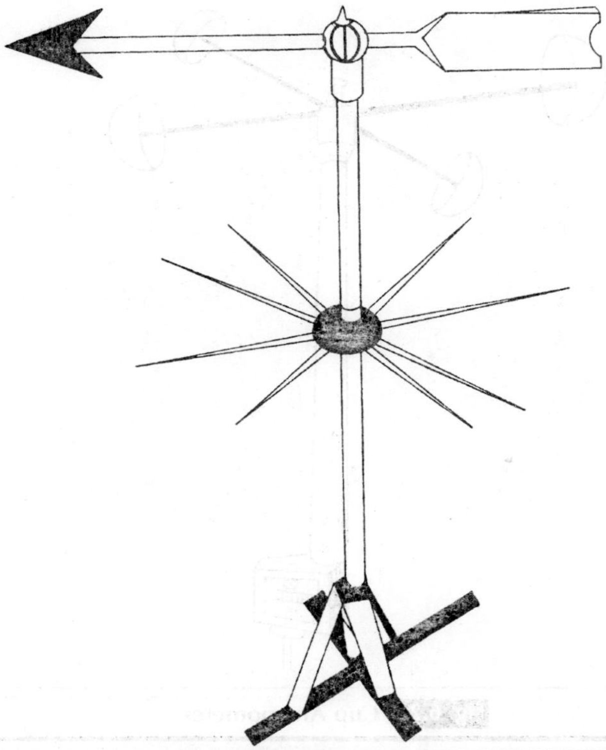

Fig. 6.23 Wind Vane

C. (i) ***Wind Vane*** : Wind vane (fig. 6.23) is also known as a weather cock. It is a common instrument used in all meteorological observatories. It is generally installed on roof tops of tall buildings where wind has a free flow. The wind should not be obstructed by trees or buildings where wind vanes are installed. There should not be any other hindrances also.

A wind vane consists of two parts :

a) An arrow which acts as a pointer. This arrow is known as the vane or cock. It is placed horizontally at the top of a vertically placed shaft. It is fitted in such a way that the arrow can rotate freely in any direction but becomes stabilized after some time.

b) The second component of the wind vane which is very essential has the eight cardinal points indicated by eight fixed rigid bars which indicate the eight directions — North, North-east, East, South-east, South, South-west, West and North-west.The arrow showing wind direction at the top of the shaft is mobile but the rods showing directions are fixed. The arrow points to the directions from which the wind blows and this principle should be remembered while noting the wind direction and it should be taken as the nearest of the sixteen points of the compass.

C. (ii) ***Anemometer*** : The cup Anemometer (fig. 6.24) is the most common instrument used for measuring the wind speed. Three or four light hemispherical metal cups are fitted at the end of horizontal axes. The axes are pivoted on a vertical shaft. On the lower end of shaft, a speedometer for measurement of speed is attached.

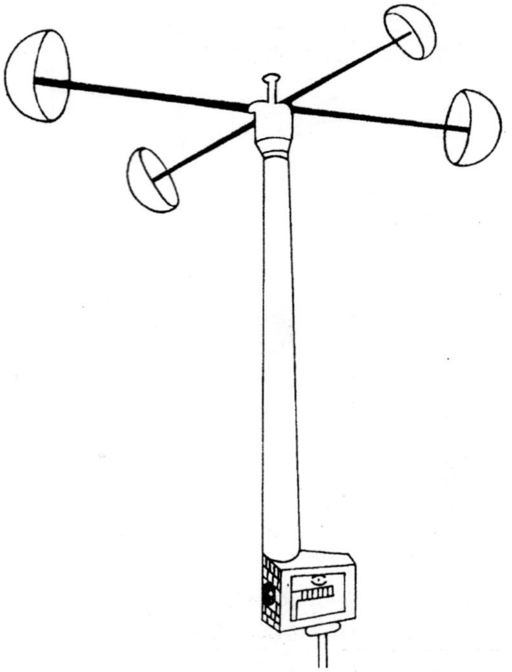

Fig. 6.24 Cup Anemometer

The speedometer is of two types :

a) Electrically operated and

b) Mechanically operated.

When wind blows, the cups provide resistance and consequently are moved due to the force of the wind causing difference of pressure between two faces of the cup. The vertical spindle about which the cups rotate, is connected to a mechanical counter through a gear system which counts the number of rotations made by the cups at a particular interval of time. The reading in the meter indicates the wind-speed in meters per second or kilometres per hour.

D. (i) ***Rain Gauge*** : Rainfall including other forms of precipitation (e.g. , snow, hail etc.) is measured by an instrument called Rain Gauge (fig. 6.25). It consists of a copper cylinder with a metal funnel either 5 inches or 8 inches in diameter, which leads to a smaller copper cylinder or a glass bottle. The hole on the funnel that leads down to the container is very small, so that evaporation of the collected water is minimised. The measurement of rainfall is done by removing the funnel, emptying the rain water in another container and in turn into a graduated cylinder which is a one and a half inches in diameter. The reading should be taken at eye-level and to an accuracy of 0.01 inch. For greater accuracy, a special kind of tapered measuring glass is available. It gives an accuracy up to 0.005 inch. A inch of rainfall means the amount of water that would cover the ground to a depth of 1 inch provided none is evaporated, streamed off, or percolated away. For meteorological recording, a rainy day occurs, when for 24 hours an amount of 0.01 inch or more rain is recorded. If the rain exceeds 0.04 inch it is considered a wet day. The daily recorded rainfall will be added at the end of the month to find out the total rainfall for the month. The total for each month is again added at the end of the year to obtain the annual rainfall.

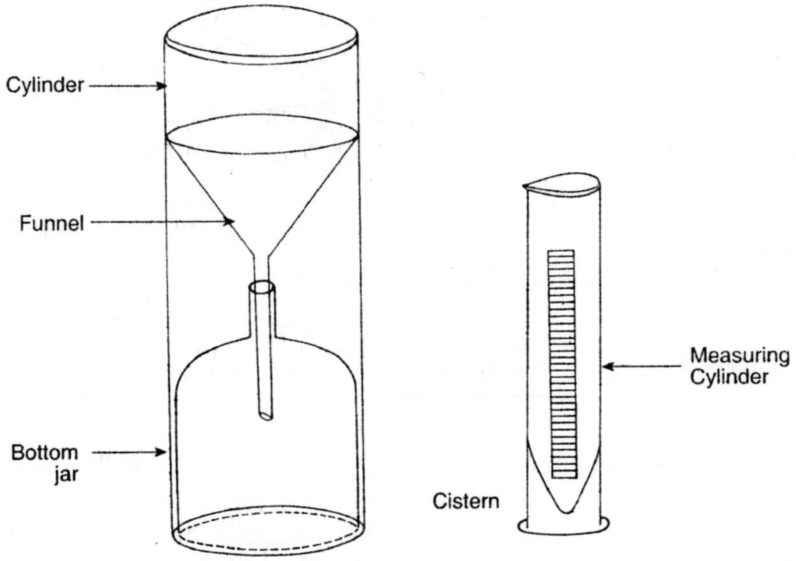

Fig. 6.25 **Rain Gange**

Precaution :

a) It should be kept on a slightly raised platform to avoid splashing of water.
b) It should be kept secured from intruding animals.
c) It should be half buried to provide stability.
d) There should be no disturbances and it should be sited well away from objects sheltering it.

While taking the record of rainfall, the rain water is poured into a measured jar at regular interval. The eyes are kept at water level. While doing so a few important conditions to be noted are :

a) No water from the outside is allowed to come in.
b) No part of the water is allowed to run off.
c) No part of water is allowed to drop on the ground.
d) It is not allowed to diminish, even invisibly due to evaporation.

Rainfall can vary from day to day, season to season. With the help of isohyets (joining places of same rainfall amount) we are able to show the rainfall distribution on the map.

E. (i) ***Evaporation Pan or Evaporimeter*** : Evaporation is measured with the help of pan evaporimeter (fig. 6.26). In this instrument the class 'A' type pan, which is approved by the World Meteorological Organisation, is 122 cm. in diameter and 25 cm. in depth (120 cm in diameter in the Indian type). It is made up of 20 gauge copper sheet which is tinned inside and painted white outside. A still well is provided inside the pan to keep the water surface undisturbed and to make the ripples broken. The well comprises a brass cylinder mounted on a heavy circular base provided with three circular holes at the bottom. The reference point for the depth of water is provided by a brass rod fixed at the centre of the still well. The top of this rod tapers at 190 mm above the base of the pan.

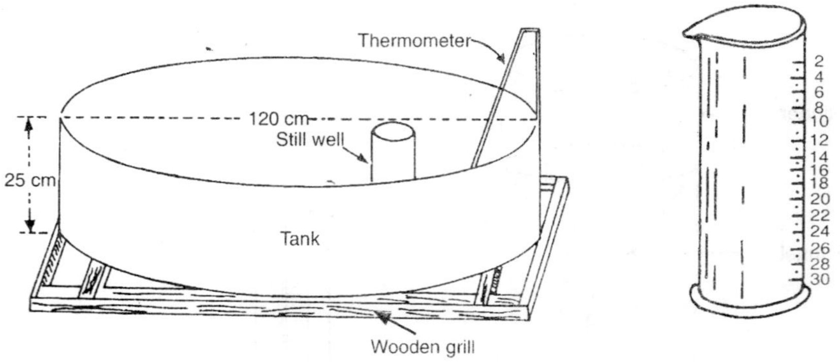

Fig. 6.26 Class "A" Pan Evaporimeter and Graduated Measuring Cylinder

The evaporation pan is filled up with clean water till the level of water touches the tip of the rod. To keep the pan out of the conduction of heat from the surrounding soil a white painted wooden grill is placed below the pan. The foundation should be firm in order to make the age of pan levelled and exactly above 36 cm. from ground. This also helps to keep it out of the reach of splinters of water bursting out from the surface at each drop of rain. The pan is provided with a standard wire mesh to prevent the loss of water from the pan by birds, animals etc. The temperature of water of the pan is measured with the help of a thermometer immersed below the water level in the pan.

To measure the amount of evaporation a graduated measuring cylinder made up of brass is also provided with this instrument. It has a scale of 0 to 20 cm. engraved inside along its height. The cross-sectional area of the measuring cylinder is exactly $\frac{1}{100}$ part of the area of the pan.

The evaporimeter should be installed at an open site where there will be no casting of shadow on the pan. Moreover, it should be noticed that the site should be free from flood or waterlogging even during heavy rains.

A few precautions should be taken to make the measurements accurate. The pan should be periodically checked for leaks. The wooden platform should be checked if the height of the rim is exactly 36 cm. above the ground level. Filling up with fresh water should be done every fortnight when cleaning of the pan will also be done. At the time of refilling it should be noticed that the temperature remains the same as that of the pan.

If on a particular day four full cylinders of water have been added to bring the water level to the reference point, the actual evaporation is determined by dividing the amount of water by 100 since the area of the pan is 100 times that of the area of the base of the measuring cylinder. Therefore, the evaporation during the day is 80 cm./100 = 0.8 cm. or 8 mm. If rainfall has occurred after the previous observation is done and if rainfall exceeds evaporation during that period, water has to be removed from the pan to make the water level reach the reference level indicated by the tip of the rod.

E. (ii) ***Atmometer*** : This instrument involves a water-filled glass-tube having an open end through which water is evaporated from a filter paper (Piche type) or porous plate (Bellani type). The tube supplying water is graduated to get evaporation in millimetre. It reflects the saturation deficit of the air. This instrument is more responsive to wind speed than radiant energy.

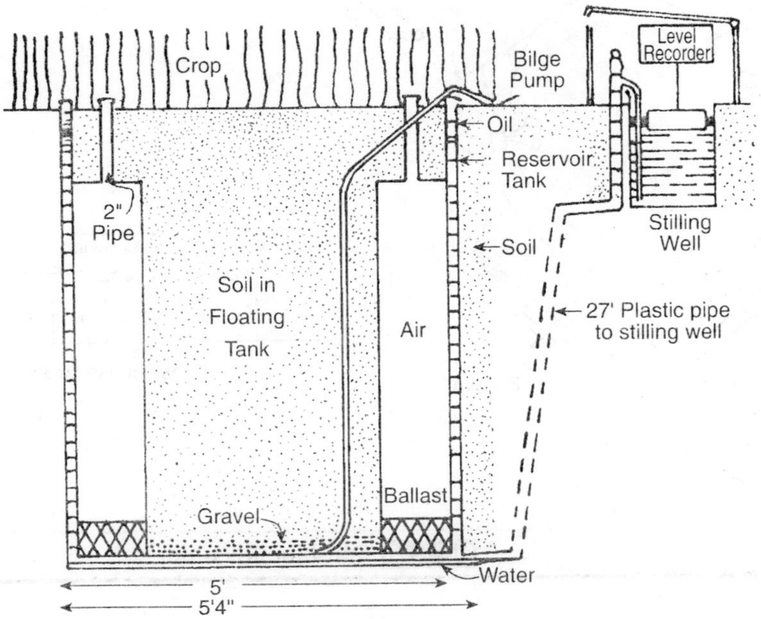

Fig. 6.27 Lysimeter

E. (iii) ***Lysimeter*** : It comprises (fig. 6.27) an enclosed block of soil with a vegetation cover (may be short grass) floating in a tank of water. The water tank itself is placed in a reservoir in which there is a layer of oil overlying a film of water. The inside bottom of the water tank is filled with gravels. One level recorder with a stilling well inside is attached to the reservoir water level with a 2.7 feet plastic pipe. Two air pipes with ballast at their bottom keeps the water tank in a balanced position. These two air containers peep through the crops. Changes of water level are recorded by the level recorder. As evaporation occurs the water level in the tank goes down and water supplied by the plastic pipe require to fill it up to the required level and that is recorded at the level recorder.

E. (iv) ***Evapotron*** : This instrument developed by C.S.I.R.O. in Australia measures the magnitude and direction of vertical eddies which transfer water vapour upwards.

F. (i) ***Sunshine recorder*** : Sunshine can be recorded by sunshine recorder (fig. 6.28) in which there is a glass sphere of 10 cm. diameter mounted in a section of a spherical bowl. Its diameter is such as the sun's rays are focussed sharply on a card held in the grooves cut into the bowl. There are three overlapping pairs of grooves each to take cards suitable in shape for different seasons of the year. The instrument is usually installed on a masonry pillar ranging in height from 1.5 to 3.05 metre approximately. There should not be any obstruction before this instrument to have an elevation of 3° above the horizon.

The cards are of three types : The short curved cards from 13th October to the end of February, the long curved cards from 13th April to 31st August and straight cards for other seasons. At the time of inserting the new sunshine card the 12 hour line should be adjusted to coincide with the noonline engraved on the bowl. The clamping screw should be tightened as well. The card is subdivided into hourly intervals. As the sun moves across the sky, its focussed image burns a trace on the card, so that by measuring the trace for the whole day, the duration of sunshine during the

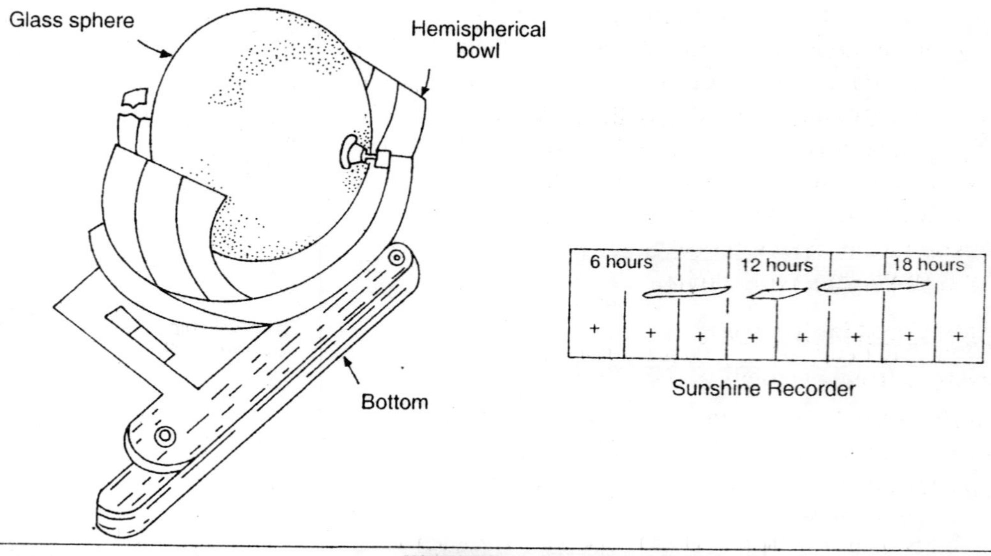

Fig. 6.28 **Sunshine Recorder**

day can be accurately recorded. A special type of plastic scale is used for this purpose. In this scale the subdivisions of the hour are also marked. By keeping the plastic scale on the trace, the total duration of the intermittent burns of the card within an hour can be added up and the total duration of sunshine can be obtained with correctness up to 0.1 part of an hour. The hours marked in a sunshine card refer to local mean time of the station. The sunshine in measured in number of hours per day. For each day's observation, sunshine card should be inserted in the recorder before sunrise and removed after sunset.

F. (ii) ***Estimation of cloud amount*** **:** The international unit for estimation of the amount of cloud of the sky is the octad or eighth of the sky. For this purpose the sky is to be divided into four quadrants. The amount of cloud is zero if the sky is completely cloudless and eight when it is completely overcast without gaps. It is estimated as how much of the total apparent area of the sky to the nearest eighth is covered with cloud.

F. (iii) ***Measurement of dew*** **:** When in cool and clear nights the air temperature through long wave radiation falls below the dew point, atmospheric water vapour in air close to the surface is condensed and dew is deposited on any surface. Formation of dew is more favoured on vegetated surface than on bare soil, as bare soil cools more slowly than vegetation. If cooling is rapid and temperature goes down below 0°, frost is formed. In this process vapour state of water is directly transformed into ice. However, frost is a hazard for agricultural and horticultural crops.

Measurement of dew is done by Duv-Devani dew gauge. The instrument (fig. 6.26) comprises a red (painted) rectangular wooden block (32 cm. × 5 cm. × 2.5 cm.) to favour retention of dew on it. It is placed on a stand and left in open air just about the sunset. The dew deposited is compared with photographs of dew album. The photographs in the dew album show dew scales and thus the proper dew scale for the day is determined. Dew scale no. 1 shows 0.02 mm and it varies up to 0.35 mm. in scale number 8.

Measurement of dew is also done at different heights above surface. For this purpose dew gauges are placed at the heights of 5, 25, 50 and 100 cm. on a single stand above the ground. The precautions which are necessary for such measurements are :

(i) after making the observation the dew gauge should be kept inside because if it is left in sunlight, it may get damaged.

(ii) after the observation wiping of the surfaces of dew gauge for removal of dew drops should be avoided; it's better to remove them by shaking or swinging in air.

(iii) touching the surface of dew gauge with greasy or dusty fingers is utterly harmful.

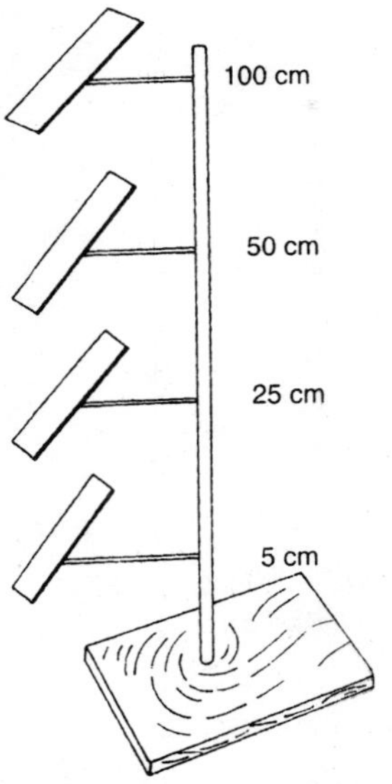

Fig. 6.29 **Dew gauge**

Geomorphological Instruments

Measurement of stream velocity and discharge :

The measurement of stream discharge is a very important work from geomorphological point of view. It involves the considering of both velocity and stage. Stream discharge is obtained by

$$Q = V \times A_C$$

Q = discharge of water

V = velocity

A_C = cross sectional area

This method is very widely used for spot measurement. Discharge is measured in volume/time unit or m^3/sec. and stream velocity is measured in units of metre/second.

As the velocity of any stream does not remain constant throughout the cross sectional area, it is slower near bed and bank, whereas, it is faster towards the mid-channel. Moreover, along the surface of the channel velocity is lower than it is at a little depth in the mid-channel. Again there are more variations if the channel bed is not smooth and stable. However, for such causes it is very difficult to have a mean velocity of channel flow. That is why a channel is often divided into segments and mean velocity for that section is taken. Then discharge for each of the segments is calculated with the help of cross sections of different segments. The sum of all these segment-wise discharges gives the total discharge of the channel. For channel cross-sections being slightly triangular in shape one or two triangular cross sectional segments can be identified and for each of them a mean velocity may be obtained.

However, a good measuring section with the following condition may be considered favourable for the measurement of velocity.

a) The cross -sectional area and the immediate upstream section of the channel should be free from aquatic growth.

b) The stream bed should be regular and stable.

c) The velocity should exceed 10–15 cm./sec.

d) The channel should have a depth of flow exceeding 30 cm.

e) Velocity lines should be parallel and normal to the cross section.

For measurement of the cross sectional area of streams having no great depth a channel cross profile with the help of staff and dumpy level can be taken (fig. 6.26a), and the width of the water surface can be taken by a tape. But the selection of points on which the staff is to be held vertical

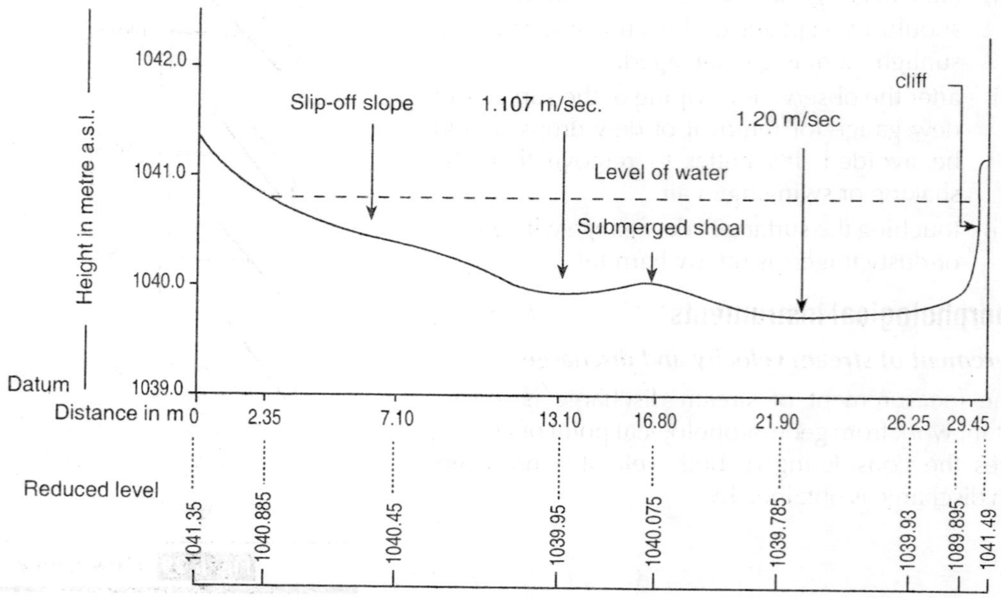

Fig. 6.30 Channel cross profile of Re chu

may either be at a regular interval of horizontal distance or, as almost all the channels possess certain irregularities, the points may be selected in a more wise way, preferably at every break of slope. As a general rule, the interval between any two verticals should not exceed 5% of the total width and the amount of discharge of any segment between two verticals should not exceed 10% of the total discharge (World Meteorological Organisation, 1965).

MEASUREMENT OF DISCHARGE BY DIVIDING THE CHANNEL INTO SEGMENTS :

As in the channel bed a smooth and a flat cross section is normally not found, the channel width should be divided into a number of segments and measurement should be done for each of the segments separately. We know that the discharge of a channel at a cross section is obtained as :

$Q = w.d.v$ [Where Q = discharge, w = width, d = depth, v = Velocity]

For the total discharge the segment values should be summed up.

$\therefore Q = \Sigma w_1 d_1 v_1 + w_2 d_2 v_2 + w_3 d_3 v_3 \ldots.. + w_n d_n v_n$

For this purpose, a rope or wire with markings for the segments can be tied across the suitable cross section of the channel bed. Almost all the segments will be of equal width except for the last one attached to the bank. The wire or rope should be placed just above the water surface. The depth should be measured in the middle of each segment. The velocity should be measured by water current meter and at least two readings will be taken at 0.2 and 0.8 depth from the water surface. For a shallower segment along the river bank only one reading can be taken at 0.6 depth. For each segment average velocity will be obtained from two or three observations at different depths.

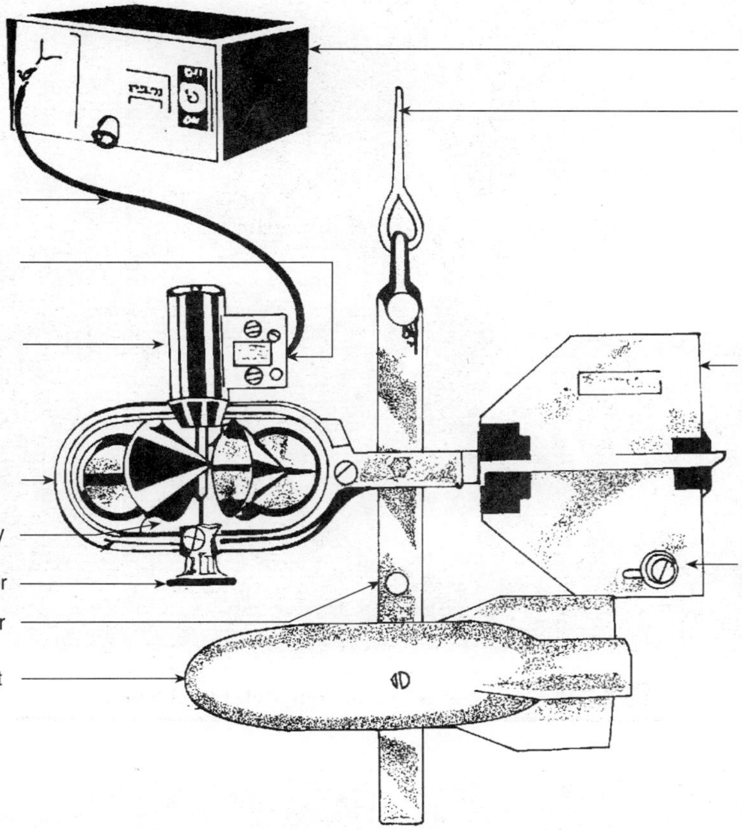

Fig. 6.31 **Magnetic water current meter**

The selection of segment-width will depend on the total width and condition of the channel at the time of measurement.

A *current meter* (fig. 6.31) is used for the measurement of velocity. Usually the Price model current meter is preferred as it is easier in operation. Two other types are Otto type and Pigmy type.

In the Price model current meter a vertically suspended bar is fitted with a metal frame at the centre of which there are four conical metal cups which rotate about a vertical axis in clockwise or anticlockwise direction. The vertical axis is connected with wires which records the number of revolutions in a digital counter. A tail fin with a weight is attached to the frame to bifurcate the flow of water. A streamlined weight is fixed at the bottom to keep the instrument in place.

The number of revolution of the conical cups within a stipulated time as recorded in the counter is compared with a calibration chart and the velocity is obtained. For determination of velocity the following calculation may also be used :

$$V = \text{Velocity equivalent} \times \frac{\text{no. of rev.}}{\text{time in sec.}} + \text{instrumental calibration}$$

[given with the instrument] of the respective instrument (Example of chart : Table 6.11)

Fig. 6.32 Placing of water current Meter in channel

Fig. 6.33 Dividing channel widths into segments

Time	Initial reading	Final reading	Number of revolution
40 sec.	23800	23826	26

$V = 0.2513 \times 26/40 + 0.0250 = 0.188$ metre/second

For individual instruments the constant will vary.

Discharge measured this way in various occasions and at variable time intervals may be used to identify the regime of a river or stream. Hydrographs are prepared using discharge in the ordinate and units of time in the abscissa. It may be an *annual hydrograph* (fig. 6.36) with monthly discharge values; may be a *storm hydrograph* with hourly discharge and amount and duration of storm rainfall; may be a *unit hydrograph* showing flood discharge reduced to lower values being divided by the depth of water spread on the basin area due to the additional amount of discharge caused by 1 inch or 1 cm of rainfall uniformly through out an hour.

A *rating curve* (fig 6.41) or a discharge - stage hydrograph can also be prepared with discharge on abscissa and gauge height along ordinate.

MEASUREMENT OF SHAPE OF PEBBLES

Rivers deposit coarse grained sediments in the river bed and in the flood plain. Of such coarse grained particles boulders and pebbles are very important because they create some resistance to the channel flow. Moreover they are mostly composed of hard rocks, though near the source some less resistant rocks also may be deposited as coarse grained bed-load. Boulders are large particles having a diameter size of 256 mm and above. Pebbles are smaller particles ranging between 2 and 64 mm in diameter size. Knighton (1998) considers, 'The size and shape characteristics of bed material at any point along a river are determined by the initial supply conditions and the subsequent transport history of the constituent grains. ....It has been generally observed that particle size (D) decreases with distance downstream (L)'.

In this part, particularly the size and shape of pebbles have been discussed and determined by specific methods of measurement. In general, all the river borne pebbles are to some extent rounded because of their rolling along the river bed as bed-load. Particle roundness may be visually determined through a comparison with standard charts. Krumbein (1941) has given one to be used for pebbles having diameter size of 16 to 32 mm.

The shape of pebbles has been more specifically determined on the basis of the relationship between the axial lengths. Zingg (1935) and Brewer (1964) have given a diagram for classification of particle shape.

The axial lengths of the pebbles are measured along the widest and longest face of the pebble. A is known as the long axis length, B is intermediate axis length and C is length of the short axis. C is basically the thickness of the pebble.

In Zingg method the two ratios are B/A (along vertical axis), and C/B (along horizontal axis being west to east direction). In this method seven categories of pebble shape are determined.

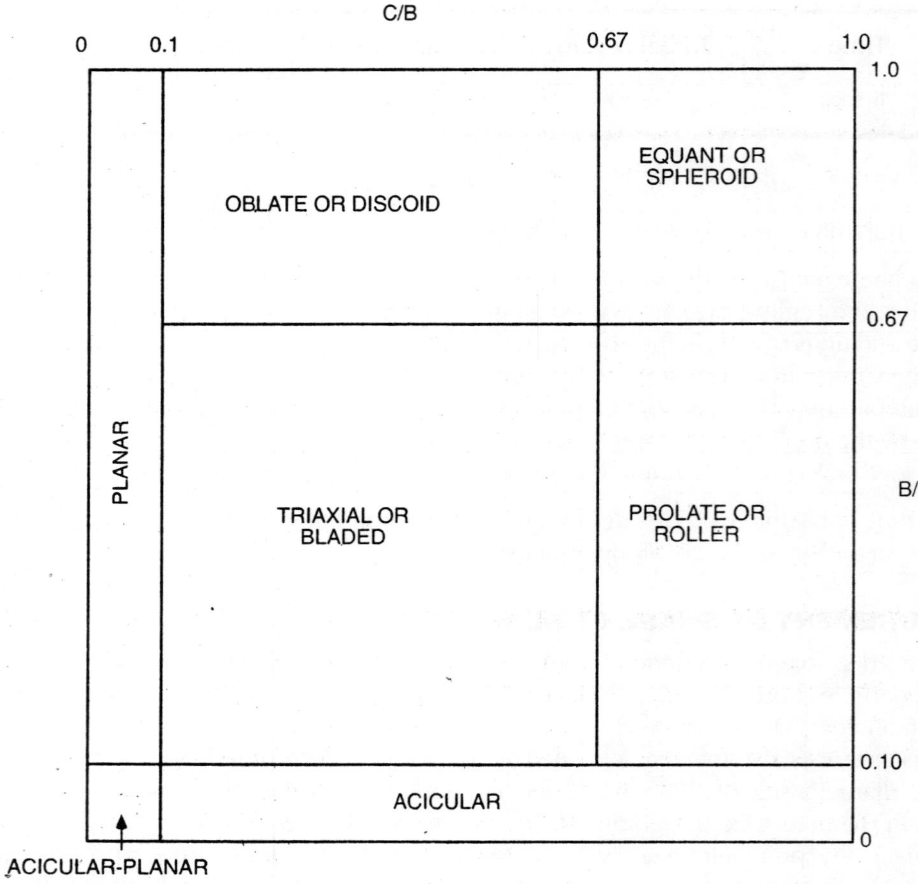

Fig. 6.34 **Zingg (1935) and Brewer (1964) method of classification of pebble-shape**

Zingg (1935) and Brewer (1964) method of classification of pebble shape.

TABLE 6.7

Calculation for pebble shape of 20 pebbles of fluvial origin (Measured by Slide Calipers)

Sample No.	Length of Axes in cm			B/A	C/B	Shape
	A	B	C			
1.	3.668	2.962	1.2	0.81	0.41	Oblate or Discoid
2.	3.04	2.354	1.798	0.77	0.76	Equant or Spheroid
3.	4.306	3.51	2.5	0.82	0.71	Equant or Spheroid
4.	8.671	3.264	1.8	0.38	0.55	Triaxial or Bladed
5.	7.68	6.638	3.54	0.86	0.53	Oblate or Discoid
6.	8.953	6.412	5.532	0.72	0.86	Equant or Spheroid
7.	1.688	1.36	0.982	0.81	0.72	Equant or Spheroid

Contd....

Sample No.	Length of Axes in cm			B/A	C/B	Shape
	A	B	C			
8.	2.658	1.95	1.18	0.73	0.61	Oblate or Discoid
9.	4.394	2.22	0.92	0.51	0.41	Triaxial or Bladed
10.	2.276	2.158	2.15	0.95	0.99	Equant or Spheroid
11.	2.806	2.12	1.324	0.76	0.62	Oblate or Discoid
12.	3.216	2.8	2.376	0.87	0.85	Equant or Spheroid
13.	5.8	3.67	1.796	0.63	0.49	Triaxial or Bladed
14.	5.773	4.64	1.821	0.80	0.39	Oblate or Discoid
15.	6.32	4.721	2.799	0.75	0.59	Oblate or Discoid
16.	6.52	3.188	3.09	0.47	0.97	Prolate or Roller
17.	6.25	2.52	1.914	0.40	0.76	Prolate or Roller
18.	4.168	3.276	1.63	0.79	0.50	Oblate or Discoid
19.	2.688	2.03	1.66	0.76	0.82	Equant or Spheroid
20	3.276	2.6	1.29	0.79	0.50	Oblate or Discoid

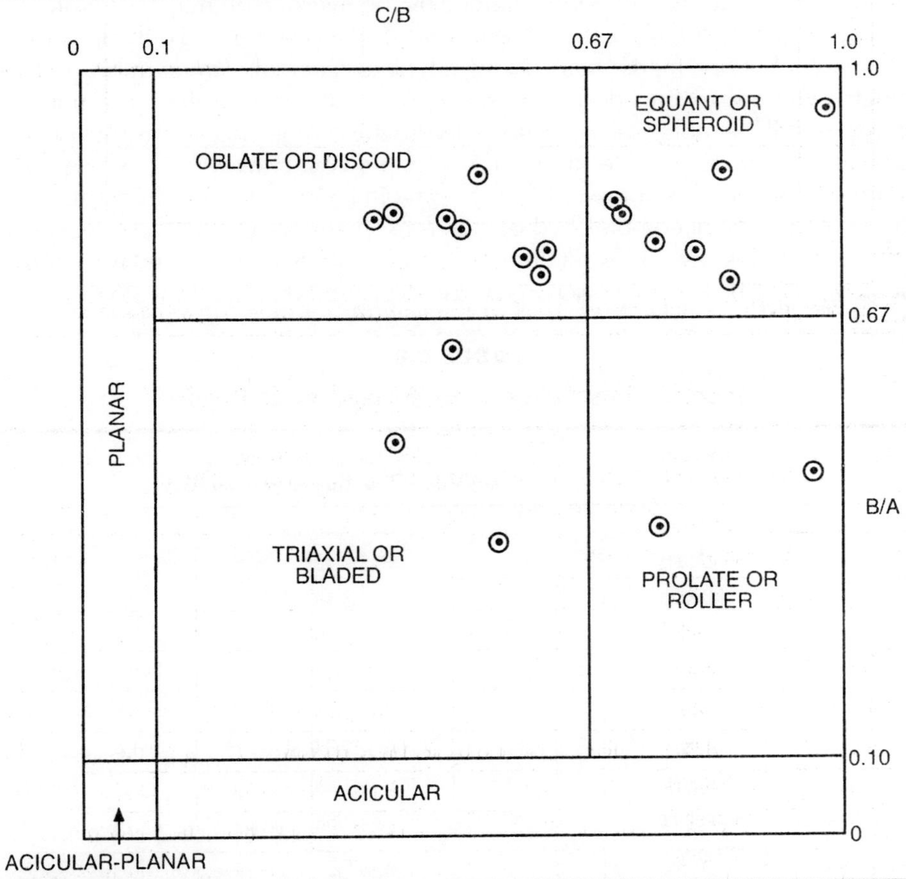

Fig. 6.35 Zingg (1935) and Brewer (1964) method of classification of pebble samples

HYDROGRAPH

A hydrograph shows correlation between time of discharge and amount of discharge of a river. The time is marked along the abscissa, whereas discharge is given along the ordinate. The unit of time may be day or month for an Annual Hydrograph. The discharge values may be given in cumec or cusec. In the case of an annual hydrograph monthly discharge may be given as the total discharge of the month.

An annual hydrograph has a few components. The curve of the annual hydrograph may mark the base flow line, a rising limb indicating concentration of flow, a peak indicating the highest discharge, an inflection point where suddenness of recession is observed and an overall recession limb reaching the base flow where the impact of excessive discharge due to rainfall ends and the minimum flow with supply of ground water is maintained. The base flow seperation line is very specific when the data of ground water contribution is known for each month, otherwise it is to same extent arbitrary particularly below the area of concentrated runoff due to rainfall or snowmelt water.

In such hydrographs, the impact of concentrated rainfall and snowmelt water with respect to time may be marked. On the basis of the source of water for discharge of the river the regime of climate can be noted. The regime may be pluvial when the source of water is rainfall, may be nival when the source is snowmelt water. It may be nivo-pluvial also. Moreover, on the basis of the source of water and the number of peaks attained by the hydrograph may be simple, complex or compound. In a simple hydrograph, there is only one source of water and only one peak. If rainfall is the major source, but one higher peak during the occurrence of summer monsoon rainfall and another, much lower one, occurs during premonsoon or autumn rainfall of postmonsoon period, the hydrograph is still a simple one. A complex hydrograph requires two distinct peaks from two different prominent sources of water during different periods. However, if the region lies within the same climatic regime, this complex hydrograph will be known as hydrograph of first degree complexity. Another type of complex hydrograph is the hydrograph of second degree complexity if the basin extends across two different climatic zones giving rise to two separate and prominent peaks, though one may be lower in discharge value than another. The Rhine River assumes such a nature.

TABLE 6.8

Monthly Discharge in Brahmaputra at Pandu

Month	Discharge Volume (Million cubic meter per second)
January	0.12
February	0.10
March	0.14
April	0.10
May	0.42
June	1.06
July	1.37
August	1.29
September	0.68
October	0.45
November	0.25
December	0.16

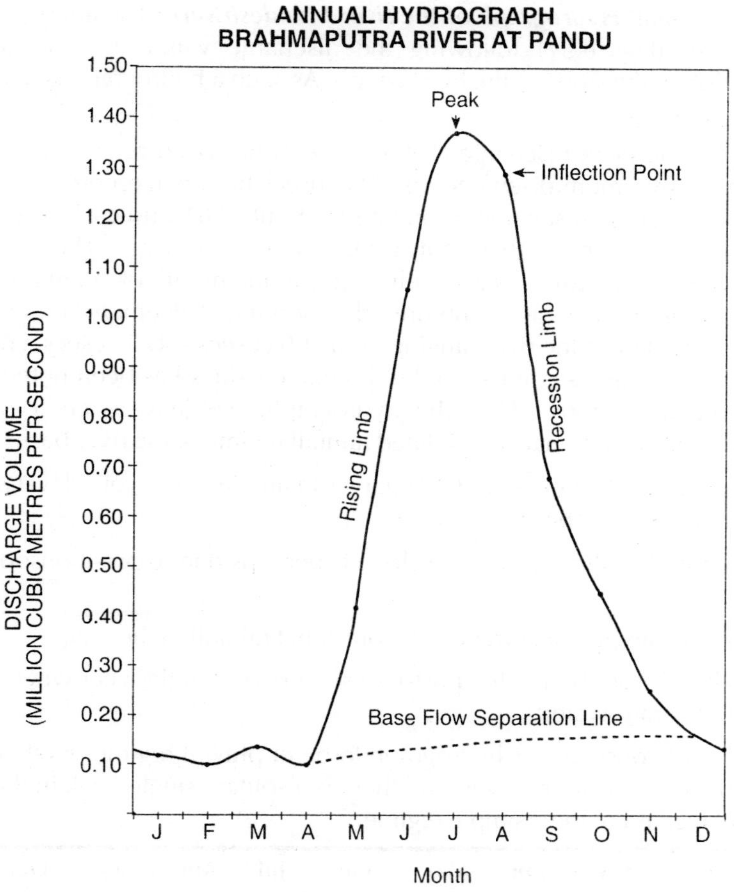

Fig. 6.36 Annual Hydrograph

Interpretation of Annual Hydrfograph of Brahmaputra River

This annual hydrograph (Fig. 6.36) shows the monthwise discharge of the Brahmaputra River at Pandu. The peak discharge i.e. 1.37 million cumec occurs in the month of July. It may be noted here that the volume of discharge is given here in terms of million units, because the Brahmaputra is one of the two or three mightiest large tropical rivers of the world and the absolute values are too high. That is why reducing of all the discharge volumes into million units is convenient for plotting. The lowest discharge i.e. 0.10 million cumec occurs in the months of February and April, whrereas January shows 0.12 and December has 0.16 million cumec.

After plotting, it reveals that the maximum concentraiton of discharge occurs between April and July marking the rising limb, whereas the recession occurs between July and December. August is the Month when the inflection point or break point is observed prior to the recession of discharge. However, the concentration of flow shows a much steeper gradient for the rising limb, whereas the recession limb is gentler in comparison with the rising limb. The concentration occurs within four months from April to July and the recession takes about six months of time to reach the base flow level.

With a sharp peak and rainfall being the source of water, this hydrograph is a simple one.

***Interpretation of Annual Hydrograph of the river Mundeshwari* :** The annual hydrograph of the river Mundeshwari (Fig. 6.37) following the discharge values for 12 months shows considerable fluctuation in the slope of the hydrograph. As such a hydrograph is a time-discharge relationship shown in the graphical way.

In this hydrograph the peak discharge (16939 cusecs) has been recorded in the month of September, whereas the minimum discharge i.e. 300 cusecs has been recorded in the month of January. However, the average discharge (monthly) is about 3661 cusecs. Therefore, the peak discharge is about 4.6 times greater than that of the average discharge. The rising limb starts sharply from the month of June onwards and culminates in the month of September where from there is a sharp fall along the recession limb upto the month of November. From December to February the base flow maintains the river ranging from 300 cusecs – 475 cusecs. From the month of March to the month of June a slight rise in the discharge values has been noted. Considering these four broadly variable slope along the hydrograph, we may reach to the following conclusions about the nature of climate and related rainfall regime of the river basin :

a) The base flow between December and February is maintained by ground water contribution when there is drought in the basin area.

b) From March to June the slight change in slope is perhaps due to pre-monsoon squalls and related rainfall.

c) The rising limb indicates the occurrence of monsoonal rainfall in the area.

d) The recession limb is ascribed to the post-monsoon period of the year when there is sharp fall in the amount of rain-water.

However, we should consider this hydrograph to be of pluvial regime. As there is only one major source of supply of water to the river, and there is a solitary single peak in the hydrograph, we may consider the river as having a simple regime.

Month	Jan	Feb	Mar	Apr	May	Jun	Jul	Aug	Sep	Oct	Nov	Dec
Discharge (in cusecs at 9 a.m.)	300	360	650	545	540	600	6395	7400	16939	7311	2425	475

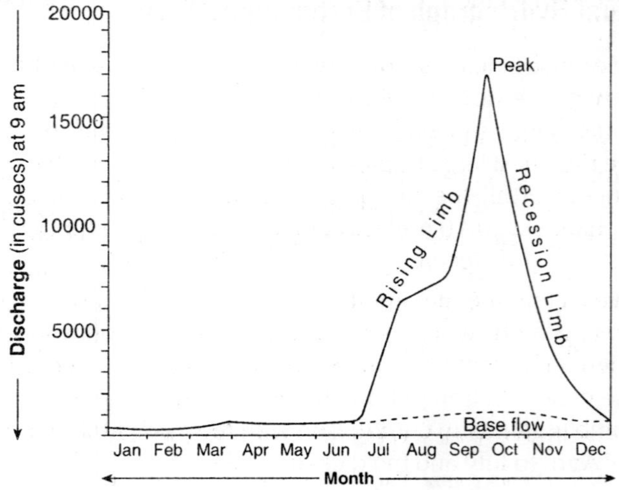

Fig. 6.37 Annual Hydrograph of the river Mundeshwari

UNIT HYDROGRAPH

A drainage basin is an open depression with a network of streams connected to a master stream or a river. Though the channels may be maintained by supply of ground water or snowmelt water, these are mostly formed and maintained by rainwater. The rainwater which falls within the basin area is not totally used by streams only. A part of it is held by the topographic depressions present on the land surface of the basin. This part of the rainwater is known as **Depression** or **Detention storage**. Another part poured on the vegetative cover of the drainage basin is held by the leaves, twigs and major branches of the trees and plants. This water is known as **Interception storage.** The land surface receiving rainwater absorbs a part of it. This is known as **Infiltration storage.**

All such sharing of rainwater amounts to the loss of precipitation and the rainwater in excess of such losses is only contributed to the channels. The total precipitation minus the losses is known as **Pnet.** In that part of the basin surface where there is no channel as such, but a sloping land exists, rainwater may flow down the slope as a sheet of water. This water also finally drains into the channels.

Basin lag : The rainwater reaches the main channel through the network of tributary streams. This process of collection requires certain length of time which is known as **Lag time** or **Basin lag**. Practically, this is a collection time of rainwater by the main channel. Piling up of rainwater after a storm causes a rise of the water level in the main channel. As a result, the gauge height of the main channel rises. Basin lag, however, denotes the time between the central time of the highest rainfall hour and highest discharge time. A strom hydrograph marks such features.

Storm hydrograph and Hyetograph : A Storm hydrograph is a graphical presentation of the discharge values with reference to the hourly duration during which rainfall occurred and the water discharge of main channel became distinctly influenced by the occurrence of rain. In this hydrograph the discharge values are marked by the ordinates and the abscissa marks the time units. As the impact of rainfall is the causative factor behind the changes in discharge values of a storm hydrograph, the amount of hourly occurrence of rain is indicated by a **Hyetograph.** A hyetograph is simply a bargraph marking the amounts of hourly occurrence of rain with its base above the height of the discharge hydrograph (Raghunath, 1988). In the hyetograph the depression storage, interception storage and infiltration storage are marked by **ϕ index** which is the uniform rate of loss and Pnet is obtained in excess of such losses. Some authors have placed the hyetograph in an inverted manner. Thus the columns of hyetograph is such cases increases downward from its base at the top (Chow, 1988; Rodda, 1967).

Unit Hydrograph : As storm hydrograph is a very useful tool for understanding the Impact of storm-rain on a drainage net, it has been widely used by hydrologists. **L.K. Sherman prepared Unit hydrograph in 1932 to develop a method of obtaining a Flood hydrograph in terms of unit depth of direct runoff resulting from a unit storm of a specified duration** (Sherman, 1932). The gauging station should be located at or near the mouth or confluence of the main channel, so that the entire basin area under the influence of storm will come into consideration.

Assumptions of Unit hydrograph : The theory of unit hydrograph has been developed with a few assumptions :

(i) The net precipitation will occur with uniform intensity over the entire basin area for one specified duration.

(ii) The ordinate values of direct runoff as a result of net rainfall (i.e., total precipitation — ϕ) of different intensities having same unit duration are proportional.

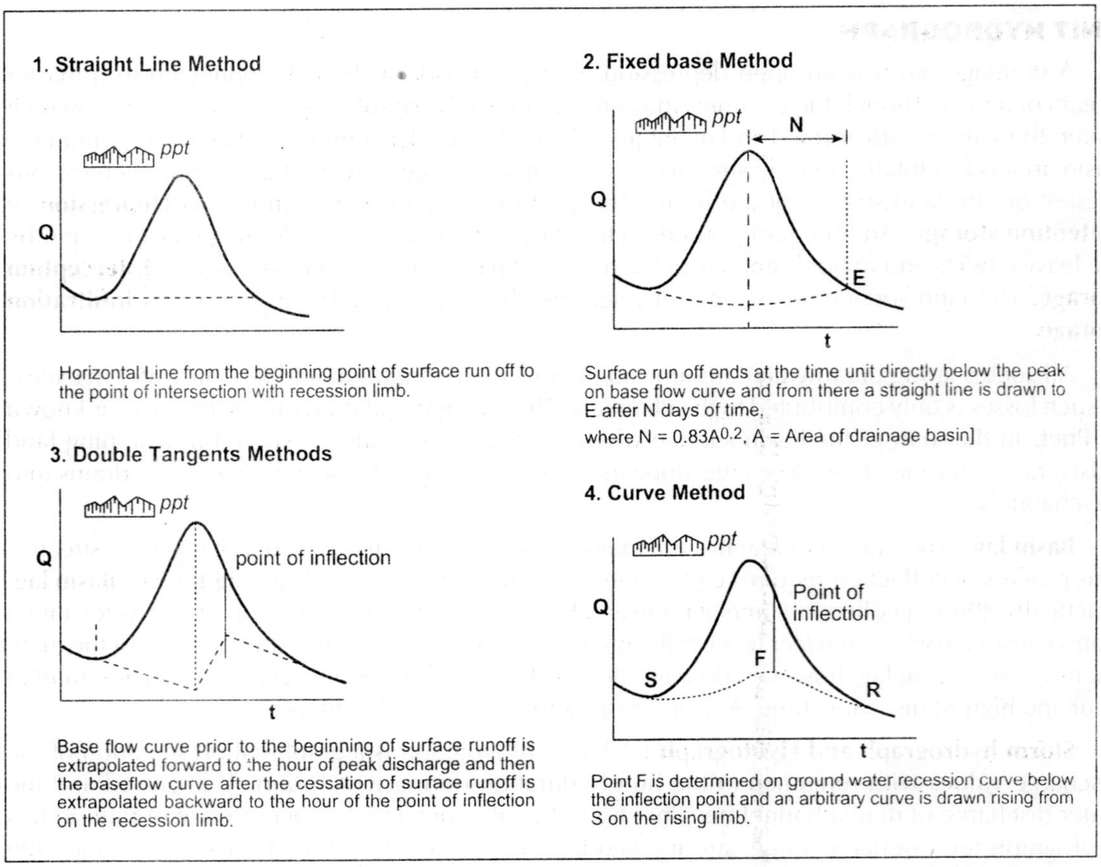

Fig. 6.38 **Four methods of separation of base flow**

(iii) The unit hydrograph takes into consideration the entire expanse of the area of basin surface and hence can reflect the physical characteristics of the drainage basin.

Preparation of Unit hydrograph : The preparation of unit hydrograph on the basis of an isolated storm should follow the steps mentioned below :

(i) First, a recorded and isolated storm creating a considerable amount of run off should be selected.

(ii) The unit duration will depend on the largeness of the drainage basin, because the larger the basin the greater will be the time required for collection of rainwater into the main channel. The unit periods, however, should range between 15% and 30% of the duration between the beginning of surface runoff or the starting hour of rain and the hour of peak discharge. Thus unit hydrographs may be of 3, 6, 8, 12 unit hours duration.

(iii) A storm hydrograph from the unit storm should be constructed with total runoff along ordinate and unit hours along abscissa.

(iv) The hyetograph should accompany this hydrograph at the upper left corner. The ϕ (phi) value should be separated from the hyetograph to get the excess amount of effective rainfall. For this purpose, a ϕ index or the constant rate of abstraction or losses (inch or cm/h) can be determined. This index will yield an **excess rainfall hyetograph** (ERH) with a total depth equal to the depth of direct runoff $\mathbf{r_d}$ over the watershed. The value of ϕ is determined by picking a time interval length Δt, judging the number of intervals **M** of rainfall that actually contribute to the direct runoff.

(v) From the total runoff ordinates (T.R.O.) the base flow ordinates (B.F.O.) will be separated, so that direct runoff ordinates (D.R.O.) can be obtained. Four methods of graphical base flow separation are there (Fig. 6.38). These are : **Straight line method, Fixed base method, Double tangents method and Curve method**. This subtraction is done because the total runoff ordinates include the base flow ordinates also. The base flow marks the lower level of water discharge immediately below the triangle of flood discharge. Base flow does not occur at a constant rate. At the beginning of a storm it maintains the channel discharge, but as the storm proceeds, the base flow or the supply of ground water is overwhelmed by direct runoff and the ground water supply gradually depletes. At the later phase, when the direct runoff or rainwater discharge is reduced following the end of the storm, the base flow again rises, because by that time the ground water storage has been recharged and the ground water table has been raised. Thus the base flow line at the lower part of the storm hydrograph may be curvilinear or of a slanting nature, being lower at the left hand side and a little higher at the right hand side. However, in absence of the base flow data, the base flow ordinates can be obtained graphically from the perpendiculars on the base line at unit hour points upto the reach of base flow separation line which separates the flood discharge triangle from the rest.

(vi) The direct runoff ordinates thus obtained should be summed up. The sum of direct runoff multiplied by time in seconds should be divided by the area of the drainage basin. Here, if the summation of the direct runoff per second is obtained in cubic feet the area should be converted into square feet units; if in cumec, the area should be in square metre.

(vii) The result obtained from this division will be in feet or metre which can be taken into inch or centimetre. This is the net precipitation depth over the entire basin.

(viii) Then each of the direct runoff ordinates be divided by net precipitation depth to get unit hydrograph ordinates.

(xi) The unit hydrograph ordinates (Initially known as U.G.O. or Unit Graph Ordinates) thus obtained will be plotted against time since the beginning hour of direct runoff. The unit hydrograph is meant for the basin of the duration of a unit storm.

For Unit Hydrograph (U.G.O.)

1. TRO — BFO = DRO where, TRO = Total runoff ordinate
   BFO = Base flow ordinate
   DRO = Direct runoff ordinate

2. $P_{net} = \dfrac{\Sigma\, Qd.t}{A}$ where, Q_d = DRO or direct runoff
   A = Area of basin

3. $\dfrac{DRO}{P_{net}} = UGO$ where, UGO = unit hydrograph ordinate.

For ϕ index first the volume of direct runoff is to be determined :

1. $Vd = \sum_{i=1}^{n} Qn.\Delta t$ [Qi .... Qn]

Vd = Volume discharge
A = Area of the basin

2. $rd = \frac{Vd}{A}$ [rd & Pnet are the same]

3. $Vd = \sum_{m=1}^{M} (Rm - \phi\Delta t$ Rm = Rainfall of certain pulse

t = time
$[m_1 \ldots\ldots M]$

[Get ϕ value from this by trial and error until ϕ is positive. For Δt it will be number of pulse multiplied by time unit in hour].

Size of Watershed : Unit hydrograph method was originally devised for large watershed areas, but it has been observed that it is applicable to small watersheds only. The preferable size of watershed is from less then 0.5 hectare to 25 square kilometre (about 1 acre to 10 square mile). A large watershed includes so many factors that the uniformity of rainfall and runoff is not expected to occur. The model is also inapplicable to runoff originating from snow or ice.

Application : The following are the rainfall and discharge data of a small river basin as affected by the occurrence of rainfall. The unit hydrograph will be prepared from this data.

TABLE 6.9

Area of discharge basin	Date	Hour	Rainfall (in cm)	Stream flow (in cumec) (TRO)	Excess rainfall (in cm)	Base flow ordinate (in cumec) (BFO)	Direct runoff (DRO)	Unit Hydrograph ordinate (UGO)
27 km²	5th June'80	18	—	6		5	—	—
		24	0.24	5	0.231	5	0	0
	6th June'80	06	2.09	13	2.081	5	8	1.45
		12	2.06	26	2.051	5	21	3.80
		18	1.36	21	1.351	5	16	2.90
		24	.02	16	0.271	5	11	1.99
	7th June'80	06	—	12		5	7	1.27
		12	—	09		5	4	.72
		18	—	07		5	2	.36
		24	—	05		5	0	0
	8th June'80	06	—	05		5	—	—
		12	—	4.5		5	—	—
		18	—	4.5		5	—	—
							$\Sigma Qd = 69m^3$	

$$P_{net} = \frac{\Sigma\, Qd.t}{A} = \frac{69 \times 6 \times 3600 m^3/S}{27 \times (1000)^2\, m^2} = \frac{1490400}{27000000}$$

$$= 0.0552 \text{ m} \times 100 = 5.52 \text{ cm.}$$

For Excess rainfall :

$$rd = \sum_{i=1}^{n} (Rm_i - \phi\Delta t)$$

where, I = Q1 ......Qn

Rm = Rainfall of certain number of pulse

t = time

(i) $5.52 = (0.24 - \phi \times 6)$ $\quad \phi = \dfrac{0.24 - 5.52}{6} = -0.88$

(ii) $5.52 = (.24 + 2.09) - \phi \times 6 \quad = -0.26$

(v) $5.52 = (0.24 + 2.09 + 2.06 + 1.36) - \phi \times 4 \times 6 \quad = 0.0095$

The unit Hydrograph is shown in Fig. No. 6.39.

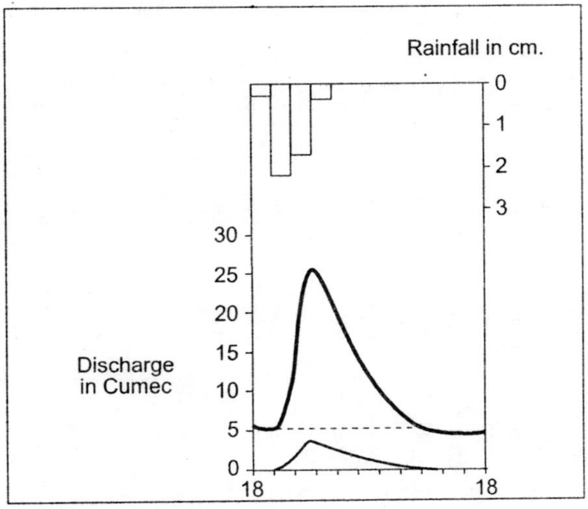

Fig. 6.39 A six hour Unit Hydrograph

TABLE 6.10

Calculation for unit Hydrograph of Ajay River

Date	Rainfall in inch	TRO (ft³/S)	BFO (ft³/S)	DRO	Excess rainfall	Basin area (mile²)	UGO
21.9.62	0.17	476	476	0	0.156		—
22.9.62	0.50	1337	1337	0	0.486	1494.59	—
23.9.62	1.42	19438	1338	18100	1.406		17075.47
24.9.62	0.01	15983	1338	14645	—		13816.03
25.9.62	0.02	8063	1363	6700	0.006		6320.75
26.9.62	0.03	3625	1425	2200	0.016		2075.47
27.9.62	—	2550	1650	900	—		849.05
28.9.62	—	1850	1850	0	—		—
29.9.62	—	1337	1337	0	—		—
				Σ=42,545			

TABLE 6.11

Ready-Reckoner for Velocity, given the Time for a specified number of revolutions

Time in secs	Velocity in M/Sec.												Time in Revs
	10 Revs	15 Revs	20 Revs	30 Revs	40 Revs	50 Revs	60 Revs	70 Revs	90 Revs	100 Revs	150 Revs	200 Revs	
40	.209	.299	.389	.568	.748	.927	1.107	1.286	1.645	1.824	2.721	—	40
41	.205	.293	.380	.555	.730	.905	1.080	1.255	1.605	1.780	2.656	3.531	41
42	.201	.286	.372	.543	.714	.884	1.055	1.226	1.568	1.739	2.593	3.448	42
43	.197	.280	.364	.531	.698	.865	1.031	1.198	1.532	1.699	2.534	3.368	43
44	.193	.275	.356	.519	.682	.846	1.009	1.172	1.465	1.625	2.422	3.220	44
45	.189	.269	.349	.508	.668	.827	.987	1.146	1.465	1.625	2.422	3.220	45
46	.186	.264	.342	.498	.654	.810	.966	1.122	1.434	1.590	2.370	3.150	46
47	.183	.259	.335	.488	.641	.794	.946	1.099	1.404	1.557	2.321	3.084	47
48	.180	.254	.329	.479	.628	.778	.917	1.077	1.376	1.525	2.273	3.020	48
49	.176	.250	.323	.469	.616	.762	.909	1.055	1.348	1.495	2.227	2.959	49
50	.174	.245	.317	.461	.604	.748	.891	1.035	1.322	1.465	2.183	2.901	50
51	.171	.241	.311	.452	.593	.734	.874	1.015	1.297	1.437	2.141	2.845	51
52	.168	.237	.306	.444	.582	.720	.858	.996	1.272	1.410	2.100	2.790	52
53	.165	.233	.301	.436	.572	.707	.842	.978	1.249	1.384	2.061	2.738	53
54	.163	.229	.296	.429	.562	.695	.827	.960	1.226	1.339	2.024	2.688	54
55	.160	.226	.291	.421	.552	.682	.813	.943	1.204	1.335	1.987	2.640	55
56	.158	.222	.286	.414	.543	.671	.799	.927	1.183	1.312	1.952	2.593	56
57	.156	.219	.282	.408	.534	.660	.785	.911	1.163	1.289	1.919	2.548	57
58	.154	.216	.277	.401	.525	.649	.772	.896	1.144	1.267	1.886	2.505	58
59	.152	.212	.273	.395	.517	.638	.760	.882	1.125	1.246	1.885	2.463	59
60	.150	.209	.269	.389	.508	.628	.748	.867	1.107	1.226	1.824	2.422	60
61	.148	.206	.265	.383	.501	.618	.736	.854	1.089	1.207	1.795	2.383	61
62	.146	.204	.262	.377	.493	.609	.725	.840	1.072	1.188	1.766	2.345	62
63	.144	.201	.258	.372	.486	.600	.714	.827	1.055	1.169	1.739	2.308	63
64	.142	.198	.254	.366	.479	.591	.703	.815	1.039	1.151	1.712	2.273	64
65	.140	.196	.251	.361	.472	.582	.692	.803	1.024	1.134	1.686	2.238	65
66	.139	.193	.247	.356	.465	.574	.682	.791	1.009	1.117	1.661	2.205	66
67	.137	.191	.244	.351	.458	.566	.673	.780	.994	1.101	1.613	2.141	67
68	.136	.188	.241	.347	.452	.558	.663	.769	.980	1.085	1.613	2.141	68
69	.134	.186	.238	.342	.446	.550	.654	.758	.996	1.070	.1590	2.110	69
70	.133	.184	.235	.338	.440	.543	.645	.748	.953	1.055	1.568	2.081	70

$$P_{net} = \frac{\Sigma\, Qd.t}{A} = \frac{42{,}545 \times 24 \times 3600 ft^3}{1494.59 \times (5280)^2\ ft^2}$$

$$= 0.088 \text{ ft} \times 12$$

$$= 1.06 \text{ inch}$$

2. (i) $rd = \sum_{i=1}^{n} (Rm_i - \phi \Delta t)$

$$1.06 = 0.17 - \phi \times 24 \times 1$$

$$\phi = -0.037$$

(ii) $1.06 = (0.17 + 0.50) - \phi \times 24 \times 2$

$$\phi = -0.0081$$

(iii) $1.06 = (0.17 + 0.50 + 1.42) - \phi \times 24 \times 3$

$$\phi = 0.014 \text{ inch}$$

The calculation for ϕ value should continue until it gives a plus (+) value. This value is infiltration loss.

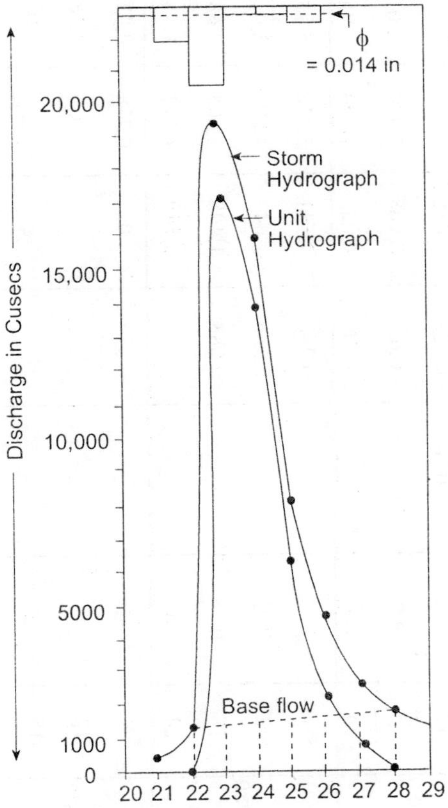

Fig. 6.40 Storm Hydrograph and Unit Hydrograph of Ajay River

TABLE 6.12

Linear Impact of Rainfall on Flood Discharge (Data Table 6.9)

Date	Hour	6 Hr. UGO	Excess R.F.	Rainfall					Composite U.GO(CUGO)	Base Flow	Flood Hydrograph Ordinate(BFO+CUGO)
				0.231	2.081	2.051	1.351	0.271			
5th June,1980	18	–	–	–	–	–	–	–	–	5	5
	24	0	0.231	0	–	–	–	–	0	5	5
6th June,1980	6	1.45	2.081	0.335	0	–	–	–	0.335	5	5.335
	12	3.8	2.051	0.878	3.018	0	–	–	3.896	5	8.896
	18	2.9	1.351	0.67	7.908	2.974	0	–	11.552	5	16.552
	24	1.99	0.271	0.46	6.035	7.794	1.959	0	16.248	5	21.248
7th June,1980	6	1.27	–	0.293	4.141	5.948	5.134	0.393	15.909	5	20.909
	12	0.72	–	0.166	2.643	4.082	3.918	1.03	11.839	5	16.839
	18	0.36	–	0.083	1.498	2.605	2.689	0.786	7.661	5	12.661
	24	0	–	0	0.749	1.477	1.716	0.539	4.481	5	9.481
8th June,1980	6	–	–	–	0	0.738	0.973	0.344	2.005	5	7.055
	12	–	–	–	–	0	0.486	0.195	0.681	5	5.681
	18	–	–	–	–	–	0	0.098	0.098	5	5.098
	24	–	–	–	–	–	–	0	0	5	5
									$\chi = 74.775$		

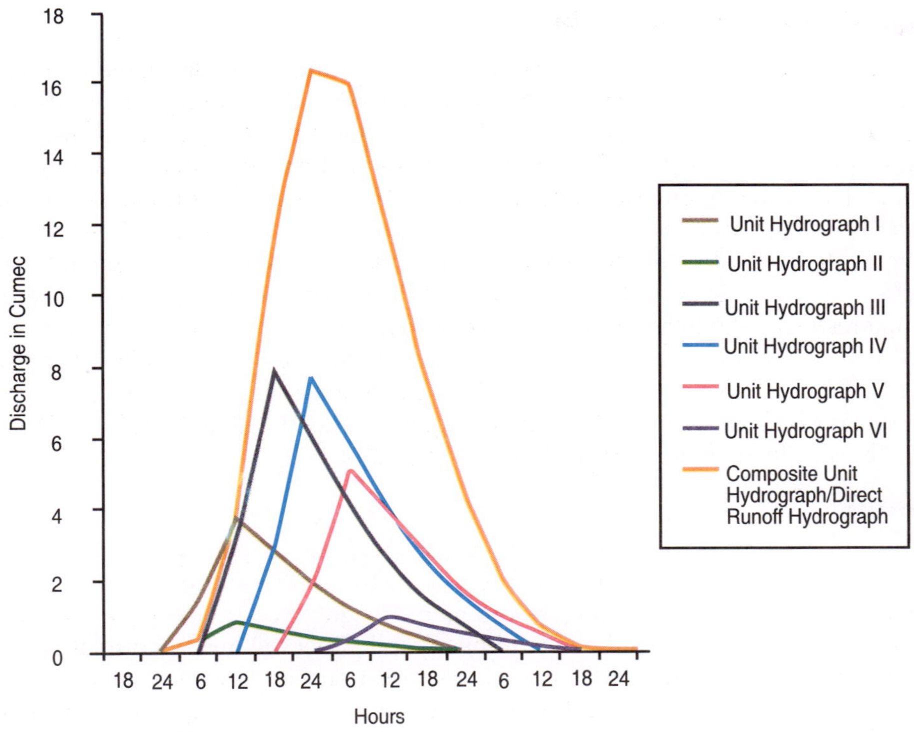

Fig. 6.41 Storm Hydrograph and Unit Hydrograph of Ajay River

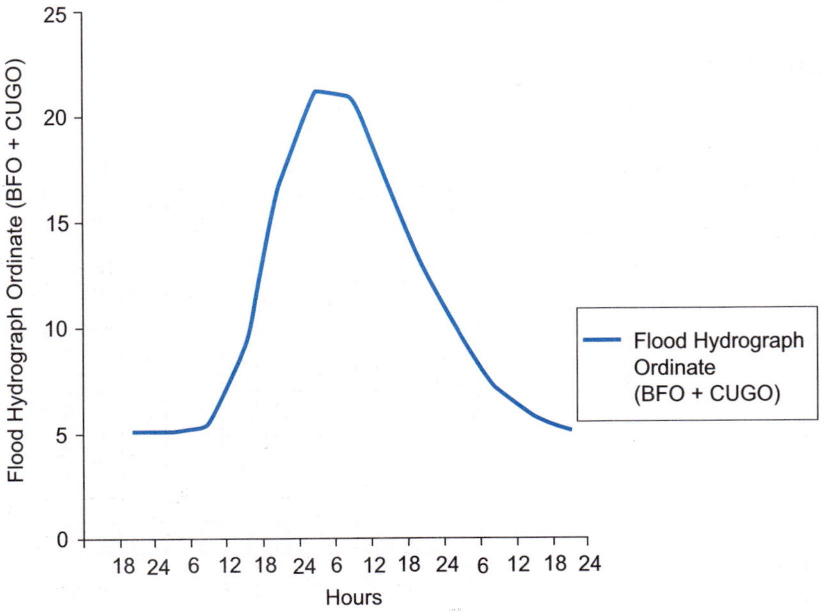

Fig. 6.42 Flood Hydrograph

Interpretation of Unit Hydrograph

Unit hydrograph shows the impact of one unit of excess rainfall on discharge of a drainage basin. The loss of precipitation through infiltration (Ö index) is 0.0095 cm. The excess rainfall amounts are 0.231, 2.081, 2.051, 1.351, 0.271 cm. As the unit hydrograph shows a linear response to precipitation, the response toward the increase in the volume of discharge should be calculated separately with reference to 6 hour time units. Hence the UGO ordinate values should be multiplied by the amount of excess rainfall, as revealed in table no. 6.9a. Individual hydrograph fig. 6.39a is constructed for response to individual excess rainfall in certain time unit. Then the entire Composite UGO (CUGO) or DRO inclusive of one unit of initial base flow is constructed. Interestingly, the total DRO, as shown in table no.6. 9, is 69 m^3 , whereas the sum total of CUGO is 74.755 cumec. It is the amount which is obtained as total DRO in linear response to the 5 showers of rainfall that occurred as a storm in the drainage basin. However, to obtain the total flood discharge the base flow (BFO) amounts should be added with DRO or CUGO as given in table no. 6. 9a. The Flood Hydrograph is shown in fig. 6.39b.

RATING CURVE

Rating Curve is a graphical presentation between discharge of a stream and its gauge height at corresponding discharge values. Discharge is shown along the abscissa (cusec/cumec), whereas a gauge height (feet/cm./m.) is marked along the ordinate. The graph can be done on normal graph paper or logarithmic graph paper. In the logarithmic graph paper the line of correlation is more steady, whereas in normal graph it gives a curvilinear relationship. However, in some cases of variable slope of channel cavity, a few dots or points of the scatter of rating curve may fall out of the line of correlation. In such cases, the rating curve may assume variable slopes.

The flatness of the segment of the rating curve with higher discharge and minimum change of gauge height indicates the flood level of the channel.

TABLE 6.13

Monthly Discharge and Gauge height data of Mundeswari at Harinkhola

Month	Discharge incusecs	Gauge height in feet
Jan	300	21.90
Feb	360	21.90
Mar	650	22.93
Apr	545	22.70
May	540	22.70
Jun	600	22.92
Jul	6395	27.78
Aug	7400	33.16
Sep	16939	34.57
Oct	7311	33.06
Nov	2425	25.12
Dec	475	21.98

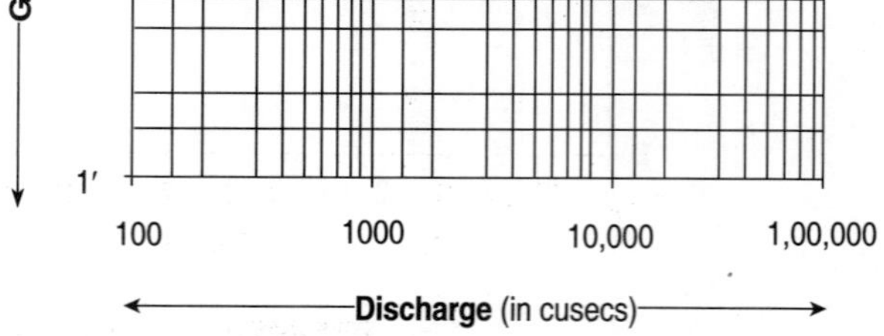

Fig. 6.43 **Rating curve of the river Mundeshwari (Reduced)**

Interpretation of rating curve of the river Mundeshwari :

The rating curve of the Mundeshwari river at Harinkhola has been prepared on the basis of discharge and gauge height values, the former shown along the abscissa and the latter shown along the ordinate. The curve drawn has shown a specific break of slope with a steeper section of slope at the later part of the year from the month of July complying with the increase in discharge values as well as gauge height due to increase in supply of water during summer monsoon season. After that from October to December there is a sudden fall and a flattening in the curve slope. In contrast, between January and June there is a gradual rise in discharge and gauge height values showing a gentle slope on the curve. Thicker sediments might have caused the rise in gauge height also.

Between July and September there has been a 1.20 times increase in gauge height and 2.64 times rise in discharge. It indicates that the walls of channel cavity are wider upward in stead of being vertical and the channel is efficient to remove the solid as well liquid discharge.

(ii) Abney Level

Abney level (fig. 6.46) is a type of clinometer. It is light, handy, compact and easily usable in field.

This instrument (a) measures angle of elevation and depression, (b) can take cross section in a rugged terrain, (c) can measure the slope of the ground directly. (d) Possessing a spirit level with bubble can act as an ordinary level instrument when the vernier is set as zero.

Components :

a) It has a square sighting tube with a mirror placed at 45° angle at one end whereas, at the other end of the tube it has small telescope.

b) There is a wire fixed at the middle of the square tube behind the mirror. This wire acts as the hairline to bisect an object.

(iii) A semi-circular graduated arc marking 0° at the middle with angles up to 90° or 60° on both sides is fixed with the main frame of the instrument.

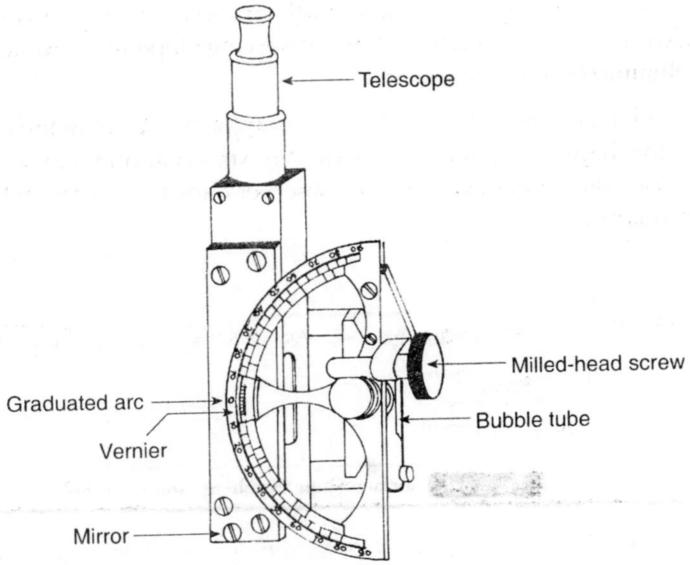

Fig. 6.44a **Abney level**

(iv) A vernier with a small bubble tube mounted on it is attached at the base of the semi-circular arc. This vernier as well at the bubble tube can be rotated with the help of a worm wheel and milled-head screw along the graduated edge of the arc. The vernier can read fractions of vertical angles to the limit of 10 minutes. The bubble of the level tube can be seen through the telescope as its image is reflected on the mirror and coincidence of the bubble image and wire can be made.

a) **Measurement of vertical angle**

The instrument is directed towards the object, and the observer makes the cross wire bisect the object by holding it properly and at the same time brings the mirror-image of the bubble at cross wire by turning the milled-head screw. Then the angle is recorded with help of vernier as accurately as possible and a small lens helps to read the graduation in an easier way.

By taking two vertical angles of an object from two points, a known distance apart, on the same vertical plane, the height of the object above ground can be measured. For this purpose the height of the observer's eye-level above ground should be known.

b) **A series of vertical angles can trace a cross section in a mountainous country.**

c) **Measurement of slope of the ground**

For this purpose a wooden board is placed flat on the hill slope or any other ground slope and the level is placed on it. After that the bubble is brought in a horizontal position where it will remain at the middle of the tube. The Abney's level is then lifted from there and the reading of the angle, indicating the ground slope, is recorded.

In another method the observer standing at one end of the slope the instrumental cross wire to bisect the mark fixed on the ranging rod at the same height as the eye of the observer. The ranging rod is held at the other end of the slope. Then the observer turns the screw to bring the bubble at the middle. After the bubble-tube comes to a horizontal position the angle is read from there.

(iii) ***Clinometer :*** This is a handy, small, rapid-working and compact instrument (fig. 6.45) which is used for (a) measuring vertical angle, and (b) observing slope on ground. The dip of the rock beds can also be obtained from clinometer.

Alike Abney Level it can read vertical angles, fixing the eye-level of the observer on a ranging rod. To determine the slope of a ground, the observer stands at one end of the of the slope. The ranging rod should be held vertically. Then the observer clips the cord with his/her thumbs. Then the angle is read from the arc.

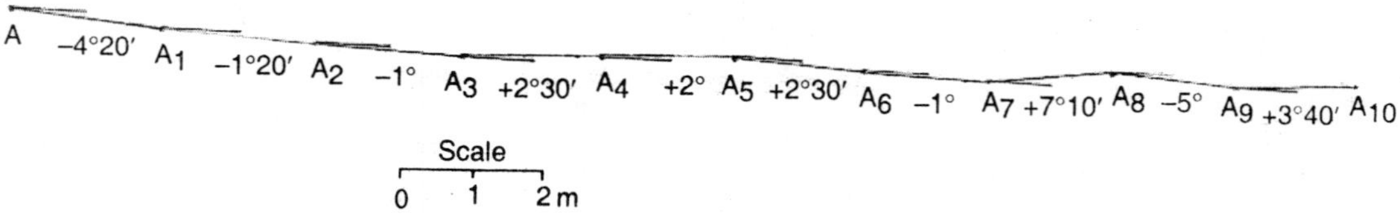

Fig. 6.44b Surface Slope Profile by Abney's Level

Interpretation : This profile done by Abney's Level shows a nearly flat ground surface where very slight change of slope is noted. A few segments of slope are in the upslope direction, whereas some others are in downslope direction depending the sheet erosion occurred along the surface.

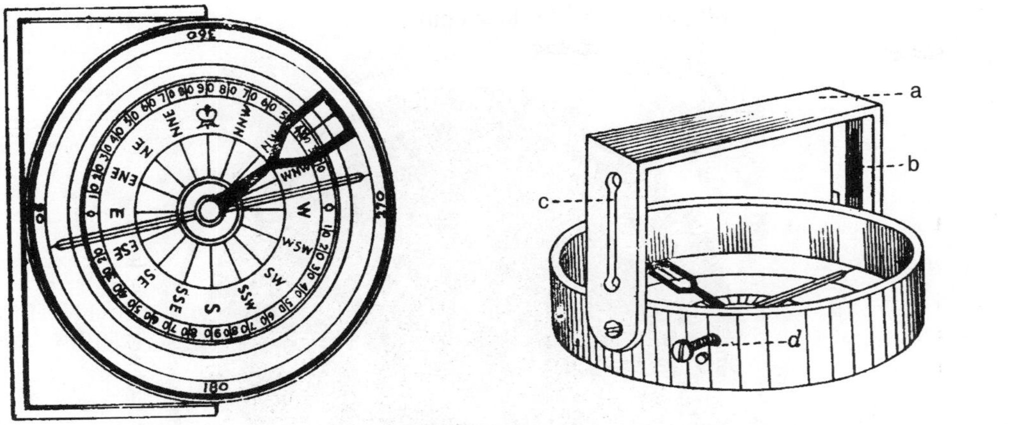

Fig. 6.45 Clinometer

MEASURING DIP AND STRIKE USING CLINOMETER

While measuring the dip and strike of a rock bed, the clinometer should be unclamped. Then the rectangular frame or handle of the instrument should be placed longitudinally (along the inclination of the rock bed) on the plane of dip and the instrument will be clamped very slowly. Then lifting it from its place, the degree of inclination of the rock bed should be obtained from the marker of the pendulous arm. It can indicate the gradient of the slope also.

To obtain the strike direction of the same rock bed the clinometer compass should be in a horizontal position placing the handle of the instrument on the dipping rock bed. it is obvious that the clinometer compass will be horizontally placed along with the handle as well. Then the magnetic needle marking the degree values of the circle showing whole circle bearing will be read as the direction of the strike. There will be two values 180° apart at the two ends of the needle. While taking the reading the instrument it should be clamped slowly. These two values indicate the strike direction which almost follows the sixteen cardinal directions. In the geological map of rock outcrops, the strike direction should be marked first following WCB or reduced bearing. Then at right angle to this line the direction of dip will be marked by a short line at the middle of strike direction with the degree value of dip given. Wheather the dip direction will be placed towards the left hand side or right hand side will be checked on the basis of right hand rule placing the thumb along the strike direction and rest of the palm towards dip direction in the field. For this the observer should turn his or her right hand side of the body in the direction of the plane of dip of the rock bed.

BRUNTON COMPASS

With the help of this instrument (Fig. 6.48) dip and strike of a rock bed can be measured. It consists of a small glass covered box, inside of which is marked by degrees. It has a vernier with a bubble tube mounted on it. The vernier can be rotated with the help of a lever on the back side. The lid of the box holds a mirror.

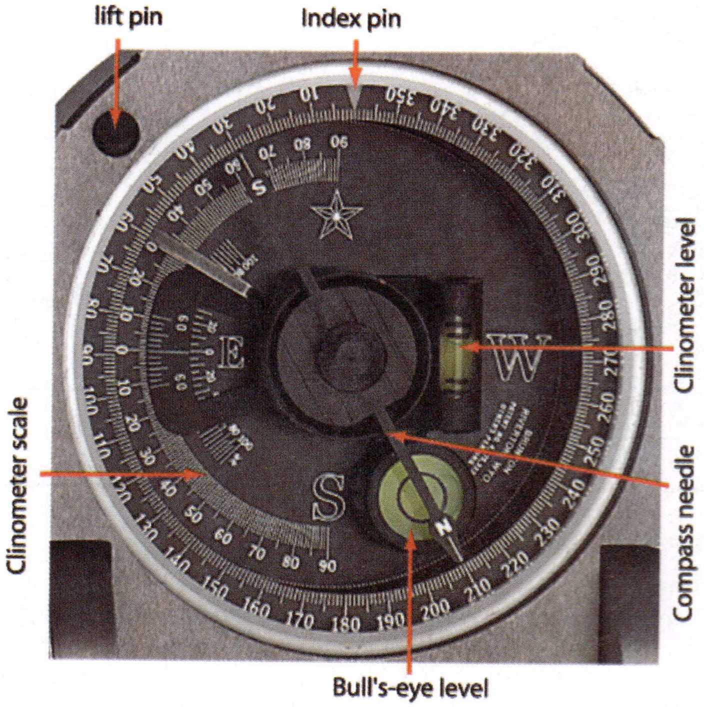

Fig. 6.46 **Brunton compass**

For observing the dip of a rock bed, the compass is held on the bedding or foliation plane placing the flat sides of the instrument on the rock bed. Then moving the bubble and vernier by the handle it is brought in a horizontal position and the reading is taken inside the box along with direction. For measuring the strike direction the instrument is held in a horizontal position. Then to bring the bull's eye bubble in proper position the lever is operated and the reading is taken.

Soil Testing Instruments

Measurement of soil temperature : Soil temperature is measured by a soil thermometer (fig. 6.49) . This is a mercury-containing glass thermometer with a bend of 120° at the bulb, and the other portion is straight. This bend is required to install the thermometer at a particular depth of soil. The thermometer is graduated for every degree of Celsius and the graduation starts from the distance of 6.5 cm., 17.5 cm. and 35.0 cm. from the bulb for 5, 15 and 30 cm. depth thermometers respectively.

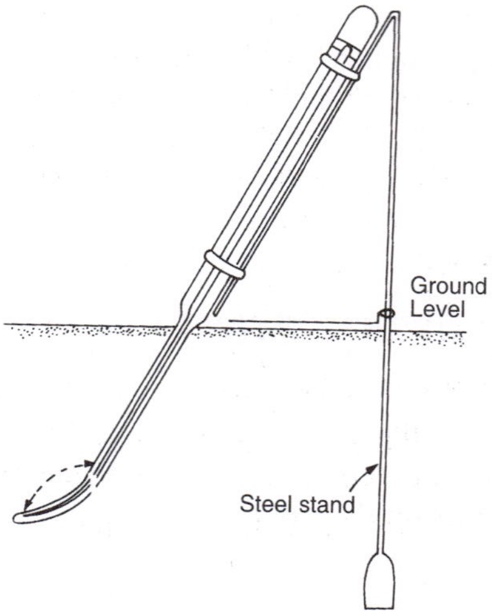

Fig. 6.47 **Soil Thermometer**

To support the thermometer at correct inclination an iron stand sloping 60° at one limb is required. The instrument is installed at a site which is sufficiently away from physical obstructions and is free from any waterlogging. No shadow should be cast on the instrument also. The soil layer should be removed at the time of installation and should again be replaced carefully in order.

The reading should be taken daily at 0700 hrs and 1400 hrs L.M.T. being correct to 0.1°C.

Measurement of length and area on map

A few minor instruments are required in connection with the measurement of length and area on maps. Topographical maps, in particular, can be used in this regard so as to work out the morphometric variables of drainage basins or of any other part of the map. The most common instruments used in this regard are i) Rotameter for measurement of length and ii) Planimeter for measurement of area.

(i) ***Rotameter*** : A rotameter (fig. 6.50) is a very simple instrument which can measure distance or length on map. It has two circular dials which can be read in different units depending on the scale of the map. There is a roller wheel at the bottom and the instrument can traverse along the measurable stretch of a stream, a road or any other linear features whose distance is to be measured. The reading is recorded by the rotary movement of the two hands places on the dial.

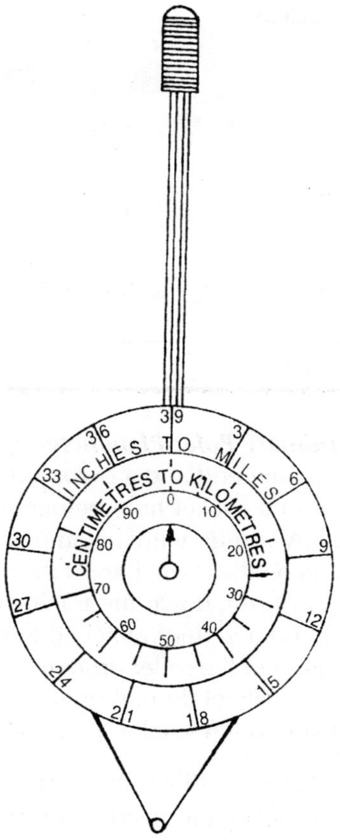

Fig. 6.48 Rotameter

On one side the dial shows inches to miles and centimetres to kilometres, the inch scale is given on the outer periphery, whereas the inner circle shows centimetres. 39 inches and 100 centimetres are measurable in one revolution of the hand which has an arrow-head on one side and a longer tapering head on the other side. If the map scale shows one inch to a mile, the length measured in inch should give the ground length in mile. Again if the map-scale reads 2 cm. to 1 km., 26 cm. reading on map will indicate 13 km. on ground.

On the other side, another dial shows statute miles, nautical miles and .... However, some of the Rotameters available in the market can convert map-scales directly into ground length on the dial and can also show conversion between scales having different units. Another type shows centimetres on the dial on one side and inches on other side.

For accuracy of measurement the distance of the linear feature measured on map should be checked at least twice. The rotameter should be held erect holding it between fore finger, middle finger and thumb at the time of measurement.

(ii) ***Planimeter*** : A Planimeter is an instrument to measure the area on map. Boundaries often show very irregular shapes and are not easily measurable graphically. For such irregular shapes the use of Planimeter is helpful. Two types of Planimeter are there : (a) Ordinary Polar Planimeter, (b) Aristo Polar Planimeter.

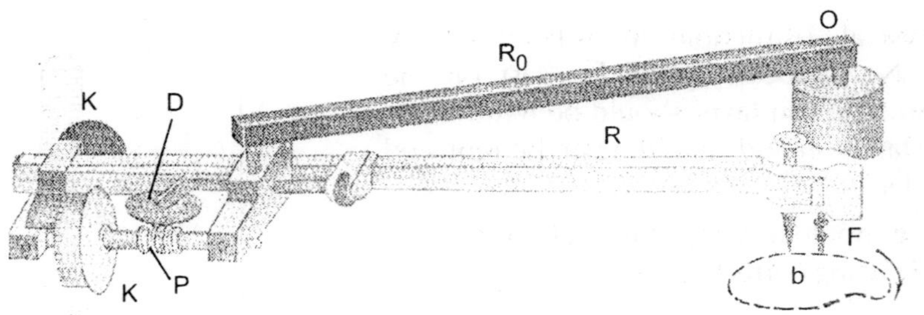

K = Wheel, R_0 = anchor arm, R = Tracer arm, O = Weight and Pin, D = Dial, P = Pinion, F = Tracer pin

Fig. 6.49 Planimeter

(i) ***Ordinary Polar Planimeter*** : This Planimeter (fig. 6.51) has one anchor bar with an anchor point at one end and a pivot point at the other end. It has a fixed length. At the pivot point it is placed in a socket hole belonging to a tracer bar which is graduated. It may be 12″ or 18″ in length. A vernier with a clamp is attached to the tracer arm to place the counting disc in proper position on the tracer bar. At the end of the tracer arm there is a tracer-point with an adjustment to lift up or bring down the tracing point. In the counting unit the components are a disc, a roller drum, and a vernier attached to the drum. The disc is divided into ten equal parts and at every revolution of the roller drum it advances one mark. This can be read with an index mark pointing on it. The wheel drum is graduated and divided into 100 parts with ten major divisions each sub-divided into ten smaller parts. The vernier can read the fractions between the smaller divisions dividing them further into ten sub-divisions. Therefore, $\frac{1}{1000}$th part of one revolution of the drum can be read by this instrument. Thus, each complete reading has four digits, one full number read on the counting disc and three figures on the right hand side of the decimal point. At the time of taking reading the roller drum may show to and fro movement and it may remain stationary too, while sliding across the map. An information card is given with the instrument indicating the map-scale, tracer bar position, actual area and area on scale for one revolution and a constant. At the time of setting up the instrument the map-scale is considered with corresponding tracer bar position and the counting unit is to be brought at the particular tracer bar position and beclamped. The scale given may not coincide with the scale of the map, but in such cases if the area is required in square centimetre, the natural scale is chosen (1 : 1) and the instrument is clamped at the corresponding tracer bar position. One revolution on such scale gives an actual area of 100 square centimetre and the value of the multiplier is also equal to 100. Thus both the actual area and area on scale covered by one revolution become equal to each other. Now if on a map of 1 : 50,000 (2 cm to 1 km and 4 cm^2 1 km^2) scale the initial reading shows 5.285 and the final reading is 6.295, it gives an amount of revolution of 1.010 as the difference between the two. Therefore, it covers an actual area of $1.010 \times 100 = 101.0$ cm^2. Now if on map- scale it is 4cm^2 to 1km^2 the area on ground will be $101.0 \div 4 = 25.25$km^2. For this method the anchor point should be placed in a convenient position outside the measurable area of the map. A check plate is supplied with this instrument to calculate the amount of probable error in the instrument. The value for one revolution of the plate is marked on the plate, any + or – value from the given one will calculate the existence of negative or positive error in percentage.

(ii) ***Aristo Polar Planimeter*:** This Planimeter (fig. 6.50) is so built that accidental damage and dust can be avoided. The measuring wheel and its axle are made off stainless nickel alloy steel and run in point bearings. The pole arm is linked with the recording unit by ball and socket joint. Some zero setting device can fix the zero just by push of a spring. The tracer point is actually a point marked in a glass vane.

In this Planimeter the tracer arm is fixed, it is 236 mm in length, whereas the pole arm is 194 mm. The vernier unit is 10 square millimetre.

TABLE 6.14

Measuring ranges of Aristo Polar Planimeter

No.	Pole outside the Figure			Pole within the figure	
	Circles	Squares	Rectangles	Circles	Squares
1100 1130 1137	320 mm^2	280 × 280 mm	920 × 550 mm	720 mm^2	50 × 500 mm
1138	660 mm^2	580 × 580 mm	430 × 950 mm	1440 mm^2	900 × 900 mm

In some other Aristo Polar Planimeters with adjustable arm the tracer bar are graduated throughout. In some Planimeters adjustment to various scales and ratios is done by a slow-motion screw and vernier. In some of them the vernier unit varies from 5 to 20 sq. mm. and the pole arm is adjustable to a constant ranging from 30,000 to 40,000.

***Use of Planimeter*:** A Planimeter is used on the basis of the following steps :

1. The index mark on the bevelled edge of the slide is set to the scale.
2. Anchor point is fixed firmly on the table outside or inside the figure depending on the smallness of the figure.
3. A definite point which is easily recognisable on the outline of the figure, is marked and the tracing point is drawn exactly on it.
4. The initial reading from the disc and wheel should be taken or in a zero setting device the wheel and dial is set to zero.
5. Tracing point should be moved exactly along the out line in a clockwise direction until it comes back to the starting point.
6. The disc and the wheel should be read as the final reading.
7. The number of times the zero mark of the dial is crossed at the time of moving the tracing point should be noted.

Finally the area should be calculated from the following formula —

Area ( ) = M (F.R. — I.R. ± 10N + C)

M = The multiplier whose value is marked on the tracing arm i.e. the number of units of area per revolution of the roller or wheel.

I.R. = Initial reading

F.R. = Final reading

N = The number of times the zero mark of the dial passes the fixed index mark

C = The constant marked on the top of the tracing arm just above the scale division.

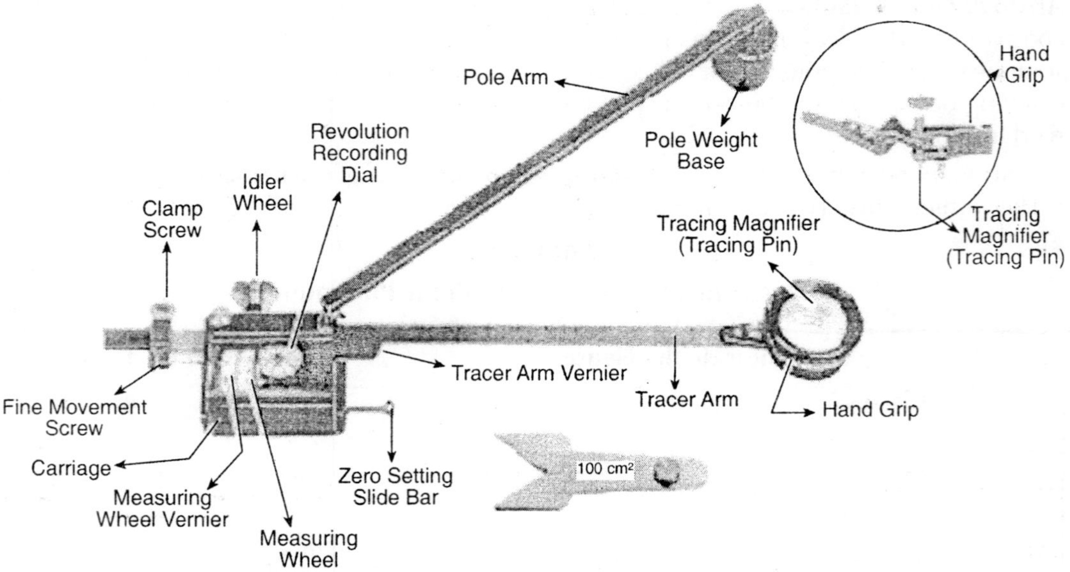

Fig. 6.50 **Aristo Polar Planimeter**

When the zero mark of the dial passes the fixed index mark in a clockwise direction, plus sign should be used, and in a counter clockwise direction minus sign is used. The constant C is added when the anchor point is fixed inside the figure.

(ii) ***Reduction or enlargement by Pantagraph*** : Reduction and enlargement for reproduction of maps is a common practice in Geography. At present reduction and enlargement have become easier through automatic photo-copying machines, but a time was there when manual reduction or enlargement of maps through a Pantagraph (fig. 6.53) was to be done to avoid exorbitant charges for photographic reduction or enlargement. It is still useful to develop the cocepts of reduction and enlargement for students. The reduction or enlargement or map-area occurs in square root or square of the time of reduction or enlargement, whereas the scale changes in square root of the area.

The instrument has four tubular bars which are square in cross section. Two of the bars are longer and hinged together at one end and two others are shorter and connected with the longer bars. The longer bars upto the length of the junction with shorter bars along with two short bars form a parallelogram having equal opposite sides. A number of castors or rollers support the instrument to remain parallel to the paper on which the reduction or enlargement is to done.

One of the long bars is graduated for various types of reduction or enlargement ratios. The vertical axis of the instrument is fixed to a triangular weight with archor pins. This is known as fulcrum. It is set at any of the graduation mark according to the required reduction ratio.

At the time of reduction the tracing point T (fig. 6.53)is placed at the end of the ungraduated long arm. This is adjustable in height with the help of a screw-roller. The pencil point P is located on a fixed point on the short arm which is hinged with the graduated arm. The tracing point is driven along the outline of the map or every line of the drawing which is being reduced, while the pencil point moves on the paper and traces out the reduced drawing on a desirable scale. The pencil point is made tightly placed in its position with the help of a card which also acts as a

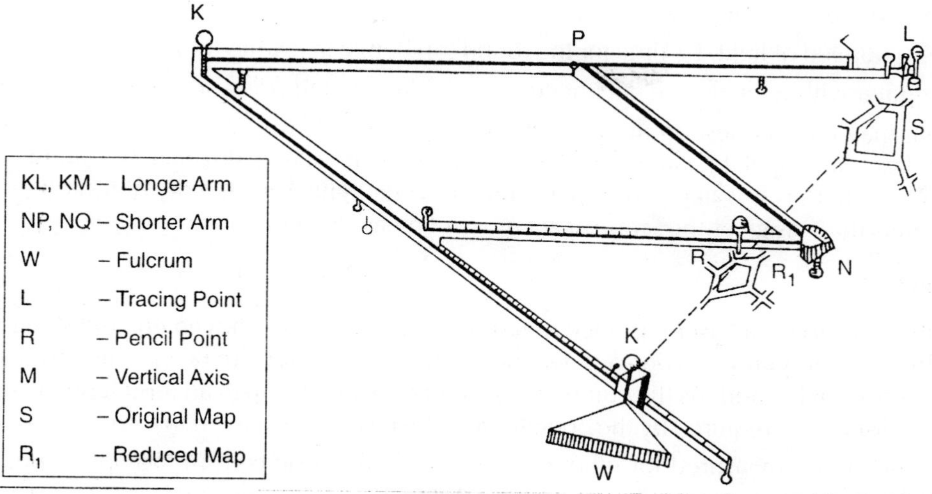

Fig. 6.51 Pantagraph

control for setting the instrument properly through its adjustable length. At the time of enlargement the pencil point and the and the tracing point are interchanged, but enlargement by Pantagraph does not give any good results.

MEASUREMENT OF DISTANCE BY LASER DEVICE

In geographical surveys, measurement of distance is an essential part. Right from the early days various survey equipments have been innovated to measure horizontal and vertical distance other than common measuring tapes.

In these days of modern technology, electronic equipments have made various works easier and faster. In connection with the measurement of distance also such devices have been innovated. Laser Distance Meter or Measurer is one of such devices used for measurement of distance, both indoor and outdoor. However, geographical surveys are outdoor in nature. Laser rays are very popular now and in many occasions the use of such rays is a common practice right from bringing extraordinary effects on performing stages to the measurement of volumes of indoor space.

A laser Distance meter throws a pulse of laser light to the target point and calculates the time taken by the reflection of laser ray to return to the equipment. It can measure various lengths of distance, but in common laser Distance meters used for geographical surveys, it measures a distance upto 30 metres, the accuracy being ±3 mm. The inbuilt processing of the device can add, subtract and calculate areas and also volumes as well as it can triangulate also. Hence, this device is versatile and convenient with a wide range of functionality, not to speak of speed, accuracy and safety.

Principles :

The speed of light rounded off is 300000 Km./Sec. So the time taken to cover 30 metre of distance is a highly fractional value of a second. A Laser Distance Meter measures the time taken between the point of time when the pulse of light is thrown and the point of time when the reflection returns from the target. The formula to measure the distance is :

Distance = A (Speed × Time) or, D = ct/2

[Where, c = Speed of light; t = time for the round trip between the device and target]

The computer within the device does accurate calculation of the distance almost instantly.

A student may face a question in his or her mind i.e. why a laser ray is used for calculating distance. A laser ray of light can travel at a fairly contant speed through the atmosphere. Moreover, a laser light is less likely to disperse unlike white light. Thus the ray of laser light does not lose its intensity. This gives the scope of accuracy of measurement.

Advantages :

As mentioned earlier, a Laser Distance Measure is fast, accurate, convenient and safe to use. Measuring by a tape requires two persons generally, but a laser meter can be operated by a single person and with a single hand. As the equipment is self-processed through an inbuilt processor, no calculation of distance is required by the operator and the result is displayed in the monitor.

The distance to be measured for otherwise less accessible points from the operator can be obtained easily. Suppose if we want to measure the distance upto the apex of a large fan deposit in a mountain valley being totally visible, we can use such a device with a longer range of measuring distance. Hence the difficulty of physical movement can be avoided while measuring distance on a rather inconvenient terrain.

The distance measured by a Laser Distance Meter is absolutely straight. The pipes or cables between the target and the operator will not hinder the course of measurement of the distance. Even in hazardous environment and poor light condition a Laser Distance Meter can measure the distance accurately.

The equipment being small in size can be easily carried to the field without any trouble. In triangulation measurement system, it can perform continuous distance measurement even for moving objects for short distances ranging from a few millimetres to several metres. However, the triangulation measurement system measures distance to a single object. Truly, it is the measurement of distance by the calculation of angle. The incident of reflected light occurs at a certain angle depending on the distance.

A Laser Distance Meter can calculate a distance in different units. Hence an operator can get the result in his or her own covenient units.

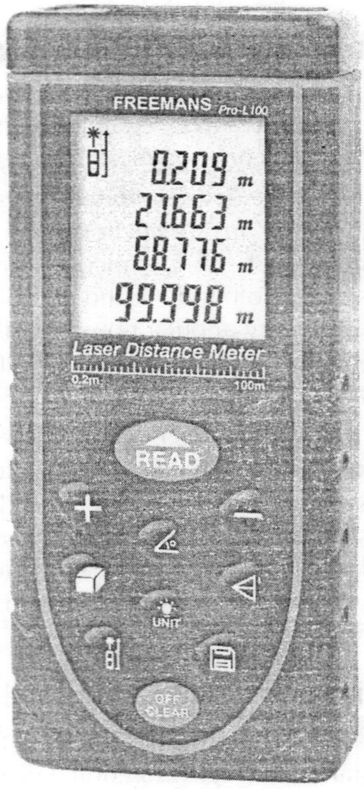

Fig. 6.52 Laser DM

How to use Laser Distance Meter :

1. First power button should be pressed to turn on the Laser Distance Meter.
2. A point will be chosen as reference position.
3. The equipment should be lined up with the target point.
4. Direct the laser beam towards the target.

5. Measure button should be released.
6. The Meter should be on until a measurement is recorded.
7. Once it is recorded the laser beam will be shut off.
8. The power button will be pressed to clear the screen.
9. Power button should be pressed and held to shut down the device.

CHAPTER 7

STATISTICAL METHODS IN GEOGRAPHY

Of the various methods applied in the analysis of geographical or spatial data statistical methods have gained much importance. Such methods are correlative, specific, and can be shown graphically too, the last attribute giving an easy visual impression to the observer. Various statistical techniques are often capable of handling a huge number of numerical data to reach a comprehensive inference, which helps to find out the clue behind the uneven distribution of data. Certain statistical parameters such as, mean, median, etc. have set some standards the deviation from which often clarifies the uneven concentration of data in different sectors of a set of apparently haphazard numericals, which are highly variable in nature.

Defining a data

Any figure or name or any quantity of an object is a data. It is transformed into an information when it is meaningful. It becomes geographical in nature when it conveys some spatial or temporal information.

In general, due to the highly variable character of a numerical data it is known as a *variate* or *variable*. Statistical techniques establish whether two or more sets of variates are dependent on or independent of each other.

Variates are distinguished in the following types :

1) Nominal, 2) Ordinal, 3) Interval, 4) Ratio, 5) Cardinal

1) ***Nominal*** : These are qualitative and their differences are indicated by name. Thus various categories of landuse, various types of rocks, soil etc. are considered as nominal data. Therefore, in general, they do not either bear any implication of quantity or show any difference of magnitude. The quality of an individual data in the nominal group is known as *attribute* (e.g. geological map).

2) ***Ordinal*** : In this type of data the relative importance of variables is understood, though the absolute values may not be known. Therefore, some sort of ranking is done in the data. Various types of hardness of minerals according to Mohs' scale may be considered as ordinal data.

3) ***Interval*** : In this type of data along with the order of magnitude the actual degree of magnitude is also known. The characteristics of rainfall data, production values, population etc. may be categorised under this type of data. Here, either exact measurement is done on the basis of some standard unit or the occurrences of a phenomenon are counted.

4) ***Ratio*** : This is a type of interval data in another form, e.g. a Santhal community may be expressed as a proportion of the total population. This ratio is converted into percentage. The ratio

values are often characterised by finite upper and lower limits. In this type the measured values may also form an index, e.g. productivity index.

5) **Cardinal :** This indicates how much or how many.

Other Classifications

Another way of distinguishing different variables is to classify the variates as *continuous* and *discrete*. In the continuous case fractions of a unit is often recorded, whereas the discrete data includes the variates having differences of whole numbers or integers. Thus a rainfall data of 5.3, 6.7 cm. etc. is continuous in character and 50 boats, 6 barges are discrete, as the latter cannot be subdivided further into fractions.

Statistical data may further be classified as *grouped* and *ungrouped* or *individual*: Grouped means grouping of individual data into a class which further contains the number of occurrences of individuals within itself. Thus grouped data divides the entire series of individuals into blocks which reflect the relative importance of classes.

When ungrouped, the individuals form the basis of the statistical process and in a grouped distribution the number of occurrences or frequency is used for calculation. A group or a class has certain range of variables confined between an upper limit and a lower limit. But in certain typical data a class may be formed without a range, e.g. wh en in a shoe-shop, 53 pairs of shoes having size number 5, 74 pairs of shoes of size 7 etc. are sold. Here, the individual size of shoes forms a class or group in which the number of sold pairs form the frequency.

A data may be *primary* or *secondary* in origin. The primary data is collected directly from field and the secondary data is the published or unpublished data collected previously by some agency.

Tabulation **:** Before any sort of statistical processing is done it is often required to organise the data into some systematic arrangement in a table in terms of rows and columns. Such an arrangement helps to visualise the significance of the data in a readily understandable way. Tabulation often reveals the inner characteristics of the data and their relative importance. For instance, while constructing an age-sex pyramid grouping of people in particular ranges of age instantly reveals the relative importance of individual age categories.

Tabulation may be simple and complex. In simple tabulation the data is tabulated on the basis of a single characteristic, whereas, in complex tabulation several characteristics of data are shown. Therefore, in a simple tabulation on a series of data which includes variates of paddy, it may show irrigated or unirrigated and some other characteristics such as high yielding or ordinary, Aus or Aman or Boro, etc. In complex tabulation students of a university may be tabulated showing their differences in terms of age, sex, religion, facility, eyesight, if they are residential or day scholar etc.

Sampling **:** A huge data is often difficult to handle and it requires selection to develop a sub-set on the basis of which inferences about the total may be made. It involves some sort of testing also when average conditions are understood from a small number of data out of a large occurrence. Various orders of magnitude distinguishing the relationship between individual data sets are observed. These are :

1) ***Universe :*** It represents the total body of the data in relation to any particular problem, viz. a series of data related to schools comprises all individual schools that exist in the world. This is hypothetical and does not bring any significance for the variable order of magnitude of them. However, this should be known as universe of schools.

2) ***Population :*** It is a part of the universe specifically related to a particular problem, e.g. English medium schools, which exclude all other different language using schools from the universe. A statistical population may be infinite, when the number of population is definite.

3) ***Target population :*** It is that part of the population which should be actually studied, e.g. I.C.S.E. Board English Medium Schools, which further separates the English Medium schools under a particular Board from schools of other boards.

4) ***Sample :*** It is the part of the target population which has been selected for study, e.g. Two schools of I.C.S.E. Board from each district of Tamil Nadu. On the basis of the study of samples, inferences that reflect the entire population, are drawn.

Types of Sampling : In general sampling methods may be accomplished in three ways :

1. Random sampling
2. Stratified sampling
3. Systematic sampling

1. ***Random sampling*** : This is also known as Simple Random sampling in which every unit of the population has an equal chance of being selected as a sample. The choice of sample is done with reference to a table of *Random Sampling Numbers.* The sample numbers can start from anywhere in the table of a large number of data and each digit or a set of digits is considered an independent sample out of the target population. Random Sampling is totally free from human bias and is also called *lottery sampling* which means a chance factor will determine if any particular unit of the population will be selected. Such a method is appropriate if the population is, more or less, homogeneous in terms of the characteristic being studied. However, Random number does not mean any haphazard selection of the digits. They have been prepared by special devices and tested for Randomness. A few famous series of Random numbers are given by Fisher and Yates (15,000 digits), Tippett (for 41,600 digits), Kendall and Babington Smith (for 1,00,000 digits), Rand Corporation (for 10,00,000 digits).

In a population of 100 any sample will be two digited and 100 will be identified as 00. It will start from 01, 02 etc. In a population of 10,000 each item will be four digited and 0000 will represent 10,000. At the time of taking the sample if any number coincides with another of same value, which has been previously drawn, the latter will be rejected.

Random sampling may be done in two ways :

(i) *With replacement* when the selected population unit is noted and then returned to the population before the drawing of the next one. Therefore, at each of the stage, population remains the same and holds equal probability. If the sample number is 'n' and the finite is 'N', the total number of possible samples with distinct permutation is N^n.

(ii) In *Random sampling without replacement* the drawn unit is not returned to the population and the size of population gradually diminishes as the sampling process continues. Therefore, the total number of possible samples with distinct permutations of numbers is ${}^NP_n = N(N-1)(N-2) \ldots (N-n+1)$. In this method no population unit can appear more than once in the samples.

For *spatial sampling* by Random method the area under study should be gridded first, from West towards East, and from South towards North, in the case of India, or any other country located in the north-east quadrant of the globe and the reference will be given on the basis of first easting and then northing. If the entire grid is taken into consideration, that is, for area sampling, two digits for the identification, one for easting and one for northing are required. In that case, the grid may be identified as rectangular or square. For point sampling the gridlines are numbered. In this case two digits may be used to locate a sample at the junction of the gridlines. For linear sampling only one number may suffice indicating the particular gridline along which the sampling will be done. In six digit point sampling by grids the third and the sixth indicate the specific point, the former for easting and the latter for northing after two digited respective gridlines.

2. ***Stratified Sampling*** : In stratified sampling different sub-sets of the target population are constructed to enable the evaluation of some spatial or regional contrast. These sub-sets are called *strata.* A sub-sample is chosen for each of them. Such samples are known as Stratified samples.

When the population is heterogeneous in character, this method is used. Some prior knowledge is required to identify the strata and there should be homogeneous data within each stratum. In a study of a drainage basin, stratification may be done on the basis of lithological differences. The sub-sets will be fixed on the basis of sub-differences. The knowledge about lithology is taken here as the prior knowledge.

The selection from each stratum may be done by Random sampling and hence the method should be known as Stratified Random sampling. The individual judgement of the sampler is important for stratification on the basis of prior knowledge. Stratified Random sampling is a mixture of Purposive and Random sampling.

3. ***Systematic Sampling*** : This method selects items at some regular intervals after all the units of population have been arranged in order. In a finite population the units may be numbered serially and thus arranged so that every tenth, fifteenth or nth sample may be selected. In field study also this may be applied. Thus, soil samples in a homogeneous field can be taken at an interval of 10 metre along gridlines and may produce Systematic sample numbers.

If any irregularities in the items being studied coincide with the regularity of the distribution of the data, the scope of misrepresentation of the situation exists. Moreover, sometimes it may not reach the required point of items, for instance while taking a cross section of a shallow stream in order to find out the exact location of shoals, pools, riffles, cliff, point bar etc., systematic sampling at regular interval may mislead. In that case stratified sampling is better.

Other methods : Besides, sampling may be *purposive* depending on the judgement of the sampler on the basis of his/her bias. *Multistage* sampling involves the carrying out of sampling operation in several stages, in each of which sub-divisions are done, mainly, on the basis of magnitude. For instance, in multistage sampling of locating the percentage of scheduled caste and scheduled tribe in total population, at the first stage, it may be a state-level, in the second stage, it may be a district-level, in the third stage, it may be a police-station level and at the ultimate it may be a village-level. The more we go downward, the probability of being selected as a sample unit becomes less and less.

Example for sampling in a Random method

If out of 87 data of population for villages of Rajnagar P.S. 15 samples are to be chosen in a Random Sampling method, all the data should be assigned an identity number (serial number in table 7.2) at first. Then following the Random Sampling table of D.V. Lindley and J.C.P. Miller (table no. XIV, XV, Appendices) 15 sample numbers are taken serially. As the numbers of population is within 100, each sample is two-digited. Therefore, the number of samples are :

20, 74, 94, 22, 93, 45, 44, 16, 04, 32, 03, 62, 61, 89, 01, 27, 49, 49, 20, 48

Any number higher than 87 has been left aside. The same has happened in the case of duplicate sample numbers. Therefore, following this order the samples selected are :

Identity no. of 15 samples (Serial no.)	20	74	22	45	44	16	04	32	03	62	61	01	27	49	48
Sample data	1533	304	606	1081	690	744	1142	274	412	525	188	578	404	416	151

Frequency distribution

What is frequency : Frequency indicates the number of occurrence of the data in a given range of items, e.g. number of buses in route 45 between 9 am and 11am. When no definite grouping is done to categorise the data into a system of intervals, it is a simple or ungrouped series, e.g. number of pairs of shoes sold in a Bata-shop for various sizes of foot.

Class determination

To reveal the inner characteristics of a data a grouped frequency distribution is required. On the basis of the total range of data the groups or classes are determined. The number of groups, which is to be selected for a particular set of a data is not fixed. The following formula may be applied for finding out the number of selected classes :

$n = 1 + 3.3 \log N$ $\qquad$ n = Number of selected classes

N = Total frequency

However, such computations may result in a fractional value from which the required number is determined by rounding up, e.g. if there are 47 items to be analysed for frequency distribution, the number of classes will be

$$n = 1 + 3.3 \log 87 = 1 + 6.40041 = 7.40041 = 7$$

But we can not say that, such a determination is totally applicable every where. The analyst should judge how many groups are required for a particular set of data in hand by a thorough examination of the given data.

We often come across a data which is regular in occurrence and in some other cases they are highly variable showing a distinctly discrete character. For both of them the same method of class determination is not applicable. The data with regular variability and moderate homogeneity may be grouped into classes at regular intervals. But for the second type classes a regular interval will not suit and any fixed interval will show number of classes without any frequency or there will be *empty classes*. For such cases classes are chosen with unequal width. It requires a jump in class interval. It is better if such jumps are done in multiple of the minimum class interval. Such an uneven group of classes may be required in a data of high degree of variability e.g. the population data of a number of police-stations, most of them being totally rural, but a few of them containing urban agglomerations. However, classes of unequal width require the computations of frequency densities to show the normal frequency distribution.

To avoid confusion about the statistical terms used in frequency distribution specific definitions of those are given below.

Class : A class is a range of data with definite limits. If one end of the class is not specified, the class may be treated as an open end class. A frequency distribution may contain one or even two open end classes. Such a class is made when the upper most value of data is far apart from the rest.

Classes are otherwise known as class-intervals. However, class interval actually means the difference between the upper limit and lower limit of the class-range or class, when the data is continuous, and it is the difference between the upper and lower boundary of the class when the data is discrete.

In this way, with the help of class-boundary, a discrete class may be converted into a continuous type. However, if any particular data coincides with the common limit between two classes, it should be considered as one of the previous class of which the upper boundary is in coincidence with the data. For instance if value of a data is 10 it will come within 0 – 10 class. Any value above 10 will come under 10 – 20 class. For continuous classes, boundaries and class-limits are the same, but for discrete classes they are different as shown in table 7.1. For discrete classes both the limits are inclusive, whereas for continuous classes the lower limit is exclusive.

TABLE 7.1

Class boundary	Class Interval	Discrete class	Class boundary	Class interval
0 – 10	10 – 0 = 10	1 – 10	0.5 – 10.5	10.5 – 0.5 = 10
10 – 20	20 – 10 = 10	11 – 20	10.5 – 20.5	20.5 – 10.5 = 10
20 – 30	30 – 20 = 10	21 – 30	20.5 – 30.5	30.5 – 20.5 = 10

Class frequency or frequency **:** As mentioned earlier frequency indicates the number of occurrences of data within the range of a class. It is determined by tally-marking in a column of frequency distribution. For the sake of convenience the number of tally marks is converted into a digit to be known as frequency. Tally marks are made in groups of five.

For uneven classes, frequency density is required to show simple frequency distribution by a *Histogram* or Frequency *Polygon* or Frequency *Curve*. It is determined by dividing the frequency by class width. However, a class width is synonymous with class interval. Therefore, it is determined by the difference between two boundaries of the same class. A class width may be much larger in comparison with the class frequency, and finding out the frequency density as ratio between frequency and class width may give a very small and fractional value which may be difficult to handle. In that case it is required to multiply the value of frequency density with any selected constant. Such a lengthy process can be avoided if the minimum class width or interval is considered as a cell and the frequency be divided by the number of cells a class contains. In that case any multiple of the minimum class width in the uneven classes will be a multiple of the number of cells. Using of the number of cells to determine the frequency density is easier and it is easy to handle also.

The summation of frequencies will give total frequency (N)

$$N=\sum_{i=1}^{n} f_i$$

N = Total frequency

f_i = frequency of the individual class upto the final nth class from the first (i = 1)

Histogram

It is an area diagram which represents the number of occurrences in each class in a frequency distribution shown in rectangles, the abscissa shows class boundaries and the ordinate shows frequency or frequency density. In uneven classes, frequency density is used instead of frequency as it standardizes the data, e.g. if in an uneven frequency distribution there is 5 as a frequency value in a class of 10 – 20 or the minimum class interval, and there is another 5 in the frequency column for a class of 50 – 80, both of them cannot show the same height in the histogram, as they do not actually have the same frequency because the base or width of the class is broader. Therefore, to standardize the data, frequency density will be calculated as

for the class of 10 – 20 :

$$\frac{5}{10(\text{class width})} = 0.5 \quad \text{or} \quad \frac{5}{1} = 5 \text{ (when } 10 = 1 \text{ cell)}$$

for the class of 50 – 80 :

$$\frac{5}{30(\text{class width})} = 0.1667 \quad \text{or} \quad \frac{5}{3} = 1.667 \text{ (when } 30 = 3 \text{ cells)}$$

However, it is easier to locate 5 and 1.667 than to locate 0.5 and 0.1667 along the ordinate, though the proportions remain the same.

On the basis of village level population of Rajnagar police-station, Birbhum district, according to 1981 census (Table 7.2) the following frequency distribution may be obtained.

TABLE 7.2

Village level population of Rajnagar P.S., Birbhum district

Serial no.	J.L. no.	Population '81	Serial no.	J. L. no.	Population '81
1	43	578	44	50	690
2	52	228	45	61	1081
3	59	412	46	01	403
4	14	1142	47	69	113
5	86	115	48	27	151
6	28	89	49	103	416
7	16	393	50	09	1154
8	20	174	51	60	1158
9	89	814	52	03	429
10	42	409	53	93	1084
11	97	207	54	73	123
12	53	113	55	55	161
13	44	589	56	45	708
14	66	781	57	25	875
15	77	468	58	15	600
16	70	744	59	08	359
17	67	7	60	26	140
18	68	10	61	29	188
19	94	135	62	56	525
20	90	1533	63	75	492
21	78	68	64	49	1167
22	12	606	65	58	626

Contd.

Serial no.	J.L. no.	Population '81	Serial no.	J. L. no.	Population '81
23	41	294	66	100	792
24	79	49	67	02	309
25	88	451	68	33	48
26	46	368	69	65	467
27	85	404	70	72	235
28	13	468	71	38	7862
29	76	913	72	11	75
30	30	1271	73	32	667
31	23	91	74	71	304
32	31	274	75	63	591
33	48	1059	76	06	381
34	80	840	77	19	642
35	07	124	78	84	639
36	18	400	79	39	1377
37	87	311	80	17	333
38	54	70	81	24	1098
39	04	547	82	96	384
40	62	269	83	05	457
41	92	90	84	51	4867
42	74	1024	85	64	359
43	40	251	86	47	319
			87	10	07

$$n = 1 + 3.3 \log N \quad = 1 + 3.3 \log 87 \quad = 1 + 6.4 \quad = 7.4 \text{ or } 7$$

Hence 7 classes are to be determined. The frequency distribution requires 7 classes of uneven width as there are a few villages having much higher population than their other neighbours. However, the frequency distribution follows table no 7.3.

TABLE 7.3

Class	Class Boundary	Class width (100 = 1 cell)	Tally Marks	Frequency	Frequency density $\frac{f}{\text{no. of cells}}$
1 – 100	0.5 – 10.5	100 (1 cell or 1)	𝍸 𝍸 /	11	11
101 – 200	100.5 – 200.5	100	𝍸 𝍸 /	11	11
201 – 700	200.5 – 700.5	500	𝍸 𝍸 𝍸 𝍸 𝍸 𝍸 𝍸 𝍸 ///	43	8.6
701 – 1200	700.5 – 1200.5	500	𝍸 𝍸 𝍸 //	17	3.4
1201 – 1700	1200.5 – 1700.5	500	///	3	0.6
1701 – 5000	1700.5 – 5000.5	3300	/	1	0.03
5001 – 8000	5000.5 – 8000.5	3000	/	1	0.033
				$\Sigma f = 87$	

From these values the following histogram has been constructed (fig. 7.1).

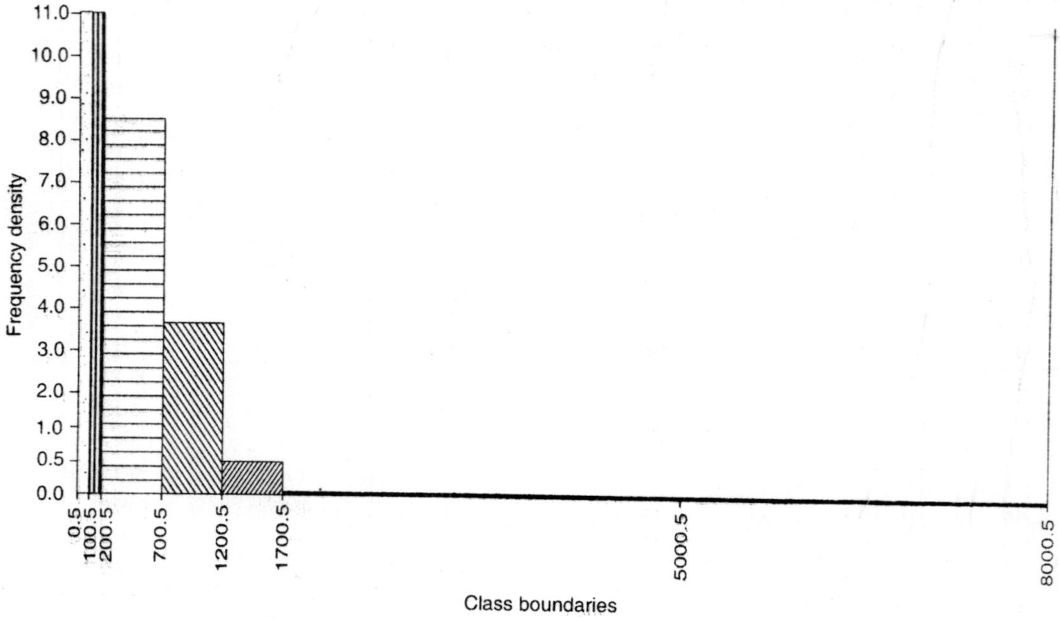

Fig. 7.1 Histogram

Frequency Polygon and Curve

Two other diagrams may be constructed with the help of simple frequency distribution. These are *frequency polygon* and *frequency curve.*

A frequency polygon is also an area diagram bounded by many sides. In a regular and normal distribution with even class widths a polygon has an area almost the same with that of a histogram. It connects through the mid-points or mid-marks of the histogram. A frequency polygon is more specific than a histogram, as it marks the particular points of frequency concentration whereas, in a histogram the number of occurrence is supposed to be uniformly distributed throughout the rectangles of the histogram.

A frequency curve on the other hand, shows a generalised trend of the frequency distribution and it does not always very specifically connect the mid-values of the histogram. However, if the series is infinite and individual classes are numerous with minimum width, the frequency curve almost coincides with a frequency polygon.

However, for drawing a simple frequency polygon and frequency curve with better results, a data with regular values is required, so that the classes are even. For the drawing of these two diagrams the data given in table 7.4 may be used.

TABLE 7.4

Police Station Level Population of Birbhum District, 1981.

Serial No.	Police Station	Population (Rural) '81
1	Muraroi	208843
2	Nalhati	194757
3	Rampurhat	224276
4	Mayureswar	187727
5	Muhammadbazar	92853
6	Rajnagar	54139
7	Khoyrasole	100817
8	Dubrajpur	113624
9	Suri	115793
10	Illambazar	99064
11	Sainthia	129318
12	Bolpur	127999
13	Labpur	130132
14	Nanoor	142952

Number of classes required :

$$\begin{aligned} n &= 1 + 3.3 \log N \\ &= 1 + 3.3 \log 14 \\ &= 1 + 3.78 \quad = 4.78 \quad = 5 \end{aligned}$$

Therefore, 5 classes are selected on the basis of regular class interval (Table 7.5).

TABLE 7.5

Class	Class Boundary	Class width	Tally marks	Frequency
54001 – 89000	54000.5 – 89000.5	35000	/	1
89001 – 124000	89000.5 – 124000.5	35000	~~////~~	5
124001 – 159000	124000.5 – 159000.5	35000	////	4
159001 – 194000	159000.5 – 194000.5	35000	/	1
194001 – 229000	194000.5 – 229000.5	35000	///	3

On the basis of this data (table 7.5) one histogram, a frequency polygon and one frequency curve have been constructed (Fig 7.2).

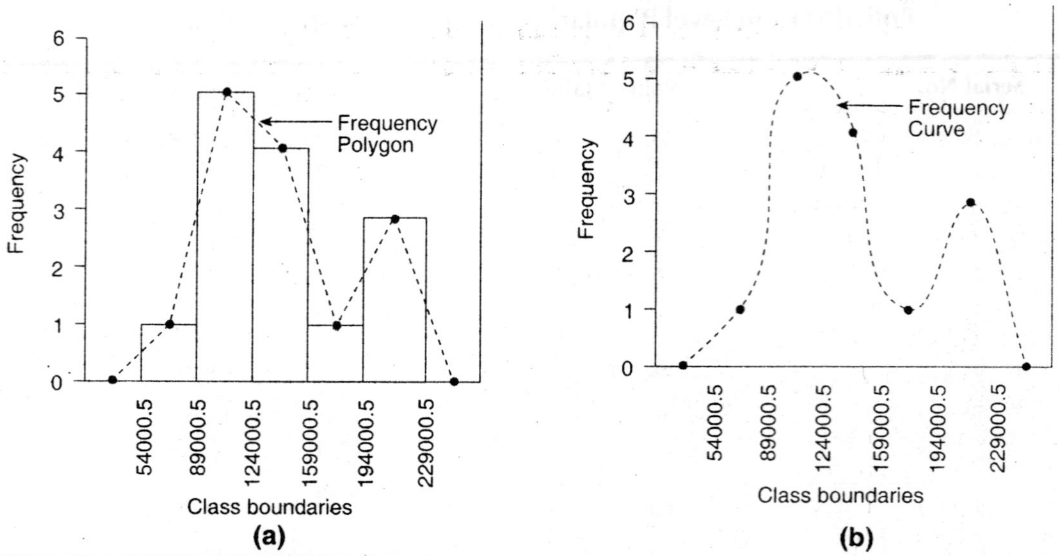

Fig. 7.2 Histogram, Frequency polygon & Frequency curve

Bi-variate distribution of frequency

In some cases the data may be bi-variate in nature having frequencies for two sets of data, which may have some sort of relationship between them. It may be height and weight of a group of people, may be ages of husbands and wives, heights and slope of unit areas etc. Such a set of data can be grouped and frequencies determined on the basis of a bi-variate table (7.6 a & b) having groups or classes along rows and columns. Each pair of data should be examined in terms of its location in rows and columns and finally the frequency table be prepared. Both row-wise and column-wise, the data will show the total frequency. Mean for both of them can be calculated.

TABLE 7.6a

Height m.	1.70	1.65	1.74	1.71	1.73	1.76	1.68	1.71	1.69	1.67
Weight in Kg.	65	60	75	80	68	85	72	72	70	68

TABLE 7.6b

x \ y	60–64	65–69	70–74	75–79	80–84	85–89	Total
1.65–1.67	1	1					2
1.68–1.70		1	2				3
1.71–1.73		1	1		1		3
1.74–1.76				1		1	2
Total	1	3	3	1	1	1	10 = N

Cumulative frequency distribution

Another graphical way of representing frequency distribution, particularly its trend between the lowest and the highest number of cumulative occurrences, is to construct an ogive or cumulative frequency polygon. It shows the gradual trend of accumulative data from one class boundary to another where the first boundary marks zero occurrence and the last class boundary specifies the total accumulation or the highest number of occurrences.

For the purpose of tabulation it is better to mark the individual class boundaries instead of writing both the lower and upper class boundaries together as in a class, because cumulative frequency always occurs upto certain class boundary.

For cumulative frequency distribution it does not matter if the frequency distribution has been calculated in equal classes or unequal classes.

Ogives are of two types, 'less than' and 'more than', the former marking the ascending order of accumulation from zero onwards, whereas the latter marks the descending order of negative accumulation from the total frequency downward. The first one ends up at the total and the second one ends at zero.

In general, an ogive and a cumulative frequency curve look like an exaggerated 'S' in the 'less than' and an exaggerated inverted 'S' in the 'more than' case. They are just like a mirror image vis-a-vis an original figure. Apart from showing the trend of accumulation of data in a grouped frequency method, a less than ogive is used to show the median, quartile, decile and percentile, but the median specifically occurs at the point of intersection between a less than and a more than ogive. Other than these graphical qualities, an ogive also marks the nature of concentration of data between two class boundaries.

Using both the village-level population of Rajnagar, and Police-station level population of Birbhum district in 1981 census, two ogives and related tables (7.7 & 7.8) for the constructions have been given here.

TABLE 7.7

Cumulative frequency distribution for Village level population of Rajnagar P.S., Birbhum

Class	Class Boundaries	Frequency	Cumulative Frequency	
			Less than	More than
	0.5		0	87
1 – 100		11		
	100.5		11	76
101 – 200		11		
	200.5		22	65
201 – 700		43		
	700.5		65	22
701 – 1200		17		
	1200.5		82	5
1201 – 1700		3		
	1700.5		85	2
1701 – 5000		1		
	5000.5		86	1
5001 – 8000		1		
	8000.5		87	0

TABLE 7.8
Cumulative Frequency Distribution for P. S. Level Population of Birbhum District, 1981

Class	Class Boundaries	Frequency	Cumulative Frequency	
			Less than	More than
	54000.5		0	14
54001 – 89000		1		
	89000.5		1	13
89001 – 124000		5		
	124000.5		6	8
124001 – 159000		4		
	159000.5		10	4
159001 – 194000		1		
	194000.5		11	3
194001 – 229000		3		
	229000.5		14	0

Hence, the two sets of C.F. *less than* and *more than* ogives are constructed (fig. 7.3 & 7.4).

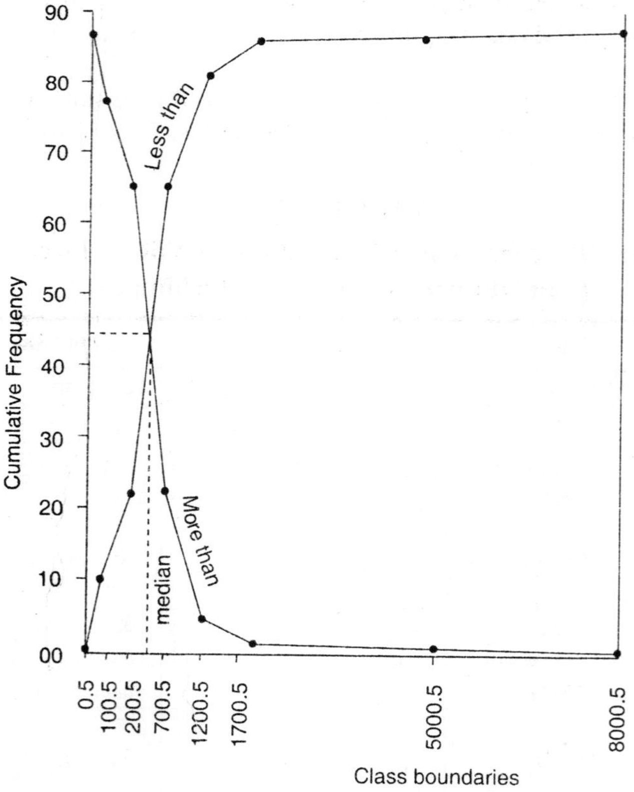

Fig. 7.3 Ogives (Less than and More than)

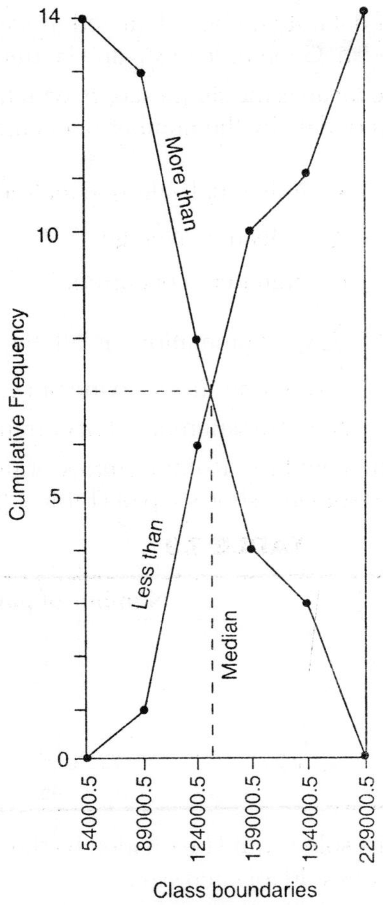

Fig. 7.4 Ogives (Less than and More than)

Measures of central tendency

Using a huge number of data comparison between two places or among countries is difficult and may often seem to be impossible. For the purpose of representation by one data or rather one value, some measures of central tendency are practised, so that one representative value with specific significance can summarise the entire set of data. For instance, in a comparison of population density among South Asian countries it is useless to consider state-wise population densities of India. It is rather helpful if the average population density for all the states is obtained and comparison is made between such central values or mean population densities for all the countries. Moreover, such measures of central tendencies clarify the distribution of data in the range of classes and mark its concentration. For this purpose *mean, median* and *mode* are calculated.

If the data is centrally concentrated, that is, if the frequency curve is symmetrical and bell-shaped, all these three will occur at the same position. When data is skewed, i.e. if the frequency curve is asymmetrical, the mean is greater than the mode, when the longer tail of the curve lies to the right and becomes less than the mode, if the longer tail lies to the left.

Mean

Mean is the average of a set of data. It can be calculated in various ways. In fact, there are three types of mean — Arithmetic mean, Geometric mean and Harmonic mean.

Of the three types the Arithmetic mean is the simplest one, which is calculated as the quotient obtained by dividing the summation of data by the number of occurrences related to it. It can be expressed as

$$\bar{X} = \frac{\sum_{i=1}^{n} x_i}{n} \quad \text{or,} \quad \bar{X} = \frac{1}{N}\sum_{i=1}^{n} x_i$$

x = Individual values in the series of data

$\bar{X}$ = Mean or average

n = Number of occurrences

$\sum_{i=1}^{n} x_i$ = Summation of all the values of x from the first one (i = 1) to the nth value or the final one

N = Total number of occurrences

An arithmetic mean may be calculated for a simple series of ungrouped data, such as, the number of pairs of shoes various sizes sold in a shoe shop of (Table 7.9).

TABLE 7.9

Sizes of Shoe	Number of pairs sold
3	12
4	8
5	7
6	10
7	9
	46

46 being the total number of pairs sold should be divided by the number of various sizes and will give an average of the pairs of shoes sold for each size.

$$\therefore \ \bar{X} = \frac{46}{5} \quad = 9.2(\text{mean})$$

Geometric mean is obtained in a set of n number of observation and is calculated as nth root of their product.

$$g = \sqrt[n]{x_1 x_2 x_3 \cdots\cdots x_n}$$

For the purpose of calculation the formula may be written in logarithm.

$$\log g = \frac{1}{n}\sum_{i=1}^{n} \log x_i$$

$$= \frac{1}{5}(\log 12 + \log 8 + \log 7 + \log 10 + \log 9)$$

$$= \frac{4.781611782}{5} \quad = 0.956322356 \quad = 9.04$$

Harmonic mean, on the other hand, is the reciprocal of the arithmetic mean of reciprocals of observations:

$$h = \frac{n}{\sum_{i=1}^{n}(1/x_i)}$$

Thus it is

$$h = \frac{5}{\frac{1}{12}+\frac{1}{8}+\frac{1}{7}+\frac{1}{10}+\frac{1}{9}}$$

$$= \frac{5}{\frac{210+315+360+252+280}{2520}}$$

$$= \frac{5}{\frac{1417}{2520}} = 5 \times \frac{2520}{1417} = 8.89$$

For any set of data the arithmetic mean is never less than the geometric mean and the geometric mean is never less than the harmonic mean

$$\text{a.m.} \geqslant \text{g.m.} \geqslant \text{h.m.}$$

When all observations are equal, it shows a.m. = g.m. = h.m.

Another way of calculating the arithmetic mean in a grouped data is by finding out the deviation from certain assumed mean of which the deviation seems to be zero. Usually the assumed mean is identified in the middle of the series, but that certainly depends on the groupwise concentration of data. For this reason in some cases it is assumed at some other value other than the middlemost, provided the data is more concentrated elsewhere. The deviations may be of two types : Cell deviation and deviation of mid-value of the assumed mean class. Cell deviation is more narrowed and specific, whereas, the deviation of mid-value of the assumed mean class from other values is usually reduced to a more specific deviation by dividing it by 'd' or common divider, by which all other mid-values are divisible. The latter is done for unequal classes.

Mean is calculated in a simpler way in regular classes :

$$\bar{x} = \bar{x}_0 + c.\frac{\sum ft}{\sum f}$$

[Here $\bar{x}_0$ = mid-value of the assumed mean class

$\sum ft$ = total deviation, which is the summation of the products of frequency and deviation of cells,

c = class interval]

For unequal classes it is better to use the following formula :

$$\bar{X} = c + d\bar{y} \qquad \text{when } y = \frac{x - c}{d} \quad \text{and } \bar{y} = \frac{\Sigma y}{\Sigma f}$$

[Here *c* = mid-value of the assumed mean class

d = common divider

$\bar{y}$ = average of the products of *y* values or total deviation and

Σf = total frequency]

In the two population data of Birbhum district the P.S. level data used before gives an equal series, whereas, the village level population of Rajnagar P.S. forms an unequal series. With these two sets of data having different characteristics the mean can be calculated in the following manner (table 7.9) :

TABLE 7.10

Class	Mid-value	Frequency (*f*)	Deviation of cell (t)	Total deviation (ft)
54001 – 89000	71500.5	1	– 2	– 2
89001 – 124000	106500.5	5	– 1	– 5
124001 – 159000	141500.5	4	0	0
159001– 194000	176500.5	1	+ 1	1
194001 – 229000	211500.5	3	+ 2	6

$\sum ft = 0$

$$\therefore \bar{x} = 141500.5 + 35000\left(\frac{0}{14}\right)$$

$$= 141500.5 + 0 \quad = 141500.5$$

Mean for unequal class (table 7.11):

TABLE 7.11

Class	Class mark	Frequency (*f*)	Deviation from class mark of mean class	$y = \frac{x - 450.5}{50}$	fy
1 – 100	50.5	11	– 400	– 8	– 88
101 – 200	150.5	11	– 300	– 6	– 66
201 – 700	450.5 (C)	43	0	0	0
701 – 1200	950.5	17	+500	+ 10	170
1201 – 1700	1450.5	3	+ 1000	+ 20	60
1701 – 5000	3350.5	1.	+ 2900	+ 58	58
5001 – 8000	6500.5	1	+ 6050	+ 121	121
					+ 255

$$\therefore\ \bar{x} = 450.5 + 50\left(\frac{255}{87}\right)$$

$$= 450.5 + 50 \times 2.93$$

$$= 597.05 \text{ (mean)}$$

When the classes are of equal width, calculation of mean is simpler.

Another simple way of deriving the arithmetic mean from a grouped data is to calculate the average of the product of mid-values and respective frequencies. This is applicable in both equal and unequal classes, though a large volume of data and big values may make it vulnerable to an erroneous calculation. This method is some what like a weighted mean, though the latter really indicates some differences in the nature of frequency from that of weight. It may be noted here that weight is the relative importance of classes, whereas, frequency calculates the absolute number of occurrence in a class. Weight and frequency are proportional to each other. However, in this method the formula may be derived as the following :

$$\bar{x} = \frac{\sum_{i=1}^{n} m_i f_i}{N}$$

[Here m_i = Class mark or mid-value of the classes starting from first to the final one :
f_i = frequency of the respective classes from first one to the final one :
N = total number of occurrences.]

Using the village level data of Rajnagar the computation for mean in this method can be done in the following way :

$$\bar{x} = \frac{(50.5 \times 11) + (150.5 \times 11) + (450.5 \times 43) + (950.5 \times 17) + (1450.5 \times 3) + (3350.5 \times 1) + (6500.5 \times 1)}{87}$$

$$= 597.05 \text{ (mean)}$$

Mean value can be graphically represented on a histogram or on a less than ogive.

Median

Another central value of a succession of statistical data is the median. It divides the data into two equal halves. In a simple series the median can be obtained by arranging the given data in order of magnitude first and then the middle-most value is selected. If the total number of occurrences is an odd number, one of the values will be the median. If the occurrences have an even number, the median will be located in the mid-way between two middle values.

For a grouped data the calculation of median can be done by using the following formula :

$$\text{Median} = \text{l.c.b.} + \frac{\frac{N}{2} - fc}{f_m}.c$$

[Here *l.c.b.* = lower class boundary of the median class.

$\frac{N}{2} - fc$ = difference between the median rank and cumulative frequency upto the lower class boundary of the median class.

f_m = frequency of the median class

c = class width or interval]

But before computation of the median, median rank should be identified first by dividing the number of occurrences by 2. The median rank would select the median class as a value occurring in the succession of less than cumulative frequency between two particular class boundaries.

Median for a simple series :

In a simple series of ungrouped data the median is simple to find out. In a data set of 12, 8, 7, 10, 9 the data should be arranged in order of magnitude first :

Number of pairs of shoes sold

7

8

(9)

10

12

After being arranged in order, '9' occupying the middle position of the odd number of occurrences should be selected as the median.

Had it been an even number of occurrences we should have to find out the median in the mid-way between two middle values, e.g.

Number of pairs of shoes sold

7	7
8	8
9	9
10	9.5 (median)
11	10
12	11
	12

Using the grouped data of P.S. level population of Birbhum district the median will be calculated as follows :

$$\text{Median rank} = \frac{14}{2} = 7$$

'7' as a cumulative value occurs in the class between 124000.5 and 159000.5 (table 7.8); therefore, this class will be selected as the class, which contains the median.

$$\text{Median} = 124000.5 + \frac{7-6}{4}.35000$$

$$= 124000.5 + 8750$$

$$= 132750.5 (\text{median})$$

The median can be taken as a partition value which divides the data into two equal parts. However, in a grouped data it is not so accurate, rather it gives an approximate value very close to the actual median.

Alternative method

Another way of calculating the median is through interpolation of cumulative frequency distribution. In this method also, the median rank is to be calculated by dividing the number of occurrences by 2. If the immediate lower and upper cumulative frequency than the median rank are marked as f_1 and f_2 respectively and the lower class boundary and upper class boundary of the class containing median are marked as l_1 and l_2 ,the median can be calculated as

$$\frac{\text{Median} - l_1}{l_2 - l_1} = \frac{\frac{N}{2} - f_1}{f_2 - f_1}$$

$$\therefore \quad \frac{\text{Median} - 124000.5}{159000.5 - 124000.5} = \frac{7-6}{10-6}$$

$$\text{or,} \quad \frac{\text{Median} - 124000.5}{35000} = \frac{1}{4}$$

$$\text{or,} \quad - 124000.5 = \frac{35000}{4}$$

$$\text{or,} \quad = 124000.5 + 8750$$

$$\therefore \quad \text{Median} = 132750.5$$

Quartile, Decile and Percentile

As median divides the data into two equal parts, some other partition values can also divide the data into four, ten and hundred parts. These are quartile, decile and percentile values. In a given series of data 3 quartile values, 9 decile values and 99 percentile values can be obtained. The second quartile, fifth decile and fiftieth percentile are equal to the median value. In fact, the methods of calculation for quartiles, deciles and percentiles are also the same with that of the median, only the ranking for each value will differ.

Calculation for quartiles : The first quartile rank can be calculated in the following manner :

(i) Quartile rank for first or lower quartile = $\frac{N}{4}$

(ii) Quartile rank for second quartile = $2\left(\frac{N}{4}\right)$

(iii) Quartile rank for third or upper quartile = $3\left(\frac{N}{4}\right)$

First quartile for P.S. level data of Birbhum :

$$\frac{N}{4} = \frac{14}{4} = 3.5 \text{ (rank for } Q_1\text{)}$$ [It occurs between 89000.5 and 124000.5 in table 7.8]

$$\frac{Q_1 - 89000.5}{124000.5 - 89000.5} = \frac{3.5 - 1}{6 - 1}$$

$$\text{or,} \quad \frac{Q_1 - 89000.5}{35000} = \frac{\cancel{2.5}}{\cancel{5}\;2}$$

$$\text{or,} \quad Q_1 - 89000.5 = \frac{35000}{2}$$

$$\text{or,} \quad Q_1 - 89000.5 = 17500$$

$$\text{or,} \quad Q_1 = 89000.5 + 17500 = 106500.5$$

Third quartile :

$$\frac{3N}{4} = \frac{3(14)}{4} = 10.5 \text{ (rank for } Q_3\text{)}$$

$$\text{or,} \quad \frac{Q_3 - 159000.5}{194000.5 - 159000.5} = \frac{10.5 - 10}{11 - 10}$$

$$\text{or,} \quad \frac{Q_3 - 159000.5}{35000} = \frac{\cancel{0.5}}{\cancel{1}\ 2}$$

$$\text{or,} \quad Q_3 - 159000.5 = \frac{35000}{2}$$

$$\text{or,} \quad Q_3 = 159000.5 + 17500 = 176500.5$$

7th decile :

$$\frac{7N}{10} = \frac{7(14)}{10} = 9.8 \text{ (Decile rank for 7th decile)}$$

$$\frac{D_7 - 124000.5}{159000.5 - 124000.5} = \frac{9.8 - 6}{10 - 6}$$

$$\text{or,} \quad \frac{D_7 - 124000.5}{35000} = \frac{3.8}{4}$$

$$\text{or,} \quad D_7 - 124000.5 = \frac{3.8 \times 35000}{4}$$

$$\text{or,} \quad D_7 - 124000.5 = 33250$$

$$\therefore \quad D_7 = 124000.5 + 33250 = 157250.5$$

33rd percentile :

$$\frac{33N}{100} = \frac{33(14)}{100} = 4.62 \text{ (percentile rank for 33 rd percentile)}$$

$$\text{or,} \quad \frac{P_{33} - 89000.5}{124000.5 - 89000.5} = \frac{4.62 - 1}{6 - 1}$$

$$\text{or,} \quad \frac{P_{33} - 89000.5}{35000} = \frac{3.62}{5}$$

$$\text{or,} \quad P_{33} - 89000.5 = \frac{3.62 \times \cancel{35000}^{\,7000}}{\cancel{5}}$$

$$\text{or,} \quad P_{33} - 89000.5 = 25340.$$

$$\therefore \quad P_{33} = 89000.5 + 25340 = 114340.5$$

Mode

Mode indicates the value, which has the maximum number of occurrence. In a grouped distribution the modal class is identified as the class having maximum frequency. More than one class may also be selected as modal classes, if they contain the highest number of frequency. Two of such classes in a data-set will characterize the distribution as bi-modal. If both of them occur in consecutive classes, there will be only one mode, even if two classes show the highest frequency.

Mode indicating the maximum number of occurrences is useful for meteorological predictions, for determination of average economic standard of people in terms of their share of expenditure from their total income etc. In a balanced distribution mode gives a substantial measure as a central value.

In a simple series the modal value can be selected just by inspection, locating the particular value which occurs for maximum number of times.

In a grouped distribution with equal classes mode in calculated from the following formula :

$$\text{Mode} = \text{l.c.b.} + \frac{f_m - f_b}{(f_m - f_b) + (f_m - f_a)} . c$$

[l.c.b. = lower class boundary of the modal class
f_m = frequency of the modal class;
f_b = frequency of the class below the modal class ;
f_a = frequency of the class above the modal class
c = Class interval.

In the P.S. level population data of Birbhum (table 7.5) the class 89001 – 124000 is identified as the modal class as it contains the maximum frequency.

$$\text{Mode} = 89000.5 + \frac{(5 - 1)}{(5 - 1) + (5 - 4)} \times 35000$$

$$= 89000.5 + \frac{4}{4+1} \times 35000$$

$$= 89000.5 + 0.8 \times 35000$$

$$\therefore \text{Mode} = 89000.5 + 28000 = 117000.5.$$

For unequal classes such a direct way of calculation of mode is not applicable. In those cases only an approximate value of mode is obtained from the inter-relation among mean, median and mode, provided the values of mean and median are already known and the distribution is not so skewed. The inter-relation between these central values can be expressed as

$$\text{Mean} - \text{Mode} = 3(\text{Mean} - \text{Median})$$

In the data of rural population of Rajnagar P.S. of Birbhum district for the grouped frequencies in unequal classes an approximate mode can be determined.

$$597.05 - \text{Mode} = 3(597.05 - 450.5)$$

$$\text{or, } 597.05 - \text{Mode} = 439.65$$

$$\text{or, } -\text{Mode} = 439.65 - 597.05$$

$$\therefore \text{Mode} = 157.4.$$

In this case the determination of mode becomes erroneous, as the frequency distribution is highly skewed. In data of low skewness and unequal classes this method may produce better results.

Graphical presentation

All the three measures of central tendency may be shown graphically too. Modal value is best shown graphically in histograms. If the two rectangles flanking the modal class rectangle are connected diagonally, the point of intersection will show the modal value.

Median can be shown at the point of intersection between the less and more than ogives.

Mean and other partition values can also be shown in histogram and on less than ogive.

MEASURES OF DISPERSION

Raw data contains variable degree of heterogeneity, be they natural values of observation or values some cultural phenomena. This degree of heterogeneity causes dispersion in the data. Thus the data shows a scattered nature which requires summarisation. Thus dispersion becomes zero, when in a given set of data all values are equal. Dispersion can be numerically identified in terms of deviation which is the distance of any value from any particular. A measure of dispersion summarizes the extent to which individual observations vary on average.

There are many of such measures of dispersion. Some of these measures are absolute in nature being specific deviation values that summarizes the dispersion considering the mean and median as the particular values from which numerical distances of individual observations are calculated in course of determining a specific deviation value.

On the other hand, some other relative measures of dispersion can also be identified. They determine the coefficients giving some variability indices which are expressed in percentage. There are further classifications of the deviation values.

Moreover, another numerical expression is also important in the regard. This is the *range*, which is expressed as the difference between the maximum value and the minimum value. It gives the specific amplitude of space on which the dispersions occur. It takes on as absolute measure of dispersion, though in practical use it lacks the specificity that is inherent in other measures of dispersion.

The coefficient of quartile deviation represents an *index of variability* and the coefficient of mean deviation is otherwise referred to as *relative variability*.

Types of deviation

Deviation represents the values as differences from mean value. Three methods may be applied for summarising a data for its deviation values, two of them are used with mean and one can be used with median.

Quartile deviation : When the condition of the scatter is presented by the median, it can be summarised by quartile deviation. It is derived as 50% of the interquartile range. Therefore, it can be expressed as

$$\frac{\text{Upper quartile} - \text{Lower quartile}}{2}$$

This method is very useful and significant values can be easily obtained by this method. It is the main exception of the deviations from mean. Here, half of the occurrences differ from the mean (median) by more than the amount and half differ by less than this amount.

The quartile deviation of the p.s. level data of Birbhum may be calculated as

$$\frac{176500.5-106500.5}{2}=35000$$

Mean deviation **:** It is the average amount by which individual values deviate from the mean. In a narrower definition the mean deviation is the average difference between various measurements and the central value, irrespective of sign, i.e. (±). It can be written as follows :

$$\text{Mean deviation}=\frac{\sum\left|X_i-\bar{X}_i\right|}{N}$$

In a simple series the mean deviation obtained among the number of five types of soap sold in a grocery is as follows :

TABLE 7.12

Type of soap	X	d (deviation)
a	12	2.8
b	7	2.2
c	8	1.2
d	9	0.2
e	10	0.8
	46/5 = 9.2	7.2/5 = 1.44

For a grouped data with frequency distribution the mean deviation is calculated by the following formula :

$$\frac{1}{N}\sum fi\left|X_i-\bar{X}_i\right|$$

Using this in table 7.12 the calculation of mean deviation may be worked out as :

TABLE 7.12A

Class boundary	X (mid value)	f	y $\frac{X-\bar{X}(141500.5)}{d(35000)}$	fy	$\left\|X-\bar{X}\right\|$	$f\left\|X-\bar{X}\right\|$
54000.5 – 89000.5	71500.5	1	– 2	– 2	70000	70000
89000.5 – 124000.5	106500.5	5	– 1	– 5	35000	175000
124000.5 – 159000.5	141500.5	4	0	0	0	0
159000.5 – 194000.5	176500.5	1	+ 1	+ 1	35000	35000
194000.5 – 229000.5	211500.5	3	+2	+ 6	70000	210000
			$\Sigma y=0$	$\Sigma fy=0$		$\Sigma f\left\|X-\bar{X}\right\|=490000$

$\bar{X} = c + d\bar{y}$

$= 141500.5 + 35000.\frac{0}{14}$

$= 141500.5$

Mean deviation $= \frac{490000}{14}$

$= 35000$

Standard deviation **:** Standard deviation, otherwise known as root mean square deviation, is the square root of the average of the squares of the deviations from the arithmetic average. It is usually expressed as sigma (σ).

The square of standard deviation is known as the variance. Therefore, the two formulae can be written as

$$\text{Variance } (\sigma^2) = \frac{\Sigma(x - \bar{x})^2}{n}$$

$$\text{Standard deviation} = (\sigma) = \sqrt{\frac{\Sigma(x - \bar{x})^2}{n}}$$

For simple series these are usable.

For frequency distribution the variance may be calculated on the basis of the following formula :

$$\sigma^2 = \frac{1}{N}\Sigma fi(x_i - \bar{x})^2$$

For frequency distribution standard deviation is calculated as

$$\sigma = c.\sqrt{\frac{\Sigma ft^2}{\Sigma f} - \left(\frac{\Sigma ft}{\Sigma f}\right)^2}$$

for standard deviation of x values for y or t values class interval (c) is not multiplied.

For the data of soaps sold :

$$\text{Variance} = \frac{(7.2)^2}{5} = \frac{51.84}{5} = 10.368$$

$$\text{S.D.} = \sqrt{10.368} = 3.21993$$

For a grouped frequency distribution (P.S. level population, Birbhum) the following table 7.13 should be prepared.

TABLE 7.13

Class	Mid-value (x)	Frequency	$t = \frac{x - c}{d}$	ft	ft^2
54001 – 89000	71500.5	1	– 2	– 2	4
89001 – 124000	106500.5	5	– 1	– 5	5
124001 – 159000	141500.5 (c)	4	0	0	0
159001 – 194000	176500.5	1	+1	+1	1
194001 – 229000	211500.5	3	+2	+6	12
				$\Sigma ft = 0$	$\Sigma ft^2 = 22$

$$\text{S.D.} = 35000 \times \sqrt{\frac{22}{14} - \left(\frac{0}{14}\right)^2}$$

$$= 35000 \times \sqrt{1.57142851 - 0}$$

$$= 35000 \times 1.25 \quad = 43750$$

or using total number of values obtained in calculator it is $35000 \times 1.253566341 = 43874.82$

Variability indices

(i) Index of variability = $\dfrac{\text{Quartile deviation}}{\text{median}} \times 100\%$

$$\therefore \frac{35000}{132750.5} \times 100\% = 26.36\%$$

(ii) Relative variability = $\dfrac{\text{Mean deviation}}{\text{Average}} \times 100\%$

$$\therefore \frac{35000}{141500.5} \times 100\% = 24.73\%$$

(iii) Coefficient of variability = $\dfrac{\text{S.D.}}{\text{Average}} \times 100\%$

$$\therefore \frac{43874.82}{141500.5} \times 100\% = 31.00\%$$

Moments, Skewness & Kurtosis

Moments are arbitrary constants about any particular value in n number of observations. The moments about mean are important in Geography. Four such central moments can be determined. These are :

	For frequency distribution it is :
First moment (m_1) abount mean = $\frac{1}{n}\Sigma(x - \bar{x}) = 0$	$\frac{1}{n}\Sigma f(x - \bar{x})$
Second moment (m_2) about mean = $\frac{1}{n}\Sigma(x - \bar{x})^2 = \sigma^2$	$\frac{1}{n}\Sigma f(x - \bar{x})^2$
Third moment (m_3) about mean = $\frac{1}{n}\Sigma(x - \bar{x})^3$	$\frac{1}{n}\Sigma f(x - \bar{x})^3$
Fourth moment (m_4) about mean = $\frac{1}{n}\Sigma(x - \bar{x})^4$	$\frac{1}{n}\Sigma f(x - \bar{x})^4$

This way further values can be determined. The second moment seems to be the square of standard deviation or variance. The third central moment is used to calculate *skewness* while the fourth central moment is a measurement of *kurtosis*.

Skewness (y_1) is measured by

$$Y_1 = \frac{m_3}{\left(\sqrt{m_2}\right)^3}$$

Kurtosis (Y_2) is measured from the following formula :

$$Y_2 = \frac{m_4}{\left(\sqrt{m_2}\right)^4} - 3$$

It may be noted here that all the important characteristics of any frequency distribution can be described by moments, e.g. the first moment about zero gives the arithmetic mean, square root of second central moment is standard deviation etc.

Calculation for moments

Using the P.S. level data of Birbhum we get

TABLE 7.14

Mid-value	f	$y = \frac{x-141500.5}{35000}$	fy	fy^2	fy^3	fy^4	$f(y+1)^4$
71500.5	1	−2	−2	4	−8	16	1
106500.5	5	−1	−5	5	−5	5	0
141500.5	4	0	0	0	0	0	4
176500.5	1	1	1	1	1	1	16
211500.5	3	2	6	12	24	48	243
	$\Sigma f = 14$	$\Sigma y = 0$	0	22	12	70	264

Charlier's check : C.V.L. Charlier observed a simple check for the calculation of moments in a grouped frequency distribution.

$\Sigma f(y+1)^4 = \Sigma fy^4 + 4\Sigma fy^3 + 6\Sigma fy^2 + 4\Sigma fy + N$

From Table 7.14

$264 = 70 + 48 + 132 + 0 + 14$

$= 264$

Hence the calculation in table 7.14 is correct.

Raw moments of y :

$m_1' = \Sigma fy/N = 0/14 = 0$ $\quad m_2' = \Sigma fy^2/N = 22/14 = 1.57$

$m_3' = \Sigma fy^3/N = 12/14 = 0.86$ $\quad m_2' = \Sigma fy^4/N = 70/14 = 5$

Central moments of y :

$m_2 = m_2' - (m_1')^2 = 1.57 - 0 = 1.57$

$m_3 = m_3' - 3m_2' m_1' + 2(m_1')^3$

$= 0.86 - 3(0) + 2(0)^3 = 0.86$

$m_4 = m_4' - 4m_3' m_1' + 6m_2'(m_1')^2 - 3(m_1')^4$

$= 5 - 4(.86)(0) + 6(1.57)(0)^2 - 3(0)^4$

$= 5 - 0 + 0 + 0 + 0 = 5$

Skewness

If the variables having equal frequencies are equidistant from the mean, the distribution is said to be symmetrical. But in most of the cases the frequency distributions are not symmetrical and the degree of asymmetry varies from one case to another. The extent of asymmetry is known as *Skewness*. A symmetrical distribution shows zero skewness.

The measurement of skewness has been done by many methods :

1. Pearson's first formula : Skewness $= \dfrac{\text{mean} - \text{mode}}{\text{Standard deviaton}}$

2. Pearson's second formula : Skewness $= \dfrac{3(\text{mean} - \text{median})}{\text{Standard deviaton}}$

3. Moment measure : Skewness $= \dfrac{m_3}{\sigma^3} = \dfrac{m_3}{\left(\sqrt{m_2}\right)^3}$

4. Bowley's measure : Skewness $= \dfrac{Q_3 - 2Q_2 + Q_1}{Q_3 - Q_1}$

It may be noted here that all the measures of skewness will show zero, when the distribution is symmetrical. Bowley's measure shows a value between –1 and +1. In Pearson's first measure there is no such theoretical limits though, but in practice a value is rarely very high. The measures of skewness in Pearson's second formula lie between –3 and +3. When in an asymmetrical frequency distribution the tail extends to the right and peak to the left, it is a case of positive skewness. If the opposite is true, it should be known as negative skewness.

Therefore, some of the measures are dependent on the relationship between mean, median and mode whereas, others are dependent on quartile values.

Calculation of Skewness from moments :

$$= \frac{m_3}{\left(\sqrt{m_2}\right)^3} = \frac{0.86}{\left(\sqrt{1.57}\right)^3} = \frac{0.86}{(1.25)^3} = \frac{0.86}{1.97} = +0.44$$

Kurtosis : Kurtosis is related to the degree of peakedness of the frequency curve. Kurtosis is measured on the basis of moments.

There are three types of kurtosis :

Platykurtic (when $\beta_2 = <3$)

Mesokurtic (when $\beta_2 = 3$)

Leptokurtic (when $\beta_2 = >3$)

The frequency curve in a platykurtic distribution is relatively flat topped, for leptokurtic distribution it has a high peak, whereas, a mesokurtic is normal and shows moderate peakedness.

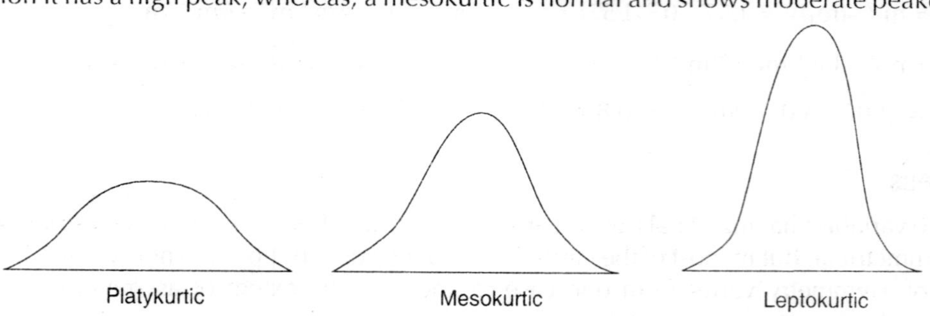

Kurtosis is calculated on the basis of moments only.

$$\text{Kurtosis} = \frac{m_4}{\sigma^4} - 3 = \beta_2 - 3 \quad \therefore \; \beta_2 = \frac{5}{(1.57)^2} = \frac{5}{2.4649} = 2.03$$

$b_2 - 3 = 2.03 - 3 = -.97$

M_4 = Fourth central moment

σ^4 = Square of Variance

$$\beta_2 = \frac{m_4}{m_2^2}$$

Therefore, the distribution is platykurtic.

Time series and determination of trend values

Geographical data or spatial data often varies with time. Such temporal variations are in many instances conclusive of geographical inferences. For instance, the recurrence of high intensity rainfall and resultant flood in a cycle of five, ten or eleven years can be detected from time series analysis. However, oscillation within the range of fluctuation may also hinder the understanding about the occurrence of trends. In such cases an average condition may be required between the high and low values to follow the trend. Moreover, a scatter diagram often disperses the dots in such a manner as it becomes difficult to find out the actual trend. For such a widely fluctuating data of temporal variation *time series analysis* is helpful. It may be accomplished on the basis of successive period of time or it may be based on semi-average method in which a straight line trend may be determined. In the period analysis of successive blocks of years, months, days, hours etc. a moving average method is used. In the semi-average method the data is divided into two parts and each of them has one average and a straight line will connect these two average values.

In the moving average method a series of arithmetic mean of successive observations are determined from the data. The moving average values are taken as periodic trend values. If the period of moving average is an odd number, the trend values correspond to the given time. If the period, for which the moving average is to be determined, is an even number, centering is required. Cyclic fluctuations are easily determined by moving average method, but at the beginning or at the end of the series, trend values can not be obtained.

The following is the discharge data of the Mundeshwari river. This has been converted into a 4 day and a 5 day moving average :

TABLE 7.15

Calculation for Moving average

Day	Discharge in cusecs	4 day moving total	4 day moving average	2 item moving total	4 day moving average (Centered)	5 day total	5 day average
7.8.93	740	—	—			—	—
8.8.93	950	—	—			—	—
		3316	829				
9.8.93	900			1660.5	830.25	4066	813.20
		3326	831.5				
10.8.93	726			1800.5	900.25	4826	965.20
		3876	969				
11.8.93	750			2750.5	1375.25	8026	1605.20
		7126	1781.5				
12.8.93	1500			5731.5	2865.75	16526	3305.20
		15800	3950				
13.8.93	4150			10250	5125	25950	5190
		25200	6300				
14.8.93	9400			13212.5	6606.25	29150	5830
		27650	6912.5				
15.8.93	10150			14537.5	7268.75	34650	6930
		30500	7625				
16.8.93	3950			14037.5	7018.75	35050	7010
		25650	6412.5				
17.8.93	7000			11275	5637.5	29600	5920
		19450	4862.5				
18.8.93	4550			9587.5	4793.75	22850	4570
		18900	4725				
19.8.93	3950			8437.5	4218.75	21850	4370
		14850	3712.5				
20.8.93	3400			6850	3425	17100	3420
		12550	3137.5				
21.8.93	2950	—	—			—	—
22.8.93	2250	—	—			—	—

Therefore, the graph for moving average may be obtained (fig 7.5).

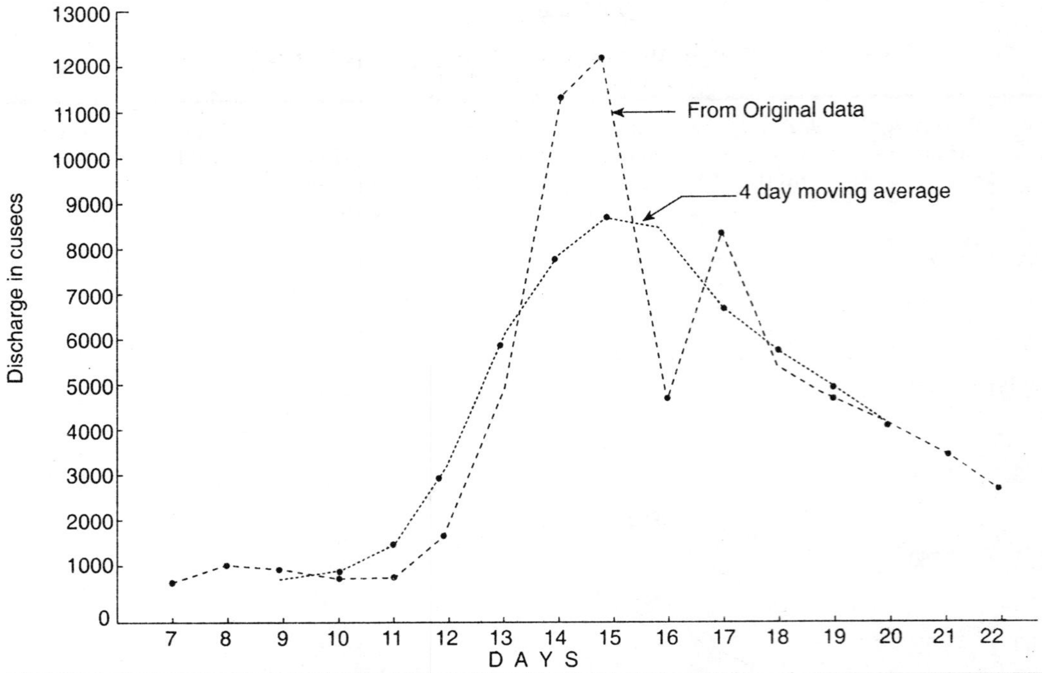

Fig. 7.5 Graph for moving average method

Time series analysis : Application of Semi Average Method

TABLE 7.16

Calculation of semi average values for fitting a straight line correlation

Census Year	Female Literacy Rate (Crude) in%	Male Literacy Rate (Crude) in %	6 year Semi Total (Female)	6 year Semi Total (male)	6 Year Semi Average	
					Female	Male
1901	0.60	9.83				
1911	1.05	10.56				
1921	1.81	12.21				
			21.62	98.04	3.60	16.34
1931	2.93	15.59				
1941	7.30	24.9				
1951	7.93	24.95				
1961	12.95	34.44				
1971	18.69	39.45				
1981	24.82	46.89				
			190.77	307.98	31.80	51.33
1991	32.17	52.74				
2001	45.15	63.24				
2011	56.99	71.22				

Graph Showing
Direct Correlation between time and changing male
Female Literacy In India

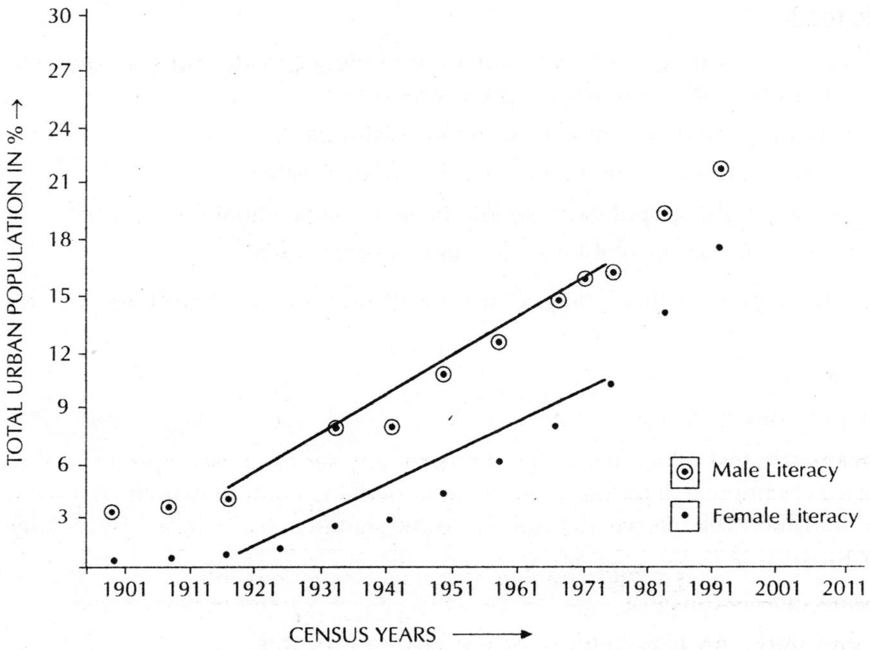

Interpretation

With the spread of education and changing perspective of human society throughout India both male and female literacy have increased with time. In different census years, the percentage of literacy has been markedly rising. In terms of male literacy it rose from 9.83% in 1901 to 71.22% in 2011. In the case of female literacy, it has risen from 0.60% to 56.99% in the census years mentioned earlier to determine a correlation in this time series of rising literacy semi avarage method is one of the simple means which can mark such temporal changes. In this method the entire set of data is divided into two groups, in the case of even number of data the division is simple and in the case of odd number one central data is taken as common in both the groups. Then the group total is averaged by number of years in the groups. The averages are placed at the middle position of the respective group. A straight line connects these two semi average values and the correlation is drawn.

In this graph, two correlations have been noted, i.e. between time and male literacy and time and female literacy. It is observed that in both the cases literacy has a steady increase with time, but in the case of male literacy the rate of increase in higher than the rise of female literacy. This difference owes its origin to the discrimination in the treatment of male and female child in Indian families.

STATISTICAL SIGNIFICANCE

While comparing between two sets of data, the method to be used will depend on the nature of data in consideration. Thus a set of nominal data can be judged by simple tests, whereas, for ordinal data certain other complicated tests may be suitable, though simple tests are also applicable. Interval data, on the other hand, requires more refined analysis. However, if nominal and ordinal data are grouped together, non-parametric tests are suitable and for interval data parametric tests are well suited.

Parametric tests

A parametric test assumes certain quality or attribute, characteristics, volume etc. otherwise implied as a parameter with the following premises in mind :

1. the population data should be normally distributed;
2. the observations should be independent of each other;
3. the comparable populations should have the same variance;
4. the variables are available on the interval or ratio scale.

The tests belonging to this category are based on variance, standard deviation etc. The common tests are :

1. Student's 't' test
2. Snedecor's 'F' test

Non-parametric test : Such tests do not require any series of assumptions in the population data, except independence. It further requires an underlying continuity in the data. Practically the ordinal, nominal and even interval data can be tested significantly in these tests. Such tests are :

1. Chi-squared test
2. One sample runs test
3. Mann-Whitney U test etc.

In two sets of data one may be statistically significant to another or it may not be too. Thus the data for average aman paddy may not be statistically significant to changing population figure whereas, marks obtained in statistics and maths may prove significant and correlated to each other.

In this connection a hypothesis may be set whether or not there lies any difference between the sets of data compared. This difference results from the fact that the data involves some samples only. Had the entire population been taken, not such difference could have occurred. The hypothesis assuming the non-existence of any real difference between the sets of data is known as the *null hypothesis.* This is marked as H_0. Through statistical testing the null hypothesis is rejected or established. If null hypothsis is rejected, the inverse of null hypothesis is accepted as H_1, which indicates that there is real difference between the data-sets as revealed from testing of samples. The null hypothesis is accepted when the observed value of test lies outside the *critical region.* Another probability lies in the occurrence of an error during the course of rejection or acceptance of null hypothesis. The maximum probability at which a null hypothesis is rejected is referred to as *Level of significance* (OC). Usually 5% or 1% level of significance is checked in terms of the *degree of freedom,* i.e. n–2, which is a measure of sample size. In graphical representation of the level of significance four predetermined critical limits are given. The lowest one among them as marked by 10% will indicate the area below it as *acceptance zone* and the area above is indicated as *rejection zone.* The point obtained in terms of the degree of freedom is on abscissa and index value on the ordinate. The location of the point in the acceptance or rejection zone will also indicate the significance level of the observed value in terms of its upper and lower limits (fig 7.6).

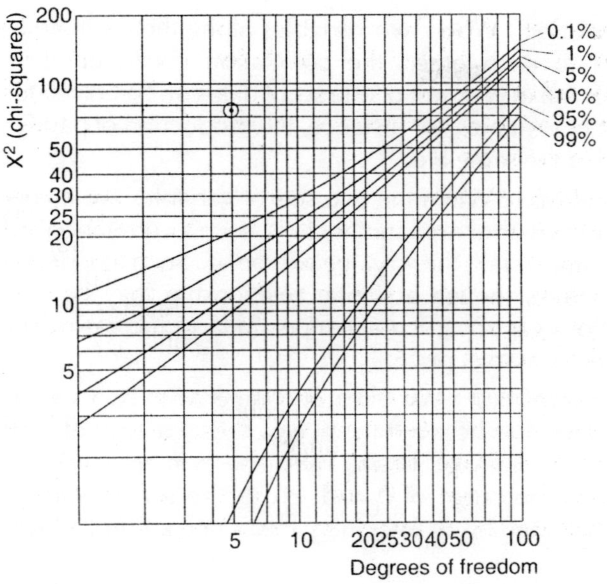

Fig. 7.6 Graph for Chi-squared test

Correlation and regression

We often come across some geographical data, which have two continuous characters that require correlation, as one of them is often dependent on the other. Such a data may be a related group of two sets of variables, e.g., height and weight of a group of persons. Geographical or spatial data often require the analysis of the interrelation between two sets of data, e.g. one may be related to the population density of an area and the other may be the number of workers of the same. Thus they require some sort of bi-variate analysis which may be a scatter representing dots marked on the basis of the data given along the ordinate and the abscissa. This relationship between two sets of variables can not be easily identifiable in every case, particularly when they develop a natural relationship between them. Such data sets may be independent of each other too, e.g., the number of literate persons of a police station and the number of workers of the same police station.

However, the extent or degree of relationship between two sets of quantitative data is measured in terms of *correlation coefficient.* This coefficient is denoted by the alphabet 'r'.

Although correlation can determine the relationship between two variables, it never proves that one particular variable alone causes the change of the other. In this connection it may be noted here that a geographical interpretation often requires some knowledge about the other untold causes apart from trying to determine the positive or negative relationship between the two given sets of variables. Thus, while interpreting a correlation between the two sets of variables the interpreter may search out in more details about the causes that may be held responsible for the variation of the data.

However, we may have, in general, five types of correlation on the basis of their direction and extent. These correlations are :

1. *Perfect positive correlation :* When two variables along the ordinate and the abscissa are directly proportional to each other, the correlation coefficient ('r') = +1. In such a relationship the rise or fall of one unit of one set of data can be correlated to one unit of rise or fall of the other set of variables, for instance, the production of paddy in one area and the supply of staple food in the same area.
2. *Perfect negative correlation :* When the two sets of variables are inversely proportional to each other, which means if one rises, another falls, such a correlation occurs. If each unit of rise is related to each unit of fall, the 'r' value will be –1. Such a perfect negative correlation is rather absent in nature, though a similar relationship may be obtained between the pressure and volume of a gas at particular temperatures or increasing supply of a perishable commodity and fall of its market price.
3. *Moderately positive correlation* : We often encounter with two sets of geographical data which have such a correlation between them, e.g., the incidence of rainfall and the amount of flood discharge in a drainage basin. Here the non-zero values of the correlation coefficient lie between the range of 0 and +1. In the scatter such moderately positive correlation may be indicated by an imaginary mean line around which the actual dots are placed.
4. *Moderately negative correlation*: In such cases the non-zero values of 'r' lie between –1 and 0. For such a case also the dots of the scatter lie in the surroundings of a mean imaginary line, which rises from the extreme values of one variable, for instance, an increase in number of govt. buses in calcutta following a partial strike of private buses in different routes of the city.
5. *No correlation* : When no linear relationship exists between two sets of variables, the 'r' value is known to be zero. Such no correlation variables occurring within the same geographical space are not uncommon, e.g. sex-ratio and birth rate of different groups of people of the same urban centre.

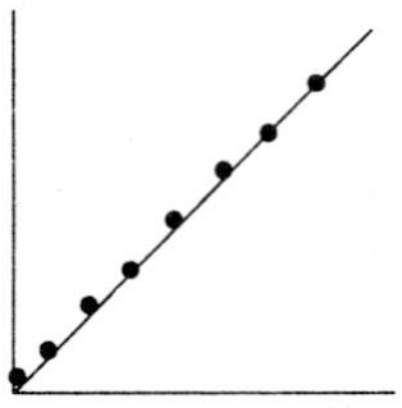
(1) [r = +1]

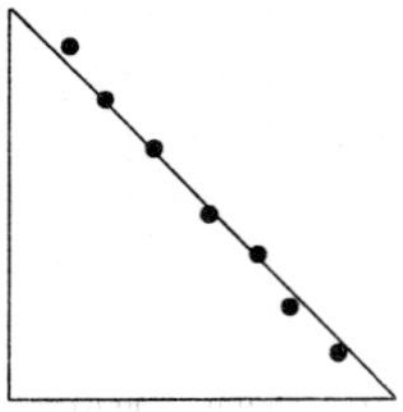
(2) [r = –1]

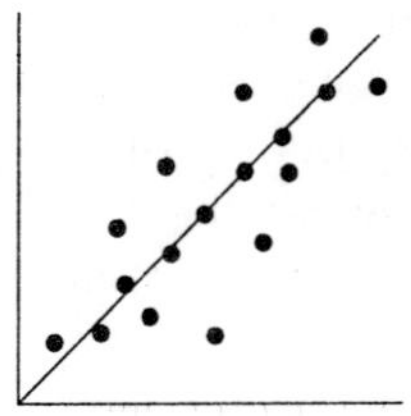
(3) [0<r<+1]

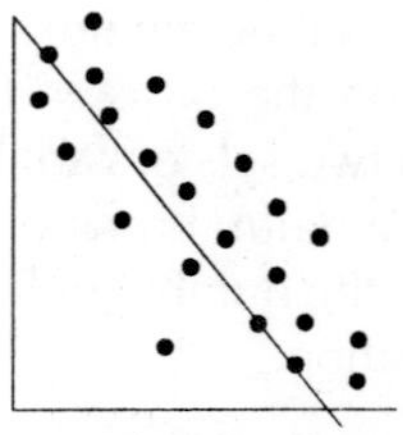
(4) [–1<r<0]

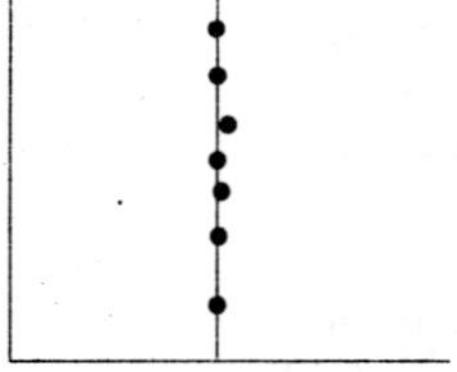
(5a) [r = 0]

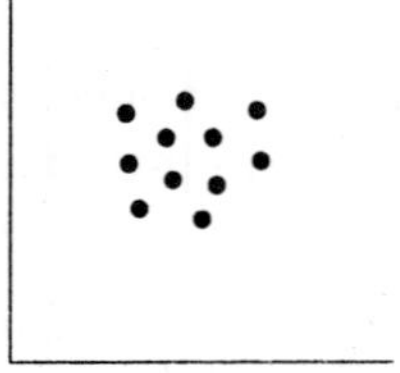
(5b) [r = 0]

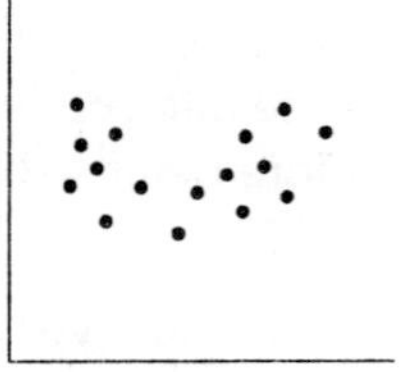
(5c) [r = 0]

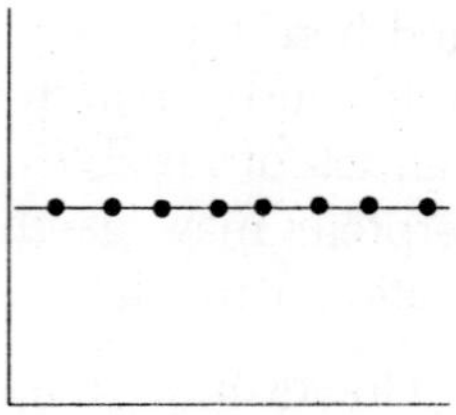
(5d) [r = 0]

Correlation Coefficient for ungrouped series

When two sets of variables are normally distributed, and they do not have a much complex relationship between them, the 'r' can be calculated as —

$$r = \frac{\Sigma(X-\bar{X})(Y-\bar{Y})}{\sqrt{\Sigma(X-\bar{X})^2\,\Sigma(Y-\bar{Y})^2}} \quad \text{or} \quad \frac{\Sigma xy}{\sqrt{\Sigma x^2\,\Sigma y^2}}$$

Here $x = (X-\bar{X}), y = (Y-\bar{Y})$

However, 'r' can also be calculated without determining the mean for the variables. It can be calculated as

$$r = \frac{\Sigma XY - \frac{\Sigma X\,\Sigma Y}{n}}{\sqrt{\left(\Sigma X^2 - \frac{(\Sigma X)^2}{n}\right)\left(\Sigma Y^2 - \frac{(\Sigma Y)^2}{n}\right)}}$$

The latter method is simple and direct and avoids the unnecessary calculation of mean, though it is more lengthy.

Calculation for correlation coefficient

The marks of 10 students in mathematics and statistics in 1998-1999 session of a school are given in table 7.16 from which the correlation coefficient has been determined.

TABLE 7.16

Roll No. of Students	Marks in Mathematics					Marks in Statistics						
	X	X^2	$\bar{X}$	$X-\bar{X}$ (x)	x^2	Y	Y^2	$\bar{Y}$	$Y-\bar{Y}$ (y)	y^2	XY	xy
1	32	1024		-11.2	125.44	30	900		-8.8	77.44	960	98.56
2	38	1444		-5.2	27.04	31	961		-7.8	60.84	1178	40.56
3	48	2304		4.8	23.04	38	1444		-0.8	0.64	1824	-3.84
4	43	1849		-0.2	0.04	43	1849		4.2	17.64	1849	-0.84
5	40	1600	43.2	-3.2	10.24	33	1089	38.8	-5.8	33.64	1320	18.56
6	22	484		-21.2	449.44	11	121		-27.8	772.84	242	589.36
7	41	1681		-2.2	4.84	27	729		-11.8	139.24	1107	25.96
8	69	4761		25.8	665.64	76	5776		37.2	1383.84	5244	959.76
9	35	1225		-8.2	67.24	40	1600		1.2	1.44	1400	-9.84
10	64	4096		20.8	432.64	59	3481		20.2	408.04	3776	420.16
Σ	432	20468		0	1805.6	388	17950		0	2895.6	18900	2138.4

According to the formula adopted :

$$r = \frac{\Sigma xy}{\sqrt{\Sigma x^2 \, \Sigma y^2}} = \frac{2138.4}{\sqrt{(1805.6 \times 2895.6)}} = \frac{2138.4}{2286.55} = 0.94$$

Following the simpler formula :

$$r = \frac{\Sigma XY - \dfrac{\Sigma X \Sigma Y}{n}}{\sqrt{\left(\Sigma X^2 - \dfrac{(\Sigma X)^2}{n}\right)\left(\Sigma Y^2 - \dfrac{(\Sigma Y)^2}{n}\right)}}$$

$$\text{or, } r = \frac{18900 - \dfrac{432 \times 388}{10}}{\left(20468 - \dfrac{186624}{10}\right)\left(17950 - \dfrac{150544}{10}\right)}$$

$$= \frac{18900 - 16761.6}{\sqrt{(20468 - 18662.4)(17950 - 15054.4)}} = \frac{2138.4}{\sqrt{1805.6 \times 2895.6}}$$

$$= \frac{2138.4}{\sqrt{5228295.36}} = \frac{2138.4}{2286.55} = 0.94$$

The observed correlation coefficient (0.94) can be tested for significance. If 'r' value of the population is zero the correlation coefficient of a large number of data should be normally distributed around zero. For determining the significance of the value the hypothesis of no correlation may be followed. This is done by

$$\frac{\text{Observed 'r' value}}{\text{S.E.}} \qquad \text{S.E.} = \text{Standard Error}$$

$$\text{or, } \frac{r}{\sqrt{\dfrac{1}{(n-1)}}} = r\sqrt{(n-1)} = 0.94\sqrt{(10-1)} = 0.94 \times 3 = 2.82$$

This value being more than 2 is significant at 5% level and hence, the hypothesis of no correlation is not to be adopted. Therefore, the score in statistics has significant correlation with the marks obtained in mathematics.

But this test is applied for a large sample data. For a small data the significance of 'r' value should be checked by 't' test.

$$t = \frac{r\sqrt{(n-2)}}{\sqrt{(1-r^2)}} \qquad t = \frac{0.94\sqrt{(10-2)}}{\sqrt{(1-0.94^2)}} = \frac{0.94 \times 2.83}{.341} = \frac{2.66}{.34} = 7.8$$

As at 5% level, at 1% level or even at 0.1% level the value is much less than the value obtained, the null hypothesis is rejected and it can be maintained that this coefficient is statistically highly significant and the marks obtained is in statistics is significantly correlated with the marks obtained in mathematics.

Regression

In some of the cases it becomes necessary to predict the value of one character or one set of data from the knowledge of the other set of data. Such variables are correlated in a linear fashion. Of the two sets the known variable is independent and the other unknown becomes dependent. The estimation of the unknown is done by finding a constant known as regression coefficient. *Regression actually means a change in the measurement of a variable character on the positive or negative side beyond the mean.* The regression coefficient is a measure of the change in the dependent set of variables (Y) with each unit of change in the independent character (X). It is detected by an alphabet 'b' which indicates relative change in Y (Y_C) from the mean of Y ($\bar{Y}$). After plotting the estimated values of Y, that is Yc_1, Yc_2 .... Yc_n corresponding to X_1, X_2, ... X_n, both are correlated.

The calculated values of Y or Y_C corresponding to any value of X is equal to $\bar{Y}$ + bx.

The calculation for Y_C is

$$Yc = \bar{Y} + bx \quad = \bar{Y} + b(X - \bar{X}) \quad = \bar{Y} + bX - b\bar{X} \quad = \bar{Y} - b\bar{X} + bX$$

However, $\bar{Y} - b\bar{X}$ being a constant may be denoted by 'a'

Therefore, $Y_C = a + bX$

According to the data of 10 students in mathematics and statistics

$$\bar{Y} = 38.8, \ \bar{X} = 43.2, \qquad b_{xy} = \frac{\Sigma xy}{\Sigma x^2} = \frac{2138.4}{1805.6} = 1.18$$

and constant a = 38.8 – 1.18 × 43.2 = –12.176

Now the Yc value corresponding the values of X are (table 7.17) :

TABLE 7.17

Yc	=	a	+	b	×	X		
Yc_1	=	– 12.176	+	1.18	×	32	=	25.584
Yc_2	=	– 12.176	+	1.18	×	38	=	32.664
Yc_3	=	– 12.176	+	1.18	×	48	=	44.464
Yc_4	=	– 12.176	+	1.18	×	43	=	38.564
Yc_5	=	– 12.176	+	1.18	×	40	=	35.024
Yc_6	=	– 12.176	+	1.18	×	22	=	13.784
Yc_7	=	– 12.176	+	1.18	×	41	=	36.204
Yc_8	=	– 12.176	+	1.18	×	69	=	69.244
Yc_9	=	– 12.176	+	1.18	×	35	=	29.124
Yc_{10}	=	– 12.176	+	1.18	×	64	=	63.344

The best fitting Regression line on the basis of the calculated values of y may thus be obtained of the following scatter (fig 7.7).

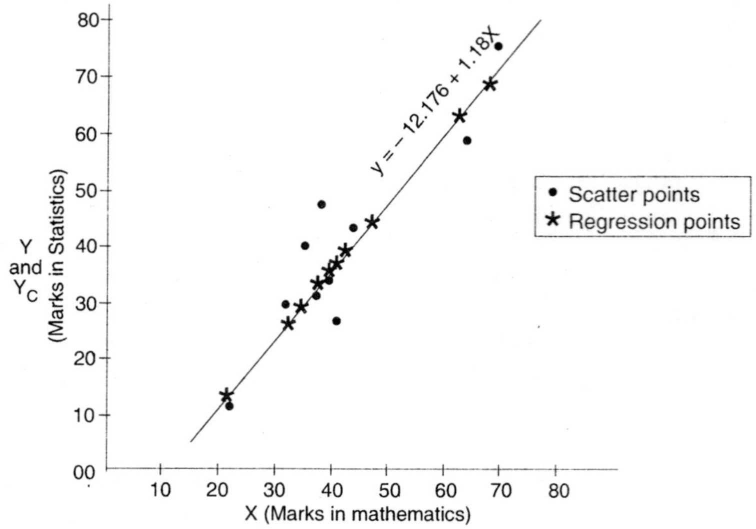

Fig. 7.7 Scatter and Regression line

The regression line is the mean line that has passed through the mean position of the scatter diagram separating five points above it and five points below. Following the trend of the line it can be inferred that the marks of statistics have a positive correlation with the marks of mathematics.

Such a calculation of correlation coefficient and regression coefficient as well as the determination of regression line on the basis of Y_C or X_C values can be applied for spatially interlinked data. Thus pairs of data sets for (i) rainfall and run off, (ii) minimum temperature and maximum temperature (atmospheric), (iii) temperature and evaporation, , (iv) texture ratio and drainage density, (v) slope and drainage density, (vi) height of land a.s.l. and paddy cultivation etc. are usable for determination of statistical significance through correlation.

Least square method

The fitting of a straight line between two sets of variables is also possible by least square method which considers that *the sum of the squares of differences lying between the observed and corresponding estimated values should be the minimum.* Thus the general equation for linking a pair of observations, i.e., Y = a+bX is also used here with a and b as constants and estimating the values of Y by substituting the corresponding values of X. Therefore, the values of a and b are determined in such a way as to minimise the sum of squares of differences, i.e. $\Sigma(Y_i - a - bX_i)^2$ i.e. i = 1

This gives us the two equations :

$$\Sigma Y = an + b\Sigma X \text{ and } \Sigma XY = a\Sigma X + b\Sigma X^2$$

Calculation

Data of Annual rainfall and run-off for 10 years of a drainage basin (table 7.18) :

X (Rainfall in cm.) 46.4. 63.0, 48.8, 60.1, 50.6, 57.5, 55.5, 57.0, 60.8, 48.3

Y (Run off in cm.) 31.9, 46.8, 34.2, 47.5, 35.2, 40.5, 41.3, 43.5, 44.8, 38.5

In this n pairs of observations the normal equations determining the constant values of a and b are :

$$\Sigma Y = an + b\Sigma X \text{ and } \Sigma XY = a\Sigma X + b\Sigma X^2$$

TABLE 7.18

X (Rainfall)	Y (Run off)	X^2	XY
46.4	31.9	2152.96	1480.16
63.0	46.8	3969	2948.4
48.8	34.2	2381.44	1668.96
60.1	47.5	3612.01	2854.75
50.6	35.2	2560.36	1781.12
57.5	40.5	3306.25	2328.75
55.5	41.3	3080.25	2292.15
57.0	43.5	3249	2479.5
60.8	44.8	3696.64	2723.84
48.3	38.5	2332.89	1859.55
$\Sigma X = 548$	$\Sigma Y = 404.2$	$\Sigma X^2 = 30340.8$	$\Sigma XY = 22417.18$

Putting the value of $\Sigma Y = 404.2$, n=10, $\Sigma X = 548$

$\Sigma XY = 22417.18$, $\Sigma X^2 = 30340.8$ in the two equations we get :

$404.2 = 10a + 548b$ .... (i)

$22417.18 = 548a + 30340.8b$ .... (ii)

Multiplying (i) by 548 and (ii) by 10 and subtracting we get

$$221501.6 = 5480a + 300304b$$

$$224171.8 = 5480a + 303408b$$

$$-2670.2 = -3104b$$

$$\therefore b = \frac{-2670.2}{-3104} = .86$$

Thus putting the value of b in (i) we get :

$$404.2 = 10a + 548 \times .86$$

$$\text{or,} \quad 10a = -404.2 + 471.28$$

$$\text{or,} \quad 10a = -67.08$$

$$\therefore a = \frac{-67.08}{10} = -6.708$$

$\therefore$ For the equation $Y = a + bX$ it is

$$Y = -6.708 + .86X$$

Putting the X value in the equation the estimated values of Y can be determined. These estimated values will fix the mean position in the scatter diagram along which the bestfit straight line can be obtained.

TABLE 7.19

Calculated y values

a	+	b	×	x	=	y_c
−6.708	+	0.86	×	46.4	=	33.196
−6.708	+	0.86	×	63.0	=	47.472
−6.708	+	0.86	×	48.8	=	35.26
−6.708	+	0.86	×	60.1	=	44.98
−6.708	+	0.86	×	50.6	=	36.81
−6.708	+	0.86	×	57.5	=	42.74
−6.708	+	0.86	×	55.5	=	41.02
−6.708	+	0.86	×	57.0	=	42.312
−6.708	+	0.86	×	60.8	=	45.58
−6.708	+	0.86	×	48.3	=	34.83

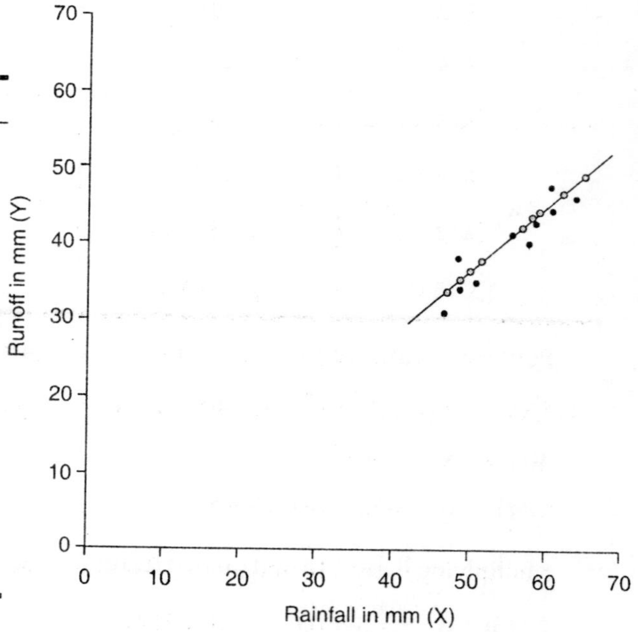

Fig. 7.8 **Correlation between rainfall and runoff through Regression**

CORRELATION IN TIME SERIES ANALYSIS

TABLE 7.20

Calculation of estimated percentrage of total urban population in India through least square method

Census Year (X)	Percentage of Total Urban Population (Y)	Coded X	X^2	XY
1901	10.84	−9	81	−97.56
1911	10.29	−7	49	−72.03
1921	11.18	−5	25	−55.9
1931	11.99	−3	9	−35.97
1941	13.86	−1	1	−13.86
1951	17.29	+1	1	+17.29
1961	17.97	+3	9	+53.91
1971	19.91	+5	25	+99.55
1981	23.34	+7	49	+163.38
1991	25.72	+9	81	+231.48
	$\Sigma Y = 162.39$	$\Sigma X = 0$	$\Sigma X^2 = 330$	$\Sigma XY = 290.29$

This least square application is temporal in nature indicating a temporal change of Y values. Census years being independent have been considered as X variable, whereas percentage of total urban population is Y. Census years are coded to obtain the X values under calculation. As there are even number of years, the mean position of X units is taken on the basis of six months as a unit instead of one year.

This method uses two normal equations for calculation of estimated Y values. The equations are —

$\Sigma Y = an + b\Sigma X$ ....(i)

$\Sigma XY = a\Sigma X + b\Sigma X^2$ ....(ii)

Putting the values in the equations from the table no. 7.20 we get —

$162.39 = 10a + 0$

$290.29 = 0 + 330b$

$\therefore a = 162.39/10 = 16.24$

and $b = 290.29/330 = 0.88$

The calculated Y_c values will be obtained on the basis of the formula :

$Y_c = a + bX$

TABLE 7.21
Calculation for Y_c values

a	+	b	×	X	=	Y_c
16.24		0.88		– 9		8.32
16.24		0.88		– 7		10.08
16.24		0.88		– 5		11.84
16.24		0.88		– 3		13.6
16.24		0.88		– 1		15.36
16.24		0.88		+ 1		17.12
16.24		0.88		+ 3		18.88
16.24		0.88		+ 5		20.64
16.24		0.88		+ 7		22.4
16.24		0.88		+ 9		24.16

CORRELATION BETWEEN TIME AND CHANGING PERCENTAGE OF TOTAL URBAN POPULATION IN INDIA, 1901 – 1991

Fig. 7.9 Correlation in time series analysis

Interpretation

During the last century India witnessed a steady growth of urbanization in the country. In different census years the urban areas as well as urban population grew steadily and a lot of rural landscapes has been changed to urban areas. This temporal change of urban population is reflected in the increase of total urban population as well as its percentage in the total population of the country.

In this graph, such temporal correlation has been drawn between the census years 1901 and 1991. The straight line marking the estimated Y_c values passing through the actual percentage of total urban population shows a positive correlation with time.

STANDARD ERROR OF REGRESSION ESTIMATE

After we obtain the regression estimates, the calculation of standard error is required to find out the range within which the actual data lies and some degree of accuracy can be obtained in this regard. The standard error of the estimate of Y or the dependent value can be calculated with the help of the following formula :

$Sy = \sigma_y . \sqrt{1 - r^2}$ Where, Sy = Standard Error of regression estimate

σy = Standard Deviation of dependent variable (Y)

r = Correlation coefficient

The standard error of the estimate shows how much variable is the data of the dependent variable. The actual values differ from the regression line but a probability of 95% is there that the variation will not be more than twice the standard error. A graphical plotting can help visualize the range of actual data with respect to the regression line. The Sy value can be determined on the basis of the Standard Deviation of the residuals also.

$Sy = \sqrt{\frac{\Sigma Z^2}{n}}$ Where, Sy = Standard Error of the Estimate

Z = Residuals $(Y - Y_c)$

n = Number of data.

The determined Sy value should be considered as percentage of the dependent variable for a distance from regression line.

TABLE 7.22

Calculation of standard deviation of residual

Rainfall in cm (X)	Runoff in cm. (y)	$Y_c = a + bX$	$Y - Y_c = Z$	Z^2
46.4	31.9	33.20	– 1.3	1.69
63.0	46.8	47.47	– 0.67	0.4489
48.8	34.2	35.26	– 1.06	1.1236
60.1	47.8	44.98	2.52	6.3504
50.6	35.2	36.81	– 1.61	2.5921
57.5	40.5	42.74	– 2.24	5.0176
55.5	41.3	41.02	0.28	0.0784
57.0	43.5	42.31	1.19	1.4161
60.8	44.8	45.58	– 0.78	0.6084
48.3	38.5	34.83	3.67	13.4689
	Σ = 404.2			Σ = 32.7944

$$Sy = \sqrt{\frac{\Sigma Z^2}{n}} = \sqrt{\frac{32.7944}{10}}$$

$$= 1.810922417 \quad = 1.81$$

$\therefore$ 2Sy = 2 × 1.81 = 3.62

Standard Error of the regression estimate = Standard Deviation of the residuals.

$\therefore$ Standard Error of the regression estimate = 1.81

$$Sy = \sigma_y . \sqrt{1 - r^2}$$

$$= 5.12. \sqrt{1 - (0.935452177)^2}$$

$$= 5.12. \times 0.353453284$$

$$= 1.809680814$$

$$= 1.81$$

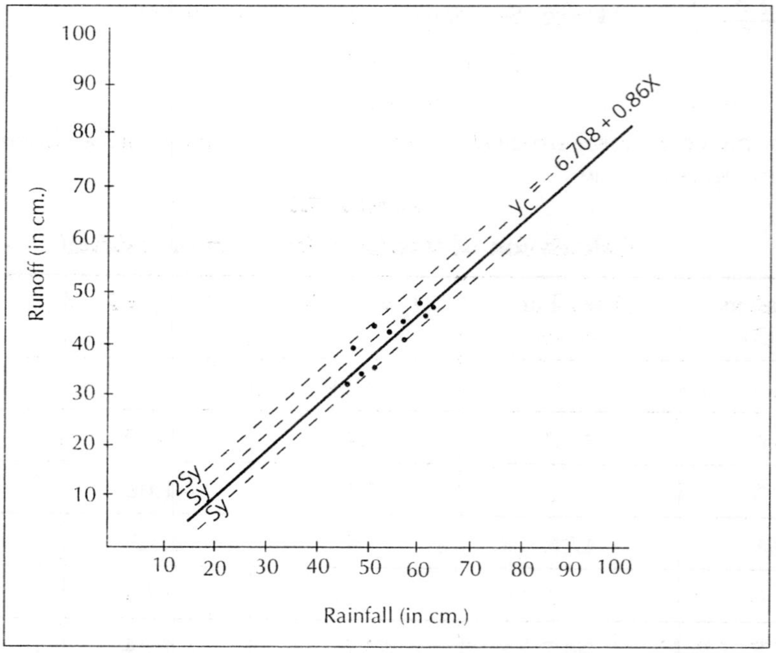

Fig. 7.10 **Plotting of standard error of regression estimate**

Interpretation

The standard Error of Regression Estimate shows how far the actual data deviates from regression estimate. The regression line may touch a few of the dots of the scatter marking the actual data. The trend line touches all the points of regressiion estimate. However, the range of data always varies towards the upper and lower areas of the regression line. The Standard Error marks the range of this deviation. Here, it is observed that towards the upper portion the actual data varies for twice the Standard Error, whereas towards the lower portion it only varies within the range of one Standard Error. It indicates that the higher values of run off are more deviating in nature.

FITTING OF A CURVE

In a bi-variate correlation, the relationship is best expressed by a straight line as an expression of the formula :

$Y_c = a + bX$

But some problems are there where the relationship between two variables is not best expressed by a straight line. Rather a non-linear function may be noted. For such relationships, the best fit regression line may be a curve which can be defined on the basis of a mathematical equation different from that of a straight line function. In geographical data, such problems often crop up from temporal variations of data or when the relationship between the two variables is a complex one. In such curves, variable slopes may be observed. When the relationship involves an increasing rate or a decreasing rate of Y, per unit of X, such curvilinear relationships may be observed also. When the rate of change varies within the range of data, not exactly at constantly increasing or decreasing rate, such curves depict the relationship. Power functions such as $Y = a + bX^n$, or $Y = a + bX^{1/n}$ and polynomial equations as $Y = a + bX + cX^2$ may be used to determine such curves.

Data for calculation

TABLE 7.23

Gross Domestic savings of West bengal

Year	Gross Domestic Savings (%)	Year	Gross Domestic Savings (%)
1990-91	22.8	1995-96	24.4
1991-92	21.5	1996-97	22.7
1992-93	21.2	1997-98	23.8
1993-94	21.9	1998-99	22.3
1994-95	24.4	1999-2000	24.8
		2000-01	23.7

TABLE 7.24

Calculation of determining points of curve

X	Y	CODED X	XY	X^2	X^3	X^4	X^2Y	$Y_C = a + bX + cX^2$
1990-91	22.8	–5	–114	25	–125	625	570	21.85
1991-92	21.5	–4	–86	16	–64	256	344	22.15
1992-93	21.2	–3	–63.6	9	–27	81	190.8	22.43
1993-94	21.9	–2	–43.8	4	–8	16	87.6	22.69
1994-95	24.4	–1	–24.4	1	–1	1	24.4	22.93
1995-96	24.4	0	0	0	0	0	0	23.15
1996-97	22.7	1	22.7	1	1	1	22.7	23.35
1997-98	23.8	2	47.6	4	8	16	95.2	23.53
1998-99	22.3	3	66.9	9	27	81	200.7	23.69
1999-00	24.8	4	99.2	16	64	256	396.8	23.83
2000-01	23.7	5	118.5	25	125	625	592.5	23.95
	$\Sigma =$ 253.5	$\Sigma = 0$	$\Sigma =$ 23.1	$\Sigma =$ 110	$\Sigma = 0$	$\Sigma =$ 1958	$\Sigma =$ 2524.7	

Putting the values from table-1 into the normal equations :

$\Sigma Y = an + b\Sigma X + c\Sigma X^2$

$253.5 = a11 + b0 + c110$ ....(i)

$\Sigma XY = a\Sigma X + b\Sigma X^2 + c\Sigma X^3$

$23.1 = a0 + b110 + c0$ ....(ii)

$\Sigma X^2Y = a\Sigma X^2 + b\Sigma X^3 + c\Sigma X^4$

$2524.7 = a110 + b0 + c1958$ ....(iii)

Calculation for a, b & c :

$a0 + b110 + c0 = 23.1$

or, $b110 = 23.1$

or, $b = \frac{23.1}{110}$

$\therefore b = 0.21$

$a11 + b0 + c110 = 253.5$ .... (i)

$a110 + b0 + c1958 = 2524.7$ ....(iii)

To get the value of c, equation no. (i) is multiplied by 110 and equation no. (iii) is multiplied by 11 :

$1210a + 0b + 12100c = 27885$

$1210a + 0b + 21538c = 27771.7$

(–) (–) (–) (–)

$-9438c = 113.3$

$$\text{or, } c = \frac{113.3}{9438}$$

or, $c = -0.012004662$

$\therefore c = -0.01$

For determining the value of a equation no. (i) is used :

$a11 + b0 + c110 = 253.5$

or, $a11 + (0.21)(0) + (-0.01)(110) = 253.5$

or, $a11 - 1.1 = 253.5$

or, $a11 = 253.5 + 1.1$

$$\text{or, } a = \frac{254.6}{11}$$

or, $a = 23.14545455$

$\therefore a = 23.15$

Thus $a = 23.15$

$b = 0.21$

$c = -0.01$

Interpretation

The data of gross domestic savings of West Bengal from 1990-91 to 2000–01 shows a temporal variation which has been used for the fitting of a curve to indicate the relationship between year of assessment and gross domestic savings. The calculated Y values are obtained on the basis of the equation :

$Y_c = a + bX + cX^2$

It shows that a best fitting gentle curve can be constructed on the Y_c values against years. It indicates that there was a gentle rise in gross domestic savings of West Bengal during the last decade of the 20th century.

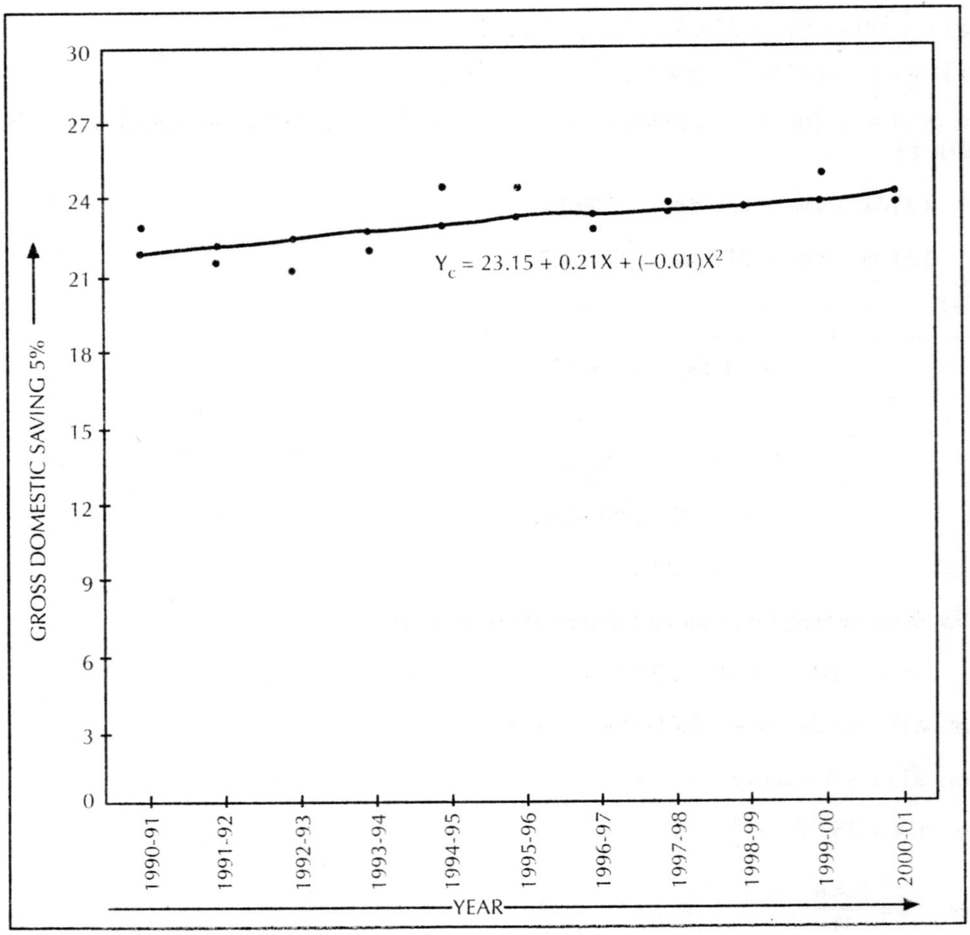

Fig 7.11 Fitting of a curve in temporal change of Gross domestic savings, West Bengal

Calculation for fitting of curve in population variation of West Bengal

Question :

1. Fit a suitable curve for the temporal variation of population in West Bengal between 1901 and 2011 on the basis of Y on X. Interpret the curve.

TABLE 7.25

Population variation of West Bengal (1931-2011)

Year	Population '000	Year	Population '000
1901	16940	1961	34926
1911	17999	1971	44312
1921	17474	1981	54581
1931	18897	1991	68078
1941	23230	2001	80176
1951	26300	2011	91348

TABLE 7.26
Calculation to determine points of curve

Year	Population (in '000) (Y)	Coded X	X^2	X^3	X^4	XY	X^2Y	$Y_c = a + bX + cX^2$
1901	16940	–6	36	–216	1296	–101640	609840	18523.09
1911	17999	–5	25	–125	625	–89995	449975	17177.54
1921	17474	–4	16	–64	256	–69896	279584	17193.11
1931	18897	–3	9	–27	81	–56691	170073	18569.80
1941	23230	–2	4	–8	16	–46460	92920	21307.61
1951	26300	–1	1	–1	1	–26300	26300	25406.54
1961	34926	1	1	1	1	34926	34926	37687.76
1971	44312	2	4	8	16	88624	177248	45870.05
1981	54581	3	9	27	81	163743	491229	55413.46
1991	68078	4	16	64	256	272312	1089248	66317.99
2001	80176	5	25	125	625	400880	2004400	78583.64
2011	91348	6	36	216	1296	548088	3288528	92210.41
	Σ = 494261	Σ = 0	Σ = 182	Σ = 0	Σ = 4550	Σ = 1117591	Σ = 8714271	

Putting the values from the table 7.26 into the normal equations :

$\Sigma Y = an + b\Sigma X + c\Sigma X^2$

$494261 = 12a + 0b + 182c$

$\therefore\ 12a + 182c = 494261$ ....(i)

$\Sigma XY = a\Sigma X + b\Sigma X^2 + c\Sigma X^3$

$1117591 = 0a + 182b + 0c$

$\therefore\ 182b = 1117591$ ....(ii)

$\Sigma X^2Y = a\Sigma X^2 + b\Sigma X^3 + c\Sigma X^4$

$8714271 = 182a + 0b + 4550c$

$\therefore\ 182a + 4550C = 8714271$ ....(iii)

Calculation for a, b and c :

$12a + 182c = 494261$ .... (i)

$182a + 4550c = 8714271$ .... (iii)

For calculation of the value of c equation no. (i) is multipled by 182 and equation no. (iii) is multipled by 12 :

$$2184a + 33124c = 89955502$$

$$2184a + 54600c = 104571252$$

$$(-) \quad (-) \quad (-)$$

$$(-)\,21476c = (-)14615750$$

$$\text{or,} \quad c = \frac{14615750}{21476}$$

$$\therefore \quad c = 680.56$$

$$182b = 1117591 \quad \ldots\ldots\ldots\ldots\ldots\ldots \text{(ii)}$$

$$\text{or,} \quad b = \frac{1117591}{182}$$

$$\text{or,} \quad b = 6140.60989$$

$$\therefore b = 6140.61$$

For determining the value of 'a' equation no. (i) is used :

$$12a + 182c = 494261$$

$$\text{or, } 12a + 182\,(680.56) = 494261$$

$$\text{or, } 12a + 123861.92 = 494261$$

$$\text{or, } 12a = 494261 - 123861.92$$

$$\text{or, } 12a = 370399.08$$

$$\text{or,} \quad a = \frac{370399.08}{12}$$

$$\therefore \quad a = 30866.59$$

Thus, $a = 30866.59$; $b = 6140.61$; $c = 680.56$

Interpretation :

As shown in the curve fitted in the variation of population figures of West Bengal between 1901 and 2011, initially there is a downward trend upto 1921 and then there is a gentle rise upto 1951. From 1951 onwards, i.e. after the independence of India there is a very steep rise which marks the tremendous growth of population in independent India, as it occurred in the influx of population in West Bengal specifically.

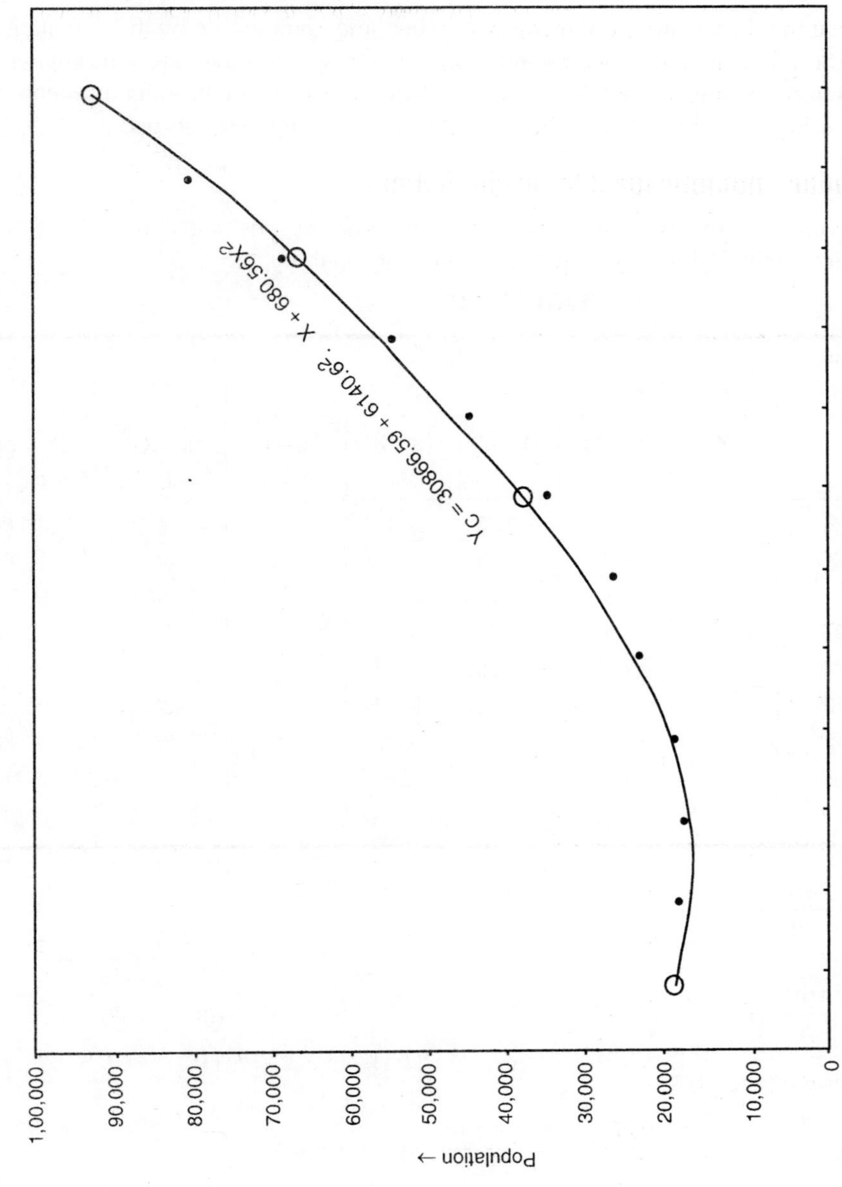

Fig. 7.12 Fitting of a curve in Changing Population Figures of West Bengal (1990-2011)

Pearson's Product Moment Correlation Coefficient

An effective measure of correlation can be obtained by Pearson's Product Moment Correlation Coefficient (r). It is calculated on the basis of the following equation :

$$r = \frac{\frac{1}{n}\Sigma(X - \bar{X})(Y - \bar{Y})}{\sigma X \ . \ \sigma Y}$$

The concept is that the fluctuation from mean values become comparable by the calculation of the amount and direction by which these values differ from their respective average, a moment being the sum of deviations from the mean raised to any power divided by n. These product moments have been further standardized by dividing them with standard deviation of the two sets of data.

Calculation for product moment correlation coefficient

The given data comprises the maximum and minimum temperatures of 8 stations. To find out the correlation coefficient the following table 7.27 has been prepared :

TABLE 7.27

Max. temp. °c		Min. temp. °C							
(X)	$\bar{X}$	*(Y)*	$\bar{Y}$	$(X-\bar{X})$	$(Y-\bar{Y})$	$(X-\bar{X})$ +	$(Y-\bar{Y})$ −	$(X-\bar{X})^2$	$(Y-\bar{Y})^2$
35°		26°		+ 6	+ 6.25	37.5		36	39.06
32°		24°		+ 3	+ 4.25	12.75		9	18.06
26°		12°		− 3	− 7.75	23.25		9	60.06
34°	29	27°	19.75	+ 5	+ 7.25	+ 36.25		25	52.56
30°		22°		+ 1	+ 2.25	2.25		1	5.06
20°		10°		− 9	− 9.75	87.75		81	95.06
24°		12°		− 5	− 7.75	38.75		25	60.06
31°		25°		+ 2	+ 5.25	10.5		4	27.56
						Σ= 249.00		Σ = 190	Σ = 357.48

$$\frac{1}{n}\Sigma(X - \bar{X})(Y - \bar{Y}) = \frac{249.0}{8} = 31.125$$

$$\sigma_X = \sqrt{\frac{190}{8}} = 23.75 = 4.87 \qquad \sigma_Y = \sqrt{\frac{357.48}{8}} = \sqrt{44.68} = 6.68$$

Putting the values we get :

$$r = \frac{31.125}{4.87 \times 6.68} = \frac{31.125}{32.53} = +0.95680$$

Interpretation

The coefficient + 0.95680 indicates that there is moderately high degree of positive correlation between the maximum and minimum temperatures of 8 stations.

Chi-squared Test

Some of the geographical data belonging to various nominal categories derive frequencies from the population. In such a multiple set of data one may require to make probabilistic value of good statistical significance, so that the comparison among different variable sets be made. One of such tests is known as Chi-squared (χ^2) test. χ^2 can test statistically if the observed frequencies differ in a significant way from the expected frequencies determined on the basis of certain hypothesis. The formula usable in this respect is :

$$\chi^2 = \Sigma \frac{(O - E)^2}{E} \qquad \text{i.e., } \chi^2 = \frac{(O_1 - E_1)^2}{E_1} + \frac{(O_2 - E_2)^2}{E_2} \; ..... \; \frac{(O_n - E_n)^2}{E_2}$$

A precondition for test is that the data must be obtained in terms of frequencies because the degree of freedom are obtained by subtracting 1 from the number of groups.

Calculation for Chi-squared test

In a landform analysis there are five groups of slope categories in which various percentages of land of varying relief are covered (table 7.21 & 7.22).

TABLE 7.28

Slope category	Slope amount	Land covered (%)	Relief covered km² (O)	Expected (E)
Flat	0° – 5°	10	40	50
Slight	5° – 10°	9	55	45
Rolling	10° – 15°	25	100	125
Moderate	15° – 20°	35	125	175
High	20° – 25°	21	180	105
		100	500	500

TABLE 7.29

O	40	55	100	125	180
E	50	45	125	175	105
O – E	– 10	+ 10	– 25	– 50	+ 75
(O – E)²	100	100	625	2500	5625
(O – E)²/E	2	2.22	5	14.28	53.57

$$\chi^2 = \Sigma \frac{(O - E)^2}{E} = 2 + 2.22 + 5 + 14.28 + 53.57 = 77.07$$

Interpretation

With n–1 degrees of freedom (i.e. 5 – 1 = 4) the χ^2 value i.e. 77.07. When compared in a graph for Chi-squared test it shows a probability value of less than 0.1%. There is thus a more than 99.9% probability that the inverse of null hypothesis is correct, i.e., there exists strong correlation between relief and steeper slope.

Comparing with table of significance points of χ^2 it is observed that at 4 degrees freedom of upper 1% point is 13.28, but the χ^2 value obtained is 77.07 (Fig. 7.6), hence the hypothesis of no correlation is rejected and a strong correlation exists.

CHI-SQUARED TEST 2

TABLE 7.30

Number of Sishusiksha Kendra by District

District	2003-04	2004-05	%Increase	Observed for 2005-06	Increased/ Decreased	Expected for 2005-06
Coochbihar	887	703	20.74	696	146	557
Jalpaiguri	1287	1109	13.83	1094	153	956
Darjeeling	1010	979	3.07	861	30	949
Uttar Dinajpur	1021	953	6.66	922	63	890
Dakshin Dinajpur	558	540	3.23	533	17	523
Maldah	587	587	0	612	0	587

$$x^2 = \frac{(O_1 - E_1)^2}{E_1} + \frac{(O_2 - E_2)^2}{E_2} \cdots\cdots\cdots \frac{(O_n - E_n)^2}{E_n}$$

$$x^2 = \frac{(O_1 - E_1)^2}{E_1} + \frac{(O_2 - E_2)^2}{E_2} + \frac{(O_3 - E_3)^2}{E_3} + \frac{(O_4 - E_4)^2}{E_4} + \frac{(O_5 - E_5)^2}{E_5} + \frac{(O_6 - E_6)^2}{E_6}$$

$$= \frac{(696 - 557)^2}{557} + \frac{(1094 - 956)^2}{956} + \frac{(861 - 949)^2}{949} + \frac{(922 - 890)^2}{890} + \frac{(533 - 523)^2}{523} + \frac{(612 - 587)^2}{587}$$

$$= 34.69 + 19.92 + 8.16 + 1.15 + 0.19 + 1.06$$

$$= 65.17$$

Points of Chi-square :

Degree of Freedom	.99	.975	.95	.05	.025	0.01
5	.0554	0.831	1.15	11.07	12.83	15.09

Interpretation

As the obtained chi-squared value is 65.17 and at (n–1) or (6–1) = 5 degree freedom of upper 1% the probability value is 15.09, The null hypothesis or hypothesis of no co-relation between the observed and expected variables is rejected and a strong co-relation exists.

ANOVA

ANOVA or Analysis of variance is a useful technique for researches in different disciplines. This technique is used when multiple sets of samples are involved in a study. R.A. Fisher (1958) first used the term variance and also developed an elaborate theory on ANOVA. Later Prof. Snedecor and many others contributed to further development of ANOVA concept and application. The essence of ANOVA is that the total amount of variation in a set of data is broken down into two types, that amount which can be attributed to chance and that amount which can be attributed to specific causes. These two types of variations are related to some questions to be answered with reference to the data and related calculation. The first question is : if the difference between the samples is significantly greater than the differences observed within the samples? If the difference is not significantly greater, it could well be the result of chance grouping. On the other hand, if observed difference between the samples is significantly greater than the within sample difference, it would assume a specific cause behind the difference.

TABLE 7.31

Data of Morphometric Variables for 10 Drainage Basins of Kalimpang District.

Sl. No.	Name of the Drainage Basin	Drainage Density (D_d) (in km/km²)	Average Bifurcation Ratio ($\bar{R}_b$)	Texture Ratio (R_t)
1.	Kali Khola (i)	3.21	2.7	1.98
2.	Bhalu Khola	4.30	2.5	2.81
3.	Tar Khola	2.75	2.6	1.18
4.	Tumthang Khola	4.09	3.3	3.04
5.	Mandam Khola	3.92	3.3	3.36
6.	Rishi Khola	4.34	3.1	3.90
7.	Rilli Khola	3.01	3.9	2.37
8.	Kali Khola(ii)	5.28	3.0	2.83
9.	Kiring Chu	2.69	2.4	0.89
10.	Jhalung Khola	3.18	3.1	1.25

TABLE 7.32

Calculation of Mean Values and Grand Mean

Sl. no.	D_d (x_1)	$\bar{R}_b$ (x_2)	R_t (x_3)	Mean Value			Grand Mean ($\bar{x}_0$)
				$D_d(\bar{x}_1)$	$\bar{R}_b(\bar{x}_2)$	$R_t(\bar{x}_3)$	
1.	3.21	2.7	1.98	3.677	2.99	2.361	3.01
2.	4.30	2.5	2.81				
3.	2.75	2.6	1.18				
4.	4.09	3.3	3.04				
5.	3.92	3.3	3.36				
6.	4.34	3.1	3.90				
7.	3.01	3.9	2.37				
8.	5.28	3.0	2.83				
9.	2.69	2.4	0.89				
10.	3.18	3.1	1.25				

In step I, the variance is to be calculated considering the grand mean, i.e. 3.677 + 2.99 + 2.361 = 9.028 ÷ 3 = 3.01.

This is actually the assumed mean $\bar{x}_0$.

TABLE 7.33

Calculation of Deviations and Variance

Sl. No.	Deviation from grand mean			Deviation Squared		
	$(x_1 - \bar{x}_0)$	$(x_2 - \bar{x}_0)$	$(x_3 - \bar{x}_0)$	$(x_1 - \bar{x}_0)^2$	$(x_2 - \bar{x}_0)^2$	$(x_3 - \bar{x}_0)^2$
1.	0.2	–0.31	–1.03	0.04	0.0961	1.0609
2.	1.29	–0.51	–0.2	1.6641	0.2601	0.04
3.	–0.26	–0.41	–1.83	0.0676	0.1681	3.3489
4.	1.08	0.29	0.03	1.1664	0.0841	0.0009
5.	0.91	0.29	0.35	0.8281	0.0841	0.1225
6.	1.33	0.09	0.89	1.7689	0.0081	0.7921
7.	0	0.89	–0.64	0	0.7921	0.4096
8.	2.27	–0.01	–0.18	5.1529	0.0001	0.0324
9.	–0.32	–0.61	–2.12	0.1024	0.3721	4.4944
10.	0.17	0.09	–1.76	0.0289	0.081	3.0976
	$\Sigma(x_1 - \bar{x}_0) = 6.67$	$\Sigma(x_2 - \bar{x}_0) = -0.2$	$\Sigma(x_3 - \bar{x}_0) = 6.49$	$\Sigma(x_1 - \bar{x}_0)^2 = 10.8193$	$\Sigma(x_2 - \bar{x}_0)^2 = 1.873$	$\Sigma(x_3 - \bar{x}_0)^2 = 13.3993$

$$\text{Overall variance} = \Sigma(x_1 - \bar{x}_0)^2 + \Sigma(x_2 - \bar{x}_0)^2 + \Sigma(x_3 - \bar{x}_0)^2$$

$$= 10.8193 + 1.873 + 13.3993$$

$$= 26.0916$$

As the deviations are calculated from an assumed mean, the application of a correction factor is needed. For this purpose, the above table 7.49 should be considered. It is calculated from the variance of sample totals.

$$\text{Correction factor (c)} = \frac{\text{Variance of sample total}}{\text{Total number of items}}$$

$$= \frac{\Sigma\{(x_1 - \bar{x}_0) + (x_2 - \bar{x}_0) + (x_3 - \bar{x}_0)\}^2}{n}$$

$$= \frac{\{6.67 + (-0.2) + (-6.49)\}^2}{30}$$

$$= \frac{\{6.67 - 0.2 - 6.49\}^2}{30}$$

$$= \frac{0.0004}{30} = 0.000013$$

The correction factor is negligible, so it is not subtracted from overall variance 26.0916.

The between sample variation should be evenly distributed between the occurrences and within sample variation can be eliminated in this way. Thus some modifications are required as :

$$\text{Elimination of within sample Differences} = \frac{\{\Sigma(x_1 - \bar{x}_0)\}^2}{n} + \frac{\{\Sigma(x_2 - \bar{x}_0)\}^2}{n} + \frac{\{\Sigma(x_3 - \bar{x}_0)\}^2}{n}$$

$$= \frac{(6.67)^2}{10} + \frac{(-0.2)^2}{10} + \frac{(-6.49)^2}{10}$$

$$= \frac{44.4889}{10} + \frac{0.04}{10} + \frac{42.1201}{10}$$

$$= 4.44889 + 0.004 + 4.21201$$

$$= 8.6649$$

Within sample sum of squares becomes the amount left after subtracting this value :

$$26.0916 - 8.6649 = 17.4267$$

Degrees of freedom :

The degrees of freedom can be obtained in the same way. As an element of safety the overall number of samples should be subtracted by 1a like the degrees of freedom in Students T test i.e. (n – 1) = (30 –1) = 29.

There are 3 types of samples. Thus the between sample degrees of freedom becomes : (3 – 1) = 2

Finally, the within sample degrees of freedom should be obtained as the difference between this value and the overall value obtained as (n –1) = (29 –2) = 27.

Snedecor's Variance Ratio Text or F value should be determined to findout the relation between two variance estimates.

For between sample condition the variance estimate is :

$$= \frac{\text{Between sample variance}}{\text{Degree of freedom}} = \frac{8.6649}{2} = 4.33245$$

For within sample condition the variance estimate is :

$$= \frac{\text{Within sample variance}}{\text{Degree of freedom}} = \frac{17.4267}{27} = 0.64543$$

Now, these estimates of variance for between sample and within sample conditions may be compared. Such a comparison is done to find out if the variance estimates are so similar that the differences between the samples may reflect the differences within the samples. This similarity indicates that no significant difference lies among the samples. For this purpose, the testing of null hypothesis may be adopted. However, as the degrees of freedom are different for between sample and within sample conditions, a direct comparison is not suggested. Hence, Snedcor's Variance Ratio Test can be applied. This test is accomplished as a simple ratio value known as Snedecor's F. Then the F value may be referred to the table fo critical probability limits on the basis of which it should be determined whether the null hypothesis should be accepted or rejected and an alternate hypothesis is to be adopted.

$$\text{Snedecor's F} = \frac{\text{Greater variance Estimate}}{\text{Lesser Variance Estimate}} = \frac{4.33245}{0.64543} = 6.71250 \quad = 6.71$$

The probability values of Snedecor's F test at different levels of significance :

At 10% level = 2.040

At 5% level = 3.238

At 1% level = 5.194

At 0.1% level = 8.30

Interpretation

At 5% level F value is 3.238 and at 1% level the probability value of F is 5.194, whereas at 0.1% level it is 8.30. The obtained value in this case is 6.71. Thus the null hypothesis is accepted at 0.1% level. Hence the relative variables of D_d, $\bar{R}_b$ and R_t do not have any significant difference between the sets of data and among the 10 basins, i.e. within sample condition.

As such, of the 3 morphometric variables drainage density and texture ratio (in Smith's Method) are directly related to each other. Thus these two areal parameters may not have much difference between them. On the other hand, the values of bifurcation ratio are close to 4.0 at the highest as is expected in mountainous or highly dissected drainage basins (Horton, 1945). Hence, the values are not exceptionally high to indicate any significant variation in the network of the drainage basins. Thus the values of bifurcation ratio also do not express any significant difference from two other sets of data.

FACTOR ANALYSIS

In different branches of Social Science including Geography bi-variate and multi-variate data are often used. Finding out the correlation between two sets of data in a bi-variate analysis, regression method determining a linear correlation between X and Y variates is common. Such bi-variate correlations are sometimes done through exponential curves, polynominal curves, and logarithmic curves. In the case of multi-variate analysis, finding out correlations is more difficult because the correlation is not so direct as in linear regression method, and variables have different characters. Basically, in bivariate analysis, one dependent variable (Y) and one independent variable (X) are selected on the basis of their relative interdependence. In such cases, X is considered as explanatory variable and Y is the criterion variable. Some other names are also given in different disciplines. Explanatory variables, however, are observable in real situations directly. Some other directly unobservable variables are there as latent variables. Sometimes standardization of the variables may be required. In such cases, the X and Y variables may be converted into standard scores of Z which has a mean as 0 and standard deviation as 1. Truly speaking, in a set of multi-variate data, determining the factor or control becomes a basic clue towards interpretation or analysis. In a multi-variate data, if there is systematic interdependence among the variables, the fundamental or latent factor is to be found out. Although such analyses are common in social and behavioural sciences, physical data can also be analysed in the same way provided some systematic interdependence underlies the situation.

Factor Analysis is widely used as it can identify the latent controls of variability in a group of connected variables. However, a factor summarizes the variables into a few ones derived by summing up the values of original variables. But the more important is that the researcher should determine the nature of relationship in terms of score and should also name the factor through subjective consideration.

Methods of Factor Analysis :

Factor Analysis can be done through different methods. Of them , the Centroid method, the Principal Components Method and the Maximum Likelihood Method are important. Only two methods have been given in this book, i.e. the Centroid method and the Principal Components Method. Before the computation through the methods of factor analysis some relevant terms should be defined for the benefit of students. These terms are common in both the methods.

As defined earlier, a factor is the latent control of the observed variables. On the other hand, factor loadnings indicate the values explaining the proximity of variables to one another of a particular set of factors identified. However, it may be negative or positive and the value is more important than sign. Normally, 0.5 is considered as the minimum value of a variable worth interpretation. Once the factors are determined, the communality (h^2) is to be calculated for the factor through summation of factor loadings. Then the eigen value being the latent root is to be derived as the sum of squared values of factor loadings. It may indicate the relative importance of each set of factors and the values become lower in subsequently derived factors as the computation is done successively. Thus the first factor is used as the data for the second factor. The structure of the data may be revealed through rotation changing the axis of the correlation between the factors. It can be graphically illustrated also.

Centroid Method

The six physical variables taken as data here are Drainage Density (D. Density), Bifurcation Ratio (B. Ratio), Texture Ratio (T. Ratio), Circularity Ratio (C. Ratio), Elongation Ratio (E. Ratio) and Erosional Satus (E. Status).

TABLE 7.34

Correlation Matrix (R) of Six Variables Obtained from Pearson's product Moment Method

	D. Density	B. Ratio	T. Ratio	C. Ratio	E. Ratio	E. Status
D. Density	1	.086	.636	.376	.352	.777
B. Ratio	.086	1	.204	.142	.080	.059
T. Ratio	.636	.204	1	.416	.464	.822
C. Ratio	.376	.142	.416	1	.885	.741
E. Ratio	.352	.080	.464	.885	1	.753
E. Status	.777	.059	.822	.741	.753	1
Column Sum	3.227	1.571	3.542	3.56	3.534	4.152

Determination of the First Centroid Factor A :

Sum of Column Sums (T) = 19.586

$\therefore \sqrt{T} = 4.426$

$$\text{First Centroid Factor A} = \frac{\text{Column Sums}}{\sqrt{\text{Sum of Column Sums}}}$$

$$= \frac{3.227}{4.426}, \frac{1.571}{4.426}, \frac{3.542}{4.426}, \frac{3.56}{4.426}, \frac{3.534}{4.426}, \frac{4,152}{4.426}$$

$$= 0.729, 0.355, 0.800, 0.804, 0.798, 0.938$$

Table 7.35

First matrix for cross product (Q_1) on the basis of first Centroid Factor A

	0.729	**0.355**	**0.800**	**0.804**	**0.798**	**0.938**
0.729	0.531	0.259	0.583	0.586	0.582	0.684
0.355	0.259	0.126	0.284	0.285	0.283	0.333
0.800	0.583	0.284	0.640	0.643	0.638	0.750
0.804	0.586	0.285	0.643	0.646	0.642	0.754
0.798	0.582	0.283	0.638	0.642	0.637	0.749
0.938	0.684	0.333	0.750	0.754	0.749	0.880

Table 7.36

First matrix of Residual coefficient (R_1) by subtracting Q_1 from R Matrix

	D. Density	**B. Ratio**	**T. Ratio**	**C. Ratio**	**E. Ratio**	**E. Status**
D. Density	0.469	–0.173	0.053	–0.210	–0.230	0.093
B. Ratio	–0.173	0.874	–0.080	–0.143	–0.203	–0.274
T. Ratio	0.053	–0.080	0.360	–0.227	–0.174	0.072
C. Ratio	–0.210	–0.143	–0.227	0.354	0.243	–0.013
E. Ratio	–0.230	–0.203	–0.174	0.243	0.363	0.004
E. Status	0.093	–0.274	0.072	–0.013	0.004	0.120

Table 7.37

Reflecting the variables having negative signs in Residual Coeffcient (R_1), the Reflected Matrix of Residual Coeffcient R'_1 is obtained

	D. Density	B. Ratio	T. Ratio	C. Ratio	E. Ratio	E. Status
D. Density	0.469	0.173	0.053	0.210	0.230	0.093
B. Ratio	0.173	0.874	0.080	0.143	0.203	0.274
T. Ratio	0.053	0.080	0.360	0.227	0.174	0.072
C. Ratio	0.210	0.143	0.227	0.354	0.243	0.013
E. Ratio	0.230	0.203	0.174	0.243	0.363	0.004
E. Status	0.093	0.274	0.072	0.013	0.004	0.120
Column Sum	1.228	1.747	0.966	1.190	1.217	0.576

Determination of the Second Centroid Factor B :

Sum of Column Sums (T) = 6.924

$\therefore \sqrt{T} = 2.631$

$$\text{Second Centroid Factor B} = \frac{\text{Column Sums}}{\sqrt{\text{Sum of Column Sums}}}$$

$$= \frac{1.228}{2.631}, \frac{1.747}{2.631}, \frac{0.966}{2.631}, \frac{1.190}{2.631}, \frac{1.217}{2.631}, \frac{0.576}{2.631}$$

$$= 0.467, 0.664, 0.367, 0.452, 0.463, 0.219$$

TABLE 7.38

Matrix of factor loadings and communality of factors

Variables	Factor Loadings		
	Centroid Factor A	Centroid Factor B	Communality (h^2)
D. Density	0.729	0.467	$(0.729)^2 + (0.467)^2 = 0.750$
B. Ratio	0.355	0.664	$(0.355)^2 + (0.664)^2 = 0.567$
T. Ratio	0.800	0.367	$(0.800)^2 + (0.367)^2 = 0.775$
C. Ratio	0.804	0.452	$(0.804)^2 + (0.452)^2 = 0.851$
E. Ratio	0.798	0.463	$(0.798)^2 + (0.463)^2 = 0.851$
E. Status	0.938	0.219	$(0.938)^2 + (0.219)^2 = 0.928$

TABLE 7.39

Determination of eigen value and proportion of factors

Variables	Factor Loadings		Communality (h^2)
	Centroid Factor A	Centroid Factor B	
Eigen Value (Common Variance)	3.461	1.261	4.722
Proportion of Total Variance	0.577 (57.6%)	0.210 (21%)	0.787 (78.7%)
Proportion of Common Variance	0.733 (73.3%)	0.267 (26.7%)	1.00 (100%)

Interpretation

In this example of factor analysis by centroid method, the minimum loading of 0.33 is the absolute value worth interpretation. However, among the six variables, four are related to spatial attributes , one is related to linear attribute and the last one is related to the sum total effect of the five variables. Of the four variables identified as spatial attributes Drainage Density and Texture Ratio belong to Drainage Characteristics, Circularity Ratio and Elongation Ratio are related to shape of the Basin. Bifurcation Ratio being a linear attribute is a network characteristic and finally all of them have certain impact on the nature of erosion of the drainage basin. Thus we may identify them into different morphometric categories.

However, in this case factor A being the general factor has all the variables with high values except for Bifurcation Ratio which is 0.355. The eigen value or common variance for this factor is 3.461 which covers 57.7% of the communality. In the next step, factor loading for centroid facor B is 1.261 which covers 21% of the total variance. Thus these two factors together cover 78.7% of the variance . It may be noted that, in centroid factor B, Bifurcation Ratio has the highest value of loading i.e. 0.664. Hence, we may consider that the four other variables are included in the primary factors, whereas the linear attribute has a secondary importance in determining the Erosional Status of the drainage basins.

TABLE 7.39

Factor analysis (Principal component method) Variables (R)

	D. Density	B. Ratio	T. Ratio	C. Ratio	E. Ratio	E. Status
D. Density	1	.086	.636	.376	.352	.777
B. Ratio	.086	1	.204	.142	.080	.059
T. Ratio	.636	.204	1	.416	.464	.822
C. Ratio	.376	.142	.416	1	.885	.741
E. Ratio	.352	.080	.464	.885	1	.753
E. Status	.777	.059	.822	.741	.753	1
Column Sum (Ua_1)	3.227	1.571	3.542	3.56	3.534	4.152

Normalizing Ua_1, Va_1 is obtained, i.e.

$$Va_1 = \frac{Ua_1}{\sqrt{\text{Normalizing factor for } Ua_1}}$$

$$\text{Normalizing factor for } Ua_1 = \sqrt{(\text{Column sum for variable 1})^2 + (\text{Column sum for variable 2})^2 + (\text{Column sum for variable n})^2}$$

$$\text{Normalizing factor for } Ua_1 = \sqrt{(3.227)^2 + (1.571)^2 + (3.542)^2 + (3.56)^2 + (3.534)^2 + (4.152)^2}$$

$$= \sqrt{67.829194}$$

$$= 8.236$$

$$Va_1 = \frac{\text{Column sum for variable 1}}{\text{Normalizing factor for } Ua_1}, \frac{\text{Column sum for variable 2}}{\text{Normalizing factor for } Ua_1}, \ldots, \frac{\text{Column sum for variable n}}{\text{Normalizing factor for } Ua_1},$$

$$Va_1 = \frac{3.227}{8.236}, \frac{1.571}{8.236}, \frac{3.542}{8.236}, \frac{3.56}{8.236}, \frac{3.534}{8.236}, \frac{4.152}{8.236}$$

$$= 0.392, 0.191, 0.430, 0.432, 0.429, 0.504$$

Ua_2 is obtained by multiplying R row by row by Va_1 and cumulating them :
1.387, 0.438, 1.511, 1.539, 1.544, 1.816
Normalizing Factor for Ua_2 is determined like previous method. Hence, it is worked out as :

$$\text{Normalizing factor for } Ua_2 = \sqrt{(1.387)^2 + (0.438)^2 + (1.511)^2 + (1.539)^2 + (1.544)^2 + (1.816)^2}$$

$$= \sqrt{12.449047}$$

$$= 3.528$$

$$Va_2 = \frac{Ua_2}{\text{Normalizing factor for } Ua_2}$$

$$= \frac{1.387}{3.528}, \frac{0.438}{3.528}, \frac{1.511}{3.528}, \frac{1.539}{3.528}, \frac{1.544}{3.528}, \frac{1.816}{3.528}$$

$$= 0.393, 0.124, 0.428, 0.436, 0.438, 0.515$$

Ua_3 is obtained by multiplying R row by row by Va_2 and cumulating them :
1.394, 0.372, 1.511, 1.549, 1.559, 1.832

$$\text{Normalizing factor for } Ua_3 = \sqrt{(1.394)^2 + (0.372)^2 + (1.511)^2 + (1.549)^2 + (1.559)^2 + (1.832)^2}$$

$$= \sqrt{12.550847}$$

$$= 3.543$$

$$Va_3 = \frac{Ua_3}{\text{Normalizing factor for } Ua_3}$$

$$= \frac{1.394}{3.543}, \frac{0.372}{3.543}, \frac{1.511}{3.543}, \frac{1.549}{3.543}, \frac{1.559}{3.543}, \frac{1.832}{3.543}$$

$$= 0.393, 0.105, 0.426, 0.437, 0.440, 0.517$$

Ua_4 is obtained by multiplying R row by row by Va_3 and cumulating them:
1.394, 0.353, 1.508, 1.548, 1.560, 1.834

$$\text{Normalizing factor for } Ua_4 = \sqrt{(1.394)^2 + (0.353)^2 + (1.508)^2 + (1.548)^2 + (1.560)^2 + (1.834)^2}$$

$$= \sqrt{12.535369}$$

$$= 3.541$$

$$Va_4 = \frac{Ua_4}{\text{Normalizing factor for } Ua_4}$$

$$= \frac{1.394}{3.541}, \frac{0.353}{3.541}, \frac{1.508}{3.541}, \frac{1.548}{3.541}, \frac{1.560}{3.541}, \frac{1.834}{3.541}$$

$$= 0.394, 0.097, 0.426, 0.437, 0.441, 0.518$$

When we compare Va_3 with Va_4, we find out that the two vectors are nearly equal. This indicates convergence. Therefore, Va_3 can be taken as the characteristic vector Va. On the basis of Va the loadings on first Principal Components are done by multiplying Va with the Square root of Normalizing factor of Ua_4.

TABLE 7.40

Calculation of Principal Components I

Variables	Characteristic vector Va	X	$\sqrt{\text{Normalizing factor of } Ua_4}$	=	Principal Components I
D. Density	0.393	X	1.882	=	0.740
B. Ratio	0.105	X	1.882	=	0.198
T. Ratio	0.426	X	1.882	=	0.802
C. Ratio	0.437	X	1.882	=	0.822
E. Ratio	0.440	X	1.882	=	0.828
E. Status	0.517	X	1.882	=	0.973

Now, the Principal components II is to be derived. For this stage, the method of calculation is similar to that of Centroid Factor B. Hence, V_b is to be calculated for second component factor II from first residual matrix of Centroid Factor R_1, rather than the original correlation matrix R.

Table 7.41

Cross Product of first matrix of factor

	0.740	0.198	0.802	0.822	0.828	0.973
0.740	0.548	0.147	0.593	0.608	0.613	0.720
0.198	0.147	0.039	0.159	0.163	0.164	0.193
0.802	0.593	0.159	0.643	0.659	0.664	0.780
0.822	0.608	0.163	0.659	0.676	0.681	0.800
0.828	0.613	0.164	0.664	0.681	0.686	0.806
0.973	0.720	0.193	0.780	0.800	0.806	0.947

Table 7.42

first matrix of Residual Coefficient (R_1)

	D. Density	B. Ratio	T. Ratio	C. Ratio	E. Ratio	E. Status
D. Density	0.452	–0.061	0.043	–0.232	–0.261	0.057
B. Ratio	–0.061	0.961	0.045	–0.021	– 0.084	–0.134
T. Ratio	0.043	0.045	0.357	–0.243	–0.200	0.042
C. Ratio	–0.232	–0.021	–0.243	0.324	0.204	–0.059
E. Ratio	–0.261	–0.084	–0.200	0.204	0.314	–0.053
E. Status	0.057	–0.134	0.042	–0.059	–0.053	0.053

Reflecting the variables having negative signs in Residual Coefficient (R_1), the reflected matrix of Residual Coefficient R'_1 is obtained :

Table 7.43

	D. Density	B. Ratio	T. Ratio	C. Ratio	E. Ratio	E. Status
D. Density	0.452	0.061	0.043	0.232	0.261	0.057
B. Ratio	0.061	0.961	0.045	0.021	0.084	0.134
T. Ratio	0.043	0.045	0.357	0.243	0.200	0.042
C. Ratio	0.232	0.021	0.243	0.324	0.204	0.059
E. Ratio	0.261	0.084	0.200	0.204	0.314	0.053
E. Status	0.057	0.134	0.042	0.059	0.053	0.053
Column sums	1.106	1.306	0.93	1.083	1.116	0.398

Sum of Column Sums = 5.939 (T)

$\therefore \sqrt{T} = 2.437$

$$\text{Hence, Principal Components II} = \frac{\text{Column Sums}}{\sqrt{\text{Sum of Column Sums}}}$$

$$= \frac{1.106}{2.437}, \frac{1.306}{2.437}, \frac{0.93}{2.437}, \frac{1.083}{2.437}, \frac{1.116}{2.437}, \frac{0.398}{2.437}$$

$$= 0.454, -0.536, 0.382, -0.444, -0.458, 0.163$$

Table 7.44

Communality and Eigen value of two sets of Principal components

Variables	Principal Components I	Principal Components II	Communality (h^2)
D. Density	0.740	0.454	$(0.740)^2 + (0.454)^2 = 0.754$
B. Ratio	0.198	–0.536	$(0.198)^2 + (-0.536)^2 = 0.327$
T. Ratio	0.802	0.382	$(0.802)^2 + (0.382)^2 = 0.789$
C. Ratio	0.822	–0.444	$(0.822)^2 + (-0.444)^2 = 0.873$
E. Ratio	0.828	–0.458	$(0.828)^2 + (-0.458)^2 = 0.895$
E. Status	0.973	0.163	$(0.973)^2 + (0.163)^2 = 0.973$
Eigen value i.e. Common variance	3.538	1.073	4.611
Proportion of total variance	0.590 (59%)	0.179 (17.9%)	0.769 (76.9%)
Proportion of common variance	0.767 (77%)	0.233 (23%)	1.000 (100%)

Interpretation

In this Principal Component Analysis on the basis of six variables, two sets of Principal Components are determined. As mentioned earlier, the value below 0.5 is not worth consideration. On such terms, the B. Ratio or Bifurcation Ratio in the network of 20 drainage basins is insignificant as Principal Component. On the other hand, all other values are much higher than 0.5 indicating that an increase in any one of the components Drainage Density, Texture Ratio, Circularity Ratio and Elongation Ratio will develop a consequent increase in others. Thus they are closely interrelated with each other. Erosional Status obtaining the highest value (0.973) has the sum total effect on all the variables of Principal Component I except for the Bifurcation Ratio.

In Principal Corponent II, only Bifurcation Ratio has a considerable value above 0.5, all other being directly correlated among them and holding a high value earlier become insignificant. However, it has a negative or decreasing nature. It can indicate how low is the value in this set of data.

The Factors on the basis of grouped variables can be named as network and shape factor for the first Principal Component and Bifurcation factor in the Second Principal Component. Together they constitute about 77% of the total variance, i.e. 6.0. The rest, i.e. about 23% is left for some other variables and factors not included in this analysis.

EXERCISE

TABLE 7.45

Marks	No. of Students
10–20	2
20–30	5
30–40	7
40–50	10
50–60	20
60–70	22
70–80	16
80–90	8

2. (a) Draw a Frequency polygon showing the marks the students achieved.
   (b) Calculate the mean and locate it on the freequency polygon.
   (c) Draw an ogive (less than type).
   (d) If the pass marks is 50 what is the percentage of student who have gotmore than the pass marks?
   (e) Calculate the median and locate it on the ogive. [Year 2001, Batch IV]

TABLE 7.46

Frequency distribution and cumulative frequency

Class boundary	Class Mark	Class Width	Freequency	Cumulative Frequency less than	Cumulative Frequency more than
				0	90
10–20	15	10	2		
				2	88
20–30	25	10	5		
				7	83
30–40	35	10	7		
				14	76
40–50	45	10	10		
				24	66
50–60	55	10	20		
				44	46
60–70	65	10	22		
				66	24
70–80	75	10	16		
				82	8
80–90	85	10	8		
				90	0
			$\Sigma f = 90$		

(a) **Frequency Polygon showing the marks the students achieved**

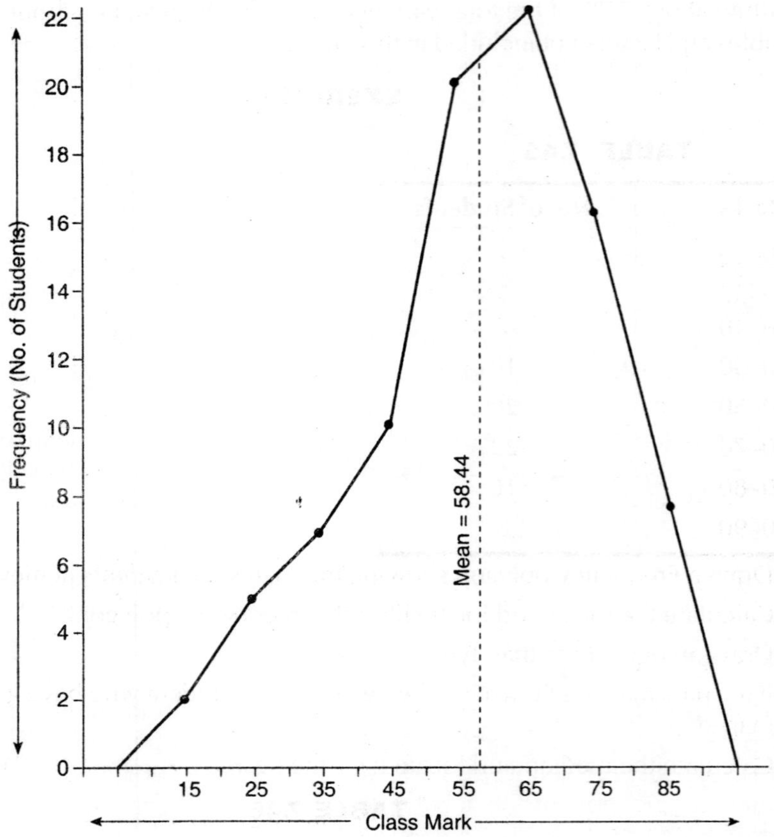

(b) **Mean :** $\bar{x} = \frac{\Sigma MV.f}{\Sigma f}$

TABLE 7.47

Class mark	Frequency	MV.f
15	2	30
25	5	125
35	7	245
45	10	450
55	20	1100
65	22	1430
75	16	1200
85	8	680
	$\Sigma f = 90$	$\Sigma MVf = 5260$

$$\therefore \bar{x} = \frac{5260}{90} = 58.44$$

(c) **OGIVE (less than type)**

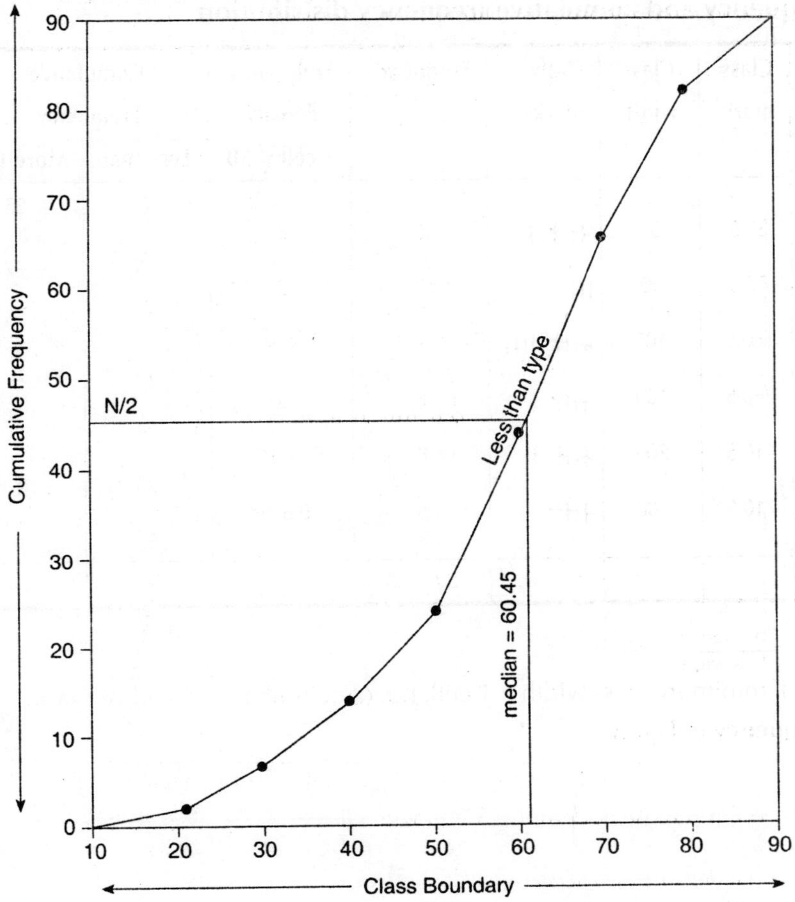

(d) Here total no of student is 90.

No. of students who have got more than pass marks is 66.

∴ the percentage of student who have got more than the pass marks is $\frac{66 \times 100}{90} = 73.33\%$.

(e) Median observation = N/2 = 90/2 = 45

median $= \text{L.C.B} + \frac{fc}{fm} \cdot c = 60 + \frac{1}{22} \cdot 10 = 60 + 0.45 = 60.45$ (median)

2. (a) Draw a histogram and frequency polygon from the given data with 6 unequal classes. Density of population per sq. km.

705, 615, 635, 402, 377, 372, 333, 292, 272, 230, 211, 216, 190, 264, 195, 194, 174, 169, 118, 100, 77, 64, 60, 59, 47, 45, 23, 20, 766, 747, 471, 401, 210, 202, 149.

(b) Draw an ogive (less than type) and interpret.

(c) Find out the median and the mode. [Year : 1999, Batch II]

TABLE 7.48

Frequency and cumulative frequency distribution

Class limit	Class Boundary	Class mark	Class width	Tally marks	Frequency	Frequency density 1 cell = 50	Cumulative Frequency Less than	Cumulative Frequency More than
							0	35
11–60	10.5 – 60.5	35.5	50	𝍸 I	6	6		
							6	29
61–110	60.5 – 110.5	85.5	50	III	3	3		
							9	26
111 – 210	110.5 – 210.5	160.5	100	𝍸 IIII	9	4.5		
							18	17
211 – 310	210.5 – 310.5	260.5	100	𝍸 I	6	3		
							24	11
311 – 510	310.5 – 510.5	410.5	200	𝍸 I	6	1.5		
							30	5
511 – 910	510.5 – 910.5	710.5	400	𝍸	5	0.625		
							35	0
					$\Sigma f = 35$			

$$\text{Frequency Density} = \frac{\text{Frequency}}{\text{Class width}}$$

(If minimum class width = 1 cell, no. of cells in a class = class width)

(a) **Histogram and Frequency polygon**

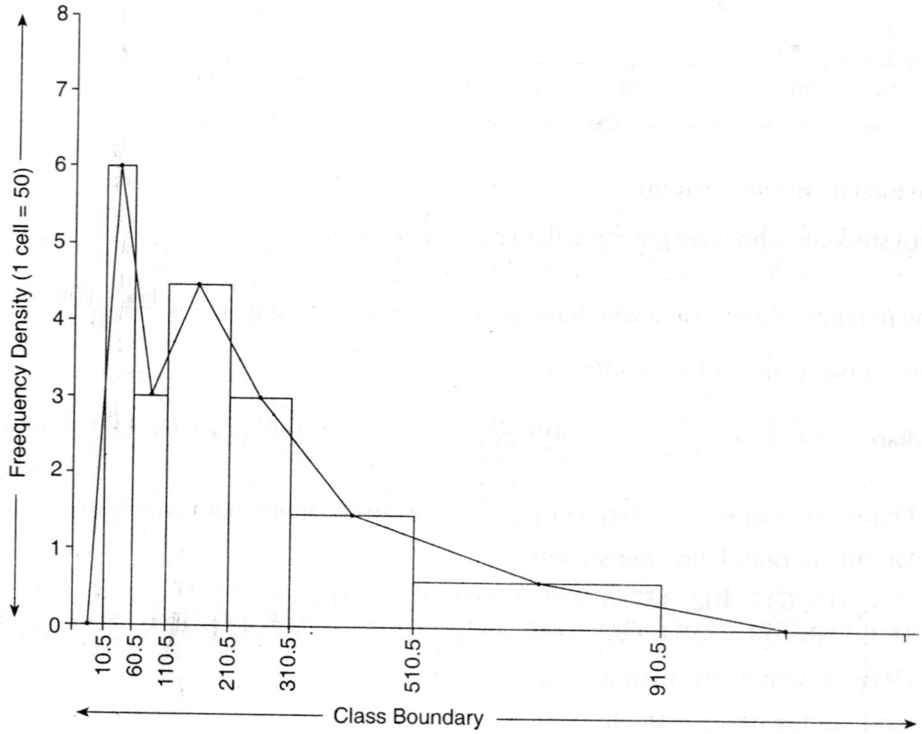

(b) **OGIVE (Less than type)**

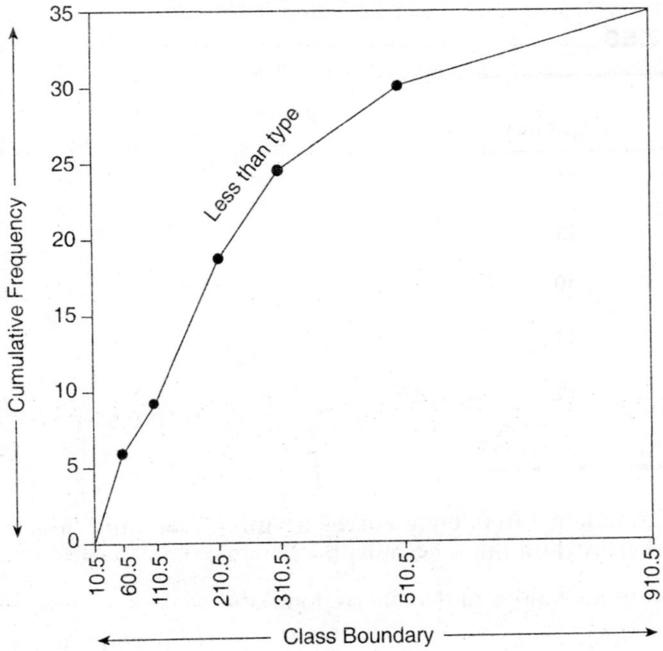

(c) **Median** $= \text{L.C.B} + \frac{fc}{fm} \cdot c$ median observation $= \frac{N}{2} = \frac{35}{2} = 17.5$

$$= 110.5 + \frac{8.5}{9} \cdot 100 = 204.94$$

Mean = $\bar{x} = \frac{\Sigma MV.F}{\Sigma F}$

Mode = Mean – mode = 3 (mean – median

or, 271.21 – mode = 3(271.21 – 204.94)

or, 271.21 – mode = 198.81

or, – mode = – 72.4

or, mode = 72.4

TABLE 7.49

Class mark	Frequency	MV.f
35.5	6	213
85.5	3	256.5
160.5	9	1444.5
260.5	6	1563
410.5	6	246.3
710.5	5	3552.5
	$\Sigma f = 35$	$\Sigma MVf = 7275.8$

$$\bar{x} = \frac{7275.8}{35} = 207.88$$

2. (a) Draw a frequency polygon on the basis of the following frequency distribution of density of population.

TABLE 7.50

Density of population persons/sq. km.	Frequency
115 – 145	15
145 – 175	21
175 – 195	10
195 – 215	14
215 – 255	16
255 – 295	4

(b) From the given data draw cumulative frequency curves of 'more than' and 'less than' types and find out median density ditribution graphically.

(c) Calculate the 6th decile and mode values of density of population.

[Year 1997, Batch III]

TABLE 7.51

Frequency and cumulative frequency distribution

Class boundary	Class Mark	Class Width	Frequency	Frequency density	Cumulative Frequency less than	Cumulative Frequency more than
					0	80
115 – 145	130	30	15	0.5		
					15	65
145 – 175	160	30	21	0.7		
					36	44
175 – 195	185	20	10	0.5		
					46	34
195 – 215	205	20	14	0.7		
					60	20
215 – 255	235	40	16	0.4		
					76	4
255 – 295	275	40	4	0.1		
			$\Sigma f = 80$		80	0

$$\text{Frequency Density} = \frac{\text{Frequency}}{\text{Class width}}$$

(a) **Frequency polygon showing Density of population**

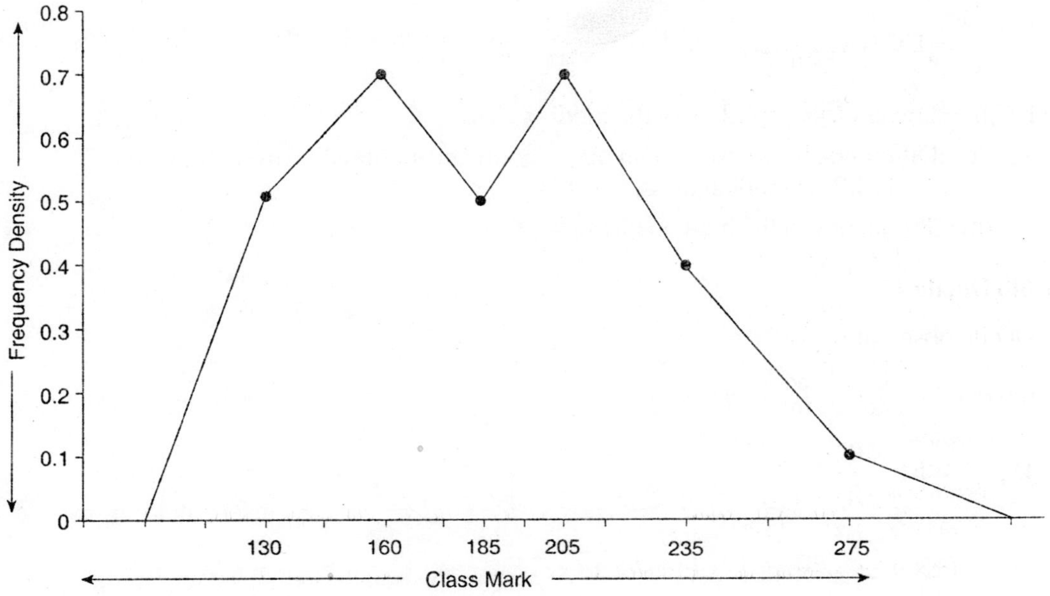

(b) **Median at point of intersection of Cumulative Frequency curves (Less than and more than type)**

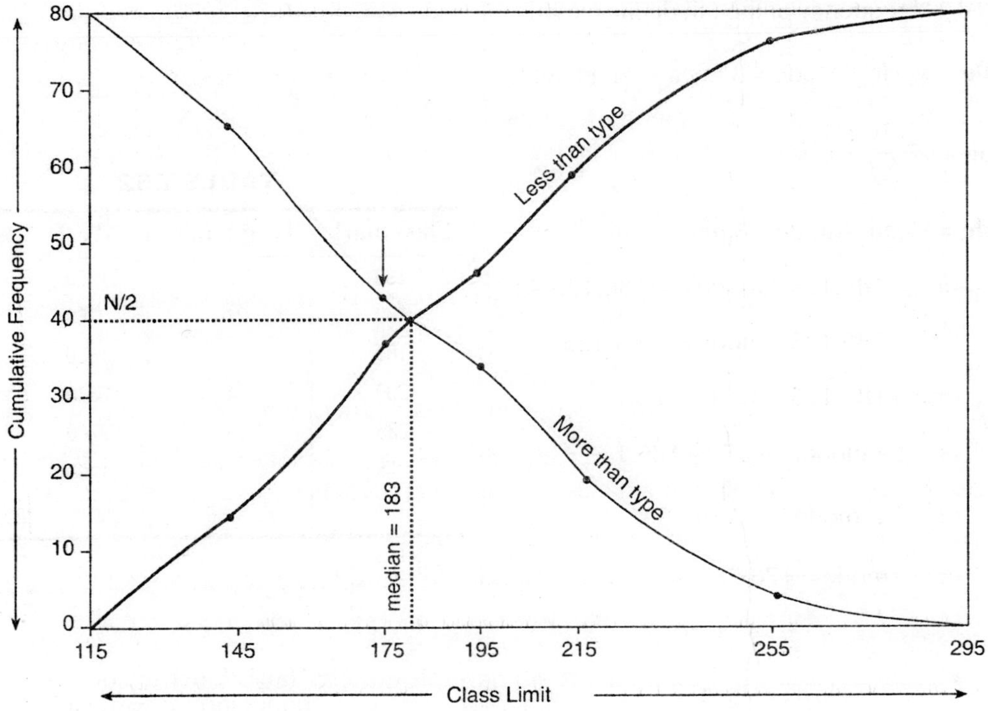

Median = median observation = $\frac{N}{2} = \frac{80}{2} = 40$

$= L.C.B + \frac{fc}{fm} \cdot c \quad = 175 + \frac{40-36}{10} \cdot 20 \quad = 175 + 0.4 \cdot 20 \quad = 183$

[L.C.B. = Lower class boundary of the median class;

fc = Difference between median observation and cumulative frequency upto L.C.B. of median class;

fm = Frequency of the median class]

(c) **6th Decile** =

Decile observation for

6th decile = $\frac{6N}{10} = \frac{480}{10} = 48$

$D_6 = L.C.B + \frac{fc}{f_{D_6}} \cdot c$

$= 195 + \frac{2}{14} \cdot 20 \quad = 197.86\ (D_6)$

[L.C.B. = Lower class boundary of the 6th decile class;

fc = Difference between decile observation and cumulative frequency upto lower class boundary;

fd_6 = Frequency of the 6th decile class]

Mode = Mean – Mode = 3 (mean – median).

Mean = $\frac{\Sigma MV.f}{\Sigma f} = \bar{x}$

TABLE 7.52

Class mark	Frequency	MV.f
130	15	1950
160	21	3360
185	10	1850
205	14	2870
235	16	3760
275	4	1100
	Σf = 80	ΣMV.f = 14890

$\bar{x} = \frac{14890}{80}$

= 186.125 density of population [$\bar{x}$ = mean]

Mode = Mean – mode = 3 (mean – median)

or, 186.125 – mode = 3(186.125 – 183)

or, 186.125 – mode = 3 × 3.125

or, 186.125 – mode = 9.375

or, – mode = 9.375 – 186.125

or, ~~–~~ mode = ~~–~~ 176.75

or, mode = 176.75

3. From the following data work out standard deviation and coefficient of variation and interpret.

TABLE 7.53

Classes	No. of units
0 – 100	39
100 – 200	48
200 – 300	52
300 – 400	102
400 – 500	115
500 – 600	80
600 – 700	34

[Year 1999, Batch II]

Standard Deviation $\sigma = C\sqrt{\frac{\Sigma ft^2}{\Sigma f} - \left(\frac{\Sigma ft}{\Sigma f}\right)^2}$

TABLE 7.54

Classes	Class Mark	Freequency	t (total deviation)	t^2	ft	ft^2
0 – 100	50	39	– 3	9	– 117	351
100 – 200	150	48	– 2	4	– 96	192
200 – 300	250	52	– 1	1	– 52	52
300 – 400	350	102	0	0	0	0
400 – 500	450	115	+ 1	1	115	115
500 – 600	550	80	+ 2	4	160	320
600 – 700	650	34	+ 3	9	102	306
	Σ = 2450	Σf = 470			Σft = 112	Σft^2 = 1336

TABLE 7.55

Class mark	Frequency	MV.f
50	39	1950
150	48	7200
250	52	13000
350	102	35700
450	115	51750
550	80	44000
650	34	22100
	$\Sigma f = 470$	ΣMV.f = 175700

$$\text{Mean} = \bar{x} = \frac{\Sigma \text{Classmark}.f}{\Sigma f}$$

$$\text{mean} = \bar{x} = \frac{175700}{470} = 373.83$$

$$\sigma = 100\sqrt{\frac{1336}{470} - \left(\frac{112}{470}\right)^2} = 100\sqrt{2.84 - (0.24)^2}$$

$$= 100\sqrt{2.84 - 0.0576}$$

$$= 100\sqrt{2.7824}$$

$$= 100 \times 1.668052757$$

$$\therefore \quad = 166.81$$

$$\textbf{Co-efficient of variation} = \frac{\text{Standard Deviation}}{\text{mean}} \times 100 \quad = 44.62\%$$

4. The rainfall in mm for Burdwan and Maldah in 1995 is given below.

Table 7.56

Months	Station : Burdwan	Station : Malda
J	19.0	8.0
F	25.0	10.0
M	0.0	4.0
A	3.0	3.0
M	87.0	53.0
J	232.0	307.0
J	302.0	363.0
A	326.0	594.0
S	324.0	720.0
O	62.0	6.0
N	87.0	86.0
D	3.0	10.0

(a) Calculate the mean deviation and standard deviation.

(b) Find out the nature of variability of the rainfall. [Year 2000, Batch II]

Table 7.57

Months	Rainfall (mm) (inascending order)	$d = \lvert X_i - \bar{X} \rvert$	$d = (X_i - \bar{X})$	d^2
Mar	0.0	122.5	−122.5	15006.25
Apr	3.0	119.5	− 119.5	14280.25
Dec	3.0	119.5	− 119.5	14280.25
Jan	19.0	103.0	−103.5	10712.25
Feb	25.0	97.5	− 97.5	9506.25
Oct	62.0	60.5	− 60.5	3660.25
May	87.0	35.5	− 35.5	1260.25
Nov	87.0	35.5	− 35.5	1260.25
Jun	232.0	109.5	+ 109.5	11990.25
Jul	302.0	179.5	+ 179.5	32220.25
Sep.	324.0	201.5	+ 201.5	40602.25
Aug	326.0	203.5	+ 203.5	41412.25
	Total Rainfall = 1470 mm	$\lvert X_i - \bar{X} \rvert$ 1230 mm		Σd^2 = 196191.00 mm

Mean $= \dfrac{\Sigma x}{N} = \bar{x}$

$$= \frac{\text{Total Rainfall}}{12} = \frac{1470}{12} \text{ mm} = 122.5 \text{ mm (mean).}$$

Mean Deviation $= \dfrac{\Sigma |xi - \bar{x}|}{N} = \dfrac{1230}{12} \text{ mm} = 102.5 \text{ mm}$

Standard Deviation $= \sigma = \sqrt{\dfrac{\Sigma(xi - \bar{x})^2}{\Sigma N}} = \sqrt{\dfrac{\Sigma d^2}{\Sigma N}}$

$$= \sqrt{\frac{196191}{12}} \text{ mm}$$

$$= \sqrt{16349.25 \text{ mm}} = 127.86 \text{ mm}$$

S.D.$\geqslant$M.D.

STATION - MALDAH

Table 7.58

Months	Rainfall (mm) (inascending order)	$\|X_i - \bar{X}\|$	$d = (X_i - \bar{X})$	d^2
Apr	3.0	177.33	– 177.33	31445.92
Mar	4.0	176.33	– 176.33	31092.27
Oct	6.0	174.33	– 174.33	30390.95
Jan	8.0	172.33	– 172.33	29697.63
Feb	10.0	170.33	– 170.33	29012.31
Dec	10.0	170.33	– 170.33	29012.31
May	53.0	127.33	– 127.33	16212.93
Nov	86.0	94.33	– 94.33	8898.15
Jun	307.0	126.67	+ 126.33	16045.29
Jul	363.0	182.67	+ 182.67	33368.33
Aug	594.0	413.67	+ 413.67	171122.87
Sep	720.0	539.67	+ 539.67	291243.71
	Total Rainfall = 2164 mm	$\Sigma\|X_i - \bar{X}\|$ = 2525.32 mm		Σd^2 = 717542.67 mm

$$\text{Mean} = \bar{x} = \frac{\Sigma X}{N}$$

$$= \frac{\text{Total Rainfall}}{12} = \frac{2164}{12} \text{ mm} = 180.33 \text{ mm (mean).}$$

$$\text{Mean Deviation} = \frac{\Sigma|xi - \bar{x}|}{N} = \frac{2525.32}{12} \text{ mm} = 210.44 \text{ mm}$$

$$\text{Standard Deviation} = \sigma = \sqrt{\frac{\Sigma(xi - \bar{x})^2}{\Sigma N}} = \sqrt{\frac{\Sigma d^2}{\Sigma N}}$$

$$= \sqrt{\frac{717542.67}{12}} \text{ mm}$$

$$= \sqrt{59795.22 \text{ mm}} = 244.53 \text{ mm}$$

(b) **Nature of variability =**

Co-efficient of variation =

Station : Burdwan

$$\frac{\text{Standard Deviation}}{\text{mean}} \times 100 = \frac{127.86 \text{ mm}}{122.5 \text{ mm}} \times 100 = 104.38\%$$

Station : Maldah

$$\frac{\text{Standard Deviation}}{\text{mean}} \times 100 = \frac{244.53 \text{ mm}}{180.33 \text{ mm}} \times 100 = 135.60\%$$

Burdwan had more consistent rainfall in 1995 as it had lower co-efficient of variation.

5. (a) Draw a scatter diagram and the line of best fit.

   (b) What will be the production of wheat when the land under it is 26 million Hectares?

   (c) Interpret the relationship giving reasons to support your answer.

Table 7.59

Area under wheat (in million Ha)	Production of wheat (in million tonnes)
22.28	36.31
23.00	47.05
24.09	58.99
23.50	49.70
24.16	54.60
23.26	55.87
24.43	56.80
24.50	58.50
25.01	62.01
25.93	69.28

[Year 2001, Batch IV]

Table for data of least square method :

TABLE 7.60

Area under wheat (in million Ha)	Production of wheat (in million tonnes)		
X	Y	X^2	XY
22.28	36.31	496.3984	808.9868
23.00	47.05	529.00	1082.15
24.09	58.99	580.3281	1421.0691
23.50	49.70	552.25	1167.95
24.16	54.60	583.7056	1319.136
23.26	55.87	541.0276	1299.5362
24.43	56.80	596.8249	1387.624
24.43	58.50	600.25	1433.25
25.01	62.01	625.5001	1550.8701
25.93	69.28	627.3649	1796.4304
$\Sigma x = 240.16$ million H.A.	$\Sigma y = 549.11$ million tonnes	$\Sigma x^2 = 5774.22$ million H.A.	$\Sigma xy = 13262.91$

Normal equations :

$\Sigma Y = an + b\Sigma X$ ....(i)

$\Sigma XY = a\Sigma X + b\Sigma X^2$ ....(ii)

$549.11 = 10a + b240.09$ ....(i)

$3262.91 = 240.09a + b5774.22$ ....(ii)

Multiplying (i) by 240.09 and (ii) by 10 and substracting (ii) from (i), we get,

$$131835.82 = 2400.9a + 57643.21b$$

$$132629.1 = 2400.9a + 57742.2b$$

$$-793.28 = -98.99b$$

$$-98.99b = -793.28$$

$$b = \frac{793.28}{98.99} = 8.01$$

Putting the value of b, we get,

$549.11 = 10a + b240.09$

or, $549.11 = 10a + 8.01 \times 240.09$

or, $549.11 = 10a + 1923.12$

or, $549.11 - 1923.12 = 10a$

or, $-1374.01 = 10a$

or, $a = \frac{-1374.01}{10} = -137.40$

Table for y_c values when $y_c = a + bx$

TABLE 7.61

a +	b	X	y_c
– 137.40	8.01	22.28	41.06
– 137.40	8.01	23.00	46.83
– 137.40	8.01	24.09	55.56
– 137.40	8.01	23.50	50.83
– 137.40	8.01	24.16	56.12
– 137.40	8.01	23.26	48.91
– 137.40	8.01	24.43	58.28
– 137.40	8.01	24.43	58.28
– 137.40	8.01	25.01	62.93
– 137.40	8.01	25.93	70.30

Best Fit Line on Scatter Diagram on Area and Production of Wheat

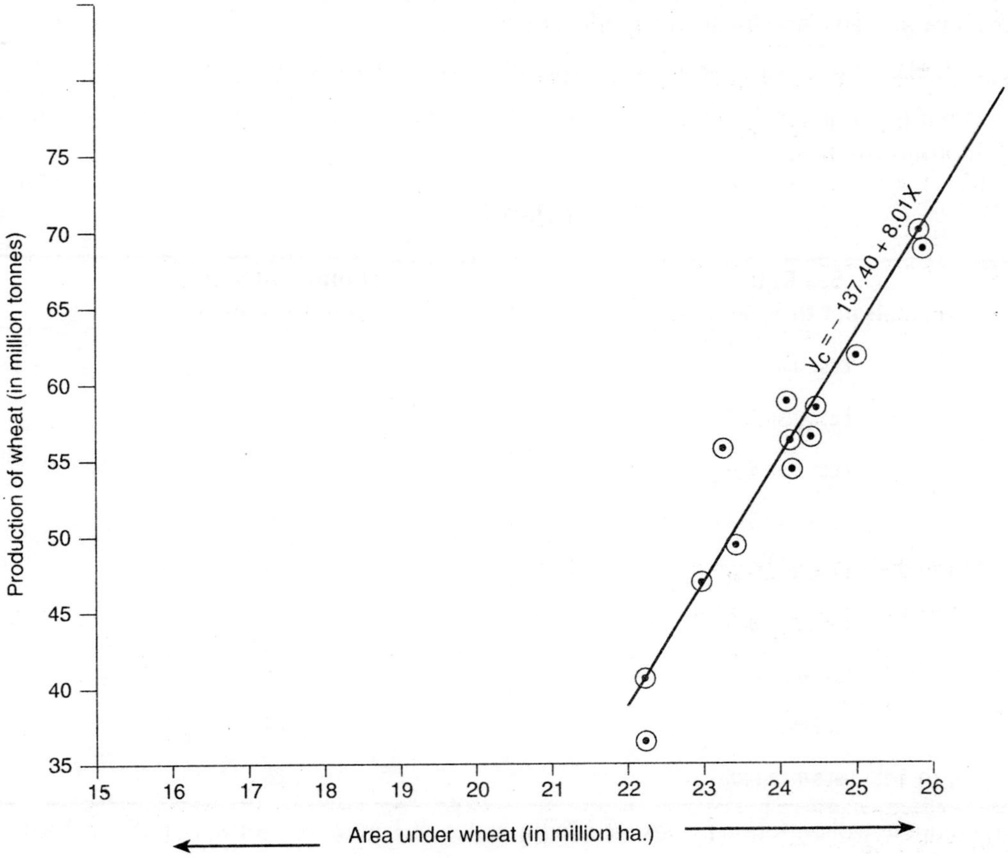

(b) we know, $y_c = a + bx$

∴ when the land under production is 26 million H.a., then the production will be

$y_c = -137.40 + b. 26$

or, $y_c = -137.40 + 8.01 \times 26$

or, $y_c = 70.86$ million tonnes.

Ans. : When the land under production of wheat is 26 million hectares, the production of wheat will be 70.86 million tonnes.

(c) From the graph it appears that there is a strongly positive relation between the area under production of wheat and production of wheat. Such a relationship is quite obvious, because the increase in land under production will eventually lead to a rise in production. The area involved must be highly fertile, because a slight rise in hectarage has given rise to multiplication in the production values. The average increase is 9.03 m. tonnes per million hectare increase in land. This is of course a high value.

6. Table No. 1 shows the cumulative frequency distribution of sex ratio in the states and union Territories of India in 2001.

(a) Prepare an ordinary frequency distribution from the given data.

(b) Draw an ogive and locate the median on it.

(c) Calculate the upper quartile, lower quartile and the sixth decile.

(d) What percentage of States and Union Territories show sex ratio below 900 females per thousand males?

[Year 2009]

Table 1

Sex Ratio (Femals per thousand males)	Number of States/ Union Territories
Less than 700	0
Less than 750	1
Less than 800	2
Less than 850	5
Less than 900	11
Less than 950	23
Less than 1000	33
Less than 1050	34
Less than 1100	35

(a) Frequency distribution for sex ratio in the states and union territories of India in 2001.

TABLE 2

Class Limit	Class Boundary	Class width (w)	Class Mark (x)	Frequency (f)
Less than 700	650–700	50	675	0
Less than 750	700–750	50	725	1
Less than 800	750–800	50	775	1
Less than 850	800–850	50	825	3
Less than 900	850–900	50	875	6
Less than 950	900–950	50	925	12
Less than 1000	950–1000	50	975	10
Less than 1050	1000–1050	50	1025	1
Less than 1100	1050–1100	50	1075	1

(b) Cumulative frequency Distribution for drawing an Ogive

TABLE 3

Class Limit	Class Boundary	Frequency	Cumulative Less than	Frequency More than
	650		0	35
Less than 700		0		
	700		0	35
Less than 750		1		
	750		1	34
Less than 800		1		
	800		2	33
Less than 900		3		
	850		5	30
Less than 950		6		
	900		11	24
Less than 950		12		
	950		23	12
Less than 1000		10		
	1000		33	2
Less than 1050		1		
	1050		34	1
Less than 1100		1		
	1100		35	0

OGIVES (Less than and more than)

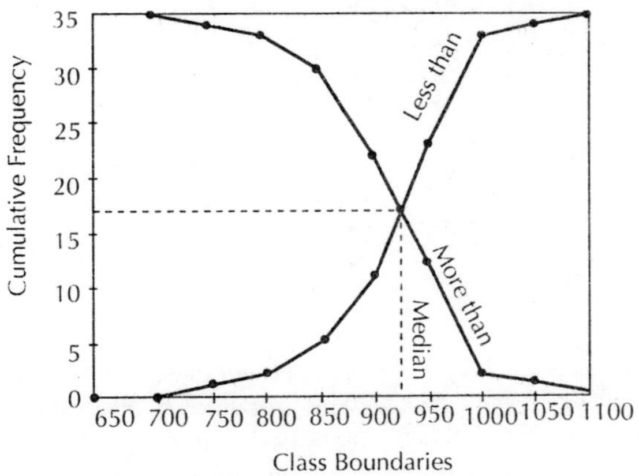

(c) Table for calculation of upper quartile, lower quartile and sizth decile :

TABLE 4

Class Boundary	Class Width	Frequency	Cumulative Frequency (less than type)
650–700	50	0	0
700–750	50	1	1
750–800	50	1	2
800–850	50	3	5
850–900	50	6	11
900–950	50	12	23
950–1000	50	10	33
1000–1050	50	1	34
1050–1100	50	1	35

Calculation of Upper Quartile (Q_3)

$$Q_3 = L_1 + \frac{3N/4 - fc}{f_Q} \times i$$

$$= L_1 + \frac{3 \times 35/4 - fc}{f_{Q_3}} \times i$$

$$= L_1 + \frac{26.25 - 23}{10} \times i$$

$$= 950 + \frac{3.25}{10} \times 50$$

$$= 950 + 16.25$$

$$= \boxed{966.25}$$

Where,
L_1 = Lower class boundary of quartile class.
N = Total no. of obervation.
fc = Less than cumulative frequency of pre-quartile class
f_Q = Frequency of particular quartile class
i = Width of the quartile class

Calculation of Lower Quartile (Q_1)

$$Q_1 = L_1 + \frac{N/4 - fc}{f_Q} \times i$$

$$= L_1 + \frac{35/4 - fc}{f_Q} \times i$$

$$= L_1 + \frac{8.75 - 5}{16} \times 50$$

$$= 850 + 31.25$$

$$= \boxed{881.25}$$

Calculation of Sixth Decile (D_6)

$$D_6 = L_1 + \frac{6N/10 - fc}{f_D} \times i$$

$$= L_1 + \frac{6 \times 35/10 - fc}{f_D} \times i$$

$$= L_1 + \frac{21 - 11}{12} \times 50$$

$$= 900 + 41.67$$

$$= \boxed{941.67}$$

Where,
L_1 = Lower class boundary of decile class.
N = Total no. of obervation.
fc = Less than cumulative frequency of pre-decile class
i = Width of the decile class

(d) Total number of states and union territories that show sex ratio = 35.

Number of states and union territories show sex ratio below 900 females per thousand males = 11

∴ The percentage of states and union territories that show sex ratio below 900 females per thousand males is :

$$\frac{11}{35} \times 100 = \boxed{31.43\%}$$

CHAPTER 8

TECHNIQUES IN REMOTE SENSING

The Remote Sensing means taking cognizance of any object from a distance. The process involves measurement of the object through the sensor. The sensor may be the human eye, camera, radiometer, spectrometer, polarimeter etc. The Remote Sensing involves the measurement of electro-magnetic energy being reflected, scattered or emitted by the objects absorbing and afterwards radiating the solar energy.

The Remote Sensing has become a key technology for ***New Cartography*** during the last few decades. Earlier the map-making was solely dependent on ground surveys, which were time consuming tedious processes and also difficult in inhospitable terrains like jungles, marshes, rugged mountains etc. With the developing technology in taking photographs from the air under cloud free condition of the atmosphere the difficulties were overcome to a large extent.

But the air-photo is not a map. Variable features of both natural and culturable landscape can be identified and processed into maps by different methods. The methods are explained by the science of photogrammetry , which make necessary correction in the distortion of shape and maintain true forms and dimension of the air-photos into maps.

In recent years images of the earth's surface taken by the satellites from the space have become important tools for map-making. The technology, though initiated in **Gemini and Apollo missions** in sixties through hand-held cameras, developed with the launching of **ERTS** or **Earth Resource Transmission Satellites** (now known as LANDSATS) in 1972. Since then the technology has remarkably advanced. Its wide application has become possible by image processing and analysis on a computer platform with the application of different user's friendly softwares. Unlike air-photos, the satellite imageries are not photographs at all. These are digital images recorded by the instruments, called sensors, which are sensitive to reflected or emitted radiation over broad electromagnetic spectrum, including microwave and thermal infra-red. Very recently Radar images are conveniently processed and analysed with the use of convenient softwares. RADARSOFT is one such software. The remote sensing images are geometrically corrected and mosaicked for transformation into planimetrically correct photo-maps.

Air-photos and their interpretation

Air-photos are taken by a specific type of camera usually on a platform of an aircraft. Various cameras, photo-sensitive films and filters are used in taking the photographs. A standard mapping camera produces a format of 9 × 9 inches (23 cm. × 23 cm.) photo. The spatial distortion of the photo can be reduced with the use of high resolution 6 inches or 12 inches focal length lenses. It is also necessary to control the advances of films in accordance with the flying height and speed of the aircraft so that a 60 per cent overlapping can be maintained between two successive exposures. For this purpose a time control device is required for the advances of motor driven films. This time-control device is known as ***Intervalometer*** and set along with the camera. The sharpness of the photographs depends upon the types of films used. An emulsion of silver salt crystals is coated on transparent plastic base. The silver salt crystals of the emulsion is exposed to photons reflected back from the objects on the ground and can record radiation energy ranging between 0.3 to 1.2 micrometers (i.e. near ultra-violet to near infra-red). Four types of emulsions are used within spectral ranges; namely panchromatic, black-white infra-red, true colour and colour infra-red.

Types of Air-photos

Air-photos may be taken at different positions of the camera. Broadly we have two types of air-photos. These are vertical and oblique types.

When the camera is focussed vertically downwards to the objects it gives the vertical air-photo. The vertical air-photo resembles the grounds plan of the earth's surface. It is just the expression of *vertical* topographic maps. So the vertical air-phot are commonly taken and used for preparation of the map.

But sometimes the camera is held tilted to get an oblique view of the ground surface. When the camera is tilted sufficiently so that the horizon of the ground surface can be shown, the air-photo is called *High oblique* type. But when tilting is not much it produces low oblique air-photos.

Determination of the Scale of the Air-photos

The scale of the air-photo can be determined by a simple equation :

$$S = f/H,$$

where f is the focal length of the camera and H is the flying height of the aircraft. Say the focal length of the camera is 6 inches and the flying height of the aircraft is 5000ft., then :

$$S = f/H = 6 \text{ inches}/5000 \text{ ft.} = 0.5 \text{ ft.}/5000\text{ft} = 1/10000$$

or it may be expressed in R.F. as 1:10000.

However in the air-photo the scale may not be shown and the flying height of the aircraft and focal length of the lens are not also shown. In such case the user can determine the scale of the photograph by identifying the horizontal distance of two objects on the air-photo and comparing this with the distance in reality. The scale of the photograph can be constructed from the ratio :

$$\frac{\text{Horizontal distance of the objects on the air-photo}}{\text{Real distance of the objects on the ground}} = \frac{PD}{GD}$$

Say, on the air-photo PD is 6 inches and GD as 6000 ft., then the scale will be :

$$6 \text{ inches}/6000 \text{ ft} = 0.5 \text{ ft.}/6000\text{ft.} = 1/12000$$

The scale may be expressed in RF 1:12000.

Arrangement of Air-photos and Stereo-vision

The aircrafts taking photographs usually fly along the flight lines arranged parallel. These are so spaced that the photographs from the adjacent lines can overlap. This overlapping is essentially required for stereo-vision.

A pair of air-photos of the same area being overlapped is viewed differently by the two eyes (LE & RE) and gives impression of three dimensional object of the area common to both photographs. Such expression is caused due to differential perception of the brain of the same area resulting in three dimensional image of the same area. Such vision is called the *Stereographic Vision* (fig. 8.1).

Fig. 8.1 Air photo

Fused Photographs or Stereo-pair

The adjacent vertical air-photos normally overlap 60% vertically and 25% laterally. The pair of air-photos is stated to be fused and is called *Fused Air-photos* or *Stereo-pair*. The overlapping of two adjacent air-photos helps in air photo interpretation.

Use of Stereoscope

The Stereoscope is the instrument which makes the stereovision of the fused photographs simply and conveniently. The cheapest and the commonest one is the *Pocket Stereoscope* or *Lens Stereoscope* (fig. 8.2). In this stereoscope two lenses are attached to a frame having the separate line of sights of the two eyes and images are slightly magnified. The stereoscope will render in the perception of two view of the same area of the fused photographs. The use of the pocket stereoscope becomes limited as only limited area of the fused photograph can be examined at one time due to its restrictive width.

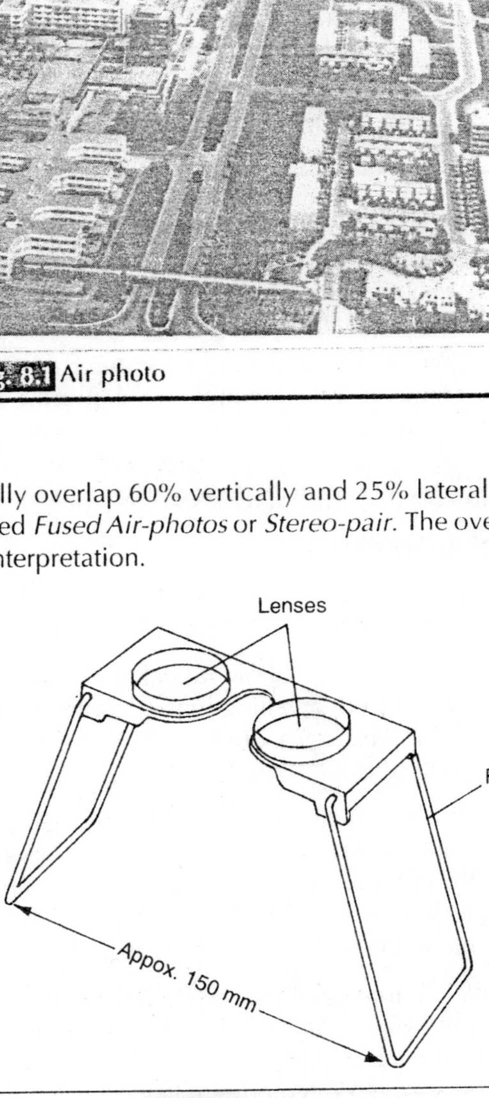

Fig. 8.2 Pocket Stereoscope

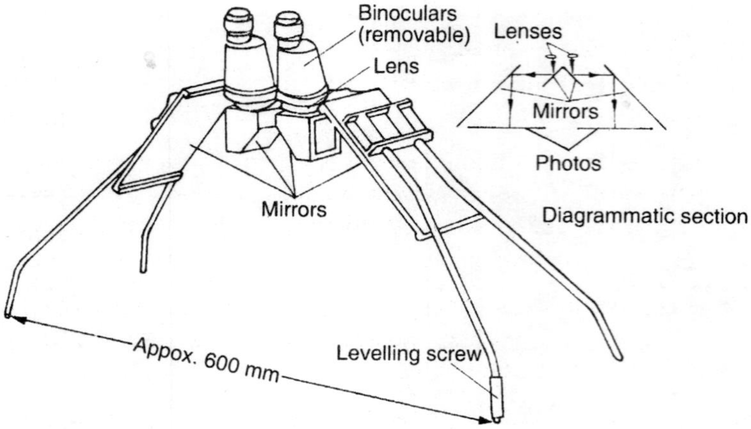

Fig. 8.3 Mirror Stereoscope

This disadvantage can be overcome with the use of *Mirror Stereoscope* (fig. 8.3). In this instrument two parallel mirrors spread the line of sight, thus allowing the whole photographs beneath it and enabling the whole of the fused photograph to be seen stereographically at one time. Binoculars are also attached to the Mirror Stereoscope for larger magnification.

The stereographic image will show the depth of the object in the photographs and determine the relief. But it requires little interpretative skill of the observer. In examining the photographs by stereoscope the vertical component of the image is exaggerated. Thus an understanding of vertical exaggeration of the stereo-pair reveals the minute details of relief and is helpful in geomorphological and terrain analysis of any region.

Properties of Air-photos

For better understanding and interpretation of the air-photos it is necessary to learn useful properties of the air-photos.

Size **:** Size signifies the stereo-photo model of any three dimensional object. From the differential sizes different objects like dwelling house, commercial building, factory etc. can be identified. Firstly the size of any recognisable object can be selected. With reference to this absolute size other objects can be distinguished.

Shape **:** Shape is a key factor in identifying any topographic expression. This is considered very important in landform interpretation. Any specific geometrical shape (rectangular, circular, polygonal etc.) indicates the cultural landscape, whether it be a farmland, roadway, railway, over head tank, reservoir park, township etc. Normally the natural landscape will show the irregular shape (i.e. the natural forest, natural lake, mountain/hill range etc.)

Tone **:** Tone of a photograph is the result of varying reflection of light by the earth's surface. Tone is expressed in the photograph (panchromatic) by the scale of black/white range or gray scale variation. Each tone has a specific value in the gray scale variation. Any object that absorbs light will exhibit a dark tone. Waterbodies (clear), forests/vegetation cover etc. will be represented as dark tonal surface. On the other hand bare land covered with sand will be of lighter tone. Waterbodies having more sediment deposits will appear lighter than the clear waterbodies. The metalled road will be shown by light line whereas the railways will be the darker line.

Pattern **:** Pattern in the air-photo gives clue whether it is natural or man-made. Orchards, housing cluster (linear, radial etc.) give an orderly systematic pattern. Different landforms like glaciers, alluvial fans, tidal flats etc. also show specific pattern. From the study of typical pattern one can identify the object from the air-photo.

Texture **:** Texture characterises the smoothness or coarseness of the image on the photograph. It is complex for identification of this property. It integrates all important properties like size, shape, tone and pattern of the photograph. This property may not be defined very accurately, but the interpreter can intutively understand the air-photo with this property as a whole.

Shadow **:** Sometimes the shadow appears very useful in identifying any object in the air-photo. The shadow is cast by obscurity of an area (say a building, forest cover etc.). The shadow as cast on the ground gives a clue in identification of the object.

Situation **:** A situation in the air-photo may help in locating a particular object in the air-photo. A building by the side of railway line will necessarily indicate a railway station, whereas warehouses near the coast may suggest the location of a port.

Interpretation Templates **:** Interpretation templates or keys are very useful for the identification of the objects and interpretation of air-photos. These keys are prepared for many features, where typical examples are classified on different types of films with written descriptions. With different keys one can identify the feature by the process of elimination and choice.

Distortion of Shape on Air-photos and Identification of Relief

Distortion of shape in air-photo is produced for two reasons : (i) Tilt displacement and (ii) Height displacement.

Tilt displacement occurs due to shifting of the camera axis from the absolute vertical. Tilt displacement can be seen most markedly on any oblique air photograph. The shapes of the buildings, rivers, roads etc. may not appear but are distorted due to perspective. In photogrammetry this perspective is referred to as ***Tilt displacement***.

The displacement related to both height of the object and its distance from the centre of the photograph or principal point is known as ***Height displacement*** or *Relief displacement*. Hills, valleys, spurs etc. display irregular relief displacement on the air-photo. The relief displacement helps to determine the elevation of the object. Positional displacements due to differences in elevation occurs radially away from the *nadir of* the air-photo. The *nadir* is a point on the photo whereas vertical line extended from the centre of the camera lens would touch the film.

The *nadir* coincides with the principal point of the photo in a true vertical air-photo. The relief displacement (rd) can be determined by the equation :

$$rd = h \times d / H,$$

where h = Local elevation, d = Radial distance and H = Flying altitude.

The relief displacement is more marked in the low altitude air-photos, than over the high-altitude air-photos and satellite imageries. In that sense low-altitude air-photos are more useful in determining the elevations of objects, particularly in the stereoscopic view of the overlapping area on two adjacent air-photos (Stereo pair).

Parallax of Aerial Photographs

The camera taking photographs of ground surface from an air craft shifts slightly between two consecutive exposures. This causes an apparent displacement in the relative position of a stationary object in the overlapping area. This apparent change in the relative position of an object, as related to the shift of the point of observation, is known as parallax. For instance, a camera positioned vertically above ground is directly above the principal or central point of the photographed landscape, but when the camera and the air craft shift their position for taking the consecutive photographs, the relative position of the object in the overlapping part changes with reference to the new position of the camera, although those can be observed still from the new position for photograph 2. This causes the occurrence of parallax.

When a pair of aerial photograph having the same focal length is considered under stereoscope and an object common in both the photographs is checked, the stereoscopic parallax of the point of the object can be determined. It is the algebraic difference between the distances of the same image in two photographs with respect to their nadir point, measurable along a horizontal plain parallel to the air base.

Measurement of Parallax

The principal point of photograph 1(P1) is marked and transferred to photograph 2 as is done for the second photographs also, i.e. the principal point of photograph 2 (P2) is transferred and marked in photograph 1. These two points are named P_1 and P_2. These are conjugate principal points. Now the principal point of each photograph is joined by a straight line to the conjugate principal point and the line of flight is marked. The position of an object *O* in P1 is also transferred to the second photograph. The distance between two actual principal points is measured as *D* and the distance between the position of *O* in two photographs is also measured as *d*.

The parallax of point *O* is $p = D - d$

Parallax bar is a device that can measure the length of parallax between two consecutive photographs.

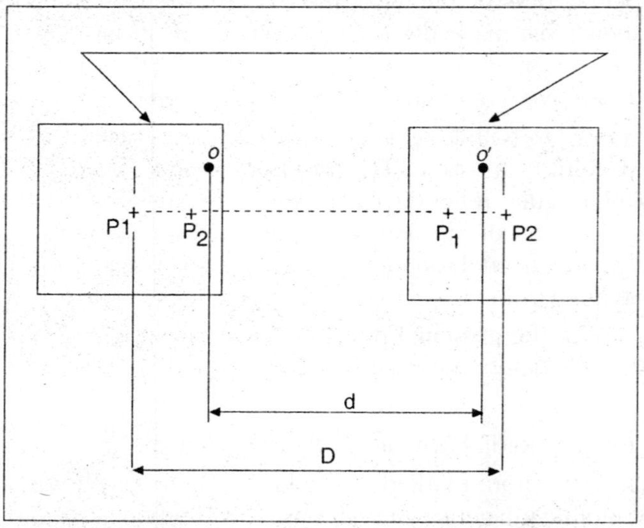

Fig. 8.4 **Measurement of parallax from vertical air photo**

Spectral Sensitivity Variation in Films and Image Identification

The photographic films of different types are used for air-photos. These are usually transparent plastic base coated on one side with an emulsion of silver salt crystals. Such crystals are sensitive are sensitive to electro-magnetic energy. Different forms of emulsions are used. Each emulsion has its own spectral sensitivity.

For black and white air-photos two principal types of films are : (i) Panchromatic film and (ii) Black and white infra-red film.

The panchromatic film is sensitive to spectral range of 0.3 to 0.7 μm. Near ultra-violet and visible energy (Red, Green, Blue) become sensitive for the film . However, haze and other atmospheric disturbance may cause loss of image contrast. The problem is now tackled with the use of different filters set in lenses of different cameras which simultaneously take photographs of the same object on ground. This process is known as *Multiband Photography.*

The gray tonal variation in the photograph help in identification of features on the photograph. The gray tone variations record the reflectance from each object. Highly reflective objects may appear lighter. On the other hand the objects absorbing light may be exposed darker air-photo. With such distinction it has become easier to identify the objects/features.

Black and white Infra-red (B/W I/R) film is similar to the panchromatic film, but has extended spectral range i.e. 0.3 to 0.9 μm. The range extends from near ultra-violet (0.3 μm.) to near infra-red (0.9 μm.) spectrum. The film is used with a filter in the camera that absorbs all ultra-violet (u/v), and visible energy. Thus the energy near the infra-red (0.7 to 0.9 μm.) is only recorded. The problem of haze can be overcome in this photography. For this reason B/W I/R film can be successfully used where the panchromatic film fails.

The greater tonal contrast is possible in B/W I/R film. The vegetative surface absorbs more infra-red energy resulting in darker tone on the photograph. Similarly the waterbodies also absorb infra-red energy greater than visible light. So the waterbodies register a darker gray tone or black colour on the air-photos for easy identification of these features. Infra-red photography is widely applied in Forest Inventory and Wetland Mapping.

True colour film is also used for taking air-photos. Initially due to high cost and low resolution the colour film was rarely used. Recently with the reduction of costs, improvement of film speed, higher image quality and greater contents of information in colour images; use of colour film has become advantageous for remote sensing. Visually different colours of the images can be identified. By understanding the subtle distinction between the colours of the images one can easily reveal the condition of natural features. Such as the maturity of crops can also be identified in true colours. For this reason colour air-photo can be effectively used for crop monitoring. It can also be conveniently applied in many other cases.

Identification of Features Based on Tonal Variations

Roads, buildings may appear light or dark on the image depending on the nature of their composition. If it is made of concrete the picture will be lighter. Whereas if it is coated with asphalt the picture will be darker. Similarly if the soil is moist the picture will be comparatively darker than the dry land. The moist ploughed land is often shown darker than the barren land. The wetlands, particularly the marshy lands appear on the air-photos with dark tone. The water flows in the rivers/streams can be distinguished. Dry river beds will appear in light tone, whereas the dark tone in the course of streams will indicate water flow. Thus different environmental and landuse features like forests, croplands, soils, rivers, wetlands and cultural landscape like buildings, reservoirs, dams, tanks, roadways, railways etc. can be distinctly identified on air-photos based on panchromatic films.

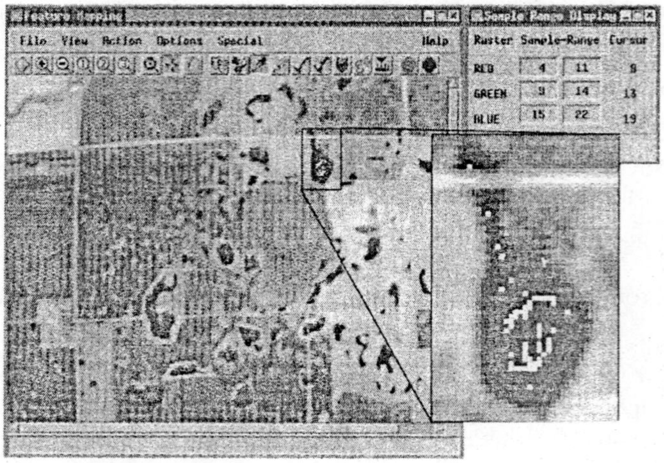

Fig. 8.5 Defining sample cells

Image Interpretation of the Air-photo on a Computer Platform

In recent years the P.C. has rendered a leap in the image analysis of the air-photo. The air-photo can be scanned digitally by a scanner and with the help of digital photogrammetry this air-photo can be generated in raster format on P.C. Many softwares have been developed to analyse the images of the air-photo. The software TNT Mips by Micro Images Inc., U.S.A. has become a useful tool for image analysis.

Air-photos are considered lower quality images than the satellite imageries. The air-photos contain such artefacts as darkening at the edges and corners of the optical image, which is called *Vignetting*. The radiometric properties of a feature at the edge and corner of the image may, thus, appear different than at the centre. TNT Mips has Feature Mapping facility to assist in the classification of lower quality images. The objective of Feature Mapping is to identify, mark and measure features in a set of processing rasters with TNT Mips processing power.

The Feature Mapping includes different processes :

(i) Launch TNT. Turn on the Air-photo Interpretation toolbar. Choose Feature Mapping.

(ii) Analysis and Reference Rasters to confirm Contrast and Colour Map Selections for Reference Raster.

(iii) Identification of a cell as representative of a particular Feature Class, known as Sample Points. The cells identified by the computer that lie within the range of values defined by the Sample Points are termed Prototypes. When a Prototype belongs to the same class as the Sample Points, it is defined as Marked Feature.

a) Define sample cells

b) Identify Prototype features

c) Add a Feature Class

d) Mark all features (fig. 8.4)

The process can be resumed. Also follow the following steps :

(i) Unmarking features

(ii) Marking features with the mouse

(iii) Generating a report

The Region of Interest may also be defined. The defined Region of Interest outlines the area considered for any subsequent classification activities and reports generated.

Creating DEMS and Ortho-photos from Air-photos

DEM, *Digital Elevation Model* is a raster object that possesses elevation values for a site. *Orthophoto* is a digital image that has been created by digital photogrammetric techniques to correct for distortions caused by camera angle, distance and surface elevation. The ortho-photos have map like geometry and give an accurate image base for many projects in geo-spatial analysis.

By using TNT Mips the Stereographic Modelling Process can generate orthophotos in five steps :

1. Geo-reference
2. Interior Orientation
3. Relative Orientation
4. DEM Extraction
5. Orthographic Creation

Stereo-image to DEM to Orthophoto

The pair of stereo air-photos when overlapped, projects stereo information that can be digitally processed to get elevation information. The *vignetting* occurs in the air-photos. The elevation information can in turn help in the correction for systematic distortions resulting due to camera perspective and surface elevation. After compensating for camera tilt, digital air-photo techniques adjust position of features inward and reduce their size, based on their elevation and their distance from the centre of air-photo.

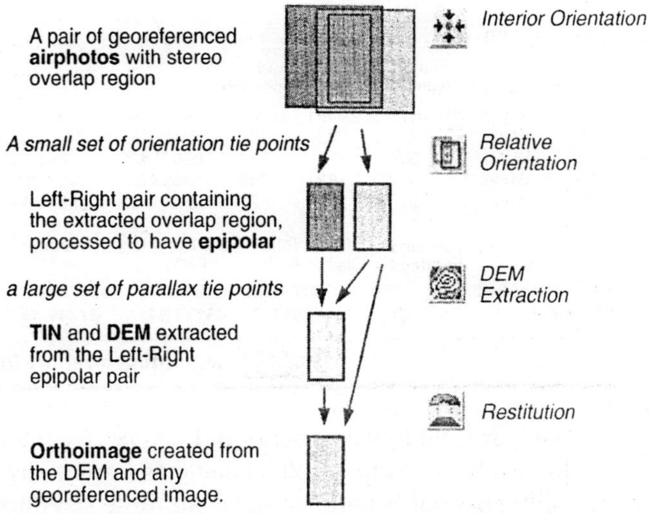

Fig. 8.6 Stereo to DEM to Orthophoto

Thus from a pair of air-photos a DEM and an Ortho-image can be created for the overlapping area. The process for the creation of a DEM and an Ortho-image has been explained in the TNT Mips (fig. 8.5).

Satellite Image Interpretation

For the last two decades images of the earth's surface taken from the space have become valuable and very useful in a wide variety of applications. In the sixties hand held cameras on board the Gemini and Apollo mission initiated the era of satellite imaging. Later on Skylab mission performed more systematic imaging. The ERTS, now known as LANDSAT 1 satellite, was launched in 1972 to cover the land surface exclusively for detailed imaging.

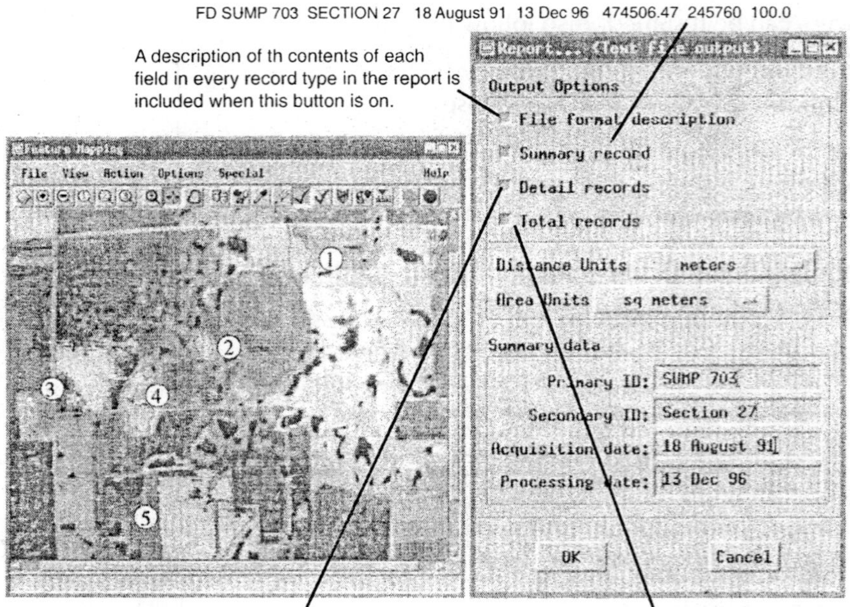

Type of Record	Class	Feature Number	Feature Centroid line	Feature Centroid column	Area	Boundary Length	Cells in Feature	Boundary Cells
FS	Water	1	334	93	13171.86	3667.89	682	821
FS	Water	2	233	188	5909.96	1652.70	306	370
FS	Water	3	111	214	66631.87	18542.53	3450	4147
FS	Water	4	162	250	19023.88	5464.64	985	1224
FS	Water	5	221	377	133920.39	35811.59	6934	8003

Class	Number of Features in Class	Total Area	Total Boundary Length	Average Area	Average Boundary Length	Percent of Area	Total Number of Cells	Total Number of Boundary Cells
FT Unclassified	1	4507848	0.00	4507848.51	0.00	95.0	233403	0
FT water	5	238657	65139.34	47731.59	13027.87	5.0	12357	14565

Fig. 8.7 Generating a report for Feature Mapping

Afterwards till to date a series of LANDSAT satellites were launched into the space equipped with Return Beam Vidicon (RBV) cameras (essentially small video cameras with high resolution) and Multi-Spectral Scanners (MSS). All these satellites orbit the earth at an altitude of 920 km. once every 103 minutes, generating image of the whole earth's surface, except the areas poleward of 82 degree, once every 18 days. The orbits are sun-synchronous so that all parts of earth's surface are exposed at the same local time on each pass.

U.S.S.R. conducted missions of Salyut 4, Salyut 5, Salyut 6 and Salyut 7 for space photography. The Soyuzkarta programme also produced images with KFA 1000, MK 4 and KATE 200 cameras. Many such images cover 120 × 120 km. areas. These are taken from an altitude of 275 km. through a 39.4 inch focal lens rendering an average photo scale of 1 : 275 ,000.

In 1986 a French satellite, SPOT (Systeme' Probatoire d'observation de la terra) was launched into a near polar 832 km. orbit. It is the first resource satellite to use *pushbroom sensors*. The sensing system has two identical High Resolution Visible (HRV) instruments that may be operated simultaneously or independently. SPOT results in a total ground swath of 117 km. being recorded when operated simultaneously. SPOT 1 passes over the same location every 26 days. SPOT provides up to 10 m. resolution (for panchromatic image). But for (false) colour images (green, red and near infra-red) the resolution is 20m.

Recently India has advanced much in the field of Remote Sensing. Remote Sensing satellites have been placed in the orbit with Multi-spectral Scanners (MSS). Multi-Spectral Scanners range from simple two channels system as on NOAA weather satellites or the Indian Bhaskara satellite to eleven channels air borne scanner available with National Remote Sensing Agency (NRSA). Indian Remote Sensing (IRS) satellites are fitted with LISS (Linear Imaging Self Scanner) cameras (scanners). These sensors can record 4 bands of data. The spatial resolutions vary in different types of IRS satellites (IRS IA, IRS IB, IRS IC, IRS P2, IRS P3).

IRS IA

Indian Remote Sensing Satellite (IRS) system was initiated with the launch of IRS IA in March 1988. It was placed in the orbit from Russia. IRS IA has two types of sensors (cameras), LISS I and LISS II with spatial resolutions of 72.5 m. and 36.25 m. respectively. LISS I possesses a swath of 148 km. and two LISS II cameras have the composite swath of 148 km.

IRS IB

IRS IB was placed in the orbit in August, 1991. IRS IB has the spatial resolution and swath like IRS IA. This satellite has been serving well in the orbit.

IRS IC

IRS IC is the second generation of Indian Remote Sensing satellites, which was launched in December, 1995. It has three sensors namely, PAN, LISS III and WiFS having different resolutions. The resolutions are 5.8 m., 23 m. and 288 m. for PAN, LISS III and WiFS respectively.

IRS IC makes 341 orbits in 24 days. On the 25th day the ground traces coincide with those of the 1st day. i.e. the 341 ground traces of the satellite orbits are repeated in each cycle. These orbits have been controlled in such a way that the actual ground traces are always within 5 km. from the nominal (fig. 8.7).

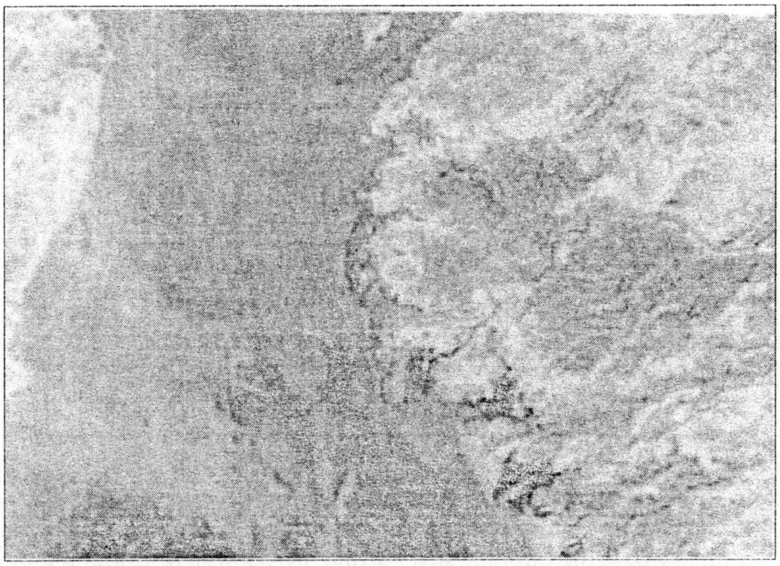

Fig. 8.8 IRS 1C LISSIII imagery of Mayurakshi Reservoir (Maithon, Bihar)

IRS IC Referencing Scheme

The ground trace of satellite is called a *path*. Along a path, the continuous stream of data is segmented into a number of scenes of a convenient size. The lines connecting the corresponding scene centres of different paths lie parallel to the equator. These are called *rows*. The *path-row* grid covers the entire globe. Each of the 341 paths has 149 rows. Path number 1 is placed at 29.7 degree west longitude at equator. The interval between successive paths is 1.055 degree. The subsequent path lie eastward. Row number 75 corresponds with the equator.

Ground Swath

The LISS II sensor records data in the form of continuous scanlines with a ground swath of 141 km. along the track. The images are obtained for a ground coverage of 141 × 141 km. area. The sidelap between two LISS III scenes in adjacent paths is 23 km. at the equator. The overlap between two successive scenes appears to be 7 km. The ground swath of Middle Infra-Red (MIR) band of LISS III is slightly larger than that of the other three bands (Red, Green and IR).

The ground swath, image sizes, overlap and sidelap for PAN and WiFS differ from LISS III. These are represented in the table below.

TABLE 8.1

IRS IC Payload Characteristics

Sensor	Resolution (m.)	Ground swath (km.)	Image size (km. × km.)	Overlap (km.)	Sidelap at the equator (km.)
LISS III Visible	23.5	141	141 × 141	7	23.5
MIR	70.5	148	148 ×148	14	30
PAN	5.8	70	70 × 70	2	–1 (opt)
WiFS	188	755	755 × 755	– 80%	– 80%

IRS P2

IRS P2 was successfully launched by PSLV (Polar Satellite Launch Vehicle) in October, 1994. It has been fitted with LISS II cameras similar to those of IRS IA and IRS IB. IRS P2 has, however, better spatial resolution of 32 m. and a swath of 148 km.

IRS P3

IRS P3 was also launched by PSLV into polar sunsynchronous orbit in March, 1996. This satellite was modelled with two remote sensing payloads for applications related to oceanography and vegetation dynamics. A Wide Field Sensor (WiFS) like IRS IC has been fitted, but includes an additional Short Wave Infra-Red (SWIR) band for the study of vegetation dynamics. Moreover it possesses a Modular Opto-electronic Scanner (MOS) and 18 channel imaging spectrometer in visible/near Infra-Red region. It has an effective ground resolution of 500 × 500 m. and a swath of about 20 km. MOS payload is specifically designed for oceanographic applications. This satellite also carried an X-ray Astronomy payload for the study of time variability and spectral characteristics of Cosmic X-ray sources and, sources and detection of transient X-ray sources.

IRS ID

IRS ID was launched into the orbit from Indian soil by an indigenous Polar Satellite Launch Vehicle (PSLV - C1) in September, 1997. It is similar to IRS IC with spatial resolution as high as 5.8 m., the highest in the world.

Many other satellites have been planned for launching in the coming years. These are all improved versions of the earlier satellites. These satellites are IRS P4 (planned to be launched in 1998-99), IRS P5 (planned to be launched in 1999-2000) and IRS P6 (to be launched in 2000-01). IRS P5 will be specifically modelled for cartographic applications with two PAN cameras providing better resolution of 2.5 m. with a steerable swath of 30 km. The cameras will provide stereo pairs of images required for the generation of Digital Terrain Model (DTM) and Digital Elevation Model (DEM). This will be very useful in getting cadastral level information up to 1:5000 scale of thematic mapping.

The comparative usefulness of IRS IC and IRS ID with respect to other R.S. satellites of the world has been noted in the following table.

TABLE 8.2

Comparative Usefulness of IRS IC and IRS ID with other R.S. Satellites in the World

Country	Satellite	Resolution
U.S.A	Landsat 5	30 m. multispectral
France	Spot 1 & 2	10 m. PAN, 20 m. multispectral
Japan	JERS1	18 m. multispectral with extended Infra-Red capability
India	IRS IC & ID	6 m. PAN, 18 m. multispectral
Russia	COSMOS	2 m./10 m. photo-digitised
Canada	Radarsat	Dynamic energy system, resolutions ranging from 8 m. to 100 m.

Image Analysis

Satellite imageries are not photographs at all. These are digital images recorded by the instruments, sensitive to reflected or emitted radiation over broad range of the electro-magnetic spectrum including micro-wave and thermal infra-red. These digital data as recorded by the satellite are beamed to the earth's receiving station, where these are stored for display, enhancement and interpretation. The satellite imaging system are capable of recording energy emitted at any desired wavelengths. The digital images can be viewed either through display on a computer platform or conversion into a photographic paper product (hard copy).

Such images can be viewed one band at a time through gray scale (black and white) reproduction. The lowest reflectance values are displayed as black, highest values as white and intermediate values as different tones of gray. On the other hand three bands of imagery may be displayed at one time to generate a colour composite image. These colours are not true. Such images are produced by projecting the green visible satellite data values with blue light, the red visible with green light and the near infra-red data with red light. These three primary colours in combination can generate all colours of the visible spectrum. Such images as produced are called *False Colour Composite (FCC)*.

Visual Interpretation

Visual interpretation of satellite imageries is a simple technique and can be done by observations of pattern/ associations, tone/colour and texture of different FCCs. This helps in the study of landuse covers. Such observations can also be made for monochrome imageries on the basis of landforms and spectral characteristics. Such techniques in conjunction with ground truth check are considered very useful for identification of landuse class and categories. Image interpretation keys are noted below for the study of IRS - LISS (FCC), LANDSAT-TM (FCC) and SPOT - HRV(FCC) imageries.

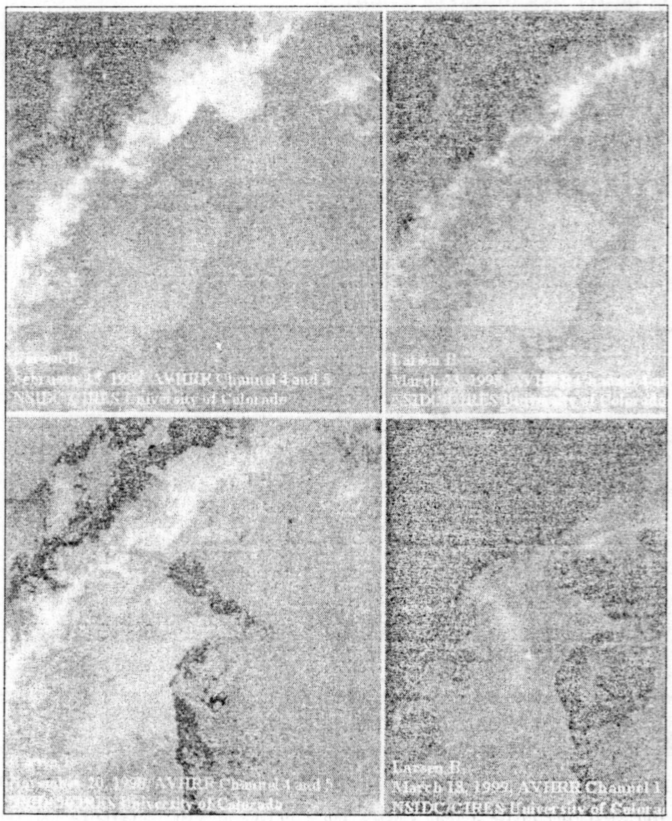

Fig. 8.9 **Break up of Larsen B Ice shelf as evidenced from AVHRR Channel I imagery**

TABLE 8.3

Image Interpretation Keys for Landuse/Land Cover Categories as Derived from Satellite Imagery

Landuse/ Cover	Pattern / Associations	IRS LISS 2B (FCC)		Landsat-TM (FCC)		Spot-HRV - 1 (FCC)	
		Tone/Colour	Texture	Tone/Colour	Texture	Tone/Colour	Texture
High density built-up	Compact, rectan gular, inner parts of city	Dark blue blackish	Medium	Dark bluish grey	Medium	Bluish grey	Medium to fine
Medium density built-up	Rectangular less compact	Bluish brown mixed	Medium	Bluish brown	Medium	Greyish-light blue mixed	Medium to fine

Landuse/ Cover	Pattern / Associations	IRS LISS 2B (FCC)		Landsat-TM (FCC)		Spot-HRV - 1 (FCC)	
		Tone/Colour	Texture	Tone/Colour	Texture	Tone/Colour	Texture
Low density built-up	Rectangular to irregular, open spaces, fringe areas	Light blue mixed brown	Coarse	Pinkish grey	Coarse	Light bluish with grey	Coarse
Rural settlement	Scattered small patches over agricultural land	Dark green brown mixed	Medium to fine	Greyish	Medium	Brown to pink	Medium to fine
Mixed built-up	Irregular, mixed residential with industries, institutions	Brown-blue mixed	Coarse	Blue-brown pinkish	Coarse	Bluish-brown patches mixed	Coarse
Built-up land under construction	Rectangular patches mainly with low built-up	Light blue bright	Medium	Bright	Medium	Bright pinkish	Coarse
Parks/ gardens	Squared/rectan-gular associated with built-up	Brownish-red	Medium	Reddish-brown	Coarse	Reddish-brown	Medium to fine
Play-ground/ stadia	do	Bright -light blue	Medium	Bright	Medium	Bright	Medium to fine
Major roads	Linear contiguous along with built-up	Dark brown blackish	Medium	Dark reddish brown	Medium	Dark brown	Medium to fine
Other important roads	do	Brownish	Coarse	Light pinkish brown	Coarse	Light brown	Medium
Railway track/ station	Linear, straight station at junctions	Brownish	Medium	Dark brown	Medium	Dark brown	Fine
Airport	Rectangular, runway linear & vacant area	Bluish brown white strip	Medium	Bluish pink white strip	Medium	Brownish white strip	Fine to medium
Vacant land	Irregular, enclosed patches	Light grey yellow mixed	Medium	Lighter	Medium	Light brown	Medium
Cultivated land	Contiguous area, rectangular fields spread throughout	Reddish with bright patches of fallow/open	Medium to fine	Reddish grey mixed	Medium to fine	Red to brown grey mixed	Fine to medium
Orchards/ plantation	Rectangular, alongwith agricul-tural land	Brownish red	Medium to fine	Reddish brown	Medium	Reddish brown	Fine to medium
Dense forest	Irregular, compact away from main built-up area	Dark reddish brown-violet mixed	Fine	Red	Medium to fine	Dark brown	Fine
Sparse vegetation	Irregular, open along dense forest	Lighter in tone than forest	Medium	Brownish light red	Medium	Light brown	Fine to medium

Landuse/ Cover	Pattern / Associations	IRS LISS 2B (FCC)		Landsat-TM (FCC)		Spot-HRV - 1 (FCC)	
		Tone/Colour	Texture	Tone/Colour	Texture	Tone/Colour	Texture
Bush/open scrub/grass	Irregular dispersed along forest/waste land	Light brownish blue mixed	Coarse	Light brownish red	Coarse	Whitish brown	Medium
River/stream	Linear, meandered	Dark blue, dark brown streams	Fine	Dark blue blackish	Fine	Bluish black	Fine
Canal	Linear, rather straight	Dark blue brownish	Fine	Light pink blue mixed	Fine	Dark blue	Fine
Tanks/ ponds	Mainly circular rectangular along settlement	Blue	Fine	Blue	Fine	Sky blue	Fine
Gullied/ eroded land	Irregular, scattered along streams	Brownish	Varying	Light with rills	Varying	Yellowish with black rills	Coarse to medium
Undulating land	Irregular, scattered patches	Yellowish brown	Varying	Pinkish	Varying	Yellowish brown	Coarse
River sands/ sandy area	Irregular patches along main river	Bright light blue	Medium to fine	Bright	Medium to fine	Bright	Fine
Salt affected land	Irregular patches along agricultural land, stream, canals	Bright bluish	Medium	Light	Medium	Bright	Medium
Water logged area/swamps	Meanders & patches along streams	Brownish black	Medium	Blackish blue pink mixed	Medium	Brownish black	Medium

The geomorphic characteristics of landforms can also be identified from the study of spectral characteristics of Landsat imageries. The key for interpretation is shown in the following table.

TABLE 8.4

The key for image interpretation of landsat images

Landforms	Landuse category	Spectral characteristics of landuse as revealed from landsat
1. Hills	Rocky and stoney waste	Bare hills appear in dark tone and vegetation due to high reflectance exhibit white tone on Landsat band 7 image and in green and red tones on FCC image
2. Rocky and gravelly pediments and plateaus	Rocky, gravelly and stony wastes and single cropped lands in pockets	The wastelands due to high reflectance exhibit white and grey tone on Landsat 5 & 7 images
3. Flat buried pediments and plateaus	Single and double cropped lands	The cropped lands due to high infra-red reflectance appear in white tone on Landsat band 7 image and in dark grey to dark tone due to low reflectance on Landsat band 5 image

Landforms	Landuse category	Spectral characteristics of landuse as revealed from landsat
4. Sandy undulating buried sediments	Single cropped lands, rainfed/ irrigated	The cultivated lands show dark grey to dark tone and the fallow lands appear in white tone on landsat band 5 image
5. Shallow to moderately deep flat aggraded older alluvial plains	Single cropped lands and gravelly wastes	Due to significant variations in Landsat spectral characteristics of the landuse patterns, the cultivated lands which exhibit dark grey to dark tone could be distinguished from the grazing lands on Landsat 5 image
6. Moderately deep to deep flat aggraded older alluvial plains	Single cropped lands under rainfed and irrigated conditions and double cropped lands in pockets	Landuse patterns due to high reflectance of crops to infra-red radiation appear in white tone and fallow lands in dark grey to dark tone on Landsat band 7 image
7. Deep flat aggraded older alluvial plains	Single cropped lands, rainfed/ irrigated	Similar to observations for No. 6
8. Deep saline flat aggraded older alluvial plains	Largely saline wastes and single cropped lands in pockets	Non-saline cropped lands due to their red tone are distinct from the saline grazing lands on Landsat and IRS FCC images
9. Deep to very deep flat aggraded older alluvial plains	Largely single cropped lands	Cropped lands appear in dark tone, while the fallow lands in white tone on Landsat band 5 image in wet season
10. Gravelly aggraded older alluvial plains	Largely rocky cropped lands	The wastelands and the cultivated lands appear in dark grey and white tones on Landsat band 7 image of wet season and are distinctly shown in green and bright red tone on FCC image
11. Sandy undulating aggraded older alluvial plains	Single cropped lands with long fallow	The cropped lands exhibit dark to dark grey tone, while the fallow lands show whitish tone on Landsat band 7 image
12. Sand dunes	Sandy wastes and single cropped lands in pockets	Sand dunes are shown in white tone, while the cropped lands in dark grey to dark tone
13. Interdune plains	Single cropped lands with short to long fallow	The cropped lands having crops and high moisture status exhibit dark grey to dark tone
14. Younger alluvial plains, subject to flooding	Cropped area along with sandy, gravelly and saline wastes	The landuse of the flood affected area shows white to grey tone, but irrigated cropped lands show darker tone on Landsat band 5 image in wet season
15. Saline depressions	Saline waste	The wastelands appear in white tone and grass covered areas exhibit dark grey tone on Landsat band 5 image

Source : *Surendra Singh, Geomorphology and Remote Sensing in Environmental Management., Jodhpur, 1992*

Image Classification on a Computer Platform

Our eye is an effective remote sensor and human visual system is a wonderful image processing system. We can sense colour, shape, texture, movement, and other visual cues to recognise and classify objects around us. Colour is the most important and effective of these visual cues. Human eyes are sensitive to the red, green and blue components of visible light.

Interestingly, as the brightness of each of these light components differs, the brain is able to synthesise the result into perception of a particular colour out of innumerable potential colours.

We can speak of optical remote sensing, which can likewise record brightness values at different wavelengths. These not only include portions of the visible light spectrum, but also photo infra-red and in few cases middle infra-red bands, which human eye cannot perceive. The brightness values for each of these bands are specifically stored in a separate grayscale raster. So in an image we record brightness values of each ground resolution cell. These values in effect represent the colour of that particular spot of the ground surface. In this way we can distinguish different patches as sensed by the respective brightness values.

By the use of TNT mips software one can attempt to classify images. The Automatic Classification process in TNT mips uses the colour or spectral patterns of raster cells in a multi-spectral image to automatically categorise all cells into specified number of spectral classes. By analysis of spectral properties of each class, the relationship between the spectral classes and different surface materials or land cover can be determined.

Methods

The spectral pattern of a cell in a multi-spectral image can be quantified by plotting the raster value from each band on a separate coordinate axis in a hypothetical *spectral space*. This spectral space has unique dimension for each band in the image. Most classification method employ the distance between input cells in this spectral space to assess their similarity. Technically the cells lying in the neighbourhood of spectral space have a close likelihood of imaging the same surface features. The methods may be either a simple unsupervised classification process, including viewing the classification result and comparing it with the input image or supervised classification of images. We are considering here the unsupervised classification (fig. 8.9).

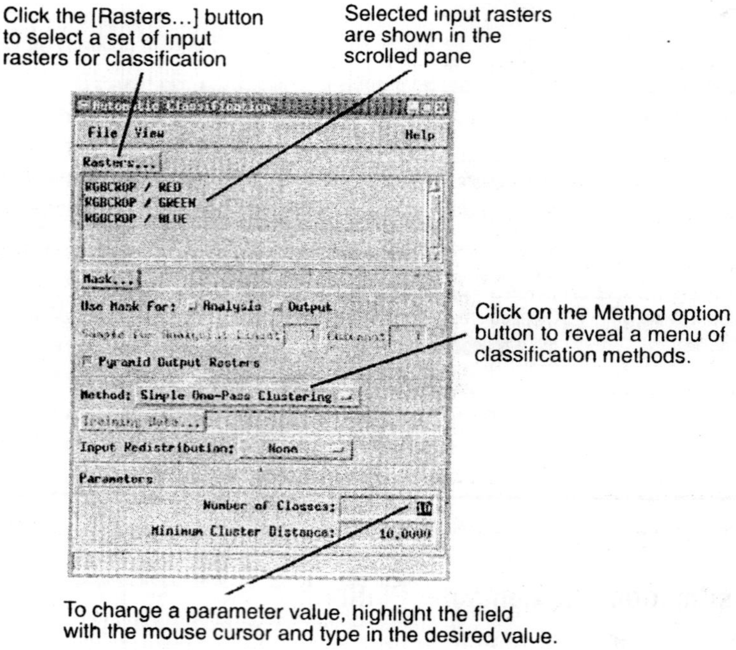

Fig. 8.10 **Unsupervised classification**

Steps

1. Select Interpret/Raster/ Classify/ Automatic from the TNT mips main menu.
2. Click the [Rasters ......] button on Automatic Classification window
3. Select raster object RED, GREEN, and BLUE from the specified project file (say RBGCROP)
4. Press the Method Option menu button and select Simple One-Pass Clustering
5. Select None from the Input Redistribution option menu
6. Change the Number of Classes to 10
7. Choose Run from the File menu
8. Use the Standard File / Object Selection procedure to create a new Project File named CROPCLAS for the output raster
9. Name the output Class and Distance rasters using the default names provided
10. Click OK on the File/Object Selection window to confirm the selection and start the classification process

The Simple One-pass Clustering method establishes initial class centres and assigns cells to classes in one processing pass by determining the spectral distance between each cell and established class centres. Each raster cell assigned to the nearest class ; a cell too far away from existing class becomes the centre of a new class (up to a specified number of classes).

Display of the Output Rasters

The main classification results lie in the Class Raster. Some classification methods help in creating Distance Raster. The standard display process (Display/Spatial Data) may be invoked to display the Class Raster CLS - SIMPLE and Distance Raster DST — SIMPLE.

The Class Raster is a categorical raster. Each numerical value in the raster is an arbitrary class identifier. This value has been assigned to the cell by the classification process. The Unsupervised Classification assigns class numbers in the order in which the classes are created. TNT uses a standard palette of colours to systematically assign a unique colour to each numbered class.

The Distance Raster is gray-scale raster. It exhibits how well each cell fits its assigned class. Each raster cell value in the Distance Raster records the distance between that cell and its class in the spectral space. Cells lying closer to their class centre (better fit) appear darker in the displayed raster than those with greater distance values (poorer fit) (fig. 8.10).

Steps

1. Select Display/Spatial data from the main menu bar.
2. Display raster object CLS — SIMPLE from the CROPCLAS Project file (earlier created) in View 1.
3. Click the Views toggle button to open the Views drop-down panel.
4. Click the New View icon button to open a second view window.
5. Display raster object DST— SIMPLE in View 2.

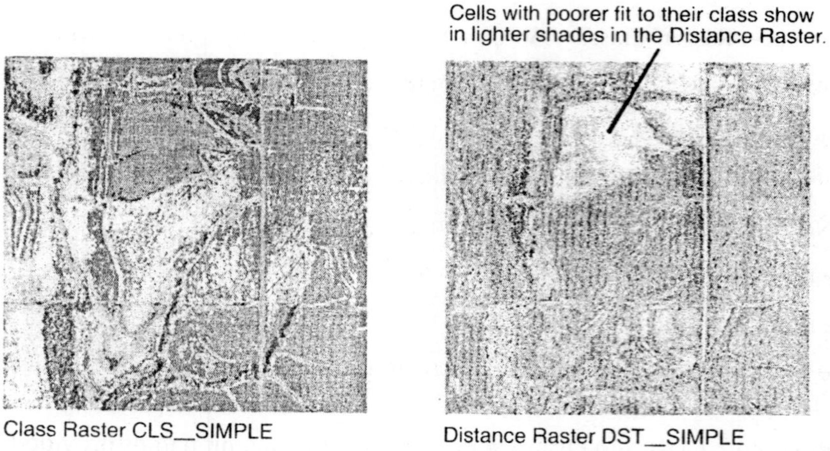

Fig. 8.11 Displaying the raster

6. Open the Raster Object Display Controls window and select Auto Normalize from the Contrast option menu.
7. Click OK to redisplay the Distance Raster.

Display of the Input Image

The Automatic Classification process is influenced by the sets of brightness values of all cells in the scene, not just the features that we intend to classify. To avoid the problem the following steps can be followed to display the input image, where we can compare to Class Raster to the input image. The views can be arranged in two windows. We find that most features include cells of two or even three classes. The class number corresponding to each colour can be determined by opening the Colour Map Editor window (Enhance/Edit Colours). The Colour Map Editor window shows colour squares for each raster value beginning with 0 in the upper left and increasing left to right and top to bottom. We can also use the Examine Raster tool to determine the class assigned to particular cells in the output Class raster.

Steps

1. Click the Open Layout icon button on the Display/Spatial Data control window.
2. Select the CROPS-LAYOUT object from the RBGCROP Project file.
3. Click on View 1 in the Views list.
4. Choose Edit Colours from the Enhance menu on the Display / Spatial Data control window.

LANDUSE AND LAND COVER MAPS

Earth's surface is covered with various types of natural vegetation, though bare exposure of rocks are also noticeable in different areas. Human society converts the natural land cover into preferred landuses. The natural landforms whichever is convenient for conversion into certain landuse type are selected and the natural land cover is removed being replaced by agricultural lands, settlements or any other type of landuse. Thus the invasion of human society continues and natural forests, grasslands etc. of river valleys, floodplains, hill slopes are depleted of their vegetative cover and the areas take the shape of a wide variety of cultural landscape.

Identification of Land Cover

As mentioned earlier, land cover denotes the natural form of land with certain cover of vegetation on it, but it has a wider range of natural characteristics other than vegetation. Thus a bare rock surface should be considered as a category of land cover and a wetland covered with water and mud, though not perennially, is also categorized into a type of land cover. A waterbody can also be taken as a category of land cover. Thus natural lakes may belong to this category, but if it is an excavated pond, an artificial lake or a reservoir behind a dam, it is not categorized as a unit of land cover. Hence, land cover is the nature of physical material on the surface of the earth and accumulation of water under human control is a type of landuse.

A land cover has a natural boundary or limit beyond which another category appears. However, a land cover type can be detected from satellite images or aerial photographs other than a physical survey into the area. In FCC some colour signatures identify different types of land cover features. For instance, broad leaf healthy vegetation may show red to magenta, whereas if it is needle leaf type, it will be reddish brown to purple. If the forest cover is stressed i.e. the natural environment under which the vegetation grew up has been partly changed and the health of vegetation deteriorates, the colour is pink to blue. A waterbody with suspended sediments appears in light blue and a deeper water with less sediment is dark blue or black. Sand dunes may appear yellow or white and the same are the bare sand bars in large rivers. A dampened ground with relatively impervious surface has distinct dark tones. This way different categories of land cover may be identified from satellite images and may be mapped on the scale of the FCC image. A proper classification is essential for identification of land cover categories. The knowledge of image resolution and the impact of climatic condition are also necessary for such mapping.

Aerial photographs being a substantive source of land cover and landuse mapping, are extensively used for the purpose. As in such photographs, alike satellite images, both land cover and landuse types are exposed, it is necessary to identify them separately and to distinguish them on the basis of certain identifiable features. It may be remembered here that tone, texture, shape association, reflectance are the basic characteristics on the basis of which landuse and land cover categories are identified. At the time of distinction between land cover and landuse certain things should be kept in mind.

(i) Man induced landuse categories may have certain *geometric shape* , whereas a land cover may not have such a shape at its boundary.

(ii) Man-made features often reflect some pattern and arrangement as well as order which may be absent in land cover features, except for structurally controlled drainage pattern.

(iii) The purpose for which a landuse type has been made should have at least some minor features to indicate its man-made status, even if it is based on certain land cover type. For instance, if a natural terrain is used as an amusement park, it should have certain buildings and other man-made features of drainage lines etc. The same principle may be applied to distinguish between a grassland and rangeland.

(iv) A large waterbody has its horizontal water surface spreading along a contour taking certain irregular shape, but if it is a man-made reservoir, the waterbody should be connected to a dam and a river or stream.

However, a proper knowledge about the real situation of the area is necessary for such distinctions because confusions and errors always come in disguise.

Field survey for mapping of land cover types is a very difficult job, as most of the categories of land cover extend over a large area. Moreover, inaccessibility is also a major hindrance. The development of the perspective about the overall spread of land cover categories is not always possible. However, we should keep in mind that without the use of any remote sensing techniques, excellent mapping has been done in a historic past. Mention can be made about Rennell's map of 'Rivers of the Eighteenth Century', 1779. Finally, it is essential to mention that field survey is highly time consuming. It may be remembered in this regard that the Survey of India's surveyors spent months and years of time during their field survey for the preparation of topographic sheets on inch to mile scale.

Identification of Landuse types

Landuse being a man-made feature is usually properly documented because all of them are linked with the land revenue department of government. Landuse is always a calculated use of land and the benefit of the use is always determined first at the planning stage. Moreover, landuse is normally done on a plot of land, large or small depending on the availability for a particular purpose.

Landuse types are dynamic in character, as the same plot of land can be used for another purpose subsequently. In this connection it may be mentioned that in these days of rapid urbanization, rural landscapes are changing into urban landscapes of built-up areas very fast. A few broad categories of landuse can be identified, though these do not cover all types of landuse in all countries. This is a broad generalization. The categories are :

- Residential buildings;
- Factories and business centres;
- Agricultural lands for crops and vegetables;
- Plantations;
- Units for transportation related to roads, railways and airlines (airports);
- Landscape for recreation and amusement related to parks;
- Cultural Wastelands;
- Reserved and protected forests;
- Man-made lakes, ponds, reservoirs and canals;
- Playgrounds (can also be categorized for recreational purpose).

Various types of landuse can be detected in satellite images as well as in aerial photographs. In the case of satellite images, certain colour signatures are identified for individual landuse categories. However, other than colour and tone, the parameters used for identification of landscape features in aerial photographs can also be used in satellite images. Agricultural plots have geometric shapes and the red tone indicating chlorophyll content varies from pink to bright red with crops on the field with a smooth texture. On the other hand, a fallow land is marked by light blue and grey colours. The built-up areas are identified by rectangular or any other geometric shape of boundary with a blue tone, though it may have a moderately grey tone also. The texture is normally coarse. However, the presence of landscape vegetation is indicated by red patches. A low density rural settlement is greyish with medium texture in Landsat-TM series (FCC), whereas if it is a low density built-up area it is pinkish grey with coarse texture.

In aerial photographs, agricultural lands are identified by geometric shapes and the grey tone varies in intensity depending on the presence of crop. If the field is cropless it has a very light, almost white tone and with crops it becomes grey with darker tone and smooth texture. Ponds have rectangular boundaries with dark grey tone, but if it is a dry pond, it is white. Urban built-up areas have geometric shapes with the buildings appearing as blocks. On the other hand, a rural settlement is often surrounded by vegetation with dark grey tone with boundaries of red and medium to coarse texture. Moreover, a rural settlement is associated with cultivated landscape.

Some of the landuse types can be identified from topographic sheets also, though these are often indicated by writing of their categories. For instance, a plantation area is indicated by its boundary and the type of plantation mentioned in writing, such as acacia plantation, bamboo plantation, teak plantation, tea garden etc. Shrubs and bushes are also indicated in topographic sheets. This way the type of forest, with the dominant species is indicated by words. Ponds are well indicated by symbols and colours, whereas rural settlements are marked by red solid squares, though the number of squares is simply symbolic and never matches with the actual number of homesteads in the village. Urban settlements are indicated by various amenities, government buildings, other important buildings with red polygons of different shapes, and presence of jail, many road connections and internal road network etc. Coloured patches of topographic sheets are also indicators of landuse, for instance, cultivated areas are coloured as yellow, whereas forests are light green.

Mapping of Landuse and land cover

The mapping of land cover and landuse is done through chorochromatic method which indicates the difference of quality from one type to another on the basis of colours. Chorochromatic methods are used for soil maps, geological maps as they include various types on the basis of the quality of the type. However, some chorochromatic maps may be of compound nature, when some symbols, lines etc. are used along with colours. Normally, different categories of land cover and landuse are indicated by some conventional colours depending on the colour scheme adopted by the mapping organization. Mention can be made about National Atlas and Thematic Mapping Organization, Govt. of India. The colour scheme adopted by this organization is given in table 8.3.

When plotwise landuse pattern is to be mapped, cadastral survey maps are taken as the base map. These are large scale maps marking the individual plots indicated by its number in the respective mouza. These maps are prepared on a scale of 16 inch to 1 mile or 1 metre to 3.96 km (1:3960). However, for mapping in the field on the basis of cadastral survey maps it requires a detailed knowledge about the village of which the mapping is done. An official personnel from land revenue office known as Amin, can be consulted for this purpose. The cadastral map survey maps are available with the land revenue office and the patwar or village head man, sometimes a panchayat chief or sarpanch.

At present, Geographical Information System softwares are used for land cover and landuse mapping. Some purpose oriented GIS softwares are available in the market, though some of them are open sources in the internet also.

The first step is to download satellite images of which the landuse and land cover mapping should be done. Google Earth images with true colours being readily available through Google Earth software can reveal the broad idea about the general landuse and land cover for an area with specific latitude and longitude extension. For a particular area, a part of Google Earth image can be saved also. However, the use of False Colour Composites (FCC) have been more common in such mapping methods, as the false colours with a specific band can give a better identification if the interpreter follows the necessary indications. Landsat images and IRS images can be downloaded for

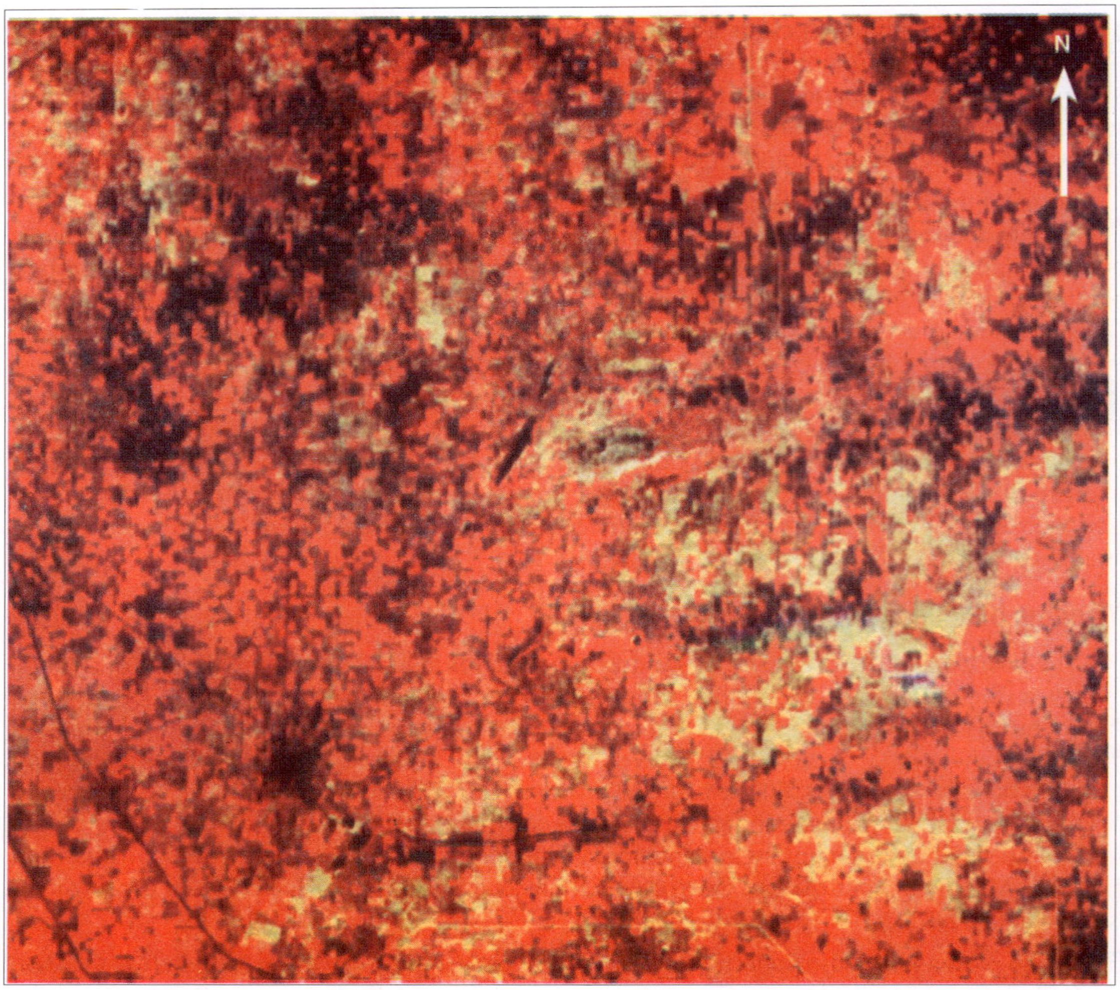

Fig. 8.12 Satellite Image

this purpose. Then an unsupervised and supervised classification can identify the particular landuse and land cover types. ERDAS IMAGINE, ARC MAP and Q-GIS (Open source) can be used as GIS softwares in this regard. However, ARC MAP is more useful for this purpose as this software helps favourably construct in index, legend etc. The use of Q-GIS is to some extent less suggestive. Whatever GIS software is used, latest versions are always better than the earlier ones.

MAPPING FROM SATELLITE IMAGE

A satellite image of TM series is usually a false colour composite which has been developed from the sensored image of a satellite. The given satellite image covers a part of Haryana and the corresponding topographic sheet is $53\frac{D}{11}$. A part of it, i.e., grid no. A_2 covering 28°20′ – 28°25′N and 76°30′ – 76°35′ E. has been selected for mapping and interpretation. The satellite image is located in Path 095 and Row 051 of landsat 3.

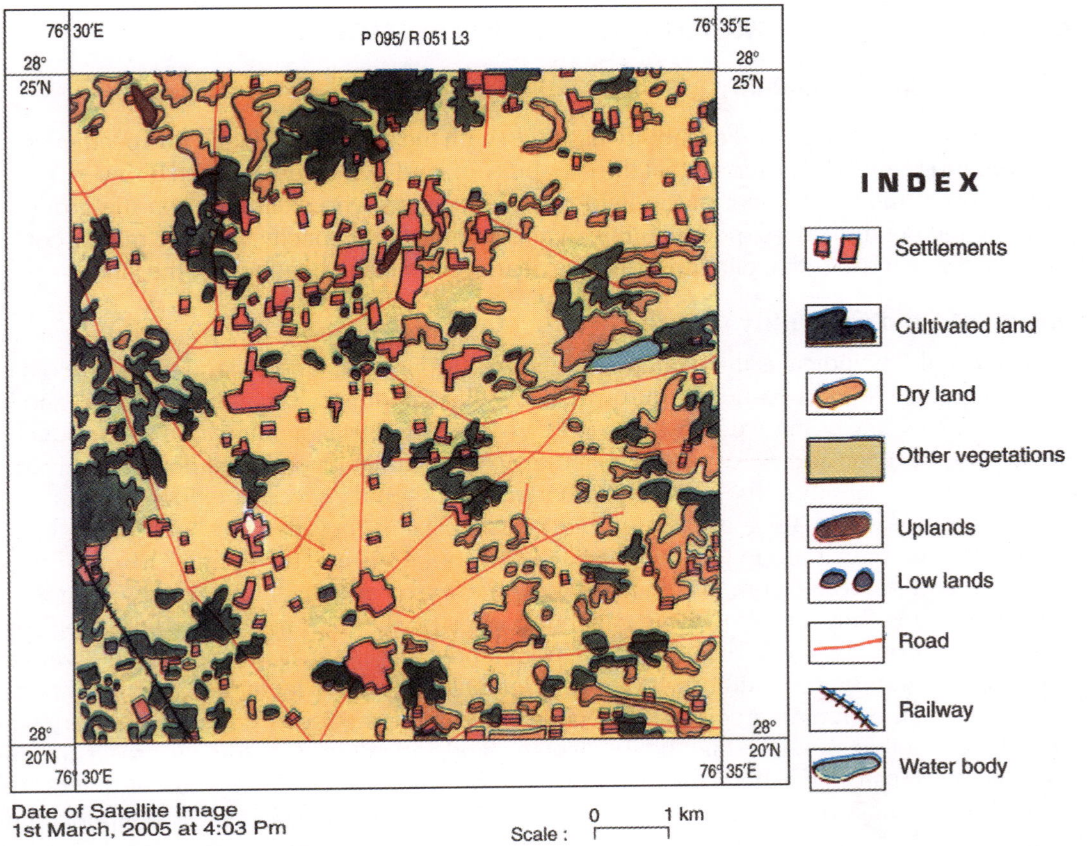

Fig. 8.13 Landform and landuse Map fom Satellite image

The area shown in the topographic sheet was surveyed in 1969–70 and the satellite image was taken on 1st March 2005 at 4:03 pm. Therefore, there is gap of 35 years and it is expected that a lot of changes should have occurred in the landuse pattern in the mean time and the same can be detected in the satellite image. In fact, while preparing a map from the given satellite image we noted that the alignment of some of the roads has been changed and some new settlements have cropped up.

However, the image being a FCC one it was difficult to identify the features, though in general, the villages appear in reddish brown, the water bodies are navy blue and vegetative areas appear red. Some other features, such as, areas with very deep water table are relatively dry and appear yellowish.

The spread of red colour over most of the areas indicates a continuous cover of tree canopies. A probe into the corresponding topographic sheet ($53\frac{D}{11}$) confirms that scattered trees are huge in number in the area and can afford a continuous spread of red colour in the satellite image. The new roads under construction have appeared yellow.

The landform and landuse map prepared from the said part of the satellite image has indicated those features as understood from the false colours of the image.

CONCEPT OF LAND CAPABILITY AND ITS CLASSIFICATION

Definition of Land Capability

As defined by USDA, 'land capability has to do with the suitability of land for specified uses.' Raychaudhuri (1966) has observed that the capability of land is to be determined by a very careful examination of the soil present in the field by soil scientists who examine it on the ground to determine the depth, texture, permeability, available moisture capacity, organic matter content and other characteristics that determine the use, management, and treatment of the land.

Concept of Land Capability

Land capability indicates the particular usability of a parcel of land. A land or a piece of land may not be suitable for a particular purpose, but at the same time it may be suited for another purpose. Usually, the primary purpose of a land is related to its use for cultivation and production of food crops but each and every parcel of land may not be suitable for the purpose of cultivation. In that case, the suitability of the land for another purpose should be recommended. Farmers have experiences about the nature of their usable landscape, but they have very limited scope of examining the particular properties and characteristics of the soil and topography. Moreover, they have social and economic compulsion for making the land productive. Hence, they do not care for examining the land in terms of its capability. Mostly, they are asked for producing some saleable crops from the land. Thus, the concept of land capability has remained useful with the Government organisations authorized to determine a firm plan in terms of suitability and management of the land. In a country like India, where the pressure of population is very high, farmers do not bother about the fine suitability of the land, rather they consider the gross suitability as dictated by climate and general nature of soil composing a particular land. Thus we find out that towards Eastern India paddy cultivation is the most common practice, even as a monoculture, whereas towards drier Western India or the North-western India the main food crop changes for less water requiring crops like jowar and bajra.

Land capability classifies all types of land into certain landuse classes which are suitable for particular landscapes. Broadly, land capability classification divide the land between two category:

1. The Land suitable for agricultural purposes;
2. The land not suitable for agriculture.

In the first category, the relative suitability of various types of agricultural land is judged and an order of class I land , class II land, class III land etc. is obtained on the basis of a descending order of rating. In the non-agricultural category, lands are selected for grazing of domesticated animals, for construction of residential and office building, for the purpose of forestry etc.

Parameters Used for Rating

The parameters on the basis of which the suitability rating is calculated include soil fertility in terms of the availability of nutrients, soil texture in terms of water retention capacity, soil structure in terms of holding the soil aggregates at the face of erosional processes, depth of soil layer in terms of easily ploughable soil, permeability of soil in terms of drainage, organic matter content, scope of management and treatment of land, stoniness of soil, salinity of soil, degree of weathering, surface slope in terms of degree or percent and length of slope. Mondal (1982) includes ruggedness number, proneness to flood etc. as some other parameters. However, the rating value thus determine the relative suitability of the land for agricultural purposes or non-agricultural purposes.

Significant Variability of Land Features As Used by USDA

The particular characteristics of the land and their significant ranges suggested are as follows:

- **Effective depth of soil (as depth over rock, tough clay, or hardpan):** Very deep, 60 inches or more(152.4 cm); deep, 36 to 60 inches (91.44 to 152.4 cm); moderately deep, 20 to 36 inches (50.8 to 91.44 cm); shallow, 10 to 20 inches (25.4 to 50.8 cm); very shallow, 0 to 10 inches (0 to 25.4 cm).
- **Texture of surface soil (fineness of constituent particles):** Very heavy (heavy clay; 60 percent or more 2 micron clay particles); heavy (clay, silty clay, sandy clay); moderately heavy (silty clay loam, clay loam, sandy clay loam); medium (silt loam, loam, very fine sandy loam); moderately light (sandy loam, fine sandy loam); light (loamy fine sand, loamy sand); very light (sand, coarse sand).
- **Permeability of subsoil:** Very slow (less than 0.05inch/0.127 cm of water percolation per hour); slow (0.05-0.20 inch/0.127-0.508 cm); moderately slow (0.20-0.80 inch/0.508-2.032 cm); moderate (0.80-2.50 inches/2.032-6.35 cm); moderately rapid (2.50-5.00 inches/6.35-12.7 cm); rapid (5.00-10.00 inches/12.7-25.4 cm); very rapid (10.00 inches/25.4 cm or more).
- **Permeability of substratum:** Very slow (less than 0.05inch/0.127 cm of water percolation per hour); slow (0.05-0.20 inch/0.127-0.508 cm); moderately slow (0.20-0.80 inch/0.508-2.032 cm); moderate (0.80-2.50 inches/2.032-6.35 cm); moderately rapid (2.50-5.00 inches/6.35-12.7 cm); rapid (5.00-10.00 inches/12.7-25.4 cm); very rapid (10.00 inches/25.4 cm or more).
- **Thickness of surface soil:** Thin (0-6 inches/0-15.24 cm); moderately thick (6-12 inches/15.24-30.48 cm); thick (12-24 inches/30.48-60.96 cm); very thick (24-36 inches/60.96-91.44 cm).
- **Available moisture capacity (inches of absorbed water per 60 inches of soil depth):** Very high (12 inches/30.48 cm or more); high (9-12 inches/22.86- 30.48 cm); moderate (6-9 inches/15.24-22.86 cm); low (3-6 inches/7.62-15.24 cm); very low (less than 3 inches/7.62 cm).
- **Reaction:** Acid (6.5 pH or less); neutral (6.6-7.3 pH); alkaline (7.4 pH or more).
- **Natural soil drainage:** Well drained (well oxidized and free from mottling of colours in surface and subsoil); moderately well drained (well oxidized and free from mottling except in lower part of subsoil); imperfectly drained or somewhat poorly drained (well oxidized surface, subsoil mottled); poorly drained (grey colour, mottling in surface and subsoil); very poorly drained (dark surface soil and grey or mottled subsoil).
- **Inherent fertility:** High; moderate; low; very low.
- **Organic content:** High; medium; low.
- **Slope:** Nearly level; gently sloping; moderately sloping; strongly sloping; steep; very steep.
- **Erosion:** No apparent or slight; moderate; severe; very severe; very severely gullied land.
- **Wetness:** Slightly wet (growth of crops slightly affected or planting dates delayed for brief periods, as less than a week); moderately wet (growth of crops moderately affected or planting dates delayed by a week or so); very wet (growth of crops seriously affected, or planting delayed as much as a month or more); extremely wet (swamp, marsh, too wet for cultivated crops or improved pastures).

- **Salinity:** Slight (crop yields slightly affected or range of crops slightly limited); moderate (crop yields moderately affected, or range of crops moderately limited); severe (crop yields seriously affected, or range of crops severely restricted); very severe (growth of useful vegetation prohibited except some salt-tolerant forms).
- **Frequency of overflow:** Occasional overflows, or overflows of short duration (crops occasionally damaged, or planting dates delayed); frequent damaging overflows, or overflows of long duration (crop frequently damaged, or range of crops limited); very frequent overflows, or overflows of very long duration (not feasible for cultivated crops).

With these facts and a knowledge of the climate of the area, the land can be classified according to its capability- its ability to produce permanently under specified uses and treatments.

For each area, one or more soil conservationists, combining the techniques of soil science, plant technology, engineering, and biology, and working with local farmers together determine how the land should be used and practices needed for each kind of land. The facts recorded on the land map, research findings, and all technical information are joined with practical farm experience in classifying the land and in working out the right combination of practices to make full use, without waste of the land resources.

Land Capability Classification for India

Professor S. P. Raychaudhuri classified the lands of India into eight capability classes and for this classification he made an extensive research wok and field work with his colleagues. Raychaudhuri observed that lands may be broadly classified into:

- Land suited for cultivation;
- Land unsuited for cultivation.

Land Suited for Cultivation

He identified four classes of land which are usable for cultivation though they differ between them in terms of relative suitability.

Class I Land

These lands can be cultivated safely with ordinary farming methods. It is nearly levelled with less than 1% slope, it is deep and productive as well as, it has easily worked soils. The land is however subject to slight erosion only by wind and water.

Such lands are well drained and are suitable for intensive cropping, as production of maize and other interfiled crop. For continued food production these lands require use of fertilizer, green manure, and crop rotation.

Class II Land

These are also good land and can be cultivated with easily applied special practices. Some of the limitations of these lands are gentle slope, moderate susceptibility to erosion, moderate depth of soil, moderate water holding capacity. Because of such limitation the lands insist on special agricultural practices such as contour binding, strip cropping, contour tillage, crop rotation which includes grasses and legumes. Green manure are to be used for suitable production, good drainage, stubble mulching and use of fertilizer may be recommended for such land.

Class III Land

These lands are moderately good in quality and may be used regularly for crop production with good rotation, intensive treatment etc. This type of land is characterised by a moderately steep slope, high susceptibility of erosion, moderate overflow, slow subsoil permeability, excessive wetness, shallow depth, formation of hardpan or clay pan, sandy or gravely textured with low moisture holding capacity and low inherent fertility

On moderately steep slopes on class III land, rotation involves the use of legumes and grasses, strip cropping etc. On nearly levelled wetland of this class better drainage system should be introduce and deep rooted legumes in rotation are needed. Addition of organic matter may increase permeability. When class III land are subject to wind erosion recommendations are done for contour farming, strip cropping, stubble mulching and terracing.

Class IV Land

This category of land is more hazardous than class III lands and requires special care in handling and proper management practices are to be carried out. The limitations of such lands include steepness of slope, attack by erosional processes, unfavourable soil characteristics and or adverse climate..These lands are suitable only for certain specialised crop.

In sub-humid regions some of the lands of this category are shallow in terms of soil layers, low in fertility, extremely sandy or moderately saline. In some of the semi arid regions class IV lands have moderately or strongly sloping surface, low fertility and may be affected by wind erosion. Hence, a special cropping system is required to conserve soil moisture and reduce soil erosion. Sometimes perennial vegetation may be used to protect the land during severe draught and to develop soil structure and maintain fertility.

Land Unsuited for Cultivation

The following categories of land are not suitable for cultivation and hence are recommended for some other purposes.

Class V Land

These lands are not suitable for cultivation because of certain limitations such as wetness, stoniness or bad drainage and wind or water erosion. These lands are not swampy, may be used for grazing. In some areas forestry can be practised favourably. With about 20% of slope such lands may be suitably used for grazing of cattle population.

Class VI Land

These lands have moderate limitations for the purpose of grazing. These are too steep, subject to severe erosion by gullies. Careful management can convert those into suitable lands for grazing and forestry.

Class VII Land

These lands are very steep, highly erodible, stony, rough, and may have shallow soils. Some of the lands may be swampy also. These lands are only recommended for woodlands with careful management practices.

Class VIII Land

These lands are identified as marshes, deserts, badlands, deep gullies or ravines or high mountains etc. These lands are only suitable for wildlife and for recreational purposes. Watershed protection uses are also recommended for such land.

Hence, the suitability of land in this classification has been considered with the main purpose of agricultural uses in mind. Some other activities such as grazing, forestry etc. which depend on natural landscapes are also included in the recommended uses, but the constructions of a residential building or a factory should never come into the consideration of land capability, because it is the natural capability of land that favours the use.

Land Capability Classification According to Kolay

A. K. Kolay classified land in terms of soil quality. For this purpose he considered all the factors of soil characteristic which can control the capability of the land. Thus the factors under consideration include soil texture, soil structure, permeability, soil colour, depth of soil, type of clay minerals present, soil reaction, soil nutrient status and salinity as well as alkalinity, but he has excluded the factors related to relief, proneness to flood or draught, stoniness of soil etc. However, Kolay also classified lands into eight capability groups.

His class I lands are recommended for sustained use in raising grain crops, oil seeds, sugarcane, or fibre crops (alluvial soils). Class II lands with moderate limitations may also be used for the same variety of crops. Though manuring and treatment of soil (red and black soil) may be required. Class III land (alluvial and black soils dominated by smectites) with severe limitations may be used for the same type of crops provided sufficient conservation measures are taken. Class IV lands (alluvial, black, saline soils) may raise grains, oil seeds or fibre crops occasionally with very careful management. Class V lands may be rocky or stony with levelled surfaces and may be used for pasture or forestry. Class VI lands are also recommended for pasture and forestry with very steep slope, saline or alkaline soil, and low moisture retention capacity. Class VII lands include dry deserts or marshy lands and soils may be highly alkaline. These are recommended for limited use of pasturing or forestry. Class VIII lands may include deserts, rugged mountains or marshy land without any usable soils and hence are recommended for wildlife and recreation.

C H A P T E R 9

COMPUTER APPLICATIONS IN GEOGRAPHY

INTRODUCTION

In recent years the development of Information Technology (IT) has resulted in broadening the base of geographical knowledge. Geographic information - both spatial and data can be stored, retrieved, manipulated and generated for reproduction of charts, maps, diagrams etc. conveniently to cater the user's need. The cost for such exercises may not be prohibitive considering the time, convenience and neatness of production.

So currently the PC with peripherals as hardware and a few user's friendly software has been turned into an important tool of the geographers. Like many other branches of science the geographers must have to learn arts and science of the computer. Such learning in some cases may be elementary, but digital mapping technology may require higher skill. The role of the computer may range from simple to complex depending upon the type of exercises.

We can specify the application of computer in various ways for exploration of spatial information and attributes. These information can be reproduced in different ways. Broadly the computer application in geography cover : (i) Preparation of graphs, charts, diagrams etc. as cartograms, (ii) Interpretation of satellite imageries and air-photos (i.e. Image Analysis), (iii) Digital mapping and (iv) Geographic Information System (G.I.S.).

The application of computer in Image Analysis has been elaborated in the earlier chapter. In this chapter we will outline the applications in the preparation of cartograms, digital mapping and G.I.S.

Computer Application in Cartograms

The geographers acquire large sets of information, which they like to represent in graphical forms. These data can be handled conveniently with the use of suitable softwares on P.C. One such user's friendly software is Lotus 1-2-3*. The Lotus 1-2-3 has three components namely, i) Electronic spreadsheet, ii) Business graphics and iii) Database management.

The electronic spreadsheets which are displayed on terminals or micro-computer screens, are made of multiple rows and columns and can store data. Moreover the electronic spreadsheet has the automatic recalculation facility. Say in a set of production data when the cost of a particular item is changed, the change automatically is registered on all the values dependent on the cost of production. Lotus 1-2-3 is made up of 8192 rows and 256 columns and can store large amount of data. These data can be depicted with convenience graphically by line, bar and pie-charts in Lotus 1-2-3. In addition the Lotus 1-2-3 has a built-in database management feature. The database management means, managing any complete set of information used by particular applications. This software can instantly retrieve and re-organise all the information without consuming much time.

* Microsoft Excel is also an useful software.

Graphics Feature of Lotus 1-2-3

The Lotus 1-2-3 presents powerful, flexible and easy to use graphics feature. With this package one can generate five different types of graphs namely, Line, Bar, XY (Correlations), Stacked Bar and pie. Moreover the graphs can be represented either in 2D or 3D forms. The X axis is considered as a horizontal label header of co-ordinates for all types of graphs, except XY graph. The Y axis supports six sets of data (A range through F range).

It is necessary to identify the type of data before one decides on the type of graph suited for the chosen data. Care must be taken not to display too many data in a graph. Graph data ranges should not contain blank cells.

The Lotus 1-2-3's powerful and flexible graphic potentialities include the following features :

1. Provisions to include up to six sets of data on the same graph.
2. Automatic scaling of the data, so that the graph fits the screen of the monitor.
3. Provision to include labels, titles, legends and data labels.
4. Provision to save the settings of a graph for later viewing.
5. Facility to save a graph as a disc file and later print it.
6. Display of graphs in black and white (monochrome) or in colour (on a colour monitor) with shading patterns (8 patterns for monochrome display, 8 patterns for EGA display and 4 patterns for CGA display).

The Geographic Information System

In the last two decades of the 20th century the cartography has been passing through a revolution – the revolution of cybernetics (information technology). New applications on a computer platform have tremendously influenced the device techniques in cartography.

For many decades the cartographers based their map-work on photography and plastic film, the technology which is known as *analog cartography*. The cartographers traditionally collected and stored data and prepared the maps using the analog technology. This technology is even today practised widely in map-making.

Using analog technology the map satisfied two functions : a) as a storage medium for spatial data and b) as a medium of communications to understand spatial relationship. A map displays geographic information of an area. In that sense the analog cartography in its traditional form may also be considered as a tool of G.I.S.

Recently digital technology has come into practice for cartographical work. The cartography has been greatly influenced by the computer revolution. The digital database is replacing the printed map as the storage medium for geographic information. Moreover the cartographic visualisations on many different media satisfy to understand the spatial pattern, relationship and complexity of the environment as derived from a map.

However the importance of analog cartography is not lost. For preparation of map it is necessary to construct a worksheet of the compilation by traditional manual or photo-chemical method, i.e. analog method. The digital database for mapping is even today very limited. An analog compilation worksheet is considered useful while using digital production methods. Usually a worksheet in traditional analog form is first created with small format map. Next this document is digitised by a scanner or digitiser and put in the file of a computer. Then with the digital version of the worksheet displayed on the V.D.U. (monitor), the final art-work could be done with the application of suitable softwares.

What is G.I.S. ?

The term G.I.S. has been defined many ways by many experts. No universal agreement has yet been reached. In some definition the focus on the map connection is highlighted, in some database, in some softwares/kit and in some application methods are considered important. However, a general consensus on the definition has been reached upon by 30 specialists in the field :

"Geographic Information System (G.I.S.) - a system of hardware, data, people, organizations and institutional arrangement for collecting, storing, analyzing and disseminating information about areas of the earth." (Ducker and Kjerne, 1989).

Fundamentally the G.I.S. is a tool - a tool in the hand of geographers and many other experts, who synthesise the spatial information to arrive at a decision. It requires the automated information system which organises the collection and storage of data, computer procedures, and individual / institutional arrangements to seek a particular solution. The tools are usually developed under a certain social and historical context to serve the changing needs and even intended to transform their environment. So the G.I.S. as a tool is the organised activity of the people that :

(i) measure aspects of geographic phenomena and processes;

(ii) represent these measurements, usually in the form of a computer database, to emphasise spatial themes, entities and relationships;

(iii) operate upon these representations to produce more measurements and to establish new relationships by integrating disparate sources and

(iv) transform these representations to conform to other frameworks of entities and relationships.

We can underline geographic information as constituted of three components - space, time and attribute. The spatial information is an intimate part of G.I.S. Our earth is a geoid, having the three dimensional shape . But for mapping the dominant spatial pattern is two dimensional. In mapping exercises and construction of G.I.S. it is initial task to format the three dimensional space into two dimensional space. Time determines the map at a given point as the map appears to be a snapshot. The time and space provide a system of reference for any phenomena. The Newtonian view considers the time and space as external absolutes. But in modern physics the space-time relationships depend on the arrangement of mass and energy within the space. So a model of relativity emerges. Likewise the relationships of objects in geographic situations can construct a relative space that varies from the abstract dimensions. The third component attributes cover a range of geographic information, from observable physical properties to aesthetic judgements. The theory of measurements delivers some structure to the realm of attributes, usually without considering space and time.

Constituents of a G.I.S.

The construction of a G.I.S. depends on four factors namely, (i) computer hardware, (ii) computer software, (iii) data and (iv) people.

Computer Hardware

The hardware in a G.I.S. must consist of at least a *personal computer* (PC) and a *graphic-input device*. It may also include a network card, one or more workstations, servers, or other PCs, a plotter and some other peripheral devices (fig. 9.1).

Fig. 9.1 Computer hardwares and peripherals

The computer is an essential platform for G.I.S. because it can accept, integrate, and archive enormous amounts of information from different sources very fast and accurately. It can do complex computations very quickly and helps to retrieve precisely the combination of information, as desired.

The graphic-input device works to transfer the information from a paper map or aerial photograph or satellite imagery (hard copy) into a digital format (of discrete decimal and binary numbers) that the PC can recognise. This process is called *digitising*.

Digitising can be attempted with devices as simple as a mouse connected to a PC. Wherever the maps are drawn freehand and traced over an image that has been scanned into the PC (heads up digitising), the mouse can perform the digitisation. Otherwise the *Digitiser* is required.

The digitiser has a number of components. These include a coordinate table or digitising surface, a moveble cursor normally containing a cross-hair and key-pad, and a computer interface. The cursor can be operated manually over the mounted material (to be digitised) on the digitising surface. The equipment can sense the cursor's positions and translate the trace of the cross-hair over the image into arbitrary x-y coordinates, which are automatically recorded in a computer file. The manual digitisers can be operated in two modes : (i) point mode and (ii) line mode. The point mode is a simple one, where clicking a certain button the operator can record point features. It is also effectively used in digitising linear features. In line the machine is present to record coordinates automatically at given time or distance intervals. Such increments, in conjunction with the scale of the source map, determine the spatial resolution of the resulting digital record.

The manual digitisers require more operator's time and computer processing time. Moreover error may creep in while digitising a complex line-work. For this reason the complicated map manuscripts are usually digitised by a *Scanner*. The objective of the scanning system is to replace the tedious and error-prone task of tracing line-work on maps with an automated method.

The scanner is a device by which the digital image of the map is obtained in the raster form. Different types of scanner are available in the market. These include i) Large format Drum scanner, ii) Electronic video system and iii) Document scanners.

The scanning process produces a digital picture of the map. The digital data are raster data and the image is the full matrix of raster data. But in some exercise the information is likely to be used in other than a simple graphic fashion. In such exercise the raster data are usually vectorised. The pixels depicting a map feature are connected and converted to a series of x-y coordinates to describe nodes, arcs and polygons.

The G.I.S. may require external data storage device as a peripheral hardware. Data may be stored on (1) disk, either hard or floppy, (2) on CD ROMs or Laser disk, (3) on Optical disk, or (4) on tape. The intended storage device will depend upon the required storage capacity, access speed, transfer rate, reliability, and portability.

The output device for the hard copy is also required as peripherals in the G.I.S. Two principal output devices are : (1) Printer and (2) Plotters. The printers may be of different types namely, dot-matrix, laser, xerographic, ink-jets or light. The plotters may be either analog or incremental.

Softwares

Many comprehensive software systems are now available, fully supported by their vendors. The cost of such softwares vary depending on their utility. The low-end G.I.S. softwares are less expensive. But such package contains only manipulation and analysis tools. These help to overlay spatial data layers and attempt limited analytical functions. The low-end G.I.S. softwares include IDRISI and GRASS. The high-end G.I.S. softwares, though expensive, possess full functionality. The two important high-end G.I.S. softwares are – i) MGE – Modular G.I.S. Environment and ii) ARC/INFO. These two systems can operate in network environment, on a large workstation or even on standalone PC.

MGE — Modular G.I.S. Environment

The MGE has been developed by Intergraph Corporation, Huntsville, USA. The MGE–PC is a software production and planning tool, intended for creating, compiling, managing, and performing analysis on geographic data. This software can be operated on DOS, Windows 3.1, Windows NT, and Windows 95 platform. MGE-PC is a complete standalone G.I.S., but may serve as an MGE satellite, expanding existing MGE systems .

As a G.I.S. technology MGE-PC can process huge amount of geographic information. Like G.I.S. the MGE-PC has three components : hardware, software and geographic information.

Hardware

The MGE-PC requires similar hardware, as required in G.I.S. These include PC in network or standalone environment, digitiser or scanner, and peripherals.

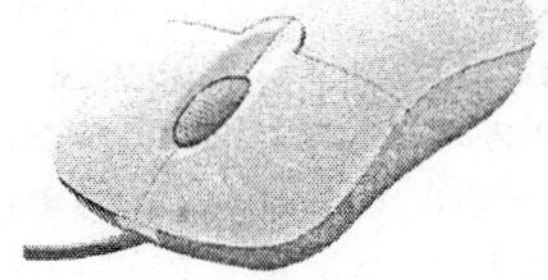

Fig. 9.2 Mouse — which controls the operation

Software

The software in a G.I.S. activates the hardware to enter, manipulate, archive, and retrieve the geographic information. MGE-PC runs the following software :

(i) MS-DOS or Windows NT as the computer operating system. It communicates with the hardware and other software.

(ii) A Relational Database Management System (RDBMS). The compatible systems are :

– Oracle, installed locally or in conjunction with Oracle SQL*Net to connect to a remote Oracle database.

– Any Relational Interface System (RIS) supported database. RIS is a relational database interface developed by Intergraph that allows switching among relational database management systems and the sharing of data among network nodes. Databases currently supported by RIS include Oracle, Infomix , Ingres, Sybase, or DB2.

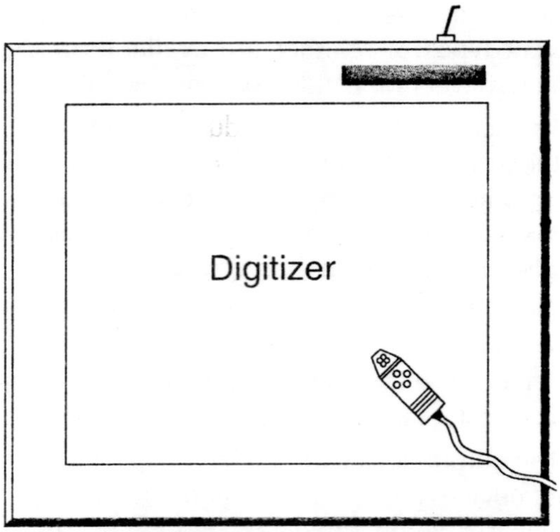

Fig. 9.3 Digitizer

– An Xbase database server, which is provided by Micro Station in creating and managing data in the file format of either FoxPro, dBASE III+, or dBASE IV.

(iii) MicroStation — it provides the graphics capabilities which help input data and draw, digitise (fig 9.3) and output maps to a plotter.

Geographic Information

Where the information has both size and spatial location, or it is an attribute of an element of both size and spatial location, is considered geographic. Size displays physical dimension – height, width, depth, area – or a relative aggregate amount such as population of a district. Spatial location signifies that it occupies a measurable position in space relative to the surface of the earth.

Sources of Geographic Information

Information may come from many sources

- Paper maps and drawings are important sources of geographic information. Maps do not have the same scale or adjacent areas that match precisely. Say a map showing the crop types in an area can hardly fit other maps showing the political boundaries and water bodies. As long as each map has some points for which accurate geographic coordinates have been measured, it can be put into MGE-PC.
- Records, charts, lists, tables, survey information, or even stacks of applications or forms are considered information. This information is generally attached in MGE-PC to certain features as attributes. The names and owners and addresses, for example, can be attached to buildings.
- Images and measurements from air-photos and satellite imageries can also provide information. If the hardware system possesses scanning equipment, then a photographic image can be put in MGE-PC for reference.

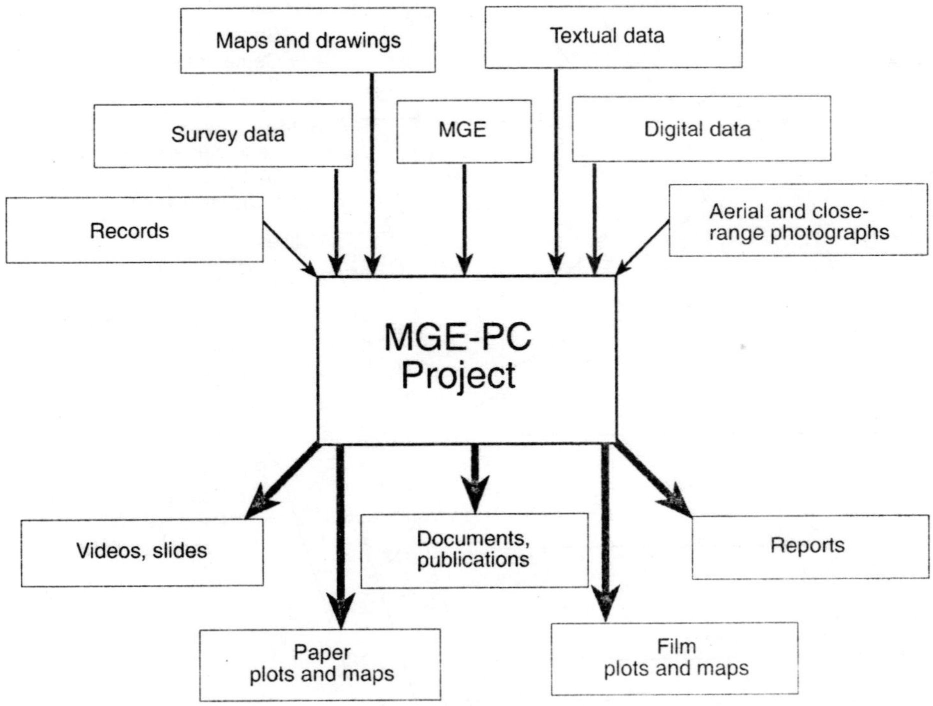

Fig. 9.4 MGE-PC project for GIS

- Geographic information from other MGE seats can be imported to MGE-PC. Similarly, MGE-PC can transform graphics created in Microstation or other digital-data sources into geographic information.
- MGE-PC possesses tools for transforming MapInfo data into MGE-PC data and also for transforming MGE-PC data into MapInfo data.

The MGE-PC project

Geographic information from all sources is combined in MGE-PC into a project. A project is a collection of geographic information of a study area. The geographic information is stored as maps and tables. Graphic information is stored as maps ; non-graphic information is stored as tables in a database. Each project may have it own database, or several projects may share a database.

In the project maps are grouped into thematically or geographically related categories. A geographic element is depicted on a map as a feature. Features are grouped into the same categories as the maps on which they appear and are stored on various levels within the categories (fig. 9.5).

This layering helps the display of any combination of features that have been placed on map in the project. Each feature on a map shows a unique look for the specification of graphic attributes, known as its symbology. However non-graphic attributes of features cannot be represented graphically on a map. They are stored in attribute tables. The name of the owner of the building and the data tax paid last are examples of non-graphic attributes of a feature.

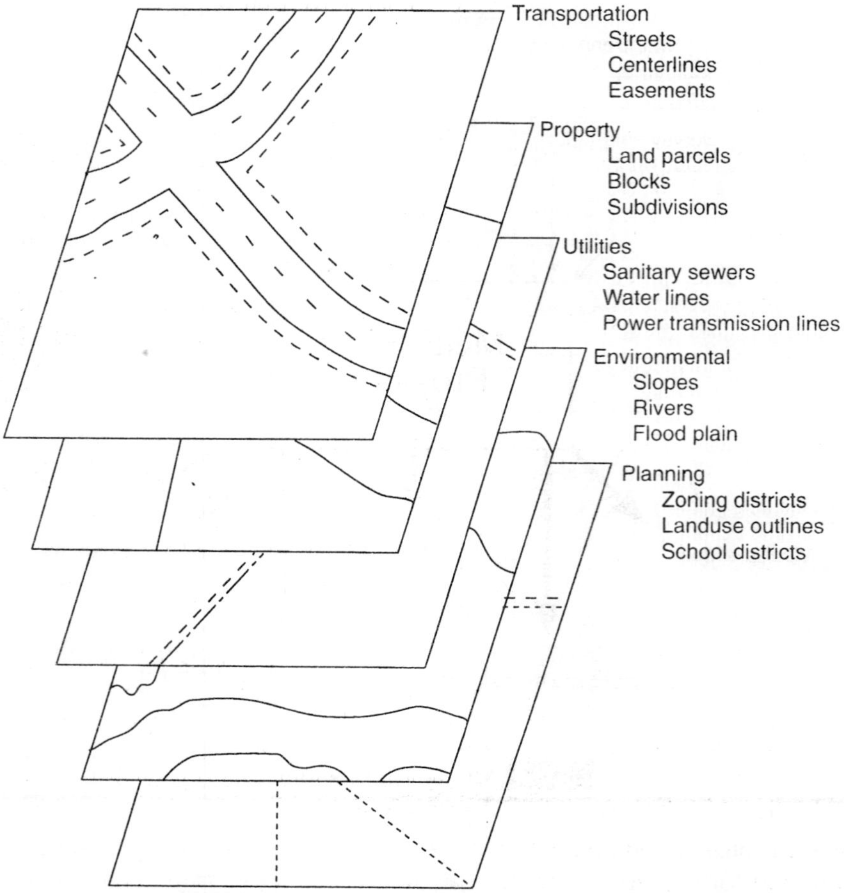

Fig. 9.5 Layering of various level

The ability to calculate and store spatial information as attributes of a feature distinguishes a G.I.S. from other interactive graphic softwares. MGE-PC can link non-graphic attributes to features automatically as they are digitised.

The basis for most G.I.S. analysis results from the relationships among features and the relationships between features and the surface of earth. So MGE-PC measures and stores spatial location with reference to a system of intersecting meridians and parallels known as coordinates.

Output of Geographic Information

As the geographic information has been entered and stored in a project, there will be output in many forms :

- As an interactive display on the monitor, one can selectively merge and display maps and features, get coordinates readouts and other measurements, query the geographic information, zoom in or out, and manipulate graphic elements.
- As map files one can print with the printer or plotter.
- As text files one can use in the form of tables in reports or documents.
- As a compressed file it can be stored on diskette or exported to another MGE seat.

Thus one can overlay and output exactly the combination of features to detect change, match patterns, create planning sceneries, or generate lists with the successful entry of information.

ARC/INFO

The Environmental Systems Research Institute, Inc. (ESRI) has developed a software, named ARC/INFO for high–end G.I.S. uses. It consists of a complete geo-processing toolbox for automation, modification, management , analysis, and display of geographic information. The ARC/INFO software along with ArcData databases provide for an unlimited variety of applications. The ARC/INFO can be run on all four major classes of computers, namely PCs, engineering workstations, minicomputers, and mainframes. It runs on more than twenty different hardware platforms.

All activities like rastering, vectoring, imaging, CAD, tabular, surface, and video data are combined in the system. The ARC/INFO possesses full analytical capabilities, including geo-processing, contiguity, coincidence, connectivity, surface modelling, logical expression, raster modelling, image processing, coordinate management, and query tools. It is also provided with a comprehensive cartographic tool kit.

WORKFLOW IN MGE - PC

1. Open MGE-PC configuration
   - give the database number and subdirectory name. Remember that this subdirectory name will be the schema name later.
2. Create New Project
   - From MGE-PC > New Project.
   - Give Schema Name.
   - Register Schema.
3. Set up Seed File
   - Project > Set Up > Seed File
   - Set the Primary Co-ordinate System
   - Set the Mapping Working Units (Put XY Resolution – 1.0 & UOR per cm)
4. Bring in the Raster Files, begin digitisation after cleaning using I/RAS B
   - Use I/RAS B & I/GEOVEC.
5. Set MGE Tables.
   - Project > Set Up > MGE Tables > OK. These are standard tables to be invoked before starting any project.
6. Set up Categories and Features.
   - Project > Set Up > Categories
   - Project > Set up > Features.

First put categories and click ADD then only it gets registered into the system. When Features are added you just select the category.

Then 'Link To Graphics' – it gives the form where tables are to be created i.e. what columns should be there.

For each Feature give the Tables. While defining the Feature you have the Option to mention the LEVEL < COLOUR, WEIGHT and STYLE. Before starting the project it is advisable to decide and jot down on a paper which Feature to put in which Level or what Colour.

7. Line Cleaning
   - Open the maps and use Line Processing Tools for cleaning the digitised work, because unless the maps are clean G.I.S. won't function properly.
8. Feature Maker for Boundary Type
   - In the options use 'Modify Symbology' so that the selected geometry will not only become a feature as defined in Set Feature but will also take the Level, Weight, and Colour as defined there (See Step 6). Thus one need not worry while digitising.
   - In option 'Blank Records' donot put a x .
9. Use Centroid Placer
   - This will place centroids in the polygons and will be visible; actually the data gets stored in the centroid.
10. Again 'Feature Maker' – this time for centroid type. Here put a x in 'Blank Record' i.e. the tables in this feature will be populated.
11. Area Loader
    - Areas for the all, the closed polygons will be calculated and stored in the tables.
12. Complexer
    - This enables the information attached with the centroid to get transferred to the boundary i.e. on clicking on the boundary one gets all the records.
13. Feature Properties
    - To see the feature and add values in the tables corresponding to that Feature i.e. actualy the data entry is done here.
14. Query Manager
    - For querying and also for creating buffer zones.

Note

a) When the feature is polygon type create two features of the same, one boundary type and other centroid type.

Eg. Category : Landuse
Feature : House – bound
Feature Type : Boundary
Tables : House – num
House – owner
House – area.

Category : Landuse
Feature : House – Centre
Feature Type : Centroid
Tables : Select the same above table and 'Add'.

b) Example of Category and Features before starting any project.

Category 1	–	*Landuse – This is the first map, say land. dgn*
Features 1	–	*Houses > LV = 1, CO = 2, WT = 1*
Features 2	–	*Commercial building > LV = 2, CO = 1, WT = 2*
Feature 3	–	*Agricultural Land > LV = 3, CO = 4, WT = 2.*
Category 2	–	*Hydrology – This is the second map, say hydro. dgn*
Feature 1	–	*Rivers > LV = 1, CO = 5, WT = 2*
Feature 2	–	*Ponds > LV = 2, CO = 3, WT = 1*
Feature 3	–	*Wells > LV = 3, CO = 4, WT = 5*

Donot worry while digitising. Run Feature Maker and Select 'Modify Symbology'. The different colours, weights and levels will be taken automatically as defined.

*LV = levels, Co = colours and WT = weights

Other G.I.S. Softwares

Several new generation softwares are now available, which are not high-end use. Of these we can mention TNTMips developed by Microimages, Mapinfo by Mapinfo Corporation and Geomedia by Intergraph Corporation and Spans Explorer/Spans Topographer by PCI Geomatics of Canada. The functions of the TNTMips as a tool have been discussed earlier for its application in the air-photo interpretation and feature class studies. The use of Mapinfo, Geomedia and Spans Explorer/Spans Topographer are now discussed which are effective tools for G.I.S. projects.

MAPINFO MANUAL

Starting Mapinfo

To start Mapinfo, double-click on the Mapinfo icon at the Programme Manager. The Quick-start dialog will appear. Here you can choose how you can start the mapping session. The Quick-start will be displayed everytime with the start of Mapinfo.

Opening a table

To open a table

1. Choose File > Open Table. The Open Table dialog will be displayed.
2. Choose the drive and directory for the table.
3. Choose the appropriate table (tab file)
4. Click Open.

A window containing the data from the table will appear.

Mapping a table

To create a new map

1. Choose Window > New Map window.
2. Choose the table you wish to display in a Map window and click OK.

Browsing a table

To browse a table

1. Choose Window > New Browser window.
2. Choose the table you intend to browse and click OK.

3. Use Browse > Pick Fields to display only the columns you want to see. Choose Expression from the Fields in Pick Fields to show information that it implicits in the base table.
4. If you intend to show or hide the browse window grid, choose Browse > Options.
5. To add arrow to the browse window, choose Edit > New Row. New records can be added to the browse window. Selecting of records can also be done.

Graphing

To create a graph

1. Choose Window > New Graph Window.
2. Choose the appropriate table or selection you like to graph.

Selecting

Mapinfo has a fundamental function in selecting objects or records. Selections are temporary tables. To convert selections into permanent tables, use the File > Save Copy as command.

Making Selections

Mapinfo offers a number of commands for making selections.

1. Selecting from the screen : Select Tool, Radius Select, Marquee Select, Boundary Select Tool, select All command.
2. Selecting with queries : Select, SQL Select.

Viewing Attached Data

1. Choose Info button from the Main Button Pad.
2. Click Map Object : The Info tool window displays the data for that map object.

If you click on a location that contains more than one map layer, the Info tool window will show a list of all objects for that location. To see the fields associated with one of the objects, click the name of the object in the window . The Info tool window expands to show all the data for the layer. Choose >> button to bring up the next object's field. The list button returns you to the list of objects for the location.

Closing Tables

Choose the Close command from the File menu to close tables. When you close a table it automatically closes all views of that table. In addition, any sub-set tables of the original will be closed. For saving choose Save Table from the File menu.

Printing and Presentation

For printing choose File > Print. Use the Print Set up option to fine-tune the look of the output.

For presentation, use the Layout menu to bring together all views of your mapping session. Choose Window > New Layout Window to display Layout window in arranging your maps, browse tables, graphs, legends, titles, logos, etc.

Creating maps in layers

Each database table that contains graphic objects can be displayed as a layer in a map window. For example one can display a table of customers, a table of streets, a table of county boundaries etc. separately as layers and superimpose each one over the other. Assume these layers as transparencies where each layer contains a different aspects of the map. The layers are stacked one on top of the other and allow to see all aspects of the map at the same time.

Creating a Map

To open a table, choose File > Open Table.

Once the tables are open, you can begin to construct the map. For example, if you like to create a map consisting of layer of Indian cities and a layer of states, it can be done in the following way :

File > Open Table

Choose File > Open Table and choose the states table. The states table will display in a map window. Choose Open Table again and open the city – 1k table. The cities table will be added automatically to the map window that contains the state's file.

You can use Layer Control Dialog to make the layers visible, editable, selectable or zoomed. By highlighting a particular layer you can also moderate these characteristics for a layer. You can reorder how layer are displayed in a map window by selecting the Reorder buttons. Layer order is also important when you use the Select tool. The Select tool selects objects from the topmost selectable layer. If there be several objects at the same location difficulty arises in selecting the exact one. In such case you can reorder your layers in Layer Control so that the layer you want to select from is the new topmost layer.

For any change to the graphic objects in a layer, it is necessary to make the layer editable. With the help of Layer Control Dialogue it is possible to draw objects, add text, combine or delete objects. Only one layer per map window can be editable at one time. To select objects for further analysis it is customary to make the layer selectable. More than one layer can be selectable at one time. If layer is editable, it is automatically selectable. To make a map layer editable or selectable, highlight the layer in the Layer Control Layer list and check the editable or selectable box.

Cosmetic Layer

Every map window has a Cosmetic Layer. It may be considered as the blank transparency that lies on the top of other map layers (transparencies). It stores labels, map titles, and other graphic objects as created. The cosmetic layer always lies on the top layer of the map. To clear objects from the Cosmetic Layer, choose Map > Clear Cosmetic Layer. If you like to save the contents of the Cosmetic Layer as a permanent layer, choose Map > Save Cosmetic Objects. You can either transfer the objects in the Cosmetic Layer to an existing layer on the map or create a new layer.

Other utilities like customizing, zooming, labelling objects in a layer are available.

Geomedia

Recently a new G.I.S. software, devised by Intergraph Corporation has become popular. The Geomedia is considered the next generation in Geographic Information System (G.I.S.). It has been based on Jupiter technology and is a desktop G.I.S. for the Windows 95 and Windows NT operating system.

The Geomedia helps in combining geographic data from different sources in various formats and with different map projections, all in a single environment. As as tool Geomedia comes to the aid of the user to perform complex queries on spatial and attribute data from different sources and generates views of highly sophisticated maps in a single workspace. Moreover integrating the Geomedia with the Imagineer Technical (a drawing software) one can print those map views on a single sheet, completed with border, marginalia, and other finishing touches. For these qualities the Geomedia has become an important viewing and analysis tool.

Basic Features of Geomedia

1. First one must create a GeoWorkspace or open an existing one. After opening the GeoWorkspace, one will have to configure to suit his need, i.e. to change the coordinate system properties or insert a map or a raster image for use as a backdrop for geographic data. The configuration is saved when one saves it and restored when opens it.
2. The dataview is stored in a *warehouse,* and one can access data by creating connections from the GeoWorkspace to one or more Warehouses. The warehouse connection wizard provides a series of dialog boxes that prompt one for the information necessary for connection. All workflows in Geomedia need at least one warehouse connection.
3. The warehouse can store both *geometric* (graphic) and *attribute* (non-graphic) information. Say, a parcel is represented by an area geometry and defined by attribute such as the owner's name and rent paid.
4. When a GeoWorkspace is connected to a warehouse, then only one can display and analyse data from it. Viewing of multiple datasets from different warehouses in various formats in a single workspace is possible in Geomedia. So spatial analysis can be performed on data from different sources in various formats creating buffer zones, spatial queries and thematic displays.
5. *Feature classes* contain features. Feature classes, images, query results, and thematic displays in the map window are collectively defined as either features or map objects. In the map windows features are displayed by geometry and in the data window represented by attributes. Multiple data or map windows can be opened simulatneously or separately. These are linked so that changes made in one window are automatically reflected in other windows.
6. Features in a map window can be displayed by adding entries to *legend.* By legends the contents of the map window can be regulated displaying characteristics of the features, including their style and display priority.
7. For insertion of images or buffer zones one must have a read/write Access warehouse connection open. Like other warehouses data written to a read/write warehouse can be displayed along with other data sets in a single GeoWorkspace.
8. Finally the results of the analysis can be customised in the map window, printed and saved for future use, all without changing the original data.

Workflow in Geomedia

Programs>Geomedia > Geomedia
GeoWorkspace Template > OK
Normal.gwt > OK

Warehouse>New Warehouse
File name : test.mdb (or any other existing file say, land.mdb)

Warehouse>Warehouse Coordinate System
#Storage Space – projection

Projection algor – Alber's Equal Area
Warehouse > Feature Class Definition
> New
General>Feature>Fishery
Geometry Type>Area

Attribute>e.g. Area, Depth, Sewage Supply etc.

Insert Image>
Image Name>give the name and open

*Interactive
OK (If the sign persists press Esc)

Go to icon – Insert Feature
Choose the Feature – say, Fishery
Draw the Feature and double click to end. Then put the values.

Legend>Add Feature Class
Shift and Select
Select the Raster Image in Legend and delete (by pressing Del button).

Lebel/Coordinate/Plot out/Import
Legend>Add Image (If further digitisation is required)

View>North Arrow

Legend>Add Thematic
Choose the Feature
Choose the Attribute (Give unique or range)

Tools>New Query
Choose the Feature and give Filter
The query result will appear

* If you want to change the Style, Select the Feature in the Legend and press right button>Properties

Exit without Saving

Opening an existing Project

Open Geomedia as normal template
– Warehouse>New Connection
Choose Access
Give the Database File Name, say Test.
Finish

Legend>Add Feature Class
Choose the Feature and say OK

Any G.I.S. Project can be opened by following the above stated workflows, whereas geometric (graphic) and attribute (non-graphic) information can be represented. This way the Geomedia becomes a user's friendly tool.

Spans Explorer

Very recently PCI Geomatics, Canada has introduced a new software for spatial analysis. The spatial analysis is of key importance in understanding the geographical characteristics of any area or region. The software is named SPANS EXPLORER, which provides "data integration, exchange, exploration, desktop mapping, and elementary analysis upto end including the popular multi-criteria model for site selection and suitability mapping".

Basic Features

Study Area Setup

The SPANS EXPLORER can –

1. Create a Study Area by defining a projection and geographic extents.
2. Support for NAD83, including the conversion of NAD27 to NAD83 and NAD83 to NAD27.
3. Maintain a list of customised map projections (add, remove, edit and copy)
4. Specity geographic extents of Study Area using either (a) a vector of the Study Area boundary, or (b) two corner points (projection, lat./long. or degrees, minutes, seconds), or (c) One centre point (projection or lat./long.) and a specified mapping resolution.
5. Optionally rotate Study Area upon creation.
6. Direct database support for SPANS tables (through dbVista) and MS Access.
7. Designate 'read only' Study Areas for users who simply intend to visualise or query information.

Displaying Spatial Data

This software also helps to –

1. Create, edit and save map compositions, afterwards conveniently open them when required. Also use multiple windows to display several map compositions of different information and scale.
2. Choose from a library of 206 point symbols, 10 line styles, 33 fill patterns (3 transparent) and 15 north arrows.
3. Display all annotations and geographic data in upto 256 colours.
4. Create aesthetically pleasant maps through colour ramping.
5. Handle all text according to size, colour and style (bold, italic, underline, strikeout and opaque).
6. Display layers within a scale range selectively.
7. Rearrange the map compositions in order to adjust priority of data layers. Annoatations will always remain on top.
8. Hide or show specific layers of the map compositions.
9. Annotate map compositions with titles, legends, scale bars, north arrows, graticules, outline and filled boxes, graphic images and a frame.
10. Tug annotations to user's defined grid.
11. Label features interactively and automatically from the attributes of an existing spatial order.
12. Control the behaviour of the annotations when zooming by choosing either a fixed or scaled font size. Scaled text can be specified by using the actual ground unit size.

13. Group annotations for manipulation of placement and text styles.
14. Rotate labels interactively or with a specified angle.
15. Cut, copy and paste.
16. Define and save zoomed views. A view is a recatangular subset of the Study Area showing a specific area of interest.
17. Zoom in or out (by specified scale factor), and pan.

Creating and Editing Geographic Data

Other functions of the SPANS EXPLORER are :

1. On screen digitising uses the mouse to create and edit spatial data layers. Existing data, including Rasters, can be displayed as backdrop. Data collected is georeferenced and full topology is maintained : (a) Points (new, move, delete, undelete), (b) Lines (new, spilt, joint, change, delete, undelete), (c) Areas (new, island, adjoining, split, change, merge, delete).
2. Connect a digitising tablet and create point or line data layers from a paper map. Compatible tablets include – (i) ALTEK AC30, AC31, AC32, Datatab IV, (ii) Calcomp 9100 Series, 9500 Series and Drawing Board II , (iii) Summagraphics MicroGrid, SummaSketch, and SummaSketch Plus, (iv) GTCO Digipad 12, and ARISTOGRID.
3. Pan, zoom and redraw hot keys can be used during digitising process, while mouse is in use.
4. Snap vectors automatically during digitising using adjustable snap and search tolerances.
5. Digitise overlapping polygons.
6. Select an subset of a layer and saving it as a new layer.
7. Identify and correct common digitising errors such as knots, dangles, overshoots and duplicating lines.
8. Clean spaghetti lines using the self intersection routine.
9. Show nodes and pseudo-nodes.
10. Build a point layer from the intersections of a line layer.
11. Join two line layers into one with edge matching.
12. Interactively connect multiple lines together into single line.
13. Four vector smoothing methods are available : B – Spline, Bezier. Interpolated and Averaging .
14. Generate a grid of geographic data. Grid options are : (a) Grid type (projection or lat./long); (b) Grid extent (input specific corner points, query screen or use in existing view); (c) Grid dimensions – grid cell resolution or number of entities, in both X and Y directions. (d) Output type – point, line or area layer.
15. Three ways to reclassify a quadtree – interactively, using an attribute table or by building a reusable template.

Creating and Editing Attribute Data

The following functions can also be performed :

1. Each point, line or area layer has an associated table of attributes ; these can be stored in SPANS format or in MS Access.
2. Basic file handling – open, close, save, save as, delete and new table.
3. Basic record and column handling – select, unselect, delete or undelete, add or edit contents.
4. Unlimited numbers of attribute columns for each record. Columns can be defined as either character (unlimited length) or numeric (integer or real).
5. Display columns left or right justified, and change the display width interactively or to a specified width.
6. Re-order the attribute columns.
7. Automatically zoom to view the feature associated with any record.
8. Save selected table information to a new layer.
9. Compute new attribute columns using mathematicals operators (+, –, *, ?), existing attribute columns and constants.
10. Protect data from unauthorised changes by making it 'read only'.
11. Change the description of a data layer.
12. Dynamic Data Exchange (DDE) on Windows platform.

Spatial Data Transformations

The SPAN Explore can also impart the following functions –

1. Automatic transformation of map projection co-ordinates upon import to ensure data consistencey and registration.
2. Automatic transformation from whole polygon topology to arc-node topology upon import.
3. Convert projection co-ordinates to lat./long to projection co-ordinates.
4. Rapid routines for transforming data from one structure to another – (a) Lines to areas, (b) Areas to lines, (c) Areas to quadtree, (d) Quadtree to line, (e) Quadtree to area, (f) Quadtree to Raster, (g) Raster to quadtree.
5. Proximity transformations include – (a) Buffers from points, lines, or areas (b) Vornoi map (theissen polygon).

Querying Spatial Data

Other features of the SPANS EXPLORER are –

1. Dynamically linked map, data and chart windows accommodate both geographic and attribute querying.
2. Query results are highlighted in the map window and in the attribute data table.
3. Toggle selection to highlight everything is 'not' currently selected.

4. Spatial searches include circular, rectangular or area boundaries.
5. Build simple or complex queries-by-example (QBE) using any combination of constant values, relational operators (=, <>, <, >, <=, >=) and logical operators (AND, OR).
6. Save and edit QBEs and the results of QBEs.
7. Nested queries select from previous query's selection, allowing spatial and attribute searches to be combined.
8. Automatic calculation of statistics for the results selected from every query (count, total, mean, minimum, maximum and standard deviation).
9. Find and replace attribute information.
10. Select all records or columns; and clear selected records or columns.
11. Query options include 'select from subset', 'select entity wholly within spatial query'.
12. Measure screen distance interactively using either metric or imperial or ordinates.
13. Query screen location interactively using either lat./long. or projection co-ordinates.
14. Display the values of multi-band Raster and quadtree layers at the cursor location.
15. Address matching with U.S. Census TIGER files, Statistics Canada Network Files (SNF) or Area Master Files (AMF). Query options include street name, number, street type, street direction and zip code.

Zoom to see the current record.

Spatial Analysis

The Spatial Analysis programme includes the following features –

1. Basis two-layer overlays. Line over line, Line over area, Area over area, Quadtree over quadtree (join, impose, or stamp).
2. Automatically generate centroids from an area (polygon) layer.
3. Point-in-polygon routine to record the area where each point falls. The area can be represented in either the Raster, quadtree or vector data structure.
4. Calculate the distance from points in one layer to points or lines in another layer with Distance-to-point function.
5. Perform proximity analysis by creating point, line, or area buffers (from 1 to 255 buffer zones).
6. Create Voronoi (thiessen) polygons from points, classifying them by an attribute.
7. Produce Area Cross-tabulation reports which includes measures of the extent of correlation between two data layers.
8. Measure the area covered by the classes of a map, reported as area, percentage of the total, the cumulative percentage.

Spatial Modelling

The Spatial Modelling illustrate the features like to :

1. Create a Multi-criteria model for suitability mapping and site selection. Uses up to 19 input maps with user-specified weights and scores.

2. Build equations interactively using relational, logical and mathematical operators to generate information.
3. Create a new map from the intersecting classes of two input maps using the Matrix Model.

Charting Spatial Data

This function includes the following;

1. Illustrate and interpret data with easy-to-use chart window. Chart types include-bar, pie, line, multi-line, radar, scatter-plot, area, horizontal bar chart and bi-value horizontal bar chart.
2. Annotate charts with X and Y axis labels, legends, titles, vertical and horizontal grids.
3. Sort chart in ascending, descending or random order.
4. Scale chart based on logarithmic, percent or standard types, with the option to fix the minimum and maximum limits on Y axis.
5. Plot the correlation between two columns of attributes using a scatter-plots with optional regressional line.
6. Save charts as images using BMP, TIFF or JPEG formats.

Advanced Operations

Advanced Operations help to :

1. Automate frequently used groups of commands with the audit function. This function captures a log of commands which can be run as batch job. The audit function provides options to create, append, suspend, resume, edit, execute and close a command file.
2. Customise the menu or toolbar. Re-arrange existing SPAN functions or add user's own command file.
3. Command files can be automatically executed on start-up.

Output

The Output functions are :

1. Print directly to any printer supported by Microsoft Windows.
2. Print to file – PostScript (PS), Windows Metafile (WMF) or Enhanced Metafile (EMF).
3. Print using a specific scale or fit to page options.
4. Page placement control provided by X and Y offsets, or horizontal and vertical alignment options.
5. Export data, statistics, graphics and text to desktop publishing and word processing softwares.
6. Save, delete, view and arrange slides for on-screen slide presentations (BMP, JPEG, TIFF and PCX formats)

Import/Export of Data

PCI softwares utilise GeoGateway technology to directly read and write raster, vector and other information from an extensive list or supported file formats. This offers the advantage of fast and direct access to data, and eliminates the need to replicate files since conversion is no longer necessary.

SPANS TOPOGRAPHER

Another useful software to the geographers is the Spans Topographer, released by PCI Geomatics, Canada. This software can perform terrain analysis from the data collected with Spans Explorer. Let us examine the salient functions of this software.

Visibility Analysis

This includes the features like :

1. Determine the unobstructed line-of-sight from a specified observation point.
2. Create a visibility raster which shows areas that are visible and not visible from the observation point.
3. Generate a distance raster which measures the distance to the terrain below the line of sight.
4. Specify the observation point in lat./long., projection co-ordinates, or by clicking or a map.
5. Specify the height of the observer above the surface in feet or meters. This could be the height of a radio antenna or observation tower.

Contouring

Contouring is a method which interpolates a surface from a numeric attribute of point data, using the Triangulated Irregular Network (TIN) method. The following functions are noted –

1. Surface is constrained to pass through the data points.
2. Allows extrapolation outside the convex hull defined by the data points.
3. Choose from six contour surface models :
   a) Elevation (weighted average of Z values)
   b) Slope (percentage)
   c) Aspect (0 - 360 degrees)
   d) X derivative (percentage)
   e) Y derivative (percentage)
   f) Incidence angle (0 - 180 degrees, i.e. azimuth and zenith angle)
4. Choice of linear or non-linear interpolation modes.
5. Ability to contour within a specified area only.
6. Use specified output resolution.

Isolines to Points

This programme provides a means to generate a digital elevation model from contour lines as noted below –

1. Isolines are converted to points which become input to surface interpolation routines such as contouring or potential mapping.
2. Optional input of additional point spot heights for a more accurate result.

3. Optional output of line layers showing valleys and ridges.
4. Interpolate values in the spaces between contour lines (search factor and sector size parameters).

Statistical Filters

A basic set of raster boxcar filters to reduce or enhance variations of the data (minimum, maximum, range, variance, mean, median and mode) has been included to :

1. Preview the effect of the filter before creating a new file.
2. Define the filter window size (3×3, 5×5, 7×7 or user specified).
3. Optionally change isolated cells only.

Convolution Filters

More advanced filters have been included for smoothening and enhancement.

1. *Laplacian*
   a) A linear edge enhancement to improve the visual interpretability of an image.
   b) Optionally apply the results of the edge enhancement back to the original image.
2. *Gaussian*
   a) Calculate the weighted mean of pixel values.
   b) Define the filter window size (3×3, 5×5, 7×7 or user specified)
3. Specify a classification scheme to apply to filter (new, existing, or unclassified)
4. Preview the effect of the filter before creating a new file.

Surface Filter

The Surface Filter function can extract four terrain measures from an elevation raster.

Slope : Mean of the slope of a terrain in either degrees or percent.

Aspect : Generate as aspect map in degrees from north (range from 0 to 360).

Illumination : For 'hill shading' or 'shadow casting ' effects – specify the zenith and azimuth of the illumination source.

Incidence Angle

1. Also known as 'self shadow'. This is the angle of the sun to the normal of the slope. The sun's position is specified by zenith and azimuth parameters.
2. Preview the effect of the filter before creating a new file.
3. Specify a classification scheme to apply to filter (new, existing, or unclassified).
4. Surface filters use a 3×3 window.

Complexity Filter

This function enhances information such as surface texture.

1. Entropy : Measure a relief or texture calculated as a logarithmic measure of the values (range from 0 to 100).
2. Diversity : Number of different values in filter window (range from 0 to n).

3. Boundaries : Number of values that are different from the centre cell of filter window (range from 0 to n–1).
4. Preview the effect of the filter before creating a new file.
5. Define the filter window size (3×3, 5×5, 7×7 or user specified).

GRAPHICAL USER INTERFACE

A user interface is an application program that facilitates the communication between the user & the computer. In the early days of electronic data processing the interface between the user & the computer took the form of job control language (JCL) commands on punch cards. When the keyboard & cathode ray tube (CRT) monitor were developed to replace punch cards as the mode of program & data input, the command line interface (CLI) became the standard method of communication between the user & the computer.

The concept of GUI was developed by Xerox's Palo Alto Research Center (Xerox PARC) of California in the early 1980s. A GUI is an audiovisual phenomenon on the computer's monitor representing the performance of a computer. The GUI for the Apple Macintosh was released in 1984. GUI is now the standard method of human-computer interaction for PCs & Unix workstations.

A typical GUI has three components : the **windowing system** creating windows & defining their characteristics, such as the X-windows system; the **windows manager** that controls the screen representation such as fonts and icons; and the **application program interface** (API) as a link to a particular program and controlling the feedback form its execution.

The graphical user interface is made consistent across different applications by adopting a standard set of elements of the graphical panel, a standard set of icons form the common, recedures, as well as standard window formats for pop-up & pull-down menu. At the application level, standard methods are used for manipulating the mouse, defining the sizes of viewing windows & the selection of individual elements in textual & graphical documents. The user is always allowed to exercise some degree of flexibility in organizing the GUI. It helps the display & hiding of particular icons, positioning of icons and the creation of special interface elements by scripting or macro programming. For GIS where specific data processing requirements can not be always met by the generic application interfaces, the GUI is particularly important. It favours the graphical user interface to be used for the specific needs of a particular application. At the same time it maintains the overall consistency of the appearence of the interface.

GUI for GIS :

Software technology has now favoured the development of customized and integrated user interfaces that can concurrently access geographic data stored in the local memory & across the internet. **Arc Explorer**, a product of ESRI (1998) is an example of such application. When connected to the internet, Arc Explorer can act as a web client application capable of browsing & downloading vector geographic data in the file format of ArcView. Once the data have been downloaded ArcExplorer becomes a local application interface for data visualization, spatial query, and map composition.

RASTER BASED PROCESSING

Raster and vector data are two different approach to representing the real world. Raster based methods are more concerned with spatio-temporal modelling in environmental applications.

Raster data have become the primary source of spatial data in geographic data bases and are used increasingly in a wide variety of GIS applications. These include topographic and thematic mapping, terrain and hydrologic analysis, wildlife habitat analysis, predictive and dispersion modelling, as well as scientific visualization.

Characteristics : The term raster data (when applied to GIS and mapping) includes scanned monochrome and coloured aerial photographs, remote sensing images, digital elevation models (DEM), as well as thematic spatial data created by manual & computer based methods.

Raster data are organized into layers, which are also called bands, themes or overlays. On the basis of the application objectives, a raster geographic data base contain multiple layers of data. Each of the layers depicts specific characteristics of Earth's surface, e.g. topography, soil type, hydrology, vegetation cover or land use.

Raster layers are best used to represent continuous spatial phenomena such as relief, temperature and pollution concentration. Discrete spatial features such as roads, rivers and lakes, land parcels and land use & land cover types may be represented too in Raster..

Raster cells are also referred to as **picture elements**, or **pixels** term. This has its origin in digital image processing. **The minimum linear dimension of the cell, expressed in terms of actual ground distance in metres or km is known as spatial resolution.**

File formats : Raster data can be stored in several ways that are formally ferred to as file formats. Raster file formats can be classified into the following categories.

1. Generic raster file format.
2. Raster data interchange format.
3. Raster data compression format.
4. Remote sensing image format.
5. Proprietory format.

Data processing : Raster based GIS data processing is made up of a sequence of processes carried out in a particular logical order that aims to generate information for scientific research or solution of spatial problems.

Raster-based GIS data processing is classified into 3 parts :

1. Input functions
2. Analysis
3. Output function.

Acquisition of raster data : Different types of raster geographic data are now obtained from **Government mapping agencies & Commercial data suppliers.**

1. **Image-to-Map rectification :** This is involves the measurement of the image co-ordinator of the reference cells & their corresponding ground co-ordinates.
2. **Image to image registration :** This is used to register one raster layer with another that has already been georeferenced by the method of image to map rectification. The rectified raster layer is now the reference for another unrectified raster layer.

Raster data Editing : Raster data editing refers to the processes that corrects geometric & pictorial characteristics. The raster data editing functions include :

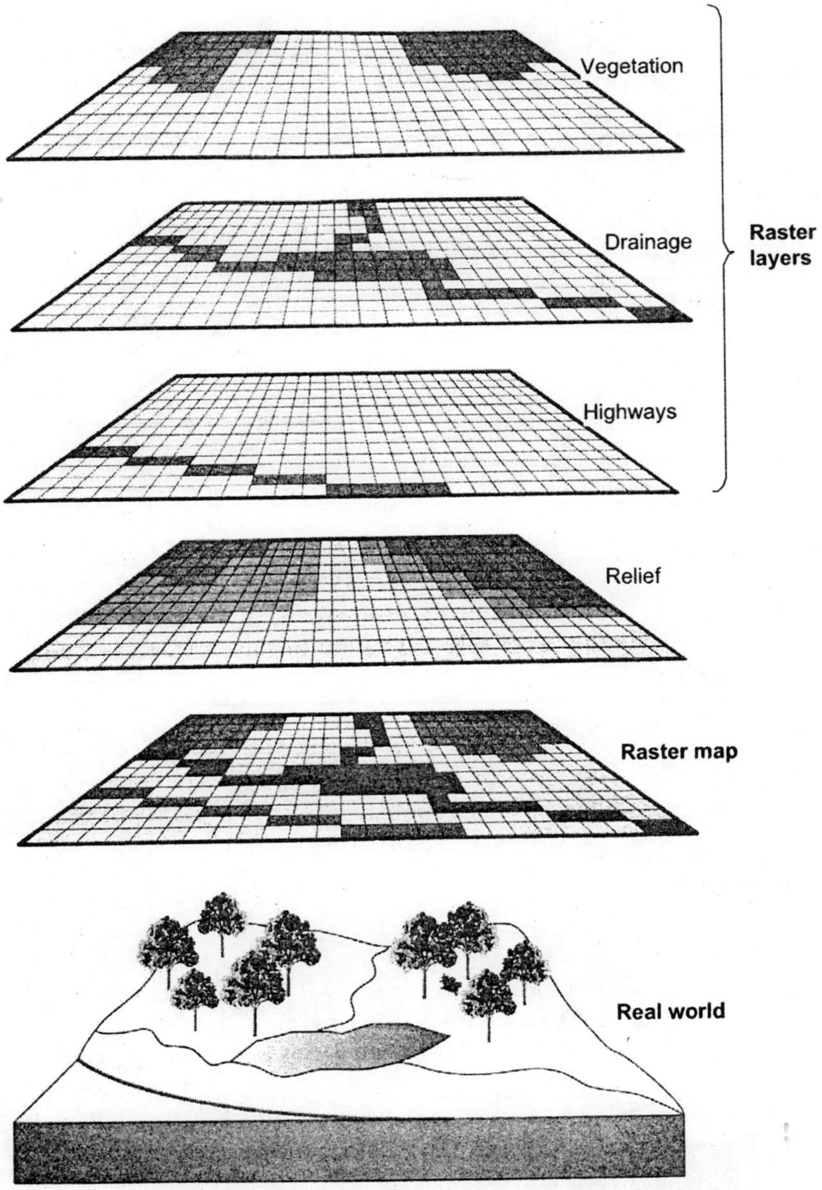

Fig. 9.6 Raster method of representing real-world features.

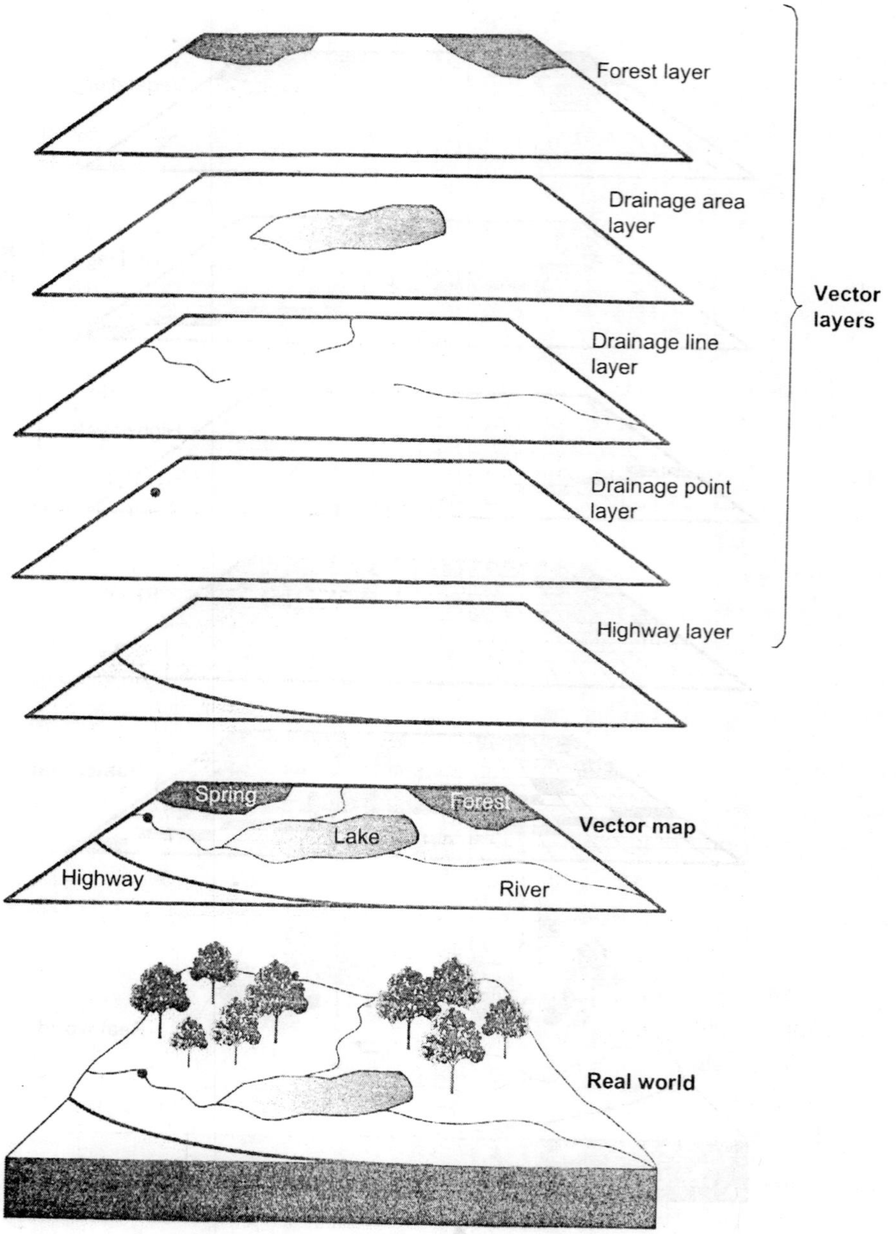

Fig. 9.7 Vector method of representing real-world features.

1. Filling holes and gaps, to fill holes an gaps that may appear;
2. Edge smoothing, removing single pixel irregularities;
3. Deskewing, to rotate the image by a small angle;
4. Speckle removal or filtering, to remove speckles;
5. Erase and Delete, to remove unwanted pixels;
6. Thinning, to reduce the representation of linear features;
7. Chipping, to cut and remove a specific portion;
8. Drawing & rasterization, to add vector graphics or text to a raster image.

Mosaicking : A mosaic is a composite picture that is made by puting together two or more aerial photographs or images to provide a continuous view of a large geographical area.

Scanning is now the most widely used method for converting hard copy maps and aerial photographs into digital images. Scanning can be used to generate data that will meet the specific requirements of various types of GIS application.

Georeferencing raster data : Raster data for GIS application must be georeferenced to a particular map coordinate system. Fundamental to the georeferencing of raster data are the concepts of raster space & raster to world relationship. A raster space is defined as the digital image of a particular area as represented by a grid of x (horizontal) by y (vertical) cells.

The position of a particular cell in raster space is referenced by row & column. This is called raster co-ordinate system. In this system the origin is normally defined at the upper left corner because the computer monitor displays an image from left to right and from top to bottom.

There are 2 approaches to georeferencing in raster based data processing.

Data Analysis : Raster-based GIS analysis tecniques can be classified in different ways. Giordano *et al* (1994) identified six categories of geographic data analysis operations.

1. *Logical operations* are processes that use logical operators ('And', or 'xor') to create a new layer from two input layers.
2. *Arithmetic operations* are processes that use arithmetic operators (i.e., '+', '–', '*', '/') to create a new layers from 2 input layers.
3. *Overlay operations* are processes that merge attribute values from two or more layers, using logical operators or arithmetic operators.
4. *Geometric property operations* are processes that compute indices that describe the geometric properties pertaining to spatial features on a layer, such as shape, size, angle & topological relationships.
5. *Geometric transformation operations* are processes that modify the spatial properties of features on a layer by applying linear transformations, such as scale changes and translation.
6. *Geometric derivation operations* are processes that create new features from existing features on a layer.

Local operations : Local operations perform raster-based data analysis on the point by point or cell by cell basis. There are 2 important groups of local operations.

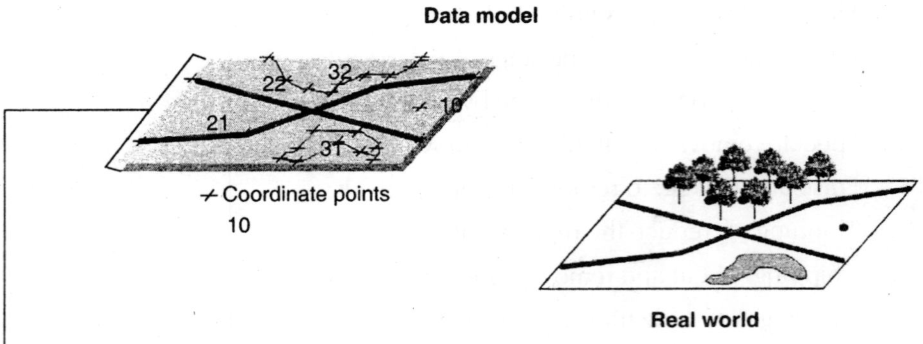

Stored data

Feature ID	Feature Type	Location
10	Point	xy
21	Line	$x_1y_1, x_2y_2, x_3y_3 \ldots\ldots\ldots\ldots x_ny_n$ (string)
22	Line	$x_1y_1, x_2y_2, x_3y_3 \ldots\ldots\ldots\ldots x_ny_n$ (string)
31	Polygon	$x_1y_1, x_2y_2, x_3y_3 \ldots\ldots\ldots\ldots x_1y_1$ (Closed loop)
32	Polygon	$x_1y_1, x_2y_2, x_3y_3 \ldots\ldots\ldots\ldots x_1y_1$ (Closed loop)

Fig. 9.8 Representation of geographic elements by coordinates

1. **Reclassifications :** The purpose of reclassification is to create a new raster layer by changing the attribute values of the cells of the input layer.
2. **Overlay analysis :** In raster based geographic data processing, overlay analysis uses either logical or arithmetic operators, to generate a new layer from two input layers.

Output : The output functions of raster data processing can be generally divided into 2 categories —

1. *Presentation graphics,* which makes use of the result of the analysis stage to generate graphics and statistical reports that are suitable for spatial decision making of publication.
2. *Raster-data conversion* – which is concerned with the restructuring of data extracted from the raster data base for export to other applications or software systems.

The emphasis of the first category, is the effective communication of presentation of spatial information to end users. On the other hand, the second category entails the conversion of raster data from one format to another.

VECTOR-BASED DATA PROCESSING

Vector-based data processing in GIS uses spatial data as discrete entities on various layers of digital data bases. Vector data also uses the three basic geographic elements i.e., points, lines and areas or polygons as spatial features. Each individual layers in vector database is meant for a particular theme of the map, i.e., topography, drainage, vegetation etc. But truely speaking, vector data are mostly represented by coordinates. Points are represented as single pairs of coordinates.

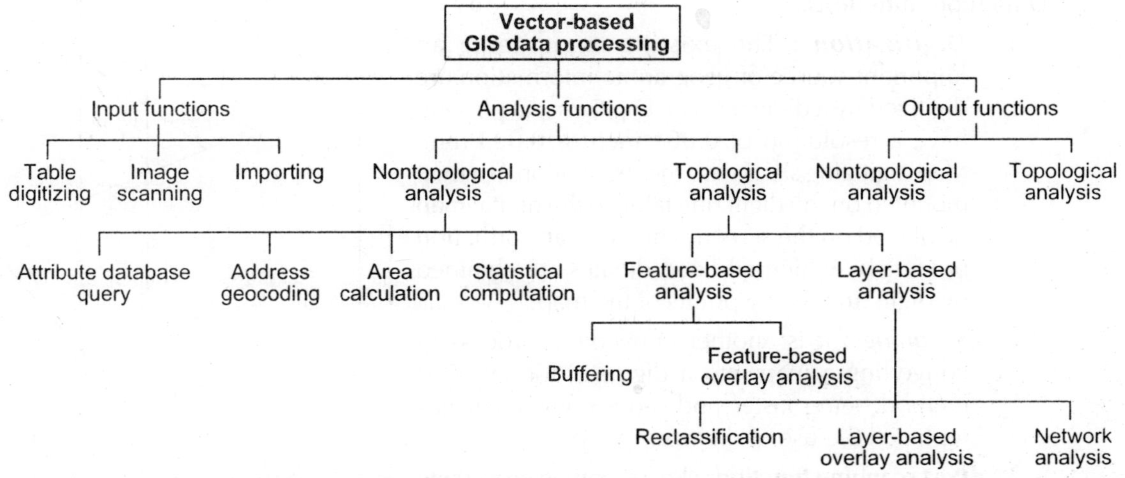

Fig. 9.9 Various Vector data processing methods.

Lines or ares are represented as string coordinates with nodes at beginning and end. Polygons or areas are represented by as closed loop of coordinates.

Vector data that is collected but not structured is known as spaghetti data model. It is obtained through map digitization. Vector data models, however, are collectively known as *topotogical data models,* since they represent geometric properties of objects and find out topological relationships among the spatial objects. As such, topology is a branch geometric figures or spaces in respect of their being one connected piece and of forming a boundary independent of shape and size. The perception of geographic space, as in mental maps, is also based on topological relationships though without any reference to the coordinates.

The topological relationship is based on three basic qualities :

1. *Adjacency* indicating information about neighbourhood of spatial objects;
2. *Containment* indicating information about inclusion of one spatial object within another spatial object;
3. *Connectivity* indicating information about linkages among different spatial objects.

Creating a topologically structured geographic database manually is a time-consuming process. It requires all points, lines and areas (polygons) to be digitized and numbered sequentially. Alike Raster-based geographic data processing Vector-bsed data processing can also be classified into input, analysis and output functions. Data input being a key function of vector data processing is accomplished through map digitizing, image scanning and geometric transformation of data stored in another format.

Data alalysis, as has already been mentioned to be topological, can also be Non-topological. Non-topological data processing includes those methods that answer spatial queries without using their relationships. Such functions include spatial and attribute database query, area calculation, statistical computation etc.

As output function of vector processing maps are composed and Vector-Raster data conversion are made. The chart (Fig. 9.9) shows the various functions of different stages of vector data processing methods.

Data Input functions:

1. ***Digitization*** : The existing maps being an important source of geographic information are digitized by a digitizer. The Digitizers, at present, have a resolution of 0.001 inch or 0.025 mm. Map digitizing starts with the registration of a map mounted on the digitizing table to the digital map displayed on the screen. This is a transformation process by which grid coordinates are obtained by digitizing the tie points of the map.
2. ***Scanning*** : It is another convenient process of converting a map into a digitized format. This method being faster and more convenient has replaced the use of digitizer in GIS.
3. ***Post scanning functions*** : Post scanning processing is carried out as a sequence of processes, i.e., raster-vector conversion, raster text conversion, raster symbol conversion. Graphical data editing and attribute data tagging.

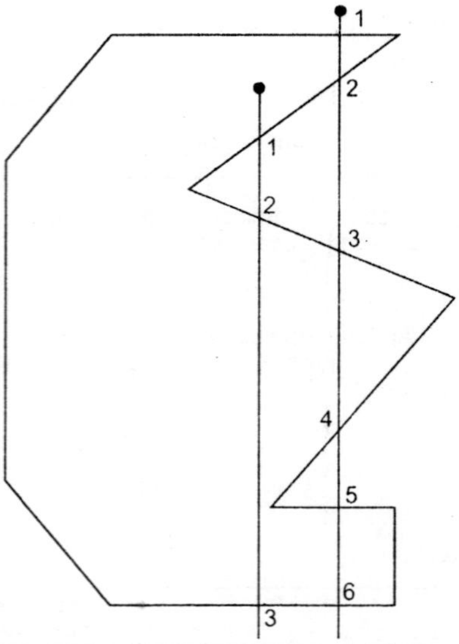

Fig. 9.10

Analysis function : Non topological

Attribute databases query : It is related to the storage of data in tables in the form of geo-relational and object-relational data models. Retrieval, Updating and Analysis of data are done by means of data-base querry.

Address geocoding : Otherwise known as address matching, address geocoding adds grid references of latitude/longitude, UTM co-ordinates and state plane co-ordinates to point locations. It can add one layer of data onto another and thus creates a new layer of spatial database.

Calculation of area : In a vector-based data of GIS the area and perimeter values of polygons can be computed on a topologically structured layer.

Statistical computation : It is practically an extended function of attribute database query. It can compute the standard measures, such as mean, maximum, minimum, standard deviation, frequency etc.

Feature-based overlay analysis : It finds out the relationship between individual features of one layer with those of another. This feature overlay function is most commonly used for matching a point in a polygon. This matching is tested by the position of the point in relation to the polygon. This is known as plumb-line algorithm. It involves dropping a line directly downward from the point and counting the number of times the line intersects the polygon boundaries. If the number is odd, the point lies within the polygon; if even, the point is outside (Fig. 9.10).

Buffering : In the context of geographic data processing a buffer is an area that is created around a particular spatial feature. This feature can be a point, line or an area (Fig. 9.11).

In raster-based geographic data processing, a buffer is defined as the raster cells that are at a specific distance from a particular cell in a linear array of cells or a cluster of cells.

Layer-based overlay analysis : In a topological overlay the layer is topologically structured and the features of the two layers are combined and new output features are developed.

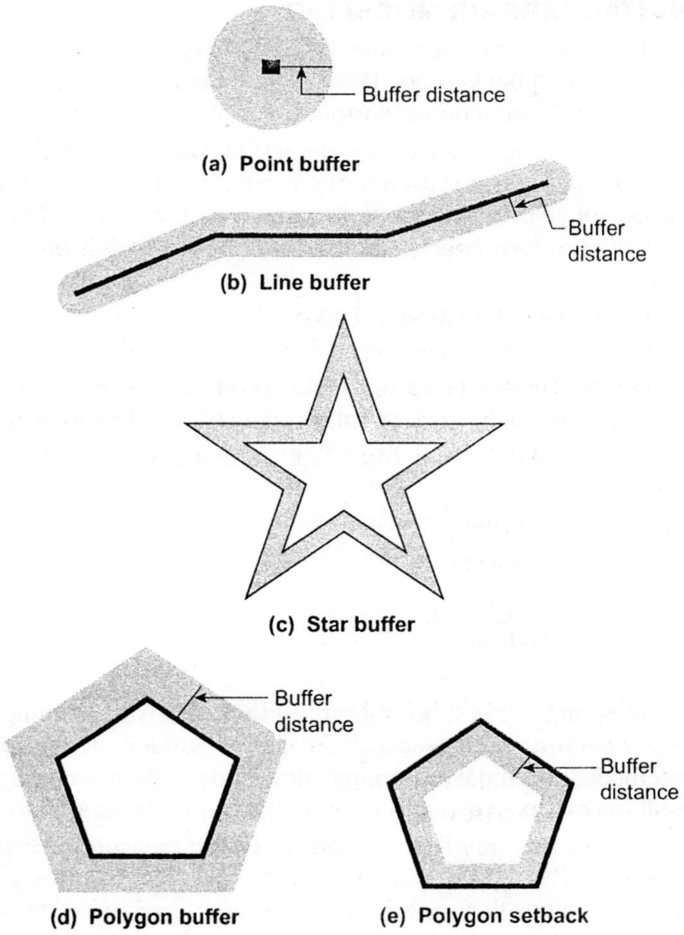

Fig. 9.11 Point, line, star and polygon buffers.

Reclassification : It is a database simplification process which reduces the number of categories of attributes on a layer.

Network analysis : A network is an interconnected set of linear features, such as streams of a drainage basin, a railway or a road network, collection routes of school buses, water supply lines, landlines telephone network etc.

For this purpose a network layer is made with topologically structured line segments and junctions. Occassionally, the turns are also included. Then network analysis algorithms are prepared on the basis of graph theories. This way using a network the shortest path between two points or locations are determined.

Output functions : The main output functions of vector-based GIS data processing is to generate maps, charts, statistical reports etc. The transformation of digital data from one form or one scale to another is a function of vector-based data processing too.

Map composition : Through the knowledge of technical training in cartographic designing maps are composed through vector-based data processing. For this purpose an efficient handling of separation layers, various types of fonts and symbols is required.

Vector-Raster format conversion : In these days of high grade integration of GIS processing and widespread use of computer-based applications the importance of vector-raster format conversion has been growing further. Since in desktop publishing and word processing softwares the proprietory format of vector-based GIS data are not accepted, conversion of vector-based data into a raster format, such as GIF and JPEG is necessary. This helps their incorporation into reports and presentation graphics.

DIGITAL TERRAIN MODELING

The history of using digital methods to represent and analyse the characteristics of topography may be traced back to the 1950s. Since then, digital terrain modeling has been a major face of research and appliction in various fields of science & technology.

The term digital terrain model (DTM) was first introduced by Miller and La Flamme (1958). They defined it as a statistical representation of the continuous surface of the ground by a large number of selected points with known X, Y & Z coordinates in an arbitrary coordinate field. Several terms have been coined to describe methods & processes pertaining to digital terrain data. These are :

Digital Elevation Model (DEM) : When the elevation values are arranged in a data file, so that it can produce an elevation model, it is known as DEM.

Digital Terrain Elevation Data (DTED): This term is used primarily as a product name for elevation data in the grid format, as given by US Defense Mapping Agency.

The 'Digital Terrain Modeling' is a multistep process that is made up of the following sequence of tasks :

1. Sampling,
2. Processing,
3. Analysis,
4. Visualisation,
5. Application.

Sampling : The acquisition of terrain data is a sampling process because it is impossible to record each and every point on Earth's surface. There are two approaches of sampling. In systematic terrain data sampling, elevation points are measured at regularly spaced intervals. The result is a matrix of elevation values that is usually referred to as a digital elevation model (DEM).

In adaptive sampling method, elevation measurements are made at selected points that are assumed to be representative of the terrain. The result is a collection of irregularly distributed elevation values that must be properly structured before they can be used for further processing. Since the method of triangulation is used to build the spatial framework for storing the elevation values, the data collected by this approach are referred to as a triangulated irregular network (TIN).

The DEM & TIN approaches to terrain data sampling are not mutually exclusive. The choice between DEM & TIN is governed more by the following considerations.

1. The nature of the terrain;
2. The purpose of modeling;
3. The needs of specific applications;
4. The method of data acquisition;

Processing : Digital terrain data processing is the manipulation of digital terrain to ensure their usability by GIS.

Analysis : Digital terrain data analysis involves the use of algorithms and procedures that restructure digital terrain data into useful geographic information.

Visualization : Digital terrain visualization entails the development of algorithms and methods that will allow the effective display of the terrain to assist in spatial problem solving and decision making.

Application : DTM application comprise the practical use of DTM in various fields of science & technology.

CHAPTER 10

HUMAN DEVELOPMENT AND ISSUES OF NATURAL AND QUASI-NATURAL HAZARDS

HUMAN DEVELOPMENT INDEX (HDI)

As GNP growth could not improve the situation of socio-economic disparities and deprivation, human development has been redefined. Human development is actually the process of enlarging people's choices, and their access to better livlihood. **Three essential keys to identify this process of development are : (i) a long and healthy life, (ii) acquiring knowledge through education and (iii) having access to resources for a decent living.**

The first indicator is life expectancy at birth, otherwise known as longevity, being related to adequacy of nutrition and good health.

The second indicator is associated with literacy, which is actually a person's access to knowledge.

The third indicator,being an access to resources required for a decent living is difficult to measure, because it should signify a person's access to land, credit, income and many other resources. Of them the most easily available indicator is per capita income, which has a wide national coverage. This indicator is supposed to reflect the diminishing returns for transforming income into human capabilities. However, it was realized that people do not require excessive financial resources for decent living. This aspect was considered to be worked out by using logarithm of real GDP per capita for the income indicator.

All these three measures of human development suffer from some common failures, as different social groups have different life

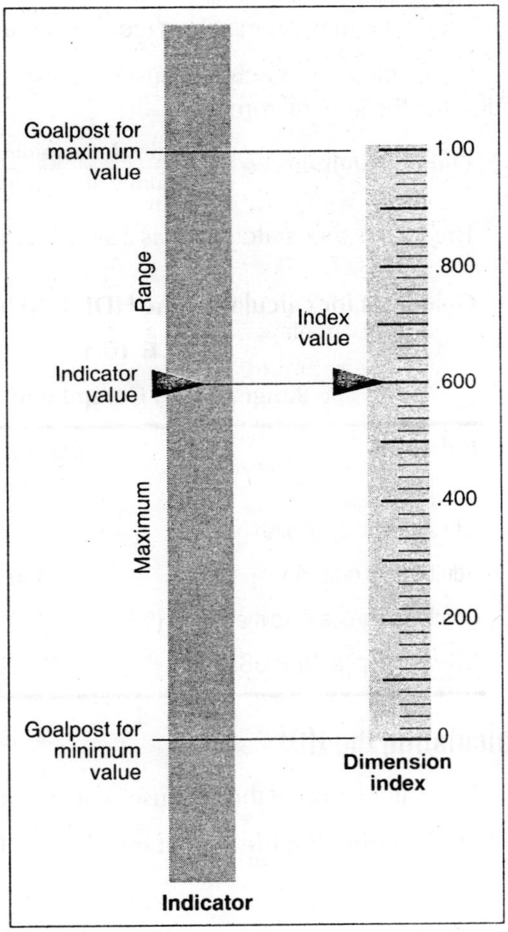

Fig. 10.1 System of indexing

expectancies, and as there is wide disparity in female and male literacy as well as the income of the people is uneven.

The construction of HDI requires mathematical formulation as is given below :

The HDI being summary measure of human development measures the average achievements in a country in three basic dimensions of human development :

- A long and healthy life, as measured by life expectancy at birth in years.
- Knowledge, as measured by the adult literacy rate (with two-thirds weight) and the combined primary, secondary and tertiary gross enrolment ratio (with one-third weight).
- A decent standard of living as messured by GDP per capita (PPP US$) on logarithmic scale.

[Purchasing power parity = PPP]

Before the HDI itself is calculated, as index needs to be created for each of these dimensions. To calculate these dimension indices — the life expectancy, education and GDP indices— minimum and maximum values (goal-posts) are chosen for each underlying indicator.

Performance in each dimension is expressed as a value between 0 and 1 by applying the following the general formula :

$$\text{Dimension index} = \frac{\text{actual value} - \text{minimum value}}{\text{maximum value} - \text{minimum value}}$$

The HDI is then calculated as a simple average of the dimension indices.

Goalposts for calculating the HDI (UNDP)

TABLE 10.1

Range of HDI Components

Indicator	Maximum value	Minimum value
Life expectancy at birth (years)	85	25
Adult litercy rate (%)	100	0*
Combined gross enrolment ratio (%)	100	0*
GDP per capita (PPP US$)	40,000	100

Calculating the HDI

This calculation of the HDI uses data the for Albania.

1. **Calculating the life expectancy index :** For Albania, with a life expectancy of 73.4 years in 2001 :

$$\text{Life expectancy index} = \frac{73.4 - 25}{85 - 25} = \mathbf{0.807}$$

2. **Calculating the education index :** The education index measures a country's relative achievement in both adult literacy and combined primary, secondary and tertiary gross

enrolment. First, an index for adult literacy and one for combined gross enrolment are calculated. Then these two indices are combined to create the education index, with two-thirds of adult literacy and one-third of combined gross enrolment. For Albania, the adult literacy rate was 85.3% in 2001 and combined gross enrolment ratio was 69% in the session 2000-2001 and the education index was 0.798.

$$\text{Adult literacy index} = \frac{85.3 - 0}{100 - 0}$$

$$= 0.853$$

$$\text{Gross enrolment index} = \frac{69 - 0}{100 - 0}$$

$$= 0.690$$

Education index = 2/3 (adult literacy index) + 1/3 (gross enrolment index)

= 2/3 (0.853) + 1/3 (0.690) = **0.798**

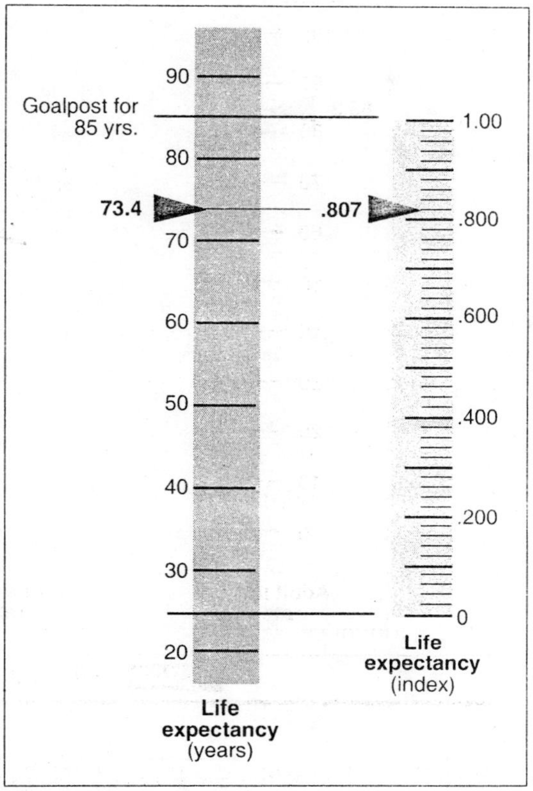

Fig. 10.2 **Index value of Albania (2001)**

3. **Calculating the GDP index :** The GDP index is calculated using adjusted GDP per capita (PPP US$). In the HDI income serves as a surrogate for all the dimensions of human development other than a long and healthy life and knowledge. Income is adjusted because achieving a respectable level of human development does not require an unlimited income. Accordingly, the logarithm of income is used. For Albania, the GDP per capita was $3,680 (PPP US$) in 2001.

$$\text{GDP index} = \frac{\log (3{,}680) - \log (100)}{\log (40{,}000) - \log (100)} = \mathbf{0.602}$$

4. **Calculating the HDI :** Once the dimension indices have been calculated, determining the HDI is a simple average of the three dimension indices.

HDI = 1/3 (life expectancy index) + 1/3 (education index) + 1/3 (GDP index)

= 1/3 (0.807) + 1/3 (0.798) + 1/3 (0.602)

= **0.735**

All such indices are marked on the Human Development Index scale.

On the scale of HD1 <0.5 indicates low development, 0.5–0.8 indicates medium development and >0.8 indicates high development.

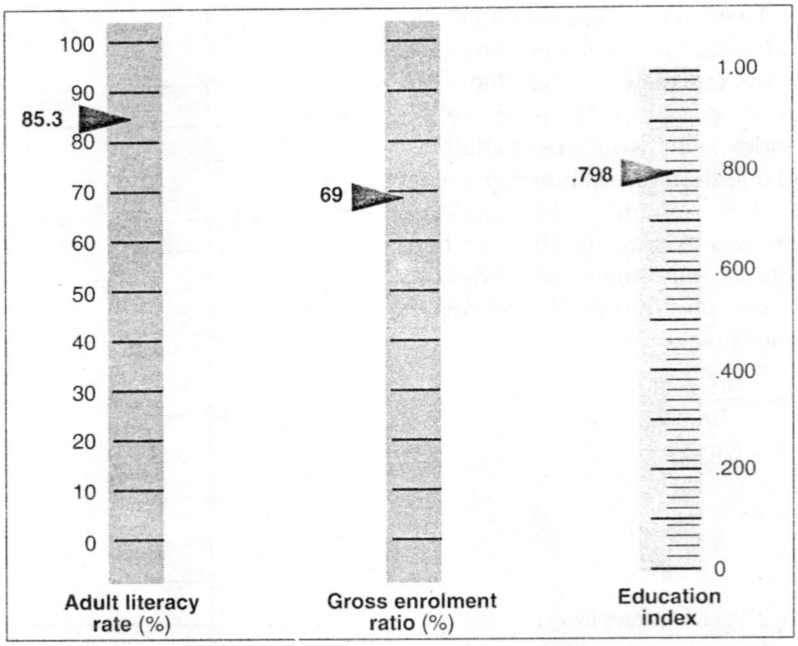

Fig. 10.3 Index Values of Albania (2001)

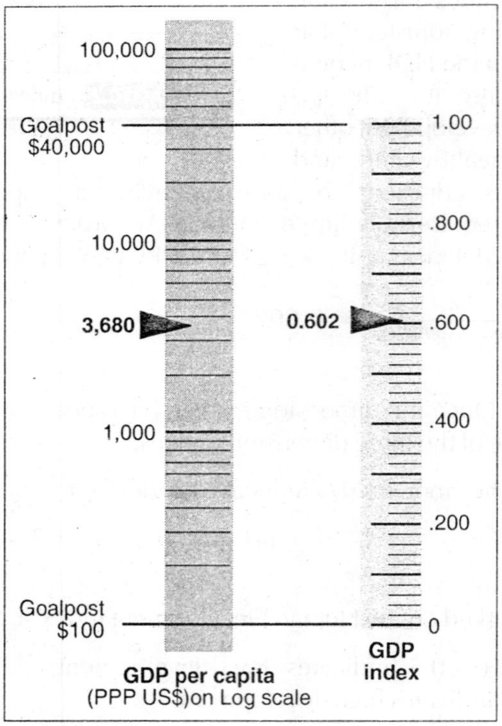

Fig. 10.4 GDP Index of Albania (2001)

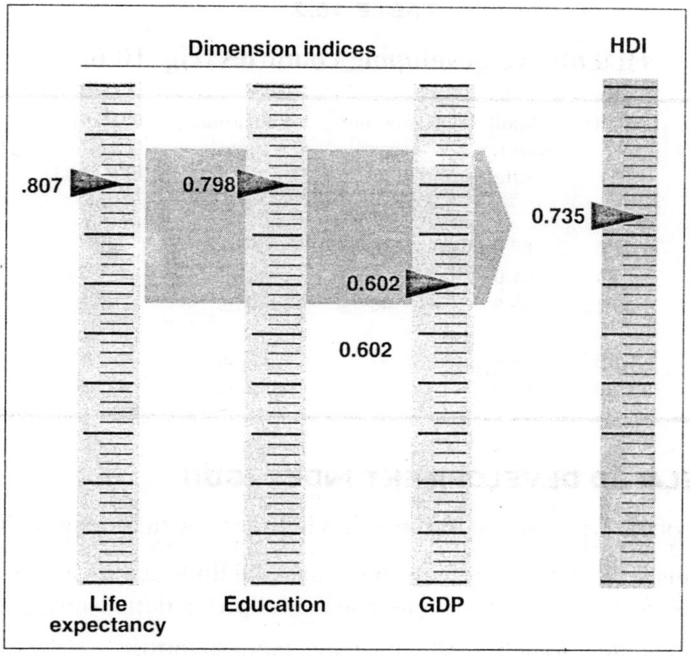

Fig. 10.5 Human Development Index for Albania

EXCERCISE

Human Development Index (HDI)

Answering a question on HDI a student should mention the Formulae for the indices first, as is given below :

1. **Life Expectancy Index (L.E.I.) :** $\frac{\text{Actual value} - \text{Minimum value}}{\text{Maximum value} - \text{Minimum value}}$

   [higher goalpost – 85, lower goalpost – 25]

2. (i) **Adult Literacy rate :** $\frac{\text{Actual value} - \text{Minimum value}}{\text{Maximum value} - \text{Minimum value}}$

   (ii) **Combined Gross Enrolment Ratio :** $\frac{\text{Actual value} - \text{Minimum value}}{\text{Maximum value} - \text{Minimum value}}$

   Education Index (E. I.) : 2/3 of Adult literacy rate + 1/3 of Gross enrolment ratio
   [Higher goalpost – 100%; lower goalpost – 0%]

3. **G.D.P. Index :** $\frac{\text{Log Actual value} - \text{Log Minimum value}}{\text{Log Maximum value} - \text{Log Minimum value}}$

   [Higher goal post - 40,000\$; lower goal post – 100\$]

4. **H.D.I. :** $\frac{1}{3}$ LEI + $\frac{1}{3}$ EI + $\frac{1}{3}$ GDPI

In the following table HDI for 5 Developing countries have been calculated.

TABLE 10.2

HDI of Five developing countries (Fig. 10.6)

Country	Life Expectancy at birth 2003	L.E.I.	Adult literacy rate	Combined gross enrolment ratio	Education Index	GDP per Capita (PPP 2003 $)	G.D.P. (Index	H.D.I.
Indonesia	66.8	0.70	87.9	66	0.81	3361	0.59	0.697
India	63.3	0.64	61.0	60	0.61	2892	0.56	0.603
Senegal	55.7	0.51	39.3	40	0.39	1648	0.47	0.456
Genia-Bissau	44.7	0.33	39.6	37	0.39	711	0.33	0.350
Argentina	74.5	0.83	97.2	95	0.96	12106	0.80	0.863

THE GENDER-RELATED DEVELOPMENT INDEX (GDI)

In every country of the world social disparity lies between the treatment of men and women.

While the HDI measures average achievement, the GDI finds out the average achievement to reflect the *inequalities* between men and women in the following dimensions :

- A long and healthy life, as measured by life expectancy at birth.
- Knowledge, as measured by the adult literacy rate and the combined primary, secondary and tertiary gross enrolment ratio.
- A decent standard of living, as measured by estimated earned income (PPP US$).

However, for determining GDI and to locate the disparity, calculations are done for both male and female population. For that purpose, the population shares for both male and female are given.

The calculation of the GDI involved three steps :

(i) First, female and male indices in each dimension are calculated according to this general formula :

$$\text{Dimension index} = \frac{\text{actual value} - \text{minimum value}}{\text{maximum value} - \text{minimum value}}$$

(ii) Second, the female and male indices in each dimension are combined in a way that penalizes differences in achievement between men and women. The resulting index, referred to as the equally distributed index, is calculated according to the following general formula :

$$\text{Equally distributed index} = [\{\text{female population share (female index}^{1-\varepsilon})] + [\text{male poulation share (male index}^{1-\varepsilon})\}]^{1/1-\varepsilon}$$

[ε = measures the aversion to inequality. If the GDIε = 2, the general equation becomes :

$$\textbf{Equally distributed index} := [\{\text{female population share (female index}^{-1})] + [\text{male population share (male index}^{-1})\}]^{-1}$$

It gives the harmonic mean of the female and male indices.

(iii) the GDI is calculated by combining the three equally distributed indices in an unweighted average.

Goalposts for calculating the GDI

TABLE 10.3

Range of Components for GDI

Indicator	Maximum value	Minimum value
Female life expectancy at birth (years)	87.5	27.5
Male life expectancy at birth (years)	82.5	22.5
Adult litracy rate (%)	100	0
Combined gross enrolment ratio (%)	100	0
estimated earned income (PPP US$)	40,000	100

Note : The maximum and minimum values (goalposts) for life expectancy are five years higher for women as they usually have longer life expectancy.

Calculating the GDI

The following calculation of the GDI has been done on the data for Thailand.

1. **Calculating the equally distributed life expectancy index :** The first step is to calculate separate indices for female and male achievements in life expectancy, using the general formula for dimension indices.

FEMALE

Life expectancy : 73.2 years

Life expectancy index $= \frac{73.2 - 27.2}{87.5 - 27.5} = 0.762$

MALE

Life expectancy : 64.9 years

Life expectancy index $= \frac{64.9 - 22.5}{82.5 - 22.5} = 0.707$

Next, the female and male indices are combined to create the equally distributed life expectancy index, using the general formula for equally distributed indices.

FEMALE

Polulation share : 0.508

Life expectancy index : 0.762

MALE

Polulation share : 0492

Life expectancy index : 0.707

Equally distributed life expectancy index $= \{[0.508\ (0.762^{-1})] + [0.492\ (0.707^{-1})]\}^{-1} = \mathbf{0.734}$

2. **Calculating the equally distributed education index :** First, indices for the adult literacy rate and the combined primary, secondary and tertiary gross enrolment ratio are calculated separately for female and male population. Calculating these indices is simple, since the indicators used are already normalized between 0 and 100.

FEMALE

Adult literacy rate : 94.1%

Adult literacy index : 0.941

Gross enrolment ratio : 69.3%

Gross enrolment index : 0.693

MALE

Adult literacy rate : 97.3%

Adult literacy index : 0.973

Gross enrolment ratio : 74.6%

Gross enrolment index : 0.746

Second, the education index, which gives two-thirds weight to the adult literacy index and one-third weight to the gross enrolment index, is computed separately for female and male.

Education index = 2/3 (adult literacy index) + 1/3 (gross enrolment index)

Female education index = 2/3 (0.941) + 1/3 (0.693) = 0.858

Male education index = 2/3 (0.973) + 1/3 (0.746) = 0.897

Finally, the female and male education indices are combined to create the equally distributed education index.

FEMALE

Polulation share : 0.508

Education index : 0.858

MALE

Polulation share : 0.492

Education index : 0.897

Equally distributed education index = $\{[0.508\ (0.858^{-1})] + [0.492\ (0.897^{-1})]\}^{-1}$ = **0.877**

3. **Calculating the equally distributed income index :** First female and male earned income (PPP US$) are estimated (for details on this calculation, see the addendum to this technical note). Then the income index is calculated for each gender. as for the HDI, income is adjusted by taking the logarithm of estimated earned income (PPP US$) :

$$\text{Income index} = \frac{\log(\text{actual value}) - \log(\text{minimum value})}{\log(\text{maximum value}) - \log(\text{minimum value})}$$

FEMALE

Estimated earned income (PPP US$) : 4,875

$$\text{Income index} = \frac{\log(4{,}875) - \log(100)}{\log(40{,}000) - \log(100)} = 0.649$$

MALE

Estimated earned income (PPP US$) : 7.975

$$\text{Income index} = \frac{\log(7{,}975) - \log(100)}{\log(40{,}000) - \log(100)} = 0.731$$

Second, the female and male income indices are combined to create the equally distributed income index :

Equally distributed GDP Index : $[\{0.508(0.649^{-1})\} + \{0.492\ (0.731^{-1})\}]^{-1} = 0.687$

4. **Calculating the GDI :** Calculating the GDI is straightforward. It is simply the unweighted average of the three component indices — the equally distributed life expectancy index, the equally distributed education index and the equally distibuted income index.

GDI = 1/3 (life expectancy index) + 1/3 (education index) + 1/3 (income index)
= 1/3 (0.734) + 1/3 (0.877) + 1/3 (0.687) = **0.766**

Why ε = 2 in calculating the GDI

The value of ε is the size of the penalty for gender inequality. The larger the value, the more heavily a society is penalized for having inequalities.

If ε = 0, gender inequality is not penalized (in this case GDI would have the same value as the HDI). As ε increases towards infinity, more and more weight is given to the lesser achieving group.

The value 2 is used in calculating the GDI (as well as the GEM). This value places a moderate penalty on gender inequality in achievement, because in all societies there is at least moderate form of gender inequality.

EXCERCISE-1

Gender Development Index (G.D.I.)

TABLE 10.4

Data for Calculation of GDI of 7 countries

Sl. No.	Name of country	Population share		Life Expectancy al birth		L.E.I		Adult Lit. rate		Gross Enrolment ratio		Education Index		G.D.P./Capita (in $)		G.D.P. Index	
		F	M	F	M	F	M	F	M	F	M	F	M	F	M	F	M
1.	China	0.485	0.515	73.2	68.8	0.762	0.772	85.5	95.1	64	69	0.790	0.864	3571	5435	0.597	0.667
2.	India	0.485	0.515	64.4	63.1	0.615	0.677	46.4	69.0	48	62	0.469	0.667	1442	3820	0.445	0.608
3.	Nepal.	0.486	0.514	59.4	59.9	0.532	0.623	26.4	61.6	55	67	0.359	0.634	891	1176	0.365	0.411
4.	Bangladesh	0.487	0.513	61.5	60.7	0.567	0.637	31.4	50.3	54	53	0.389	0.512	1150	2035	0.408	0.503
5.	Pakistan	0.488	0.512	60.7	61.0	0.553	0.642	88.5	53.4	31	33	0.693	0.466	915	2789	0.369	0.556
6.	Thailand	0.508	0.492	73.2	64.9	0.762	0.707	94.1	97.3	69.3	74.6	.858	.897	4875	7975	0.649	0.731
7.	Brazil	0.507	0.493	74.6	66.6	0.785	0.735	88.6	88.3	92.78	88.5	.900	.884	4704	10963	0.642	0.784

TABLE 10.5

GDI of 7 countries

Sl. No.	Name of country	Equally Distributed			Gender Development Index (G.D.I.)
		L.E.I.	Education Index	G.D.P. Index	
1.	China	0.767	0.826	0.631	0.741
2.	India	0.645	0.554	0.516	0.572
3.	Nepal	0.575	0.462	0.387	0.475
4.	Bangladesh	0.601	0.444	0.452	0.499
5.	Pakistan	0.595	0.555	0.446	0.532
6.	Thailand	0.734	0.877	0.687	0.766
7.	Brazil	0.759	0.892	0.705	0.785

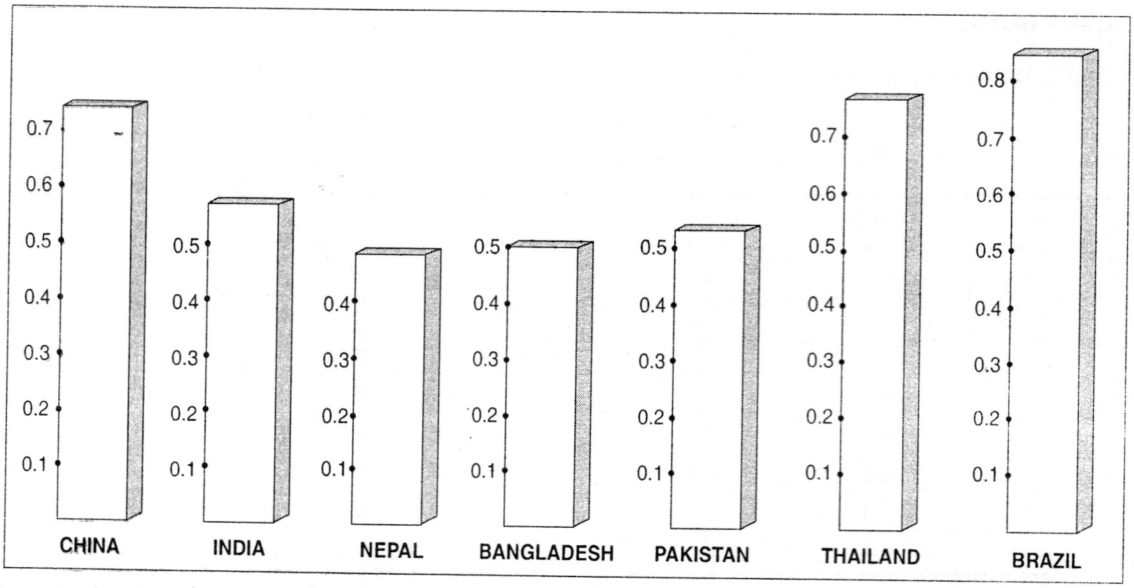

Fig. 10.7 Gender Development Index of Seven Countries

THE HUMAN POVERTY INDEX FOR DEVELOPING COUNTRIES (HPI-1)

While the HDI measures average achievement, the HPI-1 measures *deprivations* in the three basic dimensions of human development as indicated in the HDI :

- **A long and healthy life :** vulnerability to death at a relatively early age, as measured by the probability at birth of not surviving to age 40.
- **Knowledge :** exclusion from the world of reading and communications, as measured by the adult illiteracy rate.
- **A decent standard of living :** lack of access to overall economic provisioning, as measured by the unweighted average of two indicators for the percentage of the population without sustainable access to an improved water source and the percentage of children under weight for age.

Calculating the HPI-1 is more straightforward than calculating the HDI. The indicators used to measure the deprivations are already normalized between 0 and 100 (because they are expressed as percentages), so there is no need to create dimension indices as for the HDI.

Originally, the measure of deprivation in a decent standard of living also included an indicator as access to health services. *As reliable data on access to health services are lacking for recent years, in this year's Report deprivation from a decent standard of living is measured by two rather than three indicators — the percentage of the population without sustainable access to an improved water source and the percentage of children under weight for age.*

THE HUMAN POVERTY INDEX FOR SELECTED OECD COUNTRIES (HPI-2)

The HPI-2 measures deprivations in the same dimensions as the HPI-1 and also captures social exclusion. Thus it reflects deprivations in four dimensions :

- A long and healthy life — vulnerability to death at a relatively early age, as measured by the probability at birth of not surviving to age 60.

- Knowledge — exclusion from the world of reading and communications, as measured by the percentage of adults (aged 16–65) lacking functional literacy skills.
- A decent standard of living — as measured by the percentage of people living below the income poverty line (50% of the median adjusted household disposable income).
- Social exclusion — as measured by the rate of long-term unemployment (12 months or more).

Calculating the HPI-1

1. **Measuring deprivation in a decent standard of living :** An unweighted average of two indicators is used to measure deprivation in a decent standard of living.

   Unweighted average = 1/2 (population without sustainble access to an improved water source) + 1/2 (children under weight for age)

   A sample calculation : Central African Republic

   Population without sustainable access to an improved water source = 30%

   Children under weight for age = 23%

   Unweighted average = 1/2(30) + 1/2 (23) = 26.5%

2. **Calculating the HPI-1 :** The formula for calculating the HPI-1 is as follows :

   $$\text{HPI-1} = [1/3(P_1^{\alpha} + P_2^{\alpha} + P_3^{\alpha})]^{1/\alpha}$$

   Where :

   P_1 = Probability at birth of not surviving to age 40 (times 100)

   P_2 = Adult illiteracy rate

   P_3 = Unweighted average of population without sustainable access to an improved water source and children under weight for age

   $\alpha = 3$

   A sample calculation for Central African Republic

   $P_1 = 55.3\%$

   $P_2 = 51.8\%$

   $P_3 = 26.5\%$

Calculation the HPI-2

The formula for calculating the HPI-2 is as following :

$$\text{HPI-2} = [1/4(P_1^{\alpha} + P_2^{\alpha} + P_3^{\alpha} + P_4^{\alpha})]^{1/\alpha}$$

Where :

P_1 = Probability at birth of not surviving to age 60 (times 100)

P_2 = Adults lacking functional literacy skills.

P_3 = Population below income poverty line (50% of median adjusted household disposable income)

P_4 = Rate of long-term unemployment (lasting 12 months or more)

$\alpha = 3$

A sample calculation : United Kingdom

$P_1 = 8.9\ \%$

$P_2 = 21.8\ \%$

$P_3 = 12.5\ \%$

$P_4 = 1.3\ \%$

HPI-2 = $[1/4(8.9^3 + 21.8^3 + 12.5^3 + 1.3^3)]^{1/3}$ = **14.8**

Why $\alpha = 3$ in calculating the HPI-1 and HPI-2

The value of α has an important impact on the value of the HPI. If $\alpha = 1$, the HPI is the average of its dimensions. As α rises, greater weight is given to the dimension in which there is the most deprivation. Thus as α increases towards infinity, the HPI will tend towards the value of the dimension in which deprivation is greatest (for the Central African Republic, the example used for calculating the HPI-1, it would be 55.3%, equal to the probability at birth of not surviving to age 40.

In this Report the value 3 is used to give additional but not overwhelming weight to areas of more acute deprivation.

RIVER BANK EROSION : CONCEPT AND MAPPING AS ENVIRONMENT HAZARD

Definition : A river is a channelled flow of water. The channel is defined by riverbanks which delineate the cavity of a channel. The height of the bank above riverbed determines the carrying capacity of the river. As such, *a riverbank is a sloping land at the edge of a river.* it is basically an erosional feature in a rocky terrain, but in a deltaic landscape of alluvial channels it may be a depositional landform, as it is formed by the accumulation of river-borne silts.

'Bank erosion' essentially means the enroachment of a river towards outer and uninvaded areas beyond its previously defined channel and related recession of the bank further outward from its previous alignment. A change in the configuration of the bank profiles may also indicate bank erosion too. A change in the bank profile and bank alignment between too selected years can give a comprehensive idea about the extent of bank erosion. When taken into the yearly rate of encroachment, it can give the intensity of erosion too.

Why considered as a hazard ?

Recession of the bank wall towards outer areas within the drainage basin may sometimes prove hazardous as it can destroy hectares of landed property and built-up areas within a very short period of time.

Usually casualty of human life is not very frequent in this hazard, but, there are instances when sudden collapse of bank materials have taken a toll of human life. The worst thing is that a person losing his landed property to a river is not entitled to compensation from the state authority. This way bank erosion has caused great loss of immovable properties. Village after villages have been ruined during the course of shifting of a river and the losing villagers have never been able to obtain a foothold agan. The Kosi is the most notorious river in terms of bank erosion and channel shifting. The Kosi has shifted for 112 km. between 1736 and 1964.

The recent episode of the shift of the Ganga river in Maldah district due to the unforeseen consequences and unwise construction of the Farakka barage has endangered the life of people of Panchanandapur area. The shift has literally made them non-existent. 'The land eroded from left bank of Ganga in Malda is about 269 sq. km; while in Murshidabad it is about 356 sq. Km. (Kalyan Rudra, 2005). Where rivers are used as state, district or international boundaries, the shift of river course may initiate border disputes.

Process of bank erosion : Subaerial erosion is always involved in breaking and removal of earth materials in vertical and horizontal directions. Bank erosion too is related to the removal of bank materials and consequent changes occurring in the configuration of riverbanks. The process of bank erosion may include the following interactions :

1. Riverbanks being exposed to the atmosphere suffer from intensive weathering activities. Weathered debris come down the slope under the force of gravity and resultant changes occur in the form of the riverbanks.
2. Rain water directly hits the riverbanks and splash action takes place, if the banks are alluvial in nature. Sheet erosion is also common on such riverbanks.
3. High banks allow the formation of rills and gullies along their surfaces. This process is particularly significant for incising rivers.
4. Collapse of river banks occur particularly at concave banks where the river undercuts the cliff-face and the pedestal support of the bank is lost.
5. Bank erosion is of partcular significance for meandering channels. In the course of oscillation a river shifts its channel at the bends. The outer or concave bank is eroded and the inner or convex bank receives the deposition of sediments. In the middle Ganga plain the Ganga makes a huge loop beside Bhagalpur. Between Bhagalpur and Narainpur the river frequently shifts within a cycle of 40 to 50 years. The life of the villagers living on the bank of the river is frequently disturbed by such shifts. An interesting cultural feature has evolved from the course of such frequent shifts. The villages on the banks of the Ganga river have dual locations. When the river shifts towards south, new land is left towards north and people of the south bank shift to the northbank location of the same village. On the other hand, when the river shifts towards Narainpur, i.e., towards north, villages from the northern villages shift to the southbank location of the villages. The adaptation with channel shifting and related settlement dynamics have been disturbed by some landlords and mafias during last two decades, because the new depositional bars formed by the river on the convex bank are very fertile and raising of vegetable crops is very profitable on such bars and islands.
6. A braided river also erodes the banks most actively. When a river fails to accommodate an extra load of silts, pebbles and gravels along with quite high water discharge in its old channel, the river widens itself, provided the bank materials are not strong enough to resist. The flow-line of water is thus divided into many and each one passes between the channel bars formed by the deposition of sands, gravels etc. The depth of the river is reduced to a minimum at such points. Practically, an ideal braided channel is inch deep and mile wide.

Factors of bank erosion :

Riverbank erosion is favoured by certain factors which include the following :

1. **Bank materials :** If the river banks are composed of less resistant rocks, erosion of the banks becomes easier. Shale composing the river bank may be weathered and eroded away easily by the action of water. Alluviums forming a pair of river banks are also easily erodible. On

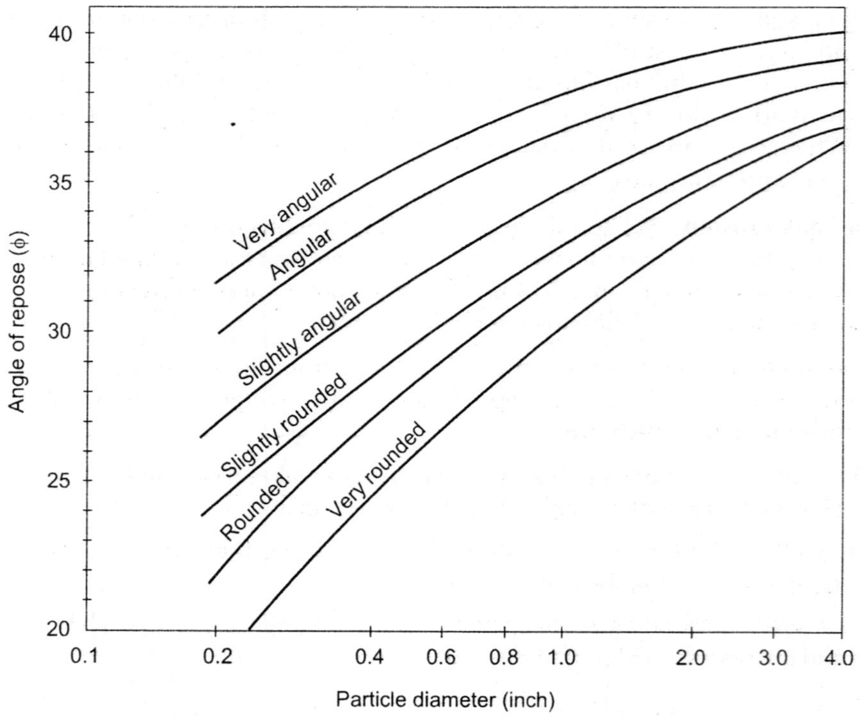

Source : Cooke and Doornkamp : Geomorphology in Environmental Management

Fig. 10.8 Ralationship of Particle size and with slope

the other hand, harder and more resistant rocks make the river banks stable, but occrrence of flood is more likely in such cases, particularly when an extra load of solid and liquid discharge is available.

2. **Slope of the banks :** The stability of river banks also depends on the angle of slope of the bank surface. As long as the angle of slope (θ) does not exceed the angle of repose (ϕ) of the bank materials, the bank slope may remain stable. The angle of repose may be related to the size sand shape of the materials involved. On a hill slope the stability largely depends on the graditational force only, *i.e.*, W Sinθ, where W is the weight of the particle. On the other hand, for river banks along which gravitational force introduce lateral force generated by the flowing water is also important. The resistance towards the movement of particles is given by :

$$\textbf{Resistance} = W \cos \theta \tan \phi$$

If the gravitational force and lateral force together exceed this resistance, erosion will result in. The graph in the previous page gives an idea about the relationship between the angle of surface slope and size of the paricle.

(c) **Amount of discharge :** Each and every channel has a normal carrying capacity. If under heavy downpour the amount of discharge suddenly rises, it may scour the channel banks because of the hydraulic force produced.

(d) **Tendency of oscillation :** As a river carries water which is highly susceptible to stress, various types of forces work together in a channel. Under such forces the channel tends to oscillate.

Oscillation or meandering thus erodes the banks as the meandering channel deviates from its previous alignment.

(e) **Human activities :** Deforestation in the catchment area may enhance the siltation problem of a river and the riverbanks may prove inadequte to hold water. This may initate bank erosion too. The loss of vegetative cover of river banks has always triggered off bank erosion at a faster rate.

(f) **Helical flow :** The helical flow or cork screw motion of river-water may also favour bank erosion, as this flow scour the pool area below the cliff and may cause collapse of channel walls.

(g) **Erection** of dam or barrage and even pillars for road or railway bridge may cause huge siltation and the resultant effect may be a shift in the course of a river in the upstream of the obstruction.

Mapping of Bank erosion hazards :

1. Find out a large scale (1:25,000 or 1:50,000) topographical sheet covering the river or part of the river for which bank erosion mapping will be done;
2. Locate a permanent point on the ground with reference to the topographical sheet;
3. Measure the map distance between the permanent point and the nearest river bank. Convert it into ground distance and measure the actual distance on the present ground. Calculate how much deviation has taken place since the survey year of the topographical sheet. The same process be repeated for the opposite bank also. This deviation or shift of the channel bank should be marked on the topographical sheet with considerable care for direction and length measured on the map scale. Taking magnetic bearings of various recognisable points on the present riverbank with the help of a prismatic compass, stationary at the permanent point and measuring the distance of such traverse lines may help locate the present riverbank.
4. For mapping the riverbank materials each type of material will be marked on the basis of a particular symbol and should be marked on the edge of the bank for the particular stretch of the channel length it is present. For instance, if may be a rock, fresh alluvial sand, old and weathered alluvium, terrace materials with gravels and pebbles etc.
5. For marking the type of bank erosion, each erosional process may be indicated by a colour ribbon and may be marked along the inner edge of the river bank for the length it is predominating.
6. The rate of bank erosion can be determined by dividing the extent of shift of the outer bank by years of time. As the two banks will have differential approach towards growth and decay of landform, the shift of the outer bank may be considered as positive departure, where as the shift of the convex or inner bank bank is negative departure from erosional point of view. This may be plotted as a deviation graph considering the previous thalweg position obtained from the map as the base line.
7. Finally, the level of severity of bank erosion may be differentially marked along the newly plotted bank-line with qualitative judgement indicating Severe, Intensive, Moderate, Low etc. For each grade a particular colour ribbon with a different colour scheme from the previous one may be given.

However, satellite images are very useful for such purposes and comparison between a topographic sheet and recent images may give a clear idea about channel shifting and bank erosion. Locating the paleo channels and reconstruction of the course of shifting may help in a great way, especially in the flood plain areas.

STUDY OF RUPNARAYAN RIVER

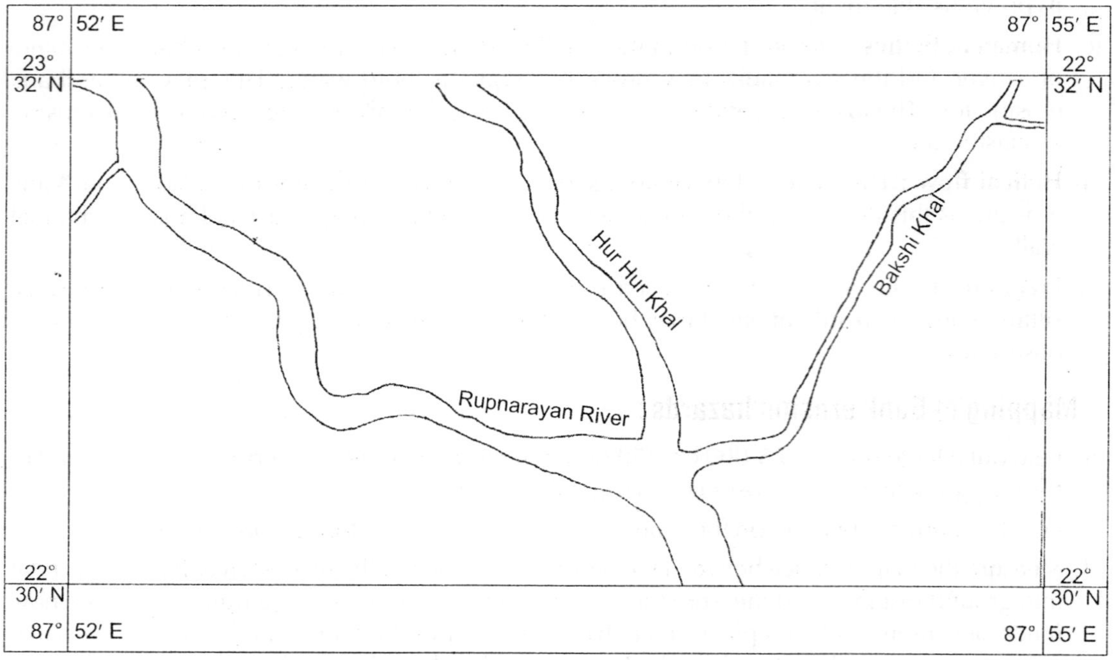

Fig. 10.9a Alignment of River Banks, 1069-70, Scale : 1:50,000

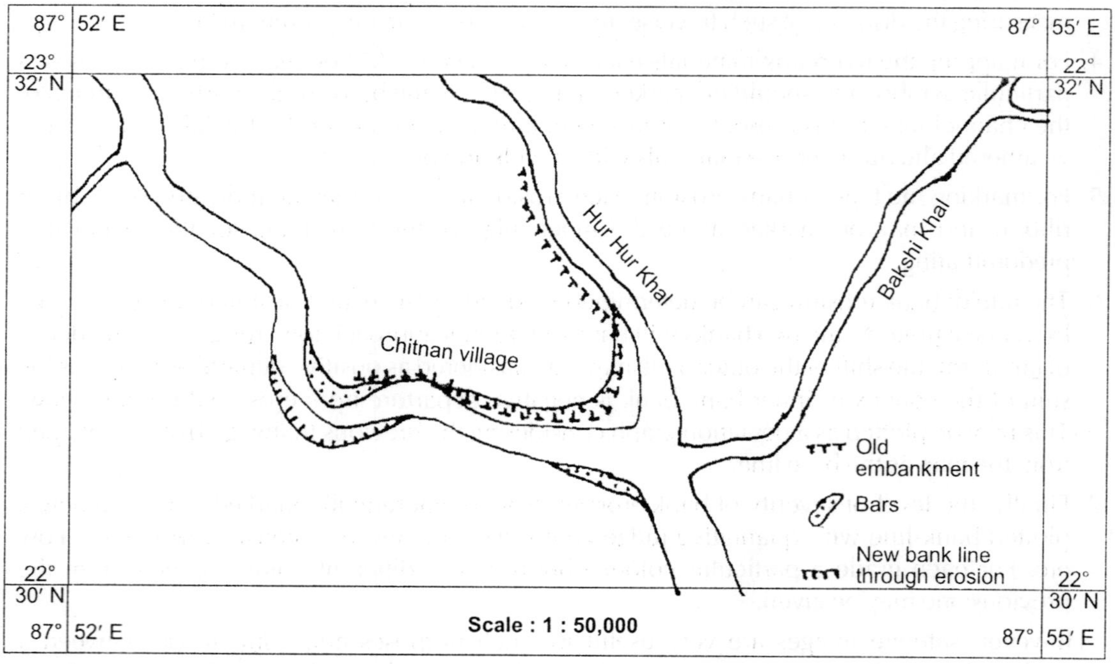

Fig. 10.9b Changed Bank Line through Erosion and Deposition

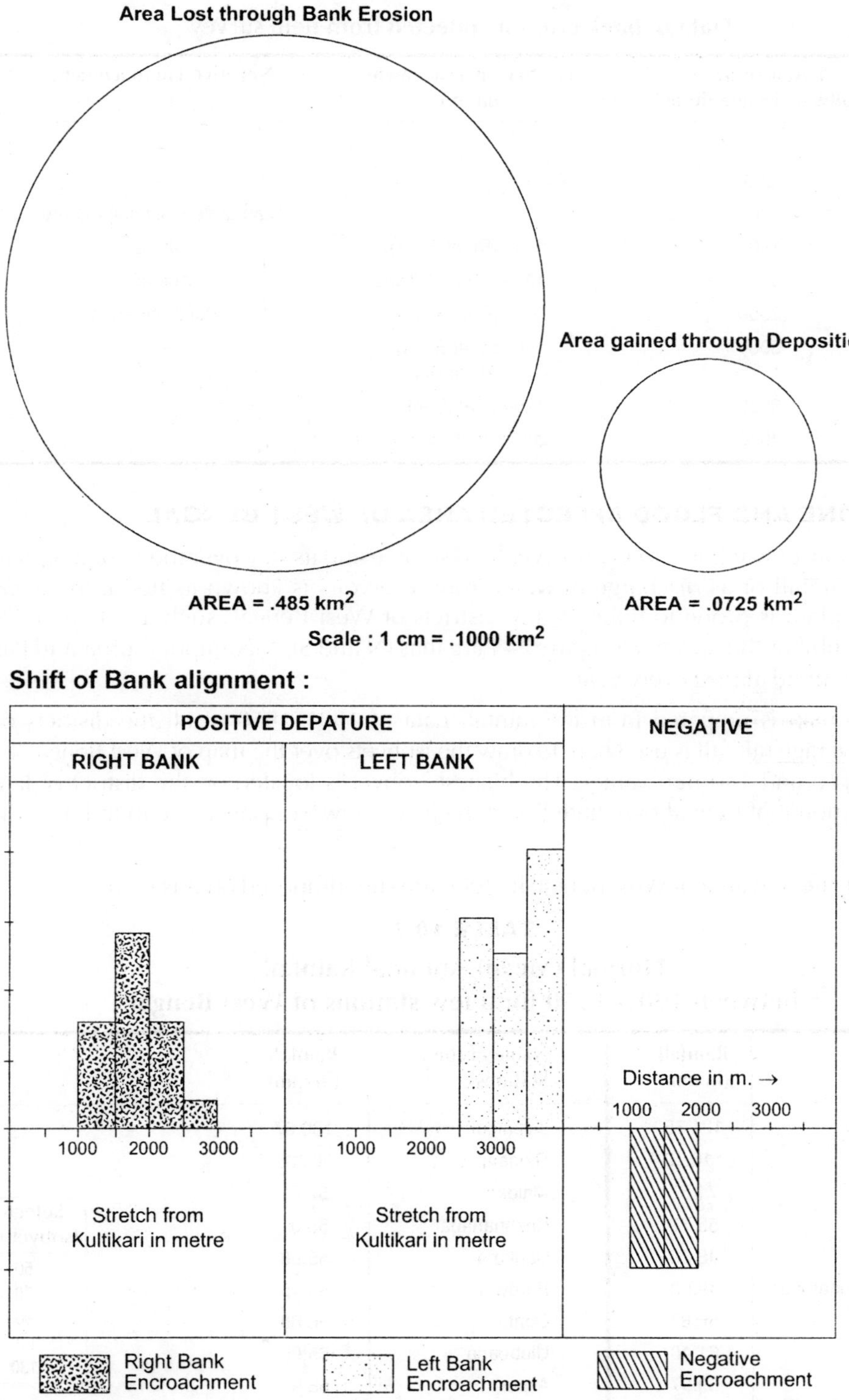

Fig. 10.10 Features of River Bank Erosion of Rupnarayan river near Chitnan Village

TABLE 10.6

Data of bank erosion collected from field survey

Distance from Kultikari village (in m.)	Positive Encroachment (in m.)	Negative Encroachment (m.)
0	—	—
500	—	—
1000	—	Start of depositional feature
1500	75 m. (Right Bank)	100 m
2000	140 m. (Right Bank)	100 m
2500	75 m. (Right Bank)	0 (Point bar ends)
3000	150 m (left Bank) 20 m (Right Bank)	—
3500	125 m (left Bank)	—
4000	200 m (Left Bank)	—

FLOOD PRONE AND FLOOD AFFECTED AREA OF WEST BENGAL

The overflow of water in a river and over land surface and its stay over there for a duration due to excessive rainfall or as discharge of water from reservoirs is known as flood. In general, the lower Ganga plain is prone to flood. Many districts of West Bengal, such as Maldah, Dakshin Dinajpur, Kochbihar, Burdwan, Hooghly, 24 Parganas (N and S), Medinipur (Purba and Paschim) are affected by flood almost every year.

A rainfall map is prepared from the rainfall data of 1901–1950 of all the districts of West Bengal. The average rainfall is used here to draw the isohyets over the map of West Bengal, being in 50 , 70, 90, 110 and 130 mm values. The highest isohyet is located on the district of Jalpaiguri because the amount of rainfall over here is very high. The lowest isohyets are found over Birbhum and Purulia.

The flood affected area of West Bengal in 2000 are superimposed on this map.

TABLE 10.7

Normal (Mean) Annunal Rainfall between 1901–1950 for a few stations of West Bengal

Name of the Stations	Rainfall (in mm)	Name of the Stations	Rainfall (in mm)
Darjeeling	121.75	Jalpaiguri	130.67
Dinhata	110.12	Raiganj	62.12
Balurghat	71.57	Maldah	57.21
Berhampur	55.77	Krishnanagar	53.01
Bolpur	48.25	Bankura	55.96
Purulia, Raghunathpur	49.50	Burdwan	60.15
Arambagh	56.83	Contai	66.69
Midnapur	61.40	Ulubearia	65.65
Barasat	59.97	Alipur	63.97
Sagar island	60.97		

Selected Isohyet mm
50
70
90
110
130

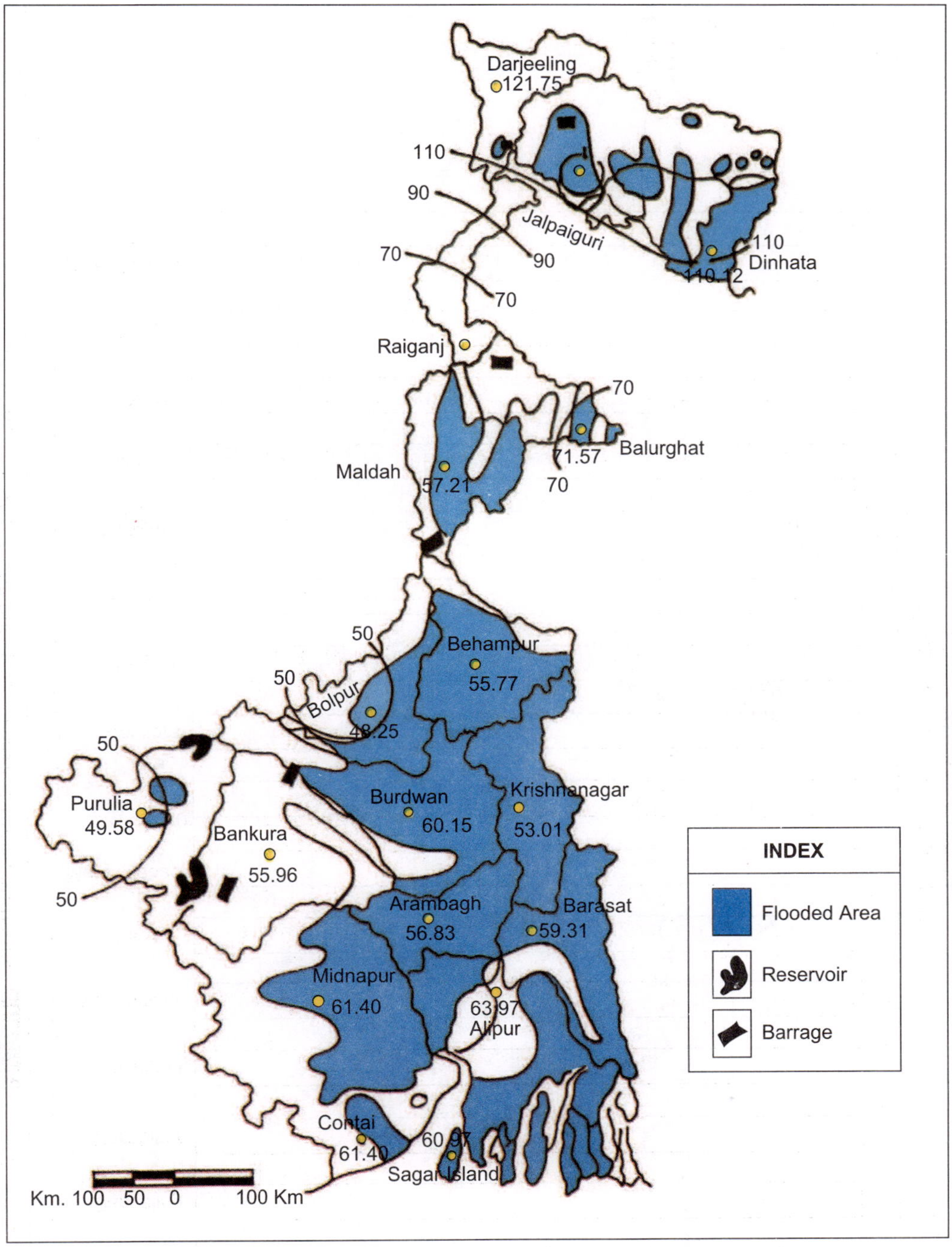

Fig. 10.11 Superimposition of Isohyets on Flood affected areas of West Bengal, 2000

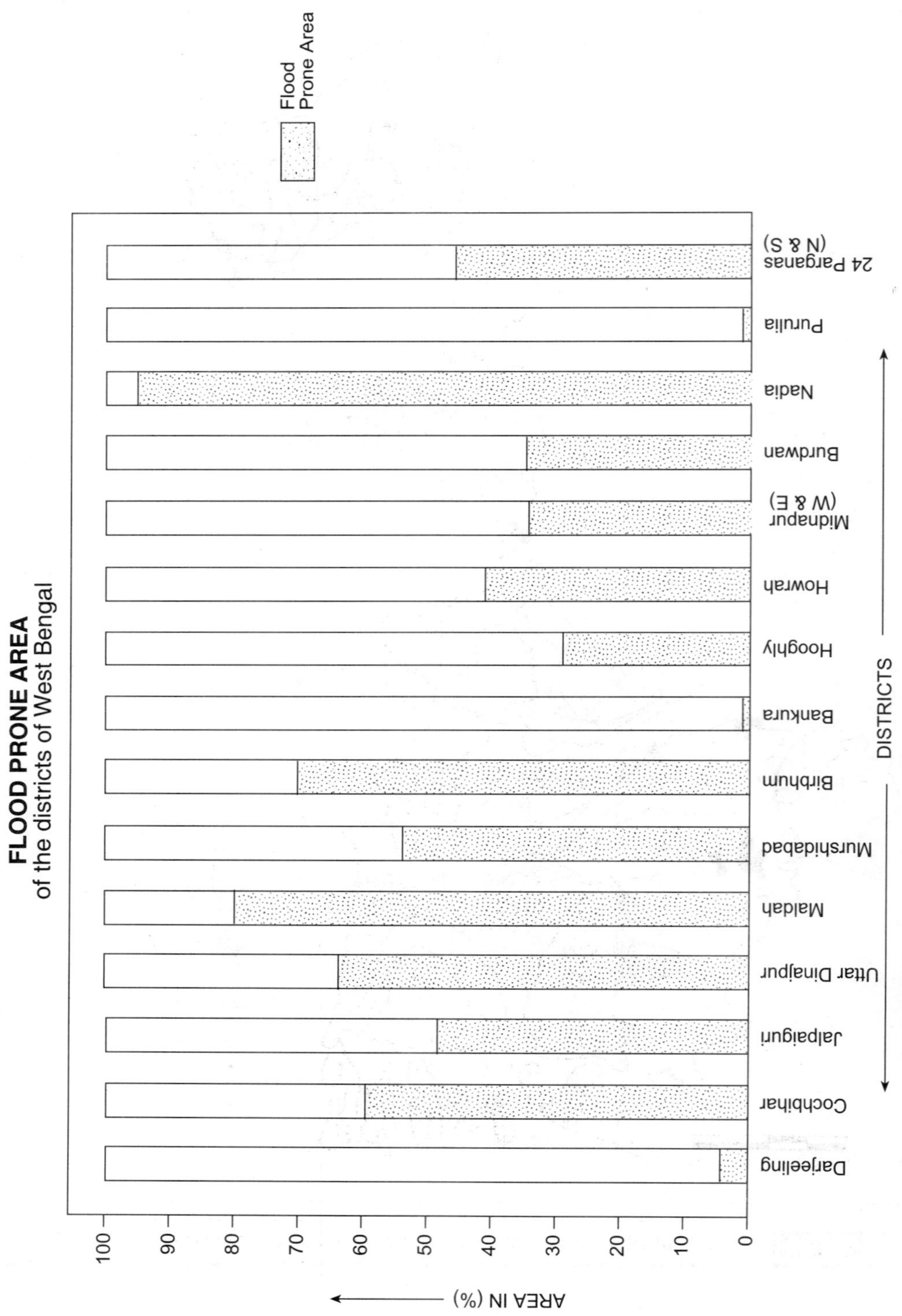

Fig. 10.12 Superimposition of Isohyets on Flood affected areas of West Bengal, 2000

Columas or bars in page no. 63 show the flood prone areas (in %) of the districts of West Bengal.

TABLE 10.8

Flood Prone Area of the Districts of West Bengal (Area usually liable to be flooded)

Sl. No.	Name of Districts	Area in Km^2		Percentage of Flood prone area
		Geographical area	Flood prone area	
1.	Darjeeling	3149	127	4.03
2.	Kochbihar	3387	2000	52.04
3.	Jalpaiguri	6227	3000	48.18
4.	Uttar Dinajpur	5358	3458	64.54
5.	Dakshin Dinajpur	—	—	—
6.	Maldah	3733	3000	80.36
7.	Murshidabad	5324	2858	53.68
8.	Birbhum	4545	3182	70.01
9.	Bankura	6882	118	1.71
10.	Hooghly	3149	912	28.96
11.	Howrah	1467	600	40.89
12.	Midnapur	14081	4823	34.25
13.	Burdwan	7024	2458	34.99
14.	Nadia	3927	3731	95.00
15.	Purulia	6259	65	1.03
16.	24 Parganas N.			
17.	24 Parganas S	14136	6428	45.47
18.	CMC area	104	—	—

Interpretation of Flood Zone Map :

In the southern part of West Bengal flood is a regular hazard either resulting from heavy rainfall or from drainage congestion and release of reservoir water. During the Summer Monsoon season of 2000 the district of Hugli suffered from intensive flood hazard due to heavy rainfall and drainage congestion. This flood zone map (Fig. 10.13 a & b) includes only spilled and flooded areas of the district. Rainfall between 18.9.2000 and 21.9.2000 was exceptionally high (Table : below) and that resulted in high intensity downpour at four stations of the district, *i.e.* Chisura, Champadanga, Arambagh and Chanditala. On the basis of the variable intensities of rainfall at these stations three isohyets (same rainfall intensity here) of 60 mm, 70 mm and 80 mm mark the pattern of the distribution of rainfall.

TABLE 10.9

Data of Rainfall at 4 stations of Hooghly District

Name of station	Dates on which rainfall (mm) occurred				Total rainfall (mm)	Intensity
	18.9.2000	19.9.2000	20.9.2000	21.9.2000		
Chinsura	61.00	125.40	24.00	19.00	229.40	57.35
Champadanga	25.00	142.00	150.00	43.75	360.75	90.187
Arambagh	2.00	112.50	125.50	37.00	276.50	69.125
Chanditala	(Individual datewise rainfall not known)				293.00	73.25

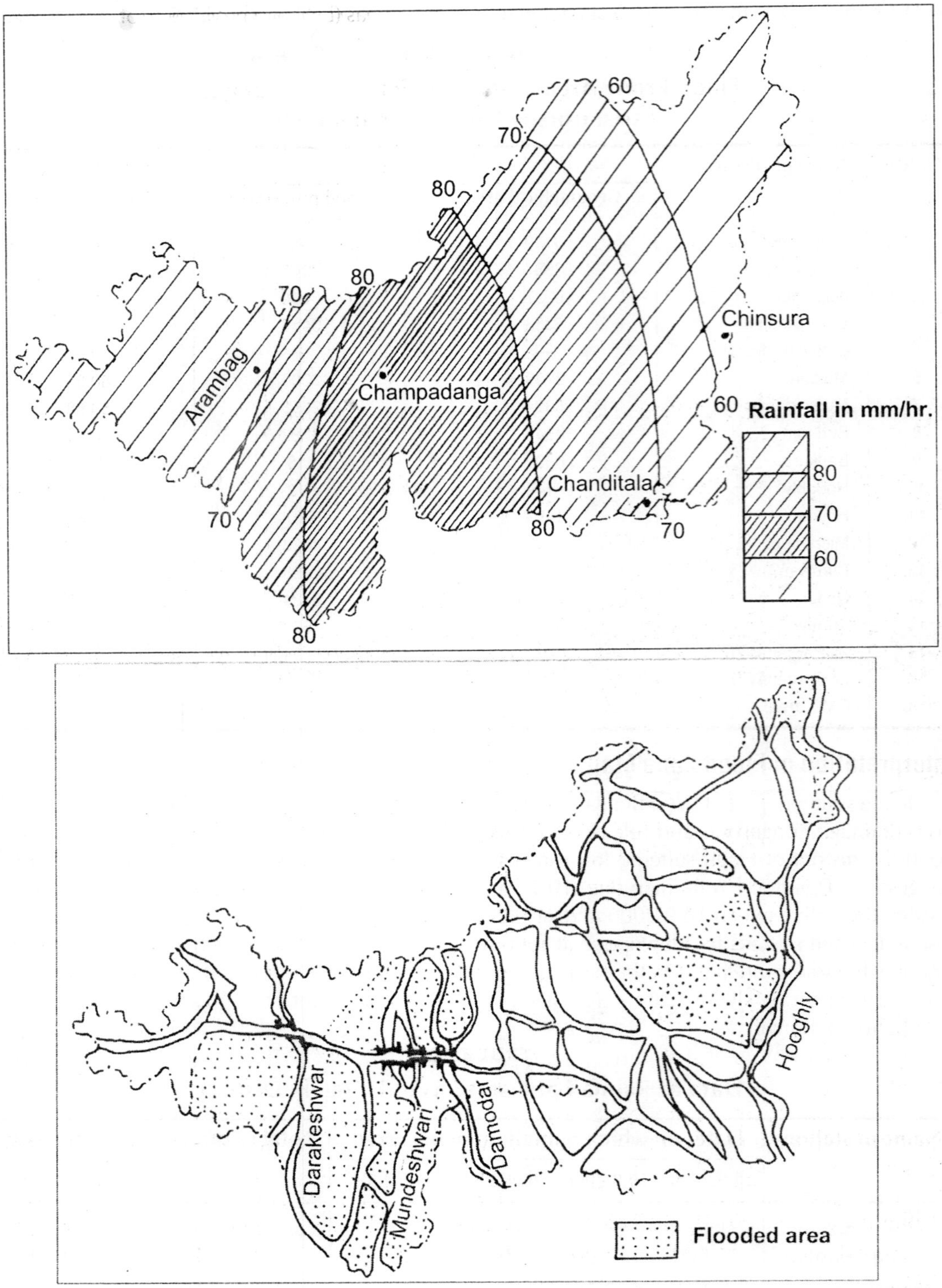

Fig. 10.13 a & b **Isohyet Map and Flood Zone Map of Hooghly District (September 2000)**

TABLE 10.10

Occurrence of Meteorological drought in the districts of West Bengal between 1901 and 1950

Stations	Normal (N) Rainfall (mm)	75% of Normal (N)	No. of years of drought with negative deviation from N	Occurrence of drought in %
Darjeeling	121.75	91.31	2 (1901, 1908, 1931)	6
Jalpaiguri	130.67	98.00	3 (1908, 1919, 1947)	6
Dinhata	110.12	82.59	2 (1908, 1942)	4
Raiganj	62.09	46.57	6(1908, 1923, 1940, 1943, 1945, 1948)	12
Balurghat	71.57	53.68	8 (1901, 03, 04, 08, 17, 21, 27, 40)	16
Malda	57.21	42.91	5 (1903, 1904, 1908, 1916, 1927)	10
Berhampur	55.77	41.83	6 (1907, 23, 27, 34, 35, 40)	12
Krishnanagar	58.01	43.51	3 (1904, 1934, 1935)	6
Bolpur	48.28	36.21	5 (1912, 19, 20, 23, 25)	10
Bankura (Raghnnathpur)	55.96	41.97	3 (1931, 1934, 1935)	6
Purulia	49.80	37.35	5(1904, 07, 15, 21, 32)	10
Burdwan	60.18	45.14	4 (1904, 1908, 1935, 1945)	8
Arambag	56.83	46.62	5 (1904, 11, 34, 35, 44)	10
Contai	66.69	50.02	3 (1918, 1935, 1943)	6
Midnapur	61.40	46.05	3 (1910, 1934, 1938)	6
Ulluberia	65.65	49.24	6 (1911, 1921, 1923, 24, 35, 45)	12
Barasat	59.38	44.54	6 (1923, 34, 35, 36, 37, 43)	12

The Flood Zone Map on the basis of actual areas of occurrence of flood with superimposition of rainfall zones shows that there is an intimate relation between the high rainfall areas and flooded areas, especially in the western half of the district. Towards east flood has occurred even with lower intensity of rainfall. This may be related to wide spread drainage congestion in this area. However, it should be noted here that flood is not the sole product of high rainfall only. There are other important factors also.

DROUGHT AS AN ENVIRONMENTAL DISASTER

Drought is almost a regular climatic incident that often turns out to be a disaster. It has the most significant correlation with agricultural cropping of a country. Crop failure is the most obvious effect that a climatic or meterological drought results in. But the definition of drought is not the same in all countries, because what is known as a drought in a humid region is obviously different from that of a drought in a dry region. A desert region may declare it a drought when a span of two years passes rainless, whereas a meteorological drought in a traditional agricultural land like India may be only a negative deviation from 75% of normal annual rainfall. Now that normal may be an one hundred years' average of annual rainfall or in the case of non-availability of data it may a fifty years' average. The frequency of drought in India had increased (11 times) during the last half of the twentieth century in comparison with the first half (5 times) (Mishra, 2005). Annual rainfall, however, may not always prove a satisfactory data for identifying a

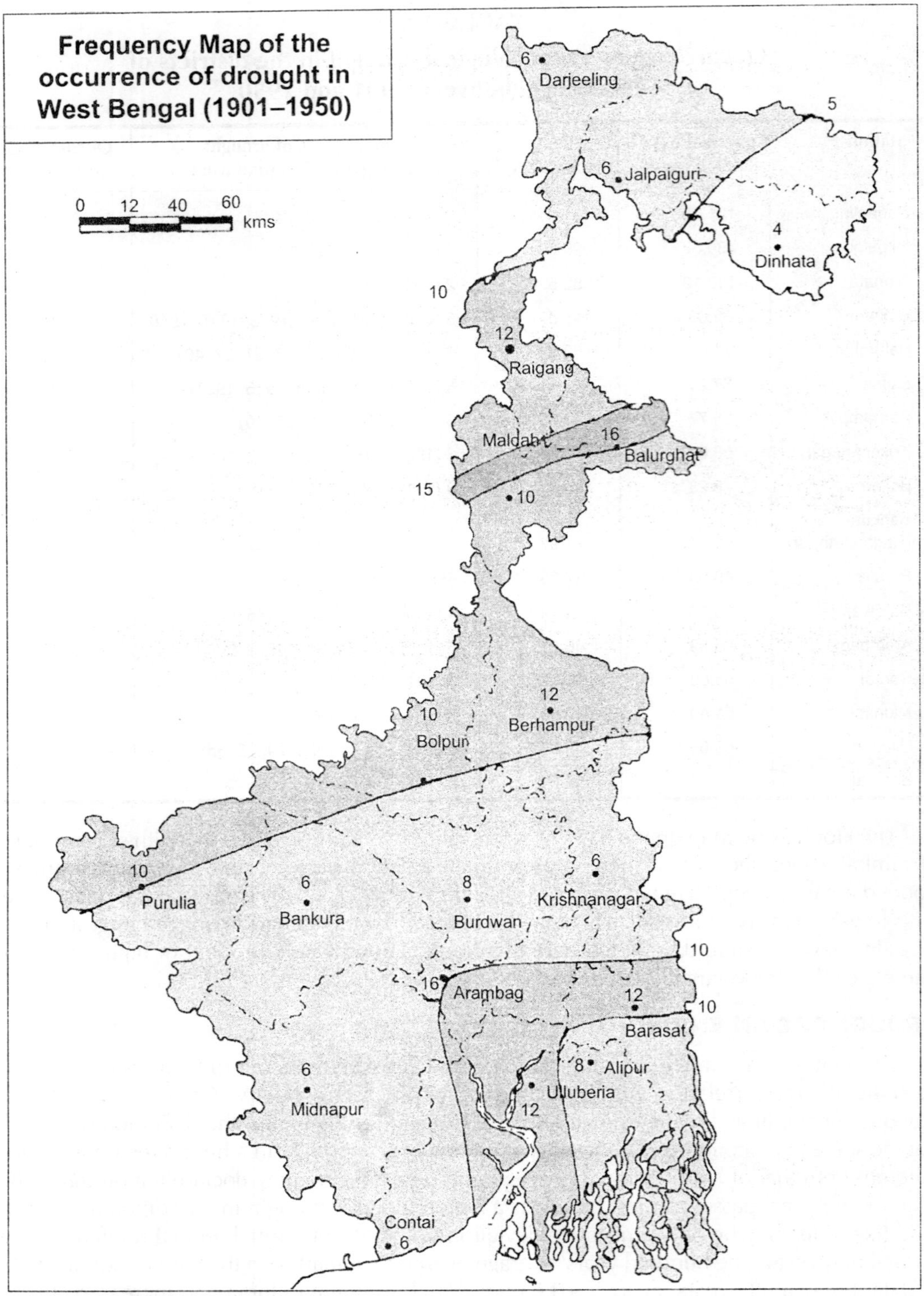

Fig. 10.14 Drought Map of West Bengal

drought, because crop failure in India is actually dependent on seasonal rainfall. Mishra (05) reports that during the twentieth century agricultural drought occurred for 30 times in the Kharif season. Hence, identifying a drought on the basis of deviation of annual rainfall may not always specify its correlation with failure of crops. Year to year checking for a meteorological drought on the basis of negative deviation of annual rainfall from 75% of the normal may, however, identify the core region of drought occurrence particularly where drought is a recurring phenomenon. In a country like India the lack of uniformity in the countrywide spatial distribution of rainfall may cause a drought. Moreover, as the rainbearing winds enter into the country from the neighbouring oceanic areas and a lot of rainfall occurs in the coastal districts as orographic rainfall, the interior districts beyond the mountain barriers often suffer from drought, e.g. Rain shadow areas of the Western Ghats, Kalahandi, Kanpur, Jalandhar, Gwalior districts etc. In West Bengal, however, the drought prone districts include Purulia, Birbhum, Hooghly, Bankura, Dinajpur etc.

The calculation for the number of occurrence of drought in West Bengal in percent values between 1901 and 1950 is incorporated in the following table.

Interpretation of drought map : The frequency map of the occurrence of drought shows that the highest frequency is obtained at Balurghat, whereas Purulia, a well known drought prone area is of middle order occurrence of drought. As Meteorological drought does not consider all the parameters like evaporation, soil moisture status etc., it may not always match our real world experience.

If we analyse the data computed in the Table 10.10 for the occurrence of meteorological drought, we understand that the normal (N) value is the highest for Balurghat. At the same time this station has maximum scope of variability. That is why it has shown maximum number of occurrence of drought. On the contrary, rainfall in drier areas in much lower in amount, though less variable.

QUESTIONNAIRES FOR SOCIO-ECONOMIC AND ENVIRONMENTAL SURVEY

Socio-economic survey is mainly an investigation into the socio-economic conditions of a human community. The social characteristics and economic status of the community are exposed in such survey works. As we know that a survey often determines the characteristics of unknown objects with reference to the known ones, a socio-economic survey is no exception too. When we find out the literacy, income status or age-sex composition of a community, we compare those with the national or international standard and draw inferences about whether the community under investigation is a backward and under developed or an advanced one. We also try to find out the crisis, the problems of the group of people we meet during our survey.

Such a survey is also useful for determining the environmental conditions as perceived by the people. Peoples' peception, their feelings, their understanding of the present socio-political scenario, the scope of availability of their amenities and basic needs etc. can be revealed through such survey works. The impact of a hazard or disaster may also be surmised through such surveys.

Usually a socio-economic survey is carried out through questionnaires and analysis of socio-economic data obtained as secondary data from official sources and as primary data form direct interaction with the people involved. The questionaries are prepared with a priliminary idea about the physical and probable socio-economic environment in the back of the mind of the surveyor. It should be kept in mind also that the questions asked to the people being surveyed may not be totally understood by them. Hence the questions should be clear and unambiguous for them. Moreover, the people may be reluctant to answer certain questions also. In that case the relevant question may be put in a different manner. Sometimes people are not willing to expose the truth, specially about their income status, socio-political conditions etc. In such cases, asking of random questions about other related phenomena, such as expenditure, savings etc. may reveal the fact indirectly.

Types of questions

The questions may be of three main types :

1. **Open end questions :** These questions do not have any hints of answer in themselves. The surveyed person has to answer it on his own. The merit of the information or inference totally depends on the answer given by the person questioned.
2. **Multiple choice questions :** These questions are suggestive. Here the choices for the answer are given and the person surveyed has to select any one of them. The statements offered as choices should be very carefully composed, so that the suitable answer lies in any one of them. The surveyor needs a lot of knowledge about the environment and the nature of the community questioned for preparing this type of questions. Sometimes these choices may be very critical, but too critical questions will be only asked to the technical and knowledgeable persons.
3. **Double choice questions :** These questions are also suggestive in nature. Usually 'yes' or 'no' is the answer. These are asked only for rapid collection of some general information for which much time is not spared and the actual situation is clear to the person under investigation.

EXAMPLE

Prepare a questionnaire for the community of people of an area which has been recently havoced by flood.

A. Open end questions :

1. When or on which day the area was flooded?
2. What was the condition of weather during the last three or four days before the flood occurred?
3. Which is the nearest river in the area?
4. Which blocks or villages had been affected by flood?
5. What was the height of water?
6. Was there any dry point in the area at the time of flood?
7. Where did the people take their refuge?
8. How long did flood water stay?
9. What are the damages?
10. Give a rough estimate of the number of death of human population and cattle population.

B. Double choice questions :

11. Was relief available at the time of flood? Yes/No
12. Who catered the flood relief, Government agencies? Yes/No
13. Was relief materials properly distributed among people? Yes/No

14. Are you satistied with the relief given to you? Yes/No
15. Does the area get flooded every year? Yes/No

C. Multiple choice questions :

16. What was the main cause of the flood?
    (a) Spilling of river water;
    (b) Release of water from reservoir;
    (c) Heavy shower;
    (d) All of the 3 previous probabilities combined.
17. What is the time internal of flood in the area?
    (a) Each year;
    (b) Every second year;
    (c) Every third year;
    (d) More than three years.
18. How can the flood be avoided?
    (a) Raising the houses on stilts;
    (b) Building a high rise building in the area with all arrangements and stay in that house at the time of flood;
    (c) To sell out and leave that flood-prone area;
    (d) To make bank embankments for the neighbouring river.
19. What is the root cause of flood in the area?
    (a) Destiny;
    (b) Siltation of river due to human interference;
    (c) Unwise daming of river and compulsory release of water;
    (d) Occasional heavy rainfall.
20. How is the reconstruction and recovery work being organised?
    (a) Satisfactorily, as Government is helping benevolently;
    (b) Government is not helping at all and people are still suffering;
    (c) Government and NGOs are working hand in hand with people;
    (d) People did not bother for help, whatever it may be, and reconstructing with the help of indigenous village organisations.

MAPPING OF LANDSLIDE HAZARD ZONES

According to the Working Party on the World Landslide Inventory (1990) a landslide is 'The movement of a mass of rock, earth or debris down a slope'. In this sense a sinking landmass because of its loss of pedestal support due to toe erosion by a mountain torrent is also a landslide. A more comprehensive definition distinguishing a landslide from other geomorphological processes is : 'the downward or outward movement of a mass of slope-forming material under the influence of gravity occurring on discrete boundaries and taking place initially without the aid of water as a transportational agent.'

Varnes (1978) classified landslides in the following manner :

Type of movement			Type of materials		
			Bed rock	Engineering soils	
				Coarse	Fine
Falls			Rock fall	Debris Fall	Earth fall
Topples			Rock topple	Debris topple	Earth topples
Slides	Rotational	Few units	Rock slump	Debris slump	Earth slump
	Translational	Many units	Rock block slide	Debris block slide	Earth block slide
			Rock slide	Debris slide	Earth slide
Lateral spread			Rock spread	Debris spread	Earth spread
Flows			Rock flow	Debris flow	Earth flow
Complex	Combination of two or more principal types of movement.				

Landslide as a hazard : Following Crozier (1989) , in unstable areas, landslides may displace materials upto 2000 m^3/Km^2/year. The assessment of a landslide hazard should be the successful prediction of a place of occurrence of the landslide event, finding out its relationship with time and to predict the impact characteristics. A landslide hazard is the probability of occurrence of a given magnitude of sliding of earth materials.

The assessment of the probable site can be done by stability analysis. The threshold conditions should consider the slope angle of terrain and its height and it would vary from terrain to terrain. A quantitative analysis of stability may compare the magnitude of resisting forces and the magnitude of shearing forces. This is expressed as the factor of safety (F_S).

$$F_S = \frac{\text{resisting stress (shear strength)}}{\text{shear stress}}$$

At the point of a land failure Fs=1.0. A landslide is worth studying individually because of the uniqueness of its characteristics. The mapping of the probable landslide hazard zones, however, can be done in many ways, such as **Parameter method, Stochastic Historical method, Triggering. Threshold method** etc. Of them Parameter method is easier. Of the two others the Stochastic

Historical method considers the records of previous landslide occurrences and the Triggering threshold method couples the forcing process with a process response. In the parameter method the type and effectiveness of causative factors are assessed. The particular parameter selected may vary from site to site, but in general, the factors include :

1. Type of bedrock and their relative strength (Fresh);
2. State of weathering;
3. Angle of landslope;
4. Presence of water;
5. Amount of dip of related rockbeds;
6. Direction of dip of related rockbeds;
7. Presence of faults, joints etc;
8. Frequency of landslide;
9. Type of landuse.
10. Local height of landform.

The impact of these factors may be standarized through the assignment of weightage to them and the summation of all will give the total amount of calculated vulnerability which can be used for zonation mapping through isopleths. While assigning weight to each of the factors relative importance of each of them should be judged. Some of them are obtained in quantified values and some others are observed as of qualitative values, but without standardization and determination of single absolute values a geographical zonation is not possible. Let us examine how we can pursue this problem of landslide hazard zonation through weightage and isoplething. The weightage should increase with an increase of vulnerability.

1. **Type of bedrock :** the intact strength of unweathered rocks can be measured on the basis of the following table of strength classification (Selby,1980) :

TABLE 10.12

Description	Strength class	Rock type
Very weak rock	5	Chalk, Rocksalt, Lignite
Weak rock	4	Coal, Siltstone, Schist
Moderately strong rock	3	State, Shale, Sandstone, Mudstone, Ignimbrite
Strong rock	2	Marble, Limestone, Dolomite, Andesite, Granite, Gneiss
Very strong rock	1	Quartzite, Dolerite, Gabbro

The variable strength of rocks can be assigned the following weightage values :

TABLE 10.13

Strength class	Weight assigned
5	25
4	20
3	15
2	10
1	5

Here the arithmetic series has been avoided because loose debris, soils, sands practically have very low strength and those materials are often subject to landslides. The higher values indicate greater susceptibility to landslides and therefore shows higher vulnerability.

2. **State of weathering :** The strength of rocks in natural landscape is often influenced by the particular state of weathering it attains, especially in the outer part which is more important in terms of landslides. Hence the state of weathering of the rock involved should be judged while assigning the weight of relative vulnerability because, we know that even quartzite may prove weak if it is highly weathered. In this regard the rockmass strength classification on the basis of the state of weathering can be taken into consideration (Selby, 1980).

TABLE 10.14

Strength class	Weight assigned
Unweathered	0
Slightly weathered	1
Moderately weathered	2
Highly weathered	3
Completely weathered	4

This classification of weightage on the basis of the state of weathering has considered the inherent strength of fresh and unexposed rock as determined by Selby (1980). A very strong rock with a relative strength of 1 should have practically no strength at all if it is completely weathered. The vulnerability value will however, increase due to weathering.

3. **Angle of landslope :** The angle of landslope for the study of an individual landslide may be determined on the basis of the angle of ground slope. But for zonation mapping average regional slope by Wentworth's method may be useful. This would determine slope on a square grid format (1 Km^2) on the basis of the following equation :

$$\text{Slope} = \frac{\text{Average no. of contour crossing} \times \text{Contour interval}}{636.6} = \tan \theta^{-1}$$

As higher degree of slope is more vuluerable for landslide hazards higher weight will be assigned to higher slope regions, but regional slope playing an indirect role can be assigned a lower value than rock strength weightage. The particular range of values should be determined on the basis of the values and number of slope regions present in a particular landscape unit.

4. **Presence of water :** The presence of water, however, plays a vital role in causing the occurrence of landslides. The pelitic rocks absorb water and get swelled up. They become slippery and soft and favour landslides. In determining the vulnerability value the range should be fixed between the presence of water along the plane of slip and the absence of this lubricating agent. As the impact of the presence of water gives a triggering effect, it should be assigned double of the general vulnerability value, whereas the absence means addition of no further vulnerability due to the absence of water and hence it should be 0.

   Toe erosion by a river may not be included in the vulnerability value as it has no direct contact with the plane of slip. Rather it is the indirect triggering factor which causes instability of slope and loss of F_S. Similarly, high intensity of rainfall has been known to be the most important causative factor for landslides in mountains, but that should not also be included as vulnerability factor.

5. & 6. **Amount and Direction of dip of related rock beds :** In general, a high angle of dip towards the valley makes a site highly vulnerable to landslides. On the contrary, a hillside dip does not favour the occurrence of landslide. The amount of dip may also play a variable role. Therefore, the amount of dip and direction of dip can be assigned the following vulnerability values.

TABLE 10.15

Vulnerability from direction and amount of slope

Amount of dip.	Direction of dip.	Vulnerability
High (50° – 80°)	Valley slide	15
Moderate (30° – 50°)	Valley slide	10
Low (<30°)	Valley slide	5

7. **Presence of faults and joints :** Faulting and jointing in rocks increases the shearing stress and causes substantial loss of F_S. Thus the vulnerability of landmass towards landslide increases and the probability of landslide is enhanced. Percolation of rainwater and even dew drops make the joints and faults planes slippery and the land becomes more susceptible to landslides. As joints and or a fault alone may be held responsible for landslides, the highest value of vulnerability will be assigned to them.

8. **Frequency of landslides :** It is rather a historical factor which can help the assessment through statistical records. The frequency of landslide records indicates the probability of further occurrence of landslides through statistical probability. This analysis, however, should not come into consideration of vulnerability, though it is useful for assessment and forecasting.

   The particular trend of a landslide may be analysed and its further encroachment may be foreseen on the basis of time–based analysis.

9. **Type of landuse :** Human interference in the form of unscientific landuse may make the landscape more vulnerable to landslides. In general, agriculture, particularly producing root crops is dangerous. Grain crop production is also detrimental, particularly when wet paddy

cultivation is done. Cultivation on highly inclined slopes, in general, makes the land vulnerable as it often requires stripping of the land. A landslope greater than 30° is not suitable for cultivation.

Deforestation of mountain slopes also increases vulnerability. On the contrary, forest cover decreases vulnerability. Shrubs and bushes can also control the probability of landslides to some extent. Built-up areas, especially high rise buildings enhance the load on slope and hence increases slope instability. The following categories of vulnerability classes on the basis of landuse may be suggested.

TABLE 10.16

Landuse and Vulnerability

Type of landuse	Vulnerability
Forest cover	5
Shrubs and bushes	10
Cultivated lands	15
Built-up areas	15
Fallow lands and open spaces with cover of grass	10

10. **Local height of landform :** The proneness of a landform towards sliding increases with increasing local height. This happens because the centre of gravity of a landmass moves upward with its increasing height and the equilibrium of stability is gradually lost. Hence a high cliff is always more prone to landslide than another with low height. However, particular weightage can be assigned on the basis of local landform characteristics and related occurrence of landslides.

The summation of the vulnerability values may be put at the centre of 1 km^2 grids and isopleths can be obtained indicating different zones of landslide hazard. If any grid includes two different values of the same factor, the average may be considered for mapping. For instance, if one grid includes two different rock outcrops, the average vulnerability can be used.

On the basis of the vulnerability zones priority can be determined as the priority for conservation is inverse to vulnerability, i.e., the highest vulnerability zone should have priority 1 and so on.

The Bureau of Indian standards (BIS, 1998), however, put forward a proposal of rating of various parameters for the preparation of Landslide Hazard Zonation Map. The following table incorporates the scheme of rating.

TABLE 10.17

Rating Scheme of Lanslide Hazard Evaluation Factors

Contributory Factors	Category	Rating	
	Lithology	Lingtse granite gneiss	2.0
		Darjiling gneiss	1.5
		Parogneiss	1.3
		Paro Quartzite	1.7
		Reyang Quartzite	0.5
		Feldspathic Greywacke	0.8
Slope	Very Gentle slope	<15°	0
	Gentle slope	15° – 20°	0.5
	Moderate slope	20° – 25°	1.0
	Steep slope	25°–30°	1.5
	Escarpment	> 30°	2.0
Relative Relief	Very Low	150 – 300	0.1
	Low	300 – 450	0.3
	Medium	450 – 600	0.5
	High	600 – 750	0.7
	Very High	> 750	1.0
Drainage Density	Very Low	1.5 – 3.00	1.0
	Low	3.00 – 4.5	0.8
	Medium	4.5 – 6.00	0.6
	High	> 6.00	0.4
Land use		Thick Forest	0.6
		Open Forest	1.3
		Tea Garden	1.1
		Agricultural Land with Settlement	0.8
		Barren Land	2.0
		Built up area	1.0
Landform		River valley	0.6
		Spur	1.0
		Ridge	0.2
Landslide Incidence		> 4/sq km	1.0
		3–4/sq km	0.8
		1–2/sq km	0.6
		< 1/sq km	0.0

However, this method of determination of LSV was proved ineffective, as Landslide incidence area was to multiply the total rating of the six parameters and if Landslide incidence was zero, the result was also zero. So a changed method has been followed. This method does not include multiplication by Landslide incidence area in percentage and considers the total rating of the six parameters only.Climatic chart and ombrothermic diagram

TABLE 10.18

Rating Scheme of Lanslide Hazard Evaluation Factors and their sub-category

Contributory factors	Description	Sub-category	Rating
1. **Lithology**	Rock type	Quartzite/Phyllite	1.8
		Schist/slate	1.3
		Quartzite	0.5
		Lingtse gneiss	0.5
		Sandstone	1.0
2. **Structure**	Lineament		1.65
	Joint		2.30
	Cleavage		1.65
	Foliation		2.0
3. **Slope morphometry**	Escarpment	> 45°	2.7
	Steep slope	30°–45°	1.7
	Moderately steep slope	20°–30°	1.0
	Gentle slope	10°–20°	0.5
	Very gentle slope	<10°	0.0
4. **Relative Relief**	Very low	<100m	0.1
	Low	100–200	0.3
	Medium	200–300	0.5
	High	300–500	0.7
	Very High	>500	1.0
5. **Landuse/Landcover**	Barren land		2.0
	Depleted forest cover		1.3
	Dense forest cover		0.8
	Cultivated land (with or without settlement)		0.6
		Drainage density	
6. **Hydrological Condition**	Dry	< 2.0 km/km^2	0.3
	Damp	2.0–4.0	0.5
	Wet	4.0–6.0	0.7
	Dripping	6.0–8.0	0.8
	Flowing	> 8.0	1.0

TABLE 10.19

Gridwise Rating for Landslide Hazard Evaluation Factors of Rillibasin and LSV values

Grid No.	Lithology	Rating	Structure	Rating	Relative Relief	Rating	Slope in degree	Rating	Landuse	Rating	Drainage Density	Rating	Total rating (L.S.V.)
A_2	Sandstone and Phyllite-schist	1.37	Foliation	2.0	<100	0.1	–	–	F	0.8	1.0	0.3	4.57
A_3	Phyilite-schist	1.55	"	"	<100	0.1	–	–	F	0.8	0.5	0.7	5.15
B_1	Phyllite-schist and sandstone	1.37	"	"	150	0.3	6	0	Ag + F	0.7	1.5	0.3	4.67
B_2	"	1.37	"	"	300	0.5	8	0	Ag + F	0.7	4.0	0.5	5.07
B_3	"	1.37	"	"	450	0.7	17	0.5	F	0.8	4.5	0.7	6.07
B_4	Phyllite-schist and quartzite	1.20	"	"	601	1	15	0.5	F	0.8	5.0	0.7	6.2
B_5	"	1.20	"	"	601	1	17	0.5	Ag + F	0.7	3.5	0.5	5.9
B_6	"	1.20	"	"	<100	0.1	2	0	Ag	0.6	4.0	0.5	4.4
B_7	"	1.20	"	"	<100	0.1	17	0.5	Ag	0.6	1.0	0.3	4.7
C_1	Phyllite-schist	1.55	"	"	450	0.7	20	0.5	Ag + F	0.7	3.5	0.5	5.95
C_2	"	1.55	"	"	150	0.3	28	1	Ag + F	0.7	4.5	0.7	6.25
C_3	"	1.55	"	"	601	1	22	1	F	0.8	4.0	0.5	6.85
C_4	Phyllite, phyllite-schist, quartzite	1.34	"	"	901	1	24	0.5	F	0.8	5.0	0.7	6.34
C_5	Phyllite-schist, quartzite	1.20	"	"	1351	1	17	0.5	Ag + F	0.7	5.0	0.7	6.1
C_6	"	1.20	"	"	450	0.7	19	0	Ag	0.6	6.5	0.8	5.3
C_7	"	1.20	"	"	450	0.7	6	0.5	Ag	0.6	6.5	0.8	5.8
C_8	"	1.20	"	"	150	0.3	11	0.5	Ag	0.6	3.0	0.5	5.1
D_1	Phyllite-schist, quartzite	1.55	"	"	300	0.5	20	0.5	Ag + F	0.7	4.5	0.7	5.95
D_2	Phyllite-schist, quartzite	1.55	"	"	601	1	20	0.5	Ag + F + W	1.7	2.0	0.3	7.05
D_3	"	1.55	"	"	601	1	28	1.0	Ag + F	0.7	5.0	0.7	6.95
D_4	Phyllite schist, quartzite	1.20	"	"	450	0.7	24	1.0	Ag + F	0.7	4.0	0.5	6.1

Contd. next page

Grid No.	Lithology	Rating	Structure	Rating	Relative Relief	Rating	Slope in degree	Rating	Landuse	Rating	Drainage Density	Rating	Total rating (L.S.V.)
D_5	"	1.20	"	"	601	1	17	0.5	Ag + F + B	1.7	4.0	0.5	6.9
D_6	"	1.20	"	"	601	1	19	0.5	Ag	0.6	2.5	0.5	5.8
D_7	"	1.20	"	"	450	0.7	19	0.5	Ag + W	1.3	6.0	0.7	6.4
D_8	"	1.20	"	"	601	1	17	0.5	Ag	0.6	5.0	0.7	6
D_9	"	1.20	"	"	601	1	2	0	Ag + F	0.7	0.25	0.3	5.2
E_1	Phyllite-schist, quartzite	1.20	"	"	901	1	6	0	Ag + F	0.7	3.0	0.5	5.4
E_2	"	1.20	"	"	450	1	24	1.0	Ag	0.6	4.5	0.7	6.5
E_3	"	1.20	"	"	<100	0.1	26	1.0	Ag	0.6	5.0	0.7	5.6
E_4	"	1.20	"	"	150	0.3	20	0.5	Ag + F	0.7	3.0	0.5	4.15
E_5	"	1.20	"	"	450	0.7	13	0.5	Ag	0.6	4.0	0.5	5.5
E_6	"	1.20	"	"	450	0.7	24	1.0	Ag	0.6	3.5	0.5	6
E_7	"	1.20	"	"	450	0.7	20	0.5	Ag	0.6	3.0	0.5	5.5
E_8	"	1.20	"	"	150	0.3	26	1.0	Ag	0.6	5.0	0.7	4.75
E_9	"	1.20	"	"	901	1.0	15	0.5	Ag + F	0.7	2.0	0.3	5.7
F_1	Phyllite-schist, quartzite	1.20	"	"	300	0.5	4	0	Ag	0.6	1.5	0.3	4.6
F_2	"	1.20	"	"	601	1.0	26	1.0	Ag + F	0.7	7.0	0.8	6.7
F_3	"	1.20	"	"	300	0.5	26	1.0	Ag	0.6	5.0	0.7	6
F_4	"	1.20	"	"	<100	0.1	17	0.5	Ag + F	0.7	5.0	0.7	5.2
F_5	"	1.20	"	"	751	1.0	15	0.5	Ag	0.6	5.0	0.7	6
F_6	Phyllite schist, Quartzite, gneiss	1.15	Lineament	1.65	450	0.7	15	0.5	Ag	0.6	6.0	0.7	5.3
F_7	"	1.15	"	"	450	0.7	19	0.5	Ag	0.6	6.5	0.8	5.4
F_8	"	1.15	"	"	300	0.5	28	1	Ag + F	0.7	5.0	0.7	5.7
F_9	"	1.15	"	"	300	0.5	20	0.5	Ag + F	0.7	3.5	0.5	5
F_{10}	"	1.15	"	"	150	0.3	8	0	Ag + F	0.7	0.5	0.3	4.1
G_2	"	1.15	"	"	450	0.7	4	0	Ag + F	0.7	1.0	0.3	4.5

Grid No.	Lithology	Rating	Structure	Rating	Relative Relief	Rating	Slope in degree	Rating	Landuse	Rating	Drainage Density	Rating	Total rating (L.S.V.)
G_3	"	1.15	"	"	601	1.0	17	0.5	F	0.8	4.0	0.5	5.6
G_4	"	1.15	"	"	300	0.5	26	1.0	Ag + F	0.7	3.0	0.5	5.5
G_5	"	1.15	"	"	<100	0.1	28	1.0	Ag	0.6	3.0	0.5	5
G_6	"	1.15	"	"	<100	0.1	17	0.5	Ag	0.6	5.0	0.7	4.7
G_7	Gneiss	0.5	"	"	601	1.0	19	0.5	Ag + F	0.7	3.5	0.5	4.85
G_8	"	0.5	"	"	450	0.7	20	0.5	Ag + F	0.7	4.0	0.5	4.55
G_9	"	0.5	"	"	601	1.0	22	1.0	Ag + F	0.7	5.5	0.7	5.55
G_{10}	Phyllite-schist, quartzite	1.20	Lineament	1.65	450	0.7	20	0.5	Ag + F	0.7	6.0	0.7	5.45
H_3	"	1.20	"	"	450	0.7	6	0	F	0.8	1.5	0.3	4.65
H_4	"	1.20	"	"	601	1.0	8	0	Ag + F	0.7	1.0	0.3	4.85
H_5	"	1.20	"	"	450	0.7	22	1	Ag + F	0.7	3.0	0.5	5.75
H_6	Phyllite-schist, quarzite, gneiss	1.15	"	"	601	1.0	26	1	Ag + F	0.7	4.0	0.5	6
H_7	Gneiss	0.5	"	"	450	0.7	20	0.5	Ag	0.6	4.0	0.5	4.45
H_8	"	0.5	"	"	601	1.0	17	0.5	Ag + F	0.7	3.5	0.5	4.85
H_9	Phyllite schist, quartzite, gneiss	1.15	"	"	<100	0.1	24	1	Ag	0.6	4.0	0.5	5
H_{10}	"	1.15	"	"	150	0.3	20	0.5	Ag	0.6	6.0	0.7	3.25
H_{11}	"	1.15	"	"	450	0.7	13	0.5	Ag + F	0.7	2.0	0.3	5
I_5	Phyllite schist, quartzite	1.20	"	"	450	0.7	4	0	F	0.8	0.5	0.3	4.65
I_6	"	1.20	"	"	450	0.7	6	0	Ag + F	0.7	2.0	0.3	4.55
I_7	Gneiss	0.5	"	"	751	1.0	14	0.5	Ag + F	0.7	2.0	0.3	4.65
I_8	"	0.5	"	"	450	0.7	13	0.5	F	0.8	4.0	0.5	4.65
I_9	"	0.5	"	"	601	1.0	20	0.5	Ag + F	0.7	3.0	0.5	4.85
I_{10}	"	0.5	"	"	300	0.5	13	0.5	Ag + F	0.7	4.0	0.5	4.35
I_{11}	"	0.5	"	"	<100	0.1	11	0.5	F	0.8	3.0	0.5	4.05

Grid No.	Lithology	Rating	Structure	Rating	Relative Relief	Rating	Slope in degree	Rating	Landuse	Rating	Drainage Density	Rating	Total rating (L.S.V.)
J_8	"	0.5	"	"	<100	0.1	4	0	Ag + F	0.7	0.25	0.5	3.95
J_9	"	0.5	"	"	601	1.0	17	0.5	Ag + F	0.7	5.0	0.7	5.05
J_{10}	"	0.5	"	"	450	0.7	11	0.5	Ag + F	0.7	2.5	0.5	4.55
K_9	"	0.5	"	"	601	1.0	13	0.5	Ag + F	0.7	3.0	0.5	4.85
K_{10}	"	0.5	"	"	450	0.7	8	0	Ag + F	0.7	4.0	0.5	4.55
L_9	"	0.5	"	"	150	0.3	8	0	Ag + F	0.7	6.5	0.3	3.45
L_{10}	"	0.5	"	"	150	0.3	11	0.5	Ag + F	0.7	7.0	0.8	4.45
L_{11}	"	0.5	"	"	751	1.0	–	–	F	0.8	2.5	0.5	4.45
M_{10}	"	0.5	"	"	300	0.5	–	–	F	0.8	2.5	0.5	3.95
M_{11}	"	0.5	"	"	150	0.3	–	–	F	0.8	2.0	0.3	3.55

Ag = Agricultural land, F = Forest ; B = Barren waste land

Interpretation :

On the basis of the L.S.V. values obtained from lithology, structure, relative relief, drainage density, slope, landuse characteristics, a landslide hazard zonation map has been prepared. This map shows the L.S.V. values to be varying from 3.25 – 7.05. Within this range, 5 zones of landslide susceptibility have been identified.

(i) very low ; 3.0 – 4.0

(ii) low : 4.0 – 5.0

(iii) moderate : 5.0 – 6.0

(iv) high : 6.0 – 7.0

(v) very high : >7.0

If we superimpose the maps of litholief, realogy, drainage and landuse, it reveals that areas under the Daling group belonging to the Gorubathan and Rayeng formation with steep precipitous slopes and high drainage density as well as spread cultivated lands have shown maximum susceptibility to landslides. On the other hand, the confluence point of the Rilli Khola with the Tista river and the upstream areas have low values, because these two areas of the basin have steeper slopes, higher relative relief and forest cover which do not allow agriculture and the lands show low L.S.V. values.

CONTOUR CONFIGURATION of

Rilli Khola Drainage Basin

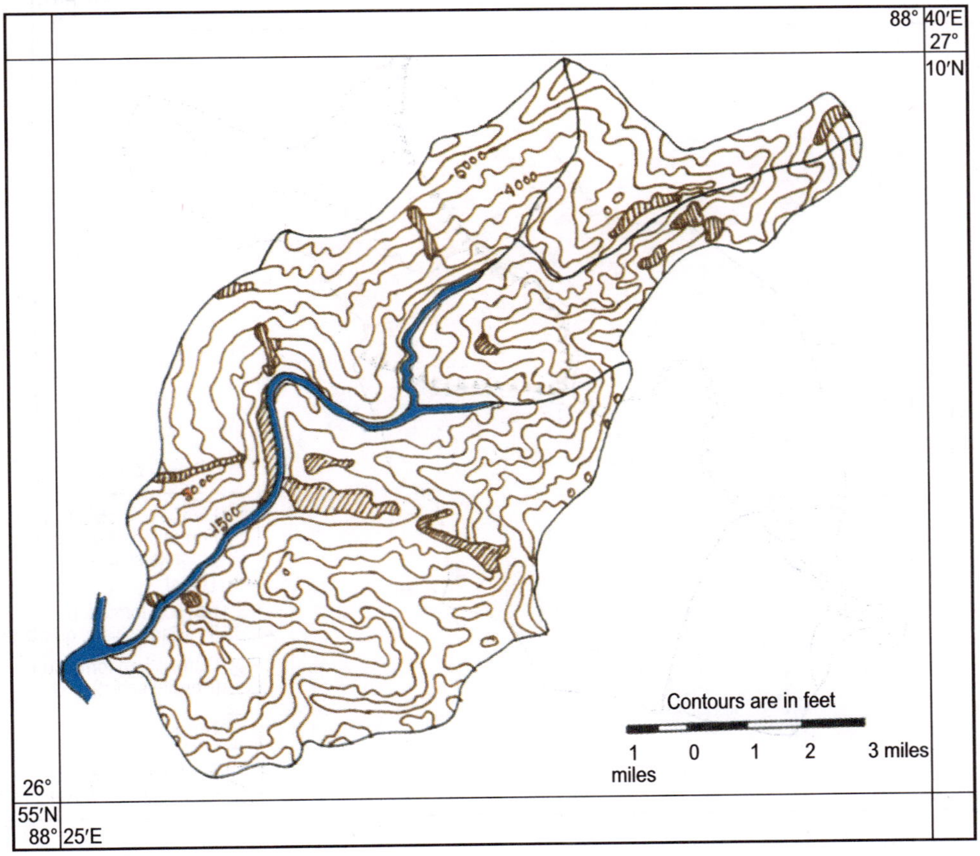

SURFACE GEOLOGY of

Rilli Khola Drainage Basin

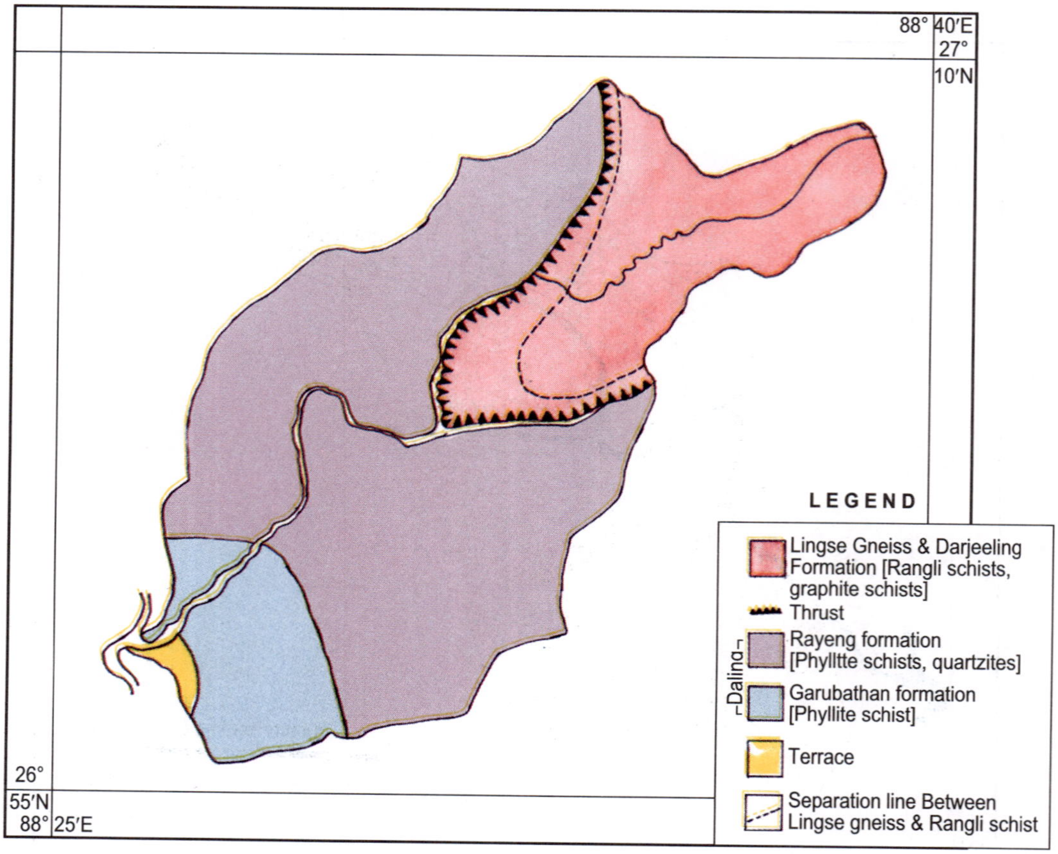

STREAM NETWORK of
Rilli Khola Drainage Brain

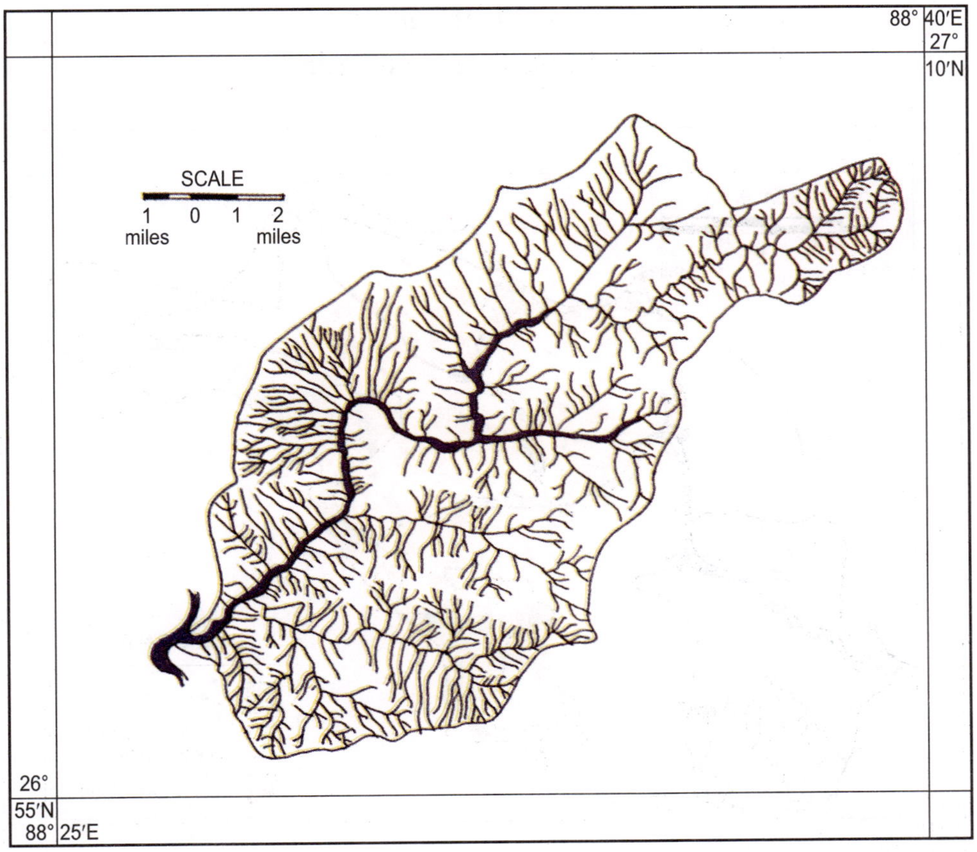

LANDUSE of
Rilli Khola Drainage Basin

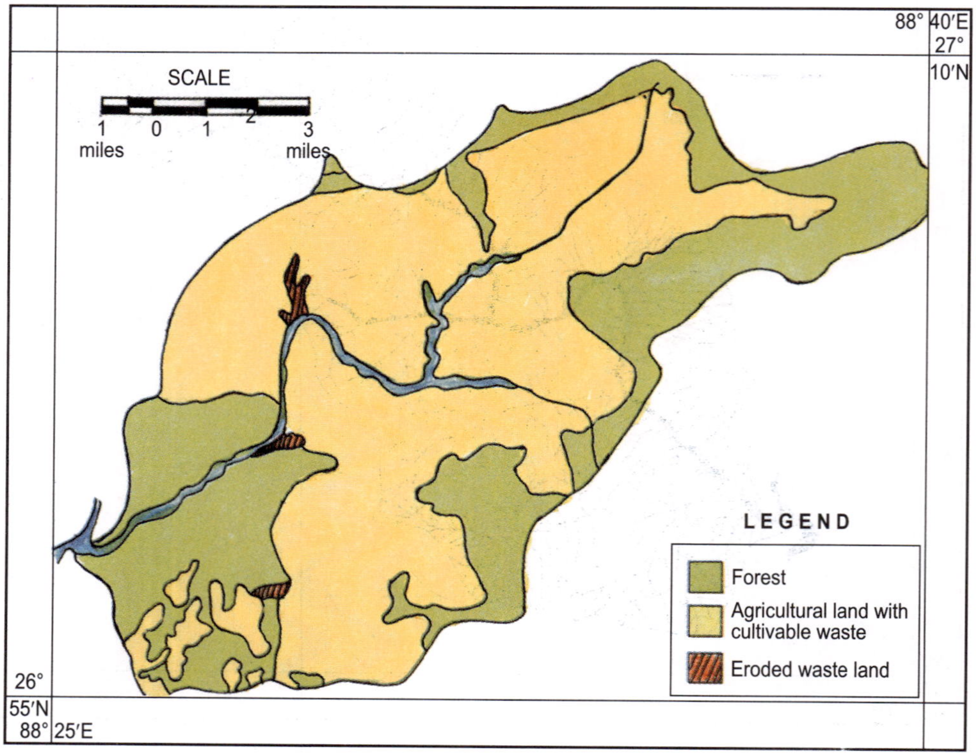

LANDSLIDE HAZARD ZONES of
Rilli Khola Drainage Basin

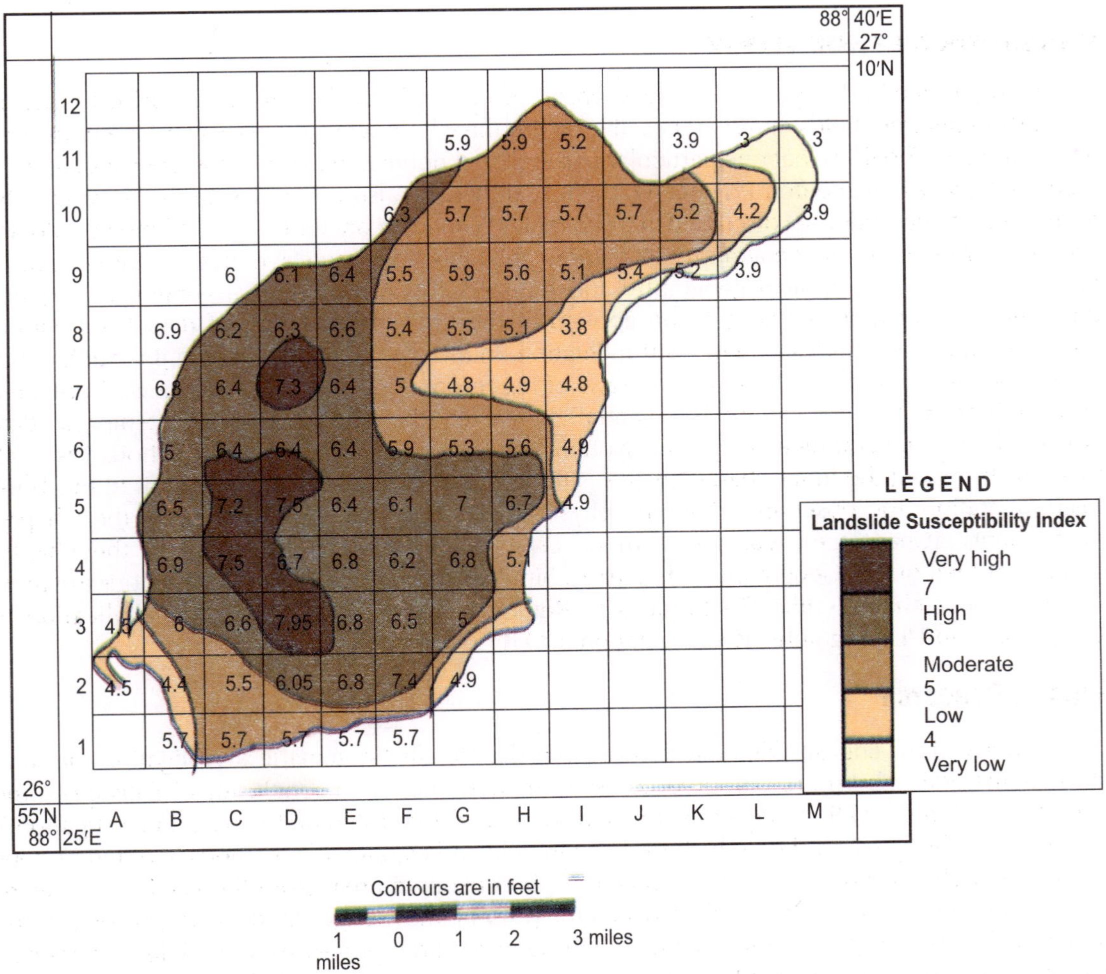

CHAPTER 11

RESEARCH METHODOLOGY

RESEARCH METHODOLOGY

Research Methodology is a comprehensive phrase which encompasses various types of methods in different fields of researches. It includes the whole set of processes and methods used in research. It is obvious that one particular research will not match another and consequently the methodology will also differ. Practically, the researches are also of various kinds. However, the term research methodology discussed in this chapter is mainly concerned with the methodologies useful for researches in geography. We know that there are two avenues of knowledge in geography, namely, physical geography and human geography. Physical geography requires different types of field methods to be applied at the time of collection of data from natural environment. This requires a lot of instrumentation. In the case of human geography, such things are not necessary. Rather taking of interviews of the respondents on the basis of a well-prepared and well-thought questionnaire is essential. However, the huge spatial and temporal data collected in a geographical research is often analysed through statistical methods, as such methods bring out the inner characteristics, similarities and differences of the data. In this book instrumentation for observing different physical elements has been given in the chapter 'Instruments' (Chapter 6). Various methods of statistical analysis are given in the chapter 'Statistical Methods in Geography' (Chapter 7). Similarly, some other required methods are there in some other chapters like 'Techniques in Remote Sensing', and 'Computer Application in Geography' and 'Cartographic Representation of Data'.

What is Research

As per Oxford English Dictionary, 'Research denotes the systematic investigation into and study of materials and sources in order to establish facts and reach conclusions.' Thus it is some sort of logical investigation into any field the researcher is interested in. By logical investigaiton it is meant that the research should be based on tangible and explainable methods in different steps of the research carried out. It takes a person to the unknown areas from the known. The word known here indicates the premises on which the present knowledge stands, and unknown is the area which is obtained as a new knowledge through research processes and related inferences. However, a research is supposed to make an original contribution to the field of knowledge which it belongs to.

Approaches to Research

A research may be **subjective** or **objective**. When the basic problem and content of research are based on some behaviours, opinions, feelings or perception of the concerned person or persons ,it requires a subjective approach where everything is not understood on the basis of some specific data, but is understood through some pattern of behaviour or response. However,a subjective approach is also sometimes substantiated through some objective observation,or data describing facts. On the otherhand, an objective approach is not influenced by personal feelings or opinions in the consideration of facts and it is substantiated by tangible data which may be qualitative or quantitative. However, a geographical research being empirical often passes through an objective approach.

Two other approaches are **simulation** approach and **experimental** approach, the former is carried out through an artificial environment to include the elements of research and to study their interactions and behaviours, whereas the latter indicates a controlled research environment to make the observations. Sometimes, in the field of geomorphology, researches are done through a natural environment on a small or local scale in order to understand some natural interactions on a much larger scale. For a research in human geography, some numerical models can help to understand the interactions and behaviours of the elements of research. For instance, the indices determined in different researches of social and economic geography can help to carry out a research in the relevant fields.

Types of Research

Researches are of various types. For almost all the geographical researches, a dual approach is observed and this favours the mode of classification of researches. On such terms, the following types of researches are observed :

1. Qualitative or Quantitative;
2. Descriptive or Analytical;
3. Fundamental or Applied;
4. Empirical or Conceptual;
5. One time Research or Longitudinal Research;
6. Historical or Contemporary;
7. Conclusive or Decisive.

Qualitative or Quantitative

A qualitative research is mainly related to the difference of quality among the elements of research. It can also be applied to the perception of the respondents or behaviour of them. It depends on the particular character of the phenomenon on which the research is done. In geographical researches, the qualitative approach is sometimes necessary as all the phenomena related to human geography are not quantifiable.

On the other hand, a quantitative research specifically indicates the analysis and inferences of the research on the basis of quantified data. In geographical researchers, this method is very relevant as geographical data is often obtained as measured values of quantity.

Descriptive or Analytical

In earlier days, geographical researches were of descriptive nature. It could only describe the state of affair of different research elements in terms of their variety.Thus an introspection is made through the qualitative differences and changes.

In an anlytical research, the analysis is done by the researcher on the basis of the available information or data. In this case, the researcher analyses the causes of differences.

Fundamental or Applied

Basically, researches are done to solve certain problems faced by the researcher or by the subject as a whole. Sometimes some researches try to generalize some specific areas of a subject for its development and for crossing the borders of limitation of the subject to open new areas of growth. These researches are fundamental in nature. For instance, when R.E. Horton introduced the concept of morphometry and two laws of drainage composition , it was a fundamental research which opened new areas of understanding in fluvial geomorphology.

On the other hand, when some practical problems require a solution and a research is done to solve the problem as well as to enhance the scope of application of the subject, it is an applied research. For instance, vanishing of water from water reservoirs (ponds) led to the investigation by geologists and geomorphologists in Bloomington', Indiana and finally the lithologic characteristics of karst landscape of the area was held responsible for the creation of the problem. Geologists recommended the shift of the reservoir to siltstone areas as the rock is relatively impervious. Initially, the suggestion was ignored, but ultimately the persistence of the problem led to the acceptance of geologial investigation and the reservoirs were shifted (Thornbury, 1954).

Empirical or Conceptual

An empirical research is related to the real data and experience. Sometimes, experiments are done to conduct the research and the observations maintained lead to the set of data evolved from the experiments. In some other occasions, as in the case of researches on hydraulics, real field data help to develop the knowledge of the researcher through its analysis. Climatologial researches are usually carried out on the basis of real observations.

Conceptual research builds theories on the basis of philosophy or hypothesis. Although it uses real database, its ultimate goal is to find out some new conceptual areas for further interpretation of the already available concepts.

One Time Research or Longitudinal Research

One time research is related to the research which uses a limited time frame. For instance, the research on the reigning period of Mughal emperor Aurangazeb is an one time research.

On the otherhand, when several time periods are involved in the research, it is longitudinal, as the research is continued over the time. For example, the study of changing demographic characteristics of India from colonial period to the post-colonial and to the present may be a longitudinal research which may be further carried on to the future time.

Historical or Contemporary

A historical research uses historical data sources and the characteristics of the subject during the period. It may reveal the nature of the subject or people associated with it during the historical point of time. The remains of the Harappa reveals the engineering capability of the people of that time in terms of the drainage system, construction of buildings, procurement of ground water.

On the other hand, contemporary research solely depends on contemporary data and much explorations are done to obtain concepts and observations into the contemporary features.

Conclusive or Decisive

A conclusive research is a terminal point to reach a conclusion about a problem within a time frame.

On the otherhand, a decisive research is partly dependent on the decision makers who control the area of research involved. In this research, the resercher cannot fix the ultimate finding as the decision makers may change partly from the premises they accepted previously. For instance, the producer is supposed to maximize his profit or production. The researcher may find out how much yield will occur on the basis of certain level of inputs into certain quality of land, but the farmers themselves may decide otherwise, and may produce less than the maximum possible.

The types of research categorized in the previous discussion is a primary consideration for the researcher. Whether it will be a purely quantitative assessment or according to the research methodology formulated by the researcher, it will be qualitative should be determined by the researcher at the initial stage. Of course the nature of the problem and the elements of the problem will decide the particular type of research to be applied.

Defining a Research Problem

A research problem is a real problem in the mind of the researcher. Sometimes it is a tangible problem for a society or a few individuals and the researcher tries to find out a solution on the basis of his recommendations. But it is not always so. The problem may lie in the gamut of a discipline where further development of knowledge is required to enhance the acceptability of a particular subject, or it may be an unexplored area where the research will be carried out. The research may be a pioneer one to initiate further discussion and growth of an area where many useful works may be accomplished.

However, a research problem should evolve in the mind of the researcher either through experience or through discussion with people, may be the commoners or the experts. It may come out at the spark of a moment, but that does not identify it fully. The researcher involved having the spark of an atom of thought should try to contemplate on it to understand the shape, and body of the problem. For this purpose, the researcher may require to go through published literature concerning the area of the problem. The researcher may discuss it with experts in the related field or if such experts are not available, he or she may even discuss it with knowledgable friends and colleagues. Moreover, the feasibility of the research should also be judged. If it is out of the means of the researcher, the selection of the problem is useless. Institutional researchers may discuss the problem in their mind with respective guide.

Inspite of all such efforts, a problem, may not really come to the surface wholly, only a part of it may be revealed at the initial stage. Thus the direction of research may be slightly modified when the entire nature of the selected problem is understood.

On the basis of the selected problem designing of the research should be done. Different types of researches may have different designs, but it depends on the problem and the researcher.

While selecting the problem, the researcher may avoid the areas which have been already explored exhaustively. Rather a less explored area for selection of problem should be considered. This will increase the importance of the research to the users. Moreover, at the time of selection of the problem, the objective of the research should be clear before the vision of the researcher. No research can be carried out without having some specific objectives.

Framing the methodology of research

Research methodology involves the total planning of the research, i.e. how is the research to be carried out scientifically, following one step after another. It reveals the entire set of logic which should be followed in the respective research. It involves the methods or techniques of research as well as the logic behind the use of particular methods for a research. It should also compare the relative suitability of the methods to be followed with alternative set of methods. In this comparison the logic behind the following of a particular methodology will be cleared. Thus methodology itself acts as a science of the steps of research, methods of research, and their scope of applicability.

In research methodology, the researcher elaborates how far the results of the research will be an acceptable product for the society or interest group. As the method to be used are scientific and already accepted in most of the cases, the result is also a scientifically reached conclusion.

In general, methodology refers to the entire course of the research with specific and brief explanations of the steps of the research and their logical suitability.

Research ethics

Research is such a work as requires some principles to follow. Apart from following the methodology of research some awareness about its ethics is also required. A research is a fundamental discovery or invention or critical appreciation which becomes the property of the society after it is complete, be it published or unpublished. The genuineness of a research work should be unquestionable. People of the society benefited from the research believe in its findings and there lies the responsibility of the researcher to maintain the ethics of research, so that the users or the beneficiaries should not be deceived in any way. Hence some ethical principles are necessary for the researcher to follow. In a general way, these may be the following, though one may suggest a few more which may also be essential.

1. **Honesty** : The first and foremost principle should be the honesty of the researcher in all scientific communications. The data a researcher uses, the methods and working procedures a researcher applies should be truly honest. He or she should never fabricate, falsify or misrepresent any of those, so that after the completion of the research when it is open to the people of the society, they can refer to the primary or secondary data which has been incorporated in the research work; the methods used in the research can be blindly followed by the successors. Moreover, when a research involves more than one person, the main researcher should not deceive his or her colleagues and should give them proper importance at the time of publication or public address. Sometimes a research involves some sponsorship. The sponsoring authority should be acknowledged and the benefit of the research should reach them earlier than others. Finally, all documentations will be presented in tangible terms.

2. **Objectivity** : A research is not supposed to be done without any specific purpose. Without any idea about the use of the result, the research becomes futile because of the lack of objectivity. Practically, objectivity of research determines the direction toward which the research should be carried out. A bias of the research may affect the process and working of it. Care should be taken to avoid such personal bias, so that the objectivity of the research can be maintained. The experimental design making and to maneuver the data design as well as data interpretation and taking of biased decisions should be avoided, so that the research follows its own way towards the objective for which the research was initiated. The real picture should come out without any manipulation. Sometimes financial interest may affect the research work. If anything of this type appears, the researcher should disclose the problem.

3. **Carefulness** : The researcher should be careful to avoid any unintentional and careless errors. No negligence is acceptable at the time of research. The researcher should be critical about his or her work as well as the work of the peers. At different stages of research, the data as well as its interpretation should be examined repeatedly so that no careless mistake is overlooked. Proper recording of the activities related to the research should be maintained for any future reference. Particular care should be given at the time of data collection because that is the basic material on which the research will be done. Towards the designing of the research work, accepted designs and models should be consulted with proper understanding. Correspondences can be made with relevant authorities, agencies and journals.

4. **Integrity** : The integrity of the researcher is a very important aspect of research, as consistency of thought and action are essential for research. Researcher might have entered into an agreement at the beginning of the research work and perhaps some promises were made. The researcher should not deviate from such agreements and promises.

5. **Respect for intellectual property** : In the course of a research work, various types of materials and literatures may be used by the researcher. The researcher should respect such intellectual properties which are marked by patent, copyrights etc. No unpublished data, methods or results can be used without author's permission. Moreover, acknowledgement of credit for all contributions of others should be properly given. Any sort of plagiarism is not acceptable in a research.

6. **Openness of research** : After the research is completed and the researcher is conferred the degree, or research-agreement is fulfilled to the full content of the authority concerned, data, results, tools and other resources can be shared with others. Moreover, a research work may face criticisms and new ideas may float beyond the scope of the present research already done. The researcher should be open to such events.

7. **Confidentiality** : The communications done at the time of research, paper submitted for publication, data and actual method of research, grants provided for the research, records of the personnel should be kept confidential during the course of research. Sometimes some trade or military secret may be involved in a research work. That should also be kept confidential. Lack of confidentiality may hinder the accomplishment of the research because the academic environment and the world related to the research may not be favourable always.

8. **Social responsibility :** A research is supposed to be related to the social good and any detrimental effect to the society should be avoided. The data or the result should not bring about any social harm; rather they should prevent or mitigate the particular social harm relevant to the research work. Advocacy and recommendations should always be directed towards the promotion of social prosperity.

9. **Competence :** The researcher should have professional competence and expertise through continuous learning and keenness toward educational process. Initially, the researcher may not possess such qualities but improvement at a personal level is earnestly required. Moreover, sometimes the research may be interdisciplinary. In such cases, the researcher should acquire the required knowledge of other disciplines relevant to the research. In fact, the researcher should have a squared knowledge, otherwise some lacuna in the research may be overlooked and the result may be erroneous.

10. **Non-discrimination :** The researcher should not discriminate on the basis of sex, race, ethnicity or some other factors like caste etc. among his or her colleagues or students. The integrity of the researcher and his or her attitude may favour the progress of research and any sort of discrimination may invite social problems and unwanted hindrances.

11. **Animal care :** Actually at the time of a research involving animals some experiments and research methods may require the use of animals, but any sort of unnecessary and poorly designed animal experiments must be avoided, so that useless loss of animals can be avoided.

12. **Protection of human subjects :** If a research is conducted on human subjects, harms and risks should be minimized and maximum benefit is to be made. In such researches, the researcher should respect human dignity, privacy and autonomy. Special precautions should be taken with vulnerable populations and the benefit of research should always be directed towards the good of human society and in any case, human subjects will not be misguided.

Apart from these ethical principles some other psychological and scientific principles may be observed by some researchers. Truly speaking, the principle to be followed as the ethics of a particular research should be determined by the researcher as well as the supervisor.

Review of Previous Works in the Related Field :

The researcher should know that some other workers in the same or associated field might have done different levels of work that had been published earlier. So, the researcher should explore those published literature relevant to the research. May be the particular case study what the researcher is working on has not been explored by any of the previous workers, but definitely there may be some published literature on the related field with some other case studies. Even if it is not a case study , the premises on which the research stands should be checked thoroughly and what are the previous findings in this regard, how far they are suitable for the research undertaken, how far the observations done by the researcher are matching a previous worker's observation, what are the lacunas of the previous works which the present research tries to fulfil, what are the new areas the present research is following as were absent in the research on the related field should all be considered in this literature review section. The reference of the previous works should be clearly mentioned in this part along with the year of publication. Sometimes, some unpublished research works and reports are also referred in a particular research. In that case also it should be mentioned properly in the literature review, so that it can be checked by someone who is willing to go through the present research.

Selection of Particular Methods

The methods or technics to be followed in a research depend largely on the subject of research and its specific requirements. Methods may be classified into field method and laboratory method. Field method is related to the quest of the researcher in actual field area. Data is generated in the field. For instance, a fluvio-geomorphological research in connection with hydraulic characteristics of a stream or river may use certain instruments to generate data on velocity, depth, width, cross-seectional area, longitudinal and transverse profiles of the channel, erosional features, depositional features and their dimensions, sediment load of the channel etc. On the other hand, a socio-economic study on a locality may require questioning the respondents on the basis of a well-prepared questionnaire. However, in both the cases sampling may be required as the entire universe of data can not be acquired because of its volume and time required for collection. That is why sampling is done with proper selection of site, selection of respondents from the locality under study, and in the case of perception research, the particular group of people vulnerable to a particlar hazard may be interviewed. Sometimes, emails, telephone, secondary source from site office may also be used for getting the data.

In the case of laboratory methods, standard technics will be applied to get the data from samples. Suppose, if composition of sediment samples is to be known, mechanical analysis through some standard methods can be done. In that case, pipetting of suspended materials may be required.

In some cases dry sieving is also useful. However , the laboratory should be well equipped for the application of necessary chemical and physical methods. If any chemical test is involved, the reagents to be applied should be in proper condition, otherwise, the result may be wrong.

Importance of Statistical Analysis

As geographical data may be huge in number, it often requires analysis by satistical methods. Which method is to be followed will depend on the intention of the researcher and purpose of research. Statistical probability can be obtained through many methods, such as chi-squared test, t-test, F-test etc. Of them, which one should be followed will depend on the nature of the data and the purpose of research. However, in all cases the nature of data, its variability, its range, its discreteness or continuity should be examined first. Then a particular method will be selected. In the case of multivariate analysis, whether the principal components are to be known or the relative importance of the factors is to be determined should be understood. Then the researcher will apply PCA or Factor analysis by Centroid method or any other multivariate analysis.

A research may start with a hypothesis according to the preliminary understanding of the researcher or a general notion. At the end of the research, this hypothesis is tested, as we have already mentioned some technics of the test of significance. However, in hypothesis testing it should be determined first whether it is a parametric test or a non-parametric test which depends on the properties of the primary population from which samples are taken. If the population data is normally distributed, the observations are independent of each other, populations being compared are having same variance, and variables are obtained on interval or ratio scale, parametric tests like Student's 't' Test, Snedecor's F Test, Dispersion diagram can be carried out. On the other hand, if there is some sort of underlying continuity of the data and the data is obtained on the ordinal scale or even on the nominal scale, non-parametric tests can be used.

Interval or ratio data may also give good results through non-parametric tests. Chi-squared Test, kolmogorov-Smirnov Test, Fisher's Exact Probability Test, Mann-Whitney U Test, One-Sample Runs Test are various non-parametric tests.

The researcher at the time of hypothesis testing begins with null hypothesis which considers that there is no real difference between two sets of data being compared. Null hypothesis is written as H_0.

If through statistical testing, the researcher reaches a conclusion that there is a real diffeence between the sets of data, the null hypothesis should be rejected and inverse of null hypothesis or alternative hypothesis should be accepted. This hypothesis is written as H_1.

However, in such testing, the degrees of freedom is to be considered depending on the test. This degree of freedom actually means the number of values which can be assigned arbitrarily. In a graph, representing the obtained data, it may have pre-determined critical limits. This limit will depend on the value of acceptance or rejection. Usually this limit is 5%, i.e., if the significance level occurs at 5%, H_0 will be rejected and H_1 accepted. In this case, the researcher takes 5% risk of error in rejecting the null hypothesis. This is known as Type I error (or α). All tests of significance have their critical limits specified as Type I error. When the researcher accepts the null hypothesis, still there is a chance of making an error. This error is referred to as Type II error (or β). Suppose, if the value comes in the acceptance zone but very close to the critical line, it cannot be interpreted as the existence of no difference. However, the method applied could not prove that there is difference. Hence, there is a chance of mistake. An anology may be drawn as 'not proven' (Gregory, 1980).

There is an opposite relation between Type I and Type II error, i.e. if the probability of Type I error is reduced, the chance of the occurrence of Type II error increases. A simultaneous reduction of these two errors is not possible. β will decrease as the size of sample increases. What will be the critical value for rejection of the null hypothesis will depend upon the aim of the researcher. If α is considered at 0.01 or 0.001 level, it may be more reliable. If the purpose is to find out as many as differences may occur, α can be fixed at a higher value i.e. 0.05 level.

Footnotes, Abbreviation and Punctuations Used in Writing a Report

While writing a report, sometimes footnotes may be required to indicate a particular reference necessary about the author or about a reference which is essential for the reader to know just at the moment. It may be related to the reader's consultation with another chapter in connection with the part given in the page. A particular word which is rarely used with reference to a particular proper noun given in the page may be indicated in the footnote. Sometimes, the meaning of a word may be necessary for the reader because the word is of antique origin. More than one footnote may be given in some cases where a superscript or subscript of the serial number should be given in the text as well as in the corresponding footnote. If some uncommon units of measurement are given in the text, it should be clarified in terms of common units which is to be included in the appendix. The reference of the particular appendix may be given in the footnote. The font size in the footnote should be very small, preferably in bourgeois.

To avoid repetition of some common words in the text as well as in the bibliography some abbreviations are used. These abbreviations originate mostly from Latin words and certain punctuations are used along with them. Usually, a fullstop is followed by a comma after the use of the abbreviation. Some common abbreviations are given in the following table.

Abbreviation	Origin	Translation in English
ante.,	ante	before
art.,	articulus	piece of writing
bk.,	book	book
bull.,	bullettino	bulletin (summary of news)
cf.,	comparare	compare
ch.,	chapitre	chapter
cap.,	capitulum	chapter
col.,	columna	column
cp.,	ceteris paribus	all other things being equal
diss.,	dissertatio	dissertation (long essay)
ed.,	editio	editor, edition, edited
ed. cit.,	editio citare	edition cited
e.g.,	exempli gratia	for example
eng.,	enlarger	enlarged
et. al.,	et alii, et alia	and others, co-workers
etc.,	et caetera	and the others
et. seq.,	et sequens	and the following
f., ff.,	folgiam	and the following
fig., fig(s).,	figura	figure(s)
fn.,	footnote	footnote
ibid.,	ibidem	in the same place
id.,	idem	the same
i.a.,	inter alia	among other things
i.e.,	id est	that is
illus., ill.,	illustrat	illustrated
intro.,	introducere	introduction
l., or ll.,	linea	line
loc. cit.,	locat, locare, lococitato	in the place cited, same page cited
M.O.	modus operandi	method of operation
MS.,	manuscriptus	manuscript
N.B.,	nota bene	note well
n.d.,	—	no date
no(s).,	numerus, nombre	numbers

Abbreviation	Origin	Translation in English
op. cit.,	opere citato	in the work cited
p.a.,	per anum	through a year
per cent.,	per centum	for each one hundred
P. or PP.	pagina	page or pages
passim.,	pass	at various places throughout the text
rev.,	reveue	review
rev.,	revisere	revised
tr., trans.,	translat	translated, translator, traslation
Q.D.,	quaque die	everyday
S.L.,	sensu lato	in the broad sense
S.S.,	sensu stricto	in the strict sense
stat.,	statim	immediately
viz.,	videlicet	namely
vol., v., vol(s)	volumen	volume (s)
vs., or v.,	versus	against
j. jour.,	jurnal	journal, magazine

Report Writing

After the analysis is done and inferences drawn, a report should be prepared as a whole. A report contains the entire course of the research right from the beginning of research to the end of it. It includes all the steps followed in the research.

Nature of report

A report may be prepared through different methods depending on the purpose of research and on its beneficiaries. A report may be technical in which a brief report is prepared on the basis of major findings only. For instance, when a geologist selects a dam site in a mountainous landscape through the examination of structure and rock strata, it may be a short report with a detailed geological map of the area of dam site. In this case, only the necessary information are given with a specific conclusion.

In a popular report, technicalities are avoided or are only given in the end part of the report in appendices. As it is meant for common and non-technical persons, the language should be very lucid, and it should include mainly the objectives of the research, the findings and possible recommendations under practical situations.

Even another type may be simply a oral presentation, where slides are prepard in Power Point and projected on screen with brief comments and elaborate oral discussions.

However, in the case of thesis writing (Ph.D.), the report is much elaborate and may follow a few specific steps. This report contains three parts :

1. Priliminary part;
2. Main text;
3. End part.

1. **Priliminary Part :** At the beginning of the report, there should be a title page where the title of the thesis will be written with proper size of lettering. This title should be exactly the same as was given at the time of registration. There will be no spelling mistakes. This title page should also contain the name of the researcher, the institution under which the research title has been registered and the date of submission of report. Then it will be followed by a preface where an overall idea of the present research and its area should be mentioned also. It may or may not be followed by a page on acknowledgement. Then the table of contents from the beginning to the end including the appendices will be given with page number. The table of content should be followed by a table for illustrations mentioning the figure number and page number. A list of tables can also be added.

2. **Main Text :** The report of the research is contained in the main text.

   It is sub-divided into three parts :

   (i) Introductory,

   (ii) Research Finding, and

   (iii) Implications and Recommendations.

   (i) *Introductory Part :* In this part, an introduction of the outline of the research is necessary. It is like an abstract in whch the summary of the research is given, so that the reader may have a brief idea about the outline of the research. The language should be very clear and unemotional, so that the reader develops his or her own impression and bias is avoided.

   The methodology of the research should be clearly given in this part. The limitations of carrying out the research can also be mentioned in this segment.

   (ii) *Research Findings* : In this section, the statement of findings should be given in a clear unambiguous language. The research findings will include analyses and their results. The logic behind the entire analysis should be clear to the reader, so that the reader does not suffer from any sort of confusion.

   (iii) *Implication and Recommendations :* The inferences drawn from the research should be given here, so that the reader may be interested towards the usefulness of the research. In fact, it is some sort of summary of the results of the research and to some extent it is a repetition of the previous section, but it is more precise.

   As the research is related to some specific natural or societal problem, it should include some recommendations towards the solution of the problem. These recommendtions are supposed to be forwarded to the appropriate authority, so that a practical solution of the problem may be sought.

3. **End Part :** In the end part of the report, appendices will be given. Appendices should contain all technical data in tabular form. All the formulae and mathematical derivations should be included in the appendices.

Bibliography should come under this part. In bibliography, all the sources of information and guidelines should be given with an alphabetical list mentioning the topic consulted, reference of the book or Journal in which it is contained, particular volume of book or journal, publisher and the place of publication, year of publication and pagination. Usually, a comma is to be put after each information of reference, but sometimes it depends on the publishing authority how the punctuations should be given in a journal. A glossary of local terminology or change of name should also be given, but in all cases glossary may not be necessary, provided no local terminology, change of name of a place are done in the research.

PLAGIARISM

In these days of widespread internet service and easy availability of information and research papers through various search engines students, professors, professionals often go through other people's works and associated write ups. Sometimes they borrow from others consciously and sometimes unconsciously without acknowledging the source. This unauthoriged pursuit of straling of ideas, thoughts, language and expressions is known as plagiarism. The term has been derived from latin *'Plagiarins'* meaning 'kidnapper', as it kidnaps the intellectuial properties another person. The concept of plagiarism at it earliest use dates back to 1601, when poet Martial reported that someone has stolen his ideas and expressions. The term was conined in English in 1604.

As research works are snappoosed to be original only, any hints of polagiarism is considered an offense. A thesis may be concelled in India with the charge of plagiarism, because in India, U.S.A, and Poland . This pursuit is unlawful. However, in all countries plagiarism is not that much offensive.

Knownledge is something which can be corrowed from others. In the the literature review of a thesis, often the concepts or ideas of previous workers are mentioned in relevance to the present research, but that, of course, acknowledges the original contributor of the ideas. This is not plagirism.

At present strict rules have been framed in India to prevent plagiarism. Many soft wares have been invented to check the percent of plagiarism in a reasearch paper. As it is customery to go through other researchers' papers before writing one's own, little bit of unconscious plagiarism often occurs. That is why diferent authorities of research organizations who publish journals are very specific about the maximum proportion of percentage of plagiarism they would allow before publishing a paper.

However, sheer plagiarism is not only offensive, but also beyond the ethries of research.

APPENDICES

I. Classification of Scales

(Serially arranged R. F. Values are given)

B (FPS)		40			M (CGS)
			20		
		xii		XII	
				2 500	1 cm = 25 m
				5 000	1 cm = 50 m
				10 000	10 cm = 1 km
6 in = 1 mi				10 560	
				20 000	5 cm = 1 km
1 in = 2 000 ft				24 000	
				25 000	4 cm = 1 km
2 in = 1 ml				31 680	
		40 000		40 000	5 cm = 2 km
		50 000		50 000	2 cm = 1 km
		62 500		62 500	8 cm = 5 km
1 in = 1 mi		63 360		63 360	
	75 000				4 cm = 3 km
	80 000				5 cm = 4 km
		100 000			1 cm = 1 km
		125 000			4 cm = 5 km
	126 000				
1 in = 2 mi		126 720			
	150 000				2 cm = 3 km
	160 000				5 cm = 8 km
1 in = 3 mi	190 080				
		200 000			1 cm = 2 km
	210 000				
		250 000			2 cm = 5 km
1 in = 4 mi		253 440			
	300 000				1 cm = 3 km
	320 000				
1 in = 6 mi	380 160				
	400 000				1 cm = 4 km
	420 000				
		500 000			1 cm = 5 km
1 in = 8 mi	506 880				
	600 000				1 cm = 6 km
	625 000				4 cm = 25 km
1 in = 10 mi	633 600				
	680 000				
	750 000				2 cm = 15 km
	800 000				1 cm = 8 km
		1 000 000			1 cm = 10 km
1 in = 16 mi	1 013 760				

II. Conversion Factors from One Scale to Another for Forty Scales

1 :	2 500	5 000	10 000	10 560	20 000	24 000	25 000	31 680	1 :
2 500	1.000	0.500	0.250	0.237	0.125	0.104	0.100	0.079	2 500
5 000	2.000	1.000	0.500	0.473	0.250	0.208	0.200	0.158	5 000
10 000	4.000	2.000	1.000	0.947	0.500	0.417	0.400	0.316	10 000
10 560	4.224	2.112	1.056	1.000	0.528	0.440	0.422	0.333	10 560
20 000	8.000	4.000	2.000	1.894	1.000	0.833	0.800	0.631	20 000
24 000	9.600	4.800	2.400	2.273	1.200	1.000	0.960	0.758	24 000
25 000	10.000	5.000	2.500	2.367	1.250	1.042	1.000	0.789	25 000
31 680	12.672	6.336	3.168	3.000	1.584	1.320	1.267	1.000	31 680
40 000	16.000	8.000	4.000	3.788	2.000	1.667	1.600	1.263	40 000
50 000	20.000	10.000	5.000	4.735	2.500	2.083	2.000	1.578	50 000
62 500	25.000	12.500	6.250	5.919	3.125	2.604	2.500	1.973	62 500
63 360	25.344	12.672	6.336	6.000	3.168	2.640	2.534	2.000	63 360
75 000	30.000	15.000	7.500	7.102	3.750	3.125	3.000	2.367	75 000
80 000	32.000	16.000	8.000	7.576	4.000	3.333	3.2000	2.525	80 000
100 000	40.000	20.000	10.000	9.470	5.000	4.167	4.000	3.157	100 000
125 000	50.000	25.000	12.500	11.837	6.250	5.208	5.000	3.946	125 000
126 000	50.400	25.200	12.600	11.932	6.300	5.250	5.040	3.977	126 000
126 720	50.688	25.344	12.672	12.000	6.336	5.280	5.069	4.000	126 720
150 000	60.000	30.000	15.000	14.205	7.500	6.250	6.000	4.735	150 000
160 000	64.000	32.000	16.000	15.152	8.000	6.667	6.400	5.051	160 000
190080	76.032	38.016	19.008	18.000	9.504	7.920	7.603	6.000	190 080
200 000	80.000	40.000	20.000	18.939	10.000	8.333	8.000	6.313	200 000
210 000	84.000	42.000	21.000	19.886	10.500	8.750	8.400	6.629	210 000
250 000	100.000	50.000	25.000	23.674	12.500	10.417	10.000	7.891	250 000
253 440	101.376	50.688	25.344	24.000	12.672	10.560	10.138	8.000	253 440
300 000	120.000	60.000	30.000	28.409	15.000	12.500	12.000	9.470	300 000
320 000	128.000	64.000	32.000	30.303	16.000	13.333	12.800	10.101	320 000
380 160	152.064	76.032	38.016	36.000	19.008	15.840	15.206	12.000	380 160
400 000	160.000	80.000	40.000	37.879	20.000	16.667	16.000	12.626	400 000
420 000	168.000	84.000	42.000	39.773	21.000	17.500	16.800	13.258	420 000
500 000	200.000	100.000	50.000	47.348	25.000	20.833	20.000	15.783	500 000
506 880	202 752	101.376	50.688	48.000	25.344	21.120	20.275	16.000	506 880
600 000	240.000	120.000	60.000	56.818	30.000	25.000	24.000	18.939	600 000
625 000	250.000	125.000	62.500	59.186	31.250	26.042	25.000	19.729	625 000
633 600	253.440	126.720	63.360	60.000	31.680	26.400	25.344	20.000	633 600
680 000	272.000	136.000	68.000	64.394	34.000	28.333	27.200	21.465	680 000
750 000	300.000	150.000	75.000	71.023	37.500	31.250	30.000	23.674	750 000
800 000	320.000	160.000	80.000	75.758	40.000	33.333	32.000	25.253	800 000
1 000 000	400.000	200.000	100.000	94.697	50.000	41.667	40.000	31.566	1 000 000
1 013 760	405.504	202.752	101.376	96.000	50,688	42.240	40.550	32.000	1 013 760

1 :	40 000	50 000	62 500	63 360	75 000	80 000	100 000	125 000	1 :
2 500	0.063	0.050	0.040	0.039	0.033	0.031	0.025	0.020	2 500
5 000	0.125	0.100	0.080	0.079	0.067	0.063	0.050	0.040	5 000
10 000	0.250	0.200	0.160	0.158	0.133	0.125	0.100	0.080	10 000
10 560	0.264	0.211	0.169	0.167	0.141	0.132	0.106	0.084	10 560
20 000	0.500	0.400	0.320	0.316	0.267	0.250	0.200	0.160	20 000
24 000	0.600	0.480	0.384	0.379	0.320	0.300	0.240	0.192	24 000
25 000	0.625	0.500	0.400	0.395	0.333	0.312	0.250	0.200	25 000
31 680	0.792	0.634	0.507	0.500	0.422	0.396	0.317	0.253	31 680
40 000	1.000	0.800	0.640	0.631	0.533	0.500	0.400	0.320	
50 000	1.250	1.000	0.800	0.789	0.667	0.625	0.500	0.400	50 000
62 500	1.563	1.250	1.000	0.986	0.833	0.781	0.625	0.500	62 500
63 360	1.584	1.267	1.014	1.000	0.845	0.792	0.634	0.507	63 360
75 000	1.875	1.500	1.200	1.184	1.000	0.938	0.750	0.600	75 000
80 000	2.000	1.600	1.280	1.263	1.067	1.000	0.800	0.640	80 000
100 000	2.500	2.000	1.600	1.578	1.333	1.250	1.000	0.800	100 000
125 000	3.125	2.500	2.000	1.973	1.667	1.563	1.250	1.000	125 000
126 000	3.150	2.520	2.016	1.989	1.680	1.575	1.260	1.008	126 000
126 720	3.168	2.534	2.028	2.000	1.690	1.584	1.267	1.014	126 720
150 000	3.750	3.000	2.400	2.367	2.000	1.875	1.500	1.200	150 000
160 000	4.000	3.200	2.560	2.525	2.133	2.000	1.600	1.280	
190 080	4.752	3.802	3.041	3.000	2.534	2.376	1.901	1.521	190 080
200 000	5.000	4.000	3.200	3.157	2.667	2.500	2.000	1.600	200 000
210 000	5.250	4.200	3.360	3.314	2.800	2.625	2.100	1.680	210 000
250 000	6.250	5.000	4.000	3.946	3.333	3.125	2.500	2.000	250 000
253 440	6.336	5.069	4.055	4.000	3.379	3.168	2.534	2.028	253.440
300 000	7.500	6.000	4.800	4.735	4.000	3.750	3.000	2.400	300 000
320 000	8.000	6.400	5.120	5.051	4.267	4.000	3.200	2.560	320 000
380 160	9.504	7.603	6.083	6.000	5.069	4.752	3.802	3.041	380 160
400 000	10.000	8.000	6.400	6.313	5.333	5.000	4.000	3.200	400 000
420 000	10.500	8.400	6.720	6.629	5.600	5.250	4.200	3.360	420 000
500 000	12.500	10.000	8.000	7.891	6.667	6.250	5.000	4.000	500 000
506 880	12.672	10.138	8.110	8.000	6.758	6.336	5.069	4.055	506 880
600 000	15.000	12.000	9.600	9.470	8.000	7.500	6.000	4.800	600 000
625 000	15.625	12.500	10.000	9.864	8.333	7.813	6.250	5.000	625 000
633 600	15.840	12.672	10.138	10.000	8.448	7.920	6.336	5.069	633.600
680 000	17.000	13.600	10.880	10.732	9.067	8.500	6.800	5.440	680 000
750 000	18.750	15.000	12.000	11.837	10.000	9.375	7.500	6.000	750 000
800 000	20.000	16.000	12.800	12.626	10.667	10.000	8.000	6.400	800 000
1 000 000	25.000	20.000	16.000	15.783	13.333	12.500	10.000	8.000	1 000 000
1 013 760	25.344	20.275	16.220	16.000	13.517	12.672	10.138	8.110	1 013 760

1 :	126 000	126 720	150 000	160 000	190 080	200 000	210 000	250 000	1 :
2 500	0.020	0.020	0.017	0.016	0.013	0.013	0.012	0.010	2 500
5 000	0.040	0.039	0.033	0.031	0.026	0.025	0.024	0.020	5 000
10 000	0.079	0.079	0.067	0.063	0.053	0.050	0.048	0.040	10 000
10 560	0.084	0.083	0.070	0.066	0.056	0.053	0.050	0.042	10 560
20 000	0.159	0.158	0.133	0.125	0.105	0.100	0.095	0.080	20 000
24 000	0.190	0.189	0.160	0.150	0.126	0.120	0.114	0.096	24 000
25 000	0.198	0.197	0.167	0.156	0.132	0.125	0.119	0.100	25 000
31 680	0.251	0.250	0.211	0.198	0.167	0.158	0.151	0.127	31 680
40 000	0.317	0.316	0.267	0.250	0.210	0.200	0.190	0.160	40 000
50 000	0.397	0.395	0.333	0.313	0.263	0.250	0.238	0.200	50 000
62 500	0.496	0.493	0.417	0.391	0.329	0.313	0.298	0.250	62 500
63 360	0.503	0.500	0.422	0.396	0.333	0.317	0.302	0.253	63 360
75 000	0.595	0.592	0.500	0.469	0.395	0.375	0.357	0.300	75 000
80 000	0.635	0.631	0.533	0.500	0.421	0.400	0.381	0.320	80 000
100 000	0.794	0.789	0.667	0.625	0.526	0.500	0.476	0.400	100 000
125 000	0.992	0.986	0.833	0.781	0.658	0.625	0.595	0.500	125 000
126 000	1.000	0.994	0.840	0.788	0.663	0.630	0.600	0.504	126 000
126 720	1.006	1.000	0.845	0.792	0.667	0.634	0.603	0.507	126 720
150 000	1.190	1.184	1.000	0.938	0.792	0.750	0.714	0.600	150 000
160 000	1.270	1.263	1.067	1.000	0.842	0.800	0.762	0.640	160 000
190 080	1.509	1.500	1.267	1.188	1.000	0.950	0.905	0.760	190 080
200 000	1.587	1.578	1.333	1.250	1.052	1.000	0.952	0.800	200 000
210 000	1.667	1.657	1.400	1.313	1.105	1.050	1.000	0.840	210 000
250 000	1.984	1.973	1.667	1.563	1.315	1.250	1.190	1.000	250 000
253 440	2.011	2.000	1.690	1.584	1.333	1.267	1.207	1.014	253 440
300 000	2.381	2.367	2.000	1.875	1.578	1.500	1.429	1.200	300 000
320 000	2.540	2.525	2.133	2.000	1.684	1.600	1.524	1.280	320 000
380 160	3.017	3.000	2.534	2.376	2.000	1.901	1.810	1.521	380 160
400 000	3.175	3.157	2.667	2.500	2.104	2.000	1.905	1.600	400 000
420 000	3.333	3.314	2.800	2.625	2.210	2.100	2.000	1.680	420 000
500 000	3.968	3.946	3.333	3.125	2.630	2.500	2.381	2.000	500 000
506 880	4.023	4.000	3.379	3.168	2.667	2.534	2.414	2.028	506 880
600 000	4.762	4.735	4.000	3.750	3.157	3.000	2.857	2.400	600 000
625 000	4.960	4.932	4.167	3.905	3.288	3.125	2.976	2.500	625 000
633 600	5.029	5.000	4.224	3.960	3.333	3.168	3.017	2.534	633.600
680 000	5.397	5.366	4.533	4.250	3.577	3.400	3.238	2.720	680 000
750 000	5.952	5.919	5.000	4.688	3.946	3.750	3.571	3.000	750 000
800 000	6.349	6.313	5.333	5.000	4.209	4.000	3.810	3.200	800 000
1 000 000	7.937	7.891	6.667	6.250	5.261	5.000	4.762	4.000	1 000 000
1 013 760	8.046	8.000	6.758	6.336	5.333	5.069	4.827	4.055	1 013 760

1 :	253 440	300 000	320 000	380 160	400 000	420 000	500 000	506 880	1 :
2 500	0.010	0.008	0.008	0.007	0.006	0.006	0.005	0.005	2 500
5 000	0.020	0.017	0.016	0.013	0.013	0.012	0.010	0.010	5 000
10 000	0.039	0.033	0.031	0.026	0.025	0.024	0.020	0.020	10 000
10 560	0.042	0.035	0.033	0.028	0.026	0.025	0.021	0.021	10 560
20 000	0.079	0.067	0.063	0.053	0.050	0.048	0.040	0.039	20 000
24 000	0.095	0.080	0.075	0.063	0.060	0.057	0.048	0.047	24 000
25 000	0.099	0.083	0.078	0.066	0.063	0.060	0.050	0.049	25 000
31 680	0.125	0.106	0.099	0.083	0.079	0.075	0.063	0.063	31 680
40 000	0.158	0.133	0.125	0.105	0.100	0.095	0.080	0.079	40 000
50 000	0.197	0.167	0.156	0.132	0.125	0.119	0.100	0.099	50 000
62 500	0.247	0.208	0.195	0.164	0.156	0.14	0.125	0.123	62 500
63 360	0.250	0.211	0.198	0.167	0.158	0.151	0.127	0.125	63 360
75 000	0.296	0.250	0.234	0.197	0.188	0.179	0.150	0.148	75 000
80 000	0.316	0.267	0.250	0.210	0.200	0.190	0.160	0.158	80 000
100 000	0.395	0.333	0.313	0.263	0.250	0.238	0.200	0.197	100 000
125 000	0.493	0.417	0.391	0.329	0.313	0.298	0.250	0.247	125 000
126 000	0.497	0.420	0.394	0.331	0.315	0.300	0.252	0.249	126 000
126 720	0.500	0.422	0.396	0.333	0.317	0.302	0.253	0.250	126 720
150 000	0.592	0.500	0.469	0.395	0.375	0.357	0.300	0.296	150 000
160 000	0.631	0.533	0.500	0.421	0.400	0.381	0.320	0.316	160 000
190 080	0.750	0.634	0.594	0.500	0.475	0.453	0.380	0.375	190 080
200 000	0.789	0.667	0.625	0.526	0.500	0.476	0.400	0.395	200 000
210 000	0.829	0.700	0.656	0.552	0.525	0.500	0.420	0.414	210 000
250 000	0.986	0.833	0.781	0.658	0.625	0.595	0.500	0.493	250 000
253 440	1.000	0.845	0.792	0.667	0.634	0.603	0.507	0.500	253 440
300 000	1.184	1.000	0.938	0.789	0.750	0.714	0.600	0.592	300 000
320 000	1.263	1.067	1.000	0.842	0.800	0.762	0.640	0.631	320 000
380 160	1.500	1.267	1.188	1.000	0.950	0.905	0.760	0.750	380 160
400 000	1.578	1.333	1.250	1.052	1.000	0.952	0.800	0.789	400 000
420 000	1.657	1.400	1.313	1.105	1.050	1.000	0.840	0.829	420 000
500 000	1.973	1.667	1.563	1.315	1.250	1.190	1.000	0.986	500 000
506 880	2.000	1.690	1.585	1.333	1.267	1.207	1.014	1.000	506 880
600 000	2.367	2.000	1.875	1.578	1.500	1.429	1.200	1.184	600 000
625 000	2.466	2.083	1.953	1.644	1.563	1.488	1.250	1.233	625 000
633 600	2.500	2.112	1.980	1.667	1.584	1.509	1.267	1.250	633 600
680 000	2.683	2.267	2.125	1.789	1.700	1.619	1.360	1.342	680 000
750 000	2.959	2.500	2.344	1.973	1.875	1.786	1.500	1.480	750 000
800 000	3.157	2.667	2.500	2.104	2.000	1.905	1.600	1.578	800 000
1 000 000	3,.946	3.333	3.125	2.630	2.500	2.381	2.000	1.973	1 000 000
1 013 760	4.000	3.379	3.168	2.667	2.534	2.414	2.028	2.000	1 013 760

1 :	600 000	625 000	633 600	680 000	750 000	800 000	1 000 000	1 013 760	1 :
2 500	0.004	0.004	0.004	0.004	0.003	0.003	0.003	0.002	2 500
5 000	0.008	0.008	0.008	0.007	0.007	0.006	0.005	0.005	5 000
10 000	0.017	0.016	0.016	0.015	0.013	0.013	0.010	0.010	10 000
10 560	0.018	0.017	0.017	0.016	0.014	0.013	0.011	0.010	10 560
20 000	0.033	0.032	0.032	0.029	0.027	0.025	0.020	0.020	20 000
24 000	0.040	0.038	0.038	0.035	0.032	0.030	0.024	0.024	24 000
25 000	0.042	0.040	0.039	0.037	0.033	0.031	0.025	0.025	25 000
31 680	0.053	0.051	0.050	0.047	0.042	0.040	0.032	0.031	31 680
40 000	0.067	0.064	0.063	0.059	0.053	0.050	0.040	0.039	40 000
50 000	0.083	0.080	0.079	0.074	0.067	0.063	0.050	0.049	50 000
62 500	0.104	0.100	0.099	0.092	0.083	0.078	0.063	0.062	62 500
63 360	0.106	0.101	0.100	0.093	0.084	0.079	0.063	0.063	63 360
75 000	0.125	0.120	0.118	0.110	0.100	0.094	0.075	0.074	75 000
80 000	0.133	0.128	0.126	0.118	0.107	0.100	0.080	0.079	80 000
100 000	0.167	0.160	0.158	0.147	0.133	0.125	0.100	0.099	100 000
125 000	0.208	0.200	0.197	0.184	0.167	0.156	0.125	0.123	125 000
126 000	0.210	0.202	0.199	0.185	0.168	0.158	0.126	0.124	126 000
126 720	0.211	0.203	0.200	0.186	0.169	0.158	0.127	0.125	126 720
150 000	0.250	0.240	0.237	0.221	0.200	0.188	0.150	0.150	150 000
160 000	0.267	0.256	0.253	0.235	0.213	0.200	0.160	0.158	160 000
190 080	0.317	0.304	0.300	0.280	0.253	0.238	0.190	0.188	190 080
200 000	0.333	0.320	0.316	0.294	0.267	0.250	0.200	0.197	200 000
210 000	0.350	0.336	0.331	0.309	0.280	0.263	0.210	0.207	210 000
250 000	0.417	0.400	0.395	0.368	0.333	0.313	0.250	0.247	250 000
253 440	0.422	0.406	0.400	0.373	0.338	0.317	0.253	0.250	253 440
300 000	0.500	0.480	0.473	0.441	0.400	0.375	0.300	0.296	300 000
320 000	0.533	0.512	0.505	0.471	0.427	0.400	0.320	0.316	320 000
380 160	0.634	0.608	0.600	0.559	0.507	0.475	0.380	0.375	380 160
400 000	0.667	0.640	0.631	0.588	0.533	0.500	0.400	0.395	400 000
420 000	0.700	0.672	0.663	0.618	0.560	0.525	0.420	0.414	420 000
500 000	0.833	0.800	0.789	0.735	0.667	0.625	0.500	0.493	500 000
506 880	0.845	0.811	0.800	0.745	0.676	0.634	0.500	0.493	506 880
600 000	1.000	0.960	0.947	0.882	0.800	0.750	0.600	0.592	600 000
625 000	1.042	1.000	0.986	0.919	0.833	0.781	0.625	0.617	625 000
633 600	1.056	1.014	1.000	0.932	0.845	0.792	0.634	0.625	633 600
680 000	1.133	1.088	1.073	1.000	0.907	0.850	0.680	0.671	680 000
750 000	1.250	1.088	1.073	1.103	1.000	0.938	0.750	0.740	750 000
800 000	1.333	1.280	1.263	1.176	1.067	1.000	0.800	0.789	800 000
1 000 000	1.667	1.600	1.578	1.471	1.333	1.250	1.000	0.986	1 000 000
1 013 760	1.690	1.622	1.600	1.491	1.352	1.267	1.014	1.000	1 013 760

III. Factors for Conversion of Areas from One Scale to Another for Forty Scales

1 :	2 500^2	5 000^2	10 000^2	10 560^2	20 000^2	24 000^2	25 000^2	31 680^2	1 :
2 500^2	1.000	0.250	0.063	0.056	0.016	0.011	0.010	0.006	2 500^2
5 000^2	4.00	1.000	0.250	0.224	0.063	0.043	0.040	0.025	5 000^2
10 000^2	16.00	4.00	1.000	0.897	0.250	0.174	0.160	0.100	10 000^2
10 560^2	17.84	4.46	1.12	1.000	0.279	0.194	0.178	0.111	10 560^2
20 000^2	64.00	16.00	4.00	3.59	1.000	0.694	0.640	0.399	20 000^2
24 000^2	92.16	23.04	5.76	5.17	1.44	1.000	0.922	0.574	24 000^2
25 000^2	100.00	25.00	6.25	5.60	1.56	1.09	1.000	0.623	25 000^2
31 680^2	160.58	40.14	10.00	9.00	2.51	1.74	1.61	1.000	31 680^2
40 000^2	256.00	64.00	16.00	14.35	4.00	2.78	2.56	1.59	40 000^2
50 000^2	400.00	100.00	25.00	22.42	6.25	4.34	4.00	2.49	50 000^2
62 500^2	625.00	156.25	39.06	35.03	9.77	6.78	6.25	3.89	62 500^2
63 360^2	642.32	160.58	40.14	36.00	10.04	6.97	6.42	4.00	63 360^2
75 000^2	900.00	225.00	56.25	50.44	14.06	9.77	9.00	5.60	75 000^2
80 000^2	1 024.00	256.00	64.00	57.39	16.00	11.11	10.24	6.38	80 000^2
100 000^2	1 600.00	400.00	100.00	89.68	25.00	17.36	16.00	9.96	100 000^2
125 000^2	2 500.00	625.00	156.25	140.12	39.06	27.13	25.00	15.57	125 000^2
126 000^2	2 540.16	635.04	158.76	142.37	39.69	27.56	25.40	15.82	126 000^2
126 720^2	2 569.27	642.32	160.58	144.00	40.14	27.88	25.69	16.00	126 720^2
150 000^2	3 600.00	900.00	225.00	201.77	56.25	39.06	36.00	22.42	150 000^2
160 000^2	4 096.00	1 024.00	256.00	229.57	64.00	44.44	40.96	25.51	160 000^2
190 080^2	5 780.87	1 445.22	361.30	324.00	90.33	62.73	57.81	36.00	190 080^2
200 000^2	6 400.00	1 600.00	400.00	358.70	100.00	69.44	64.00	39.86	200 000^2
210 000^2	7 056.00	1 764.00	441.00	395.47	110.25	76.56	70.56	43.94	210 000^2
250 000^2	10 000.00	2 500.00	625.00	560.47	156.25	108.51	100.00	62.27	250 000^2
253 440^2	10 277.09	2 569.27	642.32	576.00	160.58	111.51	102.77	64.00	253 440^2
300 000^2	14 400.00	3 600.00	900.00	807.08	225.00	156.25	144.00	89.68	300 000^2
320 000^2	16 384.00	4 096.00	1 024.00	918.27	256.00	177.78	153.84	102.03	320 000^2
380 160^2	23 123.46	5 780.87	1 445.22	1296.00	361.30	250.91	231.23	144.00	380 160^2
400 000^2	25 600.00	6.400.00	1 600.00	1 434.80	400.00	277.78	256.00	159.42	400 000^2
420 000^2	28 224.00	7 056.00	1 764.00	1 581.87	441.00	306.25	282.24	175.76	420 000^2
500 000^2	40 000.00	10 000.00	2 500.00	2 241.88	625.00	434.03	400.00	249.10	500 000^2
506 880^2	41 108.37	10 277.09	2 569.27	2 304.00	642.32	446.05	411.08	256.00	506 880^2
600 000^2	57 600.00	14 400.00	3 600.00	3 228.31	900.00	625.00	576.00	358.70	600 000^2
625 000^2	62 500.00	15 625.00	3 906.25	3 502.94	976.56	678.17	625.00	389.22	625 000^2
633 600^2	64 231.83	16 057.96	4 014.49	3 600.00	1 003.62	696.96	642.32	400.00	633 600^2
680 000^2	73 984.00	18 496.00	4 626.00	4 146.58	1 156.00	802.78	739.84	460.73	680 000^2
750 000^2	90 000.00	22 500.00	5 625.00	5 044.23	1 406.25	976. 56	900.00	560.47	750 000^2
800 000^2	102 400.00	25 600.00	6 400.00	5 739.21	1 600.00	1 111.11	1 024.00	637.69	800 000^2
1 000 000^2	160 000.00	40 000.00	10 000.00	8 967.52	2500.00	1 736.11	1 600.00	996.39	1 000 000^2
1 013 760^2	164 433.49	41 108.37	10 277.09	9 216.00	2 569.17	1 784.22	1644.33	1 024.00	1 013 760^2

1 :	$40\ 000^2$	$50\ 000^2$	$62\ 500^2$	$63\ 360^2$	$75\ 000^2$	$80\ 000^2$	$100\ 000^2$	$125\ 000^2$	1 :
$2\ 500^2$	0.004	0.003	0.002	0.002	0.001	0.001	0.001	0.0004	$2\ 500^2$
$5\ 000^2$	0.016	0.010	0.006	0.006	0.004	0.004	0.003	0.002	$5\ 000^2$
$10\ 000^2$	0.063	0.040	0.026	0.025	0.018	0.016	0.010	0.006	$10\ 000^2$
$10\ 560^2$	0.070	0.045	0.029	0.028	0.020	0.017	0.011	0.007	$10\ 560^2$
$20\ 000^2$	0.250	0.160	0.102	0.100	0.071	0.063	0.040	0.026	$20\ 000^2$
$24\ 000^2$	0.360	0.230	0.147	0.143	0.102	0.090	0.058	0.037	$24\ 000^2$
$25\ 000^2$	0.391	0.250	0.0160	0.156	0.111	0.093	0.063	0.040	$25\ 000^2$
$31\ 680^2$	0.627	0.401	0.257	0.250	0.178	0.157	0.100	0.064	$31\ 680^2$
$40\ 000^2$	1.000	0.640	0.410	0.399	0.284	0.250	0.160	0.102	$40\ 000^2$
$50\ 000^2$	1.56	1.00	0.640	0.623	0.444	0.391	0.250	0.150	$50\ 000^2$
$62\ 500^2$	2.44	1.56	1.000	0.973	0.694	0.610	0.391	0.250	$62\ 500^2$
$63\ 360^2$	2.51	1.61	1.03	1.000	0.714	0.627	0.401	0.257	$63\ 360^2$
$75\ 000^2$	3.52	2.25	1.44	1.40	1.00	0.879	0.563	0.360	$75\ 000^2$
$80\ 000^2$	4.00	2.56	1.64	1.59	1.14	1.000	0.640	0.410	$80\ 000^2$
$100\ 000^2$	6.25	4.00	2.56	2.49	1.78	1.56	1.000	0.640	$100\ 000^2$
$125\ 000^2$	9.77	6.25	4.00	3.89	2.78	2.44	1.56	1.000	$125\ 000^2$
$126\ 000^2$	9.92	6.35	4.06	3.95	2.82	2.48	1.59	1.02	$126\ 000^2$
$126\ 720^2$	10.04	6.42	4.11	4.00	2.85	2.51	1.61	1.03	$126\ 720^2$
$150\ 000^2$	14.06	9.00	5.76	5.60	4.00	3.52	2.25	1.44	$150\ 000^2$
$160\ 000^2$	16.00	10.24	6.55	6.38	4.55	4.00	2.56	1.64	$160\ 000^2$
$190\ 080^2$	22.58	14.45	9.25	9.00	6.42	5.65	3.61	2.31	$190\ 080^2$
$200\ 000^2$	25.00	16.00	10.24	9.96	7.11	6.25	4.00	2.56	$200\ 000^2$
$210\ 000^2$	27.56	17.64	11.29	10.99	7.84	6.89	4.41	2.82	$210\ 000^2$
$250\ 000^2$	39.06	25.00	16.00	15.57	11.11	9.77	6.25	4.00	$250\ 000^2$
$253\ 440^2$	40.14	25.69	16.44	16.00	11.42	10.04	6.42	4.11	$253\ 440^2$
$300\ 000^2$	56.25	36.00	23.04	22.42	16.00	14.06	9.00	5.76	$300\ 000^2$
$320\ 000^2$	64.00	40.96	26.21	25.51	18.20	16.00	10.24	6.55	$320\ 000^2$
$380\ 160^2$	90.33	57.81	37.00	36.00	25.69	22.58	14.45	9.25	$380\ 160^2$
$400\ 000^2$	100.00	64.00	40.96	39.86	28.44	25.00	16.00	10.24	$400\ 000^2$
$420\ 000^2$	110.25	70.56	45.16	43.94	31.36	27.56	17.64	11.29	$420\ 000^2$
$500\ 000^2$	156.25	100.00	64.00	62.27	41.14	39.06	25.00	16.00	$500\ 000^2$
$506\ 880^2$	160.58	102.77	65.77	64.00	45.08	40.14	25.69	16.44	$506\ 880^2$
$600\ 000^2$	225.00	144.00	92.16	89.68	64.00	56.25	36.00	23.04	$600\ 000^2$
$625\ 000^2$	244.14	156.25	100.00	97.30	69.44	61.04	39.06	25.00	$625\ 000^2$
$633\ 600^2$	250.91	160.58	102.77	100.00	71.37	62.73	40.14	25.69	633.600^2
$680\ 000^2$	289.00	184.96	118.37	115.18	82.20	72.25	46.24	29.59	$680\ 000^2$
$750\ 000^2$	351.56	225.00	144.00	140.12	100.00	87.89	56.25	36.00	$750\ 000^2$
$800\ 000^2$	400.00	256.00	163.84	159.42	113.78	100.00	64.00	40.96	$800\ 000^2$
$1\ 000\ 000^2$	625.00	400.00	256.00	249.10	177.78	156.25	100.00	64.00	$1\ 000\ 000^2$
$1\ 013\ 760^2$	642.32	411.08	263.09	256.00	182.70	160.58	102.77	65.77	$1\ 013\ 760^2$

1 :	126 000^2	126 720^2	150 000^2	160 000^2	190 080^2	200 000^2	210 000^2	250 000^2	1 :
2 500^2	0.0004	0.0004	0.000 3	0.000 2	0.000 2	0.000 2	0.000 1	0.0001	2 500^2
5 000^2	0.002	0.002	0.001	0.001	0.000 7	0.000 6	0.000 6	0.000 4	5 000^2
10 000^2	0.006	0.006	0.004	0.004	0.003	0.003	0.002	0.002	10 000^2
10 560^2	0.007	0.007	0.005	0.004	0.003	0.003	0.003	0.002	10 560^2
20 000^2	0.025	0.025	0.018	0.016	0.011	0.010	0.009	0.006	20 000^2
24 000^2	0.036	0.036	0.026	0.023	0.016	0.014	0.013	0.009	24 000^2
25 000^2	0.039	0.039	0.028	0.024	0.017	0.016	0.014	0.010	25 000^2
31 680^2	0.063	0.063	0.045	0.039	0.028	0.025	0.023	0.016	31 680^2
40 000^2	0.101	0.100	0.071	0.063	0.044	0.040	0.036	0.026	40 000^2
50 000^2	0.157	0.156	0.111	0.098	0.069	0.063	0.057	0.040	50 000^2
62 500^2	0.246	0.243	0.174	0.153	0.108	0.098	0.089	0.063	62 500^2
63 360^2	0.253	0.250	0.178	0.157	0.111	0.100	0.091	0.064	63 360^2
75 000^2	0.354	0.350	0.250	0.220	0.156	0.141	0.128	0.090	75 000^2
80 000^2	0.403	0.399	0.284	0.250	0.177	0.160	0.145	0.102	80 000^2
100 000^2	0.630	0.623	0.444	0.391	0.277	0.250	0.227	0.160	100 000^2
125 000^2	0.984	0.973	0.694	0.610	0.432	0.391	0.354	0.250	125 000^2
126 000^2	1.000	0.989	0.706	0.620	0.439	0.397	0.360	0.254	126 000^2
126 720^2	1.01	1.000	0.714	0.627	0.444	0.401	0.364	0.257	126 720^2
150 000^2	1.42	1.40	1.000	0.879	0.623	0.563	0.510	0.360	150 000^2
160 000^2	1.61	1.59	1.14	1.000	0.709	0.640	0.580	0.410	160 000^2
190 080^2	2.28	2.25	1.61	1.41	1.000	0.903	0.819	0.578	190 080^2
200 000^2	2.52	2.49	1.78	1.56	1.11	1.000	0.907	0.640	200 000^2
210 000^2	2.78	2.75	1.96	1.72	1.22	1.10	1.000	0.706	210 000^2
250 000^2	3.94	3.89	2.78	2.44	1.73	1.56	1.42	1.000	250 000^2
253 440^2	4.05	4.00	2.85	12.51	1.78	1.61	1.46	1.03	253 440^2
300 000^2	5.67	5.60	4.00	3.52	2.49	2.25	2.04	1.44	300 000^2
320 000^2	6.45	6.38	4.55	4.00	2.83	2.56	2.32	1.64	320 000^2
380 160^2	9.10	9.00	6.42	5.65	4.00	3.61	3.28	2.31	380 160^2
400 000^2	10.08	9.96	7.11	6.25	4.43	4.00	3.63	2.56	400 000^2
420 000^2	11.11	10.99	7.84	6.89	4.88	4.41	4.00	2.82	420 000^2
500 000^2	15.75	15.57	11.11	9.77	6.92	6.25	5.67	4.00	500 000^2
506 880^2	16.18	16.00	11.42	10.04	7.11	6.42	5.83	4.11	506 880^2
600 000^2	22.68	22.42	16.00	14.06	9.96	9.00	8.16	5.76	600 000^2
625 000^2	24.60	24.33	17.36	15.26	10.81	9.77	8.86	6.25	625 000^2
633 600^2	25.29	25.00	17.84	15.68	11.11	10.04	9.10	6.42	633.600^2
680 000^2	29.13	28.80	20.55	18.06	12.80	11.56	10.49	7.40	680 000^2
750 000^2	35.43	35.03	25.00	21.97	15.57	14.06	12.76	9.00	750 000^2
800 000^2	40.31	39.86	28.44	25.00	17.71	16.00	14.51	10.24	800 000^2
1 000 000^2	62.99	62.27	44.44	39.06	27.68	25.00	22.68	16.00	1 000 000^2
1 013 760^2	64.73	64.00	45.68	40.14	28.44	25.69	23.30	16.44	1 013 760^2

IV. Miles on Ground to Millimetres on Map for Twelve Major Small Scales

1 : mi	40 000	50 000	62 500	63 360	100 000	125 000	1 : mi
1	40.23	32.19	25.75	25.40	16.09	12.87	1
2	80.47	64.37	51.50	50.80	32.19	25.75	2
3	120.7	96.56	77.25	76.20	48.28	38.62	3
4	160.9	128.7	103.0	101.6	64.37	51.50	4
5	201.2	160.9	128.7	127.0	80.47	64.37	5
6	241.4	193.1	154.5	152.4	96.56	77.25	6
7	281.6	225.3	180.2	177.8	112.7	90.12	7
8	321.9	257.5	206.0	203.2	128.7	103.0	8
9	362.1	289.7	231.7	228.6	144.8	115.9	9

1 : mi	126 720	200 000	250 000	253 440	500 000	1 000 000	1 : mi
1	12.70	8.047	6.437	6.350	3.219	1.609	1
2	25.40	16.09	12.87	12.70	6.437	3.219	2
3	38.10	24.14	19.31	19.05	9.656	4.828	3
4	50.80	32.19	25.75	25.40	12.87	6.437	4
5	63.50	40.23	32.19	31.75	16.09	8.047	5
6	76.20	48.28	38.62	38.10	19.31	9.656	6
7	88.90	56.33	45.06	44.45	22.53	11.27	7
8	101.6	64.37	51.50	50.80	25.75	12.87	8
9	114.3	72.42	57.94	57.15	28.97	14.48	9

V. Miles on Ground to Inches on Map for Twelve Major Small Scales

1 : mi	40 000	50 000	62 500	63 360	100 000	125 000	1 : mi
1	1.584	1.267	1.014	1.000	0.633 6	0.506 9	1
2	3.168	2.534	2.028	2.000	1.267	1.014	2
3	4.752	3.802	3.041	3.000	1.901	1.521	3
4	6.336	5.069	4.055	4.000	2.534	2.028	4
5	7.920	6.336	5.069	5.000	3.168	2.534	5
6	9.504	7.603	6.083	6.000	3.802	3.041	6
7	11.09	8.870	7.096	7.000	4.435	3.548	7
8	12.67	10.14	8.110	8.000	5.069	4.055	8
9	14.26	11.40	9.124	9.000	5.702	4.562	9

1 : mi	126 720	200 000	250 000	253 440	500 000	1 000 000	1 : mi
1	0.500 0	0.3168	0.2534	0.2500	0.1267	0.06336	1
2	1.000	0.6336	0.5069	0.5000	0.2534	0.1267	2
3	1.500	0.9504	0.7603	0.7500	0.3802	0.1901	3
4	2.000	1.267	1.014	1.000	0.5069	0.2534	4
5	2.500	1.584	1.267	1.250	0.6336	0.3168	5
6	3.000	1.901	1.521	1.500	0.7603	0.3802	6
7	3.500	2.218	1.774	1.750	0.8870	0.4435	7
8	4.000	2.534	2.028	2.000	1.014	0.5069	8
9	4.500	2.851	2.281	2.250	1.140	0.5702	9

VI. Square Inches on Map to Hectares on Ground for Twelve Major Large Scales

1 : in²	2 500	5 000	10 000	10 560	20 000	24 000	25 000	31 680	40 000	50 000	62 500	63 360	1 : in²
1	0.403 2	1.613	6.452	7.194	25.81	37.16	40.32	64.75	103.2	161.3	252.0	259.0	1
2	0.806 4	3.226	12.90	14.39	51.61	74.32	80.64	129.5	206.5	322.6	504.0	518.0	2
3	1.210	4.839	19.35	21.58	77.42	111.5	121.0	194.2	309.7	483.9	756.0	777.0	3
4	1.613	6.452	25.81	28.78	103.2	148.6	161.3	259.0	412.9	645.2	1 008	1 036	4
5	2.016	8.064	32.26	35.97	129.0	185.8	201.6	323.7	516.1	806.4	1 260	1 295	5
6	2.419	9.677	38.71	43.17	154.8	223.0	241.9	338.5	619.4	967.7	1 512	1 554	6
7	2.823	11.29	45.16	50.36	180.6	260.1	282.3	453.2	722.6	1 129	1 764	1 813	7
8	3.226	12.90	51.61	57.56	206.5	297.3	322.6	518.0	825.8	1 290	2 016	2 072	8
9	3.629	14.52	58.06	64.75	232.3	334.5	362.9	582.7	929.0	1 452	2 268	2 331	9

VII. Square Inches on Map to Acres on Ground for Twelve Major Large Scales

1 : in²	2 500	5 000	10 000	10 560	20 000	24 000	25 000	31 680	40 000	50 000	62 500	63 360	1 : in²
1	0.996 4	3.986	15.94	17.78	63.77	91.83	99.64	160.0	255.1	398.6	622.7	640.0	1
2	1.993	7.971	31.88	35.56	127.5	183.7	199.3	320.0	510.2	797.1	1 245	1 280	2
3	2.989	11.96	47.83	53.33	191.3	275.5	298.9	480.0	765.2	1 196	1 868	1 920	3
4	3.986	15.94	63.77	71.11	255.1	367.3	398.6	640.0	1 020	1 594	2 491	2 560	4
5	4.982	19.93	79.71	88.89	318.8	459.1	498.2	800.0	1 275	1 993	3 114	3 200	5
6	5.978	23.91	95.65	106.7	382.6	551.0	597.8	960.0	1 530	2 391	3 736	3 840	6
7	6.975	27.90	111.6	124.4	446.4	642.8	697.5	1 120	1 786	2 790	4 359	4 480	7
8	7.971	31.88	127.5	142.2	510.2	734.6	797.1	1 280	2 041	3 188	4 982	5 120	8
9	8.968	35.87	143.5	160.0	573.9	826.4	896.8	1 440	2 296	3 587	5 605	5 760	9

VIII. Square Centimetres on Map to Square Kilometres on Ground for Twenty Major Scales

1 : Cm²	2 500	5 000	10 000	10 560	20 000	24 000	25 000	31 680	40 000	50 000	1 : Cm²
1	0.000 625 0	0.002 500	0.010 00	0.011 15	0.040 00	0.057 60	0.062 50	0.100 4	0.160 0	0.250 0	1
2	0.001 250	0.005 000	0.020 00	0.022 30	0.080 00	0.115 2	0.125 0	0.200 7	0.320 0	0.500 0	2
3	0.001 875	0.007 500	0.030 00	0.033 45	0.120 0	0.172 8	0.187 5	0.301 1	0.480 0	0.750 0	3
4	0.002 500	0.010 00	0.040 00	0.044 61	0.160 0	0.230 4	0.250 0	0.401 4	0.640 0	1.000	4
5	0.003 125	0.012 50	0.050 00	0.055 76	0.200 0	0.288 0	0.312 5	0.501 8	0.800 0	1.250	5
6	0.003 750	0.015 00	0.060 00	0.066 91	0.240 0	0.345 6	0.375 0	0.602 2	0.960 0	1.500	6
7	0.004 375	0.017 50	0.070 00	0.078 06	0.280 0	0.403 2	0.437 5	0.702 5	1.120	1.750	7
8	0.005 000	0.020 00	0.080 00	0.089 21	0.320 0	0.460 8	0.500 0	0.802 9	1.280	2.000	8
9	0.005 625	0.022 50	0.090 00	0.100 4	0.360 0	0.518 4	0.562 5	0.903 3	1.440	2.250	9

1 : Cm²	62 500	63 360	100 000	125 000	126 720	200 000	250 000	253 440	500 000	1 000 000	1 : Cm²
1	0.390 6	0.401 4	1.000	1.563	1.606	4.000	6.250	6.423	25.00	100.0	1
2	0.781 3	0.802 9	2.000	3.125	3.212	8.000	12.50	12.85	50.00	200.0	2
3	1.172	1.204	3.000	4.688	4.817	12.00	18.75	19.27	75.00	300.0	3
4	1.563	1.606	4.000	6.250	6.423	16.00	25.00	25.69	100.0	400.0	4
5	1.953	2.007	5.000	7.813	8.029	20.00	31.25	32.12	125.0	500.0	5
6	2.344	2.409	6.000	9.375	9.635	24.00	37.50	38.54	150.0	600.0	6
7	2.734	2.810	7.000	10.94	11.24	28.00	43.75	44.96	175.0	700.0	7
8	3.125	3.212	8.000	12.50	12.85	32.00	50.00	51.39	200.0	800.0	8
9	3.516	3.613	9.000	14.06	14.45	36.00	56.25	57.81	225.0	900.0	9

IX. Length of One Degree on Meridian in Metre as and Feet — Centred on Every Degree of Latitude

	m	ft		m	ft		m	ft
0°	110 575.4	362 780.4	30°	110 854.8	363 696.9	60°	111 417.0	365 541.3
1°	110 575.8	362 781.5	31°	110 871.9	363 753.0	61°	111 433.9	365 596.8
2°	110 576.9	362 785.1	32°	110 889.4	363 810.4	62°	111 450.5	365 651.2
3°	110 578.6	362 790.7	33°	110 907.1	363 868.4	63°	111 466.6	365 704.1
4°	110 580.9	362 798.2	34°	110 925.1	363 927.5	64°	111 482.4	365 755.9
5°	110 584.0	362 808.4	35°	110 943.3	363 987.2	65°	111 497.7	365 806.1
6°	110 587.7	362 820.5	36°	110 961.8	364 047.9	66°	111 512.6	365 855.0
7°	110 592.1	362 835.0	37°	110 980.6	364 109.6	67°	111 527.0	365 902.2
8°	110 597.1	362 851.4	38°	110 999.5	364 171.6	68°	111 541.0	365 948.2
9°	110 602.8	362 870.1	39°	111 018.6	364 234.3	69°	111 554.5	365 992.5
10°	110 609.1	362 890.7	40°	111 037.8	364 297.2	70°	111 567.4	366 034.8
11°	110 616.1	362 913.7	41°	111 057.2	364 360.9	71°	111 579.9	366 075.8
12°	110 623.7	362 938.6	42°	111 076.6	364 424.5	72°	111 591.7	366 114.5
13°	110 632.0	362 965.9	43°	111 096.1	364 488.5	73°	111 603.1	366 151.9
14°	110 640.8	362 994.8	44°	111 115.7	364 552.8	74°	111 613.8	366 187.0
15°	110 650.2	363 025.6	45°	111 135.4	364 617.5	75°	111 624.0	366 220.5
16°	110 660.3	363 058.7	46°	111 155.0	364 681.8	76°	111 633.6	366 252.0
17°	110 670.9	363 093.5	47°	111 174.6	364 746.1	77°	111 642.6	366 281.5
18°	110 682.1	363 130.2	48°	111 194.1	364 810.0	78°	111 650.9	366 308.7
19°	110 693.8	363 168.6	49°	111 213.6	364 874.0	79°	111 658.7	366 334.3
20°	110 706.1	363 209.0	50°	111 233.0	364 937.7	80°	111 665.8	366 357.6
21°	110 718.9	363 251.0	51°	111 252.3	365 001.0	81°	111 672.2	366 378.6
22°	110 732.2	363 294.6	52°	111 271.5	365 064.0	82°	111 678.0	366 397.6
23°	110 746.0	363 339.9	53°	111 290.5	365 126.3	83°	111 683.1	366 414.4
24°	110 760.2	363 386.5	54°	111 309.3	365 188.0	84°	111 687.5	366 428.8
25°	110 775.0	363 435.0	55°	111 327.9	365 249.0	86°	111 691.3	366 441.3
26°	110 790.1	363 484.6	56°	111 346.3	365 309.4	87°	111 694.4	366 451.4
27°	110 805.7	363 535.8	57°	111 364.4	365 368.8	87°	111 696.8	366 459.3
28°	110 821.7	363 588.3	58°	111 382.3	365 427.5	88°	111 698.6	366 465.2
29°	110 838.1	363 642.1	59°	111 399.8	365 484.9	89°	111 699.6	366 468.5

X. Length of One Minute on Meridian in Metres and Feet — Centred on Every Degree of Latitude

	m	ft		m	ft		m	ft
0°	1 842.9	6 046.4	30°	1 847.6	6 061.6	60°	1 857.0	6 092.4
1°	1.842.9	6 046.4	31°	1 847.9	6 062.5	61°	1 857.2	6 093.3
2°	1.842.9	6 046.4	32°	1 848.2	6 063.5	62°	1 857.5	6 094.2
3°	1 843.0	6 046.5	33°	1 848.5	6 064.5	63°	1 857.8	6 095.1
4°	1 843.0	6 046.6	34°	1 848.8	6 065.5	64°	1 858.0	6 095.9
5°	1 843.1	6 046.8	35°	1 849.1	6 066.5	65°	1 858.3	6 096.8
6°	1 843.1	6 047.0	36°	1 849.4	6 067.5	66°	1 858.5	6 097.6
7°	1 843.2	6 047.2	37°	1 849.7	6 068.5	67°	1 858.8	6 098.4
8°	1 843.3	6 047.5	38°	1 850.0	6 069.5	68°	1 859.0	6 099.1
9°	1 843.4	6 047.8	39°	1 850.3	6 070.6	69°	1 859.2	6 099.9
10°	1 843.5	6 048.2	40°	1 850.6	6 071.6	70°	1 859.5	6 100.6
11°	1 843.6	6 048.6	41°	1 851.0	6 072.7	71°	1 859.7	6 101.3
12°	1 843.7	6 049.0	42°	1 851.3	6 073.7	72°	1 859.9	6 101.9
13°	1 843.9	6 049.4	43°	1 851.6	6 074.8	73°	1 860.1	6 102.5
14°	1 844.0	6 049.9	44°	1 851.9	6 075.9	74°	1 860.2	6 103.1
15°	1 844.2	6 050.4	45°	1 852.3	6 077.0	75°	1 860.4	6 103.7
16°	1 844.3	6 051.0	46°	1 852.6	6 078.0	76°	1 860.6	6 104.2
17°	1 844.5	6 051.6	47°	1 852.9	6 079.1	77°	1 860.7	6 104.7
18°	1 844.7	6 052.2	48°	1 853.2	6 080.2	78°	1 860.8	6 105.1
19°	1 844.9	6 052.8	49°	1 853.6	6 081.2	79°	1 861.0	6 105.6
20°	1 845.1	6 053.5	50°	1 853.9	6 082.3	80°	1 861.1	6 106.0
21°	1 845.3	6 054.2	51°	1 854.2	6 083.4	81°	1 861.2	6 106.3
22°	1 845.5	6 044.9	52°	1 854.5	6 084.4	82°	1 861.3	6 106.6
23°	1 845.8	6 055.7	53°	1 854.8	6 085.4	83°	1 861.4	6 106.9
24°	1 846.0	6 056.4	54°	1 855.2	6 086.5	84°	1 861.5	6 107.1
25°	1 846.2	6 057.2	55°	1 855.5	6 087.5	86°	1 861.5	6 107.4
26°	1 846.5	6 058.1	56°	1 855.8	6 088.5	87°	1 861.6	6 107.5
27°	1 846.8	6 058.9	57°	1 856.1	6 089.5	87°	1 861.6	6 107.7
28°	1 847.0	6 059.8	58°	1 856.4	6 090.5	88°	1 861.6	6 107.8
29°	1 847.3	6 060.7	59°	1 856.7	6 091.4	89°	1 861.7	6 107.8

XI. Length of One Degree on Parallel in Metres and Feet — for Every Degree of Latitude

	m	ft		m	ft		m	ft
0°	111 324	365 236	30°	96 490	316 568	60°	55 803	183 081
1°	111 307	365 180	31°	95 508	313 346	61°	54 110	177 526
2°	111 257	365 016	32°	94 497	310 030	62°	52 401	171 919
3°	111 172	364 738	33°	93 457	306 617	63°	50 675	166 257
4°	111 055	364 354	34°	92 389	303 114	64°	48 934	160 545
5°	110 903	363 855	35°	91 292	299 514	65°	47 178	154 783
6°	110 718	363 248	36°	90 168	295 827	66°	45 407	148 973
7°	110 500	362 533	37°	89 016	292 047	67°	43 622	143 117
8°	110 248	361 706	38°	87 836	288 176	68°	41 824	137 218
9°	109 962	360 768	39°	86 630	284 219	69°	40 012	131 273
10°	109 644	359 724	40°	85 398	280 177	70°	38 189	125 292
11°	109 292	358 570	41°	84 139	276 047	71°	36 353	119 268
12°	108 907	357 306	42°	82 855	271 834	72°	34 506	113 209
13°	108 489	355 935	43°	81 545	267 536	73°	32 648	107 113
14°	108 038	354 455	44°	80 210	263 156	74°	30 781	100 988
15°	107 555	352 871	45°	78 850	258 694	75°	28 904	94 829
16°	107 039	351 178	46°	77 467	254 157	76°	27 017	88 638
17°	106 490	349 377	47°	76 060	249 541	77°	25 123	82 425
18°	105 909	347 470	48°	74 629	244 846	78°	23 220	76 181
19°	105 296	345 459	49°	73 175	240 075	79°	21 311	69 918
20°	104 651	343 343	50°	71 699	235 233	80°	19 395	63 632
21°	103 975	341 125	51°	70 201	230 318	81°	17 472	57 323
22°	103 266	338 799	52°	68 681	225 331	82°	15 545	51 001
23°	102 527	336 375	53°	67 140	220 276	83°	13 612	44 659
24°	101 756	333 845	54°	65 579	215 154	84°	11 675	38 304
25°	100 954	331 214	55°	63 997	209 964	85°	9 735	31 939
26°	100 122	328 484	56°	62 396	204 711	86°	7 792	25 564
27°	99 259	325 653	57°	60 775	199 393	87°	5 846	19 180
28°	98 366	322 723	58°	59 136	194 016	88°	3 898	12 789
29°	97 443	319 695	59°	57 478	188 576	89°	1 949	6 394

XII. Length of One Minute on Parallel in Metres and Feet — for Every Degree of Latitude

	m	ft		m	ft		m	ft
0°	1 855.4	6 087.3	30°	1 608.2	5 276.1	60°	930.0	3 051.4
1°	1 855.1	6 086.3	31°	1 591.8	5 222.4	61°	901.8	2 958.8
2°	1 854.3	6 083.6	32°	1 575.0	5 167.2	62°	873.4	2 865.3
3°	1 852.9	6 079.0	33°	1 557.6	5 110.3	63°	844.6	2 771.0
4°	1 850.9	6 072.6	34°	1 539.8	5 051.9	64°	815.6	2 675.8
5°	1 848.4	6 064.2	35°	1 521.5	4 991.9	65°	786.3	2 579.7
6°	1 845.3	6 054.1	36°	1 502.8	4 930.4	66°	756.3	2 482.9
7°	1 841.7	6 042.2	37°	1 483.6	4 867.4	67°	727.0	2 385.3
8°	1 837.5	6 028.4	38°	1 463.9	4 802.9	68°	697.1	2 287.0
9°	1 832.7	6 012.8	39°	1 443.8	4 737.0	69°	666.9	2 187.9
10°	1 827.4	5 995.4	40°	1 423.3	4 669.6	70°	636.5	2 088.2
11°	1 821.5	5 976.2	41°	1 402.3	4 600.8	71°	605.9	1 987.8
12°	1 815.1	5 955.1	42°	1 380.9	4 530.6	72°	575.1	1 886.8
13°	1 808.2	5 932.2	43°	1 359.1	4 458.9	73°	544.1	1 785.2
14°	1 800.6	5 907.6	44°	1 336.8	4 385.9	74°	513.0	1 683.1
15°	1 792.6	5 881.2	45°	1 314.2	4 311.6	75°	481.7	1 580.5
16°	1 784.0	5 853.0	46°	1 291.1	4 236.0	76°	450.3	1 477.3
17°	1 774.8	5 823.0	47°	1 267.7	4 159.0	77°	418.7	1 373.8
18°	1 765.2	5 791.2	48°	1 243.8	4 080.8	78°	387.0	1 269.7
19°	1 754.9	5 757.6	49°	1 219.6	4 001.2	79°	355.2	1 165.3
20°	1 744.2	5 722.4	50°	1 195.0	3 920.6	80°	323.2	1 060.5
21°	1 732.9	5 685.4	51°	1 170.0	3 838.6	81°	291.2	955.4
22°	1 721.1	5 646.6	52°	1 144.7	3 755.5	82°	259.1	850.0
23°	1 708.8	5 606.2	53°	1 119.0	3 671.3	83°	226.9	744.3
24°	1 695.9	5 564.1	54°	1 093.0	3 585.9	84°	194.6	638.4
25°	1 682.6	5 520.2	55°	1 066.6	3 499.4	85°	162.2	532.3
26°	1 668.7	5 474.7	56°	1 039.9	3 411.8	86°	129.9	426.1
27°	1 654.3	5 427.6	57°	1 012.9	3 323.2	87°	97.4	319.7
28°	1 639.4	5 378.7	58°	985.6	3 233.6	88°	65.0	213.2
29°	1 624.0	5 328.2	59°	958.0	3 142.9	89°	32.5	106.6

XIII. Millimetres of Mercury of Millibars

mmHg	0	1	2	3	4	5	6	7	8	9	mmHg
600	799.9	801.3	802.6	803.9	805.3	806.6	807.9	809.3	810.3	811.9	600
610	813.3	814.6	815.9	817.3	818.6	819.9	821.3	822.6	823.9	825.3	610
620	826.6	827.9	829.3	830.6	831.9	833.3	834.6	835.6	837.3	838.6	620
630	839.9	841.3	842.6	843.9	845.3	846.6	847.9	849.3	850.6	851.9	630
640	853.3	854.6	855.9	857.3	858.6	859.9	861.3	862.6	863.9	865.3	640
650	866.6	867.9	869.3	870.6	871.9	873.3	874.6	875.9	877.3	878.6	650
660	879.9	881.3	882.6	883.9	885.3	886.6	887.9	889.3	890.6	891.9	660
670	893.3	894.6	895.9	897.3	898.6	899.9	901.3	902.6	903.9	905.3	670
680	906.6	907.9	909.3	910.6	911.9	913.3	914.6	915.9	917.3	918.6	680
690	919.9	921.3	922.6	923.9	925.3	926.6	927.9	929.3	930.6	931.9	690
700	933.3	934.6	935.9	937.3	938.6	939.9	941.3	942.6	943.9	945.3	700
710	946.6	947.9	949.6	950.6	951.9	953.3	954.6	955.9	957.3	958.6	710
720	959.9	961.3	962.6	963.9	965.3	966.6	967.9	969.3	970.6	971.9	720
730	973.3	974.6	975.9	977.3	978.6	979.9	981.3	982.6	983.9	985.3	730
740	986.6	987.9	989.3	990.6	991.9	993.3	994.6	995.9	997.3	998.6	740
750	999.9	1 001.3	1 002.6	1 003.9	1 005.3	1 006.6	1 009.3	1 010.6	1 011.6	1 011.9	750
760	1 013.3	1 014.6	1 015.9	1 017.2	1 018.6	1 019.9	1 021.2	1 022.6	1 023.9	1 025.2	760
770	1 026.6	1 027.9	1 029.2	1 030.6	1 031.9	1 033.2	1 034.6	1 035.9	1 037.2	1 038.6	770
780	1 039.9	1 041.2	1 042.6	1 043.9	1 045.2	1 046.6	1 047.9	1 049.2	1 050.6	1 051.9	780
790	1 053.2	1 054.6	1 055.9	1 057.2	1 058.6	1 059.9	1 061.2	1 062.6	1 063.9	1 065.2	790
800	1 066.6	1 067.9	1 069.2	1 070.6	1 071.9	1 073.2	1 074.6	1 075.9	1 077.2	1 078.6	800
810	1 079.9	1 081.2	1 082.6	1 083.9	1 085.2	1 086.6	1 087.9	1 089.2	1 090.6	1 091.9	810
820	1 093.2	1 094.6	1 095.9	1 097.2	1 098.6	1 099.9	1 101.2	1 102.6	1 103 9	1 105.2	820
830	1 006.6	1 107.9	1 109.2	1 110.6	1 111.9	1 113.2	1 114.6	1 115 9	1 117.2	1 118.6	830
840	1 119.9	1 121.2	1 122.6	1 123.9	1 125.2	1 126.6	1127.9	1 127.9	1 130.6	1 131.9	840
850	1 133.2	1 134.6	1 135.9	1 137.2	1 138.6	1 139.9	1 141.2	1 142.6	1 143.9	1 145.2	850

mmHg	.1	.2	.3	.4	.5	.6	.7	.8	.9	mmHg
mb	.1	.3	.4	.5	.7	.8	.9	1.1	1.2	mb

XIV. Random sampling numbers

20	17	42	28	23	17	59	66	38	61	02	10	86	10	51	55	92	52
74	49	04	49	03	04	10	33	53	70	11	54	48	63	94	60	94	49
94	70	49	31	38	67	23	42	29	65	40	88	78	71	37	18	48	64
22	15	78	15	69	84	32	52	32	54	15	12	54	02	01	37	38	37
93	29	12	18	27	30	30	55	91	87	50	57	58	51	49	36	12	53
45	04	77	97	36	14	99	45	52	95	69	85	03	83	51	87	85	56
44	91	99	49	89	39	94	60	48	49	06	77	64	72	59	26	08	51
16	23	91	02	19	96	47	59	89	65	27	84	30	92	63	37	26	24
04	50	65	04	65	65	82	42	70	51	55	04	61	47	88	83	99	34
32	70	17	72	03	61	66	26	24	71	22	77	88	33	17	78	08	92
03	64	59	07	42	95	81	39	06	41	20	81	92	34	51	90	39	08
62	49	00	90	67	86	93	48	31	83	19	07	67	68	49	03	27	47
61	00	95	86	98	36	14	03	48	88	51	07	33	40	06	86	33	76
89	03	90	49	28	74	21	04	09	96	60	45	22	03	52	80	01	79
01	72	33	85	52	40	60	07	06	71	89	27	14	29	55	24	85	79
27	56	49	79	34	34	32	22	60	53	91	17	33	26	44	70	93	14
49	05	74	48	10	55	35	25	24	28	20	22	35	66	66	34	26	35
49	74	37	25	97	26	33	94	42	23	01	28	59	58	92	69	03	66
20	26	22	43	88	08	19	85	08	12	47	65	65	63	56	07	97	85
48	87	77	96	43	39	76	93	08	79	22	18	54	55	93	75	97	26
08	72	87	46	75	73	00	11	27	07	05	20	30	85	22	21	04	67
95	97	98	62	17	27	31	42	64	71	46	22	32	75	19	32	20	99
37	99	57	31	70	40	46	55	46	12	24	32	36	74	69	20	72	10
05	79	58	37	85	33	75	18	88	71	23	44	54	28	00	48	96	23
55	85	63	42	00	79	91	22	29	01	41	39	51	40	36	65	26	11
67	28	96	25	68	36	24	72	03	85	49	24	05	69	64	86	08	19
85	86	94	78	32	59	51	82	86	43	73	84	45	60	89	57	06	87
40	10	60	09	05	88	78	44	63	13	58	25	37	11	18	47	75	62
94	55	89	48	90	80	77	80	26	89	87	44	23	74	66	20	20	19
11	63	77	77	23	20	33	62	62	19	29	03	94	15	56	37	14	09
64	00	26	04	54	55	38	57	94	62	68	40	26	04	24	25	03	61
50	94	13	23	78	41	60	58	10	60	88	46	30	21	45	98	70	96
66	98	37	96	44	13	45	05	34	59	75	85	48	97	27	19	17	85
66	91	42	83	60	77	90	91	60	90	79	62	57	66	72	28	08	70
33	58	12	18	02	07	19	40	21	29	39	45	90	42	58	84	85	43
52	49	40	16	72	40	73	05	50	90	02	04	98	24	05	30	27	25
74	98	93	99	78	30	79	47	96	92	45	58	40	37	89	76	84	41
50	26	54	30	01	88	69	57	54	45	69	88	23	21	05	69	93	44
49	46	61	89	33	79	96	84	28	34	19	35	28	73	39	59	56	34
19	65	13	44	78	39	73	88	62	03	36	00	25	96	86	76	67	90
64	17	47	67	87	59	81	40	72	61	14	00	28	28	55	86	25	38
18	43	97	37	68	97	56	56	57	95	01	88	11	89	48	07	42	60
65	58	60	87	51	09	96	61	15	53	66	81	66	88	44	75	37	01
79	90	31	00	91	14	85	65	31	75	43	15	45	93	64	78	34	53
07	23	00	15	59	05	16	09	94	42	20	40	63	76	65	67	34	11
90	08	14	24	01	51	95	46	30	32	33	19	00	14	19	28	40	51
53	82	62	02	21	82	34	13	41	03	12	85	65	30	00	97	56	30
98	17	26	15	04	50	76	25	20	33	54	84	39	31	23	33	59	64
08	91	12	44	82	40	30	62	45	50	64	54	65	17	89	25	59	44
37	21	46	77	84	87	67	39	85	54	97	37	33	41	11	74	90	50

Random Sampling Number, in D.V. Lindley and J.C.P. Miller, *Cambridge Elementary Statistical tables*, 1955.

XV. Random Sampling Numbers

4062	9228	6347	1043	5824	1560	6507	2405	3832	2993
6489	7404	6051	5954	0008	5231	3311	9324	6679	0345
8163	4275	9177	9796	3253	1562	5746	8523	9118	7332
2956	8728	9335	4461	1315	0647	7177	7246	3114	0813
9203	5790	5225	7478	4920	8721	8044	1806	8271	9724
4895	7266	5890	5011	5478	6475	8887	5014	7672	3442
9388	8173	0357	1623	6416	1466	9510	0343	5816	1909
8924	9121	1570	0374	8156	1949	7720	4802	0133	4496
1829	6798	7836	8856	4001	1638	6113	8612	5795	5846
1798	2280	9290	1379	5472	0460	1544	0965	5563	5652
7306	8564	1301	7910	4952	9390	6210	5867	7018	2032
9642	5428	7002	1835	9928	5132	1453	3939	4201	6703
8194	4347	2268	0425	1026	8375	4640	7178	8317	8489
2380	1000	2259	2701	9227	1349	0647	6078	6595	6619
5491	6250	4713	5947	9580	9438	3403	3513	4613	2690
2752	3281	8909	2901	8215	2067	9589	3465	5757	3417
8767	6707	7561	1191	8583	3705	0934	2916	9749	3936
1959	8451	2771	6219	2276	5028	2750	6224	0656	6126
7943	4347	8451	5713	8193	0313	6989	0088	5867	7992
3966	1653	4509	1921	4973	9488	3410	9540	8314	0808
7056	4276	9813	9777	5686	3428	7604	0591	6542	7752
8852	3993	4048	6604	6948	5519	3769	0403	4575	3098
0298	3634	6429	2478	1197	5680	6168	9324	2506	6616
2828	6589	8721	4082	3463	1859	5918	4605	1848	0348
7973	6207	2960	8675	0536	9518	7974	9749	5723	6888

XVI. Significance Points of t

[Values of t_0 for given probabilities $P = \text{Prob.} (t > t_0) = \text{Prob.} (t < t_0)$]

Degree of freedom	Probability (P)			
	.05	.025	.01	.005
1	6.31	12.71	31.82	63.66
2	2.92	4.30	6.97	9.93
3	2.35	3.18	4.54	5.84
4	2.13	2.78	3.75	4.60
5	2.02	2.57	3.37	4.03
6	1.94	2.45	3.14	3.71
7	1.90	2.37	3.00	3.50
8	1.86	2.31	2.90	3.36
9	1.83	2.26	2.82	3.25
10	1.81	2.23	2.76	3.17
11	1.80	2.20	2.72	3.11
12	1.78	2.18	2.68	3.06
13	1.77	2.16	2.65	3.01
14	1.76	2.15	2.62	2.98
15	1.75	2.13	2.60	2.95
16	1.75	2.12	2.58	2.92
17	1.74	2.11	2.57	2.90
18	1.73	2.10	2.55	2.88
19	1.73	2.09	2.54	2.86
20	1.73	2.09	2.53	2.85
21	1.72	2.08	2.52	2.83
22	1.72	2.07	2.51	2.82
23	1.71	2.07	2.50	2.81
24	1.71	2.06	2.49	2.80
25	1.71	2.06	2.49	2.79
26	1.71	2.06	2.48	2.78
27	1.70	2.05	2.47	2.77
28	1.70	2.05	2.47	2.76
29	1.70	2.05	2.46	2.76
30	1.70	2.04	2.46	2.75

Note : These are also known as Percentage Points of t distribution. Example : For 6 degrees of freedom (d.f), the upper 1% point is 3.14, and the lower 1% point is — 3.14 (because of symmetry of the t-curve in symbols for 6 d.f.

$$t_{.01 = 3.14,\, t}99 = -3.14$$

XVII. Points of χ^2

Degree of freedom	Probability (*P*)					
	.99	.975	.95	.05	.025	.01
1	–	–	–	3.84	5.0	6.63
2	0.020	0.051	0.103	5.99	7.38	9.21
3	0.115	0.216	0.352	7.81	9.35	11.34
4	0.297	0.484	0.711	9.49	11.14	13.28
5	0.554	0.831	1.15	11.07	12.83	15.09
6	0.872	1.24	1.64	12.59	14.45	16.81
7	1.24	1.69	2.17	14.07	16.01	18.48
8	1.65	2.18	2.73	15.51	17.53	20.09
9	2.09	2.70	3.33	16.92	19.02	21.67
10	2.56	3.25	3.94	18.31	20.48	23.21
11	3.05	3.82	4.57	19.68	21.92	24.73
12	3.57	4.40	5.23	21.03	23.34	26.22
13	4.11	5.01	5.89	22.36	24.74	27.69
14	4.66	5.63	6.57	23.68	26.12	29.14
15	5.23	6.26	7.26	25.00	27.49	30.58
16	5.81	6.91	7.96	26.30	28.85	32.00
17	6.41	7.56	8.67	27.59	30.19	33.41
18	7.01	8.23	9.39	28.87	31.53	34.81
19	7.63	8.91	10.12	30.14	32.85	36.19
20	8.26	9.59	10.85	31.41	34.17	37.57
21	8.90	10.28	11.59	32.67	35.48	38.93
22	9.54	10.98	12.34	33.92	36.78	40.29
23	10.20	11.69	13.09	35.17	38.08	41.64
24	10.86	12.40	13.85	36.42	39.36	42.98
25	11.52	13.12	14.61	37.65	40.65	44.31
26	12.20	13.84	15.38	38.89	41.92	45.64
27	12.88	14.57	16.15	40.11	43.19	46.96
28	13.56	15.31	16.93	41.34	44.46	48.28
29	14.26	16.05	17.71	42.56	45.72	49.59
30	14.95	16.79	18.49	43.77	46.98	50.89

Note : These are also known as *Percentage Points* of chi-square distribution. Example : For 10 degrees of freedom (d.f.) the *upper* 5% point is 18.31, and the lower 5% point is 3.94. In symbols, for 10 d.f. $\chi^2_{.05} = 18.31$ and $\chi^2_{.95} = 3.94$.

XVIII. Area Units

Alias	UOM	Conversion Factor
ac	acres	4046.8564224 (m^2/ac)
ares	ares	100.0 (m^2/are)
centare	centares	1.0 (m^2/centare)
$chain^2$	square chains	404.68564224 ($m^2/chain^2$)
cm^2	square centimetres	0.0001 (m^2/cm^2)
deciare	deciares	10.0 (m^2/deciare)
ft^2	square feet	0.09290304 (m^2/ft^2)
hectare	hectares	10000.0 (m^2/hectare)
in^2	square inches	0.00064516 (m^2/in^2)
km^2	square kilometres	1000000.0 (m^2/km^2)
$link^2$	square links	0.040468564224 ($m^2/link^2$)
m^2	square metres	1.0
mi^2	square miles	2589988.110336 (m^2/mi^2)
mm^2	square millimetres	0.000001 (m^2/mm^2)
perch	perches	25.29285264 (m^2/perch)
rod^2	square rods	25.29285264 (m^2/rod^2)
yd^2	square yards	0.83612736 (m^2/yd^2)

XIX. UTM Zones, Central Meridians, and Longitude Ranges

Zone	Meridian	Longitude Range	Zone	Meridian	Longitude Range
1	177W	180W – 174W	31	3E	0 – 6E
2	171W	174W – 168W	32	9E	6E – 12E
3	165W	168W – 162W	33	15E	12E – 18E
4	159W	162W – 156W	34	21E	18E – 24E
5	153W	156W – 150W	35	27E	24E – 30E
6	147W	150W – 144W	36	33E	30E – 36E
7	141W	144W – 138W	37	39E	36E – 42E
8	135W	138W – 132W	38	45E	42E – 48E
9	129W	132W – 126W	39	51E	48E – 54E
10	123W	126W – 120W	40	57E	54E – 60E
11	117W	120W – 114W	41	63E	60E – 66E
12	111W	114W – 108W	42	69E	66E – 72E
13	105W	108W – 102W	43	75E	72E – 78E
14	99W	102W – 96W	44	81E	78E – 84E
15	93W	96W – 90W	45	87E	84E – 90E
16	87W	90W – 84W	46	93E	90E – 96E
17	81W	84W – 78W	47	99E	96E – 102E
18	75W	78W – 72W	48	102E	102E – 108E
19	69W	72W – 66W	49	111E	108E – 114E
20	63W	66W – 60W	50	117E	114E – 120E
21	57W	60W – 54W	51	123E	120E – 126E
22	51W	54W – 48W	52	129E	126E – 132E
23	45W	48W – 42W	53	135E	132E – 138E
24	39W	42W – 36W	54	141E	138E – 144E
25	33W	36W – 30W	55	147E	144E – 150E
26	27W	30W – 24W	56	153E	150E – 156E
27	21W	24W – 18W	57	159E	156E – 162E
28	15W	18W – 12W	58	165E	162E – 168E
29	9W	12W – 6W	59	171E	168E – 174E
30	3W	6W – 0	60	177E	174E – 180E

All values are expressed in full degrees east (E) or west (W) of Greenwich (0).

BIBLIOGRAPHY

Basu, S.R. and Majumder Paramita (2006) Landslides Scenario of the Darjeeling Himalayas in West Bengal, India; Geog. Rev. Ind., V. 68, No. 2, June 2006; Geog. Soc. Ind. pp.161-173

Bernstein, R. and D. G. Ferneyhough (1975) "Digital Image Processing, *Photogrammetric Engineering* and Remote Sensing Vol. 41

Billings, M. P. (1984) *Structural Geology;* Prentice Hall of India Pvt. Ltd; 3rd edi.

Bryant, M. (1974) *Digital Image Processing,* Chelmsford, MA, Optronics International publications

Burrogh, P.A., (1986) *Principles of Geographic Information Systems for Land Resource Assessment,* Oxford, Clarendon Press

Clarke, K. C., (1990) *Analytical and Computer Cartography,* Englewood Cliffs, N.J. Practice-Hall

Close, Col. C. F. and Cox, Capt. E. W. (1913) *Text Book of Topographical and Geographical Surveying;* His Majesty's Stationary office

Charlton, Ro (2008) Fundamentals of Fluvial Geomorphology; Routledge; London and New York.

Chorley, R. (ed.) (1987) *Handling Geographic Information,* London, Her Majesty's Stationary Office

Cole, J. P. and king, C. A. M. (1970) Quantitative Geography, *John Wiley and sons Inc., London*

Cooke, R. U. and Doornkamp, J. C. (1974) *Geomorphology in Environmental Management;* Claredon Prees, Oxford

Croxton, F. E. and Cowden, D. J. (1939) *Applied General Statistics,* Newyork and London

Dackombe, R.V. and Gardiner, V. (1983) Geomorphological Feild Manual,; Allen & Unwin; London.

Das N. G. (1991) *Statistical Method (Part 1 & 2),* M. Das & Co.;

Dalgeish, A. G. (1977) Chapter 2 of St. Joseph. J. K. S. (ed.) *The uses of Air photography, London, Baker*

Dickinson, G.C. (1979) *Maps and Air photographs.* London, Arnold-Heinmann

Govt. of India (1981 & 1991) *Census and District Census Handbooks*

Gregory. S. (1978) *Statistical Methods and the Geographer;* Longman, London and Newyork

Hinks, A. R. (1921), *Map projections,* Cambridge University Press

Kanetkar. Lt. T. P. and Kulkarni, S. V. (1980) *Surveying and Levelling (part 1 & 2),* Pune Vidyarthi Griha Prakashan

Kellaway, G. P. (1970) *Map Projections,* London, Methuen

Kidron M, and Segal, R. (1984) *The new State of the World Atlas;* Heinemann Educational; London

Kilford. K. (1973) Elementary Air Survey, London, Pitman

Lillesand, T. M. and R. W. Kiefer (1994) *Remote Sensing and Image Intepretation,* New York, John Wiley & Sons.

Lock, M. (1976) *Geography and Cartography – A Reference Handbook,* London, Bingey

Mahmood, A. (1998) Statistieal Methods in Geographical Studies; Rajesh Publications; New Delhi-2

Maling, D.H. (1973) *Co-ordinate systems and Map projections,* London, phillip

Maslov, A. V., Gordeev A. V., Batrakov, Yu. G. (1984) *Geodetic Surveying,* Mir Publishers; Moscow; Eng. Trans.

Micro Images (1999) Getting Started : TNT Mips Lincoln, Nebraska Micro Images Inc.

Mikhailov, A. Ye. (1984) *Structural Geology and Geological Mapping;* Mir Publishers; Moscow.

Monkhouse, F. J. and H. R. Wilkinson (1974) *Maps and Diagrams : Their compilation and Construction,* London, Methuen & Co. Ltd.

Mukhopadhyay, S. C. (1980) *Geomorphology of the Subarnarekha Basin;* The University of Burdwan

NRSA (1994) Reference Scheme for IRS-IC, Interface, Vol 5 No. 2, Balanagar, Hyderabad, N.R.S.A.

Petrie, G. (1977) "Orthophoto maps" *Trans. Institute of British geographers,* New series 2

Platt, J. I. and Challinor, J. (1956) *Simple Geological Structures;* Thomas Murby & Co; London

Potter, A. W. R. and Robinson, H. (1982) *Geology;* ElBS and Macdonald and Evans Ltd.

Read, H. H. (1984) *Rutley's Elements of Mineralogy;* CBS Publishers and Distrubuters; 26 edition

Robinson A. *et al* (1995) *Elements of Cartography* 6th edition, New York, John Willey & Sons.

Rodrigue, dean-Paul, Comtois Claude, and Slack Brian (2009) The Geography of Transport systems; Routeledge; London and New York.

Sabins, Floyd F. (1987) *Remote Sensing Principles and Interpretation,* New York, W. H. Freeman & co.

Sacheti, A. K. (1985) *Agricultural Meteorology;* NCERT

Sandover, J. A. and Malling, D. H. (1961) *Plane Surveying,* Edward Arnold (London) Ltd.

Short, N. M. (1982) *The Landsat Tutorial Workbook,* Washington, DC., NASA Reference Publications

Star J. , and J. Estes (1990) *Geographic Information Systems : An introduction,* Englewood Cliffs, N. J., Prentice Hall

Steers, J. A. (1971) *An Introduction to the study of Map Projections,* London, University of London Press. Ltd.

Strahlar, A. N. (1975) *Physical Geography;* John Wiley and sons; 4th edition

Thrower, N. J. W., and J. R. Jenson (1976) The Orthophoto and Orthophoto map : Characteristics, development and application, *American cartographer 3*

Tyrrell G. W. (1929) *The Principles of Petrology;* B. I. Publications;

Wentworth, C. K. (1930) *A Simplified Method of Determining the Average Slope of Land Surfaces;* Amer. Jour. Sci.; Series 5; Vol. 20

Wolf, P. R. (1974) *Elements of Photogrammetry,* New York, McGraw Hill.

VIVA-VOCE

CHAPTER 1

1. What is a map?
2. What is map scale?
3. How many types of map scales are there?
4. How do you define R.F.?
5. What is the relative advantage of R.F. scale?
6. What is the advantage of a graphical scale? What are the primary and secondary divisions?
7. Of two map scales, one at 1:50,000 and another at 1:100,000 — which one is the larger scale and how?
8. Of the two maps of the same area, one on 1:50,000 and the other on 1:100,000 — which one is larger in size?
9. What do you mean by an inset map?
10. What is the relation between the scale of a map and size of the same at the time of enlargement and reduction?
11. What is the purpose of using a large scale map?
12. Where should we use a small scale map?
13. How do you calculate the area of a triangle?
14. How do you calculate the area of a square?
15. How do you calculate the area of a cone?
16. How do you calculate the area of a polygon?
17. How do you calculate the area of a circle?
18. How do you calculate the area of a cylinder?
19. How do you calculate the area of a pyramid?
20. How do you calculate the area of a parallelopiped?
21. How do you calculate the area of a sector of a circle?
22. Why does the true north vary from the grid north?
23. How do you read a six figure grid reference?

24. What do you undestand as coordinate system?
25. Distinguish between Cartesian coordinates and Polar coordinates.
26. How can you convert cartesian coordinate to Polar coordinate?
27. What are the differences between natural scale and logarithmic scale?
28. What are the advantages of using logarithmic scale?
29. Why do we round off numbers? What are the principles of rounding off numbers?
30. How do you use log table?
31. What is the difference between geoid and spheroid?
32. What is the shape of the earth?
33. What do you mean by WGS 84?
34. What do you understand by rounding of numbers?
35. Why do we round off numbers?
36. What is the rule of rounding of numbers?
37. What is the advantage of scientific notation?
38. What is the difference between natural scale and logarithmic scale?
39. What are logarithm and anti-logarithm?
40. What is the difference between cartesian coordinate and polar coordinate?
41. What are geographical coordinates?
42. What do you mean by base of logarithmic scale?

CHAPTER 2

1. What is a map projection?
2. How does a map projection differ from the projection of a cinema?
3. What are known as parallels in a map projection?
4. What is a graticule?
5. Define a generating globe.
6. What is a developable surface?
7. How many types of developable surfaces are there?
8. What are the basic properties, which are to be maintained in a map projection?
9. What is an Aphylactic projection?
10. What is a standard parallel?
11. Why do you need a standard parallel?
12. How does the position of apex of developable surface vary in conical, zenithal and cylidrical group of projections?
13. What is the constant of a cone?

14. What is the range of values of the constant of a cone?
15. Why is the polyconic projection so named?
16. What is the difference between a polar case and an equatorial case?
17. Why is interruption used in certain projections?
18. What is orthomorphism?
19. What is a loxodrome or a rhumbline?
20. Define the term homolographic.
21. What do you mean by an antipodal position?
22. Why can't we have a loxodrome in a cylindrical equal area projection?
23. What is distortion?
24. How many types of distortions are there?
25. How many UTM-zones are there?
26. Why do we call it UTM Projection?
27. What is easting and northing?
28. Why there is no southing and westing?
29. What are the assigned values for the equator?
30. What is the assigned value for central meridian of a UTM zone?

CHAPTER 3

1. What is an outcrop?
2. What is a bedding plane ?
3. How should you choose a section line?
4. What is dip?
5. What is strike?
6. What is an unconformity?
7. What is the difference between a true dip and an apparent dip?
8. What is a series?
9. What is a fault?
10. What is throw?
11. What is heave?
12. What is the difference between a fault and a joint?
13. What is an inversion of relief?
14. What is a hidden bed?
15. What is an intrusion?

16. What is the difference between a dyke and a sill?
17. How do we know the height and nature of topography from topographical maps?
18. Can we recognize the scale of a Survey of India topographic sheet if the reference number is only known?
19. What is a planimetric map?
20. What do you mean by drainage pattern? What are the various types and their significances?
21. What is a channel pattern? What are the types?
22. What is a settlement pattern?
23. Why are settlements dispersed on a rugged terrain?
24. How are roads influenced by terrain characteristics?
25. What is the difference between a ferry and a ford?
26. What is a nodal point settlement?
27. Can we obtain 90° slope by Wentworth's method?
28. For a road density map which method is suitable, an isopleth or a gridwise shading method?
29. Where should we use an isopleth method?
30. Which method is suitable for a drainage density map, a gridwise shading method or isopleth?
31. Why do we use a transect chart?
32. Explain if it is a deterministic study?

CHAPTER 4

1. Define a mineral.
2. What is a rock?
3. What are the physical properties on the basis which the minerals are identified?
4. What is the difference between a microscopic and a megascopic examination?
5. Why are geographers interested to identify minerals and rocks?
6. How do you recognize any particular mineral? Give an example.
7. How do you recognize any particular rock? Give an example.
8. What are the major types of rocks according to their origin?
9. Distinguish between a conglomerate and a breecia.
10. What is a lamina?
11. What is foliation?
12. What is fissibility?
13. What do you understand by the presence of interlocking bands in gneiss?
14. Why does dilute or concentrated HCl react with calcite, limestone and marble?
15. What is pleochroism?

16. What is polarisation?
18. Give examples of plutonic, hypabyssal and volcanic rocks.
19. How does grain size vary in the three types of igneous rocks metioned above?

CHAPTER 5

1. What is a cartogram?
2. What is geomorphological map?
3. Distinguish between a choropleth and an isopleth.
4. What is a chorochromatic map?
5. Define an isobar.
6. Define an isotherm.
7. Define an isohyet.
8. Define an isoneph.
9. What are isomers?
10. What are isanomals?
11. What are isohypses?
12. Classify bargraphs?
13. What is a simple bar graph?
14. What is compound bargraph?
15. What types of data is suitable to be represended in a compound bargraph?
16. What is a Windrose? How do we draw it?
17. What is a Climatograph?
18. What is a Climograph and what is a hythergraph?
19. Waht is a Composite climograph?
20. What is a Columnar diagram?
21. What is a Dasymetric map?
22. Why do we use spheres to show an urbar population, whereas the rural population are conveniently shown by distribution of dots?
23. How many types of choropleths are there?
24. The particular nature of data determines the type of diagram on which it will be represented — do you agree with this statement? Justify your answer.
25. What is a pie graph?
26. What are the similarities between a compound bar graph and a pie graph?
27. What is a ergograph?
28. What is age-Sex pyramid?

29. What is a superimposed age-sex pyramid?
30. How are population potentials determined?
31. What do you understand by rank size rule?
32. How is the residual mapping done?
33. What is a Lorenz curve and what is its significance?
34. Draw a Ternary diagram marking the textural types of soil.
35. What do you mean by weighted index? What are the criteria used in determining weighted index?

CHAPTER 6

1. What is vernier?
2. Why has it been so named?
3. Why do we consider a vernier as a device?
4. What are the advantages of a diagonal scale?
5. Distinguish between the characteristics of a diagonal scale and a vernier scale.
6. Why do we use the term diagonal in diagonal scale?
7. What is surveying?
8. Why is Prismatic compass so named?
9. What is the function of a prism?
10. Why do we use a ranging rod at the time of survey?
11. How do we correct the observational errors in a prismatic compass survey?
12. Why does a plotting error occur even after the use of mathematically corrected data?
13. How do we calculate an interior angle, when the northline is outside the traverse?
14. What is a traverse?
15. Distinguish between a closed traverse and an open traverse.
16. What do you mean by levelling?
17. Why is the Dumpy Level so named?
18. What is a telescopic staff and how long is it?
19. Name another levelling instrument other than Dumpy Level.
20. Why is a telescope used in a Dumpy Level?
21. What is difference between an inverted image and an erect image telescope?
22. What is a reduced level?
23. What is datum?

24. What is bench mark?
25. What is collimation level?
26. What is a transit theodolite?
27. Why do we use a theodolite?
28. What do you understand by an accessible base and an inaccessible base?
29. What are the two methods used for determination of height if the base is inaccessible?
30. What do you mean by the term 'face' while taking readings by a transit theodolite?
31. What are the accessories of a Plane Table?
32. What is the function of a thermometer?
33. Why do we use a hygrometer?
34. Define relative and absolute humidity?
35. What is Stevenson Screen and why is it used?
36. How do we determine the atmospheric pressure by Fortin's Barometer?
37. What is an Aneroid Barometer?
38. What is a Barograph?
39. What is an anemometer?
40. How do we use a Rain Gauge?
41. What will be the direction of the arrow in a Wind vane when the wind comes from the southwest direction?
42. What is the function of an Evaporimeter?
43. What is an Atmometer?
44. What is a Lysimeter?
45. How are sunshine and dew recorded?
46. Why do we use a Water current meter ?
47. How do we calculate the velocity of river-water by a current meter?
48. How do we determine the water discharge of a river?
49. What is a discharge hydrograph?
50. What is a rating curve?
51. What are the functions of an Abney Level?
52. Why and how do we use a Clinometer?
53. Why do we use a Brunton compass?
54. How is soil temperature measured?
55. What is a rotameter or an opisometer and why is it used?
56. Why do we use a planimeter?
57. What is the function of a Pantagraph?

CHAPTER 7

1. What is a data and a variate?
2. What is an information?
3. Define nominal, ordinal, interval and ratio variates?
4. What is 'Population'?
5. What is meant by sampling? What are the methods?
6. What is a target population?
7. What is frequency and frequency density?
8. What is a grouped frequency distribution?
9. What is known as an ungrouped data?
10. How do you draw a histogram?
11. What is the difference between a bargraph and a histogram?
12. What is a class mark?
13. Distinguish between class limit and class boundary.
14. What is a continuous data in contrast to a discrete data?
15. What is the difference between a frequency curve and a frequency polygon?
16. What is an ogive?
17. What do you understand as central tendency?
18. What are the various measures of central tendency?
19. What are the various types of mean and their relationships?
20. Define mean, median and mode.
21. Distinguish between a bi-modal and a unimodal distribution.
22. What is mean deviation?
23. Why can't we get a correct mode in an unequal class distribution?
24. Express the relationship between mean, median and mode.
25. What is Standard deviation?
26. What is variance?
27. What is correlation co-efficient?
28. What is a quartile and how many of them are there in a grouped data?
29. What is a decile?
30. What is a percentile?
31. Which Quartile, decile and percentile values are equal to the median of the same data?
32. What is relative variability?
33. How is the co-efficient of variability calculated?

34. What to you understand by a bi-variate frequency distribution?
35. Of two related variables which one should be shown along the ordinate?
36. What is a scatter diagram?
37. What do you understand by a moving average? What is its relative advantage in comparison with an ordinary scatter with absolute values?
38. How do you know the significance of a small sample data?
39. What is known as a parameter?
40. What are parametric tests?
41. What are non-parametric tests?
42. What is known as 'r'?
43. What is regression?
44. What are positive, negative and neutral correlations?
45. What do you understand by Y_c?
46. Define Least square.
47. How can you calculate product moment correlation coefficient by Pearson's method?
48. What is the use of Chi Squared Test?
49. What is probability?
50. Does real conditions of geographical data exhibit perfect correlations?
51. What is null hypothesis?

CHAPTER 8

1. What is remote sensing? Give an example.
2. What is an air photo?
3. What is focal length?
4. How is the scale of an air photo determined?
5. What is 'run'?
6. What is fusion and a stereo-pair?
7. How many types of air photo are there?
8. What is a Stereoscope? How many types are there?
9. What are the visual properties observed in a stero-pair of photographs?
10. What is nadir?
11. What is Zenith?
12. Approximately how much area is overlapped in two consecutive photographs of the same run?

13. What is a fiducial mark?
14. What is tilt displacement?
15. What is relief displacement?
16. What is an orthophoto?
17. What is DEM?
18. Which energy is used in taking an air photo?
19. What is a satellite imagery?
20. What is resolution?
21. What is IRA?
22. What are the names of IRAs used by India?
23. What type of film is used for taking an air photo and a satellite imagery?
24. What is FCC?
25. What is ground control?
26. Distinguish between an air photo and a topographic map?
27. How is a satellite image interpreted?

CHAPTER 9

1. What is G. I. S.?
2. What are the equipments required for G. I. S. ?
3. What MGE?
4. What is hardware?
5. What is software?
6. What are the popular G. I. S. packages?
7. Waht are the modes in which geographic information is obtained?
8. What is a PC and What is a network?
9. What is a computer and what are its components?
10. What is cosmetic layer?
11. How is geographic data imported and exported?
12. What is a file and a directory?
13. What is Raster data?
14. What is Vector data?
15. Distinguish between Vector and Raster data?
16. What is buffering?
17. What is GUI?

18. What are three basic types of geographical data is GIS?
19. What are three major functions of Raster and Vector data processing?
20. What is UTM?

CHAPTER 10

1. What do you mean by HDI? What is the full form of HDI?
2. What is GDI? What do you mean by population share?
3. What are the three accesses required for human development?
4. What are OECD countries?
5. Who publishes Human Development Report?
6. How do you distinguish between developed and developing nations in terms of HDI?
7. How do you compute Human Poverty Index?
8. Classify hazards.
9. Why should you consider riverbank erosion as a hazard, even if it is a natural process?
10. What are the processes of riverbank erosion?
11. How do you quantify riverbank erosion?
12. What are the causes of flood in deltaic West Bengal?
13. How do you determine meteorological drought?
14. Where can you get meteorological data?
15. Define landslide.
16. How does slide or slip differ from slump?
17. What are the parameters you should take to prepare a landslide hazard zonation map?
18. Why is landuse important while mapping landslide hazard zones?
19. What is factor of safety?
20. What is crown of a landslide?
21. Distinguish between translational and rotational movements.
22. How does water favour the occurrence of landslides?
23. Which are the weak rocks vulnerable to landslides?
24. What do you mean by vulnerability?
25. What is a questionnaire in geographical survey?
26. What are open end, double choice, and multiple choice questions?
27. Who is a respondent?

28. What is the unabbreviated form of HDI?
29. What is the unabbreviated form of GDI?
30. What is the usual value of E?
31. Why do we require to calculate GDI?
32. Waht is poverty index?
33. What are the processes of river bankerosion?
34. How can we check bank erosion?
35. Define Meteorological drought?
36. How do you define a flood?
37. Why is literacy rate insufficient as an index of education?
38. Is bank embankment a permanent solution to flood?

CHAPTER 11

1. Define a research problem. How do you find it?
2. What are the various types of research?
3. Distinguish between the following typs of research?
   (a) Qualitative and Quantitative
   (b) Conclusive and decisive
   (c) Fundamental and Applied.
4. What are the research ethics?
5. Distinguish between research method and methodology.
6. Write a note on plagiarism.

INDEX

A

B

C

D

E

F

G

H

I

L

M

N

O

P

R

S

T

U

V

W

Z